Differential Diagnosis for the Chiropractor

Protocols and Algorithms

Thomas A. Souza, DC, DACBSP
Professor
Department Chair of Diagnosis
Clinic Director —Tasman
Palmer-West Chiropractic College
San Jose, California

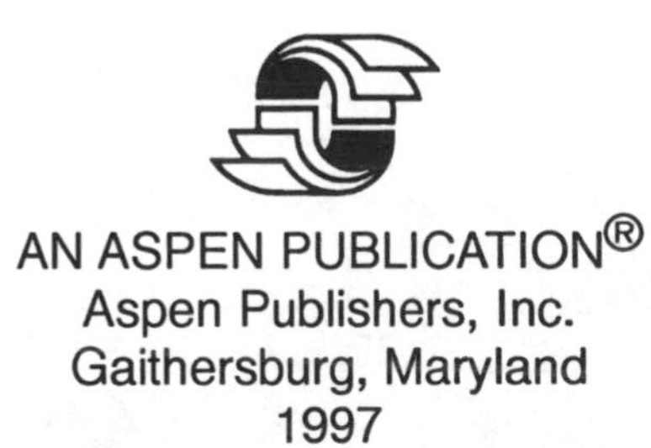

AN ASPEN PUBLICATION®
Aspen Publishers, Inc.
Gaithersburg, Maryland
1997

The authors have made every effort to ensure the accuracy of the information herein. However, appropriate information sources should be consulted, especially for new or unfamiliar procedures. It is the responsibility of every practitioner to evaluate the appropriateness of a particular opinion in the context of actual clinical situations and with due considerations to new developments. Authors, editors, and the publisher cannot be held responsible for any typographical or other errors found in this book.

Library of Congress Cataloging-in-Publication Data

Souza, Thomas A. Differential diagnosis for the chiropractor: protocols and algorithms / Thomas Souza.
p. cm.
Includes bibliographical references and index.
ISBN 0-8342-0846-6
1. Chiropractic—Diagnosis. 2. Diagnosis, Differential.
I. Title.
[DNLM: 1. Chiropractic. 2. Diagnosis, Differential. 3. Clinical Protocols. WB 905 S729d 1997]
RZ250.S68 1997
615.5'34—dc21
DNLM/DLC
for Library of Congress
97-5187
CIP

Orders: (800) 638-8437
Customer Service: (800) 234-1660

Editorial Resources: Ruth Bloom
Library of Congress Catalog Card Number: 97-5187
ISBN: 0-8342-0846-6

Printed in the United States of America

3 4 5

This text is dedicated to my wife Francie and sons Aaron and Wesley for their love and saintlike patience and understanding with what was often a major disruption to our lives.

Table of Contents

Acknowledgments

I would like to thank the photographer, John Boykin, and the models, Eric Mortensen and Tanya Slaco for their patience. I would also like to extend my heartfelt thanks to the many people at Aspen who's hard work and dedication was much appreciated. I express my deepest gratitude to the following colleagues who provided input to the development of the algorithms and text:

Ed Bifulco, DC
Department of Chiropractic Practice
The National College of Chiropractic
Lombard, Ill

Linda Bowers, DC, DABCO, DABCI, DACBN, DACAN
Department Chair of Diagnosis
Professor
Northwestern College of Chiropractic
Bloomington, Minn

Thomas A. Brozovich, DC, DACAN, DACBT
Assistant Professor
Palmer College of Chiropractic
Davenport, Iowa

William DuMonthier, DC
Director of Academic Administration
Palmer College of Chiropractic-West
San Jose, Calif

Ron Henniger, DC, DABCO
Clinical Professor
Palmer College of Chiropractic-West
San Jose, Calif

Lester C. Lamm, DC, DABCO
Dean of Postgraduate Studies
Western States Chiropractic College
Portland, Ore

Ronald LeFebvre, DC
Director of Intern Education
Western States Chiropractic College
Portland, Ore

Vincent Maples, DC
Department Chair of Diagnosis
Cleveland Chiropractic College
Los Angeles, Calif

Thomas Milus, DC, DABCO
Director of Intern Education
Professor
Palmer College of Chiropractic-West
San Jose, Calif

David Mullen, DC
Clinical Professor
Palmer College of Chiropractic-West
San Jose, Calif

Paul Mullin, DC
Department Chair of Diagnosis
Palmer College of Chiropractic
Davenport, Iowa

Dominick Scuderi, DC
Department Chair of Clinics
Clinical Professor
Palmer College of Chiropractic-West
San Jose, Calif

Greg Snow, DC
Clinical Professor
Palmer College of Chiropractic-West
San Jose, Calif

William Updike, DC
Clinical Professor
Palmer College of Chiropractic-West
San Jose, Calif

Matt E. Williams, BA, MEd, DC
Department Chair of Clinical Sciences
Life Chiropractic College
Marietta, Ga

Introduction

The role of chiropractors is distinctly different from that of medical doctors and yet similar in other ways. On the one hand we are considered specialists in spinal pain, and yet patients present with a wide variety of complaints in the hopes that chiropractic may be an alternative approach to care. This is a rather unique position. For example, a podiatrist is considered an expert in foot and lower leg disorders; however, it is unlikely that a patient would complain to the podiatrist of headache or dizziness and expect an evaluation and treatment of the complaint. In a chiropractic office, this is a rather common occurrence. Another unique aspect of chiropractic is its self-imposed restriction of management without prescription of drugs. Chiropractors are forced to be resourceful in the management of, in particular, painful conditions. Chiropractic focuses concerns on prevention through a healthy lifestyle as opposed to dependency on drug management. Realistically, this is not always possible; however, this unique perspective places chiropractors in a position of acting as healthy lifestyle advocates.

What seems to separate the student from the doctor is not so much an academic knowledge base but more the ability to have a plan of action for any given patient. What seems to strike the student is the clinician's ability to dive into an organized, directed history, sometimes following a line of questioning that initially does not connect for the student. This ability seems magical; however, it is based both on experience and a sense of the common conditions that cause a given complaint. With this knowledge, the doctor is able to search for clues and then follow a path laid out by the answers. With pain questioning is directed first by a distinction between traumatic and nontraumatic onset. With a nontraumatic onset, the distinction between overuse and insidious onset is then followed. In examining regional complaints, a knowledge of what is anatomically present in a given area helps narrow the possibilities. Examination of regions is then performed by challenging each structure in an effort to elicit pain, numbness/tingling, instability, or weakness. With more functional complaints, it is important to understand the physiologic basis of normal function in an attempt to understand what processes can interfere with function and how they might manifest clinically.

We would all like a cookbook approach that works for all patients. Given that this is not possible, an acceptable compromise would be a plan or set of markers to help direct us through the process of approaching a patient's complaint(s). This text is an attempt to provide that path. It can serve, however, only to guide the reader. No text can provide what can only be provided by experience. Experiential learning crossmatches and integrates many previously disconnected aspects of a doctor's database so that the memory is far more indelible than simply memorizing or path following. It is also difficult to mirror the dynamic, interactive process of history taking. This is due to the contingency approach that is an inherent part of the interview process. What you ask next is dependent on the previous response. This cannot be mimicked by a linear, memorized history approach. Algorithms can assist. If the answer is yes or no to a given history or examination component, the clinician proceeds down a different path.

A significant portion of this text is devoted to algorithms. Algorithms are simply road maps. The fear engendered by first view of algorithms is often with the belief that the entire algorithm must be read or memorized. This would be analogous to looking at a city street map and feeling that to be useful, the entire map must be read or memorized. Algorithms are based on what is crucial for referral purposes and what is considered common or important with any given complaint. An algorithm is therefore analogous to a road map in that you simply want to follow a path to a destination. By taking any given patient complaint and adding information (either history or examination), the path should be rather short and clear. Algorithms also serve as an important learning tool for the developer and reviewers. Although algorithms cannot fully cover all conditions and all patient presentations, they set the tone for an approach. That is all they are, an approach.

This text is formatted to present material in a redundant fashion. The redundancy may not be readily apparent because the presentation is from three perspectives: (1) a text discussion, (2) algorithms, and (3) a brief discussion of related conditions. Each section is approached first from a context point of view. This is followed by a plan, the general strategy section. Following the general strategy section is a brief discussion of the relevant anatomy, physiology, and/or biomechanics of a given area or complaint. Next a more detailed discussion of history and examination clues is given in the evaluation sections. Musculoskeletal complaints are divided into regions. For the extremities sections I felt it was important to address one of the most important clues, location. Each section has accompanying photographs of the region with a table correlating areas of pain or tenderness to specific conditions. The conditions are divided into those having a traumatic onset and those having an insidious/overuse onset. For all sections I felt it was important to provide a basic line of questioning with regard to a given complaint. Although these tables cannot mimic the interaction of real history taking, they are intended as a resource for area- or complaint-specific questions. Finally, management issues with regard to a chiropractor's role are presented. Much of this area is uncharted territory. There are some areas where literature support is available; however, many conditions are not reported in the literature, or the most that can be found are case reports. It is hoped that, by recognizing the lack of literature support for management of a given condition, chiropractors will be more interested in joining in the process of either case presentations or larger research studies to help better define chiropractic's role in the management of a given condition.

Some would argue that a little knowledge is a dangerous thing. I would argue that if that "little" knowledge contained the most common and most serious ambulatory conditions without the confusion of the other hundred possibilities, the danger is minimized. If anything, it could be argued that an attempt at too much knowledge without the ability to apply it is likely more dangerous.

It is my hope that this text will provide the groundwork for developing an approach to many patient complaints. The detail lost by such an approach can always be supplemented by other more specialized texts.

Thomas A. Souza, DC, DACBSP

PART I

Musculoskeletal Complaints

Chapter 1

General Approach to Musculoskeletal Complaints

CONTEXT

The approach to a patient's musculoskeletal complaint is a standardized, often sequential, search for what can and what cannot be managed by the examining doctor. There is always an ultimate decision: rule in or rule out referable conditions.

- The ultimate decision with acute traumatic pain is to rule out fracture (and its complications such as neural or vascular damage), dislocation, and gross instability.
- The ultimate decision with nontraumatic pain is to rule out tumors, inflammatory arthritides, infections, or visceral referral.

There appears to be a misinterpretation regarding the amount of information necessary to make diagnostic or management decisions. One error is to think of all joints as distinctly different because the names of structures, disorders, or orthopaedic tests are different for each joint. Another error is to make the assumption that the joint operates as an independent contractor without accountability to other joints. The first error leads to an overspecialization effort that often leaves the doctor unwilling to attack the vast amount of individual information for each joint. The second error leads the examiner to an approach that excludes important information that may contribute to the diagnosis of a patient's complaint. Each is an error in extremes: the first is that too much knowledge is assumed necessary; the second assumes that too little baseline information is needed for making diagnostic and treatment decisions.

A general approach to evaluation of any joint (and surrounding structures) utilizes the perspective that a joint is a joint. Although a specific joint may function differently because of its bony configuration, structurally, it is composed generally of the same tissues. All joints regions have bone, ligaments, a capsule, cartilage and synovium, surrounding tendons and muscles, associated bursae, blood vessels, nerves, fat, and skin. All of these structures may be injured by compression or stretch. Compression may lead to fracture in bones or neural dysfunction in nerves. Stretch leads to varying degrees of tendon/muscle, ligament/capsule, neural/vascular, or bone/epiphyseal damage ranging from minor disruption to full rupture. Joints can be further divided into weight bearing and non–weight bearing. Non–weight-bearing joints may be transformed into weight-bearing joints through various positions such as handstands or falls with the upper extremity, hyperextension of the spine, or any axial compression force to the joint. Weight-bearing joints are generally more susceptible to chronic degeneration and osteoarthritis.

Bones and joints are also susceptible to nonmechanical processes that involve seeding of infection or cancer as well as the development of primary cancer and the immunologically based rheumatoid and connective tissue disorders. Clues to rheumatoid and seronegative arthritides include a pattern of involvement with a specific predilection to a joint or groups of joints coupled with laboratory investigation.

The approach to evaluation of a neuromusculoskeletal complaint is also directed by a knowledge of common conditions affecting specific structures (regardless of the specific names). Following is a list of these structures and the disorders or conditions most often encountered with each:

- bone
  - —tumor—primary or metastatic
  - —osteochondrosis/apophysitis
  - —fracture

— osteopenia (osteoporosis)
— osteomyelitis

- soft tissue
  1. muscle
     - strain or rupture
     - trigger points
     - atrophy
     - myositic ossificans
     - muscular dystrophy
     - rhabdomyositis
  2. tendon
     - tendinitis
     - tendinosis
     - tenosynovitis
     - rupture
  3. ligament
     - sprain or rupture
  4. bursa
     - bursitis
  5. fascia
     - myofascitis
- joint
  — arthritis
  — subluxation/fixation (chiropractic)
  — synovitis
  — infection
  — joint mice
  — dislocation/subluxation (medical)

GENERAL STRATEGY

History

Clarify the onset.

- Is the complaint traumatic?
- Is there a history of overuse?
- Is the onset insidious?

Clarify the type of complaint.

- Is the complaint one of pain, numbness or tingling, stiffness, looseness, crepitus, locking, or a combination of complaints?
- Localize the complaint to anterior, posterior, medial, or lateral if applicable.

Clarify the mechanism if traumatic (for extremities see Table 1–1).

Table 1–1 Joint-Specific Injury Mechanism

Mechanism	*Possible Structure(s) Damaged*
Shoulder	
Fall on an outstretched arm (extended elbow)	Rotator cuff tear Glenoid labrum tear Posterior dislocation Clavicular fracture
Arm forced into abduction/external rotation	Anterior dislocation Anterior musculature strain
Blow to the shoulder area	Fracture Acromioclavicular separation Dislocation
Fall onto top of shoulder	Shoulder pointer Acromioclavicular separation Distal calvicular fracture
Traction injury to arm	Plexus injury Medical subluxation
Elbow	
Direct fall on tip of elbow or fall on hand with elbow flexed	Olecranon fracture
Fall on hand with extended elbow	Radial head fracture
Hyperextension injury to elbow	Elbow dislocation Supracondylar fracture in children

continues

Table 1–1 continued

Mechanism	*Possible Structure(s) Damaged*
Elbow continued	
Severe valgus stress	Capitellum fracture Avulsion of medial epicondyle Medial collateral ligament sprain or rupture
Sudden traction of forearm	Radial head subluxation
Wrist/hand	
Fall on dorsiflexed hand	Navicular fracture Epiphyseal and torus fractures in children Carpal dislocation, or instability
Hyperextension or abduction of thumb	Gamekeeper's thumb (ulnar collateral ligament damage)
Axial compression of thumb	Bennett's fracture Dislocation
Hyperextension of finger	Volar plate injury Jersey finger (rupture of flexor digitorum profundus) Dislocation
Hyperflexion of finger	Avulsion of central slip Mallet finger (rupture of extensor tendon)
Valgus/varus stress injury to finger	Collateral ligament or volar plate injury
Axial compression	Capsular irritation Fracture
Hip	
Fall on hip	Fracture Synovitis Hip pointer Trochanteric bursitis
Blow to flexed, adducted hip	Posterior dislocation
Knee	
Hyperextension	Anterior cruciate ligament tear
Sudden deceleration	Anterior cruciate ligament tear
Blow to a flexed knee at proximal tibia	Posterior cruciate ligament tear
Blow to anterior knee/patella	Irritation of plica Patellar fracture Bursitis Infrapatellar fat pad irritation
Valgus force	Medial collateral ligament tear Pes anserine strain
Rotational injury with foot fixed on ground	Meniscus
Rotational injury with a valgus force	Anterior cruciate ligament, meniscus, medial collateral ligament
Foot/ankle	
Plantarflexion, inversion of ankle	Ankle sprain with possible associated bifurcate ligament damage, fracture, or peroneal tendon snapping from torn retinaculum
Eversion injury to ankle	Deltoid ligament sprain or rupture Fracture Dislocation
Hyperextension of great toe	Turf-toe injury to capsular ligaments
Landing on heels	Fat pad irritation Ankle or tibial fracture

- If there was a fall onto a specific region or structure within that region consider fracture, dislocation, or contusion.
- Determine whether there was an excessive valgus or varus force, internal or external rotation, or flexion or extension. Consider ligament/capsule or muscle/tendon.
- If there was sudden axial traction to the joint consider sprain or subluxation.
- If there was axial compression to the joint consider fracture or synovitis.

Determine whether the mechanism is one of overuse.

- In what position does the patient work?
- Does the patient perform a repetitive movement at work or during sports activities? Consider muscle strain, tendinitis, trigger points, or peripheral nerve entrapment.

Determine whether the patient has a current or past history or diagnosis of his or her complaint or other related disorders.

- Are there associated spinal complaints or radiation from the spine? Consider subluxation, nerve root entrapment, or compression.
- Does the patient have a diagnosis of another arthritide, systemic disorder such as diabetes, or past history of cancer?
- Does the patient have "visceral" complaints such as abdominal or chest pain, fever, weight loss, or other complaints?

Evaluation

- With trauma, palpate for points of tenderness and test for neurovascular status distal to the site of injury; obtain plain films to rule out the possibility of fracture/dislocation.
- Palpate and challenge the ligaments and capsule of the joint.
- Challenge the musculotendinous attachments with stretch, contraction, and a combination of contraction in a stretched position.
- Measure the functional capacities of the region involved; determine any associated biomechanical faults that may be contributing to the problem.

Management

- Refer fracture/dislocation, infection, and tumors for orthopaedic management.
- Refer or comanage rheumatoid and connective tissue disorders.
- If the problem is one of instability without ligament rupture, stabilize the joint through an appropriate exercise program using a brace initially if necessary to assist.
- If the problem is weakness, strengthen the associated muscle.
- Functionally retrain the individual for a return to daily activities and occupational or sport requirements.
- Use manipulation/mobilization for articular dysfunction.

HISTORY

A mnemonic approach to patient's complaints may be helpful in organizing the vast number of possibilities. Beginning with a description of the patient's complaint, a list of common causes may be attached. WIRS Pain is a mneumonic for weakness, instability, restricted movement, surface complaints, and pain.

Weakness

Weakness may be due to pain inhibition, muscle strain, or neurologic interruption at the myoneural junction, peripheral nerve, nerve root, or spinal cord and above. Weakness may be a misinterpretation by the patient when instability or a "loose" joint is present or the patient has stiffness that must be overcome by increased muscular activity.

Instability

Instability is due to either traumatic damage to ligamentous or muscular support or due to the inherent looseness found in some individual's joints. This inherent looseness is usually global and can be identified in other joints or acquired as a result of repetitive overstretch positioning. Instability is most apparent when the joint is positioned so that muscles have less mechanical advantage (eg, overhead shoulder positions) or a quick movement demand is faster than the reaction time for the corresponding muscles (cutting or rotating knee movements).

Restricted Movement

Restricted movement may be due to pain, muscle spasm, stretching of soft tissue contracture, or mechanical blockage by osteophytes, joint mice, fracture, or effusion.

Surface Complaints

Superficial complaints include skin lesions, cuts/abrasions, swellings, and a patient's subjective sense of numbness or paresthesias.

Pain

Pain is nonspecific; however, the cause usually will be revealed by combining a history of trauma, overuse, or insidious onset with associated complaints and significant examination findings. It is important to determine local pain versus referred pain. Following are some guidelines:

- Referred pain from sclerotogenous sources: Sclerotogenous pain presents as a nondermatomal pattern with no other hard neurologic findings such as significant decrease in myotomal strength or deep tendon reflex changes. Although the term is used broadly, here we are referring mainly to facet-generated pain.
- Referred pain from visceral sources: In most cases a historical screening of patients will reveal primary or secondary visceral complaints. It is important to know the classic referral zones, such as scapular/shoulder pain with cholelithiasis and medial arm pain with cardiac ischemia.
- Bone pain: Bone pain is deep pain, commonly worse in the evening. Trauma may indicate an underlying fracture requiring radiographic evaluation. An overuse history may be suggestive of a stress fracture requiring a radiographic evaluation. If results of the radiograph are negative, but a stress fracture is still suspected, a bone scan is warranted.

A careful history will usually indicate the diagnosis or, at the very least, narrow down the possibilities to two or three. Physical examination and imaging studies more often are used as a confirmation of one's suspicion(s). Generalizing a history approach allows the doctor to address any complaint regardless of region. Generally speaking, damage to structures locally is due to (1) exceeding the tensile stress of ligaments, capsule, muscles, and tendons; (2) compression of bone; (3) demineralization of bone; or (4) intrinsic destructive processes involving arthritides (eg, pannus formation with rheumatoid arthritis (RA), crystal deposition with gout or pseudogout), infections, or cancer. Although the first two categories are almost always the result of trauma or overuse, the latter two are more commonly insidious. Traumatic and overuse disorders are classically local with regard to signs and symptoms, whereas arthritides and cancer are often either generalized or stereotypical based on the type.

Suspicion of specific structures is based on a basic knowledge of what causes damage to any similar structure regardless of which region or joint is involved. Ligament or capsular injury is often the result of excessive force on the opposite side of the ligament/capsule. For example, a valgus stress (outside to inside force) to the knee will cause an injury to the medial collateral ligament; a varus force, the lateral collateral ligament. Although more dramatically evident in an acute injury, it must be remembered that low-level, chronic stresses are often the cause of ligamentous or capsular sprain. Muscle injury can be divided into stretch injury and contraction injury. Often when ligaments are damaged, muscle/tendon groups are also involved. Muscle/tendons often act as static stabilizers simply because when they cross the joint they are in the way when outside forces stretch a joint. Additionally, muscles will often contract in an attempt to protect the joint and either incur damage or impose more damage to the joint. This occurs especially when a joint is in extension (such as the knee and elbow) or in neutral (such as the wrist and ankle). Contraction injury is divided into concentric and eccentric. Usually an overexertion problem, concentric injury often occurs when too heavy a weight is lifted or a sudden explosive muscle activity is required. Concentric injury occurs as the muscle is shortening. Eccentric injury occurs while the muscle is lengthening. Although eccentric injury may occur with lifting, this pattern is frequently seen with overuse or repetitive activity and/or injuries that challenge the decelerator or stabilizer role of the muscle.

Bursae are protective cushions placed strategically at points of friction, particularly between muscle/tendon and bone. Although there are standard bursae in most individuals, adventitious bursae may develop at sites of repetitive friction in individuals performing specific activities. Bursae may be deep or superficial. Superficial bursae are susceptible to direct traumatic forces. Deep bursae are more susceptible to compression by bone or soft tissue structures. Compression is often position specific such as during overhead movements with the shoulder. Bursitis may be secondary to other soft tissue involvement such as calcific tendinitis.

When musculoskeletal pain does not have an obvious mechanical or traumatic cause, a search is initiated for myofascial disorders, arthritides, psychologic factors, connective tissue disorders, cancer, and infection. A general historical clue approach to each is presented.

- Arthritis: Arthritis is characterized by whether inflammatory processes such as RA seronegatives (Reiter's syndrome, ankylosing spondylitis, or psoriasis) or crystalline deposits (gout) or noninflammatory processes such as osteoarthritis (OA) are present; generally RA is associated with early-morning swelling and stiffness that takes 1 hour or more to resolve, whereas OA causes an early-morning stiffness that improves with 30 minutes of activity. Each has a characteristic pattern of joint involvement.

EXAMINATION

Acute Traumatic Injury

An approach to acute injury evaluation initially focuses on neurovascular status distal to and local to the injury site. These neurovascular injuries often are secondary to fracture. Motor assessments with active and active resisted attempts evaluate both muscle and neural integrity. Sensory testing incorporates the use of a pin in an attempt to test pain perception and a paper clip for testing two-point discrimination in the fingers. Palpation of pulses is useful in determining major vascular injury. Although these tests are more applicable to extremity injury, injury to the spine requires the same diligent search for an intact neurovascular system. With these conditions reasonably eliminated, the specific sequence one uses is less important than that the approach is comprehensive.

General Approach

However complex the orthopaedic evaluation may become, the basics remain the same regardless of which joints and/or surrounding structures are involved (Table 1–2). Generally, orthopaedic testing attempts to (1) reproduce a patient's complaint (ie, elicit pain, provoke numbness/tingling, or reproduce popping or clicking); (2) reveal laxity; (3) demonstrate weakness; or (4) demonstrate restriction (orthopaedic evaluation, in the context of a chiropractor, also includes accessory motion evaluation at a joint). The possible caveats to these attempts are that pain may be due to many factors and is therefore nonspecific (localization and injury pattern help better define); laxity may be normal for an individual (especially if bilateral) or pathologic; weakness may be due to reflex inhibition caused by pain (relatively nonspecific), laxity, muscle injury, or neurologic damage; and restriction to movement may be due to soft tissue or bony blockage.

The mechanics of orthopaedic tests have similarities regardless of any assigned name. Testing involves one of three approaches: (1) stretch, (2) compress, or (3) contract. When performing a named orthopaedic test, reflection on what is the intended use coupled with the understanding of what other structures may be challenged is imperative to appreciate and interpret fully the variety of patient responses possible. Although a test is designed to stretch a ligament, also stretched are muscles, tendons, and nerves. The same maneuver may elicit a positive response through compression of tissues. For example, a valgus force stretches the medial knee, yet compresses the lateral knee. Although not the intended response, any pain response to a maneuver may provide important information if simple biomechanics are kept in mind.

Another general principle is that similar structures are tested similarly (Table 1–3).

Table 1–2 Selective Tension Approach

Condition	Active ROM	Passive ROM	Resisted Movement	Key Points
Arthritis/capsulitis	Painful at limit of range	Painful at limit of range	Usually painless within range of motion	Often specific capsular pattern of 1 or 2 restricted movement patterns
Tendinitis	Variable	Pain on stretch	Painful, especially if contracted in stretched position	Insertion of tendon is often tender or slightly proximal to insertion
Tendon rupture	None	Full; painless	Weak; painless	Note displaced muscle belly
Ligament sprain	Decreased; limited by pain	Pain on stability challenge	Painless if full rupture, painful if partial	Overpressure laxity may indicate degree of damage
Muscle strain	Painful often midrange	Passive stretch may increase pain	If resistance is sufficient pain is produced	Check with resistance throughout full range of movement
Intraarticular body	Sudden onset of pain in a specific range of motion	Sudden onset of pain in a specific range of motion is also possible	Usually painless	An "arc" of pain with a "catching" or blockage is highly suggestive
Acute bursitis (deep)	Painful in most directions	Empty end-feel is often present	Isometric testing is often painful	Positional relief is less common than with muscle/tendon injury

- Ligaments/capsules—Use direct palpation (if possible) and perform a stress test that usually involves stabilizing one bone while moving the neighboring bone on it (for example, drawer testing of the shoulder, knee, and ankle). In essence, motion palpation of a joint is the same as many ligament stability tests, yet the intent is different; locate restrictions, not instability.
- Tendons—Use direct palpation and stretch into end-range (contraction at end-range stretch may also be used).
- Muscles—Use direct palpation and contraction (although traditionally used to detect weakness, the main focus is to determine reproduction of a patient's complaint).
- Nerves—Tapping (ie, Tinsel's) and compression are direct tests for superficial nerves; indirect tests include motor and sensory evaluation of specific peripheral nerves, nerve plexus, nerve root, or central nervous system (CNS) involvement including muscle tests, deep tendon reflex testing, and sensory testing with a pin/brush or pinwheel.

Palpation is a valuable tool when accessing superficial tissues. Accessibility is limited, based on the joint and its location. The fingers and toes are thin accessible structures, whereas the hip and shoulder are not. Direct palpation of ligaments and tendons may reveal tenderness. Muscles may also be palpated for tenderness and possible associated referred patterns of pain. These trigger points have been mapped by Travell and Simons.[1] Their work serves as a road map for investigation.

The reliability of soft tissue palpation has been evaluated for the spine and the extremities. In general, it is evident that soft tissue palpation findings are not as reliable as bony palpation among examiners. When specific sites in the extremities are exposed through specific positioning, however, the reliability may increase.[2]

Although orthopaedic testing is the standard for orthopaedists, more involved investigations are usually added by the chiropractor and/or manual therapist. The first is based on the work of Cyriax,[3] which emphasizes the "feel" of soft tissue palpation, especially at end-range. Combined with this end-range determination, a selective tension approach is incorporated using the responses to active, active resisted, and passive movements to differentiate between contractile (muscle/tendon) and noncontractile (ligament/capsule and bursa) tissue. Another approach is to challenge specifically each joint to determine fixation or hypermobility. Finally, a functional approach to movement as proposed by Janda and Lewit[4,5] is often used. This approach addresses the quality of movement and the "postural" tendencies toward imbalance of strength and flexibility of muscles.

Selective Tension Approach

Cyriax[3] divided the quality of passive end-range at a joint into normal and abnormal. Some normal end-feels include the following:

- Soft tissue approximation—This is a soft end-feel that occurs when a muscle opposes another muscle, for example, when the calf muscles hit the hamstrings or the forearm hits the biceps on flexion.
- Muscular—This is an elastic end-feel that occurs when a muscle is stretched to its end-range. This occurs with straight leg raising with the hamstrings.
- Bone-on-bone or cartilaginous—This occurs when the joint anatomically stops, as occurs with elbow extension.
- Capsular—This occurs with a tight, slightly elastic feel such as occurs with full hip rotation. It is due to the elastic tension that develops in the joint capsule when stretched.

Abnormal end-feels include the following:

- Spasm—When muscle spasm is present, pain will prevent full range of motion.
- Springy block or rebound—This occurs when there is a mechanical blockage such as a torn meniscus in the knee or labrum in the shoulder. The end-range occurs before a full range of motion is attained.
- Empty—This occurs when there is an acute painful process such as a bursitis. The patient prevents movement to end-range.
- Loose—This end-feel is indicative of capsular or ligamentous damage and is in essence the end-feel that is found with a positive ligament stability test.

Probably many examiners sense these different end-range palpation findings; they have not categorized them, however, yet interpret them intuitively.

Some examiners will equate timing of the onset of pain on passive testing with staging of injury as follows:

- Pain felt before end-range is considered an acute process that would obviate the application of vigorous therapy.
- Pain felt at the same time as end-range is indicative of a subacute process and would be amenable to gentle stretching and mobilization.
- Pain felt after end-range is indicative of a chronic process that may respond to aggressive stretching and manipulation.

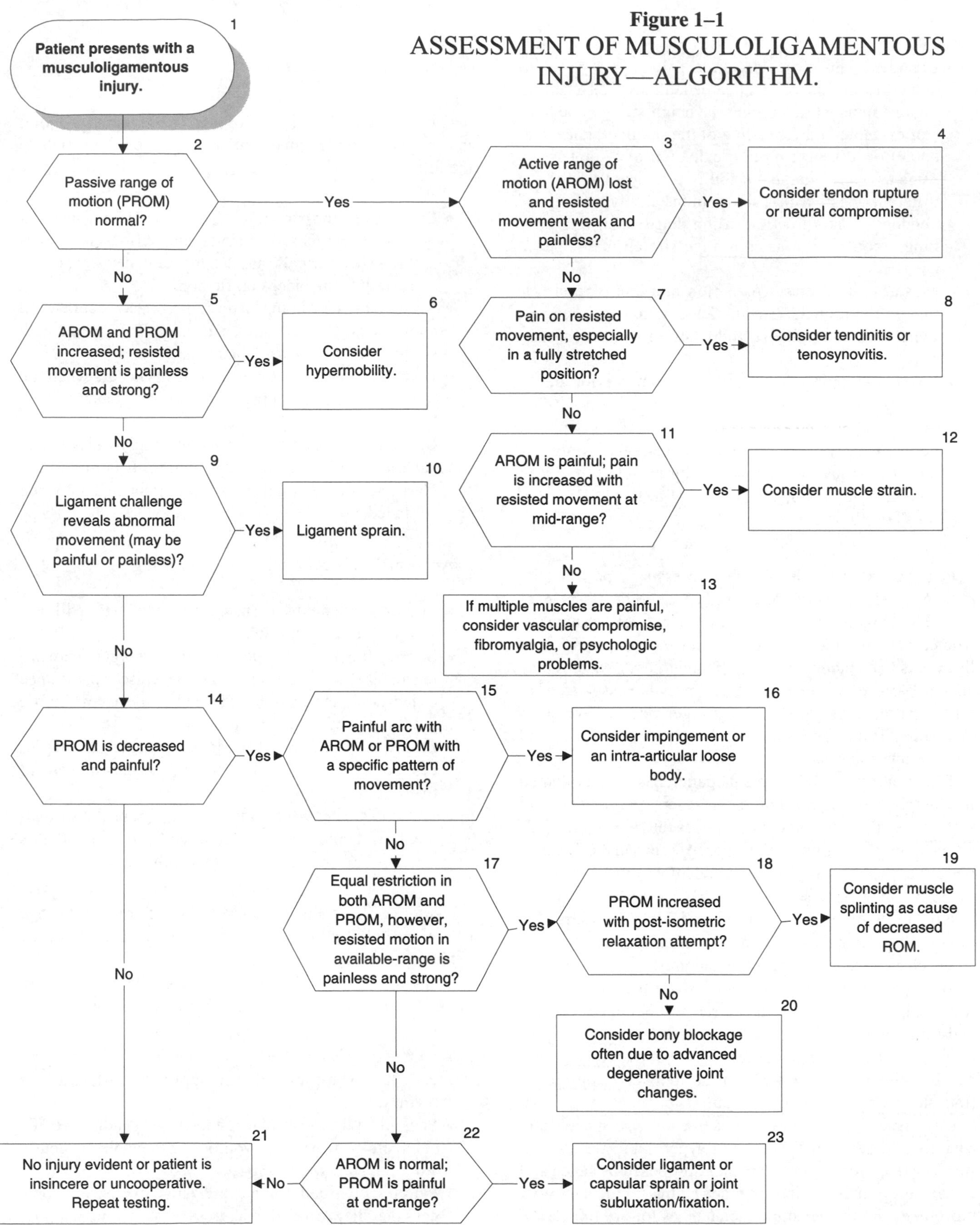

Source: Reprinted from R. Henninger and D.T. Henson, *Topics in Clinical Chiropractic,* Vol. 1, No. 4, p. 77, © 1994, Aspen Publishers, Inc.

By taking the patient through passive range of motion (PROM) and active range of motion (AROM) and testing resisted motion, a clearer idea of contractile versus noncontractile tissue may be appreciated (Figure 1–1 and Table 1–3). It should be evident that contractile tissue may be painful with either stretch or midrange contraction. If both findings are present, they should be present in opposite directions (eg, contraction into flexion hurts anteriorly while passive extension does also). If end-range stretch is not painful but contraction at end-range is, the tendon of the involved muscle is likely involved. If pain is not found with active movement but passive movement into end-range causes pain, noncontractile tissue is probably involved. Active movement should not affect most noncontractile tissue unless it is com-

Table 1–3 General Approach Based on Structure

Structure	*Initial Evaluation*	*Specific Imaging Evaluation*
Bone		
Tumor—primary or metastatic	Radiograph	MRI or CT, bone scan for metastasis (nonspecific)
Osteochondrosis/apophysitis	Local tenderness and radiograph	Possible bone scan
Fracture	Palpation, percussion, tuning fork, radiograph	CT or possibly MRI
Stress fracture	Palpation, percussion, radiograph	Bone scan, SPECT Scan
Osteopenia (osteoporosis)	Radiograph	Dual-photon absorptiometry, quantified CT, dual-energy radiograph
Osteomyelitis	Radiograph	MRI
Soft Tissue		
Muscle		
Strain or rupture	Active resistance	For rupture, sonography, or MRI
Trigger points	Palpation	None
Atrophy	Observation	Electrodiagnostic studies
Myositis ossificans	Palpation, radiograph	CT
Muscular dystrophy	Muscle testing, LDH on lab	Electrodiagnostic studies
Tendon		
Tendinitis	Stretch and contraction	Sonography
Tenosynovitis	Stretch	Sonography or MRI
Rupture	Lack of passive tension effect	Sonography or MRI
Ligament		
Sprain or rupture	Stability testing	MRI
Bursa		
Bursitis	Palpation	MRI or bursography
Fascia		
Myofascitis	Palpation	None
Joint		
Arthritis	Characteristic joint involvement, laboratory findings including rheumatoid factor, HLA-B27, ANA, and radiographic characteristics	CT for bone, MRI for soft tissue involvement
Subluxation/fixation (chiropractic)	Palpation, indirect radiographic findings	CT for facet joints (research only)
Synovitis	Capsular pattern of restriction	MRI
Joint mice	Restricted ROM, radiograph	CT or MRI
Dislocation/subluxation (medical)	Observation and radiograph	CT

Key: MRI, magnetic resonance imaging; CT, computed tomography; LDH, lactate dehydrogenase; HLA, human leukocyte antigen; ANA, antinuclear antibodies; ROM, range of motion; SPECT, single photon emission computed tomography.

pressed. This is more likely to occur at end-range. Cyriax's selective tension approach is a logical attempt to localize the involved tissue, yet until recently it has remained unchallenged. One study demonstrated a high interexaminer reliability using these methods. The interexaminer agreement was 90.5% with a kappa statistic of 0.875.[6]

An extension of the selective tension approach is to determine the effect of mild isometric contractions on restricted range of motion. If a patient provides a mild resistance for several seconds to the agonist and antagonist pattern of restriction (eg, flexion/extension) and repeats this several times followed by an attempt at stretch by the examiner, a distinction between soft tissue or bony blockage to movement may be determined. For example, if a patient presented with a restriction to abduction of the shoulder, repetitive, reciprocal contraction (minimal contraction for 5 to 6 seconds) into abduction and adduction several times will increase the available range if soft tissue is the cause (Exhibit 1–1). Bony blockage from OA, fracture, or a torn labrum will result in little or no increase in motion with the same procedure.

Functional Approach

Traditional muscle evaluation involves a test of muscle strength only. Janda and Lewit[4] and others[7] advocate an approach that takes into account not only the quantity of contraction (strength) but also the quality of movement. There is a recognized natural imbalance in muscle strength. Not all muscles are created equal. It is known that small muscles are often phasic, required to react quickly to changes in the environment, whereas larger muscles are often tonic, posturally assigned. Certain movement patterns are biased. For example, supination is stronger than pronation and internal rotation of the shoulder is stronger than external rotation. This bias is in large part due to the size or number (or both) of muscles used in the movement pattern. Strength is also positionally dependent. Certain positions place at a disadvantage some muscles of a synergistic group.

There is another perspective with regard to muscle weakness and tightness that may affect evaluation and eventually management. An observation by Janda and Lewit[4] is that there are crossed and layered patterns of weakness and tightness. For example, in the low back it is not uncommon to find a pattern of anterior weakness in the abdominal muscles associated with posterior tightness of the erector spinae (sagittal pattern). A vertical pattern is illustrated by the association of the tight erector spinae's being sandwiched between weak gluteal muscles inferiorly and weak lower trapezius muscles superiorly. These two planes create a "crossed" pattern whereby tightness of the erector spinae is associated with tightness of the iliopsoas, and weakness of the abdominal muscles is associated with weakness of the gluteal muscles.

Exhibit 1–1 Postisometric Relaxation, PNF Hold and Relax, and PNF Contract and Relax

Postisometric Relaxation

- Stretch the affected muscle to patient tolerance.
- Maintain the stretch position while the patient isometrically contracts the muscle for 6 to 10 seconds at a 25% effort against doctor's resistance.
- Instruct the patient to relax fully (taking in a deep breath and letting it out may help).
- Attempt a further stretch of the muscle with the patient relaxed.
- Repeat this procedure five or six times or until no further stretch seems possible (whichever comes first).

PNF Hold-Relax

- This technique is very similar to a postisometric relaxation approach; however, classically the patient attempts a maximum contraction of either the agonist or antagonist.
- Caution must be used with maximal contractions. The author prefers to start with a postisometric approach using a 25% contraction before proceeding to more forceful resistance.

PNF Contract-Relax

- This is a full isotonic contraction followed by a stretch into a new position.
- There are several variations of this technique. A popular one is called CRAC (contract-relax-antagonist-contract).

This pattern is relatively consistent throughout the body and is a reflection of two concepts: (1) muscles that function to resist the effects of gravity (postural muscles) have a tendency to become tight in sedentary people, and (2) muscles that function more dynamically are underused and become weak and prone to injury. Additionally, muscles that cross more than one joint are prone toward tightness (Exhibit 1–1). For example, the rectus femoris, which crosses the hip and knee, is prone toward tightness, whereas the medialis obliquus, which does not cross a joint and is primarily a "dynamic" muscle, is often weak.

With the above concepts in mind, Lewit and Janda have focused on an observation of quality of movement with an emphasis on the timing and recruitment during a movement pattern. Often these two concepts overlap when the timing of the movement is a reflection of recruitment. For example, hip extension in a lying position requires a timing of contraction beginning with the hamstrings. This is followed by gluteal contraction, then erector spinae contraction. If the hamstrings or gluteals do not participate, the erector spinae contract, causing a weak contraction and a lordotic/compressive load to the low back. In the neck, flexion may reveal an imbalance in movement. If the patient's jaw juts forward at the beginning of the pattern, weak neck flexors with associated "strong" sternocleidomastoids are indicated.

Accessory Motion

One of the indicators for manipulation or adjusting is blockage of accessory motion.[8] Accessory motion is that subtle amount of bone-on-bone movement that is not under voluntary control. For example, although the humerus moves on the glenoid during abduction, there is a degree of movement measured in millimeters that is necessary yet not under the control of the shoulder abductor muscles. Determining whether accessory motion is available involves placing the joint in a specific position and attempting passively to move one bone on another. If the end-feel is springy, then joint play is available. If there is a perceived restriction, however, movement at the joint may be restricted. It is important to distinguish between the end-range descriptions of Cyriax[3] and the end-feel of accessory motion. Cyriax is referring to the end-range of an extremity or spinal movement such as flexion, extension, abduction, or adduction. Accessory motion is palpated at the joint both with the joint in a neutral or open-packed position and also with a coupled movement pattern taken to end-range actively and passively. The joint would not be restricted by the tension of the capsule or muscle with the neutral position method. The active and passive techniques take advantage of the end-range position to determine whether the accompanying accessory motion is, in fact, occurring. There are specific guidelines for both assessment and application of treatment to accessory motion barriers.

Specific patterns of extremity and spinal movement are coupled with specific accessory motion so that restrictions in active movement may be indirectly an indicator of dysfunction of the accompanying accessory motion.[9]

Radiography and Special Imaging

When making choices regarding the need for radiographs or special imaging, it is important to keep one major question in mind: Is there a reasonably high expectation that the information provided by the study will dictate or alter the type of treatment or dictate whether medical referral is needed? If the answer is no, it is important to delay ordering expensive, unnecessary studies at that given time. As time passes, the answer to the question may change. Some secondary issues with regard to further testing are as follows:

- What are the risks to the patient?
- What is the cost? Are there less expensive methods of arriving at the same diagnosis?
- What are the legal ramifications if the study or studies are or are not performed?

The decision for the use of radiographs is based on relative risk. Patients often can be categorized into high- and low-risk groups by combining history and examination data. Many groups have developed similar standards for absolute or relative indications for the need for radiographs.[10–12] Generally, for patients with joint pain, the following are some suggested indicators:

- significant trauma
- suspicion of cancer (unexplained weight loss, prior history of cancer, patients over age 50 years)
- suspicion of infection (fever of unknown origin above 100°F and/or chills, use of intravenous drugs, recent urinary tract infection)
- chronic corticosteroid use
- drug or alcohol abuse
- neuromotor deficits
- scoliosis
- history of surgery to the involved region
- laboratory indicators such as significantly elevated erythrocyte sedimentation rate, alkaline phosphatase, positive rheumatoid factor, monoclonal spiking on electrophoresis
- dermopathy suggestive of psoriasis, Reiter's syndrome, melanoma, and the like
- lymphadenopathy
- patients unresponsive to 1 month of conservative care
- medicolegal requirements or concerns

Choice of imaging is based on the sensitivity and specificity of a given imaging tool, the cost, and the availability (see Table 1–3). In general:

- Radiography is a good screening tool. Signs of many conditions, including cancer, fracture, infection, osteoporosis, and degeneration, often are visible. The degree of sensitivity is quite low with early disease, however.
- Magnetic resonance imaging (MRI) is extremely valuable in evaluating soft tissue such as tendons, ligaments, and discs. In evaluating the volume of tumor or infection involvement, MRI is also valuable. Spinal cord processes such as multiple sclerosis or syringomyelia are well visualized on MRI (Table 1–4).
- When attempting further to clarify the degree of bony spinal stenosis, the extent of fracture, or other bony processes, computed tomography (CT) is often a sensitive

Table 1–4 Magnetic Resonance Imaging for the Chiropractor

MRI Better Than CT	*MRI Equal to CT*	*CT Better Than MRI*
MRI of the Head		
Severe headaches	Hydrocephalus	Fracture of the calvaria
Visual disturbance	Brain atrophy	Fracture of the skull base
Sensory-neural hearing loss		Cholesteatoma of inner ear
Primary brain tumor		Intracranial hemorrhage 1–3 days old
Metastatic brain tumor		Cerebral infarction 1–3 days old
Intracranial infection		Intracranial calcifications
Age-related CNS disease		
Multiple sclerosis		
Dementia		
Chronic subdural hematoma		
Posttraumatic evaluation of the brain		
Intracranial hemorrhage older than 3 days		
Cerebral infarction older than 3 days		
MRI of the Cervical and Thoracic Spines		
Tumors or masses at the level of the foramen magnum	Spinal stenosis	Occult fracture of a vertebra
Chiari I malformation		Complex fracture of a vertebra
Cervical or thoracic herniated disc		Bony foraminal encroachment
Posttraumatic syrinx		
Core or conus tumor		
Acquired immunodeficiency syndrome–related myelopathy		
Multiple sclerosis of the spinal cord		
Posttraumatic epidural hematoma		
Epidural metastatic disease		
Epidural abscess		
MRI of the Lumbar Spine		
Small lumbar herniation	Large lumbar herniation	Occult fracture
Foraminal herniation	Spinal stenosis	Hypertrophic bony overgrowth or spurring
Interruption of the posterior longitudinal ligament		Bony foraminal encroachment
Root sleeve compression		Spondylolysis
Postoperative scar versus recurrent lumbar herniation (with gadolinium)		Evaluation of posterior element fusion

continues

Table 1–4 continued

MRI Better Than CT	*MRI Equal to CT*	*CT Better Than MRI*
MRI of the Shoulder		
Posttraumatic bone bruise	Rotator cuff tear	Subtle glenoid labrum tear
Avascular necrosis of humeral head		Evaluation of the glenohumeral ligaments
Impingement syndrome		
Lipoma (or soft tissue mass)		
Tumor		
Brachial plexus tumor		
MRI of the Knee		Evaluation of the meniscus following previous meniscectomy
Posttraumatic bone bruise	Meniscal tear	
Osteochondritis dissecans		Evaluation of the articular cartilage
Anterior cruciate ligament tear		
Posterior cruciate ligament tear		
Collateral ligament tear		
Patellar tendon abnormalities		
Infection		
Tumor		

Courtesy of Murray Solomon, M.D., Redwood City, California.

tool—better than MRI in many cases. Recent cerebrovascular events and some tumors are well visualized with CT.

- When the search is for stress fracture, metastasis to bone, or avascular necrosis, bone scans often provide valuable information.
- When determining the degree of osteoporosis in a patient, dual-photon absorptiometry or dual-energy radiographic absorptiometry is more sensitive than standard radiography.

MANAGEMENT

Conservative management of a musculoskeletal problem is based on several broad principles.

- Initial management involves a greater degree of passive care with a transition into active care dominance over time.
- The goals for patient management vary based on the acuteness of the problem.
- Rehabilitation progresses in a sequence: passive motion to active motion to active resisted motion (begins with isometrics and progresses to isotonics) to functional training.

Although traditionally it was the doctor's role to be active and the patient to be passive with treatment, it is becoming clear that there is a point at which role switching is necessary. When a patient has acute pain, the goal is to reduce the pain and assist healing. Many of the treatment methods used with acute pain employ procedures that are doctor dependent. As the patient progressively improves, there should be a focus on the patient's active participation in restoring normal function. Nelson[13] has outlined some criteria for passive care (Figure 1–2). These include a history of recent trauma, acute condition or flare up, inflammation, or dependency behavior. There are generally four types of care that may overlap, as follows:

1. Care for inflammation might include the traditional approach of protection, rest, ice, and, if appropriate, compression and elevation. Modalities that are available include high-voltage galvanic stimulation, ultrasound, therapeutic heat, contrast baths, and nonsteroidal anti-inflammatory drugs (NSAIDs), or enzyme alternatives.
2. Options for care for pain include manipulation, mobilization, trigger-point therapy, transcutaneous electrical nerve stimulation (TENS), interferential stimulation, ice, cryotherapy, acupuncture, and NSAIDs.
3. Care for hypomobility includes various forms of stretch, manipulation, mobilization, and soft tissue approaches such as myofascial release techniques.
4. Care for hypermobility includes protection with taping, casts, splints, or various braces.

Figure 1–2

PASSIVE CARE MANAGEMENT—ALGORITHM.

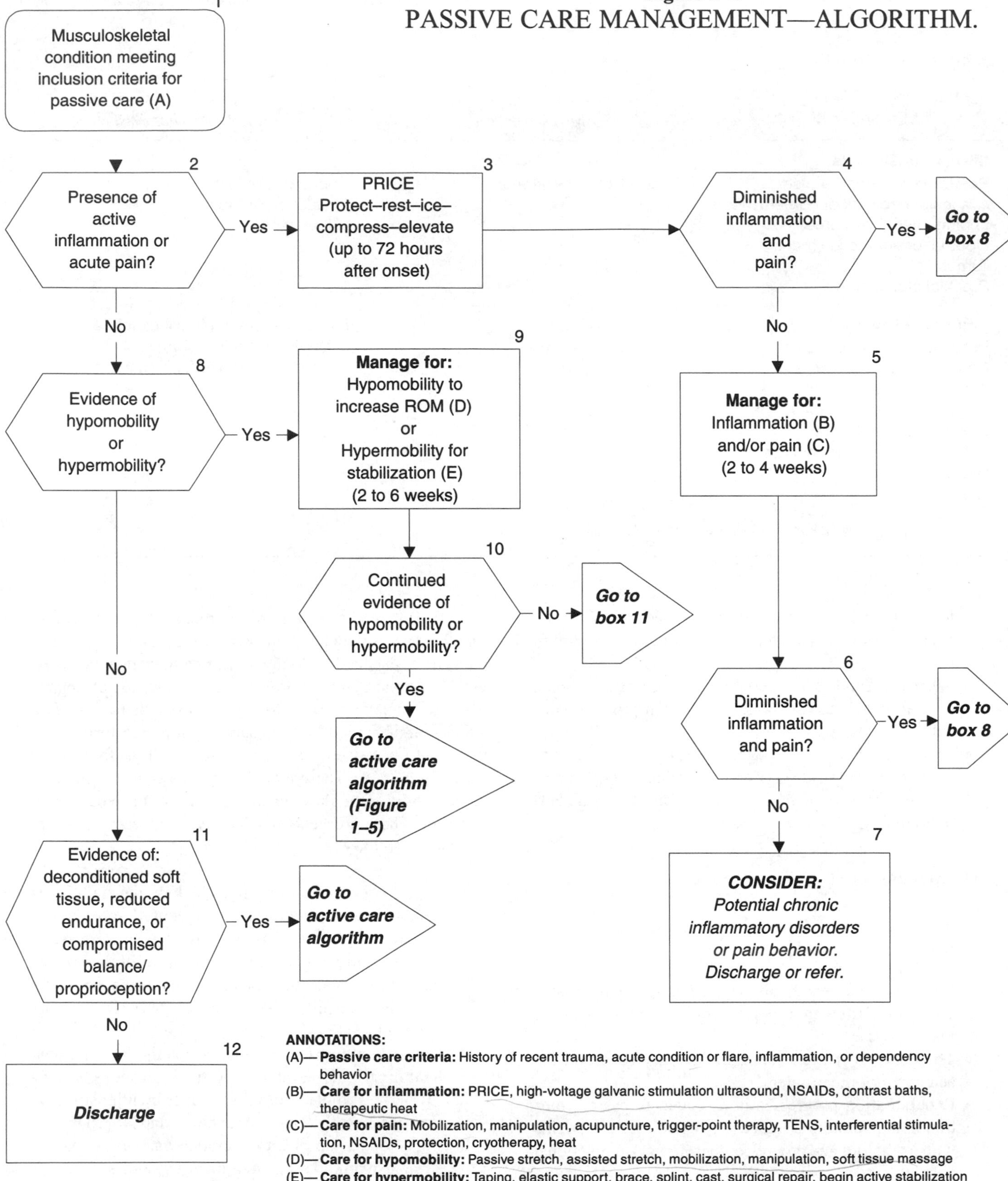

1
Musculoskeletal condition meeting inclusion criteria for passive care (A)
2
Presence of active inflammation or acute pain?
Yes
3
PRICE
Protect–rest–ice–compress–elevate (up to 72 hours after onset)
4
Diminished inflammation and pain?
Yes
Go to box 8
No
5
Manage for:
Inflammation (B) and/or pain (C) (2 to 4 weeks)
6
Diminished inflammation and pain?
Yes
Go to box 8
No
7
CONSIDER:
Potential chronic inflammatory disorders or pain behavior. Discharge or refer.
No
8
Evidence of hypomobility or hypermobility?
Yes
9
Manage for:
Hypomobility to increase ROM (D)
or
Hypermobility for stabilization (E)
(2 to 6 weeks)
10
Continued evidence of hypomobility or hypermobility?
No
Go to box 11
Yes
Go to active care algorithm (Figure 1–5)
No
11
Evidence of: deconditioned soft tissue, reduced endurance, or compromised balance/ proprioception?
Yes
Go to active care algorithm
No
12
Discharge

ANNOTATIONS:

(A)— **Passive care criteria:** History of recent trauma, acute condition or flare, inflammation, or dependency behavior

(B)— **Care for inflammation:** PRICE, high-voltage galvanic stimulation ultrasound, NSAIDs, contrast baths, therapeutic heat

(C)— **Care for pain:** Mobilization, manipulation, acupuncture, trigger-point therapy, TENS, interferential stimulation, NSAIDs, protection, cryotherapy, heat

(D)— **Care for hypomobility:** Passive stretch, assisted stretch, mobilization, manipulation, soft tissue massage

(E)— **Care for hypermobility:** Taping, elastic support, brace, splint, cast, surgical repair, begin active stabilization

Source: Reprinted from D.L. Nelson, *Topics in Clinical Chiropractic,* Vol. 1, No. 4, p. 75, © 1994, Aspen Publishers, Inc.

Exhibit 1–2 Rhythmic Stabilization

A variation of hold-relax, this technique uses a reciprocal contraction of the agonist and antagonist following the approach outlined below:

- Stretch the involved muscle to patient tolerance.
- Use a physician's contact on both sides of a joint.
- Ask the patient to contract with a 25% contraction in the direction of agonist contraction for 5 to 8 seconds.
- Without resting, ask the patient to contract into the opposite direction for 5 to 8 seconds.
- Repeat this procedure five or six times.
- Ask the patient to relax.
- Stretch into new position.
- Repeat the above five or six times or until no more stretch appears available (whichever comes first).

Exhibit 1–3 Cross-Friction Massage and Spray and Stretch

Cross-Friction Massage

Cross-friction massage is a technique popularized by Cyriax.[3] The rationale behind its use is somewhat dependent on the patient's presenting phase of injury. For example, in subacute injury the intent is to align collagen for stronger scar formation. With chronic conditions the cross-friction approach is used to break up adhesions and increase blood supply. A secondary effect of cross-friction massage is a pressure anesthesia, which occurs after a couple of minutes of application. There are several suggestions for the proper use of cross-friction massage:

- It appears to be most effective with tendon and ligaments.
- The tendon or ligament should be placed under slight tension (by stretching the involved structure) while cross-friction is performed.
- The contact is skin on skin with no lotion.
- The pressure is applied as a transverse motion (90° to the involved structure).
- Monitoring the patient every 2 minutes for a total of 6 to 9 minutes is recommended.
- Prior to application, some practitioners recommend ice; others recommend moist heat for approximately 5 minutes.
- Treatment is given every other day for 1 to 2 weeks (up to 4 weeks maximum).

Spray (Cold) and Stretch

Although the technique of using fluoromethane spray for stretching muscles was popularized by Travell and Simons,[1] concerns over damage to the ozone layer and increasing unavailability of the spray has led to a return to the use of ice. With the use of either tool, the technique of applications has several common protocol components:

- The muscle being stretched is placed in a position of mild to moderate stretch. Maintain this stretch while applying the cold stimulus.
- The cold simulus is applied in a series of linear strokes to the skin overlying the muscle and its associated pain referral zone. This is applied in the direction of pain referral.
- Gradually increase the stretch while applying cold.
- Following the stretch, the skin should be briefly rewarmed with a moist heat pack.
- The muscle should then be put through a full range of motion, passively and then actively (this is an attempt to avoid posttreatment soreness).

Numerous techniques for stretching and soft tissue pain control are used. Exhibits 1–2 through 1–4 outline many of these approaches, including rhythmic stabilization, postisometric relaxation, proprioceptive neuromuscular facilitation (PNF) hold-and-relax and contract-relax techniques, cross-friction massage, spray and stretch, and myofascial release techniques (MRT or active resistive technique [ART][14]).

Recommendations for the frequency of manual therapy generally have been outlined by the Mercy Guidelines (Figures 1–3 and 1–4).[15] A brief summary follows:

- If the condition is acute (<6 weeks) and uncomplicated (no red flags indicating referral) there may be an initial trial treatment phase of 2 weeks at a frequency of three to five times per week.
- At 2 weeks the case is reevaluated (unless there is progressive worsening); if improving, the patient is given an education program regarding activities of daily living (ADL) and a graduated program of exercise and stretching, with treatment continuing for up to 8 weeks depending on the patient's progress; if not improved, a 2-week trial with a different treatment plan is suggested.
- If after the second 2-week trial the patient has not improved, consultation or referral is suggested.
- Cases that will likely have a prolonged recovery include those with symptoms lasting longer than 8 days, severe

Exhibit 1–4 Myofascial Release Techniques

Several techniques have been developed and popularized under different technique names. Most techniques involve a stripping motion of a muscle. A combination of these techniques is found with MRT (or ART) as proposed by Leahy and Mock.[14] These techniques are best used when a muscle is determined to be dysfunctional. This is accomplished through a combination of palpation, ROM findings, and muscle testing. This technique is not intended for acute injury (within 24 to 36 hours) or for ligaments and tendons that respond better to cross-friction massage. In essence, this is an extension of other myofascial or trigger-point approaches. Skin lotion should be used when possible. Following is a summary of this approach. There are four levels. Use the highest level that patient tolerance permits.

Level 4

- Place the muscle in its shortest position.
- Apply a firm contact to the muscle just distal to the site of palpable adhesion.
- Ask the patient to move the limb actively through an antagonist pattern (if the joint is in extension, the patient flexes), elongating the muscle.
- Always maintain a fixed contact on the patient so that the adhesions are forced under the contact point.

Level 3

- Place the muscle in its shortest position.
- Apply a firm contact to muscle just distal to the site of palpable adhesion.
- Passively move the limb through an antagonist pattern, elongating the muscle.
- Always maintain a fixed contact on the patient so that the adhesions are forced under the contact point.

Level 2

- Place the muscle in a stretched position (creating tension).
- Apply muscle-stripping massage (along the direction of muscle fibers) using a broad contact, concentrating on areas of adhesion).

Level 1

- Place the muscle in a neutral position (no tension).
- Apply muscle-stripping massage, concentrating on areas of adhesion.

Treatment usually involves several passes over the muscle, treatment every other day, and resolution within the first few treatments.

Adjunctive care involves prescription of exercises for the involved muscle, starting with facilitation.

pain, more than four previous episodes, or preexisting structural or pathologic conditions.

Active care criteria include decreasing pain and inflammation and an improvement in range of motion and joint mobility (Figures 1–5 and 1–6). There is a phase where passive and active care coexist. During this stage, isometrics performed in limited arcs are helpful initiators and facilitators for a progressive exercise program. Progressing through a graded program involves settingcriteria for passing each stage. The most common criteria are range of motion, strength levels, and performance without pain.

Active care elements include training to increase range of motion, strengthening primary and secondary stabilizers of a given joint or region, increasing the endurance capabilities of the muscles, proprioceptively training for balance and reaction time, and finally, functionally training for a specific sport or occupational task. Each element involves different training strategies (Table 1–5 and Exhibits 1–5 through 1–7).

Strength and Endurance

Strengthening begins with facilitation. This is accomplished either through isometrics performed at every 20° to 30° or rhythmic stabilization using elastic tubing, performing very fast, short-arc movements for 60 seconds or until fatigue or pain limits further performance. Strengthening may then progress to holding end-range isometrics with elastic tubing for several seconds, and slowly releasing through the eccentric (negative) contraction. In some cases, these end-range isometrics may be performed against gravity only first. If these elements are strong and pain free, progressing to full-arc isotonics using weights or elastic tubing may be introduced. It is best to begin with three to five sets of high repetitions (12 to 20) using 50% to 70% of maximum weight. After 1 to 3 weeks of this training, progression through a more vigorous strengthening program may be determined by the daily adjustable progressive resistance exercise (DAPRE) approach[16] (although the exercises are performed every other day). This is a pyramid approach using lower weight with more repetitions and progressing through sets to higher weight and fewer repetitions. The last number of repetitions performed determines the working weight for the next workout.

Proprioceptive Training

Proprioceptive training incorporates various balance devices such as wobble boards, giant exercise balls, and

Figure 1–3

ACUTE/UNCOMPLICATED CASES—ALGORITHM.

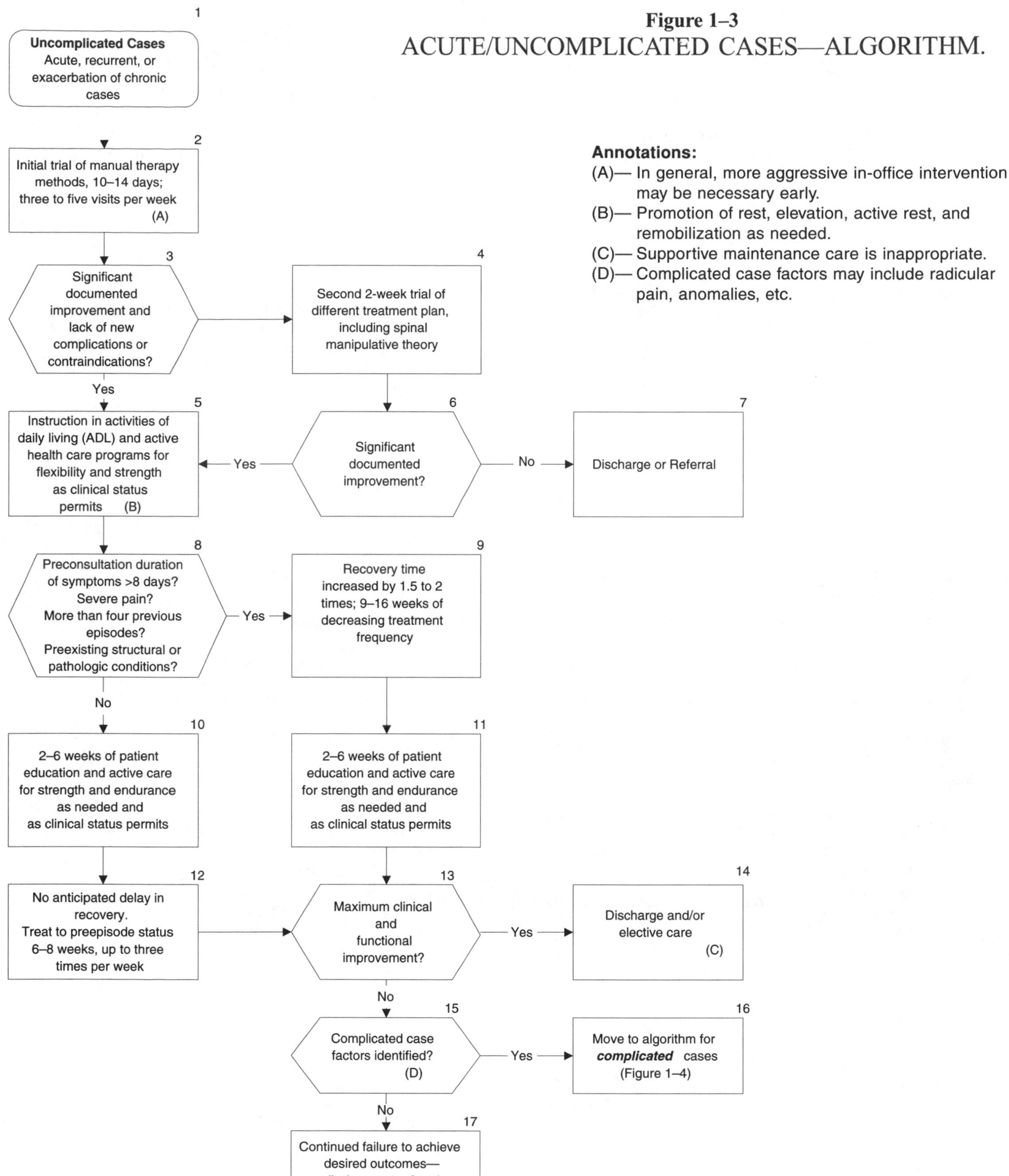

1
Uncomplicated Cases
Acute, recurrent, or exacerbation of chronic cases
2
Initial trial of manual therapy methods, 10–14 days; three to five visits per week (A)
3
Significant documented improvement and lack of new complications or contraindications?
Yes
4
Second 2-week trial of different treatment plan, including spinal manipulative theory
5
Instruction in activities of daily living (ADL) and active health care programs for flexibility and strength as clinical status permits (B)
Yes
6
Significant documented improvement?
No
7
Discharge or Referral
8
Preconsultation duration of symptoms >8 days? Severe pain? More than four previous episodes? Preexisting structural or pathologic conditions?
Yes
9
Recovery time increased by 1.5 to 2 times; 9–16 weeks of decreasing treatment frequency
No
10
2–6 weeks of patient education and active care for strength and endurance as needed and as clinical status permits
11
2–6 weeks of patient education and active care for strength and endurance as needed and as clinical status permits
12
No anticipated delay in recovery. Treat to preepisode status 6–8 weeks, up to three times per week
13
Maximum clinical and functional improvement?
Yes
14
Discharge and/or elective care (C)
No
15
Complicated case factors identified? (D)
Yes
16
Move to algorithm for *complicated* cases (Figure 1–4)
No
17
Continued failure to achieve desired outcomes—discharge or referral

Annotations:

(A)— In general, more aggressive in-office intervention may be necessary early.

(B)— Promotion of rest, elevation, active rest, and remobilization as needed.

(C)— Supportive maintenance care is inappropriate.

(D)— Complicated case factors may include radicular pain, anomalies, etc.

Source: Reprinted from D.T. Hansen, *Topics in Clinical Chiropractic,* Vol. 1, No. 4, p. 73, © 1994, Aspen Publishers, Inc.

Figure 1–4

SUBACUTE/CHRONIC COMPLICATED CASES—ALGORITHM.

Annotation:

(A)— Conditions that are exacerbated or recur, refer to algorithm for acute/uncomplicated cases (Figure 1–3).

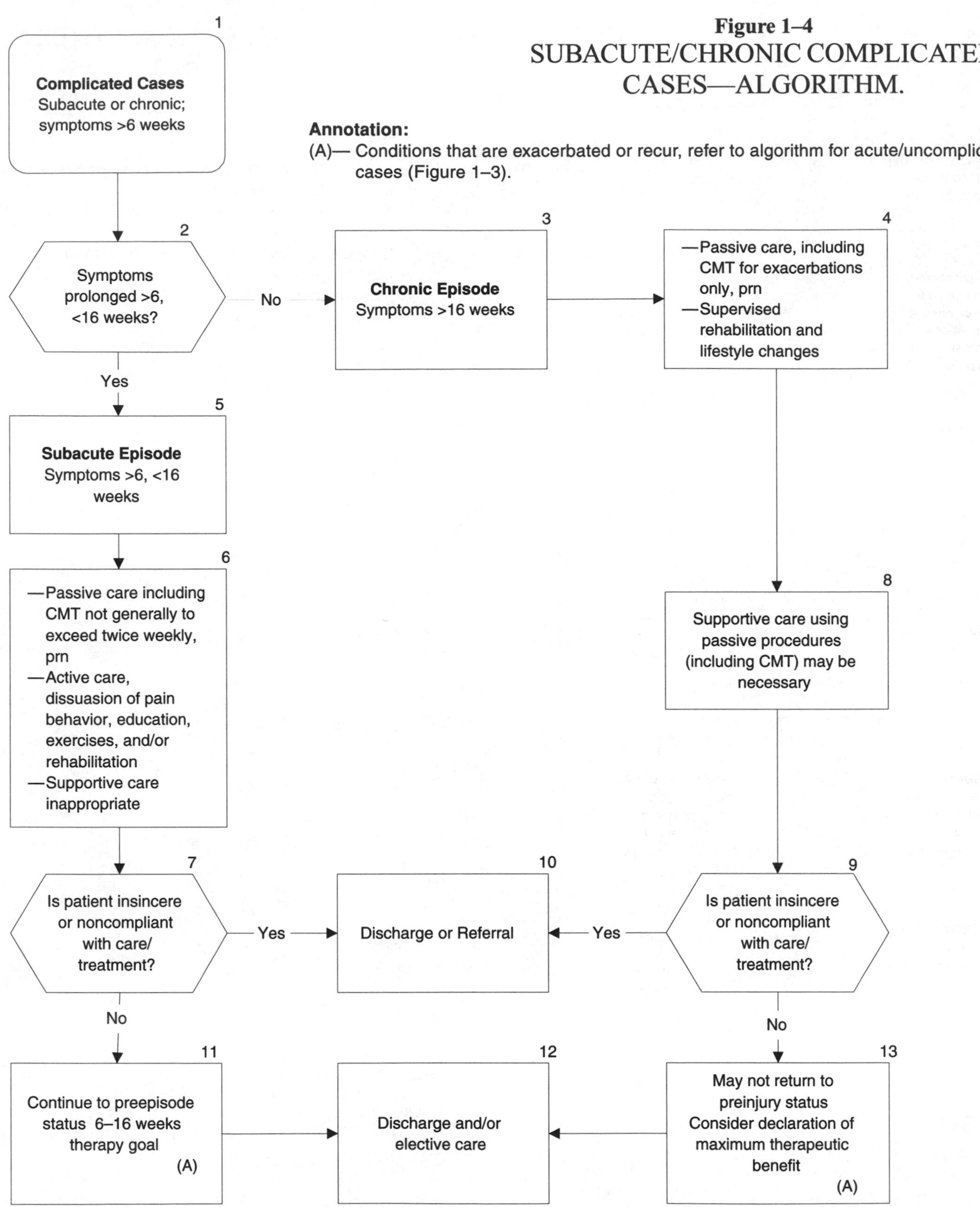

1
Complicated Cases
Subacute or chronic; symptoms >6 weeks
2
Symptoms prolonged >6, <16 weeks?
No
Yes
3
Chronic Episode
Symptoms >16 weeks
4
—Passive care, including CMT for exacerbations only, prn
—Supervised rehabilitation and lifestyle changes
5
Subacute Episode
Symptoms >6, <16 weeks
6
—Passive care including CMT not generally to exceed twice weekly, prn
—Active care, dissuasion of pain behavior, education, exercises, and/or rehabilitation
—Supportive care inappropriate
8
Supportive care using passive procedures (including CMT) may be necessary
7
Is patient insincere or noncompliant with care/ treatment?
Yes
No
10
Discharge or Referral
Yes
9
Is patient insincere or noncompliant with care/ treatment?
No
11
Continue to preepisode status 6–16 weeks therapy goal
(A)
12
Discharge and/or elective care
13
May not return to preinjury status
Consider declaration of maximum therapeutic benefit
(A)

Source: Reprinted from D.T. Hansen, *Topics in Clinical Chiropractic,* Vol. 1, No. 4, p. 74, © 1994, Aspen Publishers, Inc.

Figure 1–5
ACTIVE CARE MANAGEMENT—ALGORITHM.

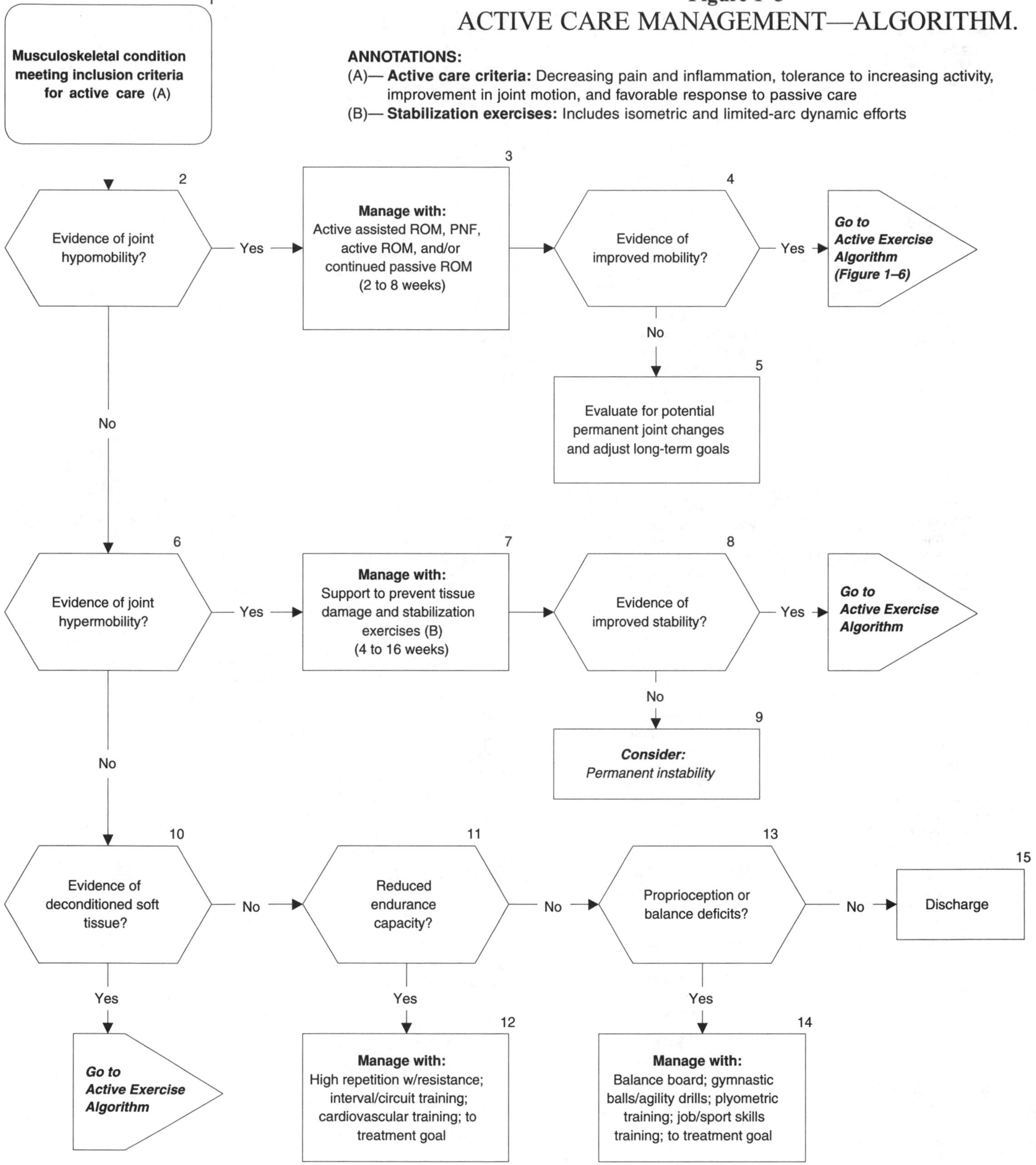
1
Musculoskeletal condition meeting inclusion criteria for active care (A)
ANNOTATIONS:
(A)— Active care criteria: Decreasing pain and inflammation, tolerance to increasing activity, improvement in joint motion, and favorable response to passive care
(B)— Stabilization exercises: Includes isometric and limited-arc dynamic efforts
2
Evidence of joint hypomobility?
Yes
3
Manage with:
Active assisted ROM, PNF, active ROM, and/or continued passive ROM (2 to 8 weeks)
4
Evidence of improved mobility?
Yes
Go to Active Exercise Algorithm (Figure 1–6)
No
5
Evaluate for potential permanent joint changes and adjust long-term goals
No
6
Evidence of joint hypermobility?
Yes
7
Manage with:
Support to prevent tissue damage and stabilization exercises (B) (4 to 16 weeks)
8
Evidence of improved stability?
Yes
Go to Active Exercise Algorithm
No
9
Consider:
Permanent instability
No
10
Evidence of deconditioned soft tissue?
No
11
Reduced endurance capacity?
No
13
Proprioception or balance deficits?
No
15
Discharge
Yes
Go to Active Exercise Algorithm
Yes
12
Manage with:
High repetition w/resistance; interval/circuit training; cardiovascular training; to treatment goal
Yes
14
Manage with:
Balance board; gymnastic balls/agility drills; plyometric training; job/sport skills training; to treatment goal

Source: Reprinted from D.L. Nelson, *Topics in Clinical Chiropractic,* Vol. 1, No. 4, pp. 76–77, © 1994, Aspen Publishers, Inc.

Figure 1–6
ACTIVE CARE: EXERCISE—ALGORITHM.

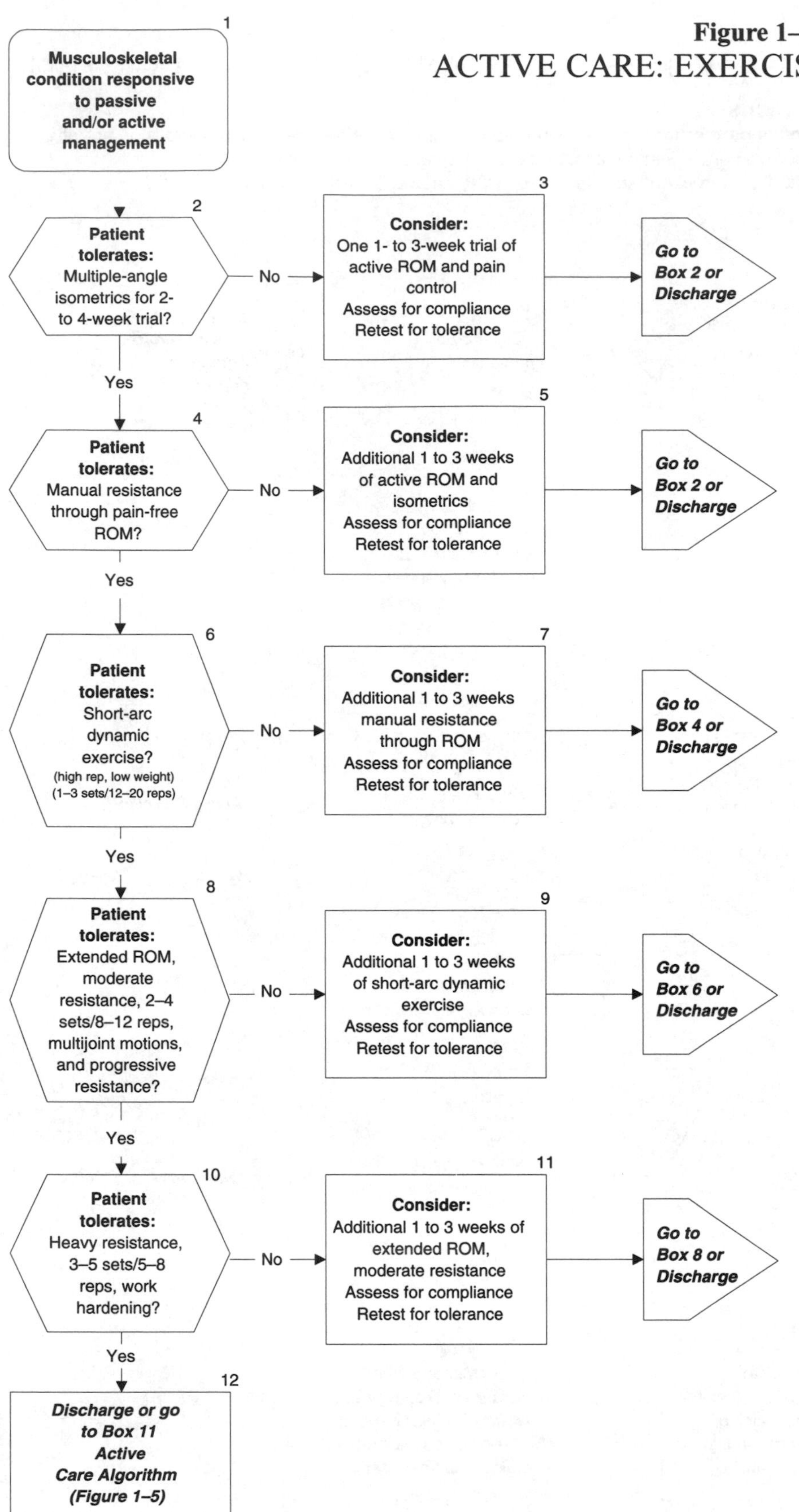

Source: Reprinted from D.L. Nelson, *Topics in Clinical Chiropractic,* Vol. 1, No. 4, p. 77, © 1994, Aspen Publishers, Inc.

Table 1–5 The Daily Adjustable Progressive Resistance Exercise (DAPRE) Approach

Set	*Weight*	*Repetitions*
1	½ working weight	10
2	¾ working weight	6
3	Full working weight	Maximum
4	Adjusted working weight (based on 3rd set)	Maximum

- Use the following table to determine working weight for 4th set (Based on 3rd set number of repetitions)
- Full working weight (3rd set) of the *next training session* is based on number of repetitions performed in the 4th set

No. of Repetitions	*For 4th set*	*Next Session Full Working Weight*
0–2	Decrease 5–10 lb	Decrease 5–10 lb
3–4	Decrease 0–5 lb	The same
5–6	The same	Increase 5–10 lb
7–10	Increase 5–10 lb	Increase 5–15 lb
11 or more	Increase 10–15 lb	Increase 10–20 lb

Exhibit 1–5 Eccentric Exercise Protocols

GENERAL COMMENTS:

- Eccentrics are usually begun in the subacute phase of healing.
- Although there is some disagreement, the initial phase begins somewhere between 3 and 7 days after injury depending on severity.
- The superiority of eccentrics over concentrics occurs only during the first 19 days postinjury.
- A load of up to 20% above a one-repetition maximum is considered safe.
- It is suggested by the literature to perform between 3 and 20 repetitions with a three-set maximum; two to three times per week. Two times per week will probably prevent delayed-onset muscle soreness (DOMS).
- Rest periods are not as important due to the low oxygen demand. Somewhere between 30 seconds to 1 minute is sufficient.
- Training begins with slow progressing to faster repetitions.
- Two concerns are chance of overload injury and DOMS.
- Generally, there are three phases of training. An example for the lower extremity follows:
    1. Two-leg concentric/eccentric training is followed by two-leg concentric/injured leg eccentric work.
    2. Slow, submaximal, single-leg eccentrics are performed. The first two phases are usually completed in 3 weeks or less.
    3. Functional eccentrics are performed in preparation for plyometrics. This phase usually takes 2 to 3 weeks to complete.

Functional Eccentrics for the Lower Extremity

A sample of a functional eccentric program would include the following:

1. One-leg step-up onto 12-inch stool; noninvolved leg steps up first, down last
2. One-leg step-up; involved leg steps up first, down last
3. Repeat with 18-inch step height
4. Slow quarter squats
5. Rapid quarter squats
6. Slow parallel squats
7. Rapid parallel squats

Curwin and Stanish[17] Eccentric Protocol for Tendinitis

1. Static stretching for 15–30 seconds is repeated three to five times.
2. Eccentric exercise is begun with gravity or light weights. For the first 2 days they are performed slowly. During days 3–5 they are performed at moderate speed. On days 6 and 7 the exercises are performed quickly. Three sets of 10 are performed.
3. After the eccentric phase, a repeat of the static stretching phase is performed.
4. Follow with 5–10 minutes of icing.

Curwin and Stanish feel that there should be some pain felt in the third set. If not, the resistance should be increased slightly. If pain is felt in the first two sets, weight should be decreased slightly.

Exhibit 1–6 Advanced Training Approaches

Russian Stimulation Protocol

- Place one electrode over the muscle and one over the associated nerve root.
- Use a 2500-Hz carrier wave; modulate at 50 pulses per second.
- Increase intensity to patient tolerance.
- Use 10-second maximum contraction with 50-second rest periods equaling 10 contractions in 10 minutes.
- Use three to five treatments per week for 5 to 7 weeks for a total of 23 to 35 treatments (2-day rest period per week).
- Protocol is used one time per year, best at night and not before or after strenuous exercise.

Plyometrics for the Lower Extremity

- Plyometrics are advanced exercises used only under the following conditions:
  1. Strength and flexibility are preinjury.
  2. Static stability is demonstrated with the following:
     — single-leg stance
     — single-leg quarter squat
     — single-leg half squat

All can be performed for 30 seconds with eyes open and closed.

- A plyometric workout should be sport specific and include the following (general conditioning):
  1. Warm-up for 10 to 20 minutes
  2. Low-intensity drills; 3 to 5 exercises; 10 to 20 repetitions
  3. Moderate-intensity drills: 3 to 4 exercises; 5 to 8 repetitions
  4. High-intensity drills: 2 to 3 exercises; 10 to 20 repetitions
- A plyometric protocol begins with horizontal and progresses to vertical movements.
- Horizontal progression is as follows:
  1. Double-leg forward hopping in a straight line
  2. Side-to-side hopping, double leg
  3. Combination of side-to-side and forward hopping
  4. Follow with single-leg progression following the above sequence
- Vertical progression is as follows:
  1. Jump from the floor to a box and back down, starting with 6 in box and progressing to 12, then 18, then 20.
  2. Jump in a line using boxes of variable height.

Never use plyometrics for an athlete with quadriceps or patellar tendinitis.

Exhibit 1–7 Classic Elastic Tubing Protocol

Facilitation

A fast midrange movement is performed for 30 to 60 seconds or until painful. The number of sets is determined by the overall status of the patient. When this can be performed pain free for 2 or 3 days, move on to the next phase.

Strength

A slow full-range movement is performed and held for an isometric contraction of up to 30 seconds at end-range. This is followed by a slow eccentric phase (at least twice as long as the concentric). Rest for 10 seconds and perform again for up to 10 repetitions (pain or fatigue dependent). When performed for 2 or 3 days pain free, move to next phase.

Endurance

A fast full-range movement is performed at the rate of one per second. This may be performed for 50 to 60 seconds or until pain or fatigue is felt. Several sets may be performed with resting phases of 30 seconds. When this is possible for 2 or 3 days pain free, the patient has the option of progressing to pulley or free-weight exercise.

Note: Always ice after any of the above exercises.

- The thickness of the tubing and the length determine the resistance.
- Thicker, shorter tubing is more resistant and requires more patient effort.
- Resistance increases throughout the concentric contraction and decreases through the eccentric phase.

Variations of Elastic Tubing Exercise Protocols

- Currently, short-arc, fast repetitions are used for stabilization. May be used every 20° or so or may focus on position of instability (eg, 20° to 30° for anterior cruciate ligament tears).
- Eccentric focus only for tendinitis. Place knee in final position of flexion or extension and resist tubing while lengthening the muscle. For example, extend knee, apply tubing behind, and gradually allow tubing to overcome resistance; end position of knee flexion.
- Sports cord training
- Closed-chain exercise: squats or seated foot dragging
- Functional PNF diagonal pattern training

minitrampolines. The intention is to have the body part react to changing support as quickly as possible and to integrate the rest of the body in this attempt.

Functional Training

Functional training is based on the requirements of a given sport or occupational activity and requires a knowledge of the biomechanics involved. Various PNF techniques may be employed. Simulated task performance is another approach for occupational retraining.

Nutritional Support

The nutritional support needed for musculoskeletal healing is based on recommendations made by Gerber.[18]

- In the inflammatory phase of healing, proteolytic enzymes, bioflavonoids, and vitamins C and E are recommended. Bromelain in doses of 1200 mg/d of 2400 μ potency taken between meals for several days may be beneficial.
- In the proliferative phase, arginine, glycine, proline, vitamins A and C, pantothenic acid, and zinc may be of benefit. Connective tissue repair may be aided with glycosaminoglycans, manganese, and chondroitin sulfate.
- Fracture healing may be enhanced with adequate dietary calcium, vitamin D, phosphorus, and magnesium; microcrystalline hydroxyapatite may also be of benefit (6 to 8 g/d).

Generally, for arthritis, dietary strategies include an approach to prostaglandin modification, including reduction of dietary animal fats and supplements with ω-3 or ω-6 fatty acids; vitamin E may also be of benefit. Free-radical reduction may include reduction of prooxidant nutrients such as polyunsaturated fats, iron, or copper and use of antioxidant enzymes such as superoxide dismutase, vitamins C and E, β-carotene, selenium, zinc, and manganese. For osteoarthritis, glucosamine sulfate may be of benefit (1500 mg/d). For rheumatoid arthritis, the focus is on ω-3 and ω-6 fatty acids, pantothenate acid supplementation and calcium (2 g/d).

REFERENCES

1. Travell J, Simons DG. *Myofascial Dysfunction: The Trigger Point Manual.* Baltimore: Williams & Wilkins; 1993.
2. Mattingly GE, Mackarey PJ. Optimal methods for shoulder tendon palpation. a cadaver study. *Phys Ther.* 1996;2:166–174.
3. Cyriax J. *Textbook of Orthopaedic Medicine.* London: Ballière Tindall; 1982.
4. Lewit K, ed. *Manipulative Therapy in Rehabilitation of the Locomotor System.* 2nd ed. Oxford, England: Butterworth-Heinemann; 1991.
5. Janda V. Evaluation of muscular imbalance. In Liebenson, C, ed. *Rehabilitation of the Spine: A Practitioner's Manual.* Williams & Wilkins, 1996:97.
6. Pellechia GL, Paolino J, Connell J. Intertester reliability of the Cyriax evaluation in assessing patients with shoulder pain. *J Orthop Sports Phys Ther.* 1996;23:34–38.
7. Liebenson C, ed. *Rehabilitation of the Spine: A Practitioner's Manual.* Baltimore: Williams & Wilkins; 1996.
8. Schafer RC, Faye LJ. *Motion Palpation and Chiropractic Technique: Principles of Dynamic Chiropractic.* Huntington Beach, CA: Motion Palpation Institute; 1989.
9. Greenman PE. *Principles of Manual Medicine.* Baltimore: Williams & Wilkins; 1990.
10. Deyo RA, Diehl AK. Lumbar spine films in primary care: current use and effects of selective ordering criteria. *J Gen Intern Med.* 1986;1:20.
11. Howard BA, Rowe LJ. Spinal x-rays. In: Haldeman S, ed. *Principles and Practice of Chiropractic.* 2nd ed. Norwalk, CT: Appleton & Lange; 1992:361–364.
12. Schultz G, Philips RB, Cooley J, Hall T, et al. Diagnostic imaging of the spine in chiropractic practice: recommendations for utilisation. *Chiro J Aust.* 1992;22:141–152.
13. Nelson DL. Assuring quality in the delivery of passive and active care. *Top Clin Chiro.* 1994;1(4):20–29.
14. Leahy PM, Mock LE III. Myofascial release technique and mechanical compromise of peripheral nerves of the upper extremity. *Chiro Sports Med.* 1992;6:139–150.
15. Haldeman S, Chapman-Smith D, Petersen DM, Jr. eds. *Guidelines for Quality Assurance and Practice Parameters.* Gaithersburg, MD: Aspen Publishers Inc; 1992.
16. Knight K. Knee rehabilitation by the daily adjustable progressive resistance technique. *Am J Sports Med.* 1979;7:336–337.
17. Curwin S, Stanish WD. *Tendinitis: Its Etiology and Treatment.* Lexington, MA: Collamore Press; 1984.
18. Gerber JM. *Handbook of Preventive and Therapeutic Nutrition.* Gaithersburg, MD: Aspen Publishers Inc; 1993.

Chapter 2

Neck Complaints

CONTEXT

The cervical spine serves a unique function as a positioner of the head in space. This requires a proprioceptive integration that results in optimization of head position through reflex setting of muscle tone. Although having the head perched atop the cervical spine allows better appreciation of the surrounding environment, this arrangement creates a potentially damaging lever arm in acute injury events that force the head to move quickly into extremes of flexion, extension, or lateral flexion. In addition to the cervical spine itself, soft tissue and neural structures may be damaged in the extremes of these movements. The lever effect also is operative in a more insidious manner when a forward head position is maintained for prolonged periods, as in a computer work environment. The demands on posterior musculature are dramatically increased by the weight of the head as it moves forward of the body.

The cervical spine is a focus for investigation of complaints that involve the head and upper extremities. The unique association between the upper cervical spinal nerves and the trigeminal nerve is postulated to have effects that result in complaints of headache, facial pain, or ear pain. Upper extremity complaints may be caused or augmented by cervical spine pathology that affects the spine, nerve roots, or brachial plexus.

Common patient presentations include the following:

- acute-injury neck and/or arm pain (ie, whiplash, cervical "stingers," etc.)
- acute, idiopathic torticollis (not a true torticollis but a painful limitation of all neck movement)
- postural pain or stiffness due to poor ergonomics in the work environment
- osteoarthritis associated stiffness or pain
- headaches

When arm complaints accompany neck pain, it is essential to make the determination of whether nerve root irritation or a referred phenomenon is the source. Chiropractors are often faced with patients who upon examination demonstrate no objectifiable neurologic deficit in the arm(s) even though numbness/tingling or weakness is part of the patient's complaint. Many of these patient appear to obtain relief from chiropractic procedures, suggesting a referral connection between what is manipulated and what causes the "phantom" symptoms. This is most likely the facet joint. Whether the complaint is local to the neck or referred to the arm, Bogduk[1] states that facet joint pain accounts for the majority of patient complaints. Neck and arm complaints also require a consideration of brachial plexus or peripheral nerve involvement.

The appropriateness of chiropractic manipulation of the cervical spine for various conditions has been addressed recently in two major reports: the 1995 Quebec Task Force on Whiplash-Associated Disorders,[2] entitled *Redefining "Whiplash" and Its Management,* and the 1996 Rand Corporation report,[3] entitled *The Appropriateness of Manipulation and Mobilization of the Cervical Spine*. Although the literature support is not as strong as for the low back, both studies recognize the potential value of manipulation in the management of some cervical spine complaints. Exhibit 2–1 is a list of randomized controlled trials for cervical manipulation and mobilization.

One of the often-quoted concerns regarding manipulation of the cervical spine is the potential of vertebrobasilar compromise. This is a difficult issue for many reasons, not the least of which is that there is no sensitive clinical premani-

Exhibit 2–1 Randomized Controlled Trials for Cervical Manipulation and Mobilization

Brodin H. Cervical pain and mobilization. *Man Med.* 1982;20:90–94.

Cassidy JD, Lopes AA, Yong-Hing K. The immediate effect of manipulation versus mobilization on pain and range of motion in the cervical spine: a randomized controlled trial. *J Manipulative Physiol Ther.* 1992;15:570–575.

Howe DH, Newcombe RG, Wade MT. Manipulation of the cervical spine: a pilot study. *J R Coll Gen Prcact.* 1983;33:574–579.

Koes BW. The effectiveness of manual therapy, physiotherapy, and treatment by the general practitioner for nonspecific back and neck complaints. *Spine.* 1992;17:28–35.

Koes BW, et al. A blinded randomized clinical trial of manual therapy and physiotherapy for chronic back and neck complaints: physical outcome measures. *J Manipulative Physiol Ther.* 1992;1:16–23.

Koes BW, et al. Randomized clinical trial of manipulative therapy and physiotherapy for persistent back and neck complaints: results of one-year follow-up. *Br Med J.* 1992; 304:601–605.

Koes BW, et al. Randomized clinical trial of manual therapy and physiotherapy for persistent back and neck complaints: subgroup analysis and relationship between outcome measures. *J Manipulative Physiol Ther.* 1993;16:211–219.

McKinney LA, Dorman JO, Ryan M. Role of physiotherapy in the management of acute neck sprains following road-traffic accidents. *Arch Emerg Med.* 1989;6:27–33.

Mealy K, Brennan G, Fenelon CC. Early mobilization of acute whiplash injuries. *Br Med J.* 1986;292:656–657.

Nordemar R, Thorner C. Treatment of acute cervical pain: a comparative group study. *Pain.* 1981;10:93–101.

Sloop PR, Smith DS, Goldenberg E, Dorse C. Manipulation for chronic neck pain: a double blind controlled study. *Spine.* 1982;7:532–535.

Vernon HT, Aker P, Burns S, et al. Pressure pain threshold evaluation of the effect of spinal manipulation in the treatment of chronic neck pain: a pilot study. *J Manipulative Physiol Ther.* 1990;13:13–16.

Source: Reprinted from L.S. Nordhoff, *Motor Vehicle Collision Injuries,* pp. 77–80, © 1996, Aspen Publishers, Inc.

pulation test with which to screen patients. Although potentially catastrophic for the patient, the incidence is quite low, reported to be between 1 in 400,000 to 1 in 10 million.[4] Management issues are discussed later.

GENERAL STRATEGY

History

- Screen the patient for "red flags" that indicate the need for either immediate radiographs/special studies or referral to or consultation with a specialist, including severe trauma, direct head trauma with loss of consciousness, nuchal rigidity, bladder dysfunction associated with onset of neck pain, associated dysphasia, associated cranial nerve or central nervous system (CNS) signs/symptoms, onset of a "new" headache, and preexisting conditions such as rheumatoid arthritis, cancer, or Down syndrome, alcoholism, drug abuse, or an immunocompromised state.
- If there is a history of trauma, determine the mechanism and severity.
- For patients involved in a motor vehicle accident (MVA), take a thorough history with regard to angle of collision, speed, use of brakes, seat belt, shoulder harness, air bag, position of the patient in the car, subsequent legal concerns with regard to police reports, and so forth (Exhibit 2–2).
- Determine whether the complaint is one of pain, stiffness, weakness, or a combination of complaints.
- Determine whether the complaint is limited to the neck or is radiating to the head or upper extremity unilaterally or bilaterally.
- Determine the level of pain and functional capacity with a questionnaire such as the Neck Disability Index (Exhibit 2–3) with a pain scale (eg, Visual Analog Scale [VAS]).

Exhibit 2–2 Automotive Crash Form

BILLING INFORMATION

Patient name: ____________________

Date of injury: ____________ Time of injury: __________ ❑ AM ❑ PM

City and street where crash occurred: ____________________

What is the estimated damage to your vehicle? $____________________

❑ Yes ❑ No Do you have automobile medical insurance coverage?

Name/address/phone ____________________

____

What is your car insurance medical coverage limit? $____________________

What is the claim number? ____________________

❑ Yes ❑ No Do you know the claims adjuster's name? ____________________

❑ Yes ❑ No Have you reported this injury to your car insurance company?

❑ Yes ❑ No Did the police come to the accident scene and make a report?

❑ Yes ❑ No Is an attorney representing you? Name/address/phone: ____________________

____

AUTO ACCIDENT DESCRIPTION

Describe how the crash happened

____

____

____

____

____

____

____

____

____

Collision Description

Check all that apply to you:

❑ Single-car crash ❑ Two-vehicle crash ❑ More than three vehicles

❑ Rear-end crash ❑ Side crash ❑ Rollover

❑ Head-on crash ❑ Hit guardrail/tree ❑ Ran off road

You were the

❑ Driver ❑ Front passenger ❑ Rear passenger

Describe the vehicle you were in

Model year and make: ____________________

❑ Subcompact car ❑ Compact car ❑ Mid-sized car

❑ Full-sized car ❑ Pickup truck ❑ Larger than 1-ton vehicle

Describe the other vehicle

Model year and make: ____________________

❑ Subcompact car ❑ Compact car ❑ Mid-sized car

❑ Full-sized car ❑ Pickup truck ❑ Larger than 1-ton vehicle

Estimated crash speeds

Estimate how fast your vehicle was moving at time of crash. _____mph

Estimate how fast the other vehicle was moving at time of crash. _____mph

continues

Exhibit 2–2 continued

At the time of impact your vehicle was
❑ Slowing down ❑ Stopped ❑ Gaining speed ❑ Moving at steady speed

At the time of impact the other vehicle was
❑ Slowing down ❑ Stopped ❑ Gaining speed ❑ Moving at steady speed

During and after the crash, your vehicle
❑ Kept going straight, not hitting anything
❑ Kept going straight, hitting car in front
❑ Was hit by another vehicle
❑ Spun around, not hitting anything
❑ Spun around, hitting another car
❑ Spun around, hitting object other than car

Describe yourself during the crash
Check only the areas that apply to you:
❑ You were unaware of the impending collision.
❑ You were aware of the impending crash and relaxed before the collision.
❑ You were aware of the impending crash and braced yourself.
❑ Your body, torso, and head were facing straight ahead.
❑ You had your head and/or torso turned at the time of collision:
❑ Turned to left ❑ Turned to right
❑ You were intoxicated (alcohol) at the time of crash.
❑ You were wearing a seat belt.
If yes, does your seat belt have a shoulder harness? ❑ Yes ❑ No
❑ You were holding onto the steering wheel at the time of impact.

Indicate if your body hit something or was hit by any of the following:
Please draw lines and match the left side to the right side.

Head	Windshield
Face	Steering wheel
Shoulder	Side door
Neck	Dashboard
Chest	Car frame
Hip	Another occupant
Knee	Seat
Foot	Seat belt

Check if any of the following vehicle parts broke, bent, or were damaged in your car
❑ Windshield ❑ Seat frame ❑ Knee bolster
❑ Steering wheel ❑ Side/rear window ❑ Other ____________________
❑ Dashboard ❑ Mirror ❑ Other ____________________

Rear-end collisions only
Answer this section only if you were hit from the rear.
Does your vehicle have
❑ Movable head restraints
❑ Fixed, nonmovable head restraints
❑ No head restraints
Please indicate how your head restraint was positioned at the time of crash.*
❑ At the top of the back of your head
❑ Midway height of the back of your head
❑ Lower height of the back of your head
❑ Located at the level of your neck
❑ Located at the level of your shoulder blades (upper back) below neck

*Estimate the distance between the back of your head and the front of the head restraint. _____ inches

continues

Exhibit 2–2 continued

All types of collisions

Answer this section regardless of the type of crash, indicating those relevant to your case.

Yes	No	
❑	❑	Did any of the front or side structures, such as the side door, dashboard, or floor board of your car, dent inward during the crash?
❑	❑	Did the side door touch your body during the crash?
❑	❑	Were your hands on the steering wheel or dashboard during the crash?
❑	❑	Did your body slide under the seat belt?
❑	❑	Was a door of your vehicle damaged to the point where you could not open the door?

Emergency department

Yes	No	
❑	❑	Did you go to the emergency department after the accident? What is name of the emergency department? ______________________________ When did you go (date and time)? ____________________________________
❑	❑	Did you go to the emergency department in an ambulance?
❑	❑	Did you or another person drive you to the emergency department?
❑	❑	Were you hospitalized overnight?
❑	❑	Did the emergency department doctor take X-rays? Check what was taken: ❑ Skull ❑ Neck ❑ Low back ❑ Arm or leg
❑	❑	Did the emergency department doctor give you pain medications?
❑	❑	Did the emergency department doctor give you muscle relaxants?
❑	❑	Did you have any cuts or lacerations?
❑	❑	Did you require any stitching for cuts?
❑	❑	Were you given a neck collar or back brace to wear?

When did you first notice any pain after injury?

❑ Immediately ❑ _____ Hours after injury ❑ _____ Days after injury

If you did not see a doctor for the first time within the first week, indicate why

Check all that apply

❑ No pain was noticed

❑ No transportation

❑ No appointment schedule available

❑ Work/home schedule conflicts

If you did not see a doctor for the first time within the first month after injury, indicate why

Check all that apply

❑ No pain was noticed

❑ No transportation

❑ I thought pain would go away

❑ I self-treated with over-the-counter drugs

❑ No appointment schedule available

❑ Work/home schedule conflicts

❑ I had no insurance or money

❑ I took hot showers, used ice, heat

Have you been unable to work since injury?

❑ Yes ❑ No If yes, you were off work ❑ partially or ❑ completely

Please list date off work: __________ to __________.

Source: Reprinted from L.S. Nordhoff, *Motor Vehicle Collision Injuries*, pp. 77–80, © 1996, Aspen Publishers, Inc.

Exhibit 2–3 Neck Disability Index

This questionnaire has been designed to give the doctor information as to how your neck pain has affected your ability to manage in everyday life. Please answer every section and mark in each section only the *one* box that applies to you. We realize you may consider that two of the statements in any one section relate to you, but please just mark the box that most closely describes your problem.

Section 1—Pain Intensity

- ❑ I have no pain at the moment.
- ❑ The pain is very mild at the moment.
- ❑ The pain is moderate at the moment.
- ❑ The pain is fairly severe at the moment.
- ❑ The pain is very severe at the moment.
- ❑ The pain is the worst imaginable at the moment.

Section 2—Personal Care (Washing, Dressing, etc.)

- ❑ I can look after myself normally without causing extra pain.
- ❑ I can look after myself normally but it causes extra pain.
- ❑ It is painful to look after myself and I am slow and careful.
- ❑ I need some help but manage most of my personal care.
- ❑ I need help every day in most aspects of self care.
- ❑ I do not get dressed, I wash with difficulty and stay in bed.

Section 3—Lifting

- ❑ I can lift heavy weights without extra pain.
- ❑ I can lift heavy weights but it gives extra pain.
- ❑ Pain prevents me from lifting heavy weights off the floor, but I can manage if they are conveniently positioned, for example, on a table.
- ❑ Pain prevents me from lifting heavy weights, but I can manage light to medium weights if they are conveniently positioned.
- ❑ I can lift very light weights.
- ❑ I cannot lift or carry anything at all.

Section 4—Reading

- ❑ I can read as much as I want to with no pain in my neck.
- ❑ I can read as much as I want to with slight pain in my neck.
- ❑ I can read as much as I want with moderate pain in my neck.
- ❑ I can't read as much as I want because of moderate pain in my neck.
- ❑ I can hardly read at all because of severe pain in my neck.
- ❑ I cannot read at all.

Section 5—Headaches

- ❑ I have no headaches at all.
- ❑ I have slight headaches that come infrequently.
- ❑ I have moderate headaches that come infrequently.
- ❑ I have moderate headaches that come frequently.
- ❑ I have severe headaches that come frequently.
- ❑ I have headaches almost all the time.

Section 6—Concentration

- ❑ I can concentrate fully when I want to with no difficulty.
- ❑ I can concentrate fully when I want to with slight difficulty.
- ❑ I have a fair degree of difficulty in concentrating when I want to.
- ❑ I have a lot of difficulty in concentrating when I want to.
- ❑ I have a great deal of difficulty in concentrating when I want to.
- ❑ I cannot concentrate at all.

Section 7—Work

- ❑ I can do as much work as I want to.
- ❑ I can only do my usual work, but no more.
- ❑ I can do most of my usual work, but no more.
- ❑ I cannot do my usual work.
- ❑ I can hardly do any work at all.
- ❑ I can't do any work at all.

Section 8—Driving

- ❑ I can drive my car without any neck pain.
- ❑ I can drive my car as long as I want with slight pain in my neck.
- ❑ I can drive my car as long as I want with moderate pain in my neck.
- ❑ I can't drive my car as long as I want because of moderate pain in my neck.
- ❑ I can hardly drive at all because of severe pain in my neck.
- ❑ I can't drive my car at all.

Section 9—Sleeping

- ❑ I have no trouble sleeping.
- ❑ My sleep is slightly disturbed (less than 1 hr. sleepless).
- ❑ My sleep is mildly disturbed (1–2 hrs. sleepless).
- ❑ My sleep is moderately disturbed (2–3 hrs. sleepless).
- ❑ My sleep is greatly disturbed (3–5 hrs. sleepless).
- ❑ My sleep is completely disturbed (5–7 hrs. sleepless).

Section 10—Recreation

- ❑ I am able to engage in all my recreation activities with no neck pain at all.
- ❑ I am able to engage in all my recreation activities with some pain in my neck.
- ❑ I am able to engage in most, but not all, of my usual recreation activities because of pain in my neck.
- ❑ I am able to engage in few of my usual recreation activities because of pain in my neck.
- ❑ I can hardly do any recreation activities because of pain in my neck.
- ❑ I can't do any recreation activities at all.

Source: Reprinted with permission from H. Vernon and S. Mior, The neck disability index: a study of reliability and validity, *Journal of Manipulative and Physiological Therapeutics*, Vol. 14, No. 7, pp. 409–415, © 1991, Williams & Wilkins.

Examination

- For patients with nuchal rigidity and/or a positive Brudzinski's or Kernig's sign, refer for medical management.
- For patients with suspected fracture or dislocation (eg, MVA, compressive or distractive injury to the neck, etc.), infection, or cancer, obtain radiographs of the cervical spine.
- For patients with neck pain only, perform a thorough examination of the neck, including inspection, observation of the patient's movements, palpation of soft and bony tissues, motion palpation of the spine, passive and active range of motion (using a goniometer or inclinometer), a functional assessment (eg, according to Janda and Lewit),[6] and a brief orthopaedic screening.
- For patients with neck and arm pain, add a thorough orthopaedic/neurologic examination, including compressive maneuvers to the neck in various positions, nerve stretch maneuvers, deep tendon reflex testing, sensation testing (include pain, temperature, light touch, and vibration), and myotome testing.
- Radiographs should be obtained for patients who have radicular findings, including an anteroposterior (AP), an AP-open mouth, a lateral, and obliques. Flexion-extension views may be added when searching for instability.
- Special imaging, including computed tomography (CT) or magnetic resonance (MR) imaging, should be reserved for the differential of radicular or myelopathic cases where there is a need for further distinction of stenosis, tumor, herniated disc, or multiple sclerosis. Electrodiagnostic studies should be reserved for cases where the cause of radicular complaints remains unclear.

Management

- Patients with clinical, radiographic, or laboratory evidence of tumor, infection, fracture, or dislocation should be sent for medical evaluation and possible management.
- Patients who appear to have a mechanical cause of pain should be managed conservatively for 1 month; if unresponsive, further testing or referral for a second opinion is suggested.

RELEVANT ANATOMY AND BIOMECHANICS

The cervical spine is often discussed as two separate yet interdependent sections: the upper cervical spine (the occiput and C1/C2) and the lower cervical spine (C2-C7/T1). This is due in part to a functional distinction based on the great degree of rotation available at the upper cervical spine, allowed by the unique articulation between the C2 and C1 vertebrae. The dens of C2 acts as a pivotal point for rotation. The intricate musculature support and control in this region is important in substituting for a generally more lax ligamentous system, compared with the thoracic and lumbar regions. Another important difference in the upper cervical region is the lack of intervertebral foramina and discs between the occiput (C0), C1, and C2. From a neurologic perspective, the upper cervical spinal cord has a unique connection with the CNS through the trigeminocervical nucleus, an intermingling of the spinal nucleus of the trigeminal nerve and the dorsal horn of the upper cervical spinal nerves.[7] This connection allows for interactions and misinterpretations postulated to be the cause of headaches, dizziness, and facial pain.

The vertebral arteries enter the transverse foramen at C6 and ascend through the other transverse foramina. At C2 they take sharp turns to reach eventually the cranium. Unfortunately, these two sites—C6 and the upper cervical region—can be tethering or compressive sites leading to occlusion or intimal tearing resulting in vertebrobasilar events (vascular accidents). These are extremely rare possibilities that have been associated primarily with rotational adjustments but also with common daily activities such as turning the head while driving and extending the head for a shampoo at the hairstylist.[8] When damage does occur it is usually due to trauma to the arterial wall leading to either vasospasm or intimal tearing. Intimal tears may occur in isolation or be complicated by embolic formation or dissection of the arterial wall.[9] The dorsolateral medullary syndrome (Wallenberg's) and the locked-in syndrome or cerebro-medullospinal disconnection syndrome are two possible consequences of vertebrobasilar injury. Wallenberg's syndrome usually involves occlusion of the posterior inferior cerebellar artery with resulting problems of vertigo, diplopia, and dysarthria. Most patients regain a significant degree of neurologic function. The locked-in syndrome is much more serious, leaving the patient conscious but paralyzed.

The Discs

Like all intervertebral discs, the cervical disc is composed of a central nucleus pulposus and an outer annulus. However, by age 40 years the nucleus pulposus is essentially nonexistent, having changed to a ligamentous-like, dry material.[10] Herniation is therefore theoretically not possible in the older patient unless small hyaline pieces become free. The cervical discs have much less weight to bear then the lumbar discs for two reasons: only the head plus gravity is borne and the distribution of load is approximately equal among the disc and the two facet joints (ie, each bears one-third the load). Like the other regions of the spine, the outer annulus fibrosus is innervated by the sinuvertebral nerves.

The Facets

The facets of the upper cervical spine are angled approximately 35° to the horizontal plane, whereas the lower cervical spine facets are oriented at approximately a 65° angle.[11] The facets (zygapophyseal) joints are surrounded by a joint capsule that is generally looser in the cervical region than in the thoracic and lumbar regions, allowing for more range of motion. The capsule is lined with synovium on the upper and lower aspects. There are often inclusions of fat-filled synovial folds and meniscoids that extend between the facets. Although they are believed primarily to be shock absorbers, these inclusions can become trapped, causing a mechanical lock. It is unlikely, however, that they are the primary cause of vertebral fixation given that meniscoids are not always present in fixed joints and that patients with rheumatoid have a higher incidence of meniscoids yet no higher incidence of fixation.[12] The facet joints are innervated by the medial branch of the posterior primary rami. Common referral patterns from the facets include neck and head pain from the C2-C3 joints, and neck and shoulder pain from the C5-C6 joints.

Ligaments and Muscles

The upper cervical spine has an intricate system of ligaments and muscles to stabilize and control fine head movements. Additionally, the muscles serve a function of providing important proprioceptive input integrated into the reflex control of the head and neck, and posture in general. Studies have demonstrated that injections into the upper cervical spine area result in various symptoms, including vertigo.[13]

Three ligaments help stabilize the dens of C2 to the anterior arch of C1. These include the alar ligament, cruciform (cruciate) ligament, and tectorial membrane. These continue down as the posterior longitudinal ligament. A prominent section of the cruciate ligament is called the transverse ligament. This ligament is the primary stabilizer of the dens. Deterioration of the transverse ligament, usually through rheumatoid processes, will allow abnormal movement between C2 and C1. The posterior longitudinal ligament (PLL) is broad in the cervical spine, providing more protection against lateral disc herniation than found in the lumbar region. The ligamentum flavum is posterior to the PLL, attaching to the laminae forming the anterior support for the facet joint capsules and protecting the spinal cord. Bogduk[1] emphasizes that the interspinous ligament is nonexistent in the cervical region and that the sagittal and superficial component of the ligamentum nuchae are simply extensions of other structures.

The muscles of the cervical spine are often divided into posterior and anterior with subdivisions of superficial and deep sections. The more superficial muscles are involved with upper extremity movement and respiration. The deeper muscles are involved more with posture and head/neck movement. The posterior muscles, including the semispinalis, spinalis, and splenius, are essential as antigravity/postural muscles, often being called upon to fire eccentrically during flexion of the neck/head, and are chronically strained during forward head positions. The four suboccipital muscles (obliquus capitis inferior and superior, and the rectus capitis posterior major and minor) plus the deep "shunt" muscles of the middle and lower cervical spine, such as the interspinales, multifidus, rotatores, intertransversarii, and longus cervicis, are important for intersegmental movement. Additionally, they play a major role in providing afferent proprioceptive input to the spinal cord that is used both for gross postural control and spinal segmental (involuntary) positioning. This is due to the high density of muscle spindles in this region.[14]

Thoracic Outlet

The thoracic outlet is the path taken by the brachial plexus and associated vasculature into the arm from the neck. Thoracic outlet syndrome (TOS) is an overdiagnosed condition. It is purported to be caused by neurologic or neurovascular compromise of the brachial plexus and/or subclavian-axillary vessels. The potential sites of entrapment or compression include, at cervical ribs (elongated C7 transverse processes), the scalene muscles, the costoclavicular interval, and the subcoracoid loop involving the pectoralis minor. When TOS is present it is most common to have involvement of the lower brachial plexus (C7-T1) with related medial arm and hand complaints. Factors that have been suggested as causes include trauma, posture (rounded shoulders), tight scalenes or pectoralis minor, and cervical ribs. Leffert[15] states however, that patients who have had stabilizing surgery for the shoulder have had accompanying TOS symptoms resolved.

Biomechanics

The various motion patterns available to the cervical spine are determined by both active and passive elements. The passive elements include the facets, discs, ligaments, and bone. The various components of functional patterns that may be affected include range of motion (ROM), coupling patterns, the instantaneous axis of rotation (IAR), and the neutral zone. Many of the biomechanical studies have focused on how the various static components contribute to movement and ROM, and therefore must be considered cautiously when extrapolated to patients. Many of the manipulative maneuvers used by chiropractors and others, however, require elimination of muscular participation; therefore the studies may have some clinical validity.

The cervical spine flexes, extends, rotates, and bends laterally. Flexion and extension occur mainly at three areas: (1) the atlantooccipital joint, (2) the C1-C2 level, and (3) between C4 and C6. Each accounts for about 20° of flexion/extension. The other segments contribute between 10° and 20°. Flexion at the atlantooccipital joint is accompanied by a coupled movement of slight anterior translation of the occiput relative to C1.

The facet orientation in the cervical spine allows for a large degree of motion. Approximately 50% to 60% of axial rotation occurs between C1 and C2.[16] This is in large part due to the pivot-shaped articulation between these segments. On the other hand, axial rotation is minimal (0° to 5°) at the atlantooccipital articulation. Lateral bending between segments increases from the upper to the lower cervical spine. In the upper cervical spine only about 5° is available, while in the middle and lower cervical spine 5° to 10° is available. With lateral bending in the middle and lower cervical regions, the spinous processes rotate to the opposite side (ie, left lateral bending causes the spinous processes to move to the right). This coupling occurs most at C2-C3 and decreases in the lower segments. With rotation, C2-C3 and segments above bend laterally in the opposite direction of rotation (ie, right rotation causes left lateral bending). Below this level, however, the cervical spine generally bends to the same side as head rotation. Another coupled pattern with rotation is flexion and extension. Above the C4-C5 level extension accompanies rotation; below this level, flexion occurs with rotation. These coupling patterns change with the beginning head position.[17] For example, if the head rotates while in full flexion, lateral flexion coupled with axial rotation decreases. These coupled patterns may be important factors for planning positioning and force application with manipulative procedures.

Because acceleration/deceleration injury to the cervical spine is a common mechanism of injury in patients seeking chiropractic care, a brief overview of the biomechanics of whiplash is presented. There is considerable research to indicate a "typical" sequence of events following a rear-end collision. These are divided into phases by Croft[18]:

- Phase one—When a vehicle is rear-ended, the patient's torso is forced back into the seat and at the same time moves upward. This upward movement is accompanied by straightening of the cervical spine as it is being compressed axially. The head and neck then begin to extend.
- Phase two—As the head and neck are extending, the vehicle has reached its peak acceleration. Energy stored in the seat from the backward movement of the body into the seat may add more acceleration to the torso as a "diving board" effect. The upward (vertical) movement of the torso may allow ramping over the headrest, adding an element of extension. If the driver's foot is taken off the brake, acceleration may be prolonged.
- Phase three—Acceleration diminishes while the head and torso are thrown forward. This may be accentuated if the driver's foot is reapplied to the brakes.
- Phase four—As the body moves forward, a seat belt and shoulder harness (if applicable) will restrain the torso, allowing the head to decelerate forward.

EVALUATION

History

The first line of business is to attempt to rule out "serious" causes of neck or neck and arm pain. It is important to consider the possibility of meningitis when there is accompanying fever and a complaint of neck stiffness. Although neck stiffness may be a common complaint with the flu, the severity of pain and the response to passive flexion of the head is usually less remarkable. When neck pain is associated with a severe headache that is "new" or worse than any headache previously experienced, a red flag should be raised for infection, tumor, or vascular causes.

When patients have a complaint of neck and arm pain, clues to the cause may be evident from the history (Table 2–1). If the complaint is of a strip of pain connecting the neck or shoulder to the hand and this strip overlaps several dermatomes or in the hand is rather diffuse, nerve root compression is unlikely. Patients with this presentation often have a referred pain that is unrelated to nerve root compression. These patients rarely complain of weakness in the arm (or if they do it is usually not objectifiable). Patients with nerve root compression will have complaints not only of pain (often localized to a dermatome) but of eventual motor weakness that can be objectified on the physical examination.

Traumatic/Overuse Injury

When there is direct trauma to the head or neck, it is important to gauge the degree of injury, the mechanism of injury, and whether there was loss of consciousness. There are some classic patterns of injury with respect to specific types of fractures (Table 2–2). When these mechanisms are evi-

Table 2–1 History Questions for Cervical Spine Injuries

Primary Question	*What Are You Thinking?*	*Secondary Questions*	*What Are You Thinking?*
Were you involved in an accident?	Sprain/strain, subluxation, dislocation, fracture, disc lesion	Was your head forced forward?	Sprain/strain of posterior neck muscles/ligaments, fracture of vertebral body, facet dislocation, disc lesion
		Was your head forced back?	Sprain/strain of anterior neck muscles/ligaments, facet compression, hangman's or teardrop fracture at C2-C3
		Was your head turned and flexed?	Facet subluxation or dislocation, sprain/strain
		Was your head stretched to the side?	Brachial plexus stretch lesion, facet fracture, nerve root compression on side of head flexion
		Was your head turned and extended?	Facet compression, articular pillar fracture, sprain/strain
		Did you hit the top of your head?	Possible Jefferson's fracture
Does the pain radiate to your arm(s)?	Disc lesion, nerve root entrapment, referred pain, myelopathy, brachial plexus damage, double crush	Is there isolated weakness or numbness?	Nerve root involvement
		Was there associated numbness/tingling or weakness that resolved over a few minutes?	Burner or stinger if involved with a lateral flexion injury
		Is there associated difficulty with walking or urinary dysfunction?	Myelopathy possible
		Is there more numbness and tingling in a diffuse or ill-defined pattern?	Referred pain from facet or trigger points
Are you unable to move your head in a specific direction?	"Torticollis," osteoarthritis, fracture/dislocation, meningitis	Did you simply wake up with this?	Acute "pseudotorticollis" due to global muscle spasm
		Is there associated fever? Is it worse with flexion?	Possible meningitis if flexion pain is severe
		Was there a gradual onset? (in an older patient)	Likely osteoarthritis
		Did this occur after head or neck trauma?	Consider fracture or dislocation
Do you have chronic pain or stiffness?	Osteoarthritis, postural syndrome, subluxation	Does work involve a forward head posture or lateral flexion while on the phone?	Postural syndrome
		Is there local pain with specific movement?	Subluxation

Table 2–2 Fractures of the Cervical Spine

Mechanism	*Fracture*	*Best Radiographic View*	*Stable/Unstable?*
Hyperflexion	Wedge fracture of vertebral body	AP and lateral views; loss of anterior body height	Generally stable; based on neurologic signs or potential risk
	Clay shoveler's (C6-T1 spinous process)	Lateral; may need swimmer's view	Generally stable; however, may require several weeks in a hard collar or in rare cases surgical excision
	Teardrop	Lateral view	Unstable; may be associated with anterior cord injury
	Burst fracture	Lateral view	Generally stable, however, requires close monitoring for neurologic compromise
	Bilateral facet dislocation	Lateral view demonstrates instability	Unstable
Flexion/rotation	Unilateral facet dislocation	Lateral view may demonstrate anterior body translation or a dysrelationship of the normal overlap of facets	May be unstable
Hyperextension	Extension teardrop fracture of anteroinferior body of C2	Lateral view	Relatively stable in flexion; unstable in extension
	Hangman's: bilateral pedicle fracture of C2	Lateral view	Highly unstable, requiring halo traction immobilization
Hyperextension/rotation	Articular pillar	Lateral view may show a double outline; AP may show a disruption of the smooth cortical line; oblique or pillar views may be necessary; if found, CT is suggested	Generally stable; however, swelling may produce some radicular signs
Hyperextension/lateral flexion	Facet fracture	Obliques	Usually neurologically stable; however, must be assessed for stability after healing
Compression	Jefferson's burst fracture of C1	Visible on AP open mouth; on lateral view increase in retropharyngeal space	Highly unstable, requiring halo traction immobilization

Source: Reprinted with permission from S.M. Foreman, Long-term Prognosis, in *Whiplash Injuries: The Cervical Acceleration/Deceleration Syndrome,* 2nd ed., S.M. Foreman and A.C. Croft, eds., © 1985, Williams & Wilkins.

dent from the history, radiographic evaluation can be more focused. If the patient was involved in an MVA, it is important to acquire detail such as type of vehicle, angle of collision, and damage to the vehicles (see Exhibit 2–2). Information to be elicited from the patient includes his or her position in the car, whether a seat belt and shoulder harness were worn, whether an air bag was triggered, and whether the head or other body parts made contact with the windshield, steering wheel, or dashboard.

Lateral flexion injury to the neck is common in sports and vehicle accidents. When a patient reports having his or her neck snapped to the side, compression injury on the side of head/neck movement and stretch injury on the side opposite are likely. When the brachial plexus is stretched, the upper section is most often involved. The patient will report a sudden onset of weakness in the arm, often with a burning or tingling pain down the outside of the arm to the hand. This type of injury is often referred to in sports as a "burner" or a "stinger." Most are transient; however, some cases may need further evaluation with electrodiagnostic studies. When a lateral flexion injury is reported, it is a caution to the chiropractor not to take the head/neck into the position of injury when adjusting the neck.

When forced flexion is the mechanism, in addition to fractures of the vertebral bodies, myelopathy from a stenotic spinal canal must be considered when the patient has arm or leg complaints. If the patient has accompanying complaints of urinary dysfunction, myelopathy must be suspected and investigated further via physical examination and radiographs.

Overuse injury is in most instances postural "injury." A line of questioning regarding occupational mechanical stresses is particularly important for patients with chronic neck pain. Questions should be asked regarding workstations, including height of chair, desk, and computer monitor, and how a phone is answered and for how long during a 1-day period. For those patients whose employment requires less sitting and more lifting, it is important to determine the degree of overhead lifting, which often requires a degree of hyperextension of the neck. Dentists, mechanics, plumbers, electricians, and others are a unique population that often works in awkward positions. It is important to have the patient give a detailed explanation of common prolonged positions or any single position that causes pain. From this description, a relationship to which anatomic structures are stretched and which are compressed can be appreciated.

Stiffness/Restricted Motion

For many patients, the biggest concern is stiffness or restricted ROM; they complain that looking over the shoulder is not possible. In an acute setting, the patient often will present with an insidious onset that began upon waking. He or she often will complain of difficulty moving the head in any direction with accompanying pain. This acute "torticollis" is most of the time not a torticollis at all, simply because all ranges are affected and the patient's head is held in neutral and not cocked to one side. Although there is no known cause, the global muscle-splinting effect makes this a painful but, in the majority of cases, benign condition.

Instability

Instability is a concern with trauma to the head or neck. The mechanism of injury often is suggested by the type of fracture (Table 2–2). Fracture should always be considered with compressive or distractive injury to the neck. Instability is always a concern with patients who have signs or symptoms or a previous diagnosis of rheumatoid arthritis, seronegative arthritides (ie, ankylosis spondylitis, Reiter's syndrome, or psoriatic arthritis), or Down syndrome.

Examination

Inspection, palpation, and ROM testing is the clinical focus when neck pain or stiffness is the primary complaint. When the complaint involves radiation into the back or extremities, specific orthopaedic and neurologic tests are added. The primary intention of orthopaedic tests is to compress or stretch pain-producing structures such as facets and nerve roots. The standard battery of orthopaedic tests includes various forms of cervical compression, cervical distraction, shoulder depression, the brachial plexus stretch test, Soto-Hall test, and Lhermitt's test. Cervical compression (Figure 2–1) is usually axially applied with the patient's head in neutral and then in all positions. Local pain felt more on extension and/or rotation indicates facet involvement while radiating pain down the arm indicates nerve root involvement. Cervical distraction is an attempt to reduce local or radiating complaints. If the maneuver is more painful, muscle splinting is likely. Shoulder depression (Figure 2–2) can cause nerve root or brachial plexus stretching on the side opposite head deviation, or nerve root compression on the side of lateral flexion. Soto-Hall and Lhermitt's tests involve passive flexion of the patient's neck. Electric shock sensations down the arm or arms is a positive Lhermitt's response and is occasionally found with multiple sclerosis or cervical myelopathy.

Vikari-Juntura and colleagues[19,20] evaluated the interexaminer reliability and validity of some common clinical evaluation procedures for the cervical spine. Inspection of atrophy of small muscles of the hand, sensitivity tests for touch and pain, and the cervical compression and distraction tests were considered reliable. Muscle strength testing and an estimation of ROM were considered fairly reliable.

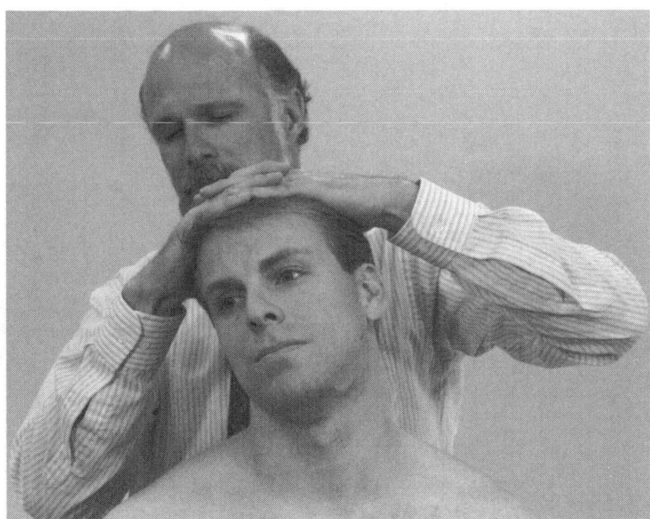

Figure 2–1 Cervical compression. The examiner delivers an axial force through the head into the neck. The compression is applied with the patient's head in various positions of flexion and extension and combined positions of rotation, lateral bending, and extension.

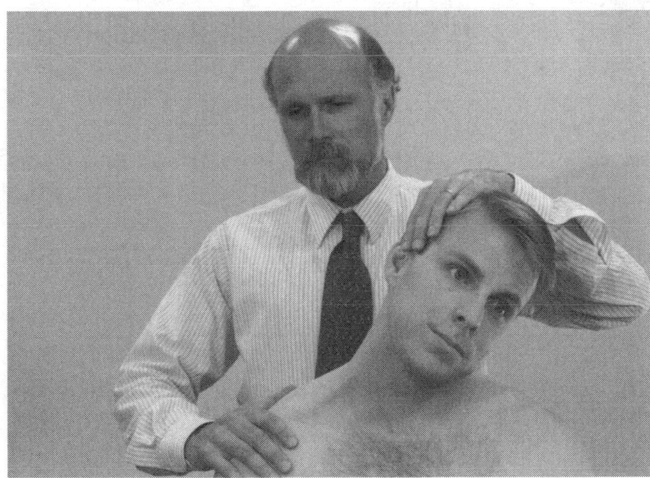

Figure 2–2 Shoulder depression. While the shoulder is being depressed with one hand, the opposite hand laterally bends the head and neck to the opposite side.

Palpation for trigger points, the brachial plexus stretch test, and the shoulder abduction relief test (relief of arm pain when holding the arm above shoulder level), however, were considered poor. When 43 patients with known cervical disc disease were tested with cervical compression, distraction, and shoulder depression the specificity was high; however, the sensitivity was low (25% to 50%). Therefore, patients with cervical disc disease did not consistently have pain provoked or relieved by these maneuvers. When the test was positive, however, it was fairly specific to a disc lesion. Adding neurologic and radiographic information raised the sensitivity to between 40% and 64%.

The standard neurologic examination attempts to differentiate the cause of associated arm pain, numbness and tingling, or weakness. This process attempts to rule in or rule out nerve root compression, peripheral nerve entrapment, referred pain, brachial plexus injury, and spinal cord injury. This is accomplished by determining whether regions specific to a nerve root or peripheral nerve have sensory or motor deficits (see Figure 2–3). Larger, more diffuse, patterns of sensory or motor loss require a search for brachial plexus or spinal cord involvement. Bilateral patterns suggests systemic polyneuropathies or spinal cord involvement.

The basic approach to detecting nerve root involvement is a search for corresponding deficits in sensory, motor, and reflex function. Following is a basic pattern for spinal levels C5-T1 (patterns may vary dependent on the source due to root overlap):

- C5—motor supply to the deltoid (shoulder abduction) and biceps (elbow flexion/supination); biceps reflex, and sensory supply to outer shoulder (axillary nerve)
- C6—motor supply to the biceps (elbow flexion/supination) and wrist extension, brachioradialis reflex, and sensory supply to the outer forearm
- C7—motor supply to the triceps (elbow extension), finger extensors and wrist flexors, triceps reflex, and sensory supply to the middle finger
- C8—motor supply to finger flexors, no reflex, sensory supply to the little and ring fingers
- T1—motor supply to the interosseous muscles of the hand (abduction/adduction of fingers), no reflex, sensory to medial arm

Part of the neurologic examination includes evaluation of grip strength. The most common device used is a Jamar dynamometer. This device has been shown to be accurate and the interrater reliability is high. There are, however, positional and postural effects on readings[21]:

- The wrist can be between 15° of palmar flexion and 30° of extension without an effect on strength; grip is stronger in supination, weaker in pronation; use neutral as the standard forearm position.
- The maximum readings are found with the second- and third-handle positions of a Jamar dynamometer.
- The first and second attempts are the strongest.
- Hand dominance may cause a 10% to 15% higher reading on that side.

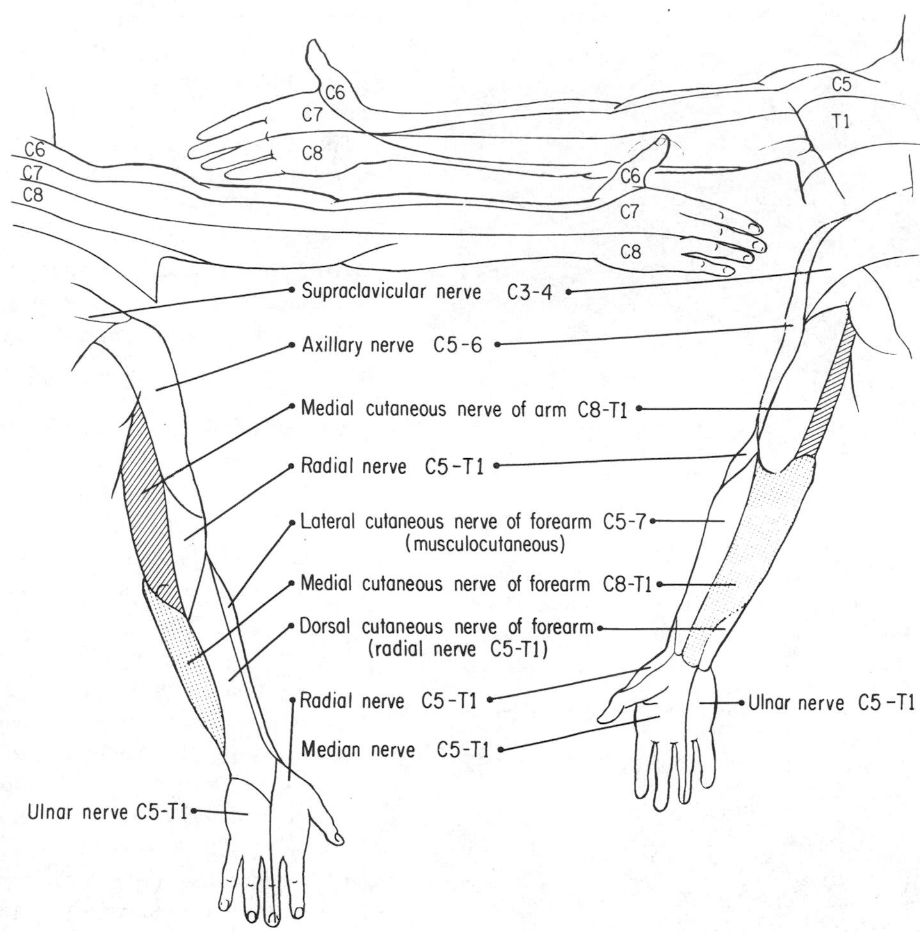

Figure 2–3 Neck Complaints. Dermatomes of the upper extremity and the cutaneous innervation of the arm by the peripheral sensory nerves.

- Test and retest reliability is best with the mean of three trials (attempts) (0.80).
- The patient should be tested in a seated position with the elbow flexed 90° at the patient's side.
- Patients test stronger in the standing position.
- If there is any question as to patient participation, it may be helpful to have the patient test with each handle position; a bell curve should appear even with neurologic weakness (ie, strongest in the middle handle positions, weakest in the shortened and lengthened positions).

Common muscle imbalances at or affecting the cervical spine include tightness of the sternocleidomastoids (SCMs); short, deep, neck extensors; upper trapezius; levator scapulae; and the pectoralis major and minor. Muscles that tend to be inhibited include the deep neck flexors and the lower stabilizers of the scapulae, including the lower and middle trapezius and the rhomboids. Taken together, these imbalances often lead to a rounded shoulder-forward head position. Functional testing as described by Janda[6] includes the spine-chin tuck test. The supine patient is instructed to tuck the chin in as much as possible and then raise the head 1 cm off the table. If the chin pokes or juts forward or if the head shifts up or down, Janda considers this an indication of substitution by the SCMs for the deep neck flexors.

TOS is often considered in the differential diagnosis of patients with arm complaints. Unfortunately, much of this testing is associated with a high level of false-positive and false-negative responses. These maneuvers are designed to compress the brachial plexus by specific structures in the hope of reproducing the patient's arm complaint. If a diminished pulse is used as a positive, however, a false-positive rate of 50% occurs.[22] Tests include Adson's, Halstead's, Eden's, and Wright's hyperabduction test. Adson's and

Halstead's attempt to isolate the anterior or middle scalenes, respectively, as compression sites. The patient's arm is passively abducted while the patient turns his or her head to one side and then the other. The examiner palpates the radial pulse for a decrease; however, a true positive is reproduction of the patient's arm complaints. Wright's hyperabduction test is similar; however, the arm is abducted and extended back. The Roos test is a functional assessment. The patient is asked to hold the hand up above the head and repeatedly grip and release for 20 to 60 seconds in an attempt to reproduce the arm complaint(s).

Vertebrobasilar testing remains controversial, not because of its need but because of the lack of an alternative. Most clinical tests are based on a vascular evaluation and a provocative maneuver. It is known that the vertebral artery is stretched between the axis and atlas with contralateral rotation. Symptoms are not produced, however, unless the other vertebral artery is already compromised. Although numerous factors have been implicated as potential predispositions to vascular injury, none have been demonstrated to be significant for vertebrobasilar risk.[23] Differences in blood pressure between sides may indicate a possible subclavian steal syndrome; however, there is no evidence that this is a risk either. Yet it would be prudent to send a patient with a difference greater than 15 mm Hg between sides for further vascular evaluation prior to manipulating them. Bruits indicate stenosis, yet are usually not audible until there is 50% occlusion; at 85% to 90% occlusion (when theoretically the risk is higher) a bruit is not heard because of the lack of blood flow. Also, bruits are normal in children under age 5 years, and a false-positive may be created by compression of a normal artery by the bell of the stethoscope. The provocative maneuver of placing the patient's head in rotation and extension is variably described. A positive finding would be mainly the production of vertigo or nystagmus. There are false positives and false negatives. In addition, there have never been tests for reliability among examiners, let alone validity. One common false-positive result occurs when the patient is asked to look as far over the shoulder as possible. This can lead to an end-range nystagmus, which is found in normally sighted individuals but particularly in myopic individuals. There is even some risk in simply placing the patient's head in the position for testing. Other forms of testing include Doppler ultrasound, CT, MR angiography, and arteriography. Unfortunately, the only viable choice as an in-office screening device (based on cost, risk, and equipment) is Doppler ultrasound. Although they found it promising, Theil et al.[24] failed to detect any decrease in vertebral blood flow in symptomatic patients or controls who were placed in the provocative position.

Routine radiography of the cervical spine is considered unnecessary unless it can potentially change the management of a case. Conditions that might warrant routine radiography include trauma, infection, gross instability, fracture/dislocation, and cancer. The decision is based on a thorough history and examination, however. Routine radiographs to evaluate degenerative changes are considered of limited value.[25] Radiographic examination of the cervical spine begins with a standard three-shot series including an AP, an AP open-mouth, and a lateral. Based on what is viewed on these basic films, a decision to complement the evaluation with obliques, flexion/extension, swimmer's, or pillar view can be made. Obliques are valuable for visualizing the intervertebral foraminae (IVFs) in search of foraminal encroachment due to osteophytes or dislocation. A bilateral or unilateral pillar view may be helpful when concerned about a possible hidden fracture of the posterior elements.[26] The unilateral view is safest with the patient's head turned 45° and slightly flexed. There is a 30° to 35° caudad tube tilt based on the degree of cervical lordosis. When segmental instability is suspected, the lateral view will provide sufficient evidence for the middle and lower cervical spine. The criteria that are used include the following:

- fanning of adjacent spinae
- a kyphotic angulation greater than 11°
- greater than 3 mm anterior displacement between the inferior posterior border of the superior vertebra and the superior posterior border of the adjacent inferior vertebra

Medical evaluation of instability may involve a radiographic traction stretch test.[27]

For the upper cervical spine, instability is often the result of rheumatoid or congenital disorders, although trauma is a possible cause. Certainly in patients with rheumatoid arthritis, the seronegative arthropathies, or Down syndrome, an evaluation of the atlantodental interspace is warranted. This is measured on a lateral view; it is most evident in flexion on a flexion/extension series. A measurement of the distance between the posterior margin of the anterior tubercle of C1 and the anterior surface of the odontoid is referred to as the atlantodental interspace (ADI) and is an indirect measure of the integrity of the transverse ligament of the atlas. For adults the normal ADI is between 1 and 3 mm; in children, 1 and 5 mm.

Intersegmental hypermobility has been suggested as a biomechanical factor worth investigating; however, the ability of examiners to agree on the criteria and the ability to detect this entity have not yet been established.[28] The standard approach is to use flexion/extension lateral views to observe or to mark intersegmental movement not visible on a neutral lateral view.

A measure of the spaciousness of the spinal canal can be estimated on the lateral cervical view. The distance is measured with a line drawn from the posterior surface of the vertebral body extending to the same level spinolaminar junction. The diameter varies based on the segmental level and between adults and children; however, a canal less than 12 mm is considered stenotic. Another approach is to take the ratio of the sagittal diameter (same as above) to the vertebral body sagittal diameter. A ratio of less than 0.82 is considered evidence of stenosis (Pavlov's or Torg's ratio).[29]

With regard to TOS, many doctors will assume that the presence of cervical ribs is diagnostic. Yet fewer than 1% of the population have cervical ribs, and of those individuals fewer than 10% will have symptoms. Also, fibrous bands not visible on a radiograph are the more common cause of TOS.[30]

Three spaces can be measured if a soft tissue mass is believed to be anterior to the cervical veterebrae. These include the retropharyngeal (at C2-C3), retrolaryngeal (at C4-C5), and retrotracheal (at C5-C7) spaces. Normal values on the neutral are 5 mm at C2, 7 mm at C3-C4, and 20 mm at C5-C7.[31]

When ordering special studies, it is always important to consider what type of tissue is best evaluated by which imaging tool. It is also extremely important to correlate clinical findings with special study findings because of the significant number of abnormal findings in asymptomatic patients. CT and MRI are valuable only when radiographs fail to determine the exact cause of a complaint of radiation of symptoms into the arms or back. Even then, it is probably worth a conservative trial prior to using these expensive tools. If stenosis is suspected, CT is quite valuable. If disc herniation, multiple sclerosis, tumor, infection, or cancer is suspected, MRI is probably more valuable in most cases.

Electrodiagnostic studies occasionally are needed in the differentiation of neck and arm pain. Electromyography (EMG) and nerve conduction studies (NCV) are valuable in differentiating nerve root compression from peripheral neuropathies. Somatosensory-evoked potentials (SEPs) and dermatomal somatosensory-evoked potentials (DSEPs) may be helpful in evaluating the patient suspected of having cervical myelopathy and determining the degree of involvement.

MANAGEMENT

The Mercy Guidelines[32] and other sources suggest that approximately 6 weeks of care is usually all that is needed in most "uncomplicated" cases. Initial high-frequency treatment ranging from three to five treatments for 1 to 2 weeks is considered appropriate. Treatment past this point is gradually decreased if the patient is responding; if not, a second 2-week trial using a different form of treatment is suggested. If then unsuccessful, special studies or referrals for medical consultation are suggested. Factors that may predict a longer recovery include a past history of four or more episodes, symptoms lasting longer than 1 week before presentation to the doctor, severe pain, and previous structural pathology. It is suggested that a questionnaire such as the Neck Disability Index (Exhibit 2–3) be used as a baseline measurement of patient status. This tool has been demonstrated to be a reliable indicator of the patient's functional improvement.[33]

Prior to the use of manipulation for the cervical spine, it has often been suggested that the patient be informed of the very rare yet potential risk of a vertebrobasilar accident. As mentioned earlier, there is no sensitive or reliable screening test, and it is not enough to rely on a past history of uncomplicated manipulation treatment.[23] It must be accepted that the risk is small but real, and there is no known clinical test to identify those who will have an accident. The patient should be informed of this rare complication, given the potential for neurologic compromise.

Postural advice regarding work and everyday posture is considered an important adjunct by many chiropractors. The focus should be to maintain a neutral head position. This often involves a focus on stretching of the short spinal extensors with strengthening of the deep neck flexors. Supportive to this attempt is correction of the factors contributing to a hyperlordotic lumbar spine or hyperkyphotic thoracic spine when possible. Exercises should include stretching of the upper trapezius/levator scapulae, pectorals, lumbar extensors, and hip flexors, followed by strengthening of the middle/lower trapezius, abdominals, and gluteals. Ergonomically, workstations should be oriented to provide a straight-ahead view of a computer screen, shoulder support or headpiece for long-term phone usage, and arm supports on the chair.

The sequence of prescribed exercises usually begins with mild isometrics, progressing to a more functional approach. Minimal contractions into all six movement patterns of flexion, extension, lateral bending, and rotation are initiated as soon as pain restriction permits. An alternative to using resistance against one's own hands is a pressurized ball. This is essentially a rubber ball that is inflated by a sphygmomanometer bulb. The patient can adjust the pressure and monitor resistance through the use of an attached pressure gauge. One study indicated markedly increased neck muscle strength in addition to a reduction in lateral-force imbalance with the use of this device.[34] Fitz-Ritson[35] suggests exercises that are based on reflex mechanisms similar to the work of Feldenkreis and Alexander. His study indicated a marked improvement in pain and a Disability Index rating compared with a group using standard (stretching/isometric/isokinetic) exercises. This approach is based on influencing the vestibular-ocular reflex (VOR), which involves a quick (phasic) coordination of the eye, head, and neck through integration and processing of vestibular, visual, and proprioceptive input.

The management of cervical disc herniation is controversial. An interesting study by Croft,[36] using a questionnaire, demonstrated among the doctors polled a "standard" of adjusting (manipulating) patients with known cervical disc herniation. This is an interesting finding given that chiropractors can be accused of causing disc herniation. The majority of chiropractors, however, would not adjust the affected level. There are several published case studies that indicate that chiropractic management of cervical disc herniation may be successful.[37]

Whiplash

Whiplash or acceleration/deceleration injuries have been classified by both Foreman and Croft[38] and the Quebec Task Force on Whiplash-Associated Disorders.[2] These two classification systems are quite similar, based in part on the classification by Norris and Watt in 1983.[39] Differentiation is based on dividing patients into those with symptoms and no objective findings, symptoms with orthopaedic but no neurologic findings, and symptoms with neurologic findings. The Quebec Task Force adds a classification including fracture or dislocation. The latter group should be referred for orthopaedic consultation in most cases (mild compression fractures of the vertebral bodies are usually stable). Foreman and Croft have used their categorization, linked with a group of modifiers, to develop a prognostic grading. These modifiers include some preexisting (canal stenosis, preexisting degeneration, and preinjury abnormal cervical curve) and some acquired (loss of consciousness, fixed segments on flexion/extension views, or postinjury change in cervical curve) elements. This is a rational, yet untested system. However, it may help guide the doctor and patient regarding expected outcomes (see Table 2–3). The difficulty with any system is the extreme variability of individual patients and the confounding issue of litigation.

Table 2–3 Whiplash Prognosis (Summary of Foreman and Croft Method)

Classifications	*Point Values*
Major injury categories (MIC)	
MIC 1: Patient has symptoms related to injury; however, there are no objective findings	10
MIC 2: Patient has a decrease in cervical ROM and MIC 1 symptoms; however, there are no neurologic signs	50
MIC 3: Patient has MIC 1 and MIC 2 symptoms plus objective neurologic signs (sensory and/or motor)	90
Modifiers	
Canal size of 10–12 mm	20
Canal size of 13–15 mm	15
Kyphotic cervical curve	15
Fixed segment seen on flexion/extension radiographs	15
Loss of consciousness	15
Straight cervical curve	10
Preexisting degeneration	10
Prognosis groups (add MIC with appropriate modifiers to determine prognosis group)	
Group 1: Excellent prognosis. This group has some minor residual problems such as muscle spasms or occipital headaches.	10–30
Group 2: Good prognosis. This group is made up of both MIC 1 and MIC 2 patients. Residual problems may occur, yet the likelihood of neurologic manifestations is small.	35–70
Group 3: Poor prognosis. This group is made up of mainly MIC 2 patients with modifiers and MIC 3 with a few modifiers. Residual symptoms such as numbness or weakness are possible.	75–100
Group 4: Guarded prognosis. This group is made up of MIC 2 patients with many modifiers and MIC 3 patients. The likelihood of persistent neurologic signs such as muscle weakness, atrophy, radiculitis, etc., is increased with the possibility of a need for surgical intervention.	105–125
Group 5: Unstable. Patients will have radiculopathy and/or myelopathy in many cases, and surgery is often indicated.	130–165

Source: Reprinted with permission from S.M. Foreman, *Long-term prognosis*, In S.M. Foreman and A.C. Croft, eds., *Whiplash Injuries: The Cervical Acceleration/Deceleration Syndrome*, 2nd ed, © 1995, Williams & Wilkins.

The Quebec Task Force on Whiplash-Associated Disorders[2] concluded that there is little or no evidence for the efficacy of soft cervical collars, corticosteroid injections of the facet joints, pulsed electromagnetic treatment, magnetic necklace, and subcutaneous sterile water injection. Use of soft collars beyond the 72 hours postinjury will probably prolong disability. The Task Force also feels that the literature did not support the use of cervical pillows, postural alignment training, acupuncture, spray and stretch, heat, ice, massage, muscle relaxation techniques, epidural or intrathecal injections, psychologic interventions, ultrasound, laser, or short-wave diathermy. It is important to note that lack of literature support often means that although many of these approaches are used, no significant research has been performed to evaluate their efficacy. In other words, it does not mean that they are ineffective, more often simply untested. This is often due to the complacency that "if it works, why question it?"

Algorithms

Algorithms for traumatic neck pain, nontraumatic neck and arm pain, nontraumatic neck pain with no radiation, and annotations are presented in Figures 2–4 to 2–7.

SELECTED CAUSES OF CERVICAL SPINE PAIN

DISC HERNIATION

Classic Presentation

The patient complains of neck and arm pain. Onset often follows neck injury; however, it may be insidious. There is often a past history of multiple bouts of neck pain following minor injuries. The patient also complains of some weakness in the hand. The pain is described as a deep ache. Some patients report some relief with the hand held behind the head.

Cause

Nerve root irritation may occur as a result of disc herniation. Osteophytic compression also may occur. In adults over age 40 years, the chance of disc herniation decreases with age because there is essentially less or no nucleus pulposus left to herniate.[9]

Evaluation

The patient often will have a painful restriction in active and passive ROM, often more on one side. Orthopaedic testing with cervical compression (Figure 2–1) may reproduce the neck and arm pain. Radiation into the medial scapular area is also possible. Cervical distraction may relieve the arm pain. Shoulder depression (Figure 2–2) may reproduce the complaint on the side of head deviation. All of these orthopaedic tests are relatively insensitive but moderately specific.[40] Some patients report some relief of the arm pain by putting the hand behind the head, thereby decreasing any traction effect. Neurologic testing should reveal a decreased corresponding deep tendon reflex, weakness in a related myotome, and sensory abnormality in a related dermatome. Radiographic evaluation of the neck should include obliques to determine the degree of bony foraminal encroachment. MRI or CT scans are reserved for patients with severe pain or those unresponsive to nonsurgical management. Electrodiagnostic studies may be helpful within 3 to 4 weeks after the onset of symptoms if a specific cause has not yet been identified or the patient is unresponsive to care.

Management

Cervical manipulation at sites other than the herniation is used by many chiropractors.[36] If osseous adjusting is to be used, it should be applied with a trial of mild mobilization impulses at the involved level to determine patient response. The degree of force applica-

Figure 2–4

TRAUMATIC NECK PAIN—ALGORITHM.

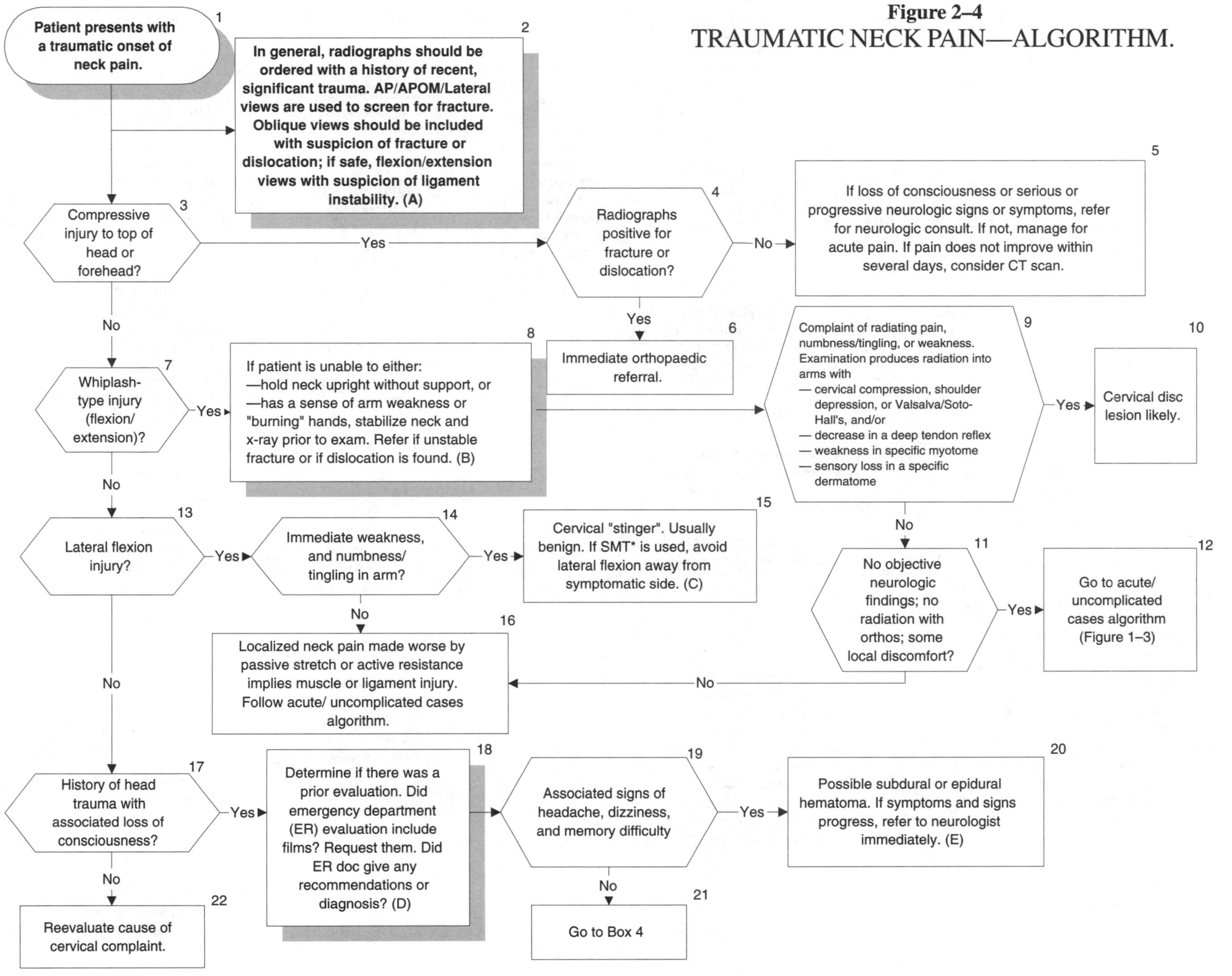

Key: SMT, Spinal manipulative therapy.

Figure 2–5

NONTRAUMATIC NECK AND ARM PAIN—ALGORITHM.

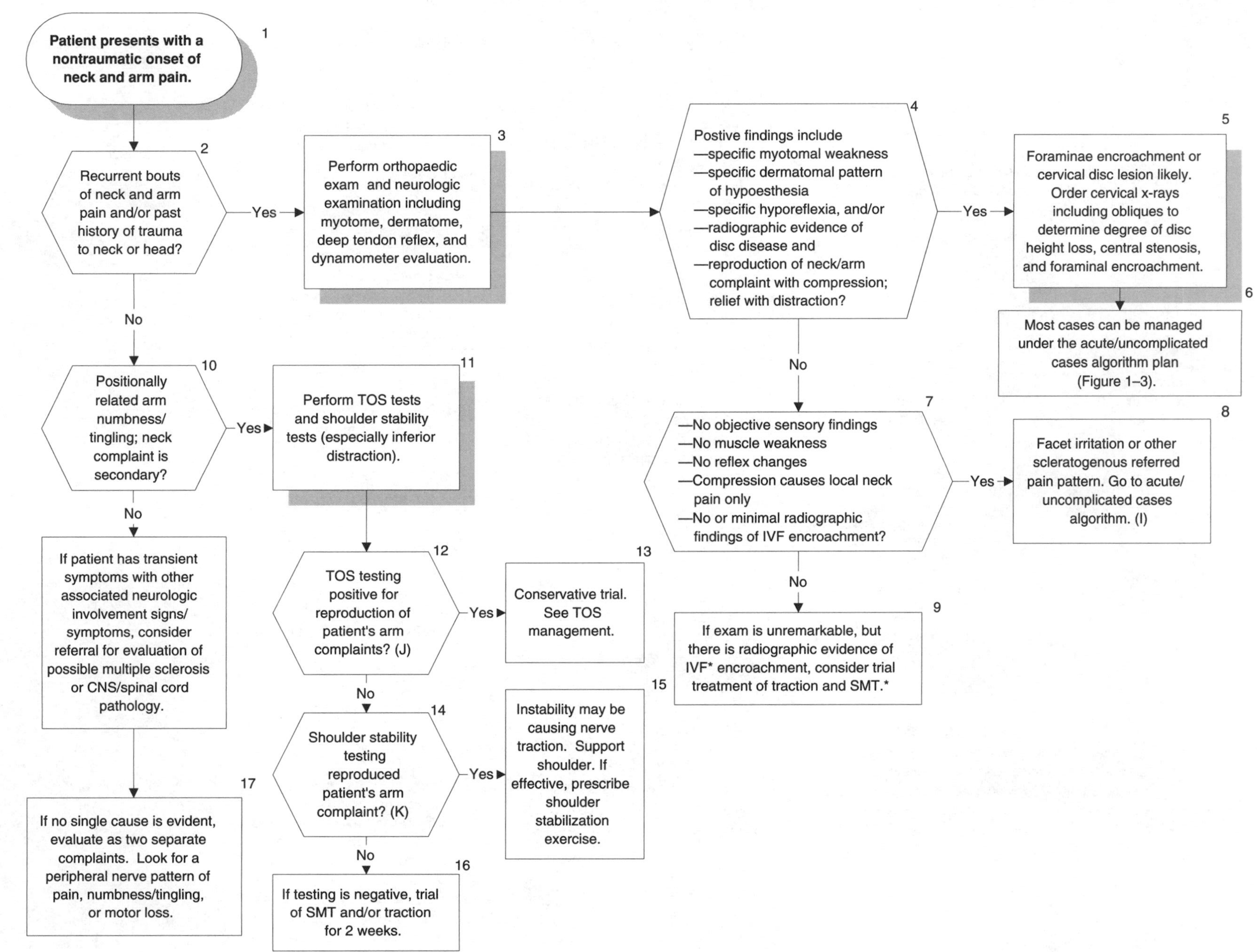

Key: IVF, intervertebral foramina; SMT, spinal manipulative therapy.

Figure 2–6
NONTRAUMATIC NECK PAIN (NO RADIATION) ALGORITHM.

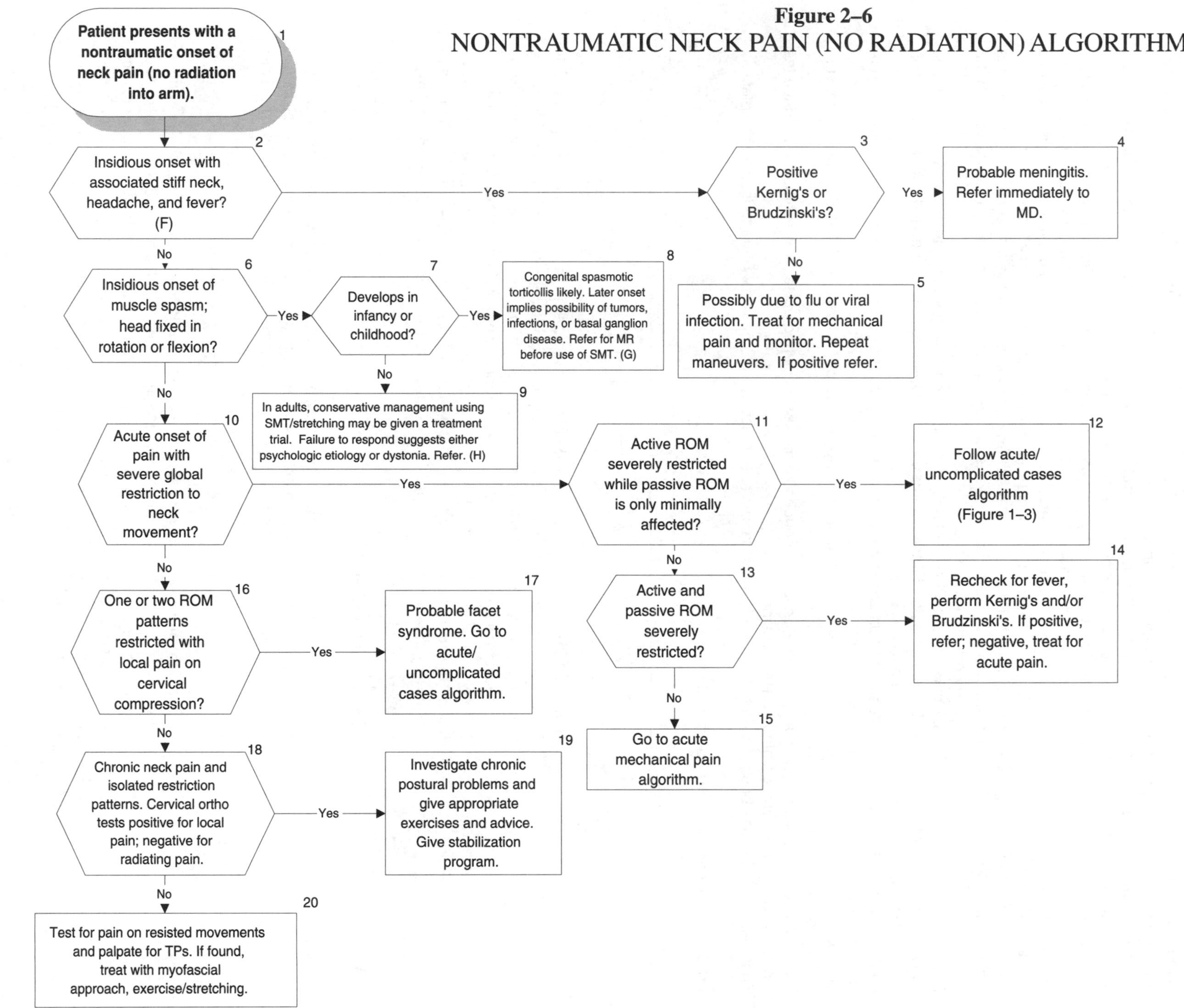

1 Patient presents with a nontraumatic onset of neck pain (no radiation into arm).
2 Insidious onset with associated stiff neck, headache, and fever? (F)
Yes
3 Positive Kernig's or Brudzinski's?
Yes
4 Probable meningitis. Refer immediately to MD.
No
5 Possibly due to flu or viral infection. Treat for mechanical pain and monitor. Repeat maneuvers. If positive refer.
No
6 Insidious onset of muscle spasm; head fixed in rotation or flexion?
Yes
7 Develops in infancy or childhood?
Yes
8 Congenital spasmotic torticollis likely. Later onset implies possibility of tumors, infections, or basal ganglion disease. Refer for MR before use of SMT. (G)
No
9 In adults, conservative management using SMT/stretching may be given a treatment trial. Failure to respond suggests either psychologic etiology or dystonia. Refer. (H)
No
10 Acute onset of pain with severe global restriction to neck movement?
Yes
11 Active ROM severely restricted while passive ROM is only minimally affected?
Yes
12 Follow acute/ uncomplicated cases algorithm (Figure 1–3)
No
13 Active and passive ROM severely restricted?
Yes
14 Recheck for fever, perform Kernig's and/or Brudzinski's. If positive, refer; negative, treat for acute pain.
No
15 Go to acute mechanical pain algorithm.
No
16 One or two ROM patterns restricted with local pain on cervical compression?
Yes
17 Probable facet syndrome. Go to acute/ uncomplicated cases algorithm.
No
18 Chronic neck pain and isolated restriction patterns. Cervical ortho tests positive for local pain; negative for radiating pain.
Yes
19 Investigate chronic postural problems and give appropriate exercises and advice. Give stabilization program.
No
20 Test for pain on resisted movements and palpate for TPs. If found, treat with myofascial approach, exercise/stretching.

Key: TP, trigger point.

A. If trauma is significant or patient is unable to move neck without significant discomfort, stabilize neck and radiograph prior to orthopaedic examination.
B. Burning hands syndrome represents spinal cord injury due to stenosis or fracture. Radiographs to determine fracture and degree of stenosis should also include lateral flexion/extension views to determine any contributory instability. Many cases are self-resolving; however, prolonged recovery is not uncommon.
C. A "stinger" usually involves a traction injury of either the nerve root or plexus. Most are brief occurrences representing a neuropraxia; however, with more severe trauma an axonotmesis can occur, requiring referral to a neurologist.
D. It is extremely important to obtain information regarding any evaluation at another facility. Often films are available and a previous diagnosis and/or patient instructions have been given, including some contraindications to manipulation.
E. Any patient with a history of head trauma should be monitored for several weeks. Epidural hematomas usually involve a temporal bone fracture and bleeding from an artery, resulting in usually a more rapid onset of neurologic signs.
F. Subarachnoid hemorrhage is essentially a brain bruise. It may result from trauma or a ruptured aneurysm or atriovenous malformation. With vessel rupture, the onset is sudden and there is no associated fever. This may help distinguish the presentation from meningitis. Immediate referral is necessary.
G. Spastic torticollis (wryneck) may be congenital and correctable within the first few months. Other causes may include basal ganglion disorders, infection, tumors, and psychiatric disorders. A thorough evaluation is needed prior to application of SMT. Note that the restriction is limited to one side.
H. Dystonia may first present with torticollis and an accompanying distortion of another body part such as the feet. It is rare yet progressive, resulting in sustained abnormal postures.
I. Sclerogenous pain patterns are less distinct than dermatomal or peripheral nerve patterns. Additionally, reflexes, sensory testing, and muscle strength are normal.
J. TOS tests may produce frequent false positives. It is not enough to obtain a diminished pulse. The test must reproduce the patient's complaint of arm pain/numbness/tingling.
K. Shoulder instability has been shown to produce symptoms similar to those of TOS because of tractioning of the plexus.

Figure 2–7 Annotations for neck pain—algorithm.

---

tion should be the least possible. It should always be kept in mind that if the patient has hard neurologic evidence of nerve root compression, the chiropractor is at risk of irritating the nerve and being accused of causing the herniation. Nonosseous techniques may be attempted for a short course to determine therapeutic effect. Cervical traction and physical therapy may also be incorporated. Home traction for 15 minutes twice a day will be of benefit to some patients. The response is usually evident within a few days.[41] Patients who are unresponsive or are simply in too much pain should be referred for medical comanagement.

MYELOPATHY

Classic Presentation

Patient presentation may differ depending on the type and degree of compression. Classically, a patient presents with complaints of bilateral symptoms of clumsiness of the hands, difficulty walking, possible urinary dysfunction, and possible shooting pains into the arms.

Cause

There are numerous causes of spinal cord compression (myelopathy), including tumor, herniated disc, and spondylotic sources. Depending on which portion of the spinal cord or whether nerve roots are also involved, the signs and symptoms will vary. Direct pressure on the posterior columns often occurs with spondylotic myelopathy, causing disturbances in vibration perception and proprioception. If compression of nerve roots also occurs, signs of a lower motor neuron problem will surface.

Evaluation

A thorough neurologic evaluation should be performed. Findings may vary; however, it is important to check for the presence of pathologic reflexes, other upper motor neuron signs, and decreases in strength, proprioception, and vibration. Tests for cerebellar function also should be included. A provocative test that utilizes passive flexion is Lhermitt's test. A positive response with spinal cord involvement is shooting pains into the arms or legs (also sometimes positive with multiple sclerosis). Radiographic measurement of spinal canal diameter may be accomplished on the lateral view of the cervical spine. The width is measured from the posterior vertebral body to the laminopedical junction. Anything less than 13 mm should warrant concern. Anything less than 10 to 11 mm is an indication of absolute stenosis. The Torg (or Pavlov) ratio uses the spinal canal width over the anterior to posterior width of the vertebral body. A ratio less than 0.82 is considered stenotic.[42] Further evaluation of bony stenosis is best seen on CT. Other causes can be visualized on MRI. Cord compression is seen as a high-signal intensity aberration on T2 weighted images.[43] Electrodiagnostic studies may be helpful in estimating the degree of involvement and perhaps the level. The most valuable tests are SEPs and DSEPs because they may determine latency of signal transmission through the spinal cord.[44]

Management

Surgery is often recommended in cases where there are "hard" lesions such as spondylosis or ossification of the posterior longitudinal ligament because of the possibility of permanent neurologic damage. "Soft" lesions such as disc lesions may resolve over time. Decompression surgery for spondylotic myelopathy has variable results between 33% and 74%.[45] Certainly, when there are indications of upper motor neuron lesion (UMNL) signs, surgical consultation is warranted. Conservative treatment may include physical therapy, neutral cervical traction, and nonosseous adjusting techniques in those cases where surgery is not an option or when signs are more of the lower motor neuron lesion (LMNL) type. Comanagement is recommended for patients who show no improvement after 1 to 2 weeks.

BURNER/STINGER

Classic Presentation

The patient reports a sudden onset of burning pain and/or numbness along the lateral arm with associated arm weakness following a lateral flexion injury of the neck/head (eg, lateral "whiplash"). The symptoms usually last only a couple of minutes.

Cause

Burner or stinger is the name given to injury of the brachial plexus or nerve roots caused by a lateral flexion injury. This is a common injury in sports and has a high percentage of underreporting (70%) because of the transient symptoms.[46] In general, lateral flexion of the head away from the involved side with accompanying shoulder distraction (depression) on the involved side causes a brachial plexopathy. Compression on the side with lateral flexion is more likely to result in nerve root compression. When the brachial plexus is involved, the upper trunk (C5-C6) is most often affected. Varying degrees of injury may occur; however, the majority of injuries are mild, with transient symptoms.

Evaluation

The most common physical finding is weakness of shoulder abduction, external rotation, and arm flexion. Both muscle weakness and sensory findings may be delayed; therefore, it is important to reexamine patients within about 1 week postinjury. Persistent symptoms require a radiographic evaluation for instability, including flexion and extension views. If arm weakness is persistent after 3 weeks, an EMG study may be helpful.[47] If a nerve root problem is suspected, an MRI may be of help. Otherwise, most cases require no special testing evaluation.

Management

It is important to avoid reproduction of the injury with a lateral-flexion type of adjustment. Given that recurrence of the injury is common in sports, athletes are encouraged to strengthen their neck muscles and wear protective gear when appropriate. Repeated episodes may lead to more damage requiring neurologic consultation.

THORACIC OUTLET SYNDROME

Classic Presentation

The patient presents with diffuse arm symptoms, including numbness and tingling. Often the patient will describe a path down the inside of his or her arm to the little and ring fingers. This is often made worse by overhead activity.

Cause

The brachial plexus and/or subclavian/axillary arteries can be compressed at various sites as they travel downward into the arm. Several common sites are possible, including an elongated C7 transverse process (cervical rib), the scalene muscles, the costoclavicular area, and the subcoracoid area (between the coracoid and the pectoralis minor). Muscular compression at the scalenes or with the pectoralis minor is believed to be due to tight muscles and/or posturally induced (forward head and rounded shoulder habit). Leffert[48] reports that in 40% of cases there is a report of inciting trauma. It is important to recognize that only 1% of the population has cervical ribs, and only 10% of those individuals have symptoms.[49] A fibrous band connecting the cervical rib to the first rib also may be the culprit in some cases.

Evaluation

Although a number of provocative tests are used, there are often false positives and false negatives. The intent of the tests is to reproduce symptoms in the arm. If the positive is based on simply a reduction of the radial pulse, many false positives will be found. When the scalenes are being tested the patient is asked to look either toward (Adson's test) or away (Halstead's test) from the involved side with the arm held in slight abduction. When the pectoralis minor is tested, the arm is lifted into abduction and horizontal abduction (Wright's test). A functional test is to have the patient raise the arms above head level and repeatedly grip and release the hands for 20 to 60 seconds (Roo's test) in an attempt to reproduce arm symptoms or weakness. It is always important to perform a neurologic evaluation in an attempt to differentiate TOS from lower brachial plexus, nerve root, or peripheral entrapment problems.

Management

Generally, management is conservative with an approach based on postural correction, stretching of tightened muscles, and strengthening of weakened muscles. This includes strengthening of the middle and lower trapezius and rhomboids, and stretching of the pectorals and scalenes. Trigger-point therapy is also advocated by Travell and Simons.[50] Taping or bracing may help with a proprioceptive training program for postural correction.

There is also a belief that a first rib subluxation may cause the signs and symptoms of TOS. Several investigators have suggested manipulation of the first rib in an attempt to correct this problem.[51–53] Surgery is suggested for a minority of patients (approximately 24%) who do not respond to conservative management.[54]

FACET/REFERRED

Classic Presentation

The patient often will report a minor (eg, sudden turning of the head) to moderate (eg, a motor vehicle accident) traumatic onset of neck and arm pain. In some patients the onset can be insidious with no recent trauma. The patient often will draw a line of pain down the outer arm to the hand. The arm and hand pain do not often fit a specific dermatome.

Cause

Irritation of the facet joints or deep cervical muscles causes a referred pain down the arm. The most common location is down the outer arm to the hand. This location often implicates segmentally related facet joints of C5-C7.

Evaluation

A standard orthopaedic and neurologic examination of the neck and upper extremity should be performed. With referred pain, there is rarely any hard neurologic evidence. Deep tendon reflexes are normal, muscle strength is normal or weakness does not fit a specific myotome, and numbness is often subjective with no objective sensory findings. Local pain may be reproduced with cervical compression (Figure 2–1) with the neck in extension and rotation to the involved side. A search for trigger-point referral should be made, including supraspinatus or infraspinatus involvement. Radiographic evaluation may be performed to detect any foraminal encroachment on the oblique views. Patients with mild foraminal encroachment, however, may still have referred pain as opposed to nerve root impingement if the neurologic examination is normal.

Management

Manipulation of the neck is the treatment of choice. If unsuccessful, cervical traction may be of benefit. Any myofascial contribution may be addressed with stretch-and-spray techniques, trigger-point therapy, or myofascial release.

TORTICOLLIS

Classic Presentation

There may be several presentations of torticollis based on age and cause. In congenital torticollis the infant will have a fixed asymmetry of the head that is seen within hours (or sometimes weeks) of delivery. In the adult version a patient presents with painful spasm of the SCM, causing the head to be held in rotation and sometimes slight flexion. In pseudotorticollis the patient presents with the inability to move the head in any direction without pain. The patient reports having awakened with the condition; there is no trauma or obvious cause. The head is held in neutral.

Cause

The congenital cause of torticollis is probably birth trauma, often breech delivery. Damage to the SCM causes it to become fibrous. The adult version may be due to a number of causes, including CNS infection, tumor, basal ganglion disease, or psychiatric disease.

Pseudotorticollis has no known cause. It differs from classic torticollis in that all movements are painful and there is no deviation of the head.

Evaluation

It is important to determine whether there is a moderate to high fever, which would be suggestive of meningitis. Kernig's or Brudzinki's signs would be positive, causing severe pain and/or flexion of the lower limbs on passive flexion of the neck. Palpation of the SCMs and the anterior neck for masses is important. Patients with pseudotorticollis often have markedly increased passive ROM when examined carefully in the supine position. The amount of passive ROM is used as the gauge as to whether or not manipulation is appropriate. A neurologic check for upper motor and lower motor neuron dysfunction will reveal any medically referable causes. Radiographs are usually not necessary. MRI or CT may be needed when CNS disease is suspected.

Management

The congenital type of torticollis may respond to physical therapy attempts to lengthen the SCM; however, the therapy must be consistent and often takes up to 1 year. For the adult who has no known cause, attempts at neck manipulation and physical therapy may help, or it may self-resolve. With pseudotorticollis, manipulation should be applied cautiously as soon as possible in an attempt to decrease the inappropriate global muscle spasm. Failure to resolve warrants a referral for medical evaluation.

REFERENCES

1. Bogduk N. The anatomical basis for spinal pain syndromes. Conference Proceedings of the Chiropractic Centennial Foundation. Presented at the Chiropractic Centennial; July 6–8, 1995; Washington, DC.
2. Spitzer WO, Skovron ML, Salmi LR, Cassidy JD, et al. Redefining "whiplash" and its management. Scientific Monograph of the Quebec Task Force on Whiplash-Associated Disorders. *Spine*. 1995;20(85):1S–73S.
3. Coulter ID, Hurwitz EL, Adams AH, Meeker WC, et al. *The Appropriateness of Manipulation and Mobilization of the Cervical Spine*. Santa Monica, CA: Rand Corporation; 1996.
4. McGregor M, Haldeman S, Kohlbeck FJ. Vertebrobasilar compromise associated with cervical manipulation. *Top Clin Chiro*. 1995;2(3):63–73.
5. Curwin S, Stanish WD. *Tendinitis: Its Etiology and Treatment*. Lexington, MA: Collamore Press; 1984.
6. Janda V. Muscles and cervicogenic pain syndromes. In: Grant R, ed. *Physical Therapy of the Cervical and Thoracic Spine*. New York: Churchill Livingstone; 1988:153–166.
7. Bogduk N. A neurological approach to neck pain. In: Glasgow EF, Twomey IV, Seall ER, et al., eds. *Aspects of Manipulative Therapy*. New York: Churchill Livingstone; 1985.
8. Weintraub M. Beauty parlor stroke syndrome: a report of 5 cases. *JAMA*. 1993;269(16):2085–2086.
9. Terrett AGJ, Kleynhans AM. Cerebrovascular complications of manipulation. In: Haldeman S, ed. *Modern Developments in the Principles and Practice of Chiropractic*. New York: Appleton-Century-Crofts; 1994:579–598.
10. Bland JH. Cervical and thoracic pain. *Curr Opin Rheumatol*. 1991;3:218–225.
11. Panjabi M, Oxland T, Parks E. Quantitative anatomy of cervical spine ligaments, part II: middle and lower cervical spine. *J Spinal Dis*. 1991:277–285.
12. Mootz RD. Theoretic models of chiropractic subluxation. In: Gatterman MI, ed. *Foundations of Chiropractic: Subluxation*. St. Louis, MO: Mosby-Year Book; 1995:176–189.
13. DeJong PTVN, DeJong JMBV, Cohen B, Jongkees LBV. Ataxia and nystagmus induced by injection of local anesthesia in the neck. *Ann Neurol*. 1977;1:240–246.
14. Richmond FJR, Vidal PP. The motor system: joints and muscles of the neck. In: Peterson BW, Richmond F, eds. *Control of Head Movement*. New York: Oxford University Press; 1988.
15. Leffert RD. Thoracic outlet syndrome and the shoulder. *Clin Sports Med*. 1983;2:439.
16. Panjabi MM, Vasavada A, White AA III. Cervical spine biomechanics. *Semin Spine Surg*. 1993;5:10–16.
17. Panjabi MM, Oda T, Crisco JJ III, et al. Posture affects motion coupling patterns of the upper cervical spine. *J Orthop Res*. 1993;11:525–536.
18. Croft AC. Advances in the clinical understanding of acceleration/deceleration injuries to the cervical spine. In: Lawrence DJ, Cassidy JD, McGregor M, et al., eds. *Advances in Chiropractic*. St. Louis, MO: Mosby-Year Book; 1995;2:1–37.
19. Vikari-Juntura E. Interexaminer reliability of observations in physical examinations of the neck. *Phys Ther*. 1987;67:1526–1532.
20. Vikari-Juntura E, Porros M, Lassomen EM. Validity of clinical tests in the diagnosis of root compression in cervical disc disease. *Spine*. 1989;14:253–257.
21. Souza TA. Which orthopedic tests are really necessary? In: Lawrence DJ, Cassidy JD, McGregor M, et al., eds. *Advances in Chiropractic*. St. Louis, MO: Mosby-Year Book; 1994;1:101–158.

22. Sieke FW, Kelly TR. Thoracic outlet syndrome. *Am J Surg*. 1988;156:54–57.
23. Ferezy JS. Neurovascular assessment for risk management in chiropractic practice. In: Lawrence DJ, Cassidy JD, McGregor M, eds. *Advances in Chiropractic*. St. Louis, MO: Mosby-Year Book; 1994:455–475.
24. Theil H, Wallace K, Donaf J, Yong-Hing K. Effect of various head and neck positions on vertebral artery blood flow. *Clin Biomech*. 1994;9:109–110.
25. Helfet CA, Stanley P, Lewis Jones B, Heller RF. Value of x-ray examinations of the cervical spine. *Br Med J*. 1983;287:1276–1278.
26. Jaeger SA, Baum CA, Linquist GR. The many faces of the facets. In: Lawrence DJ, Cassidy JD, McGregor M, et al., eds. *Advances in Chiropractic*. St. Louis, MO: Mosby-Year Book; 1995;2:331–372.
27. White AA, Panjabi MM, eds. *Clinical Biomechanics of the Spine*. Philadelphia: JB Lippincott; 1978:229.
28. McGregor M, Mior S, Shannon H, Hagino C, Schut B. The clinical usefulness of flexion-extension radiographs in the cervical spine. *Top Clin Chiro*. 1995;2(3):19–28.
29. Torg JS. Cervical spine stenosis with cord neuropraxia and transient quadriplegia. *Curr Opin Orthop*. 1994;5(11):97.
30. Karas SE. Thoracic outlet syndrome. *Clin Sports Med*. 1990;9: 297–310.
31. Sistrom CL, Southall EP, Peddada SD, et al. Factors affecting the thickness of the cervical prevertebral soft tissues. *Skeletal Radiol*. 1993;22:167.
32. Haldeman S, Chapman-Smith D, Petersen DM, Jr. *Guidelines for Chiropractic Quality Assurance and Practice Parameters: Proceedings of the Mercy Center Consensus Conference*. Gaithersburg, MD: Aspen Publishers Inc; 1993.
33. Vernon H, Mior S. The neck disability index: a study of reliability and validity. *J Manipulative Physiol Ther*. 1991;14:409–415.
34. Axen K, Haas F, Schicci J, Merrick J. Progressive resistance neck exercises using a compressible ball coupled with an air pressure gauge. *J Orthop Sports Phys Ther*. 1992;16(6):275–280.
35. Fitz-Ritson D. Phasic exercises for cervical rehabilitation after "whiplash" trauma. *J Manipulative Physiol Ther*. 1995;18:21–24.
36. Croft AC. Standards of care in cervical disk herniation: results from our nationwide survey of 3500 DCs. *SRISD Fact Sheet*. 1995;3:1–2.
37. Ben-Eliyahu D. Magnetic resonance imaging follow-up study of 27 patients receiving chiropractic treatment for cervical and lumbar disc herniations. Conference Proceedings of the Chiropractic Centennial Foundation, July 6–8, 1995; Washington DC.
38. Foreman SM, Croft AC. *Whiplash Injuries: The Cervical Acceleration/Deceleration Syndrome*. 2nd ed. Baltimore: Williams & Wilkins; 1995.
39. Norris SH, Watt I. The prognosis of neck injuries resulting from rear-end vehicle collisions. *J Bone Joint Surg Br*. 1983;65:608–611.
40. Vikari-Juntura E, Porros M, Lassomen EM. Validity of clinical tests in the diagnosis of root compression in cervical disc disease. *Spine*. 1989;14:253–257.
41. Venditti PP, Rosner AL, Kettner N, Sanders G. Cervical traction device study: a basic evaluation of home-use supine cervical traction devices. *JNMS*. 1995;3:82–91.
42. Torg JS, Pavlov H, Genuario S, et al. Neuropraxia of the cervical spine cord with transient quadriplegia. *J Bone Joint Surg*. 1986; 68(A):1354–1370.
43. Bell GR, Ross J. Diagnosis of nerve root compression. *Orthop Clin North Am*. 1992;23:405–415.
44. Swenson R. Dermatomal somatosensory evoked potentials: a review of literature. *JNMS*. 1994;2(2):45–51.
45. Yone K, Sakov T, Yanese M, Ijuri K. Preoperative and postoperative magnetic resonance image evaluation of the spinal cord in cervical myelopathy. *Spine*. 1994;17(10S):390–392.
46. Hershman EB. Brachial plexus injuries. *Clin Sports Med*. 1990;9(2):311–329.
47. Sallis RE, Jones K, Knopp W. Burners: offensive strategy for an underreported injury. *Physician Sportsmed*. 1992;20:47–55.
48. Leffert RD. Thoracic outlet syndrome: a correspondence newsletter to the American Society of Surgery of the Hand, December 12, 1988.
49. Brown SCW, Charlesworth D. Results of excision of a cervical rib in patients with thoracic outlet syndrome. *Br J Surg*. 1988;75:431.
50. Travell J, Simons DG. *Myofascial Dysfunction: The Trigger Point Manual*. Baltimore: Williams & Wilkins; 1983.
51. Grice AC. Scalenus anticus syndrome: diagnosis and chiropractic adjustive procedure. *JCCA*. 1977;5:35–37.
52. Lee R, Farquarson T, Domleo S. Subluxation and blockierung der ersten rippe: eine ursache fur das "thoracic outlet syndrome." *Manuelle Medizin*. 1993;31:126–127.
53. Lindgren KA, Leino E. Subluxation of the first rib: a possible thoracic outlet syndrome mechanism. *Arch Phys Med Rehabil*. 1988;69:692–695.
54. Swaraz ZT. The thoracic outlet syndrome: first rib subluxation syndrome. In: Gatterman MI, ed. *Foundations of Chiropractic: Subluxation*. St. Louis, MO: Mosby-Year Book; 1995:360–377.

Chapter 3

Temporomandibular Complaints

CONTEXT

Although often viewed as the domain of the specialist, many temporomandibular joint (TMJ) disorders may be sufficiently screened and managed by the chiropractor. If the TMJ is conceptually approached like any other synovial joint, most common problems can be detected. These problems include synovitis, capsulitis, disc (meniscal) derangement, tendinitis, arthritis, and associated myofascial involvement. The complexity arises when multiple factors with regard to dentition occur. Comprehensive, yet cumbersome, approaches such as the craniomandibular index (74 separate items) generally are impractical and are not weighted toward items of most importance. Screening procedures are sufficient and can provide a baseline determination of the degree of involvement without sacrificing thoroughness.

Ambiguous terminology has always hampered discussions of TMJ disorders. In general, it is important to view (no matter what the terminology) TMJ conditions as intraarticular and extraarticular. Extraarticular involvement may range from cervical spine involvement (myofascial, postural, subluxation-related dysfunction) to dental abnormalities or pathologies. Some practitioners refer to the dysfunctional cervical spine-TMJ relationship as a TMJ syndrome. Intraarticular disorders center around familiar problems such as synovitis and capsulitis with a focus on the articular disc, which is often displaced or degenerated.

One study suggests that 85% to 90% of the individuals will develop some TMJ-related symptom in their lifetime.[1] It appears that women are affected more commonly than men. Unfortunately, studies have shown a poor response to TMJ management, in the range of only 4% to 36%. An interesting subgroup of patients are professional violin and viola players who seem to have a higher than average predisposition toward TMJ problems.[2] Although osteoarthritis of the TMJ obviously is more prevalent in the elderly population, signs and symptoms of craniomandibular disorders tend to decrease in the elderly.[3] Although the TMJ may be the source of local pain, it has been accused of being a primary referral source for both neck and ear pain.[4]

GENERAL STRATEGY

History

- Determine whether the patient's complaint is one of pain, clicking/popping, crepitus, inability to open fully, or fatigue with chewing.
- Determine whether there is any history of direct trauma, episodes of jaw locking, whiplash injuries, past diagnoses of an arthritis, or significant dental pathology.
- Determine whether there are other signs or symptoms suggestive of an underlying arthritis.
- Attempt to distinguish between an intraarticular and extraarticular problem.

Evaluation

- Determine dental status.
- Measure all aspects of mandibular gait.
- Perform provocative maneuvers of stretch (capsulitis), compression (synovitis), and contraction (myofascial).
- Palpate common tender areas indicating sites for specific, commonly involved structures.
- Radiographs are not helpful; magnetic resonance imaging (MRI) may be of benefit; however, it should be reserved for patients who have severe pain or are not responsive to several months of conservative care.

Management

- Management is multifactorial. Address myofascial issues with trigger-point massage, and muscle hyperactivity or hypertonicity with myofascial release techniques. Address compressive retrodiscal problems with a splint or stretching and breaking up adhesions with short-amplitude thrusts (except in those cases listed below).
- Refer patients to a dentist who specializes in TMJ problems if dental involvement is significant, an acute lock cannot be reduced, or treatment for chronic pain is unsuccessful. Refer to a medical doctor if fracture is suspected.

RELEVANT ANATOMY AND BIOMECHANICS

The TMJ is best visualized by using both anterior to posterior and lateral to medial perspectives (Figures 3–1 and 3–2). These perspectives will assist when conceptualizing function and dysfunction. It is easiest to view the TMJ as a two-joint compartment. The superior compartment is bordered by the articular surface of the eminence of the temporal bone superiorly and the articular disc inferiorly. The superior compartment's function is to allow and govern linear movement or translation. The inferior compartment is bordered by the inferior surface of the articular disc and the superior surface of the condyle. The inferior compartment permits full rotary (open and closing) motion of the mandibular condyle if the condyle is seated under the articular disc. The articular disc, separating the TMJ into the superior and inferior compartments, is a necessary component for smooth jaw movement. If the disc is either degenerated or displaced (or both), limitation or popping/clicking of jaw movement will occur. The posterior attachment to the disc is the retrodiscal tissue. Although these two structures are connected, their composition and function are quite different. The disc is a biconcave structure consisting of dense fibrous connective tissue and, as such, is not vascularized or pain sensitive. The retrodiscal tissue, however, is mainly a large venous plexus covered with synovial membrane. It is well innervated and therefore a likely source of some TMJ pain. When irritated, the retrodiscal tissue is capable of producing synovial effusion.

The disc is connected and stabilized by the collateral discal ligaments. Together with the capsular ligaments, they are important in guaranteeing combined movement of the disc and condyle during jaw movement. Elongation or damage disengages this coupling and may allow anterior displacement of the disc.

A discussion of normal opening and closing of the jaw will illustrate the need for a balance among several structures to accomplish smooth and painless movement. As the mouth opens, there is relaxation of the closing muscles (mainly temporalis and masseters). After about 1 cm of opening, the inferior head of the external pterygoid muscle pulls

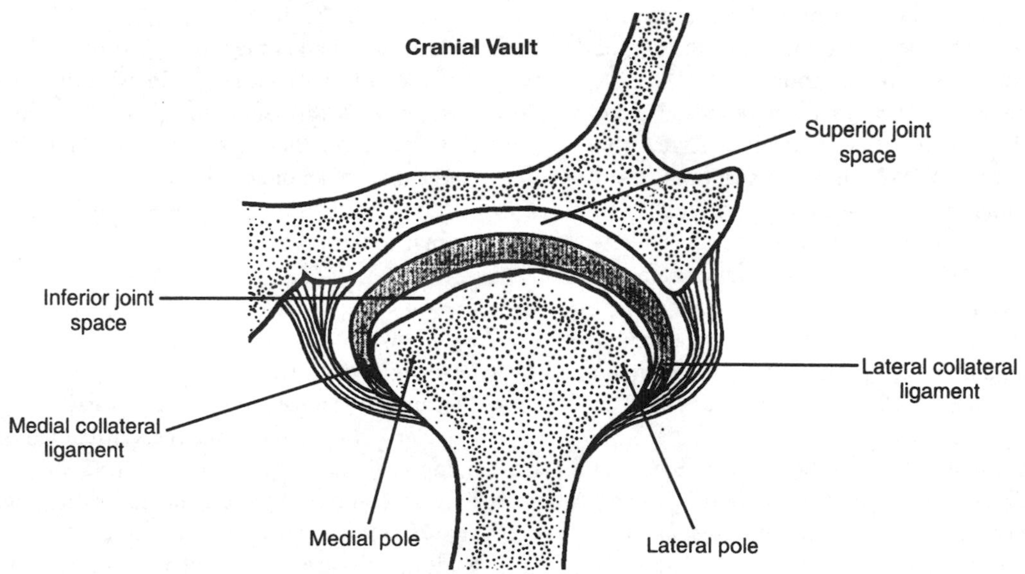

Figure 3–1 Frontal view of the TMJ showing the ligaments that tether the disc atop the condyle, dividing the TMJ space into two parts. *Source:* Reprinted with permission from S.M. Foreman and A.C. Crof, *Whiplash Injuries: The Cervical Acceleration/Deceleration Syndrome*, 2nd ed., p. 393, © 1995, Williams & Wilkins.

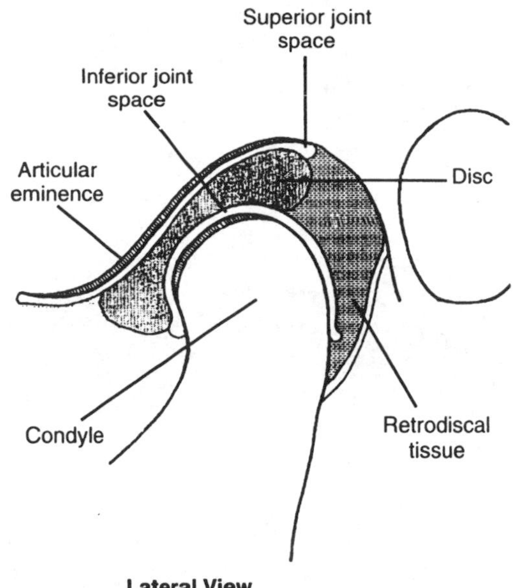

Figure 3–2 Lateral view of the TMJ. *Source:* Reprinted with permission from S.M. Foreman and A.C. Crof, *Whiplash Injuries: The Cervical Acceleration/Deceleration Syndrome*, 2nd ed., p. 393, © 1995, Williams & Wilkins.

on both the disc and the condyle. With the hyoid bone stabilized by the supra- and infrahyoid muscles, the digastric muscle helps pull the mandible downward and backward toward the end of opening. Rotation occurs primarily in the first third of opening. This movement occurs primarily between the inferior articular disc surface and the condylar head. Rotational movement is limited by tautness of the outer oblique band of the temporomandibular ligament. Further opening results in translation down the slope of the articular eminence to the point at which the condyle is slightly past the center of the eminence. During closing, the inferior head remains silent while the superior head of the pterygoid muscle stabilizes the disc and condyle as they translate posteriorly. The muscles that are primarily involved are the temporalis and masseter. Limitation of posterior movement of the condyle is provided, in part, by the inner horizontal band of the temporomandibular ligament.

Lateral movement of the mandible is caused by contraction of the ipsilateral temporalis and masseter muscles and contralateral contraction of the medial and lateral pterygoid muscles (Figure 3–3a). Protrusion is the result of forward movement of the condyles through contraction of the lateral pterygoid muscle combined with forward mandible movement caused by contraction of the masseter and medial pterygoid muscles.

Abnormal movement may be asymptomatic or result in pain, popping/clicking, or crepitus. One of the most common functional problems with the TMJ is anterior displacement of the articular disc (Figure 3–3B). When this occurs, the condylar head is positioned behind the posterior band of the disc. When viewed from the side, the articular disc looks like a stretched-out red blood cell. There is a thicker anterior band, a thin intermediate band, and a thickened posterior band. Normally, the condylar head rests in between the anterior and posterior bands in the depression formed by the intermediate area. This position is maintained from a closed-mouth to an open-mouth position. With anterior displacement, the condyle's starting position is behind the posterior band. With opening, if the condyle can override the posterior band to reach the intermediate area, a pop is often heard. When the pop is heard or felt close to full opening, marked anterior displacement and posterior ligament deterioration are suggested.[5] This characteristic pop is an indicator of anterior disc displacement with reduction. The condyle retains its normal position until full closing, when often it is again pulled back behind the posterior band of the disc. This may cause a pop or click, referred to as a reciprocal click. When the condylar head cannot reduce into the intermediate disc depression on opening, no pop is heard. This functional derangement is referred to as a closed lock. This unreduced displacement is referred to as a *lock* because condylar translation is limited by the disc/condyle relationship, preventing full opening. An open lock may occur when the condylar head extends far past the articular eminence and is not able to return posteriorly.

Although injury may be acute, many of the TMJ's problems are the result of chronic biomechanical dysrelationships. These may be complex, involving abnormalities of bone development or occlusal problems, yet many complaints are, at least in part, due to the indirect effects of soft tissue problems. As in any other joint, the capsule and ligaments are susceptible to acute or chronic stretching to the point that they no longer provide stability. In acute-stretch scenarios, further stretch often increases pain. One of the most common causes of overstretching of the capsule and ligaments is a distended joint. If this is a chronic process, the capsule and ligaments may be left in a poorly functioning overstretched position leading to hypermobility of the TMJ.

The pain-sensitive retrodiscal area is susceptible to compression. Both the compression itself and the resulting synovial fluid reaction that increases pressure in the joint may cause pain. Externally applied compression often increases the pain in this scenario. Compression of the retrodiscal tissue may be due to a number of reasons; however, there are some common culprits, as follows:

- Condylar compression due to anterior disc displacement which forces the condyle posteriorly.
- A hypertonic temporalis muscle (posterior fibers) may pull the condyle back posteriorly.

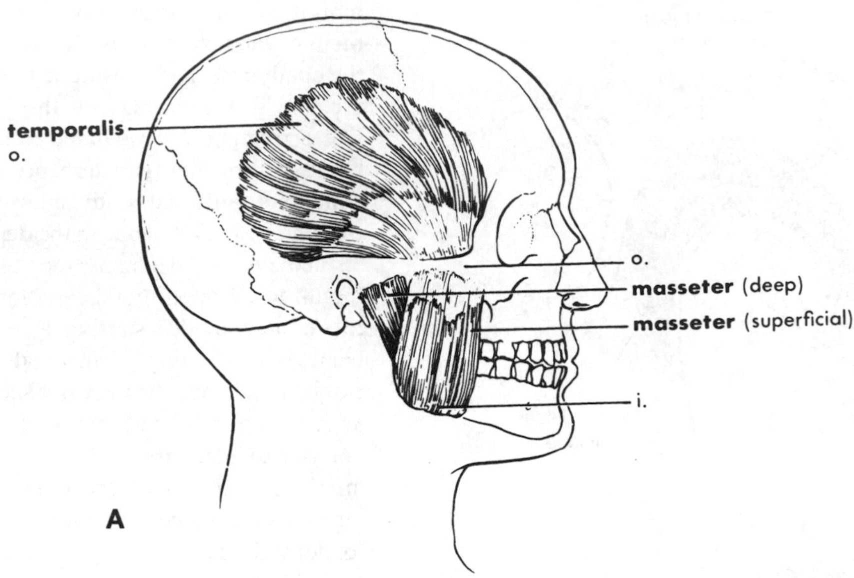

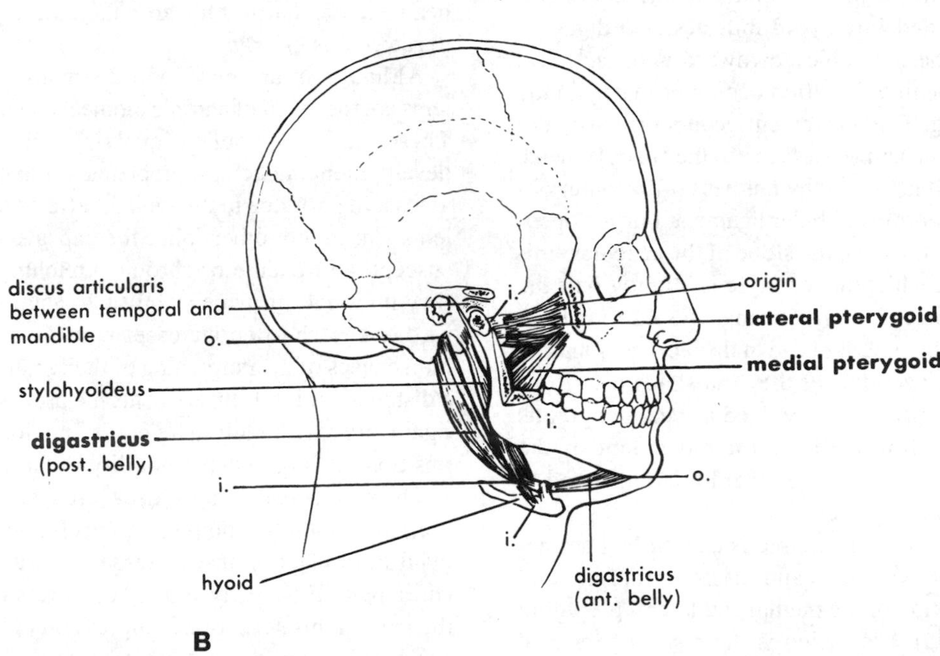

Figure 3–3A and B Muscles of mastication. Origins are indicated by *o*, insertions by *i*. *Source:* Reprinted with permission from J.E. Crouch, *Functional Human Anatomy*, 4th ed., © 1985, Lea & Febiger.

- The vertical height of the teeth, when diminished (loss of teeth or attrition), causes the condyle to be displaced up and back into the retrodiscal material.
- A blow (or an overly aggressive adjustment) to the mandible in a superior/posterior direction may jam the condyle into the retrodiscal tissue.

EVALUATION

History

It is important to determine any direct or indirect trauma to the TMJ (Table 3–1). Direct blows to the jaw can stretch or compress the same-side TMJ. A blow to the front of the jaw driving the jaw directly back will cause more of a compressive injury with a reactive synovitis. A blow to the lateral jaw may stretch the joint capsule, resulting in a capsulitis or disc derangement. Microtrauma may occur as a result of bruxism. Bruxism may be evident to the patient if he or she notices it during the day; however, if bruxism occurs at night, the patient may be unaware of grinding the teeth. A sleep partner may provide the answer.

If the patient has had a diagnosis of an inflammatory arthritis, such as rheumatoid arthritis, ankylosing spondylitis, psoriatic arthritis, Reiter's syndrome, or lupus erythematosus, it is likely that the TMJ pain is due to an inflammatory process. Pain in patients with local infections such as measles, mumps, or infectious mononucleosis are similarly affected.

Asking about provocative maneuvers may help narrow the list:

- Clicking and popping—If the jaw clicks on opening, a disc displacement with reduction is often the cause; this occurs as the translating condyle slips into its normal position under the posterior edge of the disc; a closing click indicates that a weakened posterior ligament is failing to retract the disc.
- Locking—There are two general types of lock: (1) If the patient simply cannot open fully (closed lock), the disc is probably anterior to the condyle during jaw opening (recapture not possible). (2) If the patient is unable to close the mouth (open lock), the anterior condyle has dislocated; this may occur as the result of excessive joint laxity or blunt trauma.
- Pain with excessive opening—This is the hallmark of a capsulitis; additional accompanying complaints are pain with contralateral chewing and protrusion or lateral excursion of the mandible.
- Pain with chewing—The first possibility is a dental disorder; when the TMJ is involved, a synovitis is likely; this may be due to atypical chewing habits, chronic gum chewing, or any impact injury; the patient may notice that he or she cannot close fully on the involved side so that the teeth touch.

Questioning the individual regarding associated neck pain, postural habits with regard to work and sleep, and any previous neck injuries may help establish a more myofascial or referred cause in those patients without specific complaints of clicking, popping, locking, or pain with chewing.

Examination

Examination of the TMJ focuses on two main bodies of information: (1) mandibular "gait" analysis with auscultation and (2) palpation combined with provocative maneuvers including compressive, stretch, and contractile challenge. Secondary evaluation focuses on possible involvement of dental and cervical spine contributions.

The degree of opening is measured in two ways. One is measurement with a ruler (in millimeters). The other approach is to use the patient's own knuckles as a patient-specific (accounts for patient size) approach. The general rule of thumb is that if the patient can open two or two and a half knuckles width, range of motion is considered normal. Less than two knuckles suggests hypomobility; an opening of three or more knuckles suggests hypermobility. It must be remembered that a hypermobile joint may be the result of posterior ligament stretching over a prolonged period of time.[6]

Mandibular gait analysis attempts to document visual range of motion on a cross-hair diagram. Measurement is made with a transparent straight-edge ruler in millimeters. With the horizontal line as an x-axis, laterotrusion (lateral movement to the left and right) from a starting position of neutral with the mouth closed may be documented. The vertical or y-axis line is used to document both maximum opening distance and deviation upon opening. Xs placed next to the vertical line indicate points at which clicking, crepitus, or pain occurs. Small notes indicating whether the clicking is on opening or variable should be added. The vertical line above the intersection point on the diagram represents the z-axis and is used to document the degree of protrusion of the jaw.

Muscle/tendon involvement is determined through the traditional approaches of palpation and contraction. There are distinct areas of tenderness that may correlate with involved structures. The masseter muscle may house several tender areas. The tendinous area is palpated under the zygomatic arch. Posterior to this are the deep vertical fibers of the masseter. The belly of the masseter is palpated just above the angle of the jaw. Cautious palpation should be used over the posterolateral aspect of the masseter because of the overlying parotid gland. Temporalis trigger points are not uncom-

Table 3–1 History Questions for Temporomandibular Joint Disorders

Primary Question	*What Are You Thinking?*	*Secondary Questions*	*What Are You Thinking?*
Was there a direct blow to the jaw?	Fracture, disc derangement, synovitis, capsulitis	Did you have a blow to the front of the jaw (directly back)?	Fracture, synovitis, disc derangement
		Did you have a blow to the outside of the jaw?	Same-side capsulitis; opposite-side synovitis
Does your jaw lock?	Closed lock, acute open lock	Is the lock felt as a block to full opening?	Closed lock (recapture of condyle to disc not possible)
		Does the jaw lock in full opening?	Anterior dislocation of condyle (often due to hypermobility of TMJ)
Is the complaint more one of popping or clicking?	Disc displacement, adhesions	Is there an opening and closing pop?	Disc displacement
		Is there grinding or popping throughout opening or closing?	Adhesions
Is the pain worse when opening the mouth wide?	Capsulitis, hypermobility of TMJ	Did you have either a whiplash injury or a prolonged dental procedure?	Sudden or prolonged stretching of capsule leading to capsulitis
		Do you often yawn widely?	Possible chronic stretching of capsule leading to hypermobility of TMJ
Is the pain worse with chewing?	Dental pathology, TMJ synovitis	Is the pain worse with cold, hot, or sweet foods?	Dental pathology
		Is it worse when biting down on one side?	Same-side synovitis (ask about chronic gum chewing, grinding teeth at night, or habit of chewing on one side)
Are there other joints that hurt?	Referral from cervical spine, rheumatoid arthritis (RA), rheumatoid variants, connective tissue disease	Do you have cervical spine pain or headaches?	Possible referral to TMJ (check for forward head position)
		Have you had a past diagnosis of another arthritis?	More common with inflammatory arthritides
		Do your fingers or knees also hurt?	Possible RA
		Does your low back (point to sacroiliac joint) or do your heels hurt?	Reiter's syndrome, ankylosing spondylitis
Are there current signs of local or systemic infection?	Acute otitis media, measles, mumps, or mononucleosis	Do you have associated ear pain?	Ear infection
		Do you have sore throat and fatigue?	Possible mononucleosis
		Do you have swelling of the outer cheeks?	Mumps

mon and often are found in a halo array above the ear in the belly of the muscle.

General testing of jaw opening and closing may give clues to muscle involvement due to an increased pain response. Resisting the patient's attempt at opening may cause pain when the inferior heads of the pterygoid muscles are involved. Resisted closing is accomplished by using a padded gauze contact over the incisors. Pain production implicates either the temporalis or masseter muscle.

Palpation of the TMJ should be performed both anterior and posterior to the tragus. Anterior to the tragus, a small depression is formed with jaw opening. Using a finger to palpate this depression, the examiner asks the patient to open and close the mouth. What may be appreciated is whether there is too much or too little condyle translation. Tenderness in the pretragus depression is an indicator of inflammation. Guided by the external auditory meatus to gain access to the posterior aspect of the TMJ, the examiner inserts a gloved fifth finger with the fingernail facing posteriorly. The patient is then asked to open and close slowly. The examiner may appreciate clicking or popping. If clicking or popping is felt, the examiner focuses on the involved joint and asks the patient to repeat opening until a pop or click is appreciated. Before closing, a tongue blade is placed between the teeth. The opening and closing sequence is repeated to determine whether the clicking or popping can be eliminated. If so, the disc has been recaptured, suggesting a mechanical cause of anterior disc displacement that may respond to a dental appliance. Tenderness on full closure suggests an inflamed posterior joint. Tongue blades placed posteriorly may reduce this tenderness.

Stretch testing is used to determine whether capsular irritation is present (Figure 3–4). An intraoral contact may be used to distract the mandible down and forward. An increase in pain is suggestive of capsular irritation. Compression testing is used to provoke pain when synovitis is present (Figure 3–5). Pressure on the mandible in a superior posterior direction is likely to increase pain when the retrodiscal tissue is inflamed or a synovitis is present.

Postural evaluation is an important component of TMJ evaluation. The most common postural abnormality is a forward head position with a compensatory extension of the head to correct for visual requirements. Although the initial flexion component of the forward head position causes the mandible to translate down and forward, the compensatory extension forces the mandible posteriorly, potentially irritating the retrodiscal tissue.

Radiographic evaluation of TMJ disorders may be valuable when TMJ tomograms are employed. Standard radiography of the joint rarely provides any additional information. However, two studies indicate that the addition of tomogram findings had a significant effect on clinical decision making. The most common findings that influenced either diagnosis or treatment decisions were unanticipated osseous changes and unexpected condylar position.[7,8]

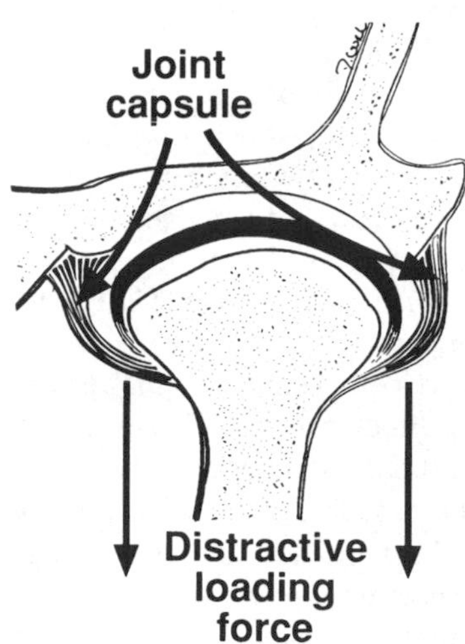

Figure 3–4 Stretch testing for capsular irritation. *Source:* Reprinted with permission from D.J. Lawrence, J.D. Cassidy, M. McGregor, et al., *Advances in Chiropractic*, Vol. 2, p. 165, © 1995, Mosby-Year Book.

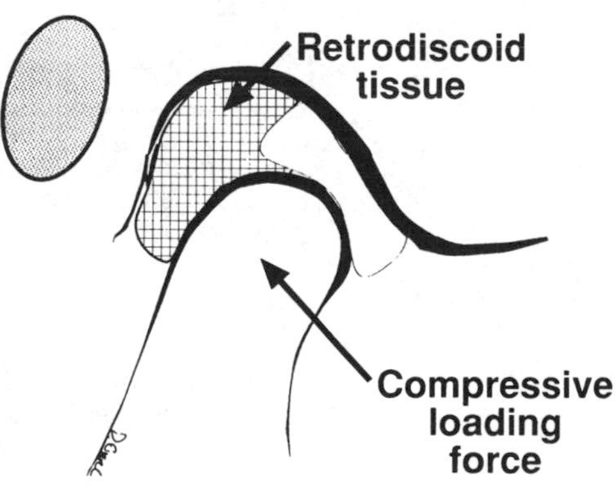

Figure 3–5 Compression testing for synovitis. *Source:* Reprinted with permission from D.J. Lawrence, J.D. Cassidy, M. McGregor, et al., *Advances in Chiropractic*, Vol. 2, p. 165, © 1995, Mosby-Year Book.

MANAGEMENT

One of the key distinctions in the determination of the appropriateness ofTMJ adjustment (manipulation) is whether the joint is inflamed or whether there are adhesions. Compressive adjustments to an inflamed joint may provoke more pain. Adhesions are likely when the patient has opening clicks. The adjustment suggested by Curl[9] is to have the patient open to the point of the click. At this point the examiner loads the TMJ with a superior/anterior compression. A quick, small amplitude thrust is then delivered parallel to the slope of the articular eminence. When the patient has an acute closed lock (not able to open fully, however, no joint clicking or popping) a distraction or gapping maneuver is used. The force is applied 90° to the slope of the articular eminence in an inferior posterior direction.

Splints are one form of conservative treatment with TMJ disorders. Splints should be considered as adjunctive therapy for TMJ disorders, given the observation that they are often no better than placebo.[10] There is a vast array of simple and complex splint products (Figures 3–6, 3–7, and 3–8). In general, they are divided into hard and soft splints. The two types of hard splints are full occlusion or pivotal. Hard, full-occlusion splints are used for repositioning or stabilization. Re-

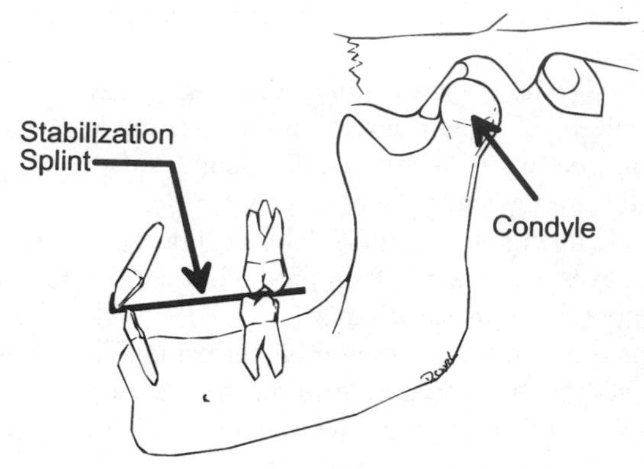

Figure 3–7 The stabilization splint is the type of splint used most often by dentists. It is a good general-purpose device for short-term therapy. *Source:* Reprinted with permission from D.J. Lawrence, J.D. Cassidy, M. McGregor, et al., *Advances in Chiropractic*, Vol. 2, p. 177, © 1995, Mosby-Year Book.

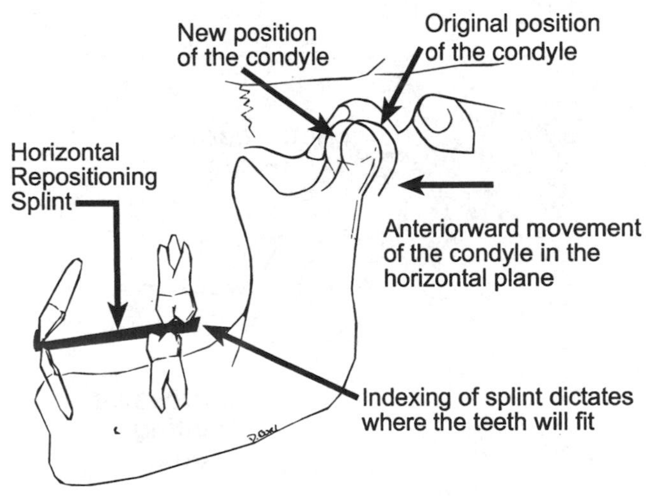

Figure 3–6 Horizontal repositioning splint. *Source:* Reprinted with permission from D.J. Lawrence, J.D. Cassidy, M. McGregor, et al., *Advances in Chiropractic*, Vol. 2, p. 178, © 1995, Mosby-Year Book.

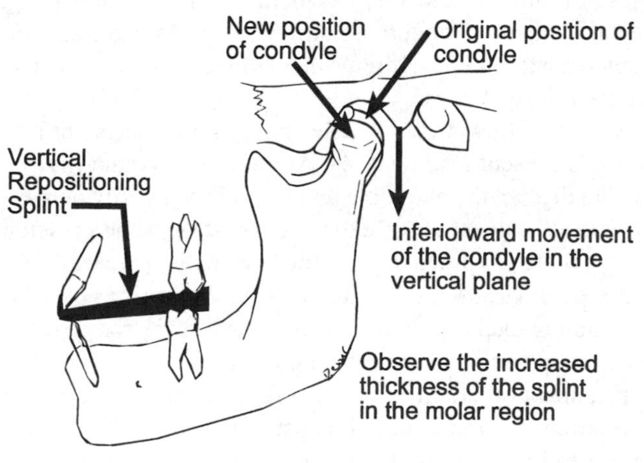

Figure 3–8 The vertical repositioning splint is used when the patient has lost vertical height to the teeth. Extreme wear from bruxing or excessively worn restorations are common causes of lost vertical height. *Source:* Reprinted with permission from D.J. Lawrence, J.D. Cassidy, M. McGregor, et al., *Advances in Chiropractic*, Vol. 2, p. 177, © 1995, Mosby-Year Book.

positioning splints attempt to alter the condylar position whereas stabilization splints do not alter dental alignment. Sato et al.[11] demonstrated in a small study group that 42% of patients with nonreducing TMJ disc displacement who opted for no treatment had resolution. Those treated with a stabilization splint had a 55% success rate. Those patients who did not have resolution naturally or respond to stabilization splinting after 19 months benefited most from surgery, with a success rate of 77%. Pivotal splints potentially are harmful and are rarely used.

Soft splints are used for protection and therefore are commonly used with a patient who grinds the teeth. The soft splints are similar to mouth guards made out of a latex type material. It appears that the use of a soft splint may be a helpful initial approach to patients with myofascial involvement of the temporalis or masseter muscle.[12,13] The soft splint does not seem to cause occlusal changes. The most popular daytime soft splint is the Aqualizer. It is inexpensive and easy to use.

Surgery is often offered as an alternative for patients with chronic TMJ disc derangement. Although there a numerous approaches, three specific surgical treatments were compared to nonsurgical treatment with regard to pain reduction and long-term effects.[10] These surgical techniques included discoplasty, discectomy without replacement, and discectomy with replacement of the disc with a Teflon implant. The long-term success rate was between 52% and 71%; however, there was a very high incidence of osteoarthritis development (93% to 100% in the discectomy groups).

Algorithm

An algorithm for evaluation of TMJ complaints is presented in Figure 3–9.

Figure 3–9

EVALUATION OF TEMPOROMANDIBULAR JOINT COMPLAINTS—ALGORITHM.

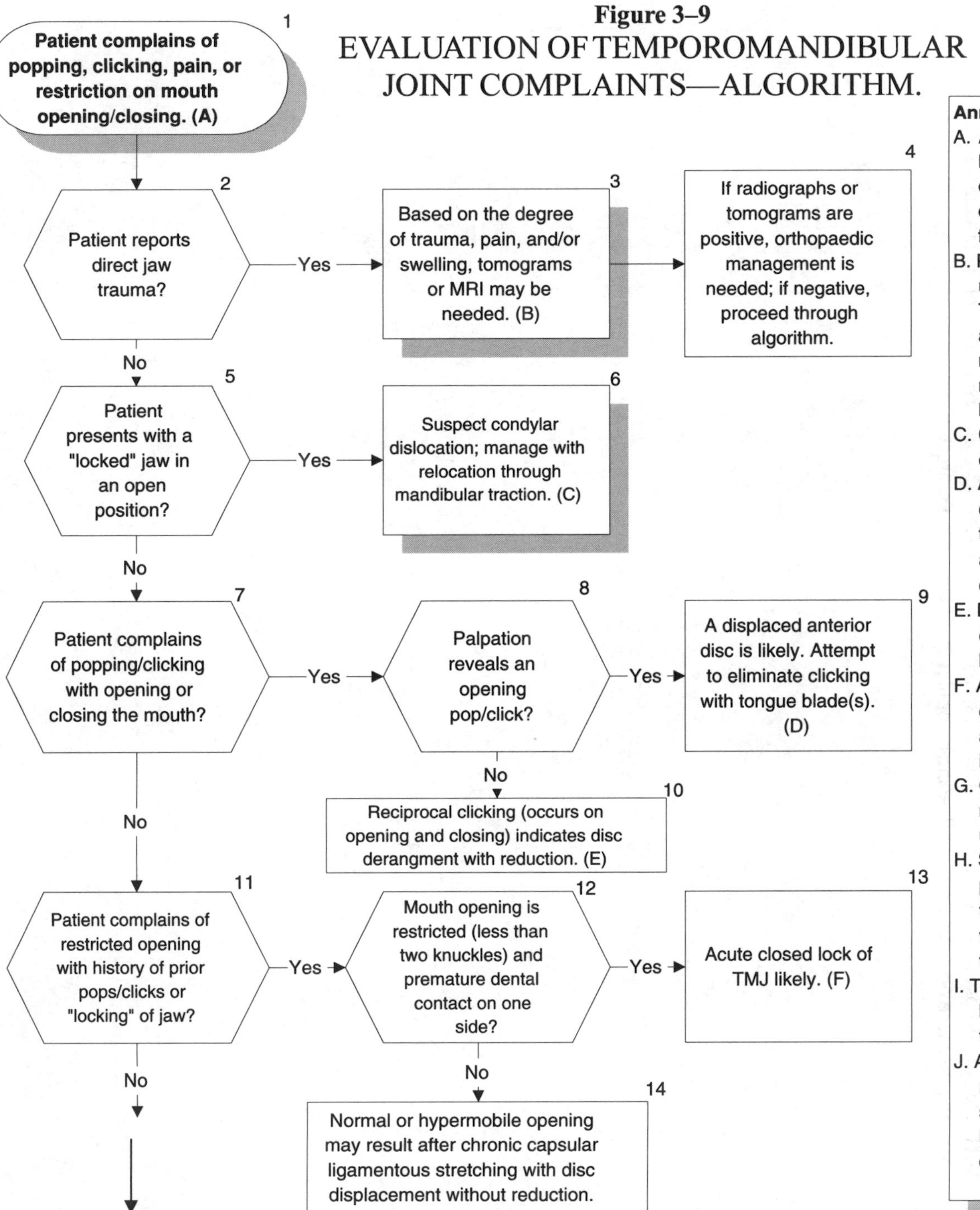

Annotations

A. Always evaluate the cervical spine and head posture with regard to TMJ complaints. Forward head position or cervical dysfunction may affect TMJ function or cause referred pain.

B. Plain film radiographs are virtually useless, except perhaps for fracture. Tomograms have limited use. 3-D volume acquisition techniques with MRI are the most sensitive. Coronal images may be necessary if the integrity of the capsule or ligaments is believed compromised.

C. Open lock usually is the result of trauma or hypermobility of the TMJ.

D. Anterior disc displacement requires the condyle to snap past the posterior part of the disc to the intermediate area, causing a click. If a tongue blade eliminates clicking, the disc is recaptured.

E. Disc displacement with reduction causes a click also on closing as the condyle snaps back to the posterior aspect of the disc.

F. Acute closed lock indicates that the condyle cannot pass over the posterior aspect of the disc to reach the intermediate area.

G. Capsulitis due to trauma associated with marked swelling may indicate an underlying fracture.

H. Synovitis may be traumatic or the result of posterior displacement of the condyle due to anterior disc displacment, loss of vertical height of teeth, or a hypertonic temporalis muscle.

I. Tendinitis and trigger points may be found by increased tenderness in the belly and tendons of the masseter and temporalis.

J. Arthritides that should be considered are rheumatoid arthritis, psoriatic, Reiter's syndrome, ankylosing spondylitis, lupus, Lyme disease, and connective tissue disorders.

continues

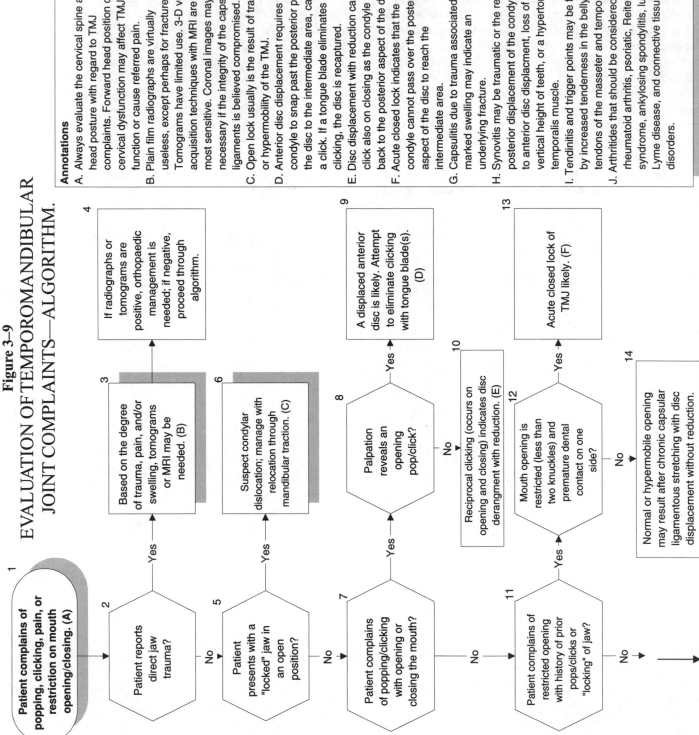

Figure 3–9 continued

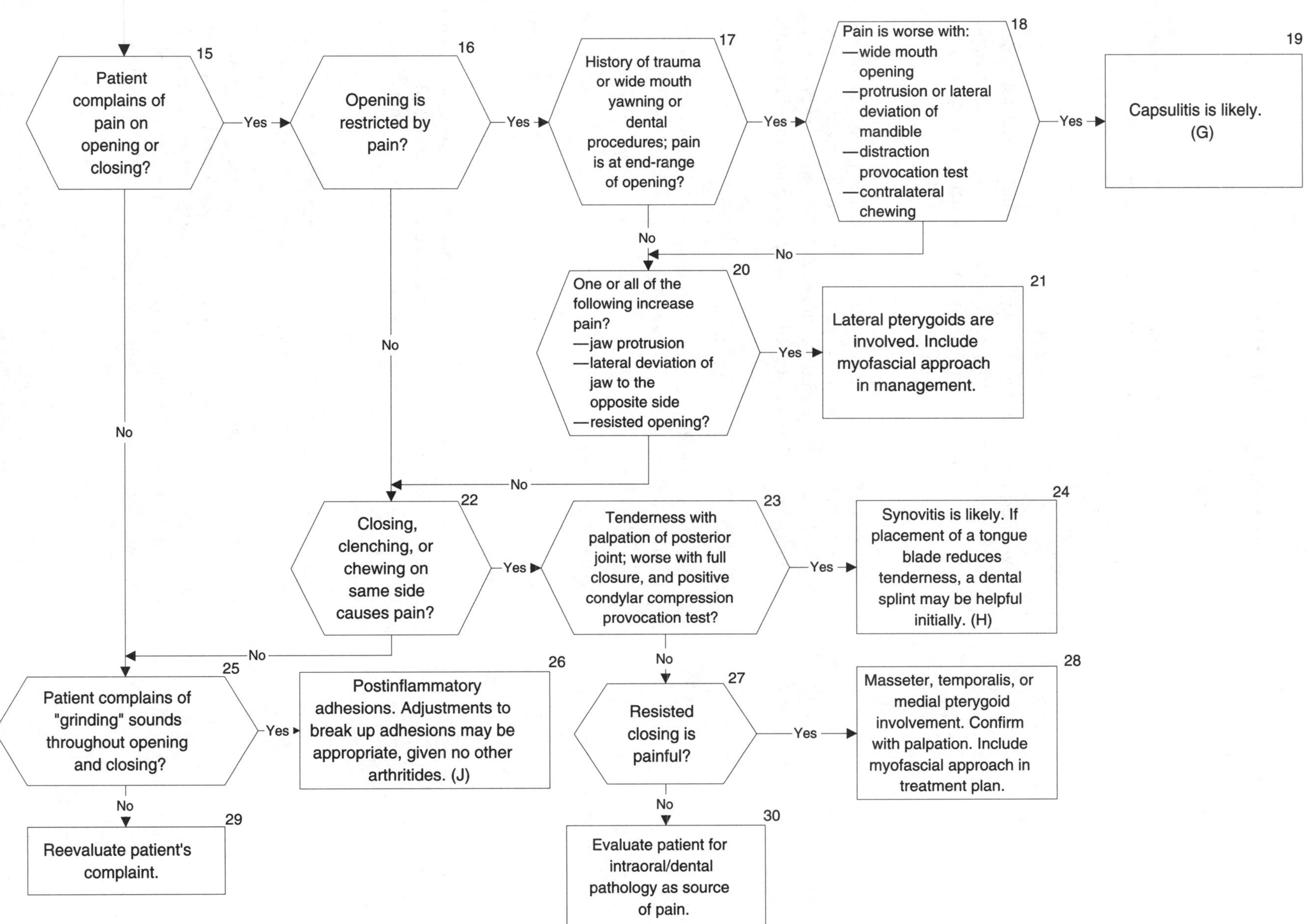

SELECTED TMJ DISORDERS

CAPSULITIS

Classic Presentation

The patient complains of pain or tenderness at the TMJ, especially with protrusion or lateral movement, chewing on the opposite side, or opening the mouth widely. There may be a history of trauma; however, most often there is not.

Cause

Overstretching of the capsule may be due to numerous causes, including wide yawning or dental procedures requiring prolonged wide opening. Microtrauma from poor chewing habits or occlusal problems may stretch and irritate the capsule.

Examination

Movements or positions that stretch the capsule often will increase pain. A condylar stretch test (pushing the mandible forward with the mouth open) may increase the pain (Figure 3–5), as will lateral deviation of the jaw to the opposite side, and wide mouth opening. Having the patient chew on the opposite side may also increase the discomfort.

Management

Avoidance of provoking maneuvers coupled with attention to proper dentition and re-education of jaw opening and chewing usually will resolve the problem. Ice and rest are used in the early stages.

SYNOVITIS

Classic Presentation

The patient complains of TMJ pain that is worse with full closure on the ipsilateral side.

Cause

Either acute direct trauma or chronic malposition may cause synovitis of the posterior TMJ. Common causes of posterior displacement of the condyle are loss of vertical height of the teeth, anterior disc displacement, and a hypertonic temporalis muscle.

Examination

Condylar compression (Figure 3–6) by the examiner will often increase pain on the side of involvement. There may be lateral deviation to the opposite side with the mandible in the rest position. While palpating the posterior joint through the external auditory meatus, tenderness is increased on full closure. Using tongue blades, a distraction force is introduced. As the patient bites down, tenderness may decrease with one or two tongue blades placed between the teeth. Another approach is to have the patient open until a click or pop is heard, indicating an anteriorly displaced disc. A tongue blade is placed between the teeth and the patient is asked to open and close. Additional tongue blades may be added in an attempt to eliminate the click, indicating recapture of the disc.

Management

If the tongue blade addition eliminates or decreases the pain or clicking, a stabilization appliance may be useful.[14] During the acute stage of synovitis, the use of mild analgesics, ice, and a soft diet with relaxation of the masticatory muscles will be helpful. If adhesions have formed as a result of chronic synovitis, adjustive maneuvers along the slope of the articular eminence may free up movement and decrease pain.

DISC DERANGEMENT WITH REDUCTION

Classic Presentation

The patient complains of popping or clicking while opening and closing the mouth.

Cause

When the articular disc is displaced anteriorly or anteromedially, the condylar head rests posterior to the disc. An opening click occurs as the condyle translates into its normal central disc location. The closing click occurs because of weakness of the posterior ligament. The disc is not pulled backward, and the condyle slips into a posterior position behind the disc.

Evaluation

Palpation in front of or inside the ear will detect the opening and closing clicks. An attempt to reduce the click can be made through the use of tongue blades. After the opening click occurs, a tongue blade or blades can be placed between the posterior teeth on the same side. If the patient closes down on the blades and no click or pop is heard or felt, reduction has occurred, indicating an underlying disc derangement.

Management

A dental appliance may help prevent displacement of the condylar head posteriorly; however, this is a temporary solution. When adhesions are present, Saghafi and Curl[15] suggest using a quick, short-amplitude thrust maneuver. The patient opens until the click is felt. To stabilize the disc and condyle together, the doctor applies an axial compression through the angle of the jaw in a superior and anterior direction. Short-impulse thrusts can then be delivered along the slope of the articular eminence in a posterior superior direction.

CLOSED LOCK

Classic Presentation

The patient complains of difficulty opening the mouth fully. There is pain and tenderness at the TMJ without current popping, although there may have been a history of prior popping on opening and/or closing. There may be an additional complaint of suboccipital pain, dysphagia, or tinnitus.

Cause

An anteriorly displaced (sometimes referred to as dislocated) articular disc is usually the cause. The condyle cannot translate to the intermediate portion of the disc. This may be due to hypermobility at the joint or trauma such as whiplash injury.[16] Often there is premature dental contact on the same side as disc displacement.

Examination

There often is tenderness at the TMJ and the patient is unable to open fully. He or she is unable to place two knuckles in between the front teeth. There is no popping on opening.

The end-feel usually is soft. Overpressure is uncomfortable but usually not very painful.

Management

Manipulation is the treatment of choice. Several maneuvers are described in the literature. Curl[17] summarizes these gapping maneuvers into three main groups: (1) downward traction with a thrust 90° to the slope of the articular eminence, (2) forward traction of the condyle under the disc, and (3) gapping with active movement by the patient. Sedative or relaxation approaches often will assist these maneuvers. Contraindications include processes that would weaken the structure of the mandible or teeth, such as tumor, infection, periodontal disease, osteoporosis, fracture, and extreme muscle splinting.

ACUTE OPEN LOCK

Classic Presentation

The patient presents with an acute locking of the jaw when it is fully open. The patient is extremely apprehensive. Pain is often due to the reactive spasm of the closing muscle. There may be history of trauma or previous occurrences when the mouth was opened too far.

Cause

Either trauma or hypermobility allows the condyle to be dislocated anterior to the articular eminence.

Examination

The patient presentation is pathognomonic: an apprehensive patient unable to close his or her mouth. If direct trauma has occurred, radiographs for fracture may be necessary.

Management

Bilateral manipulation with a downward traction is necessary to relocate the condyle.

REFERENCES

1. Solberg WK. Epidemiological findings of importance to management of temporomandibular disorders. In: Clark GT, Solberg WK, eds. *Perspectives in Temporomandibular Disorders*. Chicago: Quintessence; 1987:27–41.
2. Kovero O, Konomen M. Signs and symptoms of temporomandibular disorders and radiographically observed abnormalities in the condyles of the temporomandibular joints of professional violin and viola players. *Acta Odontol Scand*. 1995;53:81–84.
3. Ow RK, Loh T, Neo J, Khoo J. Symptoms of craniomandibular disorders among elderly people. *J Oral Rehabil*. 1995;22:413–419.
4. Blake P, Thorburn DN, Stewart IL. Temporomandibular joint dysfunction in children presenting as otalgia. *Clin Otolaryngol*. 1982;7:237–244.
5. Farar WB. Characteristics of the condylar path in internal derangements of the TMJ. *Prosthet Dent*. 1978;39:319.
6. Freidman NH, Anstendig HS, Weisberg J. Case report: treatment of a disc dysfunction. *J Clin Orthodont*. 1982;16:408.
7. Pullinger AG, White SC. Efficacy of TMJ radiographs in terms of expected versus actual findings. *Oral Surg Oral Med Oral Pathol*. 1995;79:367–374.
8. White SC, Pullinger AG. Impact of TMJ radiographs on clinician decision making. *Oral Surg Oral Med Oral Pathol*. 1995; 79:375–381.
9. Curl DD, Saghafi D. Manual reduction of adhesion in the temporomandibular joint. *Chiro Tech*. 1995;7:22–29.
10. Curl DD. The temporomandibular joint. In: Lawrence DJ, Cassidy JD, McGregor M, et al., eds. *Advances in Chiropractic*. St. Louis, MO: Mosby-Year Book; 1995;2:143–181.
11. Sato S, Kawamura H, Motegi K. Management of nonreducing temporomandibular joint disk displacement: evaluation of three treatments. *Oral Surg Oral Med Oral Pathol*. 1995;80:384–388.
12. Wright E, Anderson G, Schulte J. A randomized clinical trial of intraoral soft splints and palliative treatment for masticatory pain. *J Orofac Pain*. 1995;9:192–199.
13. Visser A, Naieje M, Hansson TL. The temporal/masseter co-contraction: an electromyographic and clinical evaluation of short-term stabilization splint therapy in myogenous CMD patients. *J Oral Rehabil*. 1995;22:387–389.

14. Friedman MH. Screening procedures for temporomandibular disorders. *J Neuromusculoskeletal Sys*. 1994;2:163–169.
15. Saghafi D, Curl DD. Chiropractic manipulation of anteriorly displaced temporomandibular disc with adhesion. *J Manipulative Physiol Ther*. 1995;18:98–104.
16. Weinberg S, La Pointe H. Cervical extension-flexion injury (whiplash) and internal derangement of the temporomandibular joint. *J Oral Maxillofac Surg*. 1987;45:653–656.
17. Curl DD. Acute closed lock of the temporomandibular joint: manipulation paradigm and protocol. *Chiro Tech*. 1991;3:13–18.

CHAPTER 4

Thoracic Spine Complaints

CONTEXT

Interest in the thoracic spine is often overshadowed by the more dramatic presentations of low back and cervical spine pain. Radicular pain into the arms and legs and its consequent functional limitations call more attention to the respective cervical and lumbar spine sources. Disc herniation is less common, as is nerve root compression in the thoracic spine, partly because of the restricted movement and stability provided by the direct attachment to the rib cage. Thoracic pain is probably as common as cervical or lumbar pain; however, it is less dramatic, due more often to the chronic consequences of postural imbalances. The pain is often of a low-grade nature and therefore less worrisome to the patient. When acute pain does occur, it is usually the result of acute muscle spasm or compression fracture. Compression fractures are usually the result of axial loading from a fall on the buttocks or, in osteoporotic individuals, minor or less memorable trauma.

Often there may be an age-related occurrence of thoracic pain or deformity. In children and adolescents scoliosis and hyperkyphosis are areas of concern (scoliosis is discussed in Chapter 5). The differential approach to hyperkyphosis should attempt to distinguish between simply poor posture habits and growth plate abnormalities as seen with Scheuermann's disease. In adults, the effects of chronic postural strain from seated work environments is predominant. Also, it appears that the long-term consequences of idiopathic scoliosis are more likely to result in pain in middle-aged adults. With senior patients, the primary concern is compression fracture, often the result of osteoporosis (osteoporosis is discussed in Chapter 31).

Although the cervical and lumbar regions require an evaluation of the limb plexuses, the thoracic spine is not involved directly (except for T1/T2). The thoracic spinal cord, however, is the home of the nerve cell bodies of the sympathetic nervous system. This relationship has not gone unnoticed by the chiropractic profession. Anecdotal stories regarding improvement of "visceral" conditions abound. The questions that still need research answers are whether these represent the normal course of these disorders, whether the pain is "referred" pain (somatovisceral), and to what degree sympathetic innervation to organs can be affected by vertebral subluxation. Some of these issues are discussed in a review article by Nansel and Szlazak.[1] From this review it appears that there are many local regulating factors that can compensate for more proximal sympathetic dysfunction. It would appear that a more reflex or referred phenomenon may be the cause of those conditions that respond to manipulation. More research is needed to compare chiropractic management of commonly reported responsive conditions such as asthma, peptic ulcer, reflux esophagitis, gallbladder disease, and various gastrointestinal and gynecologic disorders.

GENERAL STRATEGY

History

- Determine whether the patient's complaint is one of pain, stiffness, a midscapular fatigue, deformity, or a combination of complaints.
- Screen the patient for red flags such as a history of cancer, significant trauma, use of corticosteroids, or a history of infection suggestive of tuberculosis.
- If there is a history of sudden onset, attempt to elicit a description of any inciting event or trauma, no matter how minor.

Examination

- Observe the patient for deformity: buffalo hump in the upper thoracic area (Cushing's syndrome), acute-angle kyphosis (compression fracture), kyphosis (Scheuermann's disease or postural), scoliosis (many causes; however, acute-angle painful scoliosis suggests osteoid osteoma or other local processes), scapular winging (scoliosis or nerve damage causing weakness of the serratus anterior or trapezius muscle).
- Observe for skin lesions suggestive of herpes zoster (shingles) or skin cancer.
- Examine for active and passive range of motion and accessory motion.
- For patients with a kyphosis, perform a prone extension test to differentiate between a structural and a functional kyphosis.
- For patients with a scoliosis visible in the standing posture, perform an Adams' test (rib humping [angular rotation] suggests a structural curve); also observe the patient in the lying position in neutral and with maximum bending to the side of convexity (improvement indicates a functional component).
- For patients with local pain, palpate and percuss the area.
- Standard radiographs include an anterior to posterior and lateral views; oblique films are used to evaluate the ribs for fracture and the vertebral bodies for trauma to the ring apophyses.
- Special imaging, including bone scans and tomograms are reserved for evaluation of metastatic lesions and osteoid osteoma or other tumors. Magnetic resonance imaging (MRI) is also helpful with spinal infection, tumor, and the rare disc herniation.

Management

- Patients with infection, primary tumor or metastasis, unstable fracture, severe or rapidly progressive scoliosis or kyphosis, and complications of corticosteroid use should be referred for medical evaluation and possible management.
- Patients with uncomplicated compression fractures, mild to moderate idiopathic scoliosis that is not rapidly progressing, uncomplicated Scheuermann's disease, facet syndrome, postural syndrome, T4 syndrome, and other mechanical causes should be managed conservatively. If unresponsive to care, further evaluation or referral for comanagement may be indicated.

RELEVANT ANATOMY

The typical thoracic vertebrae are 2 through 8. These are heart-shaped bodies with shinglelike facets. The first thoracic vertebra is cervical-like, while the lower two thoracic vertebrae are more lumbarlike with a corresponding change in facet orientation. The typical vertebrae have two attachment sites on the body for rib articulation. The costovertebral joint is at the intervertebral disc (IVD) of the typical vertebrae, supported by a capsule and intrinsic radiate ligament. Another articulation occurs at the transverse process, with the tubercle of the rib supported by the costotransverse ligament. These ligaments are innervated by both the posterior primary rami and the anterior primary rami, indicating a neurologic priority for proprioceptive input. The superior costotransverse ligaments connect adjacent ribs. The thoracic kyphosis is a primary curve (as is the sacral angle). This means that a structural kyphosis is created by the shape of the thoracic vertebrae, whereas in the cervical and lumbar regions the lordosis is acquired.

The facets are more shinglelike overlapping at an angle of about 60° from the horizontal in the upper thoracics and up to 80° to 90° in the lower thoracics.[2] The medial branch of the dorsal rami supply the joint capsules. The intervertebral discs are quite thin in the thoracic region. Innervation is from the sinuvertebral nerve. Nerve roots exit above the IVD, making nerve root compression from disc herniation less likely.

The muscles of the thoracic region may be divided generally into two types (Figure 4–1). The more superficial muscles such as the trapezius, rhomboids, levator scapulae, and latissimus dorsi are primarily extremity muscles assisting in direct movement of the arm or assisting through positioning of the scapulae. The deeper muscles act to extend the spine; they rotate segmentally and, to a lesser degree, flex laterally. Although the middle trapezius and rhomboids act directly on the scapulae, weakness allows forward displacement of the scapulae with a tendency toward an increased kyphosis.

There are some interesting neural connections between the thoracic spine and other regions[3]:

- Portions of the T1-T3(4) nerve roots enter the brachial plexus, supplying the axillae and medial arm and forearm (may be clinically important with thoracic outlet syndrome [TOS]-like symptoms).
- The T12 nerve root enters the lumbar plexus as the iliohypogastric nerve, with lateral branches innervating the upper lateral thigh and an anterior branch to the pubic region.
- The lateral branch of the posterior primary rami of T2 descends paravertebrally to the level of T6 and then ascends to the acromion (considered with midthoracic or shoulder pain).
- The lateral branch of the posterior primary rami of T12 descends to the posterolateral iliac crest and lateral buttock (considered with "lumbar" or buttock pain).

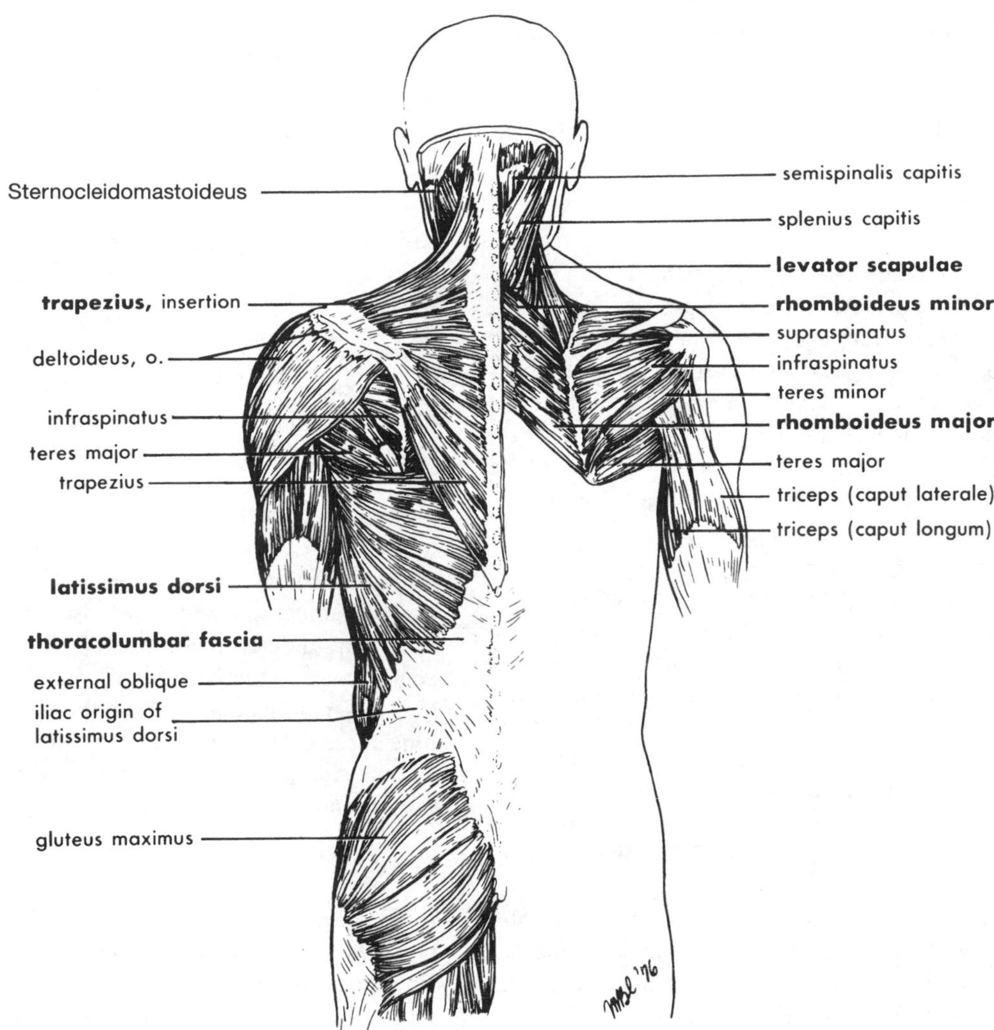

Figure 4–1 Posterior view of superficial muscles of the back and those connecting the axial skeleton to the shoulder girdle. *Source:* Reprinted with permission from J.E. Crouch, *Functional Human Anatomy*, 4th ed., p. 224, © 1985, Lea & Febiger.

The thoracic spinal cord houses the nerve cell bodies for the sympathetic nervous system. Access to other areas of the body is via the sympathetic chain. These ganglia are in close proximity to the heads of the ribs. The sinuvertebral nerve, which supplies the posterior longitudinal ligaments, epidural blood vessels, periosteum of the vertebra, and outer annulus, is made up of a somatic branch and an autonomic branch. The autonomic branch comes from the gray rami communicantes or from the sympathetic ganglia near the nerve root and as the sinuvertebral nerve reenters the intervertebral foramina. Branches of the sinuvertebral nerve may travel four or five segments in the neural canal before synapsing. Interestingly, the sympathetic neurons (for vascular supply) that follow somatic nerves into the arms may originate from as far down as T8.[4] This may account for a condition called the T4 syndrome reported in the literature on manipulation.[5] Although there is still a debate regarding the effect of manipulation on the sympathetic influence on visceral organ function, it is recognized that referred pain from organs is possible. Below are some specific organ innervations (approximate). The segmental levels may be painful when the organ is involved (viscerosomatic pain).

- heart—C8-T5(8)
- lungs—T3-T5(10)
- stomach—T5-T8(9)

- pancreas—T7-T9
- gallbladder, liver, spleen, caecum, and duodenum—T6-T10
- appendix—T9-T11
- kidneys—T9-L2

Biomechanics

Mobility in the thoracic region is somewhat restricted by the rib cage attachments. The physiologic priority appears to be protection of visceral organs rather than mobility. Only 2° to 6° per segment of sagittal movement is possible, with 60% of this movement being flexion. Lateral flexion is somewhat limited in the upper thoracic region (5° to 6° per segment per side), increasing in the lower thoracic region (8° to 9° per side). Lateral flexion involves a coupled movement pattern with rotation.[6] In the upper thoracic region, lateral bending to one side causes the spinous processes to rotate into the convexity (opposite side, similar to the cervical region), while in the lower thoracic region the spinous processes rotate into the concavity (same side; similar to the lumbar region). Rotation occurs more in the upper thoracic spine (4° to 5° per side) than in the lower (2° per side), total of about 40° per side. Rotation also causes a coupled motion with lateral flexion to the opposite side and an accompanying extension (especially in the lower thoracics). In the upper thoracics the coupled motion is lateral flexion and sagittal flexion.

During normal respiration, the rib cage moves in two patterns. The upper ribs (one to seven) move in more of a bucket-handle configuration, increasing the anterior to posterior diameter of the chest. The lower ribs move in more of a caliper action, increasing the transverse diameter. These movements are due in part to the types of articulations and angle of articulation with the vertebrae and sternum. Inspiration is more of an active process, whereas expiration is usually more passive because of the elastic recoil in the lungs.

EVALUATION

History

Careful questioning during the history taking (Table 4–1) can point to the diagnosis. Some historical red flags include a history of drug or alcohol abuse, use of corticosteroids, diabetes, or direct trauma to the chest or rib cage. In patients older than age 70 years a compression fracture or metastasis should be suspected. Combined findings of weight loss, a past history of cancer, night pain, or high fever (especially in a patient older than age 50) warrants a careful radiographic search for cancer or infection.

Trauma

Trauma to the thoracic area such as a direct blow should raise the suspicion of a rib fracture. The patient should be evaluated further with compression, percussion, vibration, and radiographs. A fall onto the buttocks with resulting thoracic pain is often due to a compression fracture. If the patient was involved in a car accident, a chance fracture may have occurred over the fulcrum of a seat belt.

Posture

Postural problems are common. There is a natural tendency for individuals who work at desks to accentuate the forward head, forward shoulder posture. Without frequent breaks or exercises to compensate, most individuals acquire a new "normal" posture. Asking the patient with an apparent kyphosis about his or her posture to determine the chronicity is important. It is possible that an adult has had the predisposition of Scheuermann's disease as an adolescent. This will be evident radiographically. For those who work at desks, it is important to determine the setup of the workstation. If the setup allows or encourages a forward head or slumped position, it is important to use this information in long-term planning for avoidance of postural pain. Adolescents often develop a slumped posture either because it is the posture of their friends or because of a lack of self-confidence.

Stiffness

Stiffness should be differentiated from a sensation or an objective loss of range of motion (ROM). Many patients who complain of stiffness have normal ROM, indicating that muscles are probably being posturally strained. When a young adult patient complains of difficulty in taking a deep breath or bending forward or to the sides, ankylosing spondylitis is suggested.

Deformity

On occasion an older patient or the parent of a child will notice a humping in the thoracic region. In the older patient, a compression fracture is likely and should be evaluated radiographically. With the child, deformity may represent simply a "bad" posture habit, Scheuermann's disease, scoliosis, or the rare Sprengel's deformity. The parent may also notice that the child with scoliosis has an unequal arm length evident by unequal sleeve length on shirts or blouses.

Examination

From a postural standpoint, there are several important clues to look for.

Table 4–1 History Questions for Thoracic Spine Injury

Primary Question	What Are You Thinking?	Secondary Questions	What Are You Thinking?
Did you injure yourself? (car accident, lifting, twisting, bending, etc.)	Sprain/strain, fracture, subluxation	Did you have a sudden flexion injury?	Compression or chance fracture
		(With older patient) Do you have pain after coughing, sneezing, stepping off a curb?	Compression fracture
		Did you suffer a blow to the chest?	Rib fracture
Does the pain radiate around to the chest?	Intercostal strain, intercostal neuritis, herpes zoster, diabetes, neurofibroma, degenerative joint disease	Do you have any associated skin lesions?	Herpes zoster
		Is the pan increased with stretching (eg, yawning)?	Intercostal strain
		Do you have diabetes?	Diabetic neuropathy
Is the pain worse at night? Is it unrelieved with rest?	Osteoid osteoma, cancer, rib fracture	Is aspirin helpful?	Dramatic relief suggests osteoid osteoma; if no relief consider cancer
		Is it more difficult to lie on your back?	Rib fracture
Is there associated chest or abdominal pain?	Referral or radiation from chest or abdominal disease	Is there associated epigastric pain?	Consider peptic ulcer, esophagitis, or pancreatitis
		Do you have upper right abdominal pain?	Cholecystitis or lithiasis
Do you have chronic pain?	Myofascial pain due to poor posture, ergonomic strain at work, fibromyalgia, or depression	Do you work in a seated, forward head position? Do you have middle or upper scapular pain?	Postural syndrome
		Do you have pain all over your body? On both sides?	Fibromyalgia
		Do you have difficulty sleeping, loss of enjoyment in any activities?	Depression
		Is the pain associated with globally restricted thoracic spine movement?	Consider ankylosing spondylitis
Are you concerned about an observed deformity?	Postural kyphosis, Scheuermann's disease, compression fracture, scoliosis, scapular winging due to nerve damage	Did you have a sudden onset of a "hunched" appearance or gradual height loss? (In a senior)	Compression fracture (osteoporosis, traumatic, or pathologic)
		(In an adolescent) Are you constantly "hunched" forward?	Scheuermann's disease or postural syndrome
		Is there curving of back with a high shoulder or bulging ribs?	Scoliosis

Scapular Winging

Scapular winging may be due to a scoliosis (convex side) or weakness of either the middle trapezius or serratus anterior (the muscle weakness is often secondary to nerve damage). Asking the patient to perform a push-up against the wall often will accentuate the winging. Winging that allows straight lateral drift of the scapula is due to weakness of the middle trapezius; flaring of the inferior border outward and of the upper border inward is indicative of serratus anterior weakness with probable damage to the long thoracic nerve. An unusually high scapula or small scapula may represent the uncommon Sprengel's deformity in which scapular muscles are underdeveloped or replaced by fibrous tissue.[7]

Buffalo Hump

A buffalo hump is the buildup of fat tissue in a patient with Cushing's disease or an individual on long-term corticosteroids; it should not be confused with a large lipoma or a Dowager's hump (compression fracture) or gibbous deformity (compression fracture or tuberculosis of the spine).

Acute-Angle Kyphosis

Acute-angle kyphosis is often seen in older women at the site of a compression fracture (called Dowager's hump or gibbous deformity); in younger athletes, an acute-angle kyphosis at the thoracolumbar region indicates atypical Scheuermann's disease.

Generalized Hyperkyphosis

A hyperkyphosis is common in adolescents for two major reasons: (1) poor posture and (2) Scheuermann's disease. To differentiate between the functional (postural) type and the structural type, the patient is asked to lie prone and then to extend the trunk with the arms behind the back, lifting the chest off the table (Figure 4–2). If the kyphosis persists it is structural. A functional examination should include an evaluation of both the lumbar and cervical curves in an effort to determine their contribution or compensation for the thoracic kyphosis. The typical pattern is weak midscapular muscles, tight pectorals, weak deep neck flexors, tight deep neck extensors, weak abdominals, and tight lumbar paraspinals.

Scoliosis

The lateral curvature of a scoliosis is often visible in the standing patient; if present, ask the patient to flex forward at the waist at three levels (90° for the lumbar region; 60° for the midthoracic, and 30° to 45° for the upper thoracic), keeping the head down and the arms hanging loosely with no trunk rotation voluntarily acquired. Prominence of one side compared with the other is indicative of a structural curve (Figure 4–3). Measurement of the degree of trunk inclination may be performed with an inclinometer such as a scoliometer. A trunk angle greater than 5° is an indication of a structural curve of at least 20°.[8] Another test for scoliosis is to observe how much correction occurs when the patient

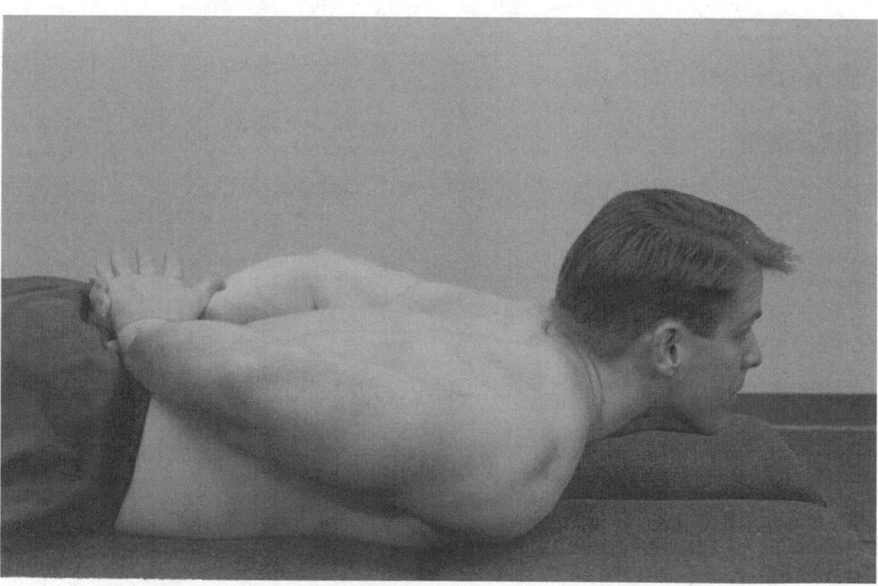

Figure 4–2 Prone extension is used to differentiate between a structural and a functional hyperkyphosis. If the kyphosis improves with extension, it is primarily functional; no improvement indicates a structural cause (eg, Scheuermann's disease).

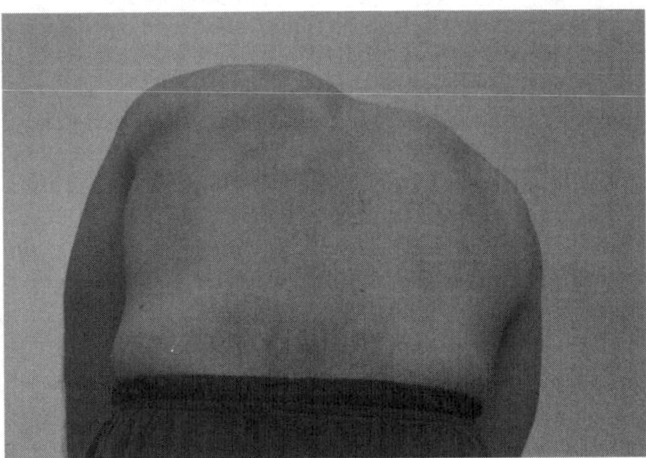

Figure 4–3 The Adams' test involves forward bending in an attempt to gain a skyline view of different areas of the back. This position of approximately 60° forward flexion demonstrates angular deformity (rib humping) in the midthoracic spine on the left.

lies prone. This can be evaluated further by asking the patient to bend maximally to the convex side of the curve. Some improvement will occur if there is a functional component to the curve.

The neurologic examination for the thoracic spine is brief, unless there is a suspicion of nerve root involvement. This rare occurrence will cause the patient to complain of pain that radiates to the front of the body, and there may be accompanying weakness of the abdominal muscles. It would be unusual for an upper motor neuron lesion to cause only isolated thoracic spine findings.

Because of the possibility of referral or radiation pain from a chest or abdominal source, it would be prudent to perform some chest and abdominal screening tests with patients complaining of both anterior and posterior pain. With costovertebral pain in the lower thoracic region, a kidney punch test might elicit a response with an inflammatory process such as pylonephritis. If the pain is more in the middle thoracic or scapular areas, Murphy's sign for gallbladder disease may be elicited.

Palpation of the thoracic spine may be helpful in finding discrete areas of tenderness. Motion palpation is commonly used. Unfortunately, one small study indicated good intraexaminer reliability but poor interexaminer reliability.[9] It is important to challenge the midthoracic area in patients with diffuse arm complaints. Reproduction of arm complaints with pressure on the spinous or transverse processes suggests T4 syndrome.

Basic radiographic evaluation of the thoracic spine requires an anteroposterior (AP) and lateral view. Additional views are required in the following scenarios:

- If rib fracture is suspected, include AP and oblique views of the involved ribs.
- If associated chest pathology is suspected, include a posteroanterior and lateral view of the chest.
- If scoliosis is suspected, begin with a full spine (14 by 36) evaluation to determine involvement of the other regions and in younger patients to determine the Risser sign; it has been recommended to take the film posterior to anterior to avoid increased radiation to the breasts and genitals; however, it is suggested that the Risser sign is not as accurate on this view and, given the technology available with regard to collimation, filtering, film speed, etc., the concern is not as strong as it once was. If a scoliosis is present, recumbent films with maximum bending into the curve convexity are important to determine the degree of functional versus structural curve (see Chapter 5). Measurements include the Cobb angle for degree of angulation, Nash-Mose measurement for degree of rotation, and the Risser sign for progression of the iliac crest apophysis (indicator of bone maturity). For the rare infantile idiopathic curve, the Mehta rib angle measurement may determine those likely to progress.
- If a compression fracture is evident, determination of stability is important. Collapse of the anterior margin to less than half the height of the posterior margin or more than 20° of wedging may indicate an unstable fracture. Loss of posterior vertebral height should raise the suspicion of a pathologic fracture often due to metastasis. Other clues may be a "missing pedicle" sign, indicating an osteolytic process such as breast cancer metastasis.

Special studies are required when tumor, unstable fracture, or osteoporosis is seen or suspected. Bone scans are helpful in determining metastatic sites in the spine and the location of osteoid osteomas. Dual-photon absorptiometry is valuable for evaluating generalized bone mass status. MRI is valuable when nerve root compression, infection, or tumor is suspected and yet the degree of involvement or cause is uncertain.

MANAGEMENT

- Patients with infection, primary tumor or metastasis, unstable fracture, severe or rapidly progressive scoliosis or kyphosis, and complications due to corticosteroid use should be referred for medical evaluation and possible management or comanagement.
- Patients with uncomplicated compression fractures, mild to moderate idiopathic scoliosis that is not rapidly progressing, uncomplicated Scheuermann's disease, facet syndrome, postural syndrome, T4 syndrome, and other

mechanical causes should be managed conservatively. If unresponsive to care, further evaluation or referral for comanagement may be indicated.

- Patients with uncomplicated compression fractures will probably have pain for 1 to 2 months during the healing phase. Bracing or restraint in the thoracic region is not recommended because of its effect on normal breathing. The same is true for patients with cracked ribs or uncomplicated rib fractures (see Chapter 39, Chest Pain).

The recommendation of the Mercy Center Guidelines[10] is that a 2-week trial of manipulative therapy at a frequency of three to five times per week (depending on severity) is appropriate for most uncomplicated mechanical problems. If unresponsive, a second 2-week trial is suggested. If the patient is responsive to either treatment trial, a reduction in frequency of care over the following several weeks is appropriate. Maintenance care may be necessary in patients with chronic problems. If the patient is still not responding after a second 2-week trial, laboratory testing, special imaging, or referral for medical evaluation should be given.

For most patients with chronic posturally induced pain, stretches, exercises, and modification of work or recreational activity patterns are the long-term approach to prevention. Stretching of the tight pectoral muscles may be performed by leaning into a corner or doorway with the arm or arms elevated to shoulder level or above. Adding a slight contraction for a few seconds followed by relaxation may allow access to more ROM. Strengthening of the midscapular muscles can be performed prone or with the back against a corner. The emphasis is to keep the arms at shoulder level, elbows bent 90°, and to maintain this position while the scapulae are squeezed together (no arm movement; only scapular movement). Patients with a kyphosis should also focus on strengthening of the lower trapezius by performing prone "superman" exercises. With the arms stretched out overhead and the hips stabilized, the patient attempts to lift the chest off the ground or table, holds for a few seconds, and slowly lowers. For generalized posture, stretching of the deep neck extensors, lumbar erector spinae, iliopsoas, and hamstrings should be coupled with strengthening of the deep neck flexors, midscapular muscles, abdominals, and gluteals.

Algorithm

An algorithm for the management of thoracic spine pain is presented in Figure 4–4.

Figure 4–4

THORACIC SPINE PAIN—ALGORITHM.

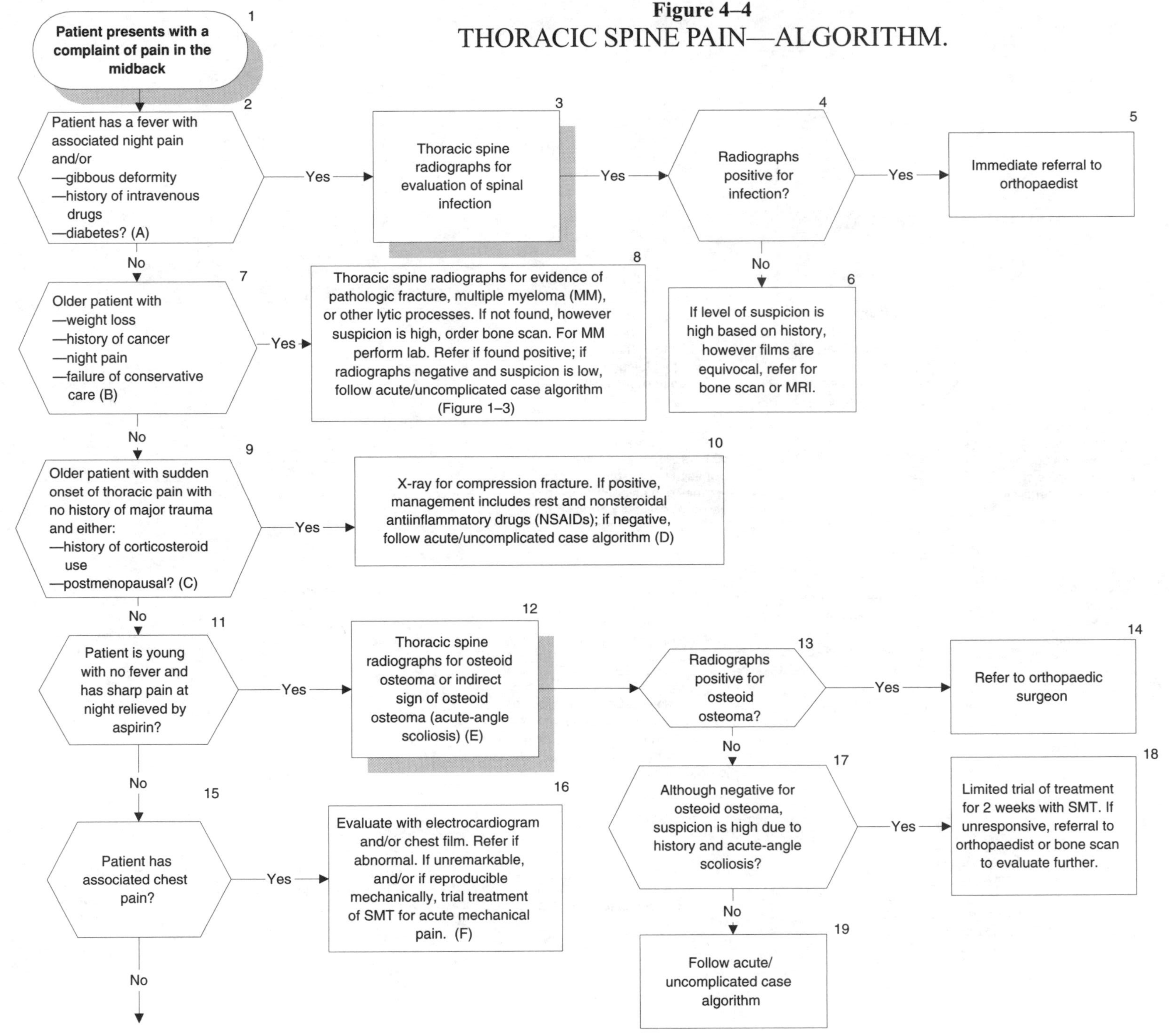

continues

Figure 4–4 continued

20 Traumatic onset of thoracic pain; pain with inspiration?
- Yes → 21
- No → 26

21 Order radiographs. Include PA chest and oblique views of area. (G) → 22

22 X-rays positive for rib fracture or pneumothorax?
- Yes → 23
- No → 24

23 If pneumothorax or complete fracture is evident, refer to ER. If rib fracture is incomplete, manage with rest and NSAIDs. If patient needs stronger medication, refer to MD.

24 If fracture is still likely due to degree of pain, manage with rest and NSAIDs. Do not adjust area. If pain is reduced substantially in a few days, consider rib subluxation and adjust the corresponding vertebra cautiously. (H)

25 Go to Box 39

26 Insidious onset of mild/moderate constant pain; is patient hyperkyphotic?
- Yes → 27
- No → 33

27 Perform prone extension test to differentiate between functional and structural kyphosis. (I) → 28

28 Patient is in teens, mainly structural kyphosis?
- Yes → 29
- No → 31

29 Order AP and lateral thoracic films. If associated scoliosis is evident, order full-spine films. (J) → 30

30 Scheuermann's disease evident on radiographs?
- Yes → 32
- No → 25

31 In a younger patient consider postural problems; evaluate and recommend exercise for correction. In older patients go to box 10.

32 If Scheuermann's disease is evident, eliminate flexion activities. Patient may benefit from wearing a brace. Give extensor-stregthening exercise.

33 Scoliosis suspected due to past history or visual observation of back?
- Yes → 34
- No → (continues)

34 Perform Adams' test. (K) → 35

35 Angular rotation (rib humping) evident; rotation >5°?
- Yes → 36
- No → (continues)

36 X-ray patient using full-spine view. If scoliosis is evident take lateral bending view. Go to scoliosis algorithm (Chapter 5). (J)

continues

Figure 4–4 continued

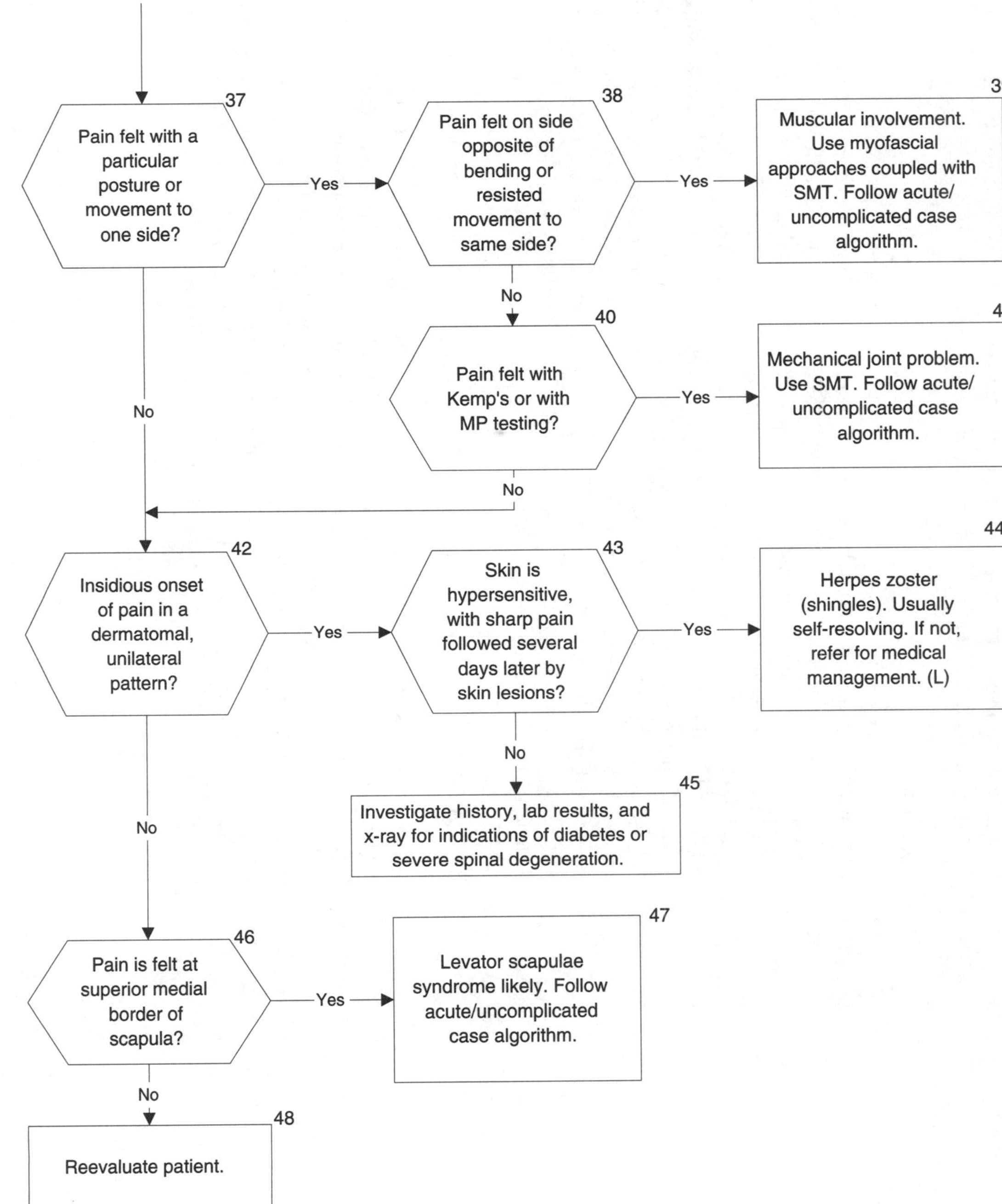

Annotations

A. Osteomyelitis is most common in diabetics and intravenous drug abusers. Fever may be present, and tenderness to spinous percussion.

B. Cancer or metastasis is suspected when there is a history of cancer, especially in patients over 50 who have experienced undesired weight loss or who have not responded to conservative care.

C. Osteoporosis-related compression fractures are most common in postmenopausal women or those on long-term steroid use without a history of significant trauma.

D. Fractures decreasing the anterior vertebral body height to <50% of posterior body height or causing more than a 20˚ angulation should be considered unstable and referred to an orthopaedist. Compression fractures are managed conservatively with rest and NSAIDs. Bracing/supports are not recommended for the thoracic area because of inhibition of normal breathing.

E. Osteoid osteoma may cause a small scoliosis due to local muscle spasm.

F. Chest pain that is noncardiac is often sharp, localized, and reproduced by stretch, contraction, or palpation.

G. Rib fracture management is generally rest and NSAIDs. Rib belts are not used because of inhibition of normal breathing.

H. Differentiating between rib fractures (cracked ribs) and subluxations of ribs is difficult; however, rib fractures do not feel substantially better in a few days.

I. A test to differentiate between structural and functional kyphosis is performed by having the patient extend the trunk from a prone position. If the kyphosis improves, the main component is functional.

J. Scoliosis x-rays are used to determine bone age using the Risser sign and the degree of curve using Cobb's angle. A lateral bending view with the patient bending as far into the convexity is used to compare Cobb's angles determining the functional amount of the curve.

K. The Adams' test coupled with scoliometer measurement is able to detect curves >20˚ when the angular rotation is >5˚.

L. Herpes zoster usually follows a single nerve root in a dermatomal pattern. Lysine and stress management may be helpful. Medical treatment may involve acyclovir.

Key: MP, metacarpalphalengeal; SMT, spinal manipulitive therapy; PA, posterior to anterior; MR, magnetic resonance.

SELECTED DISORDERS OF THE THORACIC SPINE*

SCHEUERMANN'S DISEASE

Classic Presentation

The patient is a young male or female (ages 13 to 17 years) who presents with a complaint of midback pain and fatigue. The patient has an increased kyphosis.

Cause

The cause of Scheuermann's disease has been debated for years. Scheuermann's disease is not an osteochondrosis. Currently, Scheuermann's is believed to be the result of vertebral growth plate trauma during the adolescent period with interruption or cessation of further growth.[11] In addition, end-plate fractures (Schmorl's nodes) and anterior disruption (limbus bones) are evidence of discal extrusions. The midthoracic region is affected 75% of the time. The thoracolumbar region is affected 25% of the time. The incidence is as high as 8%.[12] There is a small male predominance and an increased incidence among family members. A unique type found in female gymnasts is called atypical Scheuermann's disease. There is an acute kyphotic angulation at one or two vertebral bodies in the area of T10-L4.[13] This represents trauma to the vertebral ring apophysis.

Evaluation

An examination for posture often will reveal an exaggeration of the cervical and lumbar lordosis with a hyperkyphotic thoracic region. If the patient is asked to lie prone and extend the chest off the table, persistence of the kyphosis will indicate a structural cause, most often Scheuermann's disease in a younger individual. If the kyphosis improves, a functional cause (poor habitual posture) is probably the cause (Figure 4–2). The diagnosis is primarily radiographic with classic findings of slight anterior vertebral body wedging (at least 5° per segment), Schmorl's nodes, and decreased disc height, all occurring over at least three contiguous vertebrae.[14] Additional findings are an increased kyphosis, mild scoliosis, and limbus bones (anterior marginal Schmorl's node representing ossification in the avulsed growth plate). The classic finding with atypical Scheuermann's is an anterior Schmorl's node occurring at only one or two levels. The anterior wedging with atypical Scheuermann's can be as much as 40% to 50%.

Management

Complications such as disc herniation or nerve root compression are rare. General management for uncomplicated Scheuermann's should include postural exercises coupled with bracing or taping for proprioceptive awareness. The most important period is during the growth spurt in males. Stretching anterior muscles, strengthening interscapular muscles, spinal extension exercises, and attention to compensations in the cervical and lumbar curves are the primary focus. Atypical Scheuermann's requires restriction from all gymnastics participation and extension bracing for several months. With atypical Scheuermann's, radiographs should be retaken in 3 to 4 months to determine healing.

*See also Chapter 5, Scoliosis, and Chapter 39, Chest Pain.

COMPRESSION FRACTURE

Classic Presentation

In older patients, the onset of sudden thoracic (or lumbar) pain occurs after a minor event such as sneezing or stepping off a curb. In younger patients, the history will usually involve a fall on the buttocks and/or hyperflexion injury.

Cause

Compression fractures may be due to weakness in the bone, usually secondary to osteoporosis or cancer. Sufficient trauma may cause a fracture in normal bone. Approximately 35% of compression fractures in women over age 40 years are due to early menopause, 30% are due to long-term corticosteroid use, 8% are due to hyperthyroidism, and less than 2% are due to malignancy.[15]

Evaluation

A history of long-term corticosteroid use or age greater than 70 years is suggestive of compression fracture in patients with thoracic or lumbar complaints.[16] Pathologic fracture should be considered in patients older than 50 years with a past history of cancer, or unexplained weight loss. There is often a sharp kyphotic angle at the area of fracture. The patient will have pain on percussion and deep pressure over the involved segment. The diagnosis is essentially radiographic. The lateral view is particularly helpful in determining important differentiating factors. An anterior step defect is most common, due to the increased stress imposed by the natural kyphosis, flexion, and gravity. Collapse of the anterior margin to less than half the height of the posterior margin or more than 20° of wedging may indicate an unstable fracture. Other indicators are based on the Denis criteria.[17] Using a three-column concept, if two or more columns are disrupted, the fracture is unstable. The three columns are the anterior column (anterior longitudinal ligament [ALL] to midvertebral body), middle column (midvertebral body to posterior longitudinal ligament [PLL]), and posterior column (PLL to suspraspinous ligament). Loss of posterior vertebral body height without a history of trauma should raise the suspicion of pathologic fracture, warranting a search for metastatic cancer or multiple myeloma. Healing of noncomplicated fractures should be evident within about 3 months.

Management

Fractures due to metastatic cancer or multiple myeloma require medical referral. Stable osteoporotic fractures can be managed conservatively with rest and over-the-counter pain medication. The acute pain is often severe for 2 weeks, with persistent pain for up to 3 months. At 3 months, if pain is persistent, reradiograph the area to determine the degree of healing. If the compression fracture is in the lumbar or thoracolumbar area, a restrictive corset may be helpful to remind the patient not to bend forward or make sudden movements. All patients with osteoporosis must avoid flexion exercises. There is a dramatic increase in compression fractures among those performing flexion versus extension exercises for low back pain (see also Chapter 31, Osteoporosis).

OSTEOID OSTEOMA

Classic Presentation

The patient is usually a young male who presents with a complaint of well-localized midback pain. The pain is worse at night but relieved by aspirin (65% of patients).[18]

Cause

Osteoid osteomas are benign tumors affecting mainly the posterior elements of the vertebrae. They are not exclusive to the spine. In fact, 50% occur in the femur and tibia, and approximately 10% in the spine. Occurrence is most frequent in the lamina, followed by the pedicle, facet, and spinous processes.

Evaluation

The patient often has an acute-angle scoliosis at the site of the tumor (lesion on the concave side). The diagnosis is sometimes made from standard thoracic radiographs. The lesion is a small bony density that surrounds a smaller round, radiolucent nidus. Bone scans or tomograms often will be needed to confirm or identify the lesion.

Management

Refer the patient for surgical excision.

POSTURAL SYNDROME

Classic Presentation

The patient will present with a constant aching pain in the middle and upper thoracic regions. The pain is usually relieved by activity and made worse by working at a desk.

Cause

The natural imbalance between the anterior muscles and posterior muscles is often accentuated by various work postures that emphasize a "hunched," forward-head position. The large, tight muscles such as the pectorals become chronically shortened in adapting to the position, with associated weakness and constant strain of the midscapular muscles, which contract eccentrically.

Evaluation

Posturally the patient may present with a hyperkyphosis. There are often trigger points in the upper and middle trapezius, rhomboids, levator scapulae, and pectorals. Lower trapezius strength is minimal when the patient is asked to perform upper strength extension from a prone position with the arms held above the head (out in front of the body).

Management

The combination of manipulation of the thoracic and related regions with deep massage can be used initially to decrease discomfort. To prevent recurrence, exercises focusing on stretching the pectorals first, followed by strengthening of the midscapular muscles and lower trapezius should follow. Postural awareness may be increased with bracing or taping. The patient's work environment must be evaluated for ergonomic strengths. Redesign of the work environment and frequent breaks for stretching and mild isometrics often help.

T4 SYNDROME

Classic Presentation

The patient complains of upper back stiffness and achiness with associated signs of upper extremity numbness and/or paresthesias (often in a stocking and glove distribution). There may be associated headaches.

Cause

The cause is unknown; however, it is postulated that sympathetic dysfunction somehow related to vertebral dysfunction in the upper thoracic region (T2-T7) causes a referred or reflex phenomenon in the arms or hands. Patients may report occurrence during the night or upon rising. This syndrome is more common in women (4:1 ratio) in the age range of 30 to 50 years. Prolonged sitting, sustained reaching and pulling activities, shoveling, and overhead cleaning have all been reported by some patients.[19]

Evaluation

The patient will often have tenderness and restriction at the involved segment(s), most often T2-T7. Pressure or movement challenge at these areas may reproduce the patient's complaints. For all patients with arm complaints, a thorough neurologic examination should be performed in an attempt to differentiate nerve root, peripheral nerve, brachial plexus, or central nervous system disorders. The neurologic examination is normal in patients with the T4 syndrome. Radiographs are not diagnostic for this syndrome.

Management

Manipulation or mobilization of the involved area, coupled with postural advice and exercise, will usually resolve the patient's complaints.

REFERENCES

1. Nansel D, Szlazak M. Somatic dysfunction and the phenomenon of visceral disease simulation: a probable explanation for the apparent effectiveness of somatic therapy in patients presumed to be suffering from true visceral disease. *J Manipulative Physiol Ther.* 1995;18:379–397.
2. Valencia F. Biomechanics of the thoracic spine. In: Grant R, ed. *Physical Therapy of the Cervical and Thoracic Spine.* New York: Churchill-Livingstone; 1988:4.
3. Grieve GP. *Common Vertebral Joint Problems*. Edinburgh: Churchill Livingstone; 1981:15–17.
4. Keele CA, Neil E, eds. *Samson Wright's Applied Physiology.* 12th ed. London: Oxford University Press; 1971.
5. DeFranca GG, Levine LJ. The T4 syndrome. *J Manipulative Physiol Ther*. 1995;18:34–37.
6. White AA, Panjabi MM. Kinematics of the spine. In: White AA, Panjabi MM, eds. *Clinical Biomechanics of the Spine*. Philadelphia: JB Lippincott; 1978:61–90.
7. Carson WC, Lovell WW, Whitesides TE. Congenital elevation of the scapula. *J Bone Joint Surg Am.* 1981;63:1190.
8. Bunnell WP. An objective criterion for scoliosis screening. *J Bone Joint Surg Am.* 1984;66:1381–1387.
9. Love RM, Brodeur RR. Inter- and intra-examiner reliability of motion palpation for the thoracolumbar spine. *J Manipulative Physiol Ther*. 1987;10:1–4.
10. Haldeman S, Chapman-Smith D, Petersen, Jr., DM. *Guidelines for Chiropractic Quality Assurance and Practice Parameters: Proceedings of the Mercy Center Consensus Conference*. Gaithersburg, MD: Aspen Publishers Inc.; 1993.
11. Yochum TR, Rowe LJ. Scheuermann's disease. In : Yochum TR, Rowe LJ. *Essentials of Skeletal Radiology*. 2nd ed. Baltimore: Williams & Wilkins; 1996:1292–1295.
12. Lowe TG. Current concepts review: Scheuermann's disease. *J Bone Joint Surg Am.* 1990;72:940.
13. Blumenthal SL, Roach J, Herring JA. Lumbar Scheuermann's: a clinical series and classification. *Spine*. 1987;12:930.
14. Sorenson KH. *Scheuermann's Juvenile Kyphosis*. Copenhagen: Munksgaard; 1964.
15. Caplan GA, Scane AC, Frances RM. Pathogenesis of vertebral crush fractures. *J R Soc Med*. 1994;87:200.
16. Deyo RA, Rainville J, Kent DL. What can the history and physical examination tell us about low back pain? *JAMA*. 1992;268: 760–765.
17. Denis F. Spinal stability as defined by the three-column concept in acute spinal trauma. *Clin Orthop*. 1984;189:65.
18. Helms CA, Hattner RS, Vogler JB III. Osteoid osteoma: radionuclide diagnosis. *Radiology*. 1984;151:779.
19. McGuckin N. The T4 syndrome. In: Grieve GP, ed. *Modern Manual Therapy of the Vertebral Column*. New York: Churchill-Livingstone; 1986:370–376.

CHAPTER 5

Scoliosis

CONTEXT

Scoliosis may be the result of detectable, cause-and-effect conditions. If found as part of a composite picture of a disorder such as neurofibromatosis or poliomyelitis, scoliosis is categorized by cause. The list is long and includes neurologic, muscular, congenital bone anomalies, developmental (due to abnormal collagen, for example), and several other recognizable disorders. The majority of scolioses, however, are idiopathic. The majority of scolioses do not progress, yet for those that do, cosmesis and occasionally cardiopulmonary compromise are concerns.

Idiopathic scoliosis is truly an enigma. Etiologically disguised by apparent causes that ultimately are revealed as effects, this seemingly simple spinal deviation has remained "idiopathic" for centuries despite astounding technologic advances. Sifting through the plethora of theories, it becomes apparent that no single causative factor is or probably ever will be identifiable.

For years chiropractors have claimed success in the management of scoliosis. Yet it is unclear whether all chiropractors were dealing with idiopathic scoliosis or more the type of scoliosis that is the painful consequence of muscle spasm or the nonpainful scoliosis due to muscular imbalance that compensates for biomechanical asymmetry. Many chiropractors feel that by correcting asymmetry and keeping the spine segmentally and globally mobile, idiopathic scoliosis can be halted or reversed. Unfortunately, most studies indicate that although these are potential factors in curve progression, especially in larger curves, it is likely not the cause. Reflex mechanisms are proposed regarding proprioceptive input from the upper cervical region.[1] These factors may play a role in setting the muscular response to a perceived "normal" that is false. Yet, again, more research must be done.

IDIOPATHIC SCOLIOSIS ETIOLOGY

Although a genetic factor has been proposed, it has not yet been determined what it is. Recurrence among relatives has been reported to be between 25% and 35%.[2] With immediate relatives such as parents and grandparents, the incidence appears to be three or four times higher. When both parents are affected the number of children with significant curves was 40%, much higher than those without affected parents.[3]

The common thread running through many theories regarding the development and progression of idiopathic scoliosis is that sensory information is either aberrant or, when information is processed at the spinal cord level or more likely at higher levels such as the cortices, is misinterpreted, leading to inappropriate output information regarding body orientation in space.[4] Balance is often a problem in children with idiopathic scoliosis compared with those without.[5] Obviously, integration of proprioceptive, visual, and vestibular information is a factor.

It is known that curves greater than 30° are more likely to progress, having reached a point at which gravity has the advantage.[6] However, other concerns about progression center around the length of the spine, the length of the curve, and the size of the vertebrae.

One mechanical model that attempts to explain why females are prone to development of a progressive scoliosis has to do with the slenderness of their vertebrae. The model holds that the size of the vertebrae determines the load that can be accommodated. It is known that females, on average, have more slender spines than males. While their vertebral height increases by 50% during adolescent growth the vertebral width increases by only 15%.[7] In addition, their growth spurt occurs during a time when their kyphosis is at a minimum, thereby decreasing the absorptive effect of the sagittal curves. In contrast, males have thicker vertebrae and achieve their growth spurt during a time when their kyphosis is at a maximum, which may explain why they are more prone to the development of Scheuermann's disease.[8]

Another important concept is that the spine has a critical load capacity past which it will begin to deform. When children grow, especially when they grow rapidly, the increase in height coupled with the increased slenderness of the spine causes a decrease in the critical load needed to cause deformation. This results in a 20% decrease in the critical load level for only a 10% increase in height. Add to that any weight gain and the critical load is more likely to be exceeded while the spine is most subject to deformity.

There are several biologic models regarding the cause and progression of idiopathic scoliosis. One model states that differential pressure on end-plates leads to asymmetric growth, which results in scoliosis development. Although the Hueter-Volkmann law states that increased pressure across a growing epiphysis (end-plate) will lead to decreased growth, it has been found that the disc is more fluid in growing individuals and is able to dissipate the forces more equally across the end-plates than in the adult spine. Therefore, the effects of increased pressure due to wedging is thought to be negligible, at least in smaller curves. Dickson et al.[9] feel that the posterior elements, in particular the facets, not having the advantage of disc cushioning, are more likely to change as a result and may then be more the cause for asymmetric growth. Pressure changes in the histologic structure of the intervertebral disc has been demonstrated with effects in collagen and glycosaminoglycan content.[10,11] This occurs after the scoliosis develops, indicating that it is a response rather than a cause.

Although it may appear that an imbalance of muscular activity or strength may cause a scoliosis, the evidence suggests that any changes are reactions to the curve, not the causes. Asymmetric activity is found only in curves greater than 25°.[12] If asymmetric activity were the cause, these imbalances would be evident with lesser degrees of curvature. Comparison of bilateral muscle strength did not indicate any differences between scoliotic children and those without scoliosis.

GENERAL STRATEGY

History

- Determine whether the scoliosis onset was acute or slowly progressive.
- Determine whether there is associated acute pain at the apex (reflex muscle spasm due to a local process such as a tumor, a fracture, disc disease, etc.) or chronic pain (common in patients aged 40 years and above with idiopathic curves).
- Determine whether there was a previous diagnosis of scoliosis and whether radiographs were taken or treatment was rendered; if a brace or electrical stimulation was prescribed, determine whether the patient was compliant.
- In children and young adults, determine whether there is a family history, whether a female has reached menarche, whether a child has gone through a growth spurt, and whether indications of progression have been noticed by the parent or child.

Evaluation

- Determine whether there are any associated findings (congenital scoliosis), including clubfoot or other foot deformities, café au lait spots or patches (neurofibromatosis), or patches of hair along the spine (spina bifida).
- Observe the patient from behind for evidence of a scoliosis; perform an Adams' test; observe the patient with lateral bending into the convexity and lying prone (improvement indicates a functional component).
- Observe or measure any obvious asymmetries with regard to shoulder or hip height, winging of scapulae, or head tilt; measure with a plumb line to determine whether the scoliosis is compensated or uncompensated.
- Evaluate the patient for asymmetries of the lower extremities, including pronation, tibial torsion, femoral anteversion/retroversion, and leg length discrepancy; also test for asymmetric weakness or tightness of lower extremity musculature.
- Patients with scoliosis should be initially radiographed using a full-spine film. The films should be evaluated for signs of congenital scoliosis (ie, hemivertebrae, bar vertebrae), location of the curve, and pelvic unleveling. Measure the severity with a Cobb angle, rotation with the Nash-Moe method, and bone age with the Risser sign (iliac crest apophysis).
- To determine the degree of flexibility of the curve, films should be taken with the patient recumbent and laterally bending into the convexity and the Cobb angle measured. Subtraction of the recumbent Cobb angle standing Cobb angle and the will give an approximation of the functional component of the curve.

Management

- Most cases of congenital scoliosis should be sent for an orthopaedic consultation.
- Correlate history and examination findings to gauge the tendency to progression. The primary indicators are se-

verity of the curve and the Risser sign; important secondary indicators are age at menarche, type of curve, flexibility of curve, and familial predisposition.

- Idiopathic scoliosis may be managed within given ranges (dependent on age, tendency to progress, patient/parent choice) if there is no progression. Progression should be monitored radiographically every 3 to 4 months unless there are signs of rapid progression. Nonradiographic monitoring is appropriate using Moire topography. Curves that show signs of progression prior to age of menarche in girls should be referred for bracing; in girls past the age of menarche, large curves may require surgical progression. With boys, the relationship to a growth spurt may be helpful in determining a tendency to progress (more progression during the growth spurt).
- Idiopathic curves may become painful in patients in their 40s or older; management is for pain and correction of any obvious biomechanical or spinal dysfunction. Progression to instability or severe pain warrants an orthopaedic consultation.

EVALUATION

The prime directive with scoliosis management is to prevent progression and reverse the deformity if possible. Making decisions regarding treatment may seem easy given the limited options available. The ingredients in this decision equation are not discrete, however, and are based on risk to benefit ratios and outcome desires, which vary among doctors and patients. The primary concern for the patient is cosmetic. With severe scoliosis the physician may have additional concerns regarding cardiopulmonary function, although this is actually a rare complication.[12]

Recognition of the scoliosis at the earliest point is imperative. The first distinction that is requisite for management of a scoliosis is whether there is a known cause or whether it fits the larger group of idiopathic curves. Known causes often have associated nonspinal clues that should be screened for in all patients, not only those with an apparent curve. Bunch and Patwardham[13] have demonstrated how adequate compensation may camouflage the degree of distortion present. They use an analogy of a Christmas tree that appears to be symmetric; however, when stripped to the trunk it reveals a gross rotational distortion.

The next distinction is to determine whether a curve is primarily structural or functional. Structural curves are the end result of bone remodeling with a subsequent rotary distortion that then becomes evident superficially as a lateral curvature. This rotation is always into the concavity when using the spinous process as the reference point. In addition, structural curves do not correct with postural changes such as bending forward (Adams' test), lying down, or maximally bending into the convexity in a supine position (Figure 5–1).

Functional (nonstructural) curves have no permanent rotary component and correct or overcorrect with the positional changes noted above. Functional curves are usually compensatory to biomechanical problems or are the result of muscle spasm. The key difference is that scoliosis due to muscle spasm has a pain component that is often aggravated by bending forward. Idiopathic scoliosis is rarely the cause of spinal pain until later in life.

Curves are named by the regional location of their apices. Single curves are relatively easy to identify; however, when two or three curves are present it is necessary to determine the major curve and compensatory (minor) curves. In general, the major curve is larger and more structural (greatest degree of rotation). Minor curves are generally smaller and more flexible.

Idiopathic scoliosis is also classified according to age: infantile—birth to 3 years (males predominate); juvenile—4 to 10 years of age (female ratio higher); adolescent—more than 10 years of age (strong female to male ratio, 7:1 or higher).

Scoliosis is detected by parents or guardians, the child's doctor, or school screening. Detection by a parent is usually based on either noticing shoulder or scapula elevation or noticing that the clothes hang unevenly. Unfortunately, this is not always readily apparent and may be minimal whereby compensation has camouflaged the deformity. When scoliosis screening was introduced in the 1940s in the United States the goal was to identify scoliosis due to poliomyelitis. As the program expanded, the goal changed to identification of children at a stage of scoliosis development early enough to allow a period of bracing in the hope of avoiding surgery. At present, school screenings are mandatory in approximately one third of schools in the United States, with screening occurring between the ages of 10 and 16 years (grades 5 to 9).[14,15]

The statistical risk of having a scoliosis that progresses to the point that treatment is needed is only 0.2%. The referral rate averages 5%; however, the rate is suspected to be at least twice that because referral documentation forms are not available for a large percentage of patients.[16] Williams and Herbert[17] reviewed the results of several screening programs and found a false-positive rate of at least 60% and a false-negative rate of 23%. Viewed from a different perspective, Dickson[18] found that as little as 10% of children who screened positive for trunk asymmetry had a scoliosis that was progressive. These observations have raised serious concerns about the value of screening.

The basis of screening is to check the standing patient for signs of asymmetry and scoliosis. The patient then bends forward to enable the examiner to check for humping (Adams'

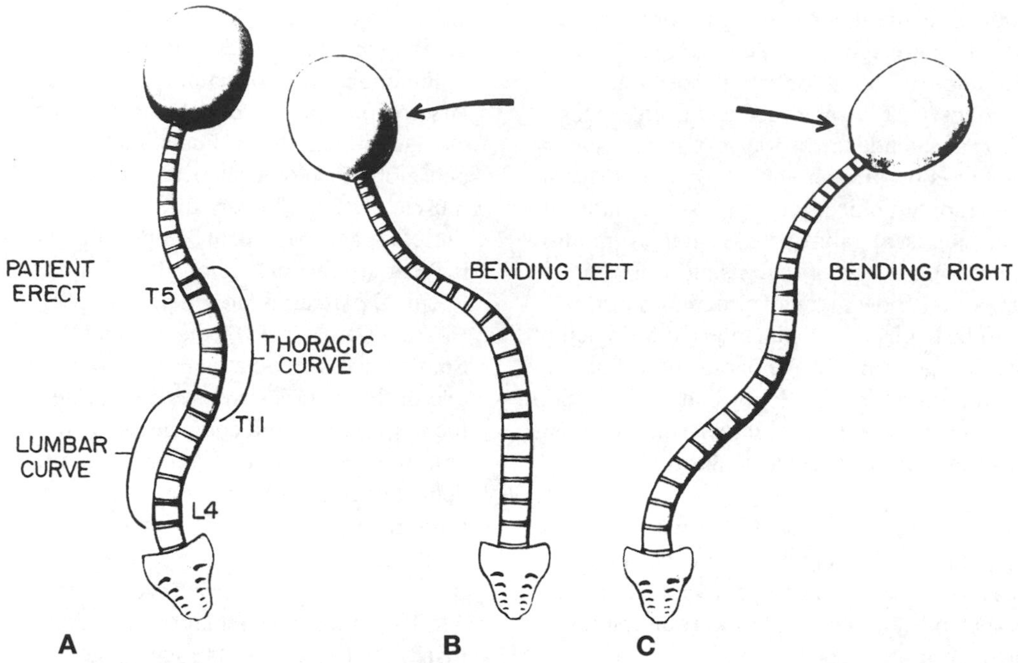

Figure 5–1 The value of the side bending to determine whether a curve is structural or nonstructural. **A**, The patient is standing erect and both curves seem to be in balance. The question is: Are both curves structural, and therefore do both require treatment, or is one of the curves secondary and functional? **B**, The patient bends to the left side and the lumbar curve straightens out and actually overcorrects. This curve is therefore a functional and nonstructural curve, and if surgery were required for the upper curve, this curve would not need to be fused. **C**, The patient is bent to the right side and the upper curve does not correct completely. This indicates that the thoracic curve is structural and does require treatment. *Source:* Reprinted with permission from H. Keim, *The Adolescent Spine*, 2nd ed., p. 114, © 1982, Springer-Verlag, New York, Inc.

test) indicating the side of convexity of a structural curve. It is felt that this is a simple process, yet many screening personnel are not adequately trained. When faced with an equivocal case, the tendency is to refer. This purely observational (subjective) approach has no support from a quantifiable measurement. In addressing these concerns, several recommendations have been made to potentially reduce the false-positive referral rate.

- Train personnel. Have them screen in the presence of a trained supervisor before being allowed to screen alone.
- View the spine in at least three positions of forward bending. As the patient bends forward he or she clasps the hands and allows them to hang dependently. The examiner views from behind first at about 45° to view the thoracic "skyline," then at a few degrees more of flexion for the thoracolumbar region, and finally at a right angle for the lumbar region.
- A scoliometer should be used to measure the degree of rib "humping," or more preferably called the angle of inclination or trunk rotation. This device is basically an inclinometer that measures in degrees the amount of rotation of the trunk. The instrument is reliable and seems to allow discrimination between curves that are greater than 20°.[19] It has been determined that if 5° of inclination is found, it is likely that 20° of structural curve exists, requiring further evaluation. Bunnell[19] feels that using the scoliometer criterion of 5° of rotation would decrease the false-positive referral rate by half.
- When the examiner is unsure, it is recommended the child be rescreened in 6 months instead of immediate referral.
- Establish several referral centers where an experienced examiner with access to radiographic facilities will examine the children at no cost. This suggestion is based on the observation that there is a very low percentage (less than one third in one study) of compliance for follow-up evaluation.[4]

Congenital Scoliosis

Congenital scoliosis, although not as common as idiopathic scoliosis, should always be screened for in a young patient.

The most common causes generally may be divided into two categories: (1) failure of formation such as occurs with hemivertebrae and (2) failure of segmentation as occurs with unilateral bar vertebrae. It is more common for these to occur in various forms of combination as opposed to discrete entities. It is extremely important to remember that these congenital abnormalities occur in all three planes and may be underestimated with regard to progression when viewed on a single radiograph. Additionally, cartilaginous tissue, not visible on the radiograph, may play a role in asymmetric growth.

Prognosis regarding progression is difficult; however, some generalizations may help guide the clinician with a warning that there are always exceptions to these generalities.[12]

- Single hemivertebrae in areas other than the thoracic spine are generally not rapidly progressive.
- Hemivertebrae on opposite sides with only a few normal vertebrae separating them are not likely to progress.
- Hemivertebrae may be further divided into fully segmented, partially segmented, or nonsegmented. The distinction is based on whether a disc space exists on both sides (fully), one side (partially), or not at all (non). In general, the disc space represents the degree of growth potential, therefore the progression potential for the scoliosis. Nonsegmented hemivertebrae are the least likely to progress.
- Predictions of progression with unilateral bar vertebrae are less difficult. The presence of a unilateral bar is strongly suggestive of progression and warrants surgical referral.
- An example of a combination of congenital deformities likely to progress would be a unilateral bar vertebra with paired hemivertebrae on the opposite side.

Unlike idiopathic scoliosis, additional diagnostic clues exist outside the spinal column and musculoskeletal system. Interference with the development of the mesoderm in utero is usually associated with multiple affected areas.

- Twenty percent of patients with congenital scoliosis were found to have genitourinary abnormalities. Six percent had serious obstructive problems.[20]
- Heart defects were found in 15% of patients with a congenital scoliosis.[21]
- Ten percent of patients with congenital scoliosis will have spinal dysraphism, with half of these being diastematomyelia.[22] The rest were found to have anomalous bands, lipomas, or a tight fila terminale. Patients fall into three groups. The first group has the scoliosis as the prominent external sign. The other two groups may show excess hair growth, dimpling, or pigmentation problems (café au lait spots) over or around the spine. All patients should be observed for these subtle indicators. Other associated findings include a clubfoot, a congenitally dislocated hip, or an anatomically short leg.

Decision Making with Congenital Curves

The clinician must be aware of the different progression rates of congenital scoliosis. Given the significant numbers of extraspinal abnormalities that may coexist with congenital scoliosis, a thorough physical examination must be performed. It would then be appropriate to refer the patient to an internist if heart or genitourinary abnormalities are present or to a neurologist if there is a suspicion of neurofibromatosis or spinal dysraphism.

If the patient has a unilateral, nonsegmented hemivertebra or bilateral hemivertebra separated by a few normal vertebrae they should be monitored radiographically every 3 to 6 months. The least likely to progress are nonsegmented hemivertebrae. However, if there is a single segmented hemivertebra in the thoracic spine or a unilateral bar vertebra, refer for orthopaedic consultation because these are likely to progress.

If there are combined defects and the curve is less than 20° or less than 40° with a balanced trunk, the patient should be monitored radiographically every 6 months for progression. Refer if progressive. If there are combined defects and the curve is between 20° and 40° with an unbalanced trunk and flexible spine, bracing is appropriate. Curves with combined defects that are progressive and those greater than 40° should be referred for orthopaedic surgical consultation.

Idiopathic Scoliosis

Prognostications regarding the natural history of an individual's idiopathic scoliosis is primarily hinged on three primary and several secondary factors. The primary gauges of progression are the severity of the curve, the apex location, and the skeletal maturity of the individual. Secondary indicators include genetic tendencies, gender, and curve flexibility.

Although the severity of the curve is relatively easy to determine radiographically, skeletal maturity is a more complex variable. Two methods are used to determine skeletal maturity: (1) the Greulich-Pyle atlas and (2) the Risser sign. The Greulich-Pyle atlas is a comparative reference to match with a patient's left wrist radiographs. It is rarely used. Risser's sign is a grading of iliac crest apophysis development (Figure 5–2). The upper pelvic rim is divided into four equal units. Radiographically the line of apophyseal growth progresses laterally to medially. It is believed that little growth (less chance for progression) occurs after a +4 Risser sign. Compared with a 36% progression with a Risser sign of 0, only 11% progressed with a Risser sign of 2.[23]

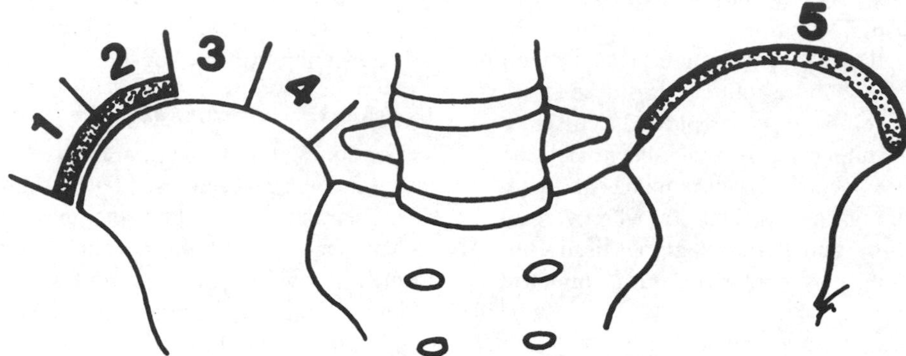

Figure 5–2 Grading the development of iliac crest apophysis according to the Risser sign. The iliac crest is divided into four quarters, and the excursion or stage of maturity is the amount of progression. In this example, the excursion is 50%; the Risser sign is 2. *Source:* Reprinted with permission from H. Keim, *The Adolescent Spine*, 2nd ed., p. 78, © 1982, Springer-Verlag, New York, Inc.

Various investigators have classified idiopathic curves into commonly occurring patterns. These curves are primarily structural and may lead to development of compensatory curves. The only way to distinguish among curves that appear to be of equal severity is to note the degree of rotation and with side-bending films to determine which curves are flexible. A list of these patterns is given with some clues to recognition.

- Double major—This includes two curves of equal or close to equal size, both of which fail to correct much on lateral-bending films. The end vertebrae for the thoracic curve is usually at T12. The pattern is consistently right thoracic/left lumbar. This is such a common pattern that when the opposite is found it is suggested that consideration for further evaluation is necessary. Furthermore, a relatively common cause is syringomyelia or the type I Arnold-Chiari syndrome.[24] Arai et al.[25] found that although the incidence was only 4% for syringomyelia and Chiari type I malformation each (total 8%), scoliosis was the only presenting complaint in 40% of these cases. Nineteen percent of these cases had a left convex thoracic curve.
- Right thoracic—This initially single curve extends from about T5 to T11 with the apex at about T8. Often confused with a double major curve, the right thoracic usually has a compensatory curve in the lumbar region that may at times be of equal size; however, it is flexible. The right thoracic curve is an excellent example that the thoracic curve is not commonly a mechanical compensation for a lumbar curve but, in fact, the reverse. This demonstrates that an unlevel pelvis or sacrum is not often the stimulus for scoliosis formation with many curves.
- Lumbar—Usually extending from about T12 to L4, this curve is usually left convex. Thoracic compensation is not uncommon; however, it occurs to a much smaller degree.
- Thoracolumbar—Extending from about T8 to L3, this single curve is less likely to have clearly compensatory curves associated with it.
- Double thoracic major—With an upper left curve extending from T2 to T7 and a lower right curve extending from T7 to L1, these two primary curves are usually compensated for in the cervical spine.

Single curves with little compensation are more deforming, as are high thoracic curves. Lumbar curves are generally far less progressive compared with the other major curve patterns.[8] The most important indicator of a good prognosis (slim chance of progression) is the closure of vertebral growth plates, generally indicating skeletal maturity. Since this event cannot currently be viewed directly we are left, as often is the case, with indirect and therefore inaccurate clues.

Age is only an indirect measure of an individual's skeletal maturity. This is so primarily because hormonal factors are variable, with one individual achieving menarche and a growth spurt at a relatively early age while another may undergo these events 2 to 3 years later. This broad difference in growth spurt is an obvious normal distinction between boys and girls and in some ways may be one reason why scoliosis is less likely to progress in boys.

Growth potential is the critical factor. If the growth potential is known, the degree of concern for progression can be approximated. In other words, when the patient has attained most of his or her adult height, there is significantly less chance of progression. The end of the adolescent growth spurt, therefore, is a good indicator of relative stability in curve size.

The growth spurt is considered to be about a 3½-year period.[26] The peak height velocity when the rate of growth is greatest occurs during the first 1½ years. The rate decreases during the last 2 years. Several studies have pointed to an apparent difference in the timing of the growth spurt. Goldberg et al.[27] noted that girls with adolescent idiopathic scoliosis appear to have an early pubertal growth spurt, but no abnormality of total growth or development. Therefore, they simply reach the adult height at an earlier age than matched controls. Numerous studies[28–31] have demonstrated that girls with idiopathic scoliosis were significantly taller than matched controls. This was most apparent in the younger groups and much less apparent in the older groups. Final adult height comparisons showed no significant differences. Several studies[32–34] indicate that there may be increased growth hormone in girls with idiopathic scoliosis, particularly in the early stages of puberty.

A good indicator of the first rapid phase of height growth is the development of secondary sex characteristics. A staging for both girls and boys has been developed by Tanner.[35] Five stages for breast development and the development of pubic hair are used for girls; for boys, genitalia development and pubic hair growth. For modesty requirements it may be necessary to use a modification of the Tanner criteria. This modification allows the patient to choose from a written description or pictorial rendition of each Tanner stage of pubic hair development.

In matching the Tanner staging to age, menarche, and peak height growth a pattern appears. In the United States the average age for menarche is 12½ years (with a standard deviation of 1 year).[6] Menarche appears to occur earlier in girls with idiopathic scoliosis. It is significant that most authors[36] support Scoles et al.[37] in finding that height increased less than 3% after menarche. Therefore, it appears to signal the slowing of the growth spurt. Menarche corresponds to stage 4 breast and pubic hair growth using the Tanner criteria. This correlates with at least a year into the peak height growth phase. Boys, however, will usually reach peak height velocity in stage 4, later than girls.

It is often stated that idiopathic scoliosis is more common in females. When the data are examined more closely, however, it is clear that there is male predominance with infantile curves, and that the ratio of male to female is generally equal with curves less than 20°.[38] Females dominate significantly with curves greater than 30°. Curves in need of surgical treatment show a dramatic female predominance of 7:1.

Flexibility is an important determination for distinguishing among the different curve patterns and may be a factor in the tendency to progress. Duval-Beaupere et al.[39] have determined two types of flexibility that must be considered: (1) collapse, the degree of increase in curvature when gravity acts as an axial force on the scoliosis (standing position), or the opposite is true, the degree to which the curve improves with recumbency; (2) reducibility, the degree of correction that occurs with corrective forces such as bracing, laterally bending into the convexity, muscle stimulation, and so forth.

It was suggested that reducibility is not a constant that helps with prediction of which curves are likely to progress; however, it was suggested that those curves with the largest collapse tendencies (corrected most when lying) had the slowest evolution rates.

Although the flexibility of the curve is screened with an Adams' test, quantification is important to determine the degree of flexibility. Radiographically this is measured by comparing the Cobb angle from the standing anterior (A) to posterior (P) (or P to A) radiograph and a recumbent radiograph with the patient bending maximally into the convexity of the curve being evaluated.

Summary of Scoliosis Evaluation

In an effort to synthesize the foregoing information a summary approach to the young scoliotic patient is presented. Physical examination of all infants, children, and adolescents should include a screen for signs of both congenital defects in vertebral development and scoliosis. Congenital problems should be suspected when bony abnormalities are evident through deformity, hip dislocation, clubfeet, and the like, and dermatologic signs such as pigmentation changes and hair growth over affected areas.

Next, a standard standing observation for asymmetry should be performed followed by an Adams' test performed in three positions. Any humping should be quantified with a scoliometer. Radiographs should be obtained for patients whose angular rotation deformity (humping) is greater than 5°. If prior radiographs are available they should be ordered for comparison purposes. If radiographs are not recent and there is a suspicion of progression, new films should be ordered. If no films are available a baseline series must be ordered.

Radiographs should include a full-spine (14 × 36) posterior to anterior (PA) or anterior to posterior (AP) if the AP incorporates rare-earth screens and appropriate shielding. The suggestion of a PA view is based on the significant reduction in radiation exposure to developing breasts. A lateral full spine should complement the AP or PA in an effort to determine the degree of sagittal effect from the scoliosis (lordosis and kyphosis) and to glean a better idea of the degree of vertebral body involvement if a congenital defect is found. Cruickshank et al.[40] have demonstrated that a lordosis or flattening is usually found at the apical region of structural curves rather than the visually perceived kyphosis. They demonstrated that this visual impression is incorrectly confirmed on the lateral radiograph. When a mean kyphosis of 41° was measured on the lateral view it was found to represent an area of lordosis when the lateral view was corrected for rotation.

Finally, recumbent, laterally bending, films should be included for each curve to determine the degree of curve flexibility. This involves the patient's maximally bending into the convexity of the curve. The Cobb angle is then compared between the standing and recumbent, laterally bending, views. Subtraction of these two values indicates the functional aspect of the curve. This helps determine which curves are major curves and which are compensatory curves.

The Cobb angle is the standard measurement of the degree of curvature. Although there are some problems with this approach, its universal acceptance allows comparison with follow-up views taken in consultation and referral. The angle is based on determining the end vertebrae. These are the upper- and lowermost vertebrae that tilt last into the concavity of the curve and demonstrate no rotation based on pedicle location. By drawing lines along the end-plates of the vertebrae toward the concavity of the curve it will be found that the first vertebrae outside the curve will have lines that diverge from the other lines (Figure 5–3A). After choosing the end vertebrae, a line across the top of the upper-end vertebra and across the bottom-end vertebra are drawn toward the concave side. Perpendicular lines are then drawn from each of these lines. The intersection of these lines equals the Cobb angle. It has been shown that there is some diurnal variation in the Cobb angle, as much as 5°.[41] This variation suggests repeating follow-up views at the same time of day if possible.

Determination of bone age (skeletal maturity) is made with the Risser sign.[42] With the iliac crest divided into four equal divisions, a determination is made regarding the extent of apophyseal fusion. Although the apophyseal advancement is from anterior to posterior and then medially, on a two-dimensional image such as a radiograph it appears as a lateral to medial growth. It has been demonstrated that the Risser sign may not be accurately viewed on a PA radiograph.[43] When the line of growth has extended through the last quadrant, a Risser sign of 4 has been reached. At this stage there is still a radiolucent separation between the apophyseal line and the crest. Closure of this space is considered a Risser sign 5, indicating full skeletal maturity. There are some flaws with this measurement; however, it still is a major indirect indicator of vertebral end-plate closure, thereby indicating the end of scoliosis progression during adolescence. The time of appearance is relatively standard; however, the time of fusion is variable. It appears that vertebral end-plate closure has probably occurred by the time a Risser sign 4 is seen in some but not all individuals.[44] So, although a Risser sign 5 is a confirmation of closure, it appears that the Risser sign may be a late indicator of end-plate closure. Still, the Risser sign is considered one of only three significant predictive factors with regard to scoliosis development.[45]

Rotation is another important observation made radiographically. The standard measurement is the Nash-Moe method. Using the pedicle shadows as reference points to a line drawn through the center of the vertebrae, the degree of deviation from the center line is determined (Figure 5–3B). A large rotational component to the curve, suggests a structural type. The degree of rotation can be so great as to give the appearance of an oblique radiograph of the region.

Rotation that does not fit the pattern of a typical structural, idiopathic curve (body toward convexity, posterior elements toward the concavity) should suggest a functional, possibly muscle spasm, cause. Also if no rotation occurs, it is likely that the curve is more flexible. Both no rotation and body rotation into the concavity indicate a functional curve, and when coupled with a patient presenting with back pain, muscle spasm is likely the cause.

Nonradiographic evaluation for progression is usually topographically based. Moire topography and integrated shape investigation system (ISIS) screening are the two most commonly used instrumentations. Moire topography uses light sources that superimpose a grid on the patient's back.[46] A Polaroid photograph is taken of this surface distortion pattern. As on a geographic map, lines that diverge indicate higher elevations (posteriority) and lines that converge indicate less height (anteriority). Although designed as a tool to replace the positional examination at school screenings, Moire topography has not been found to be significantly valuable. Moire topography is most valuable as a nonradiographic monitoring tool for detecting scoliosis progression. Although there are some problems with false positives, it is helpful in indicating in most patients when a radiographic evaluation should be performed to determine the degree of progression. ISIS screening is more high tech; therefore, it is more expensive and less available.[47] The principles are the same as those of Moire topography; however, a computer is used to generate an approximation of the coronal and sagittal curves. Again it is not a good screening tool but may help with monitoring progression.

MANAGEMENT

The literature regarding scoliosis development and progression, screening, and treatment is voluminous. The difficulty is that when criteria used for inclusion or exclusion are not held constant, meta-analysis and extrapolation based on this analysis are extremely difficult.

It would seem that decision making in scoliosis management would be a simple process. A curve exists where a

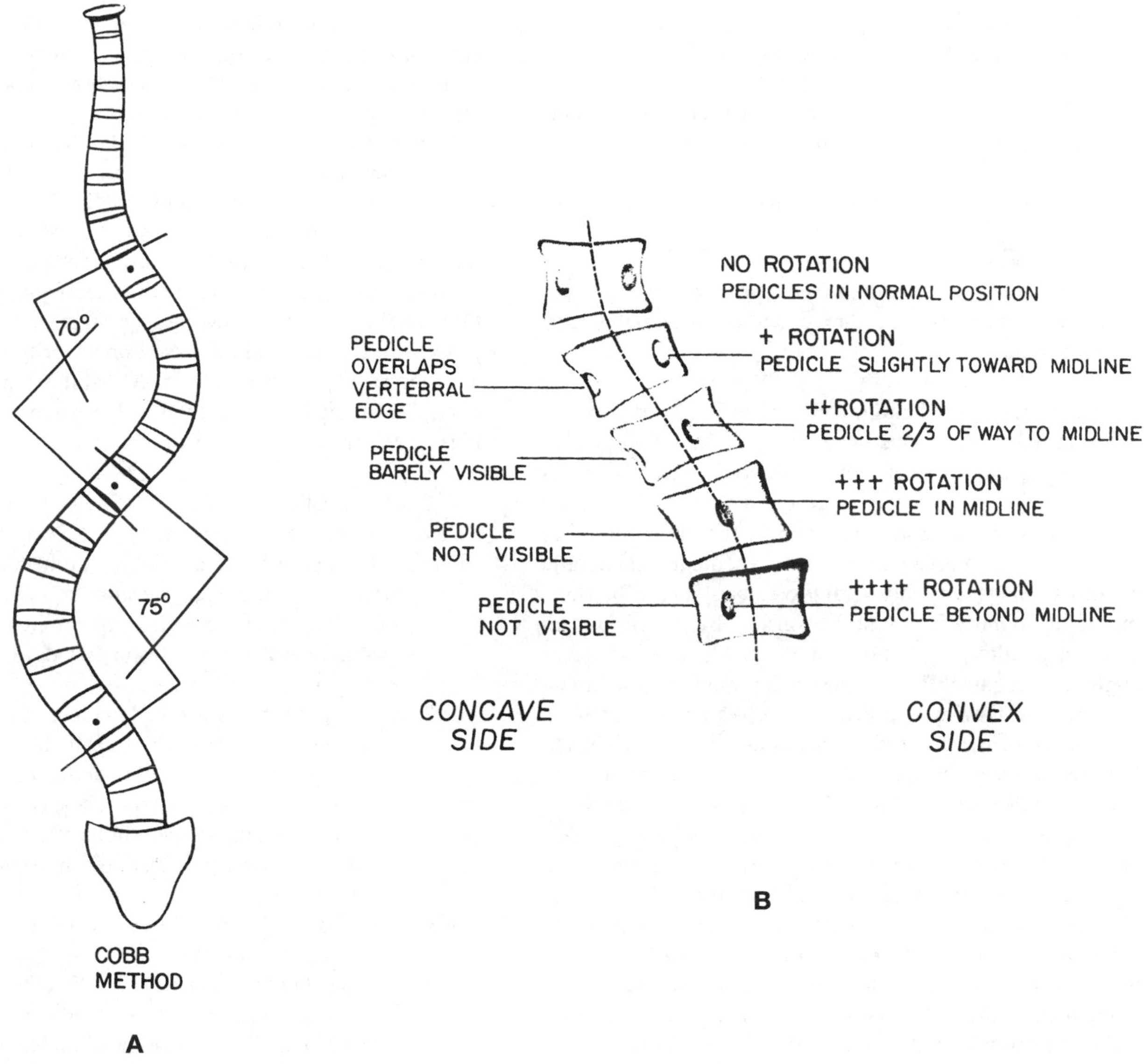

Figures 5–3A and B Measurement on a radiograph of degree of curvature in scoliosis according to the (A)Cobb angle and (B) Nash-Moe method. *Source:* Reprinted with permission from H. Keim, *The Adolescent Spine*, 2nd ed, p. 144, © 1982, Springer-Verlag, New York, Inc.

straight line should be. Push on the apices of the curve (or curves), distract the curve to assist straightening, and finally level out the base on which the spine sits, avoiding any "compensatory" curve development. This "mechanical" approach fails for two major reasons: (1) the development of a curve or curves has a mechanical component that becomes a significant factor only after the curve reaches 30°; (2) the curve is not two dimensional. A large rotational component is found with structural scoliosis also affecting the sagittal curves (kyphosis, lordosis). Individuals grow at different rates. In addition, one individual with a 30° curve may have progression while another may not for no known reason. Therefore, clinical decisions should err on the side of caution.

The key questions a clinician needs to ask himself or herself in making a decision regarding management of idiopathic scoliosis are as follows:

- What is the risk of progression?
- What is the effectiveness of various conservative options versus operative options?
- What is the risk of using chiropractic methods versus bracing or surgery regarding progression?
- If bracing or surgery is needed, what are the criteria for referral (at what level of severity or age are they most effective)?
- What are the risks of surgery?
- What outcome is desired (reduction of curve, prevention of progression, improvement of cardiopulmonary function, etc.)?

The incidence of infantile scoliosis has decreased so markedly that the condition is rarely seen.[48] This fact, coupled with the finding of a left convex thoracic curve, suggests that infantile scoliosis may represent a form separate from idiopathic scoliosis. Environmental factors are believed to be the explanation. If a clinician does encounter an infantile scoliosis, congenital and paralytic causes should be ruled out. If the infantile form is still a consideration, an orthopaedist can predict progression using the Mehta rib-vertebra angle measurement.[49] The rib-vertebra angle measurement is formed by drawing a vertical line through the center of the vertebra. Lines drawn through the long axis of the right and left ribs intersect this line. If the difference between the right and left angles is greater than 20°, progression is likely.

Although it might be easy to set a cutoff point for conservative versus surgical care based on the severity of the curve, real life contains too many variables to allow such a clean black-and-white decision. Measurements of skeletal maturity must be included in an effort to determine likelihood of progression. Outcome desires are ultimately what guide the clinician in equivocal scenarios. Outcome predictability for orthotic treatment, adapted from Bunch and Patwardham,[13] might include (1) ability to halt progression, (2) chance of progression while braced, and (3) cost and complications associated with bracing (medical and psychologic). Outcome predictability for surgical management may include (1) correction potential without complications, (2) infection and pseudarthrosis development, and (3) late complications.

In general, the predictability is fairly well known for each factor when matched with age (skeletal maturity) and curve severity. Still, there are scenarios where a "successful" outcome is fairly equal for both options. Then it is often the decision of the clinician based on the value he or she places on each of the outcome factors. For example, a 12-year-old girl with a 35° curve and a Risser sign of 3 might have an equal chance of a successful outcome with either treatment approach. However, the risk of infection, pseudarthrosis, and late complications is fairly low with surgery. A surgeon might consider this an acceptable trade-off compared with 1 or 2 years of bracing, which carries with it about a 10% chance of progression, compliance issues, and psychologic complications. In the mind of the chiropractor or conservative orthopaedist, however, the lower cost of bracing and the avoidance of some of the rare but serious complications of surgery might be more appropriate. Neither is an incorrect choice. However, the desires of the parents and the child must be factored in before a decision is made. This requires a full discussion with the parents and the child of the options and their associated advantages and disadvantages.

Always keeping in mind the complexity that may exist in individual cases, the following is a suggested baseline approach to decision making based on severity of the curve and maturity. It is important to note that these are idiopathic curves, meaning that congenital and transient curves due to muscle spasm are not included.

- Curves less than 20° may be treated chiropractically.
  1. If the patient has not reached skeletal maturity, observation using nonradiographic means should be used to determine progression. Radiographs should be taken if there are signs of progression. Radiographs may be needed during periods of rapid growth to better gauge progression.
  2. If the patient has reached skeletal maturity, treatment for progression is not needed. If biomechanical faults are present such as unilateral pronation or a significant leg length deficiency, correct them and obtain a radiograph to determine effectiveness. There is little chance of progression in this range of scoliosis, however.
- Curves between 20° and 40° are still within the conservative management range.
  1. If the patient has not reached skeletal maturity and the curve is less than 30°, initial chiropractic care may be applied; however, the clinician must be vigilant in monitoring for progression. Any signs of progression should result in referral for bracing. This is the range at which bracing has been shown to be most effective.[36]
  2. If the patient has reached skeletal maturity, progression is not likely. Correct biomechanical faults and observe periodically.
- Curves greater than 40° may require surgery.
  1. If the patient has less than a Tanner score of 2 and/or less than a Risser sign of 3, bracing should be tried for 6 months. If ineffective, refer for surgical consideration (see discussion below).
  2. If the patient has a Tanner 3 or a Risser 4, surgery is recommended.

A dilemma often exists for the chiropractor faced with a patient with a progressive or large curve who is seeking alternatives to bracing and surgery. The chiropractor is considered the last hope for the patient. It is important to explain fully to the patient and the parents the consequences of allowing the curve to progress and weigh against this the advantages of bracing or surgery. The consequences of progression are mainly cosmetic. The larger the curve at skeletal maturity, the more likely it will progress in adulthood. If cardiopulmonary function is normal as an adolescent, it is unlikely to become worse as an adult as a result of the scoliosis. It is also likely that as an adult, chronic back pain is more likely. Therefore, with cosmesis as the central issue, it is a decision that is difficult to make not knowing an individual's future adult perspective on appearance. What might help put the decision in perspective is that it has been found that scoliotic patients have a high percentage of psychosocial adjustment problems, unemployment, delayed marriage, or no marriage.[13]

Comanagement with an orthopaedist is recommended when curves enter an equivocal range wherein decisions become difficult. Finding a knowledgeable and reasonable orthopaedist for comanagement guarantees that all alternatives are explained to the patient and the doctors understand each other's rationale and concerns. The patient is then able to make more educated choices not based on fear tactics from either camp.

Conservative Treatment Options

Lateral Surface Stimulation

The principle of electrical surface stimulation is based on providing a constant load through contraction of the larger trunk muscle via the lever arm of the ribs. It was hoped that by using stimulation for 8 hours during the night the effects of creep and relaxation could be used in a positive way to effect change. The spine and its surrounding soft tissue support represent viscoelastic material. Viscoelastic material will undergo permanent change in length only when a constant load is applied over long periods of time. Although the initial reports[50] on electrical stimulation for scoliosis correction were extremely encouraging, subsequent studies have demonstrated an unacceptably low rate of success.[51]

Bracing

Bracing recently has come under attack as a viable conservative treatment option for progressive curves. The first doubts were raised when it was determined from school screening programs that curves in the 15° to 20° range that appeared to be successfully treated by bracing probably would have done as well without bracing. The study by Moe and Kettleson[52] initially indicated excellent results with bracing; however, the follow-up review of these patients by Carr et al.[53] indicated loss of correction the longer patients were off the brace. Finally, Emans et al.[54] reported on the effectiveness of part-time bracing as opposed to the tried-and-true full-time approach. This suggested to some that the concept of how bracing works was seriously flawed.

When the literature is more selectively reviewed it seems two factors surface that may help determine the patients most likely to respond to bracing:

1. Girls who were braced before and at the time of menarche had the best results. Those who were braced months or more postmenarche had the least success. It is suggested that for this latter group bracing is little more than a "holding" device.
2. The degree of curvature is crucial in determining the appropriateness of bracing. Curves less than 20° (and not progressing) probably will do as well without bracing. Curves greater than 40° are likely to lose substantial degrees of correction postbracing.

Therefore, bracing for girls who are at premenarche or menarche with curves in the 20° to 40° range have the greatest chance of success with bracing. It should be noted that although bracing was required for 23 hours a day in the past, bracing time is more commonly 16 to 18 hours with current prescriptions.

Bracing must be performed by an experienced orthotist at facilities that have experience in scoliosis brace fabrication. They are given specific design specifications by the orthopaedist. The corrective principles with bracing are based on applying pressure at the apices. This cannot be done directly, so the corrective pad is applied to the rib attached to the apical vertebra in the thoracic region. This places the pad below the apex from a surface perspective. The lumbar pad is applied to the paraspinal muscles over the transverse processes. Corrective pads are attached to the shell of the brace. Braces such as the Milwaukee brace may also apply distractive forces with a large metal superstructure extending to the occiput.

Exercise

It is agreed that exercise as a single-therapy approach is not successful in reversing or slowing the progression of scoliosis. It is agreed that exercises are a necessary adjunct to bracing therapy with a focus on abdominal strengthening, strengthening of the muscles on the convex side of the curve, and stretching of the muscles on the concave side.

Chiropractic Adjustments

Four general concepts are used in defense of chiropractic manipulative treatment of scoliosis, as follows:

1. By freeing up movement at each segmental level, the spine is kept more flexible and scoliosis is less likely to progress.
2. By a reflex reaction, adjusting (manipulation) of the cervical spine may influence righting reflexes in an effort to balance the spine.
3. Removal of segmental dysfunction may eliminate sources of aberrant sensory input and consequent output problems such as pain and accompanying muscle spasm. Proprioceptive input would then be normalized, providing an appropriate database for higher cortical decisions of body positioning.
4. By leveling the pelvis and sacrum a scoliosis can be corrected. It has been demonstrated previously, however, that although contributory, an unlevel pelvis or sacrum is not the cause of an idiopathic curve. If this were so, the first curve to develop would be a lumbar compensation followed by a thoracic curve. Another archaic belief is that by adjusting the apical vertebra toward the concavity the curve may be lessened. Force applied at this level would have to be applied for long periods of time (such as a brace) for any correction to occur. Viscoelastic tissue such as the spine has a tendency to return to its original shape unless a constant load is applied over long periods of time.

At this time there is no large-study research evidence (only a few isolated case reports) that chiropractic manipulative therapy (adjusting) affects the natural history of an idiopathic scoliosis. Certainly more research must be done to determine chiropractic's role in scoliosis management.

Surgery

It is beyond the scope of this discussion to give a detailed description or recommendation for specific surgical techniques. Some general principles are outlined. The two main goals of surgery are (1) to straighten the spine in the coronal plane and correct for sagittal contour (kyphosis or lordosis), and (2) to stabilize the spine through arthrodesis. Various surgeons have developed an array of instrumentation for these corrective procedures. The original Harrington rod implantation has been modified over the years. The rods are used for distraction to straighten the spine and for compression to correct for kyphosis if appropriate.[55] To add stability to the rods sublaminar wiring (Luque) or spinous-process wiring (Drummond[56]) was devised. The sublaminar wiring carried with it an unacceptable risk of neurologic complication.[57] It also did not produce a significant advantage in correction or stability. The Cotrel-Dubousset instrumentation focuses on correction of the rotational component in an effort to decrease rib humping.[58] This is accomplished through a cross-linking that connects the two rods. The apparatus is relatively stable in all planes.

Adult Scoliosis

Although the main discussion of this chapter has focused on idiopathic scoliosis in the growing patient, the adult patient may present with unique management problems that warrant discussion. Adult scoliosis may be a residual from earlier idiopathic development or may develop in later years.[59] If, in fact, idiopathic scoliosis is not part of the patient's history a search for cause should include the following:

- Scoliosis may be due to reactive muscle spasm. When muscle spasm is the cause, any pain-provoking entity is possible. Common causes include reactions to vertebral disc and facet injuries, visceral disorders, and spinal cord or nerve root involvement due to bony stenosis or tumor.
- Scoliosis may be due to degenerative and osteopenic disorders of the spine. When this results in instability a mechanical (compensatory or buckling) scoliosis may develop.

It is important to consider that there are generally three periods in which scoliosis may be progressive: (1) infancy, (2) adolescence, and (3) after age 50 years. Past age 50 the most common causes are bone-softening disorders and degenerative instability. Although it is more common for scoliosis to be a residual to an earlier idiopathic or congenital beginning it is possible for a new, progressive scoliosis to develop as a result of the above-mentioned structural disintegrations.

Adults have a higher incidence of nonflexible lumbar curves. In addition, pain is more likely to be a presenting complaint with adult scoliotic patients.[60] Some studies, however, demonstrate the incidence to be no higher than that in the general population.[61] If pain is reported, it is described as more of a dull, aching sensation or a sensation of fatigue in the area. Only with severe scoliosis have there been reports of direct nerve root compression.

There are several concerns that physicians traditionally have been instructed to be cognizant of. Following is a brief description of each:

- Although many physicians are concerned with cardiopulmonary function with an adult case, unless the patient had difficulty as a child or an adolescent it is not likely that new problems will develop as an adult unless he or she is also a smoker.
- An increase in mortality has been suggested by several investigators.[62] However, other studies do not support this observation.[63]

- Pregnancy has been a concern. Progression due to the increase in weight and the hormonal influences of soft tissue relaxation have been suspected. However, there is no indication that pregnancy acts as an accelerator of scoliosis development in the adult patient.[64]
- Although progression of an adult idiopathic scoliosis curve is not as aggressive over short periods of time as an adolescent curve, progression may amount to 1° per year averaged over time, with the most progression occurring after age 50. Curves greater than 50° are more likely to follow this pattern, whereas curves of 30° and less are relatively stable.[65]

Decision Making with Adult Scoliosis

Management decisions for the adult scoliotic patient are directed by the same outcome desires as for the adolescent scoliotic patient but with different response factors. Adult scoliosis is not generally as progressive, the curves are generally less flexible, pain may be a consequence of the deformity and an equal or dominant concern of the patient, correction is less dramatic, and complications of surgery are much higher, running in the range of 30% to 60%.[66]

Balancing these positive and negative factors results in a consensus that the major concern is to reduce the pain component and prevent progression. Correcting the deformity is not a primary goal not only because it is more difficult but because it is limited severely by the maturity of the spine, eliminating any adaptive structural changes and the accompanying secondary structural degenerative changes. The only component that is amenable to correction is the soft tissue component, the functional component of the curve.

Conservative management focuses on pain amelioration and strengthening of spinal and abdominal muscles with caution in the osteoporotic patient, who should avoid flexion exercises. The postmenopausal osteoporotic patient should be given exercise and diet recommendations; however, the possibility of estrogen replacement therapy also should be discussed. Chiropractic manipulative therapy should be incorporated, but radiographic evidence of instability or osteopenia should alert the clinician to modify treatment approaches and refer the patient if unresponsive.

Algorithms

Algorithms for evaluation and management of congenital, idiopathic, and adult scolioses are presented in Figures 5–4 to 5–6.

SUMMARY

Understanding that not all scolioses are idiopathic focuses the examination first on identifiable causes. One of these causes is transient muscle spasm, which will present differently. In addition to contributing to back pain the patient's scoliosis will not fit a typical pattern found in idiopathic scoliosis. Often there is little rotation or the spinous processes rotate into the convexity. When these signs are present, it is likely that chiropractic care will be beneficial. If unresponsive, consider that muscle spasm may occur as a result of serious neurologic and other pathologic processes. When a double curve pattern is evident but the apical pattern is left thoracic/right lumbar, consider referral for evaluation of possible brain stem or spinal cord abnormalities.

With idiopathic scoliosis it is important for the chiropractor to realize that justification for treating a progressive scoliosis is indefensible. Using the factors of age, skeletal maturity, severity of the curve, and location, the clinician should be able to determine adequately when to treat and monitor and when to refer. In equivocal situations it is prudent to obtain an orthopaedic consultation.

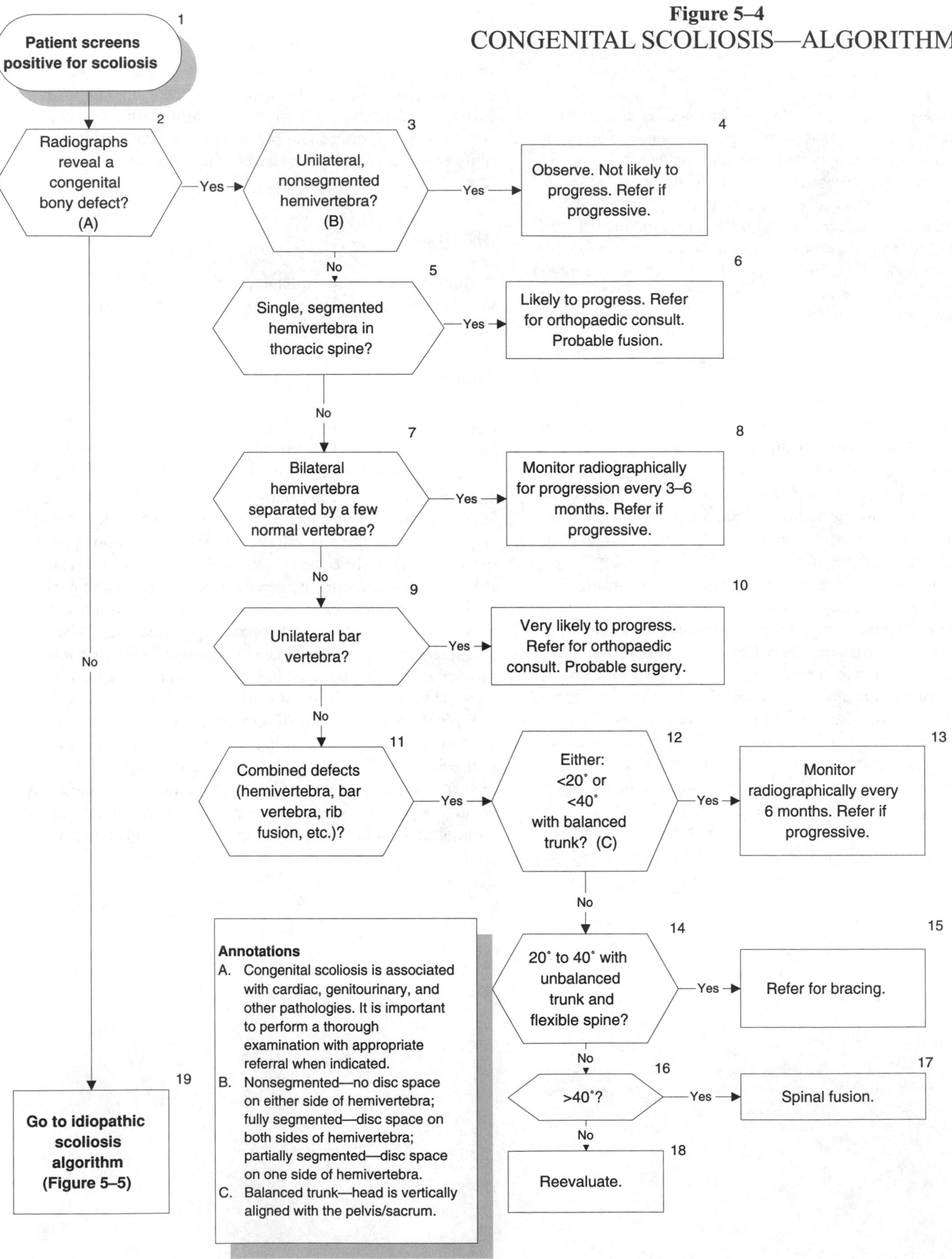
1
Patient screens positive for scoliosis
2
Radiographs reveal a congenital bony defect? (A)
Yes
3
Unilateral, nonsegmented hemivertebra? (B)
Yes
4
Observe. Not likely to progress. Refer if progressive.
No
5
Single, segmented hemivertebra in thoracic spine?
Yes
6
Likely to progress. Refer for orthopaedic consult. Probable fusion.
No
7
Bilateral hemivertebra separated by a few normal vertebrae?
Yes
8
Monitor radiographically for progression every 3–6 months. Refer if progressive.
No
9
Unilateral bar vertebra?
Yes
10
Very likely to progress. Refer for orthopaedic consult. Probable surgery.
No
11
Combined defects (hemivertebra, bar vertebra, rib fusion, etc.)?
Yes
12
Either: <20˚ or <40˚ with balanced trunk? (C)
Yes
13
Monitor radiographically every 6 months. Refer if progressive.
No
14
20˚ to 40˚ with unbalanced trunk and flexible spine?
Yes
15
Refer for bracing.
No
16
>40˚?
Yes
17
Spinal fusion.
No
18
Reevaluate.
No
19
Go to idiopathic scoliosis algorithm (Figure 5–5)
Annotations
A. Congenital scoliosis is associated with cardiac, genitourinary, and other pathologies. It is important to perform a thorough examination with appropriate referral when indicated.
B. Nonsegmented—no disc space on either side of hemivertebra; fully segmented—disc space on both sides of hemivertebra; partially segmented—disc space on one side of hemivertebra.
C. Balanced trunk—head is vertically aligned with the pelvis/sacrum.

Figure 5–4
CONGENITAL SCOLIOSIS—ALGORITHM.

Figure 5–5
IDIOPATHIC SCOLIOSIS—ALGORITHM.

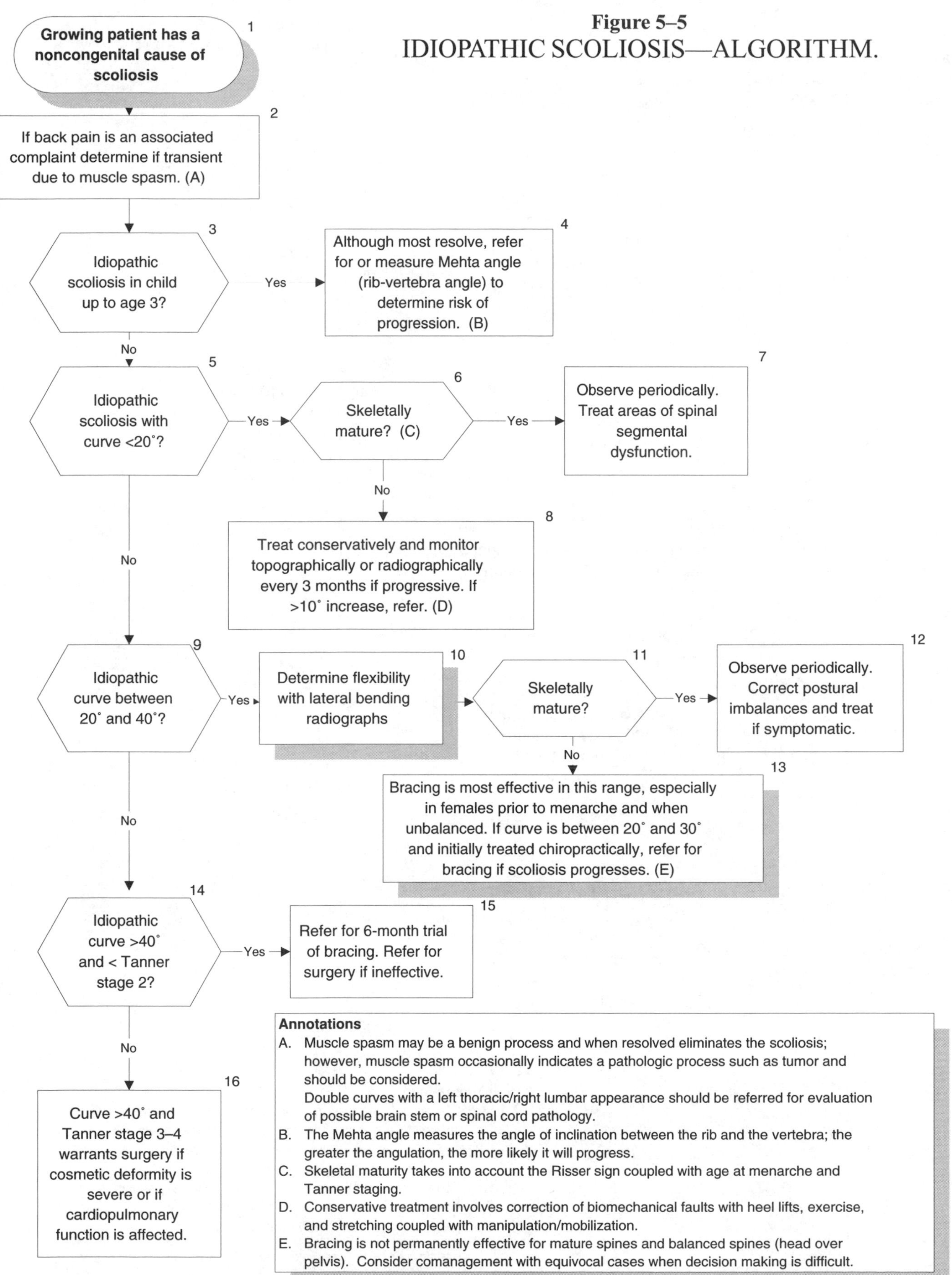

1 Growing patient has a noncongenital cause of scoliosis
2 If back pain is an associated complaint determine if transient due to muscle spasm. (A)
3 Idiopathic scoliosis in child up to age 3?
Yes
4 Although most resolve, refer for or measure Mehta angle (rib-vertebra angle) to determine risk of progression. (B)
No
5 Idiopathic scoliosis with curve <20˚?
Yes
6 Skeletally mature? (C)
Yes
7 Observe periodically. Treat areas of spinal segmental dysfunction.
No
8 Treat conservatively and monitor topographically or radiographically every 3 months if progressive. If >10˚ increase, refer. (D)
No
9 Idiopathic curve between 20˚ and 40˚?
Yes
10 Determine flexibility with lateral bending radiographs
11 Skeletally mature?
Yes
12 Observe periodically. Correct postural imbalances and treat if symptomatic.
No
13 Bracing is most effective in this range, especially in females prior to menarche and when unbalanced. If curve is between 20˚ and 30˚ and initially treated chiropractically, refer for bracing if scoliosis progresses. (E)
No
14 Idiopathic curve >40˚ and < Tanner stage 2?
Yes
15 Refer for 6-month trial of bracing. Refer for surgery if ineffective.
No
16 Curve >40˚ and Tanner stage 3–4 warrants surgery if cosmetic deformity is severe or if cardiopulmonary function is affected.
Annotations
A. Muscle spasm may be a benign process and when resolved eliminates the scoliosis; however, muscle spasm occasionally indicates a pathologic process such as tumor and should be considered.
Double curves with a left thoracic/right lumbar appearance should be referred for evaluation of possible brain stem or spinal cord pathology.
B. The Mehta angle measures the angle of inclination between the rib and the vertebra; the greater the angulation, the more likely it will progress.
C. Skeletal maturity takes into account the Risser sign coupled with age at menarche and Tanner staging.
D. Conservative treatment involves correction of biomechanical faults with heel lifts, exercise, and stretching coupled with manipulation/mobilization.
E. Bracing is not permanently effective for mature spines and balanced spines (head over pelvis). Consider comanagement with equivocal cases when decision making is difficult.

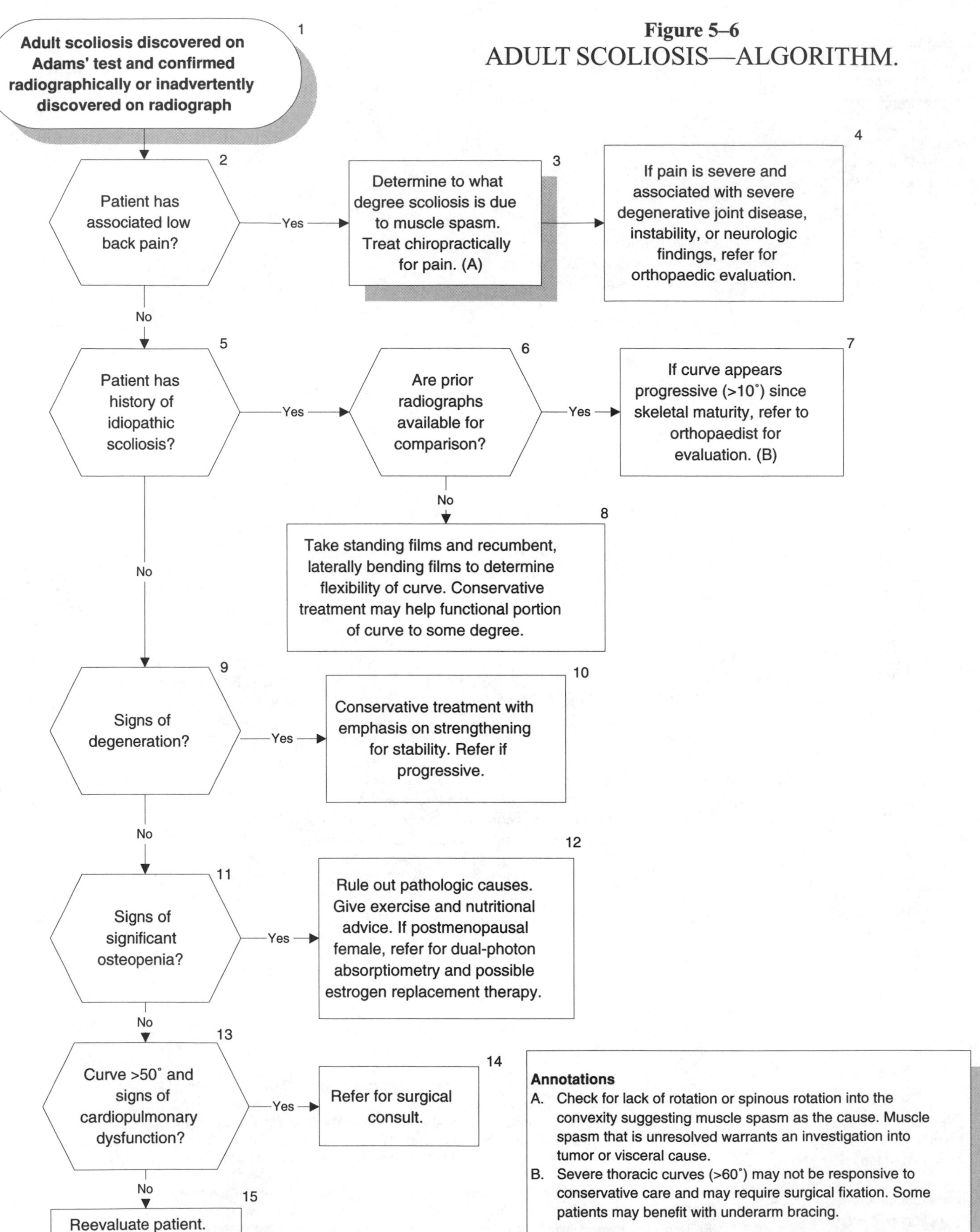
Figure 5–6
ADULT SCOLIOSIS—ALGORITHM.
1 Adult scoliosis discovered on Adams' test and confirmed radiographically or inadvertently discovered on radiograph
2 Patient has associated low back pain?
Yes
3 Determine to what degree scoliosis is due to muscle spasm. Treat chiropractically for pain. (A)
4 If pain is severe and associated with severe degenerative joint disease, instability, or neurologic findings, refer for orthopaedic evaluation.
No
5 Patient has history of idiopathic scoliosis?
Yes
6 Are prior radiographs available for comparison?
Yes
7 If curve appears progressive (>10˚) since skeletal maturity, refer to orthopaedist for evaluation. (B)
No
8 Take standing films and recumbent, laterally bending films to determine flexibility of curve. Conservative treatment may help functional portion of curve to some degree.
No
9 Signs of degeneration?
Yes
10 Conservative treatment with emphasis on strengthening for stability. Refer if progressive.
No
11 Signs of significant osteopenia?
Yes
12 Rule out pathologic causes. Give exercise and nutritional advice. If postmenopausal female, refer for dual-photon absorptiometry and possible estrogen replacement therapy.
No
13 Curve >50˚ and signs of cardiopulmonary dysfunction?
Yes
14 Refer for surgical consult.
No
15 Reevaluate patient.
Annotations
A. Check for lack of rotation or spinous rotation into the convexity suggesting muscle spasm as the cause. Muscle spasm that is unresolved warrants an investigation into tumor or visceral cause.
B. Severe thoracic curves (>60˚) may not be responsive to conservative care and may require surgical fixation. Some patients may benefit with underarm bracing.

REFERENCES

1. Nansel DD, Waldorf T, Cooperstein R. Effect of cervical spinal adjustments on lumbar paraspinal muscle tone: evidence for facilitation of intersegmental tonic neck reflexes. *J Manipulative Physiol Ther*. 1993;16:91–95.
2. Riseborough E, Wynne-Davies R. A genetic survey of idiopathic scoliosis in Boston. *J Bone Joint Surg Am*. 1973;55:974–982.
3. Czeizel A, Bellyei A, Barta O, et al. Genetics of adolescent idiopathic scoliosis. *J Med Genet*. 1978;15:424–427.
4. Herman RM, Mixon J, Fisher A, Maulucci R, Stuyck J. Idiopathic scoliosis and the central nervous system: a motor control problem. *Spine*. 1985;10:1–14.
5. Yamada K, Yamamoto H, Nakagawa Y, et al. Etiology of idiopathic scoliosis. *Clin Orthop*. 1984;184:50–57.
6. Bunnell WP. The natural history of idiopathic scoliosis. *Clin Orthop*. 1988;229:20–25.
7. Veldhuizen AG, Bass P, Webb PJ. Observation on the growth of the adolescent spine. *J Bone Joint Surg Br*. 1986;68:724–728.
8. Dickson R, Lawton I, Archer A, Butt W. The pathogenesis of idiopathic scoliosis. *J Bone Joint Surg Br*. 1984;66:8–15.
9. Dickson R, Lawton I, Archer A, Butt W. The pathogenesis of idiopathic scoliosis. In Dickson RA, Bradford DS, eds. *Management of Spinal Deformities*. London: Butterworths; 1984.
10. Oegema TR, Bradford DS, Cooper KM, Hunter RE. Comparison of the biochemistry of proteoglycans isolated from normal, idiopathic scoliotic, and cerebral palsy spines. *Spine*. 1983;8:378–384.
11. Ghosh P, Bushnell GR, Taylor TK, et al. Distribution of glycosaminoglycans across normal and scoliotic spines. *Spine*. 1980;5:310–317.
12. Schultz A. Biomechanical studies of possible causes for the progression of idiopathic scoliosis—a recapitulation of research findings. In: Jacobs E, ed. *Pathogenesis of Idiopathic Scoliosis*. Chicago: Scoliosis Research Society; 1984.
13. Bunch WH, Patwardham AG. *Scoliosis: Making Clinical Decisions*. St. Louis, MO: CV Mosby; 1989.
14. Bradford DS, Lonstein JE, Moe JH, et al. *Moe's Textbook of Scoliosis and Other Deformities*. 2nd ed. Philadelphia: WB Saunders; 1987.
15. Lonstein JE, Bjorkland H, Wamminger MH, et al. Voluntary school screening for scoliosis in Minnesota. *J Bone Joint Surg Am*. 1982;64:481–488.
16. Asher M, Beringer G, Orrick J, Halverbout N. The current status of scoliosis screening in North America. 1986. Results of a survey by mailed questionaire. Presented to Scoliosis Research Society and British Scoliosis Society; September, 1986; Hamilton, Bermuda.
17. Williams JI, Herbert MA. Is school screening reliable? *Orthop Trans*. 1985;9:110–111.
18. Dickson RA. Scoliosis in the community. *Br Med J*. 1983;286:615–618.
19. Bunnell WP. An objective criterion for scoliosis screening. *J Bone Joint Surg Am*. 1984;66:1381–1387.
20. MacEwen GD, Winter RB, Hardy JH. Evaluation of kidney anomalies in congenital scoliosis. *J Bone Joint Surg Am*. 1972;54:1341–1345.
21. Zorab P. Cardiac aspects of scoliosis. *J Bone Joint Surg Am*. 1974;56:442–447.
22. Dvonch BM, Bunch WH, Scarff TB. Spinal dysraphism. In: Bradford D, ed. *The Pediatric Spine*. New York: Thieme-Stratton; 1985.
23. Lonstein JE, Carlson MJ. The prediction of curve progression in untreated idiopathic scoliosis during growth. *J Bone Joint Surg Am*. 1984;66:1061–1071.
24. McGuire DJ, Keppler L, Kotagal S, Akbarnia BA. Scoliosis associated with type I Arnold-Chiari malformations. *Orthop Trans*. 1987;11:122.
25. Arai S, Ohtsuka Y, Moriya H, Kitahara H, Minamia S. Scoliosis associated with syringomyelia. *Spine*. 1993;18:1591–1592.
26. Marshall WA. *Human Growth and Its Disorders*. London: Academic Press; 1977.
27. Goldberg CJ, Dowling FE, Fogerty EE. Adolescent idiopathic scoliosis—early menarche, normal growth. *Spine*. 1993;18:529–535.
28. Wilmer S. A study of growth in girls with idiopathic structural scoliosis. *Clin Orthop*. 1974;101:129–133.
29. Wilmer S. A study of height, weight and menarche in girls with idiopathic structural scoliosis. *Acta Orthop Scand*. 1975;46:71–83.
30. Nicolopoulos KS, Burwell RG, Webb JK. Stature and its components in adolescent idiopathic scoliosis. *J Bone Joint Surg Br*. 1985;67:594–601.
31. Nordwall A, Wilmer S. Skeletal age in patients with idiopathic scoliosis. *J Bone Joint Surg Am*. 1974;56:1766–1769.
32. Wilmer S, Nilsson KO, Bergstrand CG. A study of growth hormone and somatomedin (sulfation factor) in girls with adolescent idiopathic scoliosis. *J Bone Joint Surg Am*. 1976;58:155.
33. Wilmer S, Nilsson KO, Kastrup K. Growth hormone and somatomedin A in girls with adolescent idiopathic scoliosis. *Acta Paediatr Scand*. 1975;65:547–552.
34. Ahl T, Albertsson-Wiklund K, Kalen R. Twenty-four hour growth hormone in pubertal girls with idiopathic scoliosis. *Spine*. 1988;13:139–142.
35. Tanner JM. *Growth at Adolescence*. 2nd ed. Oxford, England: Blackwell Scientific Publications; 1962.
36. Terver S, Kleinman R, Bleck EE. Growth landmarks and the evolution of scoliosis: a review of pertinent studies on their usefulness. *Dev Med Child Neurol*. 1980;22:675–684.
37. Scoles PV, Salvagno R, Vallalba K, Riew D. Relationship of iliac crest maturation to skeletal and chronological age. *J Paediatr Orthp*. 1988;8:639–644.
38. Rogala EH, Drummond DS, Curr J. Scoliosis incidence and natural history: a prospective epidemiological study. *J Bone Joint Surg Am*. 1978;60:173–176.
39. Duval-Beaupere G, Lespargot A, Grossiord A. Flexibility of scoliosis; what does it mean? Is the terminology appropriate? *Spine*. 1985;10:428–432.
40. Cruickshank JL, Koike M, Dickson RA. Curve patterns in idiopathic scoliosis: a clinical radiographic study. *J Bone Joint Surg Br*. 1989;71:259–263.
41. Beauchamp M, Labelle H, Grimard G, et al. Diurnal variation of Cobb angle measurement in adolescent idiopathic scoliosis. *Spine*. 1993;18:1581–1583.
42. Risser JG. The iliac apophysis: an evaluation sign in the management of scoliosis. *Clin Orthop*. 1958;11:111–119.
43. Izumi Y. The accuracy of Risser staging. *Spine*. 1995;20:1868–1871.
44. Bunch WH, Dvonch BM. Pitfalls in assessment of skeletal immaturity. *J Pediatr Orthop*. 1983;3:220–222.
45. Weinstein JN. Early results of scoliosis bracing study confirm efficacy of bracing, identify predictive factors. *Spine Lett*. 1994;1:2–8.

46. Wilmer S. Moire topography for the diagnosis and documentation of scoliosis. *Acta Orth Scand.* 1979;50:295–302.

47. Turner-Smith AR, Shannon TML, Hughston GR, Knopp DA. Assessing idiopathic scoliosis using a surface measurement technique. Surgical Rounds for Orthopaedics. Oxford, England: Orthopaedic Engineering Centre; 1988.

48. Crossan JF, Wynne-Davies R. Research for genetic and environmental factors in orthopaedic disease. *Clin Orthop.* 1986;210:99–105.

49. Mehta MH. The rib-vertebra angle in the early diagnosis between resolving and progressing infantile scoliosis. *J Bone Joint Surg Br.* 1972;54:230–243.

50. Axelgard J, Brown JC. Lateral surface stimulation for the treatment of progressive idiopathic scoliosis. *Spine.* 1983;8:242–260.

51. Sullivan JA, Davidson R, Renslaw TS, et al. Further evaluation of the Scolitron treatment of idiopathic adolescent scoliosis. *Spine.* 1986;11:903–906.

52. Moe JH, Kettleson DN. Idiopathic scoliosis: analysis of curve patterns and the preliminary results of Milwaukee brace treatment in one hundred sixty-nine patients. *J Bone Joint Surg Am.* 1970;52:1509.

53. Carr W, Moe J, Winter R, Lonstein J. Treatment of idiopathic scoliosis in the Milwaukee brace. *J Bone Joint Surg Am.* 1980;62:599–612.

54. Emans JB, Kaelin A, Bancel P, et al. The Boston bracing system for idiopathic scoliosis: follow-up results in 295 patients. *Spine.* 1986;11:792–801.

55. Harrington PR. Treatment of scoliosis, correction and internal fixation by spine instrumentation. *J Bone Joint Surg Am.* 1962;44:591–610.

56. Drummond D, Guadagni J, Keene JS, et al. Interspinous process segmental spinal instrumentation. *J Pediatr Orthop.* 1984;4:397–404.

57. Luque ER. Segmental spinal instrumentation for correction of scoliosis. *Clin Orthop.* 1982;163:192–198.

58. Cotrel Y, Dubousset J. New segmental posterior instrumentation of the spine. *Orthop Trans.* 1985;9:118.

59. Dawson EG, Moe JH, Caron A. Surgical management of scoliosis in the adult. *J Bone Joint Surg Am.* 1973;55:437.

60. Briard JL, Jegou D, Canchoix J. Adult lumbar scoliosis. *Spine.* 1979;4:526–532.

61. Nachemson A. Adult scoliosis and back pain. *Spine.* 1979;4:513–517.

62. Nilsonne U, Lundgren KD. Long term prognosis in idiopathic scoliosis. *Acta Orthop Scand.* 1968;39:456–465.

63. Collins DK, Ponseti IV. Long term follow-up of patients with idiopathic scoliosis not treated surgically. *J Bone Joint Surg Am.* 1969;51:425–445.

64. Bradford DS. Adult scoliosis: current concepts of treatment. *Clin Orthop.* 1988;229:70.

65. Weinstein SL, Ponseti IV. Curve progression in idiopathic scoliosis. *J Bone Joint Surg Am.* 1983;65:447–451.

66. Swank SM, Lonstein JE, Moe JH, Winter RB, Bradford DS. Surgical treatment of adult scoliosis: a review of 222 cases. *J Bone Joint Surg Am.* 1981;63:268–287.

Chapter 6

Lumbopelvic Complaints

CONTEXT

Low back complaints account for a majority of presentations seen in chiropractic practice. In the general population the estimated 1-month prevalence for low back pain (LBP) is between 35% and 37%.[1] Approximately 80% of adults will have LBP at some time in their lives, however, only 14% will complain of pain lasting longer than 2 weeks.[2] It has been estimated that 90% of patients with LBP will self-resolve within 1 month. Unfortunately, the remaining group account for a large financial and social burden for society.

Clinical determination of the specific tissue cause of LBP is often difficult, if not impossible. Literally any structure in the low back that is innervated could be a potential source of pain. Although clinically difficult, some diagnoses can be determined on the basis of a combination of radiographic or special studies. Approximately 39% of patients will have LBP due to disc disruption.[3] Specifically, 5% of patients will have a disc herniation, 15% to 40% (dependent on study) will have facet involvement, 4% will have a compression fracture, 3% will have spondylolisthesis, and only 0.3% will have ankylosing spondylitis.[4] Malignant neoplasms account for only 1% of all causes of LBP.[5] Spinal infection accounts for only 0.01% of LBP cases.[6] Spinal stenosis represents what is considered a common cause in the older adult as a result of the above-mentioned disorders augmented by associated congenital causes or acquired degenerative processes. The role of the sacroiliac (SI) joints in causing low back and/or leg pain has only recently begun to be investigated. However, for most chiropractors SI joint subluxation (fixation) represents a common cause of LBP that appears to respond dramatically to manipulation.[7]

The chiropractor's initial role is to identify the patient with "ominous" signs. The evaluation may require special studies or referral to a specialist. If these signs are absent, it is imperative to distinguish the patient with LBP alone or LBP with radiation into the leg(s). Focusing on the assessment of functional and neurologic status, decisions regarding management, comanagement, type of treatment, and prognosis can be broadly determined.

The effectiveness of chiropractic manipulation in the treatment of LBP has been recognized in several ways. Several past studies have demonstrated the cost effectiveness of chiropractic care.[8] Patient satisfaction has also been demonstrated.[9] The appropriateness of chiropractic management of LBP was recognized by the Rand study.[10] More recently, recommendations made by the Agency for Health Care Policy and Research (AHCPR) Guidelines strongly favor manipulation as the primary delivered care to patients with acute LBP. The British randomized study by Meade et al.[11] has set the stage for the defense of long-term effectiveness of chiropractic manipulative therapy for LBP.

GENERAL STRATEGY

History

- Screen the patient for "red flags" that indicate need for immediate radiograph/special studies or referral to a specialist: severe trauma, fever or recent bacterial infection, saddle anesthesia, severe or progressive neurologic complaints, recent onset of bladder dysfunction in association with the LBP, unexplained weight loss, prior history of cancer, intravenous drug abuse or immunosupression, or pain that is worse with recumbency or worse at night.
- Determine whether there was a history of trauma and determine the mechanism and severity.

- Determine whether the complaint is LBP alone or a combination of LBP and leg complaints such as pain, numbness or tingling, or weakness.
- If there are leg complaints, determine whether they are made worse with coughing, sneezing, or straining at stool.
- Determine the level of pain and functional capacity with a questionnaire (eg, Oswestry, Roland-Morris).

Examination

- For patients with signs of cauda equina or rapidly progressing neurologic deficits refer immediately for neurologic evaluation.
- For patients with suspected fracture (eg, those in a motor vehicle accident, those who have fallen from a height, or those with osteoporosis), infection, or cancer, radiograph the area.
- For patients with LBP only, perform a thorough examination of the low back, including inspection, observation of patients' movements, palpation of soft and bony tissues, motion palpation of the spine, passive and active range of motion (using inclinometer or Schober method), functional assessment (eg, Lewit/Janda and/or McKenzie approach), and orthopaedic examination.
- For patients with radiation of symptoms into the legs, add a thorough neurologic examination, including nerve stretch maneuvers, deep tendon reflexes, sensation testing (include pain, temperature, light touch, and vibration), and myotome testing.
- For patients with conflicting findings, inclusion of nonorganic testing may be helpful.
- Laboratory testing should be reserved for those patients suspected of having infection, cancer, or underlying diabetes.
- Patients with apparent multilevel involvement should first undergo radiographic evaluation; consideration of computed tomography (CT) or magnetic resonance imaging (MRI) should be given if the patient is unresponsive to conservative care.
- If pain appears mechanical, reserve the use of radiographs for 3 to 4 weeks unless a radiographic evaluation is likely to change the treatment approach to the patient.
- For patients who are unresponsive to care after 1 month, consideration should be given to the use of MRI, CT, or electrodiagnostic studies.

Management

- Patients with clinical, radiographic, or laboratory evidence of tumor, infection, or fracture (other than a stable compression fracture) should be sent for medical evaluation and management.
- Patients who appear to have a mechanical cause of pain should be managed conservatively for 1 month; if unresponsive, further testing or referral for a second opinion is suggested.

RELEVANT ANATOMY, PHYSIOLOGY, AND BIOMECHANICS

Many studies have attempted to localize tissues responsible for LBP and to determine where the pain is felt with regard to each of these structures. Approaches have included various relief and provocative injections, electrical stimulation, and pulling on surgically implanted strings, among others. It seems clear that when sciatica is present, it can occur only if the nerve root is already compromised by stretch, swelling, or compression.[12] This does not mean that sciatic pain cannot be mimicked by other tissues.

The Three-Joint Complex

There are essentially three joints at each functional segment of the spine: the intervertebral joint and the two facet or zygapophyseal joints. Kirkaldy-Willis[13] proposed a model of progressive dysfunction with regard to this three-joint complex whereby a shared functional relationship exists. The typical vertebra is composed of a body connected to a posterior arch via superiorly placed pedicles. The pedicles form the upper roof of the neural foramen. The vertebral canal is formed by the body, pedicles, and posterior arch. This canal can be congenitally narrowed or narrowed through acquired projection of osteophytes or disc material or by thickening of the ligamentum flavum. The flaval ligaments serve as the attachments between adjacent laminae.

The innervation of the lumbar area is primarily from the posterior ramus of the spinal nerve. The sinuvertebral nerve (also called recurrent meningeal nerve or nerve of Luschka) supplies the periosteum, posterior longitudinal ligament, the outer fibers of the annulus fibrosus, and the epidural vessels. There is a diffuse arrangement of anastomosis over several segments that may explain why localization to a specific level or side is difficult.

The Disc

The lumbar intervertebral disc (IVD) is essentially divided into two parts: (1) an inner nucleus pulposus and (2) an outer annulus fibrosus. The annulus fibrosus fibers cross each other at angles of 60° to 70° in successive layers, providing a strong resistance to rotational forces. Resistance to flexion and extension is strong with the nucleus pulposus bulging posteriorly on flexion while the annulus fibrosus bulges anteriorly.

Although the disc has been accused of being one of the major causes of LBP, it appears that it may play more a primary role than that of direct compression of nerve roots. When the disc material is large enough to compress a nerve root, frank neurologic signs become evident. The most recent theory is that the herniated disc material causes an inflammatory reaction due to the release of irritating substances, and/or an autoimmune inflammatory reaction.[14] A recent study[15] supported the growing opinion that disc herniations usually have a natural course of self-reduction through shrinkage. In this study, approximately 63% of patients had a natural reduction in the size of the disc herniation. The belief is that through resorption (caused by lack of nutrient supply), desiccation, and/or phagocytosis, the size of many disc herniations reduces over time. The old belief that herniations regress back into the annulus was not supported. It is also true that in many cases where resolution of clinical symptoms occurs, there is no change in the size of the herniation.[16] When a disc "herniates" it can either be contained (annulus fibers are intact) or not contained (outer annulus failure allows prolapse into the vertebral canal). The terminology used to describe variations on this basic distinction is often confusing. Depending on whether the describer is a radiologist or a clinician, the same term may be used to describe different events, or a different classification system entirely has been developed.

The Facets

The facet joints of the lumbar spine allow a fair degree of flexion and some extension. Lateral bending and rotation are restricted by the mainly sagittal orientation of the facets. The orientation of segments L1-L4 has been compared to a J shape, where the anterior portion is oriented more medially. The L5-S1 facets are essentially coronal, allowing more freedom in flexion with rotation resisted by the iliolumbar ligaments. Facet tropism is a congenital anomaly in which there is a turning of the orientation of the facet articulation so that a facet that should be more sagittal, for example, is more coronal. Tropism is common, being found in 21% to 37% of the entire population, most occurring at the L4-L5 or L5-S1 facets.[17] Although this must alter biomechanics at that segmental level, it has not been demonstrated to cause a higher incidence of LBP in patients who have it. The facets take up approximately 16% to 18% of compressive loading on the lumbar spine; however, the facets accept approximately 33% of the shear force across a segment.[18]

The facets are innervated by the medial branch of the dorsal rami.[19] This means that there is a unilateral distribution with some overlap between the inferior facets above and the superior facets below the segment. In other words, each facet theoretically has innervation from at least two levels. Therefore, it is theoretically possible for somewhat more localization to occur when the facet joint is the site of pain production as opposed to deeper pain-producing tissue that has an anastomosis innervation via the sinuvertebral nerve. The medial and lateral branches of the dorsal rami innervate the posterior muscles. Although the facet joints are possible sources of LBP, it is worth noting that facet joint blocks have been associated with a high placebo response rate (as much as 32%)[20]; yet facet dysfunction seems to account for a significant number of low back complaints.

Degeneration of the facet proceeds from a nonspecific synovial reaction. Both distention of the joint capsule and degeneration of the hyaline cartilage that covers the facets follow, allowing for ligament laxity. The result is a joint that may potentially subluxate and cause narrowing of the lateral canal. If the process continues, older patients may have inferior facet enlargement that often occurs in a medial direction, causing central canal narrowing. Osteophytic superior facets usually project in an anterior direction to produce narrowing of the lateral recesses. Each process is a potential source of nerve root compression.

In addition to possible contribution to LBP through laxity of the joint capsule or bony hypertrophy with possible compressive effects, another possible facet source is the trapped meniscoid.[21] The meniscoid is an intraarticular joint inclusion that may become caught between the articular surfaces. It has been proposed that manipulation releases the meniscoid—relieving LBP.

Ligaments and Muscles

It is interesting that there are few ligaments in the lumbar region. The supraspinous ligament does not exist below L3 and above this level represents more or less the aponeurosis of the erector spinae or latissimus dorsi.[22] The interspinous ligament represents more of a tendonous extension of the erector spinae. Even the iliolumbar ligament is primarily muscle before age 30 years. The posterior longitudinal ligament is less broad than it is in the cervical region, allowing posterior migration laterally.

In simple terms, the muscles of the lumbar spine are divided into three layers: (1) those passing inside the ribs, (2) those passing outside the ribs, and (3) an intermediate layer. All three layers are supplied by the anterior primary rami with the exception of the erector spinae group, which is supplied by the posterior primary rami. The innermost layer is primarily composed of flexors such as the psoas. The intermediate layer is composed of the quadratus lumborum and the internal and external intercostal muscles. The erector spinae group is subdivided into three layers. Unlike the thoracic region, the lumbar region has no deep rotators. The multifidus in the middle layer of the erector spinae group attaches from the laminar and mamillary processes to the spinous processes of the vertebra several levels above.

Biomechanics

As mentioned above, flexion is the most accessible movement pattern. Some extension and lateral bending are allowed; however, they are blocked by soft tissue and posterior joint orientation. Very little rotation occurs and is left primarily to the thoracic spine. When single-plane movements occur, there are often coupled motion patterns. With lateral flexion, there is a coupled movement of the segment so that the spinous process rotates toward the same side.[23] A small amount of flexion occurs at the segment if the lumbar lordosis is in effect. Without a lordosis, there is slight extension at the segment. This coupling pattern may vary with posture.[24] In other words, laterally bending in flexion is not the same as it is in neutral. Most important, some investigators feel that abnormal coupled patterns may occur during flexion or extension and may be a predictor of low back problems.[25]

When an individual flexes forward at the waist, the paraspinal muscles support the trunk eccentrically through the first 30° to 60° while the gluteals and hamstrings keep the pelvis locked. Then the gluteals and hamstrings relax (eccentrically contract) to allow the pelvis to rotate at the hips to allow further flexion. This may be limited by tension in the hamstrings. At full flexion, the paraspinals are relaxed, with support provided mainly by ligaments. Lifting from this position can damage ligaments or strain muscles.

It appears that there are two general mechanisms for the cause of disc herniation: (1) sudden loading with the spine in flexion and (2) degenerative failure of the annulus from repeated or prolonged mechanical stresses.[26,27] The side-posture manipulation has often been accused as a possible cause of disc herniation. It is likely, though, that the limitation imposed by the restriction of the posterior facets is sufficient to prevent excessive rotation at the disc; however, Slosberg[28] cautions the doctor that this is true only if the facets are loaded in extension by maintaining a lordosis and the degree of rotation is controlled by the adjuster.

Sacroiliac Joints

The SI joint has, after much debate, regained the status of a true diarthrodial (synovial) joint capable of some movement.[29,30] The joint is composed of an auricular shaped surface with an upper vertical and a lower horizontal section. The lower two thirds (ventral portion) is covered by a synovial membrane; the upper third (posterior) is mainly fibrous without synovial tissue. Stability is largely ligamentous. Movement has been described as nutation and counternutation. Nutation involves an anteroposterior movement around a transverse axis. Thus, when rising from a recumbent position, the sacral promontory moves forward a few millimeters.[31] This also occurs unilaterally, so that, when standing on one foot, the SI joint on the side of weight bearing reaches maximum nutation. SI joint innervation is from a broad area including both sacral and lumbar plexuses (L3-S2). This may explain the varied presentation of referred pain patterns with SI joint involvement.

EVALUATION

History

Ominous Signs

Screening the patient for ominous signs can be performed quickly, yet relatively reliable information can be gained with regard to the need for further specialized evaluation or referral (Table 6–1). Cauda equina syndrome is a rare yet serious condition. The most sensitive historical indicator is urinary retention (sensitivity = 0.90, specificity = 95%).[32] Therefore patients without urinary retention (or eventual overflow incontinence) are unlikely to have cauda equina syndrome. Although LBP is due to cancer only 1% of the time, it is obviously crucial to search for indicators of this possibility. Deyo[32] indicated in one study that the cancer patient will present with at least one of four historical findings: (1) older than age 50 (about 80% of patients with cancer-caused LBP), (2) previous history of cancer (specificity = 0.98), (3) unexplained weight loss, and (4) failure to respond to conservative therapy over a 1-month period. It is important to remember, however, that only one third of patients eventually diagnosed with cancer as the cause of their LBP have a prior history of cancer (sensitivity = 0.31%). Another sensitive but nonspecific clue is that most patients with cancer report pain that is unrelieved by bed rest.

When screening for the extremely rare occurrence of a spinal infection, it is important to ask about urinary tract infections, an indwelling urinary catheter during a recent hospital stay, injection of illicit drugs, and any indications of skin infection.[32] A fever is highly specific for infection; however, 2% of patients with mechanical back pain may have a fever (possibly virus-related).[33]

Other Possibilities

In all older patients, a suspicion of compression fracture is warranted. The factor of age is most important for patients older than 70 years; the specificity is 0.96. Although it might seem logical that there would be a report of identifiable trauma, this finding has a low sensitivity (0.30); however, long-term corticosteroid use was highly specific (0.99). The sudden onset of pain with coughing, sneezing, or sudden

Table 6–1 History Questions for Low Back Pain

Primary Question	*What Are You Thinking?*	*Secondary Questions*	*What Are You Thinking?*
Did you injure yourself (car accident, fall, lifting, etc.)?	Disc lesion, muscle strain, facet, fracture	Did you fall on your buttocks?	Compression or coccygeal fracture
		Was this a sudden hyperflexion injury?	Compression or chance fracture
		Did the pain appear while lifting or with sudden twisting?	Disc lesion or muscle strain
		Did you have a sudden extension injury?	Facet injury
Does the pain continue into the buttocks or leg?	Disc lesion, tumor, stenosis, referral from facet or trigger point (TrP)	Does the pain extend below the knee?	Nerve root pain due to disc, stenosis, or tumor; facet and TrP are less likely
		Does the pain extend into the gluteals or to the knee?	Lumbar facet, SI joint, and TrP
Do you have any difficulty with urination or defecation?	Cauda equina syndrome, prostate disease, disc lesion (Valsalva effect), constipation	Do you have any numbness around the groin or genital area?	Cauda equina syndrome
		Do you have leg pain when you defecate, cough, or sneeze?	Space occupying lesion indicating tumor or disc lesion in most cases
		Do you have to urinate often and/or have difficulty stopping or starting?	Prostate cancer is possible
Is there associated abdominal pain?	Genitourinary cause, abdominal aneurysm	Is this associated with your menstrual period?	Dysmenorrhea (if severe consider endometriosis), pelvic inflammatory disease
		Does the pain radiate around to the groin?	Kidney (infection or stone)
		Is there associated weakness in the legs?	Abdominal aneurysm
Is there marked weight loss?	Cancer, depression, diet	Do you have a past history of cancer, night pain, unrelieved with rest?	Cancer
Is there any weakness in the legs with activity?	Neurogenic or vascular claudication	Is it relieved quickly with rest?	Vascular claudication
		Is it better when flexed and/or relieved after 15–20 minutes of rest?	Neurogenic claudication (canal stenosis)

flexion unassociated with radicular complaints should warrant a radiologic search for compression fracture.[4]

Combining five screening questions, a high level of suspicion may be gained for ankylosing spondylitis (AS): (1) Is there morning stiffness? (2) Is there improvement in discomfort with exercise? (3) Was the onset of back pain before age 40? (5) Has the pain persisted for at least 3 months? If at least four positive responses are given, AS should be suspected (sensitivity as high as 0.95 with specificity as high as 0.85).[34] However, it is always important to consider the predictive value, which is dependent on the prevalence of the disorder. Because AS is relatively rare the positive predictive value is quite low (0.04).

Low Back Pain with Radiation in the Leg(s)

One of the first historical discriminators between a disc and a referred (facet or muscular) source is whether or not the pain travels below the knee. Pain below the knee is suggestive of a disc lesion. Paresthesia or numbness is more commonly found with disc lesions than with referred causes, especially in the foot or ankle area. Patients with disc lesions often will have a history of recurrent episodes of back pain without leg pain. It is likely that the patient will be between the ages of 30 and 50. This age range is due in part to the observation that the disc's nucleus pulposus dehydrates with aging, leaving little to herniate. The patient with a disc lesion may report a twisting injury accompanied by immediate leg pain. The leg pain is often more of a concern than the back pain. In the younger patient with a disc lesion, pain is often worse with sitting (due to increased disc pressure) and less with standing or walking. The older patient with leg pain is more likely to have compressive insult of a nerve root due to various forms of stenosis. The older patient has more difficulty with walking or standing because of the compressive effect created by the loading of the posterior elements (where most of the potential stenotic causes occur).

Other Factors

It is always important to screen the patient with regard to medication use. Oral corticosteroid use would suggest the possibility of compression fracture. Anticoagulant therapy may suggest epidural or spinal cord bleeding. Antidepressants may suggest an underlying psychologic component, especially in the patient with chronic pain.

If the patient is injured in a work-related accident or is involved in personal injury litigation, it is important to gain an appreciation of the patient's attitude toward employment and the desire to obtain compensation. Patient questionnaires with regard to pain and functional capacity are important baseline data, especially with these patients.

Questionnaires

Although it may seem logical that improvement is better measured with apparent objective findings through clinical examination, outcome measures through the use of questionnaires may prove to be more reliable and reproducible. Deyo[35] reviewed the reliability and reproducibility of outcome measures used in back pain trials. Standard measures such as range of motion and ankle dorsiflexion strength were far less reliable (0.50/1.00) than a questionnaire measuring the ability to perform daily activities (sickness impact profile—(0.90/1.00) or pain measurement (visual analog scale [VAS]—0.94/1.00). Passive straight-leg raising faired somewhere in between (0.78/1.00). The meta-analysis performed by Anderson and Meeker[36] also demonstrated better correlation between "functional" outcome assessment tools (questionnaires) than objective measures.

For patients with LBP, there are a number of questionnaires available. Two of the most popular that have been demonstrated to be valid and reliable are the Oswestry Disability Index for Low Back Pain and the Roland-Morris Low Back Pain Questionnaire.[37] The Oswestry Questionnaire (Exhibit 6–1) is a simple tool utilizing only 10 sections with six possible answers for each.[38] The answer choices are rated from 0 to 5, ranging from less to more disability. By scoring and adding the answer choices and multiplying by 2, a percentage disability can be calculated (Exhibit 6–2). For example, if a patient marked five answers that indicated moderate disability (eg, $3 \times 5 = 15$) and five for more severe disability (eg, $4 \times 5 = 20$) multiplying the total by 2 (2×35) results in a disability of 70%. This could then be used as a comparison for future improvement. The Roland-Morris questionnaire (Exhibit 6–3) is a behavioral measuring tool for patients with low back pain.[39] The 24-item survey is simple for the patient to complete by marking each description that fits his/her perceptions. For example, one statement is: I find it difficult to get out of a chair because of my back. When all the marked statements are added together a score is generated. The higher the score, the greater the disability. Many doctors add a VAS to the Roland-Morris.

Examination

General Evaluation

Examination "red flags" include the following:

- The patient has saddle paresthesia (cauda equina).
- Weight loss in an older patient with a prior history of cancer, and associated neurologic findings on examination suggest cancer.

Exhibit 6–1 Oswestry Questionnaire

The Oswestry Disability Index for Low Back Pain

NAME: ______________________ DATE OF BIRTH: ______________________

ADDRESS: ______________________ DATE: ______________________

______________________ AGE: ______________________

OCCUPATION: ______________________

How long have you had back pain? __________ Years __________ Months __________ Weeks

How long have you had leg pain? __________ Years __________ Months __________ Weeks

PLEASE READ:

This questionnaire has been designed to give the doctor information as to how your back pain has affected your ability to manage in everyday life. Please answer every section, and mark in each section ONE BOX that applies to you. We realize you may consider that two of the statements in any one section relate to you, but please just mark the box that most closely describes your problem.

SECTION 1—PAIN INTENSITY

- ❑ My pain is mild to moderate: I do not need pain killers.
- ❑ The pain is bad, but I manage without taking pain killers.
- ❑ Pain killers give complete relief from pain.
- ❑ Pain killers give moderate relief from pain.
- ❑ Pain killers give very little relief from pain.
- ❑ Pain killers have no effect on the pain.

SECTION 2—PERSONAL CARE (WASHING, DRESSING, ETC.)

- ❑ I can look after myself normally without causing extra pain.
- ❑ I can look after myself normally, but it causes extra pain.
- ❑ It is painful to look after myself, and I am slow and careful.
- ❑ I need some help but manage most of my personal care.
- ❑ I need help every day in most aspects of self-care.
- ❑ I do not get dressed; I wash with difficulty; and I stay in bed.

SECTION 3—LIFTING

- ❑ I can lift heavy weights without extra pain.
- ❑ I can lift heavy weights, but it gives extra pain.
- ❑ Pain prevents me from lifting heavy weights off the floor, but I can manage if they are conveniently positioned, eg, on a table.
- ❑ Pain prevents me from lifting heavy weights, but I can manage light weights if they are conveniently positioned.
- ❑ I can lift only very light weights.
- ❑ I cannot lift or carry anything at all.

SECTION 4—WALKING

- ❑ I can walk as far as I wish.
- ❑ Pain prevents me walking more than 1 mile.
- ❑ Pain prevents me walking more than ½ mile.
- ❑ Pain prevents me walking more than ¼ mile.
- ❑ I can walk only if I use a stick or crutches.
- ❑ I am in bed or in a chair for most of every day.

SECTION 5—SITTING

- ❑ I can sit in any chair as long as I like.
- ❑ I can sit in my favorite chair only, but for as long as I like.
- ❑ Pain prevents me from sitting more than 1 hour.
- ❑ Pain prevents me from sitting more than ½ hour.
- ❑ Pain prevents me from sitting more than 10 minutes.
- ❑ Pain prevents me from sitting at all.

SECTION 6—STANDING

- ❑ I can stand as long as I want without extra pain.
- ❑ I can stand as long as I want, but it gives me extra pain.

continues

Exhibit 6–1 continued

- ❑ Pain prevents me from standing for more than 1 hour.
- ❑ Pain prevents me from standing for more than 30 minutes.
- ❑ Pain prevents me from standing for more than 10 minutes.
- ❑ Pain prevents me from standing at all.

SECTION 7—SLEEPING

- ❑ Pain does not prevent me from sleeping well.
- ❑ I sleep well but only by using tablets.
- ❑ Even when I take tablets I have less than 6 hours sleep.
- ❑ Even when I take tablets I have less than 4 hours sleep.
- ❑ Even when I take tablets I have less than 2 hours sleep.
- ❑ Pain prevents me from sleeping at all.

SECTION 8—SEX LIFE

- ❑ My sex life is normal and causes no extra pain.
- ❑ My sex life is normal but causes some extra pain.
- ❑ My sex life is nearly normal but is very painful.
- ❑ My sex life is severely restricted by pain.
- ❑ My sex life is nearly absent because of pain.
- ❑ Pain prevents any sex life at all.

SECTION 9—SOCIAL LIFE

- ❑ My social life is normal and causes me no extra pain.
- ❑ My social life is normal but increases the degree of pain.
- ❑ Pain affects my social life by limiting only my more energetic interests (dancing etc.).
- ❑ Pain has restricted my social life, and I do not go out as often.
- ❑ Pain has restricted my social life to my home.
- ❑ I have no social life because of pain.

SECTION 10—TRAVELING

- ❑ I can travel anywhere without extra pain.
- ❑ I can travel anywhere but it gives me extra pain.
- ❑ Pain is bad, but I manage journeys over 2 hours.
- ❑ Pain restricts me to journeys of less than 1 hour.
- ❑ Pain restricts me to short necessary journeys under 30 minutes.
- ❑ Pain prevents me traveling except to the physician or hospital.

Source: Reprinted with permission from J.C.T. Fairbank et al., The Oswestry Low Back Pain Questionnaire, *Physiotherapy*, Vol. 66, p. 271, © 1980, Chartered Society of Physiotherapy.

- Fever (specificity = 0.98) associated with spinal tenderness to percussion (percussion sensitivity = 0.86) suggests spinal infection in a patient who has a history of intravenous drug usage, has a urinary tract infection, or is immunocompromised.

The orthopaedic-neurologic examination often can be focused based on the distribution of a patient's complaint and a suspected underlying cause. The patient with LBP only (ie, no leg pain) warrants an examination designed to determine whether the pain is reproducible and to what extent there is limitation in range of motion and/or function. If the pain is not reproducible mechanically, further tests to evaluate visceral possibilities such as genitourinary causes should be performed. Patients with radiation into the leg(s) must be categorized into those with nerve root lesions and those with referred signs or symptoms. The primary distinction between these two broad categories is that patients with referred etiologies would rarely have hard neurologic evidence. For example, although the pain projection is in the distribution of the sciatic nerve, patients with referred causes often will have pain that does not extend below the knee. Additionally, patients with referred pain would be highly unlikely to demonstrate myotome weakness, dermatome sensory abnormalities, or a decrease in reflexes (Figure 6–1).

Given that 98% of all disc lesions occur at L4-5 or L5-S1 discs, the likelihood of positive neurologic signs will be highest for the L5 or S1 nerve roots.[40] The ability to localize the nerve root and disc level is quite good. An L5-S1 disc rupture is 86% probable if three S1 signs are found: (1) pain projection into the S1 area, (2) a pathologic Achilles reflex, and (3) a sensory defect in the S1 dermatome.[41] Localization to the L4-L5 disc is 87% probable with three L5 signs: (1) extensor hallucis (EH) weakness, (2) pain projection into the L5 area, and (3) a sensory defect in the L5 dermatome. It is important to remember that pain projection into the S1 area can be found with any lumbar disc herniation; however, EH weakness and pain projection into the L5 area together are reliable indicators of an L5 nerve root lesion even when accompanied by S1 findings. With L5 nerve root involvement it is not uncommon also to find ankle dorsiflexion weakness with EH weakness. McCombe et al.[42] evaluated the reproducibility of several physical signs for LBP. Buttock wasting, toe standing, and heel standing were considered unreliable. The Achilles reflex was considered a reliable interexaminer finding; however, the patellar reflex was not. The sensory examination was considered reliable. It is important to keep in mind that numbness is usually most evident distally. In other words, although the patient may complain of pain or numbness extending down the length of the

Exhibit 6–2 Scoring the Oswestry Questionnaire

The Oswestry Questionnaire indicates the extent to which a person's functional level is restricted by pain. It is completed by the patient. It concentrates on the effects of pain rather than the nature of the pain. The patient marks the statement in each section that most accurately describes the effect of pain. If two items are marked, the more severe one is scored. When self-administered, the questionnaire takes less than 5 minutes to complete and 1 minute to score. If the questions are read to the patient, it requires about 10 minutes.

For each section, scores fall on a 0 to 5 scale, with the higher values representing greater disability. The sum of the 10 scores is expressed as a percentage of the maximum score. If a patient fails to complete a section the percentage is adjusted accordingly.

For each section, the possible score is 5; if the first statement is marked, the section score = 0; if the last statement is marked, the section score = 5. If all 10 sections are completed, the score is calculated as follows:

$$\frac{18 \text{ (total score)}}{50 \text{ (total possible score)}} \times 100 = 36\% \text{ points}$$

If one section is misused or not applicable, the score is calculated:

$$\frac{18 \text{ (total score)}}{45 \text{ (total possible score)}} \times 100 = 40\% \text{ points}$$

The originators of this scale interpreted the results as follows:

0 to 20% points—minimal disability
21 to 40% points—moderate disability
41 to 60% points—severe disability
over 60% points—the patient is severely disabled by pain in several areas of life

A further application would be to administer the questionnaire periodically throughout the patient's treatment period to monitor for changes. A reduction in the disability index would indicate improvement in the patient's perception of his or her pain problem, which would possibly be due to effective treatment.

In a randomized controlled clinical study comparing chiropractic and hospital outpatient treatment, the Oswestry Questionnaire was used as an outcome measure along with specific tests (straight leg raising and lumbar flexion range of motion). Chiropractic treatment was shown to be more effective than hospital outpatient care, mainly for patients with chronic and severe back pain.

Source: Reprinted with permission from D. Hansen and J. Ayres, Chiropractic Outcome Measures, *Chiropractic Technique*, Vol. 3, No. 1, pp. 53–54, © 1991, Williams & Wilkins.

leg to the foot, numbness may be demonstrated only distally at the foot.

Although there are well over 50 orthopaedic tests listed in the literature for the low back and more than 15 for the SI joint, most are based on a common approach with some minor variations. Using more tests does not increase the likelihood of a correct diagnosis because the reliability, sensitivity, and specificity of many tests have not been demonstrated. If they are poor tests with regard to false positives or false negatives, they can be quite misleading. Many tests can be classified as nerve tension tests, attempting to stretch a nerve or nerve root. The second group of tests attempts to increase pressure or compression at various potential pain-producing sites (eg, facet joints).

The most studied test is the straight leg raise (SLR).[43] This nerve tension test is considered quite valuable in distinguishing patients who have disc herniation from those who do not. A positive finding is reproduction of pain down the back of the leg to the foot with passive raising of the leg (Figure 6–2). Several observations are important to keep in mind while interpreting the response to an SLR[44]:

- A positive finding between 15° and 30° is a reliable indicator of disc herniation.
- A positive finding above 60° provides little diagnostic information.
- A positive finding when adding either passive dorsiflexion of the ankle (Braggard's test), medial hip rotation, or flexion of the cervical spine with active knee extension (patient seated [Figure 6–3]) (Bechterew's test) increases the likelihood of a serious disc herniation. Dorsiflexion of the ankle should reproduce the leg pain at a lower angle of elevation.

It is important to question the patient about a positive response to better guarantee that the response is not due to hamstring stretching. Medial hip rotation may also call into question possible involvement of the piriformis muscle with referred leg pain consequences. Combining the SLR findings with neurologic findings will usually be sufficient. For example, an apparently positive SLR without hard neurologic findings would be more suspect of a referral source. The well-leg raise test is less sensitive; however, it is much

Exhibit 6–3 Roland-Morris Low Back Disability Questionnaire

Instructions
When your back hurts, you may find it difficult to do some of the things you normally do. This list contains some sentences that people have used to describe themselves when they have back pain. When you read them, you may find that some stand out because they describe you *today*. As you read the list, think of yourself *today*. When you read a sentence that describes how you feel *today*, check the box next to it. If the sentence does not describe you, then leave the box blank and go on to the next one. Remember, only check the sentence if you are sure that it describes you today.

❑ 1. I stay home most of the time because of my back.
❑ 2. I change position frequently to try to get my back comfortable.
❑ 3. I walk more slowly than usual because of my back.
❑ 4. Because of my back I am not doing any of the jobs that I usually do around the house.
❑ 5. Because of my back, I use a handrail to get upstairs.
❑ 6. Because of my back, I lie down to rest more often.
❑ 7. Because of my back, I have to hold on to something to get out of an easy chair.
❑ 8. Because of my back, I try to get other people to do things for me.
❑ 9. I get dressed more slowly than usual because of my back.
❑ 10. I only stand up for short periods of time because of my back.
❑ 11. Because of my back, I try not to bend or kneel down.
❑ 12. I find it difficult to get out of a chair because of my back.
❑ 13. My back is painful almost all the time.
❑ 14. I find it difficult to turn over in bed because of my back.
❑ 15. My appetite is not very good because of my back.
❑ 16. I have trouble putting on my socks (stockings) because of the pain in my back.
❑ 17. I only walk short distances because of my back pain.
❑ 18. I sleep less well because of my back pain.
❑ 19. Because of my back pain, I get dressed with help from someone else.
❑ 20. I sit down for most of the day because of my back.
❑ 21. I avoid heavy jobs around the house because of my back.
❑ 22. Because of my back pain, I am more irritable and bad tempered with people than usual.
❑ 23. Because of my back, I go upstairs more slowly than usual.
❑ 24. I stay in bed most of the time because of my back.

Rate the severity of your pain by checking one box on the following scale.

0	1	2	3	4	5	6	7	8	9	10

NO PAIN — UNBEARABLE PAIN

Source: Reprinted with permission from M. Roland and R. Morris, A study of the natural history of back pain, *Spine,* Vol. 8, No. 2, p. 144, © 1983, Lippincott-Raven.

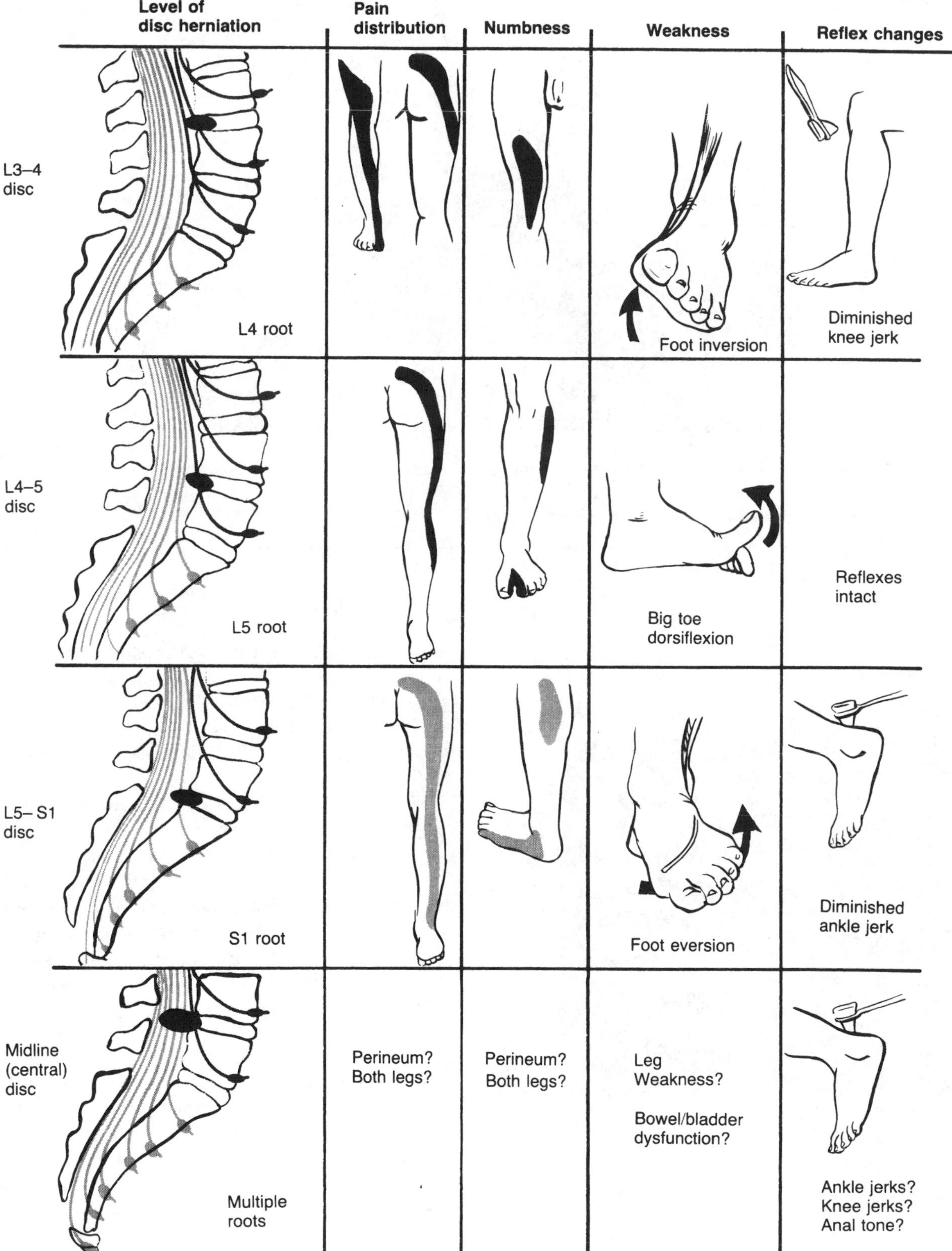

Figure 6–1 Common disc syndromes: neurologic findings. *Source:* Reprinted with permission from B.M. Reilly, *Practical Strategies in Outpatient Management*, 2nd ed., p. 915, © 1991, W.B. Saunders Company.

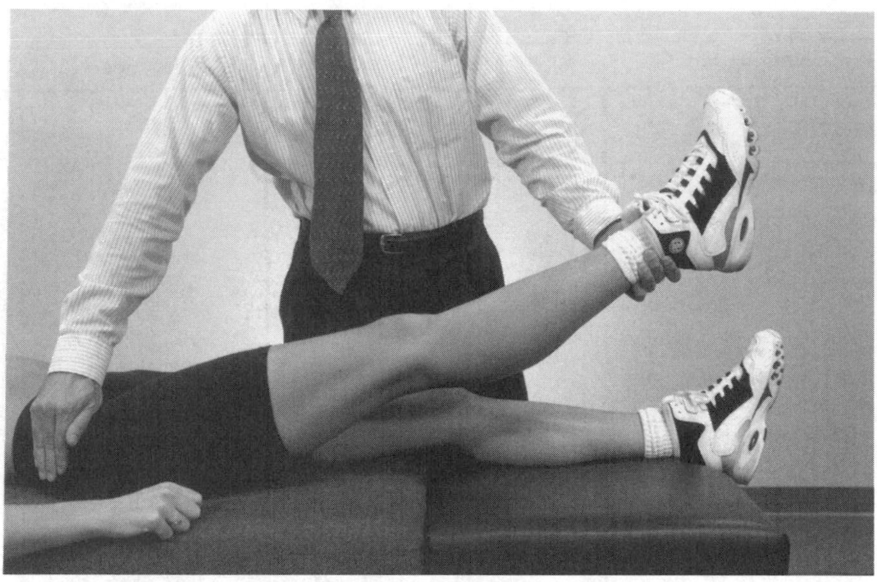

Figure 6–2 The straight leg raise test. Nerve root compression is likely when posterior leg pain is provoked below 45°.

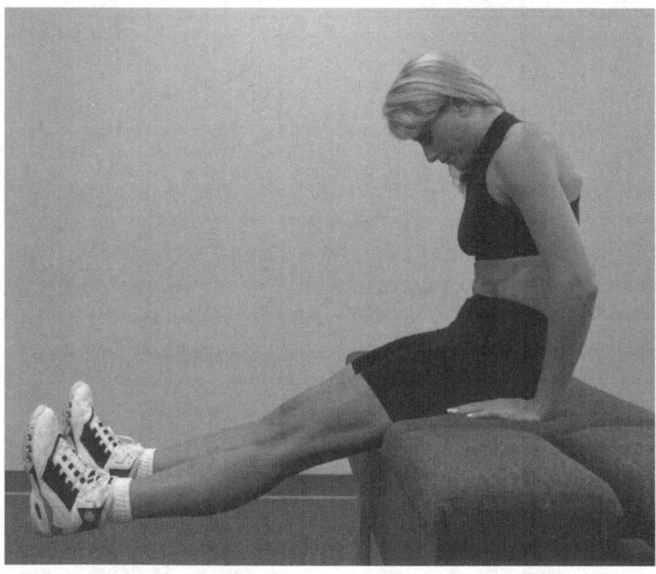

Figure 6–3 Bechterew's test. The seated patient is asked to extend the knees in an effort to determine whether leg pain is provoked. Having the patient flex the neck forward, hold his or her breath, and bear down (Valsalva maneuver) may increase the sensitivity of the test.

more specific for a disc lesion. Therefore, a positive response is virtually diagnostic for a disc lesion. Additional testing may include a Valsalva maneuver in an attempt to increase intrathecal pressure. A space-occupying lesion such as a tumor or a disc may then increase the leg pain complaint of the patient.

Facets are often challenged through compression or stretch. In the supine patient, indirect pressure at the facets may occur with flexing the heel toward the buttocks, increasing the lordosis and consequently loading the facets. Another approach is the seated or standing Kemp's maneuver. While seated, the patient is taken passively into extension and rotation to each side in an attempt to determine whether local or radiating pain is reproduced (Figure 6–4). Local pain suggests a facet cause, whereas radiating pain into the leg is more suggestive of nerve root irritation, especially if the pain is below the knee. The standing Kemp's test is a less specific test because it involves an active attempt by the patient to bend back, running the contralateral hand down the opposite leg. Therefore, muscle activation may cause spasm that is unrelated to a compressive or stretch effect.

Because leg length discrepancy has been often suspected as a biomechanical cause of LBP and other complaints, it is important to consider the reliability and validity of measurement of leg length in the physical examination. The reliabil-

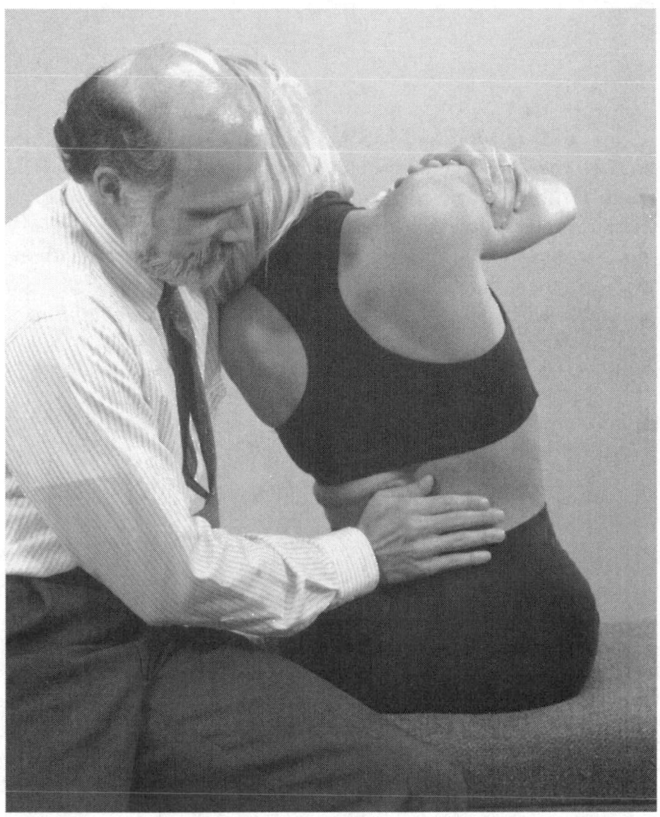

Figure 6–4 Kemp's test. Kemp's test may be performed with the patient seated or standing. While seated, the examiner applies pressure at the lumbar spine while extending and rotating the patient to one side and then the other.

ity is good if the patient is measured supine and the difference in measurement allowed for agreement among examiners is extended to 12.5 mm, with the mean value of two measurements included.[45] Estimation through palpation of the iliac crests in the standing position is considered unreliable.[46] Leg length measurement is also used as an indicator and outcome measure for successful correction of biomechanical or neurologic dysfunction. Although some studies have indicated good reliability, others question the statistical analysis used in the studies, not to mention the design, which may include telling the examiners which is the short leg side.[47] More research is needed.

Motion palpation testing of the lumbar spine is commonly used in the evaluation of low back pain. Studies have shown poor interexaminer reliability in some parts of the spine; however, Boline et al.[48] found interrater reliability at T12-L1 and L3-L4 and Mootz[49] found intrarater reliability at L4-L5.

Range of motion (ROM) may be evaluated through several procedures; however, for accurate interexaminer reliability the modified (or modified-modified) Schober method (Figure 6–5A) and the inclinometer method (Figure 6–5, B and C) are considered best.[50] The inclinometer approach uses either a single or double inclinometer; however, the principles are the same. Placing the inclinometers at the T12-L1 area and the sacrum, they are "zeroed out." The patient is then asked to flex, and the new readings are recorded. The same may be done with other movements. The bottom inclinometer readings are subtracted from the top inclinometer readings to obtain "true" lumbar participation (subtracting out the pelvic component). The modified Schober method uses a marking 5 cm and 10 cm above the lumbosacral junction (Figure 6–5A). With a tape measure held to the back, the patient is asked to flex. The difference is measured and recorded. The modified-modified Schober method involves connecting a line between the inferior margins of the posterior superior iliac spine and using a second skin marking 15 cm above the iliac line. The same procedure is then used to measure distance increases, using the closest millimeter. The finger-to-floor method is considered unreliable.

There are several commonly used approaches to functional testing of the low back. It is beyond the scope of this short discussion to cover all of these in any detail; however, the reader is encouraged to follow the references at the end of this chapter for more depth. The McKenzie approach to evaluation of LBP is to determine whether the patient has a postural problem, dysfunctional problem, or internal derangement.[51] This is accomplished by determining the position or movement that causes pain or relief. Patients who have no pain during, for example, flexion or extension (according to McKenzie) have a "postural" problem. This implies that the patient holds a particular posture during the day that needs to be interrupted to prevent the pain associated with holding any position for too long. The dysfunctional pattern is found when there is pain at end-range testing positions. McKenzie theorizes that this is due to shortened tissue. His solution is to stretch into the painful direction. The final category is the derangement syndrome. This patient has pain going through a movement pattern. More important, when the prone patient is asked to lift the trunk off the table by pushing up with the hands and keeping the pelvis on the table, pain down the leg is increased (Figure 6–6). This is referred to as peripheralization. If the same maneuver is repeated after moving the pelvis to either side and the pain is felt more in the back (centralization), then a position of relief has been determined that is used as the main form of therapy for the patient.

Especially for patients with chronic LBP or for those interested in prevention there are several functional ap-

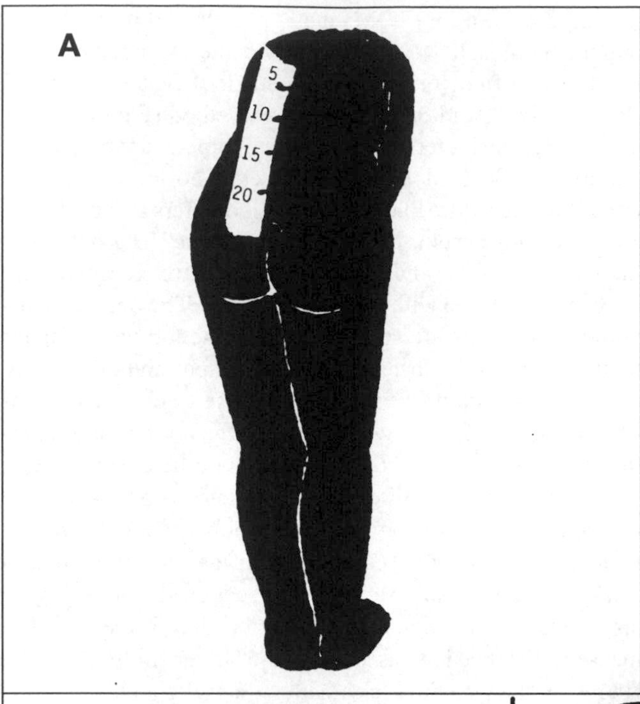

Figure 6–5 A, Modified Schober method. The modified Schober method measures the skin distraction with a tape measure. The modification of the Schober method test includes an additional third mark 5 cm below the lumbosacral junction. **B** and **C**, Inclinometer method. Lumbar spine range of motion is best measured with two inclinometers. *Source:* Reprinted with permission from C. Liebensen and R. Philips, *Chiropractic Technique Reliability of Motion Measurements for Lumbar Spine Flexion*, Vol. 1, © 1989, Williams & Wilkins.

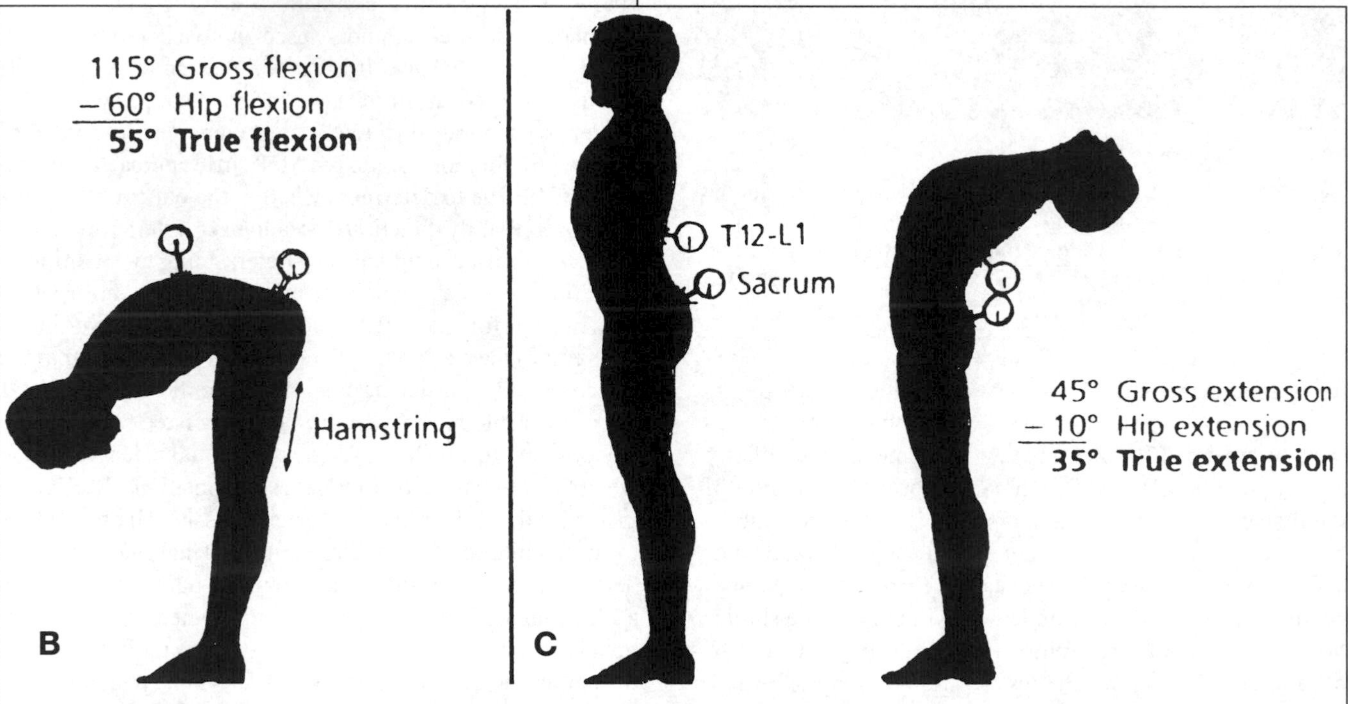

proaches that are helpful in determining exercise and stretching prescription. The Lewit/Janda approach is to search for "patterns" of muscle tightness and weakness and for dysfunctional patterns of movement.[52–54] These researchers focus on several patterns that seem to appear in layers. For the low back specifically, tight hip flexors and paraspinals associated with weak abdominals and gluteals are a common pattern. Function is also investigated by watching the timing of recruitment with specific movement patterns. For example, with active hip extension in the prone position, there is a sequential recruitment of hamstring, gluteals, and paraspinals. If the hamstrings and gluteals are dysfunctional requiring the paraspinals to contract early, facet impingement may occur as a result of the increase in lordosis.

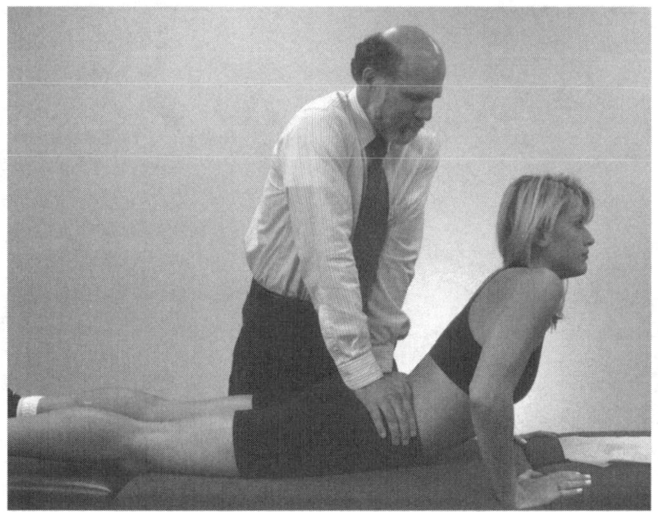

Figure 6–6 Prone extension is performed by asking the patient to lift the chest off the table by pushing up from the elbows first; if possible, then the hands. The examiner stabilizes the pelvis on the table.

Other approaches assess the patient's ability to perform predetermined exercises, rate the patient, and use the perceived weaknesses to prescribe an exercise program. Other testing involves expensive, sophisticated machines in an attempt to isolate certain muscle groups or to determine the patient's ability to lift.

Sacroiliac Tests

Two tests that appear to be reliable for SI involvement are the iliac gapping test (Figure 6–7) and the compression test (Figure 6–8).[55] These tests require a patient response. Other tests that may be valuable are the distraction (SI stretch) test (not shown), Gaenslen's test (Figure 6–9), hip extension test (Figure 6–10), and Patrick-Fabere's test (not shown). The latter tests act as compression tests and require that the hip be considered as a possible contributor to a positive response. Localization of the patient's response coupled with ROM of the hip may help localize the cause. In other words, if the pain is felt anteriorly and/or there is associated painful ROM in the hip, SI involvement is less likely. A common testing procedure used by manipulators is the Gillet or step test (Figure 6–11, A and B). Herzog et al.[56] reported that the test was reliable and a valuable indicator of the need for SI manipulation. A study by Mior[57], however, indicated poor kappa values.

Nonorganic Signs

When a patient is a chronic LBP sufferer, has potential loss of job or family breakup, or is involved in litigation, it is

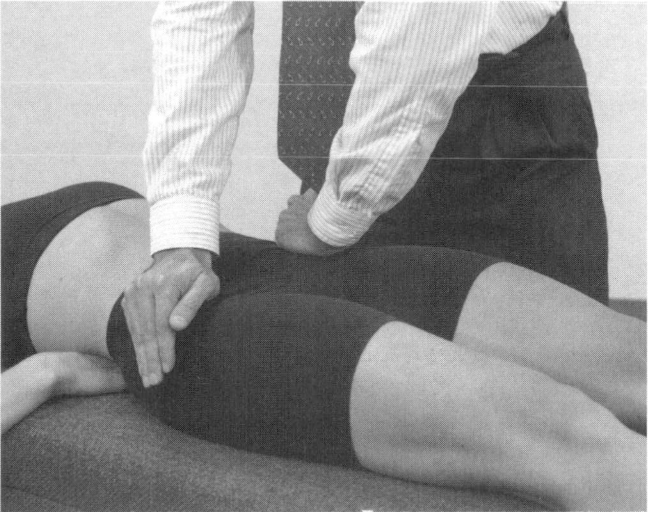

Figure 6–7 The gapping test.

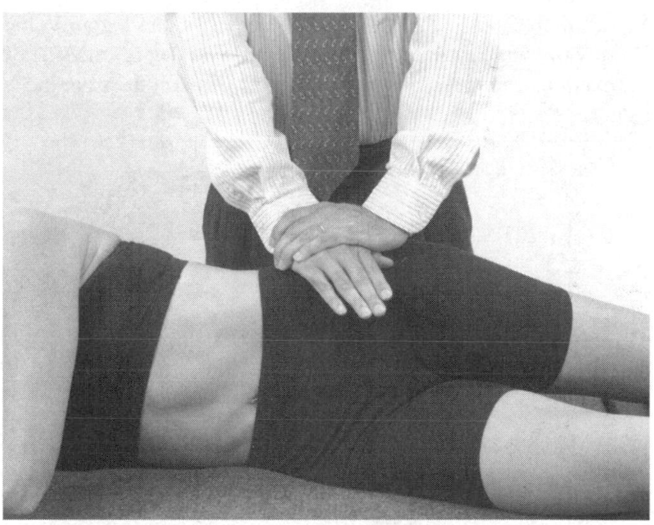

Figure 6–8 The sacroiliac compression (approximation) test.

important to consider the history with the clinical findings. In patients in whom there is a mismatch or an apparent overreaction is perceived, nonorganic testing should be included. These tests were originally designed by Waddell et al.[58] and consisted of five categories of inappropriate responses to various testing maneuvers, which included the strategies of distraction, stimulation, and evaluation of tenderness, regional disturbances, and overreaction. Finding three or more of these positive findings would indicate that the patient is somatizing or malingering. McCombe and Fairbank[42] and Fishbaine et al.[59] found that the regional disturbance category (abnormal regional sensory or motor disturbance such as the

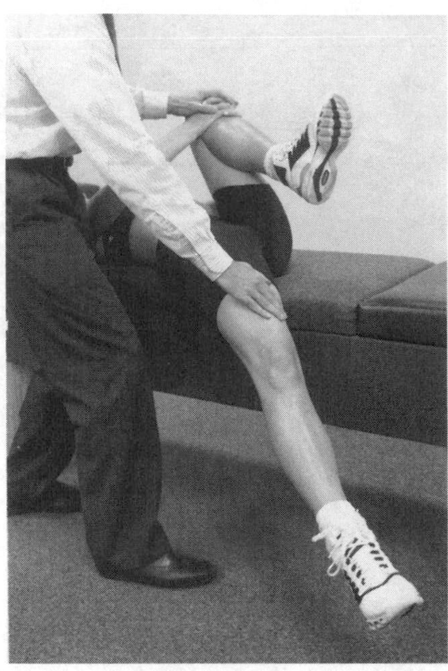

Figure 6–9 Gaenslen's test. The patient draws one leg up to the chest while the examiner distracts the opposite leg off the side of the examination table, causing SI compression on the examiner's side.

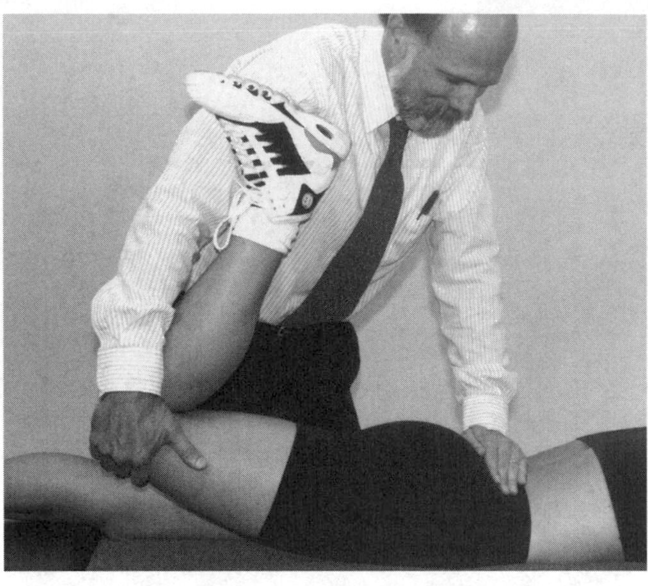

Figure 6–10 Passive hip extension may localize pain to the SI joint or lumbar facets.

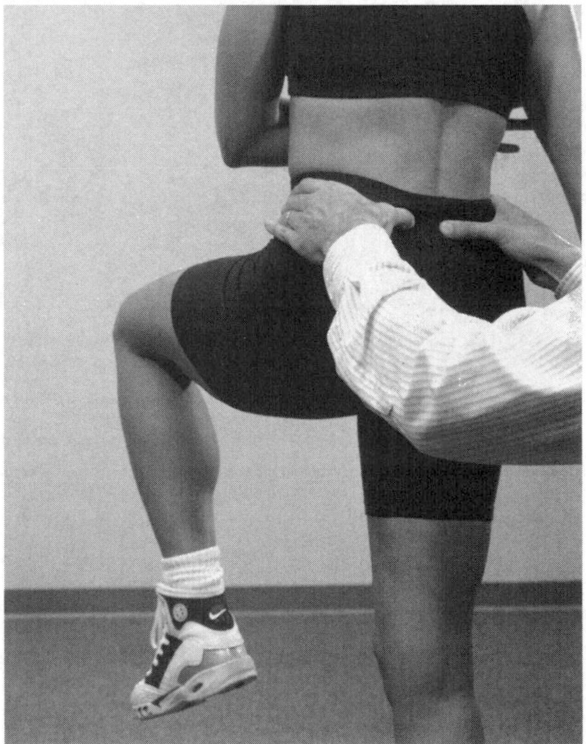

A

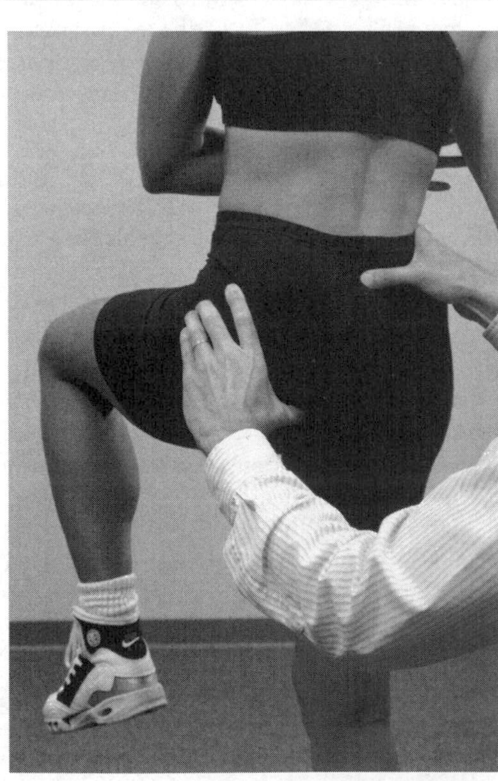

B

Figure 6–11 Testing for sacroiliac fixation. **A,** The examiner palpates the sacral spine and the posterior superior iliac spine (PSIS). The patient then lifts the leg. If the joint is fixed, the PSIS will rise on that side. **B,** The examiner palpates the sacral spine and the ischial tuberosity. With normal movement, the ischial tuberosity will move out laterally when the leg is lifted. If it moves upward, the joint is presumed fixed.

whole leg or overlapping dermatomal sensory complaints) and superficial tenderness (tenderness to light touch in a wide area) were unreliable. Part of the reason for less focus on regional disturbances is that it is possible for patients to have less discrete sensory or motor complaints with single nerve lesions and it is always possible that they have a spinal stenosis, which often can present with unusual regional disturbances. Malingering or nonorganic testing maneuvers include axial loading in the standing patient, passive flexion of the hip with the knee flexed, rotational twisting of the trunk, and forward bending in the seated position, among others.

Radiography and Special Imaging

Plain Films. The use of plain film evaluation of the patient with LBP is dictated by several factors:

- Does the patient have either a history or physical examination findings of a "high risk"?
- To what degree does the information gained alter the treatment?
- What is the relative risk and cost for the patient?

If the intention is to search for contraindications to adjusting or need for referral, it is usually clear from the history or examination when radiographs are necessary. If there are indications of cancer, infection, abdominal aneurysm, or fracture, radiographs are often the first screening test because of their high sensitivity.[60] Significant damage must occur, however, before these pathologic lesions are evident. When there are no high-risk indicators, the next need felt by many chiropractors is a biomechanical evaluation of the patient from both a gross and a segmental level. In other words, what are the relative imbalances with regard to symmetry? From a segmental perspective, static or active examination is used to search for restricted or excessive movement at a segmental level. The validity of this approach has been questioned; however, it may represent a potential source of information that may change the approach to the patient if used honestly.

Numerous lines of mensuration are used to evaluate mainly facet loading, abnormal curve, or shear stresses to the spine. Gradings of spondylolisthesis and of central canal stenosis are also possible. Following is a limited description of some of these markings:

- Central canal stenosis: Two methods are used: (1) Beuler and (2) Eisenstein.[61] A magnification factor of 0.77 is used to compensate for the magnification effect of the radiograph. Both are relatively accurate. The Beuler method is more accurate at the L3 level. The normal sagittal diameter is approximately 15 mm or more. A diameter of 12 mm is considered relative stenosis; 10 mm or less is considered absolute. On the anteroposterior (AP) view, the interpendicular distance can be measured. An AP diameter of 11.5 mm and an interpendicular distance of less than 16 mm are considered diagnostic for spinal canal stenosis.[62]
- Facet syndrome: Several lines of mensuration are used to determine vertebral inclination on lateral films in an effort to uncover excessive weight distribution to the facets. The lumbar IVD disc angle varies at each level; however, any measurement greater than 15° is likely to indicate facet syndrome in those patients with correlated clinical symptoms. This is also true of the lumbosacral disc angle. The lumbosacral angle demonstrates wide variation of normal (26° to 57°) and is probably generally not helpful. The use of MacNab's line is also not helpful because of the high incidence of abnormal findings in asymptomatic persons. Hadley's S curve is designed to indicate facet subluxation; however, displacements of 3 mm may not be visible.
- Spondylolisthesis: Meyerding's grading system is the standard for measuring the degree of spondylolisthesis. The superior surface of the base of the sacrum is divided into fourths (this can be performed with the segment below for higher spondylolisthesis). The degree of slippage is then measured and graded 1 through 4.

Some chiropractors feel that the identification of anomalies is an important reason for screening all patients with LBP. However, studies have not found a higher incidence of LBP in patients with facet tropism, transitional vertebrae, spina bifida, or Schmorl's nodes.[63,64] The other argument is that the identification of a transitional vertebra or facet tropism may alter the positioning of the adjustment (manipulation) or cause the doctor to choose a different manipulative approach. This has yet to be researched.

When pathology is suspected, it is important to begin with a limited series, including AP and lateral views. Lytic, blastic, and degenerative processes are usually well visualized on routine views. Additionally, a calcified aortic aneurysm is visible on a lateral view. Special views should be reserved for specific concerns. For example, if the patient is seen to have a spondylolisthesis on the lateral film, oblique films may allow visualization of pars interarticularis discontinuity. If the SI joint is suspected of having a sclerotic focus (eg, seronegative arthritides), angled spot-views may provide a clearer picture.

Computed Tomography. CT is usually reserved for suspected cases of fracture or stenosis. It may also be useful in imaging infection, tumor, the cause of pain in postoperative spines (recurrent disc herniation and fusion), and herniated discs in general. Because of the increased radiation exposure, MRI is often chosen as an alternative.

Magnetic Resonance Imaging. MRI has the advantage of no ionizing radiation, yet it has a higher cost. Soft tissue is well visualized. MRI is particularly valuable in evaluating disc pathology, the extent of tumor or infection invasion, and abnormalities involving the nerve root, thecal sac, or subarachnoid space. In differentiating between recurrent disc herniation or postsurgical fibrosis, MRI with gadolinium (injected) is often helpful.

Bone Scan. Bone scan is quite sensitive to bone changes and is valuable in the detection of spinal metastasis and activity of a spondylolisthesis. However, it is not specific for the cause of the increased uptake pattern. In other words, any bony inflammatory condition may cause an increased uptake. The extent of damage is also not well visualized.

Thermography. There is much controversy with regard to the use of thermography. In general, thermography can be sensitive, however nonspecific as to the cause of a patient's complaint. There are generally two types: (1) infrared and (2) liquid crystal thermography. Electronic infrared thermography is more sensitive than liquid crystal; however, the cost and need for standardization of the testing environment make it relatively unavailable. Additionally, thermography is between 78% and 94% sensitive for radiculopathy; however, it is nonspecific (20% to 44%).

Electrodiagnostic Studies. Electrodiagnostic studies (EDS) are used when there is a question as to the cause of a patient's low back and leg complaints. EDS consists of the following:

- Electromyography (EMG) is used to differentiate between nerve root causes, myelopathy, and myopathy. EMG does not become positive for 3 to 4 weeks following denervation. Positive findings include electrical hypersensitivity reactions such as fibrillation potentials and positive sharp waves.
- Nerve conduction velocity (NCV) is used to differentiate between entrapment neuropathies and radiculopathies; late responses such as the H-reflex are the electrodiagnostic equivalent of a decreased Achilles reflex and are found 90% of the time with S1 dysfunction.
- Sensory-evoked potentials (SEPs) are used to measure the sensory component of a patient's complaint in an attempt to localize the site of the pathologic lesion; dermatomal somatosensory-evoked potentials (DSEPs) may be useful in the assessment of patients with spinal stenosis.

MANAGEMENT

Important screening questions or findings with regard to possible contraindication to manipulation of a specific area include the following[65]:

- use of anticoagulants
- recent back surgery (unstable spine)
- spinal infection
- spinal cancer
- severe osteoporosis
- signs of acute myelopathy or cauda equina syndrome
- acute inflammatory arthritis

For mechanical LBP, the long-term strategy should include weight loss, smoking cessation, and exercise inclusion. Decisions regarding specific chiropractic approaches are not discussed. The broader issues of passive and active care are applicable to any approach chosen by the chiropractor. Algorithms for these areas are given in Chapter 1. Algorithms for low back pain screening and mechanical low back pain are presented in Figures 6–12 and 6–13.

Passive care involves procedures that are performed on the patient with the patient providing no more than cooperation. These include physical therapy modalities, passive ROM, massage/trigger point massage, mobilization, and manipulation. Criteria for passive care include a history of recent trauma, an acute or inflammatory condition, or dependency behavior. The primary goal is to control inflammation and pain. The frequency of manual therapy visits during the first 10 to 14 days may range from three to five visits per week dependent on the severity of the pain and disability. The patient should be reevaluated to determine whether therapy is effective. If not effective, a second 2-week trial using a different treatment approach is warranted. If this is not successful, further evaluation with special imaging or comanagement with a medical doctor is recommended. If the patient has a preconsultation duration of symptoms greater than 8 days or has severe pain, more than four previous episodes, or preexisting structural or pathologic conditions, the anticipated recovery time is often doubled.[66]

There is still and will continue to be some debate as to the appropriateness of side-posture manipulation in the treatment of disc herniations. The review of the literature by Cassidy et al.[67] supports the cautious application of this form of treatment. However, Slosberg's[28] review of the same literature points out some possible factors that may warrant a more cautious approach. Both reviews agree that premobilization attempts to determine the patient's response is a good screening procedure prior to the application of a thrust. In other words, if mild mobilization is applied at the involved segment, an increase in pain or reproduction of leg pain may be a caution against side-posture manipulation at that time.

Active care involves the patient in determining goals and objectives. Exercises and stretches, modification of diet or other lifestyle changes, and modification of work or recreational environment or performance are among the targeted areas. Exercise takes into account the fitness level of the patient, pain free ROM, strength, facilities, and motivation. In general, mild isometrics can be performed within pain-free ranges in an attempt to facilitate muscle activity and prevent atrophy. This is followed by various strategies involving isotonic exercises. The primary focus with the low back is strengthening abdominals and stretching the paraspinals. Information gained from a functional evaluation as discussed above can then lead to a more sophisticated approach at strengthening weak areas and stretching shortened areas. Following a strengthening phase, endurance and functional movement patterns are emphasized. Coupled with this approach is an attempt at proprioceptive stimulation through the use of balance exercises. For the low back, giant, balance (Swiss) ball exercise protocols have been developed.

Proper lifting is essential to avoid injury or reinjury. The primary focus is to maintain a slight lordosis when lifting. When possible the patient should be instructed to lift lower objects by bending the knees first and lifting from the legs. To reduce the effect of increasing the extensor movement, the load should be kept as close to the body as possible. Avoid twisting while lifting. The spine is most vulnerable to lifting injury after holding a prolonged flexed position or after prolonged recumbency (in the morning). Finally, all lifting should be accompanied by cocontraction of the back and abdominal muscles.

The seated position causes significantly higher disc pressure than standing. When seated, the chair should be stable with a seat-backrest angle of 95° to 105°.[68] A lumbar support may help maintain a slight lordosis. A slightly forward-sloped seat may also be helpful. Too low a seat shifts more weight onto the ischial tuberosities. Proper desk height is considered about 27 to 30 cm higher than the seat, allowing the arms to rest with the elbows bent 90° with the hand relaxed on the desk surface.[69]

Figure 6–12
LOW BACK PAIN SCREENING—ALGORITHM.

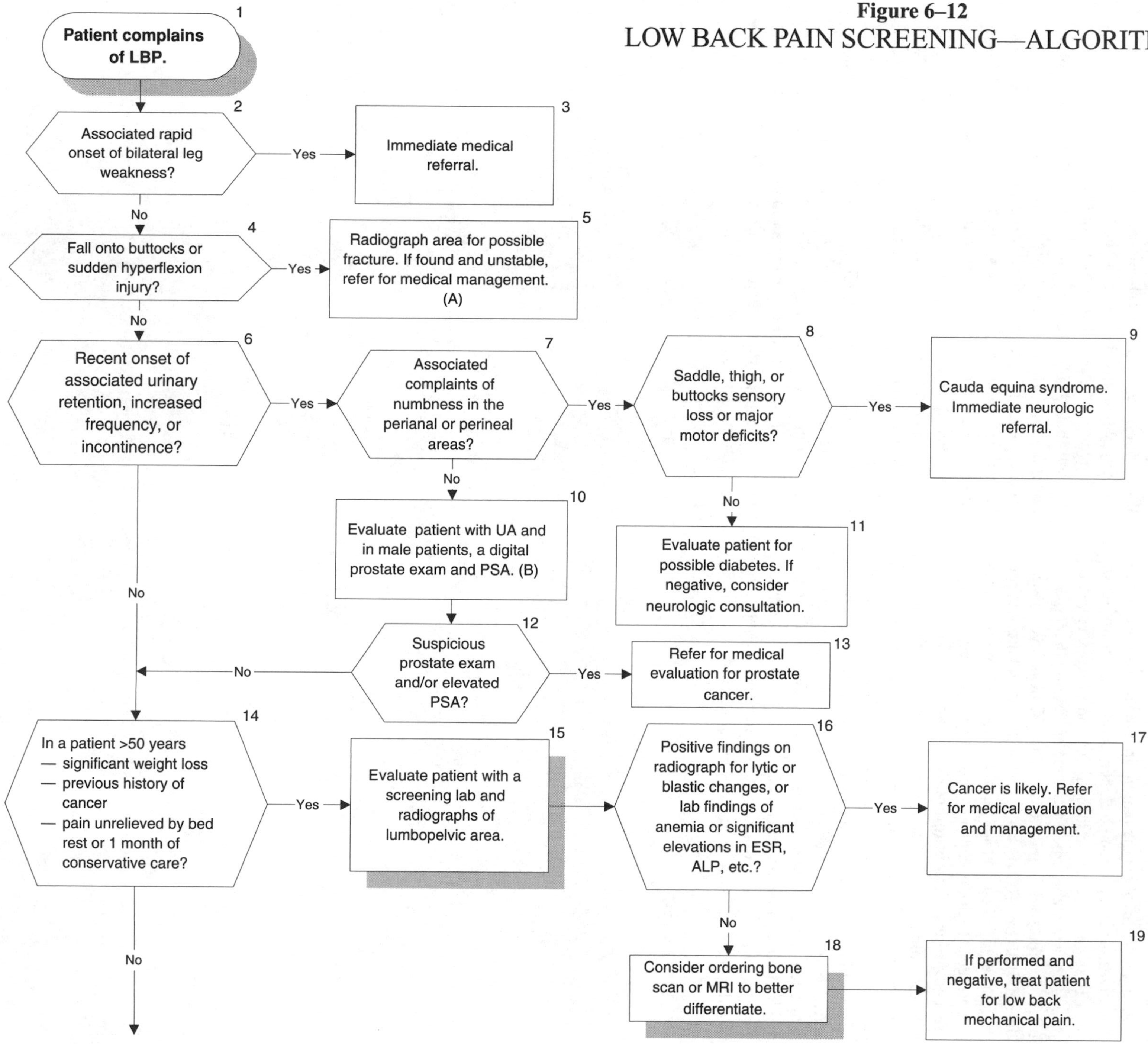

1. **Patient complains of LBP.** → 2

2. Associated rapid onset of bilateral leg weakness?
   - Yes → 3. Immediate medical referral.
   - No → 4

4. Fall onto buttocks or sudden hyperflexion injury?
   - Yes → 5. Radiograph area for possible fracture. If found and unstable, refer for medical management. (A)
   - No → 6

6. Recent onset of associated urinary retention, increased frequency, or incontinence?
   - Yes → 7
   - No → 14

7. Associated complaints of numbness in the perianal or perineal areas?
   - Yes → 8
   - No → 10

8. Saddle, thigh, or buttocks sensory loss or major motor deficits?
   - Yes → 9. Cauda equina syndrome. Immediate neurologic referral.
   - No → 11. Evaluate patient for possible diabetes. If negative, consider neurologic consultation.

10. Evaluate patient with UA and in male patients, a digital prostate exam and PSA. (B) → 12

12. Suspicious prostate exam and/or elevated PSA?
   - Yes → 13. Refer for medical evaluation for prostate cancer.
   - No → 14

14. In a patient >50 years
   — significant weight loss
   — previous history of cancer
   — pain unrelieved by bed rest or 1 month of conservative care?
   - Yes → 15
   - No →

15. Evaluate patient with a screening lab and radiographs of lumbopelvic area. → 16

16. Positive findings on radiograph for lytic or blastic changes, or lab findings of anemia or significant elevations in ESR, ALP, etc.?
   - Yes → 17. Cancer is likely. Refer for medical evaluation and management.
   - No → 18

18. Consider ordering bone scan or MRI to better differentiate. → 19

19. If performed and negative, treat patient for low back mechanical pain.

continues

Figure 6–12 continued

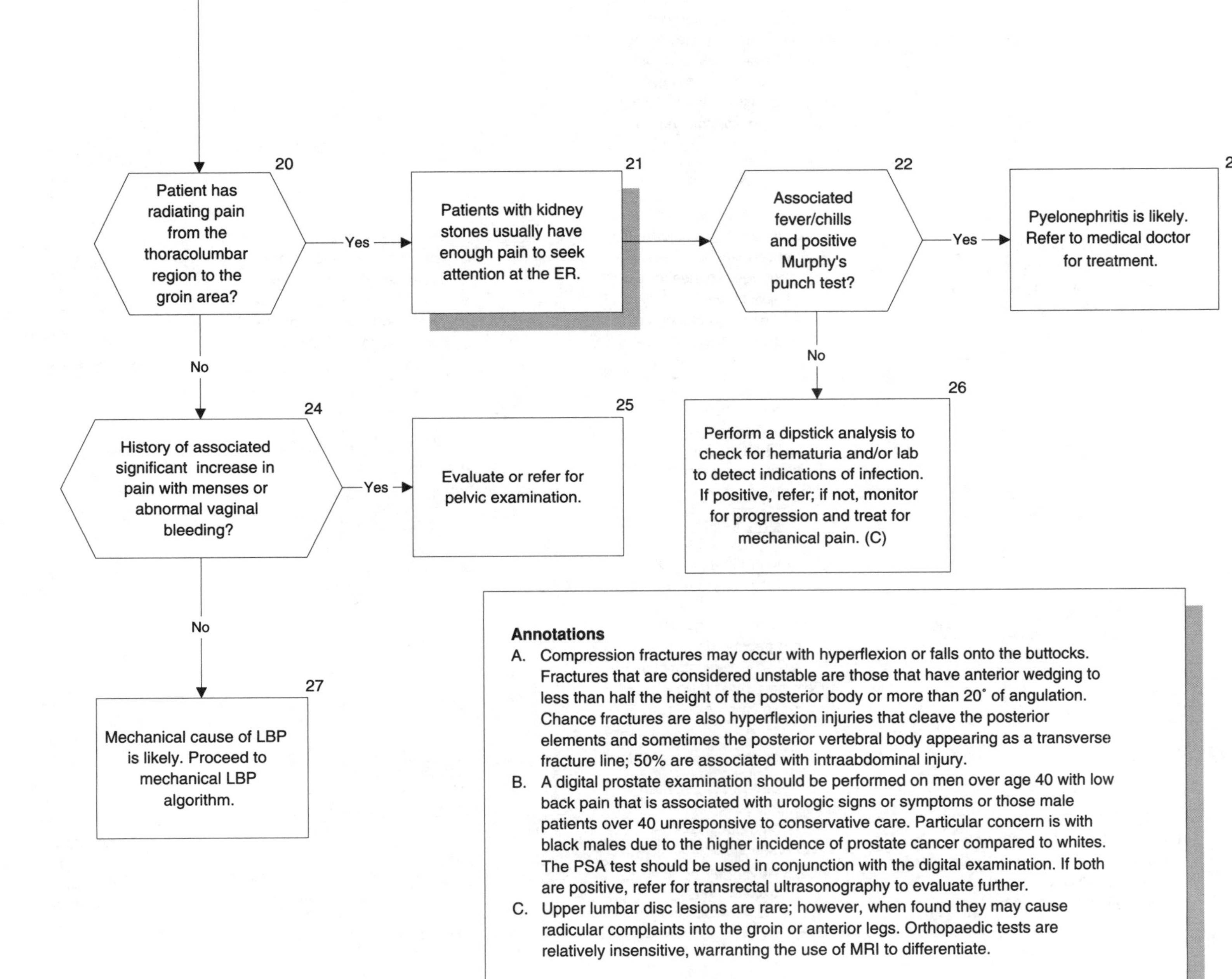

20
Patient has radiating pain from the thoracolumbar region to the groin area?
Yes
21
Patients with kidney stones usually have enough pain to seek attention at the ER.
22
Associated fever/chills and positive Murphy's punch test?
Yes
23
Pyelonephritis is likely. Refer to medical doctor for treatment.
No
26
Perform a dipstick analysis to check for hematuria and/or lab to detect indications of infection. If positive, refer; if not, monitor for progression and treat for mechanical pain. (C)
No
24
History of associated significant increase in pain with menses or abnormal vaginal bleeding?
Yes
25
Evaluate or refer for pelvic examination.
No
27
Mechanical cause of LBP is likely. Proceed to mechanical LBP algorithm.

Annotations

A. Compression fractures may occur with hyperflexion or falls onto the buttocks. Fractures that are considered unstable are those that have anterior wedging to less than half the height of the posterior body or more than 20° of angulation. Chance fractures are also hyperflexion injuries that cleave the posterior elements and sometimes the posterior vertebral body appearing as a transverse fracture line; 50% are associated with intraabdominal injury.

B. A digital prostate examination should be performed on men over age 40 with low back pain that is associated with urologic signs or symptoms or those male patients over 40 unresponsive to conservative care. Particular concern is with black males due to the higher incidence of prostate cancer compared to whites. The PSA test should be used in conjunction with the digital examination. If both are positive, refer for transrectal ultrasonography to evaluate further.

C. Upper lumbar disc lesions are rare; however, when found they may cause radicular complaints into the groin or anterior legs. Orthopaedic tests are relatively insensitive, warranting the use of MRI to differentiate.

Key: UA, urinalysis; PSA, prostate-specific antigen; ESR, erythrocyte sedimentation rate; ALP, alkaline phosphatase.

Figure 6–13

MECHANICAL LOW BACK PAIN—ALGORITHM.

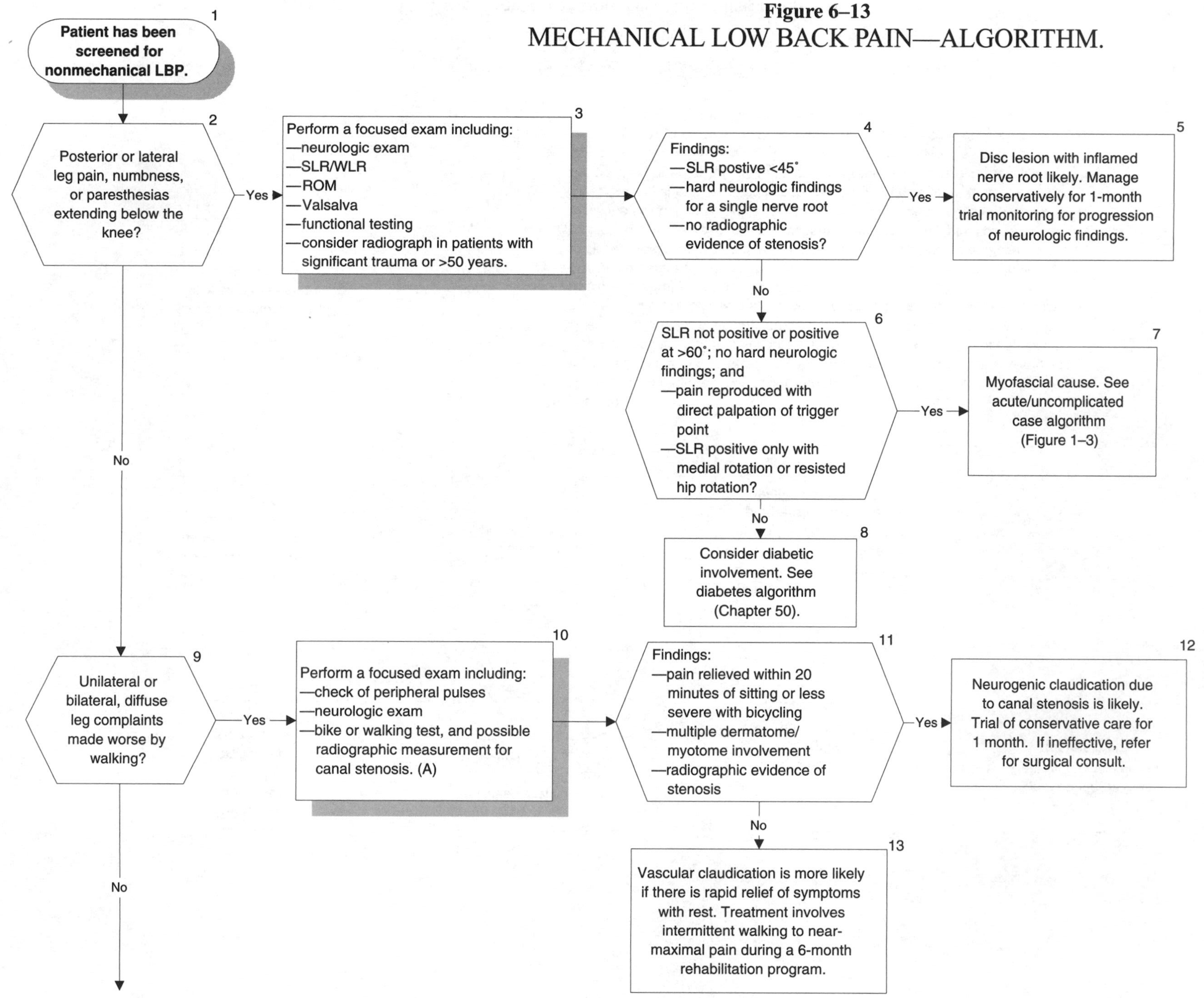

1
Patient has been screened for nonmechanical LBP.
2
Posterior or lateral leg pain, numbness, or paresthesias extending below the knee?
Yes
3
Perform a focused exam including:
—neurologic exam
—SLR/WLR
—ROM
—Valsalva
—functional testing
—consider radiograph in patients with significant trauma or >50 years.
4
Findings:
—SLR postive <45˚
—hard neurologic findings for a single nerve root
—no radiographic evidence of stenosis?
Yes
5
Disc lesion with inflamed nerve root likely. Manage conservatively for 1-month trial monitoring for progression of neurologic findings.
No
6
SLR not positive or positive at >60˚; no hard neurologic findings; and
—pain reproduced with direct palpation of trigger point
—SLR positive only with medial rotation or resisted hip rotation?
Yes
7
Myofascial cause. See acute/uncomplicated case algorithm (Figure 1–3)
No
8
Consider diabetic involvement. See diabetes algorithm (Chapter 50).
No
9
Unilateral or bilateral, diffuse leg complaints made worse by walking?
Yes
10
Perform a focused exam including:
—check of peripheral pulses
—neurologic exam
—bike or walking test, and possible radiographic measurement for canal stenosis. (A)
11
Findings:
—pain relieved within 20 minutes of sitting or less severe with bicycling
—multiple dermatome/myotome involvement
—radiographic evidence of stenosis
Yes
12
Neurogenic claudication due to canal stenosis is likely. Trial of conservative care for 1 month. If ineffective, refer for surgical consult.
No
13
Vascular claudication is more likely if there is rapid relief of symptoms with rest. Treatment involves intermittent walking to near-maximal pain during a 6-month rehabilitation program.
No

continues

Figure 6–13 continued

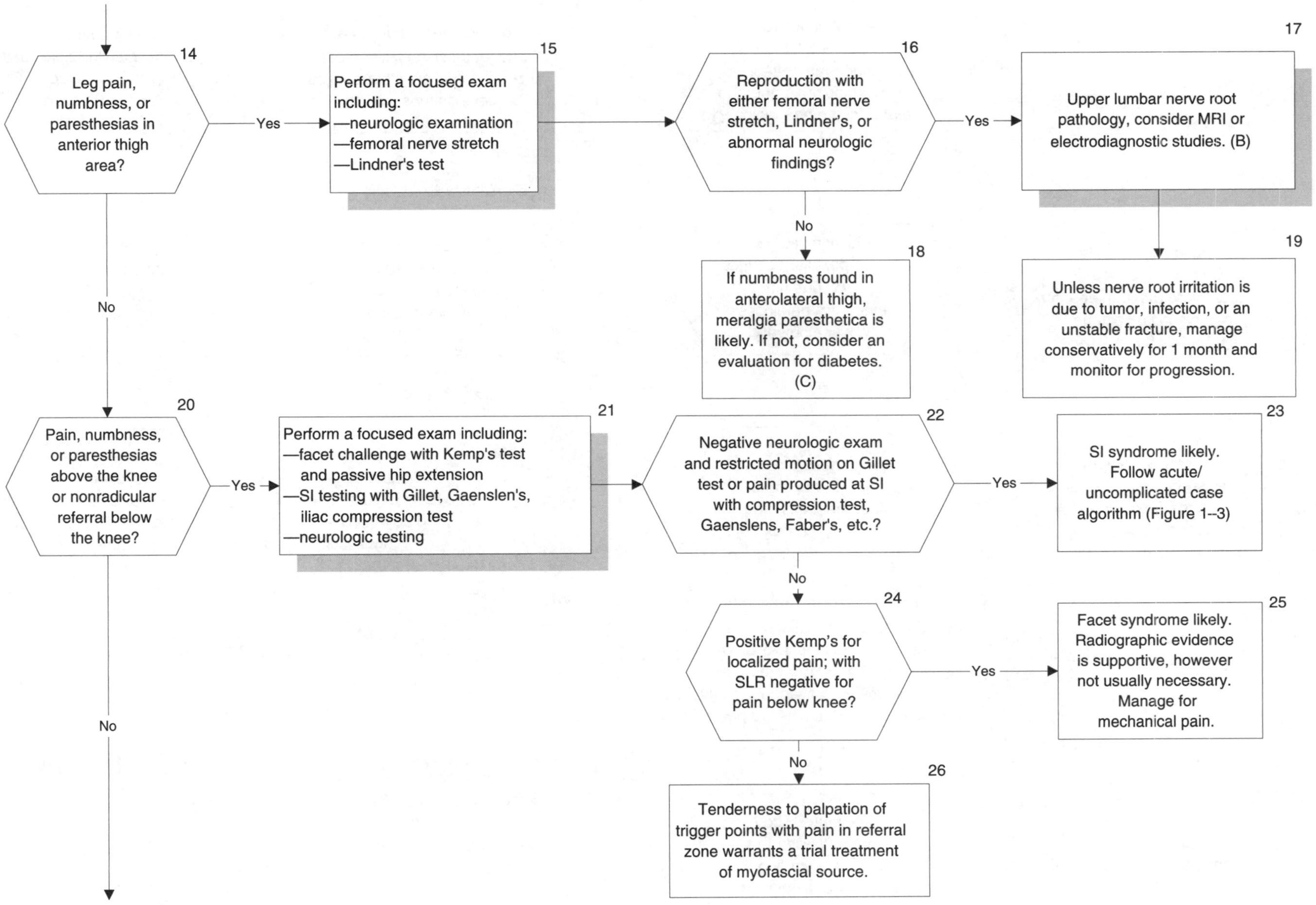

14 Leg pain, numbness, or paresthesias in anterior thigh area?
- Yes → 15 Perform a focused exam including:
  —neurologic examination
  —femoral nerve stretch
  —Lindner's test
  → 16 Reproduction with either femoral nerve stretch, Lindner's, or abnormal neurologic findings?
  - Yes → 17 Upper lumbar nerve root pathology, consider MRI or electrodiagnostic studies. (B)
    → 19 Unless nerve root irritation is due to tumor, infection, or an unstable fracture, manage conservatively for 1 month and monitor for progression.
  - No → 18 If numbness found in anterolateral thigh, meralgia paresthetica is likely. If not, consider an evaluation for diabetes. (C)
- No → 20 Pain, numbness, or paresthesias above the knee or nonradicular referral below the knee?
  - Yes → 21 Perform a focused exam including:
    —facet challenge with Kemp's test and passive hip extension
    —SI testing with Gillet, Gaenslen's, iliac compression test
    —neurologic testing
    → 22 Negative neurologic exam and restricted motion on Gillet test or pain produced at SI with compression test, Gaenslens, Faber's, etc.?
    - Yes → 23 SI syndrome likely. Follow acute/uncomplicated case algorithm (Figure 1–3)
    - No → 24 Positive Kemp's for localized pain; with SLR negative for pain below knee?
      - Yes → 25 Facet syndrome likely. Radiographic evidence is supportive, however not usually necessary. Manage for mechanical pain.
      - No → 26 Tenderness to palpation of trigger points with pain in referral zone warrants a trial treatment of myofascial source.
  - No →

continues

Figure 6–13 continued

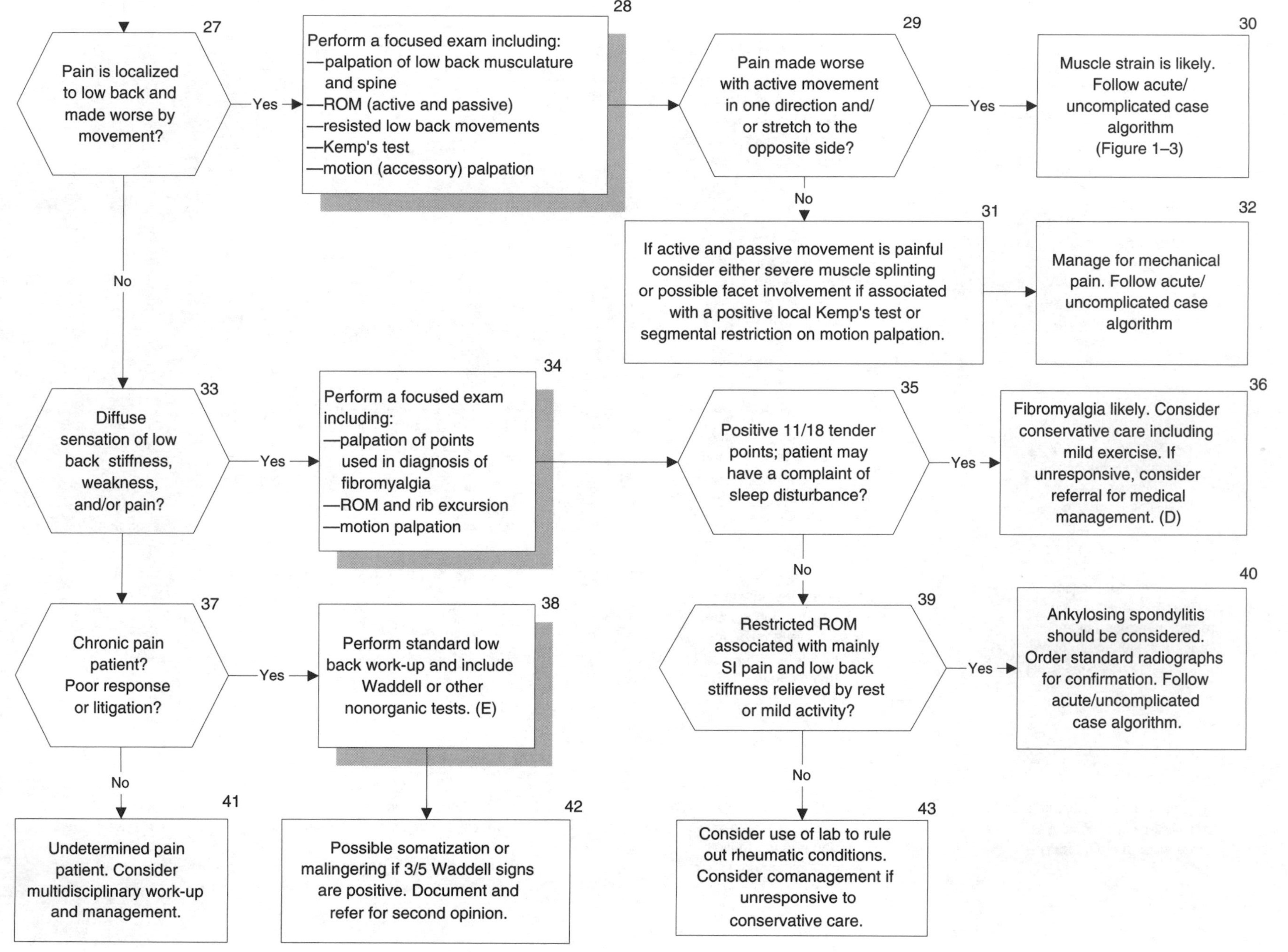

continues

Figure 6–13 continued

Annotations

A. Central canal stenosis may be estimated on a lateral lumbar radiograph using either Beuler's or Eisenstein's measurements. A normal canal is 15 mm; 12 mm is considered relative stenosis; 10 mm or less is considered absolute.

B. Upper lumbar disc lesions are rare; however, when they do occur, they often affect more than upper lumbar nerve roots. Therefore, the Achilles reflex may be affected and the patient may have some posterior leg pain.

C. Diabetes may cause distal sensory disturbances or cause unilateral peripheral nerve palsies such as in amyotrophy. With diabetic amyotrophy, involvement of the femoral nerve is most common with weakness and atrophy of the quadriceps.

D. Fibromyalgia is a more generalized, symmetric distribution of myofascitis. The American College of Rheumatology has set criteria for the diagnosis: pain in 11 of 18 tender sites in a patient with pain for at least 3 months. These bilateral points include suboccipital, lower cervical spine, trapezius, supraspinatus, second rib, lateral epicondyle, gluteals, greater trochanter, and medial fat pad of the knee.

E. Waddell's nonorganic signs include generalized or nonanatomic tenderness, positive responses to simulated orthopaedic testing (axial loading, trunk rotation), distracted SLR (flip test), regional weakness and sensory abnormalities that are nonmyotomal and nondermatomal, and overreaction to testing.

Source: Modified from K. McCarthy, Seed algorithm, *Topics in Clinical Chiropractic*, Vol. 1, pp. 79–80, © 1994, Aspen Publishers, Inc.

SELECTED DISORDERS OF THE LOW BACK*

DISC LESION WITH RADICULOPATHY

Classic Presentation

The patient complains of low back and leg pain below the knee, often of sudden onset from a bending and/or twisting maneuver. There is often a past history of several bouts of LBP that resolved.

Cause

Although in the past it was believed that all leg pain that was radicular was due to compression of a nerve root by a herniated nucleus pulposus, current thinking is that the nerve root is inflamed, but not always compressed.[70] Currently, it is theorized that herniated disc material causes the release of irritating substances or initiates an autoimmune inflammatory reaction. The disc, the corresponding inflamed nerve root, or compression of the nerve root by the disc may be the source of pain. When there is leg pain without objective neurologic evidence, the pain is often referred. When the nerve root is compressed, frank neurologic signs usually become evident.

Evaluation

Given that 98% of all disc lesions are at L4-L5 or L5-S1, the neurologic examination is focused to these areas. Weakness of dorsiflexion of the great toe and numbness on the lateral side of the lower leg are highly suggestive of an L5 nerve root lesion. An absent Achilles reflex, numbness on the back of the calf or lateral foot, and weakness on plantarflexion of the great toe or foot all implicate the S1 nerve root. The SLR is considered a reliable nerve root tension sign when positive for reproduction of leg pain below 45° of elevation (Figure 6–2). A crossed SLR or well-leg raise (WLR) is strong confirmation. Dorsiflexion of the ankle at 5° below the positive SLR range (Braggard's test) is another confirmatory test. Confirmation of nerve root involvement may be physiologic with electrodiagnostic studies or anatomic with MRI. These studies are rarely used during the first 4 weeks of a complaint unless severe, unremitting pain or progressive neurologic signs are present.

Management

There is some debate as to whether side-posture adjusting should be used in the treatment of disc herniations.[28] The primary concern is the rotary component. If the patient is adjusted in the slightly extended side-lying position, the facets will more likely provide protection. If the rotary component is minimized and the patient is pretested with mild mobilization at the segment to determine aggravation of the leg complaint, cautious side-posture adjusting is a possible alternative.[66] Other "softer" approaches involve no rotation such as flexion-distraction, blocking, and activator adjusting.

FACET SYNDROME

Classic Presentation

The patient often will complain of well-localized LBP with some hip/buttock or leg pain above the knee. The onset is often sudden after a simple midjudged movement or arising from a flexed position.

*See also Chapter 4, Thoracic Spine Complaints, and Chapter 32, Abdominal Pain.

Cause

The facet and its capsule may be the source of pain. Each facet receives innervation from two spinal levels specifically from the medial branch of the posterior primary rami. Synovial folds (meniscoids) may become entrapped or pinched, causing pain. The synovium and capsule have specific substance P–sensitive nerves in addition to small-diameter nociceptors.[71] Another process that may predispose to facet-mediated pain is degeneration, seen more often in middle-aged and older adults.

Evaluation

Although there is often difficulty in distinguishing facet from disc/nerve root irritation, there is usually a cluster of findings that help support the suspicion. These include absence of neurologic deficits, absence of nerve root tension signs/tests, pain that is rather localized with Kemp's maneuver (extension and rotation; Figure 6–4), and when reproduced with an SLR does not extend below the knee. Radiographic evidence may include signs of facet imbrication using the lumbar or lumbosacral disc angle, or Hadley's S curve. The variability of normal findings in asymptomatic patients makes the use of these markings questionable. In general, any disc angle greater than 15° is strong evidence of facet imbrication.

Management

Facet syndrome appears to be particularly responsive to adjustment (manipulation). The mechanism is still not clear; however, two major proposals are that either the adjustment frees an entrapped meniscoid tab or large-fiber input causes reflex changes, reducing muscle spasm and reflex-mediated pain.

CANAL STENOSIS

Classic Presentation

Patients often are in their 50s or older. They complain of back and leg pain. The pain can be unilateral and bilateral and often is diffuse. Patients may complain of the onset of leg complaints with walking (claudication) and relief with rest after 15 to 20 minutes or by maintaining a flexed posture.

Cause

Stenosis may be central or lateral, caused by bony or soft tissue encroachment, and may be congenital or acquired. As a result, the signs and symptoms vary widely. For leg complaints to occur, it is usually true that there are multiple levels of stenosis. Congenitally, a trefoil shape of the spinal canal leads to central canal and lateral stenosis. Pedicogenic stenosis is due to anatomically short pedicles. Acquired stenosis is due to bony outgrowths from the facets, lamina, or pedicles, degenerative spondylolisthesis, or hypertrophied and/or calcified ligamentum flavum. Postoperative stenosis may also be a consequence of decompressive surgeries (eg, laminectomies).

Evaluation

Neurologic deficits may be apparent yet cross dermatomal and other nerve root boundaries. In an older patient with multilevel findings, stenosis should be considered. Often used is the bicycle or walking test to differentiate between neurogenic and vascular claudication. Patients with neurogenic claudication often find it possible to bicycle or walk farther when flexed. This theoretically opens up the canal and intervertebral foramina, taking pressure off the neural structures. One study indicated that these tests may not be able to differentiate clearly between the two types of claudication. Although reasonably insensitive (0.60), improvement with flexion points strongly to canal senosis.[72] Central canal stenosis may be estimated on a lateral lumbar film using either the Eisenstein or Beuler method. A normal canal is 15 mm or greater; 12 mm is considered relative stenosis; 10 mm is considered absolute. CT is often used when bony canal stenosis is suspected. MRI is more valuable with soft tissue encroachment. Electrodiagnostic studies are often used when multiple nerve root levels appear to be affected. EMG is less valuable than DSEPs.[73]

Management

Treatment is based on the underlying type and cause of the stenosis. The natural history seems to suggest that many patients with stenosis may improve or remain stable (90%) without treatment.[74] If manipulative therapy is tried, caution should be used because of the possibility of increasing compression, causing an exacerbation or worsening of symptoms. The response to manipulative treatment is less predictable than for other causes of LBP. The positive response rate is approximately 36% according to a study by Cassidy et al.[7] If the patient has severe neurologic deficit or fails to respond to conservative management, surgical consultation is warranted for possible decompression of the area or areas.

SPONDYLOLISTHESIS

Classic Presentation

There are several types of spondylolistheses; however, the most common are isthmic, occurring in the young, and degenerative, occurring in older patients. Patients may be asymptomatic or have low back pain made worse with extension. In older patients, the spondylolisthesis may cause signs of stenosis.

Cause

Although congenital types and destructive (eg, tuberculosis or cancer) types are possible they are rare. The isthmic type is due to either a stress fracture of the pars interarticularis (spondylolysis) or an elongated pars; 90% of spondylolytic spondylolisthesis occurs at L5.[75] The spondylolysis type is more likely to become symptomatic in children more than 5 years old. Although slippage is more common in girls, the isthmic type is one half as common as it is in boys. Sports such as gymnastics, which require repetitive hyperextension, are more likely to cause problems. There is a high incidence in Alaskan Eskimos.

Evaluation

Spondylolisthesis is primarily a radiographic diagnosis seen best on a lateral film. However, some patients may have increased back or leg pain with a one-legged balance test. The patient is asked to balance on one leg and hyperextend at the lumbar region. Palpation may reveal a prominent spinous process at the involved level with a steep sacral base angle. The radiographic grading of spondylolisthesis is based on dividing the sacrum (if L5) or the vertebrae below (if above L5) into fourths. Each slip of one-fourth the length of the anterior to posterior body is considered a grade. Therefore, slippage three-fourths the AP length would be classified as a grade 3. Stability of the spondylolisthesis can be evaluated with a traction radiograph (the patient hangs from a bar) or a compression stress radiograph (20-kg rucksack on the shoulders). Single photon emission tomography (SPECT) is often used to distinguish athletic patients who require an anti-lordotic brace and rest from those who do not have an "active" lesion.

Management

Most grade 1 spondylolistheses are asymptomatic and stable. Progressive slippage is rare, occurring in only 2% to 3% patients.[76] The majority of slippage occurs in children under age 10 years. In adults with degenerative spondylolisthesis, progression is rarely greater than 18% anterior displacement. Grade 2 spondylolistheses may be symptomatic but are considered stable. Cassidy et al.[77] indicate a good response to manipulative management. Only when grade 3 or 4 spondylolistheses are discovered is there a need for surgical consultation. Patients with a hot SPECT bone scan are placed in a brace for several weeks. Follow-up scans should be performed in several weeks.

SACROILIAC SPRAIN AND SUBLUXATION

Classic Presentation

The patient presents with pain over one SI joint after straightening up from a stooped position, often lifting an object. The pain may radiate down the back of the leg. With a sprain the pain is often sharp and stabbing and is relieved somewhat by sitting or lying. The pain is less often affected by posture with an SI subluxation.

Cause

Although not often recognized in the medical literature as a source of LBP, SI dysfunction probably accounts for almost half the cases of LBP.[78] The SI ligamentous support is strong; however, in younger patients, pregnant patients, or those with degenerative disease, prolonged or sudden lifting or bending may cause a sprain or subluxation. Movement at the SI joint is small but existent in younger patients. The movement is primarily an anteroposterior rotary movement around a transverse axis. This is an accessory movement (involuntary) occurring mainly when attaining a standing position. The sacral promontory moves forward approximately 3 to 6 mm.[79]

Evaluation

Either direct compression (Figure 6–8) or distraction (gapping; Figure 6–7) at the joint may increase the pain or in some cases decrease the pain. Other tests include Gaenslen's test (Figure 6–9) whereby the supine patient draws the uninvolved leg to the chest while the examiner extends the involved-side leg off the side of the table. An increase in posterior pain suggests SI involvement. The Gillet test (Figure 6–11) is essentially a motion test of the SI joints in an attempt to determine restricted movement. Although the sensitivity of these tests is questioned, the combination of patient presentation, history, and SI tests will usually help define the problem. Evaluation of the patient should include signs of seronegative arthritides (ie, AS, Reiter's, or psoriatic). This would include a search for skin lesions, eye irritation, or foot pain. A prior history of painful urination or eye pain suggests Reiter's syndrome. Marked decreases in forward flexion without significant pain suggests AS; extensor skin lesions suggest psoriatic arthritis. Radiographic discrimination is usually possible.

Management

SI sprains are best managed with an SI support (brace). Adjusting of the SI joint should be performed cautiously, avoiding increased stretch to the ligaments. Patients with SI subluxation usually have dramatic pain relief with manipulation.

PIRIFORMIS SYNDROME

Classic Presentation

The patient often complains of buttock and posterior leg pain with a nontraumatic onset.

Causes

The sciatic nerve may be compressed by the piriformis muscle. In most patients, the sciatic nerve runs under the muscle; however, in approximately 15% of the population, there are two muscle bellies with the sciatic nerve coursing between them.[80]

Evaluation

Either resisted external rotation of the hip or passive medial rotation of the hip may increase the pain. Some practitioners use an SLR test with internal rotation to distinguish between nerve root or piriformis involvement. This should be interpreted cautiously because nerve root irritation also may cause pain increase with this maneuver. Direct palpation of the piriformis may cause a referred pattern down the back of the leg. Predisposition to piriformis syndrome may be an anatomically short leg, pronation, or pelvic rotation.

Management

Postisometric relaxation techniques or myofascial release techniques are often helpful. In the acute stage, it may be necessary to use adjunctive physical therapy pain modalities. In rare cases, injection of the piriformis trigger point may be needed.

ANKYLOSING SPONDYLITIS

Classic Presentation

The patient is usually a young man presenting with a complaint of chronic low back pain and stiffness with occasional radiation of pain into the buttocks, anterior, or posterior thighs. The patient feels the stiffness upon rising and has some relief of complaints with mild to moderate activity.

Cause

AS is an inflammatory arthritis that usually affects the SI joints with progressive spinal ankylosing. It is characterized by enthesopathy (inflammation at the site of ligamentous insertions). It affects about 1% of whites, 0.25% of blacks. Men are affected three times more often than women. Women are less likely to have as severe disease. In general, the earlier the onset, the more progressive the disease. With progression there is gradual stiffening, loss of the lumbar lordosis, increase in the thoracic kyphosis, and decrease in chest expansion due to costotransverse joint involvement. Heart involvement may lead to arterioventricular conduction defects and aortic insufficiency in approximately 3% to 5% of patients with chronic, severe disease. Peripheral joint involvement occurs 50% of the time, with permanent changes occurring 25% of the time. The joints most affected are the hips, shoulders, and knees.

Evaluation

AS is suspected when a patient with chronic back pain and stiffness has a global decrease in ROM of the lumbopelvic area. This is best measured with an inclinometer (Figure 6–5, B and C) or with a tape measure using the Schober method (Figure 6–5A). Orthopaedic and neurologic testing is normal. Chest expansion may be decreased with chronic involvement. In approximately 15% to 20% of patients an anterior uveitis is found. Although lab testing will reveal elevations in erythrocyte sedimentation rate (ESR) in 85% of cases and HLA-B27 in 90% of cases (compared with 6% to 8% of asymptomatic individuals) and a negative rheumatoid factor, these tests are nonspecific and not diagnostic. AS is primarily a radiographic diagnosis.[81] Early changes are seen at the SI joint with "pseudowidening," erosions, and sclerosis. In the spine, early changes include marginal sclerosis and erosion of the superior/inferior margins of the vertebral bodies, causing a "squaring" appearance on a lateral view. Calcification of spinal ligaments and the annulus fibrosus creates a "trolley track" sign and eventual fusion with a characteristic bamboo spine appearance. Peripheral joint involvement causes a periosteal reaction at ligament/tendon insertion points of the iliac crest, Achilles, and plantar fascia insertion points.

Management

AS, like other rheumatoid and rheumatoid-variant diseases, has an unpredictable course of remission and relapses.[82] Management includes manipulation to keep the spine flexible, stretching, and postural and breathing exercises. Manipulation should be as gentle as possible considering the inflammatory nature of this disease. In the early stages, the calcification present on the radiograph represents a "soft" ankylosing that allows for some intersegmental movement. With severe progression, monitoring for cardiac and pulmonary involvement should be performed. It is important that patients avoid long-term use of pain medication if possible because of the gastric and renal consequences.

REITER'S SYNDROME

Classic Presentation

A young male patient presents with a complaint of LBP that began after the onset of urethritis (burning on urination), conjunctivitis (eye pain), and skin lesions on the soles or palms.

Cause

Reiter's is a seronegative (negative for rheumatoid factor) arthropathy that follows an infection. *Chlamydia, Campylobacter, Salmonella,* and *Yersinia* have all been implicated. It appears that the HLA-B27 marker may indicate those individuals prone to a reactive arthritis following bacterial infection.

Evaluation

The diagnostic tetrad includes (1) conjunctivitis that usually resolves in a day or two, (2) mucocutaneous lesions on the tongue, palate, and penis or plantar keratogenous lesions of the foot, (3) urethritis (often one of the first symptoms and often unresponsive to antibiotics), and (4) arthritis affecting the knees and ankles asymmetrically, but the SI joint is the most common symptomatic joint. Mechanical testing of the SI joint will usually increase pain. Laboratory testing may demonstrate increases in ESR and HLA-B27l, and negative for rheumatoid factor. Radiographic changes may be subtle at the SI joint in the early stages. Unilateral involvement with joint space narrowing, erosive changes, and eburnation of subchondral bone may be seen.

Management

Antibiotics are ineffective. Management is primarily symptomatic. It must be remembered that this is an inflammatory disease, and manipulation of the SI joint may aggravate the patient's symptoms. Most of the nonarticular complaints resolve over days or weeks.

Joint involvement may be progressive and permanent, however, especially in patients who have recurrent infection.

MULTIPLE MYELOMA

Classic Presentation

The patient is older (>50 years) and complains of persistent back pain that is unrelieved by rest. The pain seems worse at night. There may be associated rib pain.

Cause

Multiple myeloma (MM) is a malignant disease characterized by proliferation of plasma cells with replacement of bone marrow, which results in osteoporosis, hypercalcemia, anemia, renal disease, and infection (often pneumonia) due to suppression of normal immunoglobulins.

Evaluation

In older patients with unexplained LBP, laboratory and radiographic evaluation may reveal signs of MM. Laboratory findings include anemia with normal erythrocyte morphology but increased rouleau formation, hypercalcemia, hyperuricemia, and increased globulins. A 24-hour urine test may reveal the presence of Bence-Jones protein (light chain). Electrophoresis will reveal a monoclonal spiking; immunoelectrophoresis usually demonstrates elevated immunoglobulin G (IgG). The definitive diagnosis is a bone marrow aspirate showing more than 20% plasma cells. Radiographic findings demonstrate osteopenia followed by widespread lytic lesions in the spine, ribs, and skull (punched out or rat-bite lesions). Unlike metastasis to the spine, MM does not usually affect the posterior elements such as the pedicles.

Management

Treatment is primarily palliative. Chemotherapy or radiation therapy is used primarily to relieve bone pain. Bone marrow transplant is curative, but the patient must be under age 55 years and therefore few patients with MM qualify. The survival rate is variable; however, some degree of prediction is based on the degree of IgG spiking on immunoelectrophoresis, anemia, and hypercalcemia. In general, patients with IgG less than 5 g/dL and no evidence of anemia, renal disease, or lytic lesions have a survival rate of 5 to 6 years.[83]

METASTATIC CARCINOMA

Classic Presentation

The patient is usually over age 50 and complains of insidious onset of pain that is persistent, worse at night, and not mechanically affected. There is often a history of weight loss and fatigue. *Note:* the patient may remain asymptomatic until late in the course of the disease or may become symptomatic after trauma because of the pathologic weakness of the vertebrae.

Cause

Metastatic involvement of the spine accounts for only 1% of LBP. The most common metastases are from the breast, prostate, lung, and kidney. Prostate cancer spreads through Batson's plexus to the vertebrae. Metastasis from the above cancers may involve the vertebral bodies, pedicles, and, less commonly, the neural arches. The sequence of changes is usually replacement of fatty bone marrow with nonfatty tumor cells, followed by either destruction of the trabeculae with a periosteal response with a lytic metastasis is involved, or osteoblastic or sclerotic response such as with prostate cancer.

Evaluation

A history of prior cancer, unexplained weight loss, or unresponsiveness to conservative care for 1 month is highly suggestive of cancer, especially in patients older than 50 years of age. Radiographically, metastatic cancer may appear as an osteolytic process (such as the missing or one-eyed pedicle seen with breast cancer) or osteoblastic (such as the ivory vertebrae seen with prostate cancer). Compression fracture of the vertebrae with posterior collapse is highly suggestive of a cancer-induced pathologic fracture. Osteolytic processes may increase the serum calcium levels, whereas the osteoblastic process may increase the alkaline phosphatase levels. Determination of total and free prostate specific antigen (PSA) with a digital rectal exam should be performed in males suspected of prostate cancer. Bone scans may help determine the degree of spinal involvement with regard to location; the volume of involvement at any individual site can be determined by MRI.

Management

Referral to an oncologic consult is necessary. Comanagement issues can then be discussed.

INFECTIOUS SPONDYLITIS

Classic Presentation

Although there is no consistency regarding a typical patient and whether fever is present, the following is a presentation not to be missed: The patient presents with a complaint of deep back pain. There is a history of a recent respiratory or urinary tract infection (or intravenous drug use or diabetes). The patient is antalgic and complains of a fever and difficulty sleeping because of the pain.

Cause

Infection involving both the disc and the vertebral body is referred to as infectious spondylitis. This is more common in adults with a prior history of urinary tract infection, intravenous drug abuse, recent use of an indwelling catheter postsurgery, or skin infection. Children are more prone to discitis (usually benign) without vertebral body involvement. Infection is spread via the arterial system, Batson's venous plexus, and direct inoculation through surgery. There are generally two types: (1) pyogenic and (2) nonpyogenic. The pyogenic type is usually due to *Staphylococcus, Streptococcus,* and gram-negative organisms. The nonpyogenic type is usually due to tuberculosis; however, *Brucella* or fungi may be the cause.

Evaluation

Adults will usually have a deep pain made worse with pressure or percussion of the spinous process. Fever is often present. Although not particularly sensitive, it is relatively specific.[32] Radiographic indications often take 3 to 4 weeks to become evident. Pyogenic causes involve more than one vertebra, often leaving the disc unaffected. Bony lysis is followed by sclerosis in the vertebral bodies. Posterior elements are rarely affected. Nonpyogenic spondylitis centers around L1. Occasionally, the posterior elements are involved. Laboratory findings include an increase in ESR, and occasionally changes in leukocyte response.

Management

Refer for orthopaedic consultation and determination of course of care.

ABDOMINAL ANEURYSM

Classic Presentation

Most abdominal aneurysms are asymptomatic until rupture. The symptomatic patient may present with mild to severe middle abdominal or low back pain. There may be an associated complaint of leg pain with exertion (claudication).

Cause

Atherosclerotic aneurysms (weakening with dilation) occur primarily below the renal arteries (95% of the time). The incidence is between 2% and 4% with a 5:1 male predominance.

Evaluation

In asymptomatic patients the most common finding is a pulsatile mid- or upper abdominal mass. Auscultation may reveal a bruit. Peripheral pulses may be prominent (due to a reactive arteriomegaly). Lateral lumbar radiographs may reveal an enlarged calcific margin of the aorta, usually between L2 and L4. A diameter exceeding 3.8 cm is considered an aneurysm.[84] Other indirect findings may include erosion of the anterior vertebral bodies behind the aneurysm.

Management

Referral for abdominal ultrasonography is warranted to demonstrate the size and extent of involvement. Those patients with a documented 4- to 6-cm diameter should have a surgical consultation. If not excised and grafted, most aneurysms will go on to rupture. However, one study indicated that in patients 65 to 80 years old with aneurysms less than 6 cm, surgery was not necessary unless the aneurysm expanded more than 1 cm.[85] Patients with acute rupture usually have a searing/tearing pain warranting immediate emergency management. Patients whose aneurysm proceeds to rupture have only a 10% to 20% survival rate.[86]

REFERENCES

1. Papagerogiou AC, Croft PR, Ferry S, et al. Estimating the prevalence of low back pain in the general population: evidence from the South Manchester back pain survey. *Spine*. 1995;17:1889–1894.
2. Deyo RA, Tsui-Wu JY. Descriptive epidemiology of low back pain and its related medical care in the United States. *Spine*. 1987;12:264–268.
3. Schwarzer AC, Aprill CN, Derby R, et al. The prevalence and clinical features of internal disc disruption in patients with chronic low back pain. *Spine*. 1995;17:1878–1883.
4. Deyo RA, Rainville J, Kent DL. What can the history and physical examination tell us about low back pain? *JAMA*. 1992;268:760–765.
5. Deyo RA, Diehl AK. Cancer as a cause of back pain: frequency, clinical presentation, and diagnostic strategies. *J Gen Intern Med*. 1988;3:230–238.
6. Sapico FL, Montgomere JZ. Pyogenic vertebral osteomyelitis: report of nine cases and review of the literature. *Rev Infect Dis*. 1979;1:754–776.
7. Cassidy JD, Kirkaldy-Willis WH, McGregor M. Spinal manipulation for the treatment of chronic low back and leg pain: an observational trial. In: Buerger AA, Greenman PE, eds. *Empirical Approaches to the Validation of Manipulative Therapy*. Springfield, IL: Charles C Thomas; 1985.
8. Manga P, Angus D, Papadopoulos C, Swan W. *A Study to Examine the Effectiveness and Cost-Effectiveness of Chiropractic Management of Low-Back Pain*. Richmond Hill, Ontario: Kenilworth Publishing; 1993.
9. Cherkin D, MacCornack F. Patient evaluations of low back pain care from family physicians and chiropractors. *West J Med*. 1989;150:151.
10. Shekelle PG, Adams AH, Chassin MR, Hurwitz EL, et al. *The Appropriateness of Spinal Manipulation for Low-Back Pain: Project Overview and Literature Review*. Santa Monica, CA: Rand Publications; 1991.

11. Meade TW, Dyer S, Browne W, Townsend J, Frank AO. Low back pain of mechanical origin: randomised comparison of chiropractic and hospital outpatient treatment. *Br Med J.* 1990;300:1431–1437.
12. Bozzao A, Gallucci M, et al. Lumbar disk herniation: MR imaging assessment of natural history in patients treated without surgery. *Neuroradiology.* 1992;185:135–141.
13. Kirkaldy-Willis WH. *Managing Low Back Pain.* New York: Churchill-Livingstone; 1983.
14. McCarron RF, Wimpee MW, Hudkins PG, Laros GS. The inflammatory effect of nucleus pulposus: a possible element in the pathogenesis of low back pain. *Spine.* 1987;8:760–764.
15. Bozzao A, Gallucci M. Lumbar disk herniation: MR imaging assessment of natural history in patients treated without surgery. *Neuroradiology.* 1992;185:135–141.
16. d'Ornano J, Conrozier T, et al. Effects des manipulations vertebrales sur la hernie discale lombaire. *Rev Med Orthop.* 1990;19:21–25.
17. Giles LGF. *Anatomical Basis of Low Back Pain.* Baltimore: Williams & Wilkins; 1989:60–97.
18. Adams MA, Hutton WC. The mechanical function of the lumbar apophyseal joints. *Spine.* 1983;8:327.
19. Giles LGF, Taylor JR. Innervation of lumbar zygapophyseal joint synovial folds. *Acta Orthop Scand.* 1987;58:43–46.
20. Schwarzer AC, Wang S, Bogduk N, McNaught PJ, Laurant R. The prevalence and clinical features of lumbar zygapophyseal joint pain: a study in an Australian population with chronic low back pain. *Ann Rheum Dis.* 1995;211:356.
21. Bogduk N, Engel R. The menisci of the lumbar zygapophyseal joints: a review of their anatomy and clinical significance. *Spine.* 1984;9:454–450.
22. Bogduk N, Twomey LT. *Clinical Anatomy of the Lumbar Spine.* 2nd ed. Melbourne, Australia: Churchill-Livingstone; 1991.
23. Pope MH, Wilder DG, Materri RE, Frymoyer JW. Experimental measurements of vertebral motion under load. *Orthop Clin North Am.* 1977;155:167.
24. Panjabi M, Yamamoto I, Oxland T, Crisco J. How does posture affect coupling in the lumbar spine? *Spine.* 1988;14:1001–1011.
25. Parmianpour M, Nordin M, Frankel V, Kahanovitz N. The triaxial coupling of torque generation of trunk muscles during isometric exertions and the effect of fatiguing isoinertial movements on the motor ouptut and movement patterns. Transaction of the Annual Meeting of the International Society for Study of the Lumbar Spine. Miami, FL; 1988:34.
26. Adams MA, Hutton WC. Prolapsed intervertebral disc: a hyperflexion injury. *Spine.* 1982;7:184–191.
27. Adams MA, Hutton WC. Gradual disc prolapse. *Spine.* 1985;10: 524–531.
28. Slosberg M. Side posture manipulation for lumbar intervertebral disk herniation reconsidered. *J Manipulative Physiol Ther.* 1994;17:258–262.
29. Bellamy N, Park W, Rooney PJ. What do we know about the sacroiliac joint? *Semin Arthritis Rheum.* 1983;12:282–307.
30. Williams PL, Warwick R, eds. *Gray's Anatomy.* 36th ed. London: Churchill-Livingstone; 1980:473.
31. Sturesson B, Selvik G, Uden A. Movements of the sacroiliac joints: a roentgen stereophotogrammetric analysis. *Spine.* 1989;14:162–165.
32. Deyo RA. Early detection of cancer, infection, and inflammatory disease of the spine. *J Back Musculoskel Rehabil.* 1991;1:69–81.
33. Waidvogel FA, Vasey H. Osteomyelitis: the past decade. *N Engl J Med.* 1980;303:360–370.
34. Calin A, Porta J, Fries JF, Schurman DJ. Clinical history as a screening test for ankylosing spondylitis. *Clin Rheumatol.* 1985;4: 161–169.
35. Deyo RA. Measuring the functional status of patients with low back pain. *Arch Phys Med Rehabil.* 1988;69:1044–1053.
36. Anderson R, Meeker WC. A meta-analysis of clinical trials of spinal manipulation. *J Manipulative Physiol Ther.* 1992;15:181–194.
37. Hsieh CJ, Philips RB, et al. Functional outcomes of low back pain: comparison of four treatment groups in a randomized controlled trial. *J Manipulative Physiol Ther.* 1992;15:4–9.
38. Fairbanks J, Davies J. The Oswestry low back pain disability questionnaire. *Physiotherapy.* 1980;66:271.
39. Roland M, Morris R. Study of natural history of back pain, I: development of reliable and sensitive measure of disability in low back pain. *Spine.* 1983;8:141.
40. Kelsey JL, Golden AL, Mundt DJ. Low back pain/prolapsed lumbar intervertebral disc. *Rheum Dis Clin North Am.* 1990;16:669–712.
41. Kortelainen P, Puranen J, Koivisto E, Larde S. Symptoms and signs of sciatica and their relation to the localization of the lumbar disc herniation. *Spine.* 1985;10:88–92.
42. McCombe PF, Fairbank JCT, Cockersole BC, Pynsent PB. Reproducibility of physical signs in low back pain. *Spine.* 1989;14:908–918.
43. Urban LM. The straight-leg raising test: a review. *J Orthop Sports Phys Ther.* 1981;2:117–133.
44. Kosteljanetz M, Flemming B, Schmidt-Olsen S. The clinical significance of straight leg raising in the diagnosis of prolapsed lumbar disc. *Spine.* 1988;13:393–395.
45. Beattie P. Validity of derived measurements of leg length differences obtained by the use of a tape measure. *Phys Ther.* 1990;70: 150–157.
46. Mann M, Glasheen-Wray M, Nyberg R. Therapist agreement for palpation and observation of iliac crest heights. *Phys Ther.* 1984;3:334–338.
47. Haas M. The reliability of reliability. *J Manipulative Physiol Ther.* 1991;14:199–208.
48. Boline PD, et al. Interexaminer reliability of palpatory evaluations of the lumbar spine. *Am J Chirop Med.* 1988;1:5–11.
49. Mootz RD. Intra- and interexaminer reliability of passive motion palpation of the lumbar spine. *J Manipulative Physiol Ther.* 1989;12:440–447.
50. Souza TA. Which orthopedic tests are really necessary? In: Lawrence DJ, Cassidy JD, McGregor M, et al., eds. *Advances in Chiropractic.* St. Louis, MO: Mosby-Year Book; 1994;1:101–158.
51. McKenzie R. *The Lumbar Spine: Mechanical Diagnosis and Therapy.* Waikanae, New Zealand: Spinal Publications; 1981.
52. Lewit K. Manipulation and rehabilitation. In: Liebenson C, ed. *Rehabilitation of the Spine: A Practitioner's Manual.* Baltimore: Williams & Wilkins; 1995.
53. Janda V. Evaluation of muscular imbalance. In: Liebenson C, ed. *Rehabilitation of the Spine: A Practitioner's Manual.* Baltimore: Williams & Wilkins; 1995.
54. Lewit K. *Manipulative Therapy in Rehabilitation of the Locomotor System.* 2nd ed. Oxford, England: Butterworth-Heinemann; 1991.
55. Potter NA, Rothstein JM. Intertester reliability for selected clinical tests for the sacroiliac joint. *Phys Ther.* 1985;65:1671–1675.
56. Herzog W, Read LJ, Conway JW, et al. Reliability of motion palpation procedures to detect sacroiliac joint fixations. *J Manipulative Physiol Ther.* 1989;12:86–92.

57. Mior SA, McGregor M, Schut B. The role of experience in clinical accuracy. *J Manipulative Physiol Ther*. 1990;13(2):68–71.

58. Waddell G, McCulloch JA, Kummel E, Venner RM. Nonorganic physical signs in low-back pain. *Spine*. 1980;5:117–125.

59. Fishbaine DA, Goldberg M, Rosomoff RS, Rosomoff H. Chronic pain patients and the nonorganic physical signs of nondermatomal sensory abnormalities (NDSA). *Psychosomatics*. 1991;32:294–302.

60. Weinstein JN, McLain F. Primary tumors of the spine. *Spine*. 1987;12:843–851.

61. Dailey EJ, Beuler MT. Plain film assessment of spinal stenosis: method comparison with lumbar CT. *J Manipulative Physiol Ther*. 1989;12:192–199.

62. Ulrich CG, Binet EF, Sanecki MG, et al. Quantitative assessment of the lumbar spinal canal by computed tomography. *Radiology*. 1980;134:137–143.

63. Nachemson AL. The lumbar spine: an orthopedic challenge. *Spine*. 1976;1:59–71.

64. Hildebrandt RW. Chiropractic spinography and postural roentgenology, I: *J Manipulative Physiol Ther*. 1980;3:87–92.

65. Haldeman S, Chapman-Smith D, Petersen, Jr., DM. *Guidelines for Chiropractic Quality Assurance and Practice Parameters: Proceedings of the Mercy Center Consensus Conference*. Gaithersburg, MD: Aspen Publishers Inc; 1993.

66. Hansen D. Determining how much care to give and reporting patient progress. *Top Clin Chirop*. 1994;1(4):1–8.

67. Cassidy JD, Thiel HW, Kirkaldy-Willis WH. Side posture manipulation for lumbar disc herniation. *J Manipulative Physiol Ther*. 1993;16:96–103.

68. Schmidt K, Ekholm J, Harris-Ringadahl K, et al. Effects of changes in sitting work posture on static neck and shoulder muscle activity. *Ergonomics*. 1986;29:1525.

69. Grandjean E. *Fitting the Task to the Man*. 4th ed. London: Taylor and Frances; 1988.

70. Kuslich SD, Ulstrom CL, Michael CJ. The tissue origin of low back pain and sciatica: a report of pain response to tissue stimulation during operation on the lumbar spine using local anesthesia. *Orthop Clin North Am*. 1991;22:181–187.

71. Giles LGF. Pathoanatomical studies and clinical significance of lumbar zygapophyseal (facet) joints. *J Manipulative Physiol Ther*. 1992;15:36–40.

72. Turner JA, Ersek M, Herron L, Deyo R. Surgery for lumbar spinal stenosis: attempted meta-analysis of the literature. *Spine*. 1992;17:1–8.

73. Stolov WC, Slimp JC. Dermatomal somatosensory evoked potentials in lumbar spinal stenosis. American Association of Electromyography and Electrodiagnosis and American Electroencephalography Society Joint Symposium, San Diego, CA; 1988:17–22.

74. Johnsson KE, Uden A, Rosen I. The effect of compression on the natural course of spinal stenosis: a comparison of surgically treated and untreated patients. *Spine*. 1991;16:615–619.

75. McKee BM, Alexander WJ, Dunbar JS. Spondylolysis and spondylolisthesis in children: a review. *J Can Assoc Radiol*. 1971;22:100.

76. Fredrickson BE, Baker D, McKollick WJ, et al. The natural history of spondylolysis and spondylolisthesis. *J Bone Joint Surg Am*. 1984;66:699.

77. Cassidy JD, Porter GE, Kirkaldy-Willis WH. Manipulative management of back pain patients with spondylolisthesis. *J Can Chirop Assoc*. 1978;22:15.

78. Kirkaldy-Willis WH, Cassidy JD. Spinal manipulation in the treatment of low back pain. *Can Fam Physician*. 1985;31:535–540.

79. Hendler N, Kozikowski JG, Morrison C, Sethuraman G. Diagnosis and management of sacroiliac joint disease. *J Neuromusc Syst*. 1995;3:169–174.

80. Pace JB, Nagel D. Piriformis syndrome. *West J Med*. 1976;124:435–439.

81. Yochum TR, Rowe LJ. *Essentials of Skeletal Radiology*. 3rd ed. Baltimore: Williams & Wilkins; 1996;2:877–892.

82. Kennedy LG, Edmonds L, Calin A. The natural history of ankylosing spondylitis: does it burn out? *J Rheumatol*. 1993;20:688.

83. Mandelli F, Avvisati G, Tribalto M. Biology and treatment of multiple myeloma. *Curr Opin Oncol*. 1992;4:73.

84. LaRoy LL, Cormier PJ, Matalon TAS, et al. Imaging of abdominal aortic aneurisms. *AJR*. 1989;152:785.

85. Scott RA. Is surgery necessary for abdominal aortic aneurysm less than 6 cm diameter? *Lancet*. 1993;342:1395.

86. Ernst CB. Abdominal aortic aneurysms. *N Engl J Med*. 1993;328:1167.

Chapter 7

Shoulder Girdle Complaints

CONTEXT

The shoulder provides a unique challenge to the chiropractor. The shoulder's dependency on an integrated, position-dependent system of ligaments, muscles, and tendons for stability, coupled with the need for coordinated interaction of a number of joints, makes it a complex region to assess. When a single-event trauma occurs, soft tissue or bony damage is usually discovered by challenge on physical examination and/or radiographs. When trauma is not evident, however, it often becomes difficult to isolate a specific structure or cause. Many shoulder problems are, in fact, multidimensional. In other words, a patient with instability may develop an impingement phenomenon, or a patient with tendinitis or restricted mobility may overload the compensatory capacity of other structures, leading to further soft tissue involvement.

The unique design of the shoulder provides a great degree of mobility; however, as a result it cannot provide substantial stability, especially at higher levels of elevation and/or extreme abduction. Therefore, local shoulder pain that occurs with these extremes of position are due to excessive demands on the stabilizing function of the muscles, ligaments, and capsule of the shoulder. Additionally, mechanical or structural predisposition may narrow the channel through which some tendons travel, resulting in an impingement phenomenon. These structures are rarely challenged in individuals whose work or play requires only minimal elevation. Shoulder complaints are common in sports such as weight lifting, swimming, and throwing, or in an occupational setting requiring overhead work. In that context, injury, when not due to a single trauma, is often due to repetitive activity or overuse. These problems can often be linked to specific positional demands. Finally, the shoulder may be the site of injury when a fall onto an extended arm transforms the shoulder into a weight-bearing joint. Fracture, dislocation, tendon, or labrum damage must be considered.

The shoulder may be the site of pain originating or caused by a variety of sources, including the following:

- referred pain from a variety of musculoskeletal sites such as cervical or thoracic spine facet joints or trigger points
- referred pain from visceral sources such as the diaphragm, gallbladder, lungs, or heart
- radicular pain from cervical nerve root compression
- peripheral nerve and brachial plexus entrapments
- local causes of pain:
  1. trauma (ie, fracture, dislocation, tendon rupture)
  2. overuse (ie, tendinitis, capsular sprain, bursitis)
  3. arthritide (ie, osteoarthritis, rheumatoid arthritis, and rheumatoid variants)
  4. other (ie, tumor or infection)

Although the above list may seem overwhelming, the primary causes of shoulder complaints generally fall into several categories with some overlap, including the following:

- instability (traumatic or nontraumatic)
- impingement syndrome (anteromedial [subcoracoid]—subscapularis; anterolateral [subacromial]—biceps, supraspinatus, and subacromial bursa; posterolateral—infraspinatus/teres minor)
- tendinitis/bursitis
- adhesive capsulitis
- acromioclavicular (AC) separations
- referred pain from the cervical spine

In the context of the chiropractic office setting, a common complaint is neck and shoulder/arm pain. With this presentation it is important to differentiate between neural referral or radiculopathy. This requires a search for objective neurologic deficits. When not present, a mechanical or referral association is more likely. When the shoulder is part of a neck and arm complaint it is also important to consider brachial plexus involvement through overstretch (stinger) or compression (thoracic outlet syndrome) and a double-crush phenomenon.

Like all joints, the shoulder is susceptible to traumatic sequelae such as fracture, dislocation, and ligament or tendon rupture. When these are suspected, a thorough radiographic and orthopaedic evaluation are necessary. If fracture or ligament/tendon rupture is found, an orthopaedic consultation is necessary. For most other conditions a conservative approach for at least 6 months is now recommended by most practitioners.[1]

In the elderly population, the accumulation of years of wear and tear leads to an end-stage of chronic irritation that results in osteoarthritis that may cycle into an impingement phenomenon. The other common problem in the senior population is stiffening of the shoulder, often due to adhesive capsulitis. Differentiating between the effects of osteoarthritis and adhesive capsulitis is an important element in approaching the stiffened senior shoulder.

Trauma, including surgery, may predispose the shoulder to early degenerative changes. Osteoarthritis may be more common than previously recognized.[2] Although it is not always evident radiographically, histologically, and clinically osteoarthritis should be considered in the senior or posttraumatic patient. Arthritides that commonly affect the shoulder are ankylosing spondylitis and rheumatoid arthritis. Advanced rheumatoid arthritis often leads to rupture of the supraspinatus tendon. The shoulder may be a site of infection, although infrequently.

GENERAL STRATEGY

History

- Determine whether the patient's complaint is one of pain, stiffness, instability, weakness, numbness, or tingling.
- Localize the complaint to anterior, posterior, lateral, or superior.
- Determine whether there was a traumatic onset; if so, determine the mechanism and the need for immediate radiographic assessment before proceeding (possible fracture or dislocation).
- Determine any relationship to activity, with focus on position, degree of restriction, and amount of repetition (overhead position suggests possible impingement).
- If stiffness is the complaint, determine whether there was a past injury; for specific ranges of restriction determine whether there was an antecedent period of moderate to severe pain that has gradually been replaced by stiffness (suggests adhesive capsulitis).
- If weakness is the complaint, determine whether this is painless (suggests instability) or painful (inhibitory effect).
- If instability is supected, determine whether the patient has a history suggestive of damaged structures (ie, anterior dislocation) or if the patient has a bilateral, multidirectional looseness indicative of generalized capsular laxity (nontraumatic).
- Determine the degree of functional impairment within the context of patient usage. Is the patient a high-end user, such as an athlete, or a low-end user such as a sedentary office worker?

Evaluation

- Perform a focus-based examination; however, begin with an evaluation of stability, since instability may be the cause of or contributor to other problems.
- Use findings to determine the need for further evaluation with regard to radiographic or special imaging, referral to a specialist, or initial management.

Management

- Dislocations should be relocated, preferably by an experienced individual; postreduction, radiographs should be taken to determine whether an associated fracture is evident; rehabilitation of the shoulder is important to avoid recurrence.
- Infections, fractures, and tumors should be referred for orthopaedic consultation. Also, if the patient is in so much pain that it is interfering with the ability to sleep and is unaffected by over-the-counter medications, referral for prescribed pain medication should be made.
- All other shoulder disorders should be managed for 6 months with conservative approaches; if unresolved, consideration for special imaging should be given.

RELEVANT ANATOMY AND BIOMECHANICS

The shoulder has the advantage of extreme mobility for the purpose of placing the upper limb in an almost infinite number of positions. For this mobility, a price is paid. From a bony support perspective, the shoulder is essentially unstable. As a result, the demand for constant integrated function is high for soft tissue structures delegated the job of providing that stability. This instability becomes even more evident at higher degrees of shoulder elevation, making unusually high demands on coordinated muscular function.

Damage to any of these soft tissue stabilizers results in increasing demands on the residual support structures. Add to this a repetitive demand from a sport or occupational perspective and the shoulder's ability to cope may be compromised (or overextended).

Depending on arm position and underlying pathologic processes, different aspects of the general capsular system are called into play. With the arm at the side, much of the support is ligamentous (superior glenohumeral ligament), with some contributions from a precarious glenoid ledge. Any relative abduction will cause an increased capsular and muscular contribution. A reciprocal contribution is most evident in the capsular structures, where stress is sequentially shared by the various capsular ligaments. With the arm at rest, the superior capsule contributes most. As the arm is elevated, the support management is shifted to the inferior capsular complex. This reciprocity also occurs with rotation. With the arm elevated, a hammocklike inferior capsule protects against inferior stress as well as anterior or posterior stress. This is accomplished by the broad aspect of the capsule's being rotated in front of the humeral head with external rotation with the cordlike aspect relaxed posteriorly. The opposite occurs with posterior support, being provided with internal rotation, again with an anterior-inferior support rotated into place. Another aspect of capsular control of movement is through a tension-dependent role in accessory movement of the humeral head. It has recently been found that capsular tightness contributes to an obligatory translation in the opposite direction of tension.[3] For example, in a normally functioning shoulder, the position of abduction with external rotation causes tension on the anterior capsule. In turn, this causes a posterior translation of the humeral head by approximately 4 mm.[4] This is also true with abduction, where tension in the inferior capsule and pull from the deltoid/supraspinatus couple cause a superior migration of the humeral head of approximately 3 to 6 mm. More is discussed under relevant clinical scenarios.

Additional support is provided passively by the fit of the humeral head into the glenoid. This is affected by the contact area, angle of the glenoid, and degree of adhesion or lack thereof. Active support is provided directly through the capsular integration of rotator cuff attachment. Indirectly, movement of the scapula provides a stable platform upon which the humeral head can function at higher elevations. This is accomplished by an exquisite cooperation between the rotator cuff and the scapular muscles. A major player in this interaction is the serratus anterior muscle.

The shoulder is part of a complex of joints that function together to provide smooth movement of the upper extremity. This complex is composed of the sternoclavicular joint, the AC joint, the glenohumeral joint, and also the pseudojoint of the scapulothoracic articulation. Through a series of levers and supports, the shoulder is allowed to function in many planes. The contribution of muscles may be categorized on the basis of several roles. First are the protectors. These are the inherently smaller rotator cuff muscles that act to compress the humeral head into the glenoid. Secondly are the pivoters. These are the scapular muscles that serve to pivot the scapula under the humeral head for proper muscle/tendon alignment and tension. Next are the positioners. These act to position the shoulder in varying degrees of elevation. This is part of the job of the rotator cuff, with the major role being played by the deltoid complex. For purposes of strength or propulsion, there are the propellers. These are the much larger adductor/internal rotator muscles consisting mainly of the pectoralis and latissimus dorsi muscles.[5] The natural imbalance between the stronger internal rotators/adductors and weaker external rotators/abductors is often made worse by occupational posture and overdevelopment.

The subscapularis, pectoralis, teres major, and latissimus dorsi are internal rotators (Figure 7–1). The external rotators include the infraspinatus, teres minor, and posterior deltoid. The abductors include the supraspinatus and deltoid group (Figure 7–2). Adduction is a large muscle movement accomplished by the pectoralis and latissimus dorsi. As stated previously, however, the rotator cuff musculature, in addition to a dynamic movement role, also serves to stabilize the shoulder. The need for this stabilization increases with arm elevation.

One of the more important anatomic or structural concepts with regard to efficient shoulder function has to do with the plane of the scapula. It is evident that the glenoid of the scapula does not face directly out. It faces between 30° and 45° forward because of the curved fit of the scapula on the bony thorax. The result is that more efficient muscle tension relationships exist in this plane.[6] This is often apparent in the patient with a painful shoulder who unconsciously selects this scapular plane as his or her elevation plane of choice.

EVALUATION

History

Careful questioning may point to the diagnosis (Table 7–1).

Pain Localization

The following are possible causes of pain based on localization (see Table 7–2 and Figure 7–3, A to C):

- anterior
  1. traumatic—fracture, dislocation, subacromial bursitis, capsular sprain, rupture of long head of biceps, labrum tear

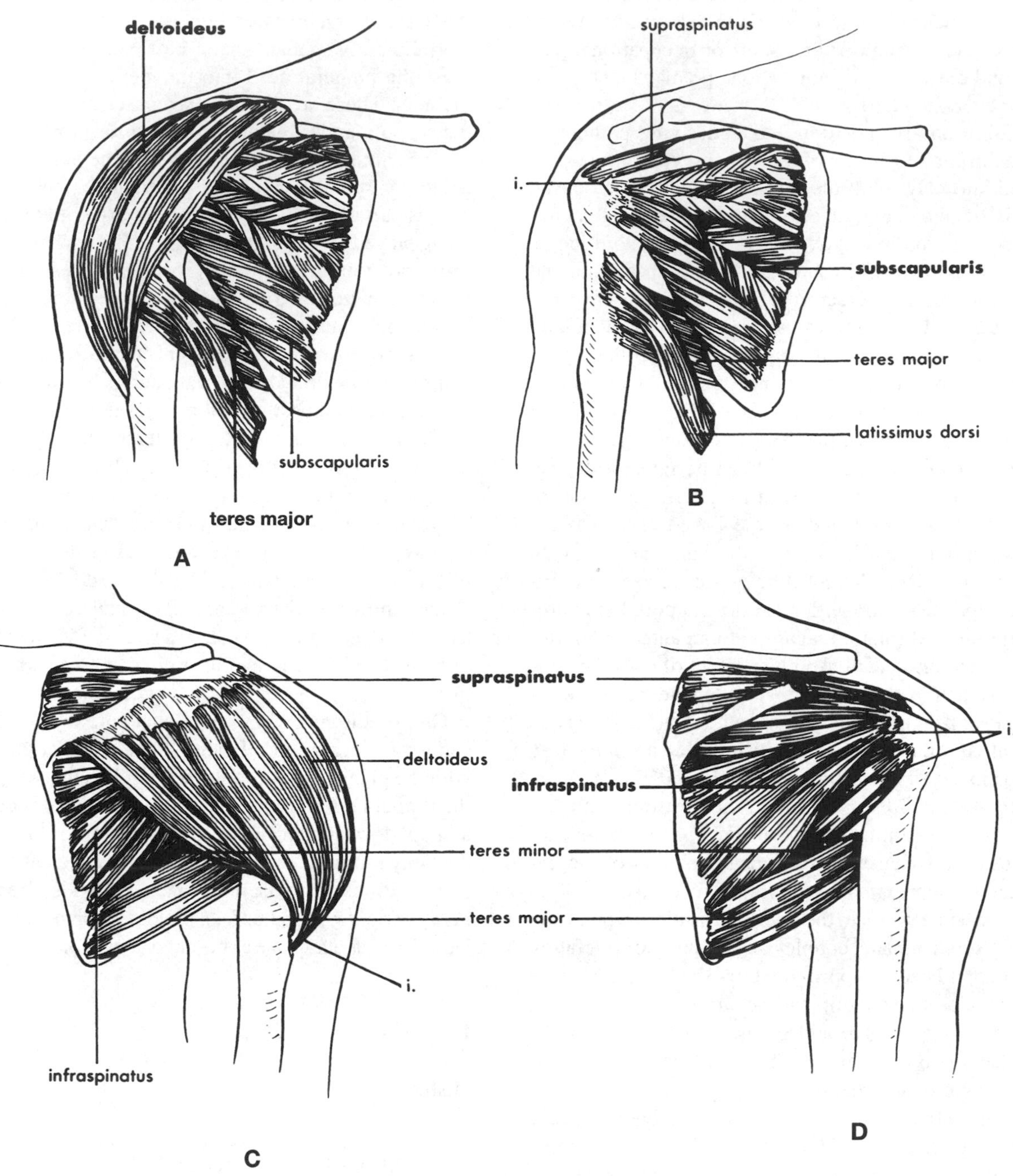

Figure 7–1 Muscles connecting shoulder girdle and arm. **A** and **B**, Anterior aspects; **C** and **D**, posterior aspects. *Source:* Reprinted with permission from J.E. Crouch, *Functional Human Anatomy*, 4th ed., p. 226, © 1985, Lea & Febiger.

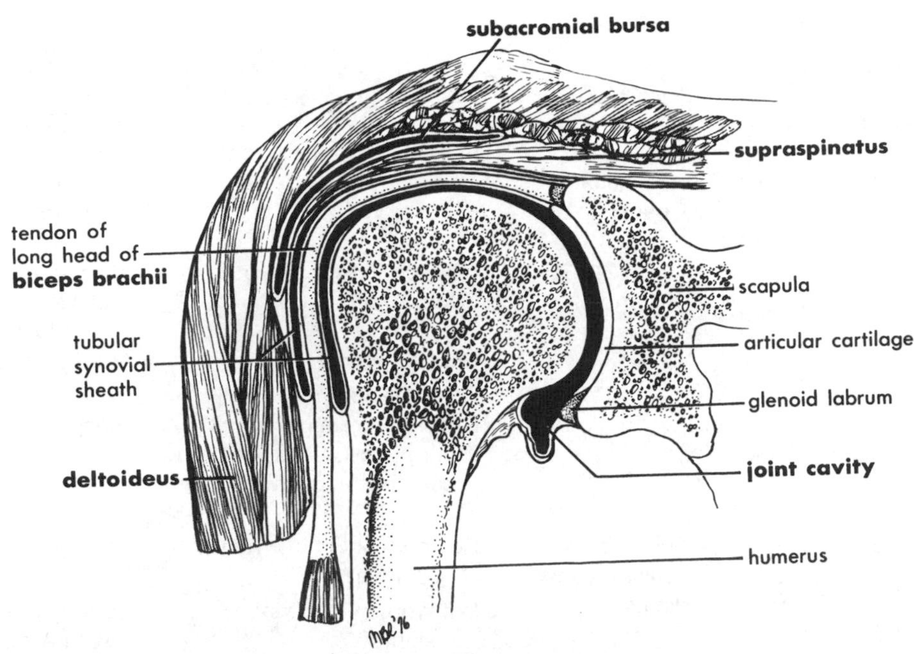

Figure 7–2 Schematic drawing of a section through shoulder joint to show joint cavity and bursa. *Source:* Reprinted with permission from J.E. Crouch, *Functional Human Anatomy*, 4th ed., p. 227, © 1985, Lea & Febiger.

2. nontraumatic or overuse—general impingement syndrome, subcoracoid impingement, biceps tendinitis, subacromial bursitis, subscapularis tendinitis, subluxation

- lateral
  1. traumatic—contusion, supraspinatus rupture, referral from cervical spine or brachial plexus injury
  2. nontraumatic or overuse—impingement syndrome, deltoid strain, supraspinatus tear or rupture, referral from cervical spine problem
- superior
  1. traumatic—AC separation, distal clavicular fracture, shoulder pointer
  2. nontraumatic or overuse—osteoarthritis of the AC joint, osteolysis of the distal clavicle
- posterior
  1. traumatic—scapular fracture, posterior dislocation
  2. nontraumatic or overuse—posterior impingement, infraspinatus or teres minor strain or tendinitis, posterior deltoid strain, triceps strain, suprascapular nerve entrapment

Traumatic and Overuse Injuries

With trauma, there are usually clear indicators of dislocation or separation. Fracture, too, may be implicated by the mechanism, magnitude of forces, and degree of pain. Common injury patterns for the shoulder include the following:

- blow to the anterior shoulder—dislocation, contusion
- fall onto top of shoulder—AC separation, distal clavicular fracture, shoulder pointer
- fall on an outstretched arm (landing on hand with elbow extended)—AC separation, clavicular fracture, posterior dislocation, glenoid labrum or rotator cuff tear
- arm forced into external rotation and horizontal abduction with shoulder flexed to 90° or above—anterior dislocation, glenoid labrum tear
- sudden traction to the arm—medical subluxation or brachial plexus traction injury
- sudden pain with weight lifting (no apparent dislocation)—consider muscle/tendon rupture, labrum tear

With frank trauma excluded, the most fruitful approach is first to distinguish the patient's complaint. Have the patient categorize his or her complaint into mainly pain, stiffness, instability, weakness, or numbness and/or tingling. Ascertain whether there are associated cervical or thoracic spine complaints. Although they are rare, determine whether there are any visceral complaints, in particular, right upper quadrant pain suggestive of biliary disease.

Table 7–1 History Questions for Shoulder Complaints

Primary Question	*What Are You Thinking?*	*Secondary Questions*	*What Are You Thinking?*
Was there trauma (Did you hurt your shoulder in an accident)?	Rule out fracture, subluxation, dislocation, separation, capsular or muscle tearing	Fall on an outstretched arm?	Clavicular fracture, posterior dislocation, supraspinatus, biceps, or labrum tear
		Land on the top of your shoulder?	AC separation, distal clavicular fracture, shoulder pointer
		Did you have your arm up and pulled back?	Anterior dislocation
		Does your arm get stuck in certain positions that you can click back in place?	Glenoid labrum tear
Do you perform repetitive activities with your shoulder?	Impingement syndrome, capsular sprain, muscle strain, tendinitis	Do you work in overhead positions?	Impingement syndrome
		Is it worse with lifting weights?	Osteolysis of distal clavicle with AC pain; labrum tear if mechanically locks or gives-out, and muscle strain
Is there any associated neck pain?	Cervical spondylosis, disc lesion, referred facet pain	Trauma to the neck?	Whiplash, and the "lateral whiplash" of a cervical burner
		Are the pains connected?	C5–C6 areas most commonly affected
Are there other problems that seemed to occur at the same time as your shoulder pain?	Arthritides, connective tissue disease, visceral referred pain	Any gastrointestinal symptoms (abdominal pain etc.)?	Gallbladder
		Any associated chest pain?	Cardiac referral
Is the complaint more of stiffness?	Adhesive capsulitis, subluxation, unrecognized posterior dislocation, arthritides	Past history of trauma?	Posterior directed force may have caused an unreduced posterior dislocation
		Did the stiffness get worse after a few weeks of pain?	Adhesive capsulitis
Is there a sense of weakness or instability?	Capsular instability, glenoid labrum tear, neurologic weakness	Past history of trauma?	Capsular, rotator cuff, or labrum damage
		Does it feel weak with your arm elevated?	Capsular looseness or damage
Have you ever been diagnosed with any kind of arthritis in the past?	Osteoarthritis uncommon unless previous surgery/trauma; RA, AS, pseudogout and others should be considered	Do you have other joint pains?	Finger joint pain might suggest RA, spine/S1 pain may suggest AS; knee/wrist pain may suggest pseudogout

When pain is the chief complaint, it is important to determine whether it is chronic or acute. An attempt to define a positional relationship is important. For example, patients who feel most of their pain while working in overhead positions may have an impingement problem. Patients who find it difficult to throw a ball or otherwise attain the cocking position of abduction/external rotation often will have instability. With chronic and insidious cases, it is important to determine the extent to which overuse or misuse is a culprit.

Weakness

A sense of weakness or instability may be an isolated or associated complaint. It is important to discover past traumas, in particular dislocations or medical subluxations. Frequently, if not rehabilitated, a progressive looseness of the capsule develops. This may lead to concomitant damage to the labrum, resulting in a downward spiral. If there is no past trauma or surgery, consider the possibility of an inherent looseness, which is likely a bilateral phenomenon. This is best determined with orthopaedic testing for instability.

Restricted Movement

With a complaint of stiffness, it is important to determine the sequence of events leading to the sense of restriction. For example, a patient complaining of an acute, unprovoked episode of incapacitating shoulder pain that lasted for weeks before resolving into stiffness is likely to have adhesive capsulitis. A patient with a past traumatic history (especially a posteriorly directed force to the humerus) must be suspected of having a posterior dislocation. Those with a general history of trauma or surgery might be expected to develop an early onset of osteoarthritic changes. In those with coexisting arthritides the shoulder may be a secondary area of involvement; the most common arthritides are rheumatoid arthritis and ankylosing spondylitis. All of these events are likely to cause stiffness in many planes. A single plane of stiffness must be qualified. Restriction due to pain and weakness is likely caused by a mechanical block resulting from bone or labrum pathology. If there is overuse or trauma to muscle, subsequent scarring may lead to an obvious restriction in the direction of stretch.

Other Complaints

Atrophy or deformity is sometimes the primary concern of patients. Atrophy of the infraspinatus is evident by a depression over the scapula. This is most often due to suprascapular nerve damage, not uncommon in overhead sports—in particular volleyball. If the patient complains of a mass in the distal arm, rupture of the long head of the biceps should be considered. The patient often will report an injury during which a pop was heard. Another cause of a mass in the arm is myositis ossificans. The patient will report having been struck on the arm, with subsequent swelling that never resolved. Radiographs will reveal the calcified muscle mass. Deformity at the top of the shoulder is often due to the instability of an AC separation or a distal clavicular fracture when trauma is reported. Without trauma and in an older individual, osteoarthritis of the AC joint is likely.

Examination

An examination of the shoulder can be problem (diagnosis) focused on generic. If the intent of the examination is to reproduce a diagnostic impression leading to further evaluation such as radiographs or special imaging, then a diagnosis-focused examination may be appropriate. This is more likely in the acute setting. With a chronic problem, two aspects of the examination become important, one being the diagnostic impression and the other being a comprehensive evaluation of the patient's biomechanical status. In other words, what are the limitations in active, active-resistive, and passive ranges of motion? How is the scapula participating in this motion? If the patient has signs of impingement, is there any underlying instability or looseness? The generic approach is best when multiple factors are suggested.

With an acute injury, mechanism of injury coupled with observation of patient positioning and shoulder contour often suggest an underlying cause:

- If the patient either was injured by a direct blow to the shoulder or was suddenly overstretched into a position of external rotation/abduction or extension, anterior dislocation is likely; significant pain causes the patient to hold the arm in slight abduction and external rotation; associated observational findings are a visibly flat deltoid, prominent humeral head anteriorly, and a prominent acromion with a posterior depression underneath.
- If the patient fell on an outstretched arm or any mechanism of posterior force was applied to a flexed arm, a posterior dislocation is likely; the patient holds the arm slightly adducted and internally rotated (sling position); a prominent coracoid with anterior shoulder flattening are associated observational signs best seen from a bird's-eye view (looking down at the shoulder of a seated patient).

Palpation of the shoulder may be revealing for many common shoulder complaints. Tenderness and deformity at the AC joint is often secondary to trauma and may represent a second- or third-degree separation or distal clavicular fracture. If there is no deformity, consider a shoulder pointer (contusion of the local muscles) or a first-degree separation of the AC joint. If there is no trauma but there is deformity,

Table 7–2 Shoulder Pain Localization

#	*Structures*	*Overt Trauma*	*Insidious or Overuse*
1	Acromioclavicular (AC) joint	AC separation, shoulder pointer, distal clavicular fracture	Osteoarthritis of AC joint, osteolysis of the distal clavicle
2	Deltopectoral triangle	Subscapularis rupture	Subscapularis tendinitis, capsulitis
3	Clavicle	Clavicular fracture	Pectoralis clavicular strain
4	Coracoid process	Coracoid fracture or bursitis	Pectoralis minor tendinitis
5	Biceps tendon	Biceps tendinitis	Biceps tendinitis
6	Pectoralis major	Pectoralis major rupture	Pectoralis major strain
7	Deltoid insertion (deltoid tubercle)	Bruise or slightly below possibility of hematoma and myositis ossificans	Common referral area for many shoulder conditions and C5 nerve root or facet irritation, deltoid strain
8	Supraspinatus insertion, subacromial bursa	Supraspinatus rupture	Impingement syndrome, bursitis, supraspinatus tendinitis
9	Infraspinatus/teres minor tendons and insertion	Contusion	Infraspinatus or teres minor tendinitis
10	Teres minor tendon, long head of triceps tendon, posterior circumflex artery, axillary nerve	Contusion	Teres minor or triceps tendinitis, quadrilateral space syndrome
11	Infraspinatus muscle, scapula	Scapular fracture	Atrophy due to suprascapular nerve entrapment
12	Levator scapulae, superior-medial border of scapula	Radiation zone for cervical disc lesions	Levator scapulae syndrome

Note: See Figure 7–3, A, B, and C, for localization of numbered areas.

consider an old AC separation or, in an older individual, osteoarthritis; tenderness may or may not be elicited. Discrete tenderness at the AC jaunt in a serious weight lifter suggests osteolysis of the distal clavicle.[7]

Tender areas often correlate well to specific tissue involvement. This is often position dependent[8]:

- The supraspinatus tendon insertion is most palpable with the patient seated and the arm held behind the back with the elbow flexed; the arm is internally rotated as much as possible and the elbow is lifted away from the back as far as possible (maximum extension of the shoulder); the supraspinatus tendon is then palpable directly anterior to the AC joint.
- The infraspinatus and teres minor tendons are most palpable with the patient seated or prone with the shoulder flexed to 90°, adducted 10°, and externally rotated 20°; the elbow is bent to about 90° during positioning; the tendons are then palpable directly inferior to the posterior acromion.
- The subscapularis tendon is palpated with the shoulder held in neutral at the patient's side; the tendon is palpable deep under the area of the clavicle just medial to the medial border of the deltoid in the deltopectoral triangle.
- The tendon of the long head of the biceps is palpated with the patient's arm internally rotated 20°; the tendon is palpable in the same deltopectoral triangle as the subscapularis; however, the internal rotation has placed the biceps tendon in an overlying position.

Range of Motion

Following are some characteristic movement pattern restrictions in range of motion (ROM):

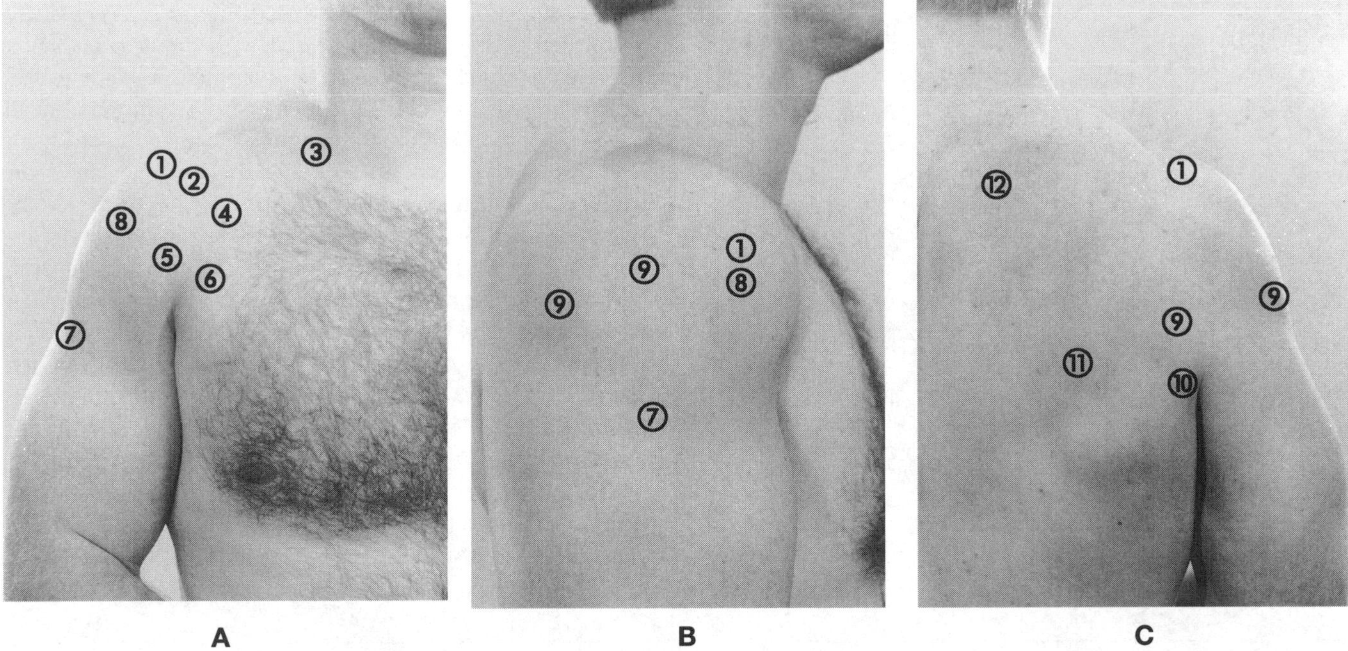

Figure 7–3 **A**, Anterior shoulder; **B**, lateral shoulder; **C**, posterior shoulder. *Note:* See Table 7–2 for explanation of numbers.

- Patients unable to perform most movements due to pain (and no history of trauma) are likely to have either an acute bursitis or the initial stage of adhesive capsulitis.
- If there is a history of trauma and the patient avoids any attempt at movement consider dislocation and/or fracture.
- If there is a history of trauma and the patient is unable to life the arm into flexion with a supinated arm, posterior dislocation should be considered.
- Pain in the midrange of abduction is referred to as a "painful arc." The painful arc is between 70° and 110° (Figure 7–4). To qualify as a painful arc, the pain must be less above this range. When patients cannot actively move beyond this range, the examiner should assist the patient to 120° and then ask the patient to continue if possible. In general, an active painful arc combined with a negative passive painful arc is suggestive of a contractile lesion (ie, muscle/tendon). If a painful arc is felt on active and passive movement, the involved structures are less clear.
- Restriction in *both* active and passive ROM preferentially affecting external rotation, abduction, and then eventually extension and flexion suggests adhesive capsulitis.
- Pain felt at a discrete point with active ROM as a sharp pain is suggestive of a labrum tear, especially if it can be relieved by avoiding the specific position.
- Inability to lower from an abducted position (drop-arm test) is suggestive of a rotator cuff (specifically supraspinatus) tear.
- The use of body leaning or shoulder hunching is often visible when patients with adhesive capsulitis, rotator cuff tear, or osteoarthritis are compensating for weakness or loss of active movement.

When the patient performs abduction maneuvers, it is important to palpate the scapula for a normal glenohumeral to scapula ratio of movement. The ratio between humeral and scapular motion is often quoted as 2:1; however, this is an average. The ratio in the first 30° is closer to somewhere between 4:1 and 7:1; from 90° to 150° it is closer to 1:1.[9,10] Thus little movement occurs in the first 30°. When excessive movement occurs at the scapula in the initial phase of abduction, weakness of the serratus anterior or other stabilizers is likely.

Instability

Testing for instability or looseness of the shoulder is not performed in the acute dislocation scenario. This testing is reserved for those patients with a past history of dislocation or medical subluxation and those individuals who are suspected of having generalized joint laxity. There are a number of tests; however, most examiners focus on three: (1) the load and shift (L&S) test, (2) the apprehension test, and

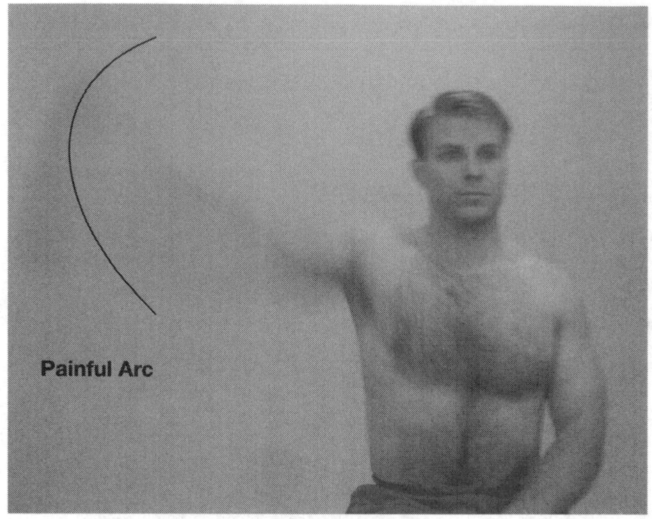

Figure 7–4 The painful arc is between 70° and 110°. The patient will feel more pain in this range and less on either side of this arc.

(3) the relocation test. The L&S test (Figure 7–5) is usually performed with the patient seated with the arm abducted slightly (20°) and the hand resting on the lap.[11] The examiner then loads the joint by compressing the humeral head into the glenoid. While stabilizing the scapula with one hand held over the spine of the scapula and clavicle, the other hand pushes the humeral head first forward to test for anterior instability, then backward for posterior stability (Figure 7–5A) and finally inferiorly (Figure 7–5B). In general, when inferior laxity is present a sulcus sign or depression will appear below the AC joint. This indicates not only inferior laxity but is suggestive of multidirectional instability. This will usually be found on the opposite shoulder, indicating an inherent looseness of the individual's shoulder capsules.

The apprehension test (Figure 7–6) may be performed with the patient seated or supine.[12] The advantage of performing supine is the ability to move directly into the relocation test, which can be used as a sequential approach. The patient's

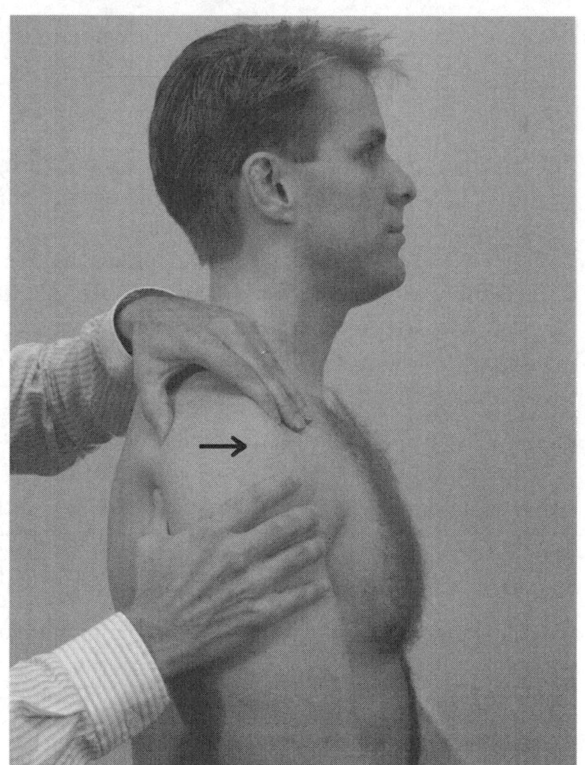

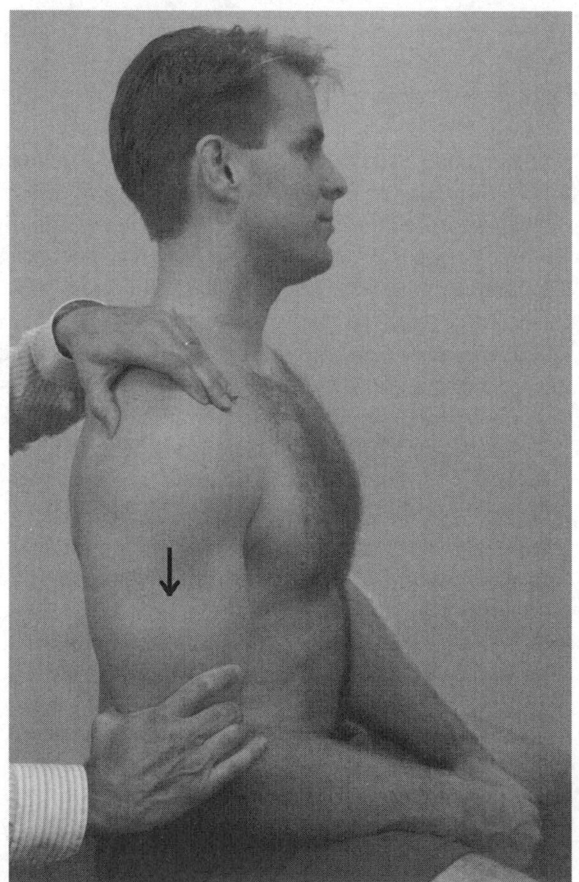

Figure 7–5 The L&S test involves stabilizing the scapula with one hand and grasping the humeral head with the other. Load the shoulder by pushing in toward the glenoid. **A**, Then push forward to test anterior stability, and pull back to test posterior stability. **B**, Pull downward on the arm to test inferior stability. A visible sulcus may appear under the acromion with a multidirectional loose shoulder.

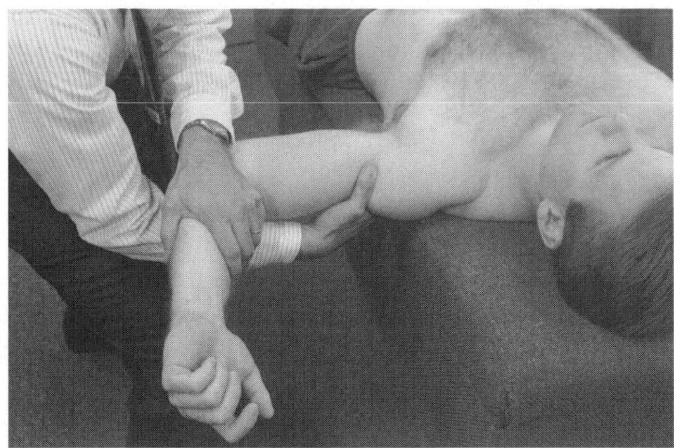

Figure 7–6 The apprehension test may be performed lying or standing. With the patient supine, the examiner extends the patient's shoulder while at 90° abduction and externally rotated while pushing the humeral head from posterior to anterior.

arm is abducted and externally rotated. A first attempt is simply to continue the arm into more horizontal abduction (extension) at about 90°. If there is no pain or sense of apprehension, continue testing at a higher elevation and add a cautious pressure in an anterior direction on the posterior humeral head. If either pain or a sense of "going out" is felt by the patient, the test is positive for anterior instability. Reperforming the test, however, by applying an anterior force to posterior force (Figure 7–7) with the examiner's hand will usually take away the sense of either pain or apprehension (relocation test).[13] When apprehension is reduced with this relocation maneuver, instability is confirmed. If pain is reduced with this test, impingement probably is present due to

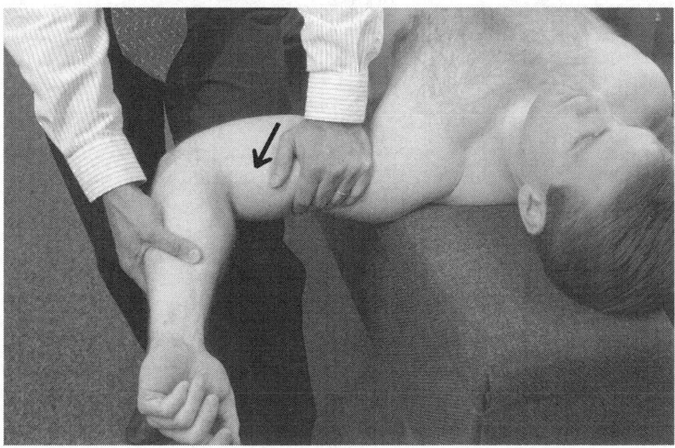

Figure 7–7 The relocation test is a repetition of the apprehension test; however, the examiner stabilizes the shoulder by applying an anterior to posterior force in an effort to relieve pain or a sense of apprehension.

an underlying instability. Cross-checking with the impingement test findings is helpful.

When instability is present or when an individual has complaints that sound like mechanical joint pain (shoulder gets stuck in certain positions or patient has a sharp pain in a specific position), labrum testing should be employed. There are two basic approaches with several variations. The original testing maneuver described in the literature is the clunk test. The patient is placed in the apprehension position with the examiner pressing the humeral head from posterior to anterior. The arm is then internally and externally rotated and circumducted in an attempt to elicit a deep "clunk" feeling or sound. Some examiners employ an axially compressive load (similar to Apley's compression test for the knee). One such test is called the crank test and involves placing the patient's arm in maximum flexion, internally rotating and externally rotating the arm with an axial force applied.[14] A positive response includes clicking with pain. The practitioners who developed the test found that when the crank test, apprehension test, and L&S test findings were combined, the sensitivity of the clinical examination for labrum tears was better than with magnetic resonance imaging (MRI). Another approach is the anterior slide test, used to locate specifically a superior labrum tear.[15] The patient is seated or standing and places the hands on the hips with the thumbs pointing posteriorly. The examiner places one hand on the top of the shoulder from behind, overlapping the index finger over the anterior acromion. The examiner's other hand takes the patient's elbow and directs an axial force superiorly into the shoulder. The patient is asked to press back against this attempt. A pop/click or pain localized to the front of the shoulder is considered positive for a superior labrum tear. Labrum tears are also suggested when popping and clicking are found on L&S testing or any distractive maneuvers coupled with internal rotation.

General Impingement

Impingement may occur under the subacromial arch, affecting mainly the supraspinatus, biceps, and subacromial bursa. Posterior impingement involves the infraspinatus and teres minor tendons. Subcoracoid impingement selectively impinges the subscapularis. Most tests designed for impingement focus on the subacromial arch. These are general tests and do not usually reveal a specific structure. One test is the painful arc discussed above in the ROM section. Other tests include the Neer test and the Hawkins-Kennedy test. The Neer test (Figure 7–8) is a passive test involving full forward flexion while holding down the shoulder (stabilizing with the other hand).[16] A positive result involves pain production at the end-range of full forward flexion, not in the midrange of motion. With the Hawkins-Kennedy test (Figure 7–9) the examiner places the patient's arm in an impingement posi-

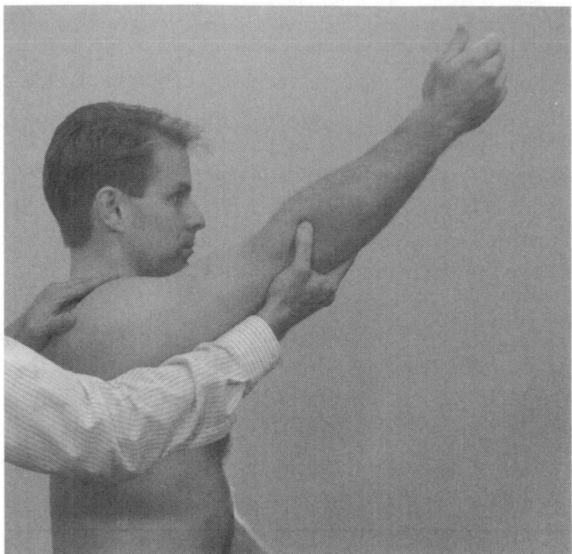

Figure 7–8 The Neer's test is performed by passively elevating the arm into forward flexion to end-range. End-range pain is a positive sign of impingement.

tion.[17] While standing behind the patient, it is important to prevent scapular elevation by hooking the hand over the top of the shoulder. The examiner's other hand lifts the arm into a position of 90° forward flexion, slight adduction, and internal rotation. The more internal rotation imposed in this position the stronger the pain response. The positive pain response for impingement is anterior pain. Posterior stretch or pain implies involvement of posterior structures such as the infraspinatus and teres minor or posterior capsule. When the general impingement tests are positive it is important to attempt to localize which structures are involved by more specific testing.

Specific Soft Tissue or Muscle/Tendon Tests

Specific testing should be incorporated after general testing has been performed. Tendinitis related to or unrelated to impingement may be detected. Palpation of tendon insertions is discussed above. Specific testing of contractile structures includes the following:

- Supraspinatus: Muscle testing of the supraspinatus is best performed as the empty can test (Figure 7–10). The patient attempts to lift the arm in the plane line of the scapula (scaption), which is 30° to 45° forward of straight abduction. The arm is maximally internally rotated. If this is not painful, the examiner adds resistance to the attempt at approximately 90° of scaption. Pain and weakness indicate a supraspinatus tear. It is important to remember that the intention of this test is to con-

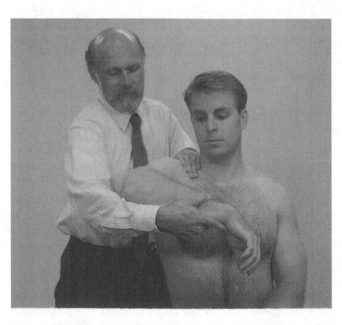

Figure 7–9 The Hawkins-Kennedy test for impingement involves passive internal rotation with the shoulder flexed forward 90° while the scapula is stabilized.

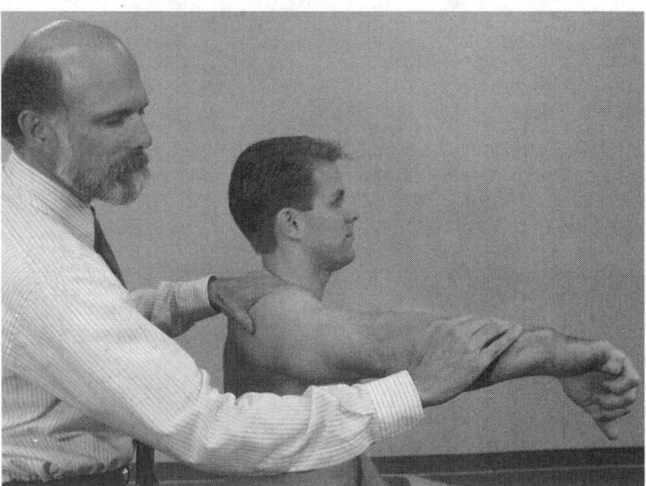

Figure 7–10 The empty can test for the supraspinatus is performed with the patient's shoulder abducted 90° in the plane line of the scapula (30° to 45° forward). With the shoulder in maximum internal rotation, the patient is asked to abduct further against resistance.

tract the supraspinatus in an impingement position; however, other muscles do participate, as with all resisted testing.[18] It has also been found that testing with the arm in a thumb's-up position recruits as much electromyographic activity; however, it is less painful than full internal rotation.[19]

- Biceps: Although there a number of tests for the biceps, the one considered most sensitive by investigators is the Speed's test.[20] Most biceps tests cause contraction of the biceps without movement of the tendon in the intertubercular groove. The Speed's test involves an isotonic contraction into forward shoulder flexion with the elbow extended. The examiner resists this attempt through a full ROM. In so doing, the intertubercular groove travels under the tendon and therefore is more likely to cause irritation if there is an underlying inflammatory process or tendinitis.
- Infraspinatus/teres minor: Contraction into external rotation may cause pain if performed with the arm in the Hawkins-Kennedy position (90° forward flexion, forearm parallel to the floor).[21] This position places a stretch on the tendons prior to contraction. Kelly et al.[19] state that there is minimal pain produced, and therefore better test-retest reliability, when the infraspinatus is tested with the arm at the side (no elevation), 90° of elbow flexion, and the shoulder internally rotated 45° from the sagittal plane.
- Subscapularis: Although the subscapularis is an internal rotator, so are many other larger muscles; therefore, resisted internal rotation is a nonselective attempt at localization. If the subscapularis is involved, the lift-off test may be positive. The patient places the hand behind the back and then attempts to lift the hand off the back. The patient must have no pain on positioning the hand for the test to be specific for the subscapularis. If she or he is unable to lift the hand away from the back or the attempt is significantly painful, the test is positive.[22] Jemp et al.[21] found the best position for isolating the subscapularis from the pectoralis major was arm elevation to 90° in the scapular plane (scaption) of 30° to 45° anterior to the coronal plane with the arm in neutral. The examiner supports the arm to allow a better attempt at internal rotation without any associated abduction or adduction attempts by the patient.

Acromioclavicular Joint

AC joint problems are usually evident from the history, observation, and direct palpation. A maneuver that may assist is compression, performed by cupping the shoulder from anterior and posterior with both palms and pressing together. Distraction using the spine of the scapula and clavicle may also cause some pain. The sulcus sign, used to indicate instability of the shoulder, is also present with second- and third-degree AC separations.

Radiography and Special Imaging

Radiographic examination of the shoulder is based on the suspected underlying pathology. General screening involves an anterior to posterior (AP) radiograph performed with the patient's arm internally and externally rotated. Following are some suggested views based on the structures or conditions suspected. Discussion of these views with illustrations of how to perform them may be found in the author's text *Sports Injuries of the Shoulder*.[23]

- Impingement: Evaluation of the subacromial outlet may be seen with the anterior oblique or outlet view (Y view); other helpful views for acromial morphology include the AP-view with 30° caudal tube tilt and the AP Acromial view (Zanca).
- Anterior dislocation: An anterior dislocation is usually visible on an AP neutral; however the AP internal rotation or anterior oblique (Y) view is best.
- Posterior dislocation: The best view is the Y view; supplementary views are the transthoracic and Velpeau or other axial projections.
- AC joint separation: Weighted and nonweighted anterior projections are often used to determine the degree of separation; these are bilateral shots; a coracoclavicular distance greater than 1.3 cm indicates third-degree separation.
- Instability: If traumatic instability is suspected, several modified axillary projections are of potential benefit in demonstrating residual Hill-Sachs and Bankart (glenoid lip avulsions associated with labrum tears) lesions; these include the West Point view and Didiée view for Bankart lesions, and the AP with internal rotation and the Stryker notch view for Hill-Sachs lesions.
- Osteolysis or fractures of the distal clavicle: The Zanca projection taken with 10° to 15° cephalad tube tilt (about half the technique of an AP shoulder projection) is used.
- Sternoclavicular (SC) joint: There are two views used to evaluate the SC joint, the Hobbs' view and the serendipity view.
- Humeral head fractures: Most fractures are visible on an AP radiograph with internal and external rotation.

In general, special imaging of the shoulder should be reserved for cases where conservative care has failed to resolve the problem. Available tools include MRI, computed tomography (CT) arthrography, and ultrasonography. The strengths of each are outlined below:

- MRI: MRI is a valuable tool when patients are unresponsive to conservative care. Full-thickness tears of

the rotator cuff are readily apparent (sensitivity and specificity at 90% or above), whereas partial-thickness tears (sensitivity 74%, specificity 87%) may require fat saturation or other techniques to help differentiate them.[24] Glenoid labrum tears are less recognizable, and the sensitivity and specificity vary depending on the investigator. It is generally accepted, however, that the sensitivity is in the range of 75% or less.[25] This varies depending on the site. Superior tears are the most discernible, followed by a poor ability to visualize inferior tears (around 40% sensitivity), and even less ability to visualize posterior tears (about 7%).[26] New approaches being investigated and used in some facilities include the use of kinematic MRI and also performing standard MRI with the addition of gadolinium.[27]
- CT arthrogram: CT arthrograms are used mainly for glenoid labrum and rotator cuff tears and are considered by many to be the imaging tool of choice. The difficulty is finding facilities that will perform them. The accuracy of CT arthrography has been reported to be as high as 95% to 100%.[28] However, other studies have not demonstrated an advantage over MRI.[29]
- Ultrasonography: Ultrasonography (diagnostic ultrasound) can be an excellent tool for detecting full-thickness cuff tears. Partial tears are sometimes detectable.[30] Interpretation may be the weak point because of the major variations in findings due to operator skill.

MANAGEMENT

In the event of an acute dislocation, relocation is accomplished with several maneuvers; however, the easiest to perform is the Milch maneuver.[31] This involves slowly elevating the arm while maintaining external rotation and superior pressure on the humeral head. Relocation may be difficult, and when not possible requires emergency department referral. Postreduction, a radiograph should be obtained to determine if there are any associated fractures. The chiropractor can play a valuable role in rehabilitation, which has been shown to reduce substantially the risk of recurrence.[32]

If radiographs reveal signs of infection, fracture, or tumor, refer the patient for orthopaedic consultation. All other problems can be addressed conservatively unless the patient's pain threshold does not allow a nonmedicated course. Acute pain may be managed by various physical therapy approaches, including high-voltage galvanic or interferrential. Over-the-counter medications may be necessary.

Support and stabilization are needed in several scenarios: AC separations, postrelocation, atraumatic instability, and acute bursitis. These may be provided by supportive strapping using various types of elastic tape or a sling. The advantage of taping is that it allows function, whereas a sling prevents use of the arm. The pain level and degree of injury dictate the better approach.

Rehabilitation of the shoulder generally proceeds through a sequential approach, beginning with a focus on the stabilizers (rotator cuff) and followed by the scapular stabilizers (serratus anterior and trapezius); the large movers such as the pectoralis major and latissimus dorsi muscles then can be addressed. Without proper stabilization, the larger muscles may cause more damage due to abnormal glenohumeral motion.

A facilitation phase using mild isometrics in various movement patterns such as internal and external rotation is helpful. Another effective tool for facilitation and stabilization is use of rapid elastic tube exercises limited to about a 20° to 30° arc (back and forth) for 60 seconds or until fatigue or pain occurs. The general program begins with light weights (5 to 10 lb) and high repetition (15 to 20), using perhaps three sets performed every day. A core group of exercises is recommended, including the following[33,34]:

- scaption (abduction in the scapular plane of 30° to 45° forward) or flexion
- horizontal abduction with external rotation performed prone
- a seated press-up
- bent-over rows
- a push-up with a plus (extending the arms at the top of the push-up)

Some disorder-specific concerns include the following:

- Initial avoidance of overhead exercise and activities is critical with impingement syndrome.
- With instability it is important to avoid the cocking position and any overhead exercise with the elbow behind the body (eg, lateral pull-downs, pectoral butterflies, etc.); the general rule with exercise is not to let the arms drift behind the body line.
- The avoidance of heavy lifting or modification of lifting routine is required for osteolysis of the distal clavicle; this includes substituting the bench press and dip with narrow grip bench presses, cable, crossovers, and include or decline press.

Algorithms

Algorithms for evaluation and management of traumatic shoulder pain, nontraumatic shoulder pain, and shoulder complaint other than pain are presented in Figures 7–11 to 7–13.

Figure 7–11
TRAUMATIC SHOULDER PAIN—ALGORITHM.*

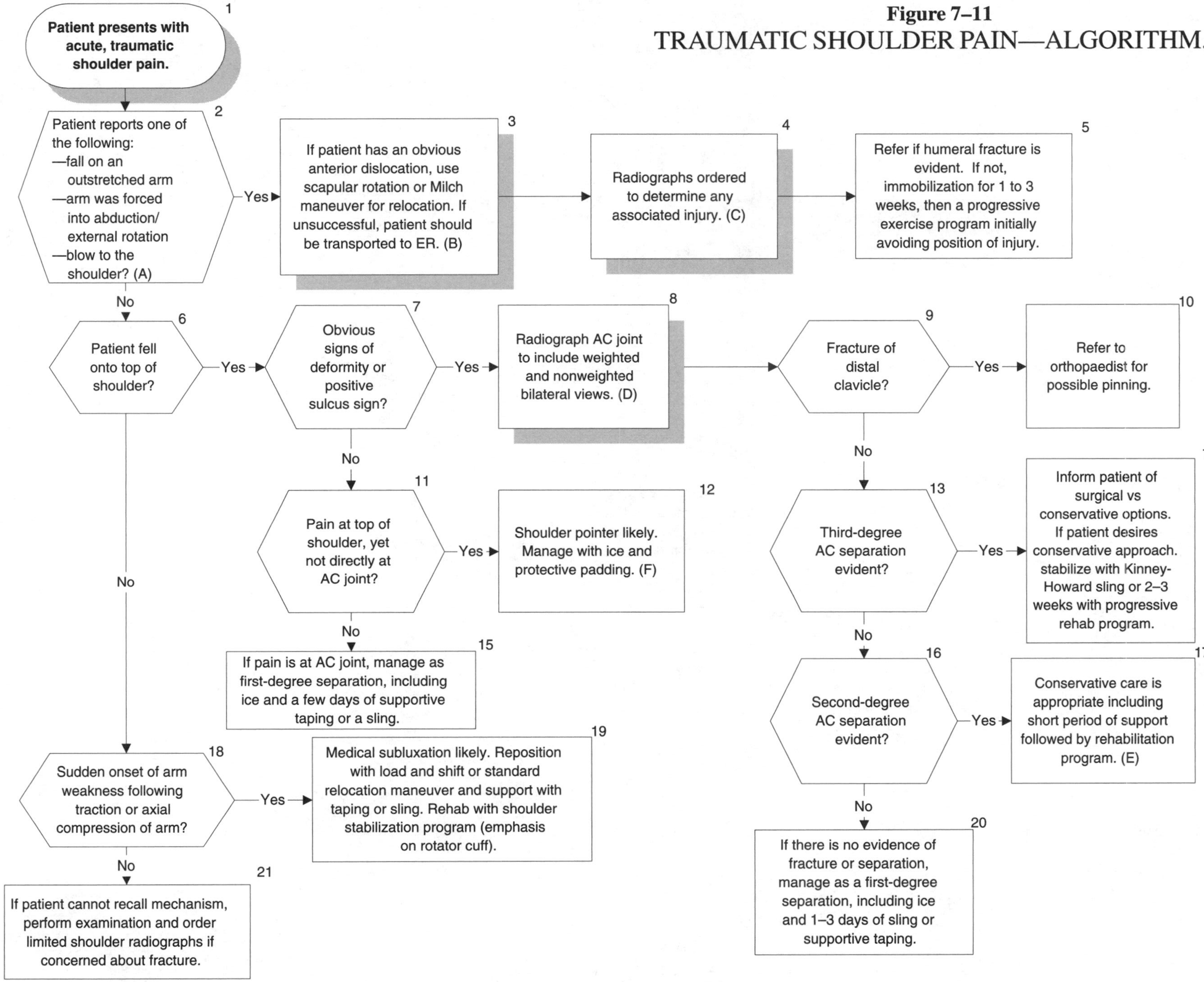

1. **Patient presents with acute, traumatic shoulder pain.**

2. Patient reports one of the following:
—fall on an outstretched arm
—arm was forced into abduction/ external rotation
—blow to the shoulder? (A)
   - Yes → 3
   - No → 6

3. If patient has an obvious anterior dislocation, use scapular rotation or Milch maneuver for relocation. If unsuccessful, patient should be transported to ER. (B) → 4

4. Radiographs ordered to determine any associated injury. (C) → 5

5. Refer if humeral fracture is evident. If not, immobilization for 1 to 3 weeks, then a progressive exercise program initially avoiding position of injury.

6. Patient fell onto top of shoulder?
   - Yes → 7
   - No → 18

7. Obvious signs of deformity or positive sulcus sign?
   - Yes → 8
   - No → 11

8. Radiograph AC joint to include weighted and nonweighted bilateral views. (D) → 9

9. Fracture of distal clavicle?
   - Yes → 10
   - No → 13

10. Refer to orthopaedist for possible pinning.

11. Pain at top of shoulder, yet not directly at AC joint?
    - Yes → 12
    - No → 15

12. Shoulder pointer likely. Manage with ice and protective padding. (F)

13. Third-degree AC separation evident?
    - Yes → 14
    - No → 16

14. Inform patient of surgical vs conservative options. If patient desires conservative approach. stabilize with Kinney-Howard sling or 2–3 weeks with progressive rehab program.

15. If pain is at AC joint, manage as first-degree separation, including ice and a few days of supportive taping or a sling.

16. Second-degree AC separation evident?
    - Yes → 17
    - No → 20

17. Conservative care is appropriate including short period of support followed by rehabilitation program. (E)

18. Sudden onset of arm weakness following traction or axial compression of arm?
    - Yes → 19
    - No → 21

19. Medical subluxation likely. Reposition with load and shift or standard relocation maneuver and support with taping or sling. Rehab with shoulder stabilization program (emphasis on rotator cuff).

20. If there is no evidence of fracture or separation, manage as a first-degree separation, including ice and 1–3 days of sling or supportive taping.

21. If patient cannot recall mechanism, perform examination and order limited shoulder radiographs if concerned about fracture.

*See Figure 7–13 for annotations.

Figure 7–12

NONTRAUMATIC SHOULDER PAIN—ALGORITHM.*

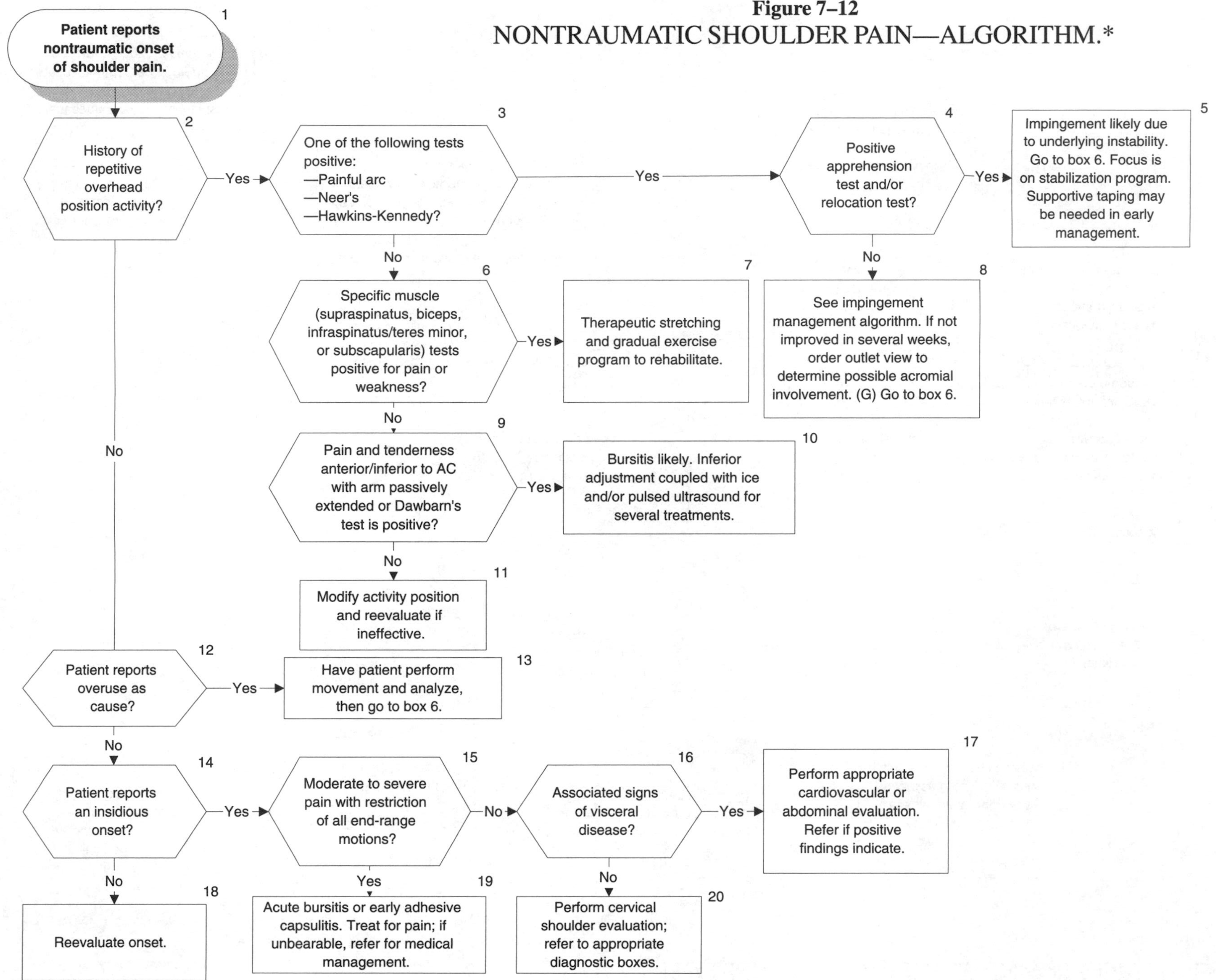

*See Figure 7–13 for annotations.

Figure 7–13

SHOULDER COMPLAINT (OTHER THAN PAIN)—ALGORITHM.

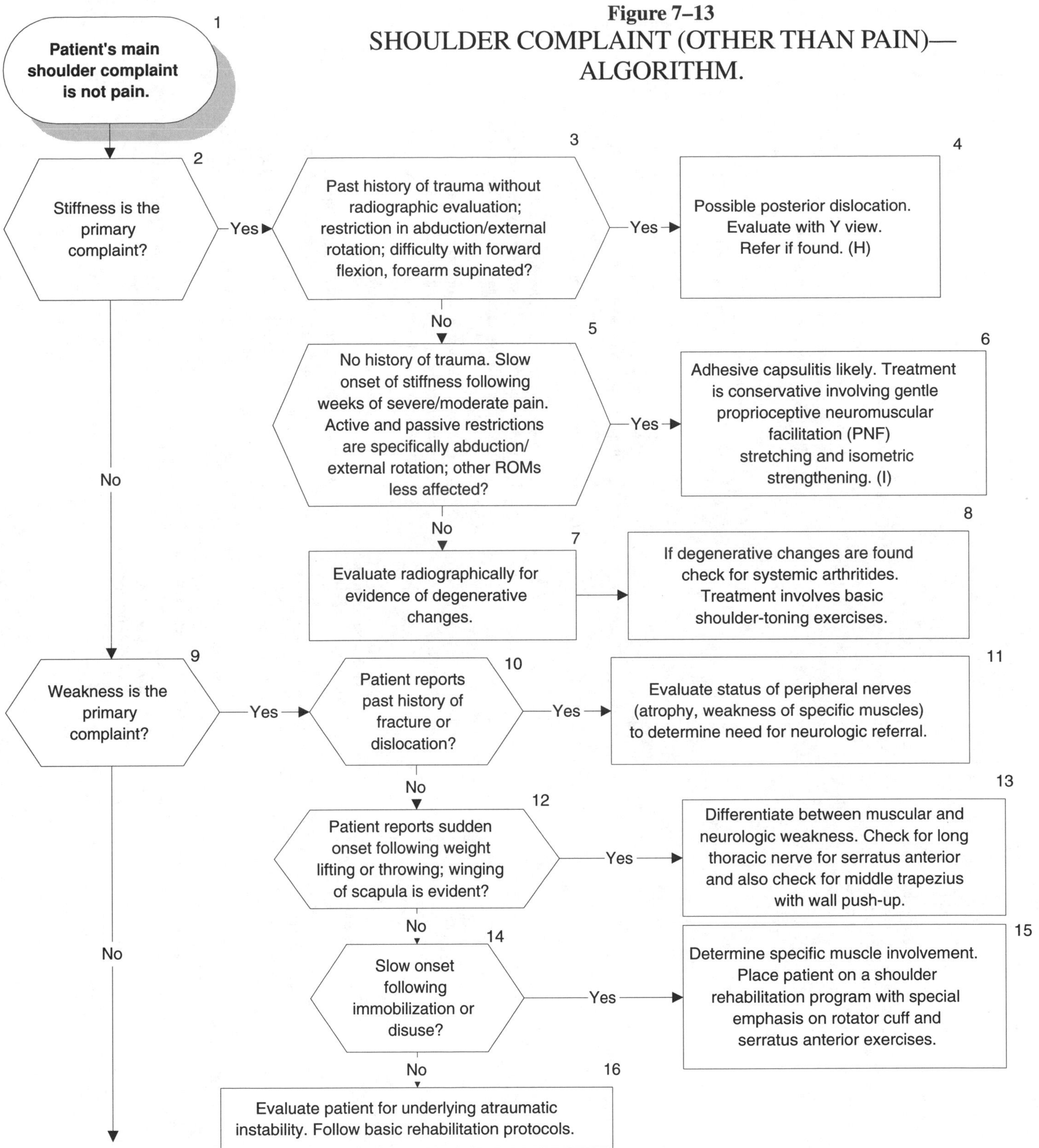

1 Patient's main shoulder complaint is not pain.
2 Stiffness is the primary complaint?
Yes
3 Past history of trauma without radiographic evaluation; restriction in abduction/external rotation; difficulty with forward flexion, forearm supinated?
Yes
4 Possible posterior dislocation. Evaluate with Y view. Refer if found. (H)
No
5 No history of trauma. Slow onset of stiffness following weeks of severe/moderate pain. Active and passive restrictions are specifically abduction/external rotation; other ROMs less affected?
Yes
6 Adhesive capsulitis likely. Treatment is conservative involving gentle proprioceptive neuromuscular facilitation (PNF) stretching and isometric strengthening. (I)
No
7 Evaluate radiographically for evidence of degenerative changes.
8 If degenerative changes are found check for systemic arthritides. Treatment involves basic shoulder-toning exercises.
No
9 Weakness is the primary complaint?
Yes
10 Patient reports past history of fracture or dislocation?
Yes
11 Evaluate status of peripheral nerves (atrophy, weakness of specific muscles) to determine need for neurologic referral.
No
12 Patient reports sudden onset following weight lifting or throwing; winging of scapula is evident?
Yes
13 Differentiate between muscular and neurologic weakness. Check for long thoracic nerve for serratus anterior and also check for middle trapezius with wall push-up.
No
14 Slow onset following immobilization or disuse?
Yes
15 Determine specific muscle involvement. Place patient on a shoulder rehabilitation program with special emphasis on rotator cuff and serratus anterior exercises.
No
16 Evaluate patient for underlying atraumatic instability. Follow basic rehabilitation protocols.
No

continues

Figure 7–13 continued

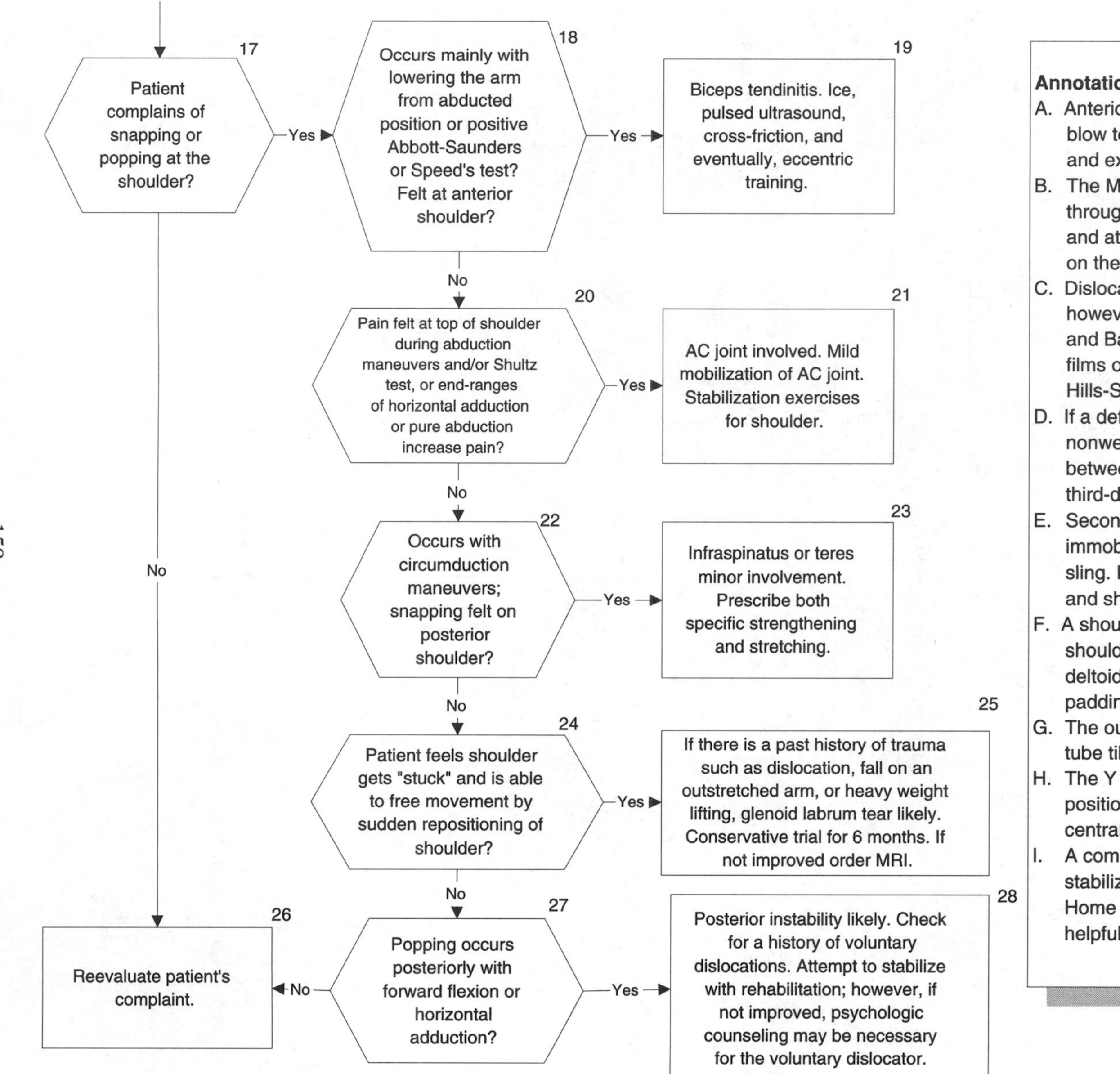

17
Patient complains of snapping or popping at the shoulder?
Yes
No
18
Occurs mainly with lowering the arm from abducted position or positive Abbott-Saunders or Speed's test? Felt at anterior shoulder?
Yes
No
19
Biceps tendinitis. Ice, pulsed ultrasound, cross-friction, and eventually, eccentric training.
20
Pain felt at top of shoulder during abduction maneuvers and/or Shultz test, or end-ranges of horizontal adduction or pure abduction increase pain?
Yes
No
21
AC joint involved. Mild mobilization of AC joint. Stabilization exercises for shoulder.
22
Occurs with circumduction maneuvers; snapping felt on posterior shoulder?
Yes
No
23
Infraspinatus or teres minor involvement. Prescribe both specific strengthening and stretching.
24
Patient feels shoulder gets "stuck" and is able to free movement by sudden repositioning of shoulder?
Yes
No
25
If there is a past history of trauma such as dislocation, fall on an outstretched arm, or heavy weight lifting, glenoid labrum tear likely. Conservative trial for 6 months. If not improved order MRI.
26
Reevaluate patient's complaint.
27
Popping occurs posteriorly with forward flexion or horizontal adduction?
Yes
No
28
Posterior instability likely. Check for a history of voluntary dislocations. Attempt to stabilize with rehabilitation; however, if not improved, psychologic counseling may be necessary for the voluntary dislocator.

Annotations

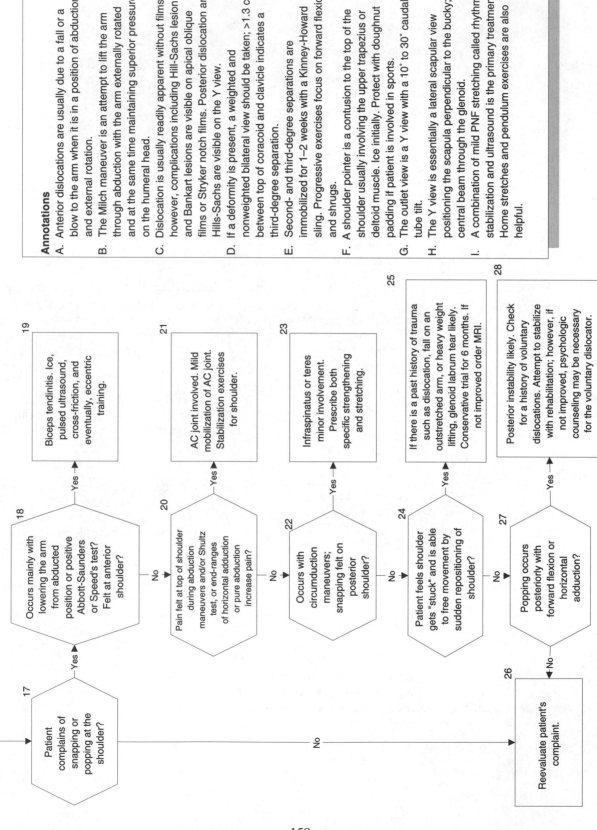

A. Anterior dislocations are usually due to a fall or a blow to the arm when it is in a position of abduction and external rotation.

B. The Milch maneuver is an attempt to lift the arm through abduction with the arm externally rotated and at the same time maintaining superior pressure on the humeral head.

C. Dislocation is usually readily apparent without films; however, complications including Hill-Sachs lesion and Bankart lesions are visible on apical oblique films or Stryker notch films. Posterior dislocation and Hills-Sachs are visible on the Y view.

D. If a deformity is present, a weighted and nonweighted bilateral view should be taken; >1.3 cm between top of coracoid and clavicle indicates a third-degree separation.

E. Second- and third-degree separations are immobilized for 1–2 weeks with a Kinney-Howard sling. Progressive exercises focus on forward flexion and shrugs.

F. A shoulder pointer is a contusion to the top of the shoulder usually involving the upper trapezius or deltoid muscle. Ice initially. Protect with doughnut padding if patient is involved in sports.

G. The outlet view is a Y view with a 10° to 30° caudal tube tilt.

H. The Y view is essentially a lateral scapular view positioning the scapula perpendicular to the bucky; central beam through the glenoid.

I. A combination of mild PNF stretching called rhythmic stabilization and ultrasound is the primary treatment. Home stretches and pendulum exercises are also helpful.

SELECTED DISORDERS OF THE SHOULDER

A summary of most of the shoulder disorders discussed below is presented in Table 7–3.

IMPINGEMENT SYNDROME

Classic Presentation

The patient reports shoulder pain that is worse with overhead activities. The patient often will have a positive history for a sports or occupational requirement to work in an overhead position.

Cause

Subacromial impingement of several structures may occur. The biceps tendon, supraspinatus tendon, and the subacromial bursa are all vulnerable to this anterolateral type of impingement. Structural causes include variant acromial types that are hooked or lengthened, degenerative changes on the undersurface of the acromion, and an inflammatory process in the subacromial space.[35] Functional considerations are primarily due to decreases in available subacromial space that occurs with elevation and internal rotation, especially at 90°. Instability is often a coexisting problem allowing excessive superior movement of the humeral head. There may also be a component of posterior capsular tightness that also causes superior-anterior migration with arm abduction. Subcoracoid impingement may cause irritation of the subscapularis. Posterior impingement may be caused by a repetitive "cocking" position of the arm, irritating the infraspinatus or teres minor.

Evaluation

The site of tenderness varies depending on the site of impingement. Subacromial impingement causes tenderness and pain at the anterior joint at the biceps tendon, supraspinatus insertion onto the greater tuberosity, or under the AC joint. More posterior tenderness suggests impingement of the infraspinatus/teres minor tendons. Tenderness or pain at the coracoid process that is made worse by passive horizontal adduction may indicate subcoracoid impingement of the subscapularis. The traditional tests include demonstration of a painful arc, the Hawkins-Kennedy test, and Neer's test.[36] The painful arc (Figure 7–4) is evident when a patient has an increase of pain in the mid-range of 90° to 110° of abduction with less or no pain above or below this range. The Hawkins-Kennedy test (Figure 7–9) passively places the patient's arm in forward flexion 90° with the elbow flexed to 90° and passively rotated internally. Neer's test (Figure 7–8) is a passive forward flexion test that is positive for pain at full end-range flexion. Another confirmatory test in patients with underlying instability is relief of pain with anterior to posterior support in the apprehension position, the relocation test (Figure 7–7).

Management

The approach is based on the severity of symptoms; however, the long-range goal is to stabilize the shoulder with a progressive rehabilitation program, stretching of the posterior capsule, and modification of sport or occupational activities (Table 7–4). If the patient is not responsive in several months, an MRI may be helpful in planning any surgical management.

Table 7–3 Summary of Shoulder Disorders

Condition	*Signs/Symptoms*	*Exam Findings*	*Treatment*
Impingement syndrome	Shoulder pain with overhead activities	Painful arc, Neer's, and Hawkins-Kennedy tests positive with secondary impingement, positive relocation test; radiographic assessment may include outlet view or Zanca view	Ice, rest from inciting activity, myofascial release to involved muscles; cross-friction to tendons; stretch posterior capsule; possible superior to inferior adjustment; exercise begins with arm slightly abducted, progressing from isometrics to isotonics with emphasis on rotator cuff
Traumatic anterior instability	History of shoulder dislocation (usually shoulder is overstretched into abduction/external rotation) or medical subluxation	Positive apprehension with improvement using relocation test; laxity evident on L&S testing; radiograph assessment may include standard views plus modified axillary views	Support in initial stage with bracing or taping; progressive strengthening program with initial avoidance of coupled abduction and external rotation
Nontraumatic instability	May have history of medical subluxation or simply overuse pain with overhead or repetitive activities	Positive for pain with the apprehension test; relieved by the relocation test; multidirectional, bilateral laxity found on L&S testing	Support in initial stage with bracing or taping; progressive strengthening program with emphasis on rotator cuff strengthening first; include scaption, flexion, and prone horizontal abduction/external rotation
Adhesive capsulitis	A period of pain lasting for weeks is followed by a period of gradual stiffening of the shoulder as the pain resolves	Restriction in both active and passive external rotation and abduction; an arthrogram is diagnostic in some cases but usually not necessary	Dependent on stage: pain stage requires efforts to reduce pain and inflammation; in the stiffening phase, rhythmic stabilization-based stretching and ultrasound are helpful
Rotator cuff tear	Sudden shoulder pain with overhead or lifting activity	Usually supraspinatus is involved—positive empty can test; tear visible with MRI, diagnostic ultrasound, or arthrography	Rest, ice, and support followed by a gradual strengthening program; with total rupture in an athletic patient, surgery is necessary
AC separation	Patient fell on the shoulder or outstretched arm	Visible bump at AC joint; weighted and nonweighted views may indicate the degree of laxity and damage	Shoulder support for 1–2 weeks with gradual strengthening program for shoulder; focus on rotator cuff and trapezius

Table 7–4 Management of Impingement Syndrome and Tendinitis

Parameter	*Acute Stage*	*Subacute Stage*	*Symptom-Free Stage*
Criteria	Painful arc, + Hawkins-Kennedy and Neer's tests, pain with overhead activity; for isolated tendinitis, pain with specific muscle action	Tests are less positive for pain	Tests are no longer positive
Goals	Decrease inflammation and pain	Increase rotator cuff strength while avoiding impingement position	Train through impingement range; functionally train for occupational or sport activity
Concerns	May be caused by a mechanical irritation from os acromiale or type III acromion	Overzealous athlete or worker unable or unwilling to rehabilitate the rotator cuff	Overzealous with progressing through exercise routine or not maintaining improvement with a routine shoulder exercise program
Requirements for progression to next stage; approximate time needed	Able to perform isometrics throughout ROM without pain, pain-free passive ROM; 1 week	Able to perform 3 sets of 15 repetitions of primary exercises pain free for several days in a row; 3–6 weeks	Able to perform functional exercises without pain
Manipulation/mobilization	Superior to inferior manipulation or mobilization may be helpful; check cervical spine and scapula for fixation	Superior to inferior manipulation or mobilization may be helpful; check cervical spine and scapula for fixation	Superior to inferior manipulation or mobilization may be helpful; check cervical spine and scapula for fixation
Modalities	Interferrential at 80–150 pps/20 minutes daily with ice	Ultrasound at 1.5 wt/cm^2 for 5 minutes; ice after exercise	Ice after exercise
External brace, support, etc.	Usually not necessary; however, shoulder support taping may be of benefit	None	None
ROM/flexibility	Codman/pendulum exercises; begin stretching of posterior shoulder capsule	Continue posterior capsular stretching	Continue posterior capsular stretching
Open-chain exercise	Isometrics performed every 20° to 30°	Begin with midrange, short arc, fast reciprocating motions into internal and external rotation. Perform daily exercise with light weight (1–5 lb), working up to 3 sets of 15 repetitions; exercises include scaption or flexion, prone horizontal abduction, bent-over rowing, internal rotation	Perform plyometric exercises if patient is an athlete and uses upper body; plyoball tosses against a wall or minitrampoline

continues

Table 7–4 continued

Parameter	*Acute Stage*	*Subacute Stage*	*Symptom-Free Stage*
Closed-chain exercise	None	Wall push-ups, press-up, push-up with a plus	Balance ball and wobble board push-ups; stair-step machine using hands
Proprioceptive training	Passive PNF diagonal patterns into flexion and extension	Being PNF diagonal patterns with accommodated resistance	Incorporate PNF functional patterns specific to sport or occupation
Associated biomechanical items	Scapular immobility, cervical or thoracic spine dysfunction	Scapular immobility, cervical or thoracic spine dysfunction	Incorporate lower body training to reduce stress on shoulder; include balance exercises on balance boards
Lifestyle/activity modifications	Avoid overhead activities; maintain aerobic capacity with bicycling or running	Gradually introduce minimal overhead activities; maintain aerobic capacity with bicycling or running	Perform every-other-day shoulder exercise routine

Key: PNF, proprioceptive neuromuscular facilitation.

TRAUMATIC INSTABILITY

Classic Presentation

The patient has a past history of shoulder dislocation. The patient currently complains of pain or weakness when the arm is placed in either an overhead position or the apprehension position of 90° flexion coupled with external rotation and horizontal abduction (horizontal extension).

Cause

Dislocation of the glenohumeral joint causes significant damage to the capsule, some ligaments, often the glenoid labrum, and the humerus itself. The result is a diminished static support system that must rely on dynamic support from the surrounding musculature. Anterior instability due to an anterior dislocation is the most common, accounting for 90% to 95% of cases.[37] Posterior instability is found in patients who chronically self-dislocate or patients who have seizures.

Evaluation

Stability should be evaluated with a load-and-shift test and the apprehension tests and its variants.[11] The L&S test (Figure 7–5) is a push-pull maneuver applied to the neutral shoulder in an attempt to determine in which direction instability is present. Inferior instability is suggestive of multidirectional instability. In other words, for there to be significant inferior displacement, much of the capsule must be damaged. The apprehension position (Figure 7–6) tests the patient for the reproduction of apprehension (a sense that the shoulder may go out of place) and pain. If either sensation is found, an anterior to posterior force is applied to the patient in the supine position as the apprehension position is acquired, the relocation test (Figure 7–7). If the apprehension is ameliorated, instability is likely. If pain is reduced, a coexisting impingement syndrome may be causing discomfort. Glenoid labrum testing should also be included. Several tests exist, including the clunk test and various shear tests in search of painful snapping or clunking felt deep in the shoulder.[15]

Management

Unfortunately, shoulders with traumatic instability are less amenable to conservative management (Table 7–5). These shoulders often have underlying mechanical interference with normal movement. Until the mechanical factor is surgically removed or repaired, the patient may continue to experience symptoms. The need for surgery is based entirely on activity level and degree of incapacitation. Prior to surgical consultation, most patients should be taken through a 6-month trial of conservative care with a focus on shoulder stabilization.

NONTRAUMATIC INSTABILITY OR LOOSENESS

Classic Presentation

The patient is usually asymptomatic. When symptoms occur, they often are the result of a sudden traction on the arm that results in pain and weakness felt in the entire arm (subluxation); symptoms are relieved by supporting the arm. Another common presentation is difficulty working in overhead positions due to a sense of fatigue rather than pain.

Cause

Most patients have an inherent looseness to their shoulder capsules (born loose).[38] This may be accentuated by sporting activities that constantly stretch the capsule, such as with throwing sports and swimming. Patients are asymptomatic unless the shoulder is subluxated with a distraction force or they develop impingement secondary to a loose capsule.

Table 7–5 Management of Chronic Anterior or Multidirectional Shoulder Instability

Parameter	*Initial Stage*	*Intermediate Stage*	*Advanced Stage*
Criteria	Instability evident on L&S or other stability tests; pain or apprehension with apprehension test; relieved by relocation test	Instability testing remains unaffected; however, pain or apprehension is reduced when performing apprehension test	Full pain-free ROM present; all muscles test strong in all ROMs
Goals	Initiate shoulder stabilization program while avoiding positions of risk	Focus on rotator cuff and scapular stabilization exercises, protected return to sporting activity if support is worn	Functionally train the shoulder to meet the demands of a given sport or occupational activity
Concerns	May be an associated glenoid labrum tear that will interfere or prevent successful rehabilitation	Possible glenoid labrum tear or too early a return to activity, noncompliance of patient with exercise program requirements and restrictions	Patient compliance with continuing exercises in a preventive program
Requirements for progression to next stage; approximate time needed	Strength present within lower ranges of shoulder movement; scapula demonstrates stability with resisted abduction or protraction; no "mechanical" pain block in active movement patterns; 1–2 weeks	Pain-free shoulder ROM; muscles test strong without pain; able to perform 3 sets of 10 reps for 2–3 weeks without pain; 3–6 weeks	Pain-free performance of sport or occupational activity: 3–6 months
Manipulation/mobilization	Mild mobilization into restricted accessory motion; however, manipulation is contraindicated; cervical spine adjusting may be helpful	Mild mobilization into restricted accessory motion; however, manipulation is contraindicated; cervical spine adjusting may be helpful	Mild mobilization into restricted accessory motion; however, manipulation is contraindicated; cervical spine adjusting may be helpful
Modalities	Ice after exercise	Ice after exercise	Ice after exercise
External brace, support, etc.	Shoulder support taping or bracing may be needed in the earlier stages while performing exercises	Shoulder support taping or bracing may be needed in the earlier stages while performing exercises	Exercises performed without bracing or taping; for high-level competition, it may be necessary to continue wearing a restriction brace for an extended period of time
ROM/flexibility/massage	Passive PNF diagonal patterns to facilitate functional movement patterns	Myofascial release technique for scapular and anterior chest muscles	As needed

continues

Table 7–5 continued

Parameter	*Initial Stage*	*Intermediate Stage*	*Advanced Stage*
Open-chain exercise	Isometrics in multiple arcs throughout a range of motion; then rhythmic stabilization in multiple arcs (reciprocal motion in a short arc performed as quickly as possible until pain or fatigue limits)	Core exercises include scaption or flexion, prone abduction, prone rowing, press-up, push-up with a plus, and prone flies (for midscapular muscles) performed with light weights or elastic tubing, performing 3–5 sets of 12–15 reps	Plyometric exercises using plyoballs against wall and minitrampoline (size of ball based on functional activity requirements)
Closed-chain exercise	None	Wall push-ups progressing to ground push-ups to push-ups with a plus	Balance on palms using balance ball stabilization approach; use balance devices to perform push-ups on; use stair-stepping machine using hands
Proprioceptive training	Taping or support is primary proprioceptive stimulus plus PNF passive diagonals	Resisted PNF diagonal patterns (incorporates patterns that combine either flexion/extension with external rotation/internal rotation, with abduction/adduction)	Accomplish to some degree by plyometrics; PNF sport-specific patterns can be emphasized; PNF exercises can be performed in various body positions that simulate the sport or occupational requirements
Associated biomechanical items	Address spinal posture as contributing factor, including hyperlordotic cervical and lumbar curves, and a hyperkyphotic thoracic curve creating a slumped position of the shoulder	Continue to address spinal posture with focus on reduction of thoracic kyphosis; begin strengthening lower extremity and trunk for need in reducing stress on shoulder muscles with throwing and other activities	Continue to address spinal posture with focus on reduction of thoracic kyphosis; begin strengthening lower extremity and trunk for need in reducing stress on shoulder muscles with throwing and other activities
Lifestyle/activity modifications	Avoid carrying objects that drag down on the arm; avoid overhead and abduction/external rotation positions	Avoid abduction and external rotation against resistance such as ball throwing or racquet hitting	Make shoulder exercises a part of every-other-day exercise routine

Evaluation

The L&S tests (Figure 7–5) are the most practical tests. Pulling the humeral head forward or backward usually indicates a large degree of movement, sometimes enough to almost subluxate the joint. Most important, inferior traction often causes the development of a sulcus sign or depression under the AC joint. These findings are bilateral. If the patient has developed secondary impingement, another finding (in addition to positive impingement tests) is pain that is produced by the apprehension test (Figure 7–6). The pain is reduced by the relocation test (Figure 7–7), in which an anterior to posterior force is applied to the proximal humerus as the arm is abducted and externally rotated (supine patient).

Management

A standard strengthening program involving initial focus on the rotator cuff and serratus anterior is necessary to substitute for the laxity of the joint capsule (Table 7–4). This may be assisted by functionally taping the shoulder. Avoidance of positions that further stretch the capsule is important. Surgical stabilization is rarely necessary.

ADHESIVE CAPSULITIS

Classic Presentation

The presentation varies depending on the stage at which the patient presents. The patient is usually over age 40 years. In the acute phase, the patient complains of moderate to severe pain that limits all shoulder movement. In most instances, the patient cannot recall any specific event that triggered the pain. The pain interferes with sleep, and in many instances causes the patient to seek prescribed pain medication. In the middle phase, the patient may present with a past history of the acute phase 1 to 3 months previously; now the pain is much less, but she or he notices that lifting the arm or turning it out is severely restricted. In the final phase, the patient may report a very slow increase in ROM, but he or she still has significant reduction.

Cause

The cause is unknown. The most accepted theory is that adhesion development occurs between or within the capsule of the shoulder; however, this is not always visible at surgery. Also, the patient often responds to stretching techniques that place little stretch on the capsule. Some individuals may be predisposed, such as those with diabetes, hyperthyroidism, or chronic obstructive or other lung disease, and those who have had a myocardial infarction.[39] It has been shown that, contrary to logic, this process is not due to immobilization. The process begins as an inflammatory process that resolves with fibrosis. The three stages are (1) an acute inflammatory stage that causes a presentation that overlaps with other conditions, leading to (2) a stiffening stage, and months to years later (3) a thawing phase wherein some of the ROM is recovered.

Evaluation

Most patients present in the stiffening phase. The classic restriction pattern is a significant and equal loss of active and passive ROM. The movements most affected are abduction and external rotation. Flexion is usually the least restricted. Muscle testing is usually strong within the available range. Loss of abduction is often substituted by shoulder shrugging or trunk leaning. Improvement of motion restriction following mild reciprocal isometric contractions (rhythmic stabilization) is confirmatory for adhesive capsulitis. Lack of improvement suggests a bony blockage possibly due to osteoarthritis or an undiagnosed posterior dislocation (if there is a history of trauma).

Management

Most patients in the acute phase do not respond to physical therapy attempts at pain control. During this phase, the pain is often disabling, requiring prescribed pain medication. The chiropractor is most effective in the later stages. In the stiffening phase, use of rhythmic stabilization, coupled with ultrasound, is usually effective in increasing ROM (Exhibit 7–1). This is supported by home exercises, including continuation of rhythmic stabilization, pendulum, and proper wall-walking exercises. Rhythmic stabilization involves taking the patient's arm to the available end-range of abduction/external rotation. The patient is then instructed to apply a minimal (15% to 25%) contraction into further abduction/external rotation for 5 or 6 seconds, followed by an immediate switch to the opposite pattern. This reciprocates back and forth several times. The patient relaxes, and the new range is passively acquired by the doctor. Mild mobilization at the joint may be helpful; however, forceful adjusting is likely to cause an inflammatory flare-up. Significant improvement should occur over a 1 to 3 month period. Failure to improve warrants referral for manipulation under anesthesia.

ROTATOR CUFF TEAR

Classic Presentation

The patient is likely to give a history of an acute traumatic event such as lifting a heavy weight or a fall on an outstretched arm. Older patients may not recall the inciting

Exhibit 7–1 Treatment of Frozen Shoulder

Stage I (acute)

In-office

- Treatment in the acute stage focuses on pain relief through the use of aspirin or nonsteroidal antiinflammatory drugs and transcutaneous electrical nerve stimulation.
- Avoid aggressive mobilization or adjustive techniques.

Home

- Use passive Codman's exercises and mild isometrics (25% contraction for 5 to 8 seconds).
- Sleep on unaffected side with affected side supported by a pillow to avoid excessive internal rotation.

Stages II and III (subacute and chronic)

In-office

- Continue treatment for pain.
- Use ultrasound for palliative pain relief and use prior to stretching.
- Use rhythmic stabilization and hold-relax techniques to increase in ROM.
- Use passive stretching with moist heat pack and gravity assistance.

Home

- Perform active Codman's and wall-walking exercises.
- Do further stretching with self-mobilization with an emphasis on inferior glide.
- Do "giant" ball exercises, pulley exercises, and wand exercises for later stages of stretching.

event. Patients usually complain of pain with overhead activities or weakness in lifting the arm.

Cause

The most common tears are in the supraspinatus. There are generally two areas where tears occur—articular sided and bursal sided. Most partial tears are articular sided and may be related to poor vascularity.[40] Tears may be due to a sudden trauma (especially a pincer action) or more likely occur secondary to chronic degenerative changes in the tendon.

Evaluation

The patient often has signs similar to those of the patient with impingement. The patient usually has difficulty raising or lowering the arm actively. For the supraspinatus, weakness is found with the empty can test (Figure 7–10); for the subscapularis, weakness is found with the lift-off test. Radiographically, there may be apparent superior head migration on an AP view. Further imaging can be accomplished with ultrasonography, MRI, or an arthrogram. Ultrasonography is accurate but operator dependent, MRI is sensitive but may require fat suppression to distinguish rotator cuff tear from other changes, and an arthrogram cannot evaluate bursal-sided partial tears.[41]

Management

Partial tears can be rehabilitated gradually, beginning with isometrics and gradually progressing through a strengthening program (Exhibit 7–2). A rest period from sports or occupational activities is required. Full-thickness tears are usually surgically repaired in younger individuals.

ACUTE CALCIFIC BURSITIS AND TENDINITIS

Classic Presentation

The patient presents with severe shoulder pain that increases with any shoulder movement, either with an insidious onset or subsequent to a fall or other major trauma.

Cause

It was once believed that acute bursitis was related to rupture of the bursa due to a calcific process in the tendon. The calcified tendon is visible on a radiograph and was thought to represent a degenerative process. Rowe,[42] however, found that calcific tendinitis did not occur in patients under age 30 or over age 60 and that many patients with radiographic evidence of calcification were asymptomatic. It appears that pain occurs on resorption of the calcium deposition. This is an inflammatory phase and causes pain. This may be the time when an acute bursitis occurs. Direct trauma and trauma subsequent to cuff rupture are other more obvious causes.

Evaluation

The patient exhibits a supportive posture, holding the arm against the side to avoid movement. All movement, active and passive, is painful. If possible, the bursa may be palpated by passively extending the shoulder and palpating in front of the AC joint for tenderness and swelling. Radiographs usually are unrevealing; however, they should be considered with trauma or when deformity is found.

Exhibit 7–2 Treatment of Acromioclavicular Joint Injury

AC Separations

Type I—Sprain (first-degree separation)

- Use ice and analgesics for pain control.
- Rehabilitative exercises may begin quickly because the AC joint is stable.
- Protective doughnut pad should be worn during contact sport participation.

Type II—Partial subluxation (second-degree separation—torn AC ligament)

- Use ice and analgesics.
- Immobilize with a Kinney-Howard sling with following recommendations:
  1. Two slings are used so that the athlete may shower with support.
  2. Changing slings should be done only with the elbow supported.
  3. Tightening of the sling also should be done with elbow support.
  4. The sling is worn 2 to 6 weeks dependent on extent of injury.
- Isometrics may be performed while in the sling, using the opposite hand (elevation of the arm or shoulder is avoided).
- After the sling, rehabilitate the shoulder muscles with emphasis on
  1. deltoid with shrugs and raises (limited to below 90° initially)
  2. trapezius with shrugs and front rows
  3. biceps
  4. pectorals with light weights and avoiding extremes of horizontal adduction initially
- Return to sport requires protective pad sown or taped in place.

Type III—Total separation (third-degree separation—torn AC and coracoclavicular ligaments)

- Use ice and analgesics for pain.
- Options suggested by various practitioners:
  1. immobilization for 4 to 6 weeks in a Kinney-Howard sling with above rehabilitation (author's choice)
  2. no immobilization with use of progressive exercises, and sports participation with protection in 2 to 4 weeks
  3. surgical repair including the following options:
     — stabilization of clavicle to coracoid with a screw
     — resection of lateral clavicle
     — transarticular AC fixation with pins
     — use of coracoacromial ligament as substitute AC ligament

Osteolysis of the distal clavicle

Suggested options include the following:

- Athlete retires from competetive weight lifting.
- Modify weight lifting activities, including the following:
  1. Substitute bench press with incline or decline press, or cross-cable exercises.
  2. Modify bench press using close grip instead of wide grip; reduce weight used.
  3. Eliminate dips and substitute with above pectoral exercises and triceps extensions.
- Athlete undergoes surgery, usually resection of lateral/distal clavicle.

Shoulder pointer and acromial apophysitis

- Use ice and analgesics for pain.
- Avoid overhead activities for several weeks, in particular with weights.
- Protect the lesion with an acromial (doughnut) pad.

Source: Reprinted with permission from T. Souza, *Sports Injuries of the Shoulder,* p. 427, © 1994, Churchill-Livingstone.

Management

An attempt at sling support and palliative physical therapy application may be made. Many patients, however, are in severe pain requiring prescription medication in the early stages.

ACROMIOCLAVICULAR SEPARATION

Classic Presentation

The patient presents with a traumatic onset of shoulder pain following either a fall on an outstretched arm or a fall onto the top of the shoulder.

Cause

AC separations are classified into three grades (however six types have been described by Rockwood et al.[43]). Grade I (first degree) indicates some tearing of the AC ligament, but no instability. Grade II (second degree) indicates rupture of the AC ligament. Grade III (third degree) involves tearing of the AC ligament and the coracoclavicular (conoid and trapezoid) ligaments. Both grades II and III are unstable.

Evaluation

The mechanism of injury and the pain/tenderness and swelling or deformity at the AC joint are classic findings. Radiographs should be obtained to rule out a distal clavicular fracture or to determine degree of injury. Weighted and nonweighted bilateral views are used to demonstrate an increased coracoclavicular space. A space greater than 1.3 cm is usually consistent with a third-degree (grade III) separation. The displacement is due less to superior migration of the distal clavicle than to inferior displacement of the glenohumeral joint.[44] In other words, this represents a different form of shoulder instability and as a result requires stabilization and support more than replacement of the clavicle into its normal position.

Management

All AC separations can be managed conservatively (see Table 7–2).[45] Grade III separations will leave a permanent bump on the shoulder, however, and for some patients may be a persistent site of minor discomfort. For those patients who require cosmetic perfection, or in those in whom conservative management has not sufficiently returned them to normal function, surgery is an option. The standard treatment of AC separations includes a short period of support with a Kinney-Howard sling (shoulder support on same side as arm sling). Mild isometrics followed by isotonics with emphasis on deltoid and upper trapezius exercises followed by biceps and pectoral exercises are usually sufficient to return to near full function. Padded protection should be worn in sports activities.

OSTEOLYSIS OF THE DISTAL CLAVICLE

Classic Presentation

Osteolysis may be secondary to AC trauma or excessive weight lifting. The weight lifter is usually a young man complaining of diffuse pain felt with the bench press, clean and jerk, or dip. The patient is a serious weight lifter who benches 300 lb or more.

Cause

The cause is unknown. However, direct trauma to the AC joint, as occurs with AC separations or repetitive compression from specific weight-lifting maneuvers, causes a resorption of the distal end of the clavicle.[7]

Evaluation

Although the patient may complain of pain when abducting beyond 90°, the orthopaedic shoulder examination findings are usually unremarkable. This fact, combined with finding a discrete area of tenderness at the AC joint or distal clavicle, should raise the suspicion. Instead of a shoulder series, the radiographic view of choice is the AC spot (Zanca) view. This involves a 10° to 15° cephalad tube tilt shot, with about half of the technique used for a general shoulder radiograph. Resorption is usually evident with an increased widening of the joint space or subchondral defects.

Management

Osteolysis requires a period of modification in weight-lifting activities. Modification includes switching to narrow-grip bench presses (instead of wide grip), cable crossovers, and incline or decline presses. The dip should be avoided. If the pain persists, however, the only conservative solution is to stop lifting heavy weights for at least 6 months. If not effective or the patient is noncompliant, resection or acromioplasty may be somewhat effective.

REFERENCES

1. Souza TA. *Sports Injuries of the Shoulder: Conservative Management*. New York: Churchill-Livingstone; 1994.
2. Ratcliffe A, Flatow EL, Roth N, et al. Biochemical markers in synovial fluid identify early osteoarthritis of the glenohumeral joint. *Clin Orthop*. 1996;330:45–53.
3. Harryman DT, Sidles JA, Clark JM, et al. Translation of the humeral head on the glenoid with passive glenohumeral motion. *J Bone Joint Surg Am*. 1990;72:1334–1343.
4. Howell SM, Galinat BJ, Benzi AJ, et al. Normal and abnormal mechanics of the glenohumeral joint in the horizontal plane. *J Bone Joint Surg Am*. 1988;70:227–232.
5. Perry J. Muscle control of the shoulder. In: Rowe CR, ed. *The Shoulder*. New York: Churchill-Livingstone; 1988:17.
6. Nuber CW, Bowman JD, Perry JP, et al. EMG analysis of classical shoulder motion. *Trans Orthop Res Soc*. 1986:11.
7. Scavenius M, Iversen BF. Nontraumatic clavicular osteolysis in weight lifters. *Am J Sports Med*. 1992;20:463.
8. Mattingly GE, Mackarey PJ. Optimal methods for shoulder tendon palpation: a cadaver study. *Phys Ther*. 1996;76:166–174.
9. Doddy SG, Waterland JC, Freedman L. Scapulohumeral goniometer. *Arch Phys Med Rehabil*. 1970;51:711.
10. Jobe FW, Moynes DR, Brewster CE. Rehabilitation of shoulder instabilities. *Orthop Clin North Am*. 1987;18:473.
11. Hawkins RJ, Schutte JP, Huckell GH, et al. The assessment of glenohumeral translation using manual and fluoroscopic techniques. *Orthop Trans*. 1988;12:727.
12. Rockwood CA. Subluxations and dislocations about the shoulder. In: Rockwood CA, Green DP, eds. *Fractures in Adults*. 2nd ed. Philadelphia: WB Saunders Company; 1984:722.
13. Jobe FW, Kvine RS. Shoulder pain in the overhand and throwing athletes: the relationship of anterior instability and rotator cuff impingement. *Orthop Rev*. 1989;18:963.
14. Liu SH, Henry MH, Nuccion S, et al. Diagnosis of glenoid labral tears: a comparison between magnetic resonance imaging and clinical examinations. *Am J Sports Med*. 1996;24:149–154.
15. Kibler WB. Specificity and sensitivity of the anterior slide test in throwing athletes with superior glenoid labral tears. *Arthroscopy*. 1995;11:296–300.
16. Neer CS. Anterior acromioplasty for chronic impingement syndrome in the shoulder: a preliminary report. *J Bone Joint Surg Am*. 1972;54:41.
17. Hawkins RJ, Kennedy JC. Impingement syndrome in athletes. *Am J Sports Med*. 1980;8:151.
18. Rowlands LK, Wertsh JJ, Prinack SJ. *Am J Phys Med Rehabil*. 1995;74:302–304.
19. Kelly BT, Kadmas WR, Speer KP. The manual muscle examination for rotator cuff strength: an electromyographic investigation. *Am J Sports Med*. 1996;24:581–593.
20. Grenshaw AH, Kilgore WE. Surgical treatment of biceps tenosynovitis. *J Bone Joint Surg Am*. 1966;48:1496.
21. Jemp YN, Malanga G, Growney ES. Activation of the rotator cuff in generating isometric shoulder rotation torque. *Am J Sports Med*. 1996;24:477–485.
22. Greis PE, Kuhn JE, Schultheis P, et al. Validation of the lift-off test and analysis of subscapularis activity during maximal internal rotation. *Am J Sports Med*. 1996;24:589–593.
23. Davis J. Radiography. In: Souza TA, ed. *Sports Injuries of the Shoulder: Conservative Management*. New York: Churchill-Livingstone; 1994:257.
24. Tuite MJ, Yandov DR, DeSmet AA, et al. Diagnosis of partial and complete rotator cuff tears using combined gradient echo and sine echo imaging. *Skeletal Radiol*. 1994;23:541–545.
25. Green MR, Christensen KP. Magnetic resonance imaging of the glenoid labrum. *Am J Sports Med*. 1990;18:229–234.
26. Legan JM, Burkhard TK, Golf WB, et al. Tears of the glenoid labrum: MR imaging of 88 arthroscopically confirmed cases. *Radiology*. 1991;179:241–246.
27. Bonutti PM, Norfray JF, Friedman RJ, Genez BM. Kinematic MRI of the shoulder. *J Comput Assist Tomogr*. 1993;17:666–669.
28. Hunter JC, Blatz DJ, Escobedo EM. SLAP lesions of the glenoid labrum: CT arthrographic and arthroscopic correlation. *Radiology*. 1992;184:513–518.
29. Neumann CH, Petersen SA, Jahnke AH, et al. MRI in the evaluation of patients with suspected instability of the shoulder joint including comparison with CT arthrography. *Rofo*. 1991;154:593.
30. Introcaso JH. Sonography. In: Souza TA, ed. *Sports Injuries of the Shoulder: Conservative Management*. New York: Churchill-Livingstone; 1994:291.
31. Milch H. Treatment of dislocation of the shoulder. *Surgery*. 1938;3:732.
32. Aronen JG, Rehan K. Decreasing the incidence of recurrence of first-time anterior shoulder dislocations with rehabilitation. *Am J Sports Med*. 1984;12:283.
33. Townsend H, Jobe FW, Pink M, Perry J. Electromyographic analysis of the glenohumeral muscles during a baseball rehabilitation program. *Am J Sports Med*. 1991;19:264.
34. Moseley JB Jr, Jobe FW, Pink M, et al. EMG analysis of the scapular muscles during a shoulder rehabilitation program. Am J Sports Med. 1992;20:128.
35. Penny JN, Welsh RP. Shoulder impingement syndromes in athletes and their surgical management. *Am J Sports Med*. 1981;9:11.
36. Souza TA. History and examination of the shoulder. In: *Sports Injuries of the Shoulder: Conservative Management*. New York: Churchill-Livingstone; 1994:167–219.
37. Post M. *The Shoulder—Surgical and Non-Surgical Management*. Philadelphia: Lea & Febiger; 1978.
38. Matsen FA, Thomas SG. Glenohumeral instability. In: Evans CM, ed. *Surgery of the Musculoskeletal System*. 2nd ed. New York: Churchill-Livingstone; 1989.
39. Souza TA. Frozen shoulder. In: *Sports Injuries of the Shoulder: Conservative Management*. New York: Churchill-Livingstone; 1994: 441–455.

40. Ozaki J, Fujimoto S, Nakagawa Y, et al. Tears of the rotator cuff of the shoulder associated with pathological changes in the acromion: a study of cadavers. *J Bone Joint Surg Am.* 1988;70:1224.
41. Unger HR, Neumann CH, Petersen SA. Magnetic resonance imaging. In: Souza TA, ed. *Sports Injuries of the Shoulder: Conservative Management.* New York: Churchill-Livingstone; 1994:299–321.
42. Rowe CR. Tendinitis, bursitis, impingement, "snapping" scapula, and calcific tendinitis. In: *The Shoulder.* New York: Churchill-Livingstone; 1988:105.
43. Rockwood CA, Williams GR, Young DC. Injuries to the acromioclavicular joint. In: Rockwood CA, Green DP, Bucholz RW, eds. *Fractures in Adults.* 3rd ed. Philadelphia: WB Saunders; 1991:1192.
44. Souza TA. Sternoclavicular, acromioclavicular, and scapular disorders. In: *Sports Injuries of the Shoulder: Conservative Management.* New York: Churchill-Livingstone; 1994:409–439.
45. Bjerneld H, Hovelius L, Thorling J. Acromio-clavicular separations treated conservatively: a 5-year followup study. *Acta Orthop Scand.* 1983;54:743.

Chapter 8

Elbow Complaints

CONTEXT

Although anatomically analogous to the knee, the elbow is injured far less often. In large part, this is due to the non–weight-bearing function of the elbow. As the link between the shoulder and the wrist/hand, the elbow is functionally challenged with repetitive activities. These overuse mechanisms account for the majority of complaints. Overstrain is common at the origin of the wrist extensors (lateral elbow) and the wrist flexors (medial elbow). With athletes, valgus stress predominates, in particular in throwing sports and in activities requiring the use of an arm extension such as a bat, racquet, or club. These devices increase the medial stress across the elbow by increasing the length of the lever arm. As with the rest of the upper extremity, the elbow becomes weight bearing when an axial force is applied acutely during a fall, or chronically with gymnastic maneuvers and with some chiropractors due to adjusting maneuvers.

GENERAL STRATEGY

History

- Clarify the type of complaint.
  1. Is the complaint one of pain, stiffness, looseness, crepitus, locking, or a combination of complaints?
  2. Localize the complaint to anterior, posterior, medial, or lateral.
- Clarify the mechanism if traumatic.
  1. Did the patient fall on an outstretched hand? Consider fracture or dislocation (in children, consider a supracondylar fracture).
  2. Did the patient fall on the tip of the elbow (olecranon)? Consider olecranon fracture.
  3. Did the patient have hyperextension of elbow? Consider dislocation and supracondylar fracture.
  4. Did the patient have sudden stretch to the inside of the elbow? Consider medial collateral ligament sprain or lateral compressive injury to the radial head or capitellum.
  5. Did the patient have sudden traction to the elbow? Radial head subluxation is likely.
- Determine whether the mechanism is one of overuse.
  1. In what position does the patient work?
  2. Does the patient perform a repetitive movement at work or with sports involving pronation and supination? Consider muscle strain, trigger points, or peripheral nerve entrapment.
  3. Does the patient perform a repetitive movement at work or with sports involving cocking or medial stretch to the elbow? Consider medial collateral ligament sprain, flexor muscle strain, or ulnar nerve stretch irritation.
- Determine whether the patient has a current or past history/diagnosis of his or her elbow complaint or other related disorders.
  1. Are there associated neck or shoulder complaints or diagnoses?
  2. Does the patient have gout, rheumatoid arthritis, chronic renal pathology, or psoriasis?

Evaluation

- With trauma, palpate for points of tenderness and obtain a radiograph for the possibility of fracture/dislocation.
- Challenge the ligaments of the elbow with varus and valgus stress.

- When nontraumatic, challenge the musculotendinous attachments with stretch, contraction, and a combination of contraction in a stretched position.
- When trauma or overuse is not present, evaluate the patient's elbow for swelling and deformity (olecranon bursitis, gouty tophi; osteoarthritis).

Management

- Refer fracture/dislocation for orthopaedic management.
- Refer cases of infection, unresolving bursitis, and gout.
- Manage soft tissue disorders and articular disorders with conservative care.

RELEVANT ANATOMY AND BIOMECHANICS

The elbow joint performs two movement patterns: (1) extension/flexion and (2) pronation/supination of the forearm. The "hinge" function of extension/flexion occurs primarily at the ulnotrochlear joint, the articulation between the distal humerus and proximal ulna and the olecranon process of the ulna and the distal fossa of the humerus. Most daily activities require elbow participation in a range of motion (ROM) between 30° and 130°.[1] Functionally, flexion is accomplished by the biceps, brachialis, and brachioradialis. Extension is primarily due to triceps contraction. As one might guess, the larger muscular contribution to flexion makes it the stronger movement. Extension is approximately 70% as strong as flexion.[1] Supination and pronation occur at the proximal radioulnar joint and the radiocapitellar joint, the articulation between the radial head and the capitellum of the distal humerus. Functionally, supination is accomplished through contraction of the biceps brachii and the supinator muscles. Supination is more effective with the elbow flexed because of the prestretch of the supinator muscle and mechanical advantage of the biceps. Pronation is accomplished by the pronator teres and less effectively by the pronator quadratus. Pronation is more effective with the elbow extended, placing a prestretch on the pronator teres. Supination is slightly stronger (15%) than pronation due to the contribution of the biceps. The biceps and triceps cross both the shoulder and elbow joints. Flexion of the shoulder decreases effectiveness of the biceps with elbow flexion and supination; extension decreases effectiveness of the triceps with extension.

As with all joints, stability is provided by a contribution of position-dependent ligamentous and capsular tension, bony congruity, and static/dynamic muscle/tendon support. Similar to the knee, a bony lock occurs in full extension, providing some protection from varus and valgus forces. In the elbow, the fit of the olecranon process of the ulna into the olecranon fossa of the distal humerus provides some stability with extension. This tongue-and-groove lock is aided by tension in the anterior capsule and collateral ligaments. The main restraint to valgus strain in extension is from the anterior oblique portion of the medial collateral ligament (Figure 8–1). With the elbow flexed to between 10° and 60°, the medial collateral ligament becomes lax. It is in this midrange position that most medial-sided injuries occur. When the elbow is flexed to 90° and beyond, the posterior aspect of the medial (ulnar) collateral ligament becomes tight.

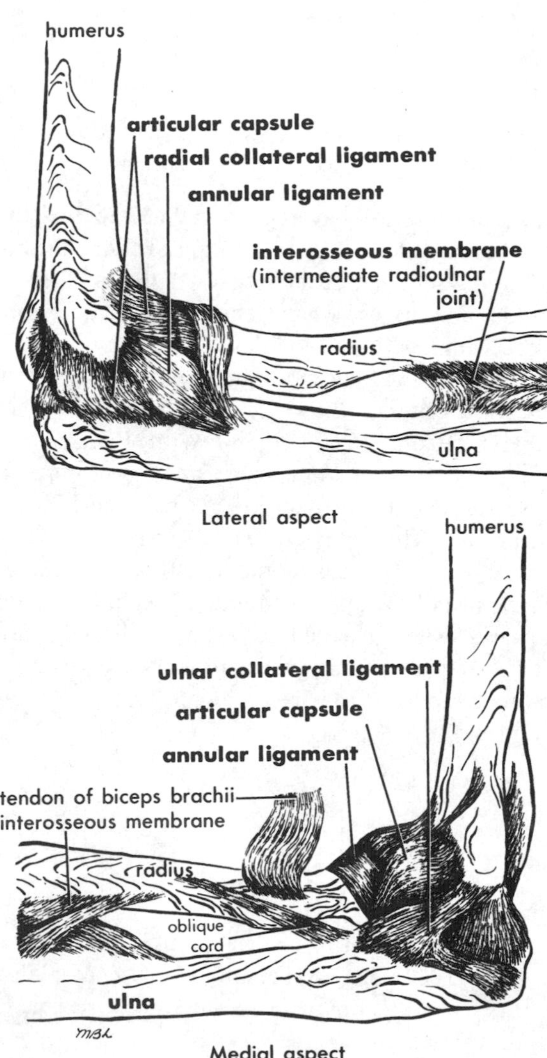

Figure 8–1 Lateral and medial aspects of the right elbow joint. *Source:* Reprinted with permission from J.E. Crouch, *Functional Human Anatomy*, 4th ed., p. 151, © 1985, Lea & Febiger.

Medial stability is statically and dynamically provided by the flexor/pronator muscle group, which takes its origin off of the medial epicondyle of the humerus. Lateral stability is provided by a very weak lateral collateral ligament, and more significantly from the anconeus muscle.[2] Lateral stability is assisted statically and dynamically by the extensor wad of muscles that take their origin off the lateral epicondyle.

Restriction to overextension is provided by stretch of the anterior capsule and biceps tendon in addition to the bony block of the olecranon in the olecranon fossa. Flexion is restricted by muscle contact, tension in the posterior capsule and the triceps tendon, and radial head and humerus contact. Pronation is restricted by the crossing of the radius and the ulna. Supination is limited by tension in the pronator muscle group.

EVALUATION

History

First, determine the type of complaint or complaints the patient has; pain, stiffness, locking, etc. Determine if there is a history of trauma (recent or distant), whether there is an overuse component, or whether the complaint had an insidious onset. Attempt to localize the complaint to the anterior, posterior, lateral, or medial aspect of the elbow. The answers to these questions should sufficiently narrow the possibilities to allow for a more focused examination (Table 8–1).

Pain Localization

The following are possible causes of pain based on location (Figure 8–2, A and B, and Table 8–2):

- anterior
  1. traumatic—anterior capsular sprain, distal biceps tendon strain, fracture, or dislocation
  2. nontraumatic—capsular sprain, biceps tendinitis, and pronator teres strain
- posterior
  1. traumatic—olecranon fracture, bursitis, triceps strain
  2. nontraumatic—olecranon bursitis, triceps tendinitis, degenerative joint disease
- medial
  1. traumatic—ulnar collateral ligament sprain, ulnar nerve traction, epicondyle avulsion, flexor/pronator strain
  2. nontraumatic—minor ulnar collateral ligament sprain, chronic ulnar nerve irritation, flexor/pronator strain (medial epicondylitis)
- lateral
  1. traumatic—radial head fracture, osteochondritis dissecans of the capitellum
  2. nontraumatic—lateral epicondylitis, osteocartilagenous fragments from the radial head or capitellum

Traumatic and Overuse Elbow Pain

As with all traumatic onsets a search for dislocation or fracture and the possible complications associated with each are the first orders of business. Dislocation and fracture are often the consequence of hyperextension of the elbow. In particular in children, the possibility of a supracondylar fracture should always be considered with a history of a hyperextension injury due to a fall on an outstretched hand or a direct blow just above the antecubital fossa.[3] These fractures account for two thirds of children's elbow fractures; one third of adult elbow fractures are distal humeral.[4] Unfortunately, these types of fractures resemble dislocations, but they are often more serious. Dislocations at the elbow are usually posterior. They also occur with hyperextension and are the result of a leverage effect. As the olecranon is blocked by the olecranon fossa, the trochlea is levered over the coranoid process. The medial collateral ligament is ruptured, and there may be associated radial head or capitellar fractures. These types of injuries are usually seen in an acute, on-the-field or playground scenario. Attempts at relocation should be tempered by the possibility that a dislocation is in fact a fracture. Attempts at relocation may cause neurovascular injury.

Valgus stress to the elbow is less often an acute injury; more often it is a chronic overuse phenomenon. If a sudden valgus force is applied to the elbow, avulsion of the medial epicondyle, medial collateral ligament sprain, and capitellum fracture should be considered. A direct fall onto the tip of the elbow with the elbow flexed may result in either an olecranon fracture or olecranon bursitis. Sudden traction on the forearm of a young child may result in a radial head entrapment phenomenon often called nursemaid's elbow.

Overuse injuries account for many of the problems presenting as medial or lateral elbow pain. Disorders associated with repetitive flexion maneuvers and medial elbow pain is suggestive of medial epicondylitis. Repetitive extension maneuvers associated with lateral elbow pain is suggestive of lateral epicondylitis. Repetitive pronation maneuvers associated with medioanterior elbow and forearm pain suggest pronator involvement, especially if associated with distal neurologic signs and symptoms. These are discussed in more detail in Chapter 9.

Repetitive sports activities are probably the most common cause of persistent elbow pain. Throwing sports or sports that require leverage at the elbow through an arm extension

Table 8–1 History Questions for Elbow and Forearm Complaints

Primary Question	*What Are You Thinking?*	*Secondary Questions*	*What Are You Thinking?*
Was there an injury?	Fracture, dislocation, sprain (capsular/ligamentous)	Hyperextended (overextended)?	Anterior capsule sprain Elbow dislocation Supracondylar fracture in children
		Fell on hand with elbow extended?	Radial head fracture
		Fell on tip of elbow?	Olecranon fracture or bursitis
		Overstretched inside of elbow?	Medial collateral ligament sprain or rupture Damage to ulnar nerve Medial epicondyle avulsion Capitellum fracture
		Sudden traction on arm?	Radial head subluxation
Was there any repetitive activity?	Overuse leading to tendinitis, trigger points (TrPs), osseous reactive changes	Throwing?	Compression injuries on lateral side; stretch on medial
		Racquet sport?	Lateral pain—lateral epicondylitis or supinator TrP Medial pain—medial epicondylitis or pronator TrP
		Pain on outside of elbow with typing, hammering, using a screwdriver?	Lateral epicondylitis or supinator TrP
Do you have weakness at the elbow?	Biceps rupture or strain, cervical disc, neural compression/entrapment	Associated with pain?	Possibly due to pain inhibition
		Any associated neck pain and/or radiation?	Cervical disc or subluxation
Do you have stiffness or restricted movement?	Osteoarthritis (OA) or other arthritide, flexor contracture, osteophytes, effusion	History of excessive throwing?	Flexor contracture
		Early-morning stiffness?	OA
		Swelling with blocked extension?	Effusion or bursitis
Do you have superficial swelling?	Bursitis or tophi (gout)	Back of elbow?	Olecranon bursitis
		Also big toe swelling?	Gout

such as a bat, racquet, or club are the main instigators. The cocking portion of the throwing act places enormous medial stretch and lateral compression stress into the elbow joint. The forearm contributions to various pitches in baseball may selectively strain the pronator or wrist flexor group of muscles. At the end of acceleration, there may be a posterior compressive force component that should be considered in athletes complaining of pain on passive and active end-range extension.

Weakness

Weakness at the elbow without associated pain should suggest the possibility of a biceps tendon rupture. There should be a history of a sudden flexion contraction with an associated proximal migration of the biceps muscle belly. Most other causes of localized elbow weakness are due to pain. Some patients with elbow flexion contracture may perceive elbow movement as weak.

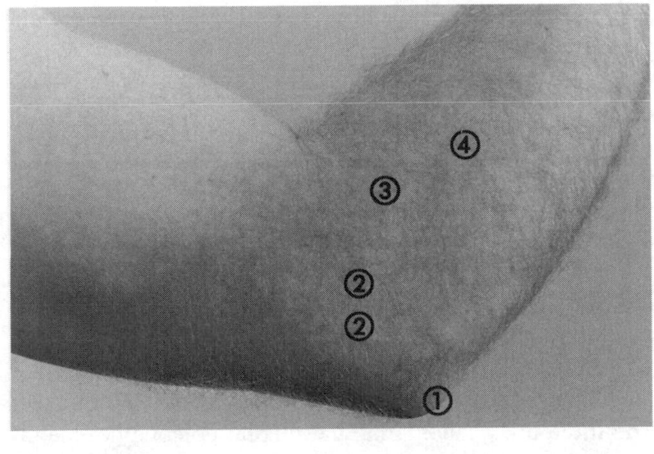

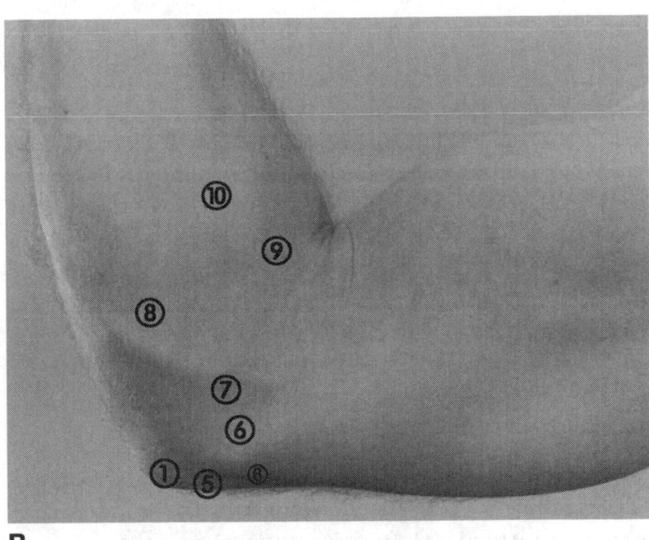

Figure 8–2 **A**, Lateral elbow; **B**, medial elbow. *Note:* See Table 8–2 for explanation of numbers.

Table 8–2 Elbow Pain Localization

#	*Structures*	*Overt Trauma*	*Insidious or Overuse*
1	Olecranon, triceps insertion	Olecranon fracture, olecranon bursitis	Triceps tendinitis, valgus-extension overload
2	Lateral epicondyle of humerus, origin of extensor wad	Supracondylar fracture (or slightly above)	Lateral epicondylitis
3	Radial head, capitellum	Radial head fracture, radial head subluxation	Radial head subluxation, osteochondritis dissecans of the capitellum
4	Supinator, proximal radius	Proximal radius fracture	Supinator syndrome, posterior interosseous nerve syndrome (palpation point)
5	Ulnar nerve	Damage from associated fracture	Ulnar neuritis, subluxating ulnar nerve
6	Medial epicondyle of humerus, origin of flexor wad	Supracondylar fracture, ulnar collateral ligament sprain	Medial epicondylitis, Little League/ pitchers elbow (apophyseal injury)
7	Ulnar collateral ligament	Collateral ligament sprain	Collateral ligament sprain
8	Wrist flexors	Contusion	Flexor tendinitis
9	Biceps tendon insertion/ tuberosity of radius	Biceps avulsion	Distal biceps strain
10	Pronator teres	Contusion	Pronator teres syndrome (palpation point)

Note: See Figure 8–2 for localization of numbered areas.

Instability

Instability will be the consequence of a past fracture, dislocation, or sudden valgus force. Following elbow dislocations, only about 1% to 2% of patients have significant instability.[5] More frequently, instability is the result of constant valgus loading of the immature athletic elbow. It is important to ask about other joints. A generalized looseness of all joints first may be noticed in the elbow. Most of these are "normal" variants based on age and female gender; however, some connective tissue disorders such as Ehlers-Danlos syndrome and Marfan's syndrome must be considered.

Restricted Motion

Restriction to passive flexion or extension coupled with a traumatic history suggest joint effusion or fracture. A nontraumatic restriction to passive extension suggests a tight biceps or anterior capsule. A history of overuse is usually found. A nontraumatic restriction to passive flexion suggests a tight triceps or posterior capsular adhesions.

Locking or Crepitus

Locking or crepitus in a young patient is suggestive of osteochondritis dissecans, whereas in an older patient is suggestive of degenerative changes. If the patient complains of crepitus or locking with pronation and supination, a search for radiocapitellar involvement is warranted. If the patient complains of crepitus on extension of the elbow, osteophytic involvement of the medial epicondyle or olecranon is possible. If there appears to be a pop with extension, the radial head is likely the source at the lateral elbow and a subluxating ulnar nerve at the medial elbow.

Superficial Complaints

The most common superficial complaints at the elbow are the skin lesions associated with psoriasis. Swellings are usually due to either gouty tophi (also seen with chronic renal failure) or an olecranon bursitis. A history of resting on the elbow or an occupation requiring constant support onto the elbow is often found.

Numbness and tingling complaints are almost always associated with a pattern including the forearm and wrist or neck and shoulder. A search for specific peripheral nerve localization findings or nerve root findings is presented in Chapter 9 and Chapter 2, respectively.

Examination

In an acute scenario, a quick check of distal neural and vascular integrity should be made with simple wrist and finger movements coupled with palpation of distal pulses while the history is being elicited.

Observation of the carrying angle of the elbow may indicate past or current bony derangement. The carrying angle for males is between 5° and 10°; for females, 10° and 15°. Cubitus valgus (greater than 20°) suggests laxity of the medial joint or possible compression injury to the lateral joint at the radial head or capitellum. Cubitus varus (less than 5°) is sometimes referred to as a gunstock deformity and may indicate fracture or epiphyseal damage. When the patient assumes a pain-relief position of about 70° of flexion and 10° of supination, joint effusion is often the cause. Note proper alignment of the posterior elbow with the elbow flexed. The three bony landmarks, the medial epicondyle, lateral epicondyle, and olecranon, should form a triangle of points; with extension they are horizontally aligned.

Swelling about the elbow is unusual unless there is an underlying fracture, bursitis, or gouty tophi deposit. Olecranon bursitis is the most common and is unmistakable due to its posterior location and size. Superficial skin lesions that are isolated to the elbow (and perhaps knees and scalp) are most often psoriatic. These lesions are silver, scaly patches found mainly on the extensor aspect of the forearm or elbow.

Palpation is useful in locating common bony or soft tissue damage sites. The olecranon process posteriorly may be tender due to a traumatic fracture (history of a fall on the elbow) or a stress fracture (excessive elbow extension). The medial epicondyle may be tender to palpation with ligament tears or flexor muscle strain. The lateral epicondyle may be tender to palpation with lateral epicondylitis or, more rarely, lateral collateral ligament sprain. Tenderness at the radial head is found with both fracture and subluxation.

Orthopaedic testing focuses on stability, internal derangement, nerve entrapment, and muscle/tendon problems. Additional testing may incorporate cervical spine testing for nerve root or referral pain sources, and biomechanical factors due to shoulder or wrist dysfunction. Following are the standard orthopaedic tests for the elbow:

- Valgus testing[6]: By flexing the elbow to 20° or 30°, the stability provided by the olecranon is eliminated and the anterior joint capsule is relaxed (Figure 8–3). The shoulder is then externally rotated to prevent any shoulder rotation during the stability testing. A valgus force is applied to the medial elbow while palpating for instability or restrictions. Opening at the joint indicates damage to the primary stabilizer, the anterior bundle of the medial collateral ligament. Pain with no instability may occur as a result of minor and/or chronic medial collateral ligament sprains or flexor/pronator muscle strains.

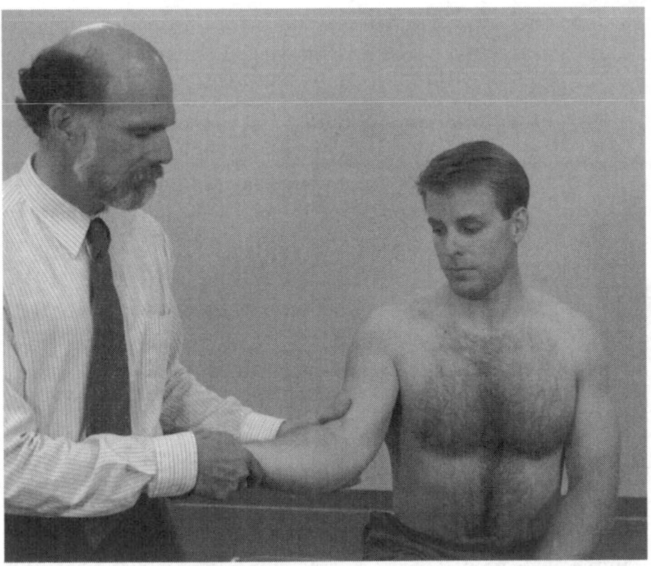

Figure 8–3 Valgus testing for stability is performed with the elbow held at 15° to 20° flexion and the forearm supinated. A force is applied from lateral to medial.

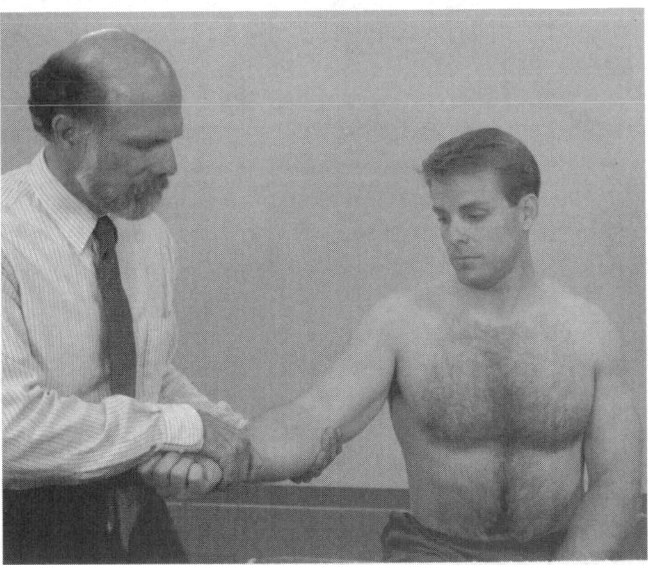

Figure 8–4 Varus testing for stability is performed with the elbow bent to 15° to 20° flexion and the arm internally rotated. A medial to lateral force is applied.

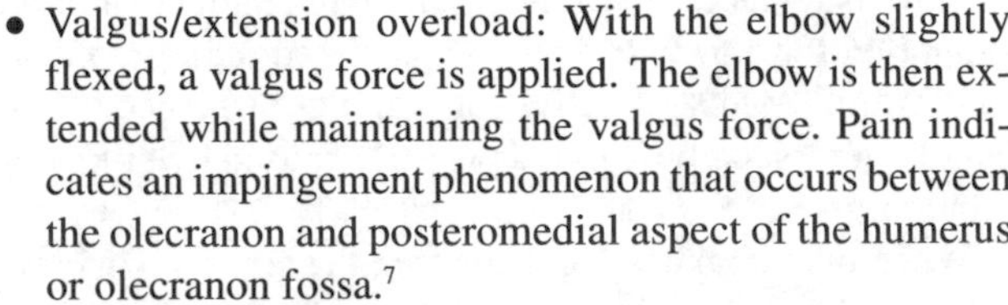

- Valgus/extension overload: With the elbow slightly flexed, a valgus force is applied. The elbow is then extended while maintaining the valgus force. Pain indicates an impingement phenomenon that occurs between the olecranon and posteromedial aspect of the humerus or olecranon fossa.[7]
- Varus testing: By flexing the elbow to 20° or 30°, a varus force will be focused more on the lateral collateral complex (Figure 8–4). The shoulder should be internally rotated to eliminate any shoulder contribution that could be misinterpreted as coming from the elbow.
- Mills' test: Lateral epicondylitis will usually be more painful with passive stretching of the extensors. This is accomplished through passive wrist flexion with the elbow extended (Figure 8–5).
- Reverse Mills' test: Medial epicondylitis will usually be more painful with passive stretching of the flexors. This is accomplished through passive wrist extension with the elbow extended.
- Cozen's test: Resisted wrist extension (with the elbow both flexed and extended) will usually increase the pain of lateral epicondylitis (Figure 8–6). Weakness on wrist extension is more indicative of radial nerve or C7 nerve root involvement.
- Tinel's test: With ulnar nerve irritation due to compression or hypermobility (subluxating or dislocating ulnar nerve), tapping over the nerve at the posterior elbow may cause pain or paresthesias down the medial fore-

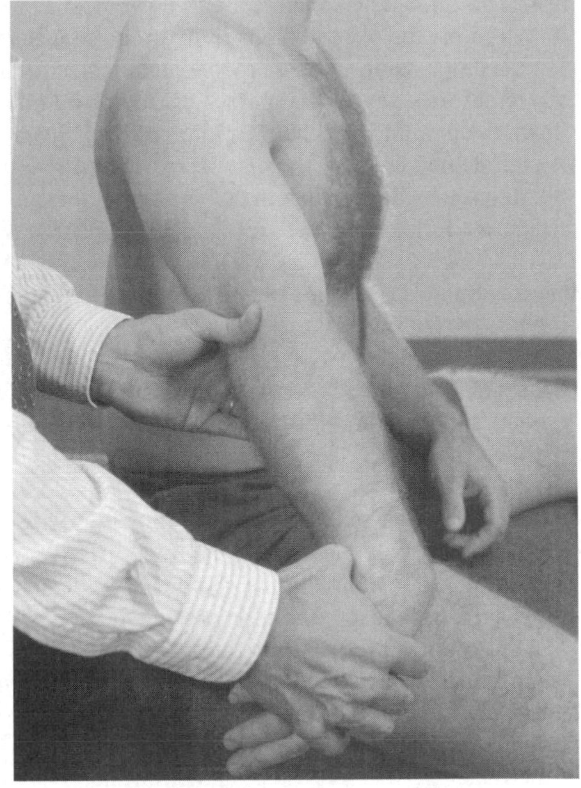

Figure 8–5 Mills' maneuver for lateral epicondylitis involves passive stretching of the extensors through passive flexion of the wrist with the elbow extended.

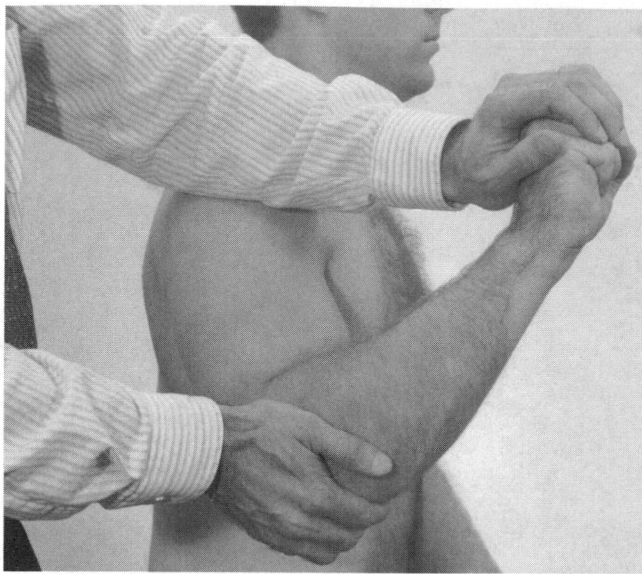

Figure 8–6 Cozen's maneuver for lateral epicondylitis is performed with the elbow flexed or extended. The patient is asked to extend the wrist against resistance.

arm. This should be compared with the opposite elbow to determine the patient's sensitivity to this maneuver.

- Ulnar compression test: Full elbow flexion held for 3 to 5 minutes may cause pain, paresthesias, or a numbness down the medial arm when the ulnar nerve is irritated. A complementary test is to palpate for ulnar nerve subluxation/dislocation when the elbow is taken from extension to full flexion.

Functional patterns that are suggestive of specific disorders include the following:

- Posterior pain on resisted extension with full shoulder flexion and/or pain with passive flexion of the elbow with the shoulder fully flexed suggests triceps tendinitis.
- Anterior pain on resisted flexion/supination with the shoulder fully extended and/or pain with passive wrist and elbow extension with the shoulder fully extended suggests distal biceps tendinitis or avulsion.
- Anterior pain on resisted pronation with the elbow in neutral and extended and/or pain with passive supination with the elbow extended suggests pronator teres strain.
- Anterolateral pain on resisted supination and/or passive pronation (sometimes with a Yergason test) suggests supinator strain.
- Lateral pain on resisted wrist extension and/or passive flexion of the wrist with the elbow extended/forearm pronated and/or resisted finger extension suggests lateral epicondylitis.
- Medial pain on resisted wrist flexion with the elbow extended and/or passive wrist extension with the elbow extended/forearm supinated and/or resisted finger flexion suggests medial epicondylitis.

Radiographic evaluation of the elbow begins with two standard views: the anteroposterior (AP) and lateral. In addition to obvious signs of fracture, indirect indicators of intra-articular fracture are positive fat pad signs. On a normal lateral view a small anterior fat pad may be visible as a small radiolucent triangle at the distal humerus. The posterior fat pad is not usually visible because of the overlap of the humeral condyles. When a patient presents with acute elbow trauma, a diligent search for an enlarged anterior fat pad (ship's sail shape) and a posterior fat pad should be made. A positive fat pad sign is indicative of intracapsular bleeding, usually due to intracapsular fracture.[8] When a positive fat pad sign is evident yet a fracture is not obvious on the two standard views, additional views should be utilized until the fracture is located. If still not visible, the patient should be supported for 5 to 7 days and reexamined radiographically to be sure.[9] A false-positive fat pad sign may occur if the lateral view is not positioned properly caused by even slight rotation.[10]

When the radial head and neck are the areas of concern, a lateral oblique view is helpful.[11] Another excellent view is the radial head-capitellum view (patient position same as for lateral view projection with a 45° tube angle toward the patient).[12] This view is also valuable in finding osteochondritis dissecans of the capitellum (Panner's), and radial head, capitellum, and coronoid process fractures. Coronoid process fracture or pathologic lesion is best visualized with the medial (internal) oblique projection. When restriction to extension is found on examination, an axial view is helpful in demonstrating osteophytes of the olecranon-trochlear joint.[13] Patients who demonstrate ulnar nerve signs should be evaluated with a cubital tunnel view in an effort to visualize medial trochlear osteophytes. This is similar to the axial view; however, the elbow is positioned in 15° of external rotation (maximally flexed).[14]

Approximately 25% patients who appear clinically to have either lateral or medial epicondylitis may demonstrate soft tissue calcification at the attachment sites of the respective muscle groups on standard elbow views.[15] However, this is not necessary for establishing a diagnosis. It is essentially an incidental finding.

MANAGEMENT

- Fractures and dislocations require referral to prevent neurovascular or long term biomechanical complications.
- Tendinitis disorders are treated with protected rest, icing, and PT modalities for pain. NSAIDs or alternatives might be helpful in the acute stage. Cross friction massage with the tendon under stretch, myofascial release techniques to the involved muscles every other day for 2 to 3 weeks should resolve most problems. Modification or elimination of an inciting activity is required for prevention of future recurrence.
- Little league elbow without radiographic evidence of damage may be managed conservatively with rest and ice. Slow return to pitching with strict adherence to Little League rules and avoidance of curve balls and side-arm pitching will usually control the problem.
- Little league elbow with radiographic evidence of medial stress or lateral compression injury should be referred or comanaged.
- Valgus-extension overload may be managed initially with taping or bracing to prevent extension. Avoidance of any forceful extension activities is required. If the patient is wanting to pursue the activity (usually sports), referral for decompression of the posterior elbow is suggested.

Algorithm

An algorithm for evaluation and management of elbow/forearm pain is presented in Figure 8–7.

Figure 8–7
ELBOW/FOREARM PAIN—ALGORITHM.

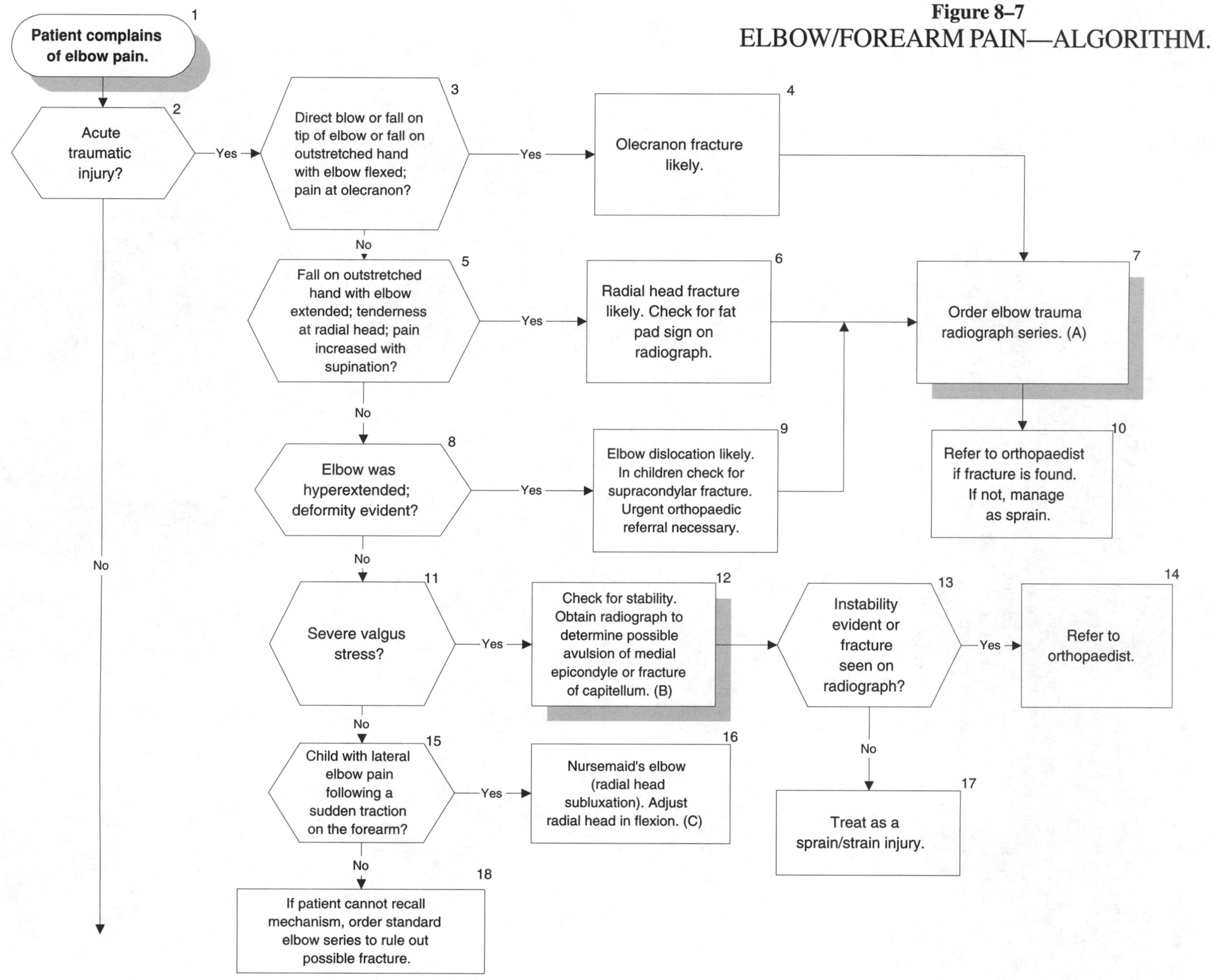

continues

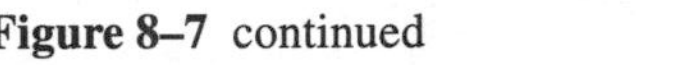

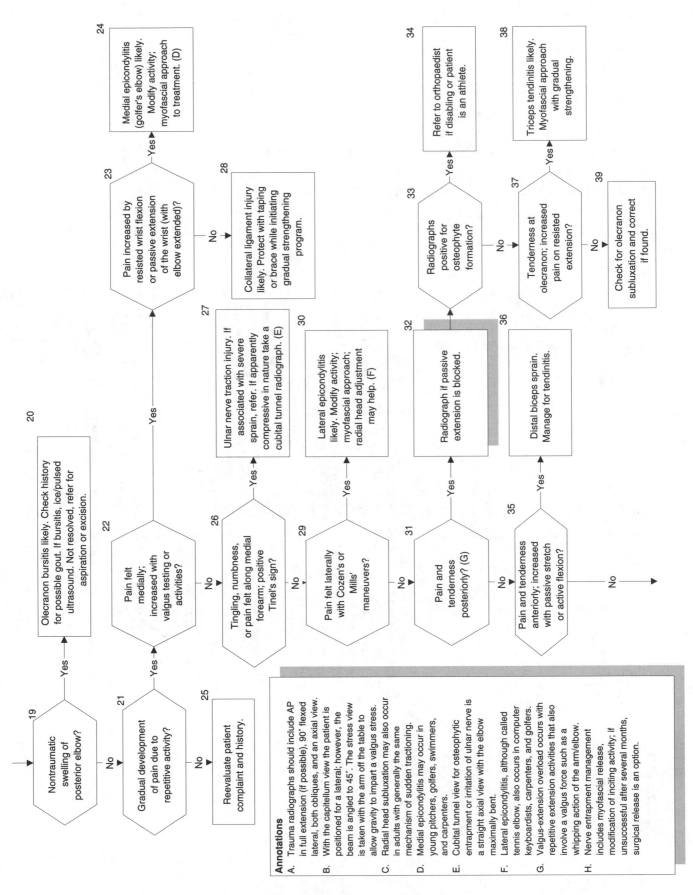

Figure 8–7 continued

19 Nontraumatic swelling of posterior elbow?
- Yes → 20 Olecranon bursitis likely. Check history for possible gout. If bursitis, ice/pulsed ultrasound. Not resolved, refer for aspiration or excision.
- No → 21

21 Gradual development of pain due to repetitive activity?
- Yes → 22
- No → 25 Reevaluate patient complaint and history.

22 Pain felt medially; increased with valgus testing or activities?
- Yes → 23
- No → 26

23 Pain increased by resisted wrist flexion or passive extension of the wrist (with elbow extended)?
- Yes → 24 Medial epicondylitis (golfer's elbow) likely. Modify activity; myofascial approach to treatment. (D)
- No → 28 Collateral ligament injury likely. Protect with taping or brace while initiating gradual strengthening program.

26 Tingling, numbness, or pain felt along medial forearm; positive Tinel's sign?
- Yes → 27 Ulnar nerve traction injury. If associated with severe sprain, refer. If apparently compressive in nature take a cubital tunnel radiograph. (E)
- No → 29

29 Pain felt laterally with Cozen's or Mills' maneuvers?
- Yes → 30 Lateral epicondylitis likely. Modify activity; myofascial approach; radial head adjustment may help. (F)
- No → 31

31 Pain and tenderness posteriorly? (G)
- Yes → 32 Radiograph if passive extension is blocked. → 33
- No → 35

33 Radiographs positive for osteophyte formation?
- Yes → 34 Refer to orthopaedist if disabling or patient is an athlete.
- No → 37

37 Tenderness at olecranon; increased pain on resisted extension?
- Yes → 38 Triceps tendinitis likely. Myofascial approach with gradual strengthening.
- No → 39 Check for olecranon subluxation and correct if found.

35 Pain and tenderness anteriorly; increased with passive stretch or active flexion?
- Yes → 36 Distal biceps sprain. Manage for tendinitis.
- No →

Annotations

A. Trauma radiographs should include AP in full extension (if possible), 90° flexed lateral, both obliques, and an axial view.
B. With the capitellum view the patient is positioned for a lateral; however, the beam is angled to 45°. The stress view is taken with the arm off the table to allow gravity to impart a valgus stress.
C. Radial head subluxation may also occur in adults with generally the same mechanism of sudden tractioning.
D. Medial epicondylitis may occur in young pitchers, golfers, swimmers, and carpenters.
E. Cubital tunnel view for osteophytic entrapment or irritation of ulnar nerve is a straight axial view with the elbow maximally bent.
F. Lateral epicondylitis, although called tennis elbow, also occurs in computer keyboardists, carpenters, and golfers.
G. Valgus-extension overload occurs with repetitive extension activities that also involve a valgus force such as a whipping action of the arm/elbow.
H. Nerve entrapment management includes myofascial release, modification of inciting activity; if unsuccessful after several months, surgical release is an option.

continues

Figure 8–7 continued

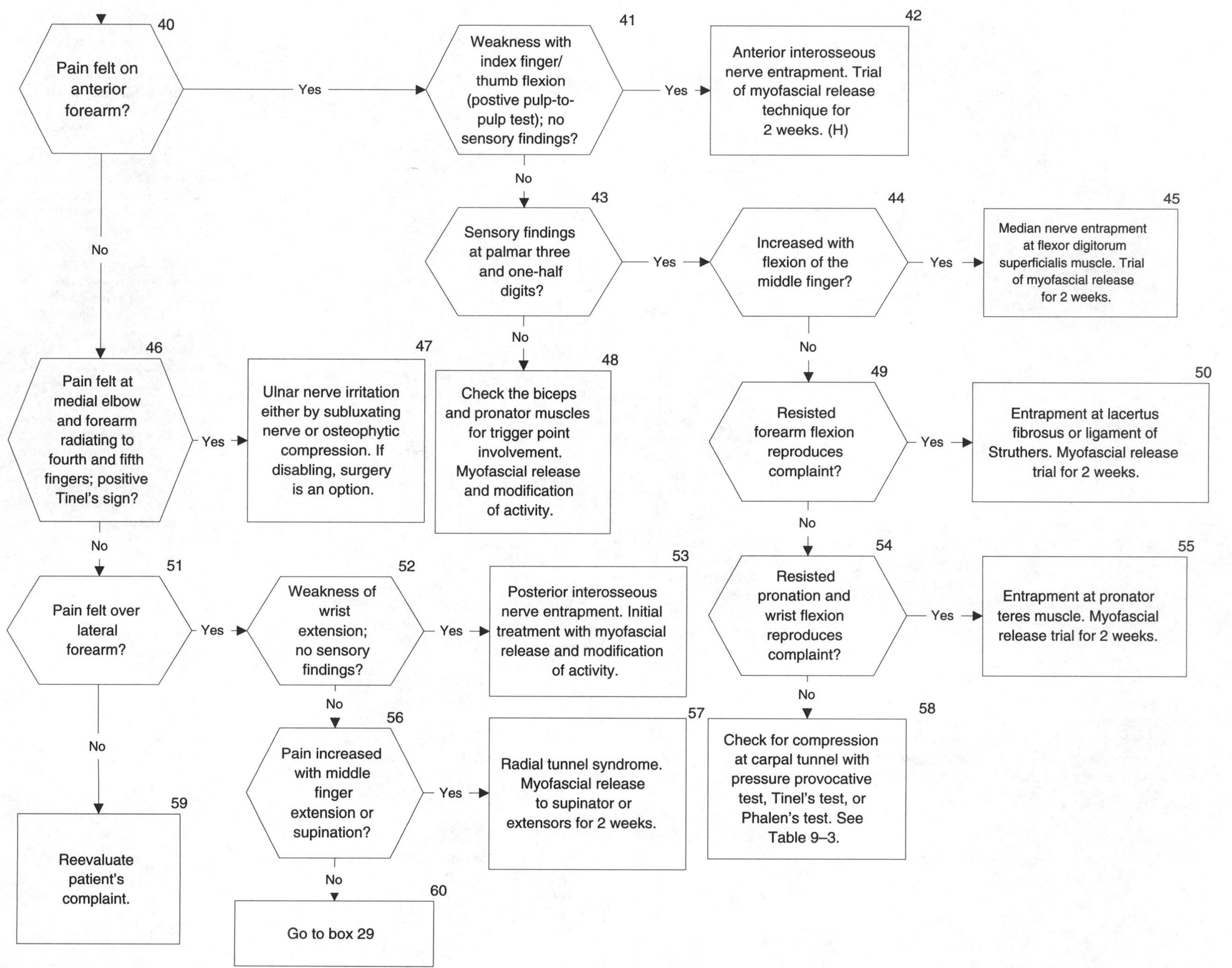

SELECTED DISORDERS OF THE ELBOW

LATERAL EPICONDYLITIS (TENNIS ELBOW)

Classic Presentation

The patient presents with lateral elbow pain associated with a repetitive sport or occupational activity.

Cause

Many theories have been proposed and many structures have been implicated; however, the currently accepted theory is that initially there is tearing of the extensor carpi radialis brevis (ECRB) origin.[16] This process may extend to the extensor digitorum communis (EDC) or the extensor carpi radialis longus (ECRL). The histologic description of the change in tissue is called angiofibroblastic hyperplasia.[17] Repetitive movements requiring forceful dorsiflexion, radial deviation, and supination are the most common causes. Although it is associated with tennis, other sports and occupational activities are also possible causes. Meat cutters, plumbers, and weavers are examples of those who may be affected. With tennis, novice players with poor backhand technique account for most cases. With professional players, the forehand or serving may be the cause. The more frequently an individual plays, the higher the risk of developing tennis elbow.

Evaluation

Tenderness is elicited at the lateral epicondyle, specifically at the origin of the ECRB. Tenderness 5 mm anterior and distal to the lateral epicondyle is most common. Provocative maneuvers include contraction of the wrist extensors with the elbow flexed or extended (Cozen's maneuver [Figure 8–6]) and stretching of the wrist extensors with passive wrist flexion with the elbow extended (Mills' maneuver [Figure 8–5]). Painful resisted middle or ring finger extension implicates the EDC. Wrist extension with radial deviation implicates the ECRB or ECRL. Another suggested test is the chair test. The patient is asked to pick up a light chair by the chair back. The patient's elbow is extended with the forearm pronated. This is usually impossible for the patient with lateral epicondylitis because of the pain. Radiographs may demonstrate calcification in as many as 25% of patients with lateral epicondylitis, although they are rarely indicated.[15]

Management

In the acute phase, ice and rest from the inciting activity are essential. Imposed rest through the use of a splint with the wrist in 30° to 45° of extension may relieve tension on the ECRB.[18] Through a graded program of slow stretching and isometric exercise progressing to isotonic exercise of the wrist extensors with an eccentric focus, resolution and prevention may be initiated. Myofascial release techniques are effective. Cross-friction massage, manipulation, and mobilization are helpful in the subacute phase.[19] During the subacute phase, the use of a tennis elbow brace may help redistribute forces distal to the ECRB. Recommendations are to use a pneumatic or Velcro type that is 3.0- to 3.5-in wide.[20] If tennis is the culprit, recommend a midsize ceramic or graphite racquet with natural gut strings. The string tension should be 3 to 5 lb below what the athlete is used to (usually 52 to 55 lb).[21] Use the Nirschl approach to proper grip size.[22]

MEDIAL EPICONDYLITIS

Classic Presentation

The patient complains of medial elbow pain following a repetitive activity such as hammering or use of a screwdriver. In athletes, the inciting activity usually involves wrist flexion and pronation such as in serving and overhead and forehand strokes. Golfing ("golfer's elbow") or throwing may also cause symptoms. Patients may also complain of pain or weakness on gripping.

Cause

Medial epicondylitis is believed to be a tendinopathy of the origin of the wrist flexors and pronator teres.

Evaluation

Tenderness is found at the medial epicondyle. Pain is reproduced with resisted wrist flexion and pronation. Passive stretching of the wrist flexors with wrist extension, keeping the elbow straight, may also elicit pain (reverse Mills' test).[6] In chronic cases, an elbow flexion contracture may occur, leading to restriction of extension and/or supination. An ulnar neuropathy may coexist with medial epicondylitis.[23] Tinel's sign may be positive over the ulnar nerve. Routine radiographs may reveal calcifications in close proximity to the medial epicondyle in 20% to 30% of patients with epicondylitis.

Management

In the acute phase, ice and rest from the inciting activity are essential. Imposed rest through the use of a splint with the wrist in 10° of flexion may relieve tension on the flexor muscle group. If the flexor carpi radialis is involved, 10° of radial deviation should be added. For pronator involvement, a splint that blocks forearm rotation may be needed. In most cases, however, myofascial release of the flexor muscle mass and pronator teres is sufficient to alleviate the patient's problem. Through a graded program of slow stretching and isometric exercise progressing to isotonic exercise of the wrist extensors with an eccentric focus, resolution and prevention may be initiated. Cross-friction massage, manipulation, and mobilization may be helpful in the subacute phase. During the subacute phase, the use of a tennis elbow brace may help redistribute forces.

TRICEPS TENDINITIS (POSTERIOR TENNIS ELBOW)

Classic Presentation

The patient complains of pain at the tip of the elbow after a repetitive extension activity or a single event involving forceful elbow extension.

Cause

Strain of the triceps insertion on the olecranon is usually due to common athletic endeavors performed by boxers, weight lifters, pitchers, shot-putters, and occasionally tennis players.[24]

Evaluation

Tenderness is found at the olecranon process. Pain is increased with resisted elbow extension, especially with a starting position of elbow flexion.

Management

Myofascial release techniques are used for the triceps. Cross-friction may be applied to the insertion point at the olecranon. Ice and rest from the inciting activity are essential. Decrease the amount of weight used in elbow extensions if the patient is working out.

POSTERIOR IMPINGEMENT SYNDROME

Classic Presentation

The patient is usually an athlete complaining of a sharp posterior elbow pain, especially on quick extension of the elbow. There may be associated complaints of popping or clicking with extension or an occasional complaint of locking.

Cause

Repetitive extension leads to posterior compression between the olecranon trochlea and olecranon fossa, which may simply cause a reactive synovitis or progress to degeneration and the production of osteophytes or loose bodies.

Evaluation

There is often a blockage to active and passive extension at end-range accompanied by pain. The valgus-extension overload test involves applying a valgus stress while extending the elbow.[7] Pain and often crepitus is produced with this maneuver. Radiographically, an axial view is required. A cubital tunnel view may also be revealing. If the radiographs are negative, computed tomography or arthrography may be necessary to reveal cartilaginous loose bodies.

Management

If loose bodies are evident, referral for surgical consultation should be made. If there appears to be primarily synovial hypertrophy or pinching, an acute pain program should be initiated with rest, ice, and use of an extension-block brace or taping.

NURSEMAID'S ELBOW

Classic Presentation

A parent presents a child (usually between ages 2 and 4 years) with lateral elbow pain after either swinging the child by his or her arms or sudden jerking of the child's arm.

Cause

The radial head is not fully formed, allowing damage or entrapment of the annular ligament by a distraction/rotation force.

Evaluation

Exquisite lateral elbow pain and tenderness in a child without obvious trauma such as a fall or a blow to the elbow is likely to have nursemaid's elbow. Palpation may reveal the malpositioned radial head.

Management

Reduction is accomplished by elbow flexion and rotation. Radiographic confirmation of reduction should be performed.

LITTLE LEAGUE ELBOW

Classic Presentation

The patient is usually an adolescent baseball pitcher who complains of either medial or lateral elbow pain.

Cause

Little League elbow is really a syndrome.[25] The repetitive valgus stress incurred with pitching causes stretch injury to the medial elbow and possible compression injury to the lateral elbow. Medial elbow pain is due to microtrauma to the medial anterior oblique ligament as well as accelerated growth and fragmentation of the medial epicondylar epiphysis. Laterally an osteochondritis dissecans of the capitellum and various degrees of radial head injury, including premature closure, may occur.[26]

Evaluation

Tenderness may be found at both the medial and the lateral elbow. Valgus testing (Figure 8–3) may reveal laxity and/or pain that must be distinguished radiographically to determine whether ligament damage or epiphyseal damage is the cause. Alternating supination and pronation performed actively or passively may cause palpable or audible crepitus at the head of the radius when osteochondritis dissecans or radial head damage is present.[27] A flexion contracture may be evident on passive ROM evaluation. Popping and clicking or locking may occur on full-range active movement. Radiographically it is important to include specialized views, including the radial head-capitellum view and the valgus stress view.[12]

Management

If radiographically apparent, referral for an orthopaedic consultation is warranted. If clinically apparent, yet radiographically normal, modification or elimination of the inciting activity is needed. Modification of pitching should include decreased time pitching (following Little League rules), avoidance of throwing curve balls, and teaching proper mechanics. Proper mechanics would include use of trunk and legs with less dependence on the elbow and wrist, avoidance of whipping or snapping of the elbow, and slow practice to accentuate proper form. The typical acute pain modalities should be used initially, and proper warm-up and stretching should be used prior to any activity.

OSTEOCHONDROSIS (PANNER'S DISEASE)

Classic Presentation

The patient is usually a young male complaining of unilateral (dominant arm) lateral elbow pain and stiffness. Associated complaints may include clicking and locking. The patient is often involved in a sport activity several times a week.

Cause

Osteochondrosis of the capitellum is caused by avascular necrosis. This may be due to trauma or other causes disturbing the circulation to the chondroepiphysis of the capitellum.[28] The vessels that supply this area pass through unossified epiphyseal cartilage and may be compressed. Also, there may be an anomalous distribution with no anastomosis decreasing the available blood supply. Other names for osteochondrosis of the capitellum include Panner's disease,[29] osteochondrosis deformans, osteochondritis, and aseptic/avascular necrosis.

Evaluation

A history of excessive throwing, as occurs in Little League pitching, or repeated weight bearing, as occurs in gymnastics, should always dictate the need for radiographs in any child with elbow pain. The diagnosis of Panner's disease is largely radiographic. The examination should include passive and active supination and pronation with the elbow extended in an effort to palpate or hear crepitus at the radial-capitellar joint. Radiographs must include obliques and a radial head-capitellum view. Fragmentation or loose body formation is a clear indicator of this condition.

Management

The best prognosis is for children with an open epiphysis. Reducing or eliminating any identifiable activity is required. A period of rest and splinting for 2 to 3 weeks should be followed by gradual stretching and strengthening. Gradual return to the activity is allowed if symptoms do not persist. If there are loose fragments or a locked elbow, referral for orthopaedic consultation is necessary. Failure of a conservative trial of several months should also warrant an orthopaedic consultation.

OLECRANON BURSITIS

Classic Presentation

The patient presents with an obvious swelling just distal to the point of the elbow.

Cause

The olecranon bursa acts as a cushion when the elbow is in contact with any surface. Therefore, a single fall on the elbow, or more commonly, repeated weight bearing or dragging of the elbow on the ground as occurs in wrestling causes irritation and swelling.

Evaluation

The goose-egg sized swelling at the elbow is difficult to miss. It must be differentiated from other swellings such as tophi in patients with gout and kidney failure. It is also crucial to distinguish between an infected or simply an inflamed bursa. Infection is more likely when there is an obvious wound near the bursitis. Additionally, the infected bursa will be warm and more tender than a simple bursitis.

Management

Protection with a doughnut support taped to the elbow, avoidance of the inciting activity when chronic, and ice or pulsed ultrasound are usually sufficient. When unsuccessful, referral for aspiration and possible excision should be made. Bursas usually grow back in 6 to 24 months. Patients with an infected bursa should be referred immediately for aspiration and antibiotic treatment.

REFERENCES

1. Morrey BF, Askew LJ, An KN, et al. A biomechanical study of normal elbow motion. *J Bone Joint Surg Am.* 1981;63:872.
2. Schwab GH, Bennett JB, Woods GW, et al. Biomechanics of elbow instability: the role of the medial collateral ligament. *Clin Orthop.*1980;186:44.
3. Whiteside JA. Field evaluation of common athletic injuries. In: Grana WA, Kalenak A, eds. *Clinical Sports Medicine.* Philadelphia: WB Saunders; 1991:130–151.
4. Griggs SM, Weis APC. Bone injuries of the wrist, forearm and elbow. *Clin Sports Med.* 1996;15:373–400.
5. Linschied RL, Wheeler DK. Elbow dislocation. *JAMA.* 1965; 194:1171.
6. Bennett JB, Tullos HS. Ligamentous and articular injuries in the athlete. In: Morrey BF, ed. *The Elbow and Its Disorders.* Philadelphia: WB Saunders; 1985:502–522.
7. Wilson FD, Andrews JR, Blackburn TA, McCluskey G. Valgus extension overload in the pitching elbow. *Am J Sports Med.* 1982;1: 83–88.
8. Murphy WA, Seigel MJ. Elbow fat pads with new signs extended differential diagnosis. *Radiology.* 1977;124:659.
9. Smith DN, Lee JR. The radiological diagnosis of post-traumatic effusion of the elbow joint and its clinical significance: the displaced fat pad sign. *Injury.* 1978;10:115.

10. Griswold R. Elbow fat pads: a radiographic perspective. *Radiol Technol.* 1982;53:303.
11. Ballinger PW. *Merril's Atlas of Radiographic Positions and Procedures.* 6th ed. St. Louis, MO: CV Mosby; 1986:82–93.
12. Greenspan A, Norman A. The radial-head-capitellum view: useful technique in elbow trauma. *AJR.* 1982;138:1186.
13. Bontrager KL, Anthony BT. *Textbook of Radiographic Positioning and Related Anatomy.* 2nd ed. St. Louis, MO: CV Mosby; 1987: 112–115.
14. St. John JN, Palmaz JC. The cubital tunnel in ulnar nerve entrapment neuropathy. *Radiology.* 1986;158:119.
15. Nirschl RP, Petrone FA. Tennis elbow: the surgical treatment of lateral epicondylitis. *J Bone Joint Surg Am.* 1979;61:832–839.
16. Plancher KD, Hallbrecht J, Lourie JM. Medial and lateral epicondylitis in the athlete. *Clin Sports Med.* 1996;15:283–305.
17. ReganW, Wold LE, Conrad R. Microscopic histopathology of chronic, refractory lateral epicondylitis. *Am J Sports Med.* 1992;20:746–749.
18. Sailer SM, Lewis SB. Rehabilitation and splinting of common upper extremity injuries in athletes. *Clin Sports Med.* 1995;14:411–446.
19. Kushner S, Reid DC. Manipulation in the treatment of tennis elbow. *J Orthop Sports Phys Ther.* 1986;7:264.
20. Froimson AI. Treatment of tennis elbow with forearm support band. *J Bone Joint Surg Am.* 1971;53:183.
21. Legwold G. Tennis elbow: joint resolution by conservative treatment and improved technique. *Physician Sportsmed.* 1984;12:168.
22. Nirschl RP. Elbow tendinosis/tennis elbow. *Clin Sports Med.* 1986;11:856–860.
23. Nirschl RP. Treatment of medial tennis elbow tendinitis. Presented at the Annual Meeting of the American Academy of Orthopaedic Surgeons, New Orleans; February, 1986.
24. Nirschl RP. Soft tissue injury about the elbow. *Clin Sports Med.*1986;5:638–644.
25. Grana WA, Girshkin A. Pitcher's elbow in adolescence. *Am J Sports Med.* 1980;82:333–336.
26. O'Neil DB, Micheli LJ. Overuse injuries in the young athlete. *Clin Sports Med.* 1988;7:602.
27. American Academy of Orthopaedic Surgeons. *Joint Motion: Method of Measuring and Recording.* Chicago: American Academy of Orthopaedic Surgeons; 1965.
28. Singer KM, Roy SP. Osteochondrosis of the humeral capitellum. *Am J Sports Med.* 1984;12:351.
29. Panner JH. A peculiar affection of the capitellum humeri resembling Calve-Perthes' disease of the hip. *Acta Radiol.* 1929;10:234.

CHAPTER 9

Wrist and Forearm Complaints

CONTEXT

The wrist is a complex of multiple joints that are required to function as the flexible link between the hand and the forearm. In essence, there are no tendon attachments that function at the wrist. Tendons cross the wrist to insert into the hand, fingers, and thumb. Stability, therefore, is inherently ligamentous. Problems affecting muscles that originate off the elbow and forearm may be manifested clinically as pain at the wrist. Biomechanical friction or inflammatory processes may affect the tendons as they cross the wrist.

Wrist complaints are often the result of direct trauma, falls, overuse, and arthritides. With trauma the most likely possibilities, other than sprains, are fractures and instability due to ruptured ligamentous support. Unfortunately, it is far too common for wrist pain to be dismissed as a simple sprain if no fracture is evident radiographically. Varying degrees of instability, however, may occur without associated fracture, and unless the examiner is testing for possible instability or is radiographically focused on the signs of instability, chronic pain and dysfunction may result from mismanagement.

In the athletic and computer operator population, overuse is common. Positions that strain muscles repetitively are likely to result in an insidious onset of wrist pain. Weight lifting, rowing, and racquetball are among the common activities that may overstrain the wrist. Cumulative trauma in the workplace has become an important Occupational Safety and Health Administration concern. Most injury is due to assembly-line movement patterns and computer use.[1] The ergonomics of these overuse problems have been studied extensively, and technologic advances in design have provided a proactive approach to these patients.

When the wrist becomes a weight-bearing joint, injury occurs. Two common scenarios of transformation from a non–weight-bearing joint to a weight-bearing joint are bracing the body for a fall and the chronic demands placed on the gymnast or chiropractor. The injury mechanism for gymnasts is obvious when handstands and other support or balance maneuvers add an element of forced, dorsiflexed weight bearing, often with torque added.[2] The mechanism for the chiropractor is repeated extension/compression injury with side-posture or double-transverse adjusting. Some chiropractors also experience wrist pain with cervical chair adjusting if the wrist is not kept straight (in neutral).

Forearm pain and wrist pain are often concomitant complaints. With a history of trauma, fracture should be ruled out. Insidious onset of forearm and wrist complaints is often due to overuse. When a complaint of pain is associated with either weakness or numbness/tingling, peripheral nerve entrapment is likely.[3] A history of overuse or misuse is usually evident, often involving repeated pronation/supination or flexion/extension. Patients who are pregnant or have metabolic disorders or rheumatoid conditions are also prone to develop reactions at the wrist, including median nerve entrapment and tendinopathies.

GENERAL STRATEGY

History

- Clarify the type of complaint.
  1. Is the complaint one of pain, stiffness, looseness, crepitus, or a combination of complaints?
- Clarify the mechanism if traumatic (see Table 9–1).
  1. For a fall on an outstretched hand, consider scaphoid fracture, carpal instability, and/or distal forearm fractures; for patients younger than age 12 years, consider epiphyseal damage or torus fracture.

Table 9–1 Fractures of the Upper Extremity

Fracture Site	*Common Mechanisms*	*Radiographs*	*Management*
Scaphoid	Fall on outstretched hand or blow to an object with the palm (60% to 70% of all carpal bone fractures)	Scaphoid series—PA, lateral, 45° pronation PA, ulnar deviation PA; optional Stecher view (PA, 20° angle from vertical, distal to proximal)	Nondisplaced fracture—cast immobilization including distal interphalangeal (DIP) joint of thumb; change every 2 weeks; switch to short-arm thumb spica (DIP of thumb not included) at 6 weeks; displaced—screw or wire fixation
Hamate	Hook of hamate due to striking a stationary object (eg, golf swing hits the ground)	Carpal tunnel view and 45° supination oblique; computed tomography (CT) may be necessary	Excision of fragment in older patient; adolescents—initial trial of cast (short arm cast with fourth and fifth metacarpophalangeal joints in flexion include base of thumb); no union after 6 weeks needs excision of fragment
Triquetral	Dorsiflexion or direct trauma; impingement of the ulnar styloid into the triquetrum (third most common carpal fracture)	Routine series including obliques	Nondisplaced fracture—short arm cast with mild extension for 4 weeks; displaced—open reduction and wired
Capitate	Forced dorsiflexion of the wrist	Routine radiographs; check for associated scaphoid fracture	Nondisplaced fracture—cast immobilization for 6 to 8 weeks; displaced—open reduction and wired
Trapezium	5% of carpal fractures; due to direct blow or forced extension of the transverse arch	Routine wrist views plus carpal tunnel and a Bett's view of the carpometacarpal (CMC) joint; CT may be needed	When associated with a dislocation or subluxation of the CMC joint reduction, excision of any fragments and casting are required
Pisiform	Direct trauma to the hypothenar eminence	Pisiform view (lateral view with wrist in 30° of supination); check for injury to distal radius	Immobilization in short arm cast; 30° of flexion and mild ulnar deviation for 4 to 6 weeks
Keinbock's	Shear stress due to ulnar minus variance leads to avascular necrosis of the lunate from repetitive activity or direct trauma in a young patient	Visible on routine views; gradual progression to lunate sclerosis with collapse and intercarpal arthritis	Surgery is only option; cast immobilization not considered useful. Ulnar lengthening or radial shortening is used. All surgical correction leads to restricted wrist motion
Distal radius: Galeazzi	Distal radial fracture with dislocation or subluxation of the distal radioulnar joint (6% of forearm injuries)	Radiographic clues are fracture at ulnar styloid base, dislocation/subluxation of ulna on true lateral view, and shortening of the radius 5 mm relative to the distal ulna	Compressive plate fixation with a minimum of five screws

continues

Table 9–1 continued

Fracture Site	*Common Mechanisms*	*Radiographs*	*Management*
Distal ulnar: Monteggia's	Fracture of the ulna with associated dislocation of the radial head. Fall on an outstretched hand with forearm forced into pronation or a direct blow	AP and true lateral elbow; radial head dislocation is missed 16% to 52% of the time	Closed reduction and long arm cast with forearm in supination with children. Adolescents and adults require internal fixation of ulna with a compression plate; radial head is a closed reduction
Capitellum	Often associated with a medial collateral ligament injury	AP and true lateral view	Open reduction and internal fixation; if more severe, excision of fragments
Coronoid	Rare	Best seen on a true lateral	
Radial head	Common fracture. Fall on an outstretched hand with the forearm pronated		

- Determine whether the mechanism is one of overuse.
  1. In what position does the patient work?
  2. Does the patient perform a repetitive movement at work or during sports activity?

Evaluation

- With trauma, palpate for points of tenderness and obtain radiographs for the possibility of fracture/dislocation or dissociation.
- If radiographs are negative for fracture, challenge the ligaments of the wrist, in particular the scapholunate (Watson's test) and the lunotriquetral (ballottement test) articulations; if unstable include stress views to the radiographic series.
- When the injury is nontraumatic, challenge the musculotendinous attachments with stretch, contraction, and a combination of contraction in a stretched position.
- When trauma or overuse is not present, evaluate the patient's wrist for swelling and deformity (discrete nodules are likely ganglions, deformities are likely arthritides: osteoarthritis [OA] or rheumatoid arthritis [RA]).

Management

- If radiographs are negative for fracture or dissociation, but, there is a high level of suspicion, place a soft cast on the patient for 2 to 3 weeks and reradiograph in 2 weeks to determine callus status.
- Refer fracture/dislocation and dissociation for orthopaedic management.
- All other soft tissue and articular disorders may be managed for a 2–3 month trial treatment period if necessary.

RELEVANT ANATOMY AND BIOMECHANICS

The wrist, as the connection between the hand and the forearm, requires a demanding degree of sophisticated movement. As always, this trade-off of movement is somewhat compromised by lack of a strong support. Although there are many interosseous ligaments that support and connect individual carpal bones, there is relatively little or no muscular support, save the support provided by tendons on their way to finger/hand attachment. As a result, when the ligamentous support is damaged, muscular support is less effective than it might be in other joints.

There is an inherent imbalance of the muscles controlling the hand and wrist. The flexors are stronger than the extensors. Few movements require the strength of the extensors; however, the flexors are required for gripping and, from an evolutionary protective standpoint, for survival. As a result, activities that do require extensor activity often result in strain.

The carpal bones have been functionally divided various ways by different investigators, yet the basic division is into a distal row (trapezium , trapezoid, capitate, and hamate) and a proximal row (scaphoid, lunate, triquetrum, and pisiform). Support is provided by extrinsic (connection between the radius/ulna and carpals or metacarpals) and intrinsic (carpal to carpal) ligaments.[4] The primary extrinsic support is from the volar intracapsular ligaments. Posterior intracapsular ligaments are thinner and less supportive. Intrinsic support is an intricate overlapping of different-length ligaments. The short intrinsic scapholunate, lunotriquetral, and capitolunate are the most important. Disruption of any of these ligaments will result in a destabilizing effect, allowing independent movement of other carpals. Because these intrinsic ligaments are shorter than the extrinsic ligaments, the reserve ability for stretch is less, leaving them more likely to be damaged.[5] The radius absorbs approximately 80% of an axial load; the ulna, 20%.[6]

The proximal and distal rows of carpal bones function together to provide a variety of precision maneuvers of the hand and fingers. With ulnar deviation, the triquetrum moves under the lunate, which dorsiflexes, taking the lunate with it; the scaphoid follows. With radial deviation, the scaphoid, lunate, and triquetrum move into palmar (volar) flexion while the distal carpal row dorsiflexes. Coupling between the proximal and distal carpal rows is guided by the scaphoid. With ligamentous damage, carpal bones are uncoupled, allowing some bones to become intercalated (unconnected).

The ulnar side of the wrist is stabilized by the triangular fibrocartilage (TFC) complex consisting of the triangular fibrocartilage (articular disc), the meniscus, the ulnar collateral ligament, the dorsal and volar radioulnar ligaments, and the extensor carpi ulnaris tendon.[7] Although anatomically on the ulnar side, this complex is extremely important for stability of the radiocarpal joint. The TFC is usually an intact structure well into the 30s; however, in gymnasts, the rate of degeneration is quite high.[8,9]

TFC perforations (traumatic or degenerative) and avulsions may occur with repetitive weight bearing or, more rarely, in a single traumatic event. A predisposition to TFC injury appears to be related to ulnar length. *Ulnar variance* is the term used to describe the relationship between the distal ends of the radius and the ulna. When the ulna extends past what is in essence a parallel line drawn across the distal radius, positive variance is demonstrated. Palmer and Werner[10] found that 81% of subjects with a positive variance had perforations of the TFC whereas only 17% of those with negative variance had perforations. Fatigue fractures and Keinbock's disease (avascular necrosis) of the lunate have been associated with a negative ulnar variance. Hypermobility and forceful repetitive wrist motions seem to be the other significant cofactors.

Muscular control of the wrist is dependent on a muscle mass that arises from the elbow and proximal forearm (Figures 9–1A and 9–1B, and 9–2A and 9–2B). Because of the need for carpal bone mobility, the insertion of the flexors and extensors is primarily on the metacarpals. The primary flexors of the wrist are the flexor carpi ulnaris and flexor carpi radialis. Each also will assist in deviating the wrist toward the named direction (ie, radialis toward the radial direction). The rotatory movement of pronation and supination are primarily forearm movements, with the wrist along for the ride. The primary pronators are the pronator teres and pronator quadratus. Pronation is more effective with the elbow straight, due to prestretch, and therefore there is a mechanical advantage for the pronator teres. Supination is accomplished by the supinator muscle and the biceps brachii. Supination is more effective with the elbow flexed because of the mechanical advantage of the biceps with flexion and the prestretch of the supinator with flexion.

Neural control of wrist movement is via the radial, median, and ulnar nerves. Wrist extension and supination are due primarily to the radial nerve. Flexion of the wrist is divided between the ulnar and median nerves. Pronation is primarily dependent on median nerve innervation. Entrapment of each of these nerves or its branches will result in weakness of related muscles, numbness/tingling, or pain in the distribution of the respective nerve. The classic entrapment neuropathy of the wrist is carpal tunnel syndrome; however, entrapment may occur proximal to the carpal tunnel, mimicking carpal tunnel syndrome. Patients who complain of numbness/tingling, weakness, or forearm pain should be suspected of having peripheral nerve entrapment, or if bilateral, a systemic neuropathy.

EVALUATION

History

Careful questioning of the patient during the history taking can point to the diagnosis (Table 9–2).

Pain Localization

The following are possible causes of pain based on location (Figure 9–3, A, B, and C, and Table 9–3):

- anterior
  1. traumatic—lunate dislocation, radial fracture, hook of hamate fracture, or distal forearm fracture
  2. nontraumatic—median or ulnar nerve entrapment
- posterior
  1. traumatic—navicular fracture (anatomic snuff-box), carpal dissociation, or distal forearm fracture
  2. nontraumatic—de Quervain's syndrome, intersection syndrome, extensor tendinitis, carpal subluxations, radial nerve entrapment

Traumatic and Overuse Injuries

With trauma, the main concern is ruling out fracture or dislocation. This requires various radiographic imaging ap-

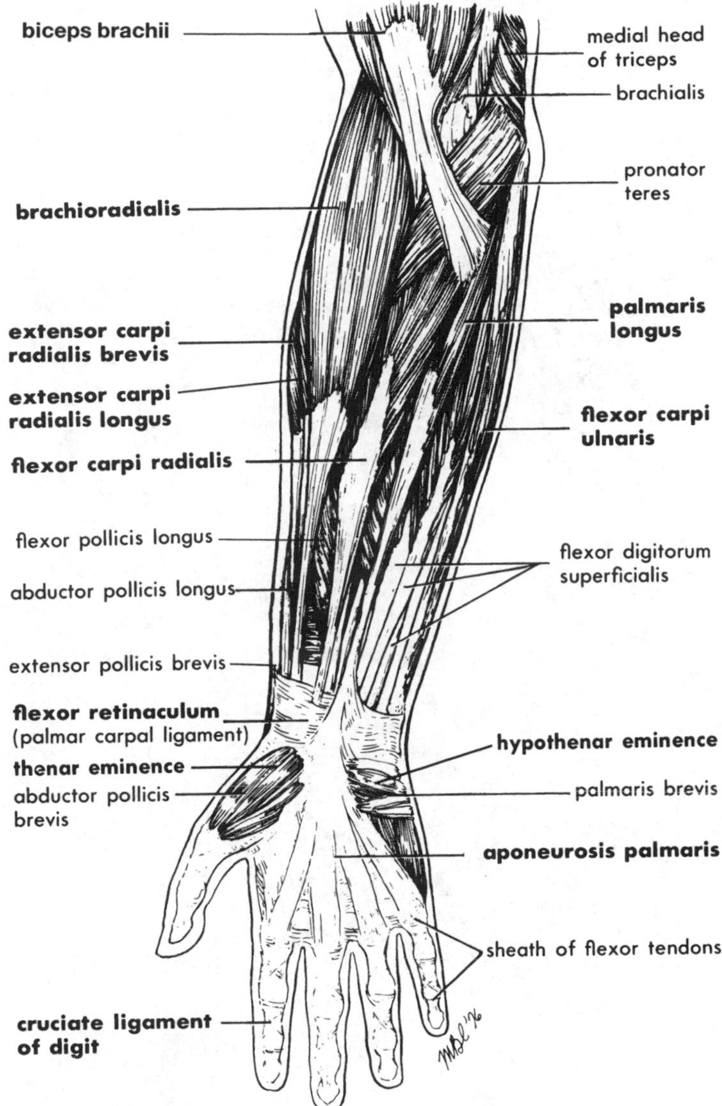

Figure 9–1A Anterior aspect of superficial muscles of the right forearm and hand. *Source:* Reprinted with permission from J.E. Crouch, *Functional Human Anatomy*, 4th ed., p. 231, © 1985, Lea & Febiger.

proaches. Determining which standard radiographic views to include is based in large part on the specific area of pain, swelling, or deformity. Additionally, the mechanism of injury may suggest a specific possibility. Following are some common injury patterns and potential sites of damage (also see Table 9–1):

- Fall on an outstretched hand: Axial loading usually occurs to the ulnar, palmar side of the wrist, creating compressive and shearing forces. Common injuries include scaphoid and distal radius fractures, scapholunate and lunotriquetral ligament damage leading to varying degrees of instability, and triangular fibrocartilage injury at the ulnar side of the wrist.
- Fall on a flexed hand: Compression injury occurs to the flexor (palmar) wrist with avulsion or stretch injury to the dorsal wrist. Structures involved are similar to those involved in dorsiflexion injuries, with slightly different fracture patterns; additionally, dorsal capsule avulsion may occur.

Accumulative trauma may occur when the wrist is used as a weight-bearing or partial weight-bearing joint. Commonly, the dorsal aspect of the wrist is irritated, leading to various

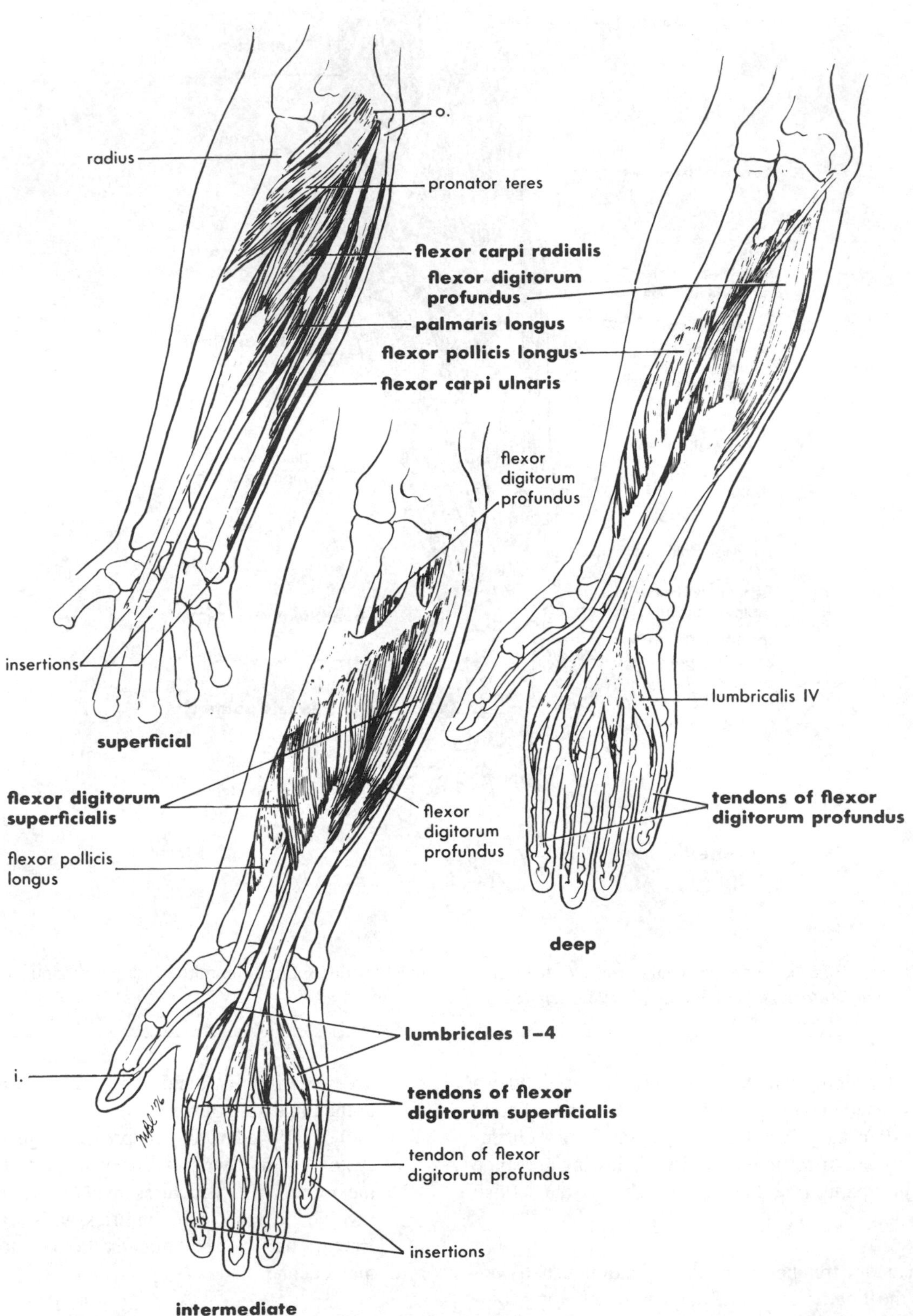

Figure 9–1B Anterior aspect of muscles of the right forearm and hand. *Source:* Reprinted with permission from J.E. Crouch, *Functional Human Anatomy*, 4th ed., p. 232, © 1985, Lea & Febiger.

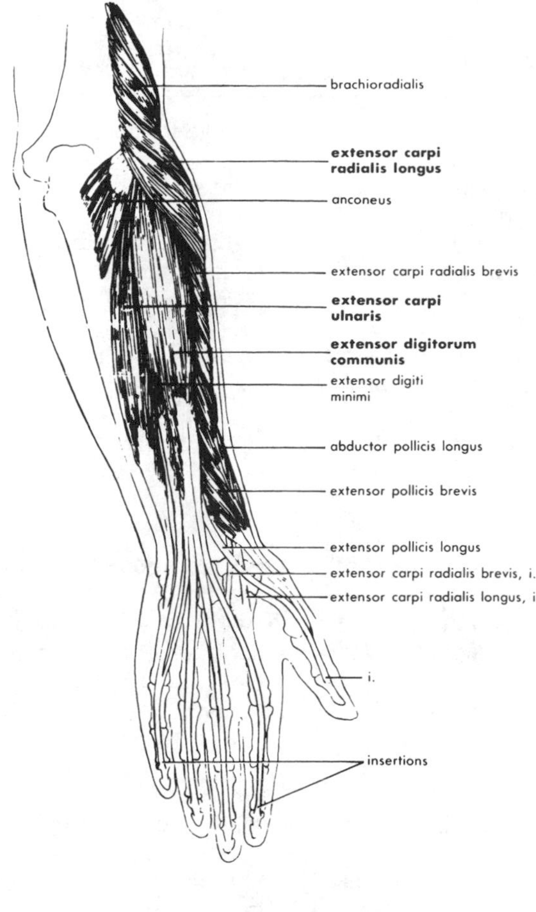

Figure 9–2A Posterior aspect of superficial muscles of the right forearm and hand. *Source:* Reprinted with permission from J.E. Crouch, *Functional Human Anatomy*, 4th ed., p. 234, © 1985, Lea & Febiger.

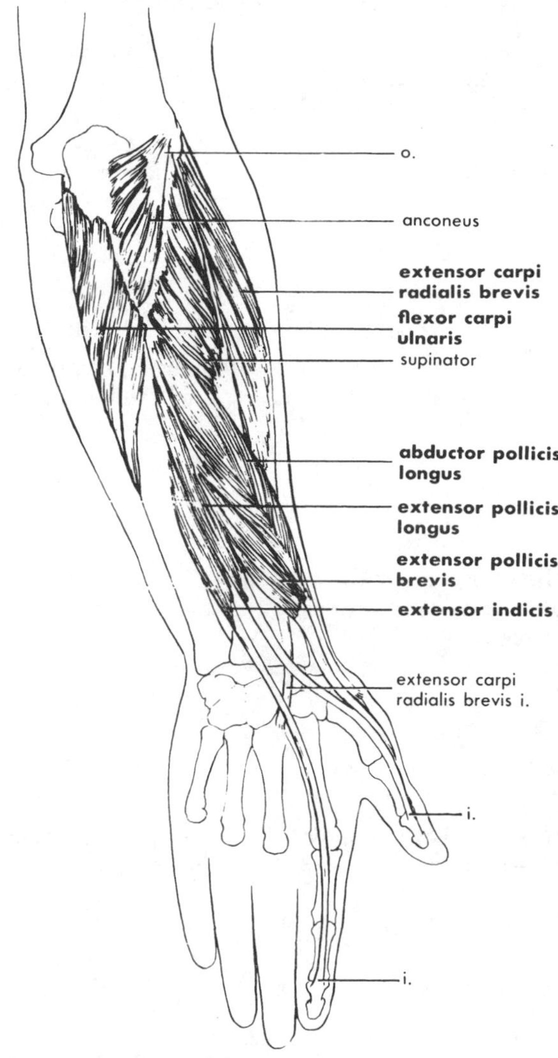

Figure 9–2B Posterior aspect of deep muscles of the right forearm and hand. *Source:* Reprinted with permission from J.E. Crouch, *Functional Human Anatomy*, 4th ed., p. 234, © 1985, Lea & Febiger.

degrees of dorsal impaction syndromes. Local synovitis, hypertrophied and/or pinched synovium, and osteocartilagenous fracture are possible with dorsal impaction.

Weakness

Weakness may be present for several reasons. Most commonly, a patient will report pain as the limiting factor with gripping. If the pain is well localized or a specific movement other than gripping is weak and painful, a specific anatomic structure may be detected through palpation and specific testing.

Most patients with a complaint of weakness will indicate some difficulty with gripping activities. These activities have been categorized by Reid.[11] The two main grip maneuvers are power grip and precision grip. Each grip maneuver requires the strength and coordination of specific joints and muscles. By determining the specific grip that feels weak, the examiner may focus on potential neural involvement. Following is a list of specific grip patterns and the main muscle/nerve control for that grip:

- Power grip includes grasping a ball, bat, bottle, or briefcase. The ulnar nerve is important for this grip as the

Table 9–2 History Questions for Wrist and Forearm Complaints

Primary Question	*What Are You Thinking?*	*Secondary Questions*	*What Are You Thinking?*
Did you fall on an outstretched hand?	Fracture, dislocation, ligamentous instability	Is there pain on the thumb side of your wrist?	Scaphoid fracture likely
		Is there any painful popping or clicking?	Ligament instability
		Is there any swelling or deformity at the wrist?	Distal radial or ulnar fracture; lunate dislocation
Did the pain begin after repetitive activity?	Tendinitis, peripheral nerve entrapment, trigger points	Do you have any associated numbness, tingling, or sense of weakness?	Peripheral nerve entrapment
		Is the pain on the thumb side of the wrist?	de Quervain's or intersection syndrome is likely
Is the complaint mainly stiffness or restricted movement?	OA, other arthritides such as pseudogout	Is there swelling in the joint?	Synovitis, traumatic or arthritic
		Have you had any past injuries or surgeries to the wrist?	Posttraumatic or surgical adhesion or accelerated OA
		Is the pain worse in the morning and improved with activity?	OA likely
Is there a chief complaint of weakness?	Painful process, neurologic cause	Does it hurt to grip objects?	Often associated with fracture and TFC damage
		Are there associated signs of numbness or tingling?	Neural involvement may be local at carpal tunnel, entrapment of motor nerve such as anterior interosseous, or from nerve root compression at the neck
		Is the weakness worse with overhead activity?	Thoracic outlet syndrome or shoulder instability likely
Do you have any known disorders such as diabetes or hypothyroidism?	Diabetes or hypothyroidism may predispose the patient to carpal tunnel syndrome	Do you have a diagnosis of any arthritis or pain in other joints?	Bilateral or symmetric joint involvement suggests an RA or connective tissue problem

primary innervation for the ulnar aspect of the wrist, for both flexion and sensation.

- Precision grip includes holding a pen, a key, or finger-tip-to-thumbtip maneuvers. The median nerve is important for this grip as the primary innervation to the radial side of the wrist.

The thumb may be important for stability with both grip patterns and is supplied by both the median and ulnar nerves. Opening of the hand from the grip position or extension is largely dependent on the radial control of extensor action.

Instability

Instability may be associated with a sense of weakness. Instability may also be the misinterpretation of a sense of clumsiness that is more suggestive of a neural cause. Finally, instability may be assumed by the patient because of constant popping and clicking about the wrist; however, clicking and popping are not necessarily pathologic unless accompanied by pain.

Restricted Motion

Restriction of both active and passive range of motion should raise the suspicion of joint effusion. With trauma, the suspicion is fracture or dislocation as the underlying cause. Without a history of trauma, it is more likely that an inflammatory arthritis is the cause. End-range passive restrictions are suggestive of subluxation.

Superficial Complaints

One of the most common superficial complaints is the presence of painful nodules on the dorsal or volar wrist. A history of chronic repetitive motion is often found, suggesting the mostly likely diagnosis—ganglions. It is also common to find a history of fluctuation in size over time. Multiple nodules and swelling over the dorsum of the wrist associated with wrist pain and stiffness is a classic presentation with established RA.

Skin lesions, when isolated to the wrist, are more likely an indication of a systemic process such as rheumatic fever (erythema marginatum) or RA. Associated signs or symptoms of each disease should be sought.

Examination

Wrist

Examination of the wrist is a standard procedure involving observation for deformities and swellings, palpation for areas of tenderness, stressing of ligamentous structures for instability, range of motion testing with overpressure, muscle testing, and accessory motion palpation. By combining these findings with the history, a preliminary working diagnosis is usually determined.

Orthopaedic testing of the wrist focuses mainly on carpal instability due to stretching or disruption of interosseous ligaments. Positive test results include a combination of popping or clunking with pain. Painless pops and clicks are common and do not represent pathologic damage or a source of a patient's wrist pain. Tests include the following:

- Watson's test (Figure 9–4) for scapholunate stability: The examiner presses the scaphoid from anterior (volar) to posterior (dorsal) with the wrist first in ulnar deviation. By moving the wrist passively into the radial direction, a painful clunk or pop may be produced, indicating that the proximal pole of the scaphoid subluxated over the posterior rim of the radius.
- Lunotriquetral ballottement (Figure 9–5) test: The examiner stabilizes the lunate between a thumb and index finger and does the same with the triquetrum. A shearing between the bones is accomplished by moving the bones in opposite directions (ie, the lunate is forced posteriorly while the triquetrum is forced anteriorly). A painful clunk or pop is indicative of lunotriquetral joint instability.
- Midcarpal instability: By having either the patient actively or the examiner passively pronate and ulnar deviate the wrist, a painful pop is felt on the ulnar aspect of the wrist. This indicates midcarpal instability.
- Axial load testing: The examiner applies an axial load through the first metacarpal of the thumb and the trapezium while adding a shear force. Fracture or joint arthrosis often will result in painful crepitus with this maneuver.
- Dynamometer testing: Although the dynamometer is most often used when trying to measure the degree of strength loss with a nerve root or peripheral nerve entrapment or compression, when a past history of wrist trauma is elicited, dynamometer testing may reveal weakness due to instability.

Soft tissue assessment of the wrist is based on a combination of palpation at the sites of insertion of major tendons, coupled with contraction, stretch, and contraction in a stretched position. For example, for the extensors carpi radialis longus and brevis, one or a combination of the following will usually increase the patient's pain complaint:

- stretching into flexion and ulnar deviation
- contraction from the above position into radial deviation and wrist extension
- palpation over the second and third metacarpals dorsally

By simply applying this approach to the remainder of tendons crossing the wrist, soft tissue involvement of a specific tendon is usually made apparent. A specific test involving the stretching concept is Finkelstein's test (Figure 9–6) for de Quervain's syndrome.[12] The patient is asked to clench the fingers over the thumb. The examiner then passively ulnar deviates the wrist, taking care not to press on the metacarpophalangeal joint of the thumb. Although this maneuver is uncomfortable it is usually not painful. Compare results with those for the opposite (hopefully uninvolved) side. This maneuver illustrates some general orthopaedic testing principles. Although the intent is to stretch the abductor policis longus and the extensor policis brevis, the position also stretches the superficial branch of the radial nerve (Wartenberg's syndrome), the flexor carpi radialis (tendinitis), and the extensors carpi radialis longus and brevis (intersection syndrome),

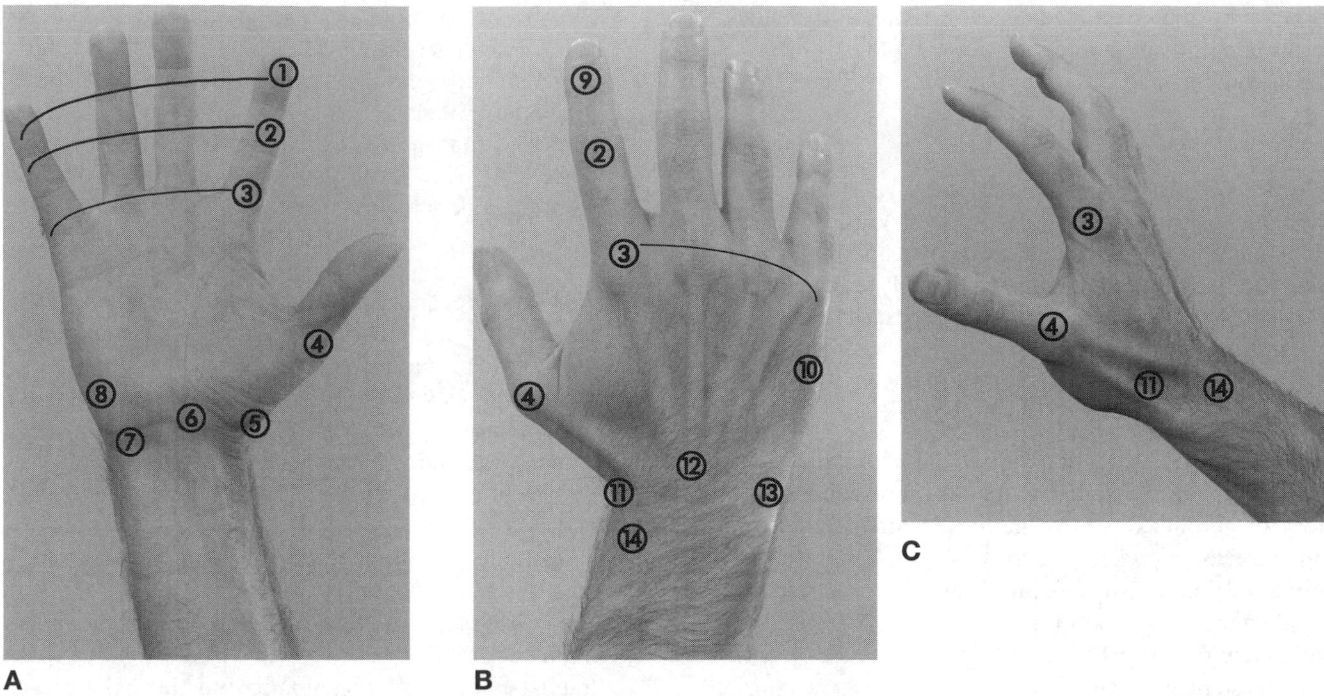

Figure 9–3 **A**, Anterior wrist and hand; **B**, posterior wrist and hand; **C**, radial wrist and hand. *Note:* See Table 9–2 for explanation of numbers.

and compresses the scaphoid (scaphoid fracture) and the metacarpophalangeal joint of the thumb (arthritis). Localization of pain and tenderness coupled with mechanism of injury should differentiate among these possibilities.

Forearm/Wrist

Patients who present with either forearm pain or forearm pain with associated hand or wrist numbness/tingling or weakness should be evaluated for peripheral nerve entrapment. Each of three peripheral nerves (median, ulnar, and radial) may be compressed or entrapped at several sites. Depending on the site of entrapment, motor weakness or sensory abnormalities may be found specific to the nerve. Additionally, if the site of entrapment is a fibrous band or hypertrophied muscle, provocative maneuvers focused on these contractile and noncontractile structures may reproduce or worsen the patient's subjective complaints. Following are some common tests, structural sites of entrapment, and findings specific to a peripheral nerve or its branches.

Median Nerve. Pronator syndrome: The median nerve may be compressed or entrapped at several locations proximal or local to the pronator teres. The most proximal site is the ligament of Struthers, an anomalous ligament that connects to the supracondylar process of the distal medial humerus. This is a rare anomaly occurring in only 1% of individuals.[13] Another site is entrapment at the lacertus fibrosus (bicipital aponeurosis) as it attaches to the pronator teres muscle. Entrapment between the two heads of the pronator teres and also at the arch of the flexor digitorum superficialis are the most common sites. Hypertrophy or fibrous bands are the cause in most cases. Each site may be localized with specific positional testing.

- Lacertus fibrosus or ligament of Struthers: Symptoms of proximal forearm aching pain with possible hand pain may be provoked by resisted elbow flexion at 120° to 130° with supination.[14]
- Pronator teres: Resisted pronation with wrist flexion may increase symptoms of proximal forearm pain; passive stretching of the proximal forearm with the elbow and wrist extended or direct deep palpation of the pronator teres may provoke symptoms.[15]
- Flexor digitorum superficialis: Resisted flexion of the middle finger may increase forearm pain symptoms.

Anterior interosseous syndrome: Compression of the motor branch of the median nerve may cause proximal forearm pain and thumb and finger weakness.[16] Numbness and tingling complaints and objective sensory loss are not found.

Table 9–3 Wrist and Hand Pain Localization

#	*Structures*	*Overt Trauma*	*Insidious or Overuse*
1	Flexor digitorum profundus (FDP) insertion	Avulsion of FDP, fracture of distal phalanx	Psoriatic arthritis
2	Proximal interphalangeal (PIP) joint	Capsular sprain or dislocation at PIP	RA, OA
3	Metacarpophalangeal (MCP) joint	Dislocation, collateral ligament sprain, capsular sprain	Mild capsular sprain, OA, trigger finger (on palmar surface)
4	First MCP joint	Dislocation, gamekeeper's thumb (ulnar collateral ligament sprain)	OA, bowler's thumb (digital neuritis), trigger thumb
5	First metacarpal base, abductor policis longus insertion	Bennett's fracture/dislocation	de Quervain's tenosynovitis
6	Carpal tunnel, lunate	Lunate dislocation, dissociation, subluxation	Carpal tunnel syndrome (palpation/ pressure point)
7	Flexor carpi ulnaris, ulna	Distal ulna fracture or dislocation	Tendinitis
8	Pisiform/hamate, tunnel of Guyon	Hook of hamate fracture	Tunnel of Guyon compression of ulnar nerve
9	Distal interphalangeal (DIP) joint and distal phalanx	Fracture of distal phalanx, mallet finger (avulsion of extensor tendon)	Psoriatic arthritis
10	Metacarpals	Metacarpal fracture	Subluxation or extensor tendinitis
11	Anatomic snuff-box, abductor policis longus (APL), extensor policis brevis (EPB) of the thumb	Scaphoid fracture, radial styloid fracture	de Quervain's, Wartenberg's syndrome (entrapment of radial sensory nerve)
12	Lunotriquetral joint, extensor tendons	Lunotriquetral dissociation, dislocation, distal forearm fracture	Ganglion, lunate subluxation, extensor tendinitis
13	Ulnar styloid process, extensor carpi ulnaris (ECU) tendon	Ulnar styloid fracture	ECU tendinitis or tendon subluxation
14	Intersection of extensor tendons and APL, EPB	Distal radial fracture	Intersection syndrome, RA

Note: See Figure 9–3 for localization of numbered areas.

Weakness may occur in the flexor policis longus, pronator quadratus, and flexor digitorum profundus of the second and third fingers. The result is an inability to perform the "OK" sign of tip-to-tip apposition of the thumb and index finger.[17] With weakness the patient presses pulp to pulp and cannot flex enough to contact the thumb and fingertips. Motor nerve compression can cause an aching pain because these peripheral nerve branches carry sensory fibers to the joints and muscles, and occasionally to skin receptors. Entrapment may be due to anomalous vessels or muscle slips; however, the most common sites are at the pronator teres and flexor digitorum superficialis muscles after the median nerve has given off the anterior interosseous motor branch.

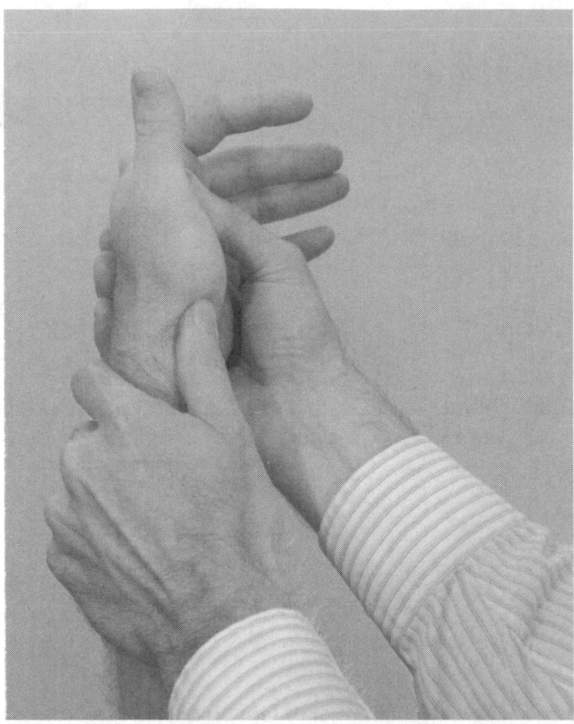

Figure 9–4 Watson's test for scapholunate dissociation. The radius is stabilized while the tubercle of the scaphoid is pushed from anterior to posterior. The wrist is then passively moved from ulnar deviation into radial deviation. A painful clunk or pop is a positive finding.

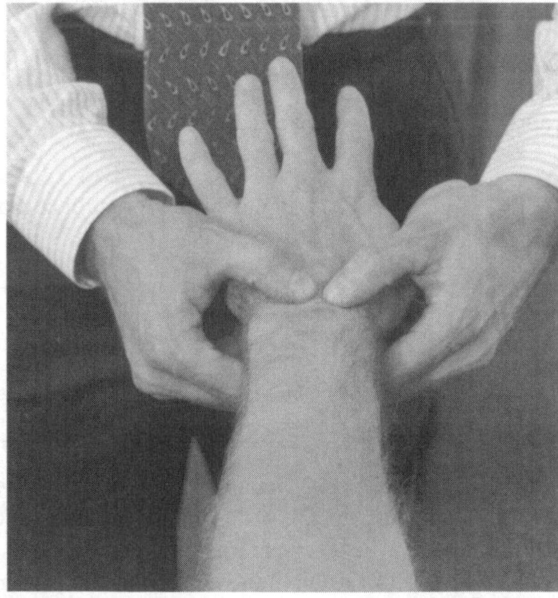

Figure 9–5 The ballottement test for lunotriquetral dissociation. The examiner stabilizes the lunate while shearing the triquetrum. A positive finding is the production of a painful clunk or pop.

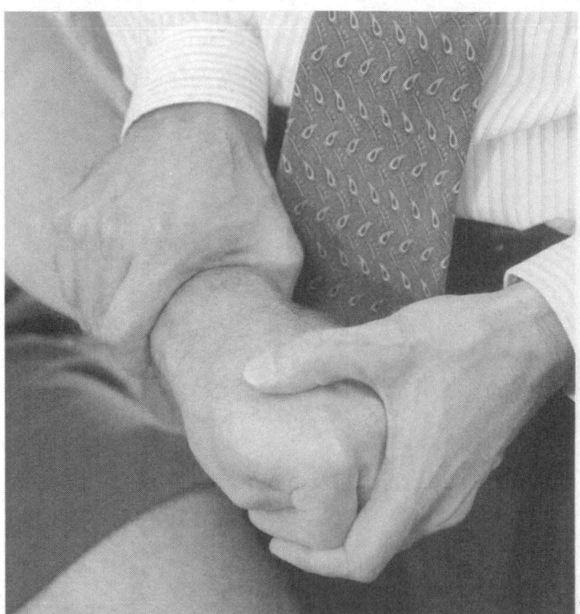

Figure 9–6 Finkelstein's test for de Quervain's tenosynovitis. The patient grasps the thumb while the examiner passively ulnar deviates the wrist. Pain at the radial wrist is a positive finding when it is notably more than the opposite wrist pain response.

Carpal tunnel syndrome: The median nerve passes through the carpal tunnel formed by the transverse carpal ligament superiorly, the pisiform-hamate bones medially, and the navicular-trapezium bones laterally. The carpal tunnel contains the flexor tendons for the fingers and thumb and occasionally anomalous vessels or muscles such as the palmaris longus. Pressure in the tunnel is increased with swelling in the tunnel or the extremes of flexion or extension. Symptoms include numbness and paresthesias over the radial three and one-half digits with sparing of the thenar eminence. Weakness or clumsiness in gripping may be reported. Eventually thenar atrophy may occur. Sensory symptoms are reproduced with several provocative tests:

- Tinel's sign: Tapping over the carpal tunnel at the wrist may elicit distal feelings of numbness or paresthesias (sensitivity, between 60% and 74%; specificity, 80%).[18]
- Phalen's test: Forced passive flexion at the wrist (pressing the backs of the hands together) or reverse Phalen's with forced passive extension (palm to palm) may elicit symptoms (sensitivity, between 49% and 64%; specificity, 55%).
- Pressure provocative test: Instead of tapping, direct pressure with a cuff or with thumb pressure at the carpal tunnel will elicit symptoms (sensitivity, close to 100%).[19]

Ulnar Nerve. Cubital tunnel syndrome: The ulnar nerve is rarely trapped in the fascia covering the triceps and an aponeurosis called the arcade of Struthers or at the ulnar groove. More frequently entrapment occurs in the tunnel just distal to where the ulnar nerve travels through the posterior condylar groove on the medial epicondyle of the humerus.[20] The floor consists of the medial trochlea and the ulnar collateral ligament; the roof consists of the triangular arcuate ligament that bridges the origins of the flexor carpi ulnaris (FCU). With flexion the arcuate ligament stretches, narrowing the tunnel, and the proximal edge of the FCU tightens; the ulnar collateral ligament can then bulge into the tunnel.[21] Excessive valgus angulation from throwing or acute trauma may stretch the nerve. Provocative tests[22] include the following:

- holding the elbow flexed between 3 and 5 minutes
- Tinel's tapping sign at the posterior elbow (this is inconsistent; however, it is occasionally helpful if compared with the opposite side)
- possible snapping or popping of the nerve with rapid extension or flexion (subluxating the ulnar nerve)

Ulnar tunnel or tunnel of Guyon Syndrome: At the wrist the ulnar nerve (and artery) pass through an osseofibrous tunnel formed by the groove between the pisiform and hook of the hamate. The floor is the pisohamate ligament; the roof is an extension of the FCU tendon. The ulnar nerve divides into a superficial nerve that is primarily sensory and a deep nerve that is exclusively motor. Sensory supply is to the fifth and ulnar half of the fourth digit. Motor supply is primarily to the hypothenar muscles, all the interossei, two medial lumbricals, the deep head of the flexor policis brevis, and the abductor policis.[23] Anastomosis between the ulnar and median nerve may lead to mixed findings. Provocation testing is with Tinel's sign or pressure at the pisiform hamate area (just distal/medial to the pisiform). Sensory testing also should be performed.

Radial Nerve. Radial tunnel syndrome (RTS): At the elbow the radial nerve lies on the anterior capsule just lateral to the lateral epicondyle. It then passes between the two heads of the supinator muscle. Prior to entering the supinator muscle the radial nerve can be compressed by fibrous bands off the anterior radial head, the sharp medial edge of the extensor carpi radialis brevis (ECRB), a fan-shaped vascular arcade, and the arcade of Frohse (the thickened edge of the superficial head of the supinator).[24] Provocative maneuvers and related sites of entrapment include the following:

- ECRB—resisted middle-finger extension with the elbow extended (found also with lateral epicondylitis) or extreme forearm pronation with passive wrist flexion
- radial head—resisted elbow flexion and forearm supination
- arcade of Frohse—extreme forearm pronation with passive wrist flexion

Posterior interosseous nerve syndrome (PINS): The literature often overlaps the description of RTS and PINS. RTS is considered more a mixed-nerve syndrome, with wrist or forearm pain as the main patient complaint. PINS is considered a pure entrapment of the motor branch of the radial nerve.[25] Testing is specifically searching for weakness in wrist extension or thumb and index finger extension. Compression of the posterior interosseous nerve may also occur at the distal radius.[26] Pain is often reproduced with forceful wrist extension or palpating the forearm with the wrist flexed.

Cheiralgia paresthetica (Wartenberg's syndrome)[27]*:* The superficial radial nerve is susceptible to trauma between the tendons of the extensor carpi radialis longus (ECRL) and the brachioradialis. Trauma or repetitive pronation and supination may cause irritation. The patient's complaints are mainly numbness and paresthesia over the dorsolateral wrist and hand. Finkelstein's test is usually negative; however, Tinel's test performed over the dorsolateral wrist may reproduce the symptoms.

Imaging

Radiographic decision making for the wrist is dictated by the degree of trauma or whether there is any suspicion of arthritis involvement based on the history and physical examination. Following are some common examples:

- A combination of anatomic snuff-box tenderness in a patient with a history of a fall on an outstretched hand suggests scaphoid injury. A scaphoid series includes a posteroanterior (PA) view, a true lateral view, a 45° pronation PA view, and an ulnar deviation PA view.[28] Another view that may be helpful is the Stecher view.[29] This is a PA shot with an angle of 20° to the vertical, angled from distal to proximal. When suspicion is high but no fracture is evident, additional angled views may help catch the fracture line. Initially, radiographs are often unrevealing even when a fracture is present. When the suspicion is high yet radiographs are negative, immobilization for 2 to 3 weeks in a thumb spica cast is recommended, followed by a second radiographic evaluation. Most fractures become apparent at this time. If immediate determination is necessary because of a particular patient's high level of use (eg, professional athlete) a bone scan should be performed at 3 days postinjury. A negative bone scan rules out fracture.[30] Computed tomography (CT) scans may also be beneficial in equivocal presentations.
- If a patient has joint line tenderness coupled with a history of a fall on a dorsiflexed hand and a positive

Watson's test, ballottement, or midcarpal stability test, scapulolunate dislocation or subluxation, lunotriquetral, or midcarpal instability, respectively, is likely. The lateral view will show a disrelationship between the radius, lunate, capitate, and third metacarpal. Two patterns may be evident: the dorsal intercalated segmental instability (DISI) pattern or the volar intercalated segmental instability (VISI) pattern (sometimes called PISI). These instability patterns are based on the position of the lunate in relationship to the radius. Several angles can be measured; however, the most common is the scapholunate angle, which normally ranges between 30° and 60°; greater than 70° indicates scapholunate dissociation. If not evident statically, stability or stress views should be added. These include the clenched fist (PA) view or a traction view, lateral views in flexion and extension, and AP views in radial and ulnar deviation.[31]

- A combination of trauma to the pisiform with local tenderness coupled with any sensory abnormalities into the fourth and fifth fingers is suggestive of a hook of hamate fracture. The PA view may demonstrate subtle signs such as absence of the hook or cortical ring, or sclerosis in the area of the hook.[32] A carpal tunnel view and/or a 45° supinated oblique view is suggested.[33] When these views are unrevealing, yet the suspicion is high, referral for a CT is warranted.[34]

MANAGEMENT

- Referral for orthopaedic consultation or management is necessary for fractures, dislocations, and carpal dissociations.
- Entrapment or compression syndromes may benefit from a conservative approach employing myofascial release and/or bracing, and patient education regarding modification of the inciting activity.
- Tendinitis not associated with an inflammatory arthritis is best managed with conservative care emphasizing rest, ice, cross-friction massage to the tendon, or myofascial release to the respective muscle. On occasion, splinting may be necessary. An eccentric exercise program may also be useful.

Algorithm

An algorithm for the evaluation and management of wrist pain is presented in Figure 9–7.

Figure 9–7

WRIST PAIN—ALGORITHM.

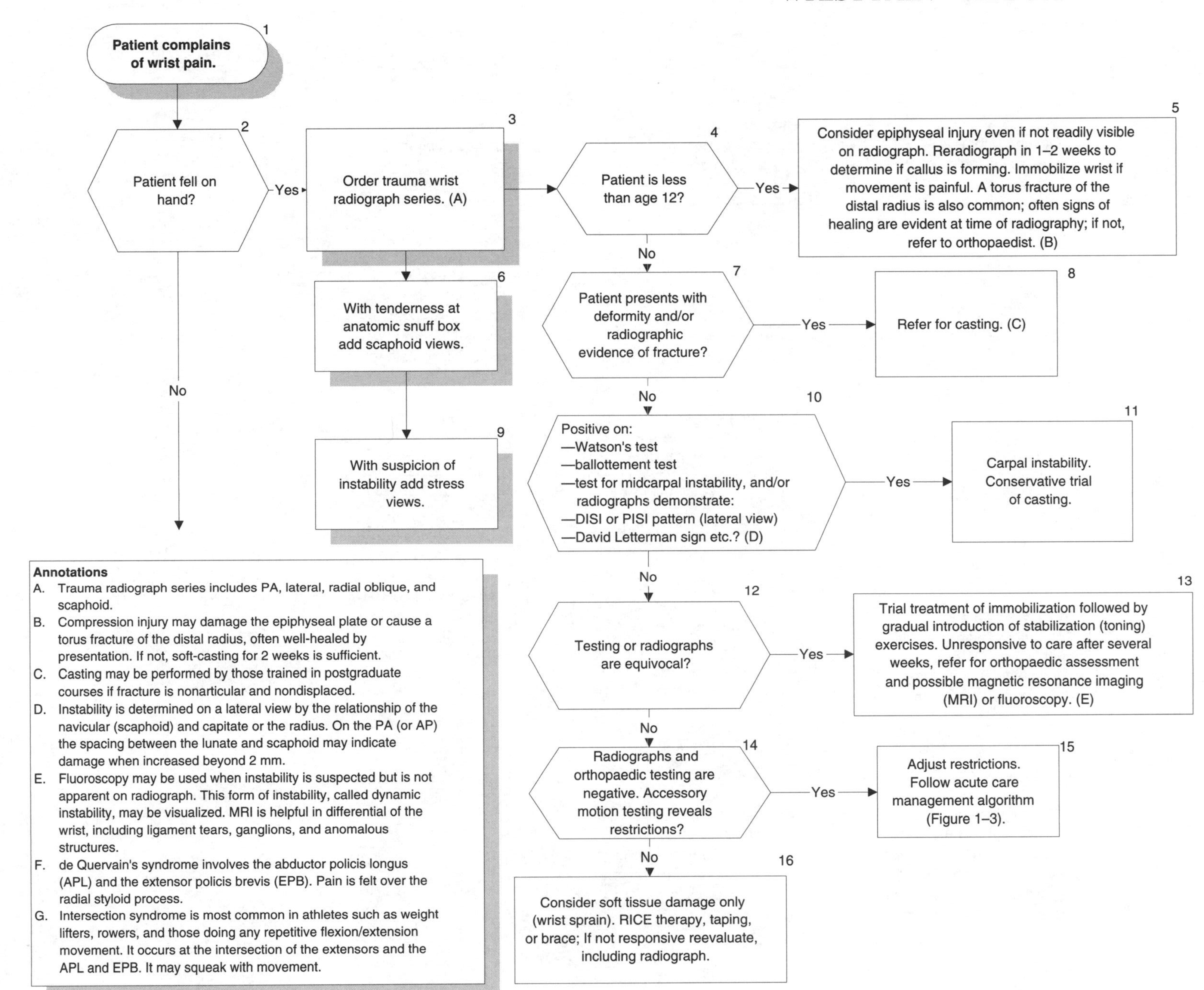

1 Patient complains of wrist pain.
2 Patient fell on hand?
Yes
No
3 Order trauma wrist radiograph series. (A)
4 Patient is less than age 12?
Yes
5 Consider epiphyseal injury even if not readily visible on radiograph. Reradiograph in 1–2 weeks to determine if callus is forming. Immobilize wrist if movement is painful. A torus fracture of the distal radius is also common; often signs of healing are evident at time of radiography; if not, refer to orthopaedist. (B)
No
6 With tenderness at anatomic snuff box add scaphoid views.
7 Patient presents with deformity and/or radiographic evidence of fracture?
Yes
8 Refer for casting. (C)
No
9 With suspicion of instability add stress views.
10 Positive on:
—Watson's test
—ballottement test
—test for midcarpal instability, and/or radiographs demonstrate:
—DISI or PISI pattern (lateral view)
—David Letterman sign etc.? (D)
Yes
11 Carpal instability. Conservative trial of casting.
No
12 Testing or radiographs are equivocal?
Yes
13 Trial treatment of immobilization followed by gradual introduction of stabilization (toning) exercises. Unresponsive to care after several weeks, refer for orthopaedic assessment and possible magnetic resonance imaging (MRI) or fluoroscopy. (E)
No
14 Radiographs and orthopaedic testing are negative. Accessory motion testing reveals restrictions?
Yes
15 Adjust restrictions. Follow acute care management algorithm (Figure 1–3).
No
16 Consider soft tissue damage only (wrist sprain). RICE therapy, taping, or brace; If not responsive reevaluate, including radiograph.

Annotations

A. Trauma radiograph series includes PA, lateral, radial oblique, and scaphoid.

B. Compression injury may damage the epiphyseal plate or cause a torus fracture of the distal radius, often well-healed by presentation. If not, soft-casting for 2 weeks is sufficient.

C. Casting may be performed by those trained in postgraduate courses if fracture is nonarticular and nondisplaced.

D. Instability is determined on a lateral view by the relationship of the navicular (scaphoid) and capitate or the radius. On the PA (or AP) the spacing between the lunate and scaphoid may indicate damage when increased beyond 2 mm.

E. Fluoroscopy may be used when instability is suspected but is not apparent on radiograph. This form of instability, called dynamic instability, may be visualized. MRI is helpful in differential of the wrist, including ligament tears, ganglions, and anomalous structures.

F. de Quervain's syndrome involves the abductor policis longus (APL) and the extensor policis brevis (EPB). Pain is felt over the radial styloid process.

G. Intersection syndrome is most common in athletes such as weight lifters, rowers, and those doing any repetitive flexion/extension movement. It occurs at the intersection of the extensors and the APL and EPB. It may squeak with movement.

Key: RICE: rest, ice, compression, elevation.

continues

Figure 9–7 continued

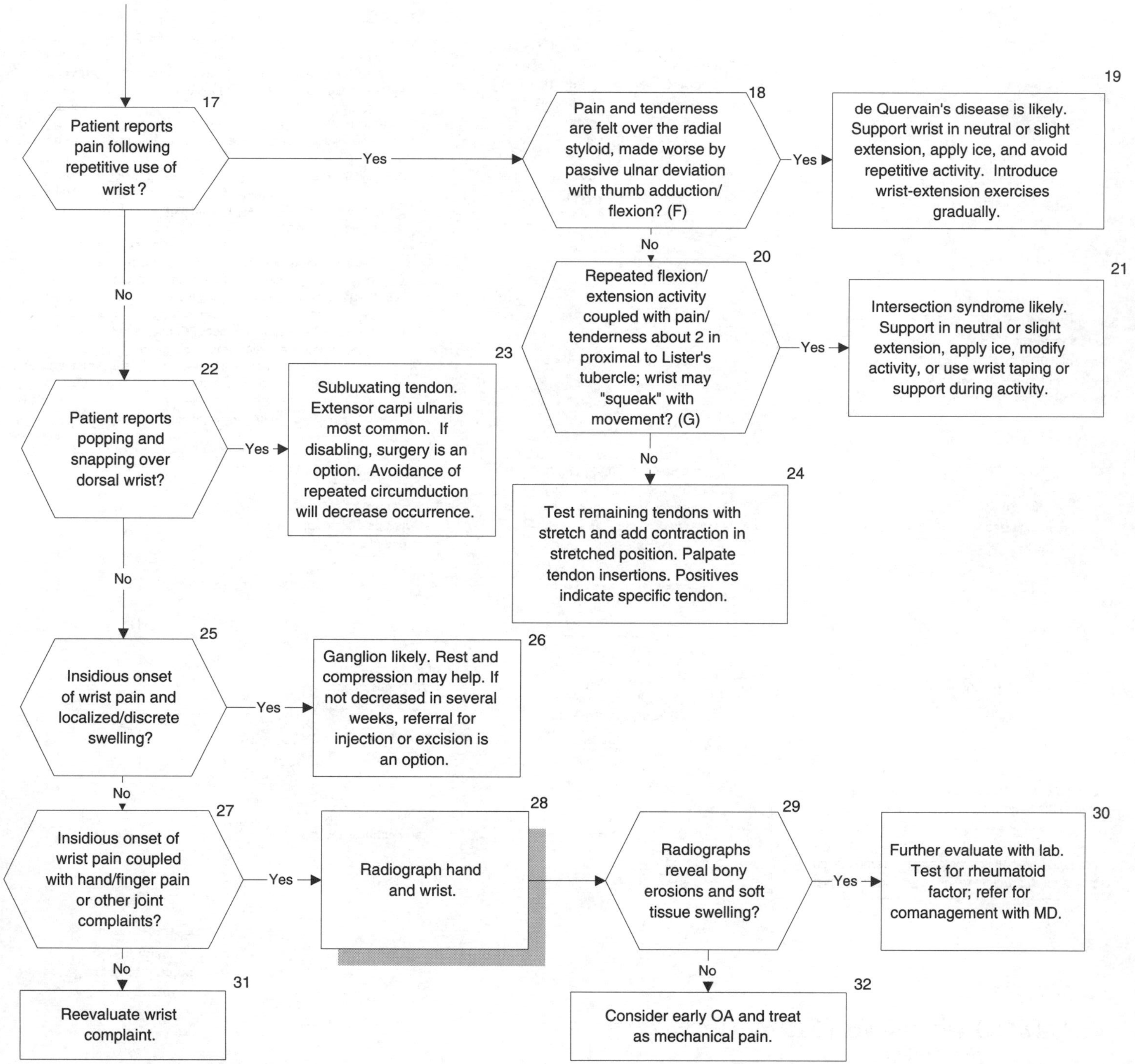

17 Patient reports pain following repetitive use of wrist?
- Yes → 18
- No → 22

18 Pain and tenderness are felt over the radial styloid, made worse by passive ulnar deviation with thumb adduction/flexion? (F)
- Yes → 19
- No → 20

19 de Quervain's disease is likely. Support wrist in neutral or slight extension, apply ice, and avoid repetitive activity. Introduce wrist-extension exercises gradually.

20 Repeated flexion/extension activity coupled with pain/tenderness about 2 in proximal to Lister's tubercle; wrist may "squeak" with movement? (G)
- Yes → 21
- No → 24

21 Intersection syndrome likely. Support in neutral or slight extension, apply ice, modify activity, or use wrist taping or support during activity.

22 Patient reports popping and snapping over dorsal wrist?
- Yes → 23
- No → 25

23 Subluxating tendon. Extensor carpi ulnaris most common. If disabling, surgery is an option. Avoidance of repeated circumduction will decrease occurrence.

24 Test remaining tendons with stretch and add contraction in stretched position. Palpate tendon insertions. Positives indicate specific tendon.

25 Insidious onset of wrist pain and localized/discrete swelling?
- Yes → 26
- No → 27

26 Ganglion likely. Rest and compression may help. If not decreased in several weeks, referral for injection or excision is an option.

27 Insidious onset of wrist pain coupled with hand/finger pain or other joint complaints?
- Yes → 28
- No → 31

28 Radiograph hand and wrist. → 29

29 Radiographs reveal bony erosions and soft tissue swelling?
- Yes → 30
- No → 32

30 Further evaluate with lab. Test for rheumatoid factor; refer for comanagement with MD.

31 Reevaluate wrist complaint.

32 Consider early OA and treat as mechanical pain.

SELECTED DISORDERS OF THE WRIST AND FOREARM

INSTABILITY

Scapholunate Dissociation

Classic Presentation

The patient complains of radial or dorsal wrist pain following a fall on an outstretched hand.

Cause

By falling onto the thenar eminence, the wrist is forced in to hyperextension, ulnar deviation, and intercarpal supination forcing the capitate between the scaphoid and lunate.[35] The result is tearing or stretching of the scapholunate interosseous and radioscaphoid ligaments, leading to various degrees of instability.

Evaluation

The standard stability test is Watson's.[36] With the patient's arm relaxed, the wrist is taken passively into ulnar deviation. The examiner presses the distal pole posteriorly as he or she passively moves the wrist into radial deviation. A painful pop or click will occur as the proximal pole is forced to subluxate dorsally. This subluxation occurs because the dorsal force of the examiner on the scaphoid prevents its normal ability to move into a vertical position.

When evaluating instability of the wrist radiographically, AP, lateral, and oblique views are supplemented with a PA clenched-fist view and, if needed, a lateral view taken in flexion and extension.[37] Scapholunate dissociation appears on the PA or AP as a 3-mm or greater space between the lunate and the scaphoid; it is sometimes referred to as the Terry Thomas[38] or David Letterman sign. Additionally, there is a vertical orientation to the scaphoid that also creates a cortical overlap, referred to as the signet ring sign. On the lateral view, a DISI pattern may be visible.[39] Normally, the scaphoid is angled between 30° and 60°. Angulation greater than 65° to 70°, coupled with a dorsiflexed lunate, indicates dissociation, lack of stability between the scaphoid and lunate.

Management

Surgery is usually necessary.

Triquetrolunate Dissociation

Classic Presentation

The patient may report a fall on either a palmar-flexed or hyperpronated wrist. Some patients present with only dorsal ulnar wrist pain and a nontraumatic history.

Cause

Stretching or disruption of the lunotriquetral ligaments allows palmar subluxation of the lunate.

Evaluation

The standard orthopaedic evaluation involves the ballottement test.[40] This test is performed by stabilizing the lunate or triquetrum and "shucking" or shearing the other bone against the stabilized bone. A painful pop is considered a positive.

Radiographic evaluation is usually normal. However, with a static instability a PISI (also known as VISI) deformity on the lateral wrist view is seen. The PISI pattern is palmar subluxation of the lunate and scaphoid with a dorsiflexed triquetrum. When the radiographs are negative for instability, either fluoroscopic evaluation or an arthrogram is necessary to reveal an underlying dynamic instability.

Management

If the ballottement test is positive, but radiographs are negative, initial treatment is immobilization in a long arm cast for 6 to 8 weeks (wrist in ulnar deviation and dorsiflexion). If instability is radiographically evident (static instability), there is some disagreement as to management. Some practitioners suggest surgery; others suggest repositioning of the lunate and scaphoid followed by immobilization.

Triquetrohamate Instability (Midcarpal)

Classic Presentation

A patient may present with a history of a fall or blow to the medial side of the hand with hyperpronation. Some patients may have wrist pain without a specific traumatic event.

Cause

Ligamentous tearing disrupts the osseous coupling between the hamate and triquetrum.

Evaluation

Reproduction may occur on either passive or active pronation coupled with ulnar deviation. Unfortunately, a host of other ulnar-sided problems may also respond with a painful click,[41] including TFC damage, lunotriquetral ligament tears, and distal radioulnar subluxation. Axial compression may also produce a click with midcarpal and other instabilities. Radiographic evaluation is usually normal. With a static instability, a DISI pattern may be visible. Videofluoroscopic evaluation is most sensitive, often revealing a sudden movement of the proximal carpal row from the normal PISI pattern in radial deviation to a DISI pattern near the end-range of ulnar deviation.

Management

Initially, immobilization may be effective for 6 weeks. If ineffective in reducing instability or pain, various forms of surgery are recommended.

Triangular Fibrocartilage Injury

Classic Presentation

A patient presents with pain on the ulnar side of the wrist made worse by pronation and supination. She or he may have a traumatic history such as a fall on an outstretched hand or no obvious trauma.

Cause

The TFC is the fibrocartilagenous structure at the distal end of the ulna. It is part of the complex that supports the ulnar side of the wrist. The TFC is injured through several mechanisms that result in either perforations (traumatic and degenerative) or avulsions. Degenerative changes occur by the third decade. Other factors include the poor blood supply limited to the peripheral 15% to 25% of the disc[42] and the association of ulnar positive variance (along ulna) that causes compression and thinning of the TFC.

Evaluation

To differentiate between damage to the distal radioulnar joint (DRUJ) and the TFC, the examiner may stabilize the radius and ulna by compressing them together proximal to the

DRUJ. Passive movement of the forearm into pronation and supination should be uneventful if only the TFC is involved. Second, ulnar deviation, axial loading, and shearing distal to the DRUJ often will produce pain and crepitus when the TFC is damaged. Radiographic evaluation is largely an attempt to determine whether the patient has positive ulnar variance. For standardization it is recommended that the PA film be taken with 90° of elbow and shoulder flexion with the hand as flat as possible.[43] A line drawn perpendicularly across the distal end of the radius should be even with the distal ulna. Referral for an arthrogram or MRI may confirm the diagnosis of TFC damage.

Management

Initial management is to immobilize the wrist in neutral for several weeks, obviously avoiding any ulnar deviation or compression maneuvers subsequent to splint removal. Failure to resolve requires arthroscopic evaluation and repair that includes resection of the distal ulna.

TENDINITIS

de Quervain's Tenosynovitis

Classic Presentation

A patient presents with a complaint of radial wrist pain with a history of activities that require either forceful gripping with ulnar deviation or repetitive use of the thumb.[44]

Cause

Stenosing tenosynovitis of the abductor pollicis longus (APL) and extensor pollicis brevis (EPL) occurs as a result of chronic microtrauma to either the tenosynovium or sheath.[45]

Evaluation

Pain is reproduced with resisted thumb extension with the wrist in radial deviation or with the standard Finkelstein test.[46] The Finkelstein test begins by having the patient grasp his or her thumb. The examiner passively deviates the wrist ulnarly. Tenderness is often found one-half inch proximal to the radial styloid.

Management

Initially, a conservative trial of activity modification, ultrasound, and nonsteroidal anti-inflammatory drugs (NSAIDs) should be attempted. Failure to improve within 2 to 3 weeks requires immobilization with a thumb spica for another 2 to 3 weeks. If ineffective, referral for local steroid injection should be made. Rarely, surgery is needed.

Intersection Syndrome

Classic Presentation

A patient (often an athlete) presents with a complaint of pain and crepitus 2 in or so above the wrist on the dorsoradial aspect. There is usually a history of repeated flexion/extension movement with either occupational or sports activity.[47]

Cause

An inflammatory response and possible adventitial bursitis occur at the crossing of two groups of tendons; the abductor pollicis longus and extensor pollicis brevis crossing over the wrist extensors. This condition is more common in canoeists, weight lifters, and recreational tennis players.

Evaluation

There is usually tenderness and swelling 4 to 6 cm proximal to Lister's tubercle.

Management

Rest, NSAIDs, and ice may help initially. Myofascial release techniques applied proximal to the tendon crossing may also be of benefit. If unsuccessful, splinting for 2 weeks may help enforce a rest period. Prevention includes modification or elimination of the inciting activity.

Other Tendinopathies

Following is a list of tendinopathies and the patient population most often associated with each:

- Extensor pollicis longus tendinitis—seen in drummers, athletes involved in racquet sports, and patients with rheumatoid arthritis.
- Extensor indices proprius syndrome and extensor digiti minimi tendinitis—due to trauma and overuse.
- Extensor carpi ulnaris tendinitis—relatively common tenosynovitis found in occupations or sports requiring repetitive wrist movement such as racquet sports, rowing, golf, and baseball. The tendon has its own sheath separate from the extensor retinaculum, which may rupture following forced supination, flexion, and ulnar deviation. This will lead to a painful snapping over the back of the wrist.

Evaluation

Palpation of the tendon or its insertion is usually painful, and there may be associated swelling. Full stretching of the tendon or contraction in a stretched position may reproduce the patient's complaint.

Management

Avoidance of the inciting activity coupled with myofascial release of the involved muscle may be helpful. If ineffective, a short period of soft cast immobilization may be necessary. For patients with RA, referral for medical management is prudent.

PERIPHERAL NERVE ENTRAPMENTS

MEDIAN NERVE

Carpal Tunnel Syndrome

Classic Presentation

The patient presents with a complaint of pain and numbness/tingling in the palmar surface of the thumb and radial two and one-half fingers; the symptoms are worse at night. There is usually also a complaint of some clumsiness with precision gripping.

Cause

The median nerve runs through an osteofibrous tunnel created by the transverse carpal ligament and carpal bones. Although direct compression from ganglions, fractures, and dislocations is possible, it is more common to have a history of direct external pressure on the tunnel or a history of prolonged wrist use in full flexion or extension. Pressure inside the tunnel increases in these extreme positions. Additional factors may have to do with fluid retention, as in pregnancy, RA, diabetes, and connective tissue disorders. Patients deficient in B vitamins may be predisposed.

Evaluation

Classically, Phalen's, reverse Phalen's, and Tinel's tests have been used clinically to provoke symptoms. These tests have variable responses. The pressure-provocative test appears to be more sensitive. Direct pressure is applied with the thumb over the carpal tunnel. Pinch and grip strength is usually weaker on the involved side. Thenar atrophy may be evident in chronic cases. Electrodiagnostic studies may indicate conduction delay at the wrist. It is important to examine other potential sites of median nerve entrapment.

Management

Initial treatment involves night splinting in extension or neutral, avoidance of compressive maneuvers or overuse as in typing, and perhaps the use of a B-complex vitamin (Table 9–3). Adjustment of the lunate may also be helpful. Ergonomic advice regarding hand and wrist position or the use of split keyboards or rest pads may be of help. When nonresponsive, surgical release of the retinaculum may be necessary.

Pronator Syndrome

Classic Presentation

The patient presents with a complaint of volar forearm pain. There is usually no history of trauma; however, there is often a history of repetitive pronation and wrist flexion such as incurred by carpenters, assembly line workers, and weight lifters.

Cause

Compression may occur at several sites, including the bicipital aponeurosis (lacertus fibrosus) that connects with the pronator teres, between the two heads of the pronator teres, and at the flexor digitorum superficialis by a thickened, fibrotic arch. Compression between the heads of the pronator is often due to hypertrophy. Other (rarer) sites are beneath the ligament of Struthers (supracondylar arch), the median artery, and a bicipital tuberosity bursa.[48]

Evaluation

- Reproduction of the patient's complaint is based on a direct or an indirect search for the compression site:
- Provocation with resisted elbow flexion and supination with maximum elbow flexion implies the lacertus fibrosus or less often the ligament of Struthers.
- Provocation with resisted pronation, keeping the elbow extended and the wrist flexed, suggests pronator teres compression (hypertrophy common).
- Provocation with resisted middle finger flexion suggests that the site of compression is the flexor digitorum superficialis.

When the lacertus fibrosus is involved, pronation may reveal indentations in the pronator teres. Direct pressure over the pronator teres often will reproduce symptoms. Electrodiagnostic studies are of little value.

Management

Initial management involves a trial of myofascial release and/or rest. If unresponsive to myofascial release after 2 to 3 weeks, splinting for 2 to 3 weeks may be necessary. If symptoms persist beyond 6 months, surgical exploration may be necessary.

Table 9–3 Conservative Management of Carpal Tunnel Syndrome

Parameter	*Acute Stage*	*Subacute Stage*	*Symptom-Free Stage*
Criteria	Numbness/tingling in palmar thumb, index, and radial half of middle finger; positive Tinel's, Phalen's, or compression test.	Frequency of numbness/tingling event is decreasing.	No complaints with moderate daily use of wrists; limited work activity does not provoke symptoms.
Goals	Reduce any internal swelling, decrease pain or numbness/tingling frequency.	Gradually retrain patient to perform activities with less stress to carpal tunnel; wean patient off daytime use of support.	Maintain proper ergonomic work environment; wean patient off night support.
Concerns	If condition progresses, atrophy of thenar muscles is likely and the need for surgery increases; patient may have irritation of the median nerve at more proximal sites; patient with diagnosis from other doctor may not have carpal tunnel syndrome.	Patient is unable to avoid aggravating activities or shows signs of progression.	Patient returns to work activities without proper ergonomic support.
Requirements for progression to next stage; approximate time needed	Improvement of frequency and intensity of numbness/tingling complaint; no progressive atrophy of thenar muscles; 1–3 weeks.	Able to perform daily activities (without brace) with minor symptoms; 2–3 weeks.	No symptoms with work activity; 2–3 months.
Manipulation/mobilization	Adjustments of the lunate and radioulnar articulation may help; evaluate the cervical spine for possible fixation.	Adjustments of the lunate and radioulnar articulation may help; evaluate the cervical spine for possible fixation.	Adjustments of the lunate and radioulnar articulation may help; evaluate the cervical spine for possible fixation
Modalities	Ice, rest, electromyographic stimulation (bipolar for 20 min/d with ice; 80–120 Hz first few days, 1–150 Hz next few days, 1–15 Hz next few days).	Underwater ultrasound at 1.5–2 wt/cm^2 for 5–7 minutes; ice after strengthening exercises for 10 minutes.	Ice after exercises.
External brace, support, etc.	Consider use of splint in neutral or slight extension.	Continue use of splint, gradually decreasing daytime use.	Continue night splinting if necessary; attempt gradual reduction of use.
ROM/flexibility massage	Mild stripping massage to flexor and extensor groups of muscles.	Grade 3 or 4 myofascial release to extensors or flexors based on findings.	Maintain flexibility with mild postisometric relaxation technique.

continues

Table 9–3 continued

Parameter	*Acute Stage*	*Subacute Stage*	*Symptom-Free Stage*
Open-chain exercise	Mild isometrics in pain-free ranges with focus on extension.	Isometrics progressing to isotonic exercises with a focus on wrist extensors, pronators, and supinators; flexor exercises should be performed but not emphasized.	Continue isotonic exercises on an every-other-day routine for maintaining wrist strength and preventing recurrence.
Associated biomechanical items	Evaluate the patient's work posture, especially with keyboard and mouse positions and padding; attempt to isolate provoking maneuvers or positions.	Follow-up of modification of workstation for patient; gradually introduce patient to activity beginning with short periods of work and frequent rest periods.	
Lifestyle/activity modifications	Avoid activities that compress the anterior wrist, such as wrist-supported typing, use of a mouse, or activities that require lifting; this may require a work-restriction request to the patient's employer. Decrease salt intake; consider use of B_6 with a B-complex vitamin; consider use of bromelain or NSAIDs.	Continue to avoid postures that compress the anterior wrist or force the wrist into hyperflexion or extension; avoid carrying heavy objects or repeated pronation supination.	

Anterior Interosseous Syndrome

Classic Presentation

The patient presents with a complaint of anterior proximal forearm pain that occurred either acutely after a single violent forearm muscle contraction or from repetitive activity. There is an associated complaint of weakness, usually isolated to pinch of the thumb and index finger and usually within 12 to 24 hours after the onset of pain.

Cause

Compression sites are similar to those for pronator teres syndrome; however, they are most commonly at the flexor digitorum superficialis or deep head of the pronator teres. At these sites, the anterior interosseous nerve, a motor branch of the median nerve, is compressed or entrapped. It may also be seen with stingers (acute stretch injuries to the brachial plexus) or after an inerscalene block.

Evaluation

Inability to pinch the tips of the thumb and index finger together results in a pulp-to-pulp pinch. This is due to weakness of the flexor policis longus (FPL) and index finger flexor digitorum profundus (FDP). The pronator quadratus may be weak when tested with resisted forearm pronation with full elbow flexion. Occasionally, there may be weakness of the hand intrinsics due to a Martin-Gruber anastomosis, which is found in 15% of the population (connection between median and ulnar nerves). Electrodiagnostic studies are considered the gold standard with denervation of the FPL and index finger FDP and pronator quadratus.

Management

Conservative treatment should be attempted for up to 8 weeks, at which time surgery should be considered. Conservative care involves myofascial release, rest, and antiinflammatory medication.

ULNAR NERVE

Cubital Tunnel Syndrome

Classic Presentation

The patient presents with a complaint of medial forearm pain and paresthesia into the ring and little finger. There is often a history of activities, such as throwing, that medially stretched the elbow.

Cause

Compression or stretch may cause irritation of the ulnar nerve. Stretch is usually due to valgus stretch to the elbow. Compression may be at the two heads of the flexor carpi ulnaris or may be due to osteophytes in the cubital tunnel. Less common causes include lipomas, ganglions, and anomalous soft tissue structures. Pressure in the tunnel is increased with elbow flexion and wrist extension (threefold), and the cocking position of throwing (sixfold).[49]

Evaluation

The symptoms are often reproduced by passive or resisted elbow flexion with the elbow in a maximally flexed position. The Tinel's sign is variable and somewhat unreliable. Electrodiagnostic studies are rarely necessary but may be helpful in differentiating among other medial forearm pain syndromes.

Management

Conservative management includes rest, ice, and antiinflammatories. Additionally, if entrapment is at the flexor carpi ulnaris, myofascial release may be of help. Night splinting with the elbow flexed to 45° in neutral rotation is recommended. Failure of conservative care should warrant a surgical consultation.

Tunnel of Guyon

Classic Presentation

The patient complains of numbness/tingling or pain in the fourth and fifth digits.

Cause

The ulnar nerve may be compressed in the tunnel of Guyon, which is an osseofibrous tunnel formed by the groove between the pisiform and the hook of the hamate. Activities that cause chronic compression at this site may result in ulnar nerve dysfunction. Constant compression on handlebars, as with cyclists, may cause this problem (handlebar of cyclist's palsy). Other causes include vascular abnormalities, fractures of the hook of the hamate, and ganglions.[50]

Evaluation

Provocation testing includes either Tinel's or pressure at the pisiform hamate area (just distal and medial to the pisiform). Compression may occur at several areas, causing either mixed motor and sensory findings or isolated motor or sensory findings. Sensory testing may reveal abnormalities in the fourth and fifth digits. Two-point discrimination may be affected in the same region. Motor involvement may be evident by testing grip strength. Weakness of the adductor policis may be evident with Froment's sign. Grasping a piece of paper between the thumb and the index finger, the patient flexes the distal thumb to substitute for the weak adductor policis. Wartenberg's sign is positive when the patient cannot fully adduct all fingers.

Management

Protection with padding and modifying any inciting activity that adds pressure to the area, such as a change in handlebar or bicycle position with cyclists, is usually sufficient. If there is an obvious neural deficit, refer to an orthopaedist when the problem persists for longer than a few weeks.

RADIAL NERVE

Radial Tunnel Syndrome

Classic Presentation

The patient complains of a dull, aching pain over the lateral forearm.

Cause

There is a disagreement with regard to whether radial tunnel syndrome (RTC) should be considered an entity separate from PINS.[51] The distinction is mainly clinical when entrapment occurs at a site where the PIN is selectively affected, leading to motor findings with no sensory deficits. As the radial nerve enters and traverses the forearm, it may be compressed or entrapped at several locations, including the radial head, the medial edge of the ECRB, a fan-shaped vascular arcade, the arcade of Frohse (thickened edge of the superficial head of the supinator), and the two heads of the supinator muscle.

Evaluation

Tenderness is distal to the lateral epicondyle (approximately four fingerbreadths below the lateral epicondyle). Provocative maneuvers are based on the site of entrapment: ECRB—resisted middle finger extension with the elbow extended; radial head—elbow flexion; supinator muscle—resisted, repeated supination with the forearm flexed; arcade of Frohse—extreme forearm pronation with wrist flexion. Weakness of the wrist extensors is often found when the PIN is involved.

Management

If the syndrome is due to repeated pronation/supination, rest from the activity and modification of the activity are required. Myofascial release technique is particularly helpful when the entrapment is at the supinator muscle. Adjusting the radial head may be of benefit in some cases.

Cheiralgia Paresthetica (Wartenberg's Syndrome)

Classic Presentation

The patient complains of numbness or tingling over the dorsolateral aspect of the wrist and hand.

Cause

The superficial branch of the radial nerve is susceptible to trauma between the tendons of the ECRL and the brachioradialis. Repetitive movements such as pronation and supination are often the cause. Wearing a wrist band or a brace or taping may cause compression. Direct blows to the dorsolateral forearm/wrist may also cause this disorder.

Evaluation

Tinel's sign is often positive over the point of compression at the dorsolateral wrist. Pain may be caused by passive ulnar deviation and flexion of the wrist.

Management

If there is a compressive culprit such as a wrist brace, support, or taping, modify use to avoid compression. If there is a repetitive movement cause, initially rest from the activity and modify the movement to avoid further irritation. Myofascial release above the area may be helpful; however, release at the area often reproduces the problem.

FRACTURES

Scaphoid

Classic Presentation

The patient presents with pain at the anatomic snuff-box after a fall on an outstretched hand. The patient often is seen 3 to 6 months after the trauma.

Cause

An impact injury with the wrist in maximum dorsiflexion (greater than 90°) will fracture the scaphoid. The radial styloid may impact the midportion of the scaphoid. The vascular supply to the scaphoid runs distal to proximal and therefore distal fractures generally heal without incident. Proximal pole fractures, however, usually result in avascular necrosis. Proximal pole fractures account for about 20% of all scaphoid fractures.

Evaluation

The clinical examination is often more revealing than radiographs. There are several tests, including axial compression of the index or middle finger, percussion on the extended thumb, forced dorsiflexion, and resisted pronation. One of the most sensitive tests is to stretch the patient's pronated hand carefully into maximum ulnar deviation. A positive test result is obtained when pain is produced at the anatomic snuff-box. The positive predictive value is 52%.

Although it may appear that radiographs are the definitive tool for detecting a scaphoid fracture, initial films are often negative. Additionally, follow-up film (2 to 3 weeks postinjury) are not always helpful. One study indicated an interpretation error of 40%.[52] However, it is prudent to use multiple views, including several oblique films at the time of injury and in 2 to 3 weeks. A scaphoid series includes the standard PA, lateral, right and left obliques, and a PA view with radial and ulnar deviation with the fingers flexed. When the suspicion is high but films are unrevealing, a bone scan or CT scan is usually diagnostic.

Management

Initial treatment of nondisplaced fractures is cast immobilization, which includes the forearm and the proximal interphalangeal joint of the thumb. If there is no visible fracture line on initial radiographs, the patient should be managed as if a scaphoid fracture is present when there is a positive scaphoid fracture test, especially if there is any associated swelling at the dorsal radial wrist. Follow-up films are taken in about 2 weeks with the cast removed. If a fracture is evident, cast immobilization is continued to 8 to 12 weeks. Out-of-cast films are taken in 6 and 12 weeks. If further healing is necessary, continue immobilization for 2 to 4 weeks. Referral is necessary if healing is not progressing or if there is a displaced fracture. Another referral is an associated perilunar dislocation where the capitate dislocates off the lunate.

Hook of Hamate

Classic Presentation

The patient presents with pain just distal and radial to the pisiform following impact to the area from a fall, a bat, racquet, or golf club.

Cause

The hook of the hamate is susceptible to direct trauma. A fall on or blow to the hypothenar eminence may result in fracture. The fracture is unstable because of the pull from the flexor carpi ulnaris (through the pisohamate ligament), the opponens digiti and flexor digiti quinti, and the transverse ligament.

Evaluation

Pain is felt 1 to 2 cm distal and radial to the pisiform. Radiographs include the carpal tunnel view and 20° supinated view. When a fracture is not visible but suspected, a bone scan or CT scan may be valuable.

Management

Fragment excision is usually successful, followed by a short arm cast for 3 to 4 months.

Kienbock's Disease

Classic Presentation

The patient presents with a stiff and painful wrist. Often there is no history of trauma.

Cause

Kienbock's disease is avascular necrosis of the lunate due to a stress or compression fracture.[53] Repetitive minor trauma is suspected as the common initiator.

Evaluation

Diagnosis is usually difficult until the lunate becomes more radiopaque than the surrounding carpal bones. CT or magnetic resonance imaging (MRI) is more sensitive, yet should be used only when the suspicion is high.

Management

If Kienbock's disease is detected, cast immobilization for about 8 weeks is necessary to allow revascularization. When this fails, surgery is used to decompress the area before collapse of the lunate. This may also include osteotomy of the radius to equal out a relatively short ulna. Following collapse, replacement with a prosthetic or autogenous material is used. Intercarpal fusion is the least desirable procedure.

Forearm

Following is a list of forearm fractures. These fractures are usually due to a fall on an outstretched hand or a blow to the area.

- Monteggia—shaft fracture of the ulna with an associated dislocated radial head
- Galeazzi—fractured distal radius and dislocated ulna
- Greenstick—an incomplete fracture, often of both the radius and the ulna, in a skeletally immature patient; healing usually occurs in 6 to 8 weeks
- Colles'—distal radial fracture with dorsal and radial angulation
- Smith's—distal radial fracture with volar (palmar) angulation

MISCELLANEOUS CONDITIONS

Dorsal Impaction Syndrome

Classic Presentation

The patient presents with a complaint of dorsal wrist pain. There is a history of repeated forced dorsiflexion with some component of concomitant weight bearing (the two groups most commonly affected are gymnasts and chiropractors).

Cause

Repeated dorsiflexion causes compression of the dorsal wrist structures, leading to a capsulitis and a number of reactive changes, including localized hypertrophic synovitis (meniscoid of the wrist), and osteocartilagenous changes in the dorsal rim of the scaphoid, lunate, capitate, or radius.

Evaluation

Tenderness is found at the middorsal aspect of the wrist, specifically at the lunocapitate area. Unfortunately, unless radiographic changes are evident, there are no indicators other than the history.

Management

Essentially an overuse (and misuse) condition, the dorsal impaction syndrome is managed by avoidance of the offending position, forced dorsiflexion. Blockage of forced passive dorsiflexion can be accomplished by the use of a wrist brace with a limiter such as taping the front of the wrist and forearm or placing padding on the back of the wrist (thick felt or multiple layers of moleskin). Flexion exercises may also be helpful. If ineffective, splinting in a soft cast for 2 to 3 weeks may allow healing. For the chiropractor, use of non-weight-bearing adjusting techniques or substitution with other soft techniques for a period of time may be the final answer.

Ganglions

Classic Presentation

The patient presents with a complaint of dorsal wrist pain. Passive dorsiflexion often makes it worse. The patient may have found a small tender nodule or knot. There is usually a history of a repetitive wrist activity occupationally or with sports. Most often, the patient is under age 35 years.

Cause

Ganglions are soft tissue tumors that arise from either the capsule or tendon sheaths. They are most common at the dorsal scapholunate ligament or at the metacarpal heads. Ganglions represent mucinous degeneration into multiple intraligamentous cysts or larger, sometimes palpable cysts.

Evaluation

Unfortunately, not all ganglions are palpable. It has been observed that often the more occult (smaller ganglion), the more symptomatic. Radiographs are useless except to rule out other causes.

Management

If the ganglion is visible, an initial attempt at compression to rupture the capsule is sometimes made. However, ganglions tend to reappear unless surgically excised. The need for surgery is based on the degree of discomfort and effect on daily activities, occupation, or sport. Ganglions often fluctuate in size.

REFERENCES

1. Bureau of National Affairs. OSHA advance notice of proposed rule-making for ergonomic safety and health management. (57 FR34192, August, 1992) OSHA Rep; 1992;310–318.
2. Weiker GG. Hand and wrist problems in the gymnast. *Clin Sports Med.* 1992;11:189–202.
3. Weinstein SM, Herring SA. Nerve problems and compartment syndromes in the hand, wrist, and forearm. *Clin Sports Med.* 1992;11:161–188.
4. Taleisnik J. *The Wrist.* New York: Churchill Livingstone; 1985.
5. Pin PG, Nowak, M, Logan SE, Young VL, et al. Coincident rupture of the scapholunate and lunotriquetral ligaments without perilunate dislocation: pathomechanics and management. *J Hand Surg Am.* 1990;15:110–119.
6. Green DP. *Operative Hand Surgery.* New York: Churchill Livingstone; 1988.
7. Kauer JMH. The distal radioulnar joint. *Clin Orthop.* 1992;275: 37–45.
8. Mikic ZD. Age changes in the triangular fibrocartilage of the wrist joint. *J Anat.* 1978;126:367–384.
9. Mandelbaum BR, Bartolozzi AR, Davis CA, et al. Wrist pain syndrome in the gymnast: pathogenetic, diagnostic, and therapeutic considerations. *Am J Sports Med.* 1989;17:305–317.
10. Palmer AK, Werner FW. The triangular fibrocartilage complex of the wrist: anatomy and function. *J Hand Surg.* 1981;6:153–162.
11. Reid DC. *Sports Injury Assessment and Rehabilitation.* New York: Churchill Livingstone; 1992:1061.
12. Thorson E, Szabo RM. Common tendinitis problems in the hand and forearm. *Orthop Clin North Am.* 1992;23:65–74.
13. Tubiana R. *The Hand.* Philadelphia: WB Saunders; 1981.
14. Spinner M. *Injuries to the Major Branches of the Peripheral Nerves of the Forearm.* 2nd ed. Philadelphia: WB Saunders; 1978:194.
15. Spinner M, Linscheid RL. Nerve entrapment syndromes. In: Morrey BF, ed. *The Elbow and Its Disorders.* Philadelphia: WB Saunders; 1985:73–91.
16. Spinner M. The anterior interosseous nerve syndrome with special attention to its variations. *J Bone Joint Surg.* 1970;52A:84–94.
17. McCue FC III, Miller GA. Soft-tissue injuries of the hand. In: Petrone FA, ed. *Symposium on Upper Extremity Injuries in the Athlete.* St. Louis, MO: CV Mosby; 1986:84.

18. Kuschner SH, et al. Tinel's sign and Phalen's test in carpal tunnel syndrome. *Orthopedics*. 1992;15:1297–1302.
19. Williams TM, et al. Verification of the pressure provocative test in carpal tunnel syndrome. *Ann Plast Surg*. 1992;29:8–11.
20. Long RR. Nerve anatomy and diagnostic principles. In: Pappas AM, ed. *Upper Extremity Injuries in the Athlete*. New York: Churchill Livingstone; 1995:47–48.
21. Vanderpool SW, Chalmers J, Lamb DW, et al. Peripheral compression lesions of the ulnar nerve. *J Bone Joint Surg Br*. 1968:50:792–803.
22. Eversmann WW. Compression and entrapment neuropathies of the upper extremity. *J Hand Surg*. 1983;8:759–766.
23. Shea JD, McClain EJ. Ulnar nerve compression syndromes at and below the wrist. *J Bone Joint Surg Am*. 1969;61:1095–1103.
24. Regan WD, Morrey BF. Entrapment neuropathies about the elbow. In: Delee JC, Drez D Jr, eds. *Orthopedic Sports Medicine: Principles and Practice*. Philadelphia: WB Saunders; 1994:844–859.
25. Spinner M. The arcade of Frohse and its relationship to posterior interosseous nerve paralysis. *J Bone Joint Surg Br*. 1968;50: 809–812.
26. Carr D, David P. Distal posterior interosseous syndrome. *J Hand Surg Am*. 1985;10:873.
27. Wartenberg R. Cheiralgia paresthetica (Isolierte neuritis des ram superficialis nerve radialis). *Z Gesamte Neurol Psychiatry*. 1932;141:145–155.
28. Leonard RN. Fractures and dislocations of the carpus. In: Brown BG, Jupiter JB, Levine AM, et al, eds. *Skeletal Trauma*. Philadelphia: WB Saunders; 1992.
29. Stechers WR. Roentgenography of the carpal navicular bone. *AJR*. 1937;37:704–705.
30. Jorgenson TM, Anderson J, Thammesen P, et al. Scanning and radiology of the carpal scaphoid bone. *Acta Orthop Scand*. 1979;50:663–665.
31. Dobyns JH, Linscheid RL, Chao EYS, et al. Traumatic instability of the wrist. Chicago: American Academy of Orhopaedic Surgeons Instructional Course Lectures. 1975;24:182.
32. Norman A, Nelson J, Gren S. Fracture of the hook of the hamate: radiographic signs. *Radiology*. 1985;154:49–53.
33. Nisenfield FG, Neviasser RJ. Fracture of the hook of the hamate: a diagnosis easily missed. *J Trauma*. 1974;14:612–616.
34. Polivy KD, Millender LH, Newberg T, et al. Fractures of the hook of the hamate: a failure of clinical diagnosis. *J Hand Surg Am*. 1985;10:101–104.
35. Mayfield JK. Wrist ligamentous anatomy and pathogenesis of carpal instability. *Orthop Clin North Am*. 1984;15:209.
36. Watson HK, Dhillon HS. Intercarpal arthrodesis. In Green DP, ed. *Operative Hand Surgery*. 3rd ed. New York: Churchill Livingstone; 1993;1:113.
37. Gilula LA, Weeks PN. Post-traumatic ligamentous instability of the wrist. *Radiology*. 1978;129:641.
38. Frankel VH. The Terry Thomas sign. *Clin Orthop*. 1977;129:121.
39. Linsheid RL, Dobyns JH, Beckenbaugh RD, et al. Instability patterns of the wrist. *J Hand Surg Am*. 1983;8:682.
40. Reagan DS, Linsheid RL, Dobyns JH. Lunotriquetral sprains. *J Hand Surg Am*. 1984;9:502.
41. Brown DE, Lichman DM. Midcarpal instability. *Hand Clin*. 1987;3:135.
42. Mikic Z. The blood supply of the human distal radioulnar joint and the microvasculature of its articular disk. *Clin Orthop*. 1992;275:19.
43. Bowers WH. The distal radioulnar joint. In Green DP, ed. *Operative Hand Surgery*. 2nd ed. New York: Churchill Livingstone; 1988.
44. Wood MB, Dobyns JH. Sports related extra-articular wrist syndromes. *Clin Orthop*. 1986;202:93–102.
45. Keifhaber TR, Stern PJ. Upper extremity tendinitis and overuse syndromes in the athlete. *Clin Sports Med*. 1969;67:116–123.
46. Finkelstein H. Stenosing tenovaginitis at the radial styloid process. *J Bone Joint Surg Am*. 1930;12:509–540.
47. Grundberg AB, Reagan DS. Pathologic anatomy of the forearm: intersection syndrome. *J Hand Surg Am*. 1985;10:299–302.
48. Posner MA. Compressive neuropathies of the median and radial nerves at the elbow. *Clin Sports Med*. 1990;9:343.
49. Glousman RE. Ulnar nerve problems in the athlete's elbow. *Clin Sports Med*. 1990;9:365.
50. Rettig AC. Neurovascular injuries in the wrists and hands of athletes. *Clin Sports Med*. 1990;9:389.
51. Plancher KD, Peterson RK, Steichen JB. Compressive neuropathies and tendinopathies in the athletic elbow and wrist. *Clin Sports Med*. 1996;15:331.
52. Corley FH. Commonly missed fractures in the hand and wrist. *J Musculoskel Med*. 1993;10:55–68.
53. Almquist EA. Kienbock's disease. *Clin Orthop*. 1986;202:68.

CHAPTER 10

Finger and Thumb Complaints

CONTEXT

Finger and thumb complaints reflect a wide spectrum of disorders ranging from local pathology to distal manifestations of systemic disease. Local pathology is usually due to trauma. Localization of pain or tenderness coupled with mechanism of injury substantially narrows down the possibilities. Radiographs are usually necessary to discover subtle bone damage not accessible through clinical examination. When a history of trauma is not evident, local finger/thumb pain is often associated with clues of systemwide involvement. Conditions such as arthritides, connective tissue disease, or vascular problems such as Raynaud's disease or reflex sympathetic dystrophy must be considered.

When a hand complaint is not local but is the extension of radiation from another site, peripheral nerve, nerve root, or spinal cord involvement must be differentiated. When numbness, tingling, or weakness is reported, peripheral nerve entrapment is likely, especially when the forearm or wrist is part of the pattern. When the neck and shoulder are part of the pathway of complaint, nerve root compression by a disc, nerve entrapment by osteophytes, or referral from the cervical facets should be considered. For a more detailed discussion of each of these possibilities see the specific section for each in this chapter.

The chiropractor's role with hand trauma is clearly to determine the degree of injury. The degree of injury often is not severe and all that is needed is appropriate splinting, taping, or a cast. Articular or displaced fractures; tendon detachments or severage; deep lacerations with risk of infection; and animal, spider, or human bites must be referred. Most nontraumatic complaints reflect chronic processes that may benefit from conservative management.

GENERAL STRATEGY

History

- Localize the complaint and determine whether it is one of pain, stiffness, numbness/tingling, weakness, popping/snapping, coldness, deformity, or a combination.
- If traumatic, determine whether the mechanism was compressive or rotational, or caused by excessive flexion, extension, abduction, or adduction.
- If traumatic, consider radiographs in most cases to determine whether there is any underlying fracture.
- If nontraumatic, determine whether there are associated complaints such as other joint complaints (arthritides), deformities (arthritides), or cervical spine or arm complaints (facet referral, nerve root, brachial plexus, or peripheral nerve).

Evaluation

- If traumatic, test for neurovascular status; examine for lacerations, swellings, or deformity; test ligamentous stability.
- If nontraumatic, examine for sites of local tenderness over joints and tendon insertions; test for accessory motion.

Management

- Displaced or articular fractures, severed or avulsed tendons, and infection should be referred for orthopaedic consultation and management.
- Many ligament injuries can be managed with taping or splints unless there is an associated articular fracture.

- Rheumatoid and connective tissue disorders may require comanagement.

RELEVANT CLINICAL ANATOMY

The fingers and thumb participate in not only simple survival functions such as gripping but complex actions that require amazing dexterity. The mechanical and neurologic integration necessary for this high functional demand is complex (Figure 10–1, A and B). An ingenious system of pulleys, redundant muscular and neural support, and varying joint design allow for an enormous degree of subtlety of motion. The general arrangement of the hand is similar to that of many joints, with a system of muscles that allow for flexion, extension, abduction, and adduction. Rotational movements are largely due to elbow/forearm and thumb movement.

Fingers

Flexion of the digits is accomplished mainly through extrinsic muscle control provided by the flexor digitorum superficialis (FDS) and flexor digitorum profundus (FDP) with assistance from the intrinsic lumbricals and interossei. The lumbricals, in fact, originate off the radial side of the FDP tendons. The FDS tendon splits at the proximal end of the first phalanx, allowing the FDP to pass through and insert onto the distal phalanx.[1] The FDS then reunites and splits again to insert on either side of the middle phalanx. The volar interossei originate off the radial side of the fourth and fifth metacarpals and the ulnar side of the second and first metacarpal, allowing adduction of the fingers (in relation to the middle finger). The dorsal interossei originate off the metacarpals and abduct the fingers. The second and third dorsal interossei abduct toward the thumb. This is important for pinch-grip stability.

Extension of the fingers is accomplished by the extensor digitorum (ED) muscle/tendons. The fifth finger is assisted by the digiti quinti and the index finger by the extensor indices. The primary insertion of the ED is onto the dorsum of the proximal phalanx. As the tendon continues distally it connects to lateral bands that are the continuation of the interossei and lumbrical muscles. The lateral bands continue distally to unite into a combined insertion into the distal phalanx. The ED tendon also inserts into the middle phalanx. Although there is an insertion into each distal phalanx, the primary functional insertion is at the proximal phalanx. When the ED tendon pulls, most of the action is at the proximal phalangeal insertion. When the proximal phalanx is extended, the interossei and lumbrical connections to the lateral bands cause these intrinsic muscles to be the primary extensors of the middle and distal phalanges. When the ED relaxes, these same muscles act as flexors. With the metacarpophalangeal (MCP) joint flexed to 90°, tension on the ED pulls the distal interphalangeal (DIP) and proximal interphalangeal (PIP) joints passively into extension without the aid of the interossei.[2]

The index and middle fingers are stable, whereas the fourth and fifth fingers are mobile (the fifth being the most mobile). This is in large part due to the unique articulation at each joint. In particular, the articulation between the fifth metacarpal and the hamate is similar to the saddle configuration at the thumb and, like the thumb, allows for greater mobility.[3] This is visible while observing the metacarpal heads during flexion and extension. The heads are in alignment with extension, allowing the palm to rest flat. With full flexion (clenched fist), the fourth and fifth heads flex beyond that of the second and third, creating a curved arch. Clinically, this is important with fracture management where more rotational or varus/valgus angularity is allowed with fourth and especially fifth metacarpal fractures. Additionally, the stability provided by the intrinsic ligaments and interossei muscles makes the metacarpals quite stable even with fracture or ligament injury.

Thumb

The thumb's mobility is due to its position and the articular configuration at the carpometacarpal and MCP joints. Nine muscles act on the thumb to allow not only flexion/extension and abduction/adduction, but opposition (abduction, rotation, and flexion). Although flexion and extension may occur at all the thumb joints, abduction and adduction occur mainly at the carpometacarpal joint (some at the MCP joint).

Flexion, extension, and abduction of the thumb are accomplished through a muscle couple made up of a long extrinsic muscle/tendon and a short intrinsic muscle. Flexion is due to the flexor policis longus (FPL) and the flexor policis brevis (FPB). Extension is accomplished with the ED and the extensor policis brevis (EPB) muscles. Abduction is governed by the abductor policis longus (APL) and abductor policis brevis (APB). The short muscles are part of the thenar group and are joined by the adductor policis and opponens policis muscles. Adduction is controlled by the first palmar interosseous muscle and adductor policis. The tendons of the EPB and the APL outline the anatomic snuffbox, a common location of tenderness with scaphoid fractures. These tendons may be involved in de Quervain's disease. Ligamentous support is provided by two collateral ligaments (similar to the other phalanges), one on each side with assistance by paired accessory ligaments. The collateral ligament on the inside web is the ulnar collateral ligament. This is often injured with a hyperextension or abduction injury referred to as gamekeeper's thumb. Support at the MCP joint is provided by the volar ligaments and plate.

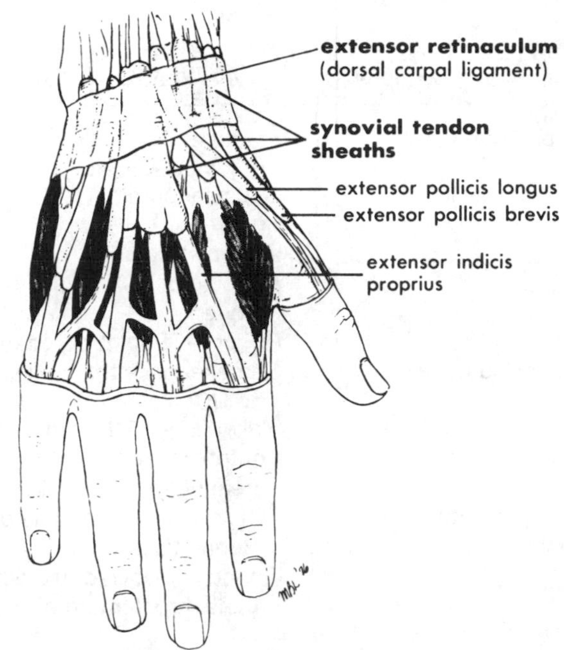

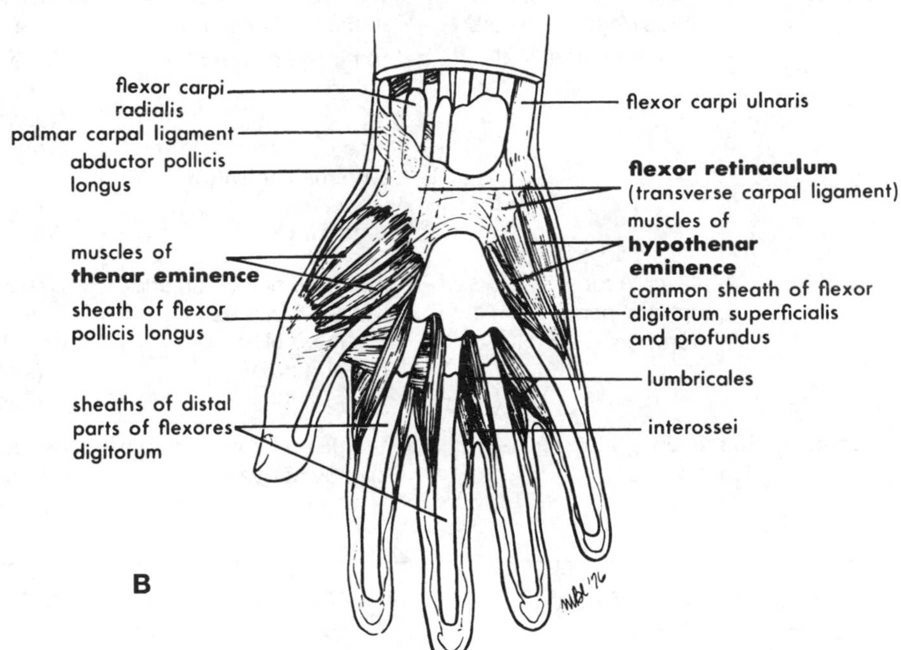

Figure 10–1 **A**, Posterior aspect of the synovial sheaths of the tendons of the right hand; **B**, anterior aspect. *Source:* Reprinted with permission from J.E. Crouch, *Functional Human Anatomy,* 4th ed., pp. 236 and 237, © 1985, Lea & Febiger.

EVALUATION

History

Careful questioning of the patient during the history taking can point to the diagnosis (Table 10–1).

Pain Localization (see Figure 9–3 A–C)

Finger.

- Metacarpophalangeal joint (MCP)
  1. traumatic—dislocation, collateral ligament sprain or rupture

Table 10–1 History Questions for Finger and Thumb Complaints

Primary Question	*What Are You Thinking?*	*Secondary Questions*	*What Are You Thinking?*
Was there an injury?	Fracture, dislocation, ligament sprain, tendon avulsion, capsular sprain	Hit on end of finger?	Fracture PIP joint dislocation
		Finger bent back?	Capsular sprain Sprain Volar plate tear Avulsion of FDP (jersey finger) PIP or MCP joint dislocation
		Thumb pulled back?	Gamekeeper's thumb (injury to UCL)
		Finger forced into flexed position?	Mallet finger (injury to DIP) Boutonnière deformity (tearing of central slip)
		Hit an object with a clenched fist?	If thumb is involved rule out Bennett's fracture If hand is involved rule out metacarpal fracture
Does your finger feel stiff?	Arthritis (OA or RA), capsular effusion or adhesion, subluxation, trigger finger	Does your finger get stuck in a flexed position?	Trigger finger likely (check for nodule)
		Can't close finger(s)?	Capsular effusion or adhesion Retinacular tightness
		Worse in morning; better with mild activity?	OA
		Associated swelling or deformity?	RA OA
Is there a sense of weakness?	C8-T1 nerve roots, peripheral nerve entrapment	Associated neck pain and/or radiation into hand?	Cervical disc, tumor, or spondylosis
		Associated elbow or forearm pain?	Peripheral nerve entrapment (distinguish by which muscles)
Do you routinely perform repetitive activity with your fingers?	Tendinitis, peripheral nerve entrapment	Is the pain at your thumb or slightly above?	de Quervain's disease Intersection syndrome

2. nontraumatic—capsular sprain, osteoarthritis (OA)
- Proximal interphalangeal joint (PIP)
  1. traumatic—dislocation (coach's finger), boutonnière deformity (hyperflexion injury)
  2. nontraumatic—rheumatoid arthritis (RA) or OA
- Distal interphalangeal joint (DIP)
  1. traumatic—mallet finger (hyperflexion), flexor digitorum avulsion (jersey finger)
  2. nontraumatic—psoriatic arthritis

Thumb.
- Traumatic—gamekeeper's thumb (ulnar collateral ligament [UCL] sprain or rupture), Bennett's fracture (first MCP base)
- Nontraumatic—OA, bowler's thumb (digital neuritis)

Traumatic Finger Pain

As distal joints, the fingers are vulnerable to all order of outside forces. Hand and finger injuries are particularly common in sports.[4] General patterns of injury occur with "hyper" movements:

- Hyperextension may simply strain the palmar surface of the fingers or hand or result in tendon avulsion of the flexor digitorum profundus, volar plate damage, or dislocation or fracture.[5]

- Hyperflexion may cause dislocation, central extensor tendon slip damage at the PIP joint, or extensor tendon avulsion at the DIP joint.
- Rotational or valgus/varus forces will often result in collateral ligament damage. With more force a dislocation or fracture is possible.
- Direct axial forces to the extended fingers may cause a synovitis or fracture. An axial force to the knuckles often results in a metacarpal fracture or simply a local contusion to the knuckle (boxer's knuckle). The examiner may need to be persistent in determining whether the patient, in a fit of anger, punched an inanimate (or animate) object.
- When the patient has a cut or laceration, a tendon or nerve may be severed. Wounds are open to infection, and questions about animal, insect, or object penetration, and recent tetanus shots should be asked.

Weakness

Weakness in the fingers may be a generalized or local problem. Clarify whether the patient feels pain with movement or gripping. Pain localization when associated with a weakness complaint may be helpful; however, a complaint of weakness with pain is itself nonspecific because of the reflex or voluntary inhibition that occurs with painful movement. The patient should be asked about weakness that is specific to a specific movement. It is important to remember that a perception of weakness may be due to stiffness or inflexibility at a joint or joints. Passive range of motion testing will often reveal this component.

Weakness in a single digit following trauma should suggest tendon avulsion, especially if associated with deformity. Weakness with specific finger/thumb gripping or pinching suggests a peripheral nerve entrapment or damage. Gross weakness with hand gripping is possible with any number of problems; however, the problem usually is neural. Ulnar or median nerve involvement will affect grip strength, as will nerve root compression. Radiation of a complaint from the forearm suggests peripheral nerve entrapment, whereas pain or paresthesia radiating from the neck suggests nerve root or a referral phenomenon. Weakness in grip may also be the result of instability at the wrist. Remember that grip strength is usually decreased with the use of thick gloves. Grip strength is also position dependent. Gripping is most efficient in neutral or slight wrist extension (less than 30°). Beyond these limits the mechanical advantage of the finger flexors is reduced.

Restriction in Movement

Movement restriction in the fingers should be divided into posttraumatic or insidious. Stiffness, especially with flexion, is not uncommon after an axial load injury to the finger with a resultant capsular sprain and reactive synovitis. Because of the inability to immobilize the fingers as easily as more proximal joints, the fingers are constantly stressed. As a result, capsulitis of the digits often takes 2 months or more to resolve.

An insidious onset suggests an arthritis. The two most common are OA and RA. Historically, there is often a distinction between the two. OA often causes the patient to complain of early-morning stiffness that improves after 20 to 30 minutes of activity. RA is often more restrictive and takes several hours to improve. Exacerbations with movement are more common with RA. A search for corroborative evidence includes the age of the patient, family history, and involvement of other joints. In an elderly patient with unilateral complaints of knee or hip pain, OA is more likely. In a middle-aged woman with a positive family history and bilateral, diffuse involvement of the PIP joints, RA is more likely.

Restriction to movement may be localized to the fourth and fifth fingers with an associated flexion contracture evident. This is likely to be Dupuytren's contracture.[6] Questioning regarding alcohol consumption or possible diabetes should be included. A unique restriction complaint is snapping of a finger or thumb upon extension. This is often due to a trigger finger or thumb. Initially, the patient may report the ability to overcome an extension restriction actively. As the condition progresses, she or he may have to extend the finger passively past the restriction, often with an audible snap.

Superficial Complaints

As the distal point of the upper extremity, the fingers and hands are often indicators of more proximal and often systemic conditions. Complaints range from numbness/tingling, coldness, skin and nail lesions, and burning sensations. If one or two fingers appear blanched and cause the patient pain when exposed to cold, Raynaud's disease or phenomenon is likely. Nail lesions are often indicators of various systemic processes. Longitudinal nail lines are seen with anemia, clubbing with chronic pulmonary disorders, and pitting with psoriasis. Many complaints of numbness or tingling are connected to a wrist, forearm, or neck complaint. See the related section in this text for a more thorough discussion. When there is localized numbness in the thumb, compression of the ulnar digital nerve of the thumb is often the cause; it is called bowler's thumb.

Examination

Traumatic Injury

When evaluation is immediately posttraumatic, a quick check of neurovascular status is warranted.[7]

Vascular.

- Allen's test for radial and ulnar arteries: The patient is instructed to open and close the hand several times. He or she is then instructed to keep the hand tightly closed in a fist. The examiner occludes both the radial and ulnar arteries at the wrist. The patient is then asked to open the hand. The examiner releases pressure on the artery and observes for filling; reddening of the distal hand within a few seconds. Repeat with the opposite artery. This test may also be used for the digital arteries at the fingers: The examiner gently squeezes the radial and ulnar sides of the volar tip with finger and thumb, sliding them proximally while maintaining the squeeze. The finger should become pale. Release pressure with the finger to determine whether the finger fills. Repeat with release of thumb pressure to check the patency of the other artery.

Neural.

- Two-point discrimination: This is the minimal distance at which a patient can discriminate between two points of stimulation. A paper clip bent to expose two points 4 mm apart may be used (testing is on the palmar surface). The two points must touch the skin simultaneously. Although the distance varies over the hand, an average of 4 to 5 mm is used for a quick check.
- Sensory testing (use a pin; check for pain perception)
  1. Ulnar nerve—volar tip of little finger.
  2. Radial nerve—dorsum of thumb web.
  3. Median nerve—volar tips of index and middle fingers.
- Motor (gross check)
  1. Ulnar nerve—cross middle finger over the back of the index finger.
  2. Radial nerve—extend thumb.
  3. Median nerve—point thumb toward ceiling (palm up on table).
- Muscle/tendon check (inability to perform may indicate a severed or avulsed tendon)
  1. Flexor digitorum profundus—with MCP and PIP joints held in extension (or held down with the patient's palm up) ask the patient to flex the DIP (often the result of a hyperextension injury).
  2. Flexor digitorum superficialis—with patient's palm up, the examiner holds down all untested fingers into extension and asks the patient to flex the unrestrained finger.
  3. Flexor policis longus—with the thumb held in extension at the MCP joint, ask the patient to flex the IP joints.
  4. Extensor digitorum—with the wrist in extension, ask the patient to extend at the MCP and IP joints.

Observation should focus on a search for deformity and swelling. This search is occurring as the above neurovascular check is being performed. Note that if there is an apparent dislocation, depending on the joint involved, an attempt at relocation should be made. See specific joints in the selected disorders section. Next, check for a rotational deformity of a finger, best seen with flexion of the fingers to the palm. Rotational or angular deformity is an indication of fracture. Tapping on an extended finger often will increase the pain if a fracture is present.[8] Further evaluation with radiographs is necessary. Tapping at the knuckle with the fingers flexed to the palm may reveal a metacarpal fracture. Swelling localized to a joint may indicate ligamentous rupture or capsular sprain with an associated synovitis. Stability testing of the PIP and MCP joints is performed in two positions: 30° and 70° of flexion. In each of these positions, a varus and valgus stress is applied to the joint.

Radiographic evaluation is necessary with most finger injuries. Standard anteroposterior (AP) and lateral views will reveal most fractures or dislocations. It is important to search for an associated dislocation when a fracture is evident. This is often best seen on a lateral view. For fractures of the metacarpal, it is useful to add a lateral view with the hand pronated about 20°. Otherwise, metacarpal fracture lines may be obscured.[9] For the thumb, AP and lateral views are required. Stress views (pulling the thumbs into abduction) are often necessary to determine the degree of injury with a gamekeeper's thumb. Greater than 30° difference between the two sides indicates rupture of the ulnar collateral ligament, as does an avulsion fracture of the proximal base.[10]

Nontraumatic

Observation of the fingers may reveal deformities or swellings. Deformities at the distal and proximal joints are most commonly associated with two arthritides, OA and RA. DIP joint involvement is referred to as Herberden's nodes; PIP involvement is referred to as Bouchard's nodes when associated with OA or RA.[11] Involvement with either arthritis is often bilateral and involves more than one digit. MCP joint involvement is rare with OA but may occur with RA and psoriatic and gouty arthritis. Psoriatic arthritis affects mainly the DIP joint and is usually associated with skin lesions on the extensor surfaces of the extremities and pitting and ridging of the nails. Swelling and tenderness of the entire involved finger (sausage finger) is found with psoriatic arthritis and Reiter's syndrome (check for associated sacroiliac pain). Clubbing of the fingers may occur with a variety of pulmonary diseases, including tuberculosis and bronchogenic carcinoma.

Severe RA will present with fusiform swelling of the PIP joints, ulnar deviation of the fingers at the MCP joints, interosseous muscle atrophy, extensor tenosynovitis, and subcutaneous nodules over the extensor surfaces of the forearm and wrist. Laboratory testing is most useful for RA, checking for rheumatoid factor (immunoglobulin [Ig] M and anti-IgG) and increases in the erythrocyte sedimentation rate. However, rheumatoid factor is found in only 70% to 80% of patients with RA.

Observation and palpation of the fingers/hand may reveal vascular compromise.

- Reflex sympathetic dystrophy—A combination of shiny, swollen skin is present (the whole arm is often involved in shoulder-arm-hand syndrome).
- Raynaud's phenomenon or disease—Often one or two fingers are "white" compared with other fingers; the condition is worse upon exposure to cold. Raynaud's disease is idiopathic; Raynaud's phenomenon is associated with an identifiable connective tissue disorder such as scleroderma or systemic lupus erythematosus.

When stiffening is the main complaint, it is important to distinguish between intrinsic muscle and capsular/collateral ligament tightness. This is accomplished by joint positioning that either tightens or relaxes these structures. For the PIP joint, the Bunnel-Littler test (Figure 10–2) is used.[12] With the MCP joint held in slight extension, the PIP joint is passively flexed toward the palm. Inability to flex fully is indicative of either joint capsule contracture or tight intrinsic muscles. If the PIP joint can be flexed after moving the MCP joint into slight flexion, the intrinsic muscles are tight. If the PIP joint cannot be flexed with MCP joint flexion, joint contracture is likely the cause. For the DIP joint, the retinacular test is used. Here the distinction is between the retinacular ligaments and the joint capsule. The retinacular test (Figure 10–3) is the distal extension of the Bunnel-Littler concept. While the PIP joint is held in neutral, the examiner attempts to flex the DIP joint passively. If it cannot be flexed, either retinacular or capsular tightness is the cause. If after flexion of the PIP joint, the DIP joint can be passively flexed, retinacular tightness is the cause. If the DIP joint still cannot be passively flexed, a joint capsule contracture is likely.

Radiographic evaluation of the hand is often a search for either fracture or typical clustered findings suggestive of each arthritis.[13]

- RA: Early signs are of soft tissue swelling; progression results in periarticular demineralization, loss of joint space, erosions of the joint margins (rat-bite lesions), and malalignment of the fingers (especially ulnar deviation at the MCP joints).
- OA: Joint space narrowing, sclerosis, subchondral cysts, and osteophytes are the hallmarks of OA. Bony enlarge-

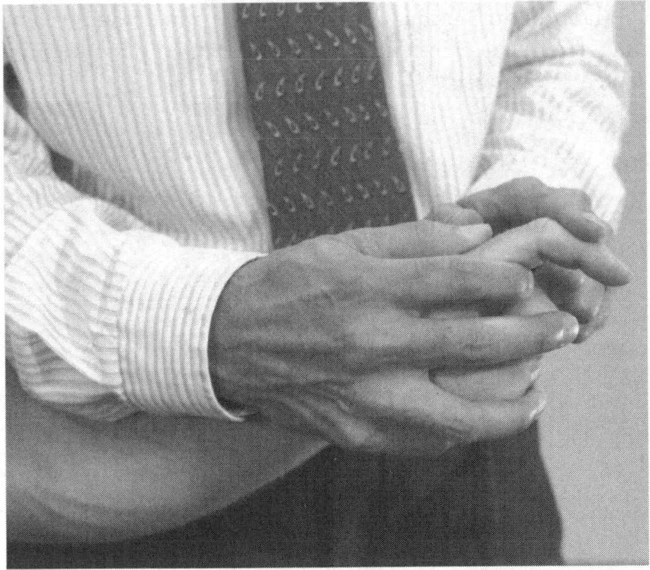

Figure 10–2 Bunnel-Littler test. With the MCP joint stabilized the examiner attempts to flex the PIP joint. If not flexible, the MCP joint is flexed and the test is repeated. Ability to flex indicates tight intrinsic muscles. Inability to flex in the second position indicates joint contracture or swelling.

Figure 10–3 The retinacular test. With the PIP joint held in neutral, the examiner attempts to passively flex the DIP joint. If unable to flex, the DIP is flexed slightly and the DIP is again flexed. If unable to flex in the second position, a joint contracture is present; able to flex indicates retinacular tightness.

ment of the DIP joints is typical (Heberden's nodes) and occasionally at the PIP joints (Bouchard's nodes). The CMC joint of the thumb is also often affected.
- Psoriatic: Bone resorption of the tufts of the distal phalanges may be seen; progression to the rest of the phalange may occur with the most severe form of psoriatic arthritis, arthritis mutilans.

There is some overlap between wrist, hand, and forearm complaints and testing. See the specific sections for each. Neurologic involvement from a proximal source is described in Chapters 2 and 9.

MANAGEMENT

Acute Traumatic Injury

Management of acute injury is as follows:

- Dislocations of the PIP and DIP joints should be relocated if possible; clinical testing for instability and radiographs for associated fracture should be performed.
- Fractures involving more than 20% to 30% of the articular surface should be referred for orthopaedic consultation.
- Nondisplaced fractures are casted (specific position dependent on joints involved).
- Displaced fractures are referred for surgical stabilization.
- Flexor tendon avulsion (mallet finger) or a suspected severed tendon requires orthopaedic referral.
- Ligament damages to the volar plate, central extensor slip, or collateral ligaments are splinted (see related conditions section for specifics).

Nontraumatic Conditions

- Rheumatoid or connective tissue disorders warrant comanagement with a rheumatologist.
- Osteoarthritic involvement requires a mild finger/hand-strengthening program; physical therapy heating modalities may be transiently beneficial; mobilization and manipulation of the involved joints when performed cautiously may also be of benefit.
- Peripheral nerve causes of numbness/tingling or pain should first be treated with a myofascial release approach for 2 to 3 weeks to determine treatment effectiveness, modification of any identifiable inciting activity, and, when necessary, splinting or soft casting for a short course of imposed rest.
- Soft tissue contracture of the intrinsic muscles may also benefit from postisometric relaxation and myofascial release.
- Joint contracture may benefit from mobilization and deep heat with passive stretching when subacute or chronic.

Algorithms

Algorithms for evaluation and management of thumb pain, traumatic hand pain, and nontraumatic hand pain are presented in Figures 10–4 to 10–6.

Figure 10–4

THUMB PAIN—ALGORITHM.

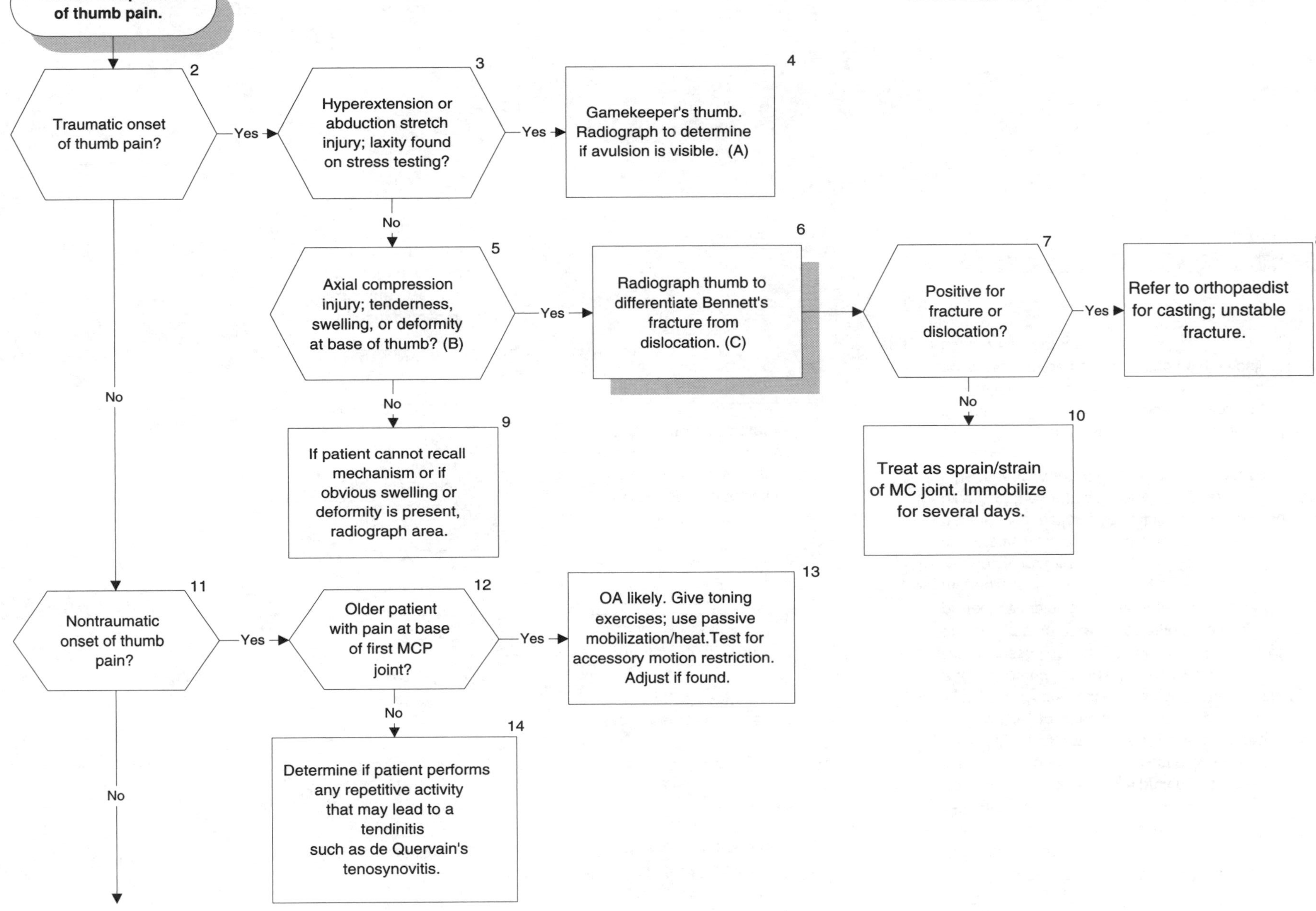

continues

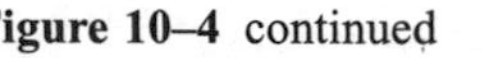

Figure 10–4 continued

15 Numbness/tingling complaint?
- Yes → 16
- No → 23

16 Localized to palmar surface of thumb?
- Yes → 17
- No → 18

17 Check for chronic history of compression such as with bowlers. Modify offending structure and/or pad thumb. (D)

18 Posterior thumb area only?
- Yes → 19
- No → 20

19 Radial nerve compression likely. Check for peripheral nerve entrapment in forearm.

20 The palmar surface of the thumb and first two fingers?
- Yes → 21
- No → 22

21 Median nerve involvement. Check for entrapment/compression at carpal tunnel, pronator teres, and other sites.

22 If more diffuse or associated with neck pain, determine areas of subluxation and adjust.

23 Reevaluate patient's complaint.

Annotations

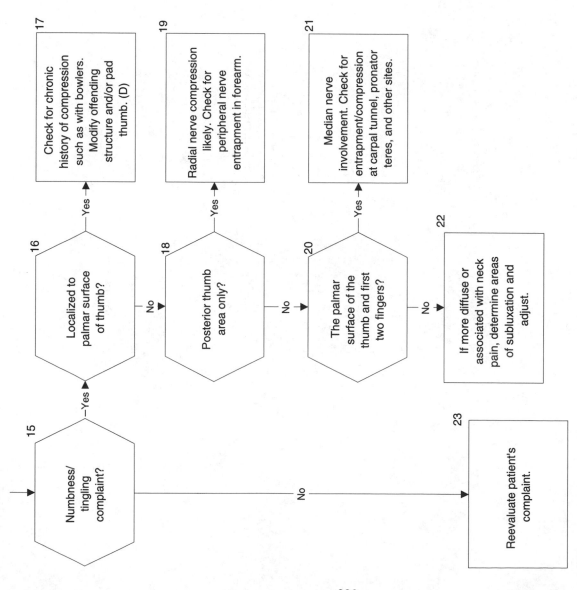

A. Gamekeeper's thumb is a tear of the ulnar collateral ligament due to hyperabduction. Stability should be tested at 0° and 30° and radiographs should be taken to determine any fracture at the base of the proximal phalanx. Stress radiographs may be used. More than 30% difference between normal and injured MCP angle indicates a complete rupture.

B. Thumb MCP dislocation may be reduced with adduction and flexion followed by traction. Unsuccessful attempt should be referred to ER. Immobilization for 3–4 weeks followed by protective taping for a few weeks is standard management.

C. Bennett's fracture is a fracture/dislocation of the first metacarpal base. It is a transarticular fracture. Reduction and stability are prevented by pull of the abductor pollicis longus. Orthopaedic referral for casting and possible surgery.

D. Compression or irritation of the digital nerve of the thumb is referred to as bowler's thumb. Protection with padding and, specifically with bowlers, enlargement of thumb hole on ball are usually sufficient.

Figure 10–5
TRAUMATIC HAND PAIN—ALGORITHM.

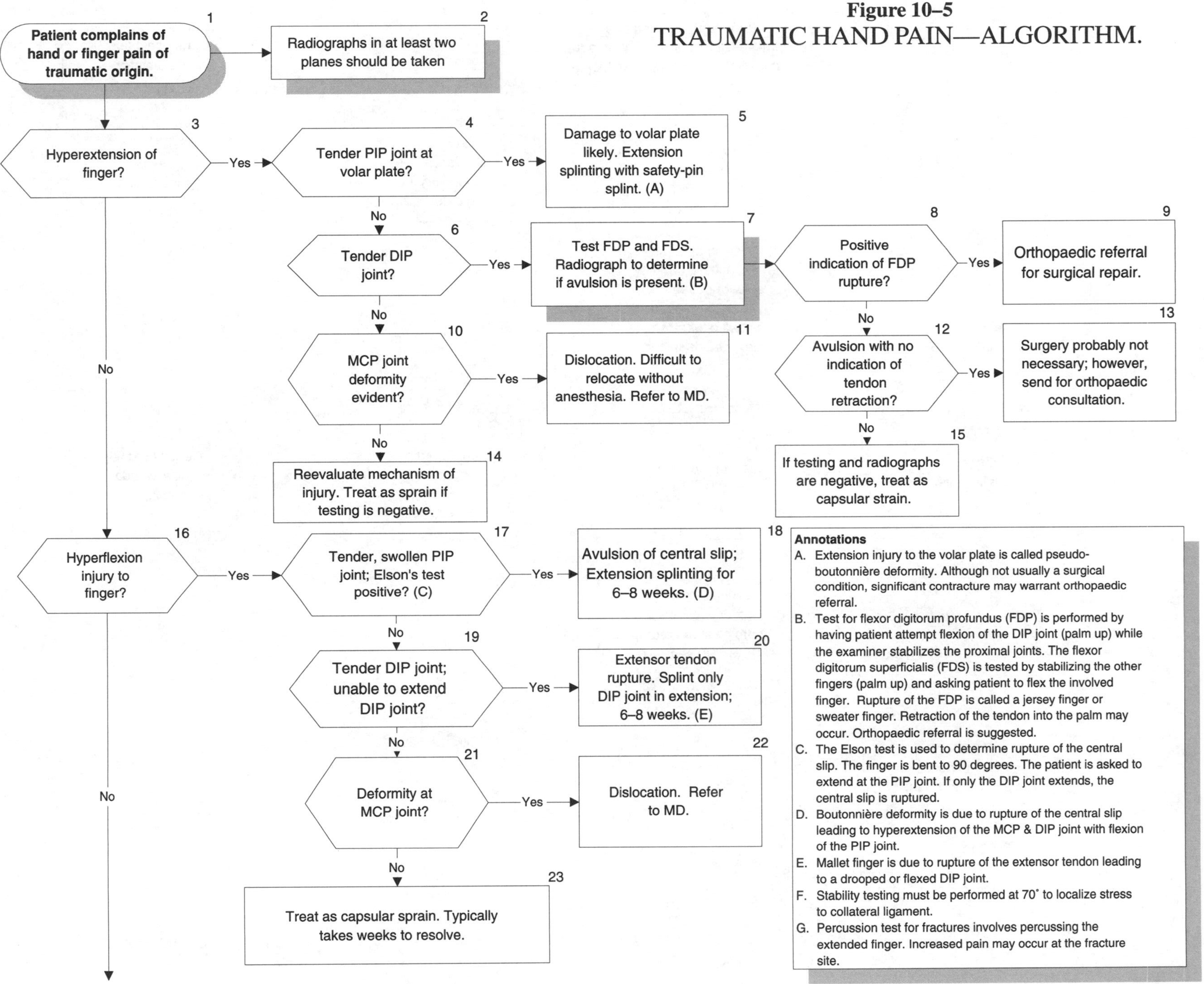

Annotations

A. Extension injury to the volar plate is called pseudo-boutonnière deformity. Although not usually a surgical condition, significant contracture may warrant orthopaedic referral.

B. Test for flexor digitorum profundus (FDP) is performed by having patient attempt flexion of the DIP joint (palm up) while the examiner stabilizes the proximal joints. The flexor digitorum superficialis (FDS) is tested by stabilizing the other fingers (palm up) and asking patient to flex the involved finger. Rupture of the FDP is called a jersey finger or sweater finger. Retraction of the tendon into the palm may occur. Orthopaedic referral is suggested.

C. The Elson test is used to determine rupture of the central slip. The finger is bent to 90 degrees. The patient is asked to extend at the PIP joint. If only the DIP joint extends, the central slip is ruptured.

D. Boutonnière deformity is due to rupture of the central slip leading to hyperextension of the MCP & DIP joint with flexion of the PIP joint.

E. Mallet finger is due to rupture of the extensor tendon leading to a drooped or flexed DIP joint.

F. Stability testing must be performed at 70° to localize stress to collateral ligament.

G. Percussion test for fractures involves percussing the extended finger. Increased pain may occur at the fracture site.

continues

Figure 10–5 continued

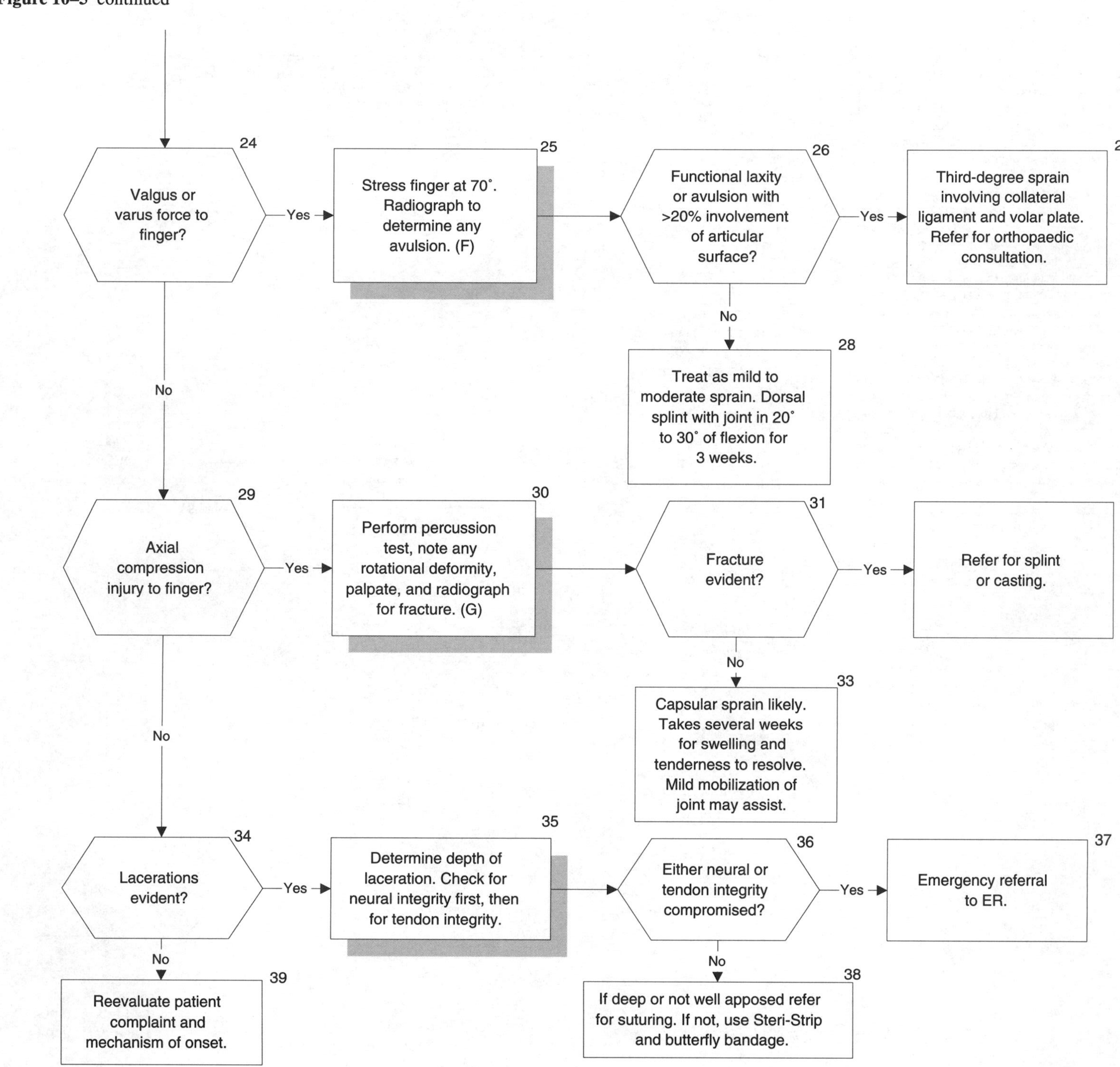

Figure 10–6

NONTRAUMATIC HAND PAIN—ALGORITHM.

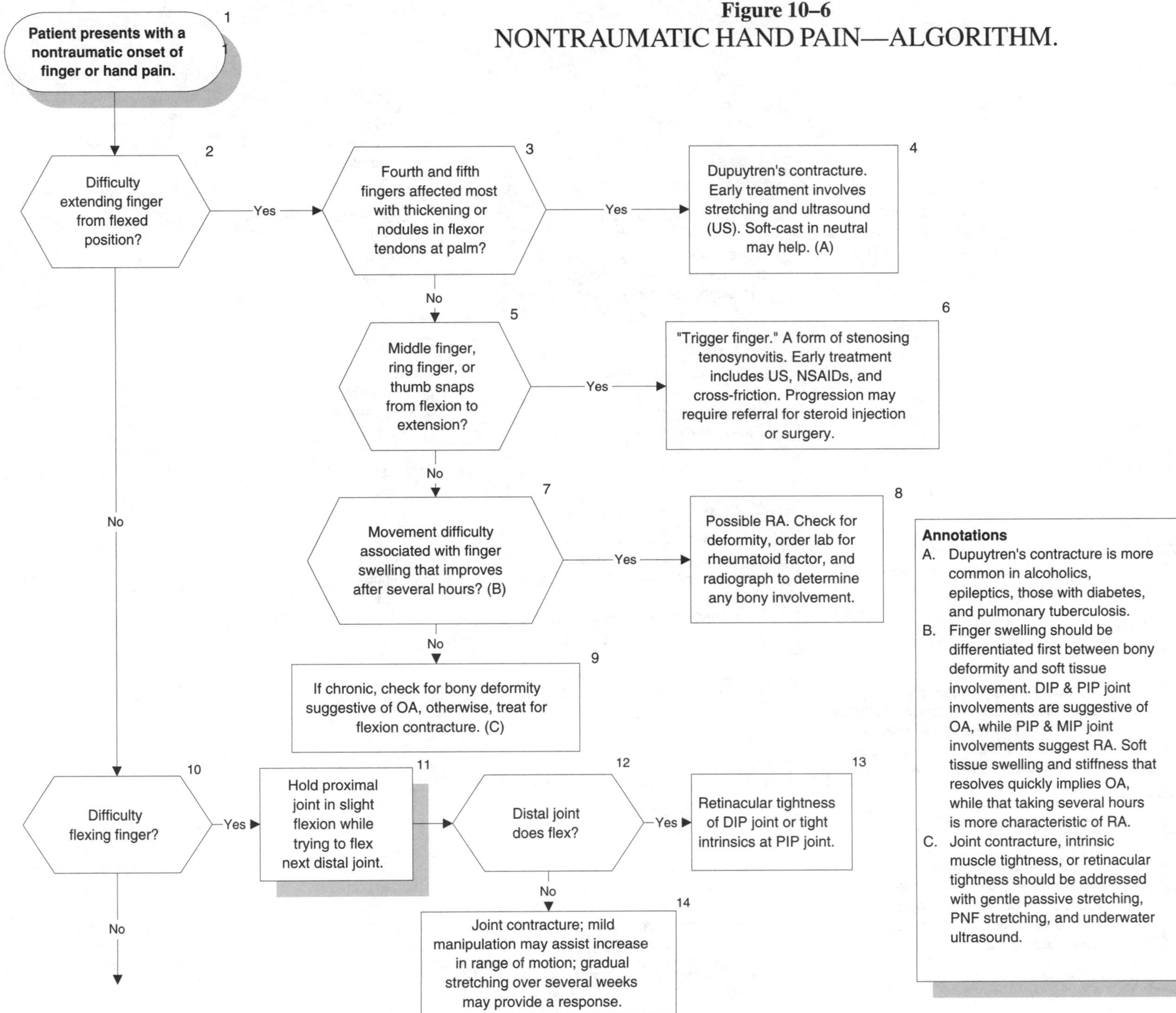

1
Patient presents with a nontraumatic onset of finger or hand pain.
2
Difficulty extending finger from flexed position?
Yes
No
3
Fourth and fifth fingers affected most with thickening or nodules in flexor tendons at palm?
Yes
4
Dupuytren's contracture. Early treatment involves stretching and ultrasound (US). Soft-cast in neutral may help. (A)
No
5
Middle finger, ring finger, or thumb snaps from flexion to extension?
Yes
6
"Trigger finger." A form of stenosing tenosynovitis. Early treatment includes US, NSAIDs, and cross-friction. Progression may require referral for steroid injection or surgery.
No
7
Movement difficulty associated with finger swelling that improves after several hours? (B)
Yes
8
Possible RA. Check for deformity, order lab for rheumatoid factor, and radiograph to determine any bony involvement.
No
9
If chronic, check for bony deformity suggestive of OA, otherwise, treat for flexion contracture. (C)
10
Difficulty flexing finger?
Yes
11
Hold proximal joint in slight flexion while trying to flex next distal joint.
12
Distal joint does flex?
Yes
13
Retinacular tightness of DIP joint or tight intrinsics at PIP joint.
No
14
Joint contracture; mild manipulation may assist increase in range of motion; gradual stretching over several weeks may provide a response.
No
Annotations
A. Dupuytren's contracture is more common in alcoholics, epileptics, those with diabetes, and pulmonary tuberculosis.
B. Finger swelling should be differentiated first between bony deformity and soft tissue involvement. DIP & PIP joint involvements are suggestive of OA, while PIP & MIP joint involvements suggest RA. Soft tissue swelling and stiffness that resolves quickly implies OA, while that taking several hours is more characteristic of RA.
C. Joint contracture, intrinsic muscle tightness, or retinacular tightness should be addressed with gentle passive stretching, PNF stretching, and underwater ultrasound.

continues

Figure 10–6 continued

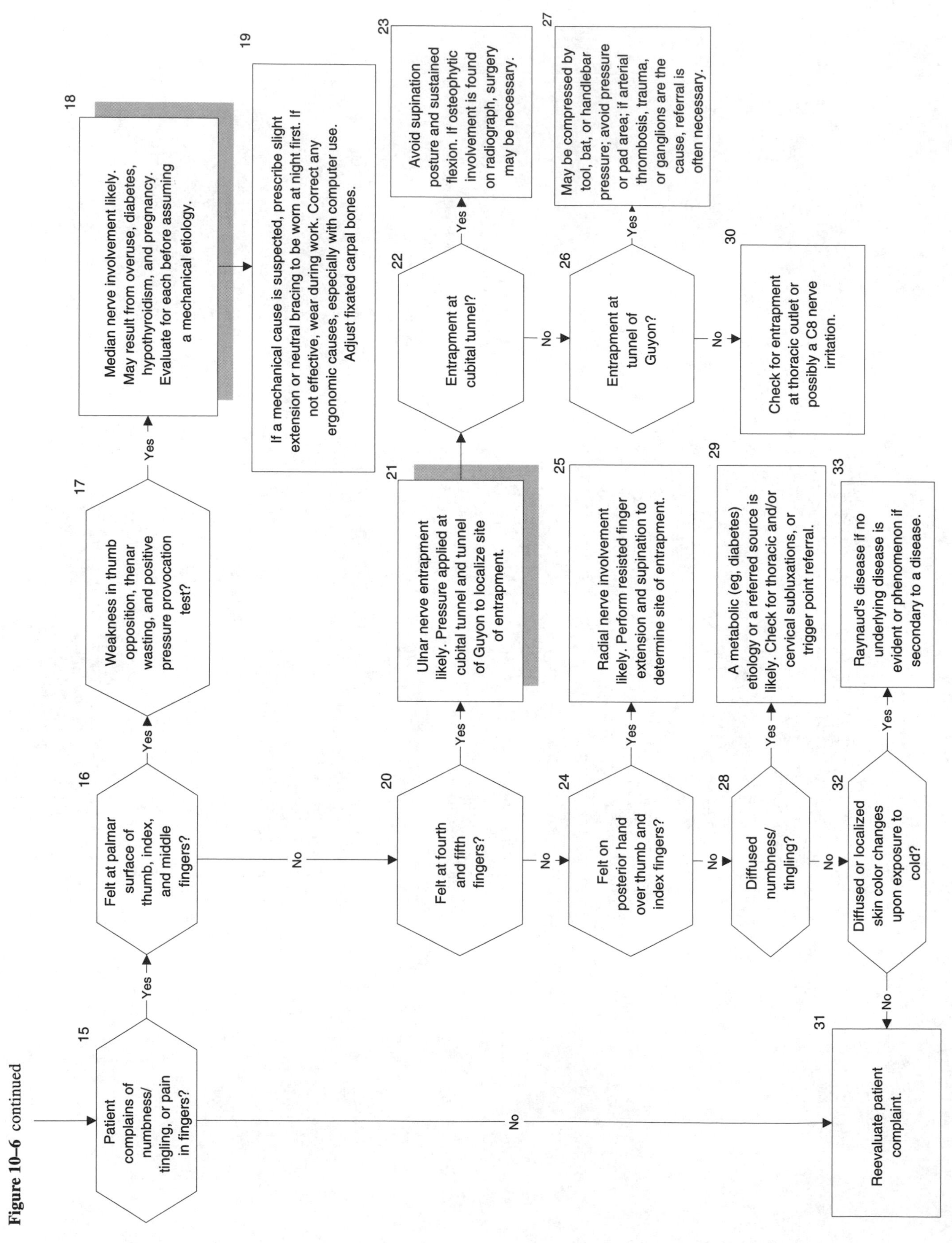

SELECTED DISORDERS OF THE FINGER, THUMB, AND HAND

A summary of the disorders discussed below is presented in Table 10–2.

FINGER

DISTAL INTERPHALANGEAL JOINT

Mallet Finger: Extensor Tendon Avulsion

Classic Presentation

A patient complains of distal finger pain after being hit on the end of the finger with a ball. The distal finger is dropped into a flexed position.

Cause

A compressive force on the tip of an extended finger, forcing it into flexion, causes avulsion of the extensor digitorum tendon. Commonly, this is due to a ball hitting the finger; often called "baseball" finger.[14] Because of the drooping deformity, another pseudonym is drop finger.

Evaluation

Active extension of the DIP joint is impossible; however, passive extension is usually accessible with some associated tenderness over the dorsum of the joint. Radiographic evaluation must include two planes of view to visualize clearly any degree of avulsion or epiphyseal fracture in immature athletes. The lateral view may also demonstrate subluxation (medial) at the joint. Two points of caution are that the DIP joint may also be injured (central slip damage) and should always be included in the examination. Second, if a large piece of bone is avulsed, surgery may be necessary.

Management

Treatment involves splinting of the DIP joint in extension (not hyperextension) for up to 6 weeks.[15] Gradual active and passive range of motion exercises may then begin. This is followed by another 6 weeks of night and, if applicable, athletic splinting.[16] The PIP joint must not be included in the splinting, to prevent contracture. It is imperative that the patient always keep the DIP joint in extension. He or she must remember this when changing finger splints.

Football or Jersey Finger: FDP Rupture

Classic Presentation

A patient complains of distal finger pain after getting his or her finger forcefully extended while grabbing a moving object.

Cause

Hyperextension of the DIP joint may result in rupture of the FDP tendon. Because of a common mechanism, this is often referred to as football or jersey finger. Apparently, the finger (often the ring finger) is caught in an opponent's jersey.[17] While the athlete is grabbing the jersey, the opponent pulls away, exerting an extension force on the flexing finger. The degree of injury is based, in part, on how far the tendon has migrated. This may be as far as the palmar crease.

Table 10–2 Summary of Hand Conditions

Name of Condition	*Injury*	*Treatment*
Boutonnière deformity	Flexion injury of PIP, tearing central slip; deformity is hyperextension of MCP and DIP with flexion of PIP.	PIP is splinted in extension for several weeks.
Pseudoboutonnière deformity	Extension injury of DIP with damage to volar plate.	Extension splinting; safety-pin splint.
Jersey finger	Avulsion of flexor digitorum profundus; hyperextension injury.	Usually surgery.
Mallet finger (baseball finger)	Hyperflexion injury to DIP.	Extension splinting of DIP for 6–8 weeks.
Collateral ligament injury	Usually ulnar stress to a flexed MCP.	Remember to stress test at 70° and radiograph for possible fracture fragment. Splint PIP at 30° of flexion.
PIP joint dislocation (coach's finger)	Axial or extension force to middle phalanx.	Immobilize at 20°–30° of flexion for several weeks.
MCP dislocation	Dorsiflexion injury, usually tearing the volar plate.	Difficult to reduce; often requires anesthesia. Immobilize for 3–4 weeks.
Gamekeeper's thumb	MCP joint sprain of ulnar collateral ligament, usually due to hyperabduction or extension.	Tape with a cinch between thumb and first finger for several weeks.
Bennett's fracture	Fracture/dislocation of first metacarpal base.	Difficult to reduce due to pull of abductor policis longus. Usually need open reduction with fixation of fracture fragment.
Boxer's fracture	Hitting an object with an unprotected fist, usually fracture to the fifth metacarpal. Look for rotation or angular deformity. Percuss distal end of finger.	Gutter splint or hand cast for 6 weeks.

Evaluation

Acute evaluation requires testing of FDP function. This is accomplished by asking the patient to flex the DIP joint fully while the PIP joint is held in extension by the doctor. Inability to flex is diagnostic for rupture.

Management

Unlike many finger injuries, this injury requires immediate referral for surgical repair. Surgery has a better prognosis within the first 3 to 4 days postinjury.

Dislocation

Classic Presentation

A patient reports having the distal finger pulled out of place by a hyperextension injury. Pain and some deformity may be evident at the DIP joint. If the patient is an athlete, he or she may have had the dislocation reduced prior to presentation.

Cause

Disruption of the volar plate allows dorsal dislocation of the distal phalanx. Associated tendon or collateral ligament damage is possible.

Evaluation

Tenderness and dorsal deformity of the distal phalanx are seen in the acute presentation. Radiographs should always be taken to rule out any associated fractures. After reduction, it is imperative to check for damage to the collateral ligaments, and for flexor/extensor tendon function.

Management

Reduction is accomplished with long-axis traction while gently increasing the deformity. After reduction, immobilization in a dorsal or volar splint (not including the PIP joint) for 2 to 3 weeks is sufficient. There is a debate as to whether to splint in 30° of flexion or full extension. Following splinting, flexion exercises are begun while maintaining protective splinting during any sporting activities.[18]

PROXIMAL INTERPHALANGEAL JOINT

Central Slip Tear (Boutonnière Deformity)

Classic Presentation

The patient presents with pain at the PIP joint and an associated deformity after having an injury that involved forced flexion of the finger.

Cause

A hyperflexion injury of the PIP joint may result in tearing of the central slip of the extensor digitorum tendon. The lateral bands drop anteriorly and maintain the PIP in flexion while the DIP joint is extended.

Evaluation

There is pain and point tenderness at the PIP with associated swelling. Functionally, the PIP joint cannot be actively extended. Eventually, a boutonnière deformity occurs as hyperextension of the DIP and flexion of the PIP. At this point the DIP cannot be actively extended. Due to volar slippage of the lateral bands, active and passive flexion is not possible at the distal joint.[19]

Management

It is imperative that the PIP joint be immobilized with a finger splint in full extension for approximately 6 weeks. If not splinted properly, there will be no apposition of the torn ends of the central slip and deformity will result. This is often the case when loss of active extension is attributed to pain and the athlete is splinted in flexion for a collateral ligament sprain by an inexperienced coach/trainer/doctor. Due to the severity of the injury, an additional 4 to 6 weeks of splinting is necessary at night and during athletic activity (if applicable). When 45° of flexion and full extension are attained, the splinting may be discontinued.

Volar Plate Injury

Classic Presentation

The patient (often an athlete) complains of finger pain after his or her finger was pulled back or overextended by a ball or from a fall on an outstretched finger.

Cause

The volar plate on the anterior surface of the PIP is injured by a hyperextension injury to the finger.[20]

Evaluation

Pain and tenderness are found at the PIP joint. If chronic, a pseudoboutonnière deformity may result due to scar tissue formation and subsequent contracture with the PIP joint held in flexion. The distinction between a boutonnière and a pseudoboutonnière deformity is that normal mobility is present at the DIP with pseudoboutonnière deformity.[21]

Management

The PIP joint is splinted in 30° of flexion for 4 to 5 weeks. If unsuccessful, surgical referral should be made.

Dislocation

Classic Presentation

The patient complains of middle finger pain following a hyperextension injury (often in ball-handling sports). It is not unusual for a coach or trainer to reduce the joint with an assumption that the individual simply "jammed" the finger.

Cause

Hyperextension with some axial loading while the PIP joint is in extension causes volar plate rupture and often an avulsion fracture of the base of the middle phalanx.

Evaluation

Tenderness and deformity are found at the PIP joint if acute. After reduction, the MCP joint should be tested for active and passive range of motion. Static stability testing for collateral ligament and volar plate integrity must also be included. Radiographs are requisite to rule out associated fractures (especially when associated with an axial load or rotation injury).

Management

Reduction is accomplished by long-axis traction with gentle hyperextension of the PIP joint. If unsuccessful, refer for reduction with a local digital nerve block. Following reduction, ice and splint. A volar splint is applied with the finger held in 20° to 30° of flexion for 2 to 3 weeks. This is followed by buddy-taping for an additional 2 weeks, especially if participating in sports. Gentle active range of motion should be prescribed after the initial 3 weeks of splinting.

Collateral Ligament Sprain

Classic Presentation

A patient presents with a sports-related injury whereby the finger was pulled sideways (usually ulnar). The patient often reports that the finger "went out," but it either reduced spontaneously or was reduced by the patient.

Cause

A varus or valgus force stretches and tears the collateral ligament support at the PIP. The index finger is most often involved. The force is often sufficient to subluxate the joint medically, however, it often reduces spontaneously or is reduced by the patient, a coach, or trainer.[22] Associated partial or complete rupture of the volar plate is possible depending on the magnitude of force.

Evaluation

Tenderness is found over the PIP collateral ligament and volar plate. Swelling is often rapid, leaving little time to test for stability. Stability testing should include varus and valgus attempts at two positions of flexion, 30° and 70°. Like all ligamentous injuries, there are varying degrees of damage. Radiographic demonstration of an avulsion fracture involving the volar plate is indicative of a rupture.

Management

With first- and second-degree sprains, the PIP is immobilized with a dorsal splint for 2 to 4 weeks in a 20° to 30° flexed position and may be buddy-taped to an adjacent finger for more stability. If a volar plate avulsion involves more than 20% of the articular surface, surgery may be indicated.[23]

METACARPAL PHALANGEAL JOINT

Collateral Ligament Sprain

Classic Presentation

The patient presents with a complaint of pain at the MCP joint after a fall on the hand that stretched the associated finger to the side. The patient initially may not have sought help. Persistent pain and swelling usually prompts the patient to seek advice.

Cause

Tearing of the radial collateral ligament of the ulnar three digits is most common. When the ligament is most taut the finger is in flexion. The finger is deviated away from the side of injury.

Evaluation

The MCP joint is most lax in full extension. Tautness increases with flexion; therefore, stress testing of the collateral ligaments with a varus and a valgus force is best accomplished at 70° of flexion. Radiographs should be taken to determine any associated fractures at the base of the proximal phalanx.

Management

Because of the support provided by the intrinsic muscles of the hand, lateral instability is not a strong concern. Immobilization in flexion for 3 weeks is followed by buddy-taping to the adjacent fingers for an additional 3 weeks. It is important not to splint in extension, which would allow shortening of the collaterals and a residual functional deficit in active and passive flexion.

Dislocation

Classic Presentation

The patient presents with pain and deformity at the MCP joint and proximal phalanx (dorsally positioned) following a hyperextension accident, often a fall on an outstretched hand.

Cause

Dislocation usually involves volar displacement of the metacarpal head through a rent in the volar plate. The metacarpal head is caught between the lumbricals, long flexors, and other soft tissue structures. Reduction is usually impossible because of this soft tissue blockage.[24] The little finger and index finger are most often involved.

Evaluation

Because of the volar displacement of the metacarpal head, the proximal phalanx is dislocated dorsally. This deformity, coupled with a prominence at the MCP joint on the palmar surface of the hand, is indicative of dislocation. Radiographs may demonstrate widening of the joint space (volar plate caught in the joint) or articular fracture at the MCP.

Management

MCP subluxations may be converted to a dislocation by an attempt at reduction. This occurs when using the standard procedure for dislocation of a phalanx; distraction with increasing the deformity into hyperextension. MCP dislocations should be referred for reductions.

Metacarpal Fractures

Classic Presentation

The patient presents with pain and often swelling over a metacarpal joint following either a direct blow or an axial compression force such as punching a wall with an unprotected hand. (*Author's note*: Patients often are embarrassed by the mechanism and often will give a fictitious history. The fracture is sometimes the result of taking out anger on an inanimate object.)

Cause

Fractures may be transverse, spiral, or oblique and may involve the base, neck, or shaft. Direct blows or axial compression forces are most common. Fracture of the neck of the fifth metacarpal is called a boxer's fracture.[25]

Evaluation

Observation should include a search for rotational deformity evident at the MCP joint and with finger flexion. This is determined by noting nail alignment. Additionally, percussion of the extended finger or of the metacarpal with the fingers flexed often will increase pain. Radiographs usually indicate the type and extent of injury.

Management

Depending on the scope of practice in a given state, management with casting or stock appliances may be acceptable if there is no fracture displacement. If not within the scope of practice and experience of a chiropractor or if there is displacement, referral for reduction and possible wire or screw fixation should be made. In general, third and fourth metacarpal fractures are inherently more stable than first and fifth. A 40° volar angulation is often considered an acceptable "functional" deformity.

Dupuytren's Contracture

Classic Presentation

The patient complains of stiffening in his or her hand so that the little and ring fingers are progressively kept in a flexed position. The patient may be a musician, often a guitarist.

Cause

The cause is unknown. However, nodular thickening occurs in the flexor tendon, usually the fourth or fifth fingers. Eventually, the fingers become flexed at the MCP and PIP joints with the DIP joint held in extension. One predisposition that has been suggested is alcoholism.[26]

Evaluation

Inspection and palpation reveal a flexion deformity with nodularity and flexor tendon/fascial thickening on the palmar aspect of the hand. Early in the course, passive stretch into extension is possible.

Management

Early management includes avoidance or modification of any possible inciting activity. Constant stretching may be of benefit. One easy stretch is to sit on the hands. If not effective, immobilization at night with a soft cast to hold the fingers in neutral has been reported to be helpful. Failure of conservative care may require surgery if the contracture is significantly affecting activities of daily living or occupation. The surgery is technically difficult, however, and should be performed by a specialist.

Trigger Finger or Thumb

Classic Presentation

The patient presents with a complaint of his or her finger's getting "stuck" when trying to extend from a flexed position. She or he often reports having to extend the involved finger or thumb passively. The patient may have a history of chronic occupational overuse, especially grasping maneuvers.[27]

Cause

The flexor tendon of the fingers or thumb pass through a soft-tissue pulley system at the base of the proximal phalanx of the thumb or finger. Through inflammation, trauma, or congenital variation, the tendon sheath enlarges proximal to the pulley system and is caught as the finger or thumb moves into extension.[28] This is a form of stenosing tenosynovitis.

Evaluation

A discrete nodule is palpated at the base of the proximal phalanx of the involved finger or thumb. The nodule may be tender to pressure or gripping. Active extension is blocked and when possible causes a snapping action. If active extension is not possible, passive movement can accomplish extension accompanied with a snap as the nodule clears under the pulley.

Management

Conservative approaches include underwater ultrasound with stretching, cross-friction massage, and avoidance of aggravating activities. Failure of conservative care (trial of several months) should result in a referral for cortisone injection. The cure rate with one to two injections is 91% according to one study.[29] Failure with cortisone injection requires a referral for surgical release under local anesthesia.

THUMB

Gamekeeper's Thumb

Classic Presentation

The patient presents with pain at the base of the thumb and reports having fallen on the thumb, bending it back.

Cause

Abduction or hyperextension causes tearing of the ulnar collateral ligament at the MCP joint of the thumb (medial side of the thumb). Common scenarios include a fall on the hand or a ski pole injury whereby the strap pulls the thumb back. Athletes who are hit on the thumb by a ball (such as in volleyball, basketball, or football) may have the thumb hyperextended.

Evaluation

Tenderness and swelling are often found at the inside web space of the thumb. Stressing the thumb into extension or abduction is painful. The pain may be too great to allow stability testing. If stability testing is possible, pull the thumb into abduction, with the thumb in extension and slight flexion. Then test extension again with the thumb in extension and flexion.[30] If a complete tear is present, pinch strength between the thumb and index finger is lost. Radiographs should be taken with stress applied. If stress views demonstrate more than 35° abduction (subtracting starting position of abduction from stress position of abduction), a rupture is likely.[31] With physical examination and radiographs, always compare with the uninjured side.

Management

First-degree and mild second-degree tears are managed with immobilization and stabilization with thumb taping, including a cinching between the thumb and index finger for a few days to a week.[32] Bad second-degree tears are immobilized with a thumb spica for 2 to 3 weeks. Complete tears are referred as soon as possible for surgery.

Bowler's Thumb

Classic Presentation

A patient complains of pain, numbness, or tingling on the palmar surface of the thumb. He or she is often a bowler.

Cause

Constant irritation of the ulnar digital nerve of the thumb leads to perineural fibrosis. The irritation is from the edge of the thumb hole in the bowling ball of bowlers, or any utensil or tool that chronically compresses the nerve. Other mechanisms include overstretch of the thumb into extension acutely or chronically.[33]

Evaluation

Tapping of the nerve causes pain and sensory symptoms in the distal thumb. Tenderness of the proximal joint is often found. Passive extension may increase symptoms.

Management

Padding of the volar thumb area will decrease any compressive force. Enlargement of the thumb hole on a bowling ball may help. Taping or bracing the thumb to prevent extension of the thumb may help if the underlying mechanism is stretch. Modification of any inciting activity is the main goal.

Dislocation

Classic Presentation

The patient presents with pain and deformity at the base of the thumb following a hyperextension injury.

Cause

Hyperextension tears the volar plate, allowing proximal phalanx dislocation dorsally.

Evaluation

Tenderness and deformity are found at the base of the thumb with posteriority of the proximal phalanx. Radiographs are necessary to determine any associated fracture.

Management

Reduction may be possible, avoiding straight traction, which may cause the volar plate to be caught in the joint. Push the dorsal aspect of the proximal phalanx in a volar direction while pushing the metacarpal dorsally to acquire reduction. If unsuccessful, refer for reduction under local block or open reduction. Postreduction, the joint is immobilized in a gutter splint or thumb spica for 2 to 3 weeks. Cautious range of motion exercises are then begun and progressively increased to resisted exercise for 2 to 4 weeks. Return to play may require a fiberglass cast for 2 weeks if allowed by the specific sport rules.

Bennett's Fracture

Classic Presentation

A patient presents in acute, severe pain following a fall or blow that caused axial compression to the thumb. There is deformity and rapid swelling.

Cause

Axial compression causes a transarticular fracture at the first metacarpal base. A triangular fragment of bone is held in place by the volar ligament while the shaft dislocates over it. The dislocated section is held out of place by the action of the abductor pollicis longus.

Evaluation

Deformity and swelling are usually severe, warranting immediate radiographic examination.

Management

Referral is required for open reduction and pinning.

ARTHRITIDES

Rheumatoid Arthritis

Classic Presentation

The patient is often a woman (aged 20 to 40 years) who complains of finger or wrist pain. She says that the joints are swollen and that in the morning it takes over an hour for her to be able to move her fingers comfortably. There is often an associated complaint of fatigue and possible weight loss.

Cause

RA is an autoimmune disorder causing an inflammatory arthritis characterized by bilateral distribution often beginning in the hand (PIP and MCP joints). At the joint a reactive pannus forms, causing swelling and eventual erosion. Genetic predisposition is based on the patient's possessing the class 2 human leukocyte antigen (HLA).

Evaluation

When the disease is active, the joints are often warm, swollen, and tender. Finding symmetric involvement adds weight to the suspicion of RA. Other joints commonly involved include the wrists, knees, ankles, and toes. Later changes include flexor contractures and ulnar deviation of the fingers. Laboratory findings include a positive rheumatoid factor (IgM antibody found in 75% of patients), elevated erythrocyte sedimentation rate (ESR), C-reactive protein, and an associated anemia (often hypochromic and normocytic). Radiographic findings usually confirm the diagnosis; however, these are not evident in the early stages of the disease. The early changes include soft tissue swelling and juxtaarticular demineralization. Eventually, uniform loss of joint space and joint erosions become apparent. Particular concern for the chiropractor is involvement of the transverse ligament at the dens of C2. This may lead to instability and would be a contraindication to upper cervical adjusting. An evaluation of the atlantodental interspace is necessary to determine stability of the C2-C1 articulation visible on a lateral view.

Management

It is important to remember two factors regarding the natural course of RA in patients: (1) those with active disease have periods of exacerbation and remission that are usually unpredictable, and (2) 50% to 75% of patients presenting with RA will experience a remission within 2 years.[34] Various medical approaches are used during acute RA episodes, including aspirin and other nonsteroidal antiinflammatory drugs (NSAIDs), methotrexate, antimalarial drugs, and—in difficult cases—gold salts (chrysotherapy). A short course of corticosteroid treatment often will dramatically improve the symptoms; however, it will not alter the course of the RA. Conservative approaches involve passive mobilization of the joints through a pain-free range of motion. Avoidance of thrusting into inflamed joints is crucial in preventing aggravation of RA.

Psoriatic Arthritis

Classic Presentation

The patient complains of unilateral finger pain of nontraumatic origin. The patient may also complain of sacroiliac pain. The patient will have either a past diagnosis of psoriasis or a secondary complaint of skin lesions on the extensor surfaces of the arms and/or legs.

Cause

Psoriatic arthritis is a seronegative arthritis, meaning it is negative for rheumatoid factor (as are Reiter's syndrome and ankylosing spondylitis). There is a genetic predisposition associated with various HLA subtypes. Only 20% of patients with psoriasis have arthritis associated with their condition.[35] The arthritis can be mild or fulminant (arthritis mutilans).

Evaluation

A search for skin lesions should be made in patients with a new, nontraumatic arthritis. Eighty percent of psoriatic arthritis patients have skin lesions prior to the onset of arthritis. The skin lesions may be quite obvious as silvery scales on the extensor surfaces of the arms and legs or subtle patches in the gluteal cleft, scalp, or umbilicus. In general, the more pronounced or involved the skin lesions the worse the arthritis (when associated with arthritis). Involvement of the fingers or toes may create a "sausage" appearance. Laboratory evaluation is negative for rheumatoid factor (seronegative). ESR and uric acid levels may be elevated during the active phase. HLA B-27 is found in almost half of patients; however, it is nonspecific, given that ankylosing spondylitis may coexist with psoriatic arthritis. HLA B-17, Bw38, and Bw39 are also found. Radiographically, marginal erosions, especially of the DIP and PIP joints, is common with tuft erosion causing a sharpened pencil appearance. Fluffy periosteal bone may be visible along the shafts of the metacarpals and phalanges. The sacroiliac involvement may be evident in 15% to 20% of patients. Atypical syndesmophytes appearing on the anterior vertebral body may be evident also.

Management

Medical treatment is similar to that for RA except that antimalarial agents may exacerbate psoriatic arthritis. In general, when skin lesions improve so does the arthritis. There are no studies discussing the chiropractic management of this arthritis.

REFERENCES

1. Lampe EW. Surgical anatomy of the hand. *Clin Symp.* 1969;21:32–33.
2. Kapandji JA. *The Physiology of the Joints.* New York: Churchill Livingstone; 1970:1.
3. Posner MA, Kaplan EB. Osseous and ligamentous structures. In: Spinner M, ed. *Kaplan's Functional and Surgical Anatomy of the Hand.* Philadelphia: JB Lippincott; 1984:23–51.
4. Posner MA. Hand injuries. In: Nicholas JA, Hershman EB, Posner MA, eds. *The Upper Extremity in Sports Medicine.* St. Louis, MO: Mosby; 1990:495–594.
5. Eaton RG. Acute and chronic ligamentous injuries of the fingers and thumb. In: Tubiana R, ed. *The Hand.* Philadelphia: WB Saunders; 1985;2:877.
6. Gonzalez SM, Gonzalez RI. Dupuytren's disease. *West J Med.* 1990;152:430.
7. Gerstner DL, Omer GE. Hand injuries: evaluation and initial management. *J Muscuoloskeletal Med.* 1988;10:19–29.
8. Ruby LK. Common hand injuries in the athlete. Symposium on sports injuries. *Orthop Clin North Am.* 1980;11:819–839.
9. Corely FH. Commonly missed fractures in the hand and wrist. *J Musculoskeletal Med.* 1993;10:55–68.
10. McCue FC III, Mayer V, Moran DJ. Gamekeeper's thumb: ulnar collateral ligament rupture. *J Musculoskeletal Med.* 1988;12:53–63.
11. Peyron JG. Osteoarthritis: the epidemiologic viewpoint. *Clin Orthop Rel Res.* 1986;213:117–123.
12. American Society for Surgery of the Hand. *The Hand: Examination and Diagnosis.* 2nd ed. New York: Churchill Livingstone; 1983.
13. Katz WA. Hands and wrists. In: Katz WA, ed. *Rheumatic Diseases: Diagnosis and Management.* 2nd ed. Philadelphia: JB Lippincott; 1988.
14. McCue FC, Baugher WH, Bourland WL, et al. Hand injuries in athletes. *Surg Rounds.* 1978;1:8.
15. Stark HH, Boyes JH, Wilson JN. Mallet finger. *J Bone Joint Surg Am.* 1962;44:1962.
16. Vetter WL. How I manage mallet finger. *Physician Sportsmed.* 1989;17:140.
17. McCue FC, Cabrera JM. Common athletic digital joint injuries of the hand. In: Strickland JW, Rettig AC, eds. *Hand Injuries in Athletes.* Philadelphia: WB Saunders; 1992:49–94.
18. Kahler DM, McCue FC III. Metacarpophalangeal and proximal interphalangeal joint injuries of the hand including the thumb. *Clin Sports Med.* 1992;11:57–76.
19. Boyes JH. *Bunnel's Surgery of the Hand.* 5th ed. Philadelphia: JB Lippincott; 1970:439.
20. McCue FC, Honner R, Gieck JH, et al. A pseudoboutonniere deformity. *J Br Soc Surg Hand.* 1975;7:166.
21. Ruby LK. Common hand injuries in the athlete. *Orthop Clin North Am.* 1980;33:819.
22. McCue FC, Andrews JR, Hakala M. The coach's finger. *J Sports Med.* 1974;2:270–275.
23. Rettig AC. Hand injuries in football players: soft tissue trauma. *Physician Sportsmed.* 1991;19:97–107.
24. Green DP, Terry GC. Complex dislocation of the metacarpophalangeal joint: correlative pathological anatomy. *J Bone Joint Surg Am.* 1973;55:1480–1486.
25. McKerrel J, Bowen V, Johnston G, et al. Boxer's fractures; conservative or operative management? *J Trauma.* 1987;27–48.
26. Burgess RC, Watson HK. Stenosing tenosynovitis in Dupuytren's contracture. *J Hand Surg Am.* 1987;12:89.
27. Osterman AL, Moskow L, Low DW. Soft-tissue injuries of the hand and wrist in racquet sports. *Clin Sports Med.* 1988;7:329–348.
28. Hueston JT, Wilson WF. The etiology of trigger finger. *Hand.* 1972;4:257–260.
29. Marks MR, Gunther SF. Efficacy of cortisone injection in treatment of trigger finger and thumbs. *J Hand Surg Am.* 1989;14:722–727.
30. McCue F, Garroway R. Sports injuries to the hand and wrist. In: Schneider RC, Kennedy JC, Plant ML, eds. *Sports Injuries: Management, Prevention, and Treatment.* Baltimore: Williams & Wilkins; 1984:752–759.
31. Gerber C, Senn E, Matter P. Skier's thumb: surgical treatment of recent injuries in the ulnar collateral ligament of the thumb's metacarpophalangeal joint. *Am J Sports Med.* 1981;9:171.
32. Gieck JH, Mayer V. Protective splinting for the hand and wrist. *Clin Sports Med.* 1986;5:801.
33. Dobyn JH, O'Brien ET, Linschied RL, et al. Bowler's thumb: diagnosis and treatment: review of seventeen cases. *J Bone Joint Surg Am.* 1972;54:751–755.
34. Hellman DB. Arthritis and musculoskeletal disorders. In: Tierney LM Jr, McPhee SJ, Papadakis MA, eds. *Current Medical Diagnosis and Treatment.* 34th ed. Norwalk, CT: Appleton & Lange; 1995:711.
35. Espinoza LR. Psoriatic arthritis: clinical response and side-effects of methotrexate therapy. *J Rheumatol.* 1992;19:872.

CHAPTER 11

Hip, Groin, and Thigh Complaints

CONTEXT

Although the hip and shoulder are the most proximal joints of their respective limbs, the hip is unique in several aspects. Unlike the shoulder, the hip is quite stable and requires a major force to cause a dislocation. Although common shoulder problems are often soft-tissue generated, the hip is more prone to bone or joint damage. As a weight-bearing joint it is commonly affected by degenerative changes and fracture in senior patients. Disorders of the hip are probably more age-related than any other joint. Many presentations fit an age-related categorization: congenital disorders in the infant, growth plate and vascular etiologies in the adolescent, trauma in the young adult, and fracture or arthritis in the elderly. The diagnosis of many of these disorders is dependent on radiographic confirmation.

Patients often claim hip pain when, in fact, the pain is in either the low back or buttocks. It is important, as with all pain, to have the patient localize the problem. Hip pain may be due to intrinsic pathology of the hip joint or referred from a number of geographically and neurally related structures. Associated pain in the lumbopelvic or abdominal areas often will identify the source, yet not always. The overlap with groin pain extends the diagnostic list substantially. Pain in the groin also may be caused by local pathology or referred from the hip, pelvis, genitals, or abdomen. Associated signs or symptoms will usually help differentiate between mechanical and visceral sources.

A common traumatic history is a fall onto the hip. This often results in soft tissue injury such as a contusion or a trochanteric bursitis. Fracture should be ruled out, in particular in the senior patient. An insidious onset of hip pain is suggestive of osteoarthritis changes in the middle-aged or senior adult. In the child or adolescent, avascular necrosis, slipped ephiphysis, or a reactive synovitis should be considered. With children it is important to remember that the knee is a common referral site for hip disorders.

Thigh pain is often differentiated on the basis of a history of either direct trauma (contusion) or sudden-movement onset (strain). When anterior numbness, paresthesias, or weakness are complaints, femoral nerve involvement should be evaluated. Lateral sensory complaints usually represent lateral femoral cutaneous nerve (meralgia paresthetica) involvement or trigger point referral. Posterior neurologic complaints suggest sciatic nerve irritation, referral from trigger points, or lumbar/sacral facet problems.

GENERAL STRATEGY

History

- Determine what the patient means by "hip" pain (groin, buttocks, hip, pelvis, etc.).
- Localize the pain to a quadrant of lateral, medial, anterior, or posterior pain.
- Determine whether any overt trauma occurred such as a fall on the hip (in younger patients suspect a slipped epiphysis or an avascular process; in the elderly, a fracture).
- If there was trauma, determine whether the patient can bear weight; if not, radiographs including anteroposterior (AP) and lateral (frog-leg) views are essential.
- If there was a sudden onset with sporting activity, determine the mechanism (in younger patients consider an apophysitis).
- Determine whether there is a history of overuse (suspicion of a stress fracture in a high-level athlete; myofascial problems in all patients).

- Determine whether there are any associated visceral complaints (radiation of pain from the back to the groin is suggestive of renal disease, from the groin to the hip suggests genitourinary disease or hernia).

Evaluation

- Determine whether there is a range of motion (ROM) restriction suggestive of capsular involvement of the hip (internal rotation and extension), a positive FABER (flexion, abduction, external rotation) test, or increased pain by axial compression into the joint (found with synovitis of various causes and with osteoarthritis [OA]).
- Determine whether there is associated anteversion/retroversion or asymmetric restrictions in either passive external or internal rotation.
- If groin pain is the complaint, test adductors and hip flexors to determine strain, palpate for tenderness at attachment sites of muscles, and palpate for hernias in patients with chronic pain made worse with straining; if pain is radiating to the groin from the back, perform a kidney punch test; palpate lymph nodes if genital complaints or lesions are present.
- If snapping around the hip is the complaint, determine the location and determine on which ROM the snapping or popping occurs (adduction for iliotibial band syndrome snapping, abduction for iliopectineal or psoas snapping).
- Determine whether there are other musculoskeletal complaints (may be a clue to hip pain's being the result of accommodation to other lower extremity or low back problem).
- Radiographs of the hip should be ordered if an obvious soft tissue cause is not evident or if pain is trauma induced; views include AP and frog-leg (lateral) views.
- Determine whether further imaging techniques are appropriate (bone scan with suspicion of stress fracture or synovitis; magnetic resonance imaging (MRI) if there is a suspicion of tumor or infection; computed tomography (CT) scan if there is a suspicion of a pelvic fracture).

Management

- Refer cases to the appropriate medical specialist if any of the following are found: fracture, avascular necrosis, dislocation, tumor, infection, or hernia.
- Management of soft tissue problems involves stretching, myofascial release techniques, appropriate exercise, and preventive approaches through correction of any underlying biomechanical faults.
- OA is managed initially with physical therapy modalities and possibly manipulation; long-term management involves a strengthening program for the hip and thigh.

RELEVANT ANATOMY

As essentiallly a ball-and-socket joint, the hip shares with the shoulder a great degree of movement capability. Unlike the shoulder, however, the hip is a primary weight bearer and as such is more prone to acute and chronic consequences of trauma such as degenerative changes, fractures, and synovitis. As a weight-bearing joint, the effect of femoral head fit and positioning is crucial to proper function. The angulation of the femoral head is referred to as *version*. When the hip is determined to be anteverted, the femoral head faces forward (with relative posterior positioning of the greater trochanter). With retroversion the angulation of the femoral head faces backward with positioning of the greater trochanter anteriorly. These angulations place a biomechanical demand on the bones and joints below. In growing children and adolescents, these demands may result in compensations that may cause torsion of the femur or tibia and foot compensations of pronation or supination. Another mechanical factor is the angulation of the neck of the femur. An increased angle (coxa valga) or decreased angle (coxa vara) is age related or may be changed by fracture or pathology of the femoral neck. The angle normally decreases from birth (average of 160°) to adulthood (average of 120°).

The hip is inherently stable because of its articulation with the pelvis and the thick support of musculature. The capsule is supported by the iliofemoral and pubofemoral ligaments anteriorly and the iliofemoral and ischiofemoral ligaments posteriorly (Figure 11–1). During standing the hips bear approximately one third of body weight. This increases to 2.4 to 2.6 times body weight when standing on one leg. During walking, the hip can bear as much as 1.3 to 5.8 times body weight. Use of a cane can reduce this load by as much as 40%.[1]

Function of the hip may be affected by pelvic motions such as anterior, posterior, or lateral tilt. These motions are affected by the cocontraction or relaxation of various muscle groups. Anterior tilt is caused by the contraction of the hip flexors. Posterior tilt can be accomplished by contraction of lumbar spine extensors, hip extensors, or trunk flexors. Lateral tilt is accomplished through contraction of hip abductors. Excessive weakness or tightness of these muscles may allow or cause abnormal mechanical function through the creation of a functionally short or long leg.

Flexion of the hip is controlled by the iliopsoas and rectus femoris (Figure 11–2). Assistance may be provided by the adductors, tensor fascia lata, and sartorius (L2-L4). Extension is primarily accomplished by contraction of the gluteus

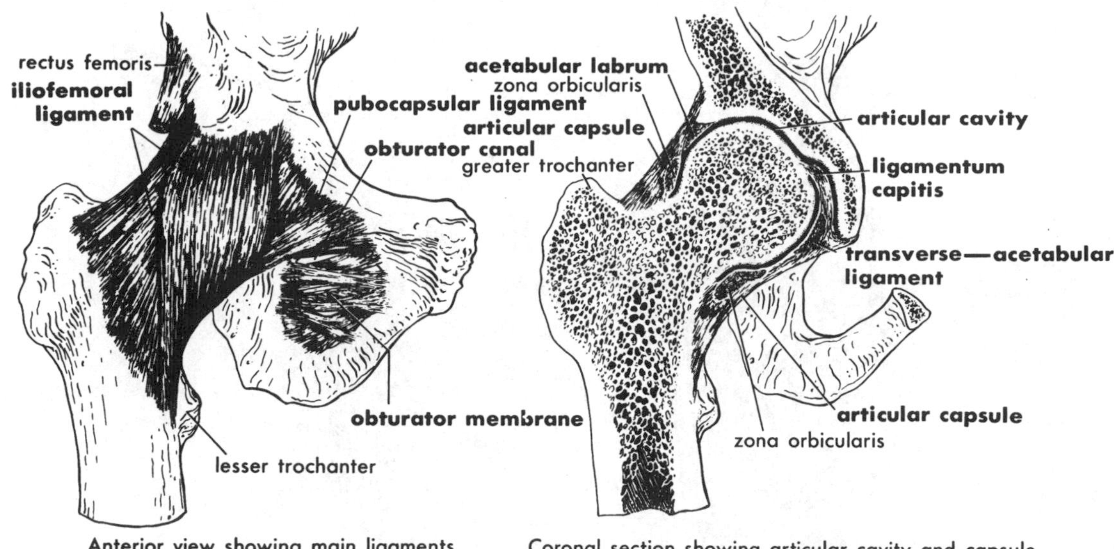

Figure 11–1 The ligamentous support of the hip. *Source:* Reprinted with permission from J.E. Crouch, *Functional Human Anatomy*, 4th ed., p. 164, © 1985, Lea & Febiger.

maximus, ischial portion of the adductor magnus, and hamstrings (L5-S2). The gluteus medius and piriformis may assist. Internal rotation and abduction are due to the contraction of the gluteus medius, gluteus minimus, and the tensor fascia lata (L4-S1). External rotation is accomplished mainly by the piriformis, gemellus, and obturator muscles (L5-S2), with some posture-dependent assistance from the iliopsoas and gluteus maximus. Adduction is primarily accomplished by the adductor group and the gracilis muscle (L3-L5). The strongest movements are extension, adduction, and external rotation. With walking, the unsupported pelvis is supported by the contralateral hip abductors (primarily gluteus medius).

EVALUATION

History

Careful questioning of the patient during the history taking can point to the diagnosis (Table 11–1).

Pain Localization

By having the patient point to the area of pain and describe whether or not the onset was traumatic, the diagnostic list can be narrowed.

Iliac Crest.

- Anterior superior iliac spine (ASIS)—sartorius strain or, in younger patients, apophysitis or avulsion
- Anterior inferior iliac spine (AIIS)—rectus femoris strain or, in younger patients, apophysitis or avulsion
- Lateral iliac crest—hip pointer (if due to a direct blow or fall); iliac crest apophysitis; oblique abdominal, tensor fascia lata, or gluteus medius strain
- Posterior iliac crest—Maigne's syndrome (from T12), strain of gluteus maximus or iliac fascia, or referral from the low back

Groin.

- Pubic bone—osteitis pubis, adductor tendinitis
- Inguinal area—hernia, abdominal strain, lymphadenopathy, iliopsoas bursitis, or tendinitis
- Lateral hip—trochanteric bursitis, tensor fascia lata, or gluteus medius trigger points
- Ischial tuberosity—hamstring sprain, ischial bursitis, or avulsion injury
- Generalized deep pain—synovitis, fracture, OA, Paget's disease

It may be frustrating to have forgotten to clarify the location of the patient's complaint. Often patients have a larger target area in mind when they describe their pain as "hip" pain. Many patients mean buttock pain or thigh pain. After it is clear that hip pain is the chief complaint, it is important to distinguish among associated complaints of snapping, crepitus, and decreased ROM or stiffness. Pain is nonspecific; however, snapping suggests a bursa or tendon source. Decreased ROM is found with many conditions; however, the pattern of restriction may be quite revealing, as discussed

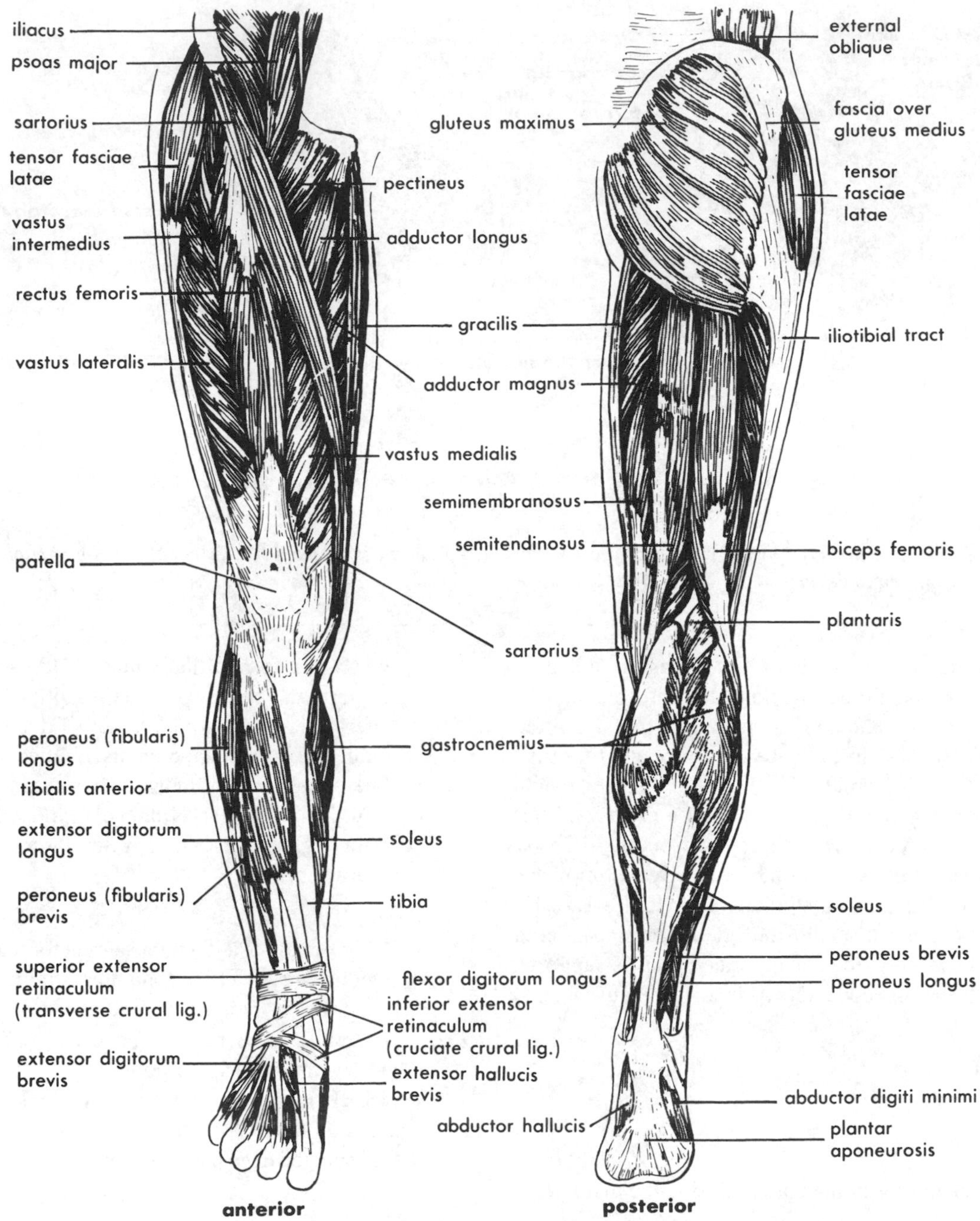

Figure 11–2 Muscles of the hip. *Source:* Reprinted with permission from J.E. Crouch, *Functional Human Anatomy*, 4th ed., p. 238, © 1985, Lea & Febiger.

Table 11–1 History Questions for Hip, Groin, and Thigh Complaints

Primary Question	*What Are You Thinking?*	*Secondary Questions*	*What Are You Thinking?*
Did you fall on your hip?	Hip pointer, hip fracture, traumatic synovitis, slipped epiphysis	Are you able to bear weight and walk?	If yes, hip pointer or contusion is likely; unable to bear weight indicates the other possibilities
Was there a blow to your thigh?	Contusion of hamstrings or quadriceps	Were you hit in the front and do you have difficulty flexing your knee?	Quadriceps contusion
		Were you hit in the back of the thigh and does it hurt to bend forward?	Hamstring contusion
Did you feel a sharp pain in your thigh or groin while performing a sport or recreational activity?	Hamstring, adductor, or quadriceps pull; in younger patients apophysitis is possible	Does it hurt to flex the knee or fully straighten the knee?	Hamstring pull
		Does it hurt to lift the leg?	Iliopsoas or adductor strain (pull)
		Does it hurt to extend the knee?	Quadriceps strain (pull)
Do you have any associated signs and symptoms?	Referral from other joints, septic or aseptic synovitis, OA or other arthritides, tumor, Paget's disease	Did you have a previous respiratory infection (especially in children)?	Septic or aseptic synovitis (needs special imaging to differentiate)
		Do you have any menstrual irregularities?	Possibly gynecologic referral
		Is the pain worse at night, and have you lost any weight recently? Any previous history of cancer?	Metastasis or primary tumor
		Is the pain in both hips and do you have any hand or finger pain?	Rheumatoid arthritis is likely
		Have you noticed a change in hat size?	Paget's disease is possible
		Have you had previous trauma or previous disease of the hip?	OA
		Does the pain radiate from the back to groin?	Renal pathology
		Do you have pain in the groin with bearing down or lifting?	Inguinal hernia

earlier in the general strategy section. Also, when there is a chief complaint of stiffness without significant pain, the diagnostic list is narrowed.

Age and Onset

By approaching the history from the perspective of age and mode of onset, a high level of suspicion for a specific cause can be gained. Many of these suspicions are quickly confirmed or eliminated with a radiographic evaluation. The following are classic presentations based on age:

Pediatric/Childhood Onset. The earliest indicator of a congenital hip disorder may be a nonpainful limp that is of concern to the parents. This would be suggestive of an undetected hip dysplasia or a congenital hip dislocation.

Adolescent/Young Adult. An insidious onset of pain in the adolescent should raise the suspicion of either a slipped femoral capital epiphysis (or preslip) or an avascular necrosis (Perthes' disease). When the onset is sudden and/or traumatic, a search for a slipped epiphysis should be followed. However, a similar presentation may be found with a transient synovitis, which is not clearly evident on radiographs. When the onset is insidious yet associated with a repetitive activity such as running, marching, dancing, or aerobics, suspicion of a stress fracture should be high.

Middle-Aged Adult. Hip pain in the middle-aged adult is unusual unless the patient has had previous problems as a child or adolescent. The obvious exceptions are pregnancy, during which hip pain may be part of the mechanical discomfort associated with extra weight bearing, and trauma. If pain began subsequent to a physical activity, such as sports, or an unaccustomed activity, such as cleaning the yard, local muscle strain should be considered. Occasionally, the answer to questions regarding the use of orthotics or heel lifts is revealing. The altered mechanics may result in strain or reactive bursitis. In the middle-aged group of patients, it is always important to distinguish between a local joint problem and one that is part of a bigger complex of joint complaints. Arthritides such as rheumatoid arthritis (RA) have their initial noticeable signs/symptoms in middle age, although they are less common in the hip. Crystalline deposition disorders, as well, may begin in middle age.

Although it may appear that the diagnosis of hip pain would be relatively straightforward based on common age-related disorders, insidious hip pain is often a dilemma. When none of the obvious causes are found, a decision as to which imaging tool is most appropriate (and cost effective) must be determined. The other complication is that the hip, more than many other joints, is dependent on proper alignment and functioning of the distal joints of the lower extremity kinematic chain. Disorders in any of these joints may cause adaptive compensation at the hip. Being the primary weight-bearing joint of the lower extremity, impact forces must be attenuated, especially in the straightened leg.

Weakness

Isolated weakness in the hips is usually a patient perception due to restricted ROM. OA or muscle contracture provides resistance to movement attempts. Further differentiation can be made by the findings of strong contractions in the midrange combined with restricted passive ROM findings upon examination. When muscle pathology is present, as in muscular dystrophy, the patient often will develop perceptible muscle weakness first in the proximal muscle around the hip and pelvis. There will be no associated complaints of pain or sensory aberrations. If weakness is associated with pain, it is important to ascertain the movement pattern to determine whether there is a specific muscle or tendon cause. Painless difficulty in standing up is suggestive of muscular dystrophy but is not specific for this disorder.

Restriction

If the patient feels that he or she has restricted movement, age and associated symptoms help distinguish the cause. In older patients, OA or perhaps Paget's disease is possible. In a younger patient, especially in males, ankylosing spondylitis is possible (due primarily to pelvic involvement). If the restriction is less discernible after moving around for a half hour or longer, OA is often the cause in older patients.

Snapping

Snapping at the hip is usually a benign problem. In addition to tendon snapping, there is often a suction affect that occurs at the hip joint, causing a pop similar to that caused by manipulation. On rarer occasions, a loose body may be present. Tendon snapping is usually evident with localization of the snapping coupled with the type of movement that creates the snapping.

- Anterior snapping with hip abduction or external rotation suggests that the psoas tendon is snapping over the lesser trochanter or iliopectineal eminence.
- Lateral snapping with hip adduction coupled with flexion or extension suggests that the iliotibial band is snapping over the greater trochanter.
- Posterior snapping with flexion or extension suggests that the biceps femoris tendon is snapping over the ischial tuberosity.
- Pubic bone snapping may occur during pregnancy or the postpartum period or, in rare cases, following a traumatic spread-eagle injury (indicates instability).

Further distinction can be made during the physical examination, palpating the area while the patient performs the provocative movement. It is important to remember that there are interposed bursae at these sites that may be inflamed and cause pain due to the constant snapping.

Groin Pain

The history is particularly important in differentiating the various causes of groin pain. When the pain follows a twisting, sudden, or forceful movement of the hip, adductor tendinitis is often the cause. If the report is that pain occurred after a lifting incident and is made worse with bearing down (Valsalva maneuver), a hernia is likely. If the patient is a man who reports an associated testicular mass, epididymitis, testicular cancer, a varicocele, or testicular torsion is possible. Testicular torsion usually causes pain severe enough to cause the patient to seek medical attention. Palpation of the testes must be performed to differentiate each. Groin pain in women that is not readily reproducible suggests a gynecologic cause. Questions regarding a relationship to the patient's menstrual period may reveal a connection.

Thigh Complaints

Thigh pain is usually due to direct trauma that results in a contusion or due to overcontraction that leads to either muscle tear or rupture. A history of a direct blow to the quadriceps or hamstrings is highly suggestive of a contusion with subsequent hematoma formation. It is important to question the patient regarding the events following the trauma. If the patient returned to a strenuous activity or applied deep heat or massage, a concern for myositis ossificans is generated.

When sudden pain follows a strenuous activity such as running to first base or sprinting, location of the pain will usually isolate a quadriceps or hamstring strain. It is important to determine whether the patient stretches or warms up prior to activity.

When the complaint is more of numbness or paresthesia into the thigh, localization to the lateral thigh suggests meralgia paresthetica. Determining whether the patient is obese, pregnant, sits for long periods, or carries keys or other objects in his or her front pockets may unearth the underlying cause. When the numbness is more anterior, the femoral nerve is involved, and it is likely that the patient is a known diabetic or has signs indicating canal stenosis (claudication signs with walking). Subjective numbness may occur with various trigger-point referrals.

Examination

Given the context of patient presentation, the evaluation of the patient on physical exam extends from very brief to extended. For example, if the patient is unable to bear weight or comfortably move the hip, it would seem prudent to begin the examination with localization of the complaint with palpation. This should be followed immediately by radiographic examination.

Direct palpation of the hip joint is not possible, causing the examiner to rely on indirect, provocative maneuvers. Orthopaedic testing for the hip is rather limited. Many tests are used as a means of differentiating the hip from other causes through a localizing response by the patient. For example, the Patrick test or FABER test is accomplished by placing the ankle of the tested leg over the well-side knee and abducting and externally rotating the hip (Figure 11–3). This test may produce pain at the hip or the sacroiliac (SI) joint. A more specific test involves applying an axial compression force through the femur into the hip joint with the knee flexed to 90° or more. This can be retested with the hip flexed and internally rotated. This is sometimes referred to as Leguerre's test. The quadrant test involves placing the hip in the same Leguerre's position while the patient is asked to resist the examiner's attempt at abduction. Most other testing is based on an effort to distinguish between hip pain of low back or SI origin (see Chapter 6).

Various stretch maneuvers can be applied to the hip joint. The Thomas test requires the supine patient to draw one leg toward the chest while the examiner observes the position of the opposite leg. If the hip or knee flexes, tightness in the hip flexors is likely. A focus on the rectus femoris can be accomplished by having the patient repeat the test with the knee hanging over the edge of the examination table. If the knee

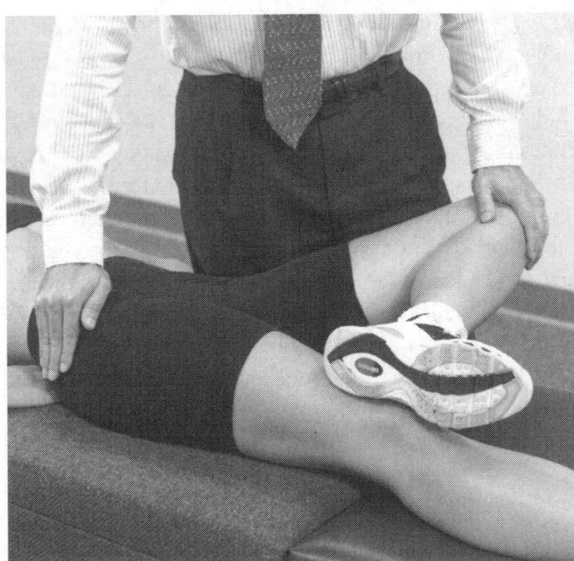

Figure 11–3 FABER test. The patient's hip is placed into flexion, abduction, and external rotation.

extends while the patient flexes the opposite hip to his or her chest, the rectus femoris is tight. A prone test for hip flexor tightness can be accomplished by passively extending the hip with the knee extended. If the hip is extended with the knee flexed, the rectus femoris is tested. This same test may stretch the femoral nerve and cause radiation of pain or other sensory complaints into the anterior thigh. Stretch testing of the abductors and adductors should also be performed. If the abductors are shortened due to contracture, a functional long leg with lowering of the ipsilateral pelvis will be created, associated with adduction of the opposite hip with a raised pelvis.[2] If the adductors are shortened, the ipsilateral leg is functionally shortened with a raised pelvis. On the opposite side, the hip abducts, lowering the pelvis.

Ober's test is often performed on patients complaining of lateral knee pain (Figure 12–10). For the hip, this test is less a provocative test and more a test of abductor flexibility. With the patient lying on his or her side and the bottom leg flexed to 90°, the examiner slowly lowers the top extended leg off the edge of the table while stabilizing at the iliac crest to avoid abdominal stretching. If the patella does not pass below the top edge of the table, tightness of the gluteus medius or the iliotibial band or its attachments (the gluteus maximus and the tensor fascia lata) is likely.

Another biomechanical factor that should be assessed is anteversion or retroversion of the femur. This refers to the angle the femoral neck forms with the femoral condyles. The degree of anteversion is based on the forward projection of the femoral neck into the acetabulum. With abnormal anteversion the femoral condyles are internally rotated with respect to the femoral neck; the reverse occurs with retroversion. Anteversion and retroversion are measured by using the Craig test. This test can be coupled with a measure of internal and external rotation of the hip. With the patient prone, the knee is bent to 90° and both active and passive internal and external rotation are measured. For the Craig test, palpation of the greater trochanter is necessary. As the patient's hip is passively internally and externally rotated, the examiner finds a point at which the greater trochanter feels parallel to the exam table (Figure 11–4). The angle formed by the lower leg and vertical is considered the angle of anteversion (if internally rotated) and retroversion (if externally rotated). The average angle is considered to be between 12° and 25° of anteversion in the adult.[3] Excessive anteversion leads to internal rotation of the femur with potential valgus forces to the knee and possible hyperpronation.

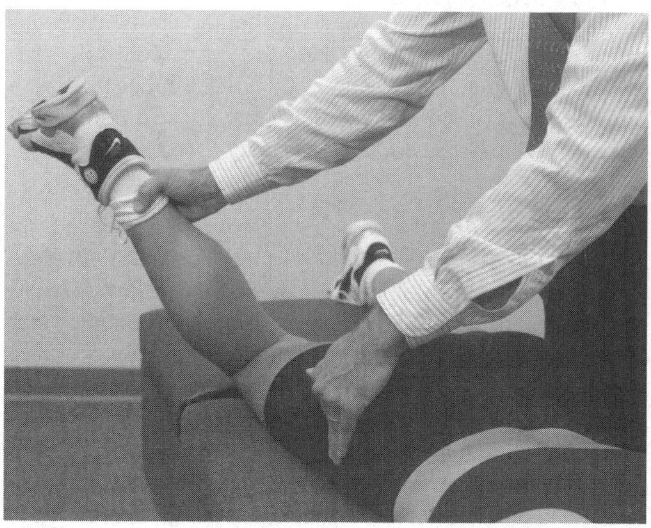

Figure 11–4 Craig test for anteversion/retroversion of the hip. While palpating the greater trochanter the patient's leg is internally or externally rotated until the greater trochanter is pointing parallel to the table. The angle formed by internal rotation with a vertical line indicates the degree of anteversion; the external rotation angle indicates retroversion.

Leg length measurement should be considered a gross but potentially valuable data source. The standard approach is to measure the supine patient from the ASIS to the medial malleolus on the same side (true or anatomic leg length) and then to measure the opposite side and compare the measurements. The same approach is repeated, but this time using the umbilicus and the medial malleolus (apparent or functional leg length). If there is a difference in the "true" leg length, an anatomic short leg (often due to a previous fracture or deforming process at the hip) is present. If the leg length deficiency is in the apparent measurement, a variety of soft tissue factors are likely involved. The interexaminer agreement is only about 40% when examiners had to be within 6 mm of each other to be considered in agreement.[4] When this was extended to 12.5 mm, the agreement increased to 86%. Also, Beattie[5] found that the reliability was high when the mean of two measurements was used. The large literature review published by Manello[6] demonstrates the continuing controversy regarding the contribution of leg length discrepancy to an increase in or predisposition to low back, pelvic, or hip pain. Generally, however, to be clinically significant, the leg length discrepancy needs to be equal to or greater than 0.5 in. This means that discrepancies beyond this range have been shown to predispose individuals to conditions such as subtrochanteric bursitis or SI dysfunction.[7] With a functionally short or long leg, recheck findings with regard to abductor, adductor, or hip flexor/extensor tightness or weakness. If the leg length appears only on weight bearing, check for unilateral pronation or supination as potential causes.

Radiographs may include the standard AP lumbopelvic film or localize for better quality with an AP hip view complemented by a lateral (frog-leg) view. Most osseous and some soft tissue abnormalities may be evident. If avulsion fractures are suspected, the AP view may require some internal or external rotation in order to view the fragment clearly. Following are some radiographic findings associated with some selected disorders[8]:

- OA—The superior acetabular joint space shows narrowing with osteophyte formation at the head/neck junction; there is subchondral sclerosis.
- RA—Early phase changes are uniform, symmetric loss of joint space with associated periarticular osteoporosis. Later changes may include subchondral cyst formation and destruction of the femoral head or acetabular roof even to the point of protrusio acetabuli (protrusion of the femoral head axially through the acetabulum into the pelvis).
- Paget's disease—The bone is thickened, with more apparent trabeculae (cross-hatching) with eventual distortion of the femoral neck or shaft shape.
- Legg-Calvé-Perthes disease (ages 4 to 8 years)—Initially changes include fissuring, flattening, and sclerosis of the epiphysis with a secondary phase of remodeling leading to the classic mushroom deformity; a varus deformity usually results.
- Slipped capital epiphysis (ages 8 to 17 years)—This is a Salter-Harris type I injury characterized by posterior-inferior displacement of the epiphysis best seen on the lateral view.
- Fractures may be due to osteoporosis, Paget's disease, metastasis, and other pathologic processes, or trauma. Femoral neck fractures are intracapsular (subcapital and transcervical regions) or extracapsular (trochanteric, subtrochanteric, and basicervical); intracapsular fractures are more serious and twice as common.[9]

Groin

- With trauma or pain following a sudden forceful maneuver of the hip, palpate for sites of tenderness (eg, adductor origin); if the history indicates a blow to the region, radiograph for possible fracture.
- If pain was insidious or due to overuse, palpate for adductor tenderness and local lymphadenopathy.
- If pain followed a lifting injury or increases with bearing down, perform a hernia evaluation.
- When a gynecologic or genital source is suspected perform or refer for a thorough examination.

When groin pain is traumatic or due to a sudden forceful movement, palpate for tenderness at the pubic bone and adductor origin. Have the patient attempt adduction, flexion, and extension against resistance to isolate specific muscle/tendon involvement. Pain with resisted hip flexion suggests iliopsoas or possibly rectus femoris strain. Pain with resisted adduction suggests adductor tendinitis. If tenderness is severe, consider radiographs to determine possible fracture. For patients with a history of pain following lifting or experience pain with bearing down, perform a hernia examination. This includes palpation for direct, indirect, and femoral hernias.

Reproduction of the pain with SI or hip testing indicates referral to the groin from these areas. If pain originates in the thoracolumbar area, perform a kidney punch test. A search for skin lesions or discharge may suggest a venereal cause.

Thigh

Trauma to the thigh requires a search for contusions. In the anterior thigh, a quadriceps contusion is likely. Palpation is important with injuries that are a few weeks old to determine the development of myositis ossificans. Posterior involvement indicates hamstring contusion. When pain follows sudden or forceful contraction of the legs such as with running, palpation for sites of tenderness is important. If the pain is posterior at the middle to distal thigh, a hamstring sprain has occurred. Occasionally a defect in the muscle can be palpated. The degree of tearing is often reflected in the patient's ability to flex the knee against resistance. The same principles apply to a quadriceps strain, with the severity based on the patient's ability to extend the knee against resistance or perform a quadriceps isometric contraction.

When thigh complaints include numbness or paresthesia it is important to determine whether the symptoms are subjective or objective. Objective numbness in the anterolateral thigh implicates the lateral femoral cutaneous nerve, suggesting meralgia paresthetica. If numbness is objectifiable in the anterior thigh, femoral nerve involvement is likely, especially if associated with weakness of knee extension.

MANAGEMENT

For more detail on management of individual disorders see Related Disorders of the Hip, Groin, and Thigh.

Medical referral is necessary when fracture, dislocation, avascular necrosis, infection, tumor, or visceral pathology is suspected or found. Acute pain is managed with physical therapy and support. With muscle strains, a compressive bandage or taping or a substituting type of elastic wrap may help decrease continued strain to the muscle. These include neoprene sleeves for hamstring and quadriceps strains and hip spica wraps for adductor or iliopsoas strains.

Management of most other complaints focuses on restoring normal mobility to the hip joint and pelvis, from both a gross ROM perspective (voluntary muscular component) and an accessory motion perspective (involuntary component). OA often results in hip joint contractures. A combination of stretching and general hip stabilization exercises coupled with hip manipulation is often effective.

Prevention of further soft tissue injury at the hip and thigh involves a routine of stretching and warming up prior to activity. For patients who have had or are at potential risk for hip fracture, evaluation of common environmental obstacles should be performed with recommendations for avoidance of falls. This would include taping down of rugs, placing nonslip strips on steps or stairs, ensuring proper lighting at night, and strategically placing balance points for use of a walker or cane.

Algorithm

An algorithm for evaluation and management of hip pain is presented in Figure 11–5.

Figure 11–5

HIP PAIN—ALGORITHM.

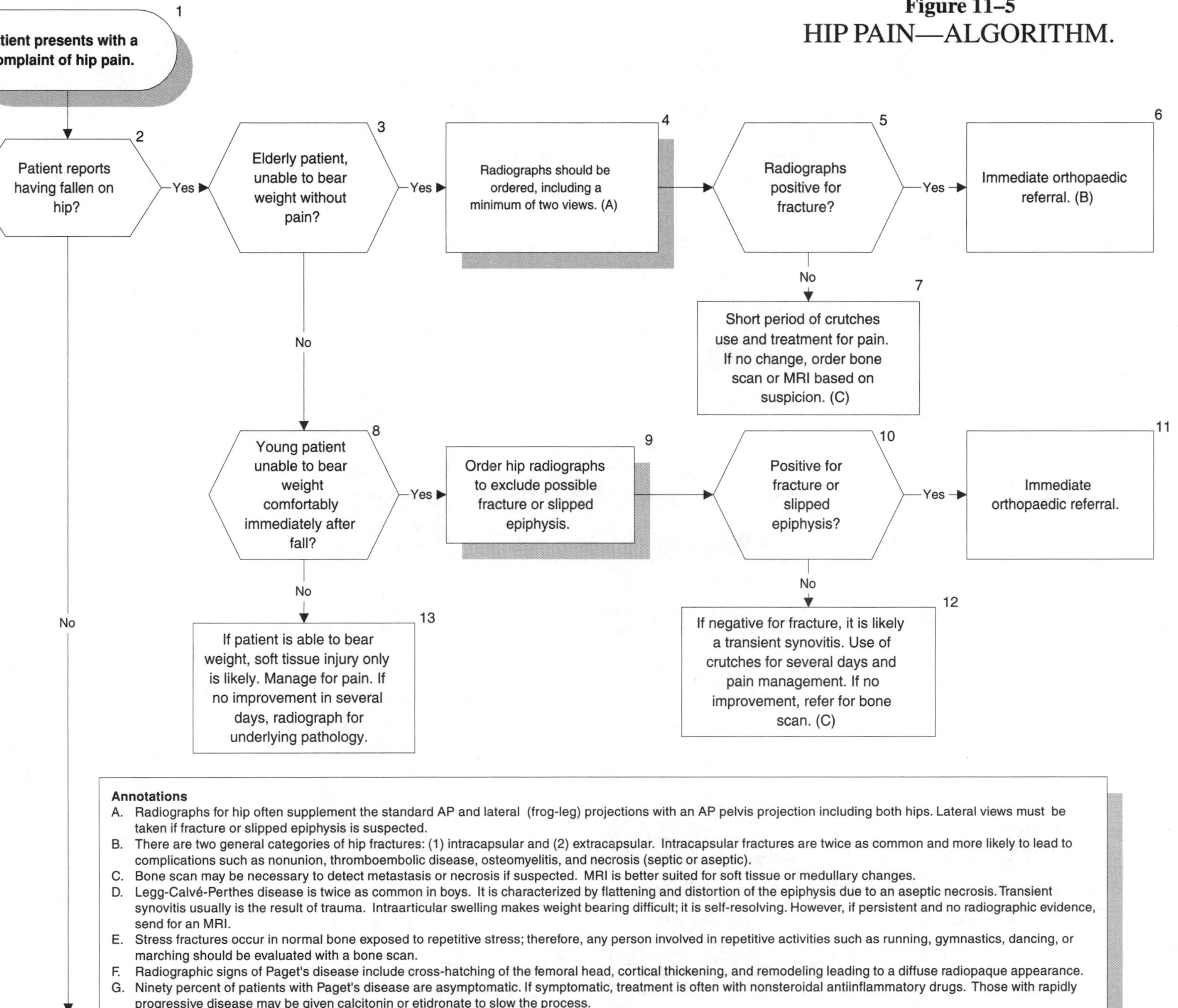

Annotations

A. Radiographs for hip often supplement the standard AP and lateral (frog-leg) projections with an AP pelvis projection including both hips. Lateral views must be taken if fracture or slipped epiphysis is suspected.

B. There are two general categories of hip fractures: (1) intracapsular and (2) extracapsular. Intracapsular fractures are twice as common and more likely to lead to complications such as nonunion, thromboembolic disease, osteomyelitis, and necrosis (septic or aseptic).

C. Bone scan may be necessary to detect metastasis or necrosis if suspected. MRI is better suited for soft tissue or medullary changes.

D. Legg-Calvé-Perthes disease is twice as common in boys. It is characterized by flattening and distortion of the epiphysis due to an aseptic necrosis. Transient synovitis usually is the result of trauma. Intraarticular swelling makes weight bearing difficult; it is self-resolving. However, if persistent and no radiographic evidence, send for an MRI.

E. Stress fractures occur in normal bone exposed to repetitive stress; therefore, any person involved in repetitive activities such as running, gymnastics, dancing, or marching should be evaluated with a bone scan.

F. Radiographic signs of Paget's disease include cross-hatching of the femoral head, cortical thickening, and remodeling leading to a diffuse radiopaque appearance.

G. Ninety percent of patients with Paget's disease are asymptomatic. If symptomatic, treatment is often with nonsteroidal antiinflammatory drugs. Those with rapidly progressive disease may be given calcitonin or etidronate to slow the process.

Key: CMT, chiropractic manipulative therapy.

continues

Figure 11–5 continued

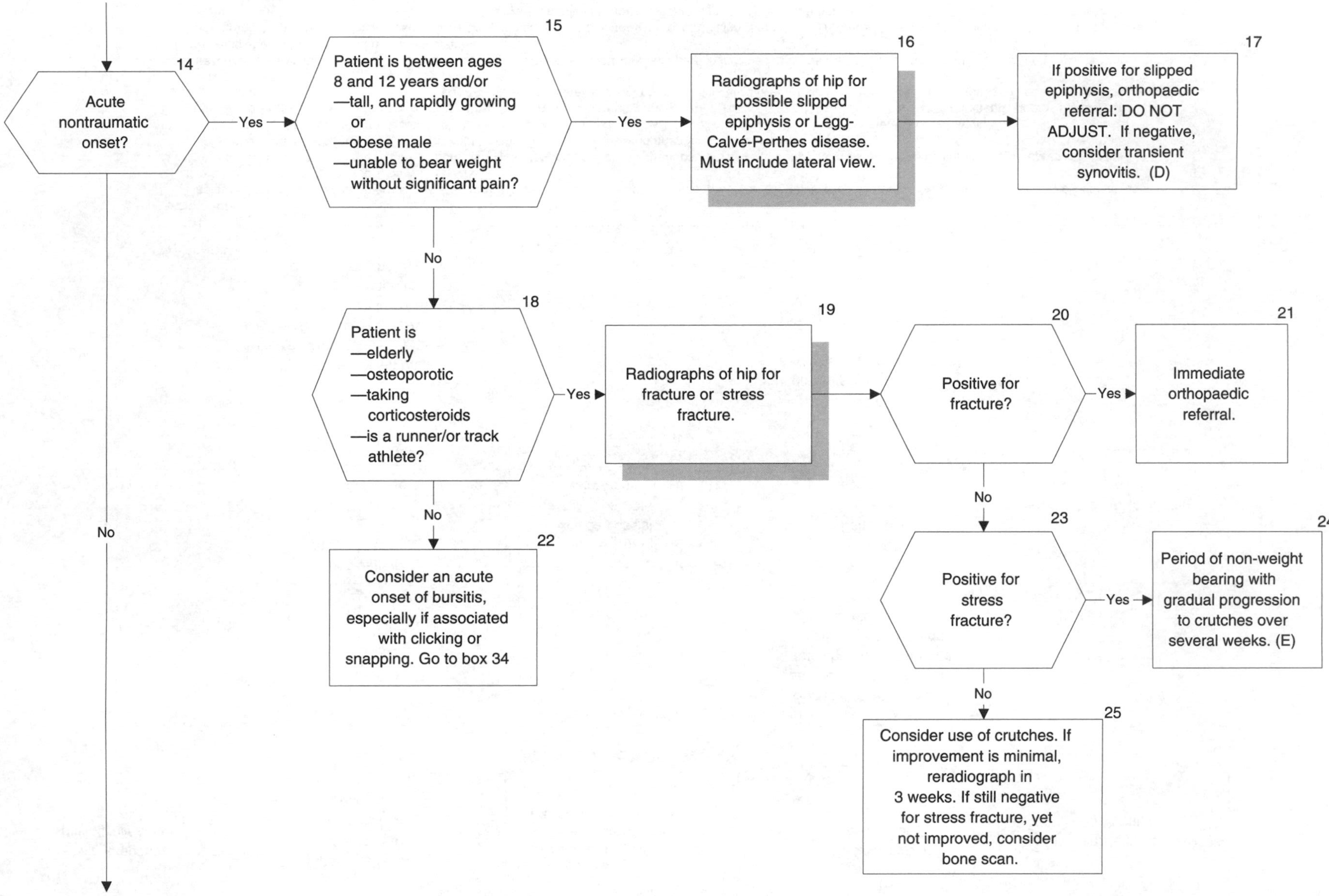

14
Acute nontraumatic onset?
Yes → 15; No → (continues)

15
Patient is between ages 8 and 12 years and/or
—tall, and rapidly growing
or
—obese male
—unable to bear weight without significant pain?
Yes → 16; No → 18

16
Radiographs of hip for possible slipped epiphysis or Legg-Calvé-Perthes disease. Must include lateral view.
→ 17

17
If positive for slipped epiphysis, orthopaedic referral: DO NOT ADJUST. If negative, consider transient synovitis. (D)

18
Patient is
—elderly
—osteoporotic
—taking corticosteroids
—is a runner/or track athlete?
Yes → 19; No → 22

19
Radiographs of hip for fracture or stress fracture.
→ 20

20
Positive for fracture?
Yes → 21; No → 23

21
Immediate orthopaedic referral.

22
Consider an acute onset of bursitis, especially if associated with clicking or snapping. Go to box 34

23
Positive for stress fracture?
Yes → 24; No → 25

24
Period of non-weight bearing with gradual progression to crutches over several weeks. (E)

25
Consider use of crutches. If improvement is minimal, reradiograph in 3 weeks. If still negative for stress fracture, yet not improved, consider bone scan.

continues

Figure 11–5 continued

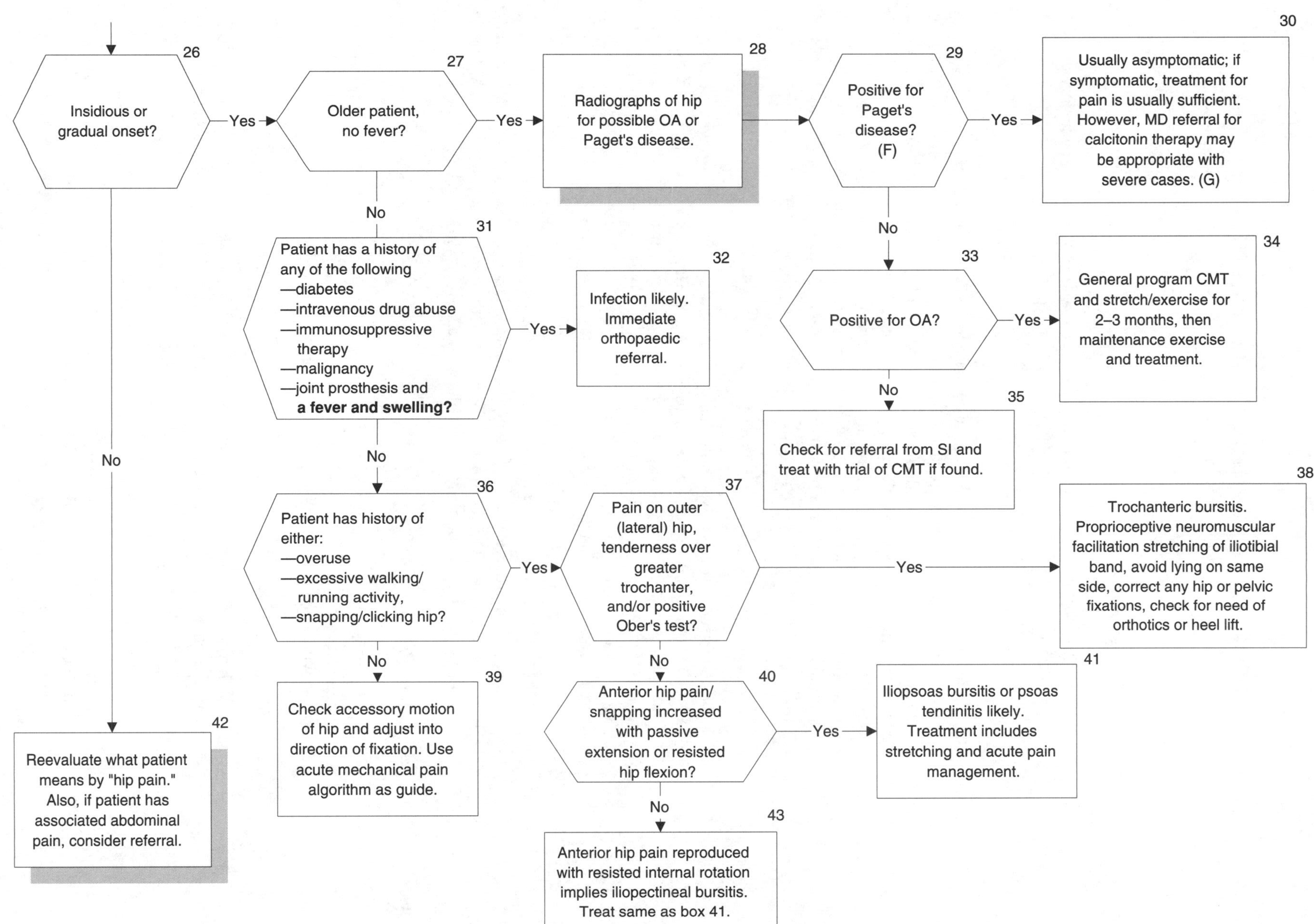

SELECTED DISORDERS OF THE HIP, GROIN, AND THIGH

HIP

Hip Fractures

Classic Presentation

An elderly patient presents with hip pain, unable to bear weight, and a history of a fall onto the hip.

Causes

In the elderly, the most common cause or predisposition of hip fracture is osteoporosis and therefore it is seen more frequently in women. One study suggests that the fracture is due to a combination of bone fatigue and axial muscular compressive forces, which then leads to falling.[10] Obviously, falls can result in fracture also. Other considerations are Paget's disease, endocrinopathies, multiple myeloma, and renal osteodystrophy.[11] In the young patient, other than a major traumatic event, pathologic fracture may be due to benign and malignant tumors. Benign tumors include a unicameral bone cyst and fibrous dysplasia. Malignant causes include osteogenic sarcoma and Ewing's sarcoma.[12]

Evaluation

In the event of trauma, beyond palpation, the next step is radiographic evaluation. A search for fractures must include both an AP view and a lateral view. Fractures are divided into intracapsular (subcapital and transcervical) and extracapsular (basicervical, trochanteric, and subtrochanteric). Intracapsular fractures are twice as common as extracapsular fractures and, unfortunately, are more likely to result in serious complications such as osteonecrosis, nonunion, thromboembolic disease, and osteomyelitis.[13]

Management

Advances in orthopaedic stabilization techniques and new advances in bone healing have helped increase the success rate of surgery. Unfortunately, the death rate following hip fracture is still approximately 15% (due to the above mentioned complications).

Stress Fractures

Classic Presentation

The patient is young and active, often participating in activities such as long-distance running, gymnastics and, less often, dancing or marching. The pain is insidious and is worse with weight bearing. The pain is often anterior and deep.

Mechanism

With repetitive stress to the femoral neck, microfractures appear. Cellular damage leads to increased remodeling. When osteoclastic activity exceeds osteoblastic activity, the bone is weakened.

Evaluation

Little is found on the examination except for perhaps end-range restriction and pain with flexion and internal rotation. Radiographs often are unrevealing. When the index of suspicion is high, a bone scan is highly sensitive.[14] If a tumor is included in the differential, MRI is valuable.

Management

There are two different types of femoral neck stress fractures. Management is different for each.

1. Transverse—Begins in the superior cortex and continues across the neck. These fractures are potentially unstable and may lead to serious complications. Therefore, percutaneous pinning is the recommended treatment.
2. Compression—Begins along the inferior cortex and may progress to sclerosis; however, it is stable. Rest and elastic support are necessary for 2 weeks, followed by non-weight-bearing exercises such as bicycling or swimming. It takes on average 4 to 6 weeks for a stress fracture to heal.

Congenital Hip Dislocation and Hip Dysplasia

Classic Presentation

Congenital hip dislocation is usually diagnosed on physical exam of the neonate; if undetected, the child would, upon weight bearing, have a limp and diminished active abduction.

Causes

Dislocation is due to acetabular deformities. Inversion of the limbus combined with capsular tightness causes dislocation and prevents a stable relocation.[15]

Evaluation

The classic tests used for early detection are Ortolani's click test and Barlow's maneuver. Radiographs may appear normal until the infant is 4 to 6 weeks of age. Radiographic identification of dysplasia is based on a triad of an underdeveloped proximal femoral epiphysis, lateral displacement of the femur, and an increased inclination of the acetabular roof (Putti's triad).[16] Severe degenerative changes are visible in chronic dislocators. MRI and diagnostic ultrasound are used to detect early dysplastic changes.[17]

Management

Management is dependent on age. In infants up to 6 months, a harness (eg, Pavlik) is used to hold the hip in flexion and prevent adduction. From ages 6 to 15 months (before walking), 2 to 3 months in a spica cast is recommended. In toddlers or in children who have not responded to closed reduction, open reduction is necessary.

Traumatic Hip Dislocations

Classic Presentation

Based on whether anterior or posterior; posterior dislocations account for 90% of sports-related hip dislocations.

- Posterior—An acute injury is reported with a major force applied to a flexed, adducted hip. After the injury, the hip is held in flexion, adduction, and internal rotation. The pain is severe. Pain down the back of the leg may indicate sciatic nerve damage.
- Anterior—Patient reports a force/blow to an extended, externally rotated leg. Immediately after injury, the leg is held in flexion, abduction, and internal rotation.

Evaluation

Visual observation and history are usually enough to raise the suspicion. Radiographs to determine the extent of damage are needed. However, these would be performed in an emergency department setting.

Management

Relocation is not possible without anesthesia. This is followed by rest, and a period of non-weight bearing with gradual return to supported walking with crutches.

Slipped Capital Epiphysis (Adolescent Coxa Vara)

Classic Presentation

An overweight child or a young, rapidly growing adolescent (8 to 17 years) presents with a traumatic (50% of the time) history, although sometimes relatively minor. Acute slippage may occur. Chronic slippage presents as a gradual hip pain with antalgia. Children may have only knee pain. This is the most common hip condition in adolescents, affecting between 0.7 and 3.4/100,000.[18]

Causes

Although trauma is reported in 50% of cases, half of cases have no obvious traumatic history. An acute slippage is a Salter-Harris type I epiphyseal fracture. Hormonal influences may play a role in obese individuals[19] (Fröhlich syndrome-like appearance) or in tall, fast-growing adolescents.

Evaluation

The physical examination may be generally unremarkable; however, sometimes when the hip is taken passively into flexion, it rotates externally.[20] The definitive diagnosis is with hip radiographs. It is essential to understand that the slippage may not be visible on the anterior view. The lateral view gives a clearer picture of the typical posterior/inferior slippage of the femoral epiphysis.[21] Bilateral views should be taken because of occurrence in the opposite hip in 10% to 20% of cases.

Management

Surgical pinning is often used. Acute slipped capital femoral epiphysis is managed with a short period of traction, followed by internal rotation to accomplish reduction, followed by pinning or screw fixation. It is imperative that there is no attempt to reduce the slippage with manipulation. The consequences can be disastrous, including avascular necrosis.

Avascular Necrosis

Classic Presentation

Legg-Calvé-Perthes disease is a form of avascular necrosis. The patient is usually male (four or five times more commonly) between the ages of 4 and 9 years (80%) presenting with a complaint of mild hip pain and an associated limp of insidious onset. Symptoms are bilateral 10% of the time[22]; 17% of patients have a traumatic history.[23] Fifteen percent of patients present with knee pain only. Avascular necrosis may be due to a multitude of other factors. The patient is more likely though, to present with a history of past trauma or metabolic disease.

Causes

Legg-Calvé-Perthes disease is believed to be due to an undetermined disruption of the vascular supply to the femoral head.[24] Other than Legg-Calvé-Perthes disease, avascular necrosis is secondary to subcapital fractures (20%), posterior hip dislocations (8%), long-term steroid use, hyperlipidemia, alcoholism, pancreatitis, and hemoglobinopathies.[25]

Evaluation

Usually there is limitation of hip abduction and internal rotation (secondary to muscle spasm). The Trendelenburg test is often positive. Over time, atrophy and limb length inequality may be evident. The definitive diagnosis is radiographic. In progression the changes begin with a small radiopaque femoral nucleus, followed by a crescent sign, fragmentation, reossification with remodeling, and deformity of the femoral head.

Management

Management is often conservative. It is generally agreed that children younger than 4 years of age or those with minor involvement (less than half of the femoral head) usually require no treatment. Children older than 4 to 5 years old who have good motion (abduction greater than 30°) may not require bracing or surgery.[26] Referral for medical consultation is required. There is no apparent evidence to support the use of crutches or non-weight bearing in most cases. When subluxation occurs due to femoral head deformation, use of a Petrie cast or ambulatory brace may help maintain needed abduction. Surgical options are rarely required but include osteotomy. Healing takes about 18 months.

Subtrochanteric Bursitis

Classic Presentation

Several bursae are capable of producing symptoms. The two major bursae are the subgluteus medius and subgluteus maximus. A smaller bursa with the gluteus minimus is less often involved. The patient presents with well-localized lateral hip pain usually with only a minor degree of limp. The patient is often between 40 and 60 years of age. Less commonly subtrochanteric bursitis may cause pain radiating to the low back, the lateral thigh, and the knee.[27–29] The patient often will not be able to sleep on the involved side.

Cause

Any condition that leads to altered hip mechanics, including low pack pain, leg length discrepancy, arthritic conditions, surgery, and neurologic conditions with paresis, may cause subtrochanteric bursitis. The result is some loss of internal rotation. The degree of discomfort is often proportional to the degree of activity. Repetitive activity can be a major cause in the younger population because the friction over the bursa causes it to be inflamed.

Evaluation

Tenderness and sometimes swelling are found over the greater trochanter. Palpation may cause a "jump" sign when localized to the lower portion of the trochanter with the knee and hip flexed. Pain may be increased with hip motion and maneuvers such as the Patrick test or Ober's test.

Management

Management includes correction of abnormal biomechanics such as leg length discrepancies combined with indicated adjustment of the pelvis or hip. Additionally, stretching of the hip abductors using proprioceptive neuromuscular facilitation (PNF) techniques should be prescribed and performed in office. Ultrasound has little applicability unless a chronic bursitis is suspected or perhaps in assisting stretching of any tight contributing muscles. Side-posture adjusting may aggravate and in rare cases cause a trochanteric bursitis. Therefore, side-posture adjusting is contraindicated for 1 to 2 weeks during acute care treatment. Alternative techniques should be employed during this time. In runners, pay particular attention to running technique and surface. They should be advised to avoid both banked surfaces and allowing the feet to cross the midline when running.

Iliopectineal and Iliopsoas Bursitis

Classic Presentation

The patient often presents with a severe, acute anterior hip pain with an antalgic gait. He or she may also report pain radiating down the anterior aspect of the leg. This is due to pressure on the neighboring femoral nerve. The patient often will assume a position of flexion and external rotation of the hip to relieve the pain.

Cause

These anterior bursitises are possibly due to hip flexor tightness coupled with repetitive activity.

Evaluation

There is often deep anterior tenderness at the hip. Specifically, the bursa is located about 1 to 2 cm below the middle third of the inguinal ligament. The iliopsoas bursa may be palpated with the supine patient's hip flexed to 90° while palpating over the lesser trochanter. Resisted hip flexion or more specific iliopsoas testing will reproduce the pain.[30]

Management

Rest and stretching of the hip flexors often will resolve the problem. Myofascial release of the iliopsoas must be performed cautiously.

Ischial Bursitis

Classic Presentation

Often the patient reports sitting for long periods of time on hard surfaces (benchwarmer's bursitis) or during horseback riding. She or he may have referral down the back of the leg mimicking sciatica. The patient may notice that pressing the foot down on the brake pedal (or gas pedal) of a car may relieve the pain. This is due to accompanying extension of the knee, which rotates the ischial tuberosity away from the sitting surface. In the younger athletic patient, speed work (sprinting) may cause a bursitis due to excessive hamstring contraction. This must be differentiated from an apophysitis.

Cause

Ischial bursitis is caused by a direct blow to the bursa, acute or chronic trauma (as in horseback riding), or prolonged irritation from hard-surface sitting. Chronic hamstring strains and occasionally prolonged standing may also cause irritation.[31]

Evaluation

The patient may list toward the affected side with an accompanying shortened stride length. Toe standing may be painful. There is well-localized tenderness over the ischial tuberosity. Straight leg raising and Patrick's test may also reproduce pain.

Management

Padding such as a small inflatable pillow may help in the acute phase. Avoidance of the inciting activity is necessary for long-term management.

Snapping Hip Syndrome

Classic Presentation

Other than snapping, many patients do not have pain. The location of the snapping is a good indicator of the offending structure. If traumatic, consider an acetabular labrum tear.

Cause

Snapping at the hip is often due to tendons that snap over bony prominences or bursae. Occasionally, abduction may cause a suction effect similar to joint gapping with manipulation. Even more rarely, a loose body may be found in the joint. However, with loose bodies, there are accompanying signs of mechanical blockage of movement.

Evaluation

The location and movement pattern are often helpful. Lateral hip snapping usually occurring on hip flexion with the hip in adduction is most often due to the iliotibial band's snapping at the greater trochanter. Anterior snapping or popping occurring with active extension of the flexed, abducted, and externally rotated hip often indicates iliopsoas tendon involvement or occasionally snapping of the iliofemoral ligaments over the anterior joint capsule. Posterior snapping in the buttocks region is probably due to the biceps femoris tendon's snapping over the ischial tuberosity.

Management

Usually these are benign and position dependent. If painful or irritating to the patient, strengthening rather than stretching the involved muscle is often helpful. Stabilization seems to reduce occurrence. If unsuccessful, stretching may be employed as a second treatment option.

Transient Synovitis

Classic Presentation

A child less than 10 years of age complains of an acute or gradual onset of pain in the inguinal area with difficulty bearing weight. The child will often hold the hip in external rotation, abduction, and flexion. Trauma is not often part of the history; however, a prior viral infection is often elicited.

Cause

The cause is unknown in many cases; however, it may be a portent of either rheumatoid disease or ensuing Legg-Calvé-Perthes disease (1.5% to 10% of cases).[32]

Evaluation

Findings of a decrease in internal rotation and some restriction of other movements with some general tenderness to palpation are commonly found; however, they are nonspecific. Radiographs are not revealing. A bone scan is often diagnostic, but the specificity is low. Ultrasound may demonstrate fluid in the joint. The primary differential is a septic hip. However, the initial history is similar, with a preceding respiratory infection. Aspiration may be needed to make the diagnosis. Septic arthritis is a medical emergency. MRI may help differentiate.

Management

In the idiopathic benign form, resolution over several weeks occurs with a non–weight-bearing period followed by crutch use over several weeks.

Osteoarthritis

Classic Presentation

In primary OA a middle-aged or elderly patient presents with hip and possibly buttock, groin, or knee pain that was insidious in onset. Additionally, the patient notes a slow stiffening (specifically internal rotation). This often results in the patient's walking with the hip held in external rotation. The patient may complain of low back pain due to excessive extension with weight bearing to compensate for limited hip extension.

In secondary OA the presentation may be similar; however, there may be a history of trauma to the hip, or the patient may have other joint involvement if crystal deposition (ie, gout) is a factor.

Cause

Primary OA is due to progressive degeneration of femoral and acetabular articular cartilage. This is presumably caused by the accumulation of microtrauma. However, primary OA of the hip is not common. It is considered when there are preexisting abnormalities of the acetabulum or femoral head (congenital or acquired).[33] Secondary OA may be due to calcium pyrophosphate dihydrate crystal deposition disease, acromegaly, hemochromatosis, neuroarthropathy, and other articular problems.

Evaluation

There is restriction to passive internal rotation and extension of the hip. Eventually, abductor or adductor contracture may develop. Pain may be produced by axially compressing the femur into the acetabulum. Nonuniform loss of joint space is found radiographically. Superior joint space narrowing with associated findings of subchondral cysts and osteophytes are the hallmark of OA. It is important to note that many patients receive the diagnosis of OA when, in fact, there are no radiographic findings to support this diagnosis.

Management

If appropriate, reduction of weight will be of benefit. Non–weight-bearing exercise is often quite beneficial, including pool exercises and bicycle riding. Strengthening of the joint often will relieve constant pain. Stretching of hip contractures may be accomplished with gentle PNF stretching or deeper myofascial release techniques. Use of a cane should be limited to those with severe pain.

Rheumatoid Arthritis

Classic Presentation

A woman between ages 25 and 55 years presents with hip pain and associated periarticular soft tissue swelling, stiffness, and ROM restriction. At some point in the presentation the pain is bilateral.

Cause

The cause is a synovial inflammatory process that creates a destructive pannus.

Evaluation

Radiographically there is uniform, symmetric joint space diminution superiorly. Eventually this is bilateral. Associated findings are periarticular osteoporosis, subchondral cysts, and osseous destruction. In later stages, ankylosis and protrusio acetabuli (femoral head protrudes through the acetabulum) may occur. Similar findings are found in other joints such as the hands, knees, ankles, and cervical spine. Positive laboratory findings include an elevated erythrocyte sedimentation rate (ESR) and a positive rheumatoid factor.

Management

Comanagement is often necessary. For acute periods, the use of nonsteroidal antiinflammatory drugs is often helpful. Mild, passive movements may be helped by maintaining hip motion and help reduce swelling. The RA hip should not be aggressively manipulated.

Tumors

Classic Presentation

A patient aged 50 or older presents with a complaint of deep bone pain (66% to 80% of cases).[34] There was an insidious onset and the pain is not relieved by rest; it is worse at night. Past history may include a previous diagnosis of lung, breast, kidney, prostate, or thyroid cancer (if metastatic).[35]

Causes

The causes are metastasis and multiple myeloma.

Evaluation

Laboratory may reveal an increase in ESR, serum calcium, alkaline phosphatase, and, if from a prostate tumor, prostate-specific antigen. Multiple myeloma has characteristic findings of Bence-Jones proteinuria, increased ESR, monoclonal spiking on electrophoresis, and an M spike on immunoelectrophoresis. Radiographic changes may be lytic or blastic, depending on the type of tumor. Breast and kidney tumors tend to be lytic, whereas a prostate tumor tends to be blastic. Multiple myeloma has a lytic presentation.

Management

Referral for oncologic consultation is needed.

Paget's Disease

Classic Presentation

Ninety percent of patients are asymptomatic. They may notice an increase in hat size or develop an insidious onset of low back and/or hip pain if symptomatic. Usually Paget's disease is found inadvertently on radiographs of middle-aged or elderly patients.

Cause

The cause is unknown; however, a viral etiology is suspected. In less than 2% of cases sarcomatous degeneration is a complication.[36]

Evaluation

Radiographic evaluation will demonstrate a cross-hatched appearance of the femoral head trabeculae. Later changes include remodeling, with increased opacity and deformation and later bowing.

Management

There is no medical treatment that prevents or cures Paget's disease. Asymptomatic patients are not treated. Those who are symptomatic are treated with a choice of various drugs. The most common drug used with pagetic pain is calcitonin, now available in a nasal spray. Other drugs include the diphosphonates, which inhibit osteoclast activity.

GROIN

Osteitis Pubis

Classic Presentation

The patient often will report either a sudden, forced adduction injury or a repetitive minor trauma seen with kicking or running. Pregnant women may be prone to irritation also.

Cause

Direct compressive or distractive injury may cause pain at the pubic joint.

Evaluation

There is tenderness at the pubic joint with compression and sometimes with compression of the two ASISs toward each other. Resisted adduction is also provocative in many cases. Occasionally a bone scan is necessary to diagnose because of the lack of sensitivity on radiographs.

Management

Management includes rest with a slow return to activity and gradual increase in flexibility; avoidance of the inciting activity, especially side-foot kicking or bilateral adduction maneuvers. Gross instability at the joint may require surgical stabilization.

Adductor Sprain

Classic Presentation

The patient is usually an athlete who is involved in kicking, sprinting, water skiing, or jumping (high jumps or hurdles). He or she reports a sudden pulling sensation in the groin that was incapacitating.

Cause

The cause of an adductor sprain is sudden contraction of the adductors from a stretched position of hip abduction or flexion. The most common site is at the myofascial junction of the adductor magnus.

Evaluation

The patient has a discrete site of tenderness in the adductor muscle group or at the pubic attachment. Resisted adduction sharply increases the pain or discomfort.

Management

Elastic figure-of-eight strapping is applied with the hip in slight extension and internal rotation. This will assist the adductor in normal walking for a week or so. Gentle stretching and a slow return to activity are suggested.

THIGH

Hamstring Strain

Classic Presentation

The patient is often an athlete or "weekend warrior" who feels a sudden pull or pop at the back of the thigh following a forceful knee extension maneuver.

Cause

The mechanism is an overcontraction of the hamstrings while in a position of stretch. Tearing occurs most often at the junction of the muscle and aponeurosis. Avulsion of the ischial apophysis is possible in younger athletes.

Evaluation

Palpation of a site of tenderness at the distal muscle belly associated with increased pain on resisted knee flexion is diagnostic. Pain is correlated to the degree of injury. Full ruptures are quite painful.

Management

Treatment includes rest, ice, use of crutches for several days, gentle stretching when tolerable, and a long-term goal of restrengthening beginning when 75% of the normal ROM is available. For first-degree strains, return to normal activity is often within a couple of weeks; for second-degree, 4 to 6 weeks; for full ruptures, it often takes 3 to 4 months to return to a normal level of activity. A focus on prevention includes preevent stretching, maintaining a proper strength ratio between the hamstrings and quadriceps (0.6:1), and proper strength balance between hamstrings.

Quadriceps Strain

Classic Presentation

The patient reports feeling a sudden pulling pain in the anterior thigh after attempting to sprint, "missing" a kick, or suddenly stopping.

Cause

Sudden contraction of the quadriceps may result in a simple pull or a full rupture. Some predispositions include tight quadriceps (or not stretching prior to a sport activity), imbalance between the quadriceps of the opposite leg, or a short leg.

Evaluation

Actively extending the knee causes pain. Inability to perform a simple quadriceps isometric contraction with the leg extended indicates moderate to severe damage. A palpable defect or muscle mass on resisted extension indicates possible rupture.

Management

Management includes ice coupled with a neoprene or elastic support wrap. Crutches may be needed for several days, depending on the degree of injury. Stretching should be initiated as early as possible but with caution. Complete ruptures require surgical repair.

Contusions and Myositis Ossificans

Classic Presentation

The most common area is the quadriceps. The patient will report a direct blow to the knee followed by swelling and decreased ability to flex the knee.

Cause

A direct blow causes damage to the underlying muscle with subsequent hematoma formation. When the hematoma is encouraged to remain, myositis ossificans may occur. The contributing factors for myositis ossificans are forcefully stretching after injury, deep massage to the area of injury, and the use of deep heat such as ultrasound.

Evaluation

There is an obvious area of swelling and often discoloration. The patient's active and passive ability to flex the knee is limited. If the injury occurred several weeks before, a painful lump may be palpable, indicating possible myositis ossificans. Radiographs often will demonstrate the degree of maturation of this calcification response.

Management

Application of a tensor bandage with an ice pack in a flexed knee position for several hours (alternating icing for 20 minutes, no ice for 10 to 20 minutes) is helpful in preventing accumulation of blood into the area. With moderate to severe contusions, use of crutches for 2 to 3 days may be helpful. Mild stretching may begin after 2 to 3 days. Treatment decisions regarding myositis ossificans development are made after several weeks, based on the deformity and degree of knee flexion restriction. Surgical excision may then be performed if deemed desirable.

Meralgia Paresthetica

Classic Presentation

The patient complains of numbness or tingling in the lateral thigh.

Cause

Compression of the lateral femoral cutaneous nerve may occur at the inguinal ligament, or slightly below, due to prolonged sitting. The patient is often either overweight or carries keys or other objects in the front pockets.

Evaluation

The symptoms may be made worse with direct pressure on the nerve where it is most superficial, about 1 in inferior to the ASIS. Maneuvers that increase symptoms include passive hip extension or forced hip flexion causing traction and compression, respectively. An area of sensory deficit or hyperesthesia may be found at a lateral patch of skin on the anterolateral thigh.

Management

Treatment and prevention include avoiding prolonged sitting, losing weight if necessary, and avoidance of carrying objects in the pockets. In the acute phase, physical therapy modalities such as interferential techniques may be helpful.

REFERENCES

1. Brand RA, Crowninshield RD. The effect of cane use on hip contraction force. *Clin Orthop*. 1980;147:181–184.
2. Steindler A. *Kinesiology of the Human Body*. Springfield, IL: Charles C Thomas; 1977.
3. Frankel VH, Nordin M. Biomechanics of the hip. In: *Basic Biomechanics of the Musculoskeletal System*. Philadelphia: Lea & Febiger; 1980.
4. Nicholas PJR, Bailey NTJ. The accuracy of measuring leg length difference. *Br Med J*. 1955;29:1247–1248.
5. Beattie P. Validity of derived measurements of leg length difference obtained by use of a tape measure. *Phys Ther*. 1990;70:150–157.
6. Manello DM. Leg length inequality. *J Manipulative Physiol Ther*. 1992;15:576–580.
7. Mondel DL, Garrison SJ, Geiringer SR, et al. Rehabilitation of musculoskeletal and soft tissue disorders. *Arch Phys Med Rehabil*. 1988;69S:130–138.
8. Taylor JAM, Harger BL, Resnick D. Diagnostic imaging of common hip disorders: a pictorial review. *Top Clin Chirop*. 1994;1(2): 8–23.
9. Yochum TR, Rowe LJ. *Essentials of Skeletal Radiology*. 2nd ed. Baltimore: Williams & Wilkins; 1996:714.
10. Cotton DW, Whitehead CL, Vyas S, et al. Are hip fractures caused by falling and breaking or breaking and falling? Photoelastic stress analysis. *Forensic Sci Int*. 1994;65:105–112.
11. DeLee JC. Fractures and dislocations of the hip. In: Rockwood CA Jr, Green DP, eds. *Fractures in Adults*. 2nd ed. Philadelphia: JB Lippincott; 1984:1211–1356.
12. Waters PM, Millis MB. Hip and pelvis injuries in the young athlete. *Clin Sports Med*. 1988;7:513–526.
13. Garden RS. Malreduction and avascular necrosis in subcapital fractures of the femur. *J Bone Joint Surg Br*. 1967;63:183–197.
14. Meaney JE, Carty H. Femoral stress fractures in children. *Skeletal Radiol*. 1992;21:173–176.
15. Resnick D, Niwayana G. *Diagnosis of Bone Disorders*. Philadelphia: WB Saunders; 1995.
16. Putti V. Early treatment of congenital dislocation of the hip. *J Bone Joint Surg Am*. 1929;11:798.
17. Miralles M, Gonzales G, Pulpeiro JR, et al. Sonography of the painful hip in children: 500 consecutive cases. *AJR*. 1989;152:579–582.
18. Stanitski CL. Acute slipped capital femoral epiphysis. *J Am Acad Orthop Surg*. 1994;2:96–106.
19. Kelsey JL, Acheson DM, Keggi KJ. The body build of patients with slipped capital femoral epiphysis. *Am J Dis Child*. 1972;124:276.
20. MacEwen GD, Bunnell WP, Ramsey PL. The hip. In: Lowell WW, Winter RB, eds. *Pediatric Orthopedics*. Philadelphia: JB Lippincott; 1986.
21. Wilson PD, Jacobs B, Schecter L. Slipped capital femoral epiphysis: an end-result study. *J Bone Joint Surg Am*. 1965;47:1128–1145.
22. Barker DJP, Hall AJ. The epidemiology of Perthes disease. *Clin Orthop*. 1986;209:89.

23. Fisher RI. An epidemiologic study of Legg-Perthes disease. *J Bone Joint Surg Am.* 1972;54:769.
24. Pires de Camago F, Maciel de Gidoy R, Tovo R. Angiography in Perthes disease. *Clin Orthop.* 1984;191:216.
25. Turek SL. *Orthopedic Principles and Their Application.* Philadelphia: JB Lippincott; 1984:1109–1268.
26. McAndrew MP, Weinstein SL. A long-term follow-up of Legg-Calve-Perthes disease. *J Bone Joint Surg Am.* 1984;66:860.
27. Swezey R. Pseudo-radiculopathy in subacute trochanteric bursitis of the subgluteus maximus bursa. *Arch Phys Med Rehabil.* 1976;57:387–390.
28. Troycoff RB. "Pseudotrochanteric bursitis": the differential diagnosis of lateral hip pain. *J Rheumatol.* 1992;18:1810–1812.
29. Baum J. Joint pain: it isn't always arthritis. *Postgrad Med.* 1989;85:311–321.
30. Rotini R, Sinozzi C, Ferrari A. Snapping hip: a rare form with internal etiology. *Ital J Orthop Traumatol.* 1991;17:283–288.
31. Swartout R, Compere EL. Ischiogluteal bursitis. *JAMA.* 1974;227:551–552.
32. Haueisen DC. The characterization of transient synovitis of the hip in children. *J Pediatr Orthop.* 1986;6:11.
33. Harris WH. Etiology of osteoarthritis of the hip. *Clin Orthop.* 1988;213:20–38.
34. Palmer E, Henrikson B, McKusick K, et al. Pain as an indicator of bone metastasis. *Acta Radiol.* 1988;24:445–450.
35. Resnick D. *Bone and Joint Imaging.* Philadelphia: WB Saunders; 1989.
36. Gallacher SJ. Paget's disease of bone. *Curr Opin Rheumatol.* 1993;5:351.

CHAPTER 12

Knee Complaints

CONTEXT

Knee complaints are common in an orthopaedic setting.[1] Although there are no available statistics on the frequency of presentation in chiropractic offices, chiropractors often serve a role as a conservative management alternative to orthopaedic consultation. In this context, the chriopractor's approach includes an evaluation of possible spinal or pelvic contributions in addition to local knee dysfunction or pathologic condition. The distinction between referred or radiating pain and local knee problems may be as obvious as a direct radiation of pain from the low back, pelvis, or hip to the knee; however, the biomechanical contribution may not be quite as evident. Inherent in the evaluation process is the need to determine any neurologic connection between a knee complaint that is associated with a low back or pelvic complaint. When knee pain is due to an obvious direct trauma, the evaluation process focuses on a regional evaluation. If, however, the knee pain is local and either insidious or due to an overuse phenomenon, biomechanical evaluation of the lower extremity and lumbopelvic region must be included to determine contributing factors.

The knee may be the site of pain originating from or caused by a variety of sources, including the following:

- referred pain from pain-sensitive structures in the low back, pelvis, and lower extremity (including facet joints, the sacroiliac and hip joints, and trigger points)
- radiating pain from nerve root compression
- peripheral nerve root entrapment (sciatic, peroneal, saphenous, etc.)
- generalized dysfucntion of the lower extremity (femoral anteversion/retroversion, genu varum/valgus/recurvatum, tibial torsion, pronation/supination, etc.)
- local causes of pain
  1. trauma
  2. overuse
  3. other (tumor, aneurysm, infection, etc.)

The knee is frequently injured based in part on its position of exposure to outside trauma. Virtually unprotected from outside forces, the knee is vulnerable to any number of impact injuries, including blows from the outside (valgus forces), dashboard injuries, and direct impact falls. Superficial damage may be readily accessible via palpation and stress testing. Internal damage is more often disguised, yielding only indirect and often delayed clues to the degree of injury. When intraarticular swelling is present, orthopaedic assessment is often delayed or the results of testing minimized because of the positional restrictions imposed on testing and the reactive muscle spasm. The stability provided by joint effusion may delay the appreciation of an unstable knee. The true residual integrity of the knee may take several weeks to become apparent following the resolution of swelling.

Soft tissue injuries are usually the result of either overuse or disuse. Overuse is usually detected through careful questioning regarding activities that require repetitive movement or prolonged or awkward positioning. This may also require an evaluation of the patient performing or acquiring the suspected inciting activity. A suspicion of disuse requires an evaluation of any biomechanical predispositions such as pronation/supination, lower extremity torsion, or patellar tracking abnormalities. If a patient presents with an insidious onset of pain with accompanying swelling, a radiographic and possibly a laboratory search for arthritides, neoplasm, or infection should be instituted. With children it is particularly important to include an evaluation of the hip. The knee is often a site of pain referral with intrinsic hip abnormalities in children.

Some common clinical presentations are

- the athlete with anterior knee pain (patellofemoral arthralgia and/or patellar tracking disorders)
- the elderly patient with a complaint of knee pain and stiffness (osteoarthritis)
- the younger athlete with a complaint of tibial tuberosity pain (Osgood-Schlatter disease)
- the patient with the complaint of instability (chronic anterior cruciate ligament [ACL] damage)

GENERAL STRATEGY

History

Clarify the Chief Complaint

- Determine whether the complaint is one of pain, stiffness, locking, swelling, instability, crepitus, or numbness and tingling.
- Localize the complaint to anterior, posterior, lateral, or medial.

Clarify the Mechanism if Traumatic

- Hyperextension: consider an isolated ACL tear or patellar dislocation.
- Sudden deceleration (stopping or cutting): consider an isolated ACL tear.
- Valgus force (no rotation): consider medial collateral ligament (MCL) tear.
- Valgus force with rotation; foot fixed on the ground: consider multiple tissue damage including ACL, MCL, and menisci.
- Blow to a flexed knee—local damage can include contusion, fat pad irritation, or patellar fracture: consider a posterior cruciate ligament (PCL) tear if significant force is applied.
- Determine the timing, location (intraarticular or extraarticular) and degree of any accompanying swelling.
- Determine whether there was or is locking, instability, or weakness associated with the injury or postinjury.

Determine Whether the Mechanism Might Be One of Overuse or Misuse

- Repetitive flexion and extension in midrange (eg, running): consider iliotibial band (ITB) syndrome or popliteus tendinitis.
- Repetitive jumping or sprinting: consider patellar tendinitis (jumper's knee); in adolescents consider apophyseal injury such as Osgood-Schlatter disease.
- Constant valgus stress applied directly or indirectly: consider chronic MCL strain or pes anserinus tendinitis.
- Constant squatting: consider meniscus injury.

Determine Whether the Patient Has a Current or Past History/Diagnosis of the Knee Complaint or Other Related Disorders

- Determine whether there are any past traumas, surgeries, or diagnoses.
- Determine whether there have been any studies such as radiography or magnetic resonance imaging (MRI) performed on the patient.
- Determine whether there are any associated low back, hip, or lower leg/foot/ankle complaints.

Evaluation

- Based on the history and presentation, perform either a region-specific or a condition-specific examination (eg, examine the lateral knee region versus perform meniscus tests).
- Determine whether radiographic views should be obtained; based on condition, determine whether specific views should be ordered.
- Avoid the initial use of MRI unless severe damage is suspected or a delayed diagnosis will affect future function; if the patient is unresponsive to conservative care, MRI may play a valuable role in determining the degree of damage and the need for surgery.

Management

- Infection, tumor, and fracture require medical referral.
- Nonisolated ACL tears require a surgical consultation.
- Isolated ACL and MCL tears may respond to conservative management, including a period of bracing and cautious rehabilitation; the decision to manage conservatively is based on age, activity level, and functional requirements of the individual and the experience of the doctor.
- Meniscus tears that are the source of unresolving signs and symptoms or are demonstrated as large tears on MRI are best managed with minimal surgical intervention.
- Most other conditions can be managed with a combination of manipulation/mobilization, rehabilitation, and activity modification.

RELEVANT ANATOMY AND BIOMECHANICS

There are three "articulations" at the knee (1) tibiofemoral, (2) tibiofibular, and (3) patellofemoral. The first two are synovial articulations. The patellofemoral "articulation" is a functional joint in which many of the same pathologic conditions found in true joints must be considered. The knee is statically supported by a peripheral system made up of the capsule, its thickenings, and the collateral ligamentous system (Figure 12–1). Internally, stability and control of rotation are provided by the meniscocruciate system. The cruciates, capsule, and collateral ligaments connect the femur to the tibia. The unique orientation of the cruciates allows tension to develop through most ranges of motion. The cruciates are named according to their tibial attachment. The ACL is smaller (about the size of the little finger) and more vulnerable than the PCL (about the size of the thumb). The middle genicular artery runs along the length of the ACL and is often torn with midsubstance tears of the ACL. The MCL is longer than the lateral collateral ligament (LCL) and has a more direct connection to the capsule. The LCL connects the distal femur to the fibular head and is separated from the joint by the tendon of the popliteus muscle. The menisci act to deepen the joint, adding static stability. They aid in shock absorption and help govern rotational movement at the knee. It has been demonstrated that neural reflexes are activated by stimulation or stretching of the knee ligaments.[2] These are important protective reflexes that cause contraction of muscles in response to a perceived stress.

The patella extends the lever arm for the quadriceps muscle, making extension of the knee much more effective. The patella is the largest sesamoid bone in the body, with the quadriceps muscles and their fascial extensions (retinacula) providing stabilizing support (Figure 12–2). The patella is attached to the tibial tuberosity via the patellar tendon. The spaces between the femur and the patella and the tibia and the patella are cushioned by the suprapatellar pouch and the infrapatellar fat pad, respectively. When the patella is not stable because of a high-riding position (patella alta) or underdevelopment of the lateral femoral condyle or posterior surface of the patella, abnormal motion occurs that may damage or irritate ligaments, muscles, and cartilage.

The primary movements of flexion and extension predominate in most functional activities. The other four movement patterns of internal/external rotation and abduction/adduction are less often voluntarily (actively) acquired or needed. Rotation and abduction/adduction at the knee are more often the consequence of voluntary hip movement. Passive abduction/adduction at the knee is not possible with the knee in full extension. As the knee flexes, these movements increase; however, they are still passively acquired. Rotation range of motion increases as the knee flexes because of the increasing mechanical advantage of the hamstrings and other secondary rotators. Flexion is primarily due to the hamstring muscles. Assistance is given by the ITB when the knee is flexed beyond 30° to 40°. Extension of the knee is performed by the quadriceps muscles with some assistance by the ITB through the last 30° to 40°. Extension is a stronger movement pattern than flexion. In the non–weight-bearing knee, internal rotation is due to the popliteus, semimembranosus, and semitendinosus muscles with some minor assistance from the sartorius and gracilis muscles. External rotation is mainly accomplished by the biceps femoris with assistance from the ITB.

Starting with the knee in extension, the bony and soft tissue components involved in stability and movement are sequenced. The knee is locked into external rotation when in full extension due in part to the lateral femoral condyle being shorter than the medial condyle. In full extension, this externally rotated position uncrosses the cruciates to some degree and places slightly more stress on the peripherally placed collateral ligaments. The tendons of the pes anserinus muscles, hamstrings, and ITB act as static stabilizers when the knee is in full extension. As the knee flexes it rotates internally. This rotation crosses the cruciates and takes some tension off the collaterals. Through the first 20° to 30° a rolling motion occurs between the tibia and the femur. Past 30° a sliding (gliding) motion occurs.

Restriction to extension is provided by tension in the posterior capsule and by the cruciates and the bony "lock" of the screw-home mechanism. Flexion is limited by approximation with the calf to the hamstring muscle group. Additional restriction may be provided by tension in the anterior capsule or tightness in the quadriceps. Rotation is limited (and governed) by the cruciates and menisci.

EVALUATION

History

Careful questioning of the patient during the history taking can point to the diagnosis (Table 12–1).

Pain Localization

The following are possible causes of pain based on localization (Figure 12–3, A through D, and Table 12–2):

- anterior
  1. traumatic—patellar fracture, fat pad irritation, contusion of other soft tissue structures, meniscus tear, pes anserinus bursitis (anteromedial)
  2. nontraumatic—extensor disorders (patellar tendinitis or Osgood-Schlatter disease), patellofemoral disorders (patellofemoral arthralgia or chondromalacia)

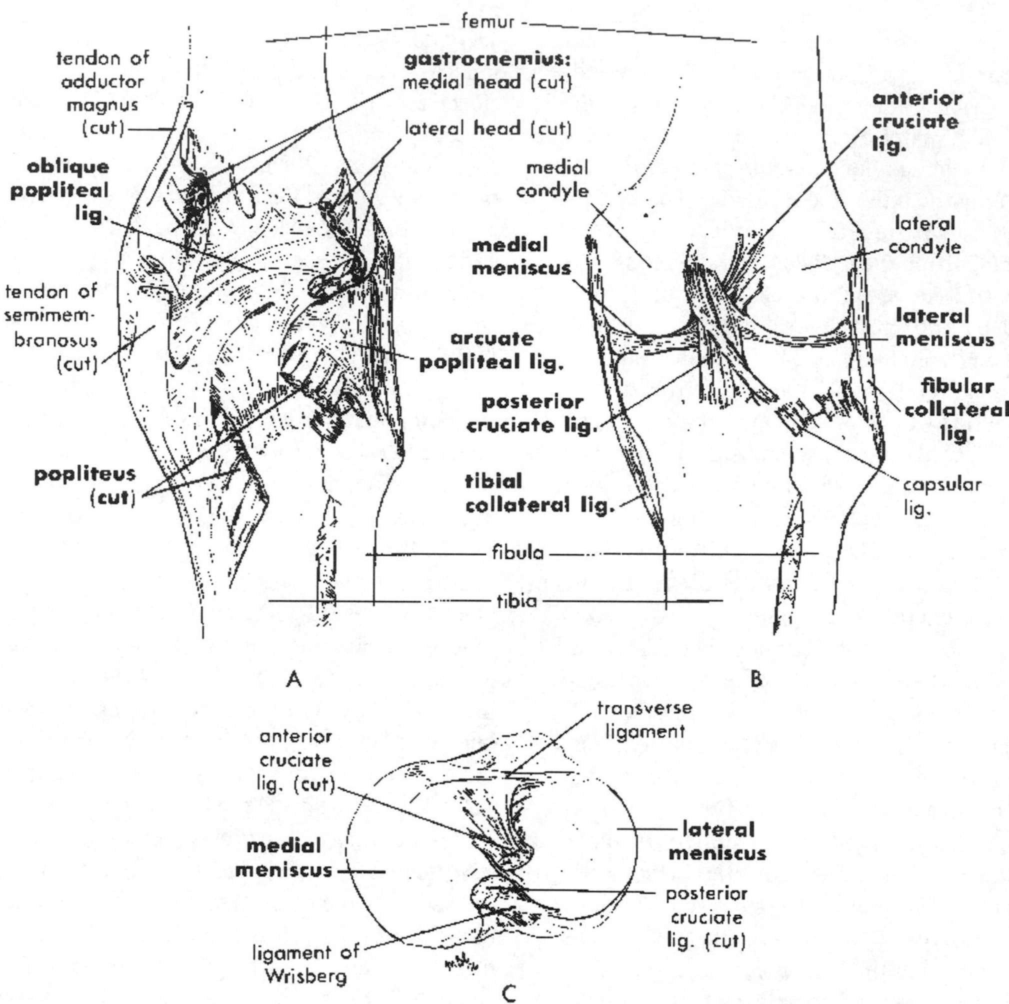

Figure 12–1 Knee joint. **A**, Posterior view showing superficial muscles and ligaments. **B**, Posterior view of deep structures and proximal tibiofibular articulation. **C**, Superior surface of tibia with menisci and cruciate ligaments. *Source:* Reprinted with permission from J.E. Crouch, *Functional Human Anatomy*, 4th ed., p. 168, © 1985, Lea & Febiger.

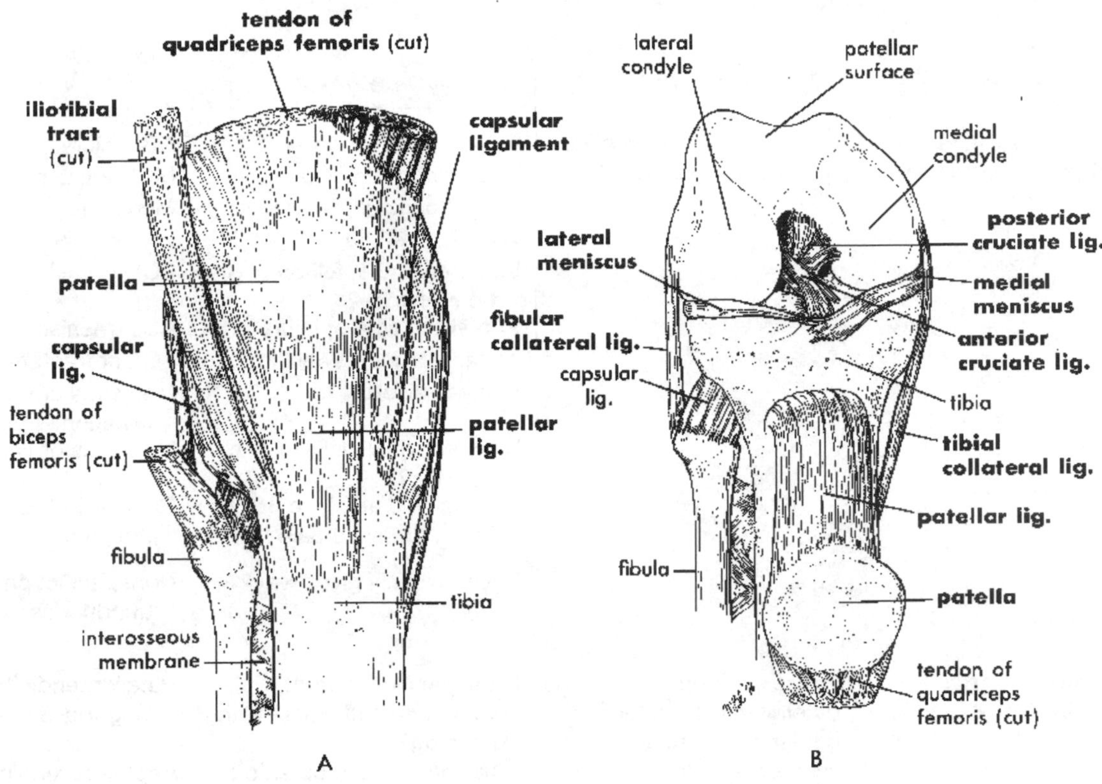

Figure 12–2 Knee joint. **A**, Anterior view showing superficial muscles and ligaments. **B**, Anterior view of deep ligaments. The patella dropped downward by cutting the tendon of the quadriceps femoris. Note the proximal tibiofibular articulation. *Source:* Reprinted with permission from J.E. Crouch, *Functional Human Anatomy*, 4th ed., p. 167, © 1985, Lea & Febiger.

Table 12–1 History Questions for Knee Pain

Primary Question	*What Are You Thinking?*	*Secondary Questions*	*What Are You Thinking?*
Was there trauma? (Did you hurt your knee in an accident or sports injury?)	Fracture, meniscal, cruciate, or collateral ligament tear	Hyperextended knee?	ACL injury
		Knee hit from outside?	MCL, ACL, or meniscus
		Weight on knee, twisted it (with or without contact)?	Meniscus
		With bent knee, fell on or hit front of knee?	PCL
		Pop at the time of injury?	ACL, meniscus, or fracture
		Immediate joint swelling?	ACL or fracture
		Delayed swelling?	Meniscus or other joint irritation
		Knee painfully locks in one position?	Meniscus or flap of ACL
		Knee is held at 20° to 30° flexion to avoid pain?	General indicator of fluid in the joint
		Knee painfully gives way?	Nonspecific; pain inhibits quadriceps
Did the pain begin after a repetitive activity?	Overuse syndromes; patellofemoral, patellar or popliteal tendinitis, ITB syndrome, mild sprain or strain	Is the pain in the front of your knee and worse with jumping?	Patellar tendinitis or Osgood-Schlatter disease
		Is the pain on the outside of your knee and worse with downhill walking?	Popliteus tendinitis or ITB syndrome
		Is the pain on the inside of your knee and worse with breaststroke kick, bicycling, or skiing?	MCL sprain; possible pes anserinus strain
Is the complaint more of stiffness?	Osteoarthritis, posttraumatic adhesions, subluxation	Do you have a past history of trauma or surgery?	Postmeniscectomy likely; trauma, adhesions from poor rehabilitation
		Age and weight of patient?	Osteoarthritis (confirm with weight-bearing films)
Is there a sense of weakness or instability?	Capsular instability, neurologic weakness	Past injury of painful swelling resolving with increasing instability?	ACL insufficiency due to past tear
		Past/current history of low back pain?	Neurologic weakness, especially if low back pain improved
Are there other problems that seemed to occur at or slightly before the beginning of your knee pain?	Arthritides, connective tissue disease, visceral referred pain	Other joints that hurt?	Check for arthritides (gout, rheumatoid arthritis, osteoarthritis, pseudogout, etc.)
		Sore throat several weeks before?	Rheumatic fever (check for murmurs)
		Abdominal pain or chronic diarrhea?	Inflammatory bowel disease arthropathy

- posterior
  1. traumatic—PCL tears, meniscus tears, gastrocnemius/soleus tears (tennis leg), semimembranosus bursitis
  2. nontraumatic—strain of gastrocnemius or soleus, semimembranosus insertion tendinitis, bursitis, Baker's cyst, popliteal thrombus, referral from other disorders
- lateral
  1. traumatic—LCL tear, ACL tear with associated fracture, meniscus tear, fibular head subluxation
  2. nontraumatic—ITB syndrome, polpliteus tendinitis
- medial
  1. traumatic—MCL tear or rupture, medial meniscus tear
  2. nontraumatic—MCL sprain, pes anserinus tendinitis, bursitis

Traumatic and Overuse Injuries

When the patient reports trauma, several clues taken together may indicate a specific damaged structure. The mechanism of injury, coupled with the associated signs or symptoms at the time of injury, may be suggestive of a characteristic pattern for a specific problem. There are four helpful questions:

1. Was there any swelling following the injury? Swelling that occurs immediately or within the first few hours is suggestive of hemarthrosis. Blood in the joint causes irritation and is usually more painful and tense than with synovial swelling. There are two strong possibilities with hemarthrosis: (1) an ACL tear and/or (2) a fracture. If swelling is delayed, taking more than several hours, and is not especially painful (unless the patient moves the knee), synovial swelling is likely. Anything that acts to irritate the synovium can cause increased pain production. Common causes include meniscus tears, ACL flaps, and loose bodies.
2. Did the knee give way at the time of injury? Giving way is a potentially helpful clue when not painful. Painful giving way often represents a reflex inhibition of the quadriceps that occurs with many painful knee conditions. If there was no pain at the time of giving way, however, instability (often ACL-related) is likely the cause.
3. Was there a pop at the time of injury? A pop at the time of injury is indicative of an ACL tear, especially if the pop was accompanied by immediate pain and swelling. Other causes include a dislocated patella and, more rarely, a meniscus tear.
4. Does the knee lock? Locking of the knee can be divided into pseudolocking and true locking. Pseudolocking occurs when the knee is held at approximately 30° of flexion in an attempt to accommodate joint effusion. The knee joint has the largest volume capacity at 30°. Therefore, less tension is developed when intraarticular swelling is present. Although it may be painful to move the knee, it is usually possible to move a few degrees into flexion or extension. True locking occurs with mechanical blockage. The knee is often in flexion and is rigidly, painfully locked in one position. No movement is possible until the knee is unlocked (often with a forced extension attempt). True locking is indicative of a meniscus tear.

The mechanism of injury may be helpful when a contact injury is reported. Outside blows to the knee in a valgus direction are likely to damage medial structures. With the knee flexed, the MCL is most vulnerable. When the knee is in extension, the pes anserinus group is also vulnerable. Rotational injuries with a fixed foot often result in a sequence of damage beginning with a meniscus tear. If combined with an outside valgus force, the MCL, ACL, and meniscus may be damaged (terrible triad/O'Donoghue triad). Hyperextension injuries are often noncontact, yet they may damage the ACL as a result of simultaneous contraction of the quadriceps. ACL damage also may occur with sudden deceleration or cutting maneuvers.

Overuse injuries are most often sports related. Running may predispose the individual to ITB syndrome. If the patient is running or walking downhill, popliteus and ITB syndrome are possible if the patient presents with lateral pain. Pronation is believed to predispose the individual to several conditions, including chronic first-degree MCL tears, patellofemoral tracking problems, ITB syndrome, and popliteus tendinitis. Jumping and sprinting activities will predispose the patient to one of several extensor disorders, including patellar tendinitis and several age-related apophyseal problems including Osgood-Schlatter disease and Sinding-Larsen disease. Pain is felt more at the tibial tuberosity with Osgood-Schlatter disease, more at the patellar tendon with patellar tendinitis, and more at the inferior pole of the patella with Sinding-Larsen disease. If pain is felt going up or down steps, patellofemoral problems such as patellofemoral arthralgia or chondromalacia should be suspected.

Weakness

The complaint of weakness must always be clarified. It is important to determine whether the patient has pain associated with the sense of weakness, or stiffness that might be misinterpreted as weakness. True motor weakness at the knee

Table 12–2 Knee Pain Localization

#	*Structures*	*Overt Trauma*	*Insidious or Overuse*
1	Quadriceps (rectus femoris)	Strain or rupture, contusion	Strain
2	Quadriceps tendon, suprapatellar pouch (deep)	Avulsion of quadriceps tendon, suprapatellar bursitis	Tendinitis, apophysitis in younger individuals
3	Vastus medialis obliquus (VMO) insertion, medial retinaculum	Sprain of medial retinaculum or strain of VMO due to patellar dislocation	Patellar tracking disorder with chronic sprain/strain of medical retinaculum or VMO
4	Patella, patellar bursa	Fracture, dislocation, bursitis	Bipartite patella, chondromalacia patella
5	Medial tibiofemoral joint, meniscus, coronary ligament, medial patellofemoral ligament, medial plica	Fracture, medial meniscus tear, traumatic plica irritation	Sprain of either coronary ligament or patellofemoral ligament, or medial plica syndrome
6	Infrapatellar fat pad	Fat pad irritation	Fat pad irritation
7	Patellar tendon, infrapatellar bursa	Bursitis	Patellar tendinitis
8	Medial proximal tibia, pes anserinus insertion	Fracture, pes anserinus bursitis	Pes anserinus bursitia
9	Tibial tuberosity, patellar tendon insertion	Fracture, avulsion fracture	Osgood-Schlatter disease in youngsters; patellar insertional tendinitis in adults
10	Tibialis anterior, extensor tendons	Contusion	Anterior shin splints, extensor strain
11	Tibia	Fracture	Stress fracture
12	MCL, medial meniscus	Medial collateral sprain or rupture, medial meniscus tear	Mild MCL sprain, osteoarthritis
13	ITB	Contusion	ITB syndrome
14	Vastus lateralis, lateral retinaculum	Contusion	Vastus lateralis strain, lateral retinaculum sprain or fibrosis
15	Lateral tibiofemoral joint, lateral meniscus	Meniscus tear, fracture	Meniscus tear, capsular sprain
16	Fibular head, LCL insertion	Subluxation, dislocation, LCL sprain	Subluxation
17	Insertion of biceps femoris onto fibular head, peroneal nerve	Direct trauma to peroneal nerve	Biceps femoris insertional tendinitis, peroneal nerve entrapment
18	Lateral meniscus, popliteus tendon, lateral gastrocnemius	Lateral meniscus tear	Popliteus tendinitis, lateral gastrocnemius strain, lateral meniscus tear
19	Semimebranosus insertion, medial meniscus, semimebranosus bursa	Medial meniscus tear	Bursitis, insertional tendinitis, medial meniscus tear
20	Medial head of gastrocnemius	Tennis leg	Strain of medial gastrocnemius

Note: See Figure 12–3 for localization of numbered areas.

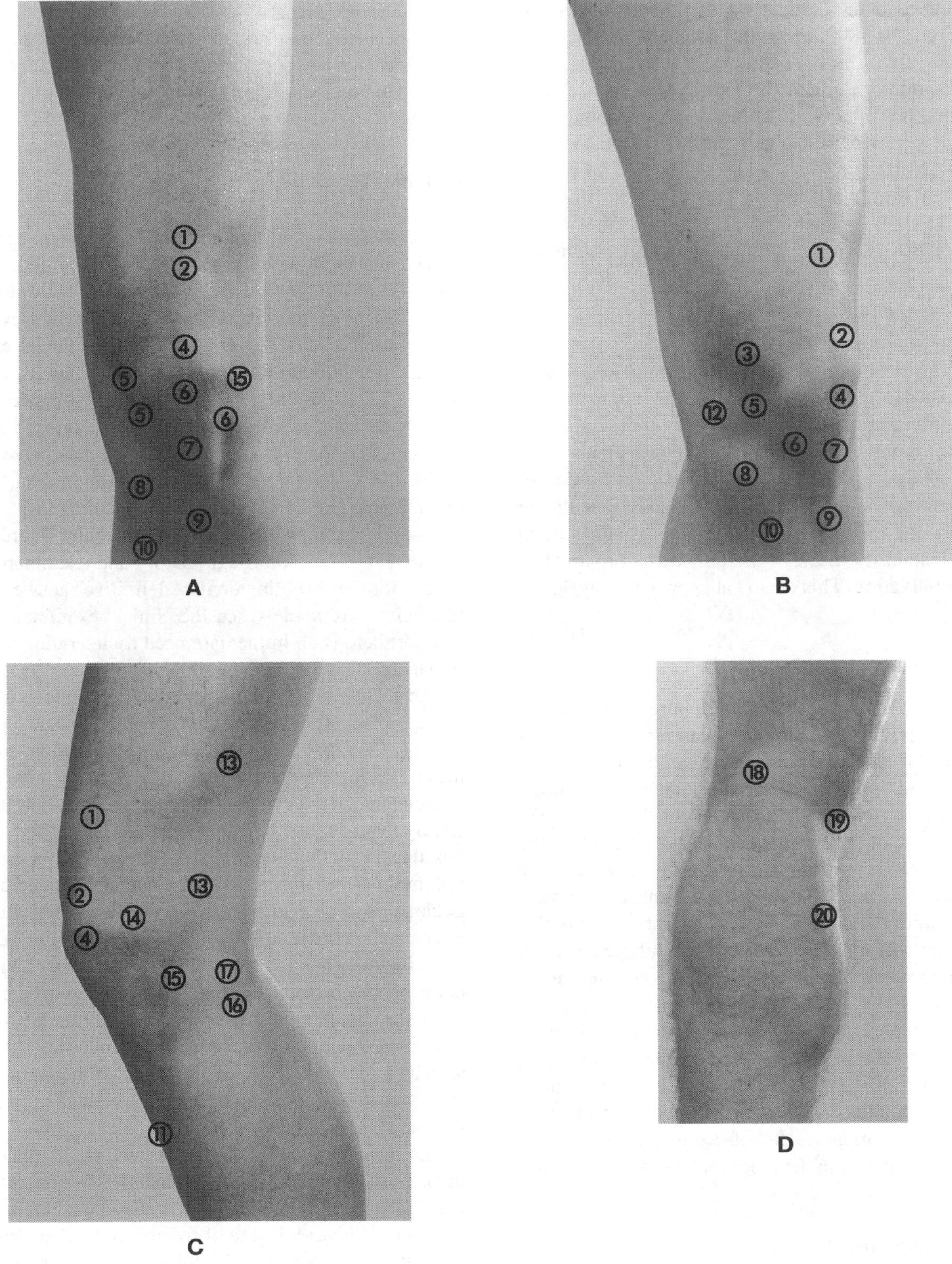

Figure 12–3 **A**, Anterior knee. **B**, Medial anterior knee. **C**, Lateral knee. **D**, Posterior knee. *Note:* See Table 12–2 for explanation of numbers.

is unusual unless found bilaterally with central nervous system/spinal cord disorders. Unilateral weakness may occur in diabetics with amyotrophy. Most lumbar disc lesions occur at the lower lumbar segments affecting more distal movement patterns; however, with L5 nerve root lesions, some patients have weakness of the hamstrings. When the knee is stiff from osteoarthritis (OA) or the patient is very inflexible, the patient must work against this restriction. This may be perceived as weakness. When pain accompanies weakness, testing should focus on contractile structures about the knee.

Instability

Instability is most often due to ACL injury. Meniscus injuries may also cause a giving way. The degree of instability may be a helpful guide. ACL instability is often nonpainful and felt with rotational movement patterns. Patients often report having to walk a particular way to lock the knee prior to placing weight on it. Instability with meniscus tears is more often painful due to mechanical interference with normal movement. Instability may also be felt with a proximal tibiofibular subluxation. This occurs at approximately 30° of flexion.

Restricted Motion

Restricted motion may be indicative of intraarticular swelling, joint mice, joint contracture, or tight musculature. Contractile causes of restricted motion are often uniplanar (ie, flexion/extension). Joint effusion causes a restricted pattern whereby full extension is not possible and flexion beyond 90° is often difficult. The historical distinction is often the difference between acute traumatic onset, acute nontraumatic onset, and insidious onset. Acute traumatic onset will almost always cause joint effusion. Acute nontraumatic onset is also likely to be joint effusion but effusion due to different causes, such as inflammatory arthritides or infection. Chronic or insidious onset is more likely due to soft tissue contracture, especially when associated with a history of immobilization or lack of activity. If the patient reports stiffness after sitting for long periods of time that resolves with 15 to 30 minutes of activity, two common possibilities are patellofemoral problems and OA. Patellofemoral disorders are more common in the younger patient, OA in the older (unless there is a previous history of trauma).

Superficial Complaints

Superficial complaints include numbness and tingling and localized swellings. Numbness and tingling local to the medial knee is often due to saphenous nerve irritation. If extending into a longer area of numbness, a nerve root lesion is possible. Localized swellings are caused by inflamed bursae, ganglions, meniscal cysts, or lipomas. When deformity is present at the joint line, especially in an older patient, OA is the likely cause. Localized swelling at the tibial tuberosity in an adolescent is highly indicative of Osgood-Schlatter disease.

Examination

The physical examination may be restricted and findings obscured by swelling or decreased range of motion. This may lead to frustration on the part of the chiropractor or the patient, leading to the desire for more expedient evaluation tools. The important contribution of the clinical examination is often undermined by the premature use of more expensive technologies such as magnetic resonance imaging (MRI) and arthrography. A recent study indicated that with traumatic knee pain, the correct diagnosis was arrived at 83% of the time when the history, clinical examination, and routine radiographs were used to make the diagnosis.[3] The diagnoses were later confirmed by arthroscopy. Therefore, focus should be on a thorough history and examination prior to resorting to or relying on the "definitive" answer of MRI. Exceptions are made when the clinical examination is not clear or there is an immediate need to determine the extent of damage.

The acute injury evaluation on the field follows a sequential approach. The first step is a search for neurologic and vascular integrity through palpation, observation, and active movement testing distal to the knee. If that is intact and no obvious fracture is evident, the next step in the evaluation is testing for collateral ligament damage. This is performed, if possible, in full extension first. If integrity of the collaterals is demonstrated, the cruciates are next challenged using the Lachman's test (or an anterior drawer test if the patient cannot extend the knee to 10° to 20° of flexion). Further evaluation includes meniscus testing and testing of the integrity of the patellar restraint system. If the athlete can bear weight, he or she should be tested sequentially through two-legged balance and squatting movements to single-legged balance with an attempt at 20° to 30° of squat. If the patient passes this evaluation, more complex skills, such as running, then stopping, are evaluated.

The in-office evaluation of the knee is first begun with palpation for specific sites of tenderness in an attempt to localize, primarily, superficial tissue. This is directed by whether the history is one of trauma or overuse. With traumatic injury, palpation of the collateral ligaments at the joint line often will indicate tenderness with sprains. Palpation of the joint line anteriorly, medially, and posteromedially may reveal tenderness with meniscus tears. In addition, anterior joint line tenderness at the medial joint line may indicate damage to the coronary ligament (capsular ligament at the joint). Tenderness on either side of the patella may indicate retinacular tearing. Tenderness on either side of the patellar tendon with the knee flexed is a strong indicator of fat pad irritation. Palpation is aided by placing the patient's knee in the Hardy or figure-four position with the involved side ankle resting on the well leg in a seated position. This position opens up the joint space and places tension on the collateral ligaments, making them more accessible.

When the history indicates no obvious trauma, palpation may focus on the insertion sites for various muscle/tendon possibilities.

- Tenderness at the lateral epicondyle of the femur or anterolateral tibia is found with ITB syndrome.
- Tenderness behind the LCL or in front of the femoral insertion of the LCL is indicative of popliteus tendinitis.
- Tenderness at the insertion of the vastus medialis obliquus (VMO) indicates a tracking abnormality; this may also be evident at the adductor tubercle.
- Tenderness at the posterior knee superior to the joint line with the knee bent may be found with gastrocnemius strain; below the joint line, with soleus strain.

The strategy for superficial soft tissue damage (in addition to palpation) is to compress, stretch, or contract the tissue. Testing for less accessible, deep intraarticular damage requires indirect tests such as compression testing for the menisci and stability testing for the cruciates. Although there are numerous variations of standardized testing, the primary tests are addressed below.

Anterior Cruciate

ACL testing is based on challenging the posterior to anterior stability of the tibia. The position of testing varies. If an anterior pull on the tibia is applied at 10° to 20° of knee flexion it is called the Lachman's test (Figure 12–4); at 90° it is called the anterior drawer test (Figure 12–5). The difference is in the sensitivity. For acute injuries, the Lachman's test is more sensitive.[4] This is primarily due to the position of slight flexion that places the hamstrings at a disadvantage. If the hamstrings are in spasm, the direct line of pull with the knee at 90° is an additional force to pull against with the anterior drawer test. Rotational testing refers to testing for damage to the ACL and other structures. When medial or lateral stabilizing structures are damaged along with the ACL, a rotational instability is created. The first evaluation for this is a modification of the anterior drawer test. By pulling forward with the knee in internal and then external rotation, the lateral and medial supporting structures, respectively, are tested (Slocum's test).

The prototype rotational test is referred to as the pivot shift test (Figure 12–6). This test takes advantage of the passive tension of the ITB.[5] This tension will pull the tibia forward into medial subluxation when an ACL tear is present along with medial or lateral damage. As the knee approaches 30° to 40° of flexion, the ITB crosses the axis of rotation (the lateral epicondyle) and now acts as a flexor. This will passively pull the tibia back into neutral. Although there are many variations of this test, this is the basic mechanism by which most of these tests function.

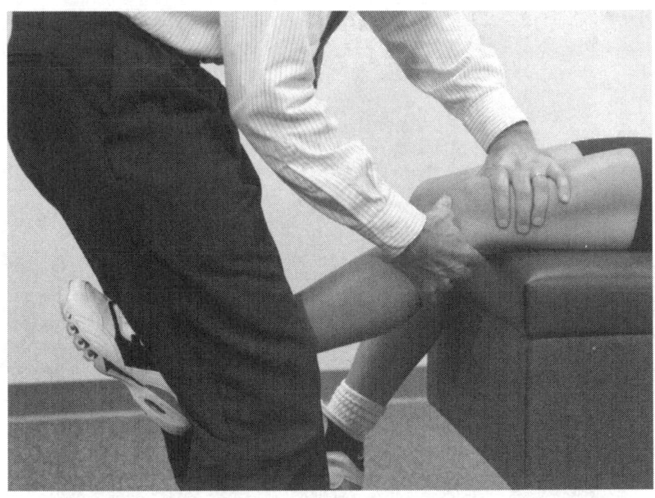

Figure 12–4 Lachman's test. To test for anterior stability, the knee is flexed about 10° to 20°. The femur is stabilized while the examiner pulls forward on the tibia.

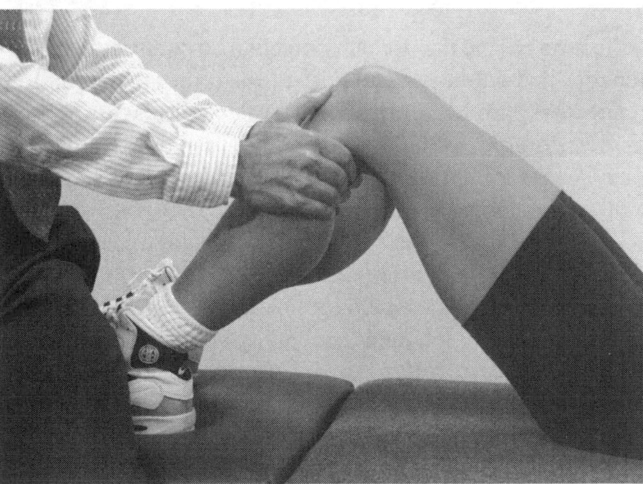

Figure 12–5 Anterior drawer test. The patient's hip is flexed to 45° and the knee is flexed to 90°. The examiner stabilizes the foot while pulling forward on the tibia. The posterior drawer test uses the same position but pushes the tibia back.

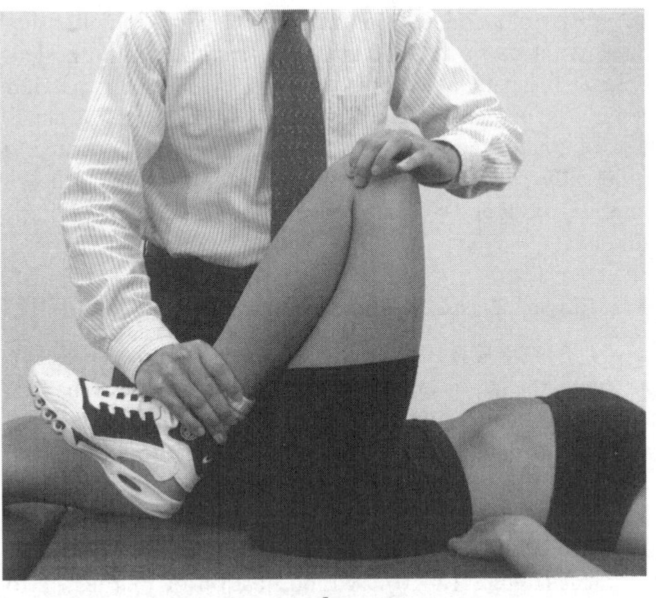

A

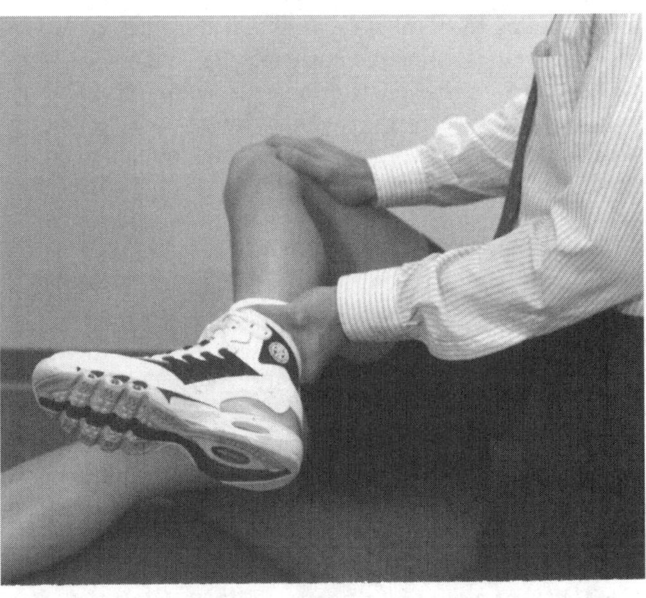

B

Figure 12–7 McMurray's test for the meniscus. **A**, The first position is full flexion. While the examiner internally and externally rotates the knee, the joint line is palpated for clicking or popping. **B**, If the first position is unrevealing, the knee is extended while applying combinations of varus, valgus, internal rotation, and external rotation.

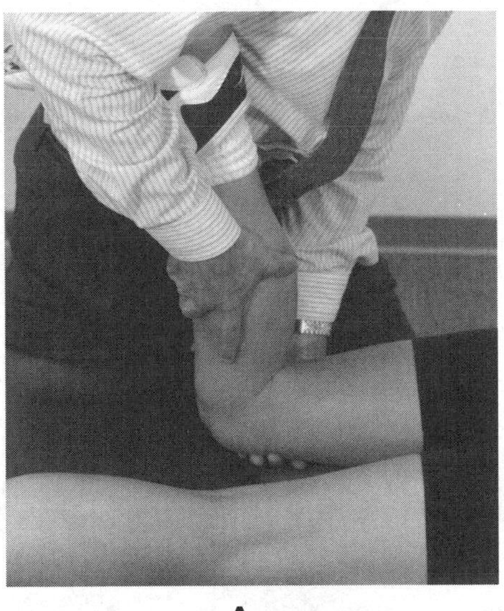

A

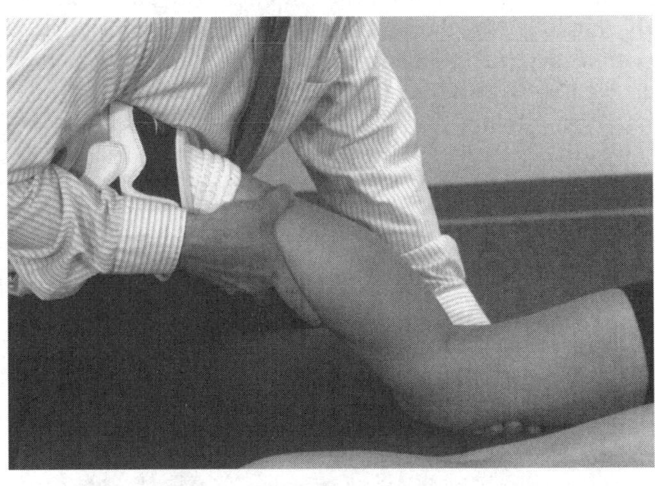

B

Figure 12–8 Apley's compression test for the meniscus. **A**, The examiner directs an axial force into the knee starting with the knee in 90° of flexion while internally and externally rotating the knee. **B**, This procedure may be continued into extension testing for the anterior portion of the meniscus.

angle, leading to strain at the patella and medial knee. Version of the hip is discussed in Chapter 11. Internal or external tibial torsion is often determined by simple observation. With the patient seated, the examiner can obtain an axial view of the knee and foot (Figure 12–9). If the foot is turned out more than 20°, external tibial torsion is likely; if internally rotated more than 15°, internal tibial torsion is likely.

One final strategy is to palpate and test for the presence of a plica, which might contribute to tracking abnormalities. There are various approaches, yet the basic idea is to press the patella from lateral to medial while the leg is either actively or passively extended. Stuttering or snapping suggests the presence of plica.

The functional portion of the knee exam focuses on tightness of lateral structures with emphasis on the ITB, and weakness of medial structures with focus on the VMO. The ITB tests are described below. The primary test is the modified Ober's test, which is designed to evaluate ITB or hip abductor tightness. VMO testing is nonspecific, yet an evaluation of tracking through the last 20° may identify a functionally "weak" VMO. This is an indirect finding indicated by stuttering of extension or inability to extend while keeping the knee in the same position (without pressing down or lifting up at the knee).

Extensor Disorders

Extensor disorders refer to damage or irritation to the quadriceps muscle and its attachment points at the patella and the patellar tendon and its attachment into the tibial tuberosity. By simply having the patient extend the knee from a flexed position against the examiner's resistance, pain is often produced at the site of the pathologic process. Pain at the tibial tuberosity in an adolescent indicates Osgood-Schlatter disease, whereas in an adult, patellar tendinitis is suggested. Pain at the patellar tendon is strong evidence for patellar tendinitis; on occasion, however, a deep infrapatellar bursitis or fat pad syndrome may cause pain. Pain at the inferior pole of the patella in an adolescent is suggestive of a process similar to Osgood-Schlatter disease, called Sinding-Larsen disease.

Specific Soft Tissue or Muscle/Tendon Tests

- ITB: The ITB is tested in two ways: (1) direct pressure over the lateral epicondyle and (2) stretching of the ITB in an attempt to determine predisposition. Direct pressure over the lateral epicondyle is performed with the knee flexed to 30° to 40° and is referred to as Noble's test. Stretching of the ITB is accomplished through passive adduction of the hip. This is referred to as Ober's test (Figure 12–10). A modification of this test is to stretch the hip with the knee extended over the side of the table. Although this maneuver may not reproduce the pain, it often indicates tightness when the patella fails to lower below the level of the top of the examination table.
- Popliteus: The popliteus is evaluated through resisted internal rotation. This may increase the lateral knee pain found with popliteus tendinitis. Palpation points of tenderness are found in front of the LCL on the distal femur or directly behind the LCL. Another approach is to have the patient bear all the body weight onto the affected side and bend the knee to 30°. If the femur is internally rotated, pain may increase with popliteus tendinitis.

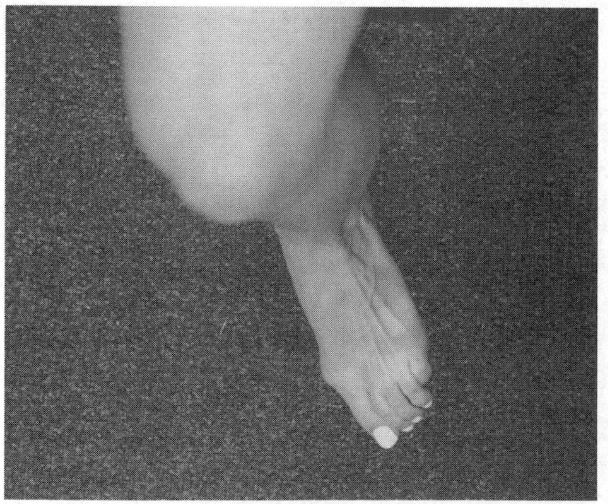

Figure 12–9 Skyline view of external torsion of the tibia.

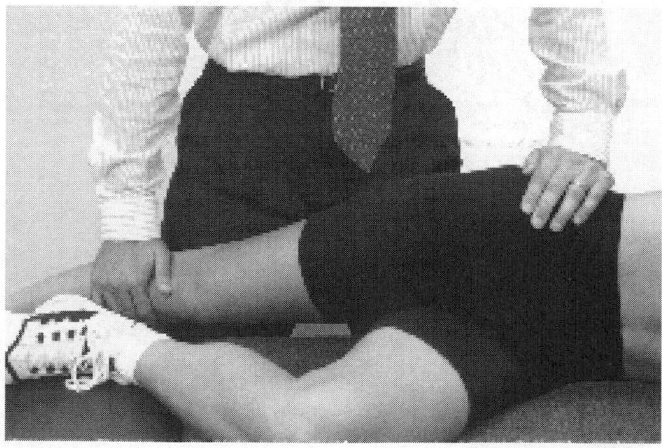

Figure 12–10 Modified Ober's test. The modified Ober's test involves extending the leg off the back of the table while stabilizing the ilium in an attempt to stretch the ITB and hip abductors.

- Semimembranosus: The semimembranosus may be involved in an insertional tendinitis. There is tenderness at the posterior attachment of the muscle or resisted knee flexion may increase pain at the posterior medial knee.
- Biceps femoris: Pain at the posterior fibular head may be increased with resisted knee flexion.

Evaluation for Stiffness

When there is restricted range of motion (ROM) at the knee, an attempt at distinguishing between soft tissue involvement and an internal pathologic process is necessary. When there is tightness in the capsule, gentle stretching of the knee in the direction of restriction will usually increase the range without a significant increase in pain. Mild contraction of an antagonist muscle followed by the restricted movement pattern will usually increase ROM when that muscle is the cause. When neither approach helps or if the attempts at increased movement are met with pain, an intraarticular process is most likely.

Radiographs/Special Studies

Standard radiographs of the knee include an anterior to posterior (AP) non–weight-bearing view and a lateral non–weight-bearing view with the knee flexed to 30°. Evaluation of the osteoarthritic knee is via a posterior to anterior (PA) view that is taken bearing weight with the knees bent to 45° and a 10° caudal tube tilt. When osteochondritis dissecans is suspected, a tunnel view is required. Patellofemoral evaluation may be performed via several tangential views. The standard sunrise view provides little information unless OA of the patella or fracture is being evaluated. Other views such as the Merchant and Lauren view are variations on this theme that are used to evaluate tracking abnormalities. Two measurements, the congruence angle and the patellar tilt, are respective lines of mensuration used with these views. MRI of the knee should be reserved for suspicion of major ACL or meniscal pathology or when the patient is unresponsive to conservative care. The ACL is best visualized on sagittal views with the knee held in external rotation of 15°. The meniscus is best visualized on the sagittal view.

MANAGEMENT

- Patients with fracture, tumor, or infection should be referred for medical management.
- Patients with isolated ACL tears with resolved swelling may be managed conservatively if they are not hard-core or professional athletes. This includes hamstring training, proprioceptive neuromuscular facilitation (PNF) training, and bracing.
- Patients with small, peripheral meniscus tears or those that are demonstrated via MRI to be vertical, stable tears may be managed conservatively first. If nonresponsive, it is important to recommend repair; when possible without meniscectomy.
- All soft tissue disorders, such as tracking disorders, first- and second-degree muscle/tendon problems, and first- and second-degree ligament disorders, can be managed conservatively. Isolated rupture of the MCL may be managed conservatively with casting and rehabilitation by experienced doctors; comanagement is recommended for those with less experience.
- When restrictions to accessory movement are found, short-arc, quick-impulse adjusting should be attempted with the knee in a distracted position. If not distracted, the knee should not be adjusted into or in full extension.

A general exercise approach begins with isometric setting exercises (Table 12–3 and Table 12–4). These are performed both in full extension (if possible) and at 20° to 30°. In this minimally flexed position, the patient pushes the heel into the ground or table to achieve a cocontraction of the hamstrings and quadriceps. When the knee is prepared with a facilitation phase of isometrics, progression to isotonics within the pain-free range is then begun, starting with a weight that allows pain-free performance of three sets of 10 repetitions. Increases in weight are dictated by the progressive resistance exercise (PRE) or daily adjustable progressive resistance exercise (DAPRE) protocols (Table 11–5). When patellofemoral problems are found, terminal extension exercises through the last 20° may be helpful. If there is instability in the knee, however, open-chain knee extension exercises should be avoided and substituted with closed-chain exercises such as partial squats or leg presses.

When using a bicycle for rehabilitation it is important to keep the seat height at a level that prevents full knee extension if there is underlying ACL insufficiency (Table 12–5). For patellofemoral problems, avoid a low-seat position that adds compressive forces to the patella. Pool or aquatic exercise is a useful approach for patients with OA of the knee, progressing to bicycle riding and finally full weight-bearing exercise.

Stretching of the hamstrings, quadriceps, gastrocnemius, and ITB (and attachments) is important to maintaining proper flexibility at the knee. This is particularly important for patellofemoral tracking problems.

Bracing is used for three purposes: (1) for those patients with ACL-deficient knees (functional brace), (2) those in need of support during rehabilitative training, and (3) prophylactic bracing used to protect against further injury. Functional braces are quite expensive. They represent a variety of

Table 12–3 General Knee Rehabilitation*

Type	*Muscles*	*Sets*	*Repetitions*	*Contractions*	*Rest Period*
Quad setting (isometrics)	Quadriceps/hamstrings	1 or 2	10–12	8 seconds	3–5 seconds
Straight leg raises *Supine* (with setting)	Quadriceps/psoas Vastus medialis Biceps femoris	2 or 3	10–12	3–5 seconds	3–5 seconds
Side-lying (abduction)	Gluteus medius Peroneals				
Side-lying (adduction)	Adductors				
Prone	Gluteals/spinal extensors				
Stretching (use PNF hold-relax approach)	Gastrocnemius/soleus Hamstrings Tensor fasciae latae Quadriceps Adductors	5	10–20	8–10 seconds	5 seconds

*Initial phase, performed three times daily. A rest period of 1 to 3 minutes between sets is recommended.

Source: Reprinted with permission from T. Souza, The Knee, in *Conservative Management of Sports Injuries*, R. Hazel, ed., p. 410, © 1994, Williams & Wilkins.

custom-fitted supports that provide a block to full knee extension and various hinge supports for both protection from further injury and control of rotational movement. Examples include the CTi and Townsend.[9] These are lighter than the prototype Lenox-Hill brace. Prophylactic bracing provides metal bars to prevent valgus or varus forces from causing further damage. Examples include the Anderson Knee Stabler and McDavid Knee Guard. Used with sporting activities, these braces may help or ironically may increase the injury rate, possibly due to an early fatigue of the involved leg or prestressing of the knee due to poor fitting.[10,11]

Rehabilitative support may be provided by taping or brace support. Patellofemoral tracking problems are in need of patellar stability and tracking control. Various braces with patella holes and strapping support or taping involving a strapping approach (McConnell taping) are used.[12] Braces for patients with Osgood-Schlatter disease incorporate a reverse horseshoe design to provide a restraint to superior pull on the tibial tuberosity. Many of these devices probably function more from a proprioceptive mechanism than from the support they are purported to provide.[13]

Algorithms

Algorithms for traumatic knee pain and nontraumatic knee complaint are presented in Figures 12–11 and 12–12.

Table 12–4 General Knee Exercise Program

Exercise/Stretch	*Activity*	*Amount*
	Beginning Phase—Begin When Patient Has 90% ROM; No Joint Irritation	
Stretch	PNF stretch for hamstrings, ITB, and gastrocnemius	3–5 sets; 10–20 reps
Isometrics	Performed every 20°	1–2 sets; 10–20 reps
Straight leg raise with weights	Supine, prone, and side-lying (5–10 lb)	2–3 sets; 10–20 reps
Functional work	Shallow knee bends, lunges, and step-downs	2–3 sets; 10–12 reps
Isotonic exercise (with elastic tubing)	All knee motions	Base on PRE or DAPRE approach
Aerobic exercise	Well-leg bicycling and rowing, upper body work	30 minutes; three times weekly at target heart rate
	Intermediate Phase—Begin When Patient Has 75% Strength and Endurance of Well Leg. Continue the stretch, functional work, and aerobic exercise and add the following:	
Isotonics	Knee and hip work (emphasize eccentrics)	Base on PRE or DAPRE approach
Sport cord training	1/3 knee bends, leg presses, and forward-backward run	Average of 3 sets, 20 reps
PNF diagonals	D1 and D2 hip flexion/extension first; knee straight, progressing to same patterns incorporating knee flexion/extension	Several sets to fatigue
Proprioceptive work	Wobble or balance boards using both legs, progressing to one-legged balance if possible	Average of 5 sets; 3–5 minutes
	Advanced Phase—Begin When Patient Has 90% Strength and Endurance of Well Leg. Continue stretch and proprioceptive work; continue above isotonic work if isokinetic machines are not available.	
Isokinetics	Knee flexion/extension patterns	10–20 reps at multiple speeds (emphasize faster speeds to decrease load)
PNF sport or activity specific	Patterns imitate patient's sport patterns	Several sets to fatigue
Agility drills	Figure-eights, cutting maneuvers, cariocas, rope jumping, side-to-side jumping, sliders	5–10 sets for total of 45 minutes
Plyometrics	Progress from two-legged to one-legged jumping; progress from straight-line to side-to-side jumping	Several sets to fatigue

Source: Reprinted with permission from T. Souza, The Knee, in *Conservative Management of Sports Injuries,* R. Hazel, ed., p. 410, © 1994, Williams & Wilkins.

Table 12–5 Exercise Program for Specific Conditions: Specific Emphasis on Modifications to the General Program

Condition	*Emphasize*	*Avoidance/Contraindication*
ITB syndrome	ITB stretching	Initially, downhill running Initially, side-posture adjusting (same side)
Patellofemoral arthralgia and chondromalacia	VMO strengthening Vastus lateralis and ITB stretching Orthotics (if pronation found) Bracing or taping initially to allow pain-free exercise	Initially, knee extension between 20° and 90° Low-seat position on bicycle
Meniscus tears	General rehabilitation	Full flexion (full squat) positions Full extension with rotation
ACL tears	Hamstring training Specific focus on vastus lateralis, biceps femoris, and tibialis anterior muscles Functional bracing Proprioceptive training PNF diagonal flexion patterns	Isometric (open-chain) exercise against resistance at 20° Isotonic exercise (open-chain) from 20° to 70° Leg extensions with heavy weight
PCL tears	Quadriceps training PNF knee extension patterns	Open-chain hamstring exercises
MCL tears	Strengthening of both abductors and adductors Strengthening of internal rotators Hinged-knee support for 1–3 weeks	Resisted knee extension from 45° to full extension initially
Patellar tendinitis	Eccentric training of quads Patellar strap or taping may have limited usefulness initially	Initially avoid jumping activities Initially avoid high-weight leg extensions
Osgood-Schlatter disease	Stretching of quadriceps, hamstrings, and gastrocnemius Bracing	Jumping and running activities should be decreased to decrease pain

Figure 12–11

TRAUMATIC KNEE PAIN—ALGORITHM.

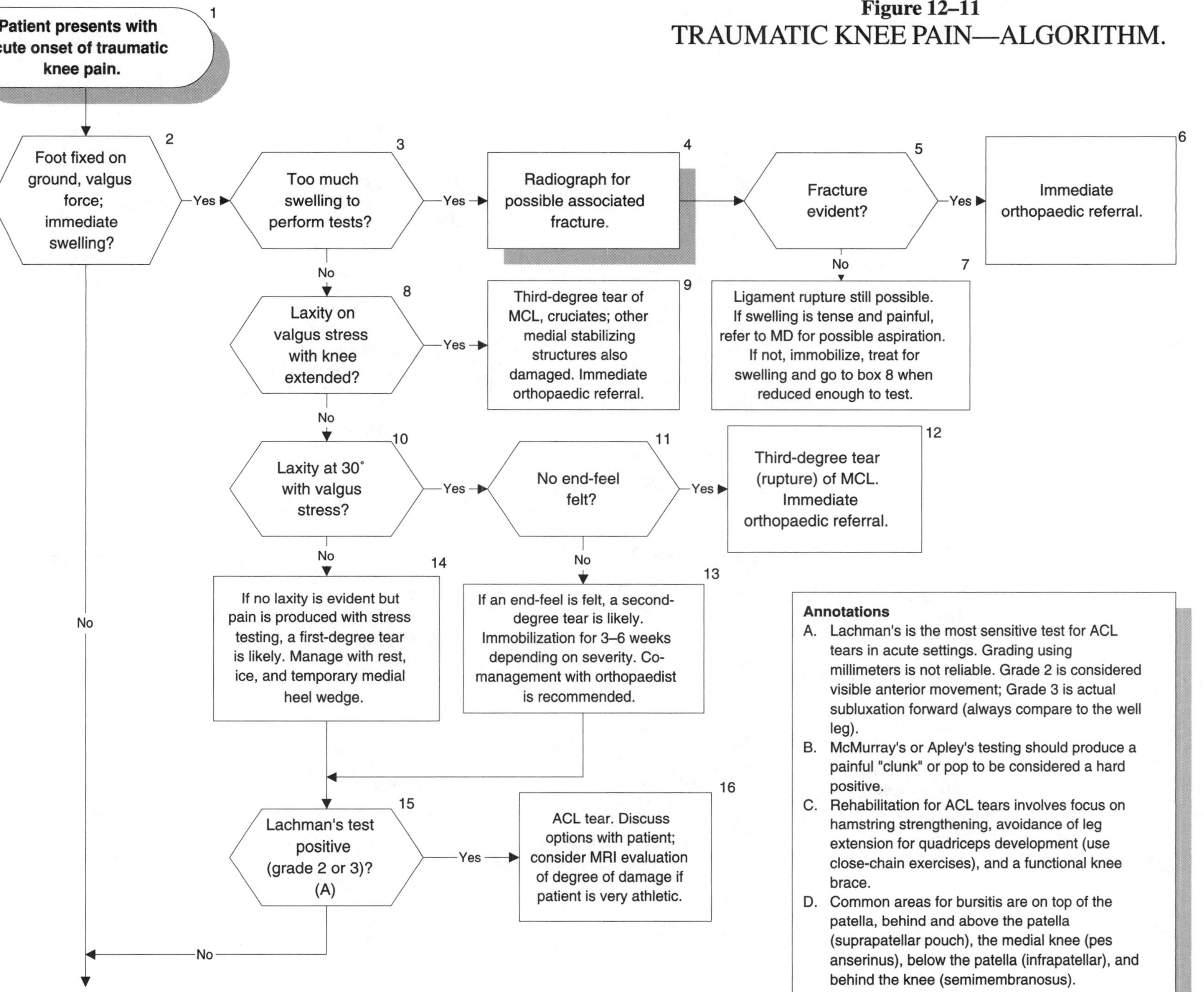

1 Patient presents with acute onset of traumatic knee pain.
2 Foot fixed on ground, valgus force; immediate swelling?
Yes
No
3 Too much swelling to perform tests?
Yes
No
4 Radiograph for possible associated fracture.
5 Fracture evident?
Yes
No
6 Immediate orthopaedic referral.
7 Ligament rupture still possible. If swelling is tense and painful, refer to MD for possible aspiration. If not, immobilize, treat for swelling and go to box 8 when reduced enough to test.
8 Laxity on valgus stress with knee extended?
Yes
No
9 Third-degree tear of MCL, cruciates; other medial stabilizing structures also damaged. Immediate orthopaedic referral.
10 Laxity at 30° with valgus stress?
Yes
No
11 No end-feel felt?
Yes
No
12 Third-degree tear (rupture) of MCL. Immediate orthopaedic referral.
13 If an end-feel is felt, a second-degree tear is likely. Immobilization for 3–6 weeks depending on severity. Co-management with orthopaedist is recommended.
14 If no laxity is evident but pain is produced with stress testing, a first-degree tear is likely. Manage with rest, ice, and temporary medial heel wedge.
15 Lachman's test positive (grade 2 or 3)? (A)
Yes
No
16 ACL tear. Discuss options with patient; consider MRI evaluation of degree of damage if patient is very athletic.
Annotations
A. Lachman's is the most sensitive test for ACL tears in acute settings. Grading using millimeters is not reliable. Grade 2 is considered visible anterior movement; Grade 3 is actual subluxation forward (always compare to the well leg).
B. McMurray's or Apley's testing should produce a painful "clunk" or pop to be considered a hard positive.
C. Rehabilitation for ACL tears involves focus on hamstring strengthening, avoidance of leg extension for quadriceps development (use close-chain exercises), and a functional knee brace.
D. Common areas for bursitis are on top of the patella, behind and above the patella (suprapatellar pouch), the medial knee (pes anserinus), below the patella (infrapatellar), and behind the knee (semimembranosus).

continues

Figure 12–11 continued

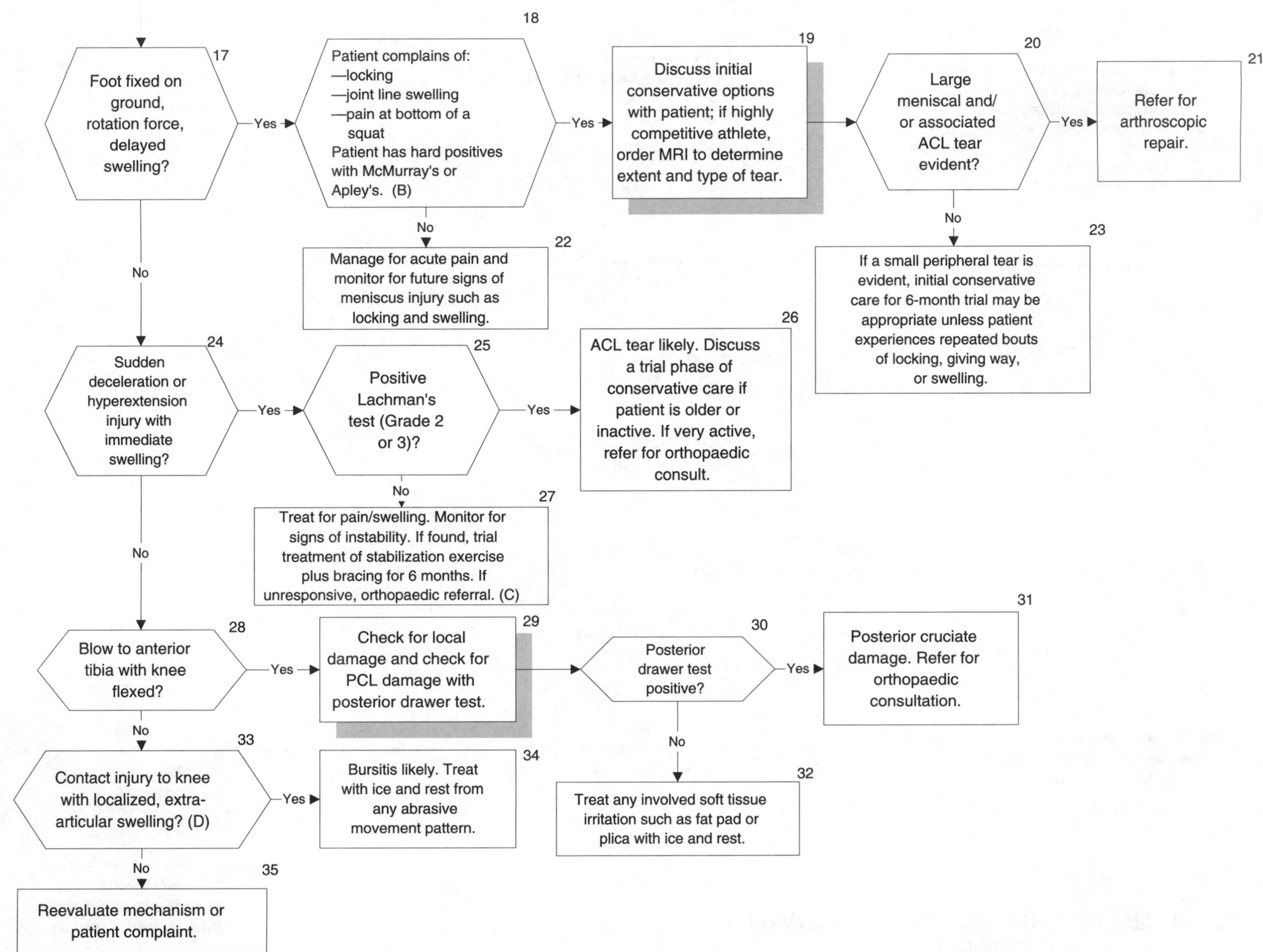

Figure 12–12

NONTRAUMATIC KNEE COMPLAINT—ALGORITHM.

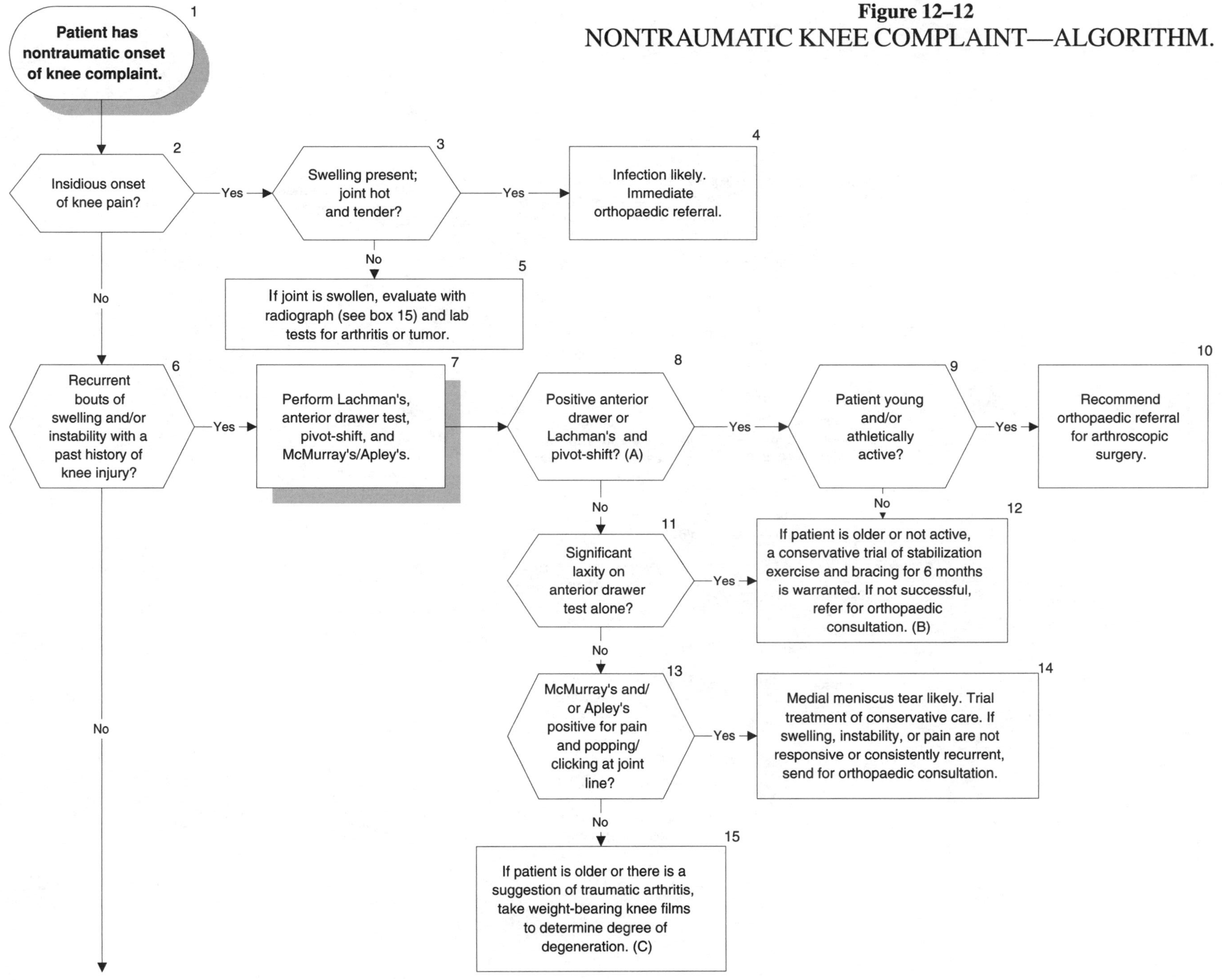

continues

Figure 12–12 continued

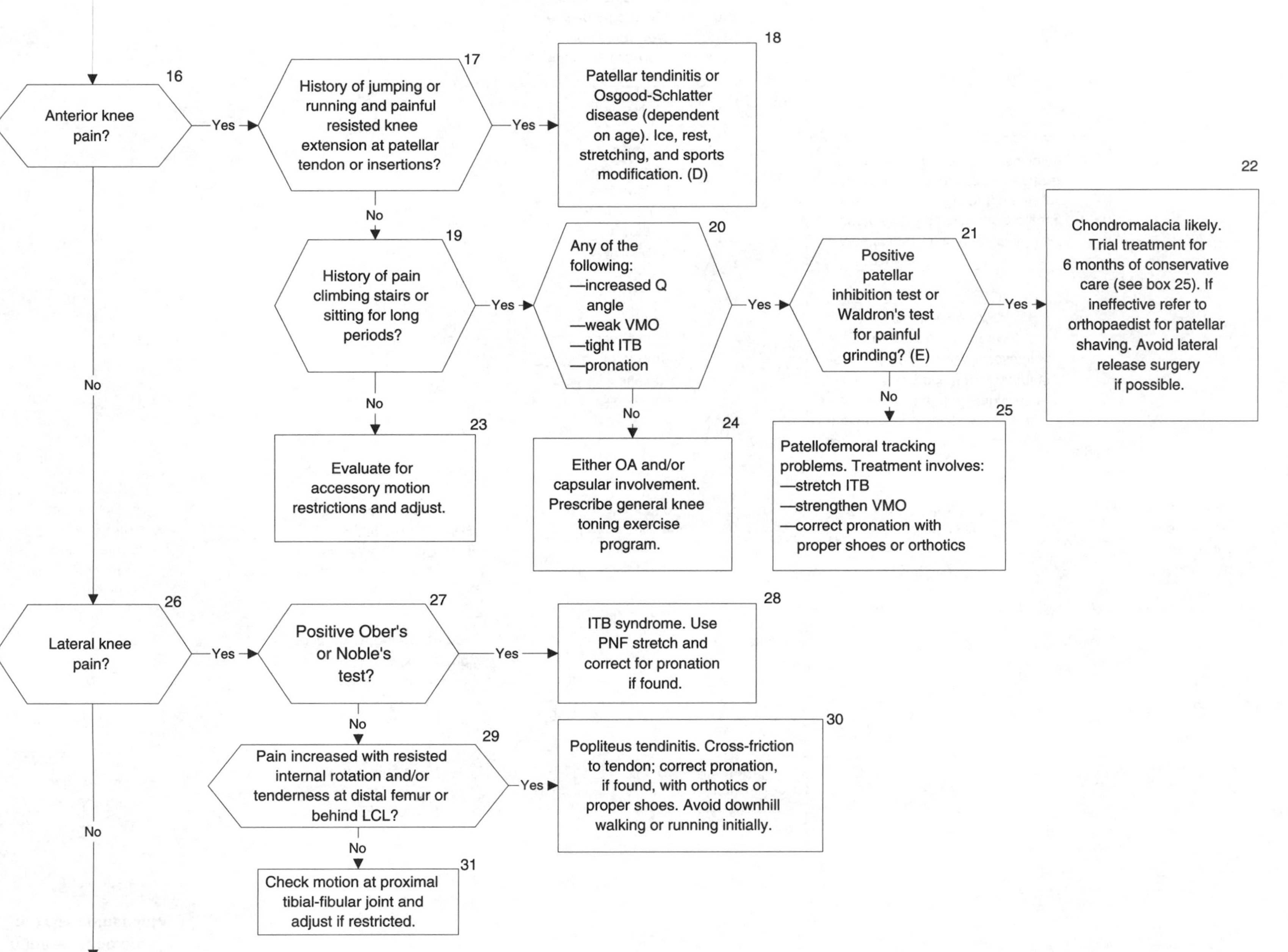

continues

Figure 12–12 continued

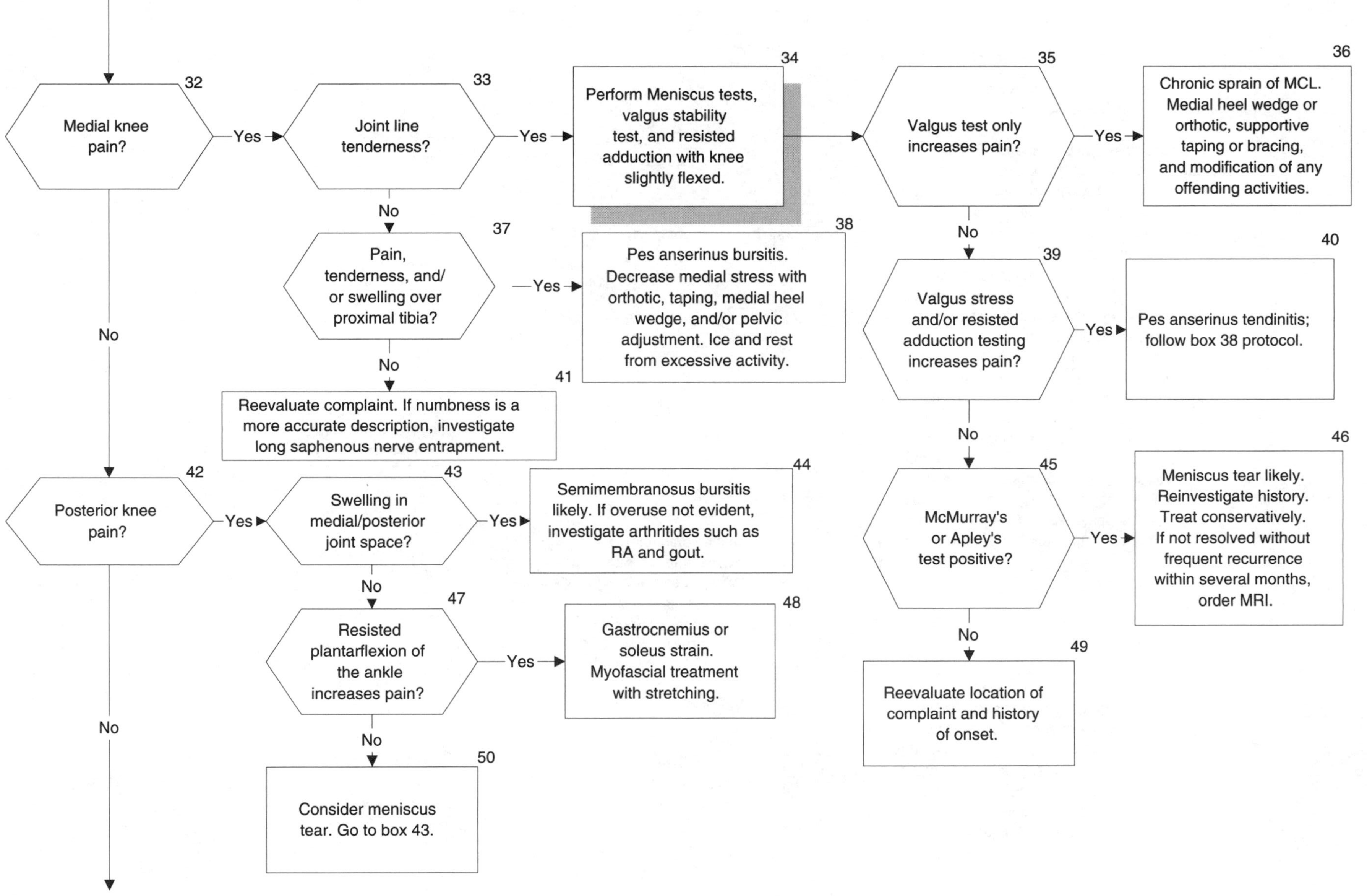

continues

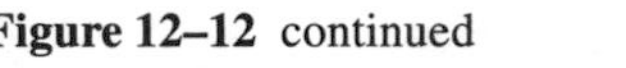

Figure 12–12 continued

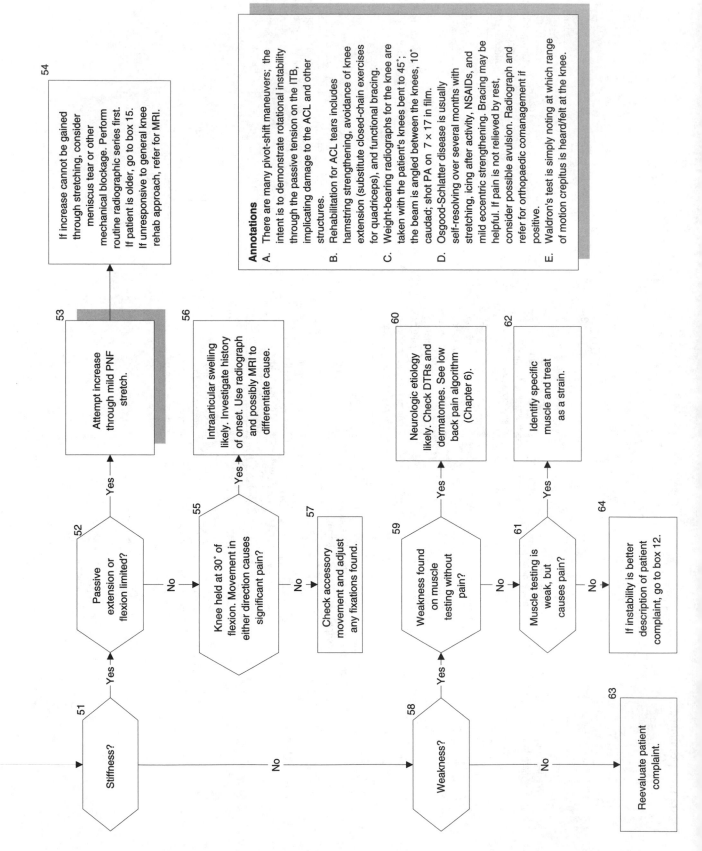

51 Stiffness?
- Yes → 52 Passive extension or flexion limited?
  - Yes → 53 Attempt increase through mild PNF stretch. → 54 If increase cannot be gained through stretching, consider meniscus tear or other mechanical blockage. Perform routine radiographic series first. If patient is older, go to box 15. If unresponsive to general knee rehab approach, refer for MRI.
  - No → 55 Knee held at 30˚ of flexion. Movement in either direction causes significant pain?
    - Yes → 56 Intraarticular swelling likely. Investigate history of onset. Use radiograph and possibly MRI to differentiate cause.
    - No → 57 Check accessory movement and adjust any fixations found.
- No → 58 Weakness?
  - Yes → 59 Weakness found on muscle testing without pain?
    - Yes → 60 Neurologic etiology likely. Check DTRs and dermatomes. See low back pain algorithm (Chapter 6).
    - No → 61 Muscle testing is weak, but causes pain?
      - Yes → 62 Identify specific muscle and treat as a strain.
      - No → 64 If instability is better description of patient complaint, go to box 12.
  - No → 63 Reevaluate patient complaint.

Annotations

A. There are many pivot-shift maneuvers; the intent is to demonstrate rotational instability through the passive tension on the ITB, implicating damage to the ACL and other structures.

B. Rehabilitation for ACL tears includes hamstring strengthening, avoidance of knee extension (substitute closed-chain exercises for quadriceps), and functional bracing.

C. Weight-bearing radiographs for the knee are taken with the patient's knees bent to 45˚; the beam is angled between the knees, 10˚ caudad; shot PA on 7 × 17 in film.

D. Osgood-Schlatter disease is usually self-resolving over several months with stretching, icing after activity, NSAIDs, and mild eccentric strengthening. Bracing may be helpful. If pain is not relieved by rest, consider possible avulsion. Radiograph and refer for orthopaedic comanagement if positive.

E. Waldron's test is simply noting at which range of motion crepitus is heard/felt at the knee.

SELECTED DISORDERS OF THE KNEE

A summary of most of the disorders discussed below is presented in Table 12–6.

TRAUMATIC

Anterior Cruciate Ligament Tears

Classic Presentation

Patients present in either an acute or a chronic phase. In an acute presentation, the patient will report a sudden onset of knee pain following either a hyperextension maneuver or a contact injury with the knee being hit from the side. He or she will remember a "pop" heard at the time of injury. Joint swelling appears quickly. The patient is unable to bear weight.

In the chronic presentation, the patient will have a past history of the above presentation with a follow-up history of gradual resolution of swelling and pain. The presenting complaint is usually more one of instability rather than pain. There may also be reported occurrences of nontraumatic joint line swelling.

Cause

ACL damage can be isolated (often a noncontact injury) usually due to hyperextension and/or sudden contraction of the quadriceps as occurs with sudden stopping or cutting. Contact injury with a rotary component is more likely to damage the ACL and other structures such as the menisci or MCL. When the ACL tears, it usually occurs in the midsubstance of the ligament. Because of the paralleling vascular supply, vascular rupture often occurs, leading to a quickly developing joint swelling that is tense and painful.

Evaluation

In an acute setting, the most helpful indicators are historical, including the mechanisms described above plus immediate swelling, and a "pop" heard at the time of injury. Evaluation in the acute setting is with the Lachman's test.[14] The test is applied by stabilizing the distal femur while the examiner attempts to pull the proximal tibia forward with the knee held at 10° to 20° of flexion (Figure 12–4). In more chronic settings, the anterior drawer test may be used. It is the same approach of pulling the tibia forward; however, the hip is flexed to 45°, knee at 90° (Figure 12–5). The disadvantage of this test is that spasmed hamstrings are in a biomechanically advantaged position, resisting the examiner's attempt at forward displacement of the tibia. It is probably not possible to detect partial tears clinically with these tests.[15] If multiple tissue damage is suspected, the examiner uses a rotary test; "pivot shift" approach (Figure 12–6). There are many variations, yet each relies on the passive tension of the ITB to pull the tibia forward when approaching extension, and to pull it back into neutral as more flexion is acquired.[5] In general, the examiner applies a valgus force at the fibular head with rotation at the tibia while flexing and extending the knee, attempting to detect not only anterior posterior movement but also rotation of the tibia. Radiographs may demonstrate a small fracture referred to as the lateral capsular sign; otherwise they are usually unremarkable. MRI is useful in determining the integrity of the ACL.

Management

If the patient is an athlete, surgery is often the only option.[16] In less active individuals, a stabilization program coupled with bracing may be sufficient (Table 12–7). The stabilization program focuses on hamstring strengthening, closed-chain quadriceps exercises (avoid-

Table 12–6 Summary of Knee Disorders

Disorder	*Signs and Symptoms*	*Positive Tests*	*Treatment*	*Avoidance*
Patellofemoral arthralgia and chondromalacia patellae	Peripatellar pain Movie sign Painful crepitus	Clarke's Waldron's Retinacular test VMO Coordination test Modified Ober's	Correct pronation Strengthen VMO Stretch lateral structures (ITB) Brace/tape for stability	Flexion/extension through crepitus range Low-seat position for bicycling
ITB syndrome	Lateral knee pain at insertion or more commonly lateral epicondyle at 30° flexion	Modified Ober's Noble's	Stretch ITB Correct pronation Rotational adjustment of knee	Downhill running Side-posture adjusting on same side
Popliteus tendinitis	Lateral knee pain with tenderness behind LCL	Resisted internal rotation Pain increased by weight bearing at 30°; internal rotation of femur	Isometric internal rotation exercises Correct pronation Cross-friction of tendon in front of or behind LCL	Downhill walking or running
Osgood-Schlatter disease	Tender and/or enlarged tibial tuberosity Tight quadriceps	Resisted extension increases pain	Stretch quadriceps Bracing Icing after activity Eccentric quadriceps training	Excessive jumping or running
Bursitis	Localized swelling/ tenderness	Compressive maneuvers	Ice Pulsed ultrasound	Pressure Direct trauma Overuse
Superior tibial fibular subluxation	Lateral knee pain with instability History of ankle injury (sometimes)	Instability at 30° full weight bearing	Fibular head adjustment (support may be needed or crutches for 1 or 2 days post-adjustment)	Excessive hamstring exercises
ACL tear	Pop at time of injury Immediate swelling Gradual instability	Lachman's Drawer's Pivot shift	Strengthen hamstrings Functional bracing Proprioceptive training Surgery (often needed for active individuals)	Knee extension exercises
MCL tear	Ligament tenderness Possible sense of instability	Stability testing at 0° or 30°	General strengthening Hinged brace for several weeks	Knee extension from 60° to full extension
Meniscus tear	Joint line tenderness Swelling Locking Giving way	McMurray's Apley's MRI	Acute pain relief Adjust with distraction Refer if signs/symptoms continue	Squatting and rotation stress
Osteochondritis dissecans	Anterior knee pain Possible locking	Wilson's test Tunnel view radiograph	Surgery if loose fragment	Manipulation

Source: Reprinted with permission from T. Souza, The Knee, in *Conservative Management of Sports Injuries*, R. Hazel, ed., p. 401, © 1994, Williams & Wilkins.

Table 12–7 Conservative Management of ACL Tears

Parameter	*Acute Stage*	*Subacute Stage*	*Chronic Stage*
Criteria for diagnosis of staging	Positive Lachman's with associated intraarticular swelling, pain; unable to bear weight; in select patients, MRI confirmation.	Positive Lachman's with reduced intraarticular swelling; able to bear weight; ROM limited.	Positive Lachman's or drawer sign; minimal or no swelling; knee feels unstable with rotation maneuvers; full or close to full ROM.
Goals	Reduce swelling, control pain, determine patient's functional needs for future planning of management.	Continue to reduce swelling and control pain; increase ROM, and develop basic strength and proprioception.	Strengthen the hamstrings to 80% of well leg quadriceps; proprioceptively train the lower extremity to react to quick changes in ground surfaces.
Concerns	The swelling is a hemarthrosis, making it painful and potentially destructive; associated damage to meniscus, capsule, and fracture must be considered and/or evaluated.	As swelling decreases, more instability than originally suspected may become evident; if unacceptable to patient or indicators of gross laxity, order MRI or refer for orthopaedic consultation.	Patient may become overaggressive in rehabilitation phase and reinjure leg through overcontraction of quadriceps or hyperextension.
Requirements for progression to next stage	Pain and swelling reduced enough to allow 50% ROM; isometric strength evident in available range.	90% ROM available; isotonic contraction through available range if capable of achieving 3 sets of 10 repetitions with minimal weight.	Full ROM; 80% strength of well leg quadriceps; able to perform complex movements such as side stepping and cuts without pain or instability.
Manipulation/mobilization	Contraindicated in the knee at this time.	Mild mobilization may assist in reducing remaining swelling and increase ROM.	Manipulation of any associated foot/ankle, hip, pelvic, or lumbar fixations; mild mobilization to the knee.
Modalities	Ice, elevation, TENS, or high-volt galvanic (80–120 Hz/20 min 3 times daily).	Ice and high-volt galvanic (1–150 Hz/20 min/day).	None needed; however, ice after activity if mild swelling still occurs.
External brace, support, etc.	Immobilization should be kept to a minimum; a long cylindrical knee immobilization device may be helpful for up to 5 days.	Protective hinge-brace allowing ROM with an extension block.	Functional knee brace is needed when performing sports activities (includes stabilization in rotation, anterior-posterior glide, protection from hyperextension and valgus forces).

continues

Table 12–7 continued

Parameter	*Acute Stage*	*Subacute Stage*	*Chronic Stage*
ROM/flexibility	Passive ROM within available range; elevation when possible.	Gradual increase in ROM with postisometric and mild PNF techniques.	Maintain flexibility of quadriceps, hamstrings, and triceps surae groups.
Open-chain exercise	Isometrics within available range.	Isotonics within available range performed as straight-leg exercises first; bicycle riding okay if well leg is used for pedaling (bad leg along for the ride); avoid high seat position.	Progressive strengthening using DAPRE or PRE approach.
Closed-chain exercise	None.	Mild quarter squats with weight on both feet with brace worn.	Three-quarter squats with resistance from weight or elastic tubing; leg presses also good.
Proprioceptive training	Electrical stimulation at quadriceps and hamstrings with minimal contraction.	Seated wobble board training; begin mild PNF diagonal training; PNF rhythmic stabilization at 30° for hamstrings.	BAPS or wobble board training; balance jumps on minitrampoline; train with full-resistance PNF diagonal patterns.
Associated biomechanical items	Avoid hyperextension or active extension through last 60°.	Avoid hyperextension.	Continue to avoid hyperextension on bicycle; avoid knee extension machines through the last 60°.
Lifestyle/activity modifications	No weight bearing, bed rest for 3–5 days with gradual attempts at partial weight bearing with crutches.	Use crutches for any stair climbing; avoid activities that cause extension of the knee, especially while standing.	Use the functional brace with sporting activities.

Key: TENS, Transcutaneous electrical nerve stimulation; BAPS, Biomechanical ankle platform system (Medipedic, Jackson, Michigan).

Source: Reprinted with permission from T. Souza, The Knee, in *Conservative Management of Sports Injuries*, R. Hazel, ed., p. 401, © 1994, Williams & Wilkins.

ing seated knee extensions), and proprioceptive training with balance devices.[17] Bracing is usually custom-fitted with a functional brace that should offer some degree of protection against hyperextension and rotational forces. Surgical options include stabilization with other local tendons or the use of Goretex or other materials.

Meniscus Tears

Classic Presentation

The patient presents with a complaint of knee pain usually following a rotational injury to the knee. The patient noticed that swelling in the knee developed over a number of hours. Since the injury, the patient may have episodes of knee locking wherein he or she experiences significant pain and is unable to move the leg for a few seconds until the involved knee is forcefully extended. Knee swelling or giving way may be the main complaint.

Cause

Most meniscus injuries are due to combined compression with rotation at the knee. There are a variety of different tears; however, they are generally divided into horizontal and vertical tears. Because of the minor blood supply, meniscus tears do not usually bleed much into the joint. The free edge of the tear, however, may cause irritation with a reactant synovial fluid production. The meniscus is often involved when the ACL is torn, in which case the predominance of signs and symptoms will come from the cruciate damage.

Evaluation

In addition to the history, it is important to challenge the knee with compression and rotation. The two primary tests are McMurray's and Apley's.[18] The combination of joint line tenderness with a positive McMurray's or Apley's test is a strong indicator of meniscal involvement; however, the tests are not very sensitive. The McMurray test begins with forced, passive flexion of the knee coupled with rotation as the examiner palpates the joint line for popping (clunking) and pain (Figure 12–7). If negative, the knee is passively extended with combined forces of internal or external rotation coupled with varus and valgus forces. Apley's compression test is performed with the patient prone (Figure 12–8). An axial force is applied through the tibia to the knee as it is passively rotated. This is performed in all degrees of flexion and extension. Further evaluation with MRI may be helpful in determining the type and extent of tear and assisting in the decision whether or not to treat surgically.

Management

Vertical, stable tears in the peripheral meniscus often will heal, especially in the younger patient.[19] Most other tears will usually progress to recurrent bouts of swelling and pain with decreasing asymptomatic periods. Arthroscopic repair or partial meniscectomy is the most common surgical approach with isolated mensical damage. The latter carries an increased risk of early degenerative changes in the knee.[20] Chiropractic manipulation may be helpful in reducing meniscus symptoms. Whether it affects the long-term course of meniscus tears remains to be seen. Manual reduction of a meniscus lock is also an important management tool.

Medial Collateral Ligament Tear

Classic Presentation

When the tear is second or third degree, the patient will report a history of contact or noncontact injury that forced the knee into valgus. There is often sharp medial pain with associated swelling at the time of injury. With first-degree tears, the patient often will have no history of trauma; however, he or she will report a history of an overuse activity with more mild to moderate pain at the medial knee.

Cause

Either traumatic outside-to-inside forces (valgus stress) or chronic strain through valgus-loading biomechanical factors (eg, pronation) will lead to partial or total disruption of the MCL fibers.

Evaluation

With trauma, it is important to test for MCL integrity. The examiner applies a valgus force to the extended knee. If there is significant opening (compared with the opposite, well leg), a third-degree tear (rupture) of the MCL has occurred in addition to other medial stabilizers such as the meniscus or cruciates. If the test is negative for instability in extension, the patient is evaluated in 20° to 30° of flexion (with the hip stabilized to prevent rotation). If the knee opens in this position without an end-feel, an isolated third-degree tear has occurred. If there is opening with a definite end-point (compared with the opposite side) a second-degree tear is likely. If there is no instability but the test produces medial joint pain, a first-degree sprain or pes anserinus tendinitis is possible. Adding an active contraction into knee flexion or medial rotation may cause pain with a pes anserinus strain.

Management

Third-degree sprains with associated meniscal or cruciate involvement should be referred for orthopaedic surgical management. Isolated third-degree tears are occasionally managed with 2 to 3 weeks of progressively less restricted bracing followed by gradual weight bearing and rehabilitation.[21] Second-degree tears are managed with 2 weeks of hinge-cast immobilization followed by rehabilitation. First-degree tears involve correcting any biomechanical predispositions such as orthotics for pronation, modification of sporting or recreational activity, and strengthening of the medial and lateral stabilizers.

NONTRAUMATIC

Patellofemoral Arthralgia and Chondromalacia

Classic Presentation

The patient complains of anterior knee pain. The pain is worse with going up and down steps and sitting for long periods of time. There is often associated crepitus and pain going through any squatting maneuver.

Cause

Patellofemoral arthralgia is thought to be primarily a soft tissue disorder associated with the consequences of a patellar tracking disorder. Stress on stabilizing structures such as the VMO and medial or lateral retinaculum may be the primary cause. Other possible involvement occurs with pinching or irritation of the infrapatellar fat pad. Chondromalacia patellae is due to degeneration of the hyaline cartilage on the back surface of the patella. A gradual deterioration occurs, often related to maltracking or instability of the patella. Underlying predispositions appear to be an increased Q (quadriceps) angle, underdevelopment of the femoral condyles or the patella, patella alta (high riding), and, more functionally, weak medial stabilizers (VMO) and tight lateral structures such as the vastus lateralis and ITB.

Evaluation

Waldron's test is performed by having the examiner listen to and feel the patella as the patient goes through a squatting maneuver. If pain and crepitus is felt during a specific range, patellar involvement is likely. If the pain is felt only at the bottom of the squat, it is more likely to be due to meniscal pathology. Other tests include the VMO coordination test, which tests the ability of the VMO to stabilize the patella through the last 15° of knee extension; Ober's test, designed to stretch the leg into adduction, thereby stretching the ITB (see below); and patellar stability tests. Palpation around the patella may reveal tenderness at the vastus insertions, retinacula, patellar meniscal ligaments, or a plica.

Management

The primary goal is to correct maltracking of the patella. This is usually accomplished through general knee-stabilizing exercises coupled with orthotic support (Table 12–8). Knee bracing at the patellar tendon may relieve some of the acute discomfort. Various patellar braces are available, based primarily on the principle of providing a support for the patella via a hole cut in the brace and/or strapping or internal padding. Taping involves the use of a strapping tape to pull the patella in the desired direction. Although this may not provide the stability intended, it does seem to provide a strong proprioceptive support to proper tracking.[12] Orthotic support may also be needed in pronated patients. Chiropractic manipulations of the foot, ankle, hip, and knee are often used to guarantee a more fully functioning integrated lower extremity. Patients with true chondromalacia who fail a conservative approach for 6 months should be referred for surgical consultation. The primary surgical procedures include shaving of the posterior patella arthroscopically and a lateral release.

Iliotibial Band Syndrome

Classic Presentation

The patient complains of lateral knee pain that gradually increased over a few days to weeks. The pain seems to be related to running (although sedentary individuals may develop similar pain). Specifically, downhill running and pain when extending the leg just before heel strike seems to be aggravating. Some patients may hear a squeaking sound with flexion-extension of the knee.

Cause

The cause of this syndrome is believed to be a tight ITB that rubs against the lateral epicondyle of the femur at approximately 30° to 40° of knee flexion. Predispositions included hyperpronation and downhill running. Recent evidence suggests the possibility that either a thicker or wider band predisposes patients to this syndrome. Additionally, it appears that not all repetitive activity is predisposing. It appears that the longer one performs a repetitive activity with the knee flexed to 30° to 40°, the more likely ITB syndrome will develop. Therefore, downhill running or slower running (jogging) may be the major factor because these activities occur primarily with the knee in the "impingement" range. Faster speed running seems less likely a cause.

Evaluation

Palpation for tenderness is targeted to the lateral epicondyle (approximately 3 cm proximal to the lateral joint line). Tenderness may be increased if pressure is applied at the lateral epicondyle while flexing and extending the knee. Tenderness increases in the "painful arc" of 30° to 40°. This is often referred to as Noble's test. Ober's test is designed mainly to detect tightness in the muscular attachments into the ITB, including the gluteus maximus and tensor fasciae latae or the band itself (Figure 12–10). The patient lies on his or her unaffected side. The examiner moves the bottom limb into flexion to avoid blocking of the following adduction movement. The top leg is then passively lowered over the back of the table to determine available adduction and any associated pain. It is crucial to stabilize the patient's iliac crest to avoid stretching above the pelvis (isolate the stretch to the

Table 12–8 Rehabilitation of Patellofemoral Disorders

Parameter	*Initial*	*Intermediate*	*Advanced*
Criteria	Anterior knee pain with going up and down stairs or after sitting for extended periods; positive tests for ITB tightness and/or VMO coordination; possible positive patellar inhibition test or pain/crepitus while squatting.	Anterior knee pain reduced, ITB tightness improved, VMO facilitated.	No pain with activity.
Goals	Reduce pain and any associated retinacular tenderness; evaluate for need of foot orthotic support.	Continue to strengthen VMO; strengthen the knee with general knee-toning exercises; train patient in stair climbing.	Functionally train individual for specific sport activity.
Concerns	Possible chondromalacia, not visible on radiograph; failure to respond is suggestive.	Patient feels better and is not compliant or not able to be compliant with stair and squat restriction.	Overenthusiastic training.
Requirements for progression to next stage	Decrease in pain with ascending/descending steps; VMO strength increasing; ITB more flexible.	Accomplished intermediate stage of knee strengthening; able to ascend/descend steps properly without discomfort; VMO coordination test is negative.	
Manipulation/mobilization	Manipulation/mobilization of the patella into restricted ranges; manipulation of any corresponding lower extremity or lumbopelvic fixations.	Manipulation/mobilization of the patella into restricted ranges; manipulation of any corresponding lower extremity or lumbopelvic fixations.	Manipulation/mobilization of the patella into restricted ranges; manipulation of any corresponding lower extremity or lumbopelvic fixations.
Modalities	Ice, rest, EMS for VMO.	Ice after activity.	None.
External brace, support, etc.	Patellar stabilizing brace or McConnell taping; cast for orthotics if necessary or use temporary trial of medial heel wedge.	Patellar stabilizing brace or McConnell taping.	Wean patient off support.
ROM/flexibility	Stretch quadriceps, hamstrings, ITB, and triceps surae group.	Stretch quadriceps, hamstrings, ITB, and triceps surae group.	Stretch quadriceps, hamstrings, ITB, and triceps surae group.

continues

Table 12–8 continued

Parameter	Initial	Intermediate	Advanced
Open-chain exercise	Extension through last 10° to 15° if tolerable; combine with adduction for better faciliation of VMO.	Extension through full range if pain and crepitus free; for additional support, strengthen abductors, adductors, and flexors using PRE or DAPRE approach.	Isokinetic exercises are added if appropriate.
Closed-chain exercise	Minisquats through crepitus/pain-free range (knee over toe).	Squats continue through an increased crepitus/pain-free range with elastic tubing resistance; perform lateral step-ups; train in single-stair-climbing technique.	Plyometrics may begin if patient passes test with single leg squats and hops.
Proprioceptive training	Begin wobble board (BAPS board) training; have patient cocontract with ramped EMS.	Progress with BAPS training and minitrampoline jumping; PNF diagonal training if patient is athletic.	Sports-specific PNF patterns.
Associated biomechanical items	Avoid low-seat position with bicycling; avoid knee extension or squats in crepitus/pain range.	Avoid low-seat position with bicycling; avoid knee extension or squats in crepitus/pain range.	Avoid low-seat bicycle positions.
Lifestyle/activity modifications	Avoid stair climbing, squatting, and prolonged sitting.	Minimal stair climbing, minisquats; take frequent breaks when having to sit for long periods (eg, driving, movies).	None.

Key: EMS, Electrical muscle stimulation; BAPS, Biomechanical ankle platform system (Medipedic, Jackson, Michigan).

ITB). Pain may also be increased by bearing full weight onto the involved side with the knee bent to 30° to 45°.

Management

The primary approach is to stretch the ITB and its muscular attachments using a postisometric relaxation technique. Modification of running/jogging activities is necessary during the acute phase. Sudden stretching of the ITB with side-posture adjusting should be avoided for 1 to 2 weeks. Because of the pelvic attachments of the ITB, tensor fasciae latae and gluteus maximus, pelvic manipulation should be considered if consistent with chiropractic evaluation findings.

Popliteus Tendinitis

Classic Presentation

The patient presents with complaints similar to those of the patient with ITB syndrome, with a report of lateral knee pain following downhill running or walking.

Cause

The popliteus functions as an internal rotator when the knee is non-weight bearing. In addition, it plays a supportive role for both the posterior PCL and the LCL, preventing forward movement of the femur on the tibia and varus angulation, respectively. Finally, the popliteus acts to pull the posterior lateral meniscus posteriorly during knee flexion. The popliteus muscle takes its origin off the back of the tibia, spiraling around as a tendon under the LCL and inserting into the distal femur just in front of the LCL.

Evaluation

A history of downhill walking or running is often found. Tenderness is found at the insertion point on the distal femur just anterior to the LCL attachment. Tenderness also may be found directly behind the LCL. Resisted internal rotation may cause pain at the lateral knee. Bearing full weight on the involved side with the knee bent 30° and then internally rotating the femur may increase the discomfort in some patients. Ancillary findings may include hyperpronation on the involved side.

Management

In addition to ice and rest, cross-friction over the tendon section of the popliteus just in front of and just behind the LCL is often effective. Orthotic support may be needed for the hyperpronated foot and adjusting of any lower extremity fixations.

Proximal Tibial-Fibular Subluxation

Classic Presentation

The patient reports the sudden onset of lateral knee pain following a sudden dorsiflexion or plantarflexion injury at the ankle. Another presentation may be a patient who experiences pain less abruptly while performing leg curls (for hamstrings). The patient may have added complaints of instability or pain radiating down the side of the lower leg.

Cause

The proximal tibial-fibular articulation is a synovial joint. Movement at this joint is influenced by movement at the ankle. When the ankle dorsiflexes, the proximal fibula moves superiorly and rotates outward; with plantarflexion, the fibula moves inferior and rotates inward. Sudden forced movements (in particular dorsiflexion) may force the fibula into a fixed position. With hamstring curls, the biceps femoris may draw the fibular head posteriorly, leading to fixation or, in some patients, chronic hypermobility. Due to the proximity of the peroneal nerve to the fibular head, compression or entrapment may occur with the result of radiating pain down the outside lower leg.

Evaluation

Joint play assessment in the supine position is accomplished with the knee extended. Palpation at the fibular head should reveal normal movement with passive dorsiflexion and plantarflexion of the ankle. With the knee bent to 90°, the examiner may pull and push the fibular head to determine any sense of fixation or hypermobility.

Management

The standard approach is to adjust the fibular head. In hypermobile joints, it may be necessary to have 1 or 2 days of non-weight bearing. Decreasing the amount of resistance on the leg curl may also be beneficial.

Patellar Tendinitis (Jumper's Knee)

Classic Presentation

The patient is often an athlete complaining of anterior knee pain with activities that involve jumping or sprinting.

Cause

Repetitive stress to the patellar tendon (ligament) is common with jumping and running sports. It appears that this is often an eccentric injury.

Evaluation

Pain is felt at the patellar tendon or at the attachments to the patella or tibial tuberosity. Resisted extension starting with the knee bent beyond 90° usually will increase pain at the tendon.

Management

The mainstays of treatment are rest, ice, and stretch. After acute symptoms have been resolved, gradual eccentric training (avoidance of plyometrics) should be initiated. Athletes who do not follow the above approach and attempt to work through the injury create a chronic, difficult, often career-limiting disorder.

Osgood-Schlatter Disease

Classic Presentation

The patient is often a young athlete complaining of pain and swelling at the tibial tuberosity.

Cause

The tibial apophysis is susceptible to repetitive stresses. When adolescents are performing demanding activities such as running and jumping, the apophysis may undergo an inflammatory reaction. It is rare for the tendon to avulse the apophysis.

Evaluation

The characteristic findings of a young athlete with tibial tuberosity pain is almost pathognomonic. Added testing may include resisted extension in an attempt to increase pain. It is not uncommon to develop Osgood-Schlatter disease bilaterally.

Management

Rest, ice, modification of the inciting sport activity, and gradual quadriceps stretching are the primary approaches. It is often helpful to use an Osgood-Schlatter brace or taping at the patellar tendon during activity. The general rule of thumb is that if the athlete is able to reduce the discomfort with rest, the injury will be self-resolving and further evaluation with a radiograph is not necessary. However, if the athlete is experiencing pain that is unrelieved by rest, radiographs should be taken in an effort to determine whether there is an avulsion. Radiographs must be reviewed by a chiropractic or medical radiologist because of the subtleties and variation of the apophyses.

REFERENCES

1. Ellison AE. *Athletic Training and Sports Medicine.* Chicago: American Academy of Orthopedic Surgeons; 1985.
2. Solomono M, Barata R, Zhou BH, et al. The synergistic action of the anterior cruciate ligament and thigh muscles in maintaining joint stability. *Am J Sports Med.* 1987;15:207.
3. O'Shea KJ, Murphy KP, Heekin D, Herzwum PJ. The diagnostic accuracy of history, physical examination and radiographs in the evaluation of traumatic knee disorders. *Am J Sports Med.* 1996;24:164–167.
4. Johnson T, Althoff L. Clinical diagnosis of ruptures of the anterior cruciate ligament: a comparison study of the Lachman test and the anterior drawer sign. *Am J Sports Med.* 1982;10:100–102.
5. Bach BR, Warren RF, Wickiewics TL. The pivot shift phenomenon: results and description of a modified clinical test for anterior cruciate ligament insufficiency. *Am J Sports Med.* 1988;16:571–576.
6. Evans PJ, Bell GD, Frank C. Prospective evaluation of the McMurray test. *Am J Sports Med.* 1993;21:604–608.
7. Apley AG. The diagnosis of meniscus injuries. *J Bone Joint Surg.* 1947;29:78–84.
8. McClure PW, Rothstein JM, Riddle DL. Intertester reliability of clinical judgments of medial knee ligament integrity. *Phys Ther.* 1989;69:268–275.
9. France EP, Cawley PW, Paulos LE. Choosing functional knee braces. *Clin Sports Med.* 1990;9:743–750.
10. Styf JR, Lundin O, Gershuni DH. Effects of a functional knee brace on leg muscle function. *Am J Sports Med.* 1994;22:6.
11. Paulos LE, France EP, Rosenberg TD, et al. The biomechanics of lateral knee bracing, I: response of the valgus restraints to loading. *Am J Sports Med.* 1987;15:419.
12. McConnell J. The management of chondromalacia patellae: a long term solution. *Aust J Phys Ther.* 1986;32:215.
13. Penau R, Frank C, Fick G. The effect of elastic bandages on human knee proprioception in the uninjured population. *Am J Sports Med.* 1995;23:2.
14. Cooperman JM, Riddle DL, Rothstein JM. Reliability and judgments of the integrity of the anterior cruciate of the knee using the Lachman's test. *Phys Ther.* 1990;70:225–233.
15. Lintner DM, Kamaric E, Mosely B, Noble PC. Partial tears of the anterior cruciate ligament: are they clinically detectable? *Am J Sports Med.* 1995;23:1.
16. Buss DD, Min R, Skyhar M, et al. Nonoperative treatment of acute ACL injuries in a selected group of patients. *Am J Sports Med.* 1995;23:2.
17. Ihara H, Nakayama A. Dynamic joint control training for knee ligament injuries. *Am J Sports Med.* 1988;14:309–315.
18. Souza TA. Which orthopedic tests are really necessary? In: Lawerence DJ, Cassidy JD, McGregor M, et al., eds. *Advances in Chiropractic.* St. Louis, MO: Mosby-Year Book; 1994;1:101–154.
19. Weiss C, Lundberg M, Maberg P, et al. Non-operative treatment of meniscal tears. *J Bone Joint Surg Am.* 1989;71:811–822.
20. Ranger C, Klestill T, Gloetzer W, et al. Osteoarthritis after arthroscopic partial meniscectomy. *Am J Sports Med.* 1995;23:2.
21. Reider B, Sathy MR,Talkington J, Blyznak N, et al. Treatment of isolated medial collateral ligament injuries in athletes with early functional rehabilitation: a five-year follow-up study. *Am J Sports Med.* 1993;22:4.

Chapter 13

Lower Leg Complaints

CONTEXT

Lower leg disorders range from the benign to life threatening. A history that includes any apparent trigger such as trauma, overuse, or disuse will usually narrow down the limited list of disorders affecting the lower leg. In older patients, calf pain should always suggest the possibility of deep vein thrombosis (DVT). This potentially life-threatening disorder is not always easily differentiated from a minor traumatic swelling or muscle strain.

Exercise-induced lower leg pain is common among athletes. Unfortunately, the terminology is confusing because of the clinical overlap and lack of identification of specific pathologic lesions in many cases. *Shin splint* is a commonly used term; however, some clinicians will include this diagnosis under the broader category of compartment syndromes or subdivide shin splints (ie, medial stress syndrome).[1] Biomechanical imbalances at the foot will often strain the calf musculature; therefore, an evaluation of excessive pronation or supination should be included in the evaluation.

In addition to pain, patients also complain of leg cramps and lower leg edema. Lower leg edema is discussed in more depth in Chapter 25. Cramps are often the result of excessive diuretic use, lack of hydration, or need for electrolytes.

GENERAL STRATEGY

History

- Determine the type of complaint: pain and/or swelling, numbness/tingling, cramping, cosmetic concern, or skin lesions.
- Distinguish between a traumatic onset and a nontraumatic onset.
- Determine whether the pain is diffuse or well localized.
- With a traumatic onset, determine whether there was minor trauma—mild sprain or DVT—or major trauma—fracture or compartment syndrome. Sudden onset without trauma would suggest muscle or tendon rupture (posteromedial knee—tennis leg; heel—Achilles rupture).
- With an overuse history determine whether the pain is felt only with activity (muscle/tendon strain or compartment syndrome) or initially with activity but now also at rest (stress fracture).
- With women ask about menstrual irregularities (stress fracture) or chronic use of birth control pills (DVT).
- With athletes determine whether there was a sudden change in training (ie, increased mileage, change in running surface, hill training).
- When swelling is the chief complaint (see Chapter 25) determine whether the onset was traumatic or nontraumatic.

Evaluation

- Attempt to pinpoint an area of tenderness or swelling.
- Test with stretch and contraction to detect a specific muscle or tendon.
- When a stress fracture is suspected obtain a radiograph first and proceed to a bone scan if necessary; for DVT refer for Doppler ultrasound; for Achilles tendon rupture or possible partial rupture, diagnostic ultrasound or magnetic resonance imaging (MRI) is appropriate; for compartment syndrome, refer for measurement of compartment pressure.

Management

- Refer cases of DVT, Achilles rupture, or acute compartment syndrome.
- Manage stress fractures with rest, increased calcium intake, and modification of inciting activity; nonhealing fractures require referral for orthopaedic consultation.
- Achilles tendinitis may be helped with temporary taping, strengthening, and activity modification.

RELEVANT ANATOMY

The lower leg is often discussed in reference to four fascial compartments:

1. anterior—tibialis anterior, extensor digitorum longus, extensor hallucis, the deep peroneal nerve, and the anterior tibial artery and vein
2. lateral—peroneus longus and brevis, and superficial peroneal nerve
3. superficial posterior—soleus muscle, and tendons of the plantaris and gastrocnemius
4. deep posterior—flexor digitorum and flexor hallucis longus, tibialis posterior, the peroneal and posterior tibial artery and vein, and the tibial nerve

Exercise and trauma-related pain may be confined to one of these compartments.[2] When hypertrophy or inflammation exceeds the accommodations of the compartment, a compartment syndrome may result. Muscle function can also be related to the compartments. The anterior compartment muscles are the extensors, the lateral evertors; superficial posterior compartment muscles cause plantarflexion, and the deep posterior compartment muscles are the primary invertors and stabilizers against over-pronation (Figure 13–1).

The anterior compartment muscles contribute to shock absorption; when they are eccentrically weak they may cause anterior shin splints.[3] The muscles in the deep posterior compartment are stabilizers; when they are eccentrically weak they may cause posterior (medial) shin splints.

EVALUATION

History

Careful questioning of the patient during the history taking can point to the diagnosis (Table 13–1).

Pain Localization

Anterior.

- proximal tibia—pes anserinus bursitis (medially), stress fracture, tumor
- middle and distal tibia—stress fracture, periostitis
- anterolateral—anterior shin splints

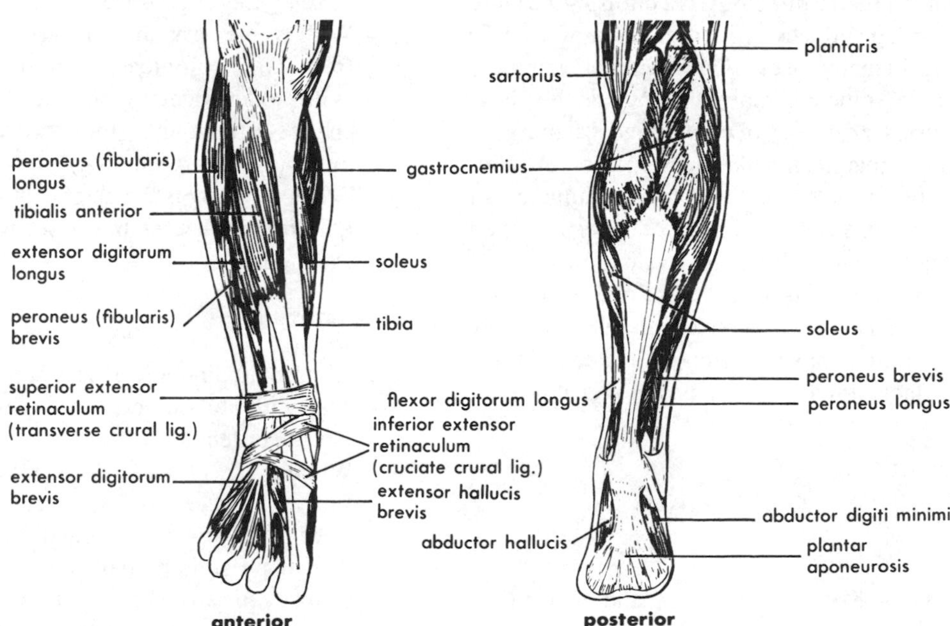

Figure 13–1 The anterior and posterior lower leg. *Source:* Reprinted with permission from J.E. Crouch, *Functional Human Anatomy*, 4th ed., p. 238, © 1985, Lea & Febiger.

Table 13–1 History Questions for Lower Leg Complaints

Primary Question	*What Are You Thinking?*	*Secondary Questions*	*What Are You Thinking?*
Did the pain occur suddenly?	Tennis leg, DVT, fracture	Did you fall on or hit your leg?	Fracture, DVT
		Did you hear or feel a pop on the back of your leg while running or playing tennis?	Tennis leg (tear of medial gastrocnemius)
Did the pain appear without any particular trauma or activity?	DVT, shin splints	Are you taking birth control pills (for females) or been immobilized for a long time?	DVT
		Do you stand or walk on hard surfaces?	Shin splints
Does the pain occur mainly with activity?	Shin splints, stress fracture, Achilles tendinitis, chronic compartment syndrome, claudication	Did this occur with running? A sudden increase in speed, distance, or duration?	Stress fracture, shin splints
		Do you work, walk, or run on hard surfaces?	Shin splints
		(For runners) Does the pain occur at a consistent distance or timing?	Compartment syndrome
		Is it worse with walking small distance; does it improve with rest?	Claudication (differentiate vascular from neurogenic causes)
		Is the pain close to your heel and worse when you go up on your toes?	Achilles tendinitis
Is the complaint one more of swelling?	Compartment syndrome, DVT, stress fracture, congestive heart failure (CHF)	Is the swelling localized to an inch or two?	Stress fracture; maybe DVT
		Is the swelling localized to one side of the lower leg?	Compartment syndrome
		Does the swelling improve with leg elevation?	Yes—vascular No—lymph
		Does the swelling involve the entire lower leg in both legs?	CHF, fluid retention due to renal problems, salt retention, liver disease

Posterior.

- upper medial tibia—tennis leg (medial gastrocnemius tear), flexor digitorum longus tendinitis
- middle and lower third of tibia—stress fracture, posterior shin splints
- calf muscle belly—muscle tear, DVT
- Achilles tendon—Achilles tendinitis
- insertion of Achilles into calcaneus—retrocalcaneal bursitis, exostosis, Achilles tendinitis

When the patient reports a sudden onset of pain in the calf, it is important to identify whether there was direct trauma or a sudden movement. Direct trauma may result from a blow to the leg or accidentally bumping the leg against an object (eg, coffee table). Minor trauma in an older patient may initiate a DVT. A strong blow to the lower leg in any patient may result in fracture and/or initiate enough swelling to produce a compartment syndrome. Tearing of the medial gastrocnemius may occur with extension of the knee coupled with dorsiflexion of the ankle. The patient often reports a "pop" associated with a severe stabbing pain.

Overuse injuries cause varying degrees of tendon irritation, bone irritation, and swelling or hypertrophy in the corresponding compartment. Patients who have just begun an exercise routine or work standing or walking on a hard surface may develop shin splints. Athletic patients who suddenly increase duration, intensity, or speed are prone to stress fractures.[4] With female athletes, it is important to determine menstrual status. Amenorrhea coupled with endurance-type training suggests stress fracture as a cause of tibial pain. Runners who complain of aching, cramping pain always occurring at a specific distance or timing is suggestive of chronic compartment syndrome. All of the above exercise-induced problems gradually will become worse. Distinction is based more on palpation findings; in some cases radiographic imaging (stress fracture), bone scans (stress fracture), or measurements of compartment pressure (compartment syndrome) are needed

Examination

The examination focuses on palpation of the tender or swollen area. A general rule of thumb is that stress fractures, although causing a diffuse tenderness, often have a discrete localized area that is extremely tender. Percussion distal or proximal to this site often will cause pain at the site of the stress fracture.

When swelling is present, the distinction between localized and diffuse swelling may be helpful. A diffuse pattern of swelling that resolves with leg elevation is indicative of a vascular cause (venous drainage). Swelling localized to a specific compartment of the leg is suggestive of compartment syndrome. Localized swelling is suggestive of DVT if found more in the belly of the triceps surae group. Localized swelling on the tibia or fibula may represent a stress fracture. Defects are occasionally visible or palpable at the medial leg with tennis leg and several centimeters proximal to the insertion of the Achilles tendon with rupture. With Achilles rupture, squeezing of the calf muscle fails to produce passive plantarflexion (Thompson test).[5]

Passive plantarflexion of the ankle may increase pain in the calf with DVT or calf strain. Adding resistance may increase the pain with muscle involvement, less with DVT. Further functional testing may indicate an involved muscle. For example, placing stretch on a tendon/muscle and then asking the patient to contract against the examiner's resistance may localize the problem.

When passive dorsiflexion causes severe posteromedial pain or when plantarflexion produces severe anterior pain, a related compartment syndrome is likely.

Further evaluation is strongly based on the suspected disorder. If a stress fracture is suspected, radiographs may demonstrate a healing callus or a periosteal reaction. However, it will often take 2 to 3 weeks for the callus to appear, if at all. Oblique views of the area may be needed to visualize the healing process. The definitive tool is a bone scan. If the suspicion is DVT, Doppler ultrasound is a decent alternative to venography, the gold standard.[6] When Achilles tendon pathology is suspected, soft tissue ultrasonography may be valuable but is operator dependent. When Achilles rupture is suspected, disruption of Kager's triangle (a radiolucent area composed of the posterior flexors, tibia, and Achilles tendon) on a lateral radiographic view may be visible.[7]

MANAGEMENT

- Suspicion of DVT requires medical referral for further evaluation and possible anticoagulant therapy.
- If compartment syndrome is suspected, referral for compartment pressure measurement is suggested.
- Achilles tendon rupture requires surgical management in most cases; if the patient is older and not active, nonsurgical management, including a period of casting and non-weight bearing may be sufficient; however, the retear rate is high in active or athletic individuals.[8]
- Achilles tendinitis can be managed with modification of activity, gentle stretching, ice after activity, and an elastic strapping support with the foot in plantarflexion; a graduated eccentric training program is often helpful.
- Stress fractures of the tibia usually will heal well with avoidance of impact loading from running or jumping for a period of a few weeks followed by low-impact conditioning for 4 to 6 weeks before returning to the full

sport activity. Calcium intake should be increased to 1 g daily during the healing process and maintained at 800 mg daily during training.[9] Shock-absorption materials in the shoes may help dissipate impact forces.

Algorithm

An algorithm for evaluation and management of calf/heel pain is presented in Figure 13–2.

SELECTED DISORDERS OF THE LOWER LEG AND POSTERIOR HEEL*

SHIN SPLINTS

Classic Presentation

The patient complains of anterior or posterior lower leg pain that is often insidious in onset. If asked, the patient may remember walking or running on a hard surface. The pain is a deep ache that is often worse with weight bearing.

Cause

Shin splints are ill-defined. It appears that tendinitis, periostitis, muscle strain, or interosseous membrane strain have all been implicated. There are generally two types. The anterior shin splint involves the tibialis anterior, extensor hallucis longus, and digitorum longus. These muscles are used for shock absorption; when they are weak or placed under increased demand as in walking or running on hard surfaces or when the shoe has no shock-absorbing quality, the force is transmitted to the tibia and its attachments. The posterior type of shin splint involves the tibialis posterior, flexor hallucis longus, and flexor digitorum longus muscles. The soleus has also been implicated. These muscles act as ankle stabilizers and appear to be overstrained when the patient is hyperpronated.[3]

Evaluation

The pain is often at the middle or lower third of the tibia. Anterior shin splints are tender just lateral to the middle tibia. Pain and tenderness for posterior shin splints is posteromedial to the middle or lower tibia. Pain may be increased by stretch or contraction of the involved muscles. It is important to check the patient's shoes for proper shock-absorption capabilities. Stress fractures may appear similarly, yet the pain is usually more localized and on the tibia itself. With shin splints, the radiographs are usually normal. If the patient does not respond to treatment or there are enough historical clues to suggest stress fracture, such as endurance training in a young athlete or menstrual irregularities in a female athlete, referral for a bone scan is warranted.

Management

The acute care of shin splints involves rest from the inciting activity, ice, and support provided by elastic tape that is applied in an upward spiral pattern toward the area of tenderness. Support at the foot is also important and can be given temporarily by foot taping and/or medial heel wedges. Orthotics will often be needed if shin splints are recurrent (Table 13–2). Simply throwing away worn-out shoes and replacing them with a good shock-absorbing pair is often all that is needed. One study indicated that dietary calcium intake should be increased in those individuals with shin splints.[9]

*See also Chapter 14, Foot and Ankle Complaints, and Chapter 25, Lower Leg Swelling.

Figure 13–2
CALF/HEEL PAIN—ALGORITHM.

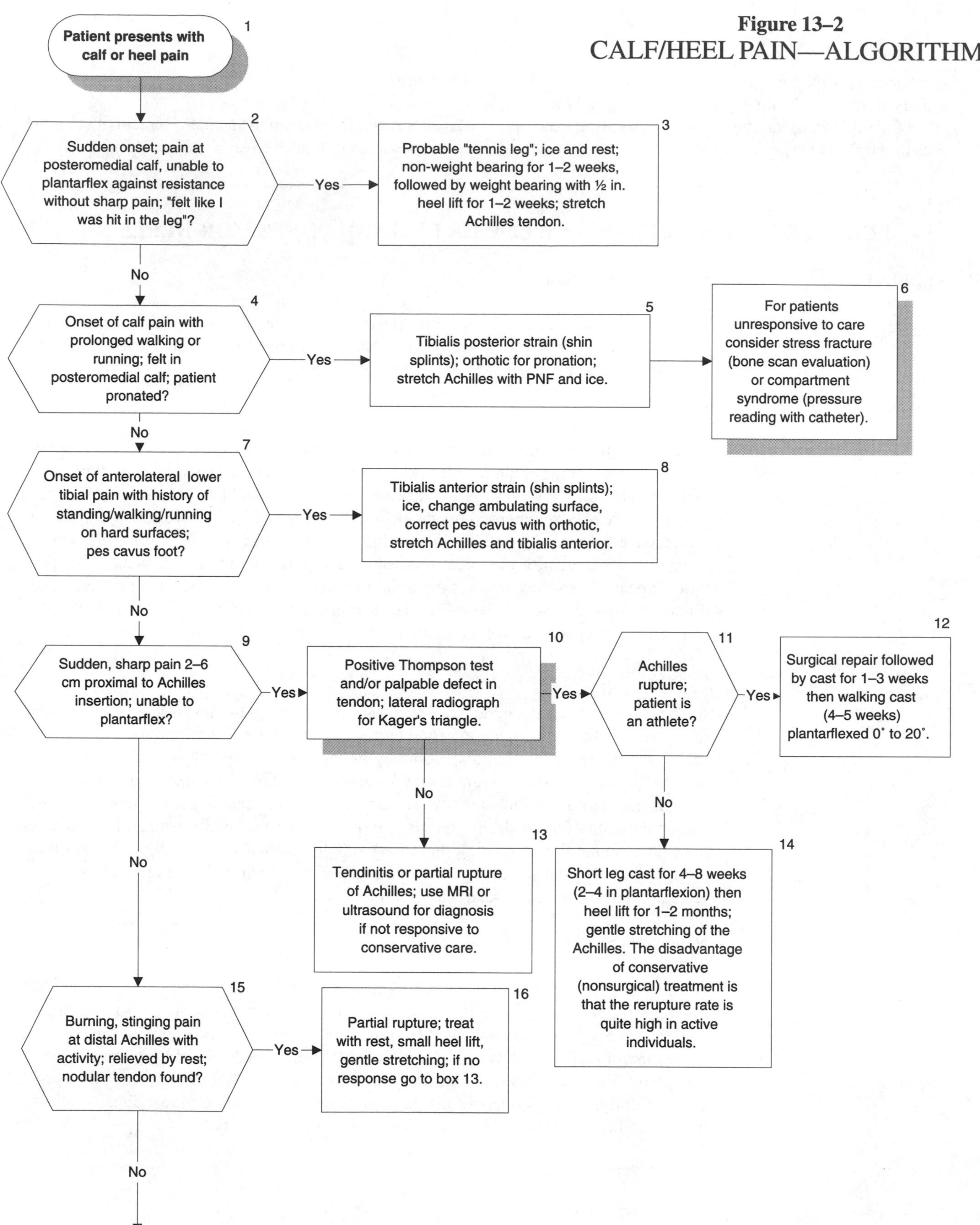
1
Patient presents with calf or heel pain
2
Sudden onset; pain at posteromedial calf, unable to plantarflex against resistance without sharp pain; "felt like I was hit in the leg"?
Yes
3
Probable "tennis leg"; ice and rest; non-weight bearing for 1–2 weeks, followed by weight bearing with ½ in. heel lift for 1–2 weeks; stretch Achilles tendon.
No
4
Onset of calf pain with prolonged walking or running; felt in posteromedial calf; patient pronated?
Yes
5
Tibialis posterior strain (shin splints); orthotic for pronation; stretch Achilles with PNF and ice.
6
For patients unresponsive to care consider stress fracture (bone scan evaluation) or compartment syndrome (pressure reading with catheter).
No
7
Onset of anterolateral lower tibial pain with history of standing/walking/running on hard surfaces; pes cavus foot?
Yes
8
Tibialis anterior strain (shin splints); ice, change ambulating surface, correct pes cavus with orthotic, stretch Achilles and tibialis anterior.
No
9
Sudden, sharp pain 2–6 cm proximal to Achilles insertion; unable to plantarflex?
Yes
10
Positive Thompson test and/or palpable defect in tendon; lateral radiograph for Kager's triangle.
Yes
11
Achilles rupture; patient is an athlete?
Yes
12
Surgical repair followed by cast for 1–3 weeks then walking cast (4–5 weeks) plantarflexed 0° to 20°.
No
13
Tendinitis or partial rupture of Achilles; use MRI or ultrasound for diagnosis if not responsive to conservative care.
No
14
Short leg cast for 4–8 weeks (2–4 in plantarflexion) then heel lift for 1–2 months; gentle stretching of the Achilles. The disadvantage of conservative (nonsurgical) treatment is that the rerupture rate is quite high in active individuals.
No
15
Burning, stinging pain at distal Achilles with activity; relieved by rest; nodular tendon found?
Yes
16
Partial rupture; treat with rest, small heel lift, gentle stretching; if no response go to box 13.
No

continues

Figure 13–2 continued

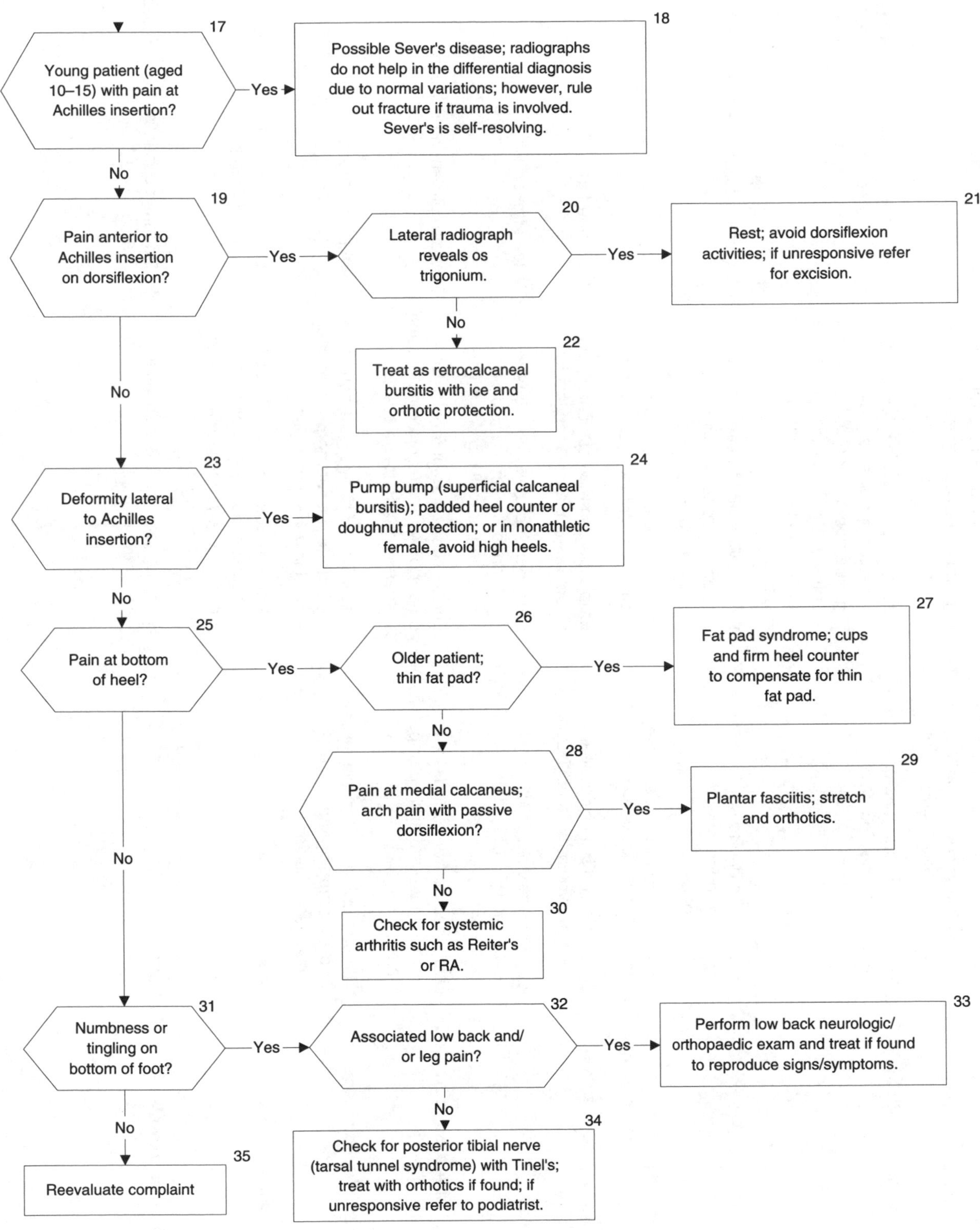

17
Young patient (aged 10–15) with pain at Achilles insertion?
Yes
18
Possible Sever's disease; radiographs do not help in the differential diagnosis due to normal variations; however, rule out fracture if trauma is involved. Sever's is self-resolving.
No
19
Pain anterior to Achilles insertion on dorsiflexion?
Yes
20
Lateral radiograph reveals os trigonium.
Yes
21
Rest; avoid dorsiflexion activities; if unresponsive refer for excision.
No
22
Treat as retrocalcaneal bursitis with ice and orthotic protection.
No
23
Deformity lateral to Achilles insertion?
Yes
24
Pump bump (superficial calcaneal bursitis); padded heel counter or doughnut protection; or in nonathletic female, avoid high heels.
No
25
Pain at bottom of heel?
Yes
26
Older patient; thin fat pad?
Yes
27
Fat pad syndrome; cups and firm heel counter to compensate for thin fat pad.
No
28
Pain at medial calcaneus; arch pain with passive dorsiflexion?
Yes
29
Plantar fasciitis; stretch and orthotics.
No
30
Check for systemic arthritis such as Reiter's or RA.
No
31
Numbness or tingling on bottom of foot?
Yes
32
Associated low back and/ or leg pain?
Yes
33
Perform low back neurologic/ orthopaedic exam and treat if found to reproduce signs/symptoms.
No
34
Check for posterior tibial nerve (tarsal tunnel syndrome) with Tinel's; treat with orthotics if found; if unresponsive refer to podiatrist.
No
35
Reevaluate complaint

Key: PNF, Proprioceptive neuromuscular facilitation; RA, rheumatoid arthritis.

Table 13–2 Shin Splint Management

Parameter	*Acute*	*Subacute*	*Symptom-Free Stage*
Criteria for diagnosis of staging	Anterior shin splints—pain/tender just lateral to middle tibia; posterior shin splints—pain/tender at posteromedial middle or lower tibia.	Pain is not constant, able to bear weight without pain; prolonged standing or walking may still cause pain.	No pain with walking and standing.
Goals and timing within each stage	Decrease pain and inflammation; approximately 1–3 days.	Strengthen and stretch lower leg muscles; increase shock absorption of shoe with anterior shin splints; support foot with posterior shin splints; about 1 week.	Emphasis on eccentric training, orthotics support, endurance training begins; 3–4 weeks.
Concerns	Pain may be due to stress fracture; consider bone scan if unresponsive.	Pain may be due to stress fracture; consider bone scan if unresponsive.	Overperformance of eccentrics.
Requirements for progression to next stage	Pain and tenderness decrease; isometric contraction not painful.	Proper shoe is chosen; concentric strength is present without pain.	No pain with eccentric training.
Manipulation/mobilization	Emphasis on tibial, calcaneal, and foot manipulation/mobilization.	Emphasis on tibial, calcaneal, and foot manipulation/mobilization.	As needed.
Modalities	Ice, compression, TENS, or high-volt galvanic (80–120 Hz/20 min/2–3 x's/1–2 days).	Ultrasound for 5–6 min/1.5 wt/cm^2 for 2–3 days; ice after any prolonged standing or walking.	Ice after activity.
External brace, support, etc.	Elastic taping from opposite side drawing around and up to painful area.	Elastic support as before; extra support with weight bearing using strapping tape for arch support.	Wean patient off support.
ROM/flexibility/massage	Mild stretching of involved muscles; gentle stripping massage of involved muscles.	Stage 3 or 4 MRT to gastrocnemius; continue postisometric stretching of all lower leg muscles.	Maintain flexibility.
Open chain exercise	Mild isometrics.	Isometrics at every 20°–30° arcs against resistance of wall or opposite leg progressing to elastic tubing training.	Continue through endurance phase of elastic tubing training.
Closed-chain exercise	None.	Standing toe raises (emphasize eccentric phase).	Continue eccentric training using 3 sets of 10.

continues

Table 13–2 continued

Parameter	*Acute*	*Subacute*	*Symptom-Free Stage*
Proprioceptive training	Diagonal PNF patterns without resistance.	Diagonal PNF patterns with resistance from examiner or elastic tubing; wobble board training begins; minitrampoline two-legged jumping.	Wobble board while bouncing a ball; minitrampoline, single-leg jumps for balance and strength.
Associated biomechanical items	Look at shoes to determine shock absorption and wear pattern.	Cast for orthotics if deemed necessary; temporarily support with taping or heel wedges.	Fit orthotics.
Lifestyle/activity modifications	Avoid running and standing for long periods on hard surfaces	Progress to jogging or minitrampoline running; avoid prolonged standing.	Avoid prolonged standing on hard surfaces; educate patient regarding shoe wear and need for buying a new pair of shock-absorbing shoes at the appropriate time.

Key: TENS, transcutaneous electrical nerve stimulation; PNF, proprioceptive neuromuscular facilitation; MRT, myofascial release technique.

TIBIAL STRESS FRACTURE

Classic Presentation

The patient is usually an active individual who develops insidious onset of tibial pain. Overuse from running or prolonged activity on hard surfaces may be evident in the history.

Cause

If a repetitive stress is applied to bone such as with running, the ability to remodel may be overwhelmed because of inadequate healing time. There is still debate as to whether stress to bone is due to weak muscles or fatigue that causes increased bone loading or more to the forceful repetitive contraction of muscles and the imposed stress at their origins onto bone. An early stage of this microtrauma event has been called the medial tibial stress syndrome; when a fracture has not occurred, however, there is enough of an inflammatory and remodeling process to cause pain.[10] Tibial stress fractures account for half of all stress fractures occurring in athletes.[11] The location varies depending on the underlying inciting activity. Runners are more likely to have middle and distal third tibial fractures; ballet dancers, the middle third; and military recruits, the proximal tibia. Middle shaft fractures as seen in dancers have a reputation for delayed union or continuing on to full fractures (sometimes called the "dreaded black line" radiographically).[12]

Evaluation

The clinical presentation of an athlete who first notices shin pain at the end of a run that gradually becomes incapacitating over several days of running is highly suggestive. Additionally, menstrual irregularities in a patient complaining of shin pain is a clue to possible underlying osteopenia. Pain is often better initially with rest, but returns with any impact loading. Tenderness is often found at a discrete area on the tibial shaft. Percussion or tuning-fork testing at a distance either proximal or distal to the site may cause reproduction or worsening of the pain at the fracture site. Radiographically, a small radiolucent line may be seen, or a localized periosteal new bone formation may be evident. Oblique films are often necessary. Definitive diagnosis may require a bone scan when radiographs are equivocal but the presentation suggests stress fracture.

Management

Most stress fractures can be managed conservatively with restriction of impact loading for several weeks. Immobilization usually is not necessary unless the athlete or patient refuses to stop the inciting activity. Crutches may be necessary in some patients who are symptomatic with walking. For the elite athlete, conditioning with bicycle riding or pool training with a water vest are good alternatives for maintaining aerobic fitness. Gradual return to activity begins with low-impact training over several weeks prior to full return.

Orthotic support, nutritional recommendations (especially calcium), and modification of activity are important for prevention. Ultrasound and pulsed electromagnetic field therapy to accelerate healing time have been suggested but are unproven at this time.

COMPARTMENT SYNDROME

Classic Presentation

The presentation varies depending on the compartment involved and whether it is acute or chronic. Typically, the patient often is an athlete complaining of aching or cramping of the leg following exercise. Pain is relieved by rest initially. There may be complaints of numbness/tingling into various parts of the foot.

Cause

The lower leg is divided into four compartments: (1) anterior, containing the tibialis anterior, extensors of the toes, anterior tibial artery and vein, and deep peroneal nerve; (2) deep posterior, containing the posterior tibialis and toe flexors and the posterior tibial artery and vein; (3) superficial posterior, containing the soleus, gastrocnemius, and plantaris; and (4) lateral, containing the peroneal muscles and nerve. Increased pressure in any of these fascial compartments may lead to damage to the muscles. Increased pressure also may cause numbness and paresthesia into the distribution of the corresponding nerve due to ischemia.[13] The most common cause is exercise induced; however, in acute situations, compartment syndrome may develop secondary to local trauma or fracture.

Evaluation

In athletes, the symptoms usually occur within 10 to 30 minutes of exercise. The pain will subside over minutes or hours following activity; initially the patient will remain pain free until the next exercise session. The examination is often normal between exacerbations. Tenderness and swelling may be evident over the involved compartment. Pulses are often normal distally; however, some sensory changes may be evident in the distal distribution of the involved nerves. Fascial defects with muscle herniation are evident in approximately 40% of patients, but they may not be evident unless the athlete runs for several minutes. The definitive tool is measurement of compartmental pressure while resting and after exercise. Elevated levels reach 80 mm Hg, compared with the normal of 30 to 40 mm Hg following exercise. Levels above 40 mm Hg that remain elevated for 15 to 30 minutes or longer indicate compartment syndrome.[2]

Management

For chronic compartment syndrome a period of rest for 4 to 8 weeks may be successful. For acute syndrome and patients who do not respond to conservative care, fasciotomy is the treatment of choice.

ACHILLES TENDINITIS

Classic Presentation

The patient is often an athlete who complains of pain in the Achilles tendon following jumping or running activities.

Cause

The Achilles tendon is covered by a peritenon composed of mainly fatty areolar tissue. The area most affected is approximately 2 cm proximal to the calcaneal insertion. The demands on the tendon are high in running and jumping sports. Interestingly, the tendon has been shown to function with as little as 25% fiber continuity. Insertional problems include irritation of the retrocalcaneal bursa and irritation leading to a Haglund's deformity. Additionally, seronegative arthritides such as Reiter's syndrome and ankylosing spondylitis cause an enthesopathy at this site. Pain and tenderness at the calcaneus may indicate Sever's apophysitis in a younger athlete.

Evaluation

Chronic degeneration may be evident as a knotty swelling, with more acute damage evident by local tenderness made worse by stretch and/or stretch and contraction. Palpable defects in the tendon may indicate impending rupture in an athlete complaining of sharp stabbing or burning pains at the site. Triceps surae tightness may be a contributing factor. Passively dorsiflexing the ankle with the knee extended should demonstrate a normal of 20° to 30°. This is a measure of gastrocnemius tightness. To test the soleus, the knee is flexed and the ankle is dorsiflexed. Thirty to 35° of dorsiflexion at the ankle should be available. The Thompson test is performed on patients suspected of having a rupture. This would occur in an on-the-field scenario. If squeezing the calf in the prone relaxed patient does not produce passive plantarflexion of the foot, Achilles rupture is likely. When partial ruptures are suspected, MRI can help differentiate between tendinitis and partial rupture.[14]

Management

Achilles tendinitis is managed with rest, ice, and modification of the inciting activity. Taping the ankle in plantarflexion with an elastic support is helpful in the early stages. Heel lifts may also decrease the stretch effect on the injured Achilles. Long-term goals are to modify faulty training activity and to gradually and consistently stretch the triceps surae group. Orthotics may be necessary in those individuals with hyperpronation. Training should consist of a graduated eccentric loading program. An example would be to begin initially with toe raises with emphasis on slowly lowering the body weight. Additional weight can be carried to increase the training effect over time. Achilles ruptures may be managed with cast immobilization in nonathletic or older individuals. However, in athletes the rerupture rate is quite high; therefore, surgery is the recommended treatment.[8]

TENNIS LEG

Classic Presentation

The patient is often a middle-aged athlete playing tennis when she or he feels a sudden pain in the back of the upper calf followed by inability to walk on the toes. The pain is often described as that of having been shot or hit on the back of the knee.

Cause

Tearing of the musculotendinous junction of the medial head of the gastrocnemius is the most common cause.[15] This occurs when the knee is suddenly extended while the foot is dorsiflexed. Another mechanism may be sudden dorsiflexion of the foot/ankle with the knee already extended.

Evaluation

Tenderness and some swelling are usually evident at the upper medial calf. The patient has increased pain on resisted plantarflexion of the foot or is unable to raise up on the sole and toes of the foot on the involved side.

Management

Management depends on the degree of damage. A full tear may require a long leg cast with the knee in 60° of flexion and the foot in 10° to 15° of plantarflexion for several weeks. More mild injuries can be managed with crutch-supported walking with gradual return to weight bearing with a temporary heel lift (6 to 12 mm) to take the stretch off the torn muscle. Gradual stretching after 1 week should progress to mild plantarflexion isometrics progressing to toe raises when tolerated.

REFERENCES

1. Clemens DB. Tibial stress syndrome in athletes. *J Sports Med.* 1974;2:81.
2. Black KP, Schultz TK, Cheung NL. Compartment syndromes in athletes. *Clin Sports Med.* 1990;9:471–487.
3. Reber L, Perry J, Pink M. Muscular control of the ankle in running. *Am J Sports Med.* 1993;21:805–810.
4. Hershman EB, Mailly T. Stress fractures. *Clin Sports Med.* 1990;9:183–214.
5. Thompson T, Doherty J. Spontaneous rupture of the tendon of Achilles: a new clinical diagnostic test. *Anat Res.* 1967;158:126.
6. Richlie DL. Noninvasive imaging of the lower extremity for deep venous thrombosis. *J Gen Intern Med.* 1993;8:271.
7. DiStefano VJ, Nixon JE. Ruptures of the Achilles tendon. *J Sports Med.* 1973;1:34.
8. Cetti R, Christensen SE, Ejsted R, et al. Operative versus nonoperative treatment of Achilles tendon rupture: a prospective randomized study and review of the literature. *Am J Sports Med.* 1993;21:791–799.
9. Myburgh KH, Srobler N, Nosakes TD. Factors associated with shin soreness in athletes. *Physician Sportsmed.* 1988;16:129.
10. Mubarak SJ, Gould RN, Lee YF, et al. The medial tibial stress syndrome. *Am J Sports Med.* 1982;10:201–205.
11. Matheson GO, Clement DB, McKenzie DC, et al. Stress fractures in athletes: a study of 320 cases. *Am J Sports Med.* 1987;15:46–58.
12. Green NE, Rogers RA, Lipscomb AB. Nonunion of stress fractures of the tibia. *Am J Sports Med.* 1985;13:171–176.
13. Martens MA, Backaert M, Vermaut G, et al. Chronic leg pain in athletes due to recurrent compartment syndrome. *Am J Sports Med.* 1984;12:148.
14. Clemens DB, Taunton JE, Smart GW. Achilles tendonitis and peritendinitis: etiology and treatment. *Am J Sports Med.* 1984;12:179.
15. Miller WA. Rupture of the musculotendinous junction of the medial head of gastrocnemius muscle. *Am J Sports Med.* 1977;5:191–193.

Chapter 14

Foot and Ankle Complaints

CONTEXT

The foot and ankle must provide support and shock absorption while at the same time balancing the body. This requires both mobility to adapt to varying terrain and stability to allow supported contact and push-off from the ground. Shock absorption occurs as a result of the dissipation of forces through complex movements at the foot and ankle and imposed adaptation through mainly rotation in the lower extremity at the knee, hip, and pelvis. Therefore, dysfunction at the feet may have consequences throughout the entire body. Foot problems may be local or referred; however, the need for lower-extremity compensation may result in more proximal pain, including low back pain.

As the most distal site of the body, the foot is also commonly affected by vascular disorders. Arterial occlusive disorders block blood flow. Valvular insufficeincy in veins, coupled with gravity, may lead to a pooling effect and vascular stasis. Neurologic dysfunction associated with metabolic neuropathies such as seen with diabetes is often felt first distally in the feet. The bare foot is exposed to possible trauma and infection. The supported foot is vulnerable to the pressure effects and biomechanical alterations of footwear. When compromised by vascular and/or sensory deficits, a patient is more prone to the long-term consequences of unnoticed or unattended lesions. This is most often seen with the diabetic patient.

The most common conditions involving the foot and ankle are biomechanical in nature and include the following:

- first toe—hallux valgus/rigidus, turf toe, gout, and sesamoiditis
- metatarsals—Morton's neuroma, metatarsalgia, "dropped metatarsal," and stess fractures
- medical longitudinal arch—pronation/supination effects, navicular subluxation, and plantar fasciitis
- lateral foot—cuboid subluxation, peroneal tendinitis, and fracture of the base of the fifth metatarsal
- ankle—inversion and eversion sprains
- Achilles tendon/heel—tendinitis, bursitis, and fat pad syndrome

The majority of foot complaints are due to lack of proper support or inappropriate footwear. Points of overpressure or irritation from shoes may result in corns or calluses, sesamoiditis or aggravation of hallux valgus at the first toe, or fat pad syndrome at the heel. Tight-fitting shoes may also cause compression of metatarsals or cause damage to toenails (ie, black toenails). If the foot is too mobile (ie, hyperpronated), lack of support may cause plantar fasciitis and strain of the tibialis posterior and other tendons. Therefore, it is requisite that shoes be examined and that the foot be evaluated for any predisposition to overstrain due to forefoot or hindfoot abnormalities (ie, varus or valgus).

Ankle sprains are common. The most common are plantar flexion/inversion sprains. Although most injuries are dismissed as a simple sprain, it is important to rule out associated injury, including various fractures and ligament ruptures. Chronic ankle pain or instability (or both) is not uncommon following repeated ankle sprains. Therefore, it is important not only to manage the acute injury but to attempt to prevent future occurrences. This often requires a determination of the needs of the associated activity or sport coupled with a strictly adhered-to postinjury rehabilitation program.

GENERAL STRATEGY

History

- Determine whether the complaint is one of pain, stiffness, popping/snapping, crepitus, locking, weakness, or numbness and tingling.
- Determine whether the patient had a traumatic onset or whether there is an obvious overuse history.
- With overuse, determine the type of activity, the types of shoes worn, and the type of surface the patient works or exercises on.

Evaluation

- With trauma, palpate for points of tenderness and obtain radiographs for the possibility of fracture/dislocation if the patient is unable to bear weight or bony tenderness is found.
- With ankle sprain, challenge for stability posterior to anterior (drawer test), into inversion (lateral ankle) and into eversion (medial ankle).
- Examine the patient's shoes and feet for signs of excessive wear on the soles of both shoes and feet.
- When the onset is nontraumatic, challenge the musculotendinous attachments with stretch, contraction, and a combination of contraction in a stretched position.
- When trauma or overuse is not present, evaluate the patient's foot and ankle for swelling and deformity (bursitis, gouty tophi, osteoarthritis [OA], etc.)

Management

- Displaced or nonhealing fractures must be referred for medical management.
- Ankle sprains can be managed with mobilization/manipulation, use of a stabilizing brace or taping, and gradual return to weight bearing with emphasis on prevention.
- Tendinitis and muscle strain can be managed conservatively with taping support, gradual stretching, ice, and activity modification.
- The patient should be educated regarding proper fitting of shoes and the special needs for specific sports requirements and type of foot (pes planus versus pes cavus).
- Orthotics may be a helpful preventive measure when biomechanical abnormalities are found, such as hindfoot or forefoot varus or valgus.
- Diabetic foot problems should be referred to the primary treating physician.

RELEVANT ANATOMY AND BIOMECHANICS

Terminology used to describe foot architecture and deformity can be confusing. Basically, the foot is divided into a hindfoot, a midfoot (midtarsal), and a forefoot. Dysfunction in one part of the foot is often accommodated or compensated by movement in another portion of the foot. Following is a brief description of the joints in each section of the foot and definitions of functional or structural deviations that may occur:

- Hindfoot—The hindfoot includes the distal tibiofibular joint. In addition to several ligaments, the two bones are joined by a flexible interosseous membrane. The distance between the bones may widen with dorsiflexion of the ankle, as the talus wedges between the malleoli. With this movement the interosseous membrane is stretched, causing superior movement of the proximal tibiofibular joint with accompanying external rotation; the opposite occurs with plantarflexion. The talar/malleolar joint is referred to as the talocrural joint. The subtalar joint consists of the talus and calcaneus. Stability of this area is provided in part by the ligamentous support of the tibia and fibula, dorsiflexion of the ankle, or supination of the subtalar joint. Ligamentous support at the ankle is provided laterally by three ligaments: (1) the anterior talofibular ligament (supports the ankle against inversion and anterior-to-posterior movement), (2) the posterior talofibular ligament (prevents mainly excessive ankle dorsiflexion and adduction), and (3) the calcaneofibular ligament (a major stabilizer for inversion). The medial side of the ankle is supported by the deltoid ligament, which consists of the tibionavicular, tibiocalcaneal, and anterior and posterior tibiotalar ligaments. These ligaments act together to prevent excessive eversion of the ankle (Figure 14–1).
- Midfoot—The midtarsal joints are the interconnections between the talus and calcaneus and the midtarsal bones, including the cuboid, navicular, and cuneiforms.
- Forefoot—The forefoot is made up of the distal articulations of the metatarsal, metatarsophalangeal (MTP), and interphalangeal joints.

The close-packed position for most of the foot is supination with the exception of the phalanges, which are close-packed in extension. Supination involves a triplanar movement of adduction, plantarflexion, and inversion. Pronation involves a triplanar movement pattern of abduction, dorsiflexion, and eversion. These movement patterns can occur independently in the foot and are often compensatory to each other. For example, supination in the hindfoot may be compensated by pronation in the forefoot.

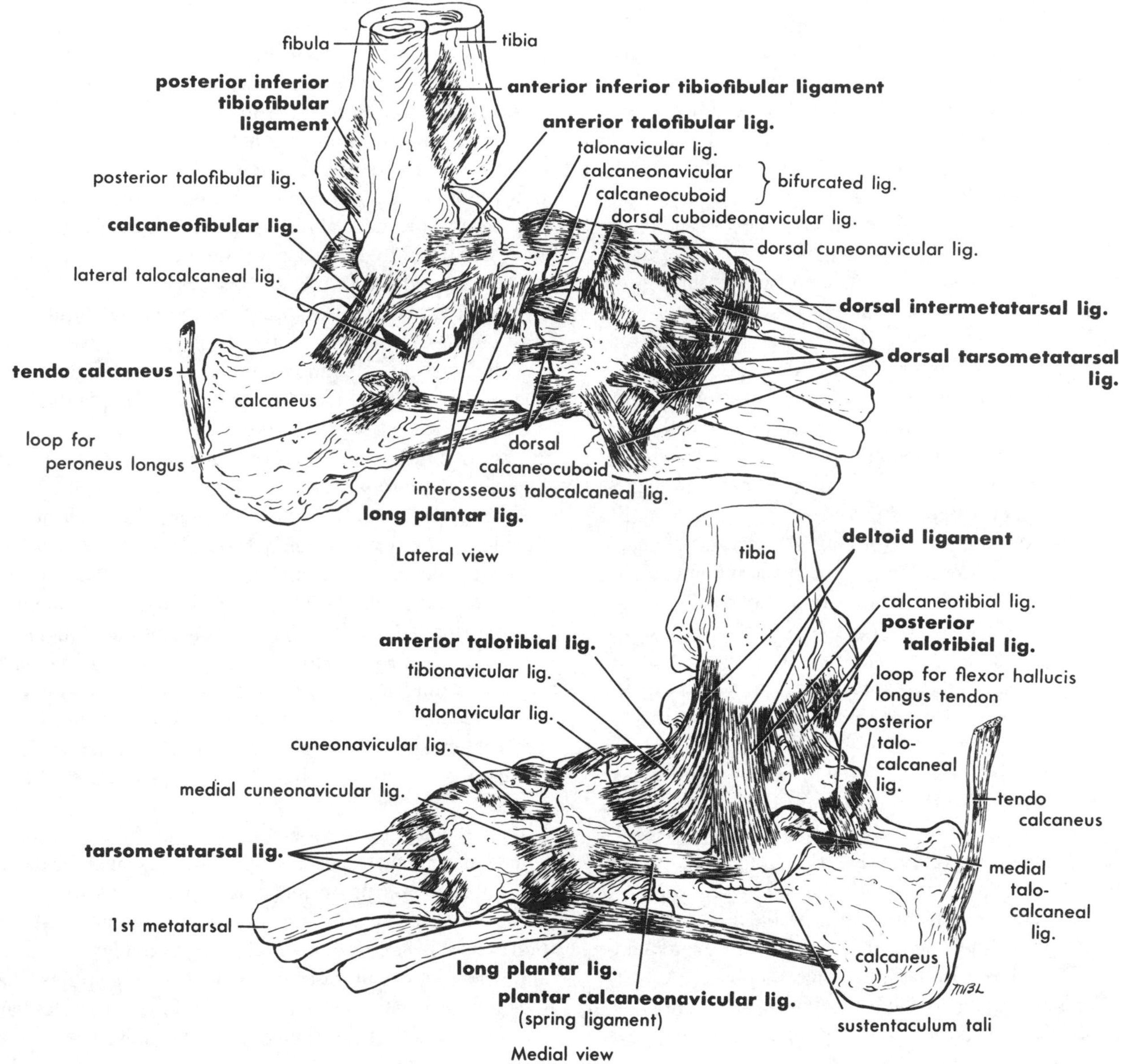

Figure 14–1 Ligamentous support of the ankle and foot. *Source:* Reprinted with permission from J.E. Crouch, *Functional Human Anatomy*, 4th ed., p. 174, © 1985, Lea & Febiger.

- Forefoot varus—When the forefoot is held in an inverted position while the subtalar joint is in a neutral position, forefoot varus occurs. This deformity occurs in only 9% of the population.[1] If not compensated for, the first toe would not reach the ground during midstance and toe-off. Forefoot varus is usually compensated for by pronation of the subtalar joint, making this clinically similar to pes planus (flattened medial longitudinal arch).
- Forefoot valgus—When the forefoot is held in an everted position while the subtalar joint is in a neutral position, forefoot valgus occurs. This deformity occurs in 44.8% of a symptomatic population.[2] The midtarsal joint must supinate in an effort to bring the fourth and fifth metatarsal heads to the ground. This will cause the foot to appear high arched (pes cavus) during ambulation.

- Hindfoot varus—The calcaneus is held in an inverted position while the subtalar joint is in neutral with hindfoot (rearfoot) varus. This is often due to a developmental abnormality of the tibia in which it is bowed outward (tibia varum). The result is that the subtalar joint must rapidly pronate through an inordinate range of motion (ROM) in an effort to bring the medial condyle of the calcaneus toward the ground during ground contact. This produces excessive torque in the foot and lower extremity.
- Hindfoot valgus—The calcaneus is held in an everted position while the subtalar joint is in neutral with hindfoot (rearfoot) valgus. The major difficulty with this position is lack of stability at heel contact.
- Equinus (talipes equinus)—Simply put, this is a restriction to dorsiflexion at the talocrural joint. Most often this is due to contracture of the soleus or gastrocnemius; however, developmental or acquired damage to the talus may also create this problem.
- Plantarflexed first ray—Normally the metatarsal heads are in alignment in the transverse plane when they are dorsiflexed. When the first metatarsal head is lower, the great toe is in contact with the ground while the other metatarsal heads are not, leading to a biomechanical problem similar to that in forefoot valgus. This problem is associated with a high-arched (pes cavus) foot.

Gait is often divided into an ipsilateral swing and a stance phase. The stance phase is divided into contact, midstance, and propulsion subphases. The time spent in each phase is dependent on whether an individual is walking, jogging, or running. With walking, the stance phase is approximately 62% of the total cycle. The contact and propulsion subphases account for 25% of the stance phase each, with the remaining 50% of time spent in the midstance subphase.[3] A basic description of the biomechanics of walking and running may help explain the impact that properly functioning feet have on the lower extremities and the rest of the body.

Support is needed for the split-second contact when the heel first touches the ground and when the foot leaves the ground at toe-off. Immediately after heel contact and during half of the foot-flat phase, the foot must dissipate the ground reaction force and accommodate to different terrain. This is accomplished through a "universal joint" reaction at the subtalar joint. The talus is everted by internal rotation of the tibia, unlocking the midtarsal, talocalcaneal joint and creating pronation. Associated with this internal rotation is flexion of the knee. The combination of these actions helps to dissipate ground forces. External rotation causes the opposite effect of talar inversion and the consequent rigid, locked position of supination.

The subtalar and midtalar joint complex (talocalcaneal, talonavicular, and calcaneocuboid joints) determines movement of most of the foot. However, the medial segment consisting of the first metatarsal and first cuneiform generally moves in a direction opposite that of the rest of the foot. Therefore, even when the hindfoot is structurally normal, compensations may result from abnormalities of the forefoot. Forefoot varus implies that the medial forefoot (the first toe in particular) does not contact the ground unless the foot pronates to bring it down. This is called a compensated forefoot varus. Forefoot valgus has the opposite effect, with the first metatarsal in contact with the ground without contact of the fifth and fourth metatarsals.

Muscle function across the foot and ankle is quite complex during ambulation. Without reference to weight bearing, the dorsiflexors of the foot/ankle are the tibialis anterior and peroneus tertius (see Figure 13–1). The plantarflexors are the peroneus longus and brevis and the tibialis posterior. Eversion of the foot/ankle is primarily due to the peroneals; inversion, primarily the tibialis anterior and posterior. These are simple uniplanar movement patterns; however, the foot functions more in a triplanar mode. From the standpoint of subtalar joint pronation and supination, tendons that pass medially to the subtalar joint axis are supinators, including the extensor hallucis longus, extensor digitorum longus, tibialis anterior and posterior, and flexors hallucis longus and digitorum longus. Those muscle tendons that pass laterally to the subtalar joint axis are pronators, including the three peroneal muscles. The peroneus longus may act as either a pronator or a supinator based on the position of the first metatarsal.

At heel contact, most lower leg muscles function eccentrically to decelerate imposed pronation. These include the tibialis anterior and posterior, extensor hallucis longus and digitorum, and the soleus/gastrocnemius group. This function indirectly acts as a shock-absorbing strategy by the body and when not optimum leads to anterior shin splints.[4] During midstance there is a dual function of many muscles based on the subphase of midstance. Early in midstance, the tibialis posterior and soleus act eccentrically and in the later phase they contract concentrically to supinate the subtalar and midtarsal joints. In the early midstance phase, the toe flexors also fire eccentrically, assisting the tibialis posterior and soleus in decelerating forward movement of the tibia. During push-off (propulsion) all of the intrinsic foot muscles act to stabilize the foot firing concentrically. The peroneus longus fires concentrically to plantarflex the first ray, as does the flexor digitorum longus. Other first toe muscles fire eccentrically to assist in stabilizing the first metatarsal joint.

EVALUATION

History

Careful questioning of the patient during the history taking can point to the diagnosis (Table 14–1).

Table 14–1 History Questions for Foot/Ankle Complaints

Primary Question	*What Are You Thinking?*	*Secondary Questions*	*What Are You Thinking?*
Did you injure your foot?	Inversion or eversion sprain, strain, fracture	Sprain your ankle?	Inversion sprain likely with lateral pain; eversion with medial pain
		Twist ankle with foot planted?	Possible distal tibial or fibular fracture or diastasis
		Did your big toe get forced backward?	Turf toe (capsular sprain of first MTP joint)
		Sudden outside foot pain with pushing-off (eg, jumping)?	Possible cuboid subluxation or metatarsal fracture (fifth)
		Stubbed toe and still painful?	Fracture of toe
		Heel pain landing from a jump?	Fat pad irritation, bone bruise, fracture
Acute onset of pain with no trauma?	Rheumatoid or crystalline arthritides, plantar fasciitis	Heel pain associated with hand pain?	Rheumatoid arthritis
		Heel pain associated with sacroiliac or low back pain?	Reiter's syndrome or ankylosing spondylitis
		Sudden pain in arch?	Plantar fasciitis
Gradual onset of first toe pain?	Hallux valgus, hallux rigidus, sesamoiditis	Hurt more when you pull your big toe back?	Hallux rigidus
		Is your big toe deviated out?	Hallux valgus (associated bunion)
		Pain on the bottom of your big toe?	Sesamoiditis
Gradual onset of pain in other parts of the foot?	Stress fracture, neuroma, tarsal subluxation, metatarsalgia	Stand for long periods of time on hard surfaces or run a lot of miles?	Stress fracture
		Pain on bottom of ball of foot?	Dropped metatarsal (subluxation) or neuroma
		Pain worse with tight shoes?	Metatarsalgia
Numbness and tingling in foot?	Nerve root, tarsal tunnel syndrome, interdigital neuritis	Associated with low back pain?	Nerve root
		On bottom of your foot?	Tarsal tunnel syndrome
		In between your toes?	Interdigital neuritis

Key: MTP, metatarsal phalangeal.

Clarify the type of complaint.

- Is the complaint one of pain, stiffness, looseness, crepitus, deformity, or a combination of complaints?
- Localize the complaint to the ankle, midfoot, or forefoot and then determine whether it is anterior, posterior, medial, or lateral.

Clarify the mechanism if traumatic.

- Plantarflexion/inversion injury to the ankle—Consider inversion ankle sprain with injury to the anterior talofibular, calcaneofibular, and (rarely) posterior talofibular ligaments.
- Dorsiflexion/eversion injury to the ankle—Eversion ankle sprains tear the deltoid ligament and are often associated with dislocation.
- Twisting injury at the ankle with foot fixed (ski boot type injury)—Consider distal tibial and fibular fracture or diastasis.
- Sudden dorsiflexion of the first toe—Turf toe is a sprain of the first MTP joint; the opposite mechanism occurs with sand toe.
- "Stubbing" the toe (especially the fifth toe)—Consider sprain or fracture.
- Lateral foot pain with push-off while jumping—Consider cuboid subluxation and metatarsal fracture.
- Heel pain when landing from a jump—Consider fat pad irritation and bone bruise to the calcaneus; when excessive force is applied, a calcaneal fracture is possible.

Determine whether the mechanism is one of overuse.

- In what position does the patient work? Does the patient stand or walk on hard surfaces?
- What type of footwear does the patient wear? Unsupportive footwear allows foot sprain/strain, high heels force the toes into the toe box and allow shortening of the Achilles tendon.
- If the patient is an athlete, determine the training program, running surface, and type of shoe.
- Are the demands of the sport or activity matched by the shoe design? Cleats may provide support in some settings and in others anchor the foot, causing injury; high-top shoes may provide some ankle stability in some sports while limiting needed motion in others.
- How often does the athlete replace his or her shoes? For high-level activity, every 4 to 6 months may be best; at the very least, every 9 months.

Determine whether the patient has a current or past history/diagnosis of the foot/ankle complaint or other related disorders.

- Are there associated low back, pelvis, hip, or knee complaints or diagnoses?
- Does the patient have gout, diabetes, arterial insufficiency, varicose veins, or familial predisposition to hallux valgus?

Pain Localization

The following are possible causes of pain based on localization (Figure 14–2, A to C, and Table 14–2):

Forefoot.

- First MTP joint
  1. Acute traumatic—turf toe, sesamoiditis
  2. Nontraumatic—hallux valgus, hallux rigidus, gout
- Fifth metatarsal
  1. Acute traumatic—transverse (Jones) fracture, avulsion fracture, spiral fracture
  2. Nontraumatic—peroneus brevis insertional tendinitis, Iselin's disease (traction apophysitis)
- Metatarsals
  1. Acute traumatic—stress fracture
  2. Nontraumatic—interdigital neuroma (between second and third interspaces), Freiberg's (second metatarsal), stress fracture

Midfoot.

- Medial
  1. Acute traumatic—fracture, rupture of plantar fascia, navicular subluxation
  2. Nontraumatic—accessory navicular, Köhler's disease, navicular subluxation, stress fracture, plantar fasciitis
- Lateral
  1. Acute traumatic—fracture, cuboid subluxation
  2. Nontraumatic—cuboid subluxation, peroneus brevis tendinitis
- Anterior
  1. Acute traumatic—fracture, subluxation
  2. Nontraumatic—talar exostosis, anterior tibial nerve compression, subluxation

Hindfoot.

- Posterior
  1. Acute traumatic—Achilles rupture, Achilles tendinitis
  2. Nontraumatic—pump bump, Achilles tendinitis, retrocalcaneal bursitis, blisters
- Plantar
  1. Acute traumatic—calcaneal fracture, bone bruise

2. Nontraumatic—fat pad syndrome, plantar fasciitis, subluxation, Sever's disease

Traumatic and Overuse Injuries

With direct trauma from a blow or dropping an object on the foot, it is always important to consider fracture of the impacted bone. When a sudden pain is felt following landing on the ball or heel, fracture should be suspected. A sudden propulsion (such as quick, forceful push-off for a sprint or jump) may on occasion cause a spiral fracture of the fifth metatarsal. When the pain is located at the first toe, it is important to determine whether there was a hyperextension or a hyperflexion of the toe, each of which is suggestive of capsular sprain.

With ankle injury it is always important to determine the position of the foot: plantarflexed/inverted (lateral stabilizing ligaments) or dorsiflexed/everted (medial stabilizing ligaments). It is extremely important to determine the ability of the patient to bear weight, and the degree and onset of swelling. All of these are important screening questions and observations in determining the need for radiographic screening for fracture. Generally, the inability to bear weight associated with significant swelling correlates with the degree of damage.

Overuse injuries are often subtle. It is important to determine the types of shoes worn by the patient and the types of ground surfaces encountered. It is important in athletes to review the specific requirements of the sport and the ability of the shoes to accommodate. How often does the athlete replace worn-out shoes? Many overuse injuries will be uncovered as a shoe problem (too flexible or loss or lack of shock absorption); too flexible or too hard a ground surface; or, in the examination, an underlying varus/valgus deformity of the rearfoot or forefoot. If there is an underlying biomechanical problem, the repetitiveness and frequency of participation become important modifiers.

Weakness

Weakness may be less appreciable directly but indirectly evident because the toes catch on rugs or hit a curb or step when climbing stairs. This indicates neural compromise, especially when the condition is nonpainful. Inability to dorsiflex the ankle indicates primarily tibialis anterior (L4-L5) weakness or perhaps inability to dorsiflex the toes (extensor digitorum) or the big toe (extensor hallucis longus, L5). The physical examination should focus on differentiating between nerve root and peripheral nerve damage. Inability to rise up onto the toes is suggestive of S1 nerve root involvement, especially when nonpainful. Other rare possibilities are rupture of the tibialis posterior in an elderly patient or a patient with rheumatoid arthritis (RA), or Achilles tendon in an athlete.

Instability

Instability is primarily an ankle-related complaint. It is important to determine the number and severity of ankle sprains in the past. It is also important to determine whether footwear relieves this complaint.

Restricted Motion

Restricted motion is not a common foot complaint. The primary occurrence is at the first MTP joint. This is suggestive of hallux rigidus, especially when dorsiflexion is stiff and painful. When the patient complains of ankle stiffness, it is important to determine whether there is any associated pain or crepitus. Pain suggests mechanical blockage from a talar or calcaneal exostosis or scar tissue from a previous ankle injury. When dorsiflexion of the ankle is limited, contracture of the Achilles is likely; however, some equinus deformities due to congenital malformation of the tarsal bones are possible. This is differentiated in the exam through postisometric attempts at increasing movement. The patient may also claim that stretching makes no difference when there is an underlying congenital cause. When end-range positions feel blocked, the examiner should be directed to test for accessory motion restrictions.

Superficial Complaints

There are numerous dermatologic complaints of the feet. It is important first to determine whether the patient is diabetic or has signs/symptoms suggestive of diabetes. Next, it is important to ask about shoe wear. Black toenails and other compressive processes are common when the shoe is too short and the patient is athletic. Fungal infection between the toes is common and is usually responsive to over-the-counter medications. The patient should be questioned regarding showering in public facilities, the environment of the shoes during activity (are the shoes made of a material that "breathes"?), and how hot/sweaty the feet become with activity. All may be predispositions for fungal growth.

When the patient complains of deformity, the location is often pathognomonic. A bunion at the first MTP indicates hallux valgus. Bony protrusion at the anterior ankle is often due to talar exostosis. Deformity at the posterior heel suggests Hagland's deformity (prominent posterosuperior lateral border of the calcaneus) or a pump bump (associated retrocalcaneal bursa).

Numbness and tingling on the bottom of the foot should suggest nerve root or peripheral nerve compression. It is again important to determine whether the patient is diabetic. When the symptom is on the bottom of the foot, an S1 nerve root problem (especially when associated with low back pain complaints) is likely. When the numbness/tingling extends across the bottom of the foot, tarsal tunnel syndrome due to poste-

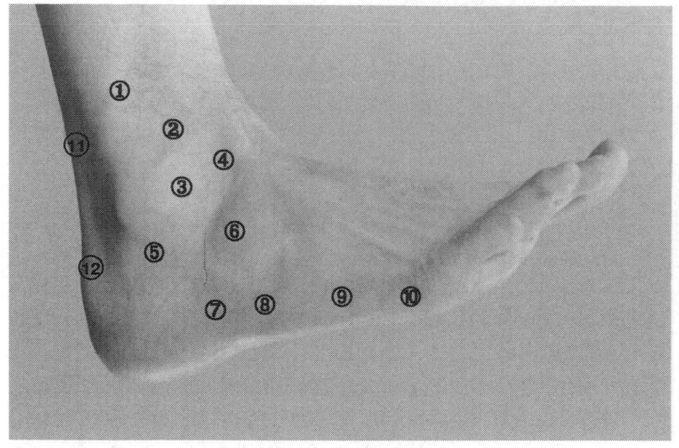

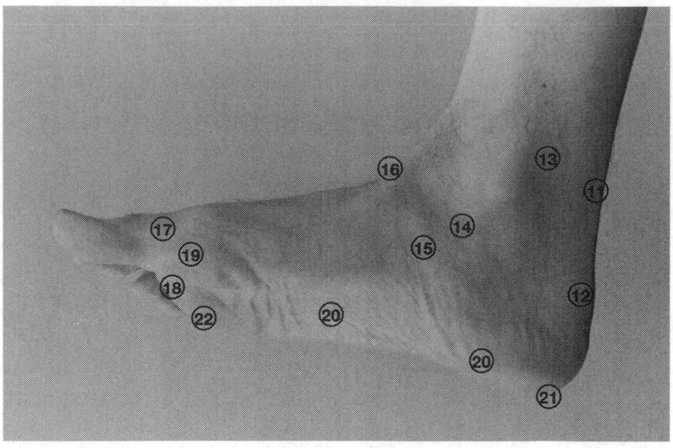

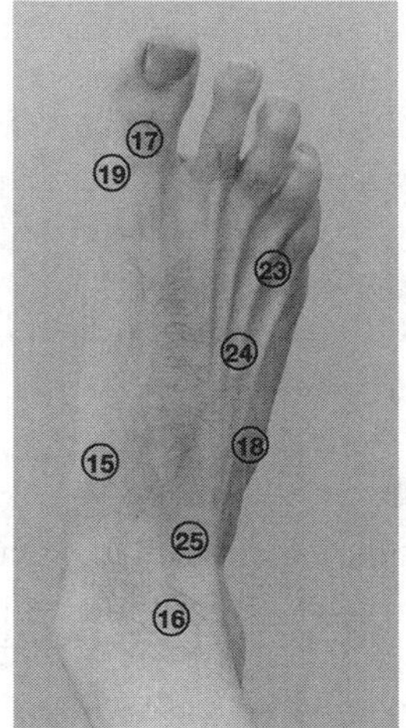

Figure 14–2 **A**, Lateral aspect of ankle and foot. **B**, Medial aspect of ankle and foot. **C**, Dorsal aspect of ankle and foot. *Note:* See Table 14–2 for explanation of numbers.

rior tibial nerve compression is likely. This is often associated with an overpronated foot. When numbness is in between the toes, interdigital neuritis due to transverse compression of the metatarsals is likely. This is often due to too narrow a shoe.

Examination

The Foot

Prior to examining the feet, it is often helpful to examine the patient's footwear. If the patient is an athlete, it is important for him or her to bring in training shoes. Looking at wear patterns on the shoe may be helpful. Generally, the normal wear pattern is at the ball of the foot and at the lateral heel. Excessive lateral wear at the heel coupled with a caved-in appearance of the inside of the shoe would suggest pes planus, the opposite for pes cavus. The inside of the shoe should be examined to determine whether any irregularities may act as friction sources to the skin or underlying tendons. Check the shoe for flexibility and shock-absorption characteristics. Is there a firm heel counter? The fit of the shoe is also important to gauge while the patient is standing. Is there sufficient toe room? Is the shoe supportive of the medial longitudinal arch? Does the lacing fit too tightly over the talus or extensor tendons?

Much can be gained through observation of the foot. Look for indications of wear and tear on the foot. These are often clues to various foot deformities.

- Callus or corn formation at the dorsal aspect of the proximal interphalangeal (PIP) joint is seen with both hammer toes (flexion deformity of the PIP joint) and claw toes (dorsal subluxation of the MTP joint). A callus is

Table 14–2 Foot and Ankle Pain Localization

#	*Significant Structures*	*Overt Trauma*	*Insidious or Overuse*
1	Peroneus longus and brevis tendons; sural nerve	Contusion of structures	Peroneal tendinitis
2	Anterior tibiofibular ligament	Diastasis with possible associated damage to interosseous membrane	Scar formation from previous ankle injury; talar subluxation
3	Anterior talofibular ligament	Inversion ankle sprain	Scar tissue from previous ankle sprains
4	Peroneus tertius, extensor tendons, superficial peroneal nerve	Contusion of structures	Peroneus tertius or extensor tendinitis
5	Calcaneofibular ligament, peroneal tendons and retinaculum	Inversion ankle sprain with possible torn ligament or retinaculum	Snapping peroneal tendons dislocating due to retinaculum looseness or rupture
6	Extensor digitorum brevis, distal calcaneus, bifurcate ligament	Bifurcate ligament rupture; avulsion fraction of distal calcaneus	Strain of extensor digitorum brevis
7	Cuboid	Cuboid subluxation	Cuboid subluxation
8	Base of fifth metatarsal; peroneus brevis insertion	Avulsion fracture (often secondary to inversion sprain); transverse (Jones) fracture	Iselin's disease (apophysitis), insertional tendinitis
9	Metatarsal shaft	Metatarsal fracture	Stress fracture
10	Fifth MTP joint	Fracture of phalange	Tailor's bunion
11	Achilles tendon	Achilles rupture	Achilles tendinitis
12	Subcutaneous and retrocalcaneal bursae, Haglund's process	Bursitis	Chronic bursitis, pump bump caused by irritation from Haglund's process
13	Tibialis posterior tendon; tibial nerve	Rupture of tibialis posterior tendon	Tibialis posterior tendinitis; tibial nerve compression
14	Deltoid ligament	Eversion ankle sprain	Ligament sprain from overpronation
15	Navicular tubercle	Secondary to eversion sprain; subluxation	Subluxation; accessory navicular, tarsal coalition
16	Tibialis anterior tendon	Strain from plantarflexion injury	Tendinitis
17	Dorsal first MTP joint	Turf toe (hyperextension) or sand toe (hyperflexion) injury to joint capsule	Hallux rigidus
18	Sesamoids	Sesamoid fracture or sesamoiditis	Sesamoiditis
19	Lateral aspect of first MTP joint	Capsular sprain	External bunion associated with hallux valgus; gout
20	Plantar fascia	Plantar fascia rupture	Plantar fasciitis
21	Calcaneus, fat pad	Calcaneal fracture	Fat pad syndrome or inflammation associated with rheumatoid arthritis and Reiter's syndrome
22	Metatarsal heads	Metatarsal subluxation	Morton's neuroma; subluxation
23	Interdigital space	Interdigital neuritis	Interdigital neuritis
24	Metatarsals; extensor tendons	Metatarsal fracture, subluxations	Stress fractures, tendinitis
25	Extensor rentinaculum, joint capsule, talus	Capsular sprain, talar subluxation, retinaculum sprain	Capsular sprain, talar subluxation, retinaculum sprain

Note: See Figure 14–2 for localization of numbered areas.

also found at the plantar MTP joint with claw toes. Mallet toe (flexion contracture of the distal interphalangeal [DIP] joint) causes callus formation at the DIP joint and distal toe.

- Bunion development on the medial aspect of the first MTP joint is indicative of hallux valgus.
- Bunion development is also seen on the fifth MTP joint and is referred to as a tailor's bunion or a bunionette. It is often due to forefoot valgus.
- Callus formation under the second through third or fourth metatarsal heads is found with forefoot varus.
- Callus formation under the first, second, and sometimes third metatarsal heads is found with forefoot valgus.

If the patient is complaining of numbness and/or tingling of the foot, a search for neural irritation begins with a test of nerve root integrity with deep tendon reflex testing and sensory testing. The foot is primarily innervated by the L4-S2 nerve roots. If intact, a search for local nerve irritation focuses on the patient's localization. When there is numbness/tingling on the bottom of the foot, Tinel's test (tapping) of the posterior tibial nerve behind the medial malleolus may reveal tarsal tunnel syndrome. If the location of the symptom is more in the toes (possible associated motor loss), Tinel's test is performed at the anterior ankle at the anterior tibial branch of the deep peroneal nerve. If the patient's symptom extends from the medial knee down through the medial foot, testing with compression at the adductor tunnel or Tinel's test performed below the medial joint line of the knee may reveal saphenous nerve involvement. If sensation is decreased between the first two toes, the deep peroneal nerve is compromised. If there is numbness between the other toes, interdigital nerve compression is likely. When there is pain and numbness and tingling on the bottom of the ball of the foot, palpation for a neuroma between the second and third or third and fourth metatarsal spaces should be performed. Passive extension of the toes may increase the complaint, and some relief may be provided by passive flexion.

Determination of forefoot and rearfoot valgus and varus is usually performed with the patient prone. The opposite leg is brought into flexion on the table to neutralize rotation of the examined extremity. The initial positioning of the foot is an attempt at finding subtalar neutral (Figure 14–3). The approach is described generally in two ways:

1. The foot is grasped at the fourth and fifth metatarsal heads and passively dorsiflexed until resistance is felt. The foot is then supinated and pronated until a point is found where slightly more movement in either direction causes the talus to "fall off" to one side or the other. This is the neutral position.
2. The foot is grasped at the fourth and fifth metatarsal heads and distracted downward to remove dorsiflexion. The foot is then passively inverted and everted while the examiner palpates the talus with the thumb and middle finger. There will be a point at which the talus is felt by both thumb and finger or not at all by either. This is the neutral position.[5]

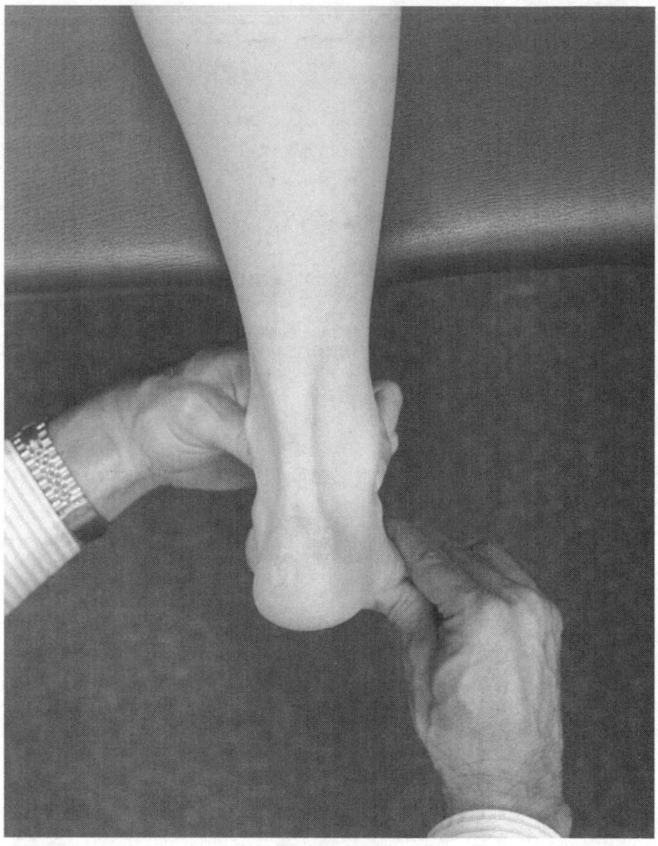

Figure 14–3 Neutral position of foot. Palpating the talus with the index finger and thumb, the examiner pronates and supinates the foot until the talus is felt equally by both contacts. The fourth and fifth metatarsal heads are then passively dorsiflexed.

At this point a determination of the degree of hindfoot varus and valgus can be determined by connecting intersecting lines through the tibia (Achilles) and the calcaneus. If the calcaneus is within 2° to 8° of varus, the leg-to-heel alignment is normal. When the heel is inverted, hindfoot varus is present; if everted, hindfoot valgus is present. Through the use of a plastic goniometer placed against the metatarsal heads, the degree of forefoot valgus or varus should be measured.[6]

The patient can also be examined from behind in the standing position. The angle formed by the lower third of the Achilles and the calcaneus can be determined, indicating statically a tendency toward pronation (hindfoot valgus) or supination (hindfoot varus). When the patient is asked to raise onto his or her toes, a medial longitudinal arch should form.

If there is no arch in this position, tarsal coalition (fibrous or bony connection between tarsal bones) or rupture of the tibialis posterior tendon is likely. Various forms of navicular positioning testing have been suggested. One is the Feiss line. This line represents a connection between the apex of the medial malleolus and the length of the first metatarsal. The navicular tuberosity is usually at a point along this line. When the patient stands with equal weight between the feet (about 6 in. apart), the navicular should remain in close proximity to this line. The farther it drops away, the more pronated the individual. A similar test is the navicular drop test (Figure 14–4, A and B). A paper card is placed alongside the foot with the patient not bearing weight. The navicular tuberosity position is marked on the card. The patient then bears his or her weight onto the foot and the distance between the original mark and the mark of the new navicular tubercle position is measured. Greater than about ½ in. implies a hyperpronated foot.

Radiographic assessment of the foot is dictated by whether the intention is a search for fracture or whether a biomechanical appreciation of the foot is desired. Fracture is usually evident on non–weight-bearing views. The standard series consists of an anteroposterior (AP [dorsiplantar]) view, an oblique (lateral aspect of foot elevated 30°) view, and a lateral view. On the AP view, the forefoot and part of the midfoot are well visualized. The oblique view gives an excellent alternate perspective of the metatarsals. The talonavicular and calcaneocuboid joints and sinus tarsi are also demonstrated on this view. Calcaneonavicular coalition (bony bridging) is best seen on the medial oblique view. The lateral view is excellent for viewing the calcaneus, talus, navicular, cuboid, first cuneiform, and head of the fifth metatarsal. In addition to fractures, bony exostosis may be seen on the talus, calcaneus, or fifth metatarsal head. Additional views are designed to visualize the phalanges, sesamoids, calcaneus, and talus.

If the intention is to obtain a more functional perspective of the foot, weight-bearing films are often used. Numerous lines of mensuration are used to evaluate the biomechanical relationship of the foot on these views, a description of which is beyond the scope of this text. However, the most commonly used is the Cyma line.[7] On the lateral view, the articulation between the talonavicular and calcaneocuboid (Chopart's joint) forms a continuous S-shaped line. A break in the line anteriorly at the talus indicates pronation; a break posteriorly indicates supination.

The Ankle

The ability to bear weight is an important screening maneuver with ankle sprains. If the patient is able to bear weight, palpation of specific bony landmarks including the malleoli, navicular, and cuboid areas will help determine the need for radiographs.[8] The ankle is tested primarily for stability. Three tests are commonly used. The first is the anterior drawer test (Figure 14–5A). This test is performed with the patient supine and the ankle plantarflexed 15° to 20°.[9] This position places the anterior talofibular ligament perpendicular to the tibia. The examiner pulls forward by stabilizing on the anterior distal tibia with one hand and the other hand pulls forward while cupping the calcaneus posteriorly. While analogous to the anterior drawer test of the knee, the more collateral ligamentous system is being tested in the ankle. With an inversion sprain the anterior talofibular ligament may be damaged. The anterior drawer test will reveal some laxity when compared with the opposite ankle. To eliminate stabilization

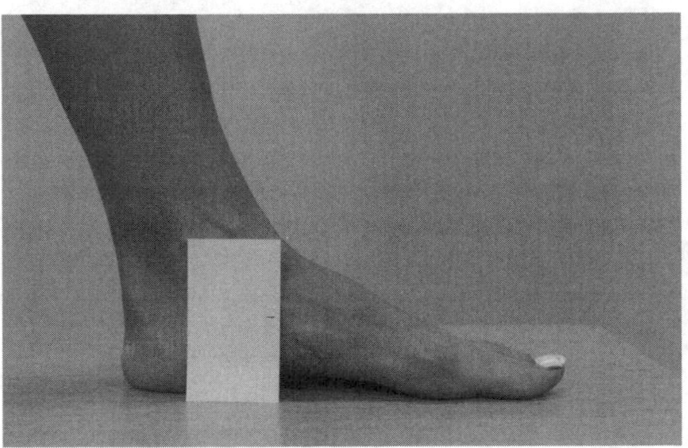

A

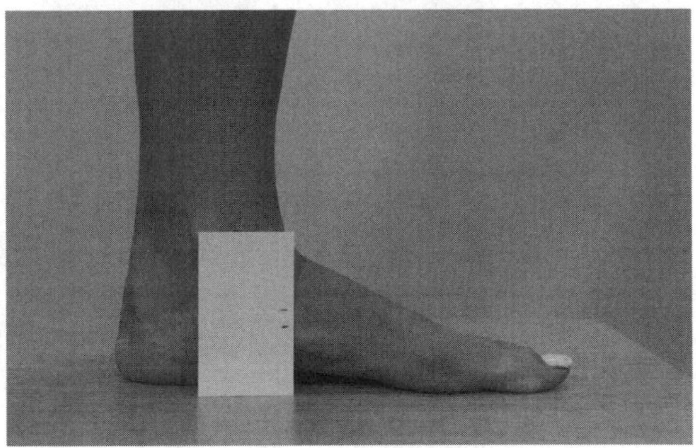

B

Figure 14–4 The navicular drop test for pronation. **A**, The patient's navicular tubercle is marked while the patient is not bearing weight. **B**, The position is then again marked when the patient bears weight onto the foot. If the difference between marks is greater than B\ , in., the patient is probably functionally a pronator.

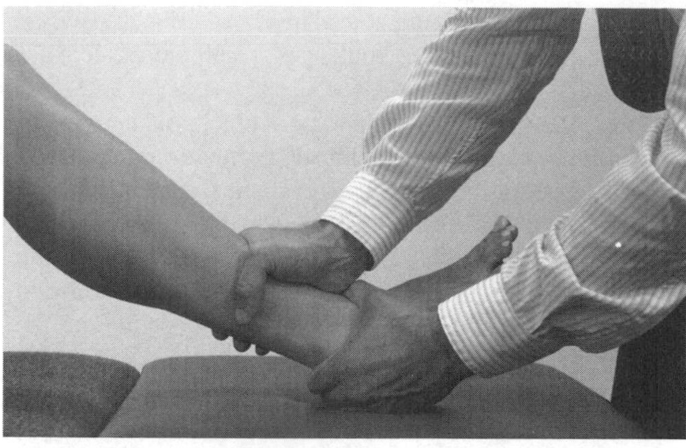

A

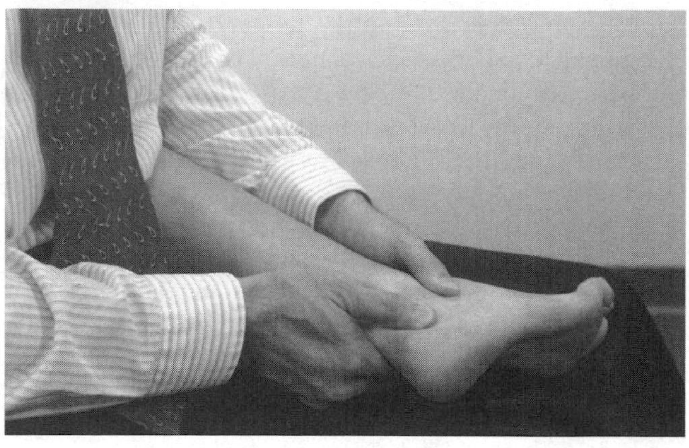

B

Figure 14–5 **A**, The anterior drawer test. With the knee flexed and the ankle flexed to 15°, the examiner stabilizes the tibia while pulling forward on the calcaneus. **B**, Inversion test for lateral ankle stability.

from the Achilles, testing with the knee in 90° of flexion may be more sensitive. If the ankle is felt to be unstable in dorsiflexion, damage to the collateral and deep system of ligaments is likely. The talar tilt test is simply an inversion stress applied to the ankle. The best position is side-lying with the patient's knee flexed 90° with the hands cupped around the ankle, imparting an inversion force (Figure 14–5B). The talar tilt tests for integrity of the calcaneofibular ligament. The Kleiger test is an eversion test of the ankle.[10] With the patient seated on the examination table, the non–weight-bearing foot is everted out to test for the medial deltoid ligament complex.

The stabilizing function of muscles and the presence of tendinitis may be evaluated by basic resisted movement patterns coupled with stretch patterns. Also, resisting the movement pattern starting from the stretched position will reveal tendinitis not evident from neutral position testing.

- Dorsiflexion/eversion—mainly due to the peroneus tertius; stretching into plantarflexion/inversion may also increase pain.
- Dorsiflexion/inversion—mainly due to the tibialis anterior; stretching into dorsiflexion/evertion may also increase pain.
- Plantarflexion/eversion—mainly due to the peroneus longus and brevis; stretching into plantarflexion usually is more painful than dorsiflexion.
- Plantarflexion/inversion—mainly due to the tibialis posterior; stretching into dorsiflexion may also increase pain.

Radiographic assessment of the ankle is primarily used to rule out associated fracture. Standard views include an AP, a lateral, and a mortise view (AP with 20° of internal rotation of the foot). Stress views may be indicated when there is a need to distinguish between a single-ligament and a two-ligament injury. The talar tilt is the degree of opening between the tibia and talus when stressed into inversion as viewed on an AP view. More than 10° of tilt indicates injury to the anterior talofibular and calcaneofibular ligaments (positive predictive value between 85% and 99%).[11] The mortise view is helpful in revealing osteochondral fracture of the talus (seen less clearly on the straight AP view) and diastasis due to interosseous membrane rupture between the tibia and fibula.

The Heel

The primary differential of plantar heel pain is between plantar fasciitis and fat pad syndrome. In patients with a history of rheumatoid conditions, radiographs may prove helpful in detecting characteristic changes, yet these conditions would rarely present solely as heel pain. The primary distinction between fat pad syndrome and plantar fasciitis is the location of tenderness. Fat pad tenderness is directly in the middle of the heel. This tenderness is decreased by squeezing the bottom of the heel together and pressing over the same tender area. By squeezing the heel together, the remaining fat pad is approximated, providing more cushioning; tenderness should decrease substantially. Plantar fasciitis is painful at the medial heel because of the attachment to the medial tuberosity of the calcaneus. Pain or tenderness may be increased through passive tension. This is accomplished by dorsiflexing the first toe and, if not positive, adding dorsiflexion of the ankle. The pain with plantar fasciitis is often across the bottom of the foot along the medial longitudinal arch.

Radiographic examination is warranted if there is trauma such as landing on the feet, if the patient is an adolescent (Sever's disease), or if there is a history of rheumatoid disease. Radiographs for plantar fasciitis are usually misleading because of the appearance of a heel spur. The heel spur is falsely accused of being the cause of the patient's pain. Resolution of pain without changes in the spur is the usual course of events. It is believed that the spur is a consequence of plantar fascial tension rather than a cause of plantar fasciitis.[12]

MANAGEMENT

Traumatic Injury

- Most fractures of the foot and ankle should be referred for reduction and casting; some exceptions include small, nondisplaced avulsion fractures at the fifth metatarsal or lateral malleolus (period of immobilization may be needed) and most toe fractures, which can be buddy-taped for 2 to 3 weeks.
- Sprains of the MTP capsules can be managed with appropriate taping, mild mobilization, and support.
- Ankle sprains are managed based on the degree of injury. Even full-ligament rupture (third degree) can be managed conservatively with a cast and graduated return to weight-bearing and activity, although comanagement or previous experience is suggested prior to following this approach (Table 14–3).

Overuse and/or Biomechanical Injury

- Overuse injuries are often treated symptomatically with ice, myofascial stretching, and modification of activity; long-term management includes modification of footwear, terrain, maintenance of proper accessory motion, functional training of supportive muscles focusing on eccentric or concentric needs, and possible prescription of orthotic support.
- Stress fractures can be managed by immobilization with non-weight bearing for 2 to 6 weeks, depending on activity level; aerobic conditioning may be continued with non–weight-bearing activities (eg, pool running).

Preventive Management

- Preventive management for ankle sprains includes isometric training of the peroneals, hip abductors, and tibialis anterior with stretching of the Achilles; proprioceptive training using taping, proprioceptive neuromuscular facilitation (PNF) techniques, or balance exercises with balance boards.
- Patient education regarding proper selection of shoes and foot hygiene is an important tool by which to avoid future problems.

An in-depth discussion of shoe design and prescription is beyond the scope of this text; however, some basics can be reviewed (see Figure 14–6). The commonly used terminology and maxims for shoe construction are as follows:

- The heel counter should be deep and firm to provide stability and cushioning.
- The shank should be strong and should not deform with weight bearing (the shank represents the portion on the bottom of the shoe that corresponds to the medial longitudinal arch).
- The toe box should be spacious enough to avoid compression of the metatarsals.
- The shoe should be long enough to avoid compression of the toes at the end of the toe box.
- If used in a sporting activity, the shoe should be specific to the sport.

The mold upon which the shoe is constructed is referred to as the last. There are essentially two types, straight last and curved last. The straight last is a better design for the pronated foot. The curved last design is for a forefoot angled medially. This shoe design is better for the supinated foot and/or those with hallux valgus. There are generally three types of last construction: (1) the board-lasted shoe, (2) the slip-lasted shoe, and (3) the combination last shoe (Figure 14–7). When a patient's foot is severely pronated, the board-lasted shoe is usually best because of the support provided by a hard fibrous material placed on the inner surface of the shoe. The slip-lasted shoe is constructed by stitching the upper into a one-piece moccasin and then gluing it to the sole. This provides a lighter, more flexible shoe; however, it has less stability. This shoe construction is probably better for the cavus foot. The combination last shoe combines a board-lasted heel with a slip-lasted forefoot, the best of both worlds. This shoe construction is best for those with rearfoot varus or mild pronators.

A prescription for orthotics is often given to the patient with foot pain. An orthotic is a device that is usually placed in the shoe to accommodate for biomechanical abnormalities or to cushion painful areas. The biomechanical orthotic can be constructed according to individual need or purchased as an off-the-shelf product. The type of orthotic is often based on the seriousness or complexity of the problem and the patient's ability to purchase the product. The three common

Table 14–3 Ankle Inversion Sprain Rehabilitation

Parameter	*Acute Stage*	*Subacute Stage*	*Chronic Stage*
Criteria	Lateral ankle swelling is dependent on degree of injury; pain and possible instability found with ankle inversion stress; radiograph to rule out fracture.	Swelling has decreased; some lateral ankle pain with inversion stress.	No swelling, mild lateral ankle pain on inversion stress.
Goals	Reduce swelling and pain; avoid full weight bearing.	Progress to full weight bearing through the use of crutches and ankle support (Air-Splint, taping, or brace).	Proprioceptively stabilize the ankle; correct any underlying predispositions; consider taping with agressive sport activity.
Concerns	Possible fracture of tibia, fibula, talus, metatarsals; bifurcate ligament rupture; peroneal tendon dislocation.	Talar dome fracture not evident on radiograph.	Too early a return to sports activity; during restrengthening athlete needs external support.
Requirements for progression to next stage including approximate time needed	Partial weight bearing possible; reduction in swelling and pain; 1–3 days.	Full weight bearing without crutches; no swelling evident; full ROM 2–3 days.	Able to balance on one leg and hop on one leg without pain; 1–2 weeks.
Manipulation/mobilization	Based on the degree of injury; general talar or tibial adjustment (opposite position of injury-dorsiflexion/eversion) may assist.	General talar or tibial adjustment may assist.	Determine need for navicular, cuboid, calcaneal, and talar adjusting.
Modalities	Ice 3–5 ×'s/day for 20 minutes (1 hour in between); rest, elevation, TENS or EMS (high-volt galvanic at 80–120 Hz with ice for 20 min/1–2 ×'s/day).	Ice after activity; combination ultrasound/EMS at 1.0 watt/cm^2, 1–15 Hz for 6–8 minutes.	Ice after activity.
External brace, support, etc.	Air-Splint or open Gibney type of ankle taping, or Unna boot splint; crutch walking with toe touching only.	Air-Splints or lace-up brace; patient weaned off crutches after 1–2 days of gradual weight bearing.	Figure-of-eight elastic bandage support with walking if necessary; taping for sports activities.
ROM/flexibility	Mild passive ROM.	BAPS board begun with the patient seated; postisometric relaxation approach to stretching.	Continue stretching with postisometric approach.

continues

Table 14–3 continued

Parameter	*Acute Stage*	*Subacute Stage*	*Chronic Stage*
Open-chain exercise	Mild isometrics in neutral.	Isometrics at end-range into dorsiflexion and eversion; passive PNF diagonal patterns; side-lying straight leg raises for peroneals and hip abductors.	Elastic tubing exercises for dorsiflexors and evertors; resisted PNF diagonal patterns.
Closed-chain exercise	None.	Gradual two-legged toe raises and half-squats.	Toe raises against resistance.
Proprioceptive training	Toe touching with crutch use.	Consider weight-bearing with TENS application; taping or support acts as a proprioceptive stimulus.	Progression to weight-bearing exercises on BAPS (wobble) board; follow progressive training.
Associated biomechanical items	Check for weakness of hip abductors; evaluate for pronation or supination.	Shoes should contain a rigid heel counter; orthotic prescription should be performed if deemed necessary and swelling has decreased enough for casting.	Orthotic fitting.
Lifestyle/activity modifications	Crutch walking only for first 1–3 days with grade 2 injuries.	Crutch walking should involve partial weight bearing, continuing to elimination of crutch use.	Stretch prior to activities such as running and jogging.

Key: TENS, transcutaneous electrical nerve stimulation; EMS, electrical muscle stimulation; BAPS, biomechanical ankle platform system (Medipedic, Jackson, Michigan).

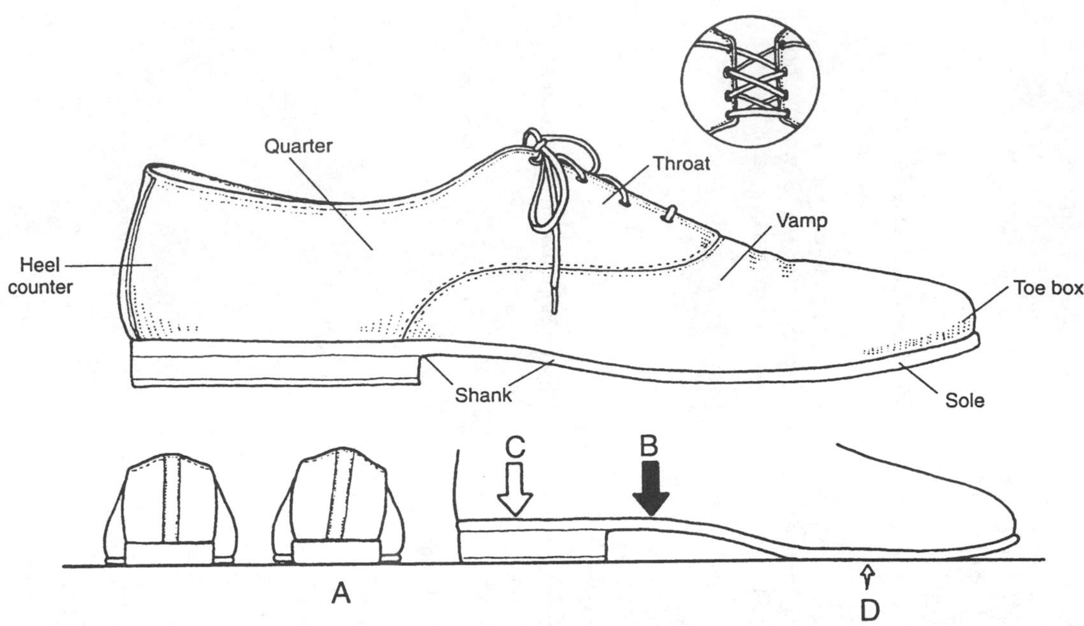

Figure 14–6 Components of a well-made shoe. The heel counter should fit securely (it may be necessary to balance Haglund's deformity with felt), and its bisection should be vertical to the supporting surface. (Poor quality control often allows for an asymmetrical heel counter that is either inverted or everted relative to the table top; see **A**. Also, the shank should be able to resist forceful compression without deforming (**B**), and it should be angled in such a way that when the heel seat is compressed (**C**), the plantar forefoot lifts no more than a few millimeters (**D**). (AP instability is present if the forefoot lifts more than this.) The toe box should provide ample space so as not to compress a dorsomedial or lateral bunion. Because it allows for greater separation of the upper, Blucher lacing may be necessary to accommodate the bulkier orthoses (**E**). If the patient complains that his or her foot is sliding forward on the orthotic (which often occurs when heel lifts are used), a strip of adhesive felt may be placed along the undersurface of the tongue that gently presses the foot posteriorly onto the orthotic, thereby preventing slippage and improving control. *Source:* T. Michaud, *Foot Orthoses and Other Forms of Conservative Foot Care,* p. 224, © 1997, T. Michaud, Newton, Massachusetts

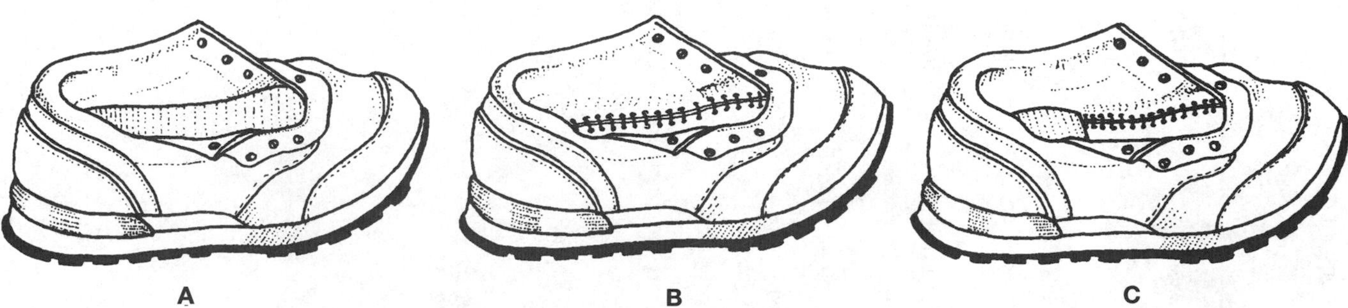

Figure 14–7 Types of shoe construction. **A**, Board-lasted shoe. **B**, Slip-lasted shoe. **C**, Combination last shoe. *Source:* T. Michaud, *Foot Orthoses and Other Forms of Conservative Foot Care*, p. 226, © 1997, T. Michaud, Newton, Massachusetts

types of customized orthotics are the non–weight-bearing, casted orthotic; the non–weight-bearing, vacuum-applied orthotic; and the weight-bearing foam impression orthotic. There is much emotional debate as to the best way to cast the feet. The foam impression orthotic supporters claim that it is a "functional" orthotic giving an individual impression of the patient's foot in a closed-packed position. The argument against this approach is that the feet are casted in an imperfect position and allowed to splay and elongate with weight bearing. The non–weight-bearing cast proponents claim that the foot is casted in the neutral "perfect" position and that the type of orthotic and the measurements used in the prescription allow for more individualized approaches through the use of forefoot and rearfoot posting. Also, if the individual has exostosis, bunions, or other abnormalities, the orthotic can be modified to accommodate.

There are generally two types of posting, rearfoot and forefoot. A varus (medial) post is used to control or limit the calcaneal eversion and associated internal rotation of the tibia shortly after heel strike. Of course, the opposite principle is used for rearfoot valgus (lateral) posting; it is used to evert the calcaneus and therefore bring the subtalar joint closer to the optimal neutral position. Forefoot varus may be compensated for by a medial post, whereas forefoot valgus is best supported by a lateral post. This is particularly helpful when rearfoot compensation occurs to accommodate for forefoot abnormalities. Heel lifts are occasionally used for problems involving the Achilles tendon. When the Achilles tendon is tight, it may augment the effect of rearfoot problems. The use of a heel lift (3 to 6 mm) may decrease the tension of the Achilles and therefore its effect on rearfoot motion. A partial heel lift, referred to as a medial or lateral wedge, may also be used temporarily as an insert to test the feasibility of posting for patients who are reluctant to purchase the more expensive casted orthotic.

Algorithms

Algorithms for traumatic or sudden onset of foot pain, nontraumatic or insidious onset of foot pain, and initial ankle sprain evaluation are presented in Figures 14–8 to 14–10.

Figure 14–8
TRAUMATIC OR SUDDEN ONSET OF FOOT PAIN—ALGORITHM.

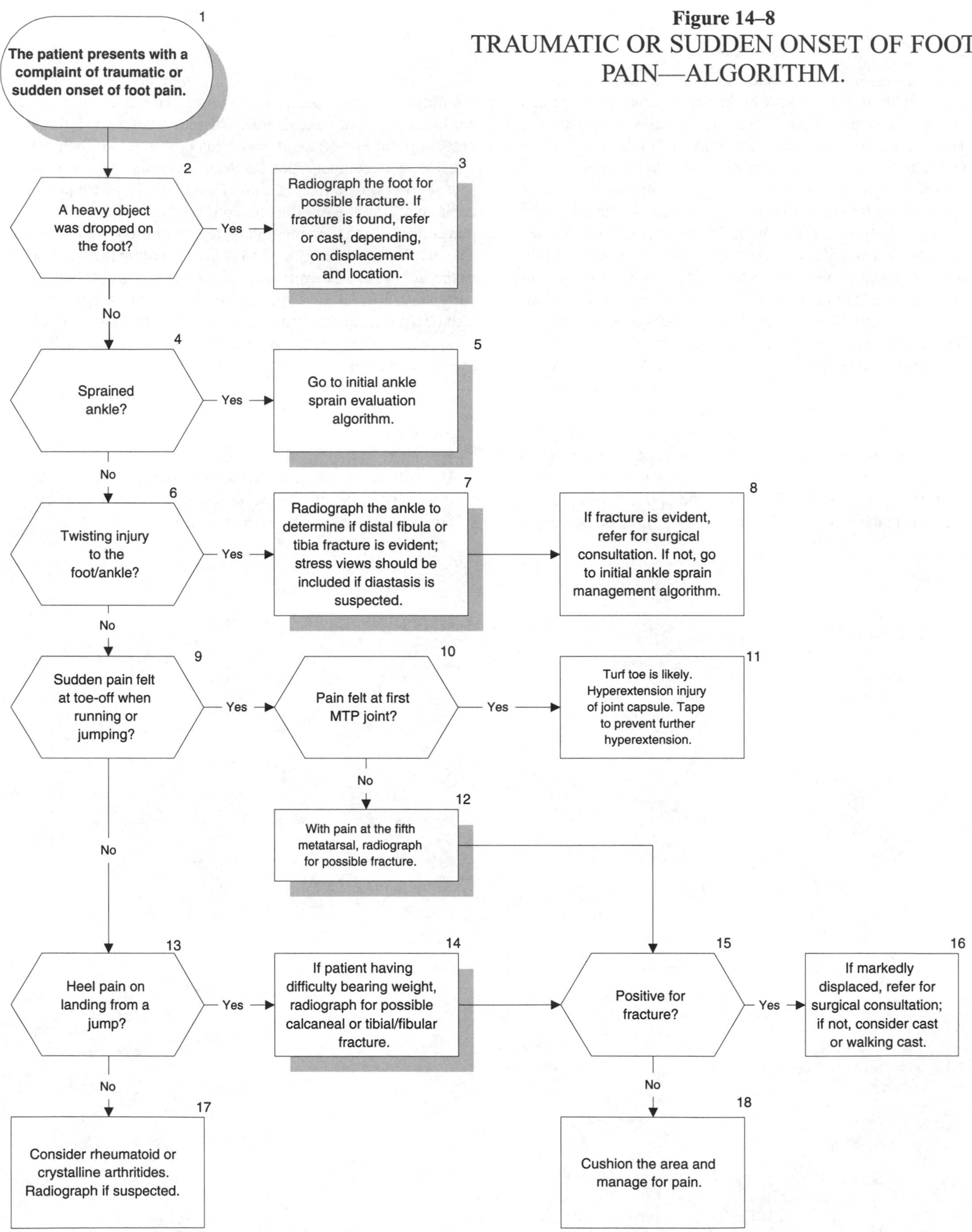

1
The patient presents with a complaint of traumatic or sudden onset of foot pain.
2
A heavy object was dropped on the foot?
Yes
3
Radiograph the foot for possible fracture. If fracture is found, refer or cast, depending, on displacement and location.
No
4
Sprained ankle?
Yes
5
Go to initial ankle sprain evaluation algorithm.
No
6
Twisting injury to the foot/ankle?
Yes
7
Radiograph the ankle to determine if distal fibula or tibia fracture is evident; stress views should be included if diastasis is suspected.
8
If fracture is evident, refer for surgical consultation. If not, go to initial ankle sprain management algorithm.
No
9
Sudden pain felt at toe-off when running or jumping?
Yes
10
Pain felt at first MTP joint?
Yes
11
Turf toe is likely. Hyperextension injury of joint capsule. Tape to prevent further hyperextension.
No
12
With pain at the fifth metatarsal, radiograph for possible fracture.
No
13
Heel pain on landing from a jump?
Yes
14
If patient having difficulty bearing weight, radiograph for possible calcaneal or tibial/fibular fracture.
15
Positive for fracture?
Yes
16
If markedly displaced, refer for surgical consultation; if not, consider cast or walking cast.
No
17
Consider rheumatoid or crystalline arthritides. Radiograph if suspected.
No
18
Cushion the area and manage for pain.

Figure 14–9

NONTRAUMATIC OR INSIDIOUS ONSET OF FOOT PAIN—ALGORITHM.

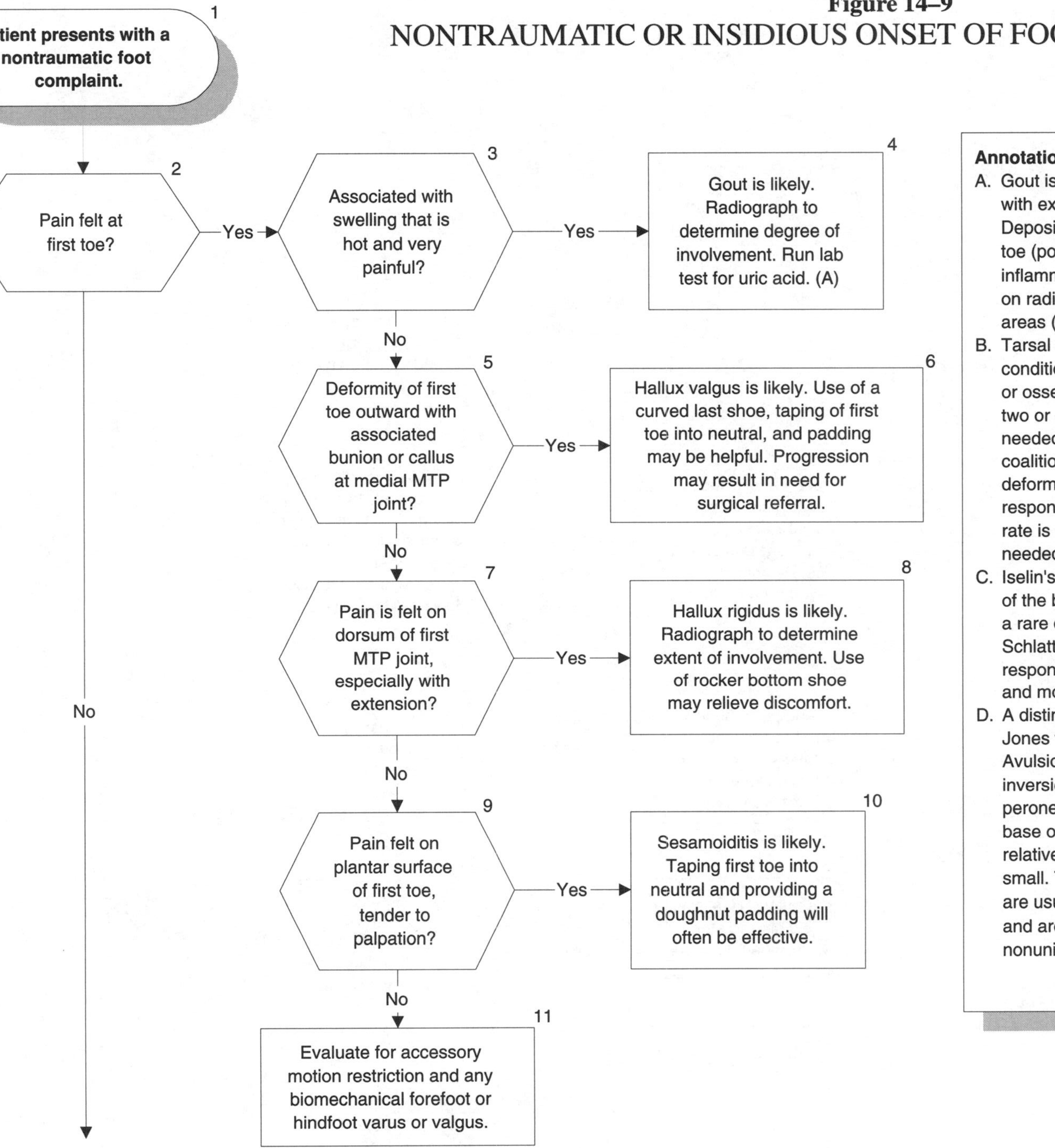

1 Patient presents with a nontraumatic foot complaint.
2 Pain felt at first toe?
Yes
No
3 Associated with swelling that is hot and very painful?
Yes
4 Gout is likely. Radiograph to determine degree of involvement. Run lab test for uric acid. (A)
No
5 Deformity of first toe outward with associated bunion or callus at medial MTP joint?
Yes
6 Hallux valgus is likely. Use of a curved last shoe, taping of first toe into neutral, and padding may be helpful. Progression may result in need for surgical referral.
No
7 Pain is felt on dorsum of first MTP joint, especially with extension?
Yes
8 Hallux rigidus is likely. Radiograph to determine extent of involvement. Use of rocker bottom shoe may relieve discomfort.
No
9 Pain felt on plantar surface of first toe, tender to palpation?
Yes
10 Sesamoiditis is likely. Taping first toe into neutral and providing a doughnut padding will often be effective.
No
11 Evaluate for accessory motion restriction and any biomechanical forefoot or hindfoot varus or valgus.

Annotations

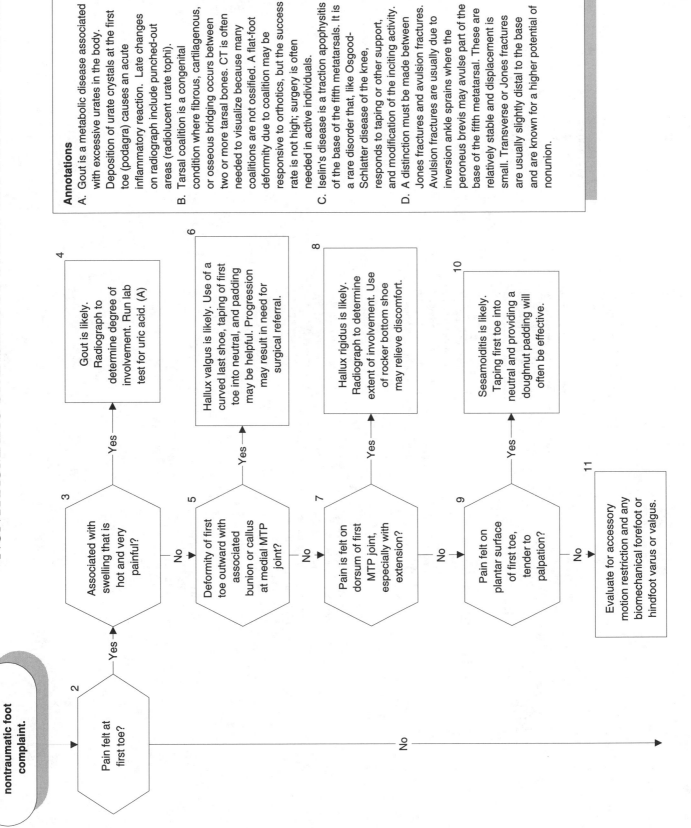

A. Gout is a metabolic disease associated with excessive urates in the body. Deposition of urate crystals at the first toe (podagra) causes an acute inflammatory reaction. Late changes on radiograph include punched-out areas (radiolucent urate tophi).

B. Tarsal coalition is a congenital condition where fibrous, cartilagenous, or osseous bridging occurs between two or more tarsal bones. CT is often needed to visualize because many coalitions are not ossified. A flat-foot deformity due to coalition may be responsive to orthotics, but the success rate is not high; surgery is often needed in active individuals.

C. Iselin's disease is a traction apophysitis of the base of the fifth metatarsals. It is a rare disorder that, like Osgood-Schlatter disease of the knee, responds to taping or other support, and modification of the inciting activity.

D. A distinction must be made between Jones fractures and avulsion fractures. Avulsion fractures are usually due to inversion ankle sprains where the peroneus brevis may avulse part of the base of the fifth metatarsal. These are relatively stable and displacement is small. Transverse or Jones fractures are usually slightly distal to the base and are known for a higher potential of nonunion.

continues

Figure 14–9 continued

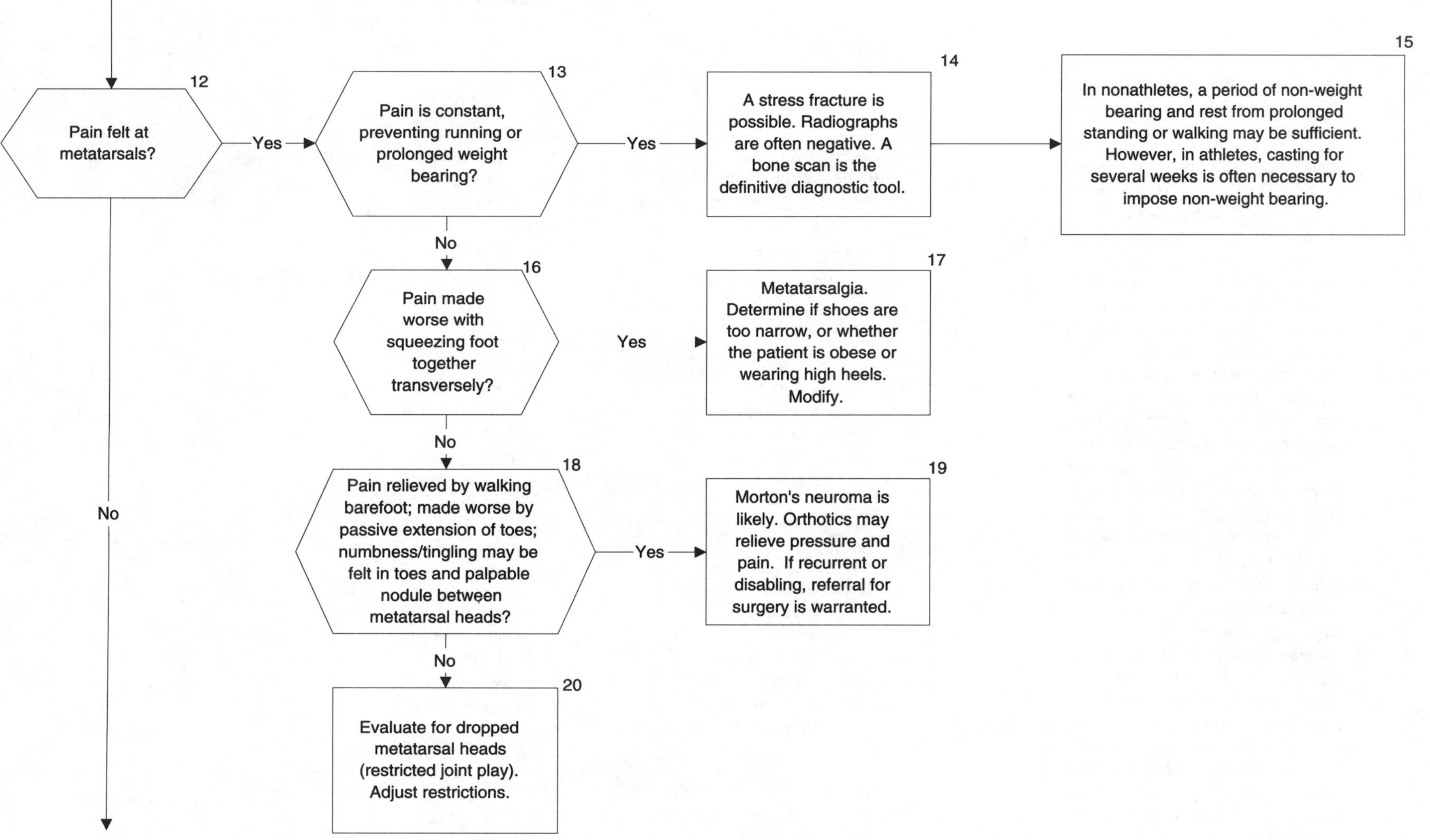

12
Pain felt at metatarsals?
Yes
No
13
Pain is constant, preventing running or prolonged weight bearing?
Yes
No
14
A stress fracture is possible. Radiographs are often negative. A bone scan is the definitive diagnostic tool.
15
In nonathletes, a period of non-weight bearing and rest from prolonged standing or walking may be sufficient. However, in athletes, casting for several weeks is often necessary to impose non-weight bearing.
16
Pain made worse with squeezing foot together transversely?
Yes
No
17
Metatarsalgia. Determine if shoes are too narrow, or whether the patient is obese or wearing high heels. Modify.
18
Pain relieved by walking barefoot; made worse by passive extension of toes; numbness/tingling may be felt in toes and palpable nodule between metatarsal heads?
Yes
No
19
Morton's neuroma is likely. Orthotics may relieve pressure and pain. If recurrent or disabling, referral for surgery is warranted.
20
Evaluate for dropped metatarsal heads (restricted joint play). Adjust restrictions.

continues

Figure 14–9 continued

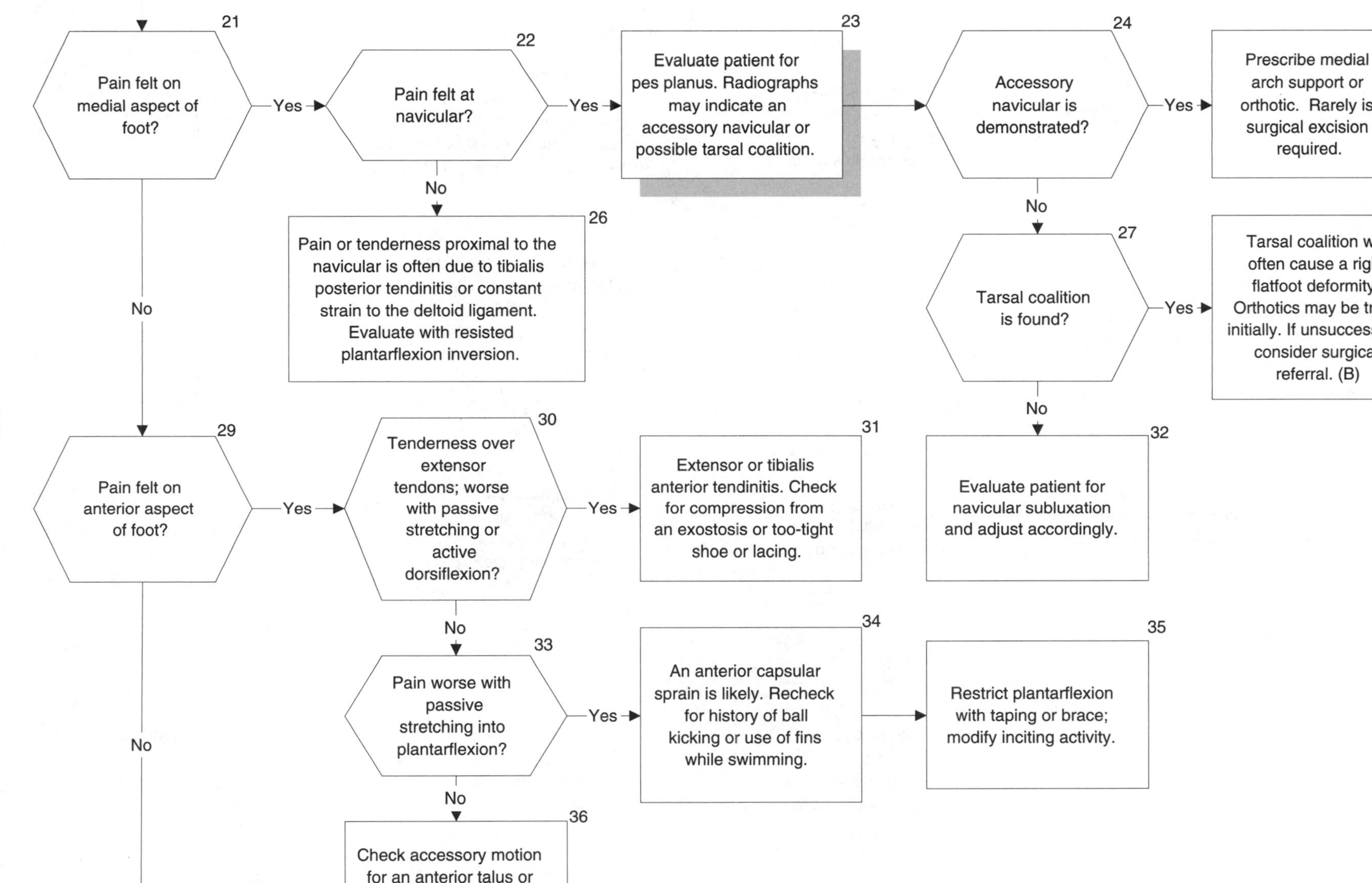

continues

Figure 14–9 continued

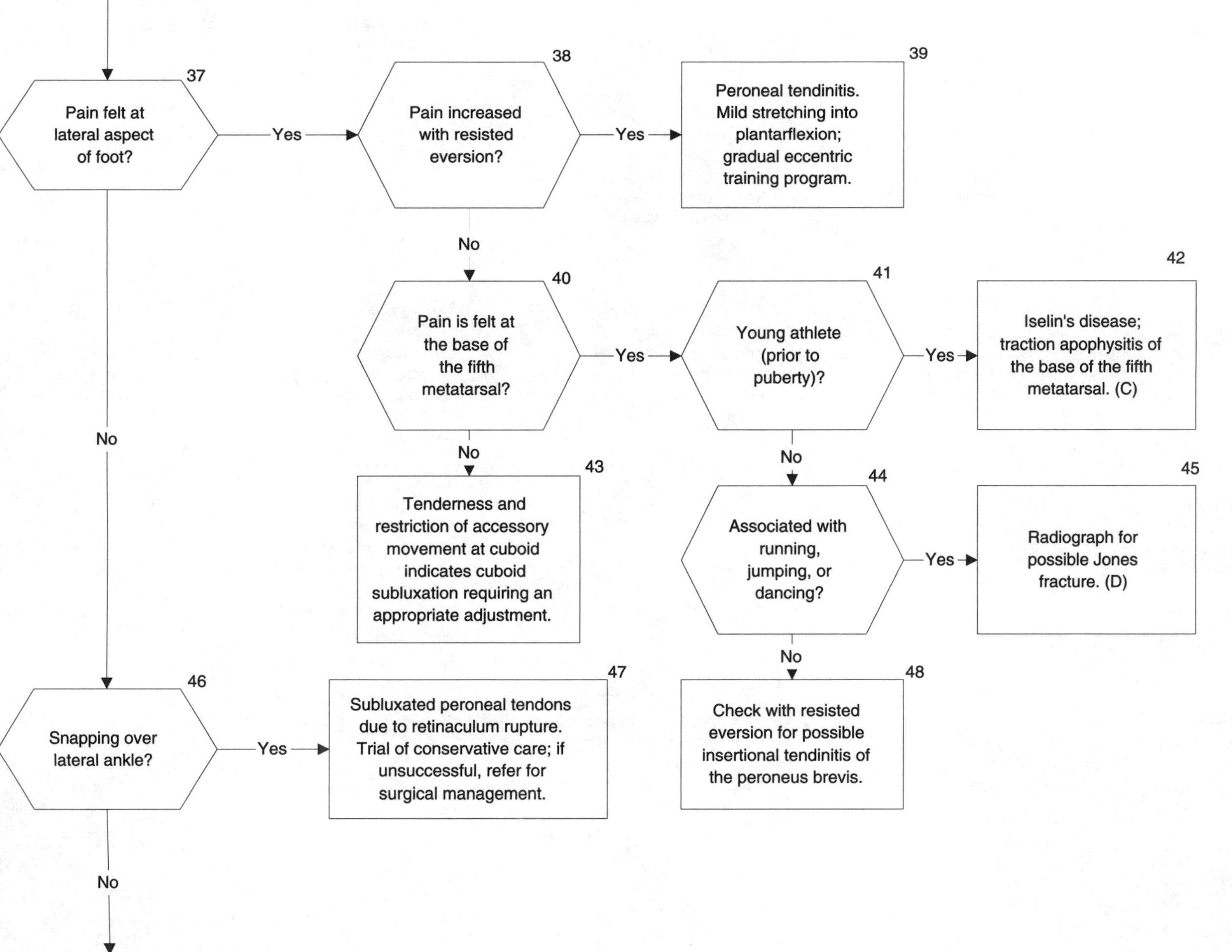

continues

Figure 14–9 continued

49 Patient complains of pain and numbness/tingling in the foot?

- Yes → 50
- No → 55

50 Pain in the foot may be the result of referred pain or radicular (nerve root) pain. Always perform a full nerve root and peripheral nerve evaluation. → 51

51 Numbness/tingling or pain on sole of foot and no evidence of nerve root involvement?

- Yes → 52
- No → 53

52 Tarsal tunnel syndrome is likely. Either the entire sole or half of the sole may be affected (medial and lateral plantar nerves). (E)

53 Numbness/tingling or pain on lateral aspect of foot/ankle and no evidence of nerve root involvement?

- Yes → 54
- No → 58

54 Superficial peroneal nerve entrapment. (F)

58 Numbness/tingling of the dorsum of the foot suggests deep peroneal nerve entrapment if no evidence of nerve root involvement. (G)

55 Patient complains of corns or calluses?

- Yes → 56
- No → 59

56 Corns are divided into soft and hard. Soft corns are extremely painful lesions between toes. Hard corns are due to friction. (H) → 57

57 Calluses indicate areas of increased pressure or friction. Often clues to forefoot or hindfoot biomechanical abnormalities. (I)

59 Patient complains of skin lesions?

- Yes → 60
- No → 62

60 Diffuse involvement of foot?

- Yes → 61
- No → 63

61 Contact dermatitis is likely. In diabetics, consider neurovascular deficit and dermatologic consequences. (J)

62 Toenail changes in athletes often represent pressure reactions; in others consider fungal infection or psoriasis. (N)

63 Local involvement in between toes suggests athlete's foot; single lesions that do not heal or bleed suggest melanoma. (K) (L) → 64

64 Hyperkeratotic lesions occur in predisposed individuals, diabetics, and those with Reiter's syndrome. (M)

continues

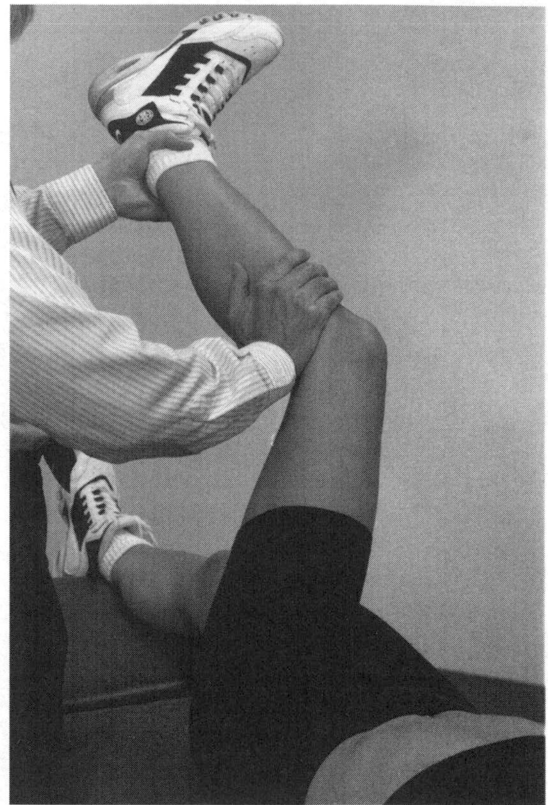

Figure 12–6 The pivot shift test for rotary instability. The patient's knee is held in 10° of flexion. While applying a valgus force at the fibular head with the knee internally rotated, the knee is passively flexed.

Meniscus

Testing for the meniscus is essentially a compressive challenge. The two most widely used tests (other than joint line tenderness) are McMurray's and Apley's. McMurray's test applies compression to the posterior and middle third of the meniscus (Figure 12–7, A and B). The first part of the test is a full-compression maneuver accomplished by passively flexing the patient's heel to the buttock. While in this end-range position the tibia is internally and externally rotated while the examiner palpates the joint line for clicking or popping. A positive test is signaled by clicking and popping with accompanying pain. Soft positives may include clicking, popping, or pain only. The next portion of the test is to apply a combination of valgus/varus and internal/external rotation while extending the leg passively to 90°. Although it is often suggested that a specific combination of forces tests a specific meniscus (medial vs. lateral), this is not borne out by studies.[6] The second test is Apley's compression and distraction test combination.[7] The advantage of Apley's test is that the anterior meniscus can be compressed because of the direct axial compression directed through the tibia (Figure 12–8, A and B). With the patient prone, the tibia is internally and externally rotated as the examiner continues to apply a compressive force while passively extending the leg. A positive test is the production of joint line pain. A confirmation of this finding may be evident with a relief of pain with distraction of the tibia in this same position.

Collateral Ligaments

The MCL is by far the most frequently injured collateral ligament. The principles used to test the MCL can easily be applied to the LCL when damage is suspected. Testing begins with the knee in full extension. A valgus force is applied through leverage against the lower leg. If the knee is unstable, there will be a palpable and visible increase in opening on the medial side of the knee. If not, the examiner proceeds to 30° of flexion and reapplies the same valgus force. If the knee opens and feels as though no end-point was reached, a third-degree rupture of the MCL has occurred. If there is opening with an end-point reached, a second-degree tear is present. If there is no opening but pain is produced, it is likely that there is a first-degree sprain. Cross-checking with contraction of the medial musculature will differentiate ligament pain from muscle pain in most cases. Only one study has tested the reliability of collateral ligament stability testing, and it does not appear to have a high interexaminer reliability.[8]

Patellofemoral Disorders

There are basically three approaches to patellofemoral testing: (1) compression, (2) stability, and (3) tracking. Compression testing involves direct compression of the patella with the knee flexed 5° to 10°. If pain is produced, chondromalacia patellae is suspected. The extension of this test is to ask the patient to contract the quadriceps while the examiner holds the patella down with a superior to inferior force. Stability testing for the patella is the reverse order of positions used for collateral ligament testing. The patient's knee is placed in 30° of flexion first while the examiner cautiously applies a lateral force to the medial patella. If this does not produce pain or apprehension, the test is cautiously repeated in full extension. Tracking is tested by having the patient go through a full squat. The patella is palpated throughout the movement and the patient is asked to identify any specific range where pain is felt. In general, if the pain is felt only at the bottom of the squat, patellar problems are less likely; meniscus problems are more likely. Tracking can also be evaluated indirectly by examining postural abnormalities that may contribute to tracking predisposition. For example, the combination of anteversion of the hip combined with external tibial torsion causes an increase in the Q (quadriceps)

Figure 14–9 continued

E. Tarsal tunnel syndrome may be due to trauma or hyperpronation. Orthotic management with appropriate foot manipulation is usually effective. However, surgical decompression may be necessary with causes other than pronation.
F. Involvement of the superficial peroneal nerve is usually due to ankle sprains. If orthotic support is ineffective, refer for lidocaine/cortisone injection.
G. The deep peroneal nerve may be compressed by tightly laced shoes or talar osteophytes. Shoe modification may be effective. Talar osteophytes may need surgical excision.
H. Hard corns are seen with hammer toes and claw toes; especially at the fifth toe. Treatment involves paring and padding the area, and shoe modification.
I. Calluses under the first metatarsal head is found with forefoot valgus; under the second, third, and fourth with forefoot varus.
J. The diabetic foot is prone to vascular insufficiency and infection. Neurologic compromise often eliminates the painful warning needed to alert the patient to a problem.
K. Athlete's foot is a fungal infection that occurs mainly in the lateral toewebs. Made worse by toe approximation from shoes, warm weather, and activity. Try OTC drugs first. Keep feet dry and use shoes that can aerate.
L. Malignant melanoma is rare; however, any bleeding lesion or nonhealing lesion requires dermatologic referral.
M. Hyperkeratosis may be hereditary or acquired. Fissures may develop and predispose the diabetic to infection. Fissures may be glued together (Krazy glue); general treatment is with topical keratolytics and buffing away thick layers.
N. When the shoe box is too tight, pressure on toenails may result in "black" toenails or other changes. Psoriatic involvement usually occurs on all the toes. Fungal infection usually occurs with "skipped" normal nails.

Key: CT, computed tomography; OTC, over-the-counter.

Figure 14–10

INITIAL ANKLE SPRAIN EVALUATION—ALGORITHM.

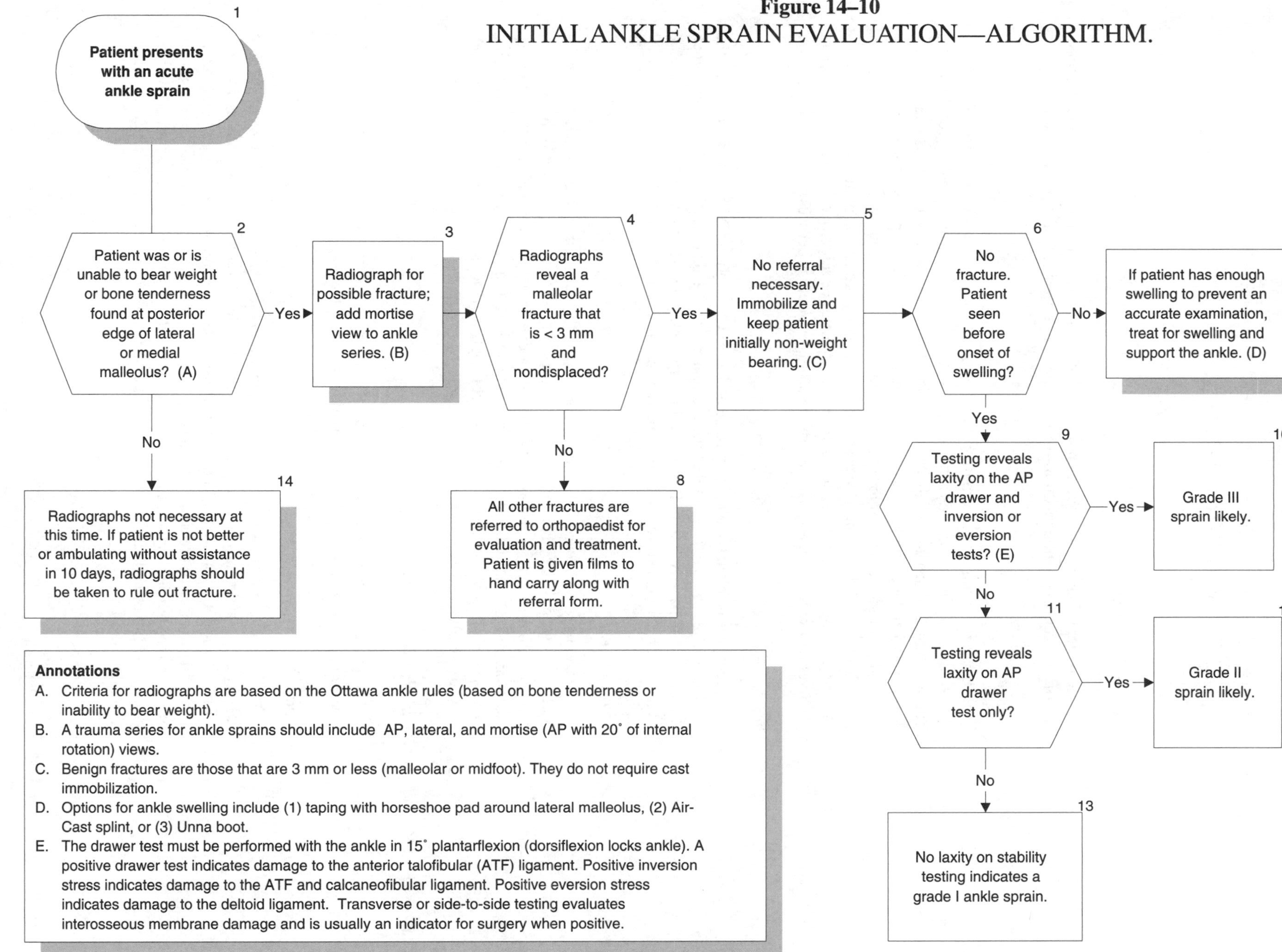

1
Patient presents with an acute ankle sprain
2
Patient was or is unable to bear weight or bone tenderness found at posterior edge of lateral or medial malleolus? (A)
Yes
No
3
Radiograph for possible fracture; add mortise view to ankle series. (B)
4
Radiographs reveal a malleolar fracture that is < 3 mm and nondisplaced?
Yes
No
5
No referral necessary. Immobilize and keep patient initially non-weight bearing. (C)
6
No fracture. Patient seen before onset of swelling?
No
Yes
7
If patient has enough swelling to prevent an accurate examination, treat for swelling and support the ankle. (D)
8
All other fractures are referred to orthopaedist for evaluation and treatment. Patient is given films to hand carry along with referral form.
9
Testing reveals laxity on the AP drawer and inversion or eversion tests? (E)
Yes
No
10
Grade III sprain likely.
11
Testing reveals laxity on AP drawer test only?
Yes
No
12
Grade II sprain likely.
13
No laxity on stability testing indicates a grade I ankle sprain.
14
Radiographs not necessary at this time. If patient is not better or ambulating without assistance in 10 days, radiographs should be taken to rule out fracture.
Annotations
A. Criteria for radiographs are based on the Ottawa ankle rules (based on bone tenderness or inability to bear weight).
B. A trauma series for ankle sprains should include AP, lateral, and mortise (AP with 20˚ of internal rotation) views.
C. Benign fractures are those that are 3 mm or less (malleolar or midfoot). They do not require cast immobilization.
D. Options for ankle swelling include (1) taping with horseshoe pad around lateral malleolus, (2) Air-Cast splint, or (3) Unna boot.
E. The drawer test must be performed with the ankle in 15˚ plantarflexion (dorsiflexion locks ankle). A positive drawer test indicates damage to the anterior talofibular (ATF) ligament. Positive inversion stress indicates damage to the ATF and calcaneofibular ligament. Positive eversion stress indicates damage to the deltoid ligament. Transverse or side-to-side testing evaluates interosseous membrane damage and is usually an indicator for surgery when positive.

SELECTED FOOT DISORDERS*

FIRST TOE

Sesamoiditis

Classic Presentation

The patient presents with pain on the bottom of the great toe. He or she may remember the onset occurring while pushing-off with the toe or after forced dorsiflexion.

Cause

Either direct trauma or overpull from the flexor hallucis brevis may cause irritation of the sesamoids. The sesamoids serve as anchors and help to form the pulley for the flexor hallucis longus. They are the attachment points for the flexor hallucis brevis and adductor hallucis and abductor hallucis. Predisposition to sesamoiditis appears related to concomitant hallux valgus, too-flexible footwear, and repetitive running or walking on hard surfaces. These small bones may be associated with many processes, including a local bursitis, chondromalacia, fracture, stress fracture, bipartite development, OA, and secondary involvement with collagen/vascular, rheumatoid, or gouty processes.

Evaluation

Tenderness is felt at the plantar surface of the first MTP joint. Of the two sesamoids, the medial is often involved and more tender to palpation.[13] This is particularly evident when the first toe is passively dorsiflexed. Radiographs may reveal an underlying process such as a stress fracture, osteochondritis, bipartite sesamoids, or OA.

Management

The treatment for sesamoiditis is to tape the toe to prevent dorsiflexion and to use initially a doughnut-shaped padding to relieve direct pressure on the sesamoids. If there is an associated hallux valgus, it may be helpful to tape the great toe into adduction. Preventive measures are to determine the need for a less flexible shoe and recommend against playing or working on hard surfaces if this is a viable option. There are surgical procedures, but they are rarely needed.

Hallux Valgus

Classic Presentation

The patient presents with a complaint of deformity and pain on the medial side of the first MTP joint. The patient often is a middle-aged woman.

Cause

Hallux valgus involves lateral deviation (abduction) of the proximal phalanx of the first toe. There is a strong hereditary component with accelerating factors such as forefoot varus, Morton's deformity, inflammatory arthritis, and the frequent wearing of high heels. The deviation causes pressure to occur at the first MTP joint with subsequent development of a localized bursitis and bunion formation. Further deviation creates a sling effect whereby pull of the flexor hallucis longus and brevis and extensor hallucis longus tendons creates more deviation.[14]

*See also Chapter 13, Lower Leg Complaints.

Evaluation

The deformity is apparent, with the first toe deviating outward and the medial MTP joint visibly enlarged. If there is an apparent inflammatory process occurring or a history of a rheumatoid condition, a radiograph may be necessary.

Management

When deviation progresses, the patient must decide whether or not to have surgery. There are many different types of surgeries, and the recovery time with each varies. Conservative options are usually an attempt to slow the process of deviation. Taping to bring the first toe into neutral and padding over the bunion area are often tried first. Keeping the joint mobile with adjustments may be beneficial. Additional approaches include paring down the bunion, buying shoes with larger toe boxes, and avoiding the wearing of high heels. Some practitioners suggest a restraining device worn during sleep.

Hallux Rigidus

Classic Presentation

The patient presents with first toe pain felt on the dorsal surface. The patient is usually elderly or may be an athlete with repetitive capsular sprains.

Cause

Osteoarthritic and capsular changes occur at the first metatarsal joint as a result of aging or repeated capsular sprains.[15] Other causes may be an underlying inflammatory arthritic or systemic disease. When this process occurs at other metatarsal heads, it is referred to as Freiberg's infraction—aseptic subchondral cancellous bone necrosis. Hallux rigidus is analogous to or may be Freiberg's infraction of the first toe.

Evaluation

The patient has decreased flexion and extension at the first MTP joint. Pain is reproduced with motion, especially into dorsiflexion. A dorsal bunion also may be evident. Radiographically, there is often a dorsal ring of osteophytes at the metatarsal head.

Management

Mobilization may free up some motion at the joint. The mainstay of conservative management is the use of a stiff-soled shoe or a rocker-bottom shoe which artificially creates toe-off through a rounded metatarsal bar. Failure to resolve usually requires surgical excision of the osteophytes.

Turf Toe

Classic Presentation

The patient often is an athlete complaining of first toe pain especially when the toe is bent back. There may be a history of a trauma that forced the toe into dorsiflexion.

Cause

Turf toe is a sports term for a hyperextension (dorsiflexion) injury of the first toe. The plantar capsule of the MTP joint is sprained.[16] The cause is either sudden dorsiflexion or chronic dorsiflexion through wearing shoes that are too flexible. It may also occur as a result of trips or falls. A similar condition found with sports played on sand, such as beach volleyball, involves forced plantarflexion that causes a sprain of the dorsal capsule (sand toe). Here the toes are rolled under during the injury.

Evaluation

The evaluation is rather straightforward with a suggestive history and pain on dorsiflexion (or plantarflexion with sand toe).

Management

Treatment involves taping of the toe to prevent the aggravating movement pattern and the use of stiff-soled shoes. If these are not successful, immobilization in a cast for several days may be necessary.

Gout

Classic Presentation

The patient is usually middle-aged or older complaining of an acute attack of first toe pain. The toe appears swollen and red.

Cause

Gout is a metabolic disease characterized by retention of urates in the body. The urates accumulate in various body sites as crystalline depositions referred to as tophi. These serve as irritative foci, causing an inflammatory arthritis with eventual bone destruction after repeated attacks. Tophi are deposited in the first toe, the knee, the olecranon bursal area, and behind the ears. Gout can be secondary to other conditions that interfere with renal clearance, such as chronic renal disease, multiple myeloma, and diuretic use.[17]

Evaluation

The location of pain and the severity of this monoarticular attack usually make the diagnosis clear. When acute, the joint is red, swollen, and very tender. Laboratory evaluation often will demonstrate a high uric acid level, especially in the acute phases (> 7.5 mg/dL). Early radiographic changes may not be visible. Later changes include punched-out areas in bone (urate tophi are radiolucent). Identification of urate crystals in joint fluid or tophi gives the definitive diagnosis.

Management

During acute attacks, the use of nonsteroidal antiinflammatory drugs is the most effective treatment. Prophylactic management involves avoidance of specific food or alcohol that appears to incite attacks; however, the general contribution of a diet high in meat is less important than once believed. One of the most important measures is consistent maintenance of a high fluid intake (not diuretic liquids such as coffee, tea, or sodas) and avoidance of diuretic medication. Medication strategy varies depending on the suspected cause. Allopurinol blocks xanthine oxidase, reducing uric acid formation, whereas colchicine inhibits the inflammatory reaction to urate crystals but does not lower uric acid levels.[18]

METATARSALS

Metatarsalgia

Classic Presentation

The patient complains of pain on the bottom of the foot, specifically at the sole.

Cause

Metatarsal pain may be due to a number of factors. It appears that chronic stretching of the transverse ligaments may be the underlying reason.[19] This may be the result of excessive weight, repetitive activity, hammer toes, or pes planus or cavus. Direct trauma from jumping or landing on the toes with running or jogging, or standing for long periods of time in high-heeled shoes may contribute to metatarsal pain. Shoes with too narrow a toe box will also cause compression and pain. Subluxated metatarsal heads may be the cause or part of the problem.

Evaluation

Increased stress at the metatarsals may be evident with calluses or corns (especially over the second metatarsal head). Evaluate the foot for pes planus/cavus, "dropped" metatarsal heads, and toe deformity.

Management

Remove or modify any underlying problems such as repetitive trauma or inappropriate footwear. During the acute phase, use of a metatarsal pad placed just proximal to the metatarsal heads, leaving room for the first and fifth metatarsal heads, is often successful. Local ultrasound may also be of some benefit. Adjustment of metatarsal heads is warranted when restricted movement is determined.

Morton's Neuroma

Classic Presentation

The patient complains of pain on the bottom of the sole. The onset was insidious. The patient notices less pain when barefoot.

Cause

The process often begins as an entrapment neuropathy with progressive degeneration and deposition of amorphous deposits on the nerve fibers.[20] Entrapment occurs most commonly on the plantar surface by the intermetatarsal ligament.

Evaluation

There is pain often in the second or third intermetatarsal space. Occasionally, a mass may be palpated in this space, representing the neuroma. Although transverse compression may increase the pain, it is nonspecific (other causes could include a stress fracture or subluxation). Passive extension of the MTP joints or interphalangeal joints may increase pain or create a sense of numbness/tingling or burning into the related toes. Plantarflexion of the joints often will relieve this response.

Management

Conservative management includes forefoot mobilization and a temporary metatarsal pad. If unsuccessful, casted orthotics may be of benefit. Acute management also may include the use of phonophoresis with cortisone (if allowed by individual state law). Preventive measures are to buy shoes that are long enough to prevent cramming of the toes and to ensure a proper-sized toe box and forefoot areas. Surgical excision is an option in recalcitrant cases.

Stress Fractures

Classic Presentation

The patient presents with a complaint of rather constant pain of the forefoot, especially with weight bearing. There is almost always a history of prolonged walking or running.

Cause

Stress fractures occur over time when the bone resorptive process exceeds osteoblastic activity. This will occur when constant stressors are applied without sufficient unstressed periods to heal or when the stresses consistently exceed the structural integrity of the bone. The second metatarsal is most affected because of its length and position in serving as a biomechanical axis.

Evaluation

The bone may be tender to touch and pain may be increased with squeezing the foot together. Tuning fork evaluation probably will not significantly increase pain. The high level of suspicion based on the history and the location of the pain warrants radiography, but it is usually unrevealing. A bone scan is the definitive tool in detecting stress fractures, revealing an increased uptake at the fracture site.

Management

For a nonathlete, it may be sufficient to use a stiff shoe or rigid orthotics for several weeks. If pain persists, non-weight bearing with crutches for a few weeks is necessary. For the athlete, it may be necessary to prescribe a walking cast or to cast the foot in order to impose a non–weight-bearing period for several weeks. Calcium intake should be increased during this period, and long-term bone status should be evaluated in serious female athletes.

Fifth Metatarsal Fractures

Classic Presentation

The patient often will complain of a sudden onset of lateral foot pain following an inversion ankle sprain. Other patients may report sudden lateral foot pain during running or jumping.

Cause

There are generally three types of fractures possible. The least common is a spiral fracture. An avulsion fracture of the styloid process of the base of the fifth metatarsal is usually the result of a sudden peroneus brevis pull during an inversion ankle sprain. A transverse fracture of the proximal diaphysis of the fifth metatarsal (Jones fracture) is usually due to repetitive stress.

Evaluation

There is point tenderness and pain at the proximal fifth metatarsal. The definitive diagnosis is radiographic.

Management

Avulsion fractures usually heal well with the symptomatic treatment of the associated ankle injury. There is a caution that if there is wide displacement of the fragment, a painful bump will form. Therefore, displacement necessitates an orthopaedic consultation. Transverse fractures have a reputation for nonunion.[21] If the patient is placed early enough in a short leg cast for 6 to 8 weeks, healing usually will be acceptable; delayed healing, however, may require as much as 3 months of casting. Spiral fractures should be referred for orthopaedic consultation because of the variety of rotational patterns that affect the healing process; however, it has been demonstrated that nonsurgical management is often possible.[22]

OTHER CONDITIONS

Osteochondrosis of the Navicular

Classic Presentation

The patient is usually a child (average age of 6 years) who complains of inner foot pain. The parent reports that the child walks on the outer side of the foot.

Cause

The cause of this condition is still being debated. Some authors believe that it is a normal variant of ossification; others think that it is an avascular necrosis. There may be a history of trauma. It is also referred to as Köhler's disease.

Evaluation

There may be tenderness at the navicular. The definitive diagnosis is radiographic. The bone will appear more radiopaque and underdeveloped. These radiographic changes develop over 2 to 4 years.

Management

The symptomatic presentation often self-resolves in 3 to 9 months.[23] During this period, use of arch supports will often relieve the discomfort. In rare cases, a below-knee walking cast is required. The natural history of the disorder is entirely benign with no apparent increase in degenerative joint disease.

Fat Pad Syndrome

Classic Presentation

An older individual presents with a complaint of heel pain. The pain is in the middle of the heel; it is much worse with weight bearing.

Cause

As an individual ages, the fat pad on the bottom of the heel degenerates, leaving little shock absorption for the calcaneus. Shoes that do not have firm heel counters and/or are too wide allow the remaining fat pad to flatten out, decreasing the thickness and therefore shock absorption.[24]

Evaluation

Pain and tenderness are found in the middle of the heel. When the fat pad is supported on either side and pressure is reapplied, the pain is decreased. Plantar fasciitis is more often at the medial aspect of the calcaneus, not in the middle. Stretching of the plantar fascia or dorsiflexors of the first toe or ankle does not increase pain with fat pad syndrome. Radiographs are rarely needed unless the patient is not responsive to care.

Management

Both support of the remaining fat pad and substitution of the pad are the two approaches used. Use of various heel cups may be helpful. The heel cup is often made of shock-absorbent material and provides some medial/lateral support. Some patients do better with a more rigid support in the heel counter of the shoe to prevent splaying of the fat pad. Misdiagnosis of plantar fasciitis is common, so that many patients are subjected to unnecessary cortisone injections and surgery.

Plantar Fasciitis

Classic Presentation

The patient complains of a sharp heel pain that radiates along the bottom of the inside of the foot. The pain is often worse when getting out of bed in the morning.

Cause

Either pronation or supination may be the cause. The flatfoot (hyperpronation) with associated forefoot abduction has a stretching effect on the plantar fascia, leading to repetitive tension overload. The high-arched foot (supinated) is relatively rigid. Forces usually absorbed through movement of the foot and ankle are transmitted to the plantar fascia and lower leg. In this way plantar fasciitis can be analogous to shin splints.

Evaluation

Pain or tenderness is increased with direct pressure over the medial tubercle of the calcaneus (the fascial insertion). This pain often will radiate along the bottom of the foot. It is also possible to reproduce the pain through stretching of the first toe into dorsiflexion alone or coupled with dorsiflexion of the ankle. Radiographs usually are not necessary. Although heel spurs often are seen, they are not the cause but the reaction to chronic fascial tension.[25] Laboratory testing is reserved for patients with known rheumatic disease or a situation where suspicion is raised by other joint complaints.

Management

Support of any underlying biomechanical predispositions includes orthotics for pronation or supination. This is based on the frequency of pain or the degree of incapacitation when pain does occur. Temporary solutions include taping the arch for support (low-dye taping) and gradual stretching. Myofascial release to the plantar fascia may be helpful. Underwater ultrasound coupled with stretching appears to be effective in many cases. Adjusting of any foot subluxations (especially navicular and first MTP joint) and strengthening of foot-support musculature should be a part of the treatment plan. Ninety-five percent of patients respond to conservative care.[26]

Tarsal Tunnel Syndrome

Classic Presentation

The patient complains of numbness and tingling across the bottom of the foot, often at the sole or first toe. The onset is insidious and not associated with low back or leg pain.

Cause

The posterior tibial nerve may be stretched or compressed in the tarsal tunnel, a fibroosseous tunnel formed by the flexor retinaculum, calcaneus, distal tibia, and malleolus. The contents of the tunnel include the tendons of the posterior tibialis, flexor digitorum longus, and flexor hallucis and the posterior tibial artery, vein, and nerve. Due to highly variable anatomy, the distal branches of the posterior tibial nerve (the medial calcaneal, medial plantar, and lateral plantar nerves) may be selectively affected.[27] Hyperpronation is often the cause of tarsal tunnel syndrome due to tightening of the flexor retinaculum or arch of the abductor hallucis. However, trauma, swelling, ganglions, and anatomic variation of blood vessels or the abductor hallucis may also cause compression.

Evaluation

Neurologic testing for nerve root involvement is negative. Numbness and tingling may be reproduced by percussion over the posterior tibial nerve just behind the medial malleolus (Tinel's sign) or along a line that continues to the navicular tuberosity, continuing down into the medial arch. Sensory deficit may occur in the medial (medial plantar nerve) or lateral (lateral plantar nerve) plantar surface of the foot. Usually two-point discrimination is decreased or hypoesthesia to pinprick are found. Motor weakness is less common. With difficult cases, nerve conduction studies may be needed.

Management

If trauma or swelling is involved, the initial course of care is to reduce the swelling with ice, compression, elevation, and physical therapy modalities. If pronation appears to be the cause, a trial use of orthotics will often solve the problem. Associated adjusting of restricted navicular, calcaneal, or talar movement may be beneficial. If a trial of several weeks is unsuccessful, referral for podiatric consultation is suggested for possible need of surgical release of the retinaculum or excision of a ganglion or other compressive structure.

Talar Osteophytes

Classic Presentation

Talar osteophytes may be anterior or posterior. Patients with anterior osteophytes complain of pain on dorsiflexion of the foot and occasionally numbness/tingling or weakness in the toes. Patients with posterior osteophytes complain of pain on forced plantarflexion of the foot.

Cause

Osteophytes on the neck of the talus or anterior tibia may cause an impingement of the local synovium leading to a hypertrophy and swelling.[28] With tight shoes, the anterior type of osteophyte may compress the deep peroneal nerve; however, this is more common with entrapment under the inferior extensor retinaculum.[29] Posterior compression may occur as a result of an os trigonium (small nonunited bone) or an elongated lateral process of the posterior tubercle of the talus (Steida's process).[30] When there is pain on forced plantarflexion or dorsiflexion, lateral radiographs will usually reveal osteophytes or accessory bones that may represent the offending structure. If sufficient trauma is involved, it is important to consider a possible avulsion fracture.

Management

Surgical excision is usually necessary for the anterior talar osteophyte, however, the posterior processes may resolve with activity modification; if not, lidocaine injection or surgery should be considered.

REFERENCES

1. McCrae JD. *Pediatric Orthopedics of the Lower Extremity.* New York: Futura Publishing; 1985.
2. McPoil TG, Knecht HG, Schuit D. A survey of foot types in normal females between the ages of 18 and 30 years. *J Orthop Sports Phys Ther.* 1989:406–409.
3. Michaud TC. Ideal motions during the gait cycle. In: *Foot Orthoses and Other Forms of Conservative Foot Care.* Baltimore: Williams & Wilkins; 1993:27–56.
4. Reber L, Perry J, Pink M. Muscular control of the ankle in running. *Am J Sports Med.* 1993;21:805–810.
5. Elveru RA, Rothstein JM, Lamb RL. Goniometric reliability in a clinical setting: subtalar and ankle joint measurements. *Phys Ther.* 1988;68:672.
6. Root ML, Orien WP, Weed JN. *Clinical Biomechanics: Normal and Abnormal Function of the Foot.* Los Angeles: Clinical Biomechanics Corp; 1977;2:26–31.
7. Weismann S. *Radiology of the Foot.* Baltimore: Williams & Wilkins; 1984.
8. Steill IG, McKnight RD, Greensburg GH, et al. Implementation of the Ottawa ankle rules. *JAMA.* 1994;271:827–832.
9. Nyska M, Amir H, Dekel S. Radiologic assessment of a modified anterior drawer test of the ankle. *Foot Ankle.* 1992;13:400–403.
10. Kleiger B. Mechanisms of ankle injury. *Orthop Clin North Am.* 1974;5:127.
11. Cox JS, Hewes TF. Normal talar tilt angle. *Clin Orthop.* 1979;140:37–40.
12. Williams PL, Smibert JG, Cox R, et al. Imaging study of the painful heel syndrome. *Foot Ankle.* 1987;6:345.

13. Richardson G. Injuries to the hallucal sesamoids in the athlete. *Foot Ankle.* 1987;7:229.

14. Hattrup SJ, Johnson KA. Hallux valgus: a review. *Adv Orthop Surg.* 1985;8:404.

15. Hattrup SJ, Johnson KA. Hallux rigidus: a review. *Adv Orthop Surg.* 1986;9:259.

16. Clanton TO, Ford JJ. Turf toe injury. *Clin Sports Med.* 1994;13:731–741.

17. Roubenoff RR. Gout and hyperuricemia. *Rheumat Dis Clin North Am.* 1990;16:539.

18. Pratt PW, Ball GV. Gout treatment. In: Schumaker HR, ed. *Primer on the Rheumatic Diseases.* 10th ed. Atlanta: Arthritis Foundation; 1993.

19. Reid DC. Selected conditions of the foot. In: Reid DC. *Sports Injury Assessment and Rehabilitation.* New York: Churchill Livingstone; 1992:129–184.

20. Graham CE, Graham DM. Morton's neuroma: a microscopic evaluation. *Foot Ankle.* 1984;5:150.

21. Zogby RG, Baker BE. A review of non-operative treatment of Jones fracture. *Am J Sports Med.* 1987;15:304.

22. O'Malley MJ, Hamilton WG, Munyak J. Fractures of the distal shaft of the fifth metatarsal: dancer's fracture. *Am J Sports Med.* 1996;24:240–243.

23. Ippolito E, Pollini PTR, Falez F. Kohler's disease of the tarsal navicular: long term follow up of 12 cases. *J Pediatr Orthop.* 1984;4:416.

24. Miller WE. The heel pad. *Am J Sports Med.* 1982;10:9.

25. Furey JG. Plantar fasciitis: the painful heel syndrome. *J Bone Joint Surg Am.* 1975;75:672.

26. Baxter DE. The heel in sport. *Clin Sports Med.* 1994;13:685–693.

27. Schon LC, Baxter DE. Neuropathies of the foot and ankle in athletes. *Clin Sports Med.* 1990;9:489–509.

28. Parks JCH, Hamilton WG, Patterson AH, et al. The anterior impingement syndrome of the ankle. *J Trauma.* 1980;20:895.

29. Murphy PC, Baxter DE. Nerve entrapment of the foot and ankle in runners. *Clin Sports Med.* 1985;4:753.

30. Reid DC. Selected lesions around the talus. *Curr Theor Sports Med.* 1990;2:241.

Part II

Neurologic Complaints

Chapter 15

Weakness

CONTEXT

As with many patient complaints, it is imperative to have the patient define his or her complaint: What does "weak" mean to the patient? Without a clear description, the doctor may be led to the assumption that a neurologic or muscular etiology is the cause when, in fact, weakness is actually fatigue associated with an infectious, metabolic, oncologic, pharmacologic, or psychologic (depression) disorder. Patients experiencing pain with movement will often express a sense of weakness. In addition, patients may interpret a sense of clumsiness, tightness, instability, or uncoordinated movement as "weakness." Determine first, then, whether the patient has general weakness or is substituting or misinterpreting another physical sign/symptom as weakness (Exhibit 15–1). If the complaint is more generalized, see Chapter 21, Fatigue, and Chapter 23, Sleep and Other Related Complaints.

In the context of chiropractic practice, it is most common to find a regional complaint of weakness with associated signs of pain and/or numbness and tingling. It would be unusual to find a patient with signs of central nervous system origin (unless previously diagnosed); the chiropractor must be vigilant, however, in searching for these findings. When weakness is associated with a concomitant complaint of region-specific pain, there must be a diligent search for an anatomic lesion. If there is an objectifiable strength deficit, a major concern is the permanency of this loss.

GENERAL STRATEGY

History

- Determine what the patient means by a complaint of "weakness." Is it a general sense of fatigue or tiredness or a specific regional or joint weakness?
- Is there a history of trauma that would lead one to suspect rupture of a muscle, ligament, or tendon? (Eventually this would be a painless weakness.)
- Is the onset sudden, with diffuse areas of neurologic weakness and/or associated signs of difficulty with speech, cognition, consciousness, or affect? (These deficits are suggestive of a cerebrovascular event.)
- Is the onset insidious with either persistence or progression of symptoms, or an addition effect of more neurologic signs? (The latter is typical of expansile lesions such as tumors.)
- Is there an improvement of neurologic signs, but recurrence? (This is suggestive of a vascular process or multiple sclerosis.)
- Has there been a period of disuse (immobilization with either a sling or cast) or support worn an extended period of time?
- With a specific regional weakness, are there associated sensory complaints such as pain, numbness/tingling, unusual sensations? (Localize and attempt to match the complaint with a specific nerve root or peripheral nerve pattern.)

Examination

- First determine whether there are signs of an upper motor neuron lesion (UMNL) or a lower motor neuron lesion (LMNL).
- If there is a single regional weakness, attempt to localize it segmentally by associating any deficits in motor or sensory function.
- If a clear distinction is not found for differentiating the site of a lesion, further studies, including electrodiagnostic studies or magnetic resonance imaging (MRI), or both, must be considered.

Exhibit 15–1 Defining Patients' Complaints of Weakness

Patient complains of weakness

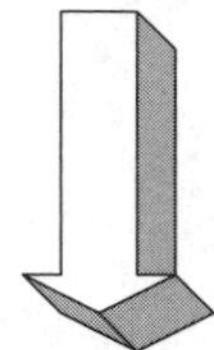

Differentiate between specific area weakness and general weakness

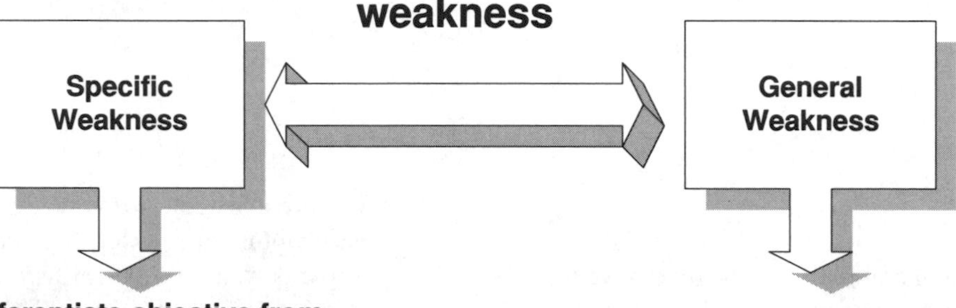

Specific Weakness

Differentiate objective from subjective if possible

Neurologic | **Muscular** | **Myoneural**

Neurologic causes usually affect the distal extremities.
Ask the patient about writing or holding a cup for the upper limb; ask about tripping over rugs or curbs for lower.
Muscular disorders generally affect the larger, more proximal muscles.
Ask the patient about gross proximal movements such as getting out of a seat for the lower extremity, combing the hair or reaching above the head for the upper.
Myoneural problems affect more the cranial nerves.
Ask questions about getting tired chewing food.

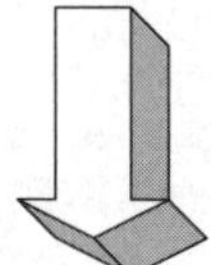

Further differentiation with electromyographic or nerve conduction velocity testing may be necessary

General Weakness

Depression | **Infection** | **Hormonal (thyroid or adrenal)**

Metabolic (drugs, anemia, or other causes of poor oxygen delivery: congestive heart failure, chronic obstructive pulmonary disease, etc.) | **Chronic fatigue syndrome**

Tiredness or fatigue associated with a loss of enjoyment in life, difficulty sleeping, and a sense of worthlessness suggests a depression.
Tiredness or fatigue that occurs only upon exertion implies metabolic causes such as anemia or poor oxygen delivery. Investigate with lab tests and auscultation.
Both hypo- and hyperthyroidism may cause a sense of tiredness.
Chronic fatigue syndrome requires certain criteria for the diagnosis:

- incapacitating decreasing ability to perform activities of daily living by 50% or more
- must have had for more than 6 months

Management

- Weakness due to a UMNL should always be referred to a neurologist immediately.
- Weakness associated with myasthenia gravis should be referred for medical management.
- Most cases of nerve root or peripheral nerve weakness can be managed conservatively for 1 month, monitoring for worsening or progression (which would warrant referral for a second opinion).

RELEVANT ANATOMY AND PHYSIOLOGY

Although integration for smooth and coordinated muscle function is a complex process involving both ascending and descending pathways, for general strength the examiner's focus is on the corticospinal (and corticobulbar) tracts. Information that has been integrated at a higher level is sent to the anterior horn cells via the corticospinal tracts. From this point, information is sent out to the spinal nerves that divide into anterior and posterior primary rami. The posterior rami innervate the deep muscles of the back. The anterior rami form four plexuses that eventually, through a process of recombination (roots to trunks to division to cords), form peripheral nerves. All peripheral nerves interact with the target muscle(s) at the myoneural junction.

Corticospinal tract function includes inhibitory influences. Increased excitability due to cortical divorce from the alpha motoneuron results in increased muscle tone with passive movement. The hyperexcitable alpha motoneuron also causes an increase in deep tendon reflexes. A number of older reflexes that disappear with maturation of the nervous system are unmasked (eg, Babinski's reflex). Although pathologic reflexes are hyperreflexic, the fact that the reflex is intact indicates a functioning alpha motoneuron and peripheral motor nerve.

An important anatomic design is the laminated arrangement of spinal tracts within the spinal cord. Fibers innervating the lower parts of the body are more superficial and lateral. Compressive lesions would present with a temporal presentation of sequential, ascending weakness. This lamination is also true of ascending sensory tracts. Therefore, an accompanying ascending sensory loss may be found.

For neurologic weakness to occur there must be a lesion somewhere along the corticospinal or corticobulbar paths (cortex, brain stem, spinal cord) or at the anterior horn cell, myoneural junction, or muscle. There are some generalizations that will guide the examiner in discriminating among the various neurologic and muscular causes. The first discrimination is whether there are any signs of a UMNL or an LMNL.

- A UMNL indicates pathology in the cerebral hemispheres, brain stem, or spinal cord. Interruption of inhibitory influences eventually leads to increased reflexes and an increase in muscle tone and spastic paralysis; pathologic reflexes such as Babinski's appear also.
- An LMNL indicates pathology in the anterior horn cell or motoneuron. Interruption of the reflex loop leads to absent or decreased deep tendon reflexes. Disconnection from the motoneuron leads to atrophy and fasciculations. Muscle tone may be normal or decreased (flaccid paralysis).

EVALUATION

History

After having the patient clarify whether he or she feels weak, tired, or fatigued, the most revealing line of questioning is in relation to daily activities (Table 15–1). Ask the patient to describe the activity that causes the feeling of weakness in an attempt to determine whether he or she means a specific regional weakness, an uncoordinated or clumsy sensation, or the exertion fatigue felt with some systemic and cardiopulmonary disorders. If it appears to be a regional complaint, further clarify by extracting a description that localizes upper or lower extremity and proximal or distal weakness. This line of questioning focuses on the generalization that neurologic diseases usually start distally, whereas myopathies usually become more evident proximally. For example, difficulty using the fingers or hands would be more suggestive of a neurologic cause, whereas difficulty with combing the hair or reaching behind the back would be more suggestive of a myopathy. In the lower extremities, tripping over rugs or curbs is more suggestive of a neural cause, whereas difficulty rising from a seated position is more often myopathic (especially if nonpainful).

Some characteristic patterns of "weakness" may help guide the examiner through questioning (see Chapter 21, Fatigue).

- Patients with an infectious cause are often tired after exertion. This may also occur with anemia or cardiopulmonary disorders.
- The weakness associated with endocrine and electrolyte disorders is often felt more proximally. Either hypo- or hyperthyroidism may cause weakness. It is more often (80% to 90%) found with hyperthyroidism. Also, hypo- or hyperadrenal disorders may present with a complaint of weakness. Electrolyte imbalances, high or low, may lead to weakness. Evaluation with a general screening lab work-up may give direct or indirect indications of these causes.

Table 15–1 History Questions for Weakness: Determining the General Cause

Primary Question	*What Are You Thinking?*	*Secondary Questions*	*What Are You Thinking?*
Do you feel weakness of your arm or leg, hands or feet?	A yes would imply a neurologic or muscular disorder; a no requires further questioning.	Do you feel generally weak (tired or fatigued)?	Think more of metabolic and endocrine problems, infection, or depression.
		Are you taking any medications?	Antihypertensives, antihistamines, and barbiturates are common culprits.
		Is this feeling always there or only when you exert yourself?	If the feeling is only with exertion consider cardiopulmonary/vascular causes (including anemia).
Are specific daily activities difficult because of weakness?	Attempt to determine whether a specific body-area weakness is upper or lower, proximal or distal.	Lower extremity • proximal—getting up from chair, toilet, car	Proximal usually indicates an endocrine or myopathic problem (painless weakness).
		• distal—tripping over rugs, curbs, cords	Distal usually indicates a neurologic disorder.
		Upper extremity • proximal—combing hair, reaching overhead • distal—writing, typing, opening jars	
		Head • whistling, blowing, chewing, speaking, swallowing, keeping soap out of eyes while showering	Cranial nerve dysfunction often implies a medullary or pontine disorder, especially if accompanied with extremity findings. Fatigue after repeated action points to myasthenia gravis.
Is there associated numbness and/or tingling?	A neurologic cause is likely. Look for a patch of skin that correlates with a dermatome or peripheral nerve pattern.	Is the numbness constant or intermittent?	*Constant* would imply a neurologic cause (possibly metabolic/endocrine); *Intermittent* would imply transient or early neurologic compression.
		Does it relate to a certain body position such as arm elevation?	Stretching or compression can increase peripheral nerve irritation (such as the brachial plexus).
Is there pain associated with the weakness?	Weakness is often the result of neurologic inhibition due to pain (example, knee gives out).	If it is not painful now, was there ever trauma (injury) to the area?	Rupture of muscles, tendons, or ligaments may result in loss of function that is eventually painless.

- Fatigue or tiredness that seems worse after eating may indicate hypoglycemic reactions, reaction to alcohol consumption, or a delayed reaction from overingestion of caffeine.
- Medications often will have a sedative affect that may be augmented by the use of alcohol or other drugs such as antihypertensives, antihistamines, codeine, and barbiturates.
- Fatigue or tiredness throughout the day may be suggestive of a sleep disorder, including the possibility of depression. A characteristic insomnia pattern is often associated with reactive depression; with endogenous (neurochemical) depression, the patient often awakens early and finds it difficult to fall back to sleep (see Chapter 20, Depression).

A sense of weakness may be a misinterpretation by the patient. For example, if a patient has hip stiffness, it may feel as if lifting the knee toward the chest is weak; muscle testing in the midrange, however, might indicate normal strength. Instability may present similarly. If a patient has laxity of the shoulder, overhead movements may feel "weak" because of the inability of the shoulder musculature to compensate for ligamentous/capsular laxity at higher levels of elevation.

Examination

Following are some pattern generalizations that may help guide the examination:

- Cerebrum—Generally a combination of UMNL and associated problems with cognitive functions or mood suggests a cortical pathologic process.
- Cerebellum—Combinations of ataxia, vertigo, and/or dysarthria suggest a cerebellar pathologic process.
- Brain stem—Cranial nerve problems are often predominant with a crossed pattern of involvement (ie, the face on the lesion side and the body on the opposite side). The corticospinal tract crosses at the lower medulla.
- Spinal cord—A spinal cord lesion usually has a sensory level; sensory disturbance is found below the level of the lesion. At the level of the lesion an LMNL is often present; below are UMNL signs. Additionally, if the lesion is expansive, loss of pain and temperature is often associated with an upper limb weakness that gradually descends to the trunk and lower extremity. Compressive lesions will produce the opposite (if anterior), an ascending pattern of motor weakness. If localized posteriorly, a loss of proprioception is evident.
- Nerve root—Weakness is often associated with low back or neck pain. Additionally, there are accompanying sensory complaints such as numbness and/or tingling. More specifically, the pain should follow a related dermatome with weakness in a specific myotome. If there is a corresponding deep tendon reflex, it will be decreased or absent.
- Peripheral nerve—Like nerve root problems, a distinctive sensory pattern often accompanies peripheral nerve irritation or compression. This pattern should be distinct from the nerve root pattern, as should the distinctive muscle weakness grouping (assuming a motor component to the nerve).
- Myoneural junction—Myoneural dysfunction is usually more evident with muscles supplied by cranial nerves. Characteristically, repeated contraction causes progressive weakness, with recovery with rest. This is typical of myasthenia gravis.
- Myopathy—Typically, myopathic weakness is evident first proximally. Examples include muscular dystrophy and inflammatory disorders of muscle. There are no sensory findings, and reflexes should be intact. Further investigation with laboratory or electromyographic (EMG) testing is necessary.

A high level of suspicion will have been gained by a thorough history. If there is a sense of a UMNL it is prudent to begin with a search for signs, including hyperreflexia, a pathologic reflex (Babinski's), and eventually changes in muscle tone (spastic weakness). If the lesion appears to be spinal, a search for a sensory level is extremely helpful. A sensory level is a combined finding where there is a sensory disturbance below the level of the lesion accompanied by signs of an LMNL at the level and signs of a UMNL below the level.

The standard grading scale for muscle strength is as follows:

- grade 5—complete range of motion (ROM) against maximal resistance
- grade 4—complete ROM against gravity and some resistance
- grade 3—complete ROM against gravity
- grade 2—complete ROM if gravity is eliminated
- grade 1—palpable or visible evidence of muscle contraction, yet no movement
- grade 0—no evidence of muscle contraction

This standard approach is based on ROM and resistance to gravity or examiner resistance. The distinction between grades 2 and 3, for example, is that with a grade 2 strength, the patient is only able to slide his or her leg across the table (gravity is eliminated), while a patient with a grade 3 strength is able to lift the leg off the table (against gravity). The faults of this system lie in the evaluation's being dependent on full ROM (isotonic contraction) and the limited choices for grading. Most patients should be examined using isometric muscle testing in an effort first to determine whether pain is causing inhibition or whether true weakness is present. Also, it is important to determine whether normal strength is present within the ROM available.

Although orthopaedic muscle testing has been used to correlate muscle weakness with other localizing neurologic findings (dermatome and deep tendon reflex), other information may be gained. When a muscle is found to be weak it is important to determine why. If the muscle tests weakly and painfully, this response serves little function as a nerve root localizer, yet it is extremely valuable as a soft tissue localizer. In other words, pain often inhibits contraction. Therefore, it is difficult to determine true neurologic function when contraction is painful. If a muscle tests weakly but is painless, there is a high level of suspicion of neurologic weakness or a tendon rupture. Often a palpable bulge or deformity, combined with other findings, clearly differentiates between the two events.

When a muscle is weak and the test is painless, the neurologic differentiation is still incomplete. What becomes apparent when trying to narrow down the possibilities is the overlap among different levels of branching of the peripheral nervous system with regard to motor innervation. For example, if a patient was found to have weakness of the triceps, the extensor carpi radialis, and the extensor carpi ulnaris, the first suspicion may be radial nerve damage. If the brachioradialis is still strong, however, and the small muscles of the thumb (such as the abductor, opponens, and adductors) are also found to be weak, radial nerve damage is not likely. The two remaining peripheral nerves (median and ulnar) may account for the small muscle weakness, but they could not account for the triceps and extensor carpi weaknesses. This is also true of the divisions and trunks of the brachial plexus. However, the common root level of all weak muscles is C8 and T1. Neither has an associated deep tendon reflex. Neither alone could account for all the weak muscles; therefore, a search for where both could be affected reveals the suspected site at the lower trunk of the brachial plexus. This would be strongly reinforced with a finding of sensory abnormality over the dermatomes for C8 and T1; medial arm down to fifth and fourth fingers.

When performing manual muscle testing, it is important to realize some inherent weaknesses. As mentioned above, pain may cause a muscle to test weakly, and although not necessarily helpful in localizing a neurologic level, it does indicate a structure in need of attention. The other variables that influence a patient's ability to contract a muscle are numerous. These include time of day, gravity, velocity of the test maneuver, technique and instructions of the examiner, ambient noise, and inability to stabilize the muscle origin.[1] Some practical examples of this variation are as follows:

- If one tests the internal tibial rotators with the knee flexed to 90°, but the hip is placed in different positions, strength will vary with hip placement even though the tibia remains the same.
- If the patient feels unstable, she or he may not be able to contract the appropriate muscle(s) fully or may recruit other muscles to assist.
- If the examiner fails to instruct or prewarn the patient, a force may be applied too quickly for the patient to react, resulting in movement at the joint that could be interpreted as weakness by the examiner.

When a pattern is not clear and a lesion site is not obvious, electrodiagnostic studies may clarify the source (Table 15–2). Electrodiagnostic studies, mainly EMG and nerve conduction velocity (NCV) studies, are limited according to the experience and expertise of the examiner. When performed appropriately, however, these studies may help differentiate and in some cases identify the degree of damage when a neuronal pathology exists. EMG uses needle insertion into muscle to test muscle and nerve.[2] The spontaneous activity generated or the response generated with contraction helps distinguish between axon injury and demyelination disorders. NCV uses surface electrodes to measure velocity and the amplitude of an evoked response to an electrical stimulus. Both motor and sensory nerves can be tested.

When an anterior horn cell (or its fibers) is damaged, a specific group of muscle fibers is affected. Surviving neurons are able to sprout collateral fibers to reinnervate the denervated muscle fibers. These changes are reflected on the EMG.

- Because denervated muscle fibers are highly irritable, prolonged activity occurs with needle insertion (this may also occur with myopathy).
- At rest with the needle inserted, spontaneous activity consisting of fibrillations, positive sharp waves, and fasciculations indicate a neurogenic abnormality.
- During contraction of the muscle a reduction in the density pattern, interference pattern, and mean amplitude of motor unit potentials (MUPs) occurs with neurogenic disorders. With myopathies, the duration and amplitude of MUPs are decreased, but the interference pattern is unaffected.

NCV studies involve electrical stimulation at one or more sites along a peripheral nerve measured at a correlated muscle. For a motor NCV, the time it takes from each point

Table 15–2 Electrodiagnostic Studies

Condition/Structure	*NCV*	*SNAP/CMAP*	*EMG*	*SSEP*
Nerve root/anterior horn (radiculopathy) (axonal degeneration)	Probably normal	Usually reduced in 2–3 weeks; SNAP normal if lesion is proximal to DRG	Fibrillation potentials, positive sharp waves, decreased recruitment; MUPs decreased.	Interpeak latency between Erb's point and dorsal columns may localize to nerve root
Peripheral neuropathy	Slowed velocity, increased latency (within 1 week)	Unaffected unless conduction block	Not segmental or specific for nerve root	May help localize based on latency
Brachial plexus lesions	Not usually useful	SNAPs decreased or absent	No fibrillation in paraspinal muscles	Sometimes valuable in localizing

Key: NCV, Nerve conduction velocity; SNAP, sensory nerve action potential; CMAP, compound muscle action potential; SSEP, somatosensory-evoked potentials; DRG, dorsal root ganglion; MUP, motor unit potential.

of stimulation to the appearance of the muscle potential is referred to as the latency. The conduction velocity is calculated by dividing the distance between two points of stimulation and the time it takes to travel between the two points. Latencies are prolonged and velocities are decreased when there is an internodal demyelination or localized axonal narrowing as seen with specific neuropathies (eg, carpal tunnel syndrome). More important, however, are the compound muscle action potential (CMAP) and the sensory nerve action potential (SNAP) amplitudes, which are more sensitive to traumatic peripheral nerve injury.[3] Following are some generalizations that may be helpful:

- Axonal degeneration will demonstrate normal velocities with NCV studies, but a reduced amplitude of evoked responses. EMG evidence takes about 3 weeks to surface, revealing spontaneous activity at rest, such as fibrillations and positive sharp waves; during contraction, there is a reduction in the density pattern, interference pattern, and mean amplitude of the MUPs.
- Demyelination disorders will demonstrate early changes in the nerve conduction velocity with relatively normal evoked amplitude responses.

When a proximal weakness pattern is found, futher testing for a myopathic cause should include laboratory testing (eg, lactate dehydrogenase) and muscle biopsy.

MANAGEMENT

Medical management is necessary for patients with UMNL, myasthenia gravis, Guillain-Barré syndrome, and drug- or toxin-induced neuropathy, or in the event that no known cause can be found. Most other causes of regional or specific weakness can be managed conservatively through a combination of spinal adjusting and muscular reeducation. The reader is directed to chapters on specific disorders for a more detailed description of conservative management recommendations.

Algorithm

An algorithm for evaluation and management of weakness is presented in Figure 15–1.

Figure 15–1

WEAKNESS—ALGORITHM.

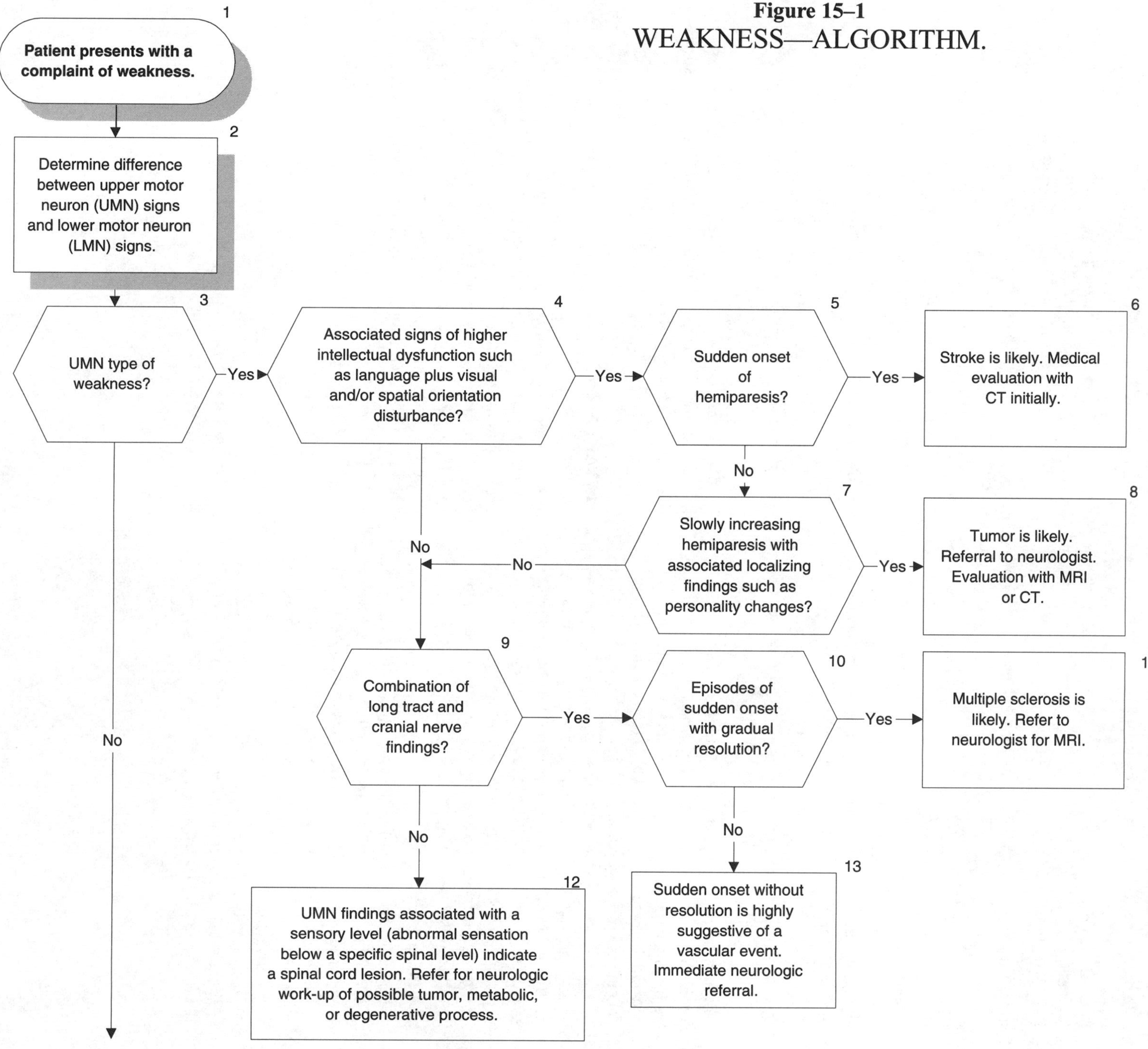

continues

Figure 15–1 continued

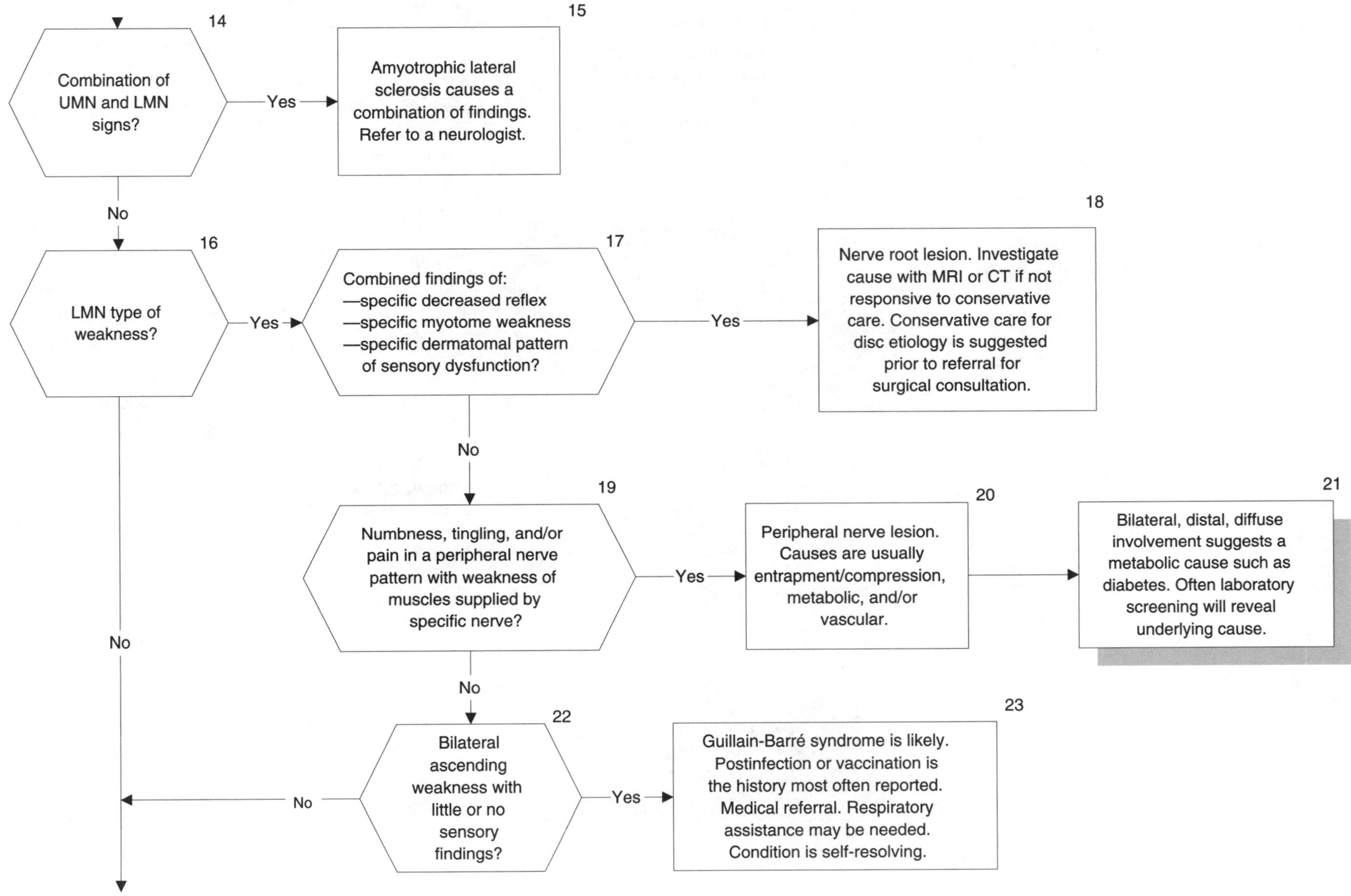

continues

Figure 15–1 continued

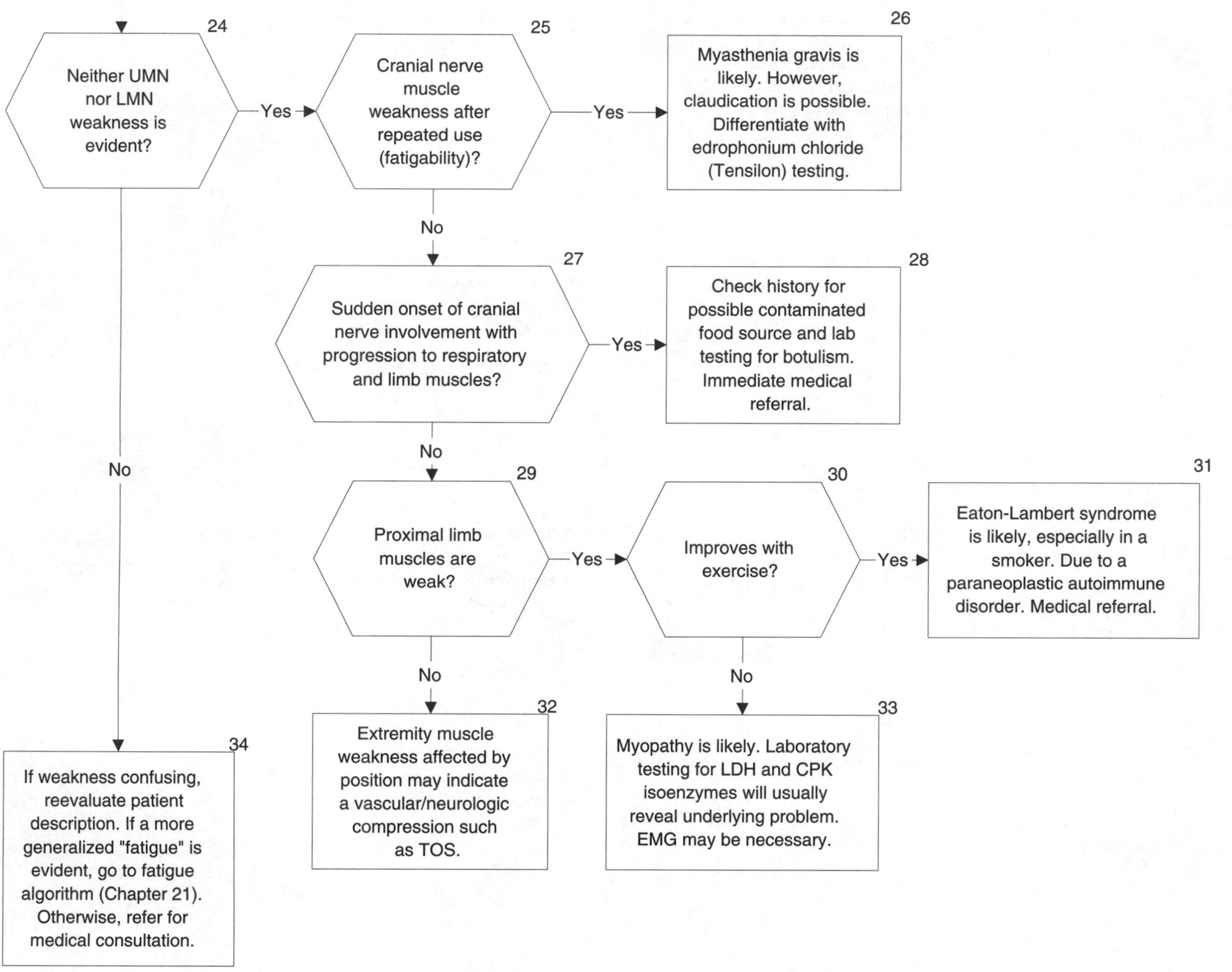

Key: CT, computed tomography; TOS, thoracic outlet syndrome; LDH, lactate dehydrogenase; CPK, creatine phosphokinase.

SELECTED NEUROLOGIC AND MUSCULAR DISEASES*

BELL'S PALSY

Classic Presentation

The patient complains of facial weakness and distortion and is unable to close one eye. There may be an associated ear pain. The patient does not recall any cause, just simply "woke up with it."

Cause

The cause is unknown; however, it is believed that a viral infection may cause an inflammatory reaction in the facial nerve near the stylomastoid foramen or in the facial nerve path through the temporal bone. Other causes of facial nerve involvement include stroke, cerebral tumor (mainly involves lower face), Ramsay Hunt syndrome (herpes vesicles visible in the ear), mastoid infection, fracture, or cerebellopontine angle tumors (associated hearing loss).

Evaluation

The patient's face appears expressionless on the involved side. If the case is severe, the palpebral fissure is widened and the patient cannot close the eye on the involved side. A deficit in taste and a hyperacusis may also be present.

Management

There is still a debate as to whether Bell's palsy should be treated initially. The general belief is that because 60% of patients recover completely without treatment and that the patients who do not usually have a more severe form, corticosteroids should be given only if the palsy is complete. It has not been demonstrated conclusively that this helps, but it does appear to reduce pain. The best approach is to monitor the degree of involvement for 2 or 3 days. If severe after this time, referral for a limited course of corticosteroids is warranted. Eye drops and a patch may be needed until eye closure is possible. Faradic stimulation or other physical therapy approaches may prevent contracture of facial muscles in long-term cases. Poorer prognosis is assumed with patients who are elderly, have hyperacusis, or severe initial pain.

PARKINSON'S DISEASE (PARALYSIS AGITANS)

Classic Presentation

The patient is older (aged 45 to 65 years) with a complaint of difficulty with movement and associated tremors. Often the patient has no specific complaint, yet on physical examination, the cardinal signs of parkinsonism are present. These include rigidity, bradykinesia, tremor, and walking difficulties.

Cause

Parkinson's disease is due to dopamine depletion caused by degeneration of the nigrostriatal system. This leads to an imbalance between dopamine and acetylcholine. The extrapyramidal system that controls the smoothness of movement is profoundly affected.

*See also regional chapters for specific neuropathies or nerve root disorders.

Evaluation

As the disease progresses, the patient appears to have a blank, emotionless facial expression. Seborrhea of the skin is also frequently seen. Although muscle strength is good, the patient is slow to react. There is often a visible tremor (four to six cycles per second) that is present at rest and is less severe with voluntary movement. Passive movement of the limbs reveals a characteristic rigidity (ie, cogwheel or ratchet). Tapping over the bridge of the nose (two times per second) creates a sustained blink response (Myerson's sign). The patient's walk will often demonstrate a classic festinating gait in which the patient takes many small, shuffling steps and has difficulty stopping. The arms do not swing automatically with walking. Some of the early signs are difficult to differentiate from signs of old age.

Management

Treatment is aimed at either blocking the effects of acetylcholine with anticholinergic drugs or restoring dopamine levels with levodopa (precursor to dopamine). Early parkinsonism is not usually treated. Mild parkinsonism is treated with amantadine. With progression, levodopa is effective in treating many of the features of parkinsonism; however, it is associated with various dyskinesias and an "on-off" phenomenon characterized by abrupt fluctuations in symptoms. Sinemet is most often given.[4] It is a combination of levodopa and carbidopa. Carbidopa-levodopa (Sinemet) is sometimes given with other medications such as bromocriptine (ergot derivative).

MUTIPLE SCLEROSIS

Classic Presentation

The patient is younger (less than age 55) presenting with a history of dizziness, numbness, tingling, or weakness that resolved over a few days. Other similar neurologic events have occurred in the past.

Cause

Mutiple sclerosis (MS) is a disease characterized by patchy demyelination with reactive gliosis in the spinal cord, optic nerve, and white matter of the brain. The cause is unknown, but MS is suspected to be an immune disorder. MS occurs mainly in individuals who live in temperate zones and especially in individuals of western European ancestry. There is an apparent genetic relationship due to the association of MS and HLA-DR2.

Evaluation

MS is characterized by episodic attacks that initially resolve but eventually leave residual neurologic deficits. The initial episode often will resolve in days, and the patient may remain symptom free for months or years. Eventually, however, symptoms reoccur. Symptoms usually will involve a region and consist of numbness, tingling, weakness, diplopia, dizziness, or urinary sphincter dysfunction (urgency or hesitancy). MRI will demonstrate multifocal areas of patchy demyelination in the brain or cervical spinal cord. Laboratory evaluation may reveal mild lymphocytosis or increased protein count in the cerebrospinal fluid (CSF) (more often in acute attacks). Immunoglobulin G and oligoclonal bands are more often seen in the CSF.

Management

There is no cure for MS. During acute exacerbations, corticosteroids are sometimes used to speed recovery. Relapses commonly occur in women 2 to 3 months after childbirth. Immunosuppresive therapy looks promising for slowing the progression of MS.[5]

GUILLAIN-BARRÉ SYNDROME

Classic Presentation

The patient complains of bilateral leg weakness following either a viral infection or immunization. The patient may also complain of distal paresthesias.

Cause

The cause is unknown; however, it is believed to be a demyelinating, autoimmune disorder.

Evaluation

The patient will have primarily motor signs, including loss of deep tendon reflexes. Because of autonomic involvement, there are fluctuations in blood pressure, abnormalities in sweating, and sphincter dysfunction. The weakness progresses variably, involving the arms and face in some patients. About 10% of patients have respiratory involvement. Examination of CSF demonstrates a high protein content; however, this may take 2 to 3 weeks to become evident.

Management

The condition is self-resolving in 80% to 90% of patients within months. During this period of time, a minority of patients will require respiratory assistance. About 10% of patients will have residual disability and about 3% will have relapses. Prednisone should not be given because of the possibility of prolonging recovery time. Plasmapheresis and intravenous immunoglobulin may be of benefit.

MYASTHENIA GRAVIS

Classic Presentation

The patient is often a young woman complaining of double vision, difficulty swallowing or weakness of the arm with repeated use or weakness of jaw muscles when chewing.

Cause

Neuromuscular transmission is blocked by autoantibodies that bind to acetycholine receptors, making them unavailable. The disease may be idiopathic or associated with a thymoma, thyrotoxicosis, rheumatoid arthritis, or lupus erythematosus. Thymomas are more common in older men.

Evaluation

Repeated muscle contraction or eye movement leads to fatigue, although initial movement or contraction is strong. Reflexes and the sensory examination are normal. In older men, a chest radiograph and/or computed tomography may be considered in a search for a thymoma. Electrophysiologic testing will reveal a decreasing response to stimulation. Laboratory testing includes a new test to assay the circulating levels of acetylcholine receptor antibodies (sensitivity is 80% to 90%). Medical evaluation involves drug testing using a short-acting anticholinesterase, which causes a temporary increase in strength.

Management

Symptomatic treatment involves the use of anticholinesterase medications such as neostigmine or pyridostigmine. Thymectomy often is dramatically effective, and is often recommended to patients under age 60 years. However, this choice should be reserved for those with progression or those unresponsive to medical management.

AMYOTROPHIC LATERAL SCLEROSIS

Classic Presentation

The patient is an adult who complains of muscle weakness and cramping in the hand. Progressively, signs and symptoms multiply, including difficulty in swallowing, chewing, coughing, or breathing.

Cause

Amyotrophic lateral sclerosis (ALS) is part of a group of motor neuron diseases with degeneration of the anterior horn cells and motor nuclei of the lower cranial nerves, corticospinal and corticobulbar tracts. The disorder occurs between ages 30 and 60 years and is progressive. Although most cases are sporadic, there are some familial cases.

Evaluation

This disorder is characterized by a combination of upper motor neuron and lower motor neuron lesion signs. Therefore, in addition to muscle atrophy and fasciculations, there are often brisk deep tendon reflexes. Sensory examination is normal and the sphincters are not affected. EMG will reveal abnormal spontaneous activity in a resting muscle and a decrease in recruitment ability.

Management

There is no treatment for ALS. The disease usually progresses to death over a period of about 2 to 2½ years in most patients. The 5-year survival rate is only 20%.

SYRINGOMYELIA

Classic Presentation

The patient is usually young. The parents are concerned about either the observation that the child injures his or her hands or arms and does not notice or the observation of a scoliosis.

Cause

A syrinx occurs in the central spinal cord either as a developmental problem or due to destruction or degeneration of gray and white matter secondary to trauma or an intramedullary tumor. Many cases are associated with herniation of the cerebellar tonsils, medulla, and fourth ventricle into the spinal canal. This developmental disorder is referred to as an Arnold-Chiari malformation. In this condition, the syrinx is actually a dilation of the central canal.

Evaluation

The patient will lose pain and temperature sense in a shawl-like distribution over the upper trunk and arms. Atrophy and areflexia also may be evident. Scoliosis is often present and sometimes represents a distinct opposite of the normal right-thoracic, left-lumbar curves, namely a left-thoracic, right-lumbar curve pattern. MRI evaluation will demonstrate both the Arnold-Chiari malformation with the cerebellar tonsils below the foramen magnum and also the level and extent of the syrinx.

Management

Treatment is surgical with decompression, including laminectomy in the upper cervical region and shunting of fluid into the peritoneum in some cases.

NEUROFIBROMATOSIS

Classic Presentation

The patient is often a child brought by parents concerned about multiple skin lesions on the trunk area. Otherwise the patient is often asymptomatic.

Cause

Neurofribromatosis is either a familial disorder that is autosomal dominant or sporadic, occurring with no known cause. The characteristic lesions involve the Schwann cells and nerve fibroblasts. There are two distinct types, type 1 and type 2. The patient with type 1 will present with multiple hyperpigmented nodules. The patient with type 2 often presents with problems with hearing or eyesight.[6]

Evaluation

Finding the characteristic café au lait lesions over the trunk, pelvis, or flexor creases of the arms is virtually diagnostic if six or more large lesions are found. The neurofibromas are slowly progressive and in type 1 may lead to the rare but deforming Recklinghausen's disease. With type 1, plexiform neuromas (overgrowth of subcutaneous tissue) and bone distortion occur. With type 2, intracranial tumors affect cranial nerves controlling eyesight, balance, and hearing.

Management

There is no known treatment. Surgical removal of tumors of the skin and nerves is the only recourse for patients at this time.

MUSCULAR DYSTROPHY (DUCHENNE TYPE)

Classic Presentation

Muscular dystrophy (MD) is a group of inherited myopathic disorders that present differently. The most common is the Duchenne type (pseudohypertrophic). The patient is between the ages of 1 and 5 years. The parents have noted that their child has difficulty in rising from a bent-over position, has a waddling gait, and falls often.

Cause

Duchenne's is an X-linked recessive gene disorder. The defective gene leads to a marked reduction or absence of an important protein, dystrophin.[7]

Evaluation

The characteristic difficulty in rising from a bent-over position may cause the patient to walk up the legs with his or her hands. Proximal muscle testing may indicate weakness. The disease affects the limbs first, then the shoulders. Pseudohypertrophy may occur as a result of fatty replacement of muscle. Mild mental retardation is also found. Laboratory studies will reveal markedly elevated creatine kinase (CK) levels.

Management

There is no treatment for the disease. Progression is rapid, leading to the need for a wheelchair. Patients progressively decline and finally die before age 20 years in most cases. Females on the maternal side of an affected child should be tested for elevations of CK or lactate dehydrogenase on several occasions. These elevated markers may indicate the need for genetic counseling. Also, genetic studies in early pregnancy can determine whether the child will have Duchenne's. In late pregnancy DNA probes can be used on fetal tissue to diagnose Duchenne's in the fetus. There may be some potential hope for the use of gene therapy in the future.[8]

REFERENCES

1. Souza TA. Which orthopedic tests are really necessary? In: Lawerence DJ, Cassidy JD, McGregor M, et al., eds. *Advances in Chiropractic.* St. Louis, MO: Mosby-Year Book; 1994;1:101–158.
2. Meyer JJ. Clinical electromyographic and related neurophysiologic responses. In: Lawerence DJ, Cassidy JD, McGregor M, et al., eds. *Advances in Chiropractic.* St. Louis, MO: Mosby-Year Book; 1994;1:29.
3. Long RR. Nerve anatomy and diagnostic principles. In: Pappas AM, ed. *Upper Extremity Injuries in the Athlete.* New York: Churchill Livingstone; 1995:43.
4. Standaert DG, Stern MB. Update on the management of Parkinson's disease. *Med Clin North Am.* 1993;77:169.
5. Weinshenker BG, Issa M, Baskerville J. Meta-analysis of the placebo-treated groups in clinical trials of progressive MS. *Neurology.* 1996;46:1613–1619.
6. Mulvihill JJ. Neurofibromatosis 1 (Recklinghausen's disease) and neurofibromatosis 2 (bilateral acoustic neurofibromatosis): an update. *Ann Intern Med.* 1990;113:39.
7. Mendell JR, Sahenk Z, Prior TW. The childhood muscular dystrophies: diseases sharing a common pathogenesis of membrane instability. *J Child Neurol.* 1995;10:150–159.
8. Karpati G, Acsadi G. The potential for gene therapy in Duchenne muscular dystrophy and other genetic muscle diseases. *Muscle Nerve.* 1993;16:1141.

Chapter 16

Numbness and Tingling

CONTEXT

Patients complaining of pain do not necessarily have pathologic involvement of neural tissue but do have a response due to trauma or irritation of nociceptive nerve fibers. Patients complaining of numbness or tingling, however, are more likely to have disease, ischemia, or injury of neural tissue. The list of possible causes is enormous and can only be narrowed down by combining the findings of location, onset, and associated neural localizing findings (ie, motor deficit or deep tendon reflex abnormality) (Exhibit 16–1). Although trauma or direct irritation often may be the source of these complaints, it is important to remember the sometimes transient response of neural tissue to ischemia (eg, diabetes) or metabolic imbalance (eg, uremia) that may occur with systemic processes.

Chiropractors are often faced with the presentation of a patient who claims numbness, but when clinically evaluated has no objectifiable loss. Important discriminators are finding associated neurologic signs indicating nerve root or peripheral nerve pathology; however, these also are often absent. Possible explanations for this lack of evidence include the presence of a transient process, misinterpretation of the sensation by the patient, a "referred" sensory abnormality, and malingering.

Sensory perversions are often divided into two categories: (1) paresthesias and (2) dysesthesias. Paresthesias are spontaneous, abnormal sensations, described by patients as "pins and needles" or tingling. Dysesthesias are irritating sensations evoked by normally nonnociceptive stimuli such as light touch. Sometimes used synonymously with dysesthesias is hyperpathia—normal stimuli are pain producing. Hypesthesia implies that there is an elevated threshold to stimulus. For example, pain is felt with a pinprick, but the applied pressure needed for pain perception is greater than would normally be required.

GENERAL STRATEGY

History

- Ask the patient to define what he or she means by a complaint of numbness, tingling, or other unusual sensations.
- Attempt to localize to a specific body region (distinguish between single and multiple areas, and whether the sensation is felt more distally in the hands or feet).
- Determine any associated symptoms such as pain or weakness.
- Determine whether the onset was abrupt or gradual and whether or not related to trauma.
- Determine whether the patient has a known diagnosis of or indications of diabetes, alcoholism, liver or renal disease, or anxiety or depression; obtain a thorough drug history.

Evaluation

- Perform a neurologic examination focusing on sensory testing; begin distally in an attempt to determine selective loss or alteration of pain, temperature, light touch, vibration, and position sense.
- Examine the motor system in an attempt to correlate findings suggestive of nerve root or peripheral nerve involvement.
- When a clear picture is not evident, it may be necessary to proceed to electrodiagnostic or other specialized testing based on the suspected cause.

Exhibit 16–1 Narrowing the Possible Causes of Numbness

Patient complains of numbness

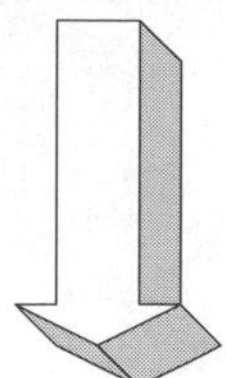

Differentiate between objective and subjective numbness with a sensory examination

Subjective numbness is suggestive of referral or a transient process (no demonstrable sensory or motor findings; often diffuse, following no specific dermatomal pattern)

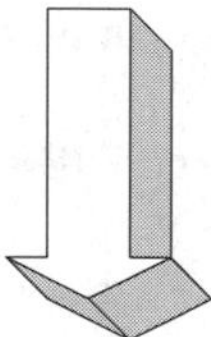

Distinguish among various neurologic possibilities

Nerve root

Often accompanied by neck pain with upper extremity numbness and low back pain with lower extremity numbness. Examination reveals
- —decrease in corresponding deep tendon reflex
- —weakness in corresponding myotome
- —hypoesthesia in corresponding dermatomal pattern

Peripheral nerve

Usually a history of overuse or direct trauma. Examination reveals weakness of corresponding muscle if there is a motor component and hypoesthesia of the peripheral nerve patch of skin.

Nerve plexus

Classic example is thoracic outlet syndrome with pressure on the neurovascular elements of the brachial plexus. Traction trauma or tumor is also a possible cause. Although symptoms may be diffuse, most plexus lesions affect a specific section such as the lower plexus with involvement, for example, of the medial arm.

Central nervous system, including spinal cord

Involvement is often bilateral. Central cord processes may also affect temperature. Patchy involvement may indicate multiple sclerosis. Complete spinal cord involvement has associated motor findings.

Management

- Most cases of isolated peripheral nerve or nerve root problems can be managed initially by the chiropractor; monitor for progression or unresponsiveness to determine need for neurologic consultation.
- Some metabolic disorders, such as uremia, often require referral for management; others, such as diabetes, can be comanaged.

RELEVANT ANATOMY

The following is a brief and generalized overview of the sensory nervous system. Participants in the sensory system include nerve cell bodies, nerve fibers, and sensory receptors. The types of sensations that are conveyed are generally divided into (1) pain and temperature, (2) touch, and (3) proprioception and vibration.

Free nerve endings are the primary receptors for pain and temperature. The signal is then carried to the first nerve cell body in the dorsal root ganglion (DRG). Fibers leaving the DRG enter the spinal cord by accessing Lissauer's tract and ascending or descending one or two segments before synapsing in the substantia gelatinosa. At this level interactions with interneurons influence transmission. From the second-order neuron A delta (small myelinated) fibers cross the anterior commissure and ascend in the contralateral lateral spinothalamic tract, ascending to the thalamus to synapse in the posterior nuclei and ventral posterolateral (VPL) thalamus. The C fibers also cross in the spinal cord to ascend primarily in the anterior spinothalamic tract and terminate in the intralaminar and parafascicular nuclei of the thalamus. Both then continue to the somatic sensory area of the cortex. The spinothalamic tract also carries touch and deep pressure sensations.[1]

Larger, myelinated fibers participate in conveying information for proprioception and vibration. The primary receptors are

- muscle spindles and Golgi tendon organs (stretch)
- skin mechanoreceptors (Meissner's corpuscles)
- joint mechanoreceptors
- vibration (pacinian corpuscles)

Fibers carry information to the dorsal root ganglion and then to the posterior column of the spinal cord and ascend without crossing to synapse in the nucleus gracilis and cuneatus in the medulla. They then cross to ascend mainly to the VPL of the thalamus. After synapsing, the neurons ascend via the internal capsule to the corona radiata, accessing the neurons of the postcentral gyrus.

The general architecture of the spinal cord may give clues to certain patterns of sensory loss or weakness. The ascending fibers are laminated such that fibers for the lower levels are more lateral and superficial, making them vulnerable to an extrinsic spinal cord lesion. Therefore, a compressive myelopathy, for example, may produce an ascending pattern of sensory loss if progressive. A spinal lesion more centrally located (eg, syringomyelia) would interrupt fibers that cross, such as those conveying pain and temperature, while sparing the dorsal column pathways, leaving vibration and proprioception unaffected.

It is believed that paresthesias and dysesthesias are the result of either damage to large fiber axons or demyelination. This is most common with structural damage that occurs with peripheral nerve or nerve root compression or toxic/metabolic disorders that cause neuropathy. Numbness is more often the result of loss or damage to smaller sensory fibers affecting both pain and temperature perception.

Neuropathies, particularly peripheral neuropathies, are often divided into two general types based on the involved structure: (1) axonal degeneration and (2) paranodal or segmental demyelination. Although many disorders do not clearly fall into one or the other category, this distinction is important from the standpoint of physiologic testing. In evaluating nerve conduction, two responses are measured: (1) the velocity (or latency) and (2) the amplitude of the evoked response. Electrodiagnostic testing can evaluate either the sensory or motor component. In general, axonal degeneration results in relatively normal conduction; the evoked amplitude of the response, however, is decreased (with eventual electromyography [EMG] changes evident). Demyelination generally causes the reverse, with conduction velocity decreased yet normal evoked amplitudes (EMG is often normal).

EVALUATION

History

The onset is often suggestive of an underlying cause.

- Sudden traumatic onset—When a related, localized area of the body is affected, a traumatic neuropathy is likely; when associated with neck or back trauma, an associated dermatome or myotome-related complaint of pain or weakness may help localize to a segmental level; bilateral complaints suggest spinal cord involvement.
- Sudden nontraumatic onset—This is more suggestive of a vascular cause. When relatively localized to a single area, vascular infarction as occurs occasionally with diabetes is likely; when more generalized or affecting a side of the body, a central vascular event is more likely (stroke or transient ischemic attack). Multiple sclerosis may also present with a rather sudden onset as either a localized or more diffuse pattern.

- Chronic onset—It is always important to ask about the patient's current medications (this may reveal a side effect of a medication or suggest a past diagnosis), and also any past diagnoses with a focus on diabetes, alcoholism, hepatic or renal disease, rheumatoid arthritis (RA), pregnancy, and depression or anxiety.

Complaints of numbness localized to the face or more generalized over the body with no apparent cause should raise the suspicion of anxiety with consequent hyperventilation. Distal numbness in a "stocking and glove" distribution is characteristic of metabolic and particularly diabetic neuropathy. This distribution is often bilateral.

If a complaint of numbness is related to a specific occupational or sports activity, it is important to identify any element of either direct compression of a specific nerve or possibly muscle or fascial entrapment. This requires the patient to demonstrate a working posture and any repetitive maneuvers employed.

Complaints associated with diabetes may have a metabolic cause (myelin affected) or be due to neural ischemia. Numbness that seems associated with pregnancy may be due to either fluid compression or vitamin deficiency. If numbness or tingling is present in a patient with RA, fluid compression is likely the primary cause.

Patients with coexisting spinal complaints often will be able to contribute localizing information with regard to pain and weakness. Coupling an outlined pain pathway or movement weakness with the area of numbness or tingling will usually discriminate between a peripheral nerve problem and a nerve root problem. This is further distinguished on the physical examination (Figures 16–1 and 16–2).

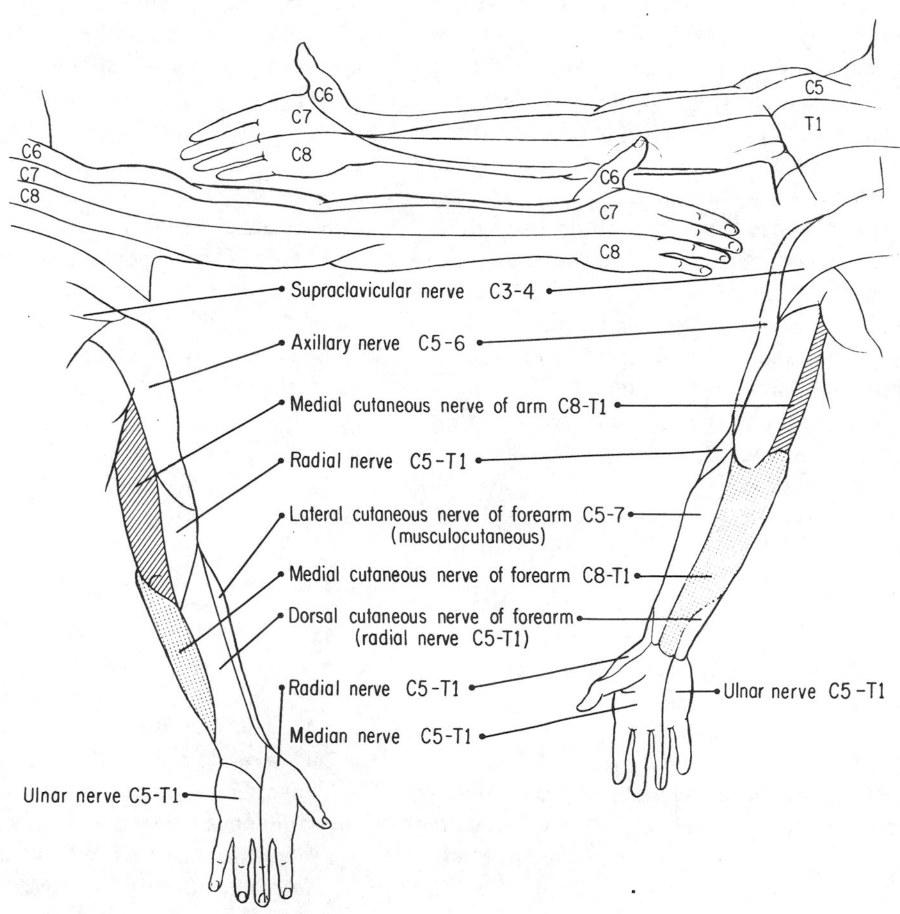

Figure 16–1 Dermatomes of the upper extremity and the cutaneous innervation of the arm by the peripheral sensory nerves. *Source:* Reprinted with permission from B.M. Reilly, *Practical Strategies in Outpatient Medicine*, 2nd ed., p. 417, © 1991, W.B. Saunders Company.

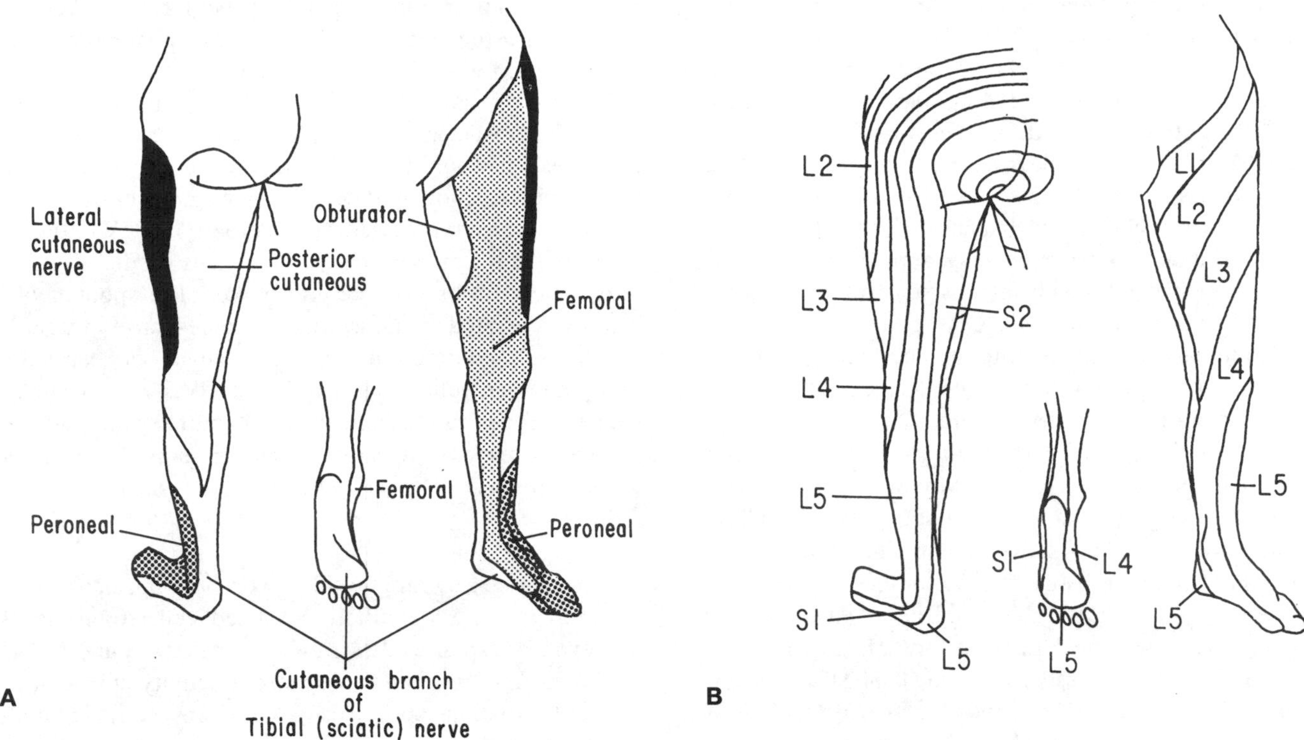

Figure 16–2 Sensory innervation of the lower extremity. **A**, Peripheral nerve innervation. **B**, Dermatomal (root) innervation. *Source:* Reprinted with permission from B.M. Reilly, *Practical Strategies in Outpatient Medicine*, 2nd ed., p. 927, © 1991, W.B. Saunders Company.

Examination

The examination must focus on finding which sensory component is affected.[2] Test the patient with his or her eyes closed and alternate the sensory stimulus, applying the stimulus in a random pattern. For example, using a pin and brush alternately touch the patient in a random fashion so that a pattern cannot be detected by the patient. Test the patient for the following:

- alternate touching with the sharp and dull edge of a pin or broken tongue blade
- light touch with a brush, wisp of cotton, or gentle touch from examiner's finger pads
- temperature with small hot and cold test tubes
- vibration with a struck tuning fork (128 vibrations per second)

Most neuropathies begin with distal sensory loss (the longer nerves affected most often). If no abnormalities are found distally, it is unusual to find proximal loss. If distal loss is found, progress upward to better define the involved area. With all sensory testing, it is important to compare sides. Specifically when testing with a pinwheel or touch, it is important to perform simultaneous testing because of the effect known as sensory extinction. Unilateral testing will be unrevealing, but when both bilateral areas are tested, a sensory deficit is exposed indicating a cortical sensory disorder. Other cortical sensory testing includes the following:

- Stereognosis—Have the patient identify an object placed in his or her hand while the patient's eyes are closed.
- Two-point discrimination—With either a two-point discriminator or a premeasured opened paper clip determine the patient's ability to feel both points of stimulation at the same time; in general, discrimination at the fingertip is 2 to 4 mm; dorsum of fingers, 4 to 6 mm; palms, 8 to 12 mm; and dorsum of hand, 20 to 30 mm.
- Graphesthesia—Write letters or numbers on the palm of the patient's hand with his or her eyes closed; ask the patient to identify what you are writing.

Proprioception is evaluated by testing joint position sense. The third and fourth digits of the upper and lower extremities have the most sparse innervation, and therefore may reveal loss earlier than other digits.[3] The joint is grasped on the lateral surfaces and separated as much as possible from the other digits, being careful not to touch the other digits. The patient, with eyes closed, is asked whether the joint is being held up or down by the examiner. Another evaluation of position sense is the Romberg test. The ability of the patient to keep his or her standing balance with the eyes closed indicates an intact proprioceptive system. If the patient is able to balance (weight equally distributed between both legs) with the eyes open, yet loses balance with the eyes closed, he or she is relying on visual input for balance control. Abnormalities of vibration or position sense indicate problems with large fiber neurons and/or dorsal column disease.

In chiropractic practice, a common presentation is neck or low back pain with associated extremity complaints of pain, numbness, or tingling. Although it is hoped that a pattern match will be made with these complaints and an objective demonstration of sensory loss, motor loss, or an associated deep tendon decrease, this is often not the case. For example, patients with neck pain may complain of a diffuse sense of numbness or paresthesias in the hand. They are unable to localize to a dermatome, and objective testing fails to clarify the diagnosis. It may be helpful first to attempt provocation maneuvers. For the nerve root, this includes standard orthopaedic testing of the related spinal area, such as cervical compression/distraction for the upper extremity or the straight leg raise or Kemp's test for the lower extremity. Additional provocation testing for peripheral nerves is accomplished by either tapping (if the nerve is superficial) or compression through direct pressure or muscle contraction. Patients who associate the complaint with an activity can be asked to repeat or hold the position (whichever is appropriate) in an attempt to reproduce the complaint.

When the area of involvement overlaps between a dermatome and a peripheral nerve skin patch, selected muscle testing, provocation tests, or an associated tendon reflex may help differentiate the source. For example, if the patient had a sensory area loss over the anterior thumb and two fingers, either median nerve involvement or a C6 nerve root lesion is possible. However, a median nerve disorder would not affect the brachioradialis reflex and a C6 nerve root disorder would not cause a positive Tinel's sign over the median nerve (unless there is a double-crush syndrome).

When the complaint is diffuse or nondermatomal, consideration of referral sources should be next. These may include facet irritation or trigger points. Reproduction may be possible with trigger point palpation, yet facet involvement is difficult to demonstrate clinically except for the relief sometimes provided by an adjustment.

If the diagnosis is still in question, consideration of electrodiagnostic or special imaging studies is warranted. In most cases it would be appropriate to treat for a 1-month period prior to utilizing these expensive procedures.

EMG and nerve conduction velocity (NCV) studies are reserved for difficult cases. EMG uses needle insertion into muscle to test muscle and nerve.[4] The spontaneous activity generated upon insertion or the response generated with muscle contraction helps distinguish between axon injury and demyelination disorders. NCV studies use surface electrodes to measure velocity and the amplitude of an evoked response to an electrical stimulus. Both motor and sensory nerves can be tested. Important concepts are as follows:

- Axonal degeneration will demonstrate normal velocities with NCV studies, but a reduced amplitude of evoked responses. EMG evidence takes about 3 weeks to surface, revealing spontaneous activity at rest, such as fibrillations and positive sharp waves; during contraction, there is a reduction in the density pattern, interference pattern, and mean amplitude of the motor unit potentials (MUPs).
- Demyelination disorders will demonstrate early changes in the nerve conduction velocity with relatively normal evoked amplitude responses.

MANAGEMENT

Management is based on the suspected cause. Most peripheral nerve and nerve root disorders can be managed by a chiropractor for 1 month, being sure to monitor for worsening or nonresponse to care. Metabolic disorders often require medical evaluation and management; diabetes, however, often can be comanaged. See more thorough discussions of individual disorders in related chapters of this text.

Algorithm

An algorithm for evaluation and management of numbness is presented in Figure 16–3.

Figure 16–3
NUMBNESS—ALGORITHM.

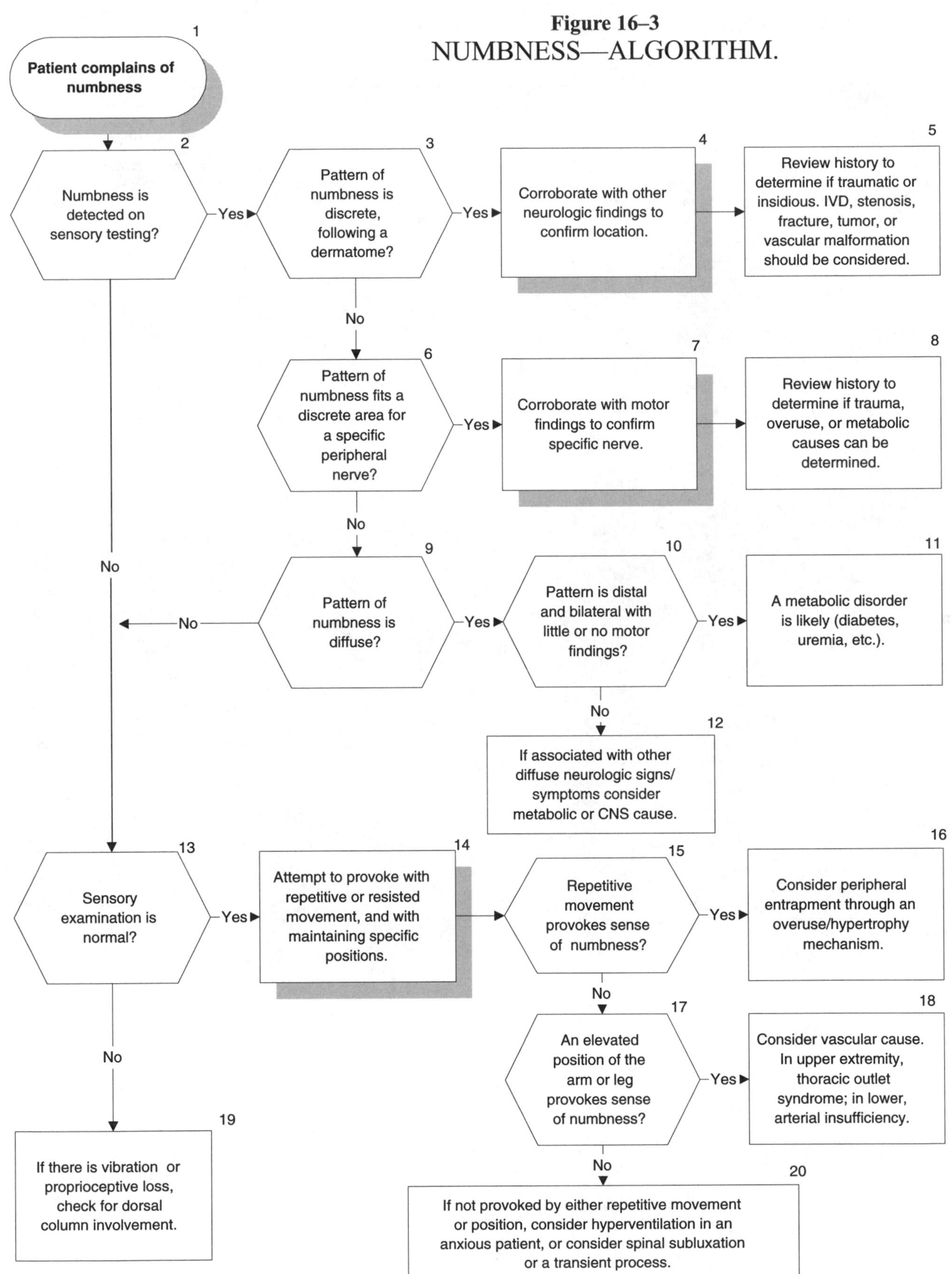

1 Patient complains of numbness
2 Numbness is detected on sensory testing?
Yes
3 Pattern of numbness is discrete, following a dermatome?
Yes
4 Corroborate with other neurologic findings to confirm location.
5 Review history to determine if traumatic or insidious. IVD, stenosis, fracture, tumor, or vascular malformation should be considered.
No
6 Pattern of numbness fits a discrete area for a specific peripheral nerve?
Yes
7 Corroborate with motor findings to confirm specific nerve.
8 Review history to determine if trauma, overuse, or metabolic causes can be determined.
No
9 Pattern of numbness is diffuse?
No
Yes
10 Pattern is distal and bilateral with little or no motor findings?
Yes
11 A metabolic disorder is likely (diabetes, uremia, etc.).
No
12 If associated with other diffuse neurologic signs/ symptoms consider metabolic or CNS cause.
No
13 Sensory examination is normal?
Yes
14 Attempt to provoke with repetitive or resisted movement, and with maintaining specific positions.
15 Repetitive movement provokes sense of numbness?
Yes
16 Consider peripheral entrapment through an overuse/hypertrophy mechanism.
No
17 An elevated position of the arm or leg provokes sense of numbness?
Yes
18 Consider vascular cause. In upper extremity, thoracic outlet syndrome; in lower, arterial insufficiency.
No
20 If not provoked by either repetitive movement or position, consider hyperventilation in an anxious patient, or consider spinal subluxation or a transient process.
No
19 If there is vibration or proprioceptive loss, check for dorsal column involvement.

Key: IVD, Intervertebral disc; CNS, central nervous system.

REFERENCES

1. Brodal A. *Neurological Anatomy.* 2nd ed. New York: Oxford University Press; 1981.
2. Walker HK, Hall WD, Hurst JW, eds. *Clinical Methods: The History, Physical, and Laboratory Examinations.* 2nd ed. Boston: Butterworth; 1980:942.
3. DeMeyer W. *Technique of the Neurological Examination: A Programmed Text.* 2nd ed. New York: McGraw-Hill; 1974:293–323.
4. Meyer JJ. Clinical electromyographic and related neurophysiologic responses. In: Lawerence DJ, Cassidy JD, McGregor M, et al, eds. *Advances in Chiropractic.* St. Louis, MO: Mosby-Year Book; 1994;1:29.

Chapter 17

Headache

CONTEXT

Severe headache has significant financial impact. Considering only the cost of lost work and productivity, migraine headaches have a price tag of between $5.6 and $17.2 billion each year.[1] This does not take into account the cost of management. Several years ago, the cost to an employer for a migraine worker was on average $5,000. Fifty-seven percent of men and 76% of women report at least one significant headache per month.[2] Approximately 23.6 million Americans have suffered from migraine headaches.[3]

Although they are a common human ailment, headaches, more often than not, do not warrant a visit to the doctor's office. Whether obviously associated with flu, excessive drinking, skipped breakfast, or other factors, the patient is quite aware of a connection to the headache. When a patient does seek an opinion or treatment, the headache has become either unbearable (affecting lifestyle) or worrisome (the patient thinks there may be a tumor), or there has been head trauma.

In the chiropractic office one of the most common headache presentations is associated with whiplash. Headache is one of the top two complaints reported postwhiplash. Many studies indicate that a high percentage of whiplash patients (70% to 90%) develop a headache.[4–9]

The categorization of headaches by the International Headache Society (IHS) distinguishes among the primary headache patterns and includes a category for cervicogenic headache.[10] The categories use specific criteria upon which to base the headache diagnosis. Unfortunately, the cervicogenic headache criteria are quite restrictive and exclusive of the other primary headache categories (Exhibit 17–1). In other words, there is a perception by the IHS that there could be no overlap or cervical contribution to the other headache types. Yet research indicates that there is likely a pure category of cervicogenic headache, another that has a significant contribution from a cervicogenic component, and yet another that is unrelated. Using the criteria set forth by the IHS, one study determined a cervicogenic headache prevalence of about 18% in a random population sample of adults.[11]

Although the vast majority of headaches are benign (not life threatening), the doctor initially must screen for secondary causes prior to assuming one of three common primary patterns: migraine, tension, and cluster headaches. Screening the patient with headaches historically is the most fruitful, time-effective, and inexpensive approach (Exhibit 17–2). Expensive imaging approaches are rarely needed.

GENERAL STRATEGY

History and Examination

- Determine whether the patient has a secondary cause for the headache, such as trauma, metabolic disease, toxic (drug) effect, infection, or intracranial pathology.
- Determine whether the patient's headache fits one of three categories of primary headache: migraine, tension, and cluster or whether cervicogenic is likely.
- Determine whether there are any obvious triggers or patterns to the headache.
- Evaluate the patient for musculoskeletal factors that may cause or influence headaches.

Management

The chiropractor should determine which cases are appropriate for referral. Referral is, in fact, rarely needed given

Exhibit 17–1 The 1995 IHS Criteria for Cervicogenic Headache

- Pain is localized to neck and occipital region. It may project to the forehead, orbital region, temples, vertex, or ears.
- Pain is precipitated or aggravated by special neck movements or sustained neck posture.
- At least one of the following occurs:
  1. resistance to or limitation of passive neck movements
  2. changes in neck muscle contour, texture, tone, or response to active and passive stretching and contraction
  3. abnormal tenderness of neck muscles
- Radiologic examination reveals at least one of the following:
  1. movement abnormalities in flexion/extension
  2. abnormal posture
  3. fractures, congenital abnormalities, bone tumors, rheumatoid arthritis, or other distinct pathology (not spondylosis or osteochondrosis)

the low incidence of serious causes. The red flags that warrant further investigation and possible referral include but are not limited to the following:

- a new headache in an older patient (tumor or temporal arteritis)
- headache due to head trauma (subdural or epidural hematoma)
- associated residual neurologic signs or symptoms (tumor or vascular event)
- cognitive changes (eg, confusion, drowsiness, giddiness)
- vomiting without nausea (indicating increased intracranial pressure)
- persistent or progressive headache
- nuchal rigidity (subacrachnoid hemorrhage or meningitis)
- suspicion of drug or alcohol dependence
- headache associated with a diastolic blood pressure greater than 115 mm Hg
- persistent or severe headache in a child

For patients without these red flags, consider the following options for conservative care:

- Modify patient behavior (sleep, diet, and exercise) when determined by history as a significant factor.
- Manage with chiropractic manipulative therapy for an initial high-frequency period of 1 to 3 weeks, followed by a gradual tapering.
- If chiropractic management is unsuccessful refer for or use nonpharmacologic treatment such as acupuncture or biofeedback.
- If nonpharmacologic management is unsuccessful, refer for medical management.

THEORIES OF CAUSATION OF PRIMARY HEADACHES

Although the treatment of headaches chiropractically has anecdotally been supported for years, only recently have models of causal relationships between headaches and cervical dysfunction and studies to confirm effectiveness been advanced. Recent research suggests that the older theories of vascular dilation with migraines[12,13] and muscle contraction with tension headaches[14] do not adequately explain how these headaches occur. It appears that a neurologic event occurs associated with an imbalance of serotonin.[15–18] This serotonin imbalance appears to be site specific. In other words, too little or too much serotonin may contribute to headache development, depending on where it occurs. In general, too little available serotonin is the primary cause.

Convergence of afferent information from cervical spinal nerves and the trigeminal nerve in the trigeminocervical nucleus may serve to explain a referred pain mechanism for both migraine and tension headaches, and perhaps for cluster headaches.[19] The trigeminocervical nucleus (Figure 17–1) is a continuous column of neurons formed by the caudal end of the spinal nucleus of the trigeminal nerve and the dorsal horn of the upper cervical spinal nerves (C1-C3). Descending fibers from the nucleus raphae magnus and other midbrain and pontine nuclei normally have an inhibitory effect on the spinothalamic neurons (directly and through interneurons), preventing transmission of pain signals. Deregulation may allow a lowering of the stimulus threshold necessary for pain perception, perhaps through a decrease in secreted serotonin. Therefore, afferent information that is not nociceptive in nature may become so due to lowering of the pain threshold and/or expansion of the receptor field. The result may be either referral to the head and face from

Exhibit 17–2 Historical Screening of the Patient with Headaches

Patient presents with a history of headaches

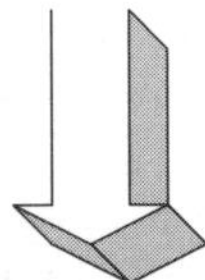

Differentiate Referral from Nonreferral Case

History Questions

History of head trauma? (Consider subdural or epidural hematoma)
Slow or insidious onset of new headache? (Consider tumor or vascular event such as an aneurysm or atriovenous malformation [AVM].)
Associated neurologic deficits? (Consider all the above.)
New temporal headache in an older patient, especially when associated with vision deficit or aching trunk area? (Consider temporal arteritis.)
Occurs only with exertion and is progressively worse? (Consider vascular cause such as aneurysm or AVM.)

Differentiate by type

Vascular/ Neurologic

Decreased blood to the brain (atherosclerosis) Increased pressure on vasculature (vasodilation or hypertension)

Migraine
Is there a family history?
Are there visual changes before the headache? (Prodrome.)
Is the headache incapacitating?
Do they last for hours or days? (Differentiate between classic and common.)
Does aspirin help?
Does the headache wake you up at night?

Cluster
Is the patient a middle-aged or young man?
Is the pain orbital and associated with tearing or drooling?
Do they last a short time (45 minutes to 2 hours)?
Does alcohol or smoking make them worse or trigger them?

Myogenic/ Cervicogenic

Direct pull on periosteum, muscle spasm, referred pain, or nerve entrapment

Is there a history of a whiplash type injury prior to headaches?
Are the headaches suboccipital or bandlike?
Are they worse in the afternoon?
Stress related?
Aspirin helpful to some degree?

Metabolic/Toxic

Decreased glucose to the brain (diabetes, hypoglycemia), increased metabolism (hyperthyroidism), drug toxicity

Is there a history of hypo- or hyperthyroid disease?
Is there a history of diabetes?
Is the patient anemic?
Is the patient taking medications?
Is there a relationship to certain foods?
Is the patient occupationally exposed to toxic materials?

Miscellaneous

Other causes such as sinus, eyestrain, cerebrospinal fluid (CSF) pressure changes, etc.

Is there a history of a spinal tap? (Possible CSF pressure cause.)
Is the headache associated with upper respiratory infection signs/symptoms or made worse by bending forward? (Possible sinus infection.)
Is the patient's eyesight normal or corrected? (Possible eyestrain or myogenic from forward head position.)

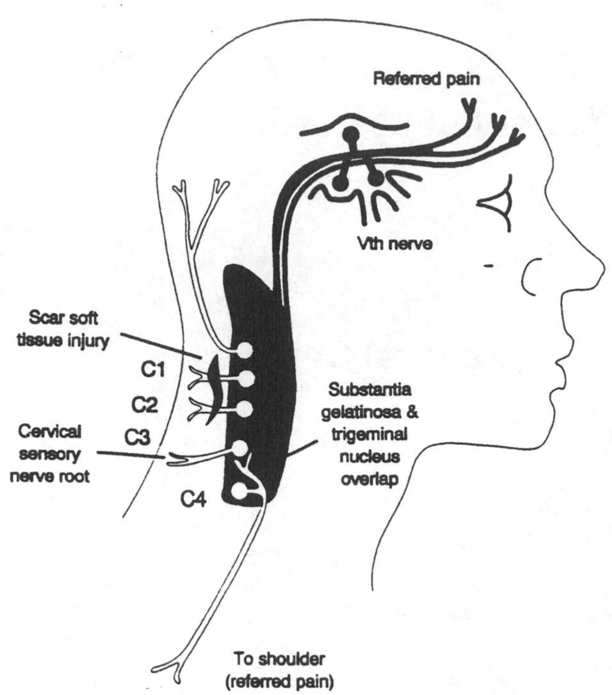

Figure 17–1 The trigeminocervical nucleus. *Source:* Adapted from Hooshmand, H., *Chronic Pain: Reflex Sympathetic Dystrophy Prevention and Management,* 52, CRC Press, Boca Raton, Florida, © 1993. With permission.

irritation in the neck or referral of neck pain from irritation of intracranial pain-sensitive structures (eg, intracerebral blood vessels causing posterior or suboccipital pain).

Hormonal influences on central serotoninergic and opioid neurons may play a role in migraine headache in women. Plasma levels of serotonin have been found to increase significantly in women with migraine with aura and those with tension headaches. This fluctuation was not evident in migraine sufferers without aura. It is unclear whether this is a reflection of central serotonin effects.[20] Menstrual migraine appears to be due to estrogen withdrawal.[21] Sixty percent of migraine attacks in women are associated with menses, but only 14% are exclusively related.[22] Sustained increased estrogen levels with pregnancy and decreased levels with menopause appear to be related to changes in headache patterns. Migraine sufferers usually improve during pregnancy, especially after the first trimester. This is suspected to be caused by sustained high levels of estrogen. However, 25% of women notice no change in their headache pattern.[23] The effect of contraceptives on migraine headache is less clear. Several studies report no difference between those who took oral contraceptives and a placebo group.[24] Other studies suggest an increased severity and incidence.[25] Migraine prevalence definitely decreases with age; menopause, however, may trigger the onset or return of migraine.[26] Again, some studies indicate that estrogen replacement therapy increases or exacerbates migraine while others indicate estrogen alone or in combination with testosterone help relieve migraine.

History

Careful questioning of the patient during the history taking can point to the diagnosis (Tables 17–1 and 17–2).

- Determine any obvious triggers or causes of headaches from environmental, dietary, or medication sources.
- Determine any red flags suggestive of referral for medical management.
- Attempt to distinguish among three primary headaches, using the patient interview and headache diary.

Although the sequence of questioning is not as important as the comprehensiveness of the questioning, it would be prudent next to rule out causes that might be obvious to the doctor but not necessarily the patient. Questions to the patient should include the following:

- Do you have signs and symptoms of flu (especially fever or cough without nuchal rigidity)?
- Have you recently been given a new prescription?
- Have you recently discontinued use of a prescription drug?
- Have you recently stopped smoking, coffee drinking, alcohol, or recreational drug use?
- Do you use recreational drugs?
- Do you get headaches after reading or have you had a recent change in eyeglass prescription?
- Are you occupationally exposed to toxic chemicals?

Exertion/Activity-Related Headaches

One of the major concerns with headache associated with exertion is the possibility of an underlying tumor or vascular weakness that may lead to sudden death. It appears as though this concern is worth addressing; however, although 50% to 60% of patients with brain tumors have headaches, only 25% experience exertion-related headaches.[27] When aneurysms rupture, the usual progression is a quick onset of headache followed by loss of consciousness and death. In patients with a slow leak, however, a severe headache may appear over several days or weeks. This "sentinel" headache appears in 30% to 60% of patients with eventual rupture.[28] Associated symptoms may include nausea, vomiting, visual disturbances and photophobia, aphasia, nuchal rigidity (without fever), and weakness. Immediate referral is necessary. Evaluation

Table 17–1 History Questions for Headache

Primary Question	*What Are You Thinking?*	*Secondary Questions*	*What Are You Thinking?*
Did you hit your head?	Fracture, subdural or epidural hematoma, postconcussion syndrome.	Did you lose consciousness and have difficulty with memory?	Postconcussion syndrome.
		Are you having difficulty with memory, walking, or talking?	Subdural hematoma.
Are you taking any medications?	Side effect of drug, drug indicates past diagnosis, withdrawal from drug.	Did you recently stop taking medication?	Withdrawal phenomenon.
		Was the medication given for your headaches?	Rebound effect.
		Were you recently prescribed a medication?	Side effect of drug (vasodilators, etc.)
		Do you use recreational drugs? Drink (alcohol) heavily?	Side effect or withdrawal phenomenon (with possible alcohol abuse use CAGE questions).
		(If the patient is taking aspirin, Tylenol, or NSAIDs) Does the drug help decrease or relieve headache?	If yes, it is unlikely that they have a migraine type headache; more likely tension headache.
Is this a "new" headache?	Especially in older persons: tumor, temporal arteritis, or CNS vascular event.	(To an older patient) Is the headache throbbing at your temple?	Temporal arteritis.
		Is there associated vision loss with this temple headache?	Temporal arteritis.
		Have you had the headache for several weeks without improvement?	Possible tumor.
		Is it worse when bending forward?	Possible tumor (especially with no signs of sinus involvement).
Do you have any disorders/diseases that you know about?	Headache is often associated with disorders such as diabetes, thyroid, COPD, hypertension, AIDS, cancer, etc. Perhaps the underlying disorder is the main cause.	Is the disorder being managed by a physician?	Disorder not well controlled.
		Do you follow the management recommendations (diet, medication, life-style changes)?	

Key: CAGE, questions asked of an alcoholic: Do you need to **C**ut down? Does your drinking **A**nnoy people? Do you feel **G**uilty about drinking? Do you use alcohol in the morning as an **E**ye opener?; NSAIDs, nonsteroidal antiinflammatory drugs; CNS, central nervous system; COPD, chronic obstructive pulmonary disease; AIDS, acquired immunodeficiency syndrome.

Table 17–2 History Questions for Suspicion of Migraine Headaches

Primary Question	*Possible Causes for Positive Response*	*Differentiating Question*	*Suspicion*
Do you have any unusual vision changes prior to the headache?	Migraine, TIA, cluster headache, glaucoma, eyestrain.	Do you see flashing lights, zigzag lines, and/or blind spots?	Migraine with aura.
		Do these go away in a short time (minutes to 1½ hours)?	Migraine with aura (longer would suggest TIA).
		Is the pain mainly around your eye with increase in tearing?	Cluster headache.
		Do you see halos around lights or lose your vision on the periphery (outsides)?	Acute glaucoma.
Are they incapacitating?	Unless new in an older patient, it is likely to be migraine or cluster headache.	Do they last for hours or days?	Migraine is likely (migraine without aura often lasts longer).
		Do they last less than 2 hours and cluster (several a day) over weeks?	Cluster headache.
Do certain foods, alcohol, or smoking bring on the headache or make it worse?	Migraine and cluster headaches.	Do you notice that wine, cheese, cured meats (extend list) cause headaches?	Migraine likely.
		Does alcohol or smoking either trigger or make your headache worse?	Cluster headache likely.
Is the headache related to sleep?	Migraine and cluster headaches.	Does either under- or oversleeping trigger a headache?	Migraine.
		Does it often wake you at night?	Cluster headache likely.
Is there a family history of similar headaches?	Migraine, tension, depression.	Has a parent, grandparent, or sibling been diagnosed with migraine headaches?	Migraine.
Have you been diagnosed with migraine and been given medication?	Migraine, rebound migraine.	Have you taken ergotamine or NSAIDs more often than twice a week or suddenly stopped taking them?	Rebound migraine.

Key: TIA, Transient ischemic attack; NSAIDs, nonsteroidal antiinflammatory drugs.

will include computed tomography (CT) for structural brain lesions and a lumbar puncture to detect a subarachnoid bleed.

It is important to screen athletes regarding some common culprits of benign exertional headaches, including dehydration, hyperventilation, hypoglycemia and/or poor diet, alcohol use, caffeine withdrawal, and heat intolerance. These are more likely to be triggering mechanisms in the poorly conditioned athlete. When headache is associated with a specific activity, clues may be found with regard to the mechanism is some cases. For example, one common presentation is weight lifter's headache.[29] There are probably two possible explanations for this occurrence: (1) increased intracranial pressure is caused by the Valsalva-like maneuver with lifting, or (2) stretching or strain occurs in the cervical musculature/tendons.

Valsalva maneuvers increase intracranial venous sinus pressure. This in turn leads to a general increase in intracranial pressure, reducing cerebral blood flow. This effect is generally short lived and benign. If the headache is persistent or severe, further evaluation with CT or magnetic resonance imaging (MRI) may be necessary. Overstrain due to maximum lift effort or abnormal posturing of the neck during activity may lead to a primarily subluxation/soft tissue–caused headache. Historical review of the mechanism of onset with regard to neck position and the onset of symptoms is valuable. Confirmation by physical examination, spinal palpation, and resolution with chiropractic care are likely with this etiology.

Migraine headaches occur in some athletes involved in short, strenuous activities, including weight lifting and short-distance running or swimming.[30] Although the mechanism is not clear, it has been proposed that hyperventilation leads to a decrease in partial pressure of carbon dioxide (Pco_2) with resulting vasoconstriction. This leads to a migraine aura followed by vasodilation leading to the headache.

Acute altitude change from 3,500 m to 5,000 m may lead to acute mountain sickness which presents as a throbbing headache that may be associated with malaise, nausea, and vomiting in some cases.[31] The onset is generally within the first 3 days after ascent. After several days of acclimation, the headache resolves.

A distinct subcategory of sport-related headaches is found in divers.[32] There is a variety of mechanisms to consider.

- Skip breathing may lead to increased Pco_2, vasodilation, and subsequent headache.
- Cervical and facial muscles may be overstrained through stabilizing the mouthpiece.
- A tight mask may compress the supraorbital and supratrochlear nerves.
- Dental cavities may be sensitive to the barometric pressure changes with deep diving.

Posttraumatic Headaches

In automobile accidents and collision or contact sports head and neck trauma is common. With direct trauma to the head, varying degrees of injury may occur, including cerebral contusion, sub- or epidural hemorrhage/hematoma, and intracranial artery dissection. Although it may seem logical that when damage is severe, headache would be immediate, this is not always the case. Slow leaks, as mentioned above, may take several hours, days, and rarely weeks to cause significant symptomatology. It would be prudent, though, to check all patients with head trauma for focal neurologic signs (in particular cranial nerves) and mental status. It is beyond the scope of this brief discussion to address the grading systems and recommendations for concussions, yet it is generally agreed that when there are signs of neurologic dysfunction and loss of consciousness (LOC), a CT or MRI (based on suspicion) should be performed.

When neurologic function is intact in a patient with head trauma and there is no history of LOC, several headaches are possible. The first type is a nonthrobbing, persistent headache often felt in the frontal or occipital areas. It is often worse upon wakening, with some resolution during the day but worsening in the late afternoon. Unfortunately, this headache has been reported to last as little as months to as much as years.

A postconcussion migraine headache has been reported especially with soccer and English football.[33] This type of migraine resembles the classic migraine (migraine with aura) and usually resolves within 48 hours. A strikingly different type of headache is one in which there are associated signs of pupillary dilation and sweating. In between attacks there may be a partial Horner's syndrome. This type of headache is sometimes called traumatic dysautonomic cephalgia and is thought to be caused by sympathetic fiber injury in the neck; it is treated medically with β-blockers.

Finally, an insidious and potentially life-threatening condition associated with head trauma and headache is the second-impact syndrome.[34] Apparently, an athlete who suffers what appears to be minor head trauma develops cerebral edema that is not resolved at the time of a second head injury. Rapid swelling and subsequent death may occur. The recognition of this condition has led to recommendations that are far more conservative than in the past. Close observation of the athlete following head trauma and restriction from participation when there is LOC or persistent amnesia are common guideline recommendations.

The New Headache

Most primary headaches have their initial onset at an early age and are recurrent. Therefore, a middle-aged or older individual complaining of a headache that feels "different" should warrant concern. A common scenario would be an older patient complaining of a temporal headache. If there are associated complaints of either an aching upper trunk area or vision difficulties, consider temporal arteritis. This systemic process becomes evident as a pulsating, hard, nodular temporal area associated with headache. Unfortunately, this process occludes other arteries and leads often to blindness. Referral for biopsy and medical treatment (corticosteroids) is necessary to identify temporal arteritis and prevent blindness, respectively.

Headaches that are constant and/or severe without reprieve are likely to indicate an intracranial process and should necessitate a referral for further evaluation prior to an attempt at chiropractic treatment.

Primary Headaches

Question the patient regarding the three primary headaches: migraine (with and without aura), tension, and cluster. There are often key clues to one of these differentials.

- Migraine (generally): There are several good clues:
  1. early onset in a female (often at menarche to early 20s)
  2. pulsatile (usually) and unilateral, often switching sides
  3. triggered by specific foods such as wines, chocolate, caffeine, cheeses, cured meats, foods containing tyramine
  4. family history of migraines
  5. over-the-counter (OTC) medication has little or no effect
  6. associated with nausea and/or vomiting (vomiting may relieve headache)
  7. associated with photophobia and phonophobia
  8. not as frequent as tension headaches (the more frequent the headache, the more likely it is to be less severe and vice versa[35])
- Migraine with aura: This type of migraine accounts for only about 10% of all migraines. Does the patient experience visual disturbances a half hour or so prior to the headache? The most common presentation is zigzag or flashing (scintillating) lines or lights around an expanding blind spot (scotoma). Other visual phenomena include distortion of curved lines into angular lines, giving a cubist appearance; a bubbling appearance or a kinetic effect that renders normal motion in an old-time movie appearance (strobelike). Other than these visual hallucinations, patients may experience temporary neurologic deficit. This ranges from numbness/tingling, to paresis of the face, a limb, or the entire side of the body. The only distinction between this and a vascular event such as a transient ischemic attack (TIA) is the hallucinatory quality of a visual prodrome and the rapid recovery of the aura (TIAs may take 24 hours). Some patients will have only the neurologic event without headache (ie, complex migraine). Other distinctive clues include the following:
  1. lasts for hours, sometimes days; often occurs after too little or too much sleep (the weekend headache)
  2. often severe, incapacitating pain
  3. trigger may include a change in sleeping (sleeping too little or much) or eating habits (skipping meals)
- Migraine without aura: the key distinction is no prodrome; however, tension headache and migraine without aura (previously common migraine) may be quite similar or coexist.
- Tension headache: Although there is a classic presentation, variation, coexistence, and migraine transformation are possible. Typical findings include the following:
  1. afternoon headache that is occipital or bandlike
  2. relieved by OTC pain medications
  3. often felt over days
- Cluster headache: This is a recurrent, orbital headache that is extremely painful (to the point of suicide attempt), lasting for 30 minutes to 2 hours, clustering over a period of a week or more (several to many times a day). The patient is usually male. There is a possible association with smoking as a trigger and alcohol as an exacerbating factor. There is associated lacrimation, rhinorrhea, and sometimes a mild Horner's syndrome.

It is important to determine past therapies and their effects on the patient's headaches. Most important is the determination of medication. When a patient with migraine takes either ergotamine or nonsteroidal antiinflammatory drugs (NSAIDs) continuously for more than 3 days or stops taking the drug suddenly, a rebound effect occurs in many patients, creating a headache often worse than the original—a common cause of emergency room visits.

Examination

- Rule out secondary causes of headaches, searching for signs indicating tumor, infection, intracranial hemorrhage, glaucoma, etc.
- Determine whether any musculoskeletal abnormalities appear to be contributing or causing (cervicogenic) a patient's headaches.
- Determine the need for radiography or special imaging.

The primary role of the standard physical examination is to rule out secondary causes of headache such as tumor, infection, intracranial hemorrhage, and glaucoma. In patients with either a history of head trauma or associated neurologic signs or symptoms, a thorough neurologic examination must be performed. Emphasis on cranial nerve, vestibular, and pathologic reflex testing is necessary to rule out referrable disorders. If the neurologic symptoms are transient, and therefore objective evidence on neurologic examination is lacking, refer for further evaluation (unless classic for the prodrome of migraine with aura). Although rarely confused with a "headache," glaucoma should be considered in patients complaining primarily of an orbital location to their pain. A quick evaluation is performed by shining a light tangentially across the eye, looking for a crescent-shaped shadow covering more than half the nasal side of the iris. This indicates a closed angle. In screening for intracranial pressure, ophthalmoscopic examination of the fundus for papilledema is necessary.

The examination process specific to those using manual therapy may provide the only clues to primary headache. The literature to date suggests that several musculoskeletal abnormalities are more prevalent in primary headache sufferers, including the following:

- intersegmental hypomobility (primarily in the upper cervical area)[36–40]
- specific tender points[41,42]
- dysfunctional motion of the cervical spine[43–45]
- postural imbalance (forward head position and round-shoulder appearance)[46,47]

Radiologic and Special Imaging for Headaches

Radiologic or advanced imaging for headache is still controversial. Although research indicates possible radiographic findings such as hypomobility or an alordotic/hypolordotic cervical curve, the addition of this information clinically may be irrelevant to the diagnosis. For patient management, it may be arguable that this information allows one to pursue correction of these apparent biomechanical associations.

The literature suggests that the use of special imaging is rarely justified with headache sufferers. This is based on the following:

- Of all the patients with tumor or other conditions requiring cranial surgery only 5% had headache as a primary complaint (other neurologic findings were suggestive).[48]
- The yield for a positive scan was as low as 1/11,200 patients with headaches.

Similar findings have been demonstrated in the pediatric population.[49] However, common sense dictates that if the headache is severe, especially in a child, or unrelenting and not responsive to medication, imaging is an important tool for ruling out serious disorders.

MANAGEMENT

- Modify lifestyle factors which may be contributors.
- Treat with chiropractic manipulative therapy and adjunctive therapies.
- Refer for other nonpharmacologic treatment if chiropractic manipulative therapy (CMT) is ineffective.
- Refer for medical management if other nonpharmacologic treatment is ineffective.

Although it is important to narrow down the diagnostic impression for purposes of referral or correction of minor triggers, it must be remembered that many primary sufferers—in particular, patients with migraine and tension headache—may have other secondary contributing factors. In addition, the chiropractic manipulative treatment of these patients has not been demonstrated to be specific to headache type. It is therefore important to tailor the treatment to the patient with a focused approach to the primary headache and a holistic approach to contributing factors, including musculoskeletal, environmental, and psychologic.

General Approach

The literature for primary headache treatment is, like many conditions, muddled by lack of definition. There are also problems with well-controlled trials. However, taken as a whole, the literature reveals a relationship between cervical dysfunction and headaches (Table 17–3).[50–56] More specifically, and most recently, studies indicate possible advantages to manipulation over the use of antidepressant medication in the treatment of chronic tension headaches.[57]

Consideration for other adjunctive or alternative therapies is based on suggestions listed below:

- Biofeedback. Biofeedback is a form of operant conditioning in which electromyographic (EMG) or thermal cues are used by the patient to attempt control of either skeletal muscle (EMG) or smooth/vascular muscle (thermal). EMG uses surface electrodes with a video display for patient monitoring. Thermal biofeedback records peripheral temperature through the use of an index finger sensor with measurements displayed on a screen. Although the mechanism is not clear, it appears that biofeedback can be a useful tool in the treatment of headaches. One study indicated a good long-term success.[58] Specifically, one study indicated a better result with trapezius biofeedback than with frontal biofeedback or relaxation therapy.[59] Biofeedback may also be helpful

Table 17–3 Literature on the Cervical Spine and Headaches

Author/Date	Headache Type	Parameters Evaluated	Results
Pozniak-Patewicz 1976	U	Neck pain & stiffness	Increased cervical paraspinal myoelectric activity in headache patients
Bakal et al. 1979	M,T	Myoelectric activity	Increased cervical paraspinal myoelectric activity in headache patients
Hudzinski 1983	T	Myoelectric activity	Reduction in cervical paraspinal myoelectric activity correlating with reduction in headaches
Bogduk et al. 1986	C	Headache pain	Resolution of headache pain in 7 of 10 patients
Inasek et al. 1987	T	Headache symptomatology	13% of patients with cervical spondylosis had headache as a prominent symptom
Winston 1987	M	Clinical observations	Temporal relationship between cervical trauma and onset of migraine headaches
Boquet et al. 1989	M	Trigger points, myoelectric activity	Trapezius tenderness & trigger points on ipsilateral side of headache in 17 & 18 patients out of 24, respectively
Jaeger 1989	C	Trigger points	Increased # of trigger points on symptomatic (headache) side
Jensen et al. 1990	T	Flexion/extension	Decreased motion associated with severity of headaches
Lebbink et al. 1991	U	Neck tightness & soreness	Increased neck tightness in headache patients
Michler et al. 1991	C	Headache & radicular pain	Relief of symptoms following surgery
Macpherson et al. 1991	M	C2 spinous process rotation	No differences between migraine patients and controls in C2 spinous rotation
Nakashima et al. 1991	M,T	Exteroceptive suppression	Decreased duration and degree of ES2 suppression
Schoenen et al. 1991	M,T	Palpable tenderness	Reduced pain thresholds in tension headache patients
Vernon et al. 1992	M,T	Tenderness, postural changes	Decreased lordosis & cervical tenderness in headache patients
Wober-Bingol et al. 1992	T	Functional & organic X-ray changes	No changes found in headache patients
Jensen et al. 1993	M,T	Pain thresholds	Increased palpable tenderness in tension headache patients
Kidd et al. 1993	M,T	Cervical ROM	Decreased ROM in headache patients
Nagasawa et al. 1993	T	Postural changes & instability	Decreased cervical lordosis, increased low-set shoulder, in headache patients
Schoenen et al. 1993	T	Myoelectric activity	Increased hypertonicity of trapezius muscles in tension headache patients
Blau et al. 1994	M	Neck & pain stiffness	32 patients reported neck pain or stiffness related to migraine

Key: M, migraine; T, tension; C, cervicogenic; U, unspecified.

Source: Reprinted with permission from Primary Headaches and Cervical Spine Dysfunction, *The Chiropractic Report*, Vol. 9, No. 3, © 1995.

in decreasing chronic headache sufferers' dependency on medication.[60]

- Exercise. Although not used specifically for headache, it is anecdotally reported and supported in one study that aerobic exercise may be of some benefit to patients with headache.[61] Perhaps the mechanism is due more to psychologic/well-being aspects than to direct measurable factors.
- Physiotherapy. When spinal pain or muscle tenderness is associated with a headache, physical therapy may be added to augment the effect of manipulation.
- Acupuncture. Although many anecdotal reports claim success with acupuncture, it appears that when compared with physiotherapy, acupuncture consistently is less effective, although it does appear to help.[62–65] One small controlled study indicated no significant difference over time between acupuncture and a placebo treatment.[66]

Specific Recommendations for Specific Headaches

Some specific recommendations are made for specific headache types with the caution that there is often overlap among these headaches and therapy that works for one may be beneficial with another.

Migraine

Patients with a prodrome to their headache can and should be managed with a treatment trial of manipulation (provided that high-risk indicators are absent such as subclavian bruits, positive vertebrobasilar testing, or extremely high blood pressure). Specific recommendations would include the following:

- Keep sleep schedule as regular as possible, avoiding under- or oversleeping.
- Avoid skipping meals.
- Avoid foods with tyramine or other food triggers.
- Manage stress through training and time-management techniques.

Tension

Management is often more difficult given that some of the factors may be external and more under patient control and choice. Following are some recommendations:

- Correct any postural imbalances, in particular in the cervicothoracic regions.
- Pay particular attention to instruction of proper ergonomics in workstation environments.
- The addition of myofascial and trigger point therapy may help.
- Educate the patient in self-stretching and exercise techniques to reduce cervicothoracic tension.

Cluster

- Avoid alcohol and smoking.
- Use of 100% oxygen (7 L/min for 10 minutes).

Sinus

- One chiropractic study suggests a technique called a nasal-specific technique[67] that is popular among a small group of chiropractors.
- Apply warm compresses or butterfly diathermy.
- OTC decongestants may help temporarily.
- If specific to airplane travel, the use of a decongestant nasal spray may help.

When a conservative approach is taken, it is important to understand the difficulties associated with treatment of asymptomatic patients. In other words, although a patient may have a history of migraines, it is often the case that he or she does not have the headache at the time of the examination and initial care. How does one determine outcome without an outcome measure? Traditionally it has been an acceptable course to attempt reduction of the associated findings of muscle hypertonicity or spinal segmental fixation (which in themselves can be considered outcome measures) and suggest appropriate lifestyle changes. The course of care often extends for 2 to 3 weeks. If the patient has infrequent headaches, it is likely that this period will not extend into the next predicted headache occurrence. If the patient has not had a headache, it would seem appropriate to discontinue constant care until the patient is symptomatic, at which time an aggressive, high-frequency approach for 2 to 3 weeks followed by a return to more of a maintenance status is appropriate. To be considered effective, treatment should have aborted the attack, decreased the intensity, or reduced the duration of an attack. If not, perhaps one more trial during a symptomatic period is reasonable. If two or three predicted headache occurrences do not occur or are reduced in intensity, treatment may have been effective. It would not seem appropriate to continue this treatment course, however, without these positive indicators. Referral for other conservative approaches or medical treatment seems appropriate when a conservative trial is ineffective.

The medical treatment of migraine headaches is primarily abortive or prophylactic. Abortive medications include mainly ergot derivatives and sumatriptan succinate (serotonin agonist). Prophylactic medications include those used for other conditions such as antihypertensives, antidepressants, and antiseizure drugs. If the patient suddenly withdraws any of these prescribed medications, he or she runs the risk of a rebound effect. This is particularly true with ergotamine and NSAIDs. Also, ergotamine, aspirin, or NSAIDs should not be taken more than a few days consecutively because of the same risk of rebound migraine.

Medical treatment for cluster headaches include many of the same medications used for abortive treatment of migraine including sumatriptan and ergots. In addition, intranasal lidocaine and prescribed oxygen may be helpful in aborting an attack.

Algorithms

Algorithms for evaluation and management of headache and chiropractic management of primary headaches are presented in Figures 17–2 and 17–3.

SELECTED HEADACHE DISORDERS

MIGRAINE WITH AURA (CLASSIC MIGRAINE)

Classic Presentation

The patient is often female and presents with a complaint of unilateral throbbing headaches that are preceded by a prodrome. The prodrome consists of a progressively increasing (fortification) scotoma (blind spot) surrounded by flashing lights (scintillation). This lasts for about one-half hour and is replaced by a disabling headache that lasts for several hours to as long as 1 to 3 days, causing the patient to seek a dark, quiet environment. There is often associated nausea and vomiting. There is a family history of similar headaches.

Cause

Once believed to be purely vascular, migraine headaches are believed to be neurogenic. Migraine with aura accounts for only 10% to 15% of all migraines. The current theories are as follows[68]:

- Trigeminal axons are prompted to release vasoactive peptides that cause vascular inflammation; this inflammation irritates meningeal nerve fibers.
- There is a dysfunction of the serotoninergic-based, central inhibitory pain system allowing a lowering of the pain threshold so that even normal stimuli may cause pain.
- The trigeminal afferent input and the upper spinal nerve (C1-C3) input converge in the trigeminocervical nucleus in the spinal cord; because of this convergence misinterpretation of the pain origin may lead to a referred headache phenomenon.

There appears to be a wide variety of triggers for migraine, including variation in sleeping or eating habits, environmental pollutants, certain medications (including vasodilators), and food. With food, the primary triggers include chocolate, caffeine, nitrates, cheese, nuts, wine, and a host of other individualized triggers. There is also a hormonal relationship, as is seen in women.

When the prodrome is the prominent feature or if it outlasts the headache, it is referred to as a complicated migraine.[69] When the prodromal signs or symptoms predominate they are often referred to as migraine equivalents. There are three types of complicated migraines: ophthalmoplegic, where the third, fourth, and sixth cranial nerves are involved, often causing diplopia and eye pain; hemiplegic, where there is paresis on one half of the body, often lasting days; and basilar, where the vertebrobasilar system is involved, leading to accompanying vertigo, diplopia, tinnitus, and ataxia.

Evaluation

The physical examination is rarely revealing and is usually used to rule out secondary causes that may resemble migraine with aura, such as a TIA or glaucoma. The combination

Figure 17–2
HEADACHE—ALGORITHM.

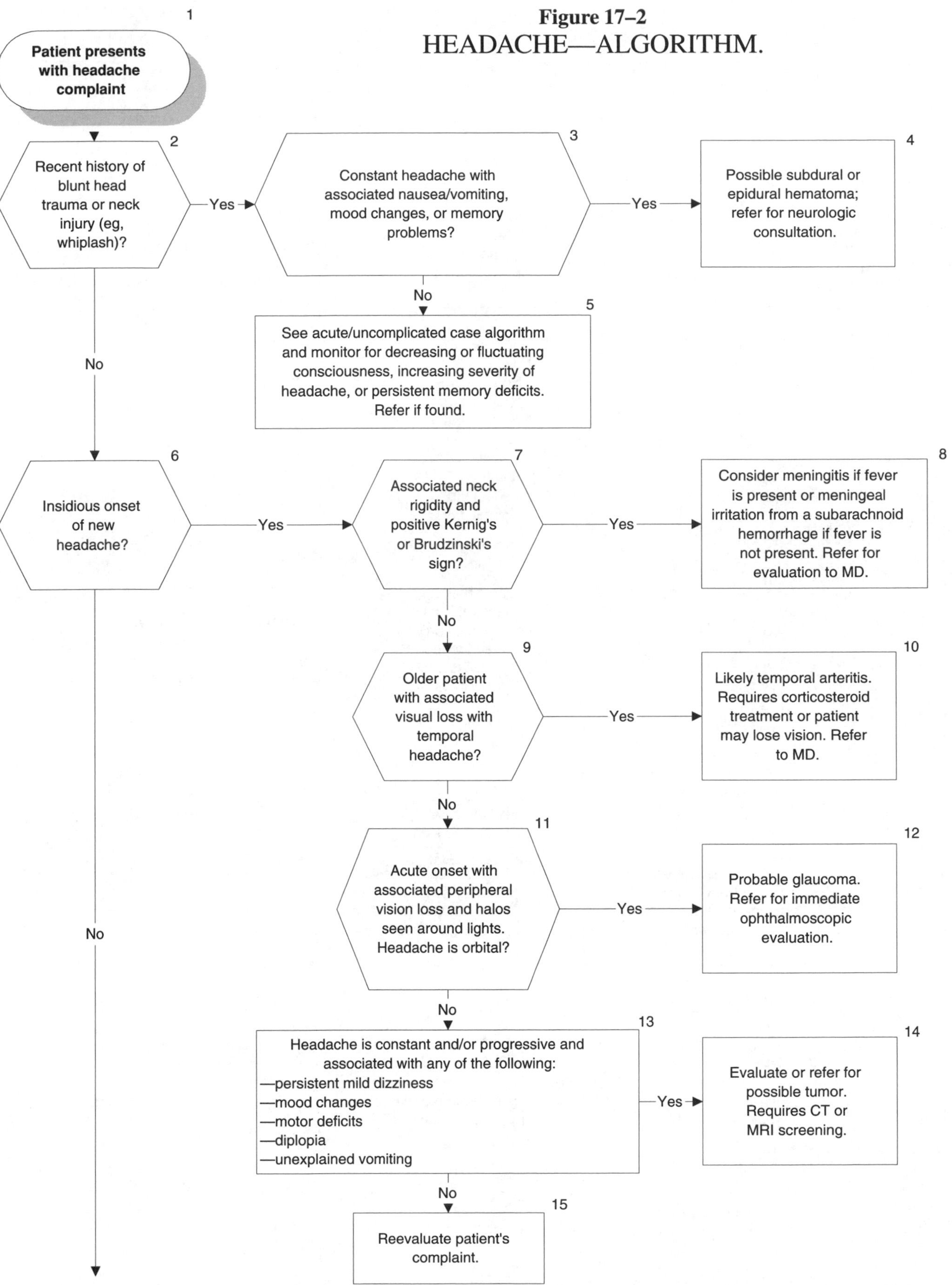

continues

Figure 17–2 continued

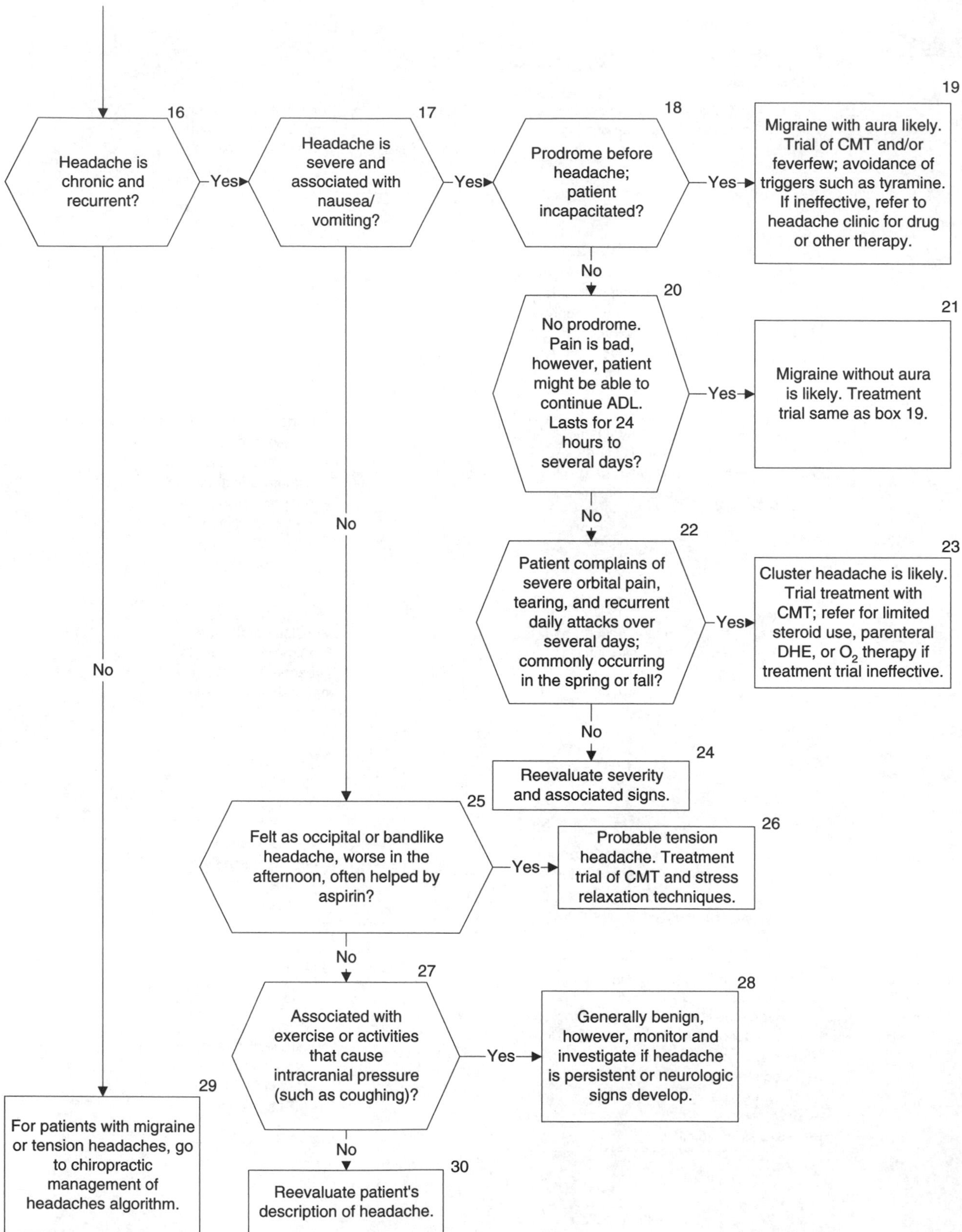

16
Headache is chronic and recurrent?
Yes
17
Headache is severe and associated with nausea/ vomiting?
Yes
18
Prodrome before headache; patient incapacitated?
Yes
19
Migraine with aura likely. Trial of CMT and/or feverfew; avoidance of triggers such as tyramine. If ineffective, refer to headache clinic for drug or other therapy.
No
20
No prodrome. Pain is bad, however, patient might be able to continue ADL. Lasts for 24 hours to several days?
Yes
21
Migraine without aura is likely. Treatment trial same as box 19.
No
22
Patient complains of severe orbital pain, tearing, and recurrent daily attacks over several days; commonly occurring in the spring or fall?
Yes
23
Cluster headache is likely. Trial treatment with CMT; refer for limited steroid use, parenteral DHE, or O2 therapy if treatment trial ineffective.
No
24
Reevaluate severity and associated signs.
No
25
Felt as occipital or bandlike headache, worse in the afternoon, often helped by aspirin?
Yes
26
Probable tension headache. Treatment trial of CMT and stress relaxation techniques.
No
27
Associated with exercise or activities that cause intracranial pressure (such as coughing)?
Yes
28
Generally benign, however, monitor and investigate if headache is persistent or neurologic signs develop.
No
30
Reevaluate patient's description of headache.
No
29
For patients with migraine or tension headaches, go to chiropractic management of headaches algorithm.

Key: ADL, Activities of daily living; DHE, dihydroergotamine.

Figure 17–3
CHIROPRACTIC MANAGEMENT OF PRIMARY HEADACHES—ALGORITHM.

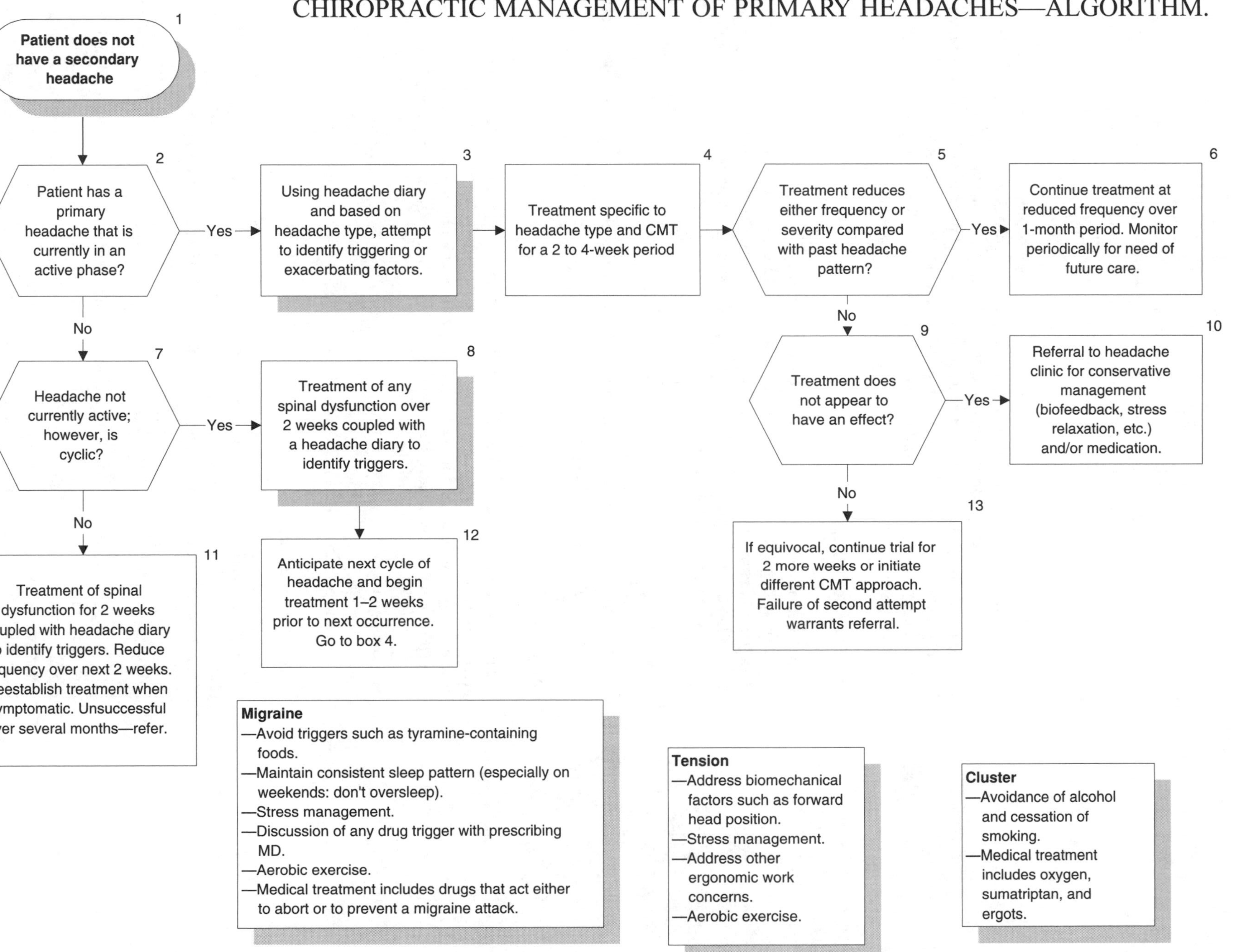

Note: Any indicators of a secondary headache or persistent or new neurologic symptoms suggest reevaluation and likely referral.

of a prodrome that is often visual that occurs prior to a severe headache and an early age onset—often in early adulthood—is highly suggestive. Migraine with aura occurs less frequently than other headaches, often only once or twice a month or less.

Management

Migraine with aura may respond to chiropractic manipulation.[70] A treatment trial is worth pursuing. Other conservative options include biofeedback and acupuncture. Medications options are primarily abortive and prophylactic.[71] The primary abortive drugs are ergotamine derivatives and sumatriptan, a serotonin agonist (avoid both during pregnancy). Patients taking ergots, aspirin, or NSAIDs for longer than 3 days should be warned of a rebound migraine that can occur. This may also occur with sudden withdrawal from other medication. Prophylactic treatments include antidepressants and antihypertensives.

MIGRAINE WITHOUT AURA (COMMON MIGRAINE)

Classic Presentation

The patient is often female complaining of a unilateral, pulsatile headache that is recurrent, having begun when she was a young adult. There are no associated visual or other neurologic signs or symptoms. The headache is severe; however, the patient is usually able to continue daily activities. Associated nausea and vomiting occur, with vomiting sometimes providing relief of the headache.

Cause

See migraine with aura above. Migraine without aura accounts for the vast majority of migraine headaches (80% to 85%).

Evaluation

The physical examination is used primarily to screen for other secondary causes. The presentation is the primary diagnostic indicator. The main difference between migraine with aura and migraine without aura is that the migraine without aura, of course, has no aura (prodrome) and is usually somewhat less severe; however, it may last longer.

Management

The same principles are applied as outlined above for migraine with aura.

TENSION

Classic Presentation

The patient describes a headache with frequent occurrence that is often worse in the afternoon or early evening. The pain is usually bilateral, often suboccipital or supraorbital. The headaches last for days or weeks. Aspirin or OTC NSAIDs seem to provide relief.

Cause

Although it was once believed that tension headaches were due to muscle tension, it is now recognized that although there are often tender trigger points in the neck and suboccipital area, there is no higher incidence of muscle hypertonicity when compared with other headache types. There is a growing group of researchers who believe that chronic tension headaches may represent part of a headache continuum.[72] These patients often begin with migraine attacks that gradually transform (transformed migraine) into more frequent, less severe, tension headaches. This may be related to chronic abuse of medication.

Evaluation

There are no diagnostic findings specific to tension headaches. It is not unusual to find tender trigger points and tight muscles in the neck, although these are not exclusive to tension headache sufferers. A history of frequent, often bilateral, attacks that are relieved by pain medication is a strong basis for a tension headache diagnosis.

Management

Studies indicate that chiropractic manipulation is beneficial for tension headache sufferers.[57] It is important for patients to avoid continual use of pain medications because of the gastrointestinal consequences.

CERVICOGENIC

Classic Presentation

The presentation is dependent on the criteria and definition of the term *cervicogenic*. The belief that other headaches have a cervicogenic component causes some overlap. Those with a pure cervicogenic headache without overlap may present with a complaint of daily headaches with no associated neurologic signs. There is often reduced movement in neck motion and/or pain.

Cause

Cervicogenic headache is due to referral from soft tissue and articular structures in the neck. Similar to the concept introduced above with migraine headaches, convergence in the trigeminocervical nucleus allows referral of pain from neck origins to the head. Vernon[73] refers to several causes, including extrasegmental (myofascial structures), intersegmental (deep muscles and ligaments), infrasegmental (nerve roots and dorsal ganglions), and intrasegmental (referral via trigeminocervical nucleus).

Evaluation

It appears that patients with cervicogenic headache may have indications of restricted movement, in particular at the upper cervical/occiput region.[70] The headache may be made worse in some patients with head movement. Radiographically, there may be indications of arthrosis, but this is not specific for cervicogenic headaches.

Management

Manipulation is recommended.

CLUSTER

Classic Presentation

The patient is often a middle-aged male complaining of incredibly painful headaches that are orbital in location. The headaches cluster over days or weeks and then end, to appear again several weeks or months later. The headaches last on an average 30 minutes and are the most painful feeling the patient has felt. The patient has a history of smoking and possibly alcohol abuse.[74]

Cause

The cause is unknown. There may be a similar dysfunction in the serotoninergic-based central inhibitory system. It is believed that an inflammatory process in the cavernous sinus and tributary veins blocks venous outflow and compresses or injures the associated sympathetic fibers.[75] Triggers during the cluster period include alcohol and some foods.

Evaluation

The physical examination is unrevealing unless the patient is seen during an attack. During an attack there is often lacrimation associated with a runny nose on the same side as the headache. In a minority of cluster patients, there may be a Horner's syndrome (ptosis, miosis, anhydrosis). Unlike the patient with migraine, the patient with cluster headaches is often agitated and animated during attacks, sometimes beating the head against a wall in an attempt for relief. Some patients commit or attempt suicide because of the severity and recurrence of the headaches.

Management

Unlike migraine and tension headaches, there is no clear literature support for chiropractic manipulation success with cluster headaches. However, given that it appears there may be a similar underlying mechanism, a trial of treatment during a cluster period seems warranted if the patient is amenable. Medical treatment is quite similar to that for migraine. Additional treatments include 100% oxygen[76] (7 L/min for 15 minutes) and intranasal cocaine (5-10% solution) or lidocaine[77] (4% solution). Oxygen therapy is less effective in older patients and those with chronic cluster attacks. Lidocaine is thought to have an anesthetic effect on the sphenopalatine ganglion.

TEMPORAL ARTERITIS

Classic Presentation

The patient is older (> 50 years) complaining of a unilateral headache in the temporal region. The headache is associated with a tender nodule at the superficial temporal artery at the side of the forehead. The patient may also complain of generalized aching and muscular fatigue in the upper trunk area. There may also be complaints of visual dysfunction or blindness of sudden onset.

Cause

Temporal arteritis (giant cell arteritis) is a generalized vasculitis affecting small and medium-sized arteries. This inflammatory process affects more than just the temporal artery; however, it is largely asymptomatic with other area involvement. When the ophthalmic artery is involved, an ischemic optic neuropathy with blindness occurs.

Evaluation

The onset of a new headache in an older patient brings temporal arteritis to the list of possibilities. Although it is called "temporal," only about half of patients feel it in the temples. However, 50% to 70% have scalp tenderness near the area of involvement.[78] Other indicators are jaw claudication and visual changes.[79] Dull, aching pain (polymyalgia rheumatica) in the upper trunk area is reported in about 40% of patients with temporal arteritis. One distinguishing feature is an elevated erythrocyte sedimentation rate. Medical biopsy of the temporal artery will confirm the presence of multinucleated giant cells.

Management

The patient with temporal arteritis must be referred because of the high likelihood of blindness if left untreated. Temporal arteritis is treated with corticosteroids.

REFERENCES

1. Osterhaus JT, Gutterman DL, Plachetka DR. Health care resource and lost labour costs of migraine headache in the United States. *Pharmacoeconomics.* 1992;2:67–76.
2. CDC Prevalence of chronic migraine headaches: United States, 1980–1989. *MMWR.* 1991;40:331–338.
3. Stewart WF, Lipton RB, Celentano DD, et al. Prevalence of migraine headaches in the United States: relation to age, income, race, and other sociodemographic factors. *JAMA.* 1992;267:64–69.
4. Balla J, Jansek R. Headaches arising from the cervical spine. In: Hopkins A, ed. *Headache-Problems: Diagnosis and Management.* London: WB Saunders; 1988:243–247.
5. Schutt CH, Dohan FC. Neck injury to women in auto accidents. *JAMA.* 1968;206:2689–2692.
6. Norris SH, Watt J. The prognosis of neck injuries resulting from rear-end vehicle collisions. *J Bone Joint Surg Br.* 1983;65:608–611.
7. Hohl M. Soft tissue injuries of the neck in automobile accidents. *J Bone Joint Surg Am.* 1974;56:1665–1672.
8. Braff MM, Rosner S. Symptomatology and treatment of injuries of the neck. *NY State J Med.* 1955;55:237–242.
9. Dies S, Strapp JW. Chiropractic treatment of patients in motor vehicle accidents: a statistical analysis. *J Can Chiro Assoc.* 1992;36:139–142.
10. Olesen J, et al. *Classification of Diagnostic Criteria for Headache Disorders, Cranial Neuralgias and Facial Pain.* Copenhagen: The International Headache Society; 1990.
11. Nilsson N. The prevalence of cervicogenic headache in a random population sample of 20–59 year olds. *Spine.* 1995;20:1884–1888.
12. Olesen J, et al. Timing and topography of cerebral blood flow, aura and headache during migraine attack. *Ann Neurol.* 1990;28:791.
13. Anderson A, et al. Delayed hyperemia following hypoperfusion in classic migraine. *Arch Neurol.* 1988;45:154.
14. Boxtel A, Goudszaard P. Absolute and proportional resting EMG levels in chronic headache patients in relation to the state of headache. *Headache.* 1984;24:259.
15. Takasha T, Shimomura T, Kazuro T. Platelet activation in muscle contraction headache and migraine. *Cephalalgia.* 1987;7:239.
16. Anthony M, Lance J. Plasma serotonin in patients with chronic tension headache. *J Neurol Neurosurg Psychiatry.* 1989;52:182.
17. Rajiv J, Welch K, D'Andrea G. Serotonergic hypofunction in migraine: a synthesis of evidence based on platelet dense body dysfunction. *Cephalalgia.* 1989;9:293.
18. Lance J, et al. 5-Hydroxytryptamine and its putative aetiological involvement in migrane. *Cephalalgia.* 1989;9(suppl 9):7.
19. Bogduk N. A neurological approach to neck pain. In: Glasgow EE, Twomey IV, Seall ER, Klehnhams AM, Edzack, eds. *Aspects of Manipulative Therapy.* 2nd ed. New York, Churchill Livingstone; 1985;136–146.
20. D'Andrea G, Hasselmark L, Cananzi AR et al. Metabolism and menstrual cycle rhythmicity of serotonin in primary headaches. *Headache.* 1995;35:216–221.
21. Silberstein SD, Merriam GR. Estrogens, progestins, and headache. *Neurology.* 1991;41:786–793.
22. Epstein MT, Hockaday JM, Hockaday TD. Migraine and reproductive hormones throughout the menstrual cycle. *Lancet.* 1975;1:543–548.
23. Ulknis A, Silberstein SD. Review article: migraine and pregnancy. *Headache.* 1991;31:372–374.
24. Raskin NH. *Headache.* 2nd ed. New York: Churchill Livingstone, 1988;35–98.
25. Philips BM. Oral contraceptive drugs and migraine. *Br Med J.* 1968;2:99.
26. Goldstein M, Chen TC. The epidemiology of disabling headache. *Adv Neurol.* 1982;33:377–390.
27. Rooke ED. Benign exertional headache. *Med Clin North Am.* 1988;52:801–809.
28. Klara PM, George ED. Warning leaks and sentinel headaches associated with subarachnoid hemorrhage. *Milit Med.* 1982;147:660–662.
29. Paulson GW. Weightlifter's headache. *Headache.* 1983;23:193–194.
30. Kinsella FP. Exercise induced migraine *Br Med J.* 1990;83:126.
31. Appenzeller O. Altitude headaches. *Headache.* 1972;12:121–129.
32. Diamond S, Solomon GD, Freitag FG. Headache in sports. In: Jordan BC, Tsairis P, Warren RF, eds. *Sports Neurology.* Gaithersburg, MD: Aspen Publishers Inc; 1989:127–132.
33. Mathews WB. Footballer's migraine. *Br Med J.* 1972;2:326–327.
34. Saunders RL, Harbaugh RE. The second impact in catastrophic contact sports head trauma. *JAMA.* 1984;525:538–539.
35. Celentano D, Stewart W, Linet M. The relationship of headache symptoms with severity and duration of attacks. *J Clin Epidemiol.* 1990;43:983.
36. Jull G. Manual diagnosis of C2-3 headache. *Cephalalgia.* 1985;5(suppl 5):308–309.
37. Jull GA: Headaches associated with the cervical spine: a clinical review. In: Grieve GP, ed. *Modern Manual Therapy of the Vertebral Column.* New York: Churchill Livingstone; 1986.
38. Jull G, Bogduk N, Marsland A. The accuracy of manual diagnosis for cervical zygapophyseal joint pain syndromes. *Med J Aust.* 1988;148:233–236.
39. Dwyer A, Aprill C, Bognuk N. Cervical zygapophyseal joint pain patterns, I: a study in normal volunteers. *Spine.* 1990;15:453–457.
40. Fligg B. Motion palpation of the upper cervical spine. In: Vernon HT, ed. *Upper Cervical Syndrome: Chiropractic Diagnosis and Management.* Baltimore: Williams & Wilkins; 1988.
41. Vernon HT, Steunab I, Hagino C. Cervicogenic dysfunction in muscle contraction headache and migraine: a descriptive study. *J Manipulative Physiol Ther.* 1992;15:418–429.
42. Bovim G. Cervicogenic headache, migraine and tension-type headache: pressure-pain threshold measurements. *Pain.* 1992;51:169–173.
43. Pfaffenrath V, Dandekar R, Mayer E, Hermann G, Pollman W. Cervicogenic headache: results of computer-based measurements

of cervical spine mobility in fifteen patients. *Cephalalgia.* 1988;8:45–48.

44. Dvorak J, Froelich D, Penning L, Baumgartner TT, Panjabi MM. Functional radiographic diagnosis of the cervical spine: flexion/extension. *Spine.* 1988;13:745–755.
45. Kidd RF, Nelson R. Musculoskeletal dysfunction of the neck in migraine and tension headache. *Headache.* 1993;33:566–569.
46. Watson DH, Trott PH. Cervical headache: an investigation of natural head posture and upper cervical flexor muscle performance. *Cephalalgia.* 1993;13:272–282.
47. Nagaszwa A, Sakakihara T, Takahashi A. Roentgenographic findings of the cervical spine in tension-type headache. *Headache.* 1993;33:90–95.
48. Weingarten S, et al. The effectiveness of cerebral imaging in the diagnosis of chronic headaches. *Arch Intern Med.* 1992;152:2457.
49. McAbee G, et al. Value of MRI in pediatric migraine. *Headache.* 1993;33:143.
50. Parker GB, Pryor DS, Tupling H. Why does migraine improve during a clinical trial? Further results from a trial of cervical manipulation for migraine. *Aust N Z J Med.* 1980;10:192–198.
51. Hoyt H. Osteopathic manipulation in the treatment of muscle contraction headache. *J Am Osteopath Assoc.* 1979;78:322–324.
52. Wight JH. Migraine: a statistical analysis of chiropractic treatment. *J Am Chiro Assoc.* 1978;12:363–367.
53. Vernon H. Chiropractic manipulative therapy in the treatment of headaches: a retrospective and prospective study. *J Manipulative Physiol Ther.* 1982;5:109–122.
54. Vernon HT. Spinal manipulation and headaches of cervical origin: a review of literature and presentation of cases. *J Managed Med.* 1991;6:73–79.
55. Whittingham W, Ellis WB, Molyneux TP. The effect of manipulation (toggle recoil technique) for headaches with upper cervical joint dysfunction: a pilot study. *J Manipulative Physiol Ther.* 1994;17:369–375.
56. Mootz RD, Dhami MSI, Hess JA, Cook RD, Schorr DB. Chiropractic treatment of chronic episodic tension-type headache in male subjects: a case series analysis. *J Can Chiro Assoc.* 1994;38:152–159.
57. Boline P, Kassak K, Bromfort G, Nelson C, Anderson AV. Spinal manipulation vs. amitriptyline for the treatment of chronic tension-type headaches: a randomized clinical trial. *J Manipulative Physiol Ther.* 1995;18:148–154.
58. Cott A, Parkinson W, Fabich M, Bedard M, Martin R. Long-term efficacy of combined relaxation biofeedback treatments for chronic headache. *Pain.* 1992;51:49–56.
59. Arena JG, Bruno GM, Hannah SL, Meader KJ. A comparison of frontal electromyographic biofeedback training, trapezius electromyographic biofeedback training, and progressive muscle relaxation therapy in the treatment of tension headache. *Headache.* 1995;35:411–419.
60. Blanchard EB, Taylor AE, Dentinger MP. Preliminary results from the self-regulatory treatment of high-medication-consumption headache. *Biofeedback Self Regul.* 1992;17:179–202.
61. Fitterling JM, Martin JE, Gamling S, Cole P. Behavioral management of exercise training in vascular headache patients: an investigation of exercise, adherence, and headache activity. *J Behav Analysis.* 1988;21:9–19.
62. Carlsson J, Fahlcrantz A, Augustinsson LE. Muscle tenderness in tension headache treated with acupuncture or physiotherapy. *Cephalalgia.* 1990;10:131–141.
63. Carksiib HM, Augustinsson LE, Blomstrand C, Sullivan M. Health status in patients with tension headache treated with acupuncture or physiotherapy. *Headache.* 1990;30:593–599.
64. Carlsson J, Rosenthall U. Oculomotor disturbances in patients with tension headache treated with acupuncture or physiotherapy. *Cephalalgia.* 1990;10:123–129.
65. Vincent CA. The treatment of tension headache by acupuncture: a controlled single case design with time series analysis. *J Psychosom Res.* 1990;34:553–561.
66. Tavola T, Gala C, Conte G, Invermizzi G. Traditional Chinese acupuncture in tension-type headache: a controlled study. *Pain.* 1992;48:325–329.
67. Folweiler DS, Lynch OT. Nasal specific technique as part of a chiropractic approach to chronic sinusitis and sinus headache. *J Manipulative Physiol Ther.* 1995;18:38–41.
68. Nelson CF. Headache diagnosis. In: Lawerence DJ, Cassidy JD, McGregor M, et al., eds. *Advances in Chiropractic.* St. Louis, MO: Mosby-Year Book; 1994;1:77–99.
69. Bartleson JD. Treatment and persistent neurological manifestations of migraine. *Stroke.* 1984;15:383–386.
70. Vernon H. Spinal manipulation and headaches: an update. *Top Clin Chiro.* 1995;2(3):34–47.
71. Kumar KL, Cooney TG. Headaches. *Med Clin North Am.* 1995;79:261–286.
72. Nelson CF. The tension headache, migraine headache continuum: a hypothesis. *J Manipulative Physiol Ther.* 1994;17:156–167.
73. Vernon HT. Vertebrogenic headache. In: *Upper Cervical Syndrome: Chiropractic Diagnosis and Management.* Baltimore: Williams & Wilkins; 1988.
74. Kudrow L. Cluster headache: clinical, mechanism, and treatment aspects. *Panminerva Med.* 1982;24:45–54.
75. Hardebo JE. How cluster headache is explained as an intracavernous inflammatory process lesioning sympathetic fibers. *Headache.* 1994;14:125–131.
76. Fagan L. Treatment of cluster headache: a double-blind comparison of oxygen by air inhalation. *Arch Neurol.* 1985;42:362–363.
77. Kittrelle JP, Grouse DS, Seybold ME. Cluster headache; local anesthetic, abortive agents. *Arch Neurol.* 1985;42:496–498.
78. Chmelewski WL, McKnight KM, Angudelo CA, et al. Presenting features and outcomes in patients undergoing temporal artery biopsy. *Arch Intern Med.* 1992;152:1690–1695.
79. Couch JR. Headaches to worry about. *Med Clin North Am.* 1993;77:141–166.

Chapter 18

Dizziness

CONTEXT

In most studies of primary care,[1] internal medicine,[2] and emergency departments,[3] dizziness ranks among the top three patient complaints. Statistics for chiropractic clinics are not as clear.[4] In the context of chiropractic practice, probably the most frequently seen cases are those associated with motor vehicle cervical spine/head injuries and in the elderly. Dizziness may be one of the top three symptoms reported after acceleration/deceleration injury to the neck.[5–8] It is unclear how many cases are due to insult to neck proprioceptors versus the vestibular apparatus or vascular supply to the head and neck.

Dizziness may occur in as many as 30% of the elderly.[9] In nearly 20% of all older persons, the dizziness is severe enough to consult a health professional. Although dizziness is a frequent complaint,[10] only a little more than half of patients received treatment.[11] The elderly population, in particular, is more prone to the vertiginous effects of medications and the lack of compensation that a younger population has for dysfunction of one of the components of balance. Vision, proprioception, and vestibular function are all integral to balance. When one is dysfunctional, the nervous system may accommodate through input and adaptation in the other systems. In the elderly, there may be a general deterioration of all neural systems, perhaps complicated by other diseases such as diabetes or atherosclerosis, making adaptation less effective and the dizziness more disabling.

Like many patient complaints, a complaint of dizziness must be further described by the patient to gain a clearer understanding of which body systems are involved. Often this simple step in evaluation will narrow down the cause into a general category (Exhibit 18–1). Dizziness may be perceived as spinning of the room or self, imbalance or lack of coordination while walking, or simply lightheadedness or the sensation of almost fainting (ie, presyncope). The sensation of spinning is generally attributed to dysfunction of the vestibular and central processing systems, whereas a sensation of imbalance or lack of coordination is more likely due to cerebellar or proprioceptive dysfunction. Lightheadedness or a sense of almost fainting suggests a vascular or psychologic cause. Some studies indicate a psychologic component in as many as 37% to 40% of patients with chronic dizziness, depending on the facility.[12,13]

GENERAL STRATEGY

History

- Obtain a more detailed description of a patient's complaint of "dizziness."
- Differentiate vertigo from nonvertiginous causes of a dizziness complaint.
- To help differentiate further, determine onset and length of attacks and whether they are recurrent.
- Determine whether the patient senses any hearing loss.
- Ask about associated neurologic or systemic complaints.
- If vertigo is likely, differentiate between peripheral and central causes.

Evaluation

- Determine whether there are any objective hearing deficits.
- Determine whether there are any associated systemic or neurologic problems.
- If nonvertiginous, determine the patient's vascular, endocrine, and psychologic status.

Exhibit 18–1 Narrowing the Cause of Dizziness

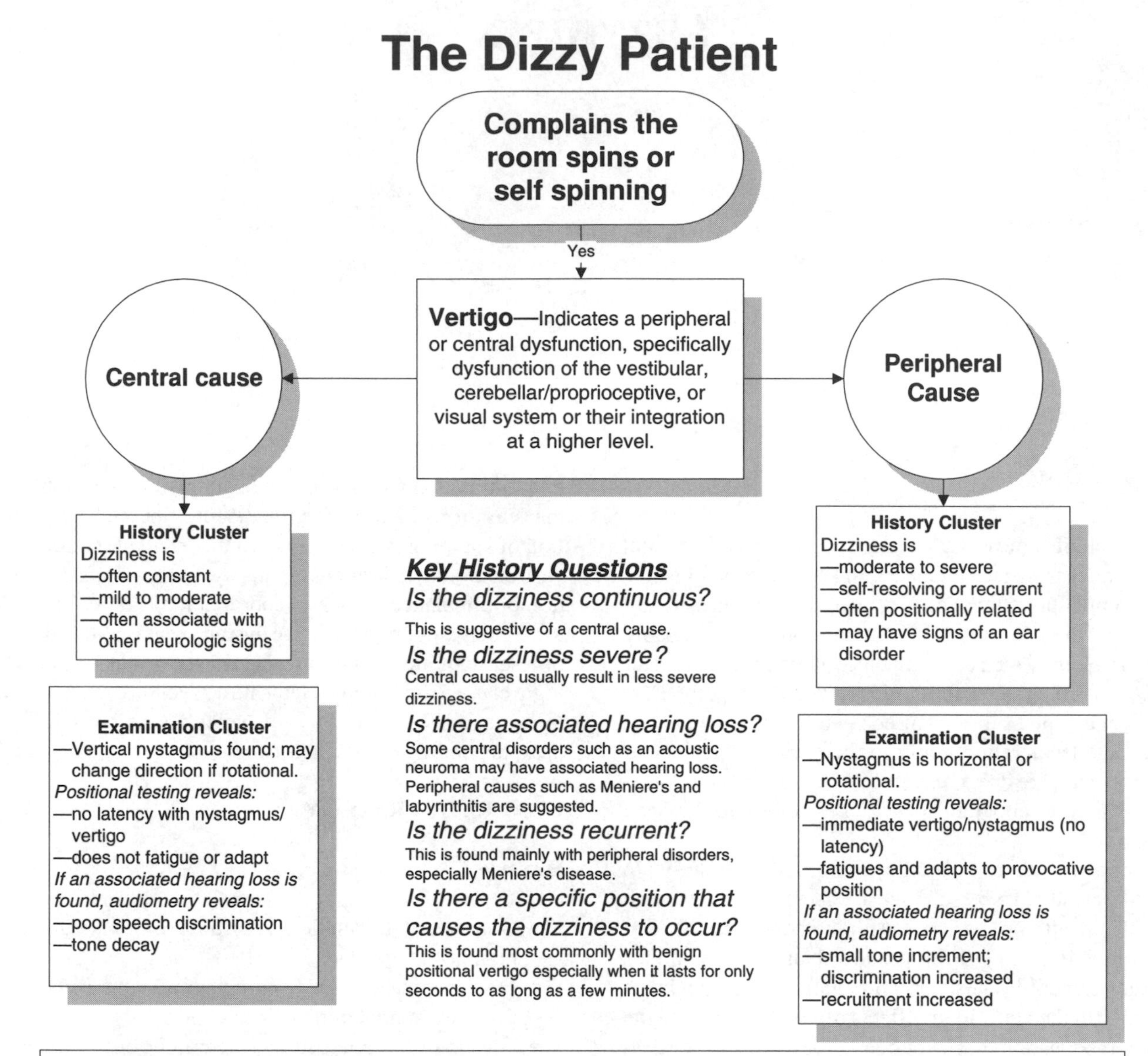

The Dizzy Patient
Complains the room spins or self spinning
Yes
Vertigo—Indicates a peripheral or central dysfunction, specifically dysfunction of the vestibular, cerebellar/proprioceptive, or visual system or their integration at a higher level.
Central cause
Peripheral Cause
History Cluster
Dizziness is
—often constant
—mild to moderate
—often associated with other neurologic signs
Examination Cluster
—Vertical nystagmus found; may change direction if rotational.
Positional testing reveals:
—no latency with nystagmus/vertigo
—does not fatigue or adapt
If an associated hearing loss is found, audiometry reveals:
—poor speech discrimination
—tone decay
Key History Questions
Is the dizziness continuous?
This is suggestive of a central cause.
Is the dizziness severe?
Central causes usually result in less severe dizziness.
Is there associated hearing loss?
Some central disorders such as an acoustic neuroma may have associated hearing loss. Peripheral causes such as Meniere's and labyrinthitis are suggested.
Is the dizziness recurrent?
This is found mainly with peripheral disorders, especially Meniere's disease.
Is there a specific position that causes the dizziness to occur?
This is found most commonly with benign positional vertigo especially when it lasts for only seconds to as long as a few minutes.
History Cluster
Dizziness is
—moderate to severe
—self-resolving or recurrent
—often positionally related
—may have signs of an ear disorder
Examination Cluster
—Nystagmus is horizontal or rotational.
Positional testing reveals:
—immediate vertigo/nystagmus (no latency)
—fatigues and adapts to provocative position
If an associated hearing loss is found, audiometry reveals:
—small tone increment; discrimination increased
—recruitment increased

Classic Presentations Not To Be Missed

1. Patient presents with a sudden onset of dizziness due to a particular head position. Vertigo lasts for at most a minute or two. The patient has a history of trauma or is older. Physical examination reveals horizontal nystagmus that fatigues and adapts.
   Diagnosis: Benign Positional Vertigo
2. Patient presents with a history of recurrent attacks of vertigo. Sudden attacks come without warning and are associated with severe vertigo. They last hours to as much as a day or two. There is often a report of fullness in the ear and tinnitus. May be a history of diabetes or problems with fluid retention.
   Diagnosis: Meniere's Disease
3. Patient presents with a sudden onset of dizziness that is constant. It slowly improves over days or weeks, often with an associated hearing loss.
   Diagnosis: Labyrinthitis
4. Same presentation as above with no hearing loss.
   Diagnosis: Vestibular Neuronitis
5. Patient presents with a history of a whiplash injury and no obvious examination findings except that dizziness is reproduced by body rotation with the head held constant.
   Diagnosis: Vertebrogenic Vertigo

- Determine to what degree cervical spine dysfunction may be contributory.

Management

- Consider referral or comanagement in the following scenarios:
  1. The patient has had head trauma and is demonstrating other associated neurologic signs, or a skull fracture is suspected.
  2. Prescription medication is suspected as the underlying cause (refer to the prescribing physician if possible).
  3. The dizziness is incapacitating, requiring medication during the symptomatic phase (comanagement may be possible).
  4. The dizziness appears to have a strong psychologic component.
  5. The patient appears to have a cardiopulmonary cause such as an arrhythmia, heart block, or congestive heart failure.
  6. The patient is suspected of having a perilymphatic fistula.
  7. The patient needs further audiologic or special imaging evaluation, especially in the consideration of brain tumors, cerebrovascular accidents, demyelinating diseases (eg, multiple sclerosis), or cerebellar or extrapyramidal disorders (eg, Parkinson's disease).
  8. The patient has hearing loss.
- Treat peripheral vertigo with chiropractic manipulative techniques, habituation exercises, and other conservative approaches.
- Refer if treatment is ineffective or the dizziness creates significant functional impairment.

RELEVANT ANATOMY AND PHYSIOLOGY

Balance and spatial orientation is maintained by an integrated, neuronal feedback loop. A slow adjustment can be made to compensate when input from any component is dysfunctional unless more than one component is involved. The components of this system are (1) vestibular, (2) visual, and (3) proprioceptive. The vestibular labyrinth sends information to the vestibular nuclei in the medulla and lower pons via the vestibular branch of cranial nerve VIII. The cerebellum, receiving input from the spinocerebellar tracts (proprioception), also sends information to the vestibular nuclei. The midline cerebellar structures have a strong inhibitory effect on the vestibular nuclei. In turn, the vestibular nuclei project to the cerebellum, to all spinal levels through the vestibulospinal tract, and to the medial longitudinal fasciculus (MLF) and the pontine reticular formation. Fibers in the MLF project to nuclei of the third, fourth, and sixth cranial nerves, stimulating reflex conjugate eye movement in reaction to head position change. The cerebral cortex, although not part of the vestibular system per se, modulates motor activity and coordination as a result of information supplied from various sensory inputs.

The three semicircular canals (anterior, posterior, and horizontal) are encased in the bony labyrinth. The horizontal canal is angled 30° cephalad to the horizontal plane with the others oriented at 90° to each other in x, y, and z axes. Stimulation in a canal causes ipsilateral stimulation of a pair of extraocular muscles with relaxation of the antagonistic pair. Stimulation is due to endolymphatic fluid (fluid in the canals) movement and its effect on sensitive hair cells on the cupula that fills the ampulla in the semicircular canals. This occurs primarily with rotational movement. Another sense organ, the macula of the utricle, is a calcium carbonate crystalline structure also referred to as the otolith. The otolith is sensitive to linear acceleration and gravity. Dislodging of otolith crystals may cause stimulation with certain head positions, causing vertigo that usually lasts for seconds to minutes. Any ipsilateral increase or decrease in labyrinth discharge will create a sense of movement.

Proprioceptive information from the upper cervical musculature and joints may play a major role in a patient's perception of balance. The high density of receptors in the upper cervical region[14] participate in several reflexes. Although it is assumed by many that these are primarily capsular afferents, the scientific basis for this has been questioned. The original study upon which this assumption is based used the vertebral joints of quadrupeds for examination. It was found that in addition to nociceptors, the capsules contained proprioceptive type I afferents (tonic discharge; function as static position detection) and type II afferents (discharge only with movement).[15] However, recent studies indicate that human facet joints contain mainly nociceptors with only a few type I or type II proprioceptors.[16–18] It appears that perhaps the majority of proprioceptors are located in other tissue, in particular the deep cervical muscles such as the interspinales, multifidus, rotator spinae, intertransversarii, and longus cervicus. The cervicoocular reflex causes the eyes to rotate to the opposite side of head rotation. It becomes especially significant as a compensation for damage to the vestibular apparatus. The vestibulocolic reflex is more of an effector reflex, allowing vestibular information to modulate cervical muscle activity. To complete the interaction, input from the neck can also modulate vestibular reflexes.[19]

Theoretically, trauma or dysfunction in the cervical spine may have effects on these reflexes or, if there is damage to the vestibular apparatus, these reflexes may help compensate. Cervicogenic vertigo is believed to be a result of cervical joint dysfunction, muscle strain, or injury from trauma such as a whiplashlike type of accident. The basic science support for this possibility comes from numerous studies that have shown ataxia, nystagmus, and/or dysequilibrium with local anesthetic injection[20] into the deep posterolateral neck, electrical stimulation[21] of strained muscles, and transection of suboccipital muscles or upper cervical root section in animals. Vibration of muscle tendons or the head can create a postural illusion leading to nystagmus and motion sickness.[22] Overstimulation from joint dysfunction or muscle spasm or damage to the upper cervical proprioceptors theoretically may result in an imbalance of proprioceptive information. Through vestibular reflexes the result may be a sense of dysequilibrium.

The vascular supply to the ear and the vestibular apparatus and nuclei may be compromised, leading to the perception of dizziness. Although it was once believed that a sympathetically mediated vascular reflex could be the cause of vertigo in patients with cervical dysfunction, it appears that vertebral blood flow is minimally responsive to sympathetic stimulation.[23] The main vascular supply to the head is from branches off the vertebral or basilar arteries (the basilar artery is formed by the two vertebral arteries). The main artery is the anterior inferior cerebellar artery. The caudal portion of the vestibular nuclei is supplied more specifically by the posterior inferior cerebellar arteries via the lateral medullary or posterior spinal arteries. The vestibular and basilar arteries supply more than the vestibular nuclei; as a result, other symptoms accompany vertebrobasilar insufficiency, including diplopia, ataxia, "drop attacks," dysarthria, and various forms of body paralysis or weakness (although dizziness is often a prominent symptom).

Generally, dizziness is caused by decreased cerebral, cerebellar, or brain stem perfusion or dysfunction of one or all of the neural balance systems: (1) visual, (2) vestibular, and (3) proprioception/cerebellar. This dysfunction is usually due to trauma, vascular compromise, infection of the labyrinths, or neural inflammation or degeneration both centrally and peripherally (such as in multiple sclerosis).

EVALUATION

History

The most important step in the evaluation of a complaint of dizziness is to ask the patient to qualify or more clearly describe his or her complaint. The patient may be reluctant or unable to describe the complaint further, and it may be necessary to prompt him or her with some common descriptions (Tables 18–1 and 18–2). Patient descriptions correlate well with four general categories of dizziness: (1) vertigo, (2) syncope or presyncope, (3) dysequilibrium, and (4) psychogenic (hyperventilation, depression). If the patient feels as though the room or he or she is spinning, one would be more likely to think of classic vertigo. The next step in evaluation would be to determine causes that are central and those that are peripheral. Peripheral vertigo refers to dysfunction of the labyrinths or vestibular nerve. Central vertigo refers to disorders affecting the central connections to the cerebellum and brain stem.

A distinction among the various types of peripheral vertigo may be evident through a comparison of common history elements with regard to onset, duration, recurrence, and associated hearing loss.

- Meniere's disease is suggested if there is an abrupt onset of severe vertigo lasting for several hours to 1 day that is recurrent and associated with attack-related tinnitus, hearing loss, and a sensation of fullness in the ear.
- Vestibular neuronitis or labyrinthitis is suggested if there is a rather abrupt onset of moderate to severe vertigo associated with a prior respiratory infection lasting for several days and gradually diminishing over weeks; the distinguishing factor is whether hearing loss is evident, suggesting labyrinthitis.
- Benign paroxysmal positional vertigo (BPPV) is suggested when there are brief episodes of moderate to severe vertigo associated with specific provocative head positioning; it gradually diminishes over a month or two without associated hearing loss.

Vertigo that is mild and/or constant is always suggestive of a central problem, especially if associated with other neurologic signs or symptoms.

Another description may be that the patient feels as though he or she is about to faint. This may also be described as lightheadedness. This description is clearly one of decreased cerebral perfusion. It would be important then to determine whether this occurs while sitting, which would be more classically a common faint position, or whether it occurs on rising, which would be more suggestive of orthostatic hypotension. With orthostatic hypotension as a suspicion, a drug history would be the first avenue of concern. This would be followed by questioning regarding signs suggestive of diabetes, anemia, or cardiopulmonary causes such as congestive heart failure.

When a patient describes his or her problem as difficulty while standing or with ambulation, it is important to determine whether the problem is one of proprioception or possibly cerebellar. An important clue that there is a proprioceptive deficit is provided if the patient says that is harder to maintain balance in dimly lighted areas or with eyes closed. This suggests a proprioceptive problem.

Table 18–1 History Questions for Dizziness

Primary Question	*What Are You Thinking?*	*Secondary Questions*	*What Are You Thinking?*
Do you or the room spin?	Vertigo. Peripheral or central causes.	Is it continuous or intermittent, coming and going?	Continuous indicates central; recurrent indicates peripheral.
Does it feel like you are about to faint or are lightheaded?	Vascular or endocrine cause.	Does this occur when you stand?	Orthostatic hypotension. Ask about medications.
		Does this occur when you haven't eaten?	Hypoglycemic reaction.
		Does this occur when you cough?	Cough syncope (glossopharyngeal).
		Does this occur when you are "stressed out"?	Anxiety. Adrenal disorder.
		Does this occur when you turn your head?	Subclavian steal, atherosclerotic cause.
		Does it occur when you wear a tight collar?	Sick sinus syndrome.
		Are you diabetic?	Patient may not know. Need to evaluate with lab.
Are you "dizzy" only when you walk?	Cerebellar or proprioception problem.	Is it worse with your eyes closed or in a dark room?	Proprioceptive problem, probably dorsal columns.
		Do you fall always to the same side?	Cerebellar cause should be investigated.
Are you taking medication?	Side effect or indication of underlying disorder that could cause dizziness.	Are you taking muscle relaxants, medication with codeine, or barbiturates?	Central nervous system depression.
		Are you taking cimetidine (Tagamet), pain medications, or high blood pressure medications?	Common drugs that may cause dizziness.

One of the most important context questions is, When does it occur? Lightheadedness on rising is suggestive of orthostatic hypotension, whereas difficulty with ambulation is suggestive of a proprioceptive problem. If the patient has more difficulty with dimly lighted areas (especially an elderly patient), a proprioceptive problem is likely. If the dizziness is apparent with certain head positions such as rotation, vertigo is more likely—more specifically benign positional vertigo.

When the patient complains of associated neurologic symptoms such as slurred speech or electric shock sensations down the arms, multiple sclerosis must be considered, especially in a middle-aged patient. Additional considerations are the use of drugs/alcohol and cervical trauma. It is important to obtain a thorough drug history to determine whether illicit use of drugs may be the cause, or the side effect of a prescription medication. Medication interactions may cause dizziness, especially in the elderly. Some drugs that may cause dizziness through central nervous system (CNS) effects are anticonvulsants, benzodiazepines, neuroleptics, and antidepressants. Drugs that are vestibulotoxic include the aminoglycosides, such as streptomycin. Antihypertensives and

Table 18–2 History Questions for Vertigo

Primary Question	What Are You Thinking?	Secondary Questions	What Are You Thinking?
Is the dizziness continuous or progressive?	If yes, a central cause is likely. If no, suspect a peripheral cause.	Is the dizziness relatively mild and not affected much by position?	Central cause such as acoustic neuroma, multiple sclerosis.
Is the dizziness recurrent?	Most commonly benign positional vertigo and Meniere's disease.	Is the onset abrupt and related to a specific position change?	Benign positional vertigo (BPV).
		Does it last for seconds to a couple of minutes?	BPV.
		Is it abrupt but last for hours to a day or so?	Meniere's disease is likely.
		Is there associated fullness and a ringing in the ear during attacks?	Meniere's disease is likely.
Is there associated hearing loss?	Peripheral causes include labyrinthitis and Meniere's disease. Central causes include acoustic neuroma and other pontine tumors.	Have you had this for weeks with a gradual decrease in dizziness?	Labyrinthitis.
		Are these recurrent attacks with associated hearing loss?	Meniere's disease.
Was there a somewhat fast onset with a slow decrease in dizziness?	Labyrinthitis and vestibular neuronitis.	Is there hearing loss?	Labyrinthitis more likely (no hearing loss with vestibular neuronitis).

antiarrhythmics may cause orthostatic hypotension or syncope.

Examination

The examination process is dictated by suspicions generated from the history. If the patient's history is suggestive of a vascular cause, evaluation of cardiopulmonary status and perhaps laboratory evaluation are warranted. If the patient's history is more suggestive of vertigo, an evaluation for nystagmus is essential, as is some form of provocative testing. If the dizziness appears to be more dysequilibrium, a search for cerebellar and proprioceptive dysfunction is the focus of the examination. Given that there is some variation and ambiguity in patient descriptions, a standard battery of screening tests should be performed on most patients in an attempt to clarify or confirm historical suspicions.

Nystagmus is a jerking eye movement that represents an external observation of a disproportional stimulus from the labyrinths. There are usually fast and slow components to this jerking eye movement. Generally, when there is a normal amount of vestibular neural output in one ear, the pathologic ear with decreased output will be the side of slow beating. It is important to recognize that some degree of end-range nystagmus is possible, especially in individuals with poor vision. Observation of nystagmus is possible visually and electrically. Electronystagmography (ENG) is a helpful adjunct to the more gross visual observation used in most offices. ENG may also detect peripheral and cerebellar nystagmus that has been hidden by gross observation because of the patient's ability to incorporate optic fixation reflexes. This is accomplished with special lenses or with the eyes closed. Gross observation can be passive, looking for spontaneous nystagmus without head movement, or active, using provocative maneuvers to elicit nystagmus. Assisting gross observation is the use of Frenzel lenses. These lenses are used to abolish the patient's ability to fixate visually on an object and have the added benefit of magnifying the patient's eyes. Generally, nystagmus accompanies a sensation of spinning. When there is no vertigo but nystagmus is present, a central neurologic cause should be suspected and a neurologic consultation sought.

The type of nystagmus may be helpful in distinguishing between peripheral and central causes. In general:

- A peripheral cause is suggested if the nystagmus is horizontal or horizontal-rotational, decreased by visual fixation, increased with gaze toward the fast phase of nystagmus, occurring in one direction yet bilateral, associated with position change, and associated with moderate to severe vertigo.
- A central cause is suggested if the nystagmus is variable, being often vertical, unaffected by visual fixation, present with the eyes open or closed, and associated with constant, mild vertigo.

Provocative testing can be positional or with the introduction of water into the ear—caloric testing. Caloric testing is cumbersome and is considered relatively insensitive for detecting inner ear causes.[24] Most chiropractors do not perform caloric testing, so the focus will be on the positional, provocative maneuvers. The classic positional test is to begin with the patient in a seated or supine position and quickly place the patient in the opposite position. The Nylen-Bárány (also called the Bárány, Hallpike, or Dix-Hallpike maneuver) test starts with the patient seated and quickly brings the patient into a supine position with the head tilted to the side of involvement and slightly extended (Figure 18–1). The responses that are monitored are as follows:

- Latency—a few seconds of latency is indicative of a peripheral cause; no latency suggests a central cause.
- Severity of dizziness—peripheral causes generally produce more severe dizziness.
- Direction of nystagmus—most peripheral nystagmus is rotational or horizontal; central causes usually produce a vertical nystagmus.
- Adaptation and fatigue—if the nystagmus decreases over 10 to 20 seconds or if the response to positioning decreases in severity with repeated attempts, a peripheral cause is suggested.

Testing for cervicogenic vertigo is performed with the rotating chair test. The examiner has the patient sit on a rotating chair. The first part of the test is to have the patient rotate his or her head from side to side several times to determine whether he or she becomes vertiginous. The examiner then stabilizes the patient's head while the patient rotates his or her body. Theoretically, the second maneuver eliminates direct semicircular canal participation yet allows stimulation of proprioceptors and the vestibular nuclei. It is suggested that vertigo reproduced with the head stationary and the body rotating indicates cervicogenic vertigo (Figure 18–1).

An attempt to differentiate vascular and other causes of dizziness may be made with a battery of tests. These tests are designed to detect vascular compromise via decreases in

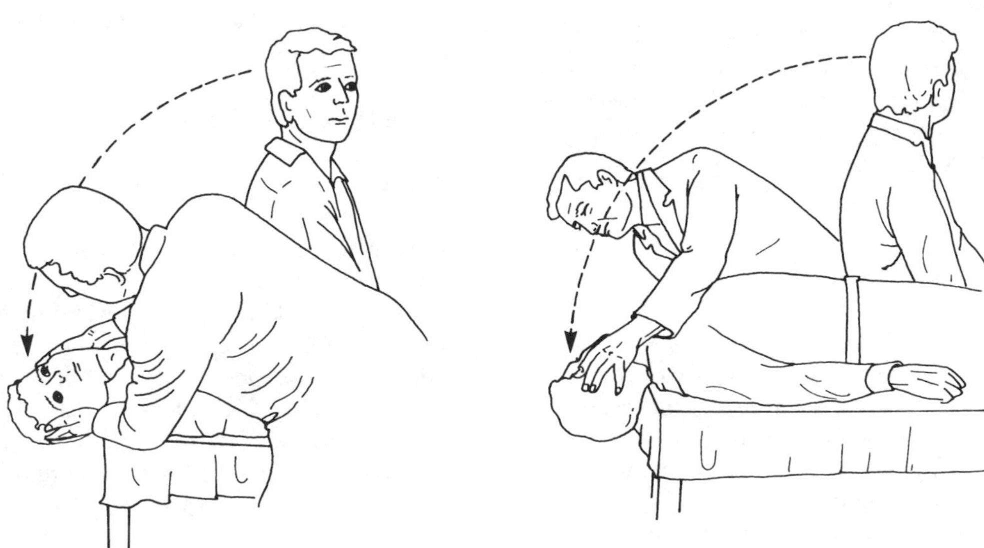

Figure 18–1 Nylen-Bárány Maneuver. *Source:* Reprinted with permission from B.M. Reilly, *Practical Strategies in Outpatient Medicine*, 2nd ed., p. 204, © 1991, W.B. Saunders Company.

blood pressure or auscultation of bruits. If absent, a position of rotation and extension to each side is performed in an attempt to provoke signs of vertebrobasilar insufficiency such as dizziness, nystagmus, or visual signs such as diplopia. Unfortunately, there is no clear evidence to support the use of these "screening" procedures.[25] They are considered insensitive and nonspecific.[26] Traditionally, chiropractors have used the maneuvers to protect the patient and also themselves (in the event of a postmanipulative vascular event). Yet there is disagreement as to whether this practice should be continued. It appears as though patients with dizziness provoked by extension or extension and rotation may, in fact, have other causes such as cervicogenic, benign positional vertigo, or a normal variant response. Brandt and Daroff[27] have demonstrated that even healthy individuals may experience a to-and-fro vertigo and postural imbalance with head extension. This effect was augmented by closing the eyes or standing on foam rubber.

Patients who complain of imbalance or unsteadiness while standing or walking should be screened with cerebellar testing. The main test is Romberg's. The inability of the patient to maintain balance with standing suggests cerebellar disease, as does the inability to hop on one foot. Variations may assist differentiation. If the patient sways or loses balance only when standing with the eyes closed, a proprioceptive problem is the cause. With the eyes open, visual input compensates.

Specialized testing options to clarify a diagnostic suspicion further include ENG, brain stem auditory evoked response (BAER), duplex Doppler scanning, dynamic posturography, and magnetic resonance imaging (MRI). In general, ENG is used to objectify a suspicion of vestibular pathology, BAER is used to identify a central lesion, duplex Doppler scanning is used to determine blood flow in extracranial (and intracranial with transcranial three-dimensional Doppler) vessels, dynamic posturography is used mainly as a research tool, and MRI is used to identify a brain tumor or multiple sclerosis.

MANAGEMENT

- Refer to a medical doctor if systemic disease, drugs, or psychologic dysfunction is suspected as the cause.
- Refer for further evaluation if hearing or other neurologic deficits are found, a tumor or bacterial infection is suggested, or a perilymphatic fistula is suspected.
- Treat peripheral vertigo with chiropractic manipulative techniques, habituation exercises, and other appropriate conservative approaches.
- Refer if treatment is ineffective or dizziness creates significant functional impairment.

Given that the vast majority of dizziness complaints are benign, initial referral often is not necessary. Obviously, if a tumor, infection, hearing deficit, or drug interaction is suspected, referral is requisite. If the patient is vomiting and disabled by the dizziness, referral for medication seems appropriate, although comanagement is often possible. Most causes of vertigo are usually due to abnormality of the vestibular nerve or labyrinth. Of these, the most common cause of vertigo is benign positional vertigo.[28,29] In patient populations of both postwhiplash and the elderly, benign positional vertigo is common. Acceleration/deceleration injuries, in addition to causing a cervicogenic form of vertigo, may simulate Meniere's disease, or in some instances cause it.

Cervicogenic Vertigo

A history of neck trauma, muscle spasm, restricted cervical range of motion (ROM), negative tests for peripheral or central causes of vertigo, or positives on the chair rotation test suggests a cervicogenic cause of vertigo. Theoretically, joint dysfunction may produce reflex muscle spasm or alter input to the vestibular nuclei. The chiropractic approach is to reduce muscle spasm and free restricted movement through manipulation, with possible adjunctive therapy such as electrical stimulation, deep heat, myofascial therapy, or traction. Some practitioners claim a high degree of success.[30,31] There are several difficulties with the designation of cervicogenic vertigo. It appears that there is often an overlap between cervicogenic vertigo and other peripheral vestibular vertigoes such as benign positional vertigo and Meniere's disease. Second, although it is called *vertigo* it appears that many patients feel more of a dysequilibrium, where they are pulled to one side.

Benign Paroxysmal Positional Vertigo

There are several conservative approaches to BPPV. One approach is habituation exercises (Exhibit 18–2). These exercises are designed to fatigue the response to the positional stimulation of vertigo. In one study in which patients acquired the provoking position several times every 3 hours, the success rate was quite high and was achieved in 3 to 14 days.[32] A more sophisticated approach, the Vestibular Habituation Therapy test battery, attempts to identify various body and head position changes to develop an individualized series of training exercises. One study indicated a 70% to 80% success rate in 6 to 8 weeks of treatment with this approach.[33]

Based on a theory of cupulolithiasis and canalithiasis, therapeutic maneuvers have been designed to "reposition" debris in the canals in an attempt to decrease inadvertent stimulation. One theory is that debris gets stuck to the cu-

Exhibit 18–2 General Habituation Exercises

The patient is taken through a structured, progressive program in an attempt to increase balance, increase independent eye-from-head movement, fatigue the peripheral response of specific head positions, and increase confidence in moving in a poorly lighted area.

The exercises are performed first seated and progress to standing. The exercises are first performed slowly and progressively increased to rapid performance. Following is a general outline of some exercises:

1. After determining the provocative head positions, have the patient either acquire the position and hold it for 30 seconds or repeatedly acquire the position several times until the sense of vertigo diminishes.
2. The patient practices moving the eyes up and down and side to side with the head remaining stationary.
3. Repeat the exercises while focusing on a finger held in front of the face.
4. Bend over to pick up objects 20 to 30 times.
5. Throw a ball from hand to hand while watching the ball (20 to 30 times).
6. Walk across a room 10 times with eyes open.
7. Walk across a room while turning the head slowly from side to side, attempting to focus on pictures or cards placed on the wall.
8. Walk across a room 10 times with eyes closed.

pula, making it heavier and more responsive to head movement. This is referred to as cupulolithiasis. The canalithiasis theory is similar; however, the debris supposedly is floating in the long arm of the posterior semicircular canal, influencing the flow of endolymph and causing a secondary movement effect on the cupula. Standard maneuvers have been developed with numerous variations employed. Several reports indicate a relatively high rate of success, often with a single treatment. The average rate of success is between 66% and 92%, depending on the type of maneuver used and the time frame in which it is measured.[34,35] Some argue that, because BPPV will resolve spontaneously in about 1 month in many cases, results measured after this time would not appear to be different from results with no treatment at all.[36] For the vertiginous patient, however, an earlier relief of symptoms is welcome. Two maneuvers are discussed below.

The modified Epley maneuver (Figure 18–2) attempts to move debris from the long arm of the posterior semicircular canal to the common crus.[37] The patient sits on the examination table with the head turned 45° toward the involved side. The examiner quickly lays the patient on his or her back, maintaining the head in 45° rotation. The patient is maintained in this position for 3 minutes, at which time the doctor rotates the patient's head to the opposite side over a 1-minute period. The patient is maintained in this position for 3 to 4 minutes and then slowly raised to a seated position.

The second approach is called the Semont's maneuver (Figure 18–3). The attempt is to remove debris from the cupula. The patient begins seated. The patient turns the head 45° away from the affected side. The patient is quickly brought down on his or her side, maintaining the previous head position. Vertigo is often experienced. The patient is maintained in this position for about 4 minutes, at which time he or she is quickly brought onto the opposite side, maintaining the same head position. If vertigo does not occur, move the patient's head through a few quick, short-arc ROM oscillations. After 4 minutes, the patient is brought back to the seated position slowly.

Following either maneuver the patient should be given the following instructions:

- Wait 10 minutes before leaving the doctor's office; avoid sudden head movement; have another person drive you home.
- For the following 2 to 3 days sleep in a half-reclined (recumbent) position either in a recliner or propped up on pillows on the couch; avoid sudden movements; avoid sleeping on the "bad" side.
- Avoid movements that will reproduce the vertigo; especially avoid head extension maneuvers such as looking to the ceiling, looking up to shave your chin (men), extension positions at the hairdresser or dentist, sporting activities (especially aerobics, sit-ups, swimming).
- After 1 week try to move slowly into the provoking position; if still dizzy see the doctor for habituation exercises.

Meniere's Disease

The basic premise for management of Meniere's disease is that there is an imbalance in the production of endolymph. A recent study suggests a dysfunction of antidiuretic hormone (ADH)-dependent control at the inner ear.[38] Medical treatment has focused on the reduction of excess endolymph with the prescription of diuretics and salt-reduction diets.

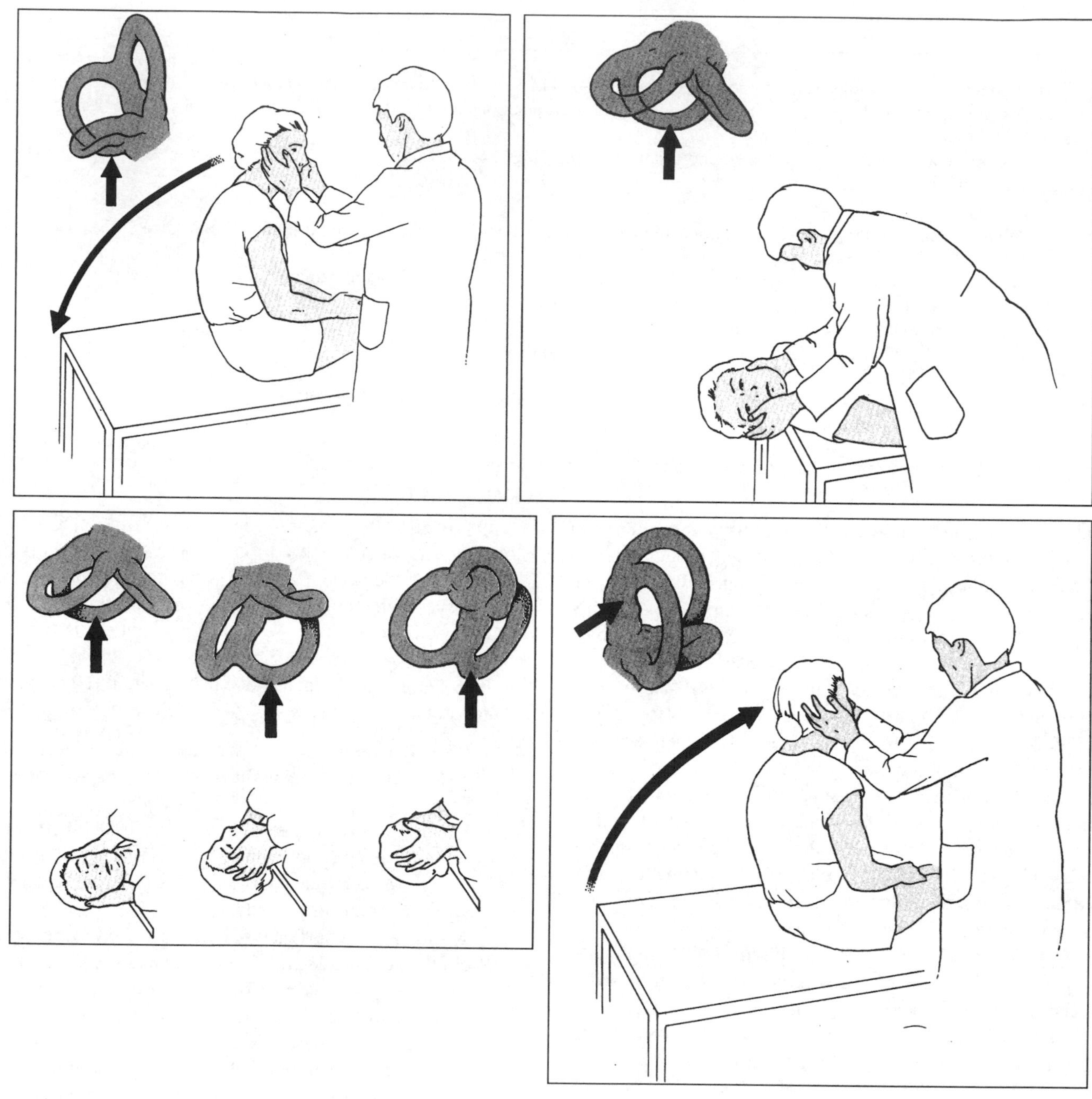

Figure 18–2 Modified Epley maneuver. *Source:* Reprinted with permission from J.J. Herdman et al., *Archives Otolaryngol Head Neck Surgery*, Vol. 119, p. 452, © 1993, American Medical Association.

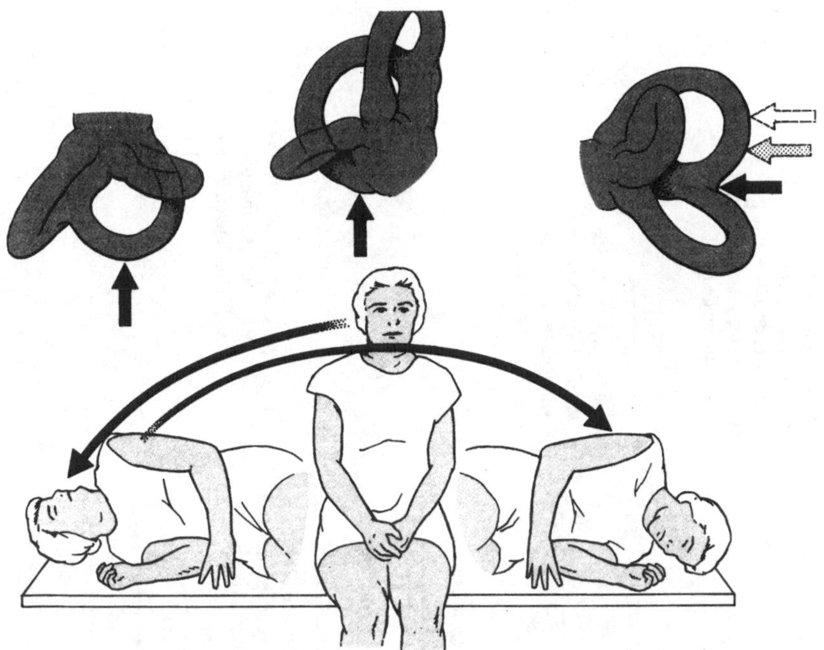

Figure 18–3 Semont's maneuver. *Source:* Reprinted with permission from J.J. Herdman et al., *Archives Otolaryngol Head Neck Surgery*, Vol. 119, p. 451, © 1993, American Medical Association.

With this approach, approximately two thirds of patients improve.

The natural course of Meniere's disease is gradually to "burn out" over months to years; however, the patient is often left with permanent hearing loss. Chiropractically, a course of nonmedical (herb) diuretic therapy coupled with a low-sodium diet may be helpful, combined with spinal manipulative therapy (SMT) for a short course to determine effectiveness. Some studies indicate the possibility of improvement with SMT.[39]

Medications used in the treatment of vertigo are usually one of several types, including antihistamines (meclizine, cyclizine), anticholinergics (scopolamine), and sedative/hypnotics (diazepam). These drugs are rarely needed except with severe attacks. It is worth mentioning that there is evidence that using these drugs in cases where there is vestibular disease decreases the ability of the CNS to compensate.

Algorithm

An algorithm for evaluation and management of dizziness is presented in Figure 18–4.

Figure 18–4

DIZZINESS—ALGORITHM.

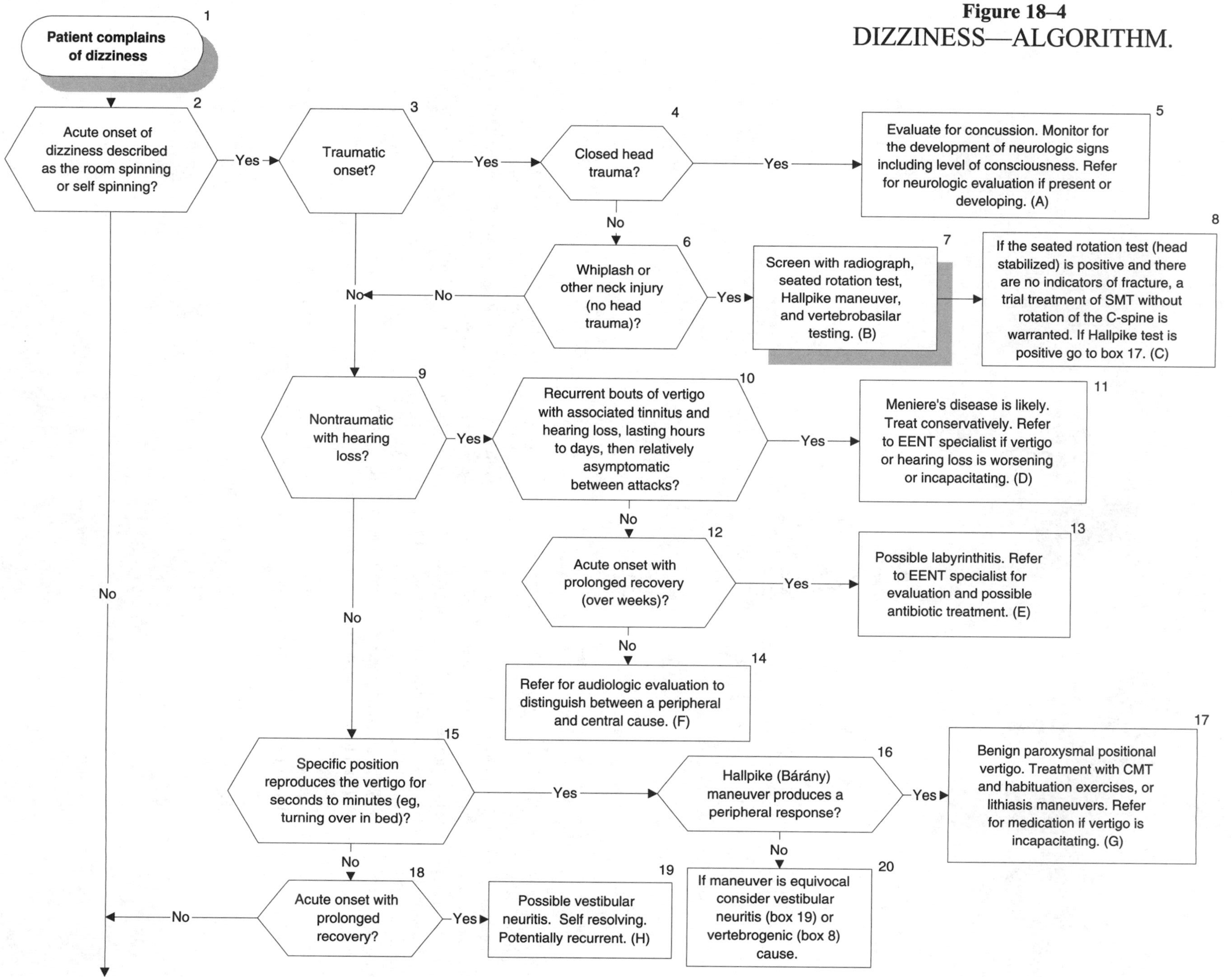

continues

Figure 18–4 continued

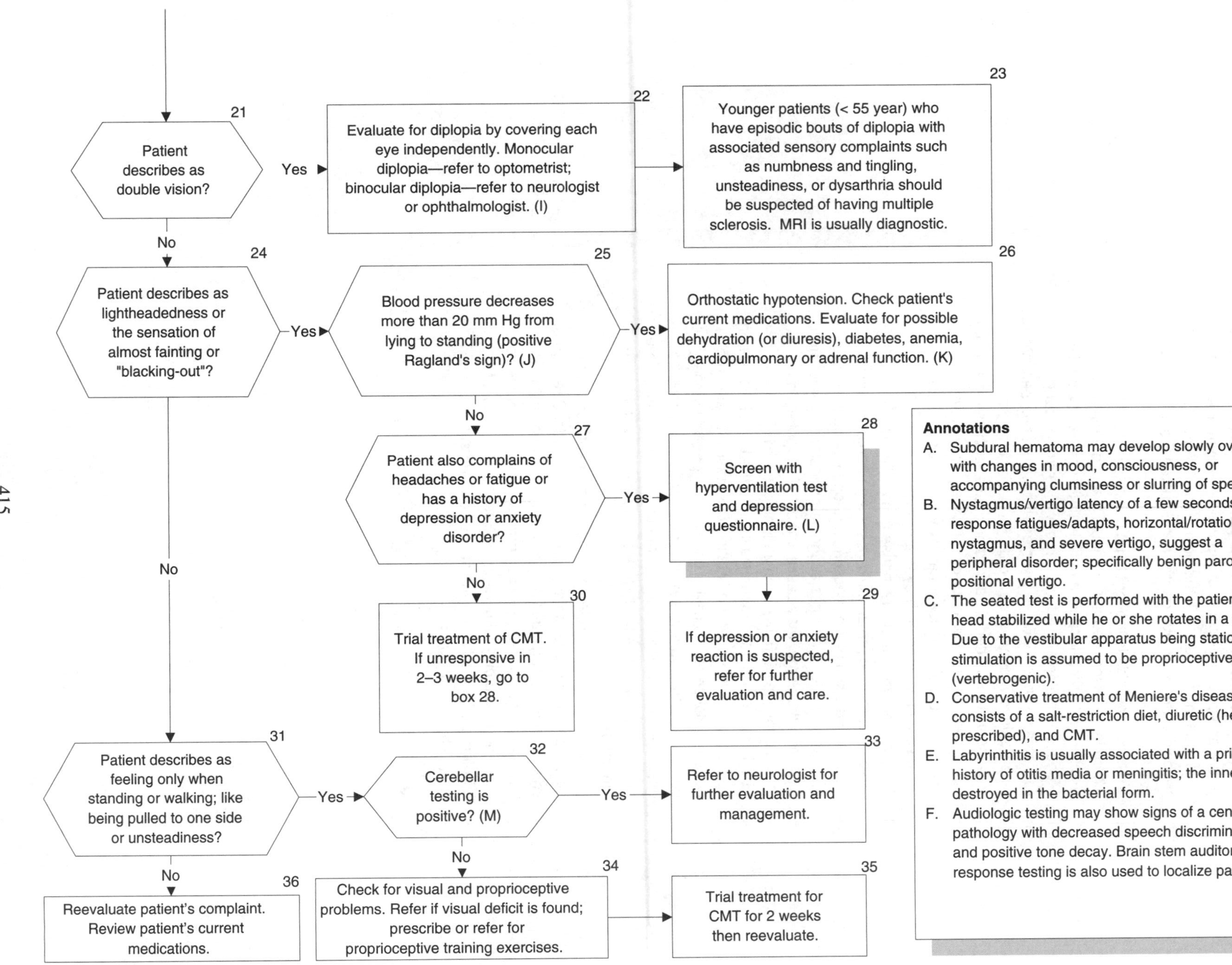
21
Patient describes as double vision?
Yes
22
Evaluate for diplopia by covering each eye independently. Monocular diplopia—refer to optometrist; binocular diplopia—refer to neurologist or ophthalmologist. (I)
23
Younger patients (< 55 year) who have episodic bouts of diplopia with associated sensory complaints such as numbness and tingling, unsteadiness, or dysarthria should be suspected of having multiple sclerosis. MRI is usually diagnostic.
No
24
Patient describes as lightheadedness or the sensation of almost fainting or "blacking-out"?
Yes
25
Blood pressure decreases more than 20 mm Hg from lying to standing (positive Ragland's sign)? (J)
Yes
26
Orthostatic hypotension. Check patient's current medications. Evaluate for possible dehydration (or diuresis), diabetes, anemia, cardiopulmonary or adrenal function. (K)
No
27
Patient also complains of headaches or fatigue or has a history of depression or anxiety disorder?
Yes
28
Screen with hyperventilation test and depression questionnaire. (L)
29
If depression or anxiety reaction is suspected, refer for further evaluation and care.
No
30
Trial treatment of CMT. If unresponsive in 2–3 weeks, go to box 28.
No
31
Patient describes as feeling only when standing or walking; like being pulled to one side or unsteadiness?
Yes
32
Cerebellar testing is positive? (M)
Yes
33
Refer to neurologist for further evaluation and management.
No
34
Check for visual and proprioceptive problems. Refer if visual deficit is found; prescribe or refer for proprioceptive training exercises.
35
Trial treatment for CMT for 2 weeks then reevaluate.
No
36
Reevaluate patient's complaint. Review patient's current medications.
Annotations
A. Subdural hematoma may develop slowly over days with changes in mood, consciousness, or accompanying clumsiness or slurring of speech.
B. Nystagmus/vertigo latency of a few seconds, response fatigues/adapts, horizontal/rotational nystagmus, and severe vertigo, suggest a peripheral disorder; specifically benign paroxysmal positional vertigo.
C. The seated test is performed with the patient's head stabilized while he or she rotates in a chair. Due to the vestibular apparatus being stationary, stimulation is assumed to be proprioceptive (vertebrogenic).
D. Conservative treatment of Meniere's disease consists of a salt-restriction diet, diuretic (herbal or prescribed), and CMT.
E. Labyrinthitis is usually associated with a prior history of otitis media or meningitis; the inner ear is destroyed in the bacterial form.
F. Audiologic testing may show signs of a central pathology with decreased speech discrimination and positive tone decay. Brain stem auditory response testing is also used to localize pathology.

continues

Figure 18–4 continued

Annotations (continued)

G. Habituation exercises require the patient to maintain the head in the provocative position or repeatedly acquire the position to fatigue the response. Lithiasis maneuvers attempt to reposition degenerative debris in the posterior semicircular canal.

H. Vestibular neuritis is thought to be due to a viral infection. There is no associated hearing loss. Recovery may be assisted with proprioceptive or habituation types of exercise.

I. Monocular diplopia suggests a refractive error or cataract (diplopia disappears when involved eye is covered; persists when uninvolved eye is covered). Binocular diplopia represents more often a neurologic cause such as extraocular muscle weakness due to tumor, diabetes, or myasthenia gravis (double vision disappears when either eye is covered; is present only when both eyes are open).

J. The normal sympathetic response to standing is vasoconstriction of splanchnic vessels (in particular veins) to maintain cerebral blood pressure. A drop in blood pressure after standing for 2 minutes suggests orthostatic hypotension.

K. Common drugs that may cause orthostatic hypotension include antihypertensives and antidepressants.

L. Short depression questionnaires include the Beck Depression Inventory and the Zung Self-Rating Depression Scale. The hyperventilation test is performed with the patient supine. The patient is instructed to breathe deeply for 2 minutes as the examiner feigns auscultation. If the patient reports the same sense of dizziness, anxiety-related hyperventilation may be the cause.

M. Cerebellar testing includes past-pointing, heel-to-shin, and quick repetitive pronation/supination of the hands. Direction of sway with Romberg's test may indicate the site of lesion in both labyrinth and cerebellar disorders. If swaying or loss of balance occurs only with the eyes closed, a proprioceptive problem peripherally or in the spinal cord (dorsal columns) should be investigated.

SELECTED CAUSES OF VERTIGO

BENIGN PAROXYSMAL POSITIONAL VERTIGO

Classic Presentation

The patient reports episodes of vertigo that occur with certain head positions. The vertigo lasts for seconds to a couple of minutes. Common head positioning changes that precipitate attacks are head extension or rotation or rolling over in bed.

Cause

It is believed that BPPV is due to degenerative debris (otoconia) floating in the posterior semicircular canal. Either the debris sticks to the cupula, making it heavier and more responsive (cupulolithiasis), or the debris floats in the long arm of the canal, inappropriately causing endolymph to move the cupula (canalithiasis).[40] Trauma and age appear to be important factors.[41] BPPV is the most common cause of vertigo.[29]

Evaluation

In addition to the patient's complaining of head positioning-specific onsets lasting for a few seconds, BPPV is also provoked by positioning maneuvers. The Hallpike (Nylen-Bárány) maneuver quickly positions the sitting patient into a supine posture with the head turned 45° to the same side.[42] A positive response is a small latency of a few seconds before vertigo and nystagmus begin. The vertigo is severe and the nystagmus is usually horizontal-rotational to the same side. If the patient is left in the position or returned to the position several times, the vertigo fatigues.

Management

There are two main approaches: habituation exercises and otoconia repositioning maneuvers. Single-treatment responses appear to be effective (55% to 70%) when using a repositioning maneuver.[34] The intention of the maneuvers is to move the debris so that it no longer causes inappropriate stimulation. The two most commonly used are the modified Epley's and Semont's maneuvers (see Figures 18–2 and 18–3). Habituation exercises take advantage of the fatigue and adaptation response of holding the head in the provocative position or repeatedly acquiring the provocative head position. In addition, exercises can be used to train independent eye movement and balance control. Rarely is medication or surgery considered a viable option.

MENIERE'S DISEASE

Classic Presentation

The patient complains of paroxysmal (sudden and recurrent) attacks of severe vertigo accompanied by low-tone hearing loss, low-tone tinnitus, and a sense of fullness in the ear. The episodes last for several hours to a day, with vertigo-free periods lasting for weeks or months. Hearing loss is progressive, while vertigo attacks appear to "burn out" over time.

Cause

Distention from either overproduction or retention of endolymph appears to be the cause in most cases. Specifically, there appears to be a problem with the endolymphatic sac's and duct's filtration and excretion function. Head trauma or previous infection may be factors. Although commonly diagnosed, Meniere's disease is considered only the fourth most common cause of vertigo.[43]

Evaluation

Recurrent, sudden onset of vertigo with associated hearing loss or tinnitus is fairly diagnostic of Meniere's disease. Hearing loss is usually low tone, and the patient may also be found to have a positive recruitment phenomenon with sensitivity to loud sounds; a small increase in sound intensity is perceived as large. Both ears are affected in 30% to 50% of patients over time.[44] Patients who fit the vertigo pattern but do not have auditory dysfunction may have recurrent vestibulopathy. Some of these patients have basilar migraine while others progress to typical Meniere's disease.

Management

The primary conservative approach is based on the theory that increased fluid causes distention and symptoms. Therefore, diuretic therapy (herbal or prescribed) in combination with a salt-restriction diet appears to be effective in managing the vertiginous component of Meniere's disease in approximately two thirds of patients.[45] For a few patients, surgical intervention using decompression of the endolymphatic sac appears effective. The possibility of an overlap between Meniere's disease and cervicogenic vertigo warrants a treatment trial of cervical manipulation in patients with Meniere's disease.

VESTIBULAR NEURONITIS (NEURITIS)

Classic Presentation

The patient complains of severe vertigo that occurred rather suddenly and lasted for days to weeks. There is often associated nausea and vomiting. The patient says that lying still may help. There is no associated hearing loss.

Cause

The cause is unknown. However, it is postulated that there is a viral infection of the vestibular nerve because of the report of an antecedent respiratory infection in some patients.[46]

Evaluation

It is important to differentiate vestibular neuritis (peripheral) from cerebellar stroke (central). Nystagmus is made worse by looking in the direction of the unaffected side (Alexander's law) and is reduced by visual fixation with vestibular neuritis. Central nystagmus is not reduced by visual fixation and may change direction. There are often other neurologic signs and symptoms with cerebellar involvement such as dysarthria, ataxia, and difficulty with repeated supination/pronation or finger-to-nose testing. Caloric testing demonstrates hyporesponsiveness or nonresponsiveness with vestibular neuritis.[47]

Management

Central compensation occurs and the condition resolves over time. During recovery, balance exercises may be helpful. Medication may be needed during the acute phase. Antihistamines such as meclizine or cyclizine or anticholinergics such as scopolamine are often prescribed.

LABYRINTHITIS

Classic Presentation

The patient complains of an acute onset of vertigo with (bacterial) or without (viral) hearing loss. Although the vertigo may improve over a week, sudden head movements may provoke the vertigo for weeks.

Cause

It is believed that either a viral or bacterial infection causes damage to the inner ear. Bacterial infection may follow otitis media or meningitis, leading to complete destruction of the inner ear. Viral infection is less fulminant and may be reversible.[48]

Evaluation

The findings are the same as for vestibular neuritis plus there is some hearing deficit. Otoscopic evaluation may reveal an otitis media.

Management

Antibiotic therapy is beneficial with bacterial labyrinthitis. With viral causes, a tapered course of oral prednisone may be helpful, but results are varied. Physical therapy training for balance control may be utilized during the recovery period.

PERILYMPHATIC FISTULA

Classic Presentation

There is no classic presentation because the onset, intensity, and frequency vary. However, many patients have a history of barometric pressure changes, as with diving or air flight, or internal pressure development through intense weight lifting.[49]

Cause

An opening develops between the middle and inner ear (oval or round window rupture), allowing leakage of perilymph. Perilymphatic fistulas are a rare cause of vertigo.

Evaluation

Findings are variable; however, there is often a response to bearing down and provocation with pressure created by a pneumatic otoscope, which causes increased pressure in the ear.[50]

Management

Surgical management is often corrective.

CERVICOGENIC VERTIGO

Classic Presentation

The patient complains of vertigo that is associated with maintaining certain head positions (not acquiring the position). There may be associated complaints of neck or suboccipital pain. There appears to be a history of trauma (such as a whiplash injury) in about one third of patients.

Cause

It is believed that either overstimulation of upper cervical proprioceptors or degeneration of these proprioceptors or their pathways may cause an imbalance of information leading to a perception of vertigo or dysequilibrium.[31]

Evaluation

Findings of upper cervical soft tissue involvement and restricted movements are possible. The Fitz-Ritson rotation test may help differentiate.[30] The examiner stabilizes the patient's head while the patient rotates his or her body in a chair. If the patient becomes dizzy, a vertebrogenic source is suggested because it is believed that vestibular stimulation is eliminated with this maneuver.

Management

Chiropractic manipulation may be beneficial and should be applied as a treatment trial.[51] It is important to consider that because of the proprioceptive input of the upper cervical area, chiropractic manipulation may serve to benefit other causes of vertigo or that there may be an overlap between cervicogenic vertigo and other types.

ACOUSTIC NEUROMA

Classic Presentation

The patient presents with a complaint of mild but constant hearing loss and dizziness sometimes with associated tinnitus. The onset is gradual and may be ignored initially. There are rarely acute attacks.

Cause

A benign schwannoma of the eighth cranial nerve is called an acoustic neuroma. It is located in the cerebellopontine angle, where other cranial nerves are susceptible to compression. As the tumor grows it may cause brain stem compression.

Evaluation

Unless the tumor is large and pressing on other cranial nerves, there are likely to be no clinical findings. Auditory testing may reveal poor speech discrimination. Caloric testing and provocative maneuvers may demonstrate a central response. When the suspicion is high, an MRI should be ordered. It is the definitive diagnostic tool.

Management

Surgical excision is necessary.

REFERENCES

1. Kroenke K, Lucas CA, Rosenberg ML, et al. Causes of persistent dizziness: a prospective study of 100 patients in ambulatory care. *Ann Intern Med.* 1992;17:898–904.
2. Kroenke K, Mangelsdorff AD. Common symptoms in ambulatory care: incidence, evaluation, therapy, and outcome. *Am J Med.* 1989;86:262–266.
3. Herr RD, Zun L, Mathews JJ. A directed approach to the dizzy patient. *Ann Emerg Med.* 1989;18:664–672.
4. National Board of Chiropractic Examiners. *Job Analysis of Chiropractic.* Greeley, CO: NBCE; 1993:64.
5. Hinoki M. Neurootological studies on vertigo due to whiplash injury. *Equilibrium Res Suppl.* 1971;1:5–29.
6. Hinoki M. Vertigo due to whiplash injury: a neurological approach. *Acta Otolaryngol (Stockh).* 1985;419:9–29.
7. Chester JB Jr. Whiplash, postural control, and the inner ear. *Spine.* 1991;16:716–720.
8. Hildingson C, Wenngren B, Bring G, Toolamen G. Oculomotor problems after cervical spine injury. *Acta Orthop Scand.* 1989;60:513–516.
9. Colledge NR, Wilson JA, MacIntyre CC, MacLennan WJ. The prevalence and characteristics of dizziness in an elderly community. *Age Ageing.* 1994;23:117–120.
10. Sullivan M, Clark M, Katon J, et al. Psychiatric and otologic diagnoses in patients complaining of dizziness. *Arch Intern Med.* 1993;153:1479–1484.
11. Jonson P, Lipsitz L. Dizziness and syncope. In: Hazzard W, Bierman J, Blass J, Ettinger W, Halter J, eds. *Principles of Geriatric Medicine and Gerontology.* 3rd ed. New York: McGraw-Hill; 1994.
12. Sloane PD, Harman M, Mitchell CM. Psychological factors associated with chronic dizziness in patients aged 60 and older. *J Am Geriatr Soc.* 1994;42:847–852.
13. Kroenke K, et al. Psychiatric disorders and functional impairment in patients with persistent dizziness. *JAMA.* 1993;810:530–535.

14. Fitz-Ritson D. Neuroanatomy and neurophysiology of the upper cervical spine. In: Vernon H, ed. *Upper Cervical Syndrome*. Baltimore: Williams & Wilkins; 1988:48–85.
15. Wyke, B. Neurology of cervical spinal joints. *Physiotherapy*. 1979;65:72–76.
16. Suzuki I, Park BR, Wilson VJ. Directional sensitivity of, and neck afferent input to, cervical and lumbar interneurons modulated by neck rotation. *Brain Res*. 1986;367:356–359.
17. Sanes JN, Jennings VA. Centrally programmed patterns of muscle activity in voluntary motor behavior in humans. *Exp Brain Res*. 1984;54:23–32.
18. Rose PK, Keirstand SA. Segmental projection from muscle spindles: a perspective from the upper cervical spinal cord. *Can J Physiol Pharmacol*. 1986;64:505–507.
19. Brink EE, Jannai K, Hirai N, Wilson VJ. Cervical input to vestibulocolic neurons. *Brain Rev*. 1981;217:13–21.
20. DeJong PTVM, DeJong JMBV, Cohen B, Johngkees LBW. Ataxia and nystagmus induced by injection of local anesthetics in the neck. *Ann Neurol*. 1977;1:240–246.
21. Suzuki M. The effect of electricity of flowing electrode. *J Physiol Soc Jpn*. 1955;17:223–234.
22. Goodwin GM, McCloskey DI, Mathews PBC. The contribution of muscle afferents to kinesthesia shown by vibration-induced illusions of movement and by the effects of paralyzing joint afferents. *Brain*. 1972;95:705–748.
23. Bogduk N, Lambert G, Duckworth JW. The anatomy and physiology of the vertebral nerve in relation to cervical migraine. *Cephalalgia*. 1981;1:1–14.
24. Moller MR, Moller AR. Vascular compression syndrome of the eighth nerve. *Neurol Clin*. 1990;8:421–439.
25. Ferezy JS. Neurovascular assessment for risk management in chiropractic practice. In: Lawerence DJ, Cassidy DJ, McGregor M, et al., eds. *Advances in Chiropractic,* St. Louis, MO: Mosby-Year Book; 1994;1:455–475.
26. Bolton PS, Stick PE, Lord RSA. Failure of clinical tests to predict cerebral ischemia before neck manipulation. *J Manipulative Physiol Ther*. 1989;12:304–307.
27. Brandt TH, Daroff RB. The multisensory physiological and pathological vertigo syndromes. *Ann Neurol*. 1980;7:195–203.
28. Drachman DA, Hart CW. An approach to the dizzy patient. *Neurology*. 1972;22:323–334.
29. Nedzelski JM, Barber HO, Milmoyl L. Diagnosis in a dizziness unit. *J Otolaryngol*. 1986;15:101–104.
30. Fitz-Ritson D. Assessment of cervicogenic vertigo. *J Manipulative Physiol Ther*. 1991;14:193–198.
31. Cote PC, Mior SA, Fitz-Ritson D. Cervicogenic vertigo: a report of three cases. *J Can Chiro Assoc*. 1991;35:89–94.
32. Brandt T, Daroff RB. Physical therapy for benign paroxysmal positional vertigo. *Arch Otolaryngol*. 1980;106:484–485.
33. Norre ME. Rationale for rehabilitation treatment for vertigo. *Am J Otolaryngol*. 1987;8:31–35.
34. Herdman SJ, Tusa RJ, Zee DS, et al. Single treatment approaches to benign paroxysmal positional vertigo. *Arch Otolaryngol Head Neck Surg*. 1993;119:450–454.
35. Harvey SA, Hain TC, Adamiec LC. Modified liberatory maneuver: effective treatment for benign paroxysmal positional vertigo. *Laryngoscope*. 1994;104:1206–1212.
36. Li JC. Mastoid oscillation: a critical factor for success in canalith repositioning procedure. *Otolaryngol Head Neck Surg*. 1995;112:670–675.
37. Herdman SJ, Tusa RJ, Zee DS, et al. Single treatment approaches to benign paroxysmal positional vertigo. *Arch Otolaryngol Head Neck Surg*. 1993;119:450–454.
38. Takeda T, Kakigi A, Saito H. Antidiuretic hormone (ADH) and endolymphatic hydrops. *Acta Otolaryngol Suppl (Stockh)*. 1995;519:219–222.
39. Lewit K. Meniere's disease and the cervical spine. *Rev Czech Med*. 1961;2:129–139.
40. Brandt T. Benign paroxysmal positional vertigo. In: Brandt T, ed. *Vertigo: Its Multisensory Syndromes*. New York: Springer-Verlag; 1991:139–151.
41. Davies RA, Luxon LM. Dizziness following head injury: a neuro-otological study. *J Neurol*. 1995;242:222–230.
42. Dix MR, Hallpike CS. The pathology, symptomatology, and diagnosis of certain common disorders of the vestibular system. *Proc R Soc Med*. 1952;45:341–354.
43. Brandt T. Vertigo—a systematic approach. In: Kennard C, ed. *Recent Avances in Clinical Neurology*. Edinburgh: Churchill Livingstone; 1990:59–84.
44. Paparella MM, Alleva M, Bequer MG. Dizziness. *Primary Care*. 1990;17:299–308.
45. Ruckenstein MJ, Rutka JA, Hawke M. The treatment of Meniere's disease: Torok revisited. *Laryngoscope*. 1991;101:211–218.
46. Schuknecht HF, Kitamura K. Vestibular neuritis: second Louis H Clerf lecture. *Ann Otol Rhinol Laryngol Suppl*. 1981;901–919.
47. Brandt T. Vestibular neuritis. In: Brandt T, ed. *Vertigo: Its Multisensory Syndromes*. New York: Springer-Verlag; 1991:29–40.
48. Paparella MM, Sugiura S. The pathology of suppurative labyrinthitis. *Ann Otol Rhinol Laryngol*. 1967;76:554–586.
49. Lehrer JF, Rubin RC, Poole DR, et al. Perilymphatic fistula—a definitive and curable cause of vertigo following head trauma. *West J Med*. 1984;141:57–60.
50. Rizer FM, House JW. Perilymph fistulas: the House Ear Clinic experience. *Otolaryngol Head Neck Surg*. 1991;104:239–243.
51. Huise M. Disequilibrium caused by a functional disturbance of the upper cervical spine. *Man Med*. 1983;1:18–23.

Chapter 19

Seizures

CONTEXT

It is important to remember that not all seizures are epileptic[1] and not all epilepsy results in convulsive activity. It is therefore requisite to make a diligent search for other causes prior to assuming that the patient has epilepsy. Patients diagnosed as epileptic often are subject to restrictions (sports, driver's license, etc.) and biases. Therefore, it is incumbent on the evaluating doctor to make an effort to distinguish epilepsy from other causes of "seizures." Epileptic seizure activity may be benign or cause death through status epilepticus (an uninterrupted seizure) or cause the deaths of others if the patient is operating a car or other potentially lethal machinery. Those with true epilepsy often can be helped through medication or surgery.

Epilepsy and unprovoked seizures affect approximately 5% (between 4.3% and 7%) of the population.[2,3] There appears to be a higher incidence in black men and in the elderly. Most of the black male increase is in middle-aged groups, possibly reflecting consequences of trauma or cerebrovascular disease.[4] In the elderly, the most common cause of seizures is stroke. Tumor accounts for the majority of seizures in patients between ages 25 and 64 years.[5] Other causes include cysts and vascular malformations. The incidence of a single, nonepileptic (nonrecurrent), unprovoked convulsive episode in children appears to be between 0.5% and 1%.[6] Most of these occur within the first year of life. Absence epilepsy (petit mal) accounts for 10% to 15% of childhood epilepsy, myoclonic epilepsy for 5%, and idiopathic localization-related epilepsy for 10%.

The total lifetime cost is $3.0 billion for all persons with an epileptic onset in 1990.[7] The average cost per person varies according to remission or intractability. The range is $4,272 to $138,602. If a patient has a family history, the chances of a second seizure within the next 2 years is 35%. Even without a family history the chance of a second seizure within the following 24 hours of a first seizure is about 15%.[8] These important facts must be kept in mind by the chiropractor, who with the best of intentions is trying to save the patient from a lifetime of medication.

Patients do not often present to chiropractic offices with a complaint of seizures. However, there is the occasional patient who has anecdotally heard of or spoken to someone with seizures who felt that he or she had been helped by chiropractic care. Such patients usually are unhappy with the side effects of medication or are not completely controlled by their medication. They present as "last hope" patients. Although the author has heard from colleagues of resolution of seizures with chiropractic care, there are unfortunately few case studies and no large studies to help support the anecdotal "miracle" cures. One of the difficulties with interpretation of therapeutic effect is that the outcome measure has been eliminated. In other words, if the outcome measure is a reduction or elimination of seizure activity, the patient on medication is often well controlled, eliminating the outcome to be measured. It is to be hoped that, within the next few years, those chiropractors who feel that they have had an effect will join together in publication to help generate interest in larger studies.

The context of a seizure patient's entering a chiropractic setting is fraught with difficulty. Often the patient is being controlled by medication and is dissatisfied with the drug's effect on his or her general sense of well-being. The chiropractor is in the position of not being able to withdraw medication gradually to determine a therapeutic effect with manipulation. If a sudden withdrawal does occur, there is a strong risk of a rebound effect with an increased severity or frequency of attacks, including status epilepticus. It is imperative that the patient understand that any changes in medication are dictated only through consultation with the prescribing physician. Neither the patient nor the chiropractor should attempt withdrawal or reduction of seizure medication.

Realistically, the chiropractor may be especially helpful if he or she is at the scene of an epileptic occurrence. With a knowledge of different seizure types, the chiropractor may assist in management of an acute seizure. A list of "do's and don'ts" is given in Table 19–1 as recommended by the Epilepsy Foundation of America.

Table 19–1 Seizure Recognition and First Aid

Type of Seizure	*Symptoms*	*First Aid*	*Don'ts*
Tonic/clonic (grand mal)	Sudden cry, fall, rigidity (grand mal) Followed by muscle jerks, shallow breathing, bluish skin, possible loss of bladder or bowel control Usually lasts a couple of minutes Person may be confused and/or fatigued, followed by return to full consciousness	Look for medical identification Protect from nearby hazards Loosen ties or shirt collars Protect head from injury Turn on side to keep airway clear Reassure when consciousness returns If brief, single seizure, ask if hospital evaluation desired If multiple seizures or if one seizure lasts longer than 5 minutes, call an ambulance If person is pregnant, injured, or diabetic, call for aid at once	Don't put any hard implement in the mouth Don't try to hold tongue; it can't be swallowed Don't try to give liquids during or just after a seizure Don't use artificial respiration unless breathing is absent after muscle jerks subside, or unless water has been inhaled Don't restrain
Simple partial	Jerking may begin in one area of body, arm, leg or face Patient stays awake and is aware Jerking may proceed from one area of the body to another, sometimes becoming a convulsive seizure May not be obvious to an onlooker Patient experiences a disturbed environment	No first aid necessary unless seizure becomes convulsive, then first aid as above No immediate action needed other than reassurance and emotional support Medical evaluation recommended	
Complex partial	Often starts with blank stare Followed by chewing, then random activity Person appears unaware of surrounding, dazed, mumbling Actions clumsy, not directed May run, appear afraid, and struggle or flail at restraint Lasts a few minutes, but postseizure confusion can last substantially longer	Speak calmly and reassuringly to patient and others Guide gently away from obvious hazards Stay with person until completely aware of environment Offer to help getting home	Don't grab unless sudden danger (such as cliff edge or approaching car) threatens Don't try to restrain Don't shout Don't expect verbal instructions to be obeyed

Source: Courtesy of Epilepsy Foundation of America, © 1989, 1996.

GENERAL STRATEGY

Look for causes other than epilepsy (Exhibit 19–1):

- Determine whether the patient lost consciousness or whether there was convulsive activity of a body part without loss of consciousness—nonepileptic causes often result in loss of consciousness due to hypoxia with associated convulsive activity.
- Determine whether the patient was given information from any witnesses detailing the length of time that he or she was unconscious.
- Determine whether the patient had any pre- or postictal signs or symptoms.
- Determine the position and environment that the patient was in and whether these are consistent with any previous episodes.
- In an infant or child, determine whether there was an associated fever.
- Always determine the patient's use of medications and alcohol, and any sudden stopping of the medication regimen.
- Is there any history of toxic exposure (specifically, lead intoxication in children)?
- Is the patient diabetic?

If epilepsy is suspected, attempt to determine the cause and any triggers.

- Determine whether there is a family history—there may be a genetic predisposition (especially with generalized absence seizures or febrile seizures).
- Did the seizures begin before age 2 years? Ask about birth trauma and metabolic causes. Specifically determine whether there is a history of cerebral palsy, mental retardation, tumors/cysts, or hydrocephalus (all are often associated with epileptic seizure activity).
- Did the seizure activity begin between ages 2 and 20 years? Idiopathic epilepsy is likely.
- Did the seizures begin later than age 30 years? If yes, consider tumor; if over age 60 consider a vascular event.
- Is there a recent or past history of head trauma?
- What accompanies the seizure? Any auras? Any postictal findings such as extreme tiredness, headaches, or incontinence during the attacks?

Determine whether further testing is necessary.

- If a nonepileptic cause is suggested, lab testing may be necessary.
- If a firm diagnosis of epilepsy is needed, an electroencephalogram (EEG) is necessary, often a 24-hour EEG.
- If a tumor is suspected, refer for neurologic consultation, which is likely to include magnetic resonance imaging (MRI).

DEFINITIONS AND CLASSIFICATIONS

Specifically, an epileptic seizure is an event characterized by excessive electrical discharge due to a hyperexcitable group of neurons. The diagnosis of epilepsy is reserved for a recurrent history of such attacks. A seizure, however, is any attack of cerebral origin regardless of the cause. It becomes clear, then, how difficult it is to use these terms always discriminately. Convulsions are involuntary contractions of muscles. They may be the result of epilepsy or a host of other causes. Convulsions do not always occur with epilepsy. Unfortunately, a patient could easily be mislabeled without a search for other causes.

The most common classification system used is that proposed by the International League Against Epilepsy (ILAE).[9] This revised classification system is complex; however, there are some general points that would be useful to the nonspecialist. There are generally two classifications of epileptic seizures:

1. Generalized—simultaneous involvement of all or large parts of both cerebral hemispheres. Generalized seizures are often metabolic in origin.
2. Localization-related (old terminology: partial)—seizures are initiated in a part of one cerebral hemisphere accompanied by related focal EEG and clinical manifestations. These seizures are further divided into simple partial seizures, in which consciousness is unimpaired, and complex partial seizures, in which consciousness is impaired.

When epilepsy results in loss of consciousness, there are two defined phases. The seizure itself is termed the *ictal phase*. The time following the seizure is referred to as the *postictal phase*.

Hallucinatory visual, auditory, olfactory, or other sensory aberrations are common. When they occur preceding loss of consciousness and last a few seconds, they are referred to as an aura. When they last longer than a few seconds, they are classified as a complex partial seizure. Additional signs of a complex partial seizure are referred to as automatisms. These include repetitive activity such as scratching an area of skin, lip smacking, or any repetitive movement.

Status epilepticus is a prolonged seizure that lasts longer than 30 minutes and may lead to death if not interrupted by medical intervention. The risk for permanent injury increases when the seizure lasts longer than 5 minutes. In children, about one third who suffer from an episode of status

Exhibit 19–1 Differentiating between Epilepsy and Other Causes of Symptoms

Patient presents with history of a "seizure"

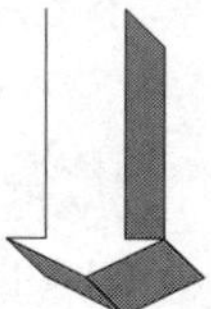

Differentiate between epilepsy and other causes of convulsive activity.

Hypoxia or hypoglycemia

Is there a relationship to eating (hypoglycemia)?
Is there a history of hyperventilation (anxiety) or fainting?
Is there a history of a heart problem (arrhythmia or mumur)?
Is there a history of breath-holding?

Fever

Do seizures only occur with a high fever?
If they occur also at other times, is there a relationship to other factors?

Drugs

Has the patient abruptly discontinued taking a precription drug?
Is there a history of "recreational" drug usage?
Has the patient acquired prescription drugs from more than one physician?

Differentiate among known causes of epilepsy.

1. **Vascular** (includes arteriovenous malformation, aneurysm, hemorrhage)
2. **Tumor**
3. **Head trauma**
4. **Metabolic**

If the patient has associated neurologic symptoms such as headache, dizziness, change in personality, changes in level of consciousness, or obvious neurologic deficits such as paralysis, weakness, or persistent numbness and tingling, an organic brain lesion is likely. Are there triggers that the patient can identify, such as use of a computer, watching a fan, specific sounds or smells, etc.?

Differentiation requires a thorough neurologic examination. Referral to a neurologist should result in an EEG, CT, or MRI evaluation, and possibly an angiogram.

epilepticus will have permanent neurologic damage (ie, hemiparesis, microcephaly, mental retardation).[10]

RELEVANT ANATOMY AND PHYSIOLOGY

A seizure involves a sudden, abnormal electrical discharge in the brain. The normal asynchronous interaction of the cortical neurons suddenly becomes synchronous. Although the etiology of seizure activity is often unclear with epilepsy, generally it can be said that a decrease in either oxygen or glucose, an imbalance in electrolytes, or generalized toxic events may lead to a seizure episode. Other causes are direct damage through pressure or scarring of an area of the brain. Pressure is often due to either a tumor or vascular event, whereas scarring is often due to infection. The result is a dysfunctional cortical area that is in many instances hyperexcitable. With infection or trauma, it is not uncommon for the seizure to occur after 6 months to as much as several years later, after scar tissue has formed. During a seizure, transmission of neural impulses is accelerated. Electrical discharges traveling at, for example, 80 per second are suddenly increased to 500 per second. In addition, this increased activity is uncoordinated. The resulting seizure activity is dependent on the specific area affected. Therefore, an epileptic "seizure" runs the gamut of emotional, motor, and sensory manifestations with and without loss of consciousness.

EVALUATION

History

Important aspects of the history that might suggest a nonepileptic form of seizure include the following (Table 19–2):

- loss of consciousness that was brief, with no postictal complaints
- no aura prior to loss of consciousness
- history of arrhythmias, diabetes, use of antidepressants and other medications, use of recreational drugs, psychologic problems, or possible electrolyte imbalance

There are generally two history findings that confuse the distinction between epileptic and nonepileptic seizures: (1) loss of consciousness (LOC) and/or (2) convulsions. Obtaining an eyewitness account and the patient's recollection of presyncope and postsyncope events go a long way in differentiating between epilepsy and other causes. If LOC occurred upon standing, after prolonged standing (especially in a hot environment), or after feeling lightheaded and nauseated, the cause is less likely to be epilepsy. If the patient collapsed as opposed to falling stiffly when passing out, the cause again is less likely to be epileptic. Finally, if the patient did not experience significant ictal or postsyncopal signs or symptoms such as tongue biting, urinary or fecal incontinence, extreme fatigue, headache, or persistent achiness, the cause probably is not epileptic. Movement disorders such as shuddering attacks, nonepileptic myoclonus, tics and spasms, and paroxysmal choreoathetosis may be mistaken for epilepsy. Betts[11] feels that as many as 20% of patients referred to specialist centers for intractable epilepsy have nonepileptic seizures.

Febrile seizures are alarming to parents. However, very few cases proceed to tonic-clonic seizures, and only 5% of children will have status epilepticus.[12] Although the cause may be direct, such as with meningitis, most seizures are benign and do not indicate a propensity for future epilepsy or other neurologic dysfunction.[13] A family history is often found. With generalized absence seizures a family history is also found, often suggesting an inherited tendency toward a low-seizure threshold reaction to physiologic stresses such as sleep deprivation, fever, psychic stress, and repetitive stimulation (eg, light flashes/photosensitivity).[14] One study of inducing factors found that in adolescents, common triggers were fatigue after exercise (15.2%), sleep disturbance (9.1%), and psychic stress and emotional change (15.1%).[15]

The following are important facts about seizures and related causes or triggers:

- One rare but significant cause of seizure activity is an arrhythmia such as ventricular tachycardia of the torsades de pointes type. It is identified on an electrocardiogram as a P/long or prolonged QT interval (idiopathic QT syndrome).[16]
- Although antidepressants (and other drugs) have been targeted as causes of seizures, the rate is only 0.3% to 0.6%.[17] Predictive risk factors include a previous history of seizures, alcohol or sedative withdrawal, or multiple drug usages.
- One of the causes of nonepileptic seizures is a response to sexual abuse in childhood.[18] Two reactions have been studied. One is referred to as a "swoon," considered a cutoff reaction. The other is referred to as an abreactive type that may represent an acting out of the memory of abuse.
- Although video games have been accused of increasing the occurrence of epileptic seizures, one study indicates that the risk is no greater than that for the general population.[19]
- Seizures that are likely to be epileptic are those that are recurrent and often stereotypic for that patient.
- Recent evidence suggests a relationship between migraine headache and epilepsy.[20] Migraine is particularly

Table 19–2 History Questions for Seizures

Primary Question	*What Are You Thinking?*	*Secondary Questions*	*What Are You Thinking?*
Did you lose consciousness?	Epilepsy, hypoxia, head trauma, syncope.	Were you out for less than a minute?	Syncope. Seizure due to hypoxia.
		Did you hit your head?	Posttraumatic seizure or subdural/epidural hematoma. Warrants neurologic referral.
		Did you feel any unusual feelings before passing out?	An epigastric sensation or confusion would suggest epilepsy; lightheadedness suggests syncope.
		How did you feel after regaining consciousness?	Extreme fatigue, soreness, headache, incontinence, tongue bleeding suggest grand mal seizure.
		Were you out longer than a couple of minutes?	Epileptic attack usually lasts 3–5 minutes.
		Were there any witnesses?	Describe sequence; especially how the person fell; any automatisms.
		Any history of irregular heart rhythm or do you feel any chest symptoms?	Arrhythmia may cause LOC with convulsions due to hypoxia.
		(For a child) Did the child hold breath before passing out?	Breath-holding is possible with children when they are angry.
Are you taking medications?	Side effect, withdrawal symptom.	Have you had a recent change in your prescription?	Check Physicians' Desk Reference for side effect of medication.
		Have you recently stopped taking the medication?	Antiseizure medication will often cause seizures when abruptly stopped.
		Do you use recreational drugs or alcohol? How much?	If abuse is suggested, refer to a counseling or specialized center.
(For infants or children) Did this occur with a high fever?	Febrile seizures.	Do they occur only with fever or at other times?	Febrile seizures usually do not indicate progression to epilepsy.
Is there a family history?	Epilepsy, inherited metabolic problems.	Any known metabolic disorders?	These usually occur in infancy. If epilepsy, chance of more seizures is increased.
Did this occur while you were conscious?	Partial epileptic seizures.	Did the seizure happen in your arm/leg?	Especially if it moves slowly up the arm it is suggestive of partial seizure.

prevalent in patients with centrotemporal epilepsy (63%) (rolandic epilepsy). In patients with absence seizures, 33% had migraine, 7% had partial epilepsy, and 9% had a history of cranial trauma.[21]

Examination

The examination of a seizure patient should focus on nonepileptic causes first. This would include a cardiovascular examination, including blood pressure after lying for 3 minutes and then standing (check for orthostatic hypotension), auscultation for any obvious chronic lung or heart abnormalities, and a thorough neurologic evaluation to determine any underlying neurologic disease. Further evaluation would include laboratory testing to determine the possibility of a metabolic association. Electrolyte, glucose, and blood cell evaluation should be used as an initial screen. Further evaluation is warranted when a specific metabolic disorder is suggested; this is best performed by the medical specialist. More and more, a reaction to use of or discontinuation of illicit drugs and alcohol is found, especially in the adolescent, young, and middle-aged adult in whom no other obvious cause has been found. Laboratory evaluation is often helpful. When pseudoseizures are suspected (due often to psychologic factors), a postictal prolactin estimation may help clarify whether a "true" seizure has occurred. After a major tonic/clonic seizure, there is usually a significant rise in serum prolactin levels.[22] This is not as noteworthy with partial seizures. If a baseline can be established and a subsequent level taken postseizure, an elevated level would be more suggestive of a true seizure.

The primary diagnostic tool in evaluating seizures is EEG. EEG coupled with clinical findings is likely to distinguish between generalized and localization-related (partial) seizures. Epileptiform EEG patterns (spikes and sharp waves) are characteristic of epileptic seizures. Although only 29% to 50% of patients with epilepsy show abnormalities on the first EEG, multiple testing yields abnormal findings in 59% to 92% of patients. This is increased with the use of sleep EEG and sleep deprivation–induced procedures.

When structural brain disorders are suspected (often based on the finding of localization-related seizures), MRI and other specialized imaging procedures may be helpful. MRI is usually more sensitive than computed tomography (CT) in uncovering cerebral lesions as causes of epilepsy.[23] Positron-emission tomography (PET) may demonstrate abnormalities in about 70% of patients with temporal lobe epilepsy.[24] However, its use is probably more valuable for research purposes because it is generally unavailable and does not provide information beyond that gained from other imaging techniques.

MANAGEMENT

If the patient is having a seizure, based on a knowledge of the most common seizure types, quickly determine intervention needs based on recommendations from the Epilepsy Foundation of America (see Table 19–1).

If the patient is not having a seizure but has had a past diagnosis of epilepsy, review the history to determine whether the patient has had a full evaluation to differentiate between nonepileptic and epileptic seizures. If the patient has had a recent episode that has not been evaluated prior to presentation in your office, obtain a thorough history to determine any indicators of seizure type and refer the patient with your recommendations. If the patient wants chiropractic care, it is important to comanage the case with the prescribing physician to avoid patient misinterpretation and resultant changes in medication schedule.

The majority of epileptic cases are managed with medication. Those that are unresponsive and fit other criteria may be successfully treated with a variety of surgical procedures. The only predictors of seizure intractability are short-term unresponsiveness to medication, history of status epilepticus, and an initially high seizure frequency.[25] Most cases will resolve over time. The debate is whether the resolution is due to medication or the natural history. Some studies indicate that when epilepsy was untreated or minimally treated in some societies, the remission or inactivity rate was quite high (44%).[26,27] With medical care, about 50% of children on medication for 2 years will remain seizure free with gradual withdrawal of the drug(s) over a period of 6 weeks to 1 year. In 4 years, this rate increases to 70%.[28] Those who do not have remission over time are usually patients for whom the following factors apply[29]:

- there is a high frequency of seizures
- there was a long period of time before medical therapy was initiated or before the seizures could be controlled through medication
- there are associated neurologic problems such as mental retardation

The major concern with medical management of epilepsy are the chronic effects on psychomotor and cognitive function.[30] Two drugs in particular are of concern with long-term usage, phenytoin and phenobarbital. With phenytoin, gum hyperplasia, hirsutism, and coarsening of the fasciae are known effects. With phenobarbital, hyperkinesis, reduction of attention span, and learning and memory impairment are concerns.[31] Fewer side effects are found with single-drug therapy and (especially with children) use of carbamazepine and sodium valproate. The specific prescription must account for several other variables, however, including seizure type, age of patient, ability to control with one medication, and other concomitant systemic or neurologic disorders (other medications, diabetes, other diseases).

Another concern with antiepileptic medication is the risk to pregnant patients of having malformed infants. Although 90% of all pregnancy outcomes are unremarkable, the remaining 10% are abnormal and may be attributed to the possible teratogenic effect of seizure medication.[32] Unfortunately, none of the four major medications has been identified as the single culprit. Suggestions for pregnant epileptics are to seek monotherapy drug treatment at the lowest effective dosage and to adhere to a diet with adequate amounts of folate (or supplement).

For intractable childhood seizures, a diet developed in the 1920s, referred to as the ketogenic diet, may be of benefit. This radical diet is almost the antithesis of the "healthy" diet. A ketogenic approach consists of a diet high in fat and low in protein and carbohydrate.[33] The success rate in intractable patients is reported to be as high as 67%. These are patients in whom drug therapy was not effective. Apparently the diet must be strictly adhered to for long periods of time for the effect to be significant.

Surgery is reserved for a special subgroup of epileptic patients. If it appears that the cortical area that is the cause of the seizure is identifiable and that surgical excision can safely remove this epileptogenic region without significant neurologic impairment, surgery may be an option. Most often these patients will be those with complex partial seizures and unilateral temporal lobe seizures. The procedures vary; however, the three most common procedures are cortical resection, corpus callosotomy, and "functional" cerebral hemispherectomy. With correct patient selection, about half of patients remain seizure free while another quarter or more have a significant reduction in seizure activity.[34]

Debate over the recommendations for driving privileges will continue. In 1994, the Joint Commission on Drivers' Licensing of the International Bureau for Epilepsy and the International League Against Epilepsy made joint recommendations.[35] They recommended against physicians' being required to report all cases of epilepsy. They suggested an individual case-by-case assessment with the general recommendation that there be a seizure-free period of 1 to 2 years. However, they felt that physicians should report those patients whom they believe pose a danger to themselves and to public safety.

Algorithm

An algorithm for evaluation and management of seizure is presented in Figure 19–1.

Figure 19–1
SEIZURE—ALGORITHM.

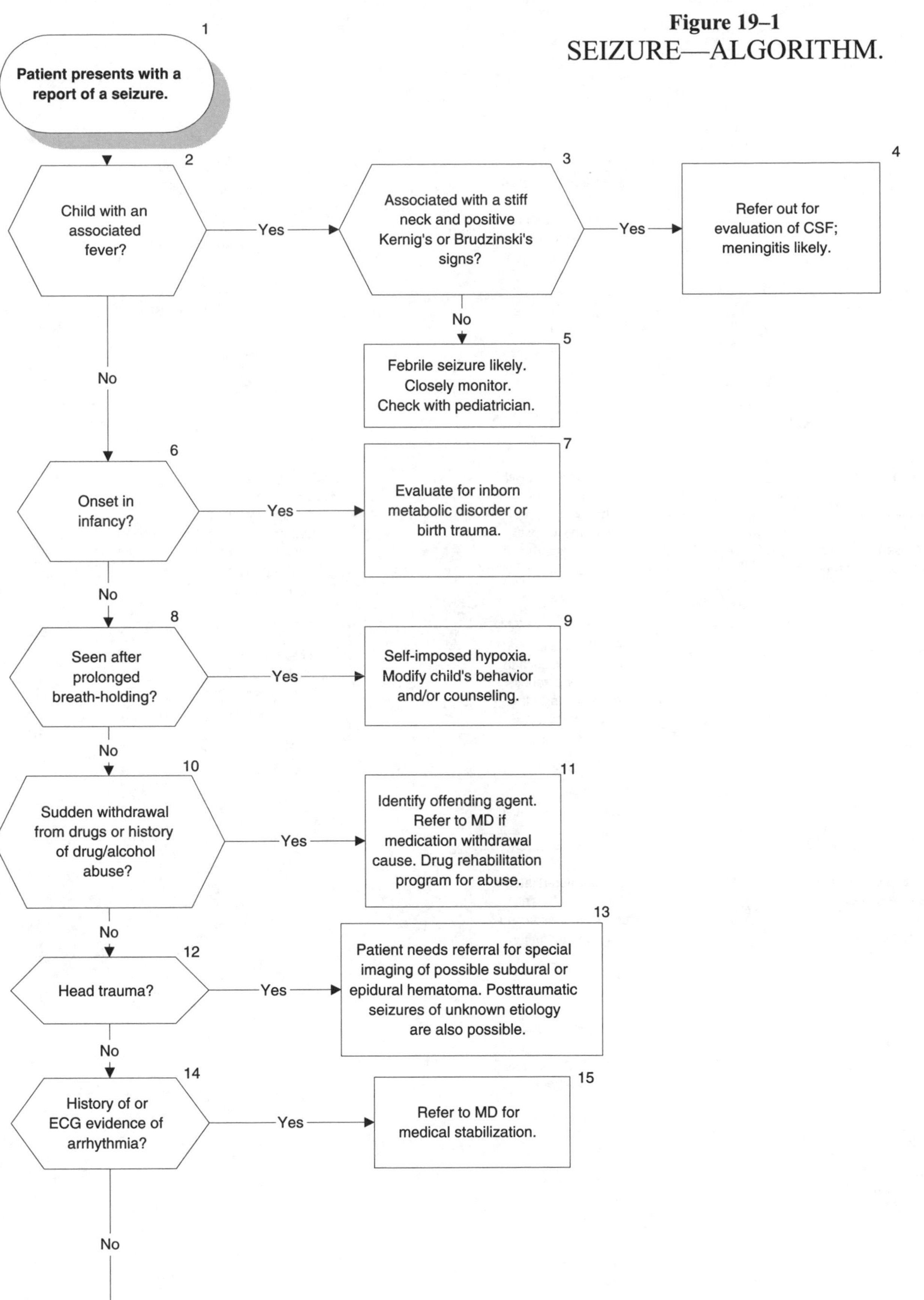

continues

Figure 19–1 continued

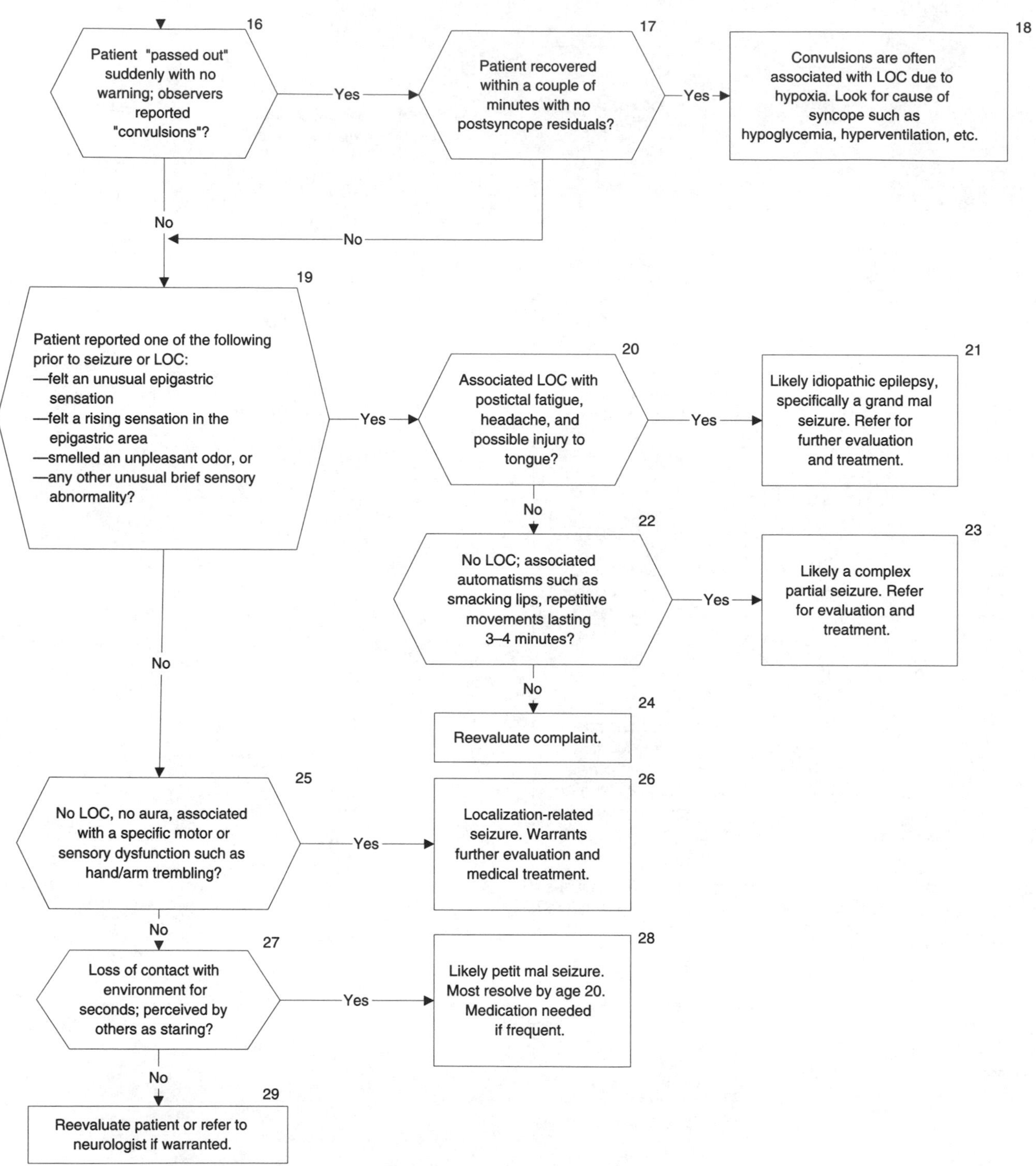

Key: ECG, electrocardiogram; CSF, cerebrospinal fluid.

REFERENCES

1. Betts T. Pseudoseizures: Seizures that are not epilepsy. *Lancet.* 1990;336:163–164.
2. Cockerell OC, Eckle I, Goodridge DM, Sander JW, Shorwon SD. Epilepsy in a population of 6,000 reexamined: secular trends in first attendance rates, prevalence, and prognosis. *J Neurol Neurosurg Psychiatry.* 1995;58:570–576.
3. Hauser WA, Annegers JF, Kurland LT. Incidence of epilepsy and unprovoked seizures in Rochester, Minnesota: 1935–1984. *Epilepsia.* 1993;34:453–468.
4. Hauser WA, Headorffer DC. *Epilepsy: Frequency, Causes and Consequences.* New York: Epilepsy Foundation of America; 1990.
5. Ettinger AB. Structural causes of epilepsy: tumors, cysts, stroke, and vascular malformations. *Neurol Clin.* 1994;12:41–56.
6. Hauser WA. The prevalence and incidence of convulsive disorders in children. *Epilepsia.* 1994;35(suppl):2P:S1–6.
7. Begley CE, Annegers JF, Lairson DR, Reynolds TF, Hauser WA. Cost of epilepsy in the United States: a model based on incidence and prognosis. *Epilepsia.* 1994;35:1130–1143.
8. Hart YM, Sanders JWAS, Johnson AL, et al. National General Practice Study of Epilepsy: recurrence after a first seizure. *Lancet.* 1990;336:1271–1274.
9. Proposal for revised classification of epilepsies and epileptic syndromes: Commission on Classification and Terminology of the International League Against Epilepsy. *Epilepsia.* 1989;30:389–399.
10. Aicardi JM, Chevrie JJ. Convulsant status epilepticus in infants and children: a study of 239 cases. *Epilepsia.* 1970; 111:187–197.
11. Betts T. Pseudoseizures: seizures that are not epilepsy. *Lancet.* 1990;336:163–164.
12. Hauser WA. Status epilepticus frequency: etiology and neurological sequelae. *Adv Neurol.* 1983;34:3–13.
13. Smith MC. Febrile seizures: recognition and management. *Drugs.* 1994;47:933–944.
14. Monetti VC, Granieri E, Casetta I, et al. Risk factors for idiopathic generalized seizures: a population-based case control study in Copparo, Italy. *Epilepsia.* 1995;36:224–229.
15. Konishi T, Naganuma Y, Hongo K, et al. Seizure inducing factors in patients with childhood epilepsy. *No To Hattatsu.* 1992;24:238–243.
16. Hordt M, Haverkamp W, Oberwittler C, et al. The idiopathic QT syndrome as the cause of epilepsy and nonepileptic seizures. *Nervenarzt.* 1995;66:282–287.
17. Rosenstein DL, Nelson JC, Jacobs SC. Seizures associated with antidepressants: a review. *J Clin Psychiatry.* 1993;54:289–299.
18. Betts T, Boden S. Diagnosis, management, and prognosis of a group of 128 patients with non-epileptic attack disorder, II: Previous childhood sexual abuse in the aetiology of these disorders. *Seizure.* 1992;1:27–32.
19. Quirk JA, Fish DR, Smith SJ, et al. First seizures associated with playing electronic screen games: a community-based study in Great Britain. *Ann Neurol.* 1995;37:733–773.
20. Lipton RB, Ottman R, Ehrenberg BL, Hauser WA. Comorbidity of migraine: the connection between migraine and epilepsy. *Neurology.* 1994;44(suppl 7):S28–S32.
21. Septien L, Pelletier JL, Brunote F, Giroud M, Dumas R. Migraine in patients with history of centrotemporal epilepsy in childhood: a Hm-PAO sPECT study. *Cephalalgia.* 1991;11:281–284.
22. Rao ML, Stefan H, Bauer J. Epileptic but not psychogenic seizures are accompanied by simultaneous elevation of serum pituitary hormones and cortisol levels. *Neuroendocrinology.* 1989;49:33–39.
23. Theodore WH, Dorwan R, Holmes M, et al. Neuroimaging in refractory partial seizures: comparison of PET, CT, and MRI. *Neurology.* 1986;36:750–759.
24. Henry TR, Engel JM, Marziotta JC. PET studies of functional cerebral anatomy in human epilepsy. In: Meldrum BS, Ferrendelli JA, Wieser HG, eds. *Anatomy of Epileptogenesis.* London: John Libbey; 1988;155–178.
25. Sillampaa M. Remission of seizures and predictors of intractability in long-term follow-up. *Epilepsia.* 1993;34:930–936.
26. Placencia M, Sander JW, Roman M, et al. The characteristics of epilepsy in a largely untreated population in rural Ecuador. *J Neurol Neurosurg Psychiatry.* 1994;57:320–325.
27. Watts AE. The natural history of untreated epilepsy in a rural community in Africa. *Epilepsia.* 1992;33(3):464–468.
28. Thurston JH, Thurston DL, Hixon BB, Keller AJ. Prognosis in childhood with epilepsy: additional follow up of 148 children 15 to 23 years after withdrawal of anti-convulsant therapy. *N Engl J Med.* 1982;306:831–836.
29. Emerson R, D'Souza BJ, Vining EP, et al. Stopping medication in children with epilepsy: predictors of outcome. *N Engl J Med.* 1983;304:1125–1129.
30. American Academy of Pediatrics Committee on Drugs. Behavioral and cognitive effects of anticonvulsant therapy. Elk Grove Village, IL: American Academy of Pediatrics; 1985;76:644–647.
31. Stores G. Behavioral effects of antiepileptic drugs. In: Nelson KB, Ellenberg JH, eds. *Febrile Seizures.* New York: Raven Press; 1981:185–192.
32. Delgado-Escueta AV, Janz D. Consensus guidelines: preconception counseling, management, and care of the pregnant woman with epilepsy. *Neurology.* 1992;42(suppl 5):149–160.
33. Kinsman SL, Vining EP, Quaskey SA, et al. Efficacy of the ketogenic diet for intractable seizure disorders: a review of 58 cases. *Epilepsia.* 1992;33:1132–1136.
34. Engel J Jr, ed. *Surgical Treatment of the Epilepsies.* New York: Raven Press; 1987:553–571.
35. Fisher RS, Parsonage M, Beaussart M, et al. Epilepsy and driving: an international perspective. Joint Commission on Drivers' Licensing of the International Bureau for Epilepsy and the International League Against Epilepsy. *Epilepsia.* 1994;35:675–684.

PART III

General Concerns

CHAPTER 20

Depression

CONTEXT

Depression is thought of by most individuals as a reaction to an unfortunate and emotionally painful occurrence in one's life. However, this is not the clinical entity referred to as major depression. The physician expecting his or her patients to complain of depression or to account for a "sad" feeling with a cause-and-effect narrative will miss the diagnosis in many cases. Almost half of adult patients with a major depression are not diagnosed by their primary care physician. It is obvious that it is difficult to diagnose a disorder for which one does not understand the criteria. Patients with a major depressive disorder will account for between 5% and 13% of patients seen in a primary care setting[1] (Zung[2] reports this estimate as high as 30% of patients). Approximately 25% of women and 10% of men will experience depression at some time in their lives.

Chiropractors may feel that depression is outside their scope of practice. The chiropractor, however, can play an important role in developing a diagnostic impression of depression and perform an appropriate referral. It may be that the treatment of major depression is the domain of the medical specialist, but comanagement may be appropriate when associated with musculoskeletal complaints. More important, when treating a depressed patient for a musculoskeletal complaint, the outcome of treatment may be seriously affected by underlying depression.

Depression has a major impact on the quality of life and the productiveness of the individual. Suicide is more common in depressed patients, with a suicide rate eight times that of the general public.[3] The societal impact of depression can be enormous. The annual indirect and direct costs of depression have been estimated at $44 billion.[4]

GENERAL STRATEGY

History and Evaluation

- Ask the patient about mood disturbance: feeling "blue," "sad," "low," "not right."
- Determine whether the patient can associate a life event with this feeling, such as loss of a loved one, moving, divorce, leaving home, getting married, or occupational or school stress.
- If depression is suspected, screen with questions regarding sleep disturbances, appetite changes, energy level, and loss of interest in previously enjoyed activities.
- Observe all patients for suggestive signs in appearance, behavior, and thought content.
- Determine any past history or family history of mental illness and any past suicide attempts.
- Determine whether there are any current medical conditions that have been diagnosed. Some disorders associated with depression include rheumatoid arthritis, multiple sclerosis, chronic heart conditions, AIDS, and Parkinson's disease.
- Determine whether the patient has given birth within the last year.
- Obtain a thorough drug history. Some drugs that may cause affective changes are glucocorticoids, anabolic corticosteroids, oral contraceptives, antihypertensives (especially methyldopa, guanethidine, and clonidine), H_2 antagonists such as cimetidine, anticonvulsants, antiparkinsonian drugs, and digitalis. Always investigate the possibility of alcohol abuse (CAGE questions, discussed later). Always check for use of any stimulants; they may cause depression upon withdrawal.

- Consider using a questionnaire for patients suspected of having depression. Choose from the Beck Depression Inventory (BDI), Center for Epidemiologic Studies Depression Scale (CES-D), or the Zung Self-Rating Depression Scale (SDS).

Management

- Patients who appear to have a reactive depression should be referred for counseling if the depression appears to be disabling or causing a major disruption in job performance.
- Patients who appear to have a major depressive disorder, bipolar disorder, or mood disorder secondary to another illness or drug or alcohol abuse should be referred for medical evaluation and management of the depression.

TERMINOLOGY AND CLASSIFICATION

The terminology and criteria used to describe mental illness may be confusing. Terminology is often updated with new terminology; however, the older terminology is still used. Many psychologic disorders are overlapping, making distinct diagnosis difficult. An attempt at standardization has been made by the American Psychiatric Association (APA) through a task force that has provided updated classification and criteria for mental disorders in a manual called *Diagnostic and Statistical Manual of Mental Disorders* (DSM). The fourth (latest) edition (DSM-IV) was published in 1994.[5]

Depression fits under a broad category of mood disorders characterized by disturbances in emotional, behavioral, cognitive, and somatic function. Depression is further divided into the following main types:

- adjustment disorders with depressed mood
- depressive disorders
- bipolar disorders
- organic mood disorders

Adjustment Disorders

Adjustment disorder is the new terminology for what was called exogenous, reactive, or situational depression. This is a common occurrence when a stressful life situation such as moving, divorce, job stress, or physical illness is "reacted to" with depression. This is considered a maladaptive reaction when the degree of response and type of response are out of proportion to the stressor. Depression is usually mild and lacks some of the diagnostic criteria for major depression.

Another similar type of depression is bereavement or grief reaction. Although it is a normal reaction to be depressed at the loss of a loved one, there appears to be a natural course of incapacitation that does not usually exceed 6 months. A prolonged grief reaction is disabling for more than 6 months. The patient demonstrates signs of a major depression disorder (loss of sleep, loss of weight, overwhelming sadness with crying, and isolation from friends/relatives) indicating the need for medication and psychotherapy.

Depressive Disorders

Depressive disorders are divided into major depression disorders (MDD) and dysthymia. Major depression may occur as a single episode or recurrently. The hallmark of MDD is a major depressive episode (MDE). Major depression is believed to be due to an imbalance in neurotransmitters, possibly genetically determined. The diagnostic criteria for MDE require that an individual experience a minimum of five out of nine symptoms almost continuously for 2 weeks; the nine symptoms are as follows:

1. depressed mood that lasts most of the day, often worse in the morning; felt by the individual or observed by others
2. loss of interest in previously enjoyable activities; unable to have fun, disinterest in sex, or previously enjoyed hobbies
3. disturbed appetite or change in weight; involuntary loss of more than 5% of weight in a 1-month period
4. fatigue or loss of energy felt every day
5. disturbed sleep indicated by insomnia or hypersomnia; the classic pattern is terminal insomnia—the person wakes up several hours early and cannot get back to sleep
6. psychomotor retardation or agitation
7. feelings of guilt, worthlessness, or self-reproach
8. suicidal thoughts or focus on death
9. inability to concentrate or make decisions

The major required criteria are depressed mood and loss of interest or pleasure in life. The criteria are also exclusive in that the patient must also not have an underlying secondary cause such hypothyroidism, drug effect, stress at work, another mental illness, or bereavement. An MDE is also seen with bipolar disorders.

Dysthymia is a more chronic condition in which many of the same symptoms for MDE are present in a more mild form for at least 2 years in adults or 1 year in children and adolescents. Other types of major depression are seasonal affective disorder (SAD) and postpartum depression.[6] SAD appears to be a dysfunction of circadian rhythms occurring more frequently in the winter. These patients respond to full-spectrum light. Postpartum depression must be differentiated from postpartum blues. Within the first month postdelivery there are large fluctuations of hormones in the mother. This may lead to periods of sadness and emotional lability; however, it is self-resolving within weeks. Postpartum depression, however, is more likely to occur months or a year after delivery and is characterized by thoughts about harming the baby or feelings of incompetence with regard to taking care of the infant. This disorder may occur in varying degrees in approximately 20% of pregnancies. Postpartum depression is possibly more related to neurotransmitter imbalance than hormonal imbalance and requires medical management.

Bipolar Disorders

Bipolar disorders are often alternating episodes of depression and mania. Manic episodes are characterized by feelings of elation or euphoria, overactivity, constant offerings of plans or new ideas, and easy distractibility. Although these are not inherently bad traits, the individual is prone toward lability with regard to mood, becoming easily agitated. Quick decisions and commitments are often regretted and abandoned, leaving a track of alienated friends and relatives. The onset of bipolar disorders is generally at an earlier age than unipolar depression. Spring and summer appear to be periods when manic episodes surface. When the cycle of mania and depression occurs four or more times per year, the patient is referred to as a "rapid cycler." Substance abuse is often found in manic depressives in an attempt to keep the "highs" of the disorder.

Like major depression, bipolar disorders may manifest as a milder, yet more chronic dysfunction. For manic depression this is called a cyclothymic disorder. Like dysthymia, the symptoms are milder, yet are constant for a period of 2 years.

Organic Mood Disorders

Organic mood disorders have an identifiable cause. The major categories are concurrent illness and medication induced. Many illnesses, especially chronic illnesses, can cause depression. Disorders such as rheumatoid arthritis, multiple sclerosis, cancer, AIDS, Parkinson's disease, and chronic heart disorders are commonly associated with depression. Depression may also occur in response to hormonal changes.

Drugs are an important cause of depression. Drugs may cause depression as part of normal usage or as part of a substance abuse pattern. Common medications that have been noted as potential causes of depression are corticosteroids, oral contraceptives, antihypertensives, antiparkinsonian drugs, and digitalis. All stimulant drugs potentially can cause a limited cycle of depression associated with withdrawal, including caffeine.

EVALUATION

The Agency for Health Care Policy and Research (AHCPR) has through the Depressive Guideline Panel developed the *Clinical Practice Guidelines: Depression in Primary Care.*[7] A suggested approach to diagnosis and management is given. The focus of the AHCPR approach is detection of depression via a systematic evaluation that begins with a patient's appearance, behavior, and thought process and content. Therefore, both examination and history are occurring simultaneously in the evaluation of depression.

History

It is important for primary care or first-contact physicians to be cognizant of the symptoms of depression. Suspicion should be raised when a patient presents with multiple complaints, especially if these include complaints of coexisting mild headaches, dizziness, chest pains, and multiple joint pains. Depression is more common in women and in those who are single, divorced, or separated or who have a serious disease or a personal or family history of depression.[8] It is equally important to realize that patients may not voluntarily report the symptoms of depression, and a subtle fishing expedition is often needed. The characteristic indicators are mood depression and a loss of enjoyment of activities that used to be enjoyable (anhedonia). While interviewing the patient, statements indicating a sense of guilt or worthlessness may surface. The patient may also be slow to respond and have difficulty concentrating or even remembering information. This has led to the term *pseudodementia,* which should be considered as an alternative to Alzheimer's disease as a cause of "forgetfulness" in the elderly.

When depression is suspected, a distinction among the various types should be made when possible. Questions regarding life stressors such as relationships and occupation are good beginning points. Common causes include loss of a loved one, postpartum periods, moving, leaving home, performance expectations at work, loss of money/property, and being a victim of abuse or violence. Reactions to these adverse situations may become overreactive or prolonged, requiring psychologic counseling, or evolve into major depression requiring medical care.

In looking for secondary causes, it is important to ask about coexisting disease and to perform a review of systems to determine the possibility of an undiagnosed condition. Questioning regarding substance or alcohol abuse is important. The CAGE questionnaire[9] should be considered if alcohol abuse is suspected. It includes the following questions:

- Have you ever felt you ought to **C**ut down on your drinking?
- Have people **A**nnoyed you by criticizing your drinking?
- Have you ever felt bad or **G**uilty about your drinking?
- Have you ever had a drink first thing in the morning to steady your nerves or get rid of a hangover (**E**yeopener)?

A medication history is important in determining a side effect of medication or a reaction from withdrawal of stimulants. An endogenous source is suggested when there are indicators for depression but no identifiable cause. A familial tendency may be evident.

Examination

The initial part of examination begins while interviewing the patient. If the patient appears to be unkempt, and if his or her movements demonstrate either a slowness or conversely restlessness or agitation, depression should be suspected.

The examination of a patient suspected of having depression is largely a search for underlying, secondary causes. Thyroid screening may be appropriate when physical signs and history are supportive. Also, anemia, vitamin deficiency, cancer, or endocrine disorders may be unmasked by appropriate laboratory examination.

MANAGEMENT

The following are suggestions with regard to suspected depression. When the depression appears to be a reaction to an outside stressor and the symptoms are prolonged or acute, psychologic counseling is warranted. If the depression appears to be the result of a medication, referral to the prescribing physician is imperative with a letter of explanation. When the cause is a secondary disorder, referral to the primary physician, if already diagnosed, is needed. If undiagnosed but suspected, referral to the appropriate specialist is necessary for proper management. If the suspected problem is major depression or manic depression, referral to a psychologist first may facilitate the referral to a psychiatrist. Many patients are reluctant to see a psychiatrist immediately.

Medical management is dictated by the type of depression. The types of management include psychotherapy, pharmacologic therapy, electroconvulsive shock therapy, and light therapy. Drug therapy alone is not a complete treatment for depression. Some form of psychotherapy should be combined with drug therapy or used as an initial approach with dysthymia. Psychotherapy approaches vary; however, the intention is to provide a supportive environment for management of the emotional component of dealing with depression. Cognitive and behavioral therapists use a directed approach, guiding the patient through assignments that target negative behavior and help direct appropriate responses.

Psychoanalytic approaches attempt to focus the patient's attention on the past in order to interpret his or her current feelings in the context of his or her whole life experience.

Pharmacologic approaches fall into several broad categories of medications:

- tricyclic antidepressants such as amitriptyline
- selective serotonin reuptake inhibitor (SSRI) such as fluoxetine (Prozac)
- monoamine oxidase (MAO) inhibitors
- lithium
- antianxiety drugs

For major depression without mania, most physicians will begin with a single tricyclic medication. It takes a minimum of 3 to 4 weeks and as much as 6 to 8 weeks for the medication to be effective. If not effective, a second tricyclic or SSRI is used. Failing a response, MAO inhibitors are the next course of care. Antidepressants do work in approximately 80% of cases. The argument against drug therapy is that major depression may resolve without therapy in 6 to 12 months. Therefore, in those cases, drug therapy is simply assisting the person through a very difficult emotional period. Given that major depression may be self-resolving, it is recommended that the prescribing physician gradually reduce medication starting 6 to 12 months after symptoms have resolved. It should be noted that sexual dysfunction may be a side effect with many antidepressant medications.

It is not unusual for a patient with a depressive disorder to have accompanying anxiety or a panic disorder. Up to 20% of patients with an MDD have a panic disorder. The panic disorder precedes MDD in about half of cases. It appears that these individuals are less responsive to therapy and are more prone to suicide attempts. Antianxiety drugs are often used as an adjunct to antidepressant medication. For patients with manic depression, the standard medication is lithium.

Electroconvulsive shock therapy, although sounding barbaric, is often an effective, painless approach to recalcitrant, disabling depression. The patient is anesthetized for a short time while the shock therapy is administered. The most common side effect is some memory loss.

REFERENCES

1. Coulehan JL, Schulber HC, Block MR, et al. Medical cormorbidity of major depressive disorder in a primary medical practice. *Arch Intern Med*. 1990;150:2363–2367.
2. Zung WWK. Prevalence of depressive symptoms in primary care. *J Fam Pract*. 1993;37:337.
3. Monk M. Epidemiology of suicide. *Epidemiol Rev*. 1987;9:51–68.
4. Greenberg PE, Stiglin LE, Finkelstein SN, Berndt ER. The economic burden of depression in 1990. *J Clin Psychiatry*. 1993;54: 405–418.
5. American Psychiatric Association. *Diagnostic and Statistical Manual of Mental Disorders*. 4th ed. Washington, DC: APA; 1994:339–345.
6. Rosenthal NE. Diagnosis and treatment of seasonal affective disorder. *JAMA*. 1993;270:2717.
7. Agency for Health Care Policy and Research. *Clinical Practice Guidelines: Depression in Primary Care*. Bethesda, MD: National Institutes of Health; 1993.
8. Weissman MM. Advances in psychiatric epidemiology: rates and risk for depressioon. *Am J Public Health*. 1987;77:445–451.
9. Ewing JA. Detecting alcoholism. The CAGE questionnaire. *JAMA*. 1984;252:1905–1907.

Chapter 21

Fatigue

CONTEXT

How often do patients complain of feeling tired? It may seem to many practitioners that most do most of the time. Some studies indicate as many as one out of four or five patients have a complaint of constant tiredness.[1] As a primary complaint, fatigue ranks seventh among all patient complaints in primary care. Statistically, this represents approximately 5% of patients in a primary care setting in the United States; studies in Canada indicate 7%.[2,3] Although patients often arrive self-diagnosed with chronic fatigue syndrome, it is extremely important to realize that this diagnosis is a difficult one, even for the physician; however, there are defined criteria. It is also important to note that some studies indicate that 50% to 80% of patients with chronic fatigue have a psychiatric problem, most often depression.[4]

The causes of fatigue are generally divided into organic and psychogenic. Each accounts for up to half of all cases (20% to 45% have an organic cause; 40% to 45% have a psychogenic cause).[5,6] In approximately 10% to 30% of cases, however, no cause is identified. The good news is that approximately 75% of patients improve within a 1- to 3-year period.[7,8] These are not necessarily the patients for whom a diagnosis was made. One study provided interesting insight into the psychology of the doctor-patient relationship with regard to diagnosis of chronic fatigue syndrome (CFS). Seventy-five percent of doctors were reluctant to give their patients a diagnosis of CFS because of the uncertainty of the scientific understanding of the etiology and treatment. They also feared that the diagnosis might be a self-fulfilling prophecy if patients believed they had the disorder. Patients, however, felt that the negative effects of not having a diagnosis outweighed the negative effects of the diagnosis of CFS.[9]

GENERAL STRATEGY

History

Determine what the patient means by a complaint of fatigue. Determine the following:

- Is the complaint more of tiredness (relieved by rest) as opposed to fatigue?
- Is the fatigue or tiredness disabling? Does it interfere with more than 50% of daily activities? If so, consider CFS.
- Consider the timing of the fatigue or tiredness. If felt more in the morning it is suggestive of a functional cause; if it is worse as the day progresses it is more suggestive of a physiologic cause.
- If the sense of fatigue is felt only with exertion, a physiologic cause is suggested.
- Determine the patient's typical daily schedule, including eating habits, work habits, and sleep habits (not enough or interrupted sleep, skipping breakfast, drinking large amounts of coffee in the morning, a large lunch, alcohol consumption during the day, athletic training schedule is excessive, etc.).
- Are there any signs of infection such as fever, upper respiratory symptoms such as sore throat or cough?
- Is the patient taking medication(s)?
- Have there been any past diagnoses for the fatigue by any other physicians?
- Are there signs or symptoms suggestive of endocrine disorders such as thyroid problems, diabetes, cancer, anemia, or depression?
- Consider the use of a depression questionnaire if suspected.

Evaluation

- Based on the history, perform a focused examination.
- Order laboratory studies based on history and examination findings; Epstein-Barr testing is not recommended.

Management

- Management is based on the underlying cause.
- Half of all cases of CFS will self-resolve in 2 years; supportive advice and recommendations involve diet, rest, and exercise.
- Patients suspected of endocrine or oncologic causes should be referred to the appropriate specialist.
- For anemia, see Chapter 53.

GENERAL DISCUSSION

The more common causes of tiredness and fatigue are usually easily recognized by patients. These include strenuous activity, lack of sleep, flu, pregnancy, and overwork. Often, though, patients do not associate fatigue with stress. Although the first list illustrates situations of increased demand or lack of rest (physiologic), stress borders the categories of physiologic and functional causes. Physiologic stress is often more acute, and therefore, more easy to associate to a specific cause. Functional or psychologic causes are often without an identifiable match (Exhibit 21–1).

CFS is a popular label for patients who feel fatigued or who have no other identifiable cause for their complaint. There are, however, specific criteria that may help separate CFS as a cause.[10,11] The case definition requires that the patient have a "new" onset of fatigue (not lifelong). This is not the result of ongoing exertion nor is it substantially relieved by rest. The sense of fatigue causes a significant reduction in previous levels of occupational, educational, social, and personal activities. To fit the criteria, other symptoms such as short-term memory loss, postexertion fatigue lasting more than 24 hours, sore throat, or headache must persist for 6 months or more. These criteria alone will eliminate the majority of patients with a complaint of fatigue in an ambulatory setting. It is important to explain to patients that there is no single laboratory or physical examination finding by which to diagnose CFS.

CFS has had many names, including Epstein-Barr virus (EBV) disease, yuppie flu, neuromyasthenia, postviral fatigue syndrome, royal free disease, Iceland disease, and encephalomyelitis; it is often confused with fibromyalgia.[12] There is little support for most theories for CFS. There is no clear evidence that EBV or chronic yeast infection is the cause. Evidence does suggest a chronic immunologically mediated inflammatory process involving the central nervous system.[13] The immune response is believed to be sec-

Exhibit 21–1 Etiology of Fatigue

Acute infection: influenza, hepatitis
Chronic infection: tuberculosis, infectious mononucleosis, brucellosis, subacute infectious hepatitis, subacute bacterial endocarditis, asymptomatic urinary tract infection, hookworm, parasitic infection
Autoimmune condition: systemic lupus erythematosus, rheumatoid arthritis
Neurologic disorder: Parkinson's disease, multiple sclerosis, posttraumatic syndrome
Primary muscle disorders: polymyositis, muscular dystrophy, myasthenia gravis
Endocrine and metabolic disease: adrenal or aldosterone insufficiency, panhypopituitarism, Cushing's disease, hypothyroidism, hyperthyroidism, hypogonadism, hyperparathyroidism, hypercalcemic and hypocalcemic states, hyperaldosteronism, potassium depletion, uncontrolled diabetes mellitus, hypoglycemic states, renal insufficiency
Anemia or blood dyscrasia
Nutritional deficiency
Circulatory disorders: silent myocardial infarction, congestive heart failure, cardiomyopathy
Pulmonary insufficiency: emphysema, chronic bronchitis
Neoplastic disorders: lymphomas, carcinomas, occult tumors
Psychologic: depression, anxiety
Chronic drug intoxication
Lack of sleep

Source: Reprinted from L.J. Bowers, *Topics in Clinical Chiropractic*, Vol. 1, No. 1, p. 27, © 1994, Aspen Publishers, Inc.

ondary to a number of infectious and psychiatric illnesses. Interest in human herpesvirus 6 (hHV 6) is based on lymphocyte cell cultures. This finding, however, probably is not an indication of primary infection but reactivation of a latent infection.[14,15]

An association between neurally mediated hypotension (NMH) and chronic fatigue has been recognized. Initially, NMH was identified as a cause of unexplained syncope in some individuals. In one study the patients had postexertional fatigue, whereas another study tested a sample of patients who met the criteria for CFS. Both groups had an abnormal response to the upright tilt test and good response to therapy using antihypertensive medication.[16,17] The upright tilt test is designed to detect an abnormal cardiovascular reflex.

CFS and depression are related. Studies suggest that in many cases, depression precedes CFS; however, depression is found with all CFS patients. For this reason, the original criteria for CFS, which excluded patients with psychiatric disorders have been modified to include those with nonpsychotic depression, somatoform disorders, and generalized anxiety or panic disorders.[18] In one study, suicidal thoughts were found in 55% of CFS patients.[19]

Two other interesting studies should be mentioned. The first illustrates a possible relationship between hypofunctioning of the corticotropin-releasing hormone neurons and CFS. The authors suggest a central deficiency of a potent arousal-producing neuropeptide.[20] In the second study, the authors suggest that the immunosupportive role of sleep is key to the understanding of the sleepiness associated with chronic fatigue.[21] They point out that some viruses cause excessive sleepiness and postulate that some infections may cause a dysfunction in the sleep/wakefulness cycle.

EVALUATION

History

The initial focus of the history is to determine exactly what the patient means by a complaint of fatigue. Patients may describe their complaint as being weak, weariness, boredom, lack of energy, exhaustion, unwillingness or aversion to work, sleepiness, and dyspnea upon exertion, among others. It is important for the chiropractor to listen patiently to this explanation. Although obtaining the history is time consuming, there are often valuable clues that will lead to a more expedient diagnosis with more judicious use of laboratory testing (Table 21–1).

The key initial distinction is between organic/physiologic causes and functional/psychologic causes. In general, the history clues that would point toward a functional cause include the following:

- Fatigue or tiredness is felt more in the morning and improves as the day progresses.
- Although the patient may feel like sleeping, sleeping does not improve his or her fatigue.
- The sense of fatigue is associated with work or situations that are perceived as stressful, improvement with avoidance.
- There is a past or current history of depression, anxiety, or somatization disorder.

Clues that would point toward a physiologic cause include the following:

- Complaints of insomnia or disrupted sleep improve with napping.
- The patient feels best in the morning and feels worse with activity or as the day progresses; complaints improve with sleep.
- The patient has dyspnea or weakness on exertion.
- The patient attributes fatigue to a work or sports activity that is strenuous.
- The patient describes the fatigue as worse in the afternoon and has a history of large caffeine ingestion in the morning, a large lunch, skipped breakfast, or daytime alcohol ingestion.
- The patient is taking a medication such as anti-hypertensives, antipsychotics, chemotherapy for cancer, anticonvulsants (for seizure), tricyclic antidepressants, benzodiazepines, and antihistamines (antihistamines are the main ingredients in most over-the-counter sleep-inducing medications).
- The patient has a history of drug or alcohol abuse.

Examination

The examination focuses on a search for systemic, metabolic, or neurologic conditions that may cause fatigue. Often the symptoms elicited with the history will be suggestive of a particular system. Following are some of the more common causes with associated examination clues:

- infection—fever, lymphadenopathy, associated upper respiratory complaints such as cough, urinary tract complaints such as burning on urination, and abdominal complaints such as nausea/vomiting, abdominal pain, or diarrhea
- hypothyroidism—thyroid nodules or enlargement, coarse hair, dry skin, loss of outer third of eyebrows
- hyperthyroidism—thyroid nodules or enlargement, moist skin, fine tremor, fine hair, occasionally pretibial myxedema

Table 21–1 History Questions for Fatigue

Primary Question	*What Are You Thinking?*	*Secondary Questions*	*What Are You Thinking?*
How long have you had a sense of fatigue?	Fatigue of recent onset is more likely physiologic and/or transient.	Have you had the fatigue for longer than 6 months and does it significantly affect your performance of daily activities?	More likely CFS unless other condition has been diagnosed.
(For more recent onset) Are you taking any medications?	Medications may be the cause or may be prescribed for an underlying disorder that can cause fatigue.	Are you taking antidepressants, antiseizure medicine, or antihistamines? Do you use illicit drugs such as cocaine?	Side effect of medications.
Does your fatigue occur only after exertion?	Physiologic cause, likely postinfectious or cardiopulmonary.	Have you had a recent infection that included a sore throat, fever, and/or lymph node swelling?	Postinfectious; consider mononucleosis.
		Is it difficult for you to breathe while lying on your back at night?	Congestive heart failure or obesity.
		Are you a high-level athlete training multiple hours a week?	Overtraining.
Is the fatigue more a sense of tiredness in the afternoon?	Consider dietary cause or sleep disturbance.	Do you eat a large meal at lunch or have alcohol with lunch?	Postprandial hypoglycemia.
		Do you drink multiple cups of coffee in the morning but not in the afternoon?	Rebound effect of caffeine.
		Do you or your sleep partner notice any problems with sleep?	Sleep disorder.
Do you feel "blue" or depressed?	Depression.	Do you relate this feeling to a specific life event (eg, loss of a loved one)?	Reactive depression.
		Do you feel that activities that used to bring you enjoyment no longer do?	Depression.
		Have you noticed a change in eating or sleeping habits (increase or decrease in either)?	Depression.
Do you have a diagnosed condition?	Hyperthyroidism, cancer, depression, etc., cause fatigue.	Have you had a significant loss of weight over the last 6 months?	Possible cancer, especially in an older patient.
		Have you noticed a change in heat/cold tolerance, tremor, fast heart rate, or change in skin or hair?	Possible thyroid disorder.

- chronic renal failure—hypertension, cardiomegaly, edema, or pericardial friction rub
- congestive heart failure—lower leg edema, ascites, adventitial lung sounds, hepatojugular reflux, cardiomegaly
- chronic obstructive pulmonary disease—cyanosis, barrel chest, prolonged respiration, FEV_1 reduction, rhonchi, wheezes
- cancer—weight loss, blood in stool, persistent or localized lymphadenopathy
- anemia—tachycardia, conjunctival pallor, fatigue on exertion (step test), glossitis
- acquired immunodeficiency syndrome (AIDS)—persistent lymphadenopathy, muscle wasting, leukoplakia

Laboratory evaluation of a fatigued patient is often unrevealing because of the high percentage of psychologically related complaints. However, a general screen often will reveal direct or indirect signs of a physiologic cause if present. The National Institutes of Health recommended in 1991 that the following be included on an initial laboratory examination of the fatigued patient[22]:

- complete blood cell count with differential
- serum chemistries (including electrolytes, blood urea nitrogen, glucose, and creatinine)
- thyroid function tests
- antinuclear antibody (ANA) test
- urinalysis
- tuberculin (TB) skin test

The majority of the above tests are done in a standard screening laboratory; however, the ANA test, thyroid function tests, and the TB skin test are not. The expense of adding these tests should be considered, and the decision to order based on relevant historical or examination clues.

Tests that should be run if clinically indicated include the following:

- serum cortisol (Addison's disease)
- immunoglobin levels (chronic fatigue syndrome and connective tissue disorders)
- rheumatoid factor (rheumatoid arthritis)
- Lyme serology (Lyme disease in endemic areas)
- human immunodeficiency virus (HIV) antibody (AIDS)

The study did not recommend testing for EBV in evaluating a patient suspected of having chronic fatigue syndrome because 95% of adults over age 30 years have serologic evidence of a past EBV infection.[23,24] The study, however, did recommend the use of screening questionnaires for depression or other psychiatric problems (see Chapter 20).

When an underlying sleep disorder is suggested, referral to a sleep laboratory for confirmation is needed to determine the degree of involvement. Many patients feel they sleep poorly; however, they are demonstrated to sleep adequately with a sleep laboratory investigation.

MANAGEMENT

Management of fatigue is based on an identifiable cause. When there is an obvious lifestyle factor, such as diet, work, or stress, modification is often all that is needed. The chiropractor can play a clear role in advice regarding proper diet and exercise, stress management, and avoidance of excess in alcohol and drugs. When the underlying cause is suspected to be a medication, referral to the prescribing physician with a letter of explanation is necessary. All other patients with identifiable or suspected diseases should be referred to a primary care or specialist physician for comanagement.

A number of different approaches have been used in the treatment of CFS, but there has been no consistent, reproducible benefit with any. Of note is that a study comparing immunologic therapy, psychiatric counseling, and placebo demonstrated no difference in effect among groups.[25] The literature is full of therapeutic trials using essential fatty acids,[26] magnesium,[27] liver extract-folic acid/vitamin B_{12},[28] gamma globulin,[29] and acyclovir.[30] None has demonstrated a consistent effect superior to the natural course of CFS or placebo.

Algorithm

Algorithms for evaluation and management of initial fatigue screening and organic fatigue screening are presented in Figures 21–1 and 21–2.

Figure 21–1

INITIAL FATIGUE SCREENING—ALGORITHM.

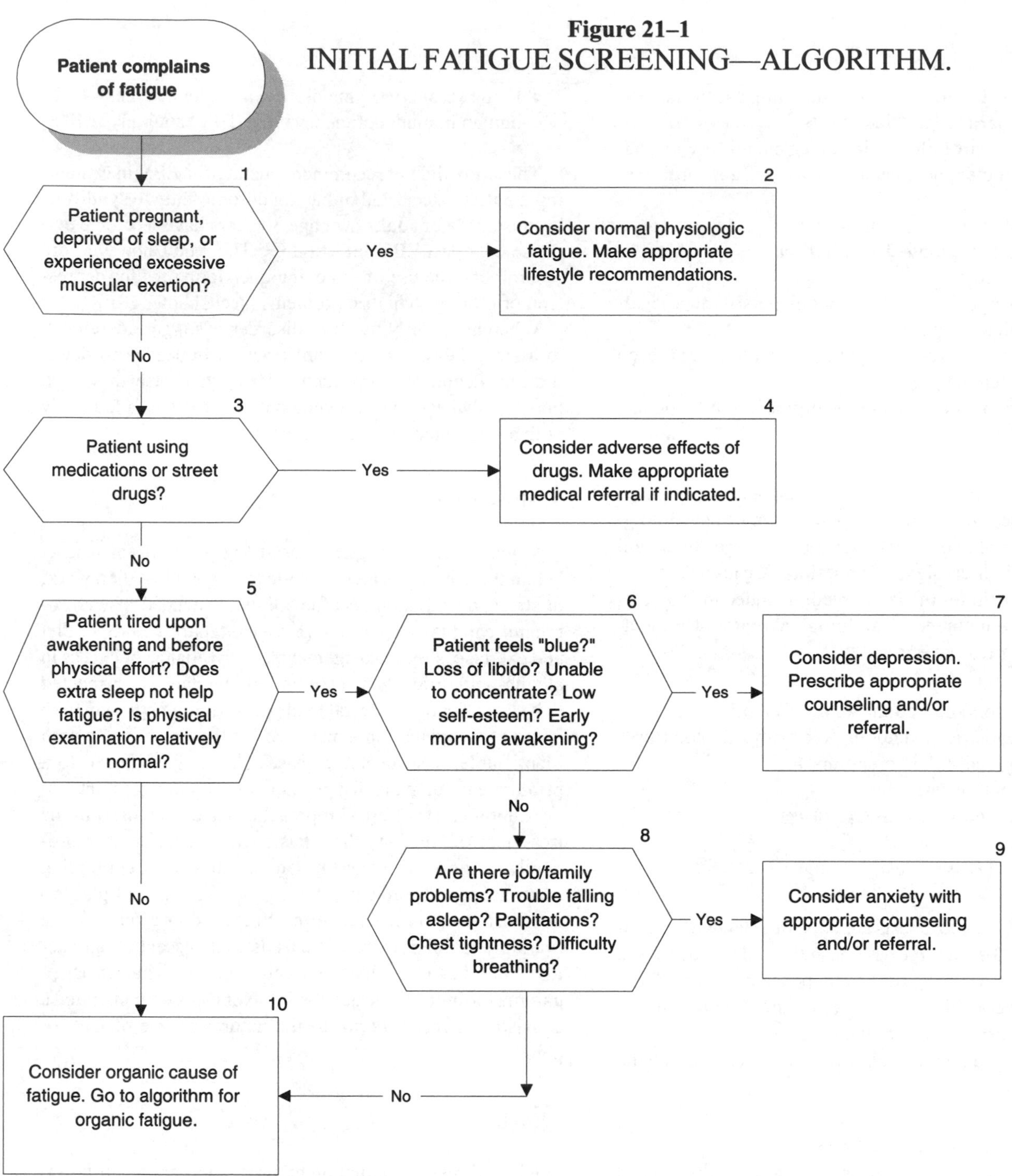

Source: Reprinted from L.J. Bowers, *Topics in Clinical Chiropractic*, Vol. 1, No. 1, p. 73, © 1994, Aspen Publishers, Inc.

Figure 21–2
ORGANIC FATIGUE SCREENING—ALGORITHM.

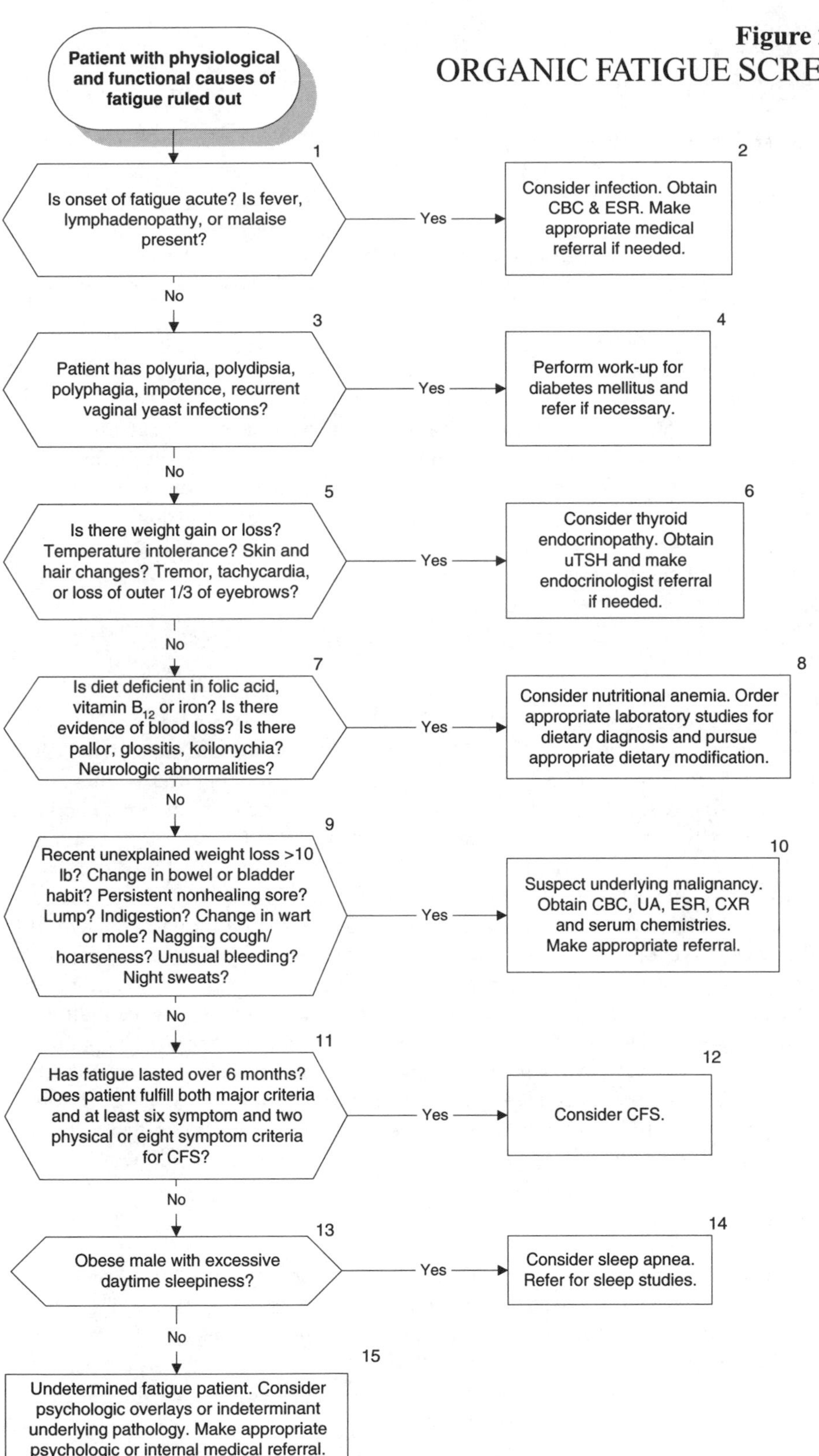

Patient with physiological and functional causes of fatigue ruled out
1
Is onset of fatigue acute? Is fever, lymphadenopathy, or malaise present?
Yes
2
Consider infection. Obtain CBC & ESR. Make appropriate medical referral if needed.
No
3
Patient has polyuria, polydipsia, polyphagia, impotence, recurrent vaginal yeast infections?
Yes
4
Perform work-up for diabetes mellitus and refer if necessary.
No
5
Is there weight gain or loss? Temperature intolerance? Skin and hair changes? Tremor, tachycardia, or loss of outer 1/3 of eyebrows?
Yes
6
Consider thyroid endocrinopathy. Obtain uTSH and make endocrinologist referral if needed.
No
7
Is diet deficient in folic acid, vitamin B_{12} or iron? Is there evidence of blood loss? Is there pallor, glossitis, koilonychia? Neurologic abnormalities?
Yes
8
Consider nutritional anemia. Order appropriate laboratory studies for dietary diagnosis and pursue appropriate dietary modification.
No
9
Recent unexplained weight loss >10 lb? Change in bowel or bladder habit? Persistent nonhealing sore? Lump? Indigestion? Change in wart or mole? Nagging cough/ hoarseness? Unusual bleeding? Night sweats?
Yes
10
Suspect underlying malignancy. Obtain CBC, UA, ESR, CXR and serum chemistries. Make appropriate referral.
No
11
Has fatigue lasted over 6 months? Does patient fulfill both major criteria and at least six symptom and two physical or eight symptom criteria for CFS?
Yes
12
Consider CFS.
No
13
Obese male with excessive daytime sleepiness?
Yes
14
Consider sleep apnea. Refer for sleep studies.
No
15
Undetermined fatigue patient. Consider psychologic overlays or indeterminant underlying pathology. Make appropriate psychologic or internal medical referral.

Key: CBC, complete blood count; ESR, erythrocyte sedimentation rate; TSH, thyroid stimulating hormone; UA, urinalysis; CXR, chest X-ray.

Source: Reprinted from L.J. Bowers, *Topics in Clinical Chiropractic*, Vol. 1, No. 1, p. 74, © 1994, Aspen Publishers, Inc.

SELECTED DISORDERS PRESENTING AS FATIGUE*

CHRONIC FATIGUE SYNDROME

Classic Presentation

The patient complains of fatigue that has persisted for several months. This is not something felt before. It is disabling enough to interfere with normal activities of daily living. Rest feels good, but does not seem to make any difference.

Cause

The cause is unknown. In the past there was a belief that a specific viral agent such as Epstein-Barr was the cause. However, there is no evidence that there is a single cause. It appears that the cause is a dysfunction in immune function, often in reaction to an acute illness. One finding that helps support this theory is the persistence of high levels of cytokines (ie, inferferons and interleukins) after a viral infection in patients with chronic fatigue.[31] Confusing the diagnostic picture is that other conditions coexist, such as fibromyalgia, depression, or other illness.

Evaluation

The diagnostic criteria have changed. The 1988 case definition was revised in 1994 to a much more abbreviated list of criteria.[11] The case definition requires that the patient have a "new" onset of fatigue (not lifelong). This is not the result of ongoing exertion nor is it relieved substantially by rest. The sense of fatigue causes a significant reduction in previous levels of occupational, educational, social, and personal activities. To fit the criteria, other symptoms, such as short-term memory loss, postexertion fatigue lasting more than 24 hours, sore throat, and headache, must persist for 6 months or more. The clinical search for other causes of fatigue involves a thorough history and evaluation for possible thyroid or adrenal disease, psychologic cause or overlay (ie, depression), somatization, Lyme disease, mononucleosis, anemia, cancer, or any chronic disease. The choice of laboratory or imaging testing is based on the suspected cause. The clinical examination can help differentiate fibromyalgia, and questionnaires may help reveal depression. Specific laboratory testing, such as a Monospot for mononucleosis, anemia panel for anemia, general screen for cancer or chronic disease, and enzyme-linked immunosorbent assay (ELISA) testing for Lyme disease, should be used only after a thorough history and examination have suggested their need. Epstein-Barr or other specific viral testing is not suggested.

Management

Fifty percent of patients will recover in 2 years.[32] During recovery several strategies may help, including a proper diet, adequate rest periods, and mild exercise. To treat the sleep dysfunction associated with CFS, low doses of tricyclic antidepressants (eg, doxepin hydrochloride [Sinequan] 10 mg/d) are prescribed. It is important to help support the patient emotionally through the illness and to manage musculoskeletal complaints when necessary.

FIBROMYALGIA

Classic Presentation

The patient is often a woman complaining of both fatigue and generalized musculoskeletal pain.

*See also Chapter 20, Depression, Chapter 51, Thyroid Disorders, and Chapter 53, Anemia.

Cause

It is believed that an interruption of stage 4 (nonrapid eye movement)) sleep due to intrusions of alpha rhythms is the underlying cause.[33]

Evaluation

The American College of Rheumatology set criteria for the diagnosis of fibromyalgia in 1990.[34] These include persistence of generalized musculoskeletal pain (both sides of the body, above and below the waist) for at least 3 months. There must also be tenderness at 11 of 18 sites (nine bilateral sites). These include the suboccipital area, the lower cervical spine (transverse processes of C5-C7), upper trapezius, supraspinatus, second rib (costochondral junction), lateral epicondyle (2 cm distal), gluteals, greater trochanter of the femur, and the medial fat pad at the knee, (proximal to the joint line). The sensitivity of this approach is 88%; specificity is 81%.[35] Other symptoms include fatigue, sleep disturbance, persistent early morning stiffness, paresthesia, and headache.

Management

Unfortunately, there is no consistent effect with any therapy. However, approximately three quarters of all patients with fibromyalgia will recover over a 1-year period.[36] It appears that the use of low-dose tricyclic antidepressants will help approximately half of patients. Although many other conservative approaches have been suggested, including the use of oral malate and magnesium, vitamin E, exercise, physical modalities, homeopathy, and manipulation, none has been demonstrated in large studies to indicate a significant difference compared with control groups.[37]

MONONUCLEOSIS

Classic Presentation

The patient is usually young (age range 10 to 35 years) and complains of fever, fatigue, and sore throat.

Cause

Infection by Epstein-Barr virus (human herpesvirus 4) is the cause of mononucleosis. It appears to be most often transmitted via saliva, with an incubation period of 5 to 15 days.

Evaluation

The patient usually has a fever, enlargement of the posterior cervical chain lymph nodes, and, in about half of cases, splenomegaly. Inspection of the throat will usually reveal an exudative pharyngitis or tonsillitis. All of the above findings may be nonspecific, yet suggest a laboratory evaluation. This may include a screen, which will reveal atypical lymphocytes, or suggest the need for specific testing including the heterophile antibody test (or the related Monospot test), which will be positive for mononucleosis. It may take several weeks after acquiring the infection for these tests to become positive, however.

Management

Management is largely palliative for most patients. The sore throat may last several weeks while the fatigue may last for 1 to 3 months. Rare complications occur in older or immunosuppressed patients and include enlargement of lymphoid tissue compromising breathing (refer for corticosteroids), hepatitis, myocarditis, or encephalitis. These select patients should be managed medically.

CHRONIC MYELOGENOUS LEUKEMIA

Classic Presentation

The patient is usually middle-aged and complains of fatigue, night sweats, and a low-grade fever.

Cause

Overproduction of myeloid cells that are capable of differentiation is due to an abnormality of the Philadelphia chromosome (reciprocal translocation of long arms of chromosomes 9 and 22).

Evaluation

The patient will have splenomegaly at some point. The diagnosis is based on laboratory findings of a markedly elevated white blood cell count (>150,000/mm^3). Blasts are less than 5% and a basophilia may be present. Uric acid levels may be elevated.

Management

The disease is eventually fatal unless the patient has a bone marrow transplant. Palliative treatment includes chemotherapy and recombinant interferon alpha. The success rate is 70% to 80% for bone marrow transplant in patients under age 40 years who have the transplant within 1 year of the diagnosis.[38]

REFERENCES

1. Buchwald D, Gantz NM, Katon WJ, Manu P. Tips on chronic fatigue sydrome. *Patient Care.* 1991;25:45–58.
2. Kroenke K, Wood DR, Mangelsdorff D, et al. Chronic fatigue in primary care. *JAMA.* 1988;260;929–934.
3. Kroenke K. Chronic fatigue: frequency, causes, evaluation, and management. *Compr Ther.* 1989;15(7):3–7.
4. Cathebras PJ, et al. Fatigue in primary care: prevention, psychiatric comorbidity, illness, behavior, and outcome. *J Gen Intern Med.* 1992;7:276.
5. Morrison JD. Fatigue as a presenting complaint in family practice. *J Fam Pract.* 1980;10:776–781.
6. Kirk J, Douglass R, Nelson E, et al. Chief complaint of fatigue: a prospective study. *J Fam Pract.* 1990;30:33–41.
7. Levine PH, et al. Clinical, epidemiologic, and virologic studies in four clusters of the chronic fatigue syndrome. *Arch Intern Med.* 1992;152:1611.
8. Elnicki DM, Schockcor WT, Brick JE, et al. Evaluating the complaint of fatigue in primary care: diagnoses and outcomes. *Am J Med.* 1992;93:303–306.
9. Woodward RV, Broom DH, Legge DG. Diagnosis of chronic illness: disabling or enabling—the case of chronic fatigue syndrome. *J R Soc Med.* 1995;88:325–329.
10. Holmes GP, Kaplan JE, Ganz NM, et al. Chronic fatigue syndrome: a working case definition. *Ann Intern Med.* 1988;108:387–389.
11. Fukuda K, Straus SE, Hickie I, et al. The chronic fatigue syndrome: a comprehensive approach to its definition and study. *Ann Intern Med.* 1994;121:953–959.
12. Shafran SD. The chronic fatigue syndrome. *Am J Med.* 1991;90: 730–739.
13. Holmes GP, Kaplan JE, Stewart JA, et al. A cluster of patients with a chronic mononucleosis-like syndrome. *JAMA.* 1987;257:2297–2302.
14. Krupp LB, Mendelson WB, Freidman R. An overview of chronic fatigue syndrome. *J Clin Psychol.* 1991;52:403.
15. Centers for Disease Control. Inability of retroviral tests to identify persons with chronic fatigue syndrome. *MMWR.* 1993;42:183.
16. Bou-Holaigah J, Rowe PC, Kan J, Calkins H. The relationship between neurally mediated hypotension and the chronic fatigue syndrome. *JAMA.* 1995;274:961–967.
17. Rowe PC, Bou-Holaigah J, Kan J, Calkins H. Is neurally mediated hypotension an unrecognized cause of chronic fatigue? *Lancet.* 1995;345:623–624.
18. Schleudelberg A, et al. Chronic fatigue syndrome research: definition and medical outcome assessment. *Ann Intern Med.* 1992;117:325–331.
19. Lane TJ, Mann P, Mathew DA. Depression and somatization in the chronic fatigue syndrome. *Ann Intern Med.* 1991;91:335.
20. Gold PW, Licino J, Wong ML, Chrousos GP. Corticotropin releasing hormone in the pathophysiology of melancholic and atypical depression and in the mechanism of action of antidepressant drugs. *Ann N Y Acad Sci.* 1995;771:716–729.

21. Pollmacher T, Mullington J, Korth C, Hinze-Selche D. Influence of host defence activation in sleep in humans. *Adv Neuroimmunol.* 1995;5:155–169.
22. Gunn WJ, et al. Epidemiology of chronic fatigue syndrome: the Centers for Disease Control study. *Ciba Found Symp.* 1993;173.
23. Sumaya SV, et al. Seroprevalence study of Epstein-Barr virus infection in a rural community. *J Infect Dis.* 1975;131:403–408.
24. Buchwald D, Sullivan JL, Kormaroff AL. Frequency of "chronic" active Epstein-Barr virus infections in general medical practice. *JAMA.* 1987;257:2303–2307.
25. Lloyd AR, Hickie I, Brockman A, et al. Immunologic and psychogenic therapy for patients with chronic fatigue syndrome: a double-blind, placebo controlled trial. *Am J Med.* 1993;94:187–203.
26. Behan PO, Behan WMH, Horrobin D. Effect of high doses of essential fatty acids on the postviral fatigue syndrome. *Acta Neurol Scand.* 1990;82:209–216.
27. Cox IM, Campbell MJ, Dowson D. Red blood cell magnesium and chronic fatigue syndrome. *Lancet.* 1991;337:757–760.
28. Kaslow JF, Rucker L, Onishi R. Liver extract-folic acid-cyanocobalamin versus placebo for chronic fatigue syndrome. *Arch Intern Med.* 1989;149:2501–2503.
29. Lloyd AR, Hickie I, Wakefield D, et al. A double-blind, placebo controlled trial of intravenous immunoglobulin therapy in patients with chronic fatigue syndrome. *Am J Med.* 1990;89:561–568.
30. Strauss SF, et al. Acyclovir treatment of the chronic fatigue syndrome. *N Engl J Med.* 1988;319:1692–1698.
31. Bates DW, Buchwald D, Lee J, et al. Clinical laboratory test findings in patients with chronic fatigue syndrome. *Arch Intern Med.* 1995;155:97–103.
32. Hicks JE, Jones JF, Renner JH, Schmaling K. Chronic fatigue syndrome: strategies that work. *Patient Care.* 1995;5:55–73.
33. Smythe H. Fibrositis syndrome: a historical perspective. *J Rheumatol.* 1989;16(suppl 9):2–6.
34. Wolfe F, Smythe HA, Yunus MB, et al. The American College of Rheumatology 1990 criteria for classification of fibromyalgia: report of the Multicenter Criteria Committee. *Arthritis Rheum.* 1990;33:160–172.
35. Bennett RM. Nonarticular rheumatism and spondyloarthropathies—similarities and differences. *Postgrad Med.* 1990;87:97–104.
36. Mitchell RI, Carmen GM. The functional restoration approach to the treatment of chronic pain in patients with soft tissue and back injuries. *Spine.* 1994;19:633–642.
37. St. Claire SM. Diagnosis and management of fibromyalgia syndrome. *J Neuromusculoskeletal Sys.* 1994;2(3):101–111.
38. Clift RA. Treatment of chronic myeloid leukemia by marrow transplantation. *Blood.* 1993;34:1954.

CHAPTER 22

Fever

CONTEXT

Although fever may not be a common presenting complaint to a chiropractic office, its presence among other signs or symptoms, or lack thereof, provides an important clue in differential diagnosis. Temperature should be measured in:

- children on an initial visit who appear to have low energy, loss of appetite, or decreased playfulness
- all patients with signs of infection or generalized inflammation
- all seniors on initial presentation

Fever of unknown origin (FUO) is a temperature greater than 101°F that is present several times over a 3-week period (undiagnosed after 1 week) or a persistent fever for 10 to 14 days that remains undiagnosed.[1] It is unlikely but possible that this scenario may present to a chiropractor's office. If so, it is important to recognize the potential seriousness of this presentation. One study estimated that approximately 41% of children with true FUO had a chronic or fatal disease.[2] The primary focus of the following discussion is on proper assessment of temperature and a generalized approach to narrow possibilities.

There are many misconceptions with regard to fever. It is important to bear in mind the following:

- Fever is a protective response and is not in and of itself bad.
- Fever does not always indicate infection.
- Although there is a reference normal temperature of 98.6°F, this does not represent a "fixed" normal.
- Fever is often regarded as a symptom; however, it is possible to feel "feverish" and not have a fever, or to feel normal and have a fever. It is also possible for someone with a fever to appear normal, sometimes even hyperactive; therefore, fever must be objectified.

The standard normal temperature of 98.6°F was established over 130 years ago by Wunderlich.[3] Recently, this has been called into question and reexamined. Mackowiak determined that the mean body temperature was not 98.6°F, but 98.2°F (close enough!).[4] More important is the recognition that there is a normal range of temperature that varies. Temperature is usually the lowest in the morning, highest in the late afternoon–early evening. This diurnal variation is as much as 1° to 1.5°F. According to Mackowiak's study, fever in young and middle-aged adults is classified as a reading at or above 37.2°C (99.0°F) in the early morning; in the evening, at or above 37.8°C (100°F). There are other normal variations that must be acknowledged, as follows:

- Women have a rise in temperature at ovulation of 0.5°F to 0.75°F due to production of progesterone. The temperature returns to the normal basal reading at the beginning of menstruation.
- Children often have an exaggerated response to infection, generating a much higher temperature than adults with the same infection or cause.
- Senior patients generally have a lower mean temperature (average of 36.2°C [97.2°F]); their response to a pyrogenic stimulator is often less remarkable than that of a younger adult; seniors often do not feel that they have a fever when, in fact, they have one.
- Exercise can raise the body temperature.

FUO is a worrisome phenomenon. Five to thirty-five percent of FUO cases go undiagnosed, with approximately 75%

of these resolving without incident (the majority having an infectious etiology).[5] However, there are still concerns. As with a standard self-remitting fever, the most common cause of FUO is infection. The most common causes are tuberculosis and endocarditis. Other common infections that may not have obvious associated signs are sinus infections and urinary tract infections. The second most common cause of FUO is neoplasms, especially leukemias, lymphomas, and solid tumors of the abdomen. Obviously, a patient with FUO must be referred for a medical evaluation to determine these potentially life-threatening and often curable disorders.

GENERAL STRATEGY

History

Screen for patients at risk, including those with a history that might suggest an infectious, inflammatory, hemorrhagic, or cancerous process.

Evaluation

- Determine the temperature using a mercury, electronic, or infrared device (rectal temperature readings are reserved for infants, or athletes suffering from hypo- or hyperthermia).
- Attempt to match other physical signs that localize to a specific organ system or process.

Management

- Refer the patient if an underlying serious process is discovered, if the fever is persistent for more than 10 days, if the fever is greater than 104°F, or if the fever is present off and on over a period of 3 weeks (FUO).
- Minor fevers (101°F or less) associated with signs of gastroenteritis, flu, or other common infections can be managed with time and monitoring; if necessary, aspirin (not for children) or acetaminophen every 4 hours is effective.
- Fevers of 102° to 104°F do not usually require treatment; however, cold sponges, ice packs, or cold baths may help in reducing body temperature.

RELEVANT PHYSIOLOGY

Phagocytic leukocytes release endogenous pyrogens (proteins) into the blood stream in response to a host of pyrogenic triggers. The endogenous proteins reach the thermoregulatory center in the anterior hypothalamus, causing the production and release of prostaglandins. The result is a new set-point for the body requiring measures to raise body temperature, including shivering and vasoconstriction. Following is a general list of conditions that may cause fever:

- infections
- connective tissue disorders
- thromboembolic hemorrhage
- various metabolic conditions
- neoplasms
- vascular events

Table 22–1 gives a more extensive list under each category. Generally, infection is the most common cause resulting in a fever that is gone within 1 week. When fever persists beyond this time frame, the other categories of disorders should be considered.

EVALUATION

Examination

Although generally the history is the starting point in evaluation, the order has been switched to emphasize the need for an accurate, consistent measurement of body temperature. The armamentarium for body temperature evaluation has expanded beyond the simple mercury thermometer.[6] Now available are mercury-in-glass, electronic, infrared, and strip thermometers. Mercury thermometers can be used orally, rectally, and in the axillary region. (The least reliable and most susceptible to variation is the axillary reading; it has largely been avoided when possible.) Oral mercury thermometers are accurate when properly used; however, readings take between 4 and 8 minutes depending on whether or not the patient is febrile. Electronic thermometers take only about 30 seconds in comparison. They also use disposable, unbreakable probe covers. The new infrared thermometers have recently become less expensive and provide an accurate measurement in a few seconds. Paper strip thermometers are convenient, but they are not considered very reliable.

The standard for medical recording is in degrees Celsius (centigrade) (C). The conversion formulas are

- degrees C = 5/9 (degrees F - 32)
- degrees F = (9/5°C) + 32

Following is a suggested technique for taking an oral temperature with a mercury thermometer:

- If the patient has just had hot or cold liquids, wait 15 minutes prior to evaluation.

Table 22–1 Causes of Fever

Infection	Autoimmune disease	Neoplasms
Bacterial	Systemic lupus erythematosus	Primary neoplasms
Viral	Polyarteritis nodosa	• Colon
Rickettsial	Rheumatic fever	• Rectum
Fungal	Polymyalgia rheumatica	• Liver
Parasitic	Giant-cell arteritis	• Kidney
Mycobacterial	Still's disease	Neuroblastoma
	Relapsing polychondritis	Liver metastasis
Hematologic	Dermatomyositis	
Lymphomas	Adult rheumatoid arthritis	**Abdominal disease**
Leukemias		Inflammatory bowel disease
Hemolytic anemias	**Cardiovascular disease**	Liver abscess
	Myocardial infarction	Alcoholic hepatitis
Endocrine disease	Pulmonary embolism	Granulomatous hepatitis
Hyperthyroidism		
Pheochromocytoma	**Central nervous system disease**	**Chemical**
	Cerebral hemorrhage	Drug reactions
Miscellaneous	Head injuries	
Sarcoidosis	Brain and spinal cord tumors	
Familial Mediterranean fever	Degenerative CNS disease	
Factitious fever	Spinal cord injury	

Source: Reprinted from Evans, R., *Topics in Clinical Chiropractic*, Vol. 2, No. 1, pp. 30–36, © 1995, Aspen Publishers, Inc.

- If the patient has just smoked, wait 2 minutes.
- Shake the thermometer down to a temperature of 35.5°C (96°F).
- Make sure the thermometer has been sterilized and/or has a disposable probe slip in place.
- Place the thermometer at the base of the tongue on either side of the posterior sublingual pockets (not in the middle of the tongue).
- Instruct the patient to keep his or her lips closed.
- Leave the thermometer in place for 3 to 4 minutes if the patient is afebrile.
- Leave the thermometer in place for up to 8 minutes if the patient is febrile.

For an infrared thermometer:

- Gently place the covered probe tip in the patient's ear.
- Do not force the thermometer into the ear or fully block the canal.
- Activate and read the temperature in approximately 2 to 3 seconds.

Rectal temperature is considered to be a more accurate measure; however, it is less convenient in most cases. When other devices are not available or when measuring for hypo- or hyperthermia, rectal temperature is preferred.

- Wear gloves.
- Lubricate the probe end of the rectal thermometer (it has a more short, blunt probe compared with the oral thermometer).
- Insert the thermometer about 1 in toward the umbilicus.
- Leave the thermometer in for 2½ minutes.
- Rectal readings are generally 0.5°C (1°F) higher than oral readings.

A factitious fever should be suspected in patients who are emotionally disturbed. These patients are often women working in health care positions. Clues to a factitious fever include the following:

- The fever is out of proportion to patient's general appearance—no loss of weight, no prostration, no sweating.
- The pulse rate does not increase proportionately with fever.
- The urine temperature does not match the rectal temperature (rectal temperature is significantly higher).

The remainder of the examination is a generalized approach looking first for clues such as the following:

- examination of the skin for patterns of lesions (and in the history a sequence of appearance) (found with common childhood diseases, venereal disease, and rheumatoid and connective tissue disorders)
- auscultation of the heart for murmurs
- auscultation of the lungs for rales
- palpation of the calves for localized swelling (thrombophlebitis)
- examination for tophi at the big toe, knees, elbows, and ears
- examination of the abdomen with a complaint of associated abdominal pain

This generalized approach should provide clues that narrow the possibilities. Further testing with laboratory, radiographs, or special studies should be justified by the history and physical exam findings.

History

Given the enormous numbers of pyrogenic stimulators, the diagnostic approach is a search for the above-listed categories. The approach is a broad-based evaluation looking for any clue that may suggest the underlying cause. It is highly unusual to have fever as the only indicator of a disease or disorder. Localizing findings by organ or system is usually revealing. See the applicable chapters of this text based on these accompanying signs or symptoms.

General indicators of a viral infection in an adult are a low-grade fever and associated general aches and pains, a headache, malaise or fatigue. An adult with a bacterial infection presents with a fever above 103°F and the general symptoms of a viral infection plus some localizing findings in the throat, abdomen, or chest. Children, on the other hand, may run high temperatures with almost any illness, including viral infections, otitis media, measles, and roseola. Very high readings (>105°F) are medical emergencies suggesting intracranial hemorrhage or tumor, pancreatitis, or a bad urinary tract infection. If the temperature remains at this elevation, significant brain damage or malignant cardiac arrhythmias may occur.

When the fever is not obviously tied to a flu or upper respiratory infection, a potential valuable avenue of questioning is recent travel within or outside the United States.[7] Certain fungal infections are endemic to specific regions of the United States. Following the same line of questioning, contact with certain animals such as birds, dogs, cats, rats or other rodents, or livestock suggests a specific infectious organism.

In the past, it was recommended to determine a time curve for fever presentation in an attempt to attach a specific diagnosis to a specific pattern of fever activity. This approach is now not considered useful as a match-type approach. The temporal sequence, however, may provide valuable clues to the underlying cause.

MANAGEMENT

There are two overlapping goals of management: (1) control for excessive fever and ensure adequate hydration and (2) treat the underlying cause if it poses a health risk to the patient. Control of fever is rarely necessary unless it reaches the range of 103° to 104°F. At this level of fever it may be necessary to use cold packs, alcohol or cold sponges, or cold baths. Generally, this level of fever is well tolerated. If medication is used it is important to give aspirin or acetaminophen every 4 hours without a break in routine. Giving it only at night may cause a reactionary occurrence of chills or sweats. It is important not to give aspirin to children, especially those with flu or chicken pox, because of the risk of Reye's syndrome (leads to brain and liver damage or death).

REFERENCES

1. Everett MT. Definition of FUO in general practice. *Practitioner*. 1977;218:388–393.
2. Kimmel SR, Gemmill DW. The young child with fever. *Am Fam Physician*. 1988;37:196–206.
3. Kluger MJ. *Fever: Its Biology, Evolution, and Function*. Princeton, NJ: Princeton University Press; 1979.
4. Mackowiak PA, Wasserman SS, Levine MM. A critical appraisal of 98.6 degrees F: the upper limit of the normal body temperature, and other legacies of Carl Reinhold August Wunderlich. *JAMA*. 1992;268:1578–1580.
5. Greenberg SB, Taber L. Fever of unknown origin. In: Mackowiak PA, ed. *Fever: Basic Mechanisms and Management*. New York: Raven Press; 1991.
6. Jarvis C. *Physical Examination and Health Assessment*. Philadelphia: WB Saunders Co; 1992:200.
7. Strickland GT. Fever in the returned traveler. *Med Clin North Am*. 1992;76:1375–1392.

Chapter 23

Sleep and Related Complaints

CONTEXT

If asked, most patients would have a complaint of disrupted sleep at some time. Often they can relate this to a specific event such as a stressful incident, alcohol ingestion, or pain. When it is a prolonged or chronic problem, the patient becomes concerned. The conscious effort to initiate sleep often may worsen the condition. It is interesting to note that underreporting is the standard for one of the most common sleep disorders: insomnia. A 1991 Gallup survey found that only 5% of insomniacs consulted a physician. Approximately 30% had mentioned it when presenting to a doctor for other complaints.

It is not always obvious what a person does or does not do during sleep. This is important when considering that the result of sleep dysfunction is excessive sleepiness often without a complaint of disrupted sleep. Instead the primary complaint is tiredness or fatigue. With excessive tiredness or fatigue, there is the obvious disruption of functional ability with daily activities; however, the larger concern is the potential danger when driving a car or operating other potentially dangerous machinery.

Although many sleep problems are transient and/or benign, when a primary sleep disorder is detected, further evaluation at a sleep laboratory is necessary to identify clearly the cause and plan for subsequent management.

GENERAL STRATEGY

History and Evaluation

- Determine whether the patient is able to describe the complaint, attempting to clarify whether the difficulty is falling asleep, constant interruption of sleep, inability to fall back to sleep after early morning awakening, "light" sleep, or other difficulty.
- Determine associated problems such as excessive daytime sleepiness.
- Determine possible causes or contributing factors, including the following:
    1. diet related—alcohol, caffeine, food allergy
    2. smoking (more than one pack per day)
    3. drugs—cocaine, over-the-counter (OTC) stimulants such as nasal sprays, abuse of OTC sleep medications, prescription drugs
    4. underlying disorders such as asthma, hypo- or hyperthyroidism, chronic obstructive pulmonary disease, congestive heart failure
    5. painful conditions (headaches; hip, knee, shoulder, low back, and/or neck pain)
    6. restless legs or muscle cramps
    7. amount of sleep, jet lag, work habits
    8. stress and possible depression
    9. moderate exercise prior to sleep
    10. past diagnosis or treatment of a psychologic/psychiatric disorder
- If the patient is presenting with a complaint of fatigue or tiredness, it may be necessary to obtain an eyewitness account of his or her sleep pattern.

Management

- If a primary sleep disorder is suspected, referral to a sleep laboratory is warranted.
- Make recommendations regarding sleep hygiene (Exhibit 23–1).
- Conservative management may be appropriate when sleep hygiene is the primary cause; however, specific

Exhibit 23–1 Sleep Hygiene

- Go to bed at a consistent time.
- Sleep in a comfortable room that is cool and free of stimulation (noise, light, restless sleep partner).
- Sleep on a comfortable bed (more firm is suggested).
- Do not eat large amounts of food prior to sleeping.
- Avoid alcohol, smoking, and caffeine prior to sleeping.
- Do not exercise heavily before sleeping.
- Avoid daytime napping.
- If focused on a bothersome mental concern, write it down and deal with it in the morning if possible.
- If unable to sleep after 30 minutes, get up and have a light snack or listen to soothing music; then return to bed.
- Avoid the use of OTC sleep medications.
- Weight reduction may be helpful to those with central sleep apnea.

sleep disorders should be referred to a specialist for management.

RELEVANT ANATOMY AND PHYSIOLOGY

Sleep is a complex interactive function coordinated by many parts of the brain. The structures that facilitate sleep include the basal forebrain, the dorsal raphe nuclei, the midline thalamus, and the area around the solitary tract in the medulla. Waking is facilitated by the reticular activating system (pons and midbrain) and the posterior hypothalamus. This interaction is dependent on changing levels of serotonin, catecholamines, acetylcholine, and a host of other neurotransmitters. During sleep there are also fluctuations of hormonal levels that may play a role in the quality of sleep and wakefulness. One example is the decrease in epinephrine and cortisol coupled with elevated histamine and other mediator levels between midnight and 4 AM. These changes correlate with worsening of asthma at night.[1]

Sleep is generally divided into two phases in relationship to changing eye movement and other electrophysiologic events: rapid eye movement (REM) sleep and non–rapid eye movement (NREM) sleep. These two distinct states cycle throughout the night at about 90-minute intervals. They are not equal, however. NREM accounts for approximately 80% of total sleep.

NREM sleep is divided into four stages. Stages 3 and 4 are referred to as delta sleep. NREM is characterized by slowing of the electroencephalogram (EEG), with accompanying muscle relaxation, and slow, rolling eye movements. EEG activity slows dramatically during stages 3 and 4. This deep sleep occurs mainly in the first few hours of sleeping. During this delta sleep, dreaming is less vivid than it is during REM. Patients awakened during delta sleep recall more thought fragments than actual dreams. Only 5% of patients recall vivid dreams.[2]

REM sleep is more analogous to wakefulness in that there is a faster EEG rate combined with an increase and variability of autonomic nervous system function. Heart rate, respiration, blood pressure, and penile erections vary widely throughout REM sleep. Peripheral voluntary muscles, however, are paralyzed with the exception of the eyelids. This accounts for the phenomenon of sleep paralysis wherein, upon wakening, an individual is temporarily not able to move. When persistent and recurrent, narcolepsy, a disorder of REM sleep, is suggested.

NREM begins first, cycling through its four stages. This is followed approximately 80 to 120 minutes later with the first REM sleep, lasting only about 5 to 10 minutes. As the night progresses, the intensity and duration of REM sleep increases to about 15 to 45 minutes. Vivid dreaming is a characteristic event of REM sleep. Given that REM sleep becomes more intense and lasts longer as the night progresses, the majority of dreaming occurs in the last few hours of sleeping.

There is a maturation phenomenon associated with time spent in REM or NREM. Newborns spend 50% of their time in REM and enter REM soon after sleep initiation.[3] The time spent in REM decreases as the newborn matures to as little as 20% by 6 months of age. The corresponding switch to an adult pattern of REM/NREM cycling begins at around 4 months and is associated with a concomitant increase in the production of melatonin. This connection between melatonin and sleep has led to the recent use of melatonin in the elderly to help "normalize" sleep. In the elderly the amount of REM remains the same; however, there is a marked decrease in deep sleep (stages 3 and 4).

CLASSIFICATION SYSTEM

The *International Classification of Sleep Disorders* has created two primary categories. Insomnias are disorders that affect the ability of the patient to fall asleep or disorders that result in excessive daytime sleepiness.[4] Insomnias are further classified by cause into intrinsic, extrinsic, and circadian. The type of disorder can be further categorized by whether it prevents the patient from falling asleep, causes difficulty falling back to sleep after early-morning awakening, or causes sleep fragmentation whereby the patient has constant interruption of sleep. Dyssomnias are disorders that interrupt sleep but do not result in excessive sleepiness during the day. These major categories do not include sleep disorders due to psychologic or other medical cause.

EVALUATION

History

- Obtain a detailed history of the patient's complaint with regard to length of the problem and any recognizable contributing lifestyle events.
- Obtain a detailed history from the sleep partner if available (personal videotaping may be feasible).

Difficulty Falling Asleep

At some time in everyone's life, difficulty falling asleep has occurred. When this is chronic, it is important to ask questions regarding lifestyle and environment. The most productive avenue of investigation is to ask what occurs prior to going to bed, such as stimulation from exercise, caffeine, smoking, alcohol, stimulating reading, nasal sprays (active ingredient is often ephedrine), argument with family member, or paying bills. If this line of questioning is unproductive, a search for daily activities may yield a possibility. Does the patient take naps; smoke more than a pack of cigarettes during the day; or take steroids, dopaminergic agents, xanthine derivatives other than caffeine (eg, theophylline for asthma), β-agonists, appetite suppressants, or decongestants?

A curious but distressing disorder is restless legs syndrome. The patient complains of a dysesthesia that is relieved only by moving the legs. In fact, the urge to move the legs is irresistible. The dysesthesia can occur as often as every 20 to 30 seconds and delay sleep well into the early morning. Because of the associated hereditary tendency, it is important to ask whether relatives experience the disorder or have been diagnosed with a similar condition.

Early Morning Awakening with Difficulty Falling Back to Sleep

Questioning directed at possible depression should be initiated with any patient who reports waking up early and not being able to get back to sleep. A quick screening question is, "Are there activities/hobbies/relationships that used to give you pleasure, events that you would look forward to, but no longer hold any interest?" If it seems that the patient has lost interest in past hobbies or activities and feels a lack of drive or energy, endogenous depression is a possible cause when associated with this pattern of sleep disturbance.

Other possibilities include drug-induced early-morning waking. This is more likely to occur with the use of some short-acting benzodiazepines. Alcohol may cause a rebound REM effect, which also will result in early-morning waking. Another condition that may manifest similarly is advanced sleep phase syndrome. This is frequently seen in the elderly.

Frequent Awakenings (Interrupted Sleep)

Secondary effects of drugs, pain, an uncomfortable environment, alcohol, abuse, or stress could all result in frequent awakenings. If a screening for the causes of these complaints is unrewarding, however, it is likely that the patient has a primary sleep disorder. Those that cause frequent awakenings are divided into those that result in excessive daytime sleepiness and those that may not.

Does the patient notice repetitive, uncontrolled, muscle jerks throughout the night? Some patients with sleep-related (nocturnal) myoclonus are aware of the jerks and partial awakenings throughout the night. Others are aware of waking often but do not recall the muscle jerks. In these cases, it is extremely helpful to have the report of a sleep partner to corroborate your suspicion. Another possibility is restless legs syndrome. This is characterized by an irresistible urge to move the legs because of a sensation of "creeping" inside the calves. Many of these patients also have nocturnal myoclonus. Patients with restless legs syndrome may have an underlying cause. Therefore, it is important to determine whether a deficiency of iron or folate exists or whether the patient is pregnant or has uremia or a peripheral neuropathy. A common misinterpretation is the presence of hypnic jerks, which occur in many people sporadically. This phenomenon is the sudden jerking that occurs as one is falling asleep and does not represent a sign of myoclonus. Persistent leg cramps may also be a cause of frequent awakenings and may be due to excessive exercise, inadequate hydration, or deficiencies in potassium or calcium.

Excessive Daytime Sleepiness

Excessive daytime sleepiness (EDS) is caused by sleep apnea syndrome (43%), narcolepsy (25%), and insufficient sleep.[5] Sleep apnea that is central is not as likely as obstructive sleep apnea to result in EDS. Obstructive sleep apnea causes the patient to increase abdominal pressure as he or she recovers from an apneic episode. As a result the patient may have an apparently unrelated list of associated problems, including the following:

- early-morning headache
- urge to void early in the morning or often throughout the night
- esophageal reflux
- early-morning hypertension

Examination

The primary evaluation tool for sleep disorders is a polysomnogram.[6,7] This consists of a series of measurements that are superimposed to present a composite picture of various sleep activities, including the following:

- an EEG
- an electrooculogram (EOG)
- an electromyogram (EMG)
- arterial oxygen saturation (SaO_2)
- oral airflow (N/OT)
- thoracic movement (TSG)
- heart rate (by a cardiotachometer)
- an electrocardiogram (ECG)

REM and NREM sleep are distinguished by characteristic patterns, especially with the EEG and EOG. These are summarized in Table 23–1.

MANAGEMENT

- Alter aspects of the patient's lifestyle that might assist sleep, such as reducing smoking, alcohol, caffeine, or OTC stimulants; keeping regular sleeping hours; or decreasing stress (see Exhibit 23–1).
- Refer to sleep disorders clinic for evaluation and management of primary disorders.
- Refer for psychologic evaluation when sleep disturbance is typical of depression, such as early-morning waking with difficulty falling back to sleep.
- Treat any coexisting musculoskeletal complaints.

Some general measures apply to most patients with sleep difficulties. These include keeping a regular sleep cycle, avoiding stimulation such as exercise, reducing medications (nasal sprays, caffeine, smoking, etc.), and decreasing stress. If the patient has a more severe problem or a clear-cut primary or secondary sleep disorder, referral for sleep analysis and treatment is needed. Below are some selected conditions and the options for management.

Sleep Apnea

Sleep apnea may be central or obstructive. Obstructive sleep apnea is characterized by periods of apnea due to mechanical or functional blockage to airflow.

Specifically for those patients with obstructive sleep apnea disorders, several conservative measures are recommended. It is realistic to state that many of these alterable factors are only effective in mild cases and when the patient is or can be compliant. Given that two thirds of patients with sleep apnea have moderate to severe obesity,[8] a loss of weight often will subjectively and objectively improve breathing.[9,10] This is due to increased lung volumes and decreased pharyngeal collapse. Maintaining the weight reduction, however, is notoriously elusive. Sleep position change may help with the caveat that it is difficult to avoid certain positions while asleep. It has been demonstrated that apnea occurs less often in the lateral decubitus (sidelying) position than the supine position.[11] Avoidance of alcohol may eliminate a compounded effect on sleep apnea. Alcohol has been shown to depress hypoglossal nerve activity with genioglossal and other support muscle decreases in tone, leading to increases in upper airway resistance even in nonapneic sleepers.[12,13] If sedatives (or narcotics) are used to assist sleep, they should be discontinued if the patient has obstructive problems.

Other conservative options include oral appliances and nasal continuous positive airway pressure (CPAP). Although many oral appliances have been utilized, little information on criteria for the device or the specific patient group that would benefit has been provided. A fairly comprehensive study suggests, however, that an oral appliance may be beneficial with some patients.[14] Both snoring severity and apnea were improved. Overexcitement is tempered by the additional observation that 35% of patients still had breathing difficulty significant enough that they needed additional therapy. The compliance rate is approximately 75%. Although side effects are minimal, long-term effects on the temporomandibular joint might occur. The device evaluated in the study caused the mandible to advance and rotate downward, thereby enlarging the posterior airway. This may have a secondary effect on the soft palate.

Nasal CPAP was introduced in 1981 as a potential treatment option for obstructive sleep apnea. The general principle is simple: maintain air pressure through a mask that delivers a continuous stream of room air under high pressure, thereby creating a "pneumatic splint." Although the device appears to be extremely effective, there are several compliance issues that render it far less effective than had been hoped. The mere presence of the machine, the loudness of the blower, and the irritation to the mucosa from constant air have led to a poor compliance rate after several months. Patients complain of nasal problems, throat soreness, and headaches, among other side effects. Patients who remain on CPAP for a minimum of several weeks have improvement in NREM and REM sleep and particularly in daytime function, with much less daytime tiredness. Improvements in technology may allow adjustment of pressure and

Table 23–1 Characteristic EEG Findings with Various Causes and Disorders of Sleep

Disorder or Substance	*Characteristic EEG Findings*
Depression	Decreased total sleep time Fragmented sleep Early onset of REM sleep Shift of REM sleep to first half of night Decreased slow-wave sleep
Bipolar disorder	Total sleep time decreased Shortened REM latency Increased REM activity
Sleep panic attacks	Occurs in transition from stage 2 to stage 3 (NREM) in patients with a longer REM latency
Acute alcohol intake	Decreased sleep latency Reduced REM sleep in first half of night Increased REM in second half of night (REM rebound) Increase in stages 3 and 4 sleep Vivid dreaming and frequent awakenings
Chronic alcohol intake	Increase in stage 1 Decreased REM sleep
Alcohol or sedative withdrawal	Delayed onset of sleep REM rebound
Smoking (other stimulants)	Decreased total sleep time (mainly NREM) Increased sleep latency
Sedatives/hypnotics	Increased total sleep time Decreased sleep latency Decreased awakenings Variable effects on NREM sleep Antidepressants decrease REM

oxygen concentration, decreasing some side effects and increasing compliance.

For those patients who do not improve, various forms of surgery are an option. Removing nasal polyps; correcting a deviated nasal septum; or removing tonsils, adenoids, or simply the uvula is often a first attempt. More radical approaches involve mandibular restructuring. A new technique using a laser to remove the uvula has a dramatic effect on snoring; however, the effect on apnea is variable.

Narcolepsy

Narcolepsy is characterized by rather sudden sleeping episodes during the day. This is a condition whereby the patient drops into REM sleep without warning.

It appears that narcolepsy has an autoimmune basis due to the strong association with human leukocyte antigens (HLA) DQw6 and DRw15.[15] Treatment includes central nervous system stimulants for the hypersomnolence (eg, amphetamine or methylphenidate) and anticholinergics for the cataplexy (eg, imipramine or protriptyline).

Restless Legs Syndrome

Although many cases are benign, some patients have severe dysesthesia and irresistible leg movements in an attempt at temporary relief. These abnormalities can lead to serious sleep deprivation in some patients because of a prolonged

Figure 23–1

INSOMNIA OR OTHER COMPLAINTS OF SLEEP—ALGORITHM.

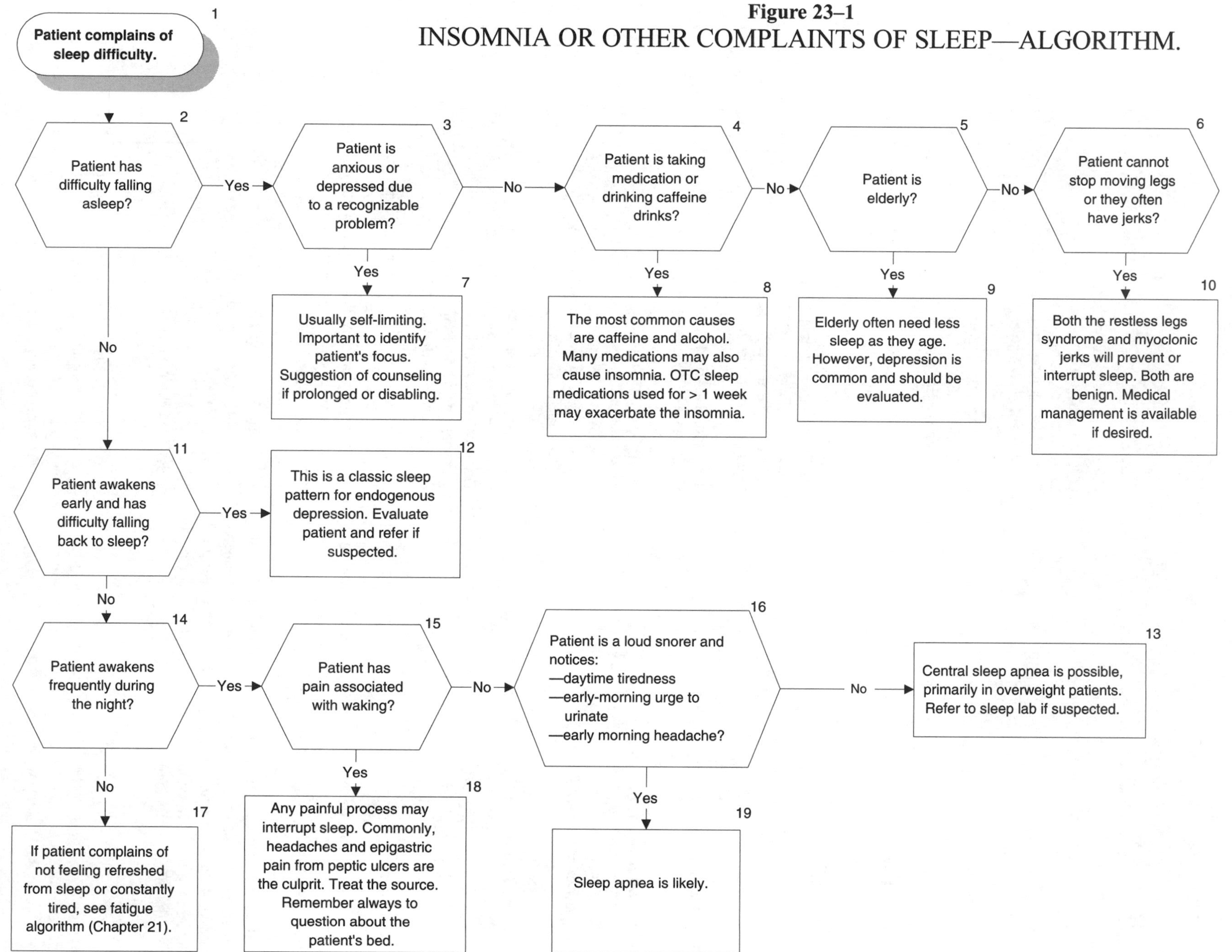

sleep latency until after 3 AM. The treatment considered most effective is a tablet containing 25 mg of carbidopa and 100 mg of levodopa (Sinemet) taken before bedtime and occasionally a second dose during the night or during the day.[15] Other drugs include L-dopa or bromocriptine mesylate. It is important to caution the doctor that these are not muscle cramps and will not respond to the usual recommendations. The disorder is quite distressing and requires medication in most serious cases.

Algorithm

An algorithm for insomnia or other complaints of sleep is presented in Figure 23–1.

REFERENCES

1. Kraft M, Martin RJ. Chronobiology and chronotherapy in medicine. *Dis Mon.* 1995;41:501–575.
2. Kovasevic-Ristanovic R. Sleep disorders. In: Weiner WJ, Goetz CG, eds. *Neurology for the Non-Neurologist.* 3rd ed. Philadelphia: JB Lippincott Co; 1989:281.
3. Sandyk R. Melatonin and maturation of REM sleep. *Int J Neurosci.* 1992;63:105–114.
4. Diagnostic Classification Steering Committee: *International Classification of Sleep Disorders: Diagnostic and Coding Manual.* Rochester, MN: American Sleep Disorders Association; 1990.
5. Buchholz D. Sleep disorders. In: Bayless TM, Brain MC, Chermick RM, eds. *Current Therapy in Internal Medicine.* Philadelphia: BC Decker; 1987;2.
6. Iber C, O'Brien C, Schluter J, et al. Single night studies in obstructive sleep apnea. *Sleep.* 1991;14:383–385.
7. Thorpy MJ, McGregor PA. The use of sleep studies in neurologic practice. *Semin Neurol.* 1990;10:11.
8. Kales A, Cadieux RJ, Bixler EO, et al. Severe obstructive sleep apnea: onset, clinical course, and characteristics. *J Chronic Dis.* 1985;38:419–425.
9. Wittels EH, Thompson S. Obstructive sleep apnea and obesity. *Otolaryngol Clin North Am.* 1990;23:751–760.
10. Bray GA. Barriers to the treatment of obesity. *Arch Intern Med.* 1991;115:152–157.
11. Cartwright RD, Diaz F, Lloyd S. The effects of sleep posture and sleep stage on apnea frequency. *Sleep.* 1991;14:351–353.
12. Robinson RW, White DP, Zwillich CW. Moderate alcohol ingestion increases upper airway resistance in normal subjects. *Ann Rev Respir Dis.* 1985;132:1238–1241.
13. Scrima I, Broudy M, Nay K, et al. Increased severity of obstructive sleep apnea after bedtime alcohol ingestion: diagnostic potential and proposed mechanisms of action. *Sleep.* 1982;5:318–328.
14. Schmidt-Norwara WW, Meade TE, Hays MB. Treatment of snoring and obstructive sleep apnea with a dental orthosis. *Chest.* 1991;99:1378–1385.
15. Farney RJ, Walker JM. Office management of common sleep-wake disorders. *Med Clin North Am.* 1995;79:391.

Chapter 24

Hypertension

CONTEXT

As a primary contact doctor, chiropractors are well positioned for detecting patients with high blood pressure/hypertension (HTN). Given that the majority of these patients will be asymptomatic for HTN, it is important to include screening on all new patients. HTN is found in as many as 43 to 50 million Americans, 18% of the adult white population and 35% of the adult black population.[1] Sixty percent of these individuals have a blood pressure (BP) in the high-normal range. The patients with BP in the high-normal range can be managed initially with diet and exercise prior to referral for drug management. These patients have been demonstrated to have a 40% increase in risk for cardiovascular disease, however, so their management is not to be taken lightly.[2]

The risk of HTN increases with age and is greater in blacks than in whites.[1] Although some cases of HTN are due to secondary causes (5%), primary (essential) hypertension accounts for 95% of cases with no identifiable cause. Secondary causes include the following:

- estrogen use (5% of women taking oral contraceptives chronically)
- renal disease and renal vascular hypertension (1% to 2% of hypertensive patients)
- primary aldosteronism and Cushing's disease (or chronic corticosteroid use) (0.5% of hypertensive patients)
- coarctation of the aorta (prevalence is 0.1 to 0.5/1,000 children)[3]
- pheochromocytoma
- pregnancy (preeclampsia/eclampsia)
- disorders associated with hypercalcemia such as thyroid conditions

Uncontrolled hypertension puts an individual at risk for coronary heart disease (CHD), congestive heart failure, cerebrovascular events, aortic aneurysms, renal disease, and retinopathy. Obviously, many of these disorders are life threatening. Fortunately, the death rate from CHD and stroke has been reduced 50% or more over the last two decades.[4] This decline has been attributed to public awareness leading to improvements in diet, exercise, and medical intervention.

RELEVANT PHYSIOLOGY

Blood pressure is the result of cardiac output and peripheral vascular resistance (PVR). There are numerous factors that can influence either. Basically, the PVR can be increased by smooth muscle contraction or intrinsically elevated through blockages as seen with athero- and arteriosclerosis. Cardiac output increases as a result of sympathetic discharge from stress or increased metabolic demand. Output also increases with an increased vascular volume; there is more fluid to pump.

PVR is predominantly determined by an interplay among the autonomic nervous system, renal system, and neuroendocrine/hormonal actions. Sympathetic activity increases BP through both increase in PVR and cardiac output. The renin-angiotensin system also plays a key feedback role. Decreases in renal perfusion, increased sympathetic activity, hypokalemia, and arteriolar stretch all may act as initiators of this sequence. Renin secreted by the juxtaglomerular cells causes angiotensinogen to create angiotensin I that is then converted to angiotensin II. Angiotensin II is a potent vasoconstrictor and also causes the release of aldosterone, another vasoconstrictor.

The underlying cause of essential hypertension is unknown; however, it appears to be multifactorial. There appears to be a genetic predisposition most evident when both parents are hypertensive. Other factors that influence HTN are those that influence the development of atherosclerosis, such as diet and exercise, diabetes mellitus, and smoking. Salt intake is a factor in some patients; however, it is usually only one component of an individual's BP increase.[5] Obesity influences HTN through several mechanisms, the most obvious being an increase in intravascular volume with a consequent higher cardiac output.[6] Alcohol consumption also influences BP. An increase in BP is thought to be due to increased levels of catecholamines.[7] Patients with HTN who drink excessively have HTN that is more difficult to control. Smoking has a similar effect, possibly due to increased levels of norepinephrine.[8]

Theories regarding underlying pathology with essential HTN patients include the following[9]:

- sympathetic nervous system hyperactivity or decrease in sensitivity of baroreflexes
- renin-angiotensin system dysfunction
- intracellular increases in sodium

GENERAL STRATEGY

- Screen all patients for HTN.
- Check for possible signs and symptoms suggestive of a secondary cause of hypertension: in young patients, renal insufficiency, renal artery stenosis, or coarctation of the aorta are possible causes; in adults, renal artery stenosis, Cushing's disease, hyperthyroidism, and pheochromocytoma should be considered.
- Use proper cuff size and procedure; make sure the patient has avoided alcohol for 12 hours and smoking at least 30 to 60 minutes prior to examination.
- Recheck high findings at least two other times over the next week to confirm original reading (Exhibit 24–1); if severely high on the initial reading, refer for medical evaluation.
- Refer patients with moderate to severe HTN.
- Manage or comanage patients with mild HTN with diet and exercise.

EVALUATION

History

Historical clues are important in determining underlying causes of hypertension and any end-organ dysfunction as a result of hypertension. A significant finding in younger patients is a family history, especially if both parents have hypertension. Other familial findings that are significant include stroke, diabetes, cardiovascular disease, and hyperlipidemia. Important personal history information to be elicited include the following:

- Note any symptoms suggestive of end-organ problems (congestive heart failure, stroke, kidney dysfunction, peripheral vascular problems).
- Determine whether there are indicators of a secondary cause (mainly renal, cardiac, or endocrine factors) or a history of oral contraceptive use; alcohol abuse; use of corticosteroids, nonsteroidal antiinflammatory drugs, or monoamine oxidase (MAO) inhibitors.
- Ask about any past levels of BP, cholesterol, and other lipids. Ask about a previous diagnosis of cardiovascular, cerebrovascular, or renal disease.
- Obtain a dietary history; ask the patient to keep a diary indicating intake of sodium, fat, and alcohol.
- Determine other lifestyle factors such as exercise, work and family environment, and general response to stress.

Examination

Key to the diagnosis of HTN is an accurate BP measurement. Many factors can influence this reading, thus sequential measurements are required for confirmation. These variables can be classified as extrinsic or intrinsic to the patient. If the patient has smoked, drunk alcohol, or exercised, or is nervous, BP may be increased transiently. Although it is generally recommended to wait 30 minutes after the patient has smoked or ingested alcohol, some authors recommend waiting an hour after a patient has smoked and 12 hours after ingesting alcohol. Otherwise the patient should rest at least 5 minutes prior to examination. Equipment errors may occur if the sphygmomanometer is not calibrated, the pressure leaks, the stethoscope has defects, or the wrong size cuff is used. To accommodate different arm sizes, pediatric, adult, and oversized cuffs should be available. The bladder portion should cover four fifths of the patient's arm circumference. Using too small a cuff will increase the BP reading, often substantially. Procedurally, it is important to do the following:

- Make sure the arm is bare and at heart level.
- Always wait at least 2 minutes between readings on the same arm.
- Measure the BP twice on one arm when the patient is seated or supine; take the BP twice again after the patient has stood for 2 minutes (2 minutes between each reading).
- Follow the same procedure on the opposite arm.
- Recheck high readings on the following 3 days (same time of day).

Exhibit 24–1 Screening for Hypertension

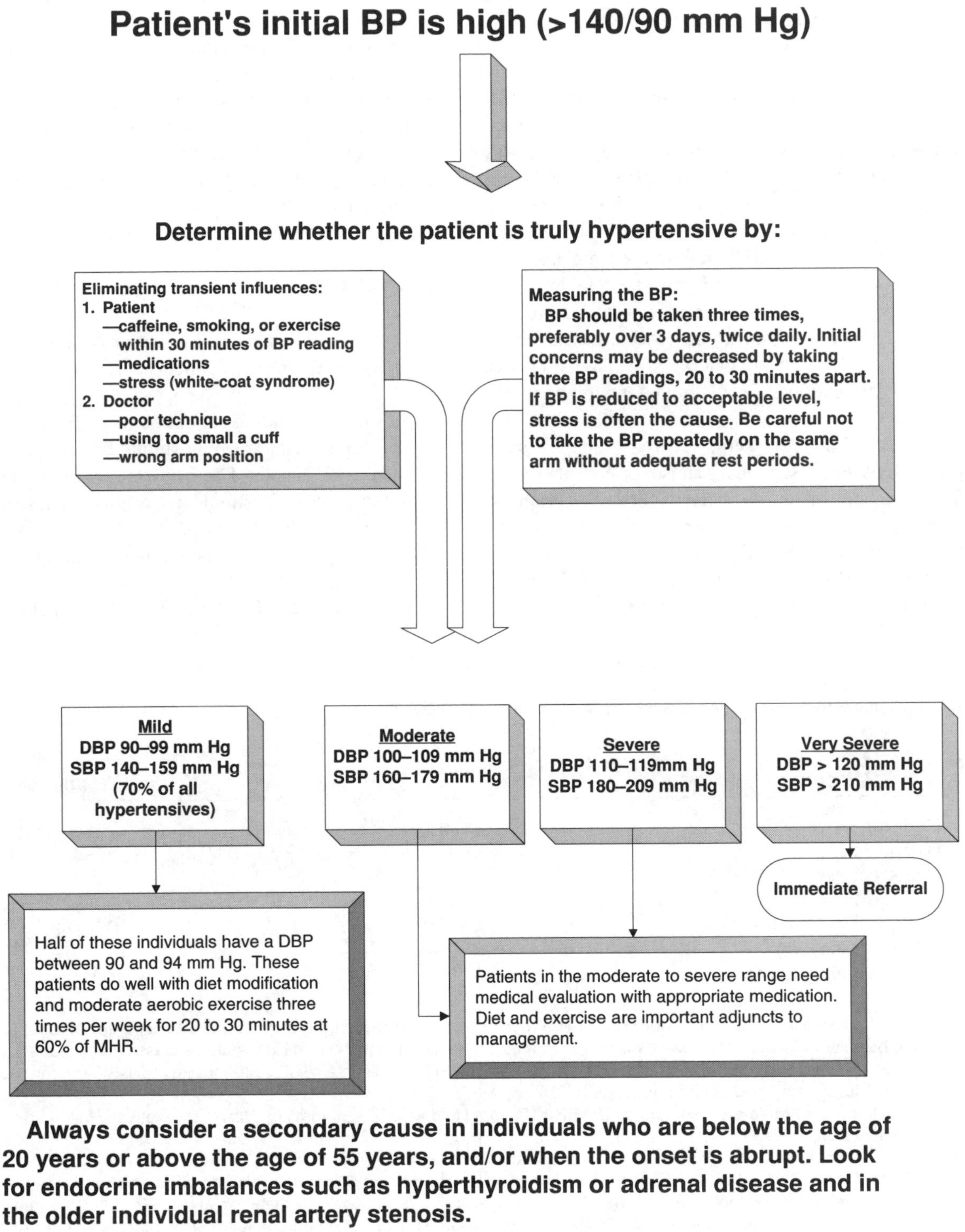

Patient's initial BP is high (>140/90 mm Hg)

Determine whether the patient is truly hypertensive by:

Eliminating transient influences:
1. Patient
   —caffeine, smoking, or exercise within 30 minutes of BP reading
   —medications
   —stress (white-coat syndrome)
2. Doctor
   —poor technique
   —using too small a cuff
   —wrong arm position

Measuring the BP:
BP should be taken three times, preferably over 3 days, twice daily. Initial concerns may be decreased by taking three BP readings, 20 to 30 minutes apart. If BP is reduced to acceptable level, stress is often the cause. Be careful not to take the BP repeatedly on the same arm without adequate rest periods.

Mild
DBP 90–99 mm Hg
SBP 140–159 mm Hg
(70% of all hypertensives)

Moderate
DBP 100–109 mm Hg
SBP 160–179 mm Hg

Severe
DBP 110–119mm Hg
SBP 180–209 mm Hg

Very Severe
DBP > 120 mm Hg
SBP > 210 mm Hg

Immediate Referral

Half of these individuals have a DBP between 90 and 94 mm Hg. These patients do well with diet modification and moderate aerobic exercise three times per week for 20 to 30 minutes at 60% of MHR.

Patients in the moderate to severe range need medical evaluation with appropriate medication. Diet and exercise are important adjuncts to management.

Always consider a secondary cause in individuals who are below the age of 20 years or above the age of 55 years, and/or when the onset is abrupt. Look for endocrine imbalances such as hyperthyroidism or adrenal disease and in the older individual renal artery stenosis.

Key: DBP, Diastolic blood pressure; SBP, systolic blood pressure; MHR, maximum heart rate.

While auscultating it is important to record an ausculatory gap, and to use the first sound heard as systolic (unless there is an ausculatory gap) and the last sound heard as the diastolic. Do not use the movement of the indicator as the measure of systolic or diastolic readings.

A decade ago, the diastolic BP (DBP) was used as the prime indicator of high or low BP. Currently, both the DBP and the systolic blood pressure (SBP) are used in classification and management criteria. This new grading system was developed by the Joint National Committee on the Detection, Evaluation, and Treatment of High Blood Pressure (JNC). The categories include normal, high-normal, and HTN. HTN is divided into mild, moderate, severe, and very severe (stages 1 through 4, respectively) (see Table 24–1). The JNC guidelines for categorization are used as the framework for management decisions. These guidelines are illustrated in Table 24–2. It appears that the SBP may be a better predictor of complications to HTN in patients over the age of 50.[10]

In addition to BP measurement, a search should be made for physical signs due to secondary causes or contributors to HTN. Measurement of height and weight is important to determine any level of obesity. Atherosclerosis may diminish pulses. Atherosclerosis and/or high volume or turbulent flow may cause bruits. Auscultation for thyroid, subclavian, aortic, and renal bruits should be performed. Auscultation of the heart may indicate murmurs, S3 or S4 sounds, and arrhythmias. Indication of congestive heart involvement is found with distended neck veins, bilateral lower leg edema, and ascites. Fundoscopic evaluation includes a search for arteriovenous nicking, cotton-wool patches, or papilledema. The thyroid should be palpated and the patient examined for possible hyperthyroidism if indicated.

Laboratory evaluation may be helpful if an underlying cardiac or renal problem is suspected. Diabetes is an important cause of HTN and should be screened for in high-risk individuals. Additionally, a serum cholesterol and lipid panel is helpful in determining hyperlipidemia.

MANAGEMENT

Following is a general outline of the JNC recommendations for management of patients based on BP measurement[2]:

- A normal reading should be rechecked in 2 years.
- A high-normal reading should be checked in 1 year.
- Mild HTN should be confirmed within 2 months.
- Moderate HTN should be evaluated and sent to a source of care within 1 month.
- Severe HTN should be evaluated and sent to a source of care within 1 week.
- Very severe HTN should be referred out immediately.

Table 24–1 Classification of BP for Adults Aged 18 Years and Older*

Category	*Systolic (mm Hg)*	*Diastolic (mm Hg)*
Normal†	<130	<85
High normal	130–139	85–89
Hypertension‡		
Stage 1 (mild)	140–159	90–99
Stage 2 (moderate)	160–179	100–109
Stage 3 (severe)	180–209	110–119
Stage 4 (very severe)	≥210	≥120

*Not taking antihypertensive drugs and not acutely ill. When systolic and diastolic pressures fall into different categories, the higher category should be selected to classify the individual's BP status. For instance, 160/92 mm Hg should be classified as stage 2, and 180/120 mm Hg should be classified as stage 4. Isolated systolic hypertension (ISH) is defined as SBP ≥140 mm Hg and DBP <90 mm Hg and staged appropriately (eg, 170/85 mm Hg is defined as stage 2 ISH).

†Optimal BP with respect to cardiovascular risk is SBP <120 mm Hg and DBP <80 mm Hg. However, unusually low readings should be evaluated for clinical significance.

‡Based on the average of two or more readings taken at each of two or more visits following an initial screening.

Note: In addition to classifying stages of hypertension based on average blood pressure levels, the clinician should specify presence or absence of target-organ disease and additional risk factors. For example, a patient with diabetes and a BP of 142/94 mm Hg plus left-ventricular hypertrophy should be classified as "Stage 1 hypertension with target-organ disease (left ventricular hypertrophy) and with another major risk factor (diabetes)." This specificity is important for risk classification and management.

Source: Reprinted from *The Fifth Report of the Joint National Committee on Detection, Evaluation, and Treatment of High Blood Pressure*. NIH Publication 93-1008, 1993, National Institutes of Health.

Table 24–2 Recommendations for Follow-up Based on Initial Set of BP Measurements for Adults Aged 18 Years and Older

*Initial Screening BP (mm Hg)**		
Systolic	*Diastolic*	*Follow-up Recommended†*
<130	<85	Recheck in 2 years.
130–139	85–89	Recheck in 1 year.‡
140–159	90–99	Confirm within 2 months.
160–179	100–109	Evaluate or refer to source of care within 1 month.
180–209	110–119	Evaluate or refer to source of care within 1 week.
≥210	≥120	Evaluate or refer to source of care immediately.

*If the systolic and diastolic categories are different, follow recommendation for the shorter time follow-up (eg, 160/85 mm Hg should be evaluated or referred to source of care within 1 month).

†The scheduling of follow-up should be modified by reliable information about past BP measurements, other cardiovascular risk factors, or target-organ disease.

‡Consider providing advice about lifestyle modifications.

Source: Reprinted from *The Fifth Report of the Joint National Committee on Detection, Evaluation, and Treatment of High Blood Pressure.* NIH Publication 93-1008, 1993, National Institutes of Health.

Patients with moderate to very severe HTN should be referred for medical management. The conservative management options for the chiropractor hinge mainly on lifestyle modification, including diet and exercise. This approach may be successful in high-normal or mild hypertensives; however, failure to reduce BP after a reasonable trial of perhaps 6 months should warrant referral for comanagement. Although there have been several isolated studies reporting reduction in HTN following adjustments of the spine, the current evidence suggests that these effects do not appear to be consistent or permanent.[11] Further research is needed.

Following are modifications that may assist in lowering BP:

- reduction of calorie and alcohol intake
- reduction in salt intake
- exercise

Recent evidence suggests that folic acid may be helpful in reducing hypertension. The foods highest in folic acid are broccoli, asparagus, and spinach. There have also been studies that suggest that calcium supplementation may lead to a small reduction in systolic BP.[12]

Pregnant women appear to be at increased risk of preeclampsia/eclampsia with calcium deficiency. Either supplementation at 2 g of calcium per day or drinking one or two glasses of milk per day have been shown to decrease the risk of hypertension during pregnancy.[13] Interestingly, one study demonstrated an increased risk when women drank three or more glasses of milk per day.[14]

For normotensive patients, the American College of Sports Medicine (ACSM) and the Centers for Disease Control and Prevention (CDC) have made similar recommendations for exercise including aerobic exercise three or four times per week. The CDC recommended a duration of 20 to 30 minutes per session, whereas the ACSM recommended 20 to 60 minutes per session at an intensity of 60% to 85% of the maximum heart rate (MHR). Several studies indicate that moderate exercise in the range of 50% to 65% of MHR decreases diastolic pressure 15 to 20 mm Hg in patients with mild HTN. Exercise at levels of 70% or above demonstrated an abrupt increase in diastolic BP. One study indicated that patients with mild hypertension (DBP, 90 to 105; SBP, 140 to 180 mm Hg) showed no difference between those on an aerobic program and those on a waiting list with regard to blood pressure reduction.[15] However, these patients were exercising at 70% or above the maximum oxygen consumption ($\dot{V}o_2max$). When HTN is in the moderate range, or when the patient has diabetes mellitus and/or signs of end-organ damage, medication is often recommended. However, if the patient is going to exercise, the choice of medication may have an effect on performance.

Medication Summary

Medications reduce the pressure in the cardiovascular system by reducing the force of contraction of the heart, reducing the amount of fluid in the system, or reducing the tension in the arteries/veins. This is accomplished by the following general classes of medications:

Figure 24–1
HYPERTENSION—ALGORITHM.

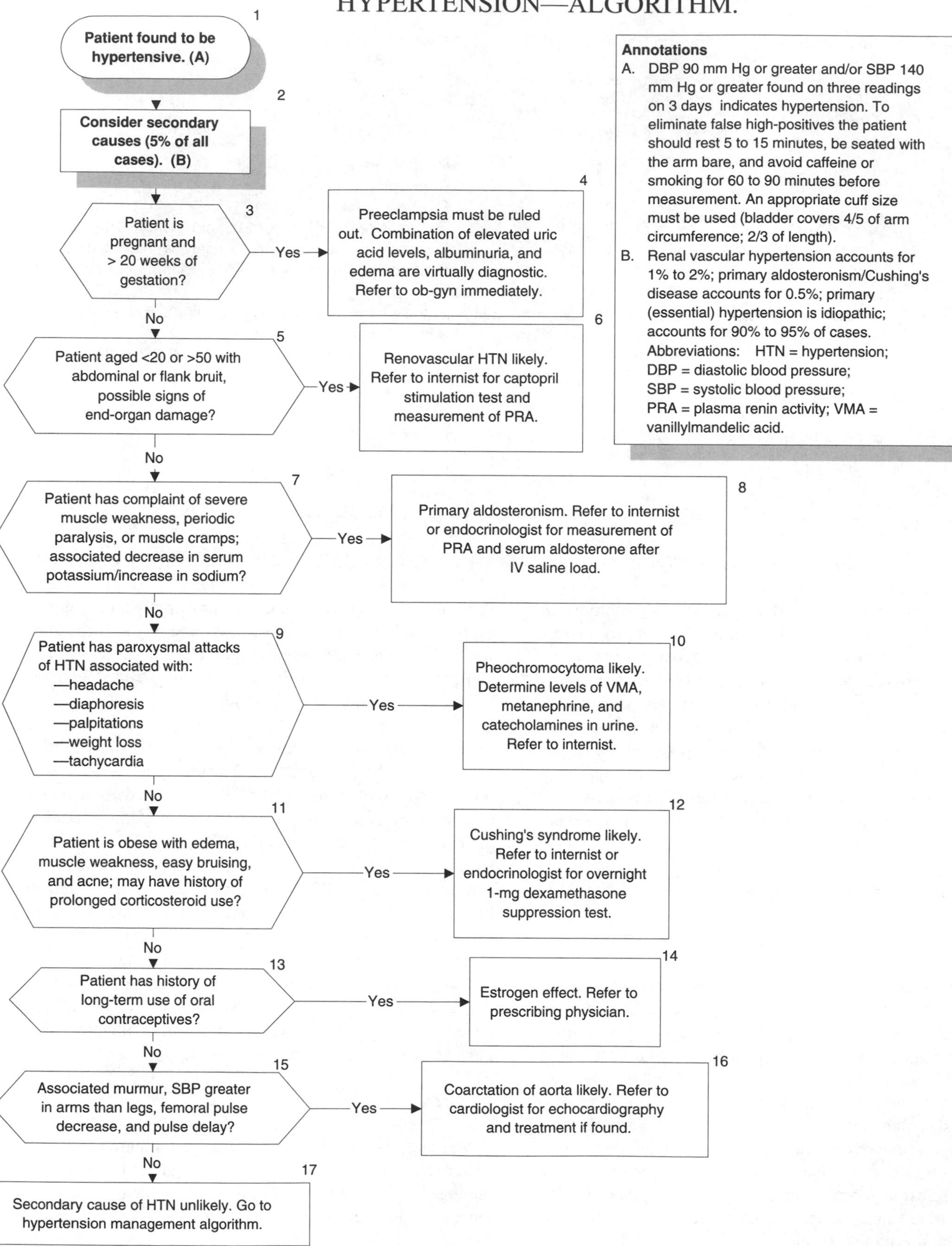

Figure 24–2
HYPERTENSION MANAGEMENT—ALGORITHM.

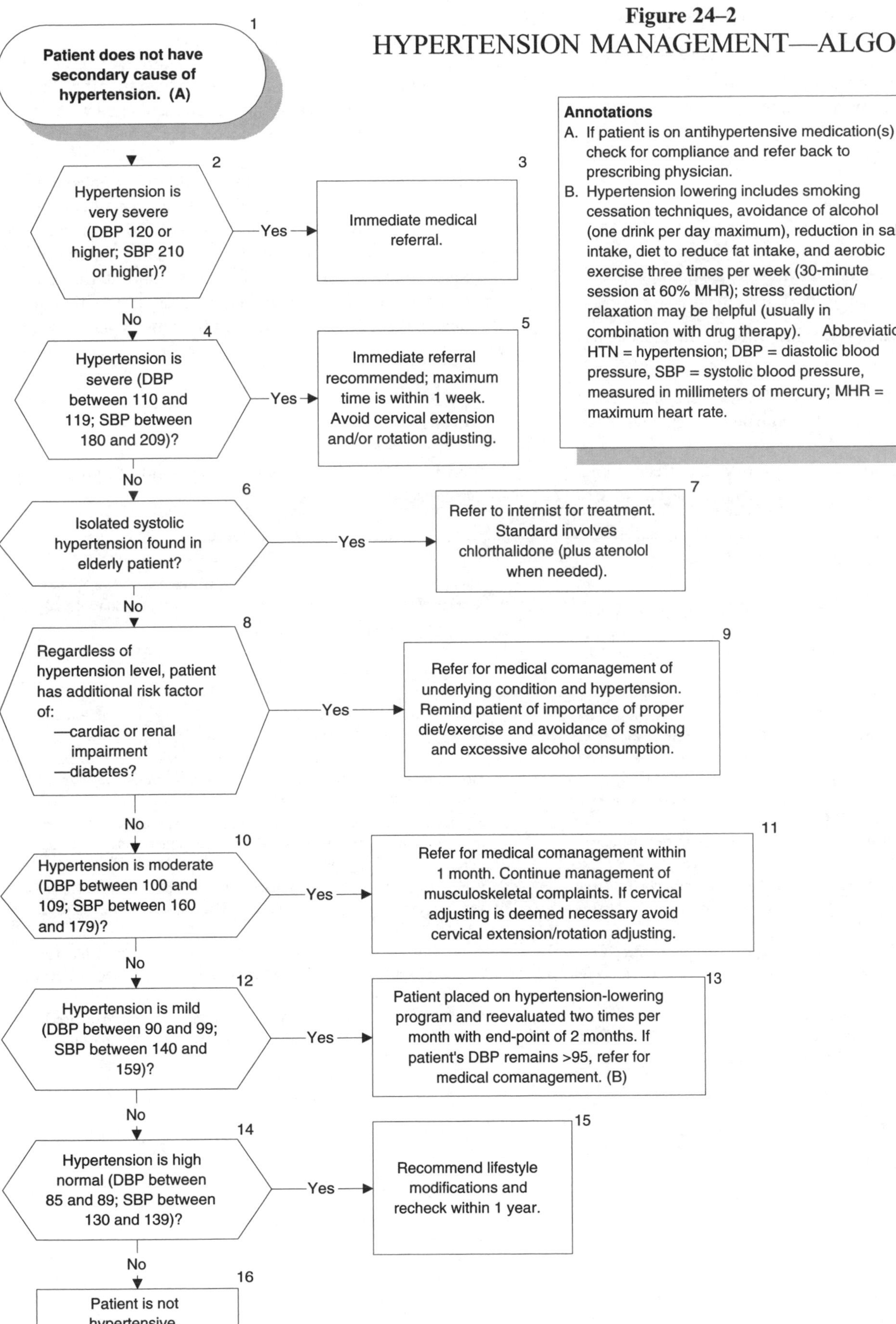

1 Patient does not have secondary cause of hypertension. (A)
2 Hypertension is very severe (DBP 120 or higher; SBP 210 or higher)?
Yes
3 Immediate medical referral.
No
4 Hypertension is severe (DBP between 110 and 119; SBP between 180 and 209)?
Yes
5 Immediate referral recommended; maximum time is within 1 week. Avoid cervical extension and/or rotation adjusting.
No
6 Isolated systolic hypertension found in elderly patient?
Yes
7 Refer to internist for treatment. Standard involves chlorthalidone (plus atenolol when needed).
No
8 Regardless of hypertension level, patient has additional risk factor of:
—cardiac or renal impairment
—diabetes?
Yes
9 Refer for medical comanagement of underlying condition and hypertension. Remind patient of importance of proper diet/exercise and avoidance of smoking and excessive alcohol consumption.
No
10 Hypertension is moderate (DBP between 100 and 109; SBP between 160 and 179)?
Yes
11 Refer for medical comanagement within 1 month. Continue management of musculoskeletal complaints. If cervical adjusting is deemed necessary avoid cervical extension/rotation adjusting.
No
12 Hypertension is mild (DBP between 90 and 99; SBP between 140 and 159)?
Yes
13 Patient placed on hypertension-lowering program and reevaluated two times per month with end-point of 2 months. If patient's DBP remains >95, refer for medical comanagement. (B)
No
14 Hypertension is high normal (DBP between 85 and 89; SBP between 130 and 139)?
Yes
15 Recommend lifestyle modifications and recheck within 1 year.
No
16 Patient is not hypertensive.

Annotations

A. If patient is on antihypertensive medication(s) check for compliance and refer back to prescribing physician.

B. Hypertension lowering includes smoking cessation techniques, avoidance of alcohol (one drink per day maximum), reduction in salt intake, diet to reduce fat intake, and aerobic exercise three times per week (30-minute session at 60% MHR); stress reduction/relaxation may be helpful (usually in combination with drug therapy). Abbreviations: HTN = hypertension; DBP = diastolic blood pressure, SBP = systolic blood pressure, measured in millimeters of mercury; MHR = maximum heart rate.

- diuretics (decrease fluid in system)
- drugs that affect the sympathetic nervous system such as β-blockers and α-adrenergic blockers (reduce force of contraction of the heart and/or tension in the vascular system)
- general vasodilators
- calcium channel blockers (similar effect on heart and vasculature as sympathetic drugs)
- angiotensin-converting enzyme (ACE) inhibitors (inhibit the renin-angiotensin-aldosterone cycle)

Each drug has its potential side-effects. The most characteristic are as follows:

- Diuretics—Some diuretics will cause loss of potassium or magnesium and lead to some increase in low-density lipoprotein cholesterol.
- β-Blockers—β-Blockers often have an effect of causing a decrease in energy or inducing general malaise.
- Calcium channel blockers—some of the older types of calcium channel blockers have been associated with an increased risk for certain cancers.

It is important that the patient consult his or her physician prior to decreasing or increasing the dose of medication. Older patients may forget to take their medication (or with diuretics, potassium supplementation) or decide to stop taking medication because of the cost. It is important to ask questions regarding any change in medication, in particular with those patients who appeared to be under control, yet now have a high BP.

Algorithms

Algorithms for evaluation and management of hypertension are presented in Figures 24–1 and 24–2.

REFERENCES

1. Burt VL, Whelton P, Rocella EJ, et al. Prevalence of hypertension in the U.S. adult population: results from the Third National Health and Nutrition Examination Survey, 1988–1991. *Hypertension.* 1995;25:305–313.
2. Joint National Committee on Detection, Evaluation, and Treatment of High Blood Pressure. *The Fifth Report of the Joint National Committee on Detection, Evaluation, and Treatment of High Blood Pressure.* NIH Publication 93-1008. Bethesda, MD: National Institutes of Health, National Heart, Lung, and Blood Institute; 1993.
3. Buyse M, ed. *Birth-Defects Encyclopedia.* St. Louis, MO: Blackwell Scientific Publications; 1990:156.
4. Garraway WM, Whisnant JP. The changing pattern of hypertension and the declining incidence of stroke. *JAMA.* 1987;258:214–217.
5. Cutler J, Follman D, Eliot P, Suh I. An overview of randomized trials of sodium reduction and blood pressure. *Hypertension.* 1991;17(suppl 1):127–133.
6. Pan W, Nanas S, Dyer A, et al. The role of weight in the positive association between age and blood pressure. *Am J Epidemiol.* 1986;124:612–623.
7. Smith W, Crombie I, Tavendale R, et al. Urinary electrolyte excretion, alcohol consumption, and blood pressure in the Scottish heart health study. *Br Med J.* 1988;297:329–330.
8. Mann S, James G, Wang R, Pickering T. Elevation of ambulatory systolic blood pressure in hypertensive smokers: a case control study. *JAMA.* 1991;265:2226–2228.
9. Massie BM. Systemic hypertension. In: Tierney LM Jr, McPhee SJ, Papadakis MA, eds. *Current Medical Diagnosis and Treatment.* 34th ed. Norwalk, CT: Appleton & Lange; 1995:373.
10. Saige A, Larson MG, Levy D. The natural history of borderline isolated systolic hypertension. *N Engl J Med.* 1993;329:1912.
11. Goertz C, Mootz RD. A review of conservative management strategies in the care of patients with essential hypertension. *J Neuromusculoskel Sys.* 1993;1:91–108.
12. Bucher HC, Cook RJ, Guyatt GH, Lang JD, et al. Effects of dietary calcium supplementation on blood pressure. A meta-analysis of randomized controlled trials. *JAMA.* 1996;275:1016–1022.
13. Cong K, Chi S, Liu G. Calcium supplementation during pregnancy for reducing pregnancy induced hypertension. *Chin Med J.* 1995;108:57–59.
14. Richardson BE, Baird DO. A study of milk and calcium supplement intake and subsequent preeclampsia in a cohort of pregnant women. *Am J Epidemiol.* 1995;141:667–673.
15. Blumenthal JA, Siegel WC, Appelbaum M. Failure of exercise to reduce blood pressure in patients with mild hypertension. *JAMA.* 1991;266:2098–2104.

Chapter 25

Lower Leg Swelling

CONTEXT

Lower leg swelling may be the result of a variety of causes via a variety of mechanisms. In general, swelling is usually vascular, muscular, fatty, myxedematous, or tumorous. Bilateral leg swelling is suggestive of a systemic process and is often the result of fluid retention and stagnation due to congestive heart failure, salt-retaining drugs, liver or kidney disorders (hypoproteinemia), primary lymphedema, and dependency. Unilateral leg swelling is usually secondary to trauma, requiring a differentiation between thrombosis and a muscular tear, a task not always as simple as first imagined.

GENERAL STRATEGY

Unilateral Acute Leg Swelling

- Determine whether trauma was involved.
- Determine whether there is a history of contraceptive use or immobilization.
- Determine whether there was a sudden or gradual onset of pain with exercise.

Bilateral Chronic Leg Swelling

- Determine whether the onset was at an early age.
- Determine the patient's cardiopulmonary status.
- Determine whether the patient is taking drugs that cause salt retention or has a high-salt diet.
- Determine whether the patient stands for many hours at a time.
- Determine whether the patient has varicosities and, if so, test to determine which part of the venous system is involved.

RELEVANT PHYSIOLOGY AND ANATOMY

Review of simple physiologic principles reveals most of the common causes of edema (Exhibit 25–1). Fluid within the vascular system remains in the system unless drawn or forced outward by two processes. One process is simply pressure within the system. Hypertension, gravity, venous valvular incompetence, and venous or lymph blockage will increase hydrostatic pressure, forcing fluid into the interstitium. The second mechanism involves onconic pressure. Key to the retention of fluid is the osmotic influence of protein, specifically albumin. Low albumin states are usually due to loss or decreased production. Production of albumin occurs in the liver. Albumin is usually retained by the kidney, yet in some pathologic states, such as long-term diabetes or chronic renal failure, albumin is lost in the urine.

Veins allow unidirectional (toward the heart) movement of blood. This is dependent on one-way valves. When these valves are incompetent or pressure and dilation exceed their restraining ability, blood flows retrograde and can be forced into the interstitium. The venous system has two levels of veins that connect via communicating veins. Blood in the deep system is pumped toward the heart through muscular contraction. Lack of muscular contraction or blockage in the deep system forces blood to flow retrograde through the communicating system to the superficial veins. The superficial system does not have the advantage of muscular contraction to aid in transport and as a result is more likely to demonstrate superficial signs of incompetence—varicosities.

Salt either in the diet or due to drugs or hormones, such as estrogen, that cause the retention of salt can increase vascular fluid and cause lower leg edema.

Exhibit 25–1 Common Causes of Edema

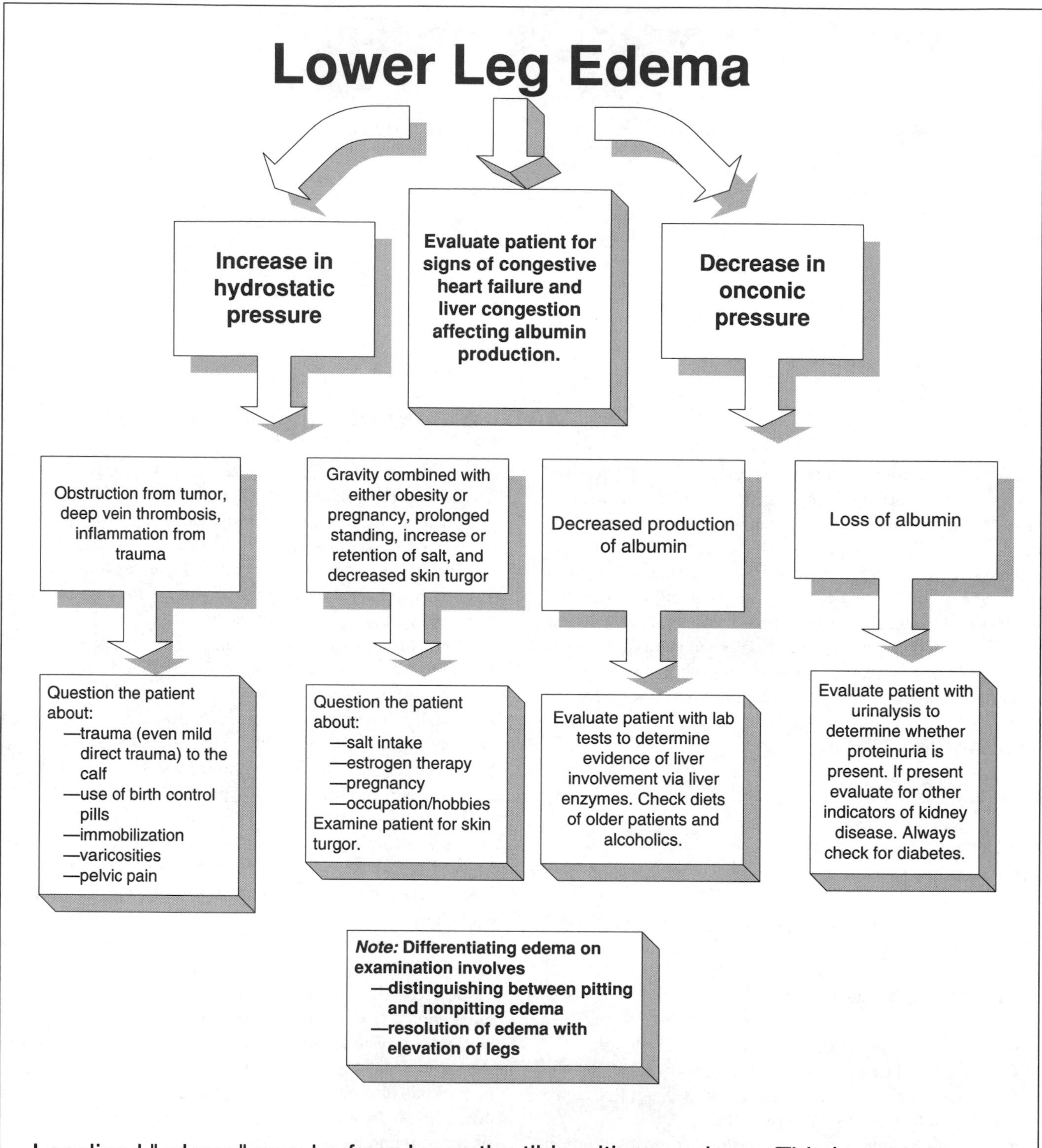

Lower Leg Edema
Increase in hydrostatic pressure
Evaluate patient for signs of congestive heart failure and liver congestion affecting albumin production.
Decrease in onconic pressure
Obstruction from tumor, deep vein thrombosis, inflammation from trauma
Gravity combined with either obesity or pregnancy, prolonged standing, increase or retention of salt, and decreased skin turgor
Decreased production of albumin
Loss of albumin
Question the patient about:
—trauma (even mild direct trauma) to the calf
—use of birth control pills
—immobilization
—varicosities
—pelvic pain
Question the patient about:
—salt intake
—estrogen therapy
—pregnancy
—occupation/hobbies
Examine patient for skin turgor.
Evaluate patient with lab tests to determine evidence of liver involvement via liver enzymes. Check diets of older patients and alcoholics.
Evaluate patient with urinalysis to determine whether proteinuria is present. If present evaluate for other indicators of kidney disease. Always check for diabetes.
Note: Differentiating edema on examination involves
—distinguishing between pitting and nonpitting edema
—resolution of edema with elevation of legs
Localized "edema" may be found over the tibia with myxedema. This is not true edema, but a deposition of mucoid material.

EVALUATION

History

Timing and position are helpful discriminators. Acute, unilateral swelling of the calf is most often due to deep vein thrombosis (DVT) or muscle tear. Associated indicators of DVT are a history of immobilization, use of birth control pills, or minor trauma to the area (especially in an older patient). It is more likely that a muscle strain occurred when the patient can identify a sudden onset with activity, especially with plantarflexion of the ankle. Slow onset of swelling that is relieved by elevation of the legs is suggestive of venous insufficiency or congestive heart failure. Diffuse swelling that is unrelieved by elevation suggests lymph blockage. Calf pain and swelling that appears with exercise is more likely due to a compartment syndrome in a younger person and DVT in an older person.

A review of medications and diet may indicate a salt-retaining mechanism for swelling. Substances such as estrogen promote salt retention (this occurs as a natural consequence of estrogen production during a regular menstrual cycle).

Examination

Observation for the degree of swelling and whether it is localized may be extremely helpful, for example, in the following cases:

- In obese women, swelling that spares the ankles is often due to fat deposition (lipedema), especially if bilateral.
- Localized swelling that appears rather hard and sometimes tender may indicate an underlying bone or soft tissue tumor.
- Swelling localized behind the knee may indicate bursal swelling, a Baker's cyst, or a medial gastrocnemius rupture.
- Swelling localized to the tibial crest probably represents myxedema, which is found in some patients with hyperthyroidism.
- Swelling in the calf may represent thrombophlebitis.

Skin texture and appearance may be characteristic for some causes of leg swelling.

- Lymphedema—The skin becomes dry and scaly with progressive thickening.
- Chronic venous insufficiency—The skin may become golden brown (hemosiderin deposition) at the medial ankle or more diffusely.
- Cellulitis—Diffuse redness and warm skin or red streaks appear on the leg.
- Erythema nodosum—Discrete, nummular areas that are warm appear on the anterior leg.
- Reflex sympathetic dystrophy—In the early stage, the skin is hypersensitive and cool; later, the skin is taut, shiny, and thin.
- Gastrocnemius tear—Bluish purple discoloration appears at the medial malleolus.
- Congenital venous malformations—Flat, purplish red angiomata or dark purple verrucous lesions appear.
- Lymphatic obstruction—Eventually the skin is indurated with the texture of an orange peel (peau d'orange).

Another distinguishing factor is whether the swelling is pitting or nonpitting. Pitting edema is often found in conditions that produce a less viscous fluid, for example, the edema found with congestive heart failure. Swelling that is nonpitting is more often associated with lymph blockage as may occur with tumors. The excess proteinaceous fluid that is normally cleared from the interstitium by the lymphatics is allowed to accumulate.

Improvement of swelling with leg elevation may also help distinguish between lymphedema and edema due to venous involvement. There is a marked improvement with elevation when venous engorgement is the main problem. There is little improvement when the lymphatics are involved. Additionally, venous insufficiency is evaluated with several tests. Trendelenburg's test is used to determine whether varicosities are due to incompetence of the superficial, communicating, or deep veins. The patient's leg is elevated to drain the venous system. A tourniquet is tied tightly enough to occlude the superficial veins at the proximal thigh. The patient stands. If the varicosities fill, the deep and communicating systems are responsible (usually deep vein obstruction). If the varicosities do not appear, yet do develop with removal of the tourniquet, the incompetency is in the superficial system.

If the patient has history and examination results suggestive of DVT, referral for noninvasive Doppler ultrasound is needed to confirm the suspicion. Doppler ultrasound is replacing the gold standard of venography in most cases. A positive finding is identification of an area of noncompressibility along the suspected vein.

MANAGEMENT

- Acute unilateral swelling that is suggestive of DVT should be referred immediately for evaluation with Doppler ultrasound or a venogram; if positive, medical management would include immobilization with elevation for approximately 1 week and anticoagulant therapy for 3 months or longer.

- Congestive heart failure should be referred for co-management. Long-term management should include the use of natural diuretics, when possible; reduction of salt; and a graduated, supervised diet and exercise program.
- Varicose veins may be treated conservatively through advice, including use of elastic stockings, use of frequent breaks with leg elevation, loss of weight, and avoidance of prolonged standing; if unsuccessful or unacceptable by the patient, referral for a discussion of surgical options should be made.

Algorithm

An algorithm for evaluation and management of lower extremity edema is presented in Figure 25–1.

SELECTED CAUSES OF LOWER LEG SWELLING

ACUTE UNILATERAL

Deep Vein Thrombosis

Classic Presentation

The patient may complain of calf pain or tightness that is worse with walking. There may be a history of a minor trauma to the calf or a prolonged period of rest due to a chronic illness.

Cause

Eighty percent of thrombosis occurs in the deep veins of the calf, although other sites may include the femoral and iliac veins. Predispositions include prolonged rest, surgery (especially hip surgery), use of oral contraceptives in women, and cancer.

Evaluation

The clinical examination is often unrevealing. In fact, 50% of patients are not even symptomatic. When symptomatic, there may be mild swelling and tenderness in the calf. Other findings that are relatively nonspecific include a slight fever and tachycardia. The standard Homan's test, which involves passive dorsiflexion of the ankle in an attempt to increase pain, is nonspecific in an ambulatory population. When the suspicion is high, plethysmography or Doppler ultrasound is an acceptable noninvasive screening tool.[1] The definitive diagnosis may require the gold standard of ascending contrast venography.

Management

The medical approach is to prevent the lethal consequence of pulmonary embolism through the use of anticoagulant therapy (ie, heparin) for several months. In addition, elevation of the legs for approximately 1 week is needed with the knees slightly flexed. Return to weight bearing is gradual.

Cellulitis

Classic Presentation

The patient complains of a diffuse, hot, swollen area on the leg. There may be a history of a break in the skin.

Cause

Cellulitis is due primarily to gram-positive organisms; however, *Escherichia coli* may also be a cause. Cellulitis may be seen as a complication of chronic venous stasis.

Figure 25–1

LOWER EXTREMITY EDEMA—ALGORITHM.

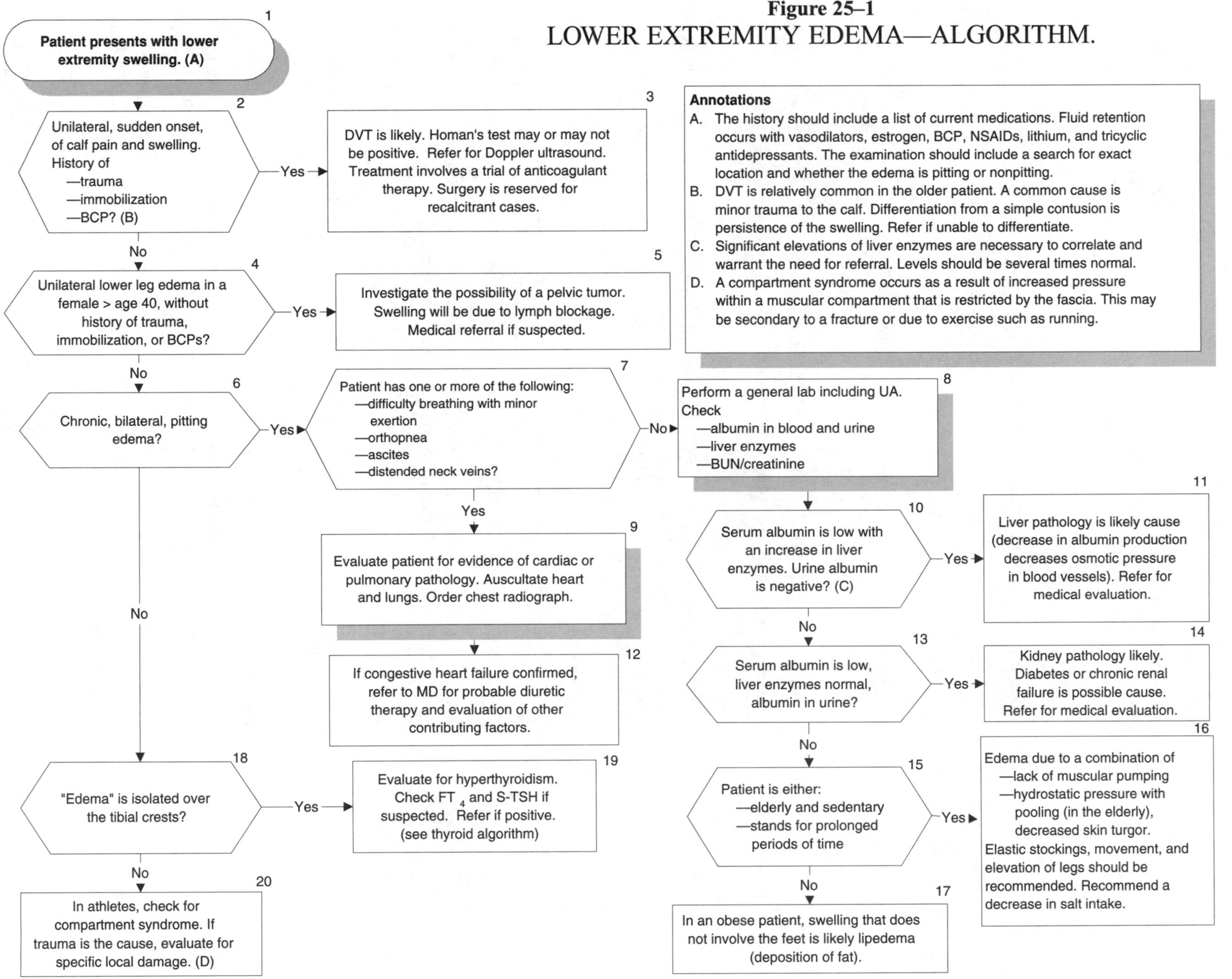

1 Patient presents with lower extremity swelling. (A)
2 Unilateral, sudden onset, of calf pain and swelling. History of —trauma —immobilization —BCP? (B)
Yes
3 DVT is likely. Homan's test may or may not be positive. Refer for Doppler ultrasound. Treatment involves a trial of anticoagulant therapy. Surgery is reserved for recalcitrant cases.
No
4 Unilateral lower leg edema in a female > age 40, without history of trauma, immobilization, or BCPs?
Yes
5 Investigate the possibility of a pelvic tumor. Swelling will be due to lymph blockage. Medical referral if suspected.
No
6 Chronic, bilateral, pitting edema?
Yes
7 Patient has one or more of the following: —difficulty breathing with minor exertion —orthopnea —ascites —distended neck veins?
Yes
9 Evaluate patient for evidence of cardiac or pulmonary pathology. Auscultate heart and lungs. Order chest radiograph.
12 If congestive heart failure confirmed, refer to MD for probable diuretic therapy and evaluation of other contributing factors.
No
8 Perform a general lab including UA. Check —albumin in blood and urine —liver enzymes —BUN/creatinine
10 Serum albumin is low with an increase in liver enzymes. Urine albumin is negative? (C)
Yes
11 Liver pathology is likely cause (decrease in albumin production decreases osmotic pressure in blood vessels). Refer for medical evaluation.
No
13 Serum albumin is low, liver enzymes normal, albumin in urine?
Yes
14 Kidney pathology likely. Diabetes or chronic renal failure is possible cause. Refer for medical evaluation.
No
15 Patient is either: —elderly and sedentary —stands for prolonged periods of time
Yes
16 Edema due to a combination of —lack of muscular pumping —hydrostatic pressure with pooling (in the elderly), decreased skin turgor. Elastic stockings, movement, and elevation of legs should be recommended. Recommend a decrease in salt intake.
No
17 In an obese patient, swelling that does not involve the feet is likely lipedema (deposition of fat).
No
18 "Edema" is isolated over the tibial crests?
Yes
19 Evaluate for hyperthyroidism. Check FT 4 and S-TSH if suspected. Refer if positive. (see thyroid algorithm)
No
20 In athletes, check for compartment syndrome. If trauma is the cause, evaluate for specific local damage. (D)
Annotations
A. The history should include a list of current medications. Fluid retention occurs with vasodilators, estrogen, BCP, NSAIDs, lithium, and tricyclic antidepressants. The examination should include a search for exact location and whether the edema is pitting or nonpitting.
B. DVT is relatively common in the older patient. A common cause is minor trauma to the calf. Differentiation from a simple contusion is persistence of the swelling. Refer if unable to differentiate.
C. Significant elevations of liver enzymes are necessary to correlate and warrant the need for referral. Levels should be several times normal.
D. A compartment syndrome occurs as a result of increased pressure within a muscular compartment that is restricted by the fascia. This may be secondary to a fracture or due to exercise such as running.

Key: BCPs, Birth control pills; UA, urinalysis; BUN, blood urea nitrogen; FT_4, free thyroxine; TSH, thyrotropin; NSAIDs, nonsteroidal antiinflammatory drugs.

Evaluation

Finding an area that is red and swollen, with either a history or evidence of a break in the skin, is a classic presentation. If the patient has a history of venous statis, finding a new area of tenderness is also suggestive. Attempts at isolating the organism are usually unsuccessful.

Management

Refer for antibiotic treatment in suspected cases.

SUBACUTE OR CHRONIC

Venous Insufficiency

Classic Presentation

The patient complains of chronic lower leg swelling. There is itching and a dull ache in the area that is worse with prolonged standing. There may be a history of phlebitis or leg trauma.

Cause

Damage to the deep vein valves is usually secondary to DVT or trauma.

Evaluation

The patient will have edema that is reduced by elevation of the leg. Associated findings include varicosities and leg lesions. When the valves are incompetent, resulting venous stasis will eventually lead to the development of skin lesions around the medial ankle and anterior lower leg. These may include nonhealing ulcers.

Management

Like primary varicosities, the long-term management involves avoiding prolonged standing, elevating the legs as often as possible, wearing supportive elastic stockings, and reducing weight and salt intake. When acute stasis dermatitis is present, compresses using isotonic saline, Burow's solution (buffered aluminum), or boric acid may be applied for 1 hour four times daily. Over-the-counter corticosteroid creams may be helpful. Ulcerations require a medical consultation to determine the need for grafting.

Primary Varicosities

Classic Presentation

The patient may complain of cosmetic and/or painful discrete swellings on the inside of the leg. The pain is a dull, aching heaviness in the lower extremity that is worse with prolonged standing. Cramping may also occur; it is relieved by leg elevation.

Cause

Varicosities are abnormally dilated, tortuous superficial veins. Primary varicosities occur due to incompetence of the valves in superficial veins, communicating veins (veins that connect the deep and superficial venous system), occurring most often in the long saphenous vein (inside of leg) and its tributaries. Patients who are overweight or pregnant or who stand for prolonged periods of time are more often affected. There does appear to be a genetic predisposition.

Evaluation

The diagnosis is primarily through visual inspection. The Trendelenburg test is an attempt to differentiate between deep vein occlusion and superficial vein valve incompetence. The patient's leg is elevated for 20 to 30 seconds. A tourniquet is tied around the upper thigh (enough to occlude the superficial venous system). The patient is then asked to stand. If the varicosities become apparent with the tourniquet still applied, deep vein occlusion or communicating vein incompetence is the cause. If varicosities appear only after removal of the tourniquet, superficial vein valve incompetence is the cause. Doppler ultrasound or duplex scanning may identify the sites of valve incompetence and help in planning surgery (if performed).

Management

Conservative management includes taking frequent breaks to elevate the legs, the use of elastic stockings, losing weight, and avoidance of prolonged standing. If conservative management is ineffective or cosmetically unacceptable by the patient, surgery involves ligation or removal of involved segments, preserving uninvolved segments for the potential need of vein grafting with cardiac bypass surgery. Sclerotherapy is reserved for small varicosities. The vein is injected with a sclerosing agent and compressed, obliterating the vein.

Congestive Heart Failure

Classic Presentation

The patient complains of bilateral leg edema. He or she has associated complaints of difficulty breathing with exertion or lying fully supine at night (orthopnea).

Cause

Right-sided heart failure is often secondary to left-sided failure. Pressure increases into the venous system, delaying return to the heart from the lower extremities.

Evaluation

The edema is reduced by elevation of the legs. Rales are often apparent on auscultation. The chest radiograph provides important confirmation of cardiac failure with a demonstration of cardiomegaly, dilation of the upper-lobe veins, haziness of vessel outlines, and interstitial edema. Electrocardiography may reveal associated arrhythmias or hypertrophy.

Management

Comanagement is recommended. The standard approach is the use of diuretics for early-stage failure. However, long-term management should include a change to a strict, low-fat diet, with gradual supervised exercise.

Reflex Sympathetic Dystrophy

Classic Presentation

The patient will report having persistent pain and swelling following an episode of trauma.

Cause

There are many theories regarding reflex sympathetic dystrophy (RSD). Some investigators question the existence of this disorder. It is believed that sympathetic nervous system (SNS) dysfunction is at the core of this syndrome. Theories include hyperactivity of the SNS, abnormal connection between the sympathetic and sensory neurons, nerve sprouting following injury, or abnormal activation of receptors.[2]

Evaluation

RSD may progress through stages. In the early stage, the patient may complain more of a burning, sharp pain in the area. In the "moderate" stage, sympathetic signs may appear, including atrophic skin changes with cold, moist, or mottled skin. The generalized area becomes hypersensitive to stimuli and the pain becomes continuous. In more severe stages, the pain becomes throbbing and aching. Dystrophic changes become visible in the skin and nails. Muscular atrophy and contracture may become evident. Radiographically, localized osteoporosis (ie, Sudeck's atrophy) occurs in the later stages of RSD. Bone scans will demonstrate an increased uptake on the involved side. Thermography will usually demonstrate a temperature differential between the two sides, but it is nonspecific.

Management

Conservative management would include manipulation of spine-related segments, physical therapy, and elevation to decrease swelling. Two reports suggest that chiropractic manipulation may increase distal blood flow; however, the reports are not specific to RSD.[3,4] Stress reduction may be helpful for some patients. Medically, sympathetic blockades through injectable blocks (eg, bretylium and lidocaine),[5] ganglion blocks, implanted neurostimulators, and α- and β-adrenergic blocker drugs are all approaches that are employed.[6]

REFERENCES

1. Ritchlie DL. Noninvasive imaging of the lower extremity for deep venous thrombosis. *J Gen Intern Med.* 1993;8:271.
2. Vernon HT. Reflex sympathetic dystrophy and chiropractic. In: Lawerence DJ, Cassidy JD, McGregor M, et al, eds. *Advances in Chiropractic.* St. Louis, MO: Mosby-Year Book; 1995;2:183–194.
3. Figar S, Stary O, Hladka V. Changes in vasomotor reflexes in painful vertebrogenic syndromes. *Rev Czech Med.* 1964;10:238–246.
4. Stary O, Figar S, Andelova E, et al. The analysis of disorders of vasomotor reactions to lumbrosacral syndromes. *Acta Univ Carol Med Monogr (Praha).* 1965;21:70–72.
5. Hord AH, Rooks MD, Stephens BO, et al. Intravenous regional bretylium and lidocaine for treatment of reflex sympathetic dystrophy: a randomized, double-blind study. *Anesth Analg.* 1992;74: 818–821.
6. Charlton JE. Management of sympathetic pain. *Br Med Bull.* 1991;47:601–618.

Chapter 26

Lymphadenopathy

CONTEXT

Patients present with a concern of either an enlarged or a tender lymph node or upon examination the examiner discovers a suspicious enlargement. The patients' common concern is whether this is an indication of cancer. Statistically, their concern may be justified if they are over age 50 years, when approximately 60% of lymphadenopathy represents a malignancy. However, if they are under age 30, there is approximately an 80% chance that the cause is benign.[1]

The chiropractor's role is to determine whether an enlarged lymph node is simply an inadvertent discovery. For the patient this represents a "new" or enlarged nodule; however, in reality it represents a chronic, benign node or group of nodes unnoticed by the patient in the past. Additionally, it is important to attempt to differentiate among other causes of "nodules" (especially in the head and neck area in thin individuals), including the following:

- sebaceous or dermoid cysts
- a cervical transverse process or cervical rib
- the carotid body (high cervical area)
- nodularity in the brachial plexus

The next two important steps in the process of evaluation are first to distinguish among generalized, regional, and localized involvement. Second, it is important to determine whether there are associated signs of infection or indicators of malignancy. In general, follow-up with specific laboratory procedures should be reserved for specific suspicions or when there is little evidence to indicate a specific cause.

GENERAL STRATEGY

History

Determine whether the following apply:

- the patient's onset was acute or chronic
- the patient has associated signs of infection
- the complaint is generalized, more regional, or localized
- the patient has been exposed to others with similar signs
- the patient has been exposed to birds, cats, or dogs or their excrement
- the patient is taking medications that may cause a hypersensitivity reaction
- the degree of exercise is associated with the degree of inguinal enlargement

Evaluation

- Palpate the lymph nodes in an effort to distinguish the texture and whether or not the nodes are fixed.
- Determine the degree of involvement: a single node, all regional nodes, or generalized.
- Consider specific laboratory investigation when a specific disorder is suspected such as mononucleosis, hyperthyroidism, tuberculosis (TB), human immunodeficiency virus (HIV), connective tissue disorder, or fungal infection.
- Consider radiographs when TB, sarcoidosis, lung disease, or fungal infection is suspected.
- Refer for biopsy if the patient has indicators of high risk (eg, solitary supraclavicular node).

Management

- Many causes are benign and self-resolve.
- When lymphadenopathy is an indicator of an underlying serious or medically responsive condition, referral for consultation is suggested.
- When lymphadenopathy is persistent beyond 3 weeks with no identifiable cause, refer for medical evaluation.

RELEVANT ANATOMY AND PHYSIOLOGY

The lymphatic system includes the lymph nodes, the lymphatic channels, and the spleen. The function of the lymphatic system is to remove excess protein-rich fluid and return it to the vascular system. The lymph nodes are sites of immune response. There are more than 500 lymph nodes in the body. Certainly, not all are peripherally located and therefore are not accessible. Hilar lymph nodes, for example, require radiographic or invasive investigation to determine involvement. Children have as much as twice the amount of lymphoid tissue as adults and are more likely to respond to an infectious, inflammatory, or other inciting reaction than adults, and in a more dramatic way.

Node involvement is found with a variety of processes including infectious, inflammatory, and neoplastic diseases; metastatic carcinomas; connective tissue disorders; endocrine/metabolic disorders; hypersensitivity reactions; and infiltrative disorders. It would seem impossible to narrow this large list down; however, there are some anatomic predispositions and some classic presentations that may help. Generalized lymphadenopathy usually represents a systemic process involving infection, connective tissue disease, or hematologic neoplastic disease. Lymphomas and leukemias are two general categories to consider. Lymphocytic leukemia is more likely to produce a generalized response. Carcinomas are more likely to cause a regional lymphadenopathy; however, carcinomas are more likely than sarcomas to produce general involvement. Sarcomas are much more likely to disseminate hematogenously and are therefore less likely to cause lymph node involvement.

When investigating enlargement of lymph nodes, it is important to understand the watershed area of the node(s). Draining for common involved areas is listed below:

- occipital, postauricular, and posterior cervical nodes—the scalp
- preauricular—the face and eye
- high superficial and deep cervical nodes, submaxillary, and submental—the pharynx and mouth
- supraclavicular and scalene—the head and neck, arms, mediastinum, and abdomen
- axillary nodes—arm and breast
- epitrochlear—arm and hand
- inguinal-femoral nodes—most of the lower extremity and buttocks, lower anus, genitalia, perineum, and the lower anterior abdominal wall (ovarian and testicular cancer do not usually enlarge the inguinal nodes)

Additionally, certain regional presentations represent systemic processes:

- posterior cervical and postauricular—viral infections, intraarticular pathology, mononucleosis
- preauricular—eyelids and conjunctivae
- high cervical nodes—carcinoma of the oral cavity (often submaxillary)
- supraclavicular and scalene—often represents a neoplastic process (ie, Virchow's node)
- axillary—metastatic breast carcinoma, cat-scratch disease, streptococcal and staphylococcal infections of the arm, brucellosis, tularemia
- epitrochlear—infections of the hand and forearm; occasionally mononucleosis and non–Hodgkin's lymphoma
- inguinal—lymphogranuloma venereum, venereal disease, excessive exercise (ie, marathon running or heavy lower extremity workouts)

EVALUATION

History

Timing may be an important discriminator. Nodes that appear abruptly and are tender more often will represent an infectious or inflammatory process. Chronic or recurrent node enlargement often represents a neoplastic or connective tissue disorder. Associated signs of infection such as cough, sore throat, and fever are common in children with cervical lymph node enlargement.

Associated signs and symptoms often will help narrow down the possibilities:

- night sweats, fever, and weight loss suggest either lymphoma or tuberculosis
- joint pains, skin rash, and muscle weakness suggest a connective tissue disorder (eg, lupus erythematosus)
- fever, sore throat, and cervical lymphadenopathy suggest mononucleosis

Determining the patient's exposure to particular environments or with others having similar signs and symptoms may be helpful in the following cases:

- HIV—homosexual contact among gay or bisexual men (although heterosexual contact is also a possibility), sharing needles (use of contaminated needles) with drug abuse (also consider syphilis)
- mononucleosis—saliva transmission
- cat-scratch fever or toxoplasmosis—contacts with cats or cat litter, respectively
- fungal infection—travel to specific areas or contact with soil or bird excrement (eg, coccidioidomycosis in the San Joaquin Valley of California)

Examination

It is recommended that the chiropractor palpate as many "normal" individuals as possible to gain a sense of the variation in lymph node presentation. Palpation of the area of enlargement is performed with a focus on the area of drainage and the most common causes of regional involvement. These are listed above. Additionally, it may be important to determine whether the lymph nodes are tender. This is more indicative of an inflammatory or infectious cause. Hard and matted lymphadenopathy that is fixed to underlying muscle is suggestive of cancer. If the nodes are more rubbery in consistency, lymphoma is more likely. The distinction between the two is not always easily made.

Evaluation of the throat, skin, and joints is essential in differentiating common upper respiratory infection from generalized connective tissue disease or fungal infections. The spleen and liver must be palpated for enlargement. These may be enlarged in several conditions, such as mononucleosis (cervical lymph node enlargement), lymphomas, and leukemias. Axillary lymph node involvement in a woman warrants a breast examination and follow-up mammography or biopsy if suspicious.

Some lymph node involvement is not palpable but is visible radiographically. Sarcoidosis is more often characterized by hilar lymphadenopathy visible on a chest radiograph. This is also true of bronchogenic carcinoma of the lungs. A chest radiograph may add evidence to a suspicion of fungal infection such as coccidioidomycosis or histoplasmosis if it demonstrates diffuse granulomatous involvement.

Determining which laboratory evaluations to perform is important given the large number of disease processes possible and the separate laboratory evaluation for each. Following are some examples[2]:

- mononucleosis—heterophil antibody or monospot test
- HIV—enzyme-linked immunosorbent assay (ELISA) test confirmed by Western blot test (testing may be performed by the patient through a mail service if desired)
- lupus erythematosus and mixed connective tissue disease—antinuclear antibody (ANA)
- TB—purified protein derivative (PPD) skin test and if positive, culture and smear
- coccidioidomycosis, histoplasmosis, lymphogranuloma venereum—complement fixation test

Biopsy of lymph nodes is often needed to determine the cause in persistent lymphadenopathy. Therefore, patients without an identifiable cause after 2 to 4 weeks or with a suspicious single node involvement in the supraclavicular area or axilla should be referred for biopsy. Lymph node biopsy is not entirely sensitive; however, a second attempt will often raise the positive yield. Biopsy is important in diagnosing neoplastic and fungal causes. Reactive hyperplasia is a nonspecific finding with viral and connective tissue disease causes. It must be remembered that lymph node biopsy of the neck in an elderly patient has been shown to increase the incidence of distant metastasis.

Sometimes it is necessary to biopsy other areas of the body when a specific disease is suspected, including the following:

- transbronchial lung biopsy for sarcoidosis
- renal biopsy for systemic lupus erythematosus
- bone aspiration and biopsy for leukemia

MANAGEMENT

Because of the large list of lymphadenopathy causes, there is no common management approach. Treatment is specific to the underlying cause. Chiropractically, it is important to act as a watchdog for lymphadenopathy, pursue a rationale diagnostic approach, and consider referral when evidence suggests a serious disorder requiring further evaluation or amenable to medical management. Persistence of lymphadenopathy beyond 3 weeks with no identifiable cause is reason for medical consultation.

Algorithm

An algorithm for evaluation and management of lymphadenopathy is presented in Figure 26–1.

Figure 26–1
LYMPHADENOPATHY—ALGORITHM.

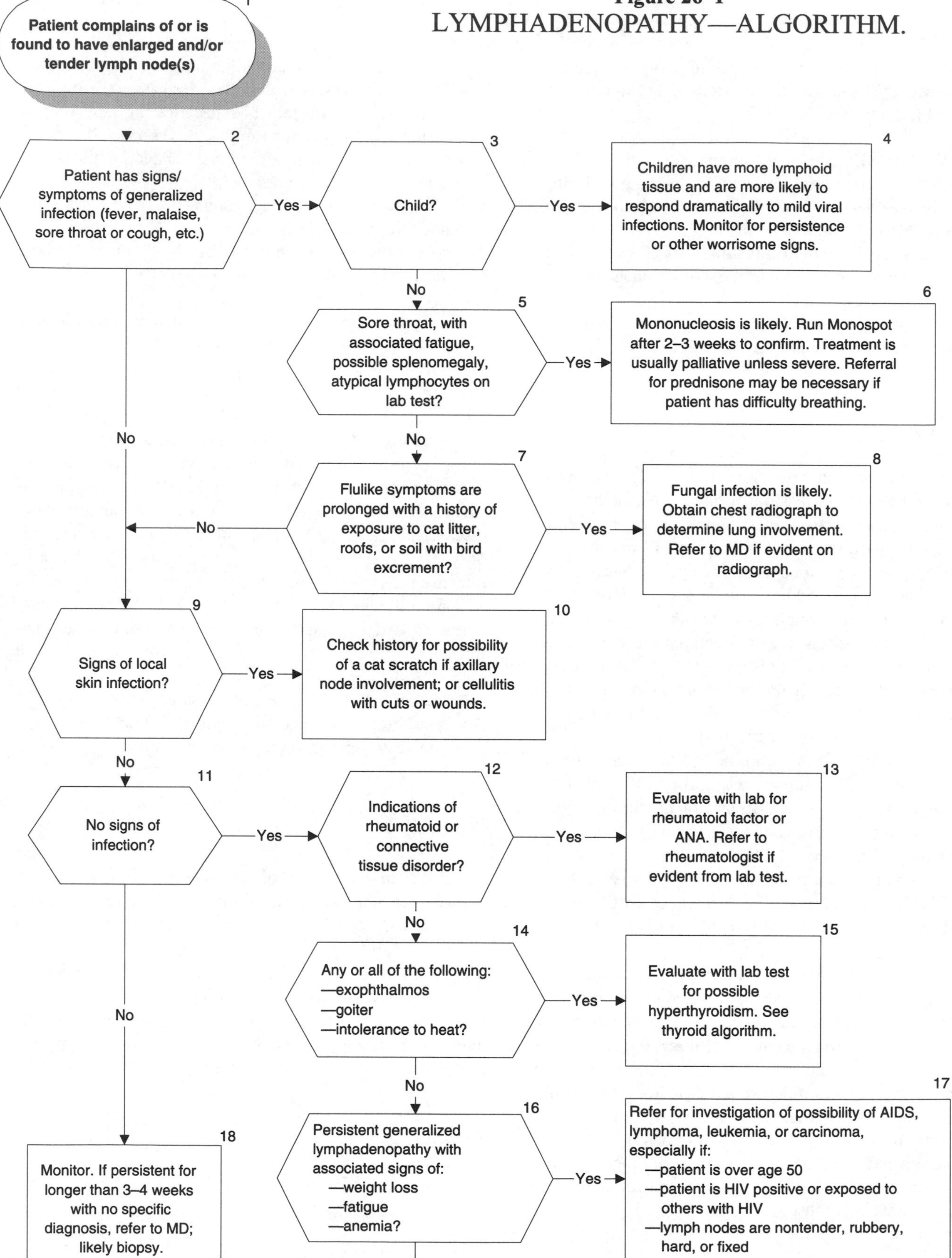

1
Patient complains of or is found to have enlarged and/or tender lymph node(s)
2
Patient has signs/ symptoms of generalized infection (fever, malaise, sore throat or cough, etc.)
Yes
3
Child?
Yes
4
Children have more lymphoid tissue and are more likely to respond dramatically to mild viral infections. Monitor for persistence or other worrisome signs.
No
5
Sore throat, with associated fatigue, possible splenomegaly, atypical lymphocytes on lab test?
Yes
6
Mononucleosis is likely. Run Monospot after 2–3 weeks to confirm. Treatment is usually palliative unless severe. Referral for prednisone may be necessary if patient has difficulty breathing.
No
No
7
Flulike symptoms are prolonged with a history of exposure to cat litter, roofs, or soil with bird excrement?
Yes
8
Fungal infection is likely. Obtain chest radiograph to determine lung involvement. Refer to MD if evident on radiograph.
No
9
Signs of local skin infection?
Yes
10
Check history for possibility of a cat scratch if axillary node involvement; or cellulitis with cuts or wounds.
No
11
No signs of infection?
Yes
12
Indications of rheumatoid or connective tissue disorder?
Yes
13
Evaluate with lab for rheumatoid factor or ANA. Refer to rheumatologist if evident from lab test.
No
14
Any or all of the following:
—exophthalmos
—goiter
—intolerance to heat?
Yes
15
Evaluate with lab test for possible hyperthyroidism. See thyroid algorithm.
No
No
16
Persistent generalized lymphadenopathy with associated signs of:
—weight loss
—fatigue
—anemia?
Yes
17
Refer for investigation of possibility of AIDS, lymphoma, leukemia, or carcinoma, especially if:
—patient is over age 50
—patient is HIV positive or exposed to others with HIV
—lymph nodes are nontender, rubbery, hard, or fixed
No
18
Monitor. If persistent for longer than 3–4 weeks with no specific diagnosis, refer to MD; likely biopsy.

SELECTED CAUSES OF LYMPHADENOPATHY

ACQUIRED IMMUNODEFICIENCY SYNDROME

Classic Presentation

The presentation of acquired immunodeficiency syndrome (AIDS) varies dependent on the staging of the disease. Following is the earliest presentation. The patient is often a homosexual man (however, this is not always true; see below) who complains of generalized symptoms such as fever, sore throat, lymphadenopathy, and headache. The symptoms resolved, but there is persistent lymph node swelling.

Cause

The HIV is a retrovirus that infects mainly T cells and cells related to monocytes. The major factor for immune dysfunction is the progressive depletion of T lymphocytes (primarily CD4+ lymphocytes), leading to decreased ability to fight disease. Lymphocyte functions such as cytotoxic and natural killer cell function are impaired. The antibody response to antigens is reduced.[3] There are several groups at risk including: sexually active, unprotected individuals, particularly homosexual males; drug users who share needles; hemophiliacs and others who received blood transfusions from 1978 through 1985; sexual partners of high-risk individuals; and children born to HIV-infected mothers.

Evaluation

Physical examination may reveal few signs in the early stages. Persistent generalized lymphadenopathy (PGL) is one of the few indicators. Later in the course of disease progression, acquisition of minor opportunistic infection is common, followed by progressive susceptibility to more life-threatening infections. Oral manifestations include thrush and leukoplakia. HIV may be tested by a screening for antibodies to viral protein using an ELISA. A positive test is then confirmed with a Western blot test. Home kits are now available, allowing the person to send a sample to a lab. An indicator of progression is the CD4 cell numbers. These numbers correlate well with the acquisition of common opportunistic infections. The correlations are TB in patients with a count of 300; *Pneumocystis carinii* pneumonia with counts less than 200; cytomegalovirus and mycobacterium avium complex (MAC) when counts are less than 50.[4] HIV-related malignancies are common causes of death, including Kaposi's sarcoma and non–Hodgkin's lymphoma.

Management

AIDS is managed medically with zidovudine (AZT) (antiviral drug).[5] Alternative drugs include didanosine, zalcitabine, protease inhibitors, stavudine, or a combination of these drugs. Treatment of an acquired disease is specific to the disease, but is more difficult in these immunosuppressed individuals. Prevention is crucial to further spread. This includes condom protection and the use of sterilized needles.

NON–HODGKIN'S LYMPHOMA

Classic Presentation

The patient may present with lymphadenopathy alone or complain of constitutional symptoms such as night sweats, fever, or weight loss.

Cause

Non–Hodgkin's lymphoma represents a broad array of lymphocytic cancers. The classification is based on the degree of aggressiveness, including low-grade, intermediate-grade, and high-grade classifications. Patients with HIV disease are particularly prone to non–Hodgkin's lymphoma.

Evaluation

Finding regional or disseminated lymph node involvement warrants referral for biopsy if persistent. Laboratory results vary and may include increased levels of serum lactate dehydrogenase and occasionally a leukemic response.

Management

Indolent lymphomas are not usually curable, but high-grade lymphomas may respond to chemotherapy. The survival period for indolent lymphoma is between 6 and 8 years. The disseminated large-cell lymphomas can be cured in about half of patients.[6]

HODGKIN'S DISEASE

Classic Presentation

Because of the bimodal age distribution, the patient may be in the 20s or over age 50 years. The patient complains of constitutional symptoms such as fever, weight loss, night sweats, or generalized pruritus. He or she may have noticed a painless mass in the neck and is concerned.

Cause

Hodgkin's disease is characterized by lymphoreticular proliferation of unknown cause.

Evaluation

The patient presentation is nonspecific. Suspicion requires referral to a hematopathologist who can determine whether there is the presence of Reed-Sternberg cells on lymph node biopsy. Additionally, it is important to stage the disease. This is done with two approaches: (1) degree of involvement and (2) whether or not symptomatic (A = asymptomatic; B = symptomatic). Stage I indicates one lymph node region involved, stage II indicates involvement of two lymph node regions, stage III indicates lymph nodes involved on both sides of the diaphragm, and stage IV is disseminated involvement of bone and liver.

Management

Treatment is often based on staging. Stage IA and stage IIA diseases are treated with radiotherapy, with a 10-year survival rate of 80%. Chemotherapy is used in patients with stages IIIB and IV (5-year survival rate of 50% to 60%).[7]

CHRONIC LYMPHOCYTIC LEUKEMIA

Classic Presentation

The patient is older than age 50 and complains of fatigue and lymph node swelling.

Cause

The cause is mainly a malignancy of B lymphocytes. The cells are immunoincompetent, leading to a predisposition to infection. Additionally, there is bone marrow failure and organ infiltration. Ninety percent of cases occur over the age of 50. The disease is slowly progressive.

Evaluation

About half of patients have splenomegaly or hepatomegaly. Patients with fatigue and lymphadenopathy should be screened with a laboratory evaluation. The white blood cell count is usually more than 20,000 with the majority of cells being lymphocytes.

Management

No treatment is used initially. Advanced stages are treated with chemotherapy and prednisone. The 5-year survival rate is about 50%; the 10-year survival rate is 25%. Patients discovered with advanced disease usually survive less than 2 years.[8]

REFERENCES

1. Strauss GM. Lymphadenopathy. In: Greene HL, Fincher RME, Johnson WP, et al, eds. *Clinical Medicine*. 2nd ed. St. Louis, MO: Mosby-Year Book; 1996:383–387.
2. Hayes BF. Enlargement of lymph nodes and spleen. In: Branswald E, ed. *Harrison's Principles of Internal Medicine*. 12th ed. New York: McGraw-Hill; 1991.
3. Pantaleo G. The immunopathogenesis of human immunodeficiency viral infection. *N Engl J Med*. 1993;328:327.
4. Stein DS. CD4+ lymphocyte enumeration for prediction of clinical course of human immunodeficiency virus disease. *J Infect Dis*. 1992;165:352.
5. Cooper DA. Zidovudine in persons with asymptomatic HIV infection and CD4+ cell counts greater than 400 per cubic millimeter. *N Engl J Med*. 1993;329:297.
6. Armitage JO. Treatment of non-Hodgkin's lymphoma. *N Engl J Med*. 1993;328:1023.
7. Urba WJ, Longo DL. Hodgkin's disease. *N Engl J Med*. 1992;326:678.
8. Foon KA, Rai KR, Gale RP. Chronic lymphocytic leukemia: new insights into biology and therapy. *Ann Intern Med*. 1990;113:525.

Chapter 27

Skin Problems

CONTEXT

Dermatologic problems can be very difficult to diagnose because of the enormous number of causes and the variety of presentation. Yet chiropractors may serve a role as either a referral source or source of assurance to the patients with many common, benign skin conditions. A discussion of skin problems is hampered without an atlas of color plate examples. The reader is encouraged to compare the following verbal descriptions with an atlas to compare better with a specific patient presentation. The intention of the following discussion is to focus on several common scenarios in a chiropractic setting without a comprehensive discussion of all dermatologic possibilities.

It is extremely important for the chiropractor to recognize the following skin presentations:

- generalized skin changes such as pallor, cyanosis, jaundice, brown-tannish discoloration
- danger signs with pigmented lesions
- the rashes associated with "childhood" diseases such as measles, chickenpox, and rubella
- common causes of pruritus (itching)
- lesions associated with venereal disease
- lesions associated with rheumatoid/arthritic disorders

It is also extremely important for the chiropractor to have a working knowledge of the vocabulary used to describe skin lesions to facilitate an intelligent discussion with a dermatologist in the course of consultation or referral. Following is a list of these terms (see Figures 27–1 and 27–2 for illustrations).

Primary Lesions

Primary lesions develop on previously normal skin due to a specific causative factor. *Note:* Primary lesions often evolve from flat, nonpalpable lesions to fluid-filled palpable lesions or may coexist, leading to combined descriptions such as maculopapular or vesiculopustular.

Flat and Nonpalpable

- Macule—small (up to 1 cm) and circumscribed. Examples: freckles, flat nevi, petechiae, hypopigmentation
- Patch—larger than 1 cm. Examples: mongolian spot, café au lait spot, vitiligo, chloasma

Palpable (Raised) and Solid

- Papule—small (up to 0.5 cm). Examples: mole, wart, lichen planus
- Nodule—large (0.5 to 2 cm) and deeper than a papule. Examples: fibroma, xanthoma
- Tumor—larger (> 2 cm) benign or malignant, hard or soft. Examples: lipoma, hemangioma
- Plaque—papules coalesce, forming a flat, elevated lesion larger than 0.5 cm. Examples: lichen planus, psoriasis
- Wheal—local, transient, skin erythema due to an allergic reaction, mosquito bite, dermatographism.
- Urticaria (hives)—wheals coalesce to form a large reaction that is pruritic.

Palpable, Fluid-Filled Lesions (Rupture Releases Pus or a Clear Fluid)

- Vesicle—small, elevated lesion full of clear serum. Examples: chickenpox, shingles (herpes zoster)
- Bulla—larger lesions that are usually single-chambered. Examples: burns, friction blister, pemphigus, a contact dermatitis
- Pustule—circumscribed lesion filled with pus. Examples: acne, impetigo

MACULE
Solely a color change, flat and circumscribed, less than 1 cm. Examples: freckles, flat nevi, hypopigmentation, petechiae, measles, scarlet fever.

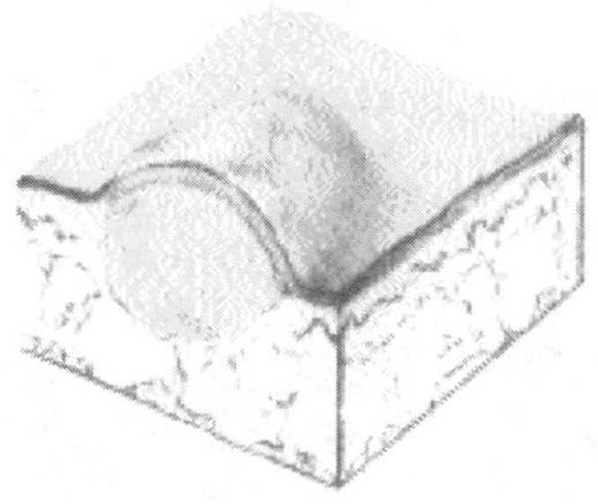

PAPULE
Something you can feel, ie, solid, elevated, circumscribed, less than 1 cm diameter, due to superficial thickening in the epidermis. Examples: elevated nevus (mole), lichen planus, molluscum, wart (verruca)

PATCH (not illustrated)
Macules larger than 1 cm. Examples: mongolian spot, vitiligo, café au lait spot, chloasma, measles rash

PLAQUE (not illustrated)
Papules coalesce to form surface elevation wider than 1 cm. A plateau-like, disc-shaped lesion. Examples: psoriasis, lichen planus

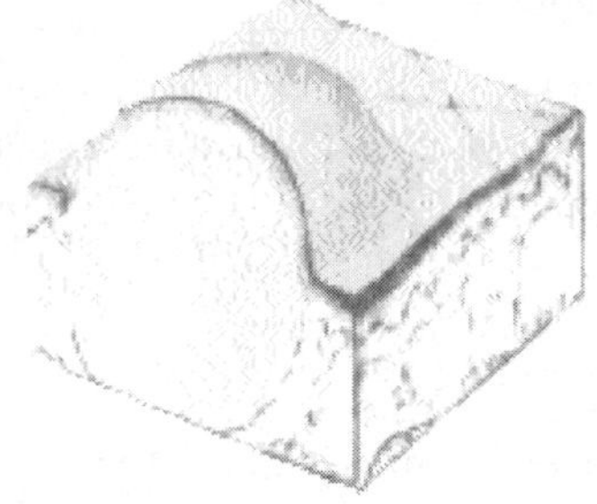

NODULE
Solid, elevated, hard or soft, larger than 1 cm. May extend deeper into dermis than papule. Examples: xanthoma, fibroma, intradermal nevi

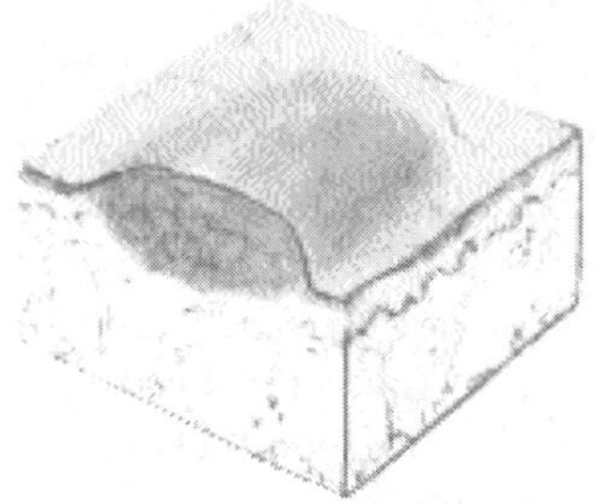

WHEAL
Superficial, raised, transient, and erythematous; slightly irregular shape due to edema (fluid held diffusely in the tissues). Examples: mosquito bite, allergic reaction, dermatographism.

continues

Figure 27–1 Primary skin lesions. *Source:* Reprinted with permission from C. Jarvis, *Physical Examination and Health Assessment*, 2nd ed., pp. 249–252, © 1996, W.B. Saunders Company.

Figure 27–1 continued

TUMOR
Larger than a few centimeters in diameter, firm or soft, deeper into dermis; may be benign or malignant, although "tumor" implies "cancer" to most people. Examples: lipoma, hemangioma

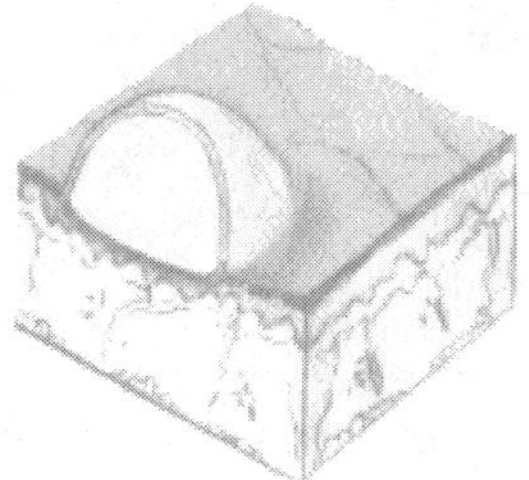

VESICLE
Elevated cavity containing free fluid, up to 1 cm. Clear serum flows if wall is ruptured. Examples: herpes simplex, early varicella (chickenpox), herpes zoster (shingles), contact dermatitis

BULLA
Larger than 1 cm diameter; usually single-chambered (unilocular); superficial in epidermis; it is thin walled, so it ruptures easily. Examples: friction blister, pemphigus, burns, contact dermatitis

URTICARIA (HIVES)
Wheals coalesce to form extensive reaction, intensely pruritic.

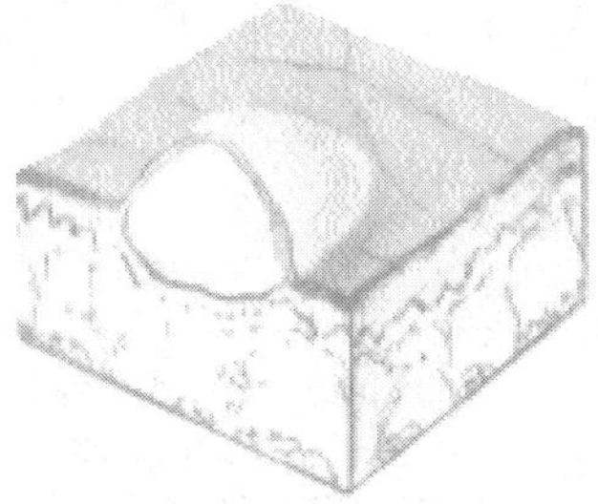

PUSTULE
Turbid fluid (pus) in the cavity. Circumscribed and elevated. Examples: impetigo, acne

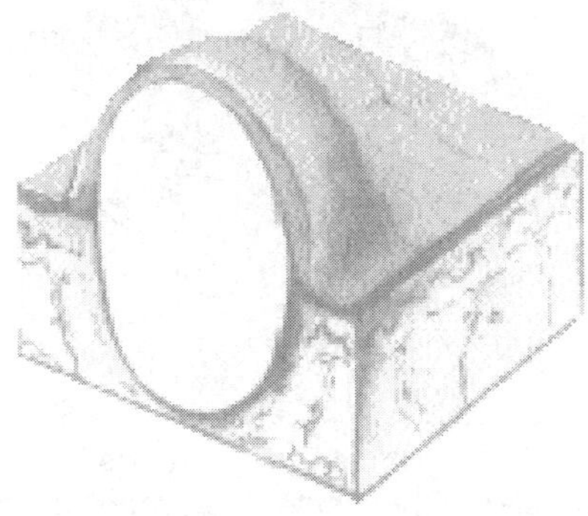

CYST
Encapsulated, fluid-filled cavity in dermis or subcutaneous layer, tensely elevating skin. Examples: sebaceous cyst, wen

- Cyst—encapsulated, fluid-filled lesion that may be in the dermis or subcutaneous. Example: sebaceous cyst

Other

Lesions involving hair include furuncle and carbuncle or comedo (blackhead).

Secondary Lesions

Secondary lesions are due to evolutionary changes in primary lesions.

Below-the-Skin Lesions

- Erosion—a superficial lesion involving only the epidermis, therefore no bleeding; heals without a scar; a scooped-out depression. Example: the appearance of skin after a vesicle has ruptured
- Ulcer—a deeper depression involving the dermis, therefore may bleed and heals with a scar; lesion is irregular. Examples: pressure sore, stasis ulcer, chancre
- Fissure—a linear crack extending into dermis; may be dry or moist. Examples: cheilosis (corners of mouth) or athlete's foot

DEBRIS ON SKIN SURFACE

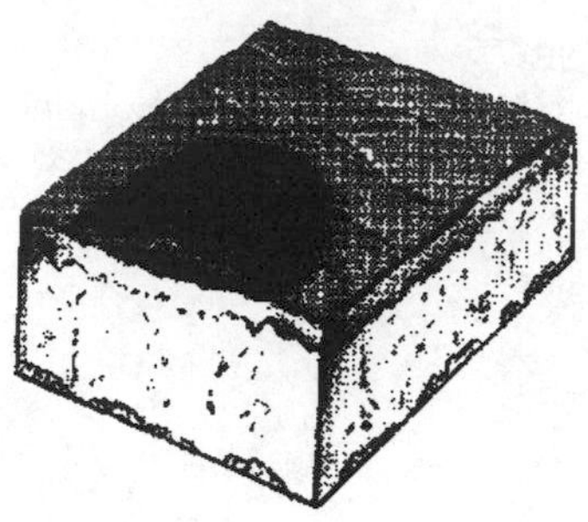

Crust
The thickened, dried-out exudate left when vesicles/pustules burst or dry up. Color can be red-brown, honey, or yellow, depending on the fluid's ingredients (blood, serum, pus). Example: impetigo (dry, honey colored), weeping eczematous dermatitis, scab following abrasion

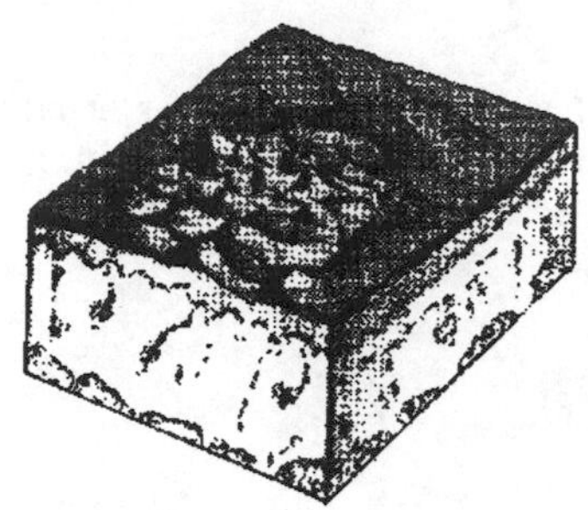

SCALE
Compact, desiccated flakes of skin, dry or greasy, silvery or white, from shedding of dead excess keratin cells. Examples: following scarlet fever or drug reaction (laminated sheets), psoriasis (silver, micalike), seborrheic dermatitis (yellow, greasy), eczema, ichthyosis (large, adherent, laminated), dry skin

BREAK IN CONTINUITY OF SURFACE

Fissure
Linear crack with abrupt edges, extends into dermis, dry or moist. Examples: Cheilosis—at corners of mouth due to excess moisture; athlete's foot

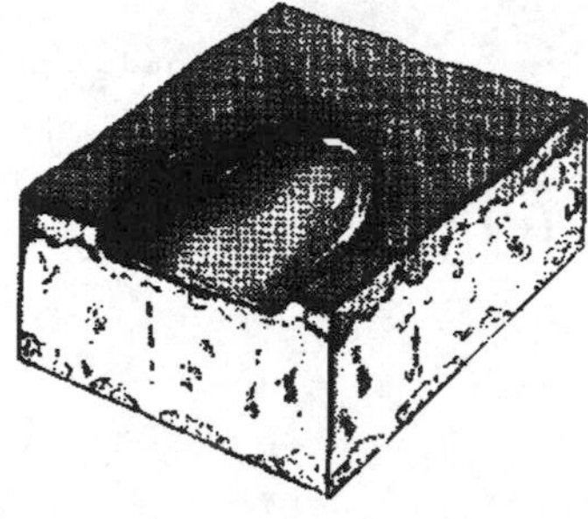

Erosion
Scooped out but shallow depression. Superficial; epidermis lost; moist but no bleeding; heals without scar because erosion does not extend into dermis

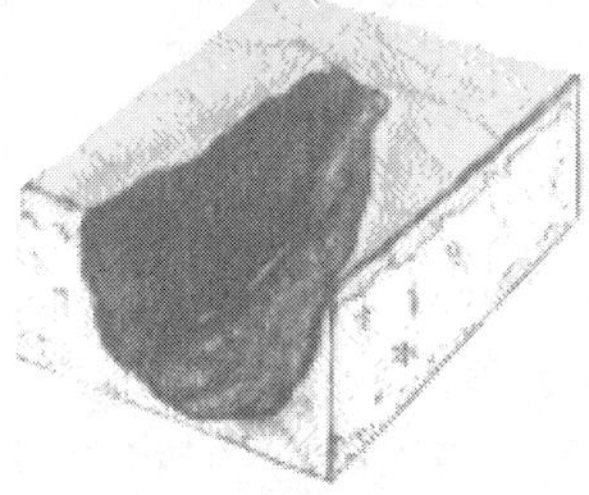

Ulcer
Deeper depression extending into dermis, irregular shape; may bleed; leaves scar when heals. Examples: stasis ulcer, pressure sore, chancre

Excoriation
Self-inflicted abrasion; superficial; sometimes crusted; scratches from intense itching. Examples: insect bites, scabies, dermatitis, varicella

continues

Figure 27–2 Secondary skin lesions. *Source:* Reprinted with permission from C. Jarvis, *Physical Examination and Health Assessment*, 2nd ed., pp. 249–252, © 1996, W.B. Saunders Company.

Figure 27–2 continued

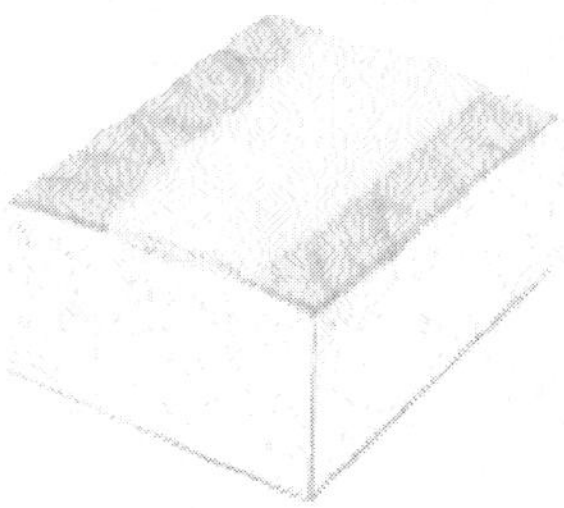

Scar
After a skin lesion is repaired, normal tissue is lost and replaced with connective tissue (collagen). This is a permanent fibrotic change. Examples: healed area of surgery or injury, acne

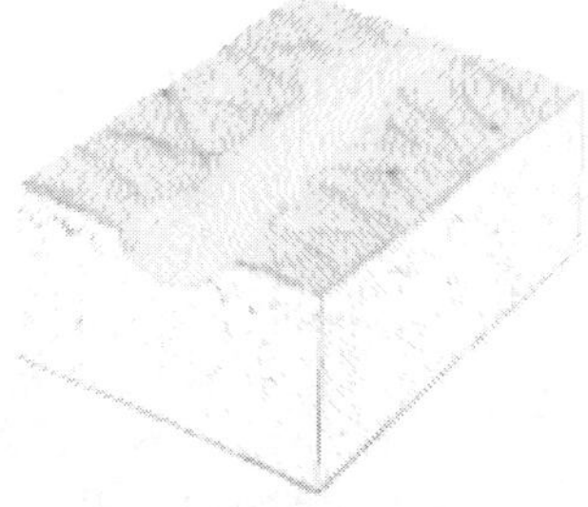

Atrophic Scar
Resulting skin level depressed with loss of tissue; a thinning of the epidermis. Example: striae

Lichenification
Prolonged intense scratching eventually thickens the skin and produces tightly packed sets of papules; looks like surface of moss (or lichen).

Keloid
A hypertrophic scar. The resulting skin level is elevated by excess scar tissue, which is invasive beyond the site of original injury. May increase long after healing occurs. Looks smooth, rubbery, "clawlike," and has a higher incidence among blacks.

- Excoriation—an abrasion that is self-inflicted, usually due to scratching from intense itching. Examples: insect bites, scabies, varicella, dermatitis
- Atrophic scar—thinning of epidermis with associated depression. Examples: striae or injection site for insulin
- Scar—when normal tissue is replaced with connective tissue (collagen) the area is fibrotic. Examples: healed wound from surgery, injury, or acne; a hypertrophic scar (common in blacks) is called a keloid

Above-the-Skin Lesions

- Scaling—flakes of skin from dead epidermis that may be dry or greasy, silvery or white. Examples: psoriasis (silver), seborrheic dermatitis (yellow, greasy), eczema, or simply dry skin
- Crusting—when pustules or vesicles erupt they leave a thickened, dried-up exudate. Examples: impetigo, scab formation following abrasion, weeping eczematous dermatitis
- Lichenification (lichen = mosslike appearance)—an intermediate skin lesion due to prolonged, intense scratching leading to a thickened area of skin characterized by tightly packed papules.

GENERAL STRATEGY

If the patient has a skin complaint, determine whether it is a lesion, pruritus, or skin color change. For skin lesions, do the following:

- Determine whether there is a single lesion or multiple lesions (always check for sites not always visible to the patient).
- Determine whether the onset was associated with other signs such as fever, malaise, or joint pains.

- Determine whether the initial lesions appeared in one area and spread or moved to another.
- Determine whether there is associated pruritus.
- Determine whether there are other contact individuals with similar presentations.
- Elicit a medication history, including topical skin applications.
- Determine whether a rash occurred after sun exposure (miliaria [heat rash]).
- Determine whether the patient was exposed to dyes or color film developers (lichen planus).
- With single pigmented lesions, determine any "danger signs," such as enlargement, change in color, ulceration, or change in sensation (melanoma).

With pruritus as the chief complaint (no obvious skin lesions):

- Determine whether the patient lives or works in an environment that is dry or whether central heating is used.
- Determine whether the patient may have been exposed to fiberglass.
- Determine whether the patient has signs or past diagnosis of renal failure.
- Determine whether the patient has signs of hypo- or hyperthyroidism.
- If the patient complains of specific itching of face, scalp, and genitalia without skin lesions, consider depression.

With skin color changes (not a color change of a lesion; see above):

- Determine whether the patient has had signs of flu and the skin color is yellow (jaundice).
- Determine whether the patient has associated signs of fatigue and has a brown-tan appearance without exposure to the sun (Addison's disease).
- Determine whether the color change is localized to an area of skin and whether this occurred at birth or was acquired (mongolian spots, café au lait spots, vitiligo, some vascular nevi).

EVALUATION

Contact and Allergic Dermatitis

One should first attempt to identify a contact allergen, especially when skin lesions appear to be regional (Table 27–1). Any environmental contact is a potential source. The most common are soaps, lotions, clothing, and poison oak or poison ivy. The onset and relationship to the potential contact allergen are usually clear.

Drug reactions are rare; however, they do occur in 2% to 3% of hospitalized patients. The onset is usually abrupt, resulting in a maculopapular rash involving the entire body or symmetrically the extremities. This may be accompanied by severe itching. The most common drugs are amoxicillin, trimethoprim-sulfamethoxazole, penicillin, or ampicillin. Fixed, single, or multiple lesions that become hyperpigmented are seen with reactions to barbiturates and tetracycline.

Childhood Diseases

With children, maculopapular rashes are caused by common childhood diseases, including chickenpox (varicella) , measles (rubeola), German measles (rubella), and roseola. One helpful clue is a history of exposure to a patient with known disease (incubation period for most is 2 to 3 weeks). Second, the initial location of the rash and its evolution will usually make the diagnosis clear. A brief description of each follows:

- Varicella—Mild, generalized symptoms of malaise, fever, or headache are followed by lesions that first appear on the trunk and then spread to the face and extremities; the sequence of evolution is important, starting as maculopapules, changing in hours to vesicles, pustules, and crusting (new lesions may appear over 3 to 5 days).
- Rubeola—The rash is preceded usually by a high fever (104° to 105°F); 2 days before the rash, Koplick spots (resembling table-salt crystals) appear on the mucus membranes of the mouth (these are pathognomonic for measles); the rash appears on the face and behind the ears about 4 days after the onset of symptoms and spreads to the trunk and extremities (including soles of feet and palms).
- Rubella—Preceded by mild symptoms, the rash first appears on the face as a fine, pink rash that spreads to the trunk and extremities quickly over 2 to 3 days; the rash disappears over 1 day in each area (some patients do not have a rash).
- Roseola—Roseola is most common in infants between ages 6 and 18 months; it is heralded by a high fever (103° to 105°F) for 4 to 5 days followed by a faint macular rash on the trunk that lasts a few days.

When erythematous lesions follow an upper respiratory infection or flu (especially in children), two possibilities should be investigated: (1) erythema multiforme and (2) erythema nodosum. Erythema multiforme lesions are symmetric and may be bullous lesions involving the distal

Table 27–1 Contact Dermatitis

Body Area	*Cause*
Face and neck	
Scalp	Hair sprays, shampoos, conditioners, hair dyes
Sides of neck	Perfumes, hair sprays, insect sprays
Forehead	Hatband
Around the mouth	Lipstick, mouthwashes, toothpaste
Earlobes	Metal earrings
Face	Soaps or cosmetics
Hands and forearms	
Fingers/hands	Soaps, soap under rings, rings, fingernail polish
Forearms	Soaps, insect spray, wrist bands or tennis elbow brace, tape
Axillae	Deodorants, dress shields, dry cleaning solutions
Trunk	Any new clothing (especially wool or clothing with a dye) or clothing with attached metal or rubber
Anogenital	Douches, contraceptive creams, dusting powder, colored toilet paper, medications used to treat pruritus ani or fungal infections in infants
Feet	Shoe or foot powders, treatment for athlete's foot
Generalized	Bath soaps, clothing, drug allergy

extremities or mucous membranes. They are referred to as target or iris lesions forming a concentric ring with a central purpura (grayish discoloration). Erythema nodosum commonly involves the pretibial area or arms. Red, tender nodules are found. There are numerous other causes in adults. Treatment of the above is mainly for the underlying disease; antibiotics are often used.

Scaling

When scaling is prominent there are a few common disorders to consider. Their distribution and characteristic presentation are often helpful. Following is a list with a brief description of each:

- Eczema (atopic dermatitis)—There is often a personal or family history of allergies or asthma; itching may be a prominent symptom with dermal inflammation occurring on the face, neck, upper trunk, hands and wrists, popliteal area of the knees, and antecubital area of the elbows. Constant itching may lead to lichenification. Eczema is chronic and recurrent.
- Psoriasis—silvery scaling or red plaquing that is usually not itchy appears on the scalp and extensor surfaces of the extremities, particularly the knees and elbows (although some patients may have inverse psoriasis in body folds that is itchy); associated findings include pitting of fingernails or onycholysis (nail separation); some patients may have an associated arthritis of the fingers or sacroiliac joint. Psoriasis is chronic and recurrent.
- Seborrheic dermatitis—This disorder presents as either a dry or oily scaling with a predilection for the scalp, eyebrows, body folds, and presternal or intrascapular areas; it is possibly yeast related. Factors such as stress, nutrition, and seasonal effects (drier humidity in winter due to heated homes) play a role. Patients who are more prone include those with Parkinson's disease, those who are chronically hospitalized, and those with HIV. Seborrheic dermatitis is chronic and recurrent.
- Pityriasis rosea—This disorder appears as oval-shaped, fawn-colored, scaly eruptions. A single patch, called a herald patch, appears 1 to 2 weeks prior to more extensive involvement of the cleavage lines of the trunk; the

center of the lesions has a cigarette-paper appearance. Pityriasis rosea is more common in women and in the spring or fall (may be due to a virus); it is self-resolving over 1 to 2 months.
- Tinea capitis—a presentation similar to that of seborrheic dermatitis occurring in children is tinea capitis due to head lice. There are often small areas of hair loss (alopecia), with broken off or short stubs of hair visible. Accompanying cervical lymphadenopathy is often present. Tinea capitis is more common in African-Americans.

Pruritus

Many skin disorders have itching as an accompanying complaint; however, when the main complaint is itching, a search may be narrowed by location or associated findings. Following are some common presentations:

- Dry skin—Dry skin from environmental causes is more common in the winter, with low-humidity environments in heated homes. Skin may also become dry from frequent bathing or use of soaps with some individuals. Dry skin is also part of the presentation of hypothyroidism.
- Metabolic disease—Uremia occurring with kidney failure (or with hemodialysis), obstructive liver disease, or malignant disorders (leukemia, lymphoma, or other cancers) may cause itching.
- Psychiatric disorder—Patients who complain of burning and itching that involve primarily the face, scalp, and genitalia with no obvious skin lesions may have an underlying depression.
- Genital/anal itching—In addition to the above-mentioned depression, anal itching may be due to irritation from toilet paper, contact dermatitis, extension of psoriasis or seborrheic dermatitis, irritation from fecal content or diarrhea, or pinworm in children. Localized vaginal itching suggests yeast infection in women (frequent occurrence in diabetics); in athletes and in the obese, "jock itch" (tinea cruris) is a common cause of groin pruritus (sparing the scrotum in men).
- Scabies—When the itching is primarily at night, scabies should be considered. Scabies is caused by mite infestation acquired through bedding or an infested individual. The most common location of lesions is on the sides of fingers and on the palms, appearing as vesicles and pustules occurring as "runs" or "burrows."
- Urticaria—Urticaria is a hypersensitivity reaction mediated by immunoglobulin E with quickly changing wheals or hives. The common causes are drugs, insect bites, heat (including hot showers) or cold, exercise or excitement, or reactions to vaccines or food (shellfish or strawberries). The response may be mild or lead to difficulty breathing; severe responses require epinephrine.
- Ringworm (tinea corporis or circinata)—Ring-shaped lesions appear on the face or arms after exposure to an infected cat (some patients have only scaly patches).
- Lichen planus—Violet lesions along scratch marks with a symmetric distribution in a patient exposed to color dyes or in color film developers is suggestive.

Acne Vulgaris

Acne vulgaris is probably the most common skin condition; it is caused by sebaceous overactivity with subsequent plugging of follicles, leading to infection with the acne bacillus (*Propionibacterium acnes, Staphylococcus albus,* or *Pityrosporon ovale*). Overspill of sebum and fatty acids causes local irritation. Acne vulgaris often begins at puberty and is much more common and severe in males. A similar problem, rosacea, may occur in middle-aged patients and is associated with a higher incidence of migraine headaches. These patients may complain of burning or stinging of the face associated with flushing. It should be kept in mind that large, muscular, young men with acne may be abusing steroids.

The lesions with acne vulgaris are commonly found on the face and upper trunk area. The most common lesion is a comedone (blackhead). Papules, pustules, and cysts may also be seen. The general approach to treatment involves avoidance of touching the lesions, using an over-the-counter benzoyl peroxide cleanser, and avoidance of foods that seem to increase the occurrence. With moderate acne, antibiotic creams or oral antibiotics may be used. With severe acne, isotretinoin (Accutane) is often used.

Warts

Warts are a common complaint representing single or multiple papules often on the hands or feet. Anogenital warts are not uncommon in homosexual men. Warts are due to a viral infection and often heal spontaneously. Large, chronic warts in older individuals may represent squamous cell carcinoma and should be biopsied. Treatment for warts is usually with over-the-counter salicylic acid products or liquid nitrogen, or surgical or laser removal.

Venereal Disease

Venereal disease does not always present with skin lesions; however, those that do should be recognized and referred.

Chancroid is caused by *Haemophilus ducreyi,* beginning with a vesicopustule that breaks down and forms a soft, painful ulcer with a necrotic base. The chancre of syphilis, in contrast, is clean, painless, and characterized by a hard base. Granuloma inguinale produces painless nodules with a bright-red friable base. Lesions tend to spread out and can become infected secondarily. Lymphogranuloma venereum is caused by *Chlamydia trachomatis,* producing a quickly vanishing ulcerative lesion on the external genitalia. The characteristic associated finding is inguinal lymphadenopathy producing soft, matted nodes. A patient with herpes simplex virus type 2 will usually present with burning and stinging in a patch of skin in the genital or buttocks area that evolves into a lesion made up of small, grouped vesicles that eventually crust and fall off. Inguinal lymph nodes are often enlarged. Although only a brief introduction, any of the above descriptions or any genital lesions in a sexually active person should be considered suspicious, and referral for laboratory confirmation should be achieved through medical referral. Antibiotics are used for the bacterial causes, and acyclovir is used for herpes simplex virus type 2.

Skin Lesions Associated with Polyarthritis/Rheumatic Conditions

Skin lesions are sometimes associated with conditions that cause joint pain and, therefore may present to a chiropractic office. The most common conditions are rheumatoid arthritis, seronegative arthritides, and connective tissue disorders. Most conditions have characteristic regional joint involvement and radiographic findings that support the diagnosis. However, skin involvement may assist in the diagnosis or, in a patient already diagnosed, may represent an indicator of disease activity. Following is a brief list:

- Reiter's syndrome—keratogenous lesions on the feet, oral ulcers (also uveitis and conjunctivitis)
- ankylosis spondylitis (although not specifically skin)—uveitis and conjunctivitis
- psoriatic arthritis—psoriatic lesions (usually extensor surfaces), pitting of nails
- rheumatoid arthritis—subcutaneous nodules (often extensor surfaces)
- systemic lupus erthythematosus (SLE)—malar erythema, rash, hair loss, oral ulcers
- scleroderma—atrophic, edematous thickening of the skin
- sarcoidosis—erthythema nodosum (tender nodules over pretibial area)
- dermatomyositis—discoloration of upper eyelids

Skin Cancer

Patients and chiropractors should be aware of the relative risks of developing skin cancer. They are[1]:

- a history of childhood sunburns
- excessive exposure to sunlight as a child
- excessive exposure through occupation and recreational activities
- fair skin, light hair, and light-colored eyes, especially Irish or Scottish descent
- the presence of more than 50 moles
- a poor ability to tan or tendency toward sunburn
- a family history of skin cancers
- exposure to therapeutic radiography (acne, cancer) or ultraviolet light (psoriasis)
- immunosuppression such as in acquired immunodeficiency syndrome or organ transplantation

Probably the single most important role the chiropractor may play in the evaluation of a patient's skin is the detection of suspicious lesions in need of dermatologic referral. The most important is malignant melanoma. The distinction between a benign lesion and a malignant lesion is summarized by the American Cancer Society mnemonic ABCD (Asymmetry, Border irregularity, Color variation, and Diameter > 6 mm). Therefore, a mole that is burning, stinging, itching, changing shape or color, or growing or bleeding requires a dermatologic evaluation. Unfortunately, in the elderly and the diabetic, these lesions are often ignored by physicians who assume that they are the consequence of poor healing. Basal cell carcinoma is more common in fair-skinned, young adults with chronic sun exposure. The lesions are found on areas of skin exposed to sun and appear as papules or nodules with a characteristic "pearly" or translucent appearance. Squamous cell carcinoma, although occurring in a similar group of patients, is not as easily detected. The lesions are usually small, red, hard nodules that ulcerate.

The incidence rate for malignant melanoma has risen 4% per year since 1975, so that the rate of melanoma has gone from 1/1,500 persons in 1935 to a predicted risk of 1/75 in the year 2000 for those living in the United States.[2] However, the 5-year survival rate has gone from 40% in the 1940s to a current rate of 87%. The smaller the lesion the higher the predicted rate of survival. If the lesion is less than 1 mm thick, the survival rate approaches 95%; however, if the lesion is greater than 4 mm thick, the survival rate drops to 50% over 5 years.[3]

The ability of nondermatologists to detect skin cancer is not impressive. By testing with color pictures, one study indicated that malignant melanoma was correctly identified by only 12% of nondermatologists; an atypical mole by 42%

(98% of dermatologists correctly identified).[4] Another limiting factor is that malignant melanoma occurs in exposed areas only 20% of the time, requiring a full body examination. Many patients are embarrassed by full body examination. Even if the examination is performed (with a patient same-sex "chaperone") a lesion may still be missed. More education in detection of skin cancer is needed in the education of nondermatologist health care providers.

Self-examination may be helpful in detecting some of the "danger" signs. One study indicated that patients instructed on self-examination for palpable arm nevi and larger (> 5 mm) nevi scored specificities of 63% and 68%, respectively.[5] The recommendation for self-examination, coupled with an annual examination in patients over 40 and every 3 years in younger patients, is important in detecting skin cancer.

MANAGEMENT

- If the underlying cause is obviously a contact dermatitis—unless complicated by infection—time and the use of over-the-counter medications such as corticosteroid creams, diphenhydramine hydrochloride (Benadryl), or calamine lotion for poison ivy are usually sufficient.
- For drug-reaction dermatitis, refer back to the prescribing physician or, if over-the-counter, have the patient discontinue use.
- Common childhood diseases (measles, rubella, chickenpox) usually resolve with minimal palliative care; all common childhood diseases should be monitored, and exposed individuals or institutions such as schools should be contacted. Each state has a list of reportable diseases; check individual state for reporting criteria. Monitor for complications.
- Seborrheic dermatitis and acne, if mild, may be helped minimally with over-the-counter medication; however, dermatologic referral is necessary in more involved cases.
- Refer all cases of venereal-related skin disease.
- Comanagement of collagen-vascular cases or referral is suggested.
- Refer all cases of suspected skin cancer to a dermatologist.
- Refer all cases that are not identifiable and worrisome to the patient to a dermatologist.

REFERENCES

1. Daniel CR III, Dolan NC, Wheeland RG. Don't overlook skin surveillance. *Patient Care.* 1996;30:90–107.
2. American Cancer Society. *Cancer Facts and Figures—1996.* Atlanta; 1996.
3. Drake LA, Ceilley RI, Cornelisen RL, et al. Guidelines of care in malignant melanoma. *J Am Acad Dermatol.* 1993;28:638–641.
4. Wagner RF, Wagner D, Tomich JM, et al. Diagnosis of skin cancer: dermatologists vs nondermatologists. *J Dermatol Surg Oncol.* 1985;11:476–479.
5. Gruber SB, Roush GC, Barnhill RL. Sensitivity and specificity of self-examination for cutaneous malignant melanoma risk factors. *Am J Prev Med.* 1993;9:50–54.

Chapter 28

Vaccination: A Brief Overview

The subject of vaccination is likely to touch off a strong emotional reaction by many chiropractors who are concerned about the need and safety of this approach to disease. Many chiropractors "philosophically" support the idea of "naturally" acquired immunity over "imposed" immunity. They feel that it is not harmful, and perhaps that it is important for the body to fight its own battles; by preventing this occurrence, the body may be impaired in its ability to react to other invaders. Specifically, the main concerns as outlined by Anderson[1] are as follows:

- Some vaccinations are for diseases that do not carry with them serious consequences for most individuals.
- Some vaccines are not entirely effective.
- Vaccinations may be dangerous themselves.
- The data or the author of studies that support vaccination are flawed (biased, uncontrolled, underreported adverse effects, etc.).

When asked for specifics in defense of nonvaccination, most chiropractors will admit to ignorance. Often the answer is, "It just doesn't seem right!" The debate will continue; however, it is important to have a general sense of the issues. Following is a brief list of concerns that are addressed below:

- Are all the diseases that vaccines are designed to prevent equally serious?
- How effective are vaccines?
- What is the relative risk of using vaccines?
- What are the comparable rates of morbidity and mortality with nonvaccination?
- Are all vaccinations equally effective or risky?
- What has the government done to determine the answers to these concerns?
- What should a chiropractor advise his or her patients?

The recommended vaccinations for children without known contraindications include the following[2]:

- DTP (also called DPT)—diphtheria-tetanus-pertussis (immunization schedule is at ages 2, 4, and 6 months; DTP at 12 to 18 months or DTPaP at 15 to 18 months and between the ages of 4 and 6 years; a Td booster at age 11 or 12)
- OPV—oral poliovirus (immunization schedule at 2 and 4 months, 6 to 18 months, and 4 to 6 years)
- MMR—measles-mumps-rubella (immunization schedule at age 12 to 15 months, 4 to 6 years of age, or 11 to 12 years of age as an option)
- conjugate *Haemophilus influenzae*, type b (Hb) (immunization schedule generally at 2, 4, and 6 months with a booster at 12 to 15 months)
- hepatitis B—(immunization schedule is first at 0 to 2 months, the second 1 to 2 months after the first, and the third at 6 to 18 months [at least 4 months after the second])
- varicella—(immunization schedule is between 12 and 18 months; however, the duration of immunity may allow infection as an adult with more serious consequences, requiring a booster shot [or no vaccination in the first place])

For children at high risk, the following vaccinations have been recommended:

- hepatitis A
- pneumococcal
- annual influenza

A movement began in the 1980s among average citizens questioning the safety and efficacy of vaccination. This also involved an increased number of lawsuits against vaccine manufacturers. In response to these concerns the US Congress passed the National Childhood Vaccine Injury Act (Pub. L. No. 99-660) in 1986. In addition to having impact on vaccination policies and programs, this act provided a federally funded compensation program for individuals injured by vaccines. Another mandate of the act was the establishment of two review committees conducted under the Institute of Medicine. The first review, *Adverse Effects of Pertussis and Rubella Vaccines,* was published in 1991.[3] The second review, *Adverse Events Associated with Childhood Vaccines: Evidence Bearing on Causality*, was published in 1994.[4] With regard to causality, the committee found the following[5]:

- insufficient evidence to indicate the presence or absence of causal relation between DTP vaccine and chronic neurologic damage, aseptic meningitis, erythema multiforme or other rash, Guillain-Barré syndrome, hemolytic anemia, "juvenile" diabetes, learning disabilities or attention deficit disorder, peripheral neuropathy, or thrombocytopenia
- insufficient evidence to indicate the presence or absence of causal relation between rubella vaccine and radiculoneuritis and other neuropathies or thrombocytopenia purpura
- no causal relation between diphtheria and tetanus toxoids and encephalopathy, infantile spasms, or sudden infant death syndrome
- no evidence for increased susceptibility to Hb disease and conjugate Hb vaccines
- causal relation between DTP vaccine and anaphylaxis and between the pertussis component of DTP and uncontrollable crying and screaming
- causal relation between rubella vaccine and acute arthritis in women; weaker evidence for chronic arthritis in women
- causal relation (but weaker evidence) between DTP and acute encephalopathy and hypotonic, hyporesponsive episodes
- causal relation between diphtheria and tetanus toxoids and anaphylaxis, Guillain-Barré syndrome, and brachial neuritis
- causal relation between measles vaccine and anaphylaxis and death
- causal relation between unconjugated Hb vaccine and susceptibility to Hb disease
- causal relation between MMR vaccination and thrombocytopenia and anaphylaxis
- causal relation between OPV and paralytic polio and death

It is important to caution the reader that some of these were implicated from case studies, and the number of adverse reactions is actually extremely low. For example, the MMR vaccine has been used for 20 years, yet there were only two well-documented cases of anaphylaxis (neither was fatal) in the literature.

OPV (POLIO)

Probably 90% of individuals exposed to polio show no symptoms and rarely do the paralytic consequences occur. Yet when looked at from the perspective of total numbers of cases, the perception of a benign disease changes. In 1952, the reported number of paralytic cases was 20,000. The incidence of paralytic poliomyelitis from vaccine is approximately 1 case in 500,000 first doses and 1 case per 12 million subsequent doses. This averages to 1 paralytic reaction out of 2.5 million vaccine doses. In the United States since 1980, the average number of cases per year is eight. The efficacy of the OPV vaccine using all three doses is 95% to 100% in children for all three poliovirus types. The relative risk of developing Guillain-Barré syndrome in adult vaccinations was low.

MMR (FOCUS ON MEASLES)

Most measles cases in the United States will resolve without complications. One in 3000 cases develop postmeasles encephalomyelitis (PMENM) resulting in a 15% death rate.[6] Another 25% of patients developing PMENM have lasting disability. One of 100,000 measles cases develops subacute sclerosing panencephalitis (SSPE) leading to death. Measles leading to secondary infection is the cause of a worldwide death rate of 1.5 million per year.[7] Measles may also cause deafness.

Between 1989 and 1994, the number of vaccine failures appeared to be approximately 20%, due to a single dose after 12 months of age.[8] Using a two-dose program virtually eliminates this failure rate. The number of reactions to MMR vaccine appears to be quite low. The number of cases of thrombocytopenia was approximately 3/100,000 vaccinated persons; for anaphylaxis, 0.1-5/100,000.[3] There are only a few reported deaths, all occurring in immunocompromised children (none in human immunodeficiency virus [HIV]-infected children). The risk of SSPE due to vaccination is ⅕ to 1/40 the risk of developing SSPE following measles by natural infection.[4]

DTP (FOCUS ON PERTUSSIS)

The pertussis portion of the DTP vaccine is associated with higher reaction rates than other vaccines. DTP has been associated with febrile seizures in about 57/100,000 doses and hypotonic/hyporesponsive episodes in 3.5 to 291/100,000 doses.[4] Febrile seizures appear to be more likely to occur in children with a personal or family history of seizures. The vast majority of febrile seizures were benign. Acute neurologic reaction will usually occur within the first 7 days after receiving the DTP. One large British study[9] indicated a severe neurologic reaction in 6.8 per million doses and acute encephalopathy in 2.7 per million doses. It is important to point out that the incidence of serious neurologic illness is 10 times higher with pertussis than with the DTP vaccination. However, the incidence of reactions has led to the development of less reactive acellular forms. The acellular pertussis-component DTaP appears to cause far fewer side effects.

SUMMARY

Although this is a brief discussion, it is to be hoped that it has demonstrated the multifactorial nature of the issues. In addition to a philosophic reaction, chiropractors may bolster their reaction with broad statements that do not appear to be supported in the literature. In other words, a list of adverse reactions is given without a comparison to the numbers of adverse reactions with naturally acquiring the illness. Ironically, the chance of contracting a disease if not immunized is quite low, yet this is due to the campaign of immunization that has successfully decreased the incidence. Conversely, the literature may suffer from bias or underreporting.[10] Some parents may wish to let nature take its course and accept the consequences. However, issues that must be considered are the worldwide effect of immunization, the effect of parents' individual decisions not to immunize their children on other children, and the risks of certain groups such as immunocompromised children and those with a family history of seizures or other disorders. Therefore it would seem prudent to provide patients with a presentation of what is and what is not known, the relative risk, and the government's recommendations. It is this author's recommendation that the patient not be misled by personal bias. Allow the patient to make his or her own educated decision after presenting both sides. Obviously, some vaccines are more important than others in preventing serious disease.

SOME CHILDHOOD DISEASES*

MEASLES (RUBEOLA)

Classic Presentation

The patient presents with a history of a high fever (103° to 105°F), runny nose, sore throat, and cough several days before the appearance of a bright-red rash. The rash began on the face and behind the ears and then spread to the trunk and extremities.

Cause

Infection is by paramyxovirus acquired through inhalation of droplets. Measles is most communicable before the rash appears and is essentially noncommunicable when the rash disappears. The incubation period is 10 to 14 days. Worldwide, 1 million children per year die of measles.

Evaluation

Prior to the onset of the rash, the patient may have a pathognomonic finding of tiny white spots on the mucous membranes in the mouth called Koplik's spots. The spots are still present when the rash appears. Laboratory testing is usually not necessary. A serum hemagglutination inhibition antibody level that is found to be four times normal is diagnostic for measles. Standard laboratory tests demonstrate leukopenia and possible proteinuria.

Management

Treat measles symptomatically.

*For these diseases, check local state health regulations regarding reporting requirements.

GERMAN MEASLES (RUBELLA)

Classic Presentation

The patient may report having had a mild fever or malaise up to a week prior to the appearance of a light rash that appeared on the face first and then spread to the trunk and extremities. The rash faded (or is fading) quickly over 1 day per site.

Cause

Rubella is caused by inhalation of droplets of togavirus. The incubation period is between 2 and 3 weeks. Communicability occurs 1 week before the rash and continues for up to 2 weeks.

Evaluation

There is a characteristic cervical and postauricular lymphadenopathy in most patients. The rash does not appear in all cases and without its appearance, the diagnosis would be difficult to make unless there was a history of exposure. Laboratory testing with rubella virus hemagglutination inhibition and fluorescent antibody tests is usually not necessary except in the case of pregnancy. A pregnant female infected with rubella during the first trimester carries the risk of conveying congenital rubella 80% of the time.[11]

Management

Treat rubella symptomatically.

VARICELLA (CHICKENPOX)

Classic Presentation

The patient presents with a history of mild malaise, anorexia, mild headache, and fever followed in 24 hours by the appearance of a pruritic, vesicular rash that began first on the trunk (and oropharynx), spread to the face, and spread less to the extremities. New vesicles are appearing as the older ones are crusting (over 1 to 5 days).

Cause

Chickenpox is a highly contagious infection with human herpesvirus 3 (the same organism for herpes zoster [shingles]). Infection is through either inhalation of infective particles or direct contact with lesions. The incubation period is 10 to 20 days.

Evaluation

The rash is usually diagnostic. Laboratory evaluation could include a Tzanck test of vesicle scrapings for confirmation, although it is rarely necessary.

Management

The patient should be isolated because of the contagious nature of the vesicles. Topical calamine lotion or over-the-counter antihistamines may help with the itching. It is important to keep the skin clean and to avoid scratching, preventing minor scarring. Aspirin for children should be avoided because of the possibility of Reye's syndrome.

MUMPS

Classic Presentation

The patient presents with painful, swollen parotid glands. Mild malaise or fever may be present.

Cause

Paramyxovirus is the cause of mumps. Inhalation of infective droplets is the mechanism. The salivary glands become inflamed. Complications such as orchitis, pancreatitis, and meningitis are more likely to occur when the patient is older. The incubation period is 2 to 3 weeks.

Evaluation

The presentation of parotid gland swelling is usually quite clear, often beginning with one gland first and in 1 to 3 days the other. A headache and stiff neck suggest meningeal involvement. Abdominal pain with nausea and vomiting suggests pancreatitis. Testicular pain suggests orchitis. Lymphocytosis and an elevated serum amylase (with or without pancreatitis) are often found. The organism may be tested in saliva; if present, there is a sharp increase in complement-fixing antibodies.

Management

Isolate the patient while the glands are swollen. If the patient has a fever, require bed rest because of the strong possibility of aseptic meningitis. Watch for complications.

REFERENCES

1. Anderson R. Chiropractors for and against vaccines. In: *Medical Anthropology.* New York: Gordon and Breach Science Publishers; 1990;12:169–186.
2. U.S. Preventive Services Task Force. Childhood immunizations. In: U.S. Preventive Services Task Force. *Guide to Clinical Preventive Services*. 2nd ed. Baltimore: Wiliams & Wilkins; 1996:767–790.
3. Howson CP, Howe CJ, Feinberg HV, eds. *Adverse Effects of Pertussis and Rubella Vaccines*. Washington, DC: National Academy Press; 1991.
4. Stratton KB, Howe CJ, Johnston RB Jr, eds. *Adverse Events Associated with Childhood Vaccines: Evidence Bearing on Causality*. Washington, DC: National Academy Press; 1994.
5. Stratton KB, Howe CJ, Johnston RB Jr. Adverse events associated with childhood vaccines other than pertussis and rubella: summary of a report from the Institute of Medicine. *JAMA*. 1994;271: 160–165.
6. Bloch AB, Orenstein SG, Wassilak CS, Harrison PM, et al. Epidemiology of measles and its complications. *Monogr Epidemiol Biostat*. 1986;9:5–20.
7. Johnson RT, Griffin DE. Virus induced autoimmune demyelination disease of the central nervous system. In: Motkins AL, Oldstone MBA, eds. *Concepts in Viral Pathogenesis*. New York: Springer-Verlag; 1986;2:203–209.
8. Centers for Disease Control and Prevention. Measles—United States 1994. *MMWR*. 1995;44:486–487, 493–494.
9. Miller D, Wadsworth J, Diamond J, et al. Pertussis vaccine and whooping cough as risk factors in acute neurological illness and death in young children. *Dev Biol Stand*. 1985;61:389–394.
10. Coulter H, Fisher B. *DPT: A Shot in the Dark*. New York: Avery Publishing Group; 1985.
11. Less SH. Resurgence of congenital rubella syndrome in the 1990's. *JAMA*. 1992;267:2616.

CHAPTER 29

Weight Loss

CONTEXT

Rapid or excessive weight loss is often viewed as an ominous sign indicating life-threatening cancer. It is true that 25% of patients die within the first year of significant weight loss detection. However, studies indicate that although a significant percentage of patients (7% to 36%) have cancer, very few are occult malignancies.[1–4] Another significant percentage of patients (9% to 18%) are diagnosed as depressed. Fourteen to seventeen percent of patients have a gastrointestinal disorder such as inflammatory bowel disease, malabsorption, or peptic ulcer. Twenty-three to thirty-five percent of patients have no identifiable cause for their weight loss.

Weight loss is a comparative measurement. Past documentation as a base reference is necessary to establish true weight loss. When this information is not available, the next reliable source is family members. The severity of weight loss with regard to significance is not clearly defined. An accepted standard is loss of more than 5% of total body weight within 6 months or 10% within 1 year. It is interesting to note that as many as 50% of patients who complain of significant weight loss are unsupported by past medical records or family members.[2] Only about one third of patients with significant weight loss report it as the chief complaint. The remainder have systemic complaints that are elevated to a higher level of concern because of an associated weight loss.

The significance of weight loss increases with age. Either low body weight or unintentional loss of weight factors into increased morbidity and mortality.[5] Obviously, this is a multifactorial occurrence given that the elderly have a naturally higher morbidity and mortality rate. Compared with risk to seniors who are at ideal or high body weight, the risk of death is significantly higher with very low body weight. In a sense, those with higher body mass are protected because of an available "reserve" that buffers them from reaching the critical threshold beneath which skeletal and cardiac muscle wasting occur.

GENERAL STRATEGY

History

- Attempt to document a significant loss of weight from past medical records or corroborate the patient's report with family member support or at the very least a change in clothes or belt size.
- Determine whether weight loss is intentional. If it is, determine whether the patient is educated in proper dieting.
- If weight loss is intentional, determine whether the patient feels that although he or she appears thin, the patient's perception is that he or she is overweight.
- If weight loss is unintentional, determine whether the patient's food intake is normal or decreased.
- If food intake is normal, determine whether there is associated diarrhea.
- If food intake is decreased, determine whether the patient has pain or discomfort associated with eating.
- Obtain a full medication, drug, and alcohol history.
- Screen the patient for depression or other psychologic problems.
- Determine if there are any symptoms that might suggest cancer, hyperthyroidism, diabetes, or gastrointestinal pathology, including peptic ulcer disease or inflammatory bowel disease.
- Determine the patient's ability to feed themselves (financially, functionally, environmentally).

Evaluation

- Attempt to document true weight loss greater than 5% over 6 months or 10% over a year, comparing with any available past medical records.
- Look for indications of "occult" disease through examination of the mouth, skin, and lymph nodes.
- Look for any indications of hyperthyroidism, including a fine tremor, exophthalmos or lid lag, increased pulse, and respiratory rate.
- Evaluate the patient for chronic obstructive pulmonary disease (COPD) if suggested from history (chronic cough in a smoker for 3 consecutive months for 2 years).
- Evaluate the patient with laboratory testing for any suspected underlying metabolic problems such as anemia, diabetes, hyperthyroidism, cancer, liver, and kidney disease.
- Evaluate the patient with a chest radiograph (especially in smokers) and stool Hemoccult tests.
- Radiography of painful joints may reveal a metastatic or primary process. If negative yet the suspicion is high, a bone scan is warranted (especially in a patient with a past history of cancer).
- Refer for upper gastrointestinal studies, endoscopy, or colonoscopy in patients with suspected upper and lower gastrointestinal disease.

Management

- If occult processes are discovered or still suspected after evaluation, refer to an internist.
- Refer to a psychiatrist for depression and other psychologic problems.
- Refer to an eating disorders clinic if anorexia nervosa is suspected.
- Refer to a medical physician for evaluation of medication-induced weight loss or possible medical control of anorexia or cachexia if needed.

RELEVANT PHYSIOLOGY

Weight loss occurs because of a decrease in caloric intake, increase in utilization, or loss in the stool or urine. A number of factors may contribute to weight loss when caloric intake is the cause, including anorexia, nausea, altered sense of taste or smell, and altered perception of satiety. High on the list of causes are cancer, depression, and medications. Following are some proposed mechanisms in these patients:

- Humoral substances (bombesin and somatostatin) may cause early satiety or anorexia in patients with cancer, possibly due to a distension effect.[6]
- Cytokines (tumor necrosis factor, methyl *N*-methylnipecotate [Adipsin], and interleukin 1) are causes of anorexia in patients with cancer, acquired immunodeficiency syndrome (AIDS), and infection.[7]
- Decreased norepinephrine and increased corticotropin-releasing factor levels may play a role in an early satiety effect or food aversion with depression.[8]
- In the elderly, the satiety effect of cholecystokinin is increased; zinc deficiency may cause anorexia.

Of course, a decrease in caloric intake may be voluntary, as is the case with anorexia nervosa, or involuntary because of isolation or economic hardship.

Increased utilization may be due to demands of increased physical exertion as is seen in marathon runners and triathletes. Internal metabolic demands may come from hypermetabolic states such as hyperthyroidism (more rarely pheochromocytoma) or cancer. Weight loss may be the most common presenting complaint of the elderly with hyperthyroidism. Patients with either congestive heart failure or chronic pulmonary disease may lose weight due to an increased workload of breathing.

Medications may lead to significant weight loss through a variety of mechanisms. Following are some common examples:

- Nonsteroidal antiinflammatory drugs (NSAIDs), theophylline, quinidine, procainamide, and other drugs may cause nausea.
- Digoxin toxicity causes stimulation of the "vomit" center in the medulla, leading to anorexia, nausea, and vomiting.
- Angiotensin-converting enzyme (ACE) inhibitors may alter taste or smell.
- Tricyclic antidepressants, diuretics, and clonidine may cause dry mouth, which adversely affects swallowing.
- Amphetamines and other stimulants inhibit the appetite center in the hypothalamus, as does smoking.
- Alcohol may be used as a substitute for food.

Loss of calories may occur through several processes, as follows:

- maldigestion and malabsorption
- diarrhea
- renal excretion of glucose and protein

Significant loss of weight may carry with it the following consequences:

- increased rate of infection
- cardiac and muscle wasting
- decreased sensitivity to chemotherapy in patients with cancer

EVALUATION

History

Careful questioning of the patient durng the history taking can point to the diagnosis (Table 29–1).

Intentional weight loss is due to a limited number of causes. Questioning first determines the patient's knowledge of proper dieting. Second, if the patient is thin, it is important to determine whether he or she has a distorted image of self. If patients feel that they are overweight and yet their weight is 15% below normal, anorexia nervosa is likely. Another subgroup of patients may be wrestlers. To meet certain weight classifications, wrestlers often resort to short-term approaches to weight loss through water loss.

Unintentional weight loss is often accompanied by other signs or symptoms that help lead to the diagnosis. The most logical line of questioning begins with a discrimination between those patients who have a normal or increased appetite and those who do not. Patients who have a normal or increased appetite may be further subdivided into those with chronic diarrhea and those without. Patients with diarrhea are likely to have inflammatory bowel disease, malabsorption, parasitic infection, or pancreatic disease. These patients often will have other abdominal symptoms that help differentiate further (see Chapter 34). Patients with or without di-

Table 29–1 History Questions for Weight Loss

Primary Question	*What Are You Thinking?*	*Secondary Questions*	*What Are You Thinking?*
Are you intending to lose weight?	Dieting, anorexia nervosa	(With a thin patient) Do you feel you are overweight and need to restrict your diet?	Possible anorexia nervosa, especially with a young female
		(With an overweight patient) What kind of diet are you on?	Determine whether the patient understands the nutritional requirements and the yo-yo effect of many diet fads
Is your appetite normal or increased?	Conscious decision not to eat due to pain, poverty, or endocrine or hypermetabolic states if increased food intake	Is it painful to eat?	Temporomandibular joint (TMJ) or dental problems are most common; ask about ill-fitting dentures and painful oral lesions
		Do you have diarrhea?	Increased loss; determine underlying cause (inflammatory bowel disease likely)
		Do you have any back pain unrelieved by rest or past history of cancer?	Cancer
Is your appetite decreased?	Side effect of medications, depression, cancer	What medications are you currently taking?	Check drug handbook to determine effect on appetite
		Do you feel sad or depressed, not enjoying life's activities as you used to?	Depression
		Do you have a chronic history of smoking?	Possible lung cancer
		Blood in stools	Possible colorectal cancer

arrhea should be screened for common symptoms related to the following:

- diabetes—polyphagia, polydipsia, polyuria, numbness and tingling in the hands or feet, or visual changes
- hyperthyroidism—nervousness, weakness, tremor, menstrual dysfunction, heat intolerance, etc.
- excessive exercise
- decreased eating—check for painful conditions associated with eating, including peptic ulcer, oral or anal conditions, and dysphagia; also check for limited diet and alcoholism

Patients who do not have a normal appetite should be questioned regarding medications, COPD, congestive heart failure, liver disease, and kidney disease. Certainly, the combination of weight loss and spinal pain that has been unresponsive to conservative care for 1 month in a patient over age 50 years with a history of prior cancer is highly suggestive of metastasis.

Examination

The physical examination is less revealing than the history. Documentation of weight loss is the initial task. If convinced that there is significant weight loss, examination for signs of hyperthyroidism, congestive heart failure, COPD, and other lung pathology is warranted. Patients suspected of having anorexia nervosa may have coexisting signs of bulimia. These are usually the result of the erosive action of gastric juices or the loss of protein. Swollen parotid glands, hoarseness unrelated to respiratory symptoms, calluses on the backs of fingers, tooth erosions, or swollen hands or feet may be clues.

Given the broad list of possibilities, a general screening lab testing, including urinalysis, may indicate the underlying problem if anemia, kidney, liver, or diabetic disorders are the cause. Chest radiographs are often very revealing. One study indicated that 41% of cases had a significant abnormality on chest films, including a lung mass or infiltrate, congestive heart failure, or adenopathy.[2]

MANAGEMENT

The chiropractor may serve in a primary care role by referring cases to appropriate specialists, and comanaging other cases. Comanagement involves a supportive and an educational role. Instruction on proper diet, assistance with access to financial assistance programs, and food programs such as Meals on Wheels are among the many adjunctive tools that can be used. Patients who are depressed or suffering from prolonged bereavement due to the loss of a loved one will benefit from referral to a psychologist or psychiatrist. Patients with dental problems should be referred to a dentist. Those with motor skill or memory deficits should be referred to a therapist who specializes in these areas. Patients suspected of having anorexia nervosa must be referred to an eating disorders clinic. It is far beyond the scope of most health care professionals to manage this disorder. Simple advice or counseling is useless.

Neuropsychologic disorders need a minimum of comanagement. Conditions such as Parkinson's disease, various causes of dementia, stroke, depression, and alcoholism require specialized care.

One option for some patients is referral to a medical physician for prescription of medication that increases appetite. There are several drugs, as follows:

- Cyproheptadine (antiserotoninergic drug), although generally effective, has not been shown to affect weight gain in patients with advanced cancer.
- Corticosteroids are used in patients with advanced cancer; however, it has yet to be demonstrated that the weight gain is not primarily fluid; in addition, side effects including oral candidiasis and Cushing's-like effects occur often.
- Megestrol acetate (progestational agent) is an expensive, yet effective, medication with few side effects for patients with cancer.

Algorithm

An algorithm for evaluation and management of weight loss is presented in Figure 29–1.

Figure 29–1

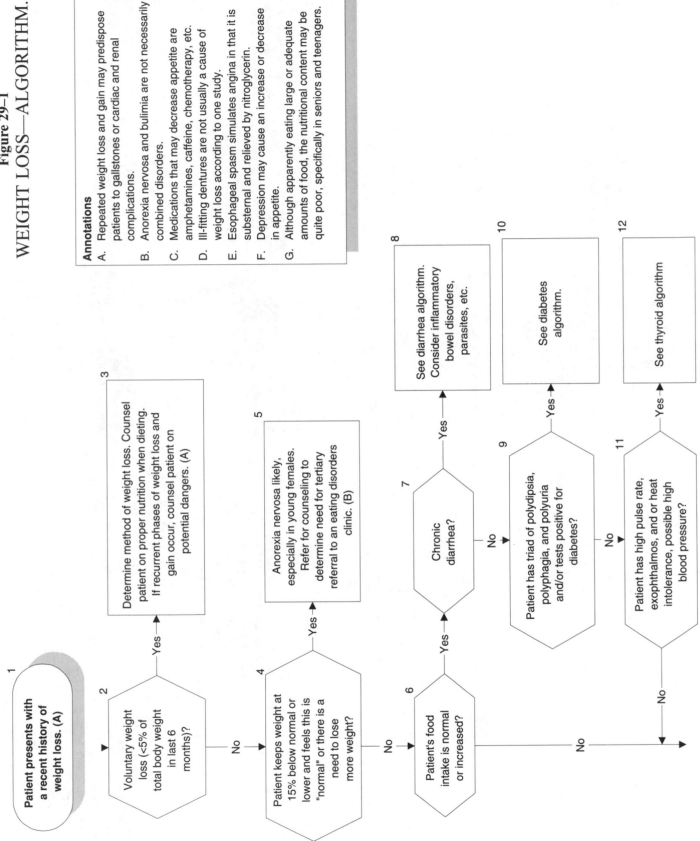

WEIGHT LOSS—ALGORITHM.

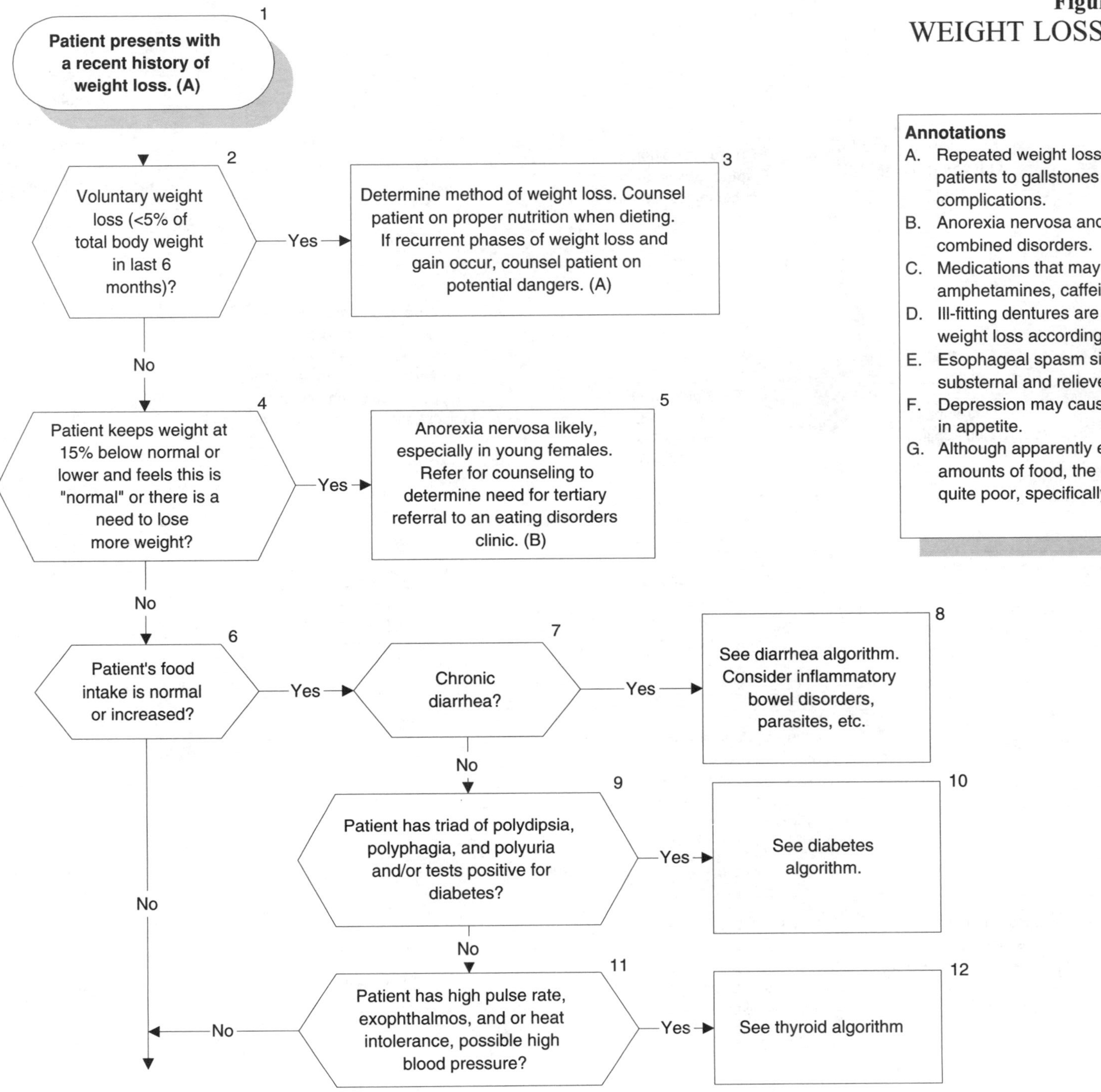

1 Patient presents with a recent history of weight loss. (A)
2 Voluntary weight loss (<5% of total body weight in last 6 months)?
Yes
3 Determine method of weight loss. Counsel patient on proper nutrition when dieting. If recurrent phases of weight loss and gain occur, counsel patient on potential dangers. (A)
No
4 Patient keeps weight at 15% below normal or lower and feels this is "normal" or there is a need to lose more weight?
Yes
5 Anorexia nervosa likely, especially in young females. Refer for counseling to determine need for tertiary referral to an eating disorders clinic. (B)
No
6 Patient's food intake is normal or increased?
Yes
7 Chronic diarrhea?
Yes
8 See diarrhea algorithm. Consider inflammatory bowel disorders, parasites, etc.
No
9 Patient has triad of polydipsia, polyphagia, and polyuria and/or tests positive for diabetes?
Yes
10 See diabetes algorithm.
No
11 Patient has high pulse rate, exophthalmos, and or heat intolerance, possible high blood pressure?
Yes
12 See thyroid algorithm
No
No

Annotations

A. Repeated weight loss and gain may predispose patients to gallstones or cardiac and renal complications.
B. Anorexia nervosa and bulimia are not necessarily combined disorders.
C. Medications that may decrease appetite are amphetamines, caffeine, chemotherapy, etc.
D. Ill-fitting dentures are not usually a cause of weight loss according to one study.
E. Esophageal spasm simulates angina in that it is substernal and relieved by nitroglycerin.
F. Depression may cause an increase or decrease in appetite.
G. Although apparently eating large or adequate amounts of food, the nutritional content may be quite poor, specifically in seniors and teenagers.

continues

Figure 29–1 continued

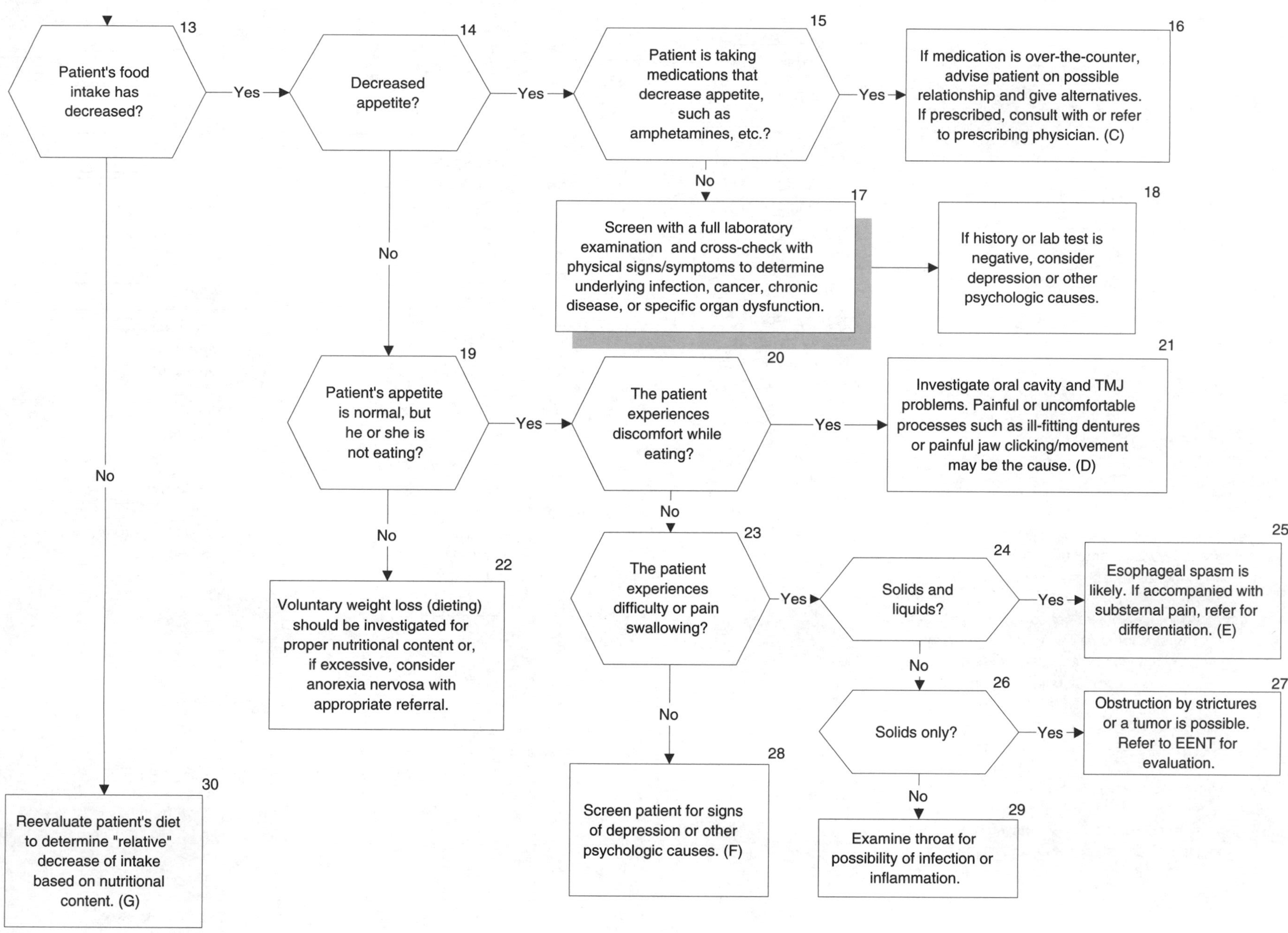

REFERENCES

1. Rabinovitz M, Pitlik SD, Leifer M, et al. Unintentional weight loss: a retrospective analysis of 154 cases. *Arch Intern Med.* 1986;146:186–187.
2. Marton KI, Sox HC, Krupp JR. Involuntary weight loss: diagnostic and prognostic significance. *Ann Intern Med.* 1981;95:568–574.
3. Wiley MK, Zahn PE. Evaluation of weight loss in the elderly. *Clin Res.* 1987;35:93.
4. Thompson MP, Morris LK. Unexplained weight loss in the ambulatory elderly. *J Am Geriatr Soc.* 1991;39:497–500.
5. Hardy C, Wallace C, Khansur T, et al. Nutrition, cancer, and aging: an annotated review. *J Am Geriatr Soc.* 1986;34:219.
6. Morley JE. Neuropeptide regulation of appetite and weight. *Endocr Rev.* 1987;8:256–278.
7. Lowry SF, Moldawer LL. Tissue necrosis factor and other cytokines in the pathogenesis of cancer cachexia. *Cancer Prin Pract Oncol Updates.* 1990;4:1–12.
8. Morley JE, Silver AJ. Anorexia in the elderly. *Neurobiol Aging.* 1988;9:9–16.

CHAPTER 30

Weight Gain

CONTEXT

Simply put, the most common cause of weight gain is an increase in caloric intake or a decrease in energy expenditure. Fluctuations in weight are common within a few pounds and generally reflect fluid retention and loss. Cyclic fluctuations are common in women in relation to menstruation. Substances that cause salt retention such as estrogen and steroids and appetite-stimulating drugs such as some antidepressants are less common causes. Familial obesity and low resting metabolic rates are uncommon. As few as 10% of obese patients have an underlying neurologic, endocrine, or genetic cause. Hypothyroidism may account for small increases in weight due to a slowed metabolic rate; however, significant weight gain is found in only 60% of patients and usually when the disease is advanced. Eighty percent of patients with adult-onset diabetes are obese.[1]

Obesity, to some extent, is a relative term. In the past a patient's weight was compared with actuarial tables that reflected averages based on height, weight, and gender. This simple approach was found to be misleading, not accounting for body build and the amount of muscle mass and body fat. A newer approach is to combine two methods. A determination of the body mass index (BMI) coupled with a body fat measurement accounts for some of these variables. These are discussed in more detail below.

Another issue regarding obesity is cultural perception. It may be acceptable, and sometimes desirable, to be overweight as one ages. This is often perceived as a sign of prosperity. It is important to recognize this cultural variation and be sensitive to a different perspective. However, morbid obesity carries with it enough risk that some degree of weight loss would need to be suggested.

Being obese carries some increased risk in several areas[1]:

- Mortality rates are higher for patients who weigh 30% more than ideal weight compared with normal-weight age- and sex-matched controls, mainly because of the increased incidence of coronary and cerebrovascular disease and associated hypertension and hyperlipidemia.
- The obese are 3 to 10 times more likely to develop adult-onset diabetes (insulin resistance increases with weight gain).
- The obese are more likely to have sleep apnea or hypersomnolence syndrome, which carries with it the risk of arrhythmias, hypoxemia, cor pulmonale, and pulmonary hypertension.
- The obese are more likely to have degenerative joint disease, especially in the hips and knees; it is also a risk factor for low back pain.
- Increased risk for cholelithiasis, thromboembolism, varicose veins, and blunted growth hormone response have also been demonstrated in obese patients.

GENERAL STRATEGY

History

- Determine the amount of weight gain and specify over what period of time.
- Determine what constitutes the patient's diet; follow with a diet diary.
- Determine whether the patient is taking any medications that may increase fluid retention or appetite.
- Determine whether the patient has recently stopped smoking.

- Determine any changes in exercise levels.
- Determine whether the patient is under stress and uses food for relaxation or reward.
- Determine whether the patient has any symptoms of hypoglycemia (insulinoma; rare).

Examination

- Weigh the patient.
- Determine the patient's percentage of body fat with skin calipers or an impedance device (referral for water immersion method is less practical, but most accurate).
- Examine the patient for signs of fluid retention in abdomen and legs.
- Examine the patient for congestive heart failure if suspected from history (difficulty breathing while lying recumbent) and obtain a chest radiograph.
- If the patient has historical and/or physical signs of diabetes, Cushing's disease, or hypothyroidism, laboratory evaluation is warranted.

Management

- The majority of obese patients can be managed with a healthful diet and a graduated exercise program.
- It may be necessary to work with a team including a specialist in weight loss to better guarantee compliance with suggestions and provide a support network for those making substantial lifestyle changes.

EVALUATION

History

It is extremely important to approach the obese patient from a health risk perspective and not be perceived as being judgmental or addressing the more cosmetic aspects of excess weight. As mentioned above, weight gain over a day or two is most often due to fluid retention. Therefore minor gain in weight over a number of days or during a woman's menstrual period is of little concern. The patient who is dieting, however, may feel discouraged. Also when patients are exercising, they must keep in mind that developing muscle weighs more than fat.

Examination

Estimation of a patient's relative body weight is best accomplished with a formula to determine the BMI. Additionally, an estimate or measurement of body fat content is crucial to determining the degree to which weight is due to fat and muscle. The BMI is calculated by dividing kilograms of weight by meters of height. The conversion for pounds and inches is 750 × lb/sq in. A BMI over 27 is equal to being about 20% overweight and warrants further investigation and management.

MANAGEMENT

Given that the most common cause of weight gain is overeating or eating an unbalanced diet, the chiropractor must decide how much time, investment, and interest can be donated to patient management. There are many centers that specialize in weight loss. These centers do not focus on diet alone but address issues of mental attitude and motivation, and exercise. Quick fixes with diet drinks or fad diets is to be avoided. Statistically, most patients who diet eventually gain back weight over a period of a year or two. The solution is total management with inclusion of a sensible exercise routine coupled with a sensible diet (see Exhibits 30–1 to 30–3). The time demand for education, exercise and diet prescription, and counseling/support may be well beyond the time availability and expertise of the chiropractor. Comanagement with a medical doctor or a clinic specializing in weight loss is often more appropriate.

Referral for medical consultation is warranted when drugs are suspected as the underlying cause or when metabolic problems such as Cushing's disease or hypothyroidism are suspected.

REFERENCE

1. Report of the U.S. Preventive Services Task Force. Screening for obesity. In: *Guide to Clinical Preventive Services*. 2nd ed. Baltimore: Williams & Wilkins; 1996:219.

Exhibit 30–1 Eating Guide

Anytime	*In Moderation*	*Now and Then*
Milk products (three to four servings per day for children, two for adults)		
Buttermilk (from skim milk)	Cocoa with skim milk[5]	Cheesecake[4,5]
Low-fat cottage cheese	Cottage cheese, regular[1]	Cheese fondue[4,(6)]
Low-fat milk (1 percent)	Frozen yogurt[5]	Cheese soufflé[4,(6),7]
Low-fat yogurt	Ice milk[5]	Eggnog[1,5,7]
Nonfat dry milk	Low-fat milk (2 percent)[1]	Hard cheeses: blue, brick, Camembert, cheddar, Muenster, Swiss[4,(6)]
Skim milk cheeses	Low-fat yogurt, sweetened[5]	Ice cream[4,5]
Skim milk	Mozzarella, part skim[1,(6)]	Processed cheeses[4,6]
Skim milk and banana shake		Whole milk[4]
		Whole-milk yogurt[4]
Poultry, fish, meat, and eggs (two servings per day; vegetarians should eat added servings from other groups)		
Cod	Fried fish [1 or 2]	Fried chicken, commercial[4]
Flounder	Herring[3,6]	Cheese omelet[4,7]
Gefilte fish[(6)]	Mackerel, canned[2,(6)]	Whole egg or yolk (limit to three a week)[3,7]
Haddock	Salmon, canned[2,(6)]	Bacon[4,(6)]
Halibut	Sardines[2,(6)]	Beef liver, fried[1,7]
Perch	Shrimp[7]	Bologna[4,6]
Pollock	Tuna, oil-packed[2,(6)]	Corned beef[4,6]
Rockfish	Chicken liver[7]	Ground beef[4]
Shellfish, except shrimp	Fried chicken in vegetable oil (homemade)[3]	Ham, trimmed[1,6]
Sole	Chicken or turkey, boiled, baked, or roasted (with skin)[2]	Hot dogs[4,6]
Tuna, water-packed[(6)]	Flank steak[1]	Liverwurst[4,6]
Egg whites	Leg or loin of lamb[1]	Pig's feet[4]
Chicken or turkey, boiled, baked, or roasted (no skin)	Pork shoulder or loin, lean[1]	Salami[4,6]
	Round steak or ground round[1]	Sausage[4,6]
	Rump roast[1]	Spareribs[4]
	Sirloin steak, lean[1]	Red meats, untrimmed[4]
	Veal[1]	
Fruits and vegetables (four or more servings per day)		
All fruits and vegetables except those at right	Avocado[3]	Coconut[4]
Applesauce (unsweetened)	Coleslaw[3]	Pickles[6]
Unsweetened fruit juices	Cranberry sauce[5]	
Unsalted vegetable juices	Dried fruit	
Potatoes, white or sweet	French fries[1 or 2]	
	Fried eggplant[2]	
	Fruits canned in syrup[5]	
	Gazpacho[2,(6)]	
	Glazed carrots[5,(6)]	
	Guacamole[3]	
	Potatoes au gratin[1,(6)]	
	Salted vegetable juices[6]	
	Sweetened fruit juices[5]	
	Vegetables canned with salt[6]	

[1]Moderate fat, saturated. [2]Moderate fat, unsaturated. [3]High fat, unsaturated. [4]High fat, saturated. [5]High in added sugar. [6]High in salt or sodium. [(6)]May be high in salt or sodium. [7]High in cholesterol. [8]Refined grains.

continues

Exhibit 30–1 continued

Anytime	*In Moderation*	*Now and Then*
Beans, grains, and nuts (four or more servings per day)		
Bread and rolls (whole grain)	Cornbread[8]	Croissant[4,8]
Bulgur	Flour tortilla[8]	Doughnut[3 or 4,5,8]
Dried beans and peas	Granola cereals[1 or 2]	Presweetened cereals[5,8]
Lentils	Hominy grits[8]	Sticky buns[1 or 2,5,8]
Oatmeal	Macaroni and cheese[1,(6),8]	Stuffing (with butter)[4,(6),8]
Pasta, whole wheat	Matzo[8]	
Rice, brown	Nuts[8]	
Sprouts	Pasta, refined[8]	
Whole-grain hot and cold cereals	Peanut butter[3]	
Whole-wheat matzo	Pizza[6,8]	
	Refined, unsweetened cereals[8]	
	Refried beans[1 or 2]	
	Seeds[3]	
	Soybeans[2]	
	Tofu[2]	
	Waffles or pancakes with syrup[5,(6),8]	
	White bread and rolls[8]	
	White rice[8]	

[1]Moderate fat, saturated. [2]Moderate fat, unsaturated. [3]High fat, unsaturated. [4]High fat, saturated. [5]High in added sugar. [6]High in salt or sodium. [(6)]May be high in salt or sodium. [7]High in cholesterol. [8]Refined grains.

Source: Copyright 1991 CSPI. Reprinted from *Nutrition Action Health Letter* (1875 Connecticut Ave., N.W., Suite 300, Washington, DC 20009-5728. $24.00 for 10 issues).

Exhibit 30–2 Reading Labels—Making Choices

The following list shows some foods to choose more often, plus ways to prepare and serve them to reduce your fat intake. Other ways to cut down on fat include the following:

1. Eat more breads and cereals, vegetables, and fruits each day.
2. Choose lean meats and low-fat products when you shop.
3. Select low-fat or skim milk products often.
4. Try low-fat meals such as salads, low-fat soups, bean dishes, lean meat or fish, and vegetable mixed dishes.
5. Trim all visible fat from meats before and after cooking.
6. Remove skin from poultry.
7. Broil, poach, or roast meats and drain the fat from the pan.
8. Substitute broth for grease in cooking main dishes and accompaniments.
9. Cut down on the amount of salad dressings, fats, creams, and rich sauces you add to foods in cooking and at the table.

CHOOSE MORE OFTEN

Whole grain products:
- Bakery products, including whole-wheat crackers; bran muffins; brown, rye, oatmeal, pumpernickel, bran, and corn breads; whole-wheat English muffins, bagels
- Breakfast cereals such as bran cereals, shredded wheat, whole grain or whole-wheat flaked cereals, others that list dietary fiber content
- Other foods made with whole grain flours such as waffles, pancakes, pasta, taco shells
- Other foods made with whole grain including barley, buckwheat groats, bulgur wheat

Fruits:
- Apples, pears, apricots, bananas, berries, cantaloupes, grapefruit, oranges, pineapples, papayas, prunes, raisins

CHOOSE LESS OFTEN

Refined bakery and snack products:
- Bakery products, including refined flour breads, and quick breads, biscuits, buns, croissants, snack crackers and chips, cookies, pastries, pies

CHOOSE MORE OFTEN

Vegetables:
- Carrots, broccoli, potatoes, corn, cauliflower, Brussels sprouts, cabbage, celery, green beans, summer squash, green peas, parsnips, kale, spinach, other greens, yams, sweet potatoes, turnips

All dry peas and beans:
- Black, kidney, garbanzo, pinto, navy, white, lima beans
- Lentils, split peas, black-eyed peas

Snack foods:
- Fruits and vegetables
- Unbuttered popcorn
- Whole grain and bran cereals, breads, crackers

Lower fat poultry, fish, and meat:
- Chicken, turkey, Rock Cornish hens (without skin)
- Fresh, frozen, water-packed canned fish and shellfish
- Reduced fat luncheon meats such as bologna and hot dogs
- Beef, veal, lamb, and pork cuts with little or no marbling (visible fat), trimmed of all fat

Low-fat or skim milk dairy products:
- Low-fat or skim milk and buttermilk
- Low-fat yogurt

CHOOSE LESS OFTEN

Higher fat poultry, fish, and meat:
- Duck and goose
- Poultry with skin
- Frozen fish sticks, tuna packed in oil
- Regular luncheon meats, sausage
- Beef, veal, lamb, and pork cuts with marbling, untrimmed of fat

Nuts and seeds:
- Peanut and other nut butters
- Nuts and seeds
- Trail mix

Full-fat dairy products:
- Whole milk
- Butter
- Yogurt made from whole milk

CHOOSE MORE OFTEN

Low-fat dairy products:
- Skimmed evaporated milk, nonfat dry milk*
- Low-fat cheese (ricotta, pot, farmer, or cottage, mozzarella, or cheeses made from skim milk)
- Sherbet, frozen low-fat yogurt, ice milk

Fats and oils:
- "Diet" and low-fat salad dressings
- Low-fat margarine

continues

Exhibit 30–2 continued

CHOOSE LESS OFTEN

High-fat dairy products:
- Sweet cream, sour cream, half-and-half, whipped cream, other creamy toppings (including imitation)
- Full-fat soft cheeses such as cream cheese, cheese spreads, Camembert, Brie
- Hard cheeses such as cheddar, Swiss, bleu, American, jack, Parmesan, etc.
- Ice cream
- Coffee creamers (including non-dairy)
- Cream sauces, cream soups

Fats and oils:
- Vegetable and salad oils, shortening, lard, meat fats, salt pork, bacon
- Mayonnaise and salad dressings
- Margarine
- Gravies, butter sauces

CHOOSE MORE OFTEN

Snack foods:
- Fruits and vegetables
- Breads and cereals

Food preparation:
- Baking, oven-broiling, boiling, stewing (skimming off fat), poaching, stir frying, simmering, steaming
- Use nonstick cookware to avoid extra fat
- Season vegetables with herbs, spices, or lemon juice

CHOOSE LESS OFTEN

Snack and bakery foods:
- Donuts, pies, pastries, cakes, cookies, brownies
- Potato chips and snack crackers
- Canned puddings, icings, candies made with butter, cream, chocolate
- Granola
- Croissants

Food preparation:
- Batter and deep-fat frying, sautéeing
- Use of fatty gravies and sauces
- Adding cream or butter to vegetables

*Infants less than one year old should not be given low-fat or skim milk.

Source: Reprinted from *Diet, Nutrition, & Cancer Prevention: A Guide to Food Choices*, Publication No. 85-2711, 1984, National Institutes of Health.

Exhibit 30–3 Low-Fat Foods

HERE ARE SOME LOW-FAT FOODS TO CHOOSE MORE OFTEN:

	Serving	*Calories*	*Grams of Fat*
Dairy Products			
Cheese:			
Low-fat cottage (2%)	½ cup	100	2
Mozzarella, part skim	1 oz	80	5
Parmesan	1 Tbsp	25	2
Milk:			
Low-fat (2%)	1 cup	125	5
Nonfat, skim	1 cup	85	trace
Ice milk	1 cup	185	6
Yogurt, low-fat, fruit flavored	1 cup	230	2
Meats			
Beef:			
Lean cuts, such as trimmed bottom round, braised or pot-roasted	3 oz	190	8
Lean ground beef, broiled	3 oz	230	16
Lean cuts, such as eye of round, roasted	3 oz	155	6
Lean and trimmed sirloin steak, broiled	3 oz	185	8
Lamb:			
Loin chops, lean and trimmed, broiled	3 oz	185	8
Leg, lean and trimmed, roasted	3 oz	160	7
Pork:			
Cured, cooked ham, lean and trimmed, baked	3 oz	135	5
Center loin chop, lean and trimmed, broiled	3 oz	195	9
Rib, lean and trimmed, roasted	3 oz	210	12
Shoulder, lean and trimmed, braised	3 oz	210	10
Veal:			
Cutlet, braised or broiled	3 oz	185	9
Poultry Products			
Chicken, roasted:			
Dark meat without skin	3 oz	175	8
Light meat without skin	3 oz	145	4
Turkey, roasted:			
Dark meat without skin	3 oz	160	6
Light meat without skin	3 oz	135	3
Egg, hard cooked	1 large	80	6
Seafood			
Flounder, baked, no butter or margarine	3 oz	85	1
Oysters, raw	3 oz	55	2
Shrimp, boiled or steamed	3 oz	100	1
Tuna, packed in water, drained	3 oz	135	1
Other Foods			
Salad dressing, low calorie	1 Tbsp	20	1

Source: Reprinted from *Diet, Nutrition & Cancer Prevention: The Good News*, Publication No. 87-2878, 1986, National Institutes of Health.

CHAPTER 31

Osteoporosis

CONTEXT

The signs of osteoporosis often appear suddenly with the development of a painful kyphosis or hip fracture. Over half of women over age 50 years will have a fracture due to osteoporosis.[1] A decade ago, estimates for the number of fractures related to osteoporosis were as high as 1.3 million, with an estimated cost of $3.8 billion.[2] The chiropractor's role with osteoporosis is both diagnostic and preventive. It is estimated that 50% of osteoporotic hip fractures and 90% of vertebral compression fractures are preventable.[3] Prevention should not be thought of as crisis intervention but a lifelong attempt at development and preservation of bone mass.

Osteoporosis is generally divided into bone loss associated with age, called senile or senescent osteoporosis (type II) and postmenopausal osteoporosis (type I). Women are susceptible to both types. Radiographically, osteoporosis is classified based on the area or region of involvement. Generalized osteoporosis is the most common form found with both senile or postmenopausal causes. A regional osteoporosis may occur that is restricted to a bone or a portion of a limb. This is most often found with immobilization and Sudeck's atrophy (associated bone changes found with reflex sympathetic dystrophy). Localized osteoporosis may occur in specific areas of bone as a result of infection, neoplasm, or an inflammatory arthritis.

Osteoporosis is often classified as primary or secondary. Primary causes include senile and postmenopausal types. Secondary causes include hormonal dysfunction such as hyperthyroidism and hyperparathyroidism as well as the effect of reduced bone mass associated with the use of thyroid medication, corticosteroids, smoking, and alcohol.

The difficulty with diagnosing and managing osteoporosis is that it is radiographically hidden until 30% to 50% of bone mass is lost. It is therefore important to be aware of more sensitive imaging options that allow for screening of high-risk patients. When osteoporosis is inadvertently discovered on radiographs, it is necessary to include a list of less common but possible differentials. The main differentials include osteomalacia, renal osteodystrophy, hyperparathyroidism, Paget's disease, and multiple myeloma. When an underlying pathologic process is discovered, referral for medical management or comanagement is warranted.

GENERAL STRATEGY

History

- Differentiate osteopenia caused by osteoporosis from other diffuse processes such as hyperparathyroidism or osteomalacia, and more regional processes such as reflex sympathetic dystrophy or bone cancer.
- Determine whether the patient has any known risk factors.
- Determine whether the patient has any indications of hormonal dysfunction.
- Determine whether the patient is taking corticosteroids, thyroid supplementation, estrogen, or calcium supplementation or has adequate calcium content in his/her diet.
- Determine the patient's exercise routine, if any.
- Determine whether there is any history of cancer.

Evaluation

- Evaluate radiographs for vertebral compression fractures.
- Determine the degree of osteopenia via dual-photon absorptiometry to establish a baseline for future determinations.

Management

- Refer patients with a suspicion of cancer, hyperthyroidism, adverse effects of corticosteroids, alcohol abuse, or hyperparathyroidism.
- Educate the patient with primary osteoporosis regarding management options such as estrogen replacement, calcitonin, or alendronate.
- Comanage patients with primary osteoporosis with an emphasis on exercise, diet, and precautions for falling.

RELEVANT ANATOMY AND PHYSIOLOGY

Osteoporosis is a consequence of bone quantity loss without an associated decrease of bone quality (mineralization is normal). Generally it is the result of increased resorption in the face of normal bone formation. The process of bone formation and resorption is a delicate balance governed by the interplay of a number of environmental, nutritional, and hormonal factors.

A productive imbalance occurs in early life when bone formation exceeds resorption. This peaks during and soon after puberty, gradually declining in the mid-20s to early 30s. A relatively small period of balance occurs when production equals resorption. Particularly in women, an imbalance in favor of resorption begins in the late 30s and early 40s. The rate of bone loss in women exceeds that of men, so that women lose about 50% of their total bone mass in a lifetime; men lose only about 25%.

Bone is composed of two-thirds mineral (mainly hydroxyapatite) and the remaining one third a combination of collagen, water, proteoglycans, and other noncollagenous proteins. Type I collagen acts as a framework for deposition of minerals. The process of bone formation and repair is determined by an interaction of three cell types: osteoblasts, osteocytes, and osteoclasts. The role and cross-talk of these cells is not completely understood. Osteoblasts secrete the precursors that help form type I collagen. Osteocytes appear to be osteoblasts that serve more of a coordinating function, perhaps helping to mobilize bone minerals. Osteoclasts are multinucleated giant cells that use collagenases and proteolytic enzymes to break down bone. Osteoclasts are stimulated by a number of factors, including parathyroid hormone (PTH), cytokines (interleukin 1 and tumor necrosis factors), growth factors, and prostaglandin E_2.

Calcium metabolism is an important link in the chain of bone formation. Calcium intake must meet the demands of peak bone formation and exceed the daily loss of 100 to 250 mg. Calcium absorption is dependent on a normally functioning gastrointestinal environment. Key to absorption is adequate amounts of vitamin D (more closely resembles a hormone). Vitamin D is produced by the body through several conversion reactions beginning with ultraviolet stimulation of epidermal 7-dehydrocholesterol, which forms an unstable form of vitamin D. Further conversions in the liver and subsequently the kidney produce a potent form of vitamin D. Without sufficient sunlight, vitamin D production is halted, requiring supplementation.

EVALUATION

History

Known risk factors for osteoporosis include the following:

- female gender
- white or Asian background
- early menopause
- family history
- lean body habitus
- lack of exercise or excessive exercise in the young
- glucocorticoids, phenytoin, alcohol, smoking, low calcium intake, more than four cups of coffee per day, carbonated drinks (several a day), and possibly a high animal-protein diet.

In many patients, osteoporosis is a silent disorder until fracture occurs. Physical examination findings are usually the result of these fractures. An increased, acute-angle kyphosis is suggestive, especially if associated with an acute onset of spine pain following sneezing, coughing, or a sudden jolt to the body such as stepping heavily off a curb. Additional examination findings will be found if the underlying cause of the osteoporosis is, for example, endocrine. Hyperthyroidism may be associated with osteoporosis, and either a history of previous diagnosis or physical examination findings may be suggestive. If the patient complains of intolerance to heat, fatigue, palpitations, and/or a change in the appearance of the eyes (exophthalmos), hyperthyroidism should be investigated. Hyperparathyroidism may also be associated with osteoporosis. Physical signs are generally absent with the exception of joint pains, especially of the knee, hip, wrist, or shoulder. Radiologic confirmation is necessary.

Examination

The primary tools for evaluation of osteoporosis are radiographic. Physical examination focuses on indirect indicators of compression fractures such as an increased kyphosis. Signs of secondary causes of osteoporosis focus on hyperthyroidism and Cushing's disease or cushingoid appearance due to long-term corticosteroid use.

From a preventive perspective, it is important to screen the elderly for proprioceptive deficits. This would include an evaluation of balance, vision, and sensory function.

There are classic radiographic findings with osteoporosis; however, their appearance indicates advanced involvement. Loss of between 30% and 50% is necessary before osteopenia becomes radiographically evident as an increase in radiolucency. Additional findings are cortical thinning (pencil-thin cortex) and trabecular changes. Trabecular resorption may leave the remaining stress-surviving trabeculae more visible, in contrast to a background of radiolucency. The remaining trabeculae of the spine are the vertical, stress-bearing ones. The horizontal trabeculae are preferentially lost. Changes in the vertebral shape with osteoporosis include vertebra plana (pancake vertebra), wedged vertebra, and bioconcave (fish, hourglass) vertebra.

More sensitive and less radiographically abusive techniques include single- and dual-photon absorptiometry (DPA), quantitative computed tomography (QCT), and dual-energy X-ray absorptiometry (DEXA).[4] Single-photon absorptiometry measures only the appendicular skeleton. Although DPA, QCT, and DEXA measure both types of bone, DEXA is not readily available. QCT requires a long scan time, resulting in more irradiation than with DEXA and DPA. Most major medical groups do not recommend screening all women with these techniques.[5] Recommendations for the use of one of these specialized tools include the following:

- as an aid in the decision making regarding the need for estrogen replacement therapy (high-risk individuals)
- for monitoring patients on long-term glucocorticoids
- for monitoring patients with hyperparathyroidism who are at risk for skeletal disease (ie, those who may need parathyroid surgery)

Laboratory evaluation is valuable only in the differential evaluation. Most bone-related lab levels, such as calcium, phosphorus, and alkaline phosphatase, are usually normal unless there has been a recent fracture. Urinary hydroxyproline levels may be elevated.

MANAGEMENT

- When a secondary cause of osteoporosis or a compression fracture is found or suspected (ie, cancer, Paget's disease, hyperparathyroidism, or osteomalacia) medical consultation is necessary.
- If a compression fracture appears radiographically unstable, refer for medical consultation (see Chapter 6 for details).
- For all other osteoporotic patients, a comprehensive program is needed, including patient education, appropriate exercise, and appropriate nutrition coupled with psychosocial support.

Education of the osteoporotic patient is a key component to management. In addition to the educational advice of the doctor, several organizations such as the National Osteoporosis Foundation (NOF), the Older Women's League (OWL), and the National Dairy Council provide educational pamphlets and materials to patients and doctors.

Although there is some debate as to the degree of effect, it has been demonstrated that a combination of calcium supplementation and exercise can, at the very least, reduce bone loss in the majority of postmenopausal females. The amount of calcium intake is generally recommended to be 1,000 mg for premenopausal women and 1,500 mg for postmenopausal women. Although dairy products are a common source of calcium, other options exist for those patients with lactose intolerance or a concern about the high cholesterol/calorie content of some dairy products.

The debate over which calcium supplementation is best continues. Part of the prescription decision is clarified when considering the following:

- Calcium lactate may not be tolerated by those with lactase deficiency.
- Calcium carbonate is an acceptable choice because it is inexpensive and relatively effective; however, it may cause bloating or constipation.
- Supplements derived from bone meal or dolomite sometimes have been found to contain contaminants such as lead, mercury, and arsenic.[6]
- Calcium citrate is a good alternative and is available in some orange juices; however, citric acid may not be tolerated by some patients.

It is important that patients be educated about the misleading trappings of advertising. For example, although the product may be labeled as containing 1,500 mg of calcium carbonate, it may contain only 500 mg of elemental calcium.

For the elderly or homebound patient it is important to consider the need for vitamin D supplementation. The recommended daily allowance is between 400 and 800 IU. A cup of milk will provide only 100 IU of vitamin D. This is a significant factor that is often overlooked.

Medical options for postmenopausal women include three drug options:

1. estrogen
2. calcitonin
3. alendronate

Estrogen replacement therapy (ERT) is controversial. Some physicians feel that all postmenopausal women should be placed on ERT; others feel that it should be a decision based on risk. There are some known contraindications to ERT, including the following:

- undiagnosed vaginal bleeding
- pregnancy
- breast cancer
- estrogen-dependent neoplasm
- active thromboembolic disorders or past history of thrombus related to estrogen

Relative contraindications include gallbladder and liver diseases and a history of menstrual migraines. To reduce the chance of uterine cancer, estrogen is combined with progesterone in women with an intact uterus.

Calcitonin appears to have two effects. In addition to increasing bone density, calcitonin appears to reduce pain significantly in some patients. The infrequent complaints of nausea and flushing are usually managed by beginning with a low dose given at bedtime.

The newest approach, recently approved in the United States, is alendronate. It has none of the side effects of estrogen, yet has been demonstrated to increase bone density in the spine (average of 8%) and to reduce vertebral compression fracture by almost 50% in postmenopausal osteoporotic women.[7] Currently, it is not considered first-line therapy but as an alternative for women who may have contraindications to estrogen therapy or do not tolerate it.

Exercise prescription for the osteoporotic patient should meet two goals. First, it is important to stimulate bone production and prevent loss. Second, it is important to strengthen muscles to provide support and to train the patient proprioceptively to prevent falls. Spinal exercises should focus on extension with avoidance of the compressive effects of flexion exercises.

In addition to the prevention of further bone loss, it is equally important to prevent falls in the elderly. An assessment of physical risks that are the consequence of the individual's health status and those that are a consequence of the patient's living environment should be identified and utilized in patient education. Addressing the patient's balance, posture, and muscle strength, combined with modification of environmental hazards, can decrease the risk of falling by as much as 30%.[8]

REFERENCES

1. Chrischelles EA, Butler CD, Davis CS, et al. A model of lifetime osteoporosis impact. *Arch Intern Med.* 1991;2026–2032.
2. National Institutes of Health, Consensus Panel. Consensus development conference on osteoporosis. *JAMA.* 1984;252:799.
3. Lindsay R. Sex steroids in the pathogenesis and prevention of osteoporosis. In: Riggs BL, Melton LI, eds. *Osteoporosis: Etiology, Diagnosis and Management.* New York: Raven Press; 1988:333–358.
4. Kellie SE. Diagnostic and therapeutic technology assessment (DATTA): measurement of bone density with dual-energy x-ray absorptiometry. *JAMA.* 1992;267:286–294.
5. Report of the U.S. Preventive Services Task Force. Screening for postmenopausal osteoporosis. In: *Guide to Clinical Preventive Services.* 2nd ed. Baltimore: Williams & Wilkins; 1996:509.
6. National Osteoporosis Foundation. *Boning Up on Osteoporosis: A Guide to Prevention and Treatment.* Washington, DC: National Osteoporosis Foundation; 1991:26.
7. Liberman UA, Weiss SR, Broil J, et al. Effect of oral alendronate on bone mineral density and incidence of fractures in postmenopausal osteoporosis. *N Engl J Med.* 1995;333:1437–1443.
8. Tineti ME, Baker D, McAvay G, et al. A multifactorial intervention to reduce the risk of falling among elderly people living in the community. *N Engl J Med.* 1994;331:821–827.

PART IV

Gastrointestinal Complaints

Chapter 32

Abdominal Pain

CONTEXT

Chiropractors are sometimes faced with a dilemma regarding whether or not to accept a patient. A patient may present with a chief complaint or secondary complaint of abdominal pain. The first concern is whether the pain is due to a visceral source, and the second concern is whether the chiropractor can appropriately manage the patient. Delayed referral for appropriate diagnostic testing and care may have serious consequences for the patient (and inevitably for the chiropractor). Inappropriate or unnecessarily early surgical referral may result in nonessential or inappropriate surgery with its consequences. At the core of this issue, for many chiropractors, is the belief or experience that management of apparently viscerally caused abdominal pain results in successful resolution under chiropractic care. A debate of whether spinal dysfunction is the cause of referred abdominal pain or an actual dysfunction of an organ still ensues. This issue is well addressed in a review by Nansel and Szlazak.[1] The reader is referred to this source for a more in-depth discussion. The issue is clouded when a patient presents with a back complaint associated with a "viscerally" associated symptom. Is the back pain the cause of the visceral symptom or is it the reverse? The remainder of this discussion is based on the assumption that serious, surgically treatable disease is the domain of the surgeon and will more likely present to the emergency department and rarely present in the chiropractic setting. The remaining conditions that do present may be in need of medical treatment, may respond to conservative measures, or are self-resolving. The task for the chiropractor is to determine which of these conditions the patient has.

GENERAL STRATEGY

Acute Abdominal Pain

Determine whether the condition requires referral:

- Determine the onset and severity of the pain (abrupt pain suggests rupture or blockage of a nonintestinal lumen such as a ureter [kidney stones] or the gallbladder [gallstones]).
- Determine whether other acquaintances of the patient have similar symptoms (flu or food poisoning).
- Determine any relationship to ingestion of food (food poisoning).
- In women, determine recent history of sexual contact (pelvic inflammatory disease) and menstrual history (ectopic pregnancy).
- Determine whether there is any past history of surgery (postsurgical adhesions causing obstruction).
- Does the patient maintain a position of relief (fetal position indicates pancreatitis; flexed hip position may indicate appendicitis).
- Attempt to localize the pain by patient description and palpation.
- Determine whether there are any peritoneal signs (pain with movement or jarring, central pain that has progressively localized, rebound tenderness, or rigid abdomen suggests appendicitis, perforated ulcer, or another peritoneal problem).
- Determine the timing of associated symptoms such as vomiting, constipation, or diarrhea.
- Attempt to narrow the differentials to a system, such as genitourinary (radiation from thoracolumbar area to

groin, or associated dysuria, increased frequency, hesitancy, or hematuria), gastrointestinal (nausea, vomiting, constipation, diarrhea, or rectal bleeding), gynecologic (change in menstrual period, vaginal discharge or bleeding, or dyspaerunia), or cardiovascular (history of hypertension, atrial fibrillation, or sickle cell disease).
- Determine whether laboratory tests (for acute infection or urinary tract involvement) or radiographic studies (free air or obstruction) are necessary.

Chronic, Recurrent Abdominal Pain

Determine the following:

- Determine whether the pain is associated with the timing of meals (empty stomach implies ulcer; full stomach implies reflux) or meal content (similar foods affect both ulcer and reflux).
- Is the pain relieved by passing gas (gas distention)?
- Determine whether the patient has traveled recently, locally on camping trips (giardiasis, amebic dysentery) or abroad to a foreign country (parasitic infection).
- Determine whether there is a relationship to a woman's menstrual cycle (primary dysmenorrhea or endometriosis).
- Obtain the medication history of the patient (use of nonsteroidal antiiflammatory drugs [NSAIDs] or aspirin suggests gastric bleeding; use of antacids or H_2 receptor antagonists that help the pain suggests esophageal, gastric, or duodenal pathology).
- Ask about any associated diarrhea (inflammatory bowel disorders, parasitic infections, or a drug reaction) or alternating diarrhea and constipation (irritable bowel syndrome).
- Ask about any blood in the stool, weight loss, change in caliber of stool (colon or other cancer).

RELEVANT ANATOMY AND PHYSIOLOGY

Visceral pain is characteristically different from somatic pain. There may be overlaps, however. Visceral afferent receptors serve a function different from that of somatic receptors. Somatic receptors signal the brain about external threats and in so doing need to have a high degree of localization and reflex response capabilities. Visceral receptors are designed more to provide information that helps maintain homeostasis. In the abdominal area, the most important information for homeostasis is distention, constriction, and vascular status. Whether these nerve endings or specific nociceptors relay pain is still unknown. It is known, however, that the types of stimuli that will produce a sensation of pain are often extreme events of normal stimuli such as overdistention (eg, gas in the intestine or a stone in a nonintestinal lumen) or ischemia. This is in part due to the fact that nerve endings are located in muscular walls of the gut and organs such as the gallbladder and urinary bladder. Other irritating factors causing visceral pain are probably chemical in nature, such as pH changes or toxic irritation. This pain reaction is probably stimulated by local release of bradykinin, serotonin, histamine, and other substances. Also, the rate at which distention occurs often determines whether pain is felt at all. For example, gradual distention that occurs from malignancy (such as malignant biliary obstruction) may be painless, whereas acute blockage from cholelithiasis is painful. If the capsule of an organ such as the liver (Glisson's capsule) is involved, pain will be produced somatically. The organ itself, having no muscular component, is insensitive to pain. This is true not only of the liver, but the lungs, brain, kidneys, and intestines. Interestingly, the walls of most organs are insensitive to malignant involvement unless obstruction or ulceration also occurs.

The quality and location of visceral pain are in part determined by the neurology of the afferent supply. Localization to the center of the body is known to occur initially with most organ pain. Embryologically, the gastrointestinal tract and related structures originate as midline organs that receive bilateral innervation. Therefore, if a visceral afferent is activated, transmission occurs to both the right and the left sides of the spinal cord, making localization (lateralization) impossible. In other words, most stimulation is projected so that only a central recognition is possible. Overlapping of innervation to more than one organ and the multilevel input at the spinal cord make vertical localization difficult. For example, the lower esophagus, stomach, proximal duodenum, gallbladder, liver, and pancreas are innervated from the same levels of the spinal cord (T5-T10). This overlap in segmental innervation also accounts for the phenomenon of referred pain, either somatovisceral or viscerosomatic. About 75% of thoracic and lumbar dorsal horn neurons receive both somatic and visceral input. It appears that no specific group of spinal neurons responds to visceral input.[2]

The quality of pain is also a reflection of the neurologic logic behind a system designed for retreat and one for homeostasis. Somatic pain is often sharp and localized, with a reflex response of retreat. Visceral pain is usually due to an existing process such as inflammation or infection. Given that an individual cannot escape from his or her body, the purpose seems more to provide a reflex splinting resulting in immobilization. The quality is often dull and aching (prior to peritoneal or capsular irritation), and there is no retreat response.

The afferent supply to internal organs follows a path similar to that of the sympathetic nervous system, often in close proximity to blood vessels. The nerve cell bodies are located in the dorsal root ganglion (similar to the somatic system). The fibers of these splanchnic nerves follow the sympathetic chains and enter the cord via the white rami communicants. The fibers enter the dorsal horn, and, through the tract of Lissauer, travel several segments cranially and caudally to end in laminae I and V. There is a small number of visceral fibers and receptors compared with those in the somatic system (such as the skin or even peritoneum). This sparse innervation often allows small, localized damage to be asymptomatic. The stimulus must be strong enough to involve an area large enough to stimulate enough receptors to produce a conscious perception of pain.

Organ pain may become somatic pain and allow localization. This occurs when a somatic structure around an organ is stimulated, such as the peritoneum, pleura, pericardium, or capsule (liver and kidneys). These somatically innervated structures allow cortical or thalamic localization as a result of the unilateral innervation afforded by the spinal nerves of the thoracolumbar area and the phrenic nerve. Specifically, the phrenic nerve (C3-5) innervates portions of the pericardium, the biliary tract, and the central zone of the diaphragm. The thoracic and upper lumbar spinal nerves innervate the parietal pleura, the parietal peritoneum, the outer diaphragm, and the roots of the mesentery of the intestines. The parietal peritoneum and the segmentally related dermatome (skin), sclerotome (bone), and myotome (muscle) are truly overlapping. Irritation of one of these structures may refer pain to its segmentally related partner(s). (Figure 32–1).

The appendix serves as a review of the above concepts. If the appendix is distended or inflamed, visceral afferents will be stimulated, usually leading to a perception of periumbilical, central pain. This is more likely to occur if the distention is rapid. If, however, the appendix were inflamed or distended enough to irritate the local peritoneum, somatic afferents would be stimulated, localizing the pain to the right lower quadrant (McBurney's point). Similar events could occur with the gallbladder with an extra component of referred pain to the scapula due to a segmentally related overlap.

EVALUATION

History

Pain localization is often quite valuable in narrowing down the possibilities. Figure 32–2 summarizes some possible causes based on pain localization to a specific quadrant.

Acute Abdominal Pain

Acute abdominal pain is a generic term. In other words, a patient may present with a pain that began within a few seconds, a few minutes, or over hours to days; all are called acute. This distinction may be a relevant starting point in deciding whether or not to make a medical referral. Abrupt pain that begins within seconds to a matter of minutes is often due to a serious disorder, such as the following:

- rupture of an organ (perforated ulcer, ruptured abdominal aneurysm, or ectopic pregnancy)
- torsion (testicular or ovarian)
- blockage of a nonintestinal lumen (cholelithiasis, ureteral stone, and rarely acute appendicitis)
- vascular occlusion (mesenteric infarction in the elderly or sickle cell crisis)

The seriousness of the situation is not lost on the patient who calls 911 or rushes to the emergency department.

Pain that appears rather abruptly over minutes and builds over hours to a few days is characteristic of a number of processes such as cholecystitis, pancreatitis, appendicitis, pelvic inflammatory disease, food poisoning, and diverticulitis. Also, many of the conditions that become chronic and recurrent have their advent as an acute pain such as in peptic ulcer, endometriosis, diverticulitis, and inflammatory bowel disorders. Pain that grows slowly over days or longer suggests an underlying inflammatory process or intestinal obstruction.

Still, the majority of patients with pancreatitis, cholecystitis, and appendicitis will have a belated trip to the emergency department, not the chiropractor's office. If the chiropractor inadvertently is present at the time of onset (or has had a personal attack of acute abdominal pain), however, it is important to determine what was eaten within 24 hours, past history of similar attacks, alcohol ingestion, and any premonitory signs.

The quality and location of the pain are obviously important. Dull, aching central pain in the epigastric, umbilical, or hypogastric area is nonspecific, but it indicates visceral involvement. If this pain migrates to a specific quadrant and especially if this is accompanied by a change in the quality of the pain, local peritoneal or capsular involvement is likely. The classic example, as mentioned above, is the sequence of appendicitis that begins in the central abdomen and localizes to the right lower quadrant when the local peritoneum is irritated. If the appendix ruptures into the peritoneum, a more diffuse, peritoneal response with a rigid abdomen will result. Pain that begins anteriorly and radiates to the back is often felt in a region segmentally related to the organ. For example, pain from a perforated ulcer is referred to the T6-T10 area; uterus, to the lumbopelvic area; esophagus, to the central midthoracic area; and gallbladder, to the inferior angle of the right scapula.

Associated symptoms may be useful indicators of the underlying process. Although it may appear as though vomit-

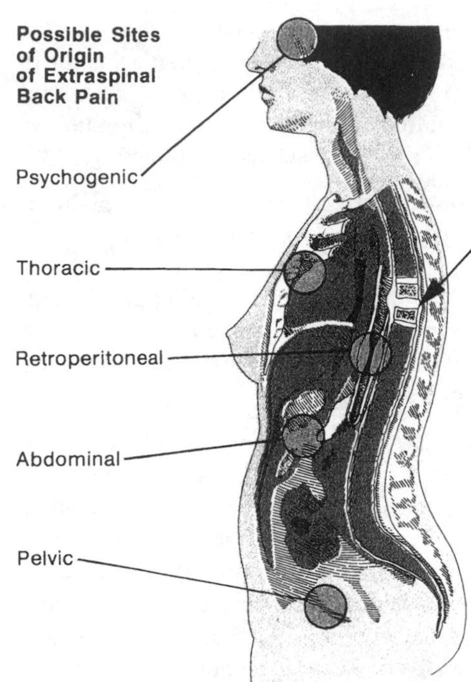

Keep in Mind:

- Back pain may at times be the earliest and only manifestation of visceral disease.
- Pain due to metastatic lesions may be severe before x-ray findings are positive.
- Conversely, do not overlook possible visceral origins of pain because spinal x-rays reveal benign changes.
- Consider visceral origin of back pain particularly when muscular spasm, tenderness, and impaired mobility are *absent*.
- Persistent backache due to extraspinal pathology is rare in children, common in adults.

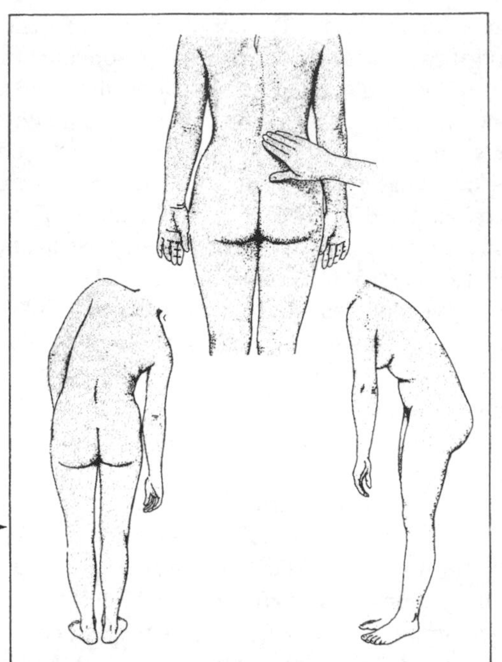

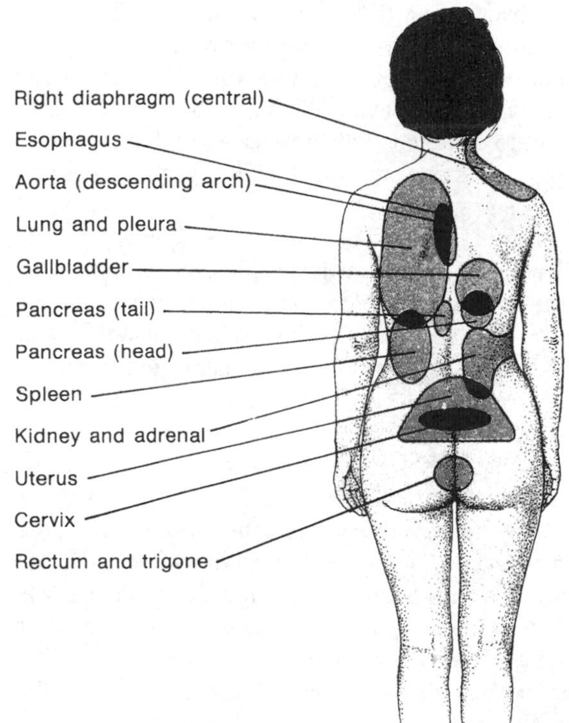

Keep in mind:

- A careful general history and physical examination in backache is of the utmost importance.
- Associated symptoms have differential value.
- Backache may occur in any acute systemic infection.
- Myocardial infarction can also cause back pain.
- Lumbar spasm may accompany the severe pain of certain retroperitoneal diseases (renal tumor, abscess, stone, lymphoma, etc).
- Radicular pain may occur with visceral lesions, as in sciatic radiation due to hypernephroma.
- Just as visceral disease may suggest spinal pathology, so may the radiation of spinal lesions suggest a visceral origin of pain.
- Do not overlook the possibility of rectal and bladder lesions in persistent coccygodynia.
- Check the breasts of all females with back pain. Pain due to metastasis is not infrequently the first sign of a breast lesion.

Figure 32–1 (Top) Extraspinal causes of back pain: some basic considerations. **(Bottom)** General visceral map in backache. *Source:* Reprinted by permission of QUADRANT HEALTHCOM Inc. from "Extraspinal Causes of Back Pain," *Hospital Medicine,* Vol. 18, No. 12, p. 95, Copyright 1982 by QUADRANT HEALTHCOM Inc.

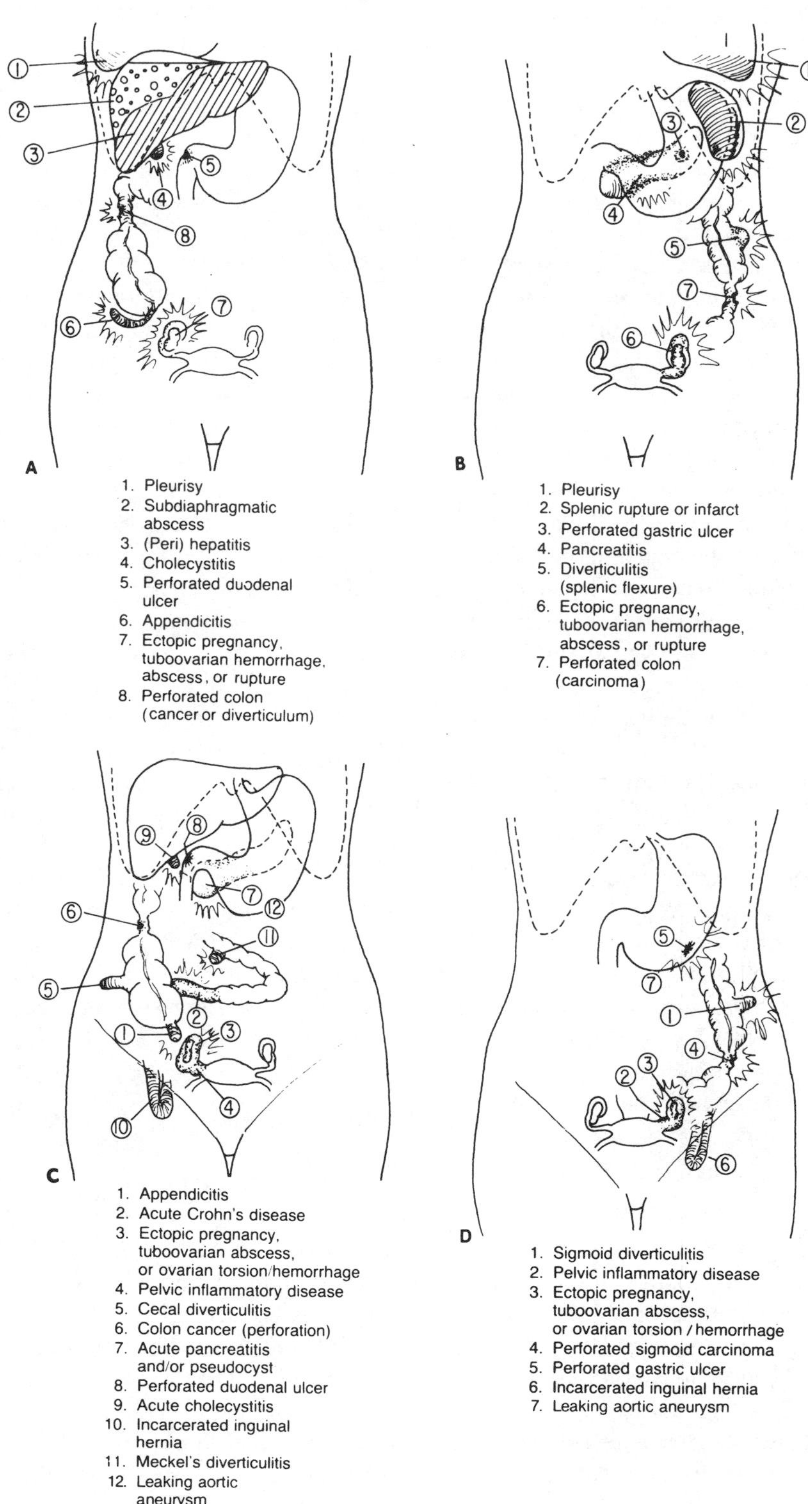

Figure 32–2 Common and uncommon conditions that may cause "parietal" pain and localized peritonitis in the various quadrants of the abdomen. **A**, Right upper quandrant. **B**, Left upper quandrant. **C**, Right lower quandrant. **D**, Left lower quandrant. *Source:* Reprinted with permission from B.M. Reilly, *Practical Strategies in Outpatient Medicine*, 2nd ed., p. 703, © 1991, W.B. Saunders Company.

ing is a purely gastrointestinal (GI) symptom, it is important to remember that in addition vagal stimulation, intracranial pressure, vestibular dysfunction, and metabolic processes (uremia, acidosis, chemotherapy, hypoxia, and toxins) may also induce vomiting. The timing of vomiting may be important. If vomiting occurs before abdominal pain, a "surgical" cause is less likely. Early gastroenteritis, food poisoning, and drugs may present this way. If vomiting relieves abdominal pain, peptic ulcer disease (less commonly upper intestinal obstruction) is often the cause in a patient with epigastric pain. Vomiting does not relieve the pain of many other acute abdominal conditions such as pancreatitis and cholecystitis. The content of vomit may indicate where the process is located in the alimentary tract. If the vomit contains undigested food, gastroesophageal obstruction is likely. If the vomit smells like feces, intestinal obstruction is high on the list. Coffee-ground vomit indicates GI bleeding.

Constipation and diarrhea are less specific indicators. If constipation precedes abdominal pain, the rectum or colon is probably involved. However, abdominal pain often causes a decrease in peristalsis; therefore, many patients with abdominal pain are constipated. For the same reason, anorexia is also nonspecific; however, if the patient has an appetite, serious disease is unlikely.

When the patient reports that family members or friends who shared a common meal have similar symptoms, food poisoning is likely. The onset of symptoms is highly variable depending on the underlying causative organism. This time frame varies from as little as 2 hours to as much as 48 hours; however, the average time is between 4 and 8 hours.

In the female patient, the relationship to the menstrual cycle may be helpful. For example, a missed period or spotty last period may be a clue to ectopic pregnancy. Increase in pain during or soon after menstruation is suggestive of pelvic inflammatory disease in a sexually active female. Pain between menstrual periods may represent mittelschmerz, indicating an ovarian cyst or rupture.

Recurrent Abdominal Pain

When abdominal pain is recurrent, the differential list is decreased substantially. It is important to ask some general questions regarding alcohol abuse (pancreatitis, esophageal, and gastric problems), medication intake (NSAIDs or other drugs causing gastric bleeding), predominance of diarrhea or constipation (irritable bowel syndrome versus inflammatory bowel disease), and a menstrual history (primary or secondary dysmenorrhea) (Table 32–1).

With epigastric pain, reflux esophagitis, peptic ulcer, or (much less commonly) pancreatitis is possible. Historical clues that help differentiate reflux from peptic ulcer include the relationship to meals. In general, food will relieve the pain of a duodenal ulcer (depending on the food type), whereas with reflux, pain is increased after a heavy meal and especially with tight garments or recumbency. Antacids may help both. It is important to question the patient regarding diet. Common foods may irritate a duodenal ulcer and increase reflux. Foods that lower the tone of the lower esophageal sphincter, leading to reflux, include chocolate, caffeine, fat, garlic, onions, and alcohol. Other substances include nicotine, theophylline, calcium channel blockers, and anticholinergic drugs.

Severe upper abdominal pain lasting for several hours and associated with nausea and sometimes vomiting is highly suggestive of cholelithiasis. A profile of female, fat, forty, and flatulent may be found; however, it is not an exclusive descriptor of the patient with biliary colic. The association of onset with a fatty meal also is not consistent.

With the exception of menstrually related pain, recurrent lower abdominal pain generally can be grouped historically into those with bowel habit change and those without. Irritable bowel syndrome commonly causes alternating bouts of diarrhea and constipation. Usually constipation is the predominant symptom, with a characteristic passage of small, marble-sized stool in the morning that is associated with some mild diarrhea that may have mucus attached. The inflammatory bowel diseases often have diarrhea as a major complaint, often more than the abdominal pain with ulcerative colitis. Diverticulitis usually does not cause a change in bowel movement.

Recurrent cyclic pain in menstruating women is usually dysmenorrhea. Dysmenorrhea may be a "normal" problem that has established a baseline of pain for most females by their 20s. Any change in this pattern to a more severe menstrual pain is suggestive of secondary causes. High on this list is endometriosis.

Examination

Acute Abdominal Pain

With acute abdominal pain there are several clues with regard to the patient's posturing. Patients who are cautious to move for fear of increasing pain may have a peritoneal problem. Patients doubled over in pain or seeking relief by the fetal position are likely to have pancreatitis if the pain is upper abdominal. A patient who keeps the right leg in flexion and avoids extension may have appendicitis with irritation of the psoas muscle. Patients who cannot find a comfortable position and continue to move around or are writhing in pain will probably have a ureteral stone (if associated with radiation into the groin), or cholecystitis (if the pain is upper abdominal).

Although a rare chiropractic office presentation, a patient with acute abdominal pain should be evaluated immediately

Table 32–1 History Questions for Recurrent Abdominal Pain

Primary Question	*What Are You Thinking?*	*Secondary Questions*	*What Are You Thinking?*
Is the pain in your upper abdomen?	Reflux esophagitis, peptic ulcer, pancreatitis, cholecystitis, or cholelithiasis	Is the pain worse on an empty stomach?	Duodenal ulcer likely
		Are you taking large doses of aspirin or other NSAIDs?	Gastric irritation, possible ulcer
		Do you drink alcohol often? (Perhaps use CAGE approach.)	Alcohol-related pancreatitis or ulcer irritation
		Do you feel worse after lying down after a heavy meal?	Reflux esophagitis
		Did a severe pain occur rather suddenly and last for several hours, associated with nausea or vomiting?	Biliary colic (cholecystitis)
		Did you notice a relationship to fatty meals?	Possibly cholecystitis if severe; if epigastric and less severe consider reflux esophagitis
		Does vomiting relieve the pain?	Peptic ulcer if it does; if it does not, consider pancreatitis or cholecystitis
		Did others in your family or did your friends also become sick after eating the same food?	Food poisoning
Is the pain lower in your abdomen?	Irritable bowel syndrome, inflammatory bowel diseases, dysmenorrhea, diverticulitis	Do you have constipation that alternates with diarrhea?	Irritable bowel syndrome likely
		Do you mainly have recurrent diarrhea?	Inflammatory bowel disease (most likely ulcerative colitis)
		(For females in reproductive years) Is the pain associated with your period?	Dysmenorrhea
		If the pain is related to your period, is it much worse than previously felt pain?	Secondary dysmenorrhea (most likely endometriosis)
		Lower left quadrant abdominal pain (in an older patient) with apparent change in stools?	Consider diverticulosis or colon cancer

for shock. Hypotension, tachycardia, impaired mentation, and oliguria are indications of volume loss from intraabdominal bleeding or fluid loss. Shock requires an emergency department evaluation.

The yield on plain abdominal films (scout, kidney/ureter/bladder [KUB], flat plate) is usually quite low. Even in an emergency department setting, one study indicated positive findings on only 10% of films.[3] Most GI pathology is not visible on film. Free air from a perforated organ and bowel obstruction are the only non–stone indicators visible. Radiopacities indicating stones occur with gallstones, kidney stones, and fecaliths (with appendicitis). The yield is approximately 70% of the time with kidney stones, 10% to 15% with gallstones, and only 5% with fecaliths.[3] With gallstones, it is also important to recognize that finding stones does not always mean that the cause of the patient's abdominal pain has been found. There are significant numbers of asymptomatic patients with radiographic evidence of gallstones.

Laboratory studies may give general or very specific indications of an underlying process. On a general screen, findings of leukocytosis with a shift to the left is an important indicator of an inflammatory reaction and, coupled with the history and location of pain, often will point to appendicitis or cholecystitis. Many acute inflammatory reactions may cause a similar finding, however. Acute pancreatitis also will raise the white blood cell (WBC) count and may have associated hyperglycemia, increased lactate dehydrogenase (LDH), and increased aspartate transaminase (AST) levels. With pancreatitis measurement of the specific isoenzyme *p*-amylase or, when measured later, lipase may assist in the diagnosis, but this is often performed in the hospital.

More specific are the urinalysis findings that may demonstrate an increase in red blood cells (RBCs) or WBCs. Microscopic hematuria (more than three cells per high-power field) is strong evidence of a ureteral stone in a patient with flank pain. Microscopic pyuria (more than five WBCs per high-power field) is suggestive of a urinary tract infection (UTI). Therefore, in a patient with pyuria, hematuria, and flank pain, pyelonephritis is likely. For patients with suspected ectopic pregnancy, a serum human chorionic gonadotropin (hCG), β-subunit test (pregnancy test) should be performed.

The abdominal examination is a sequential approach beginning with auscultation, progressing to percussion, then palpation.[4] The primary purpose of auscultation is to determine whether bowel sounds are present or absent. This may require up to 3 minutes. Complete absence is found with peritonitis and paralytic ileus. Although it may seem logical that bowel obstruction would also be a consideration, partial bowel obstruction often causes high-pitched rushes of bowel sounds. When bowel sounds are "hyperactive," gastroenteritis or intestinal bleeding should be considered. Percussion may be used to distinguish between air and fluid in the abdomen; however, it is more commonly used to detect referred tenderness. A positive rebound tenderness is often found at McBurney's point with appendicitis. Palpation is used to differentiate among masses that are superficial and deep. Superficial masses are still present with abdominal contraction. This is most common with incisions, umbilical hernias, or diastasis of the abdominals. Next, deeper palpation may distinguish among fat/feces, fluid, and masses that represent a tumor or fetus. In general, if there is lower abdominal tenderness that improves with a sustained pressure, feces or gas is likely the cause (especially when the patient reports relief with either passage of gas or a bowel movement).

The chiropractor should be conscious of the need for pelvic, testicular, and rectal exams in patients with acute abdominal pain. If the chiropractor is unfamiliar or uncomfortable with these procedures, it is imperative that they be performed by a trained health professional. All indicators of pelvic inflammatory disease, testicular or ovarian torsion, and rectal masses indicating cancer will be missed without this portion of the examination.

Occasionally, mechanical testing will reproduce or exacerbate abdominal pain. Two apparently muscular responses may indicate underlying visceral irritating processes. The psoas sign is sometimes seen in patients with appendicitis.[5] The patient keeps the hip flexed and is reluctant to extend the leg. Resisted flexion or passive extension increases the pain. Another sign is the obturator sign. This is found more often with pelvic pathology in women. Internal rotation of the flexed hip may increase the abdominal pain in these patients.

Further evaluation with more sophisticated testing such as ultrasound, radionuclide scans, computed tomography (CT), or magnetic resonance imaging (MRI) is dependent on one's underlying suspicion based on a thorough history and examination. In general, ultrasound is often used for appendicitis and cholelithiasis and in women in a search and differentiation among various pelvic processes such as tumors and ectopic pregnancy. Ultrasound is between 85% and 90% accurate for the diagnosis of gallstones.[6] Radionuclide scanning may also be used as the definitive tool for cholelithiasis. CT is reserved for abscess, tumors, or unexplained causes.

Recurrent or Chronic Abdominal Pain

The examination of chronic abdominal pain is often unrevealing. Lower abdominal tenderness that is improved by slow sustained palpation pressure is suggestive of irritable bowel syndrome (IBS). A stool sample is important in the evaluation for parasites, occult blood, mucus, polymorphonuclear leukocytes (PMNs), and unprocessed food. Hemocult testing must include three samples in an effort to increase the yield of the test.

Occult blood in the stool is not found with IBS but may be found with colon cancer and inflammatory bowel disease (IBD). Crohn's disease often has associated findings of fistulas and other anorectal disease. The stool sample will help differentiate between IBD and other causes of colitis such as parasitic infections (see Chapter 34).

Referral for sigmoidoscopy or colonoscopy is necessary with persistent diarrhea or suspicion of colorectal cancer or diverticulitis. Barium studies are occasionally used, but not during an acute attack of diverticulitis. Ultrasound may be helpful in the diagnosis of secondary dysmenorrhea, specifically with endometriosis. More recently, MRI with gadolinium may be used to accentuate the locations of endometrial implantation.

MANAGEMENT

A general rule of thumb is that if the pain has been present for 2 to 3 days and the physical examination shows no signs of abdominal distention, localized peritoneal irritation, or palpable masses, it is highly unlikely to be a "surgical" case.

Referral is still necessary when the pain is severe, or there are related signs of GI or genitourinary infection. Cases of gastroenteritis or food poisoning are often self-resolving, but the degree and abruptness of symptoms may cause the patient to seek medical attention.

The chiropractor's role in management of acute cases is to determine the need for referral for surgery or further investigation. The role in chronic or recurrent pain is to do the same; however, comanagement of patients with irritable bowel syndrome, inflammatory bowel syndromes, and diverticulitis may be appropriate. The focus of comanagement is the suggestion of or support of medical recommendations for lifestyle modifications and treatment of associated musculoskeletal complaints. These may include the following:

- high-fiber diet for diverticulosis
- avoidance of alcohol for pancreatitis
- avoidance or substitution for NSAIDs and other causes of gastric bleeding
- stress relaxation techniques and a balanced diet for patients with IBS
- for reflux, avoidance of smoking, tight garments, high-fat meals, chocolate, and caffeine; recommending that the patient eat more frequent, smaller meals

An interesting phenomenon has developed with regard to management of peptic ulcer disease. Previously prescription-only medications, H_2 antagonists are now available over the counter. The effectiveness of these medications in peptic disease and esophageal disease may make the patient reluctant to seek medical care. If the underlying cause of epigastric discomfort is peptic ulcer disease, however, the most effective treatment for long-term cure is a triple medication regimen that includes an antibiotic. Endoscopic evaluation is often suggested in patients over age 40 years or with an atypical pain response to rule out gastric carcinoma.

Algorithm

An algorithm for initial screening for abdominal pain is presented in Figure 32–3.

SELECTED CAUSES OF ACUTE ABDOMINAL PAIN

APPENDICITIS

Classic Presentation

The classic presentation of acute appendicitis follows a sequence. The patient develops anorexia and poorly localized pain over the midabdomen that is followed by nausea or vomiting (75% of patients).[7] The pain then localizes to the right lower quadrant over the next 2 to 12 hours. At this point there is constant pain made worse by coughing or jarring. If the patient is not seen at this point, there may be a sudden relief of pain indicating rupture, usually followed by an increase in pain.

Cause

The appendix is obstructed by a fecalith, inflammation, or tumor in most cases. It affects approximately 6% of the population, with the major occurrence in males between the ages of 10 and 30.[8] The appendix may be located in different areas, affecting the clinical presentation.

Figure 32–3

ABDOMINAL PAIN: INITIAL SCREENING—ALGORITHM.

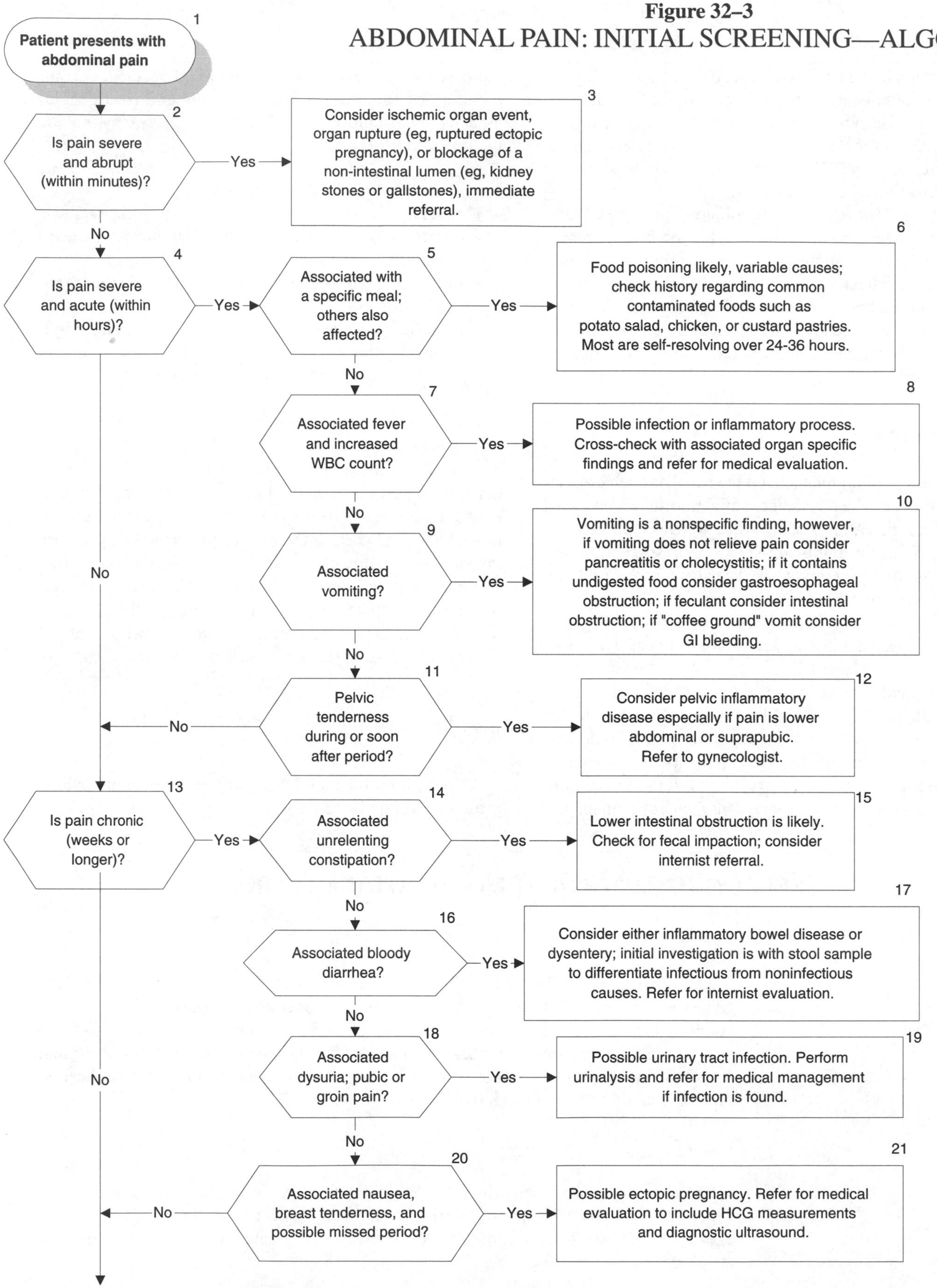

1 **Patient presents with abdominal pain**

2 Is pain severe and abrupt (within minutes)?
- Yes → 3 Consider ischemic organ event, organ rupture (eg, ruptured ectopic pregnancy), or blockage of a non-intestinal lumen (eg, kidney stones or gallstones), immediate referral.
- No → 4

4 Is pain severe and acute (within hours)?
- Yes → 5
- No → 13

5 Associated with a specific meal; others also affected?
- Yes → 6 Food poisoning likely, variable causes; check history regarding common contaminated foods such as potato salad, chicken, or custard pastries. Most are self-resolving over 24-36 hours.
- No → 7

7 Associated fever and increased WBC count?
- Yes → 8 Possible infection or inflammatory process. Cross-check with associated organ specific findings and refer for medical evaluation.
- No → 9

9 Associated vomiting?
- Yes → 10 Vomiting is a nonspecific finding, however, if vomiting does not relieve pain consider pancreatitis or cholecystitis; if it contains undigested food consider gastroesophageal obstruction; if feculant consider intestinal obstruction; if "coffee ground" vomit consider GI bleeding.
- No → 11

11 Pelvic tenderness during or soon after period?
- Yes → 12 Consider pelvic inflammatory disease especially if pain is lower abdominal or suprapubic. Refer to gynecologist.
- No → 13

13 Is pain chronic (weeks or longer)?
- Yes → 14
- No → (continues)

14 Associated unrelenting constipation?
- Yes → 15 Lower intestinal obstruction is likely. Check for fecal impaction; consider internist referral.
- No → 16

16 Associated bloody diarrhea?
- Yes → 17 Consider either inflammatory bowel disease or dysentery; initial investigation is with stool sample to differentiate infectious from noninfectious causes. Refer for internist evaluation.
- No → 18

18 Associated dysuria; pubic or groin pain?
- Yes → 19 Possible urinary tract infection. Perform urinalysis and refer for medical management if infection is found.
- No → 20

20 Associated nausea, breast tenderness, and possible missed period?
- Yes → 21 Possible ectopic pregnancy. Refer for medical evaluation to include HCG measurements and diagnostic ultrasound.
- No → (continues)

continues

Figure 32–3 continued

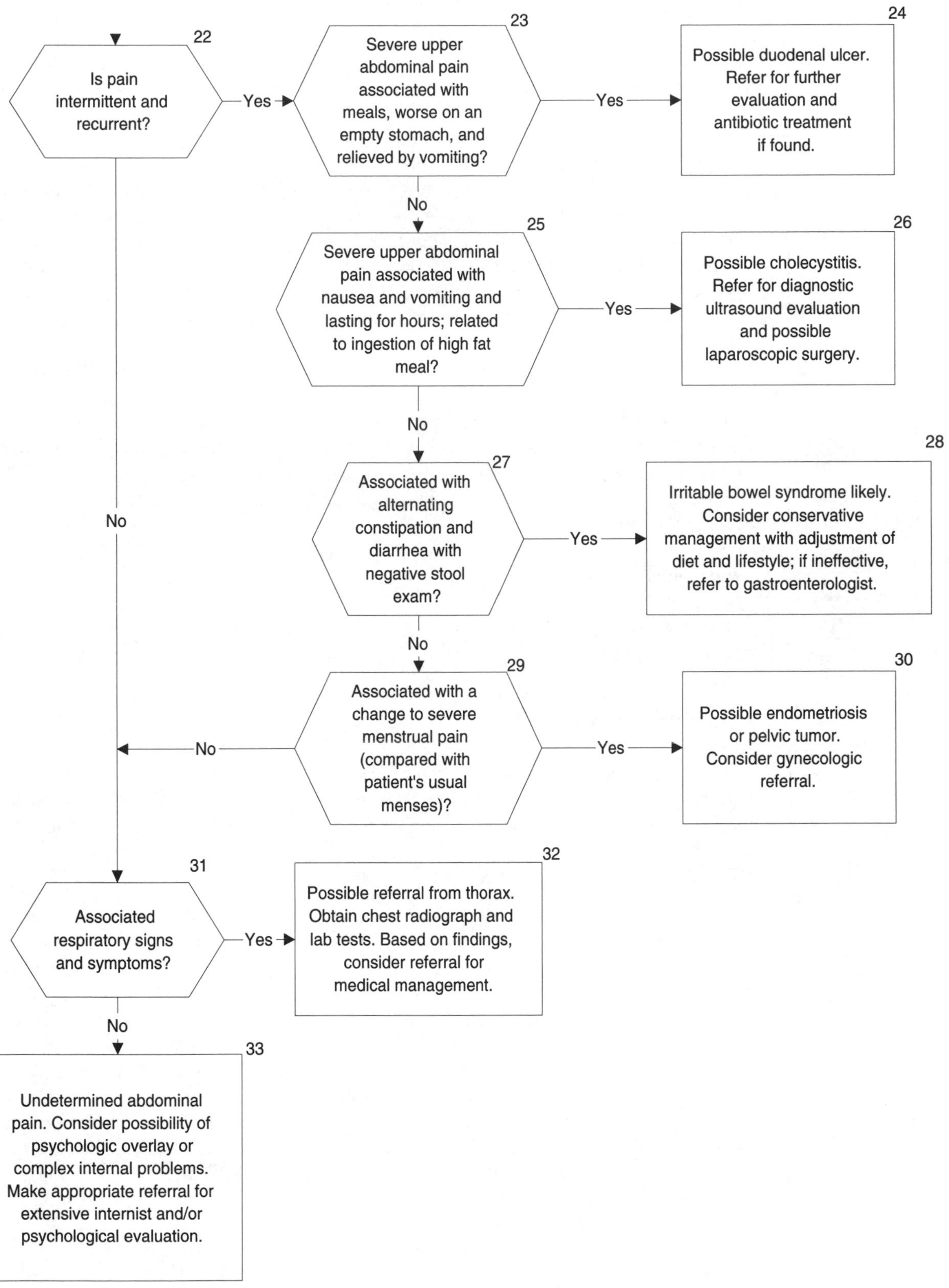

Source: Reprinted from T.A. Souza, *Topics in Clinical Chiropractic*, Vol. 1, No. 1, pp. 68–69, © 1994, Aspen Publishers, Inc.

Evaluation

The patient is anorexic and probably has vomited a couple of times. There is often a low grade fever (<102°F). Higher temperatures may indicate perforation or another disorder. The patient may move cautiously to avoid jarring and when lying keep the right hip flexed if the psoas muscle is irritated. Examination focuses on eliciting a peritoneal reaction of rebound tenderness. This may be accomplished by percussion or pressure over McBurney's point or even in the left lower quadrant (Rovsing's sign). Bowel sounds are not hyperactive as would be found with gastroenteritis. Because of the various locations of the appendix, some of the classic presentation and peritoneal findings may not be evident. If the appendix is retrocecal, it is hidden from the peritoneum, producing few peritoneal clues. If the appendix extends over the pelvic brim, it is less accessible to abdominal palpation and pain may be more easily provoked with a rectal examination. In the elderly, only two thirds of patients had right lower quadrant (RLQ) pain.[9] Laboratory findings are nonspecific, indicating a mild leukocytosis. The diagnosis in female patients is complicated by possible gynecologic causes. A pelvic examination should always be performed by an experienced professional on all women with abdominal pain of unknown origin. In one study the false positive laparotomy rate was twice as high in women.[10] This rate has been much improved, however, with the use of ultrasound. The definitive diagnostic tool is high-resolution, real-time ultrasonography. It has a sensitivity rate of 90% with a specificity of 98%; overall accuracy is approximately 96%.[11]

Management

Laparoscopic appendectomy is the standard treatment. Some patients survive an attack of appendicitis but may suffer from further attacks. The perforation rate in delayed diagnosis or treatment is quite high.

CHOLECYSTITIS/ CHOLELITHIASIS

Classic Presentation

A middle-aged or older woman complains of severe abdominal pain associated with nausea and vomiting that occurred rather abruptly after eating a fatty meal. The patient may report having had similar attacks in the past that resolved (60% to 75% of patients).[12]

Cause

The cause of cholecystitis (acute inflammation of the gallbladder) is blockage of the cystic duct by gallstones (90% of the time). Other causes may include pancreatitis or vascular abnormalities of the cystic duct. There are particular patient populations and risk factors to consider. Cholecystitis is more common in women. Estimates are that 10% of men and 20% of women over age 65 years have gallstones. Ethnic groups at high risk are Native Americans of both North and South America. Blacks are at less risk unless they have sickle cell disease. Patients who are obese, lose substantial weight, or take birth control pills or estrogen are at higher risk. Patients who are pregnant or who have Crohn's disease, cirrhosis, or diabetes are also at increased risk. Gallstones are usually classified as cholesterol stones or calcium bilirubinate stones. The cause for cholesterol stone development is suspected to be increased biliary secretion of cholesterol, delayed emptying of the gallbladder, or other factors that allow precipitation of cholesterol. Calcium bilirubinate stones are caused by the breakdown products of hemolysis.

Evaluation

Most patients will have an attack of severe pain with nausea and vomiting that lasts between 12 and 18 hours and then resolves. Twenty-five percent of patients are jaundiced, which represents a possible complication of common duct obstruction. Tenderness is in the right upper quadrant (RUQ) with a positive Murphy's sign. This test involves gradually palpating under the lower right rib margins anteriorly and determining whether patient inspiration dramatically increases pain. The patient often has rebound tenderness in the RUQ (essentially the same as a Murphy's sign). The patient may also have referred pain to the inferior border of the scapula. The gallbladder may be palpable 15% of the time. Laboratory evaluation reveals a mild leukocytosis with a shift to the left. Higher ranges suggest gangrene or other complications. Alkaline phosphatase may also be elevated.

Management

There are several treatment options; however, the standard is laparoscopic cholecystectomy.[13] The patient is released in 1 day and returns to daily activities in a few days. Another option is dissolution therapy with bile salts. The success rate is variable, and half of patients have recurrence within 5 years after stopping therapy. It may take up to 2 years for dissolution, and the medication often is expensive. Lithotripsy is available for patients with single stones less than 20 mm in size.[14]

URETERAL STONE

Classic Presentation

The patient reports a sudden onset of pain that is severe and often episodic. The pain is often felt at the costovertebral area of the lower ribs posteriorly, radiating anteriorly, often into the groin (testes in men, labia in women). There is associated nausea and vomiting.

Cause

Stones develop for two main reasons: lack of appropriate hydration and dietary factors. There are three common types of stones. The most common are calcium oxalate, uric acid, and cystine. An environment for stone precipitation is created by excessive intake of calcium, oxalates, or protein.[15] This in combination with insufficient water intake sets the stage for stone formation in predisposed individuals. Stone formation is much more common in men (4:1) than women, usually occurring in the 30s or 40s. In the elderly, the ratio is almost even. An environmental factor that may play a role is a humid, hot area. Stones are more likely to form in the summer months.

Evaluation

The patient is often constantly moving or writhing in pain, unable to find a position of relief. The location of the pain, a urinalysis indicating hematuria, and a plain film of the abdomen indicating a corresponding radiopacity are usually diagnostic. If not, ultrasound is often necessary if the stone is at the ureterovesical junction.

Management

The pain is usually severe enough to warrant an emergency department visit. Management is often symptomatic with follow-up monitoring. Stones that appear to be 6 mm or less on plain film often will pass without need of intervention. It is important to know that overhydration during an attack will not force the stones out. If the stone is large enough or caught at an anatomic juncture, lithotripsy or ureteroscopic stone extraction is utilized.[16] The key to prevention is hydration and dietary management. The patient should be advised to double water intake, to drink water between meals, with meals, and before going to bed at night. It is important that patients understand that water intake, not caffeine or alcohol, is needed. Coffee, tea, and alcohol act as diuretics and may worsen the predisposition. Fifty percent of those who do not follow this advice will have symptomatic stones again within 5 years. Those with uric acid stones may have a return attack within months if therapy is not initiated and fluid advice is not heeded.[17]

PANCREATITIS

Classic Presentation

The patient is often an alcohol abuser who develops a sudden onset of epigastric pain associated with nausea and vomiting. The pain often radiates to the back. The patient is in a bent-forward or fetal position to relieve pain.

Cause

It appears that edema or obstruction of the ampulla of Vater causes a reflux of bile into the pancreatic ducts or acinar cells. The result is the release of pancreatic enzymes into the surrounding tissue. This sequence is initiated by heavy alcohol intake. In a small percentage of cases other causes may need to be considered, including viral infections, hypercalcemia, hyperlipidemias, trauma, and drugs (sulfonamides and thiazides).[18]

Evaluation

There is often a mild fever, a tender and often distended upper abdominal region, and possible signs of hypotension. Because the pancreas is retroperitoneal, a palpable mass or rebound tenderness is not a common feature. Bowel sounds are often absent, and the patient may demonstrate a mild degree of jaundice. Although the laboratory indicates mild leukocytosis, proteinuria and glycosuria (25%), hyperglycemia and elevated bilirubin, the classic tests are serum amylase and lipase. Although sensitive to pancreatitis, these tests are not always specific. The isoenzyme *p*-amylase is more specific. Imaging is not as valuable as with other abdominal problems. Plain films usually show indirect signs, including an air-filled small intestine or transverse colon. CT may demonstrate an enlarged pancreas. Ultrasound is less valuable because of the artifact of gas distention. A grading system developed by Ranson is often used to estimate the prognosis with pancreatitis.[19] The more positive criteria met, the higher the morbidity rate. In general in an older patient with high glucose and elevation of liver enzymes, the prognosis is poorer.

Management

There are two main complications of acute pancreatitis: (1) hypovolemia secondary to intravascular fluid loss to the bowels and (2) adult respiratory distress syndrome (ARDS). These usually occur within a few days to 1 week after the acute attack. In general the treatment for pancreatitis is bed rest with no food or fluids by mouth, and pain medication. A nasogastric tube is often required. After resolution, the preventive program is simply avoidance of alcohol. Continued attacks may lead to chronic pancreatitis. This may be demonstrated on radiographs as pancreatic calcification.

PELVIC INFLAMMATORY DISEASE

Classic Presentation

The patient is a woman of child-bearing years who is sexually active (often with multiple partners) and who presents with a complaint of lower abdominal pain with associated chills and fever, dyspareunia (painful intercourse), and vaginal (cervical) discharge.

Cause

There are several major organisms that cause pelvic inflammatory disease (PID) of the upper genital tract in women. The primary organisms are *Chlamydia* trachomatis and *Neisseria* gonorrhoeae. Other organisms include *Haemophilus influenzae* and some enteric organisms. PID is more likely to occur in nonwhites and those who smoke or douche. Oral contraceptives or barrier methods of protection may help prevent infection. However, use of an intrauterine device (IUD) will increase the risk of PID for several months after insertion.

Evaluation

The diagnosis may be difficult because many women are relatively asymptomatic. When the presentation is acute, the differentiation includes appendicitis as well as other gynecologic possibilities. The patient may describe a slow onset of pain that begins during or soon after menstruation. The presentation of lower abdominal pain is relatively nonspecific; however, a pelvic examination will usually reveal adnexal and cervical motion tenderness or a palpable mass. Sometimes the presentation is bilateral lower abdominal pain and suprapubic pain. Laboratory testing is rarely helpful; however, if a woman with lower abdominal pain, adnexal tenderness, fever, and an elevated WBC count also presents with cervical discharge, PID is high on the list. Culdocentesis or Gram staining of discharge may reveal the underlying cause. Most patients will undergo ultrasound, which may help differentiate any masses felt on examination. The definitive diagnosis is with laparoscopy, but most women are treated with antibiotics with an assumption of PID. One study indicated that the diagnoses of only 65% of women with PID were confirmed laparoscopically.[20]

Management

Treatment is with appropriate antibiotics. Failure to recognize the diagnosis or to treat the disease may result in an ascending infection to the capsule of the liver called the Fitz-Hugh–Curtis syndrome. Also, the long-term consequences may include scarring that interferes with fertility or leads to an ectopic pregnancy. Chronic pelvic pain is also more likely in these patients.

ECTOPIC PREGNANCY

Classic Presentation

The patient is a woman of childbearing years who complains of lower abdominal pain and a missed or "spotty" period over 6 to 8 weeks prior to the pain onset.

Cause

Implantation of the ovum outside the uterine cavity occurs in approximately 1% of pregnancies. Ninety-eight percent of the time this is in the fallopian tubes. Predispositions include prior PID, IUD use (especially with progesterone), progesterone-only contraceptives, endometriosis, or tubal ligation.[21]

Evaluation

The classic findings include adnexal tenderness on the pelvic examination coupled with a positive pregnancy test (β-hCG). The β-hCG level is higher than 5,000 to 6,000 mIU/mL with uterine pregnancies; ectopic pregnancy usually produces levels less than 3,000 mIU/mL. Also, if the test is followed over several days, the levels will rise slowly with an ectopic pregnancy, whereas they usually double with a normal pregnancy. A low hCG level (<1,500 mIU/mL) with an associated low progesterone level (<10 ng/mL) is highly supportive of an ectopic pregnancy.[22] For further differentiation, an ultrasound examination is used in an effort to visualize an ectopic mass.

Management

Treatment is usually through laparoscopy. Recent studies indicate a role for methotrexate to destroy the placenta.[23]

SELECTED CAUSES OF RECURRENT ABDOMINAL PAIN

UPPER ABDOMINAL PAIN

Peptic Ulcer (Duodenal and Gastric)

Classic Presentation

Usually onset begins in a young man (teenage or the 20s; however, may occur from ages 30 to 50 years with duodenal ulcer; over age 50 years for gastric ulcer) and is felt as epigastric pain that is often reported as waking the patient from sleep. The pain is intermittent and recurrent. Antacids and over-the-counter (OTC) H_2 antagonist seem to provide relief. Classic presentations and classic relationships to pain on an empty stomach that is relieved by food are not consistent. Sixty percent of patients with complications such as bleeding or perforation have had no prior history of symptoms. As many as half of patients with NSAID ulcers are asymptomatic.

Cause

The major cause of gastric ulcers is NSAID use. The main cause of duodenal ulcer is *Helicobacter pylori* infection. Although gastric ulcers are due to a breakdown of the protective mechanisms in the stomach against acid and pepsin, the *H pylori* role with duodenal ulcers is not yet defined. Ninety-five percent of duodenal ulcers occur at the bulb or pyloric channel. Benign gastric ulcers occur mainly at the antrum.

Evaluation

The physical examination is usually unrevealing. Laboratory testing may reveal anemia from blood loss or leukocytosis if the ulcer is perforated. The most accurate diagnostic procedure is endoscopy with biopsy for *H pylori* and cytologic brushings of ulcer margins for potentially (5%) malignant gastric ulcers. If an upper GI series is performed in lieu of endoscopy, any gastric lesions should be followed up with endoscopy in 2 to 3 months.

Management

There is now a general consensus that an antibiotic regimen to eradicate *H pylori* is the most effective means of dealing with duodenal ulcer. Compared with standard therapy of H_2 antagonists, antibiotic therapy demonstrated only a 5% recurrence (largely due to use of NSAIDs), compared with a 70% to 85% recurrence in the standard H_2 group.[24,25] This "triple therapy" is a combination of bismuth (Pepto-Bismol) with metronidazole (Flagyl) and tetracycline. For gastric ulcers, discontinuing NSAIDs combined with a 2- to 3-month course of H_2 antagonists or sucralfate (a drug that acts locally as a mucus bandage) is usually effective. Discontinuing smoking is often necessary. If the ulcers do not heal, Zollinger-Ellison syndrome is suspected.

Gastroesophageal Reflux

Classic Presentation

The patient is often older and complains of epigastric pain after eating large meals and lying down.

Cause

The tone of the lower esophageal sphincter (LES) may decrease with age and also with ingestion of certain foods, including chocolate, caffeine, fat, and alcohol. Additionally, smoking, theophylline, calcium channel blockers, and anticholinergic medications also will decrease the tone of the LES, leading to reflux.[26]

Evaluation

The diagnosis is mainly historical. The patient may report that by eating smaller, frequent meals; going to bed on an empty stomach; and avoiding chocolate, caffeine, and alcohol, the pain is better. Antacids or the newer OTC H_2 antagonists (Tagamet, Zantac, etc.) usually help. A hiatal hernia may predispose the individual to a reduced LES tone. This may be seen on a chest or anterior-posterior thoracic film indicated by an air lucency above the diaphragm. The main differential is peptic ulcer. If the patient's pain is not relieved with the modifications suggested above, referral for a barium study or endoscopy is probably warranted.

Management

Recommend to the patient that he or she avoid alcohol, caffeine, fatty meals, smoking, and eating large meals. Switching to smaller meals eaten more frequently and going to bed with a partially full stomach may help. If there is an associated hiatal hernia, chiropractic manipulation in the epigastric region may help reflexly. Weight loss is important for obese patients.

LOWER ABDOMINAL PAIN

Irritable Bowel Syndrome

Classic Presentation

Generally patients present with complaints of abdominal pain (usually lower left or suprapubic) and distention that is relieved with defecation. Patients often report early-morning constipation that results in the passage of small-sized feces. Signs and symptoms often begin in late teens or 20s. Manning et al.[27] have determined six symptoms that occur together more often in patients with IBS than in patients with other GI disorders. Recent studies confirm this observation and add that the likelihood increases with the number of positive criteria; the predictive value decreases with age and is less valuable with men.[28,29] These criteria are as follows:

- pain relief with bowel movement
- more frequent stools with the onset of pain
- looser stools with the onset of pain
- passage of mucus
- sensation of incomplete defecation
- abdominal distention sensed through tight clothing or visibly evident

Symptoms compatible with IBS are found in 10% to 22% of adults.[30,31] Only 14% to 50% of this group seek medical advice. Some studies have classified patients into two subgroups: (1) abdominal pain predominant and seems to be related to meals and stress;

(2) bowel-habit predominant and usually constipation is the main complaint, but diarrhea may be; abdominal pain is not the chief complaint. Some studies describe a prototype patient who is often angry, depressed, or stressed.[32,33]

Cause

The cause is unknown. However, there appears to be abnormal myoelectric activity in the intestines (and sometime other structures) that result in a change in peristaltic activity. Studies indicate that a normal six-cycle per second slow-wave rate is more often three cycles per second in patients with IBS. Colonic spike activity peaks about 1 to 1½ hours after meals, which seems to correlate with a common complaint of pain after meals.[34] It also appears that patients may have a lower visceral pain threshold, perceiving what would be considered normal bowel distention as pain.[35]

Evaluation

IBS is largely a historical diagnosis and one of exclusion. The patient should have had symptoms for at least 3 to 6 months before considering IBS in the differential. Other causes of constipation should be screened historically, and education in proper fluid/fiber intake combined with proper bowel habits should be used initially for patients who are constipation predominant. Patients with bowel-predominant symptoms should have a rectal and stool examination. Stool that is nonbloody (occult or frank) and free of fecal leukocytes, parasites, and ova suggests ITB as probable. Mucus is often found in the stool of patients with IBS. In older patients, sigmoidoscopy is sometimes warranted if colon cancer is suspected.

Management

The patient should be counseled regarding the chronicity of IBS, and that there will be periods of exacerbation and remission. Primary conservative focus is on stress relaxation and dietary factors. Keeping a diary with relation to the onset of symptoms may be helpful. Generally, patients often benefit by avoidance of lactose, fructose, and sorbitol. Additionally, gas-producing foods such as cabbage, cauliflower, raisins, grapes, raw onions, sprouts, coffee, red wine, and beer should be eliminated initially to determine effect. A high-fiber diet may help, although if the fiber is bran, increased gas production may worsen symptoms. Pharmacologically, it is interesting that placebo agents result in improvement in up to 70% of patients. When medication is used, anticholinergic agents are often used. Antidiarrheal or anticonstipation agents are sometimes prescribed.

Diverticulitis

Classic Presentation

Usually, the patient will be elderly with complaints of left lower abdominal pain and tenderness and associated low-grade fever; nausea and vomiting may occur. Most patients will have symptoms mild enough that they will wait a few days before seeking medical attention. Patients with a large perforation will present with generalized abdominal pain and peritoneal signs.

Cause

Diverticula are herniations of the mucosa and submucosa into the colonic muscle wall at the site of mesenteric vessel penetration. Diverticular disease appears to be the result of years of colonic high pressure due to contracted segments of bowel that are undistended; thus it is believed that a chronic fiber-deficient diet is the cause. The prevalence is higher in Western countries. Diverticular disease occurs in approximately one third of patients over age 60 years; more than two thirds of this group are asymptomatic.

Evaluation

Lower-left abdominal tenderness with a palpable mass are common findings. A low-grade fever, occult blood, and a mild to moderate leukocytosis often are found. A plain film may be used to determine free air (evidence of perforation) or obstruction. Referral for medical management will usually result in a limited hospitalization followed 7 to 10 days later with an outpatient barium study and sigmoidoscopy.

Management

In patients who have diverticular disease discovered incidentally, a high-fiber diet is recommended. For those with active diverticulitis, antibiotic therapy and intravenous fluids are initial approaches. Twenty to 30% of patients eventually will require surgery.

INFLAMMATORY BOWEL DISEASE

Ulcerative Colitis

Classic Presentation

Generally a younger patient presents with complaints of frequent bloody diarrhea, lower abdominal cramping, mild pain, and rectal urgency. Approximately 10% to 20% will complain of multiple joint pain. Variation in presentation is based on the number of bowel movements per day from less than four (mild) to more than six (severe).

Cause

The cause of ulcerative colitis (UC) is unknown. It appears that there may be some predisposition that somehow interacts with environmental factors to create varying degrees of inflammatory reaction. Half of all patients with UC have involvement of the distal colon, 30% of patients have extension to the splenic flexure, with 20% of patients extending into the more proximal bowel.[36] An association with HLA-B27 explains the occurrence of peripheral arthropathies in some patients and a higher risk of colorectal cancer.

Evaluation

The patient with mild ulcerative colitis may have no more discriminating findings clinically than patients with other causes of colitis such as infection or antibiotic colitis. However, those with severe UC may also have signs of hypovolemia such as an increased pulse rate. Severe forms will also cause weight loss, a decreased hematocrit and albumin, and an increased erythrocyte sedimentation rate (ESR) and temperature.

The diagnosis is established with sigmoidoscopy with characteristic findings of a granular mucosa with edema, erosions, and friability. Colonoscopy is reserved for patients who are not acutely ill to determine the extent of involvement. Laboratory testing of the stool is used to rule out other causes of colitis, usually infectious.

Management

Exacerbations seem related to stressful events, but they may occur without an obvious cause. The mainstay of medical management is similar to that for Crohn's disease, consisting of antiinflammatory (sulfasalazine and corticosteroids), antidiarrheal, and (rarely) immunosuppressive drugs. Dietary advice is generic. Avoiding lactose during acute exacerbations may help some patients. The prognosis in most patients is good. Those acquiring the disease in infancy or after the age of 60 have the poorest prognosis. Pregnancy often worsens UC; however, the use of medication does not seem to affect the fetus.

Crohn's Disease (Regional Enteritis)

Classic Presentation

The patient is often young with an insidious onset of intermittent bouts of right lower quadrant pain, some diarrhea, and a low-grade fever. In some patients, the initial presentation is with extraintestinal manifestations such as perianal fistulas, fissures, or abscesses. Eventually, the patient may appear anemic with weight loss.

Cause

The cause is unknown. It appears that there may be some predisposition that somehow interacts with environmental factors to create varying degrees of inflammatory reaction. Specifically, it appears that there is an environment that allows chronic T-cell activation, which causes damage through secondary macrophage activation.[37] As to what activates the T cells remains controversial. Current interest is on the role of measles and the measles vaccine as one potential instigator.[38,39] There is transmural involvement with extension possible through to the serosa. This patchy, segmental involvement is isolated to the ileum in about one third of patients, with half of patients also having involvement of the colon. In 15% to 20% of cases only the colon is affected. The process may extend, however, from the mouth to the anus. The inflammatory reaction includes infiltration of lymphocytes and plasma cells. Fibrosis is often extensive, causing obstruction. Sarcoidlike granulomas occur in 30% to 40% of patients within involved intestinal segments. An association with HLA-B27 explains why some patients have peripheral arthropathies.

Evaluation

Evaluation findings are contingent on the degree and location of involvement. The abdominal examination may reveal a tender right quadrant, anal-rectal disease, and weight loss. Laboratory examination is relatively nonspecific, showing an increase in ESR, macrocytic anemia (with terminal ileum involvement), leukocytosis, and occasionally decreased albumin. Stool examination for ova, parasites, and other pathogens is used to differentiate from other causes of diarrhea. Colonoscopy and barium studies are diagnostic. Colonoscopy allows direct visualization and biopsy. Barium studies may demonstrate "slip" lesions (areas of involvement adjacent to normal mucosa).

Management

In the National Cooperative Crohn's Disease Study, it appears that one third of patients on a placebo went into remission within 4 months and remained in remission for 2 years.[40] This is important information for all who attempt to treat Crohn's disease with alternative approaches. Medical care varies based on patient presentation. In the armamentarium of medications the primary drugs are antiinflammatory (sulfasalazine and prednisone), immunosuppressive (azathriopine), and various antidiarrheals.

Dietary management is important because of malabsorption. Vitamin supplementation is often necessary, often including parenteral vitamin B_{12}. However, this does not appear to alter the disease course. Approximately 70% of all patients with Crohn's disease must have some surgery.

DYSMENORRHEA

Primary

Classic Presentation

The patient is often 1 to 2 years postmenarchal with increasing pain associated with menses. The pain is felt in the lower abdomen and pelvis, sometimes radiating to the back or inner thighs.[41]

Cause

Pain is mediated via prostaglandins. The cause is a combination of vasoconstriction and myometrial contraction. Increased discomfort may be caused by fluid retention (estrogen causes salt retention).

Examination

No examination usually is necessary unless the pain is "new" or suddenly increased. Then a pelvic examination is warranted. With primary dysmenorrhea there are no obvious pathologic findings, but the exam may be more uncomfortable during menses.

Management

Medical management focuses on decrease of certain prostaglandins. NSAIDs (ibuprofen, ketoprofen, naproxen) are usually helpful. Conservative approaches may also include manipulation of the lumbar spine, pelvis, or sacrum. Stimulation of sacral and low-back reflex points may provide relief. Dietary formulas, including omega-3 polyunsaturated fatty acids, and B_{12} may provide relief.

Secondary

Classic Presentation

A female patient in her late 20s or 30s (as late as 40s) presents with a complaint that her menstrual pain is much worse than it had been previously. Suspicion is increased when the patient is infertile. Depending on sites of endometrial implantation, endometriosis may also cause dyspareunia and/or rectal pain with bleeding.[42]

Cause

The two most common causes are endometriosis (implantation of uterine tissue outside the uterus) and pelvic inflammatory disease (salpingitis). Endometriosis appears to be somewhat dependent on a dysfunction of cell-mediated immunity. One study observed that women with endometriosis were more sensitive to the stimulatory effects of peripheral blood monocytes on proliferation of endometrial tissue.[43] Other causes include submucous myoma, IUD use, and cervical stenosis (often post–induced abortion).

Examination

The pelvic examination may reveal pelvic tenderness or discrete nodules in the cul-de-sac (with endometriosis). However, the definitive diagnosis may rest on laparoscopy to differentiate between PID and endometriosis. Cervical stenosis should be suspected with a presentation subsequent to an induced abortion.

Management

The focus of management is to suspend ovulation for 4 to 9 months. This is accomplished via a regimen similar to birth control pills or danazol (androgenic effects). This will usually result in a decrease in size of the endometrial implants. When extensive, surgery is often necessary. The approach is dictated by age and desire for reproductive function. Under age 35 years, resecting lesions and freeing adhesions allows fertility in about 20% of patients. After age 35 years or for those not wishing to conceive, treatment involves bilateral salpingo-oophorectomy and hysterectomy if the disease is extensive.[44]

REFERENCES

1. Nansel D, Szlazak M. Somatic dysfunction and the phenomenon of visceral disease stimulation: a probable explanation for the apparent effectiveness of somatic therapy in patients presumed to be suffering from true visceral disease. *J Manipulative Physiol Ther.* 1995;18:379–397.
2. Foreman RD. Spinal substrates of visceral pain. In: Yaksh TL, ed. *Spinal Afferent Processing.* New York: Plenum Publishing; 1986.
3. Eisenberg RL, Heinekin P, Hedcock MW, et al. Evaluation of plain abdominal radiographs in the diagnosis of abdominal pain. *Ann Intern Med.* 1982;97:257–261.
4. Cope Z. *The Early Diagnosis of the Acute Abdomen.* 14th ed. London: Oxford University Press; 1972.
5. Vitello JM, Nyhus LM. The physical examination of the abdomen. In: Nyhus LM, Vitello JM, Condon RE, eds. *Abdominal Pain: A Guide to Rapid Diagnosis.* Norwalk, CT: Appleton & Lange; 1995:31–48.
6. Laing FC. Ultrasonography of the acute abdomen. *Radiol Clin North Am.* 1992;30:389–404.
7. Manning RT. Signs that point to appendicitis. *Diagnosis.* 1982;2: 88–90.
8. Vitello JM. Appendicitis. In: Nyhus LM, Vitello JM, Condon RE, eds. *Abdominal Pain: A Guide to Rapid Diagnosis.* Norwalk, CT: Appleton & Lange; 1995:83–104.
9. Peltokallio P, Janhainen K. Acute appendicitis in the aged patient: study of 300 cases after the age of 60. *Arch Surg.* 1970;100: 140–143.
10. Lews FR. Appendicitis: a critical review of diagnosis and treatment in 1,000 cases. *Arch Surg.* 1975:110:677–684.
11. Skane P, Amland PF, Nordshus T, et al. Ultrasonography in patients with suspected appendicitis: a prospective study. *Br J Radiol.* 1990;63:787.
12. Diehl AK, Sugarek NJ, Todd KH. Clinical evaluation of gallstone diseases: usefulness of symptoms and signs in clinical diagnosis. *Am J Med.* 1990;89:29–34.
13. NIH Consensus Development Panel on Gallstones and Laparoscopic Cholecystectomy. Cholecystectomy: gallstones and laparoscopic cholecystectomy. *JAMA.* 1993;269:1018.
14. Strasberg SM, Clavien PA. Cholecystolithiasis: lithotherapy for the 1990's. *Hepatology.* 1992;16:820.
15. Coe FL, et al. The pathogenesis and treatment of kidney stones. *N Engl J Med.* 1992;327:1141.
16. Assimos DG et al. A comparison of anatrophic nephrolithotomy and percutaneous nephrolithotomy with and without extracorporeal shock wave lithotripsy for management of patients with staghorn calculi. *J Urol.* 1991;145:710.
17. Riese RJ, Sakhaee K. Uric acid nephrolithiasis: pathogenesis and treatment. *J Urol.* 1992;148:765.
18. Burns GP, Bank S. *Disorders of the Pancreas: Current Issues in Diagnosis and Management.* New York: McGraw-Hill; 1992.
19. Marshall JB. Acute pancreatitis: a review with an emphasis on new developments. *Arch Intern Med.* 1993;153:1185.
20. Jacobson L, Westron L. Objective diagnosis of acute pelvic inflammatory disease. *Am J Obstet Gynecol.* 1969;105:1088–1098.
21. Stabile I, Grudzinkas JG. Ectopic pregnancy: a review of incidence, etiology and diagnostic aspects. *Obstet Gynecol Surv.* 1990;45:335.
22. Vajaranant M. Acute pelvic pain in women. In: Nyhus LM, Vitello JM, Condon RE, eds. *Abdominal Pain: A Guide to Rapid Diagnosis.* Norwalk, CT: Appleton & Lange; 1995:191–206.
23. Ory SJ. New options for diagnosis and treatment of ectopic pregnancy. *JAMA.* 1992;267:534.
24. Graham DY, et al. Effect of treatment of *Helicobacter pylori* infection on the long-term recurrence of gastric and duodenal ulcer: a randomized controlled study. *Ann Intern Med.* 1992;116:705.
25. Graham DY, et al. Effect of triple therapy (antibiotics plus bismuth) on duodenal ulcer healing. *Ann Intern Med.* 1992;115:256.
26. Jackson SB. Gastroesophageal reflux disease. *Topics Clin Chiro.* 1995;2(1):24–29.
27. Manning AP, Thompson WP, Heaton KW, et al. Towards positive diagnosis of the irritable bowel. *Br Med J.* 1978;2:653.
28. Jeong H, Lee HR, Yoo BC, et al. Manning criteria in irritable bowel syndrome: its diagnostic significance. *Korean J Intern Med.* 1993;8:34.
29. Talley NJ, Philips SF, Melton MJ, et al. Diagnostic value of the Manning criteria in irritable bowel syndrome. *Gut.* 1990;31:77.
30. Crossman DA, Zhiming L, Andruzzi E, et al. U.S. housholder survey of functional gastrointestinal disorders: prevalence, sociodemography, and health impact. *Dig Dis Sci.* 1993;38:1569.
31. Jones R, Lydeard S. Irritable bowel syndrome in the general population. *Br Med J.* 1992;304:87.
32. Lynn RB, Friedman LS. Irritable bowel sydrome. *N Engl J Med.* 1993;329:1940.
33. Welgan P, Meshkinpour H, Beeler M. Effect of anger on colon motor and myoelectric activity in irritable bowel syndrome. *Gastroenterology.* 1988;94:1150.
34. Kellow JE, Phillips SF. Altered small bowel motility in irritable bowel syndrome is correlated with symptoms. *Gastroenterology.* 1987;92:1885.
35. Camilleri M, Prather C. The irritable bowel syndrome: mechanisms and a practical approach to management. *Ann Intern Med.* 1992;116:1001.
36. Podolsky DK. Inflammatory bowel disease. *N Engl J Med.* 1991;325:928–1008.
37. MacDonald TT, Murch ST. Aetiology and pathogenesis of chronic inflammatory bowel disease. *Baillieres Clin Gastroenterol.* 1994;8:1–34.
38. Ekborn A, Wakefield AJ, Zack M, Adami HO. Perinatal measles infection and subsequent Crohn's disease. *Lancet.* 1994;344:508–510.
39. Thompson NP, Montgomery SM, Pounder RE, Wakefield NJ. Is measles vaccination a risk factor for inflammatory bowel disease? *Lancet.* 1995;345:1071–1074.
40. Singleton J, et al. The National Cooperative Crohn's Disease Study. *Gastroenterology.* 1979;7:53.
41. MacKay HT, Chang RJ. Dysmenorrhea. In: Rakel RE, ed. *Current Therapy 1993.* Philadelphia: WB Saunders Co; 1993.
42. Olive DL, Swartz LB. Endometriosis. *N Engl J Med.* 1993;24:1759.
43. Dmowski WP, Gebel HM, Braun DP. The role of cell-mediated immunity in the pathogenesis of endometriosis. *Acta Obstet Gynecol Scand Suppl.* 1994;159:7–14.
44. Witt BR, Barad DH. Management of endometriosis in women older than 40 years of age. *Obstet Gynecol Clin North Am.* 1993;20: 349.

Chapter 33

Constipation

CONTEXT

Although many patients complain of constipation, it is important to remember that constipation is a relative term. Most physicians would classify a normal bowel movement as one bowel movement per day without straining; others may find passage every 3 to 5 days acceptable. The answer lies in the patient's history. If the patient has always had bowel movements every 3 days, this may likely be his or her normal pattern. In one study that used the criteria of no more than two bowel movements per week and/or straining on more than one in four bowel movements, only 62% of self-reporters met the criteria, although 47% of all patients reported constipation.[1] Self-reporters took twice as many laxatives as those who did not report constipation. The self-reported rate of constipation is as high as 60% among the elderly. Thirty percent of healthy elderly persons report using laxatives, although the majority of these patients have never gone more than 3 days without a bowel movement ($400 million per year in cost for laxatives).[2]

Most causes of constipation are benign and are the result of external or internal influences that are easily identifiable. In the context of chiropractic practice, it is a common observation that patients with low back pain are also constipated. The assumption is that this is due to either increased pain with bearing down or simply neural inhibition without straining. In either case, it is important for the chiropractor to rule out more serious causes. When not present, assist the patient with what may be an aggravating factor to his or her low back pain.

GENERAL STRATEGY

History

Careful questioning of the patient during the history taking can lead to appropriate management (Table 33–1).

- Determine the patient's definition of constipation.
- Determine the degree of constipation and whether it is acute or chronic.
- Determine any additional signs or symptoms that may indicate a systemic disorder such as hypothyroidism or diabetes.
- Determine the patient's current medication history, including over-the-counter (OTC) drugs.
- Determine the amount of dietary fiber and fluid intake and also iron supplementation.
- Determine whether laxatives are being used and how often.
- Note whether the patient is pregnant.
- Determine the patient's status with regard to abdominal muscle tone; immobilized, incapacitated, or sedentary individuals may have less propulsive ability.
- Determine whether there is any soiling of undergarments (may be more suggestive of constipation than fecal incontinence).

Evaluation

- On physical examination determine whether any anorectal disease is present and the status of the rectum (empty

Table 33–1 History Questions for Constipation

Primary Question	*What Are You Thinking?*	*Secondary Questions*	*What Are You Thinking?*
How often do you have a bowel movement?	Determine what is normal for the individual.	How long have you had constipation? Did it occur over the last few weeks, months, or years?	Determine in an older patient whether there is a gradual decrease in the frequency of bowel movements as opposed to a recent change.
Is it painful to defecate?	Local pathology is causing pain; pain is increased due to muscle contraction or increase in intrathecal pressure.	Do you have hemorrhoids or other local problems around the anorectal area?	Pain inhibits defecation urge or there is conscious inhibition due to fear of pain.
		Does bearing down cause local back pain?	Muscle spasm or other local irritation.
		Does bearing down cause pain radiating into the legs?	Consider intrathecal pressure increase indicating disc lesion or tumor.
Do you take medications?	Direct action of medication or medication indicates underlying medical condition associated with decreased bowel function.	Do you take medication for diabetes or depression?	Underlying disease may be cause of constipation.
		Do you take iron supplements, or medication for Parkinson's disease, hypertension, seizures, or depression?	All may cause constipation as a side effect.
		Do you take laxatives?	Many seniors take laxatives out of habit, not necessarily because they need them; also some laxatives can *cause* constipation.
What are your eating and drinking habits?	Low-fiber diet.	Describe what you eat on an average day.	Get a sense of dietary fiber intake.
(For children) Do you go to the bathroom when you feel the urge?	Too busy, does not like bathroom facilities, defecation hurts.	Does it hurt to go to the bathroom?	Either too little fiber or hydration causes hard stools; or an anal fissure causes local pain.
		Do you not go to the bathroom because you are playing or are too busy or because the bathroom is dirty?	Suppression of urge will lead to a habit that causes constipation.

or impacted); 25% of colorectal cancer may be found on rectal examination.
- Testing for occult blood is often warranted; referral for sigmoidoscopy is warranted in chronic constipation.

Management

- If the bowel is impacted, use digital disimpaction or an enema, or refer for disimpaction.
- Educate the patient on proper bowel habits, including proper fluid and dietary fiber intake, mild exercise, avoidance of laxatives, strengthening pelvic/abdominal musculature, allowing enough time for bowel movement, and avoiding inhibition of gastrocolic reflex.

RELEVANT ANATOMY AND PHYSIOLOGY

For the regular, unstrained passage of stool, it is necessary to have the proper balance of fluid, dietary fiber, and normal motility and transit time. The colonic mucosa usually absorbs 95% of intestinal sodium and water.[3] Interestingly, this function is usually normal in constipated patients. Increased desiccation, however, may occur as a result of increased mucosal contact due to slowed colonic transport time.[4] It would seem logical that this would be due to a decrease in colonic motor activity; however, investigators have actually found contraction of the pelvic colon to be increased.[5] The colonic myoelectric activity of patients with idiopathic constipation is usually normal, but this activity seems to be abnormally responsive to several outside stimuli, such as emotional stimulation, eating a meal, and hormonal stimulation. The intestinal smooth muscle cells have an inherent property that results in cyclic depolarization and repolarization. This occurs at what is referred to as a slow wave rate. There are two observed rates of six and three cycles per minute. Although normal individuals have an almost exclusive six-cycle per minute frequency in the colon and rectum, patients with irritable bowel syndrome have almost half the contractions occurring at three cycles per minute.[6]

Diseases that affect the central nervous system (CNS), spinal cord, and autonomic nervous system may have an effect on intestinal motility. A common example is the ileus that develops after abdominal surgery. This is due to effects of anesthesia (CNS depression) and manipulation of the organs. Diabetes may also affect bowel movements through dysfunction of the autonomic nervous system.

Most cases of constipation can be assigned to two general problems: ineffective filling and ineffective emptying. Ineffective filling is most often due to inadequate amounts of fluid and/or dietary fiber. Other common causes are CNS depression, which is usually the effect of medications or clinical depression.

The main stimulus to defecate is distention of the rectum by the colon contents. This initiates the rectoanal inhibitory reflex and internal sphincter relaxation.[7] The resultant urge to defecate is voluntarily controlled. Through contraction of the external sphincter and pelvic musculature, defecation can be prevented. To defecate, a combination of intraabdominal pressure through bearing down and external sphincter and pelvic floor muscle relaxation is voluntarily employed. Ineffective emptying is usually due to suppression of the defecation urge. This suppression may be due to painful anorectal disorders or circumstantial detractors. For example, children who are playing rarely want to interrupt their play to go to the bathroom. Additionally, they may find a restroom away from home unpleasant, which causes them to suppress the urge to defecate. In adults, commuting at the time of the defecation urge, being in a meeting, exercising, and a host of other interferences may be a reason to suppress the urge. Unfortunately, in all cases, this suppression becomes a habit, which then eventually decreases the sense of urge.

EVALUATION

History

For most cases of constipation a simple line of questioning will quickly uncover the cause. Determining a patient's dietary fiber, fluid, and medication intake often will reveal the problem. Most patients do not understand that coffee, tea, and sodas do not have the same hydrating effect as water and often result in a diuretic effect. Dietary fiber is harder to determine; however, the amounts of fruits, vegetables, and fiber substitutes will give a general indication of inadequacy. Medications may cause or aggravate constipation through several mechanisms. Many drugs, such as anticholinergics, anticonvulsants, antidepressants, antiparkinsonians, and tranquilizers, act as central or peripheral neural depressants. Nonsteroidal antiiflammatory drugs (NSAIDs) may inhibit motility through prostaglandin blockade. Diuretics decrease the water content of stool. Calcium channel blockers and angiotensin-converting enzyme (ACE) inhibitors decrease smooth muscle contraction. Several laxative types (especially anthraquinones) may cause megacolon and decreased response to distention; sometimes with damage to the intramural nerve plexuses (Table 33–2).

The next avenue of investigation is the degree to which the urge to defecate is suppressed. Children, in particular, will avoid defecation, although adults may be found to have similar habits. Usually this falls into three categories: (1) too busy or having too much fun to stop to go to the bathroom, (2) unpleasant bathroom environment (while traveling or at school), and (3) painful defecation. Overriding the defecation reflex will eventually lead to a habit that is difficult to

Table 33–2 Laxatives

Type	*Important Considerations*
Bulk—psyllium, husk, methylcellulose	Natural and semisynthetic polysaccharides and cellulose derivatives. Form emollients and gels when mixed with intestinal water. May produce colonic gas (especially bran), causing distention and pain. Risk of impaction if fluid intake is not increased.
Lubricants—mineral oils	Nonabsorbable hydrocarbons lubricate the colon, allowing easier passage. These have limited use because chronic use may decrease absorption of fat-soluble vitamins or cause perianal inflammation.
Osmotic—two types: saline cathartics (Milk of Magnesia) and synthetic disaccharides (lactulose)	Salts or nonabsorbable sugars act to draw fluid into the intestines. Lactulose is safe, but sorbitol is less expensive. Both are considered safe for the elderly. The saline cathartics also stimulate the release of cholecystokinin (CCK). Watch electrolyte levels, especially calcium and magnesium. Magnesium and phosphase laxatives should be avoided with renal insufficiency.
Stimulants and surface active—castor oil, anthraquinones (senna; Senokot), diphenlymethane derivatives, docusate	Decrease colonic absorption and increase secretion. Stimulate adenylate cyclase and synthesis of prostaglandin E, inhibit sodium-potassium absorption, and alter mucosal permeability. Castor oil may cause cramping. Docusate is a stool softener and is usually only effective when patients must avoid straining (postsurgically). Docusate side effects are largely due to an increased absorption of toxic drugs (gastritis with aspirin ingestion).
Enemas—glycerin, bisacodyl, tap water, saline, or soapsuds (castile soap)	Must be watchful of electrolyte losses, mucosal damage with repeated use of soaps, and hyperphosphatemia with abuse of Fleet enemas.

reestablish. If defecation is painful, questions regarding the aggressive use of rough toilet paper can often expose the cause of anal fissures.

Examination

- Determine whether there is any anorectal disease that might suppress the urge to defecate.
- Determine whether there is an empty rectum (ineffective filling disorders) or a full rectum and whether this is impacted.
- Laboratory testing is usually not necessary unless there is a suspicion of either an ionic imbalance or a specific underlying disorder such as diabetes or hypothyroidism.
- If radiographs are taken for low back pain, determine whether there is evidence of gas and fecal stasis.

Although generally it has been assumed that constipation leads to hemorrhoids, which then prolong the constipation, a recent study suggests that constipation is not a risk factor for hemorrhoids, but diarrhea may be.[8]

MANAGEMENT

- Bowel habit education for all patients
- Diet recommendations for fiber and fluid intake
- Referral if significant anorectal pathology is evident
- Referral if indicators of colon cancer are present
- Referral if impacted and digital release or enema is ineffective

The approach to management is usually conservative. When it appears that there is no evidence of a secondary cause such as medication, laxative abuse, or anorectal disease, patient education regarding proper bowel habits is usually effective. Fluid intake should be at least 1.5 L/d. It is important to define "fluid" as water and not coffee, tea, and sodas, which act more as diuretics and will usually worsen the problem. At least 30 g of fiber should be included in the daily diet. This is preferably provided by bran and vegetables. If the patient admits to a sedentary lifestyle or has been bedridden, activity and exercise (when appropriate) should be encouraged. With inactivity or illness, it is also likely that the tone of abdominal and pelvic musculature is weak. Abdominal exercises need not be strenuous. With the patient lying supine, ask her or him to bend the knees and place the feet flat on the floor or table. Then the patient is asked to lightly press the palms of the hands against his or her thighs. This is enough to give a starting contraction of the abdominals. Sit-ups are the next step, but they are not necessary if the patient is elderly, overweight, or frail.

It is imperative that patient education include a discussion of how important timing and relaxation are to proper bowel movements. The patient should understand the importance of comfort, privacy, sufficient time to defecate, and the need to "heed the call" of the defecation urge. Setting aside a regular time for bowel movements is helpful. Elevating the legs while on the toilet may also assist.[9]

When medication appears to be the culprit, referral back to the prescribing physician with a note regarding the suspected connection to the patient's constipation complaint should be made.

If fecal impaction is evident, an attempt at digital removal or recommendation for an enema is usually sufficient. If not, referral to a medical doctor for use of medications or surgery is warranted. When there is evidence of painful but mild anorectal disease (hemorrhoids or anal fissures), correction of dietary habits and bowel habits are usually sufficient; however, referral for medical management is recommended when the patient is noncompliant or the changes are ineffective.

Laxative abuse is certainly an example of too much of a good thing. Although laxative use occasionally may be needed, it is not a recommended method of bowel control. Apparently half of patients who use laxatives chronically would establish a normal bowel habit if the laxative use was discontinued.[10] The effects of laxatives generally can be divided into several categories. Table 33–2 lists these categories and gives examples of various agents and their effects. Bulk-forming agents act similarly to fiber. When ingested these agents form emollients and gels when they mix with intestinal water, expanding their size. This distention increases peristaltic activity. One side effect with these agents is that they may contribute to gas production, causing distention and discomfort. Lubricants (ie, mineral oils) are of limited value. Chronic use may impair fat-soluble vitamin absorption and lead also to a chronic perianal inflammatory response. Salts are used for their osmotic effects of drawing in fluid and increasing reflex colon contractions. They are usually the sulfate or phosphate salts of sodium and magnesium ions (saline cathartics). A similar action occurs with lactulose; however, lactulose has no effect on the small bowel. Another group of agents is referred to as surface-active agents. They act to decrease colonic absorption and increase secretion. Stimulation of adenylate cyclase and prostaglandin E, inhibition of sodium absorption, and alteration in mucosal permeability are all possible mechanisms of these agents. Castor oil is an example of a surface-acting agent.

Rectal enemas or suppositories are usually in the form of glycerin, bisacodyl, water (tap and saline), and soaps (usually castile). These should be reserved for the patient with impaction. Chronic use may lead to colitis.

Pregnancy often results in a complaint of constipation. Although this may be multifactorial, an increase in progesterone has an effect of decreased gut motility. Aggravating this may be the increased weight, which may result in hemorrhoids. Finally, iron supplementation, which often is used in pregnancy, will have a constipating effect.

Algorithm

An algorithm for evaluation and management of constipation is presented in Figure 33–1.

REFERENCES

1. Harari D, Gurwitz JH, Avorn J, et al. Constipation assessment and management in an institutionalized elderly population. *J Am Geriatr Soc.* 1994;42:947–952.
2. Harari D, Gurwitz JH, Minaker KL. Constipation in the elderly. *J Am Ger Soc.* 1993;41:1130–1140.
3. Schultz SG, Frizzel RA, Nellans HN. Ion transport by mammalian small intestine. *Annu Rev Physiol.* 1974;36:51–91.
4. Devroede G, Soffe M. Colonic absorption in idiopathic constipation. *Gastroenterology.* 1973;64:552–561.
5. Connell AM. The motility of the pelvic colon, 2: paradoxical motility in diarrhea and constipation. *Gut.* 1962;3:342–448.
6. Snape WJ Jr, et al. Evidence that abnormal myoelectric activity produces colonic motor dysfunction in the irritable bowel syndrome. *Gastroenterology.* 1977;72:383.
7. Usbach TJ, Tobon F, Hambrecht T, et al. Electrophysiological aspects of human sphincter function. *J Clin Invest.* 1970;49:41–48.
8. Johanson JF, Sonnenberg A. Constipation is not a risk factor for hemorrhoids: a case-control study of potential etiological agents. *Am J Gastroenterol.* 1994;89:1981–1986.
9. Bueono-Miranda F, Cerull M, Schuster MM. Operant conditioning of colonic mobility in irritable bowel syndrome. *Gastroenterology.* 1976;70:867.
10. Zimring JG. High fiber diet versus laxatives in geriatric patients. *N Y State J Med.* 1978;78:2223–2234.

Figure 33–1
CONSTIPATION—ALGORITHM.

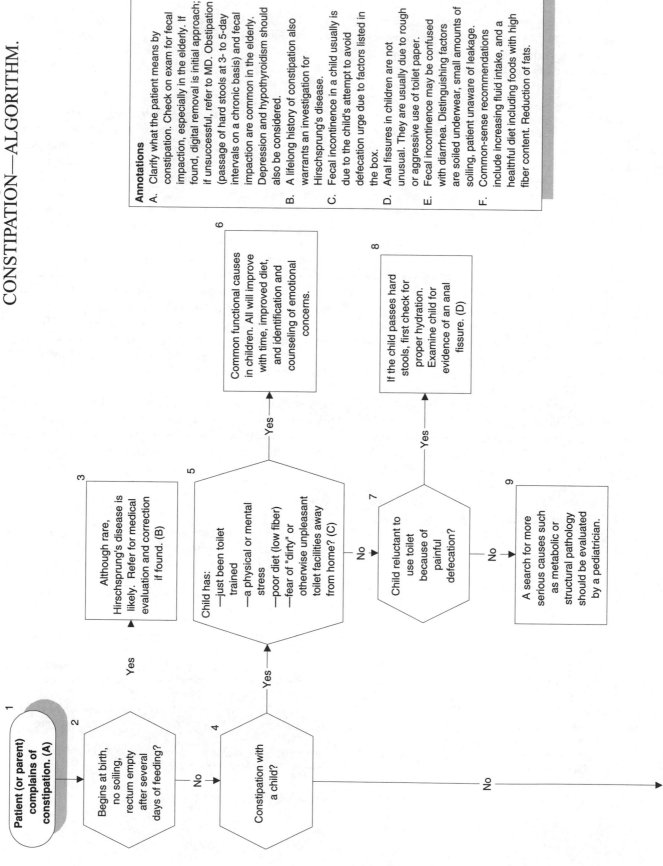

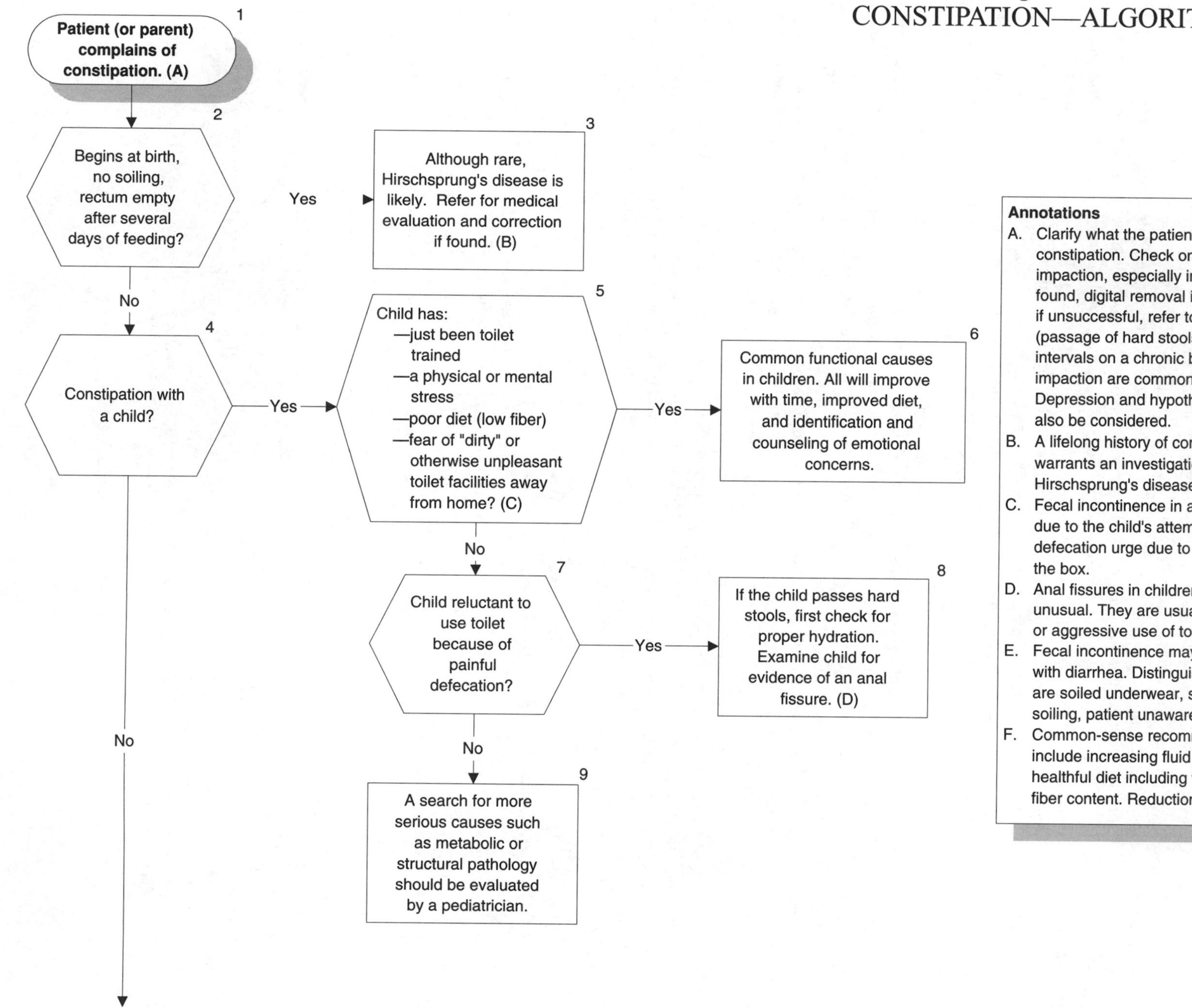
1
Patient (or parent) complains of constipation. (A)
2
Begins at birth, no soiling, rectum empty after several days of feeding?
Yes
3
Although rare, Hirschsprung's disease is likely. Refer for medical evaluation and correction if found. (B)
No
4
Constipation with a child?
Yes
5
Child has:
—just been toilet trained
—a physical or mental stress
—poor diet (low fiber)
—fear of "dirty" or otherwise unpleasant toilet facilities away from home? (C)
Yes
6
Common functional causes in children. All will improve with time, improved diet, and identification and counseling of emotional concerns.
No
7
Child reluctant to use toilet because of painful defecation?
Yes
8
If the child passes hard stools, first check for proper hydration. Examine child for evidence of an anal fissure. (D)
No
9
A search for more serious causes such as metabolic or structural pathology should be evaluated by a pediatrician.
No
Annotations
A. Clarify what the patient means by constipation. Check on exam for fecal impaction, especially in the elderly. If found, digital removal is initial approach; if unsuccessful, refer to MD. Obstipation (passage of hard stools at 3- to 5-day intervals on a chronic basis) and fecal impaction are common in the elderly. Depression and hypothyroidism should also be considered.
B. A lifelong history of constipation also warrants an investigation for Hirschsprung's disease.
C. Fecal incontinence in a child usually is due to the child's attempt to avoid defecation urge due to factors listed in the box.
D. Anal fissures in children are not unusual. They are usually due to rough or aggressive use of toilet paper.
E. Fecal incontinence may be confused with diarrhea. Distinguishing factors are soiled underwear, small amounts of soiling, patient unaware of leakage.
F. Common-sense recommendations include increasing fluid intake, and a healthful diet including foods with high fiber content. Reduction of fats.

continues

Figure 33–1 continued

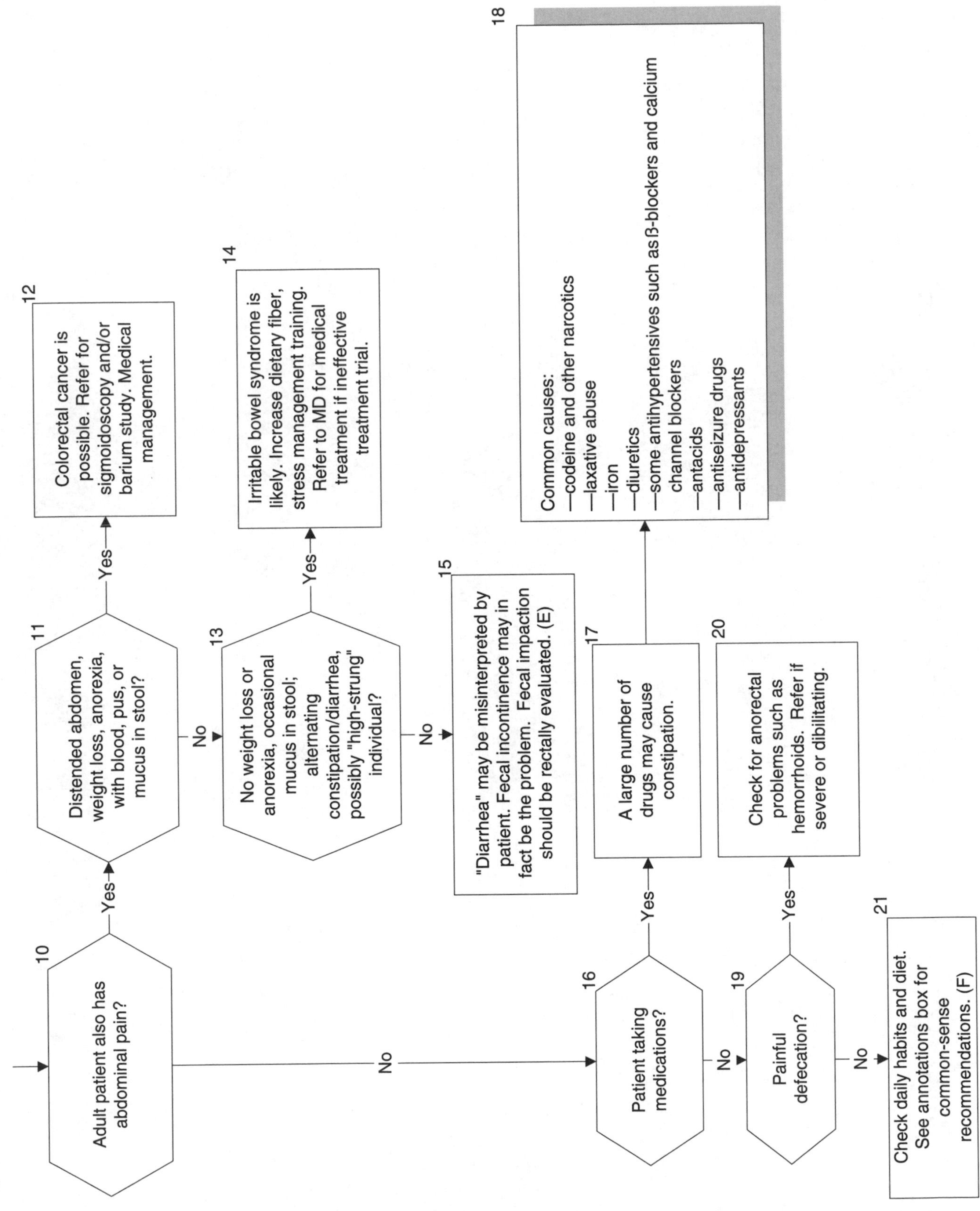

10
Adult patient also has abdominal pain?
Yes
11
Distended abdomen, weight loss, anorexia, with blood, pus, or mucus in stool?
Yes
12
Colorectal cancer is possible. Refer for sigmoidoscopy and/or barium study. Medical management.
No
13
No weight loss or anorexia, occasional mucus in stool; alternating constipation/diarrhea, possibly "high-strung" individual?
Yes
14
Irritable bowel syndrome is likely. Increase dietary fiber, stress management training. Refer to MD for medical treatment if ineffective treatment trial.
No
15
"Diarrhea" may be misinterpreted by patient. Fecal incontinence may in fact be the problem. Fecal impaction should be rectally evaluated. (E)
No
16
Patient taking medications?
Yes
17
A large number of drugs may cause constipation.
18
Common causes:
—codeine and other narcotics
—laxative abuse
—iron
—diuretics
—some antihypertensives such as β-blockers and calcium channel blockers
—antacids
—antiseizure drugs
—antidepressants
No
19
Painful defecation?
Yes
20
Check for anorectal problems such as hemorrhoids. Refer if severe or dibilitating.
No
21
Check daily habits and diet. See annotations box for common-sense recommendations. (F)

CHAPTER 34

Diarrhea

CONTEXT

Diarrhea is second only to respiratory infections as a health complaint in the United States.[1] However, the vast majority of patients have a self-limited, familiar problem that does not warrant enough concern to seek the advice of a doctor. Self-treatment with over-the-counter (OTC) medications is used effectively by many patients with acute diarrhea. Diarrhea is more a nuisance, and only when it becomes disruptive or life threatening are answers sought by the patient or parent. Diarrhea is a concern when it is chronic and/or when it occurs in a frail individual, infants and immuno-compromised patients in particular.

Diarrhea is considered acute when it lasts less than 2 weeks; it is considered chronic when it lasts more than 2 weeks. Common culprits with acute diarrhea are infections, lactose (and other deficiencies), and medications. Less commonly, but more important, diarrhea may represent part of a syndrome with gastrointestinal (GI) disease such as inflammatory bowel disease, dysentery, irritable bowel syndrome, or cancer. One helpful distinguishing factor is whether blood is present in the stool.

GENERAL STRATEGY

History

Determine the following according to Exhibit 34–1:

- Determine whether diarrhea is acute (< 2 weeks), chronic (> 2 weeks), or recurrent.
- Determine whether there are associated signs of infection (ie, fever, abdominal pain, vomiting) and whether any family members or friends have similar symptoms (viral gastroenteritis likely).
- Determine the volume and consistency of the stool (large-volume, watery stool suggests small bowel problem; small-volume stool indicates colon problem).
- Determine whether the diarrhea is bloody (consider inflammatory bowel disease, dysentery, and cancer).
- Determine any recent ingestion of medications, in particular, antibiotics or magnesium-containing antacids (a side effect of medication with some antibiotics is overgrowth of *Clostridium difficile*).
- Determine whether there is a history of lactose intolerance (more common in patients with Mediterranean and African ancestry, in the elderly, and after acute gastroenteritis transiently).
- Determine whether diarrhea persists if the patient fasts (if present after fasting, secretory diarrhea is likely).
- Determine whether the patient has traveled to a foreign country (*Escherichia coli* or parasitic infection).

Evaluation

If chronic, check patient for electrolyte loss with lab testing and have stool evaluated for blood, mucus, fecal leukocytes (enteroinvasive bacteria), undigested food (pancreatic or small-bowel disease), and ova or cysts (parasites).

Management

- If diarrhea is in an infant, recommend electrolyte substitution drink, avoidance of milk, and cold unfiltered juices. If not effective after 2 days refer to pediatrician.

Exhibit 34–1 Diarrhea

Diarrhea

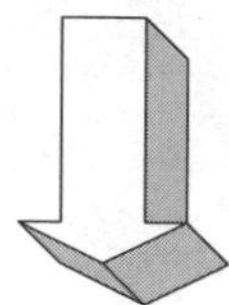

Secretory	Osmotic	Exudative	Metabolic	Motility and Transit Disorders
Bacterial toxins, viral agents, and hormones	Nonabsorbable or osmotically active substances	Invasive bacteria or other ulcerative or infiltrative processes	Hyperthyroidism, diabetes, adrenal insufficiency, and hyperparathyroidism	Hyperthyroidism and various forms of gastrointestinal (GI) surgery
Usually large-volume, watery stool. Fasting has no effect because the cause is usually independent of food ingestion.	Most common causes are laxatives (containing magnesium, sulfate, or phosphate) and lactose intolerance. Improvement occurs when causative food is avoided.	The diarrhea may have blood and mucus. The patient often will have a high fever, abdominal pain, and tenesmus. Invasion is usually in the colonic mucosa; referred to as dysentery.	Associated signs and symptoms (or a previous diagnosis) will be suggestive. Also under metabolic are various drug-induced causes.	This category overlaps with metabolic in that diabetes, hyperthyroidism, and drugs may affect transit time. It is important to gain a full history of any past GI surgical procedures that can affect intestinal flora and transit time.

Diarrhea is further distinguished by being acute or chronic, bloody, or nonbloody, and whether there are single or recurrent episodes.

Relief of abdominal cramping with defecation with passage of small stool implies colonic disease.

Recurrent bloody diarrhea is suggestive of inflammatory bowel disease or in older patients, cancer.

- For adults, recommend Imodium or other OTC medication coupled with elimination of milk products and cold, unfiltered juices to determine effectiveness. If ineffective, refer to medical doctor for further work-up such as with proctosigmoidoscopy.

RELEVANT ANATOMY AND PHYSIOLOGY

Motility of the GI tract is dependent on an intact and functioning autonomic nervous system, appropriate digestive tract flora, an appropriate transit time, and an appropriate diet. Additionally, the osmotic balance is important in maintaining a proper fluid ratio in the stool. Two general causes of diarrhea are osmotic imbalance and secretory stimulus. Osmotic diarrhea occurs when material is nonabsorbable, acting as a fluid magnet. Examples include lactose, sorbitol, mannitol, and magnesium-containing antacids. Secretory diarrhea is due to irritation of the intestinal wall by bacterial toxins and viruses. Exudative diarrhea indicates mucosal ulceration, exudation, and bleeding. A common cause is direct bacterial invasion by organisms such as shigella and salmonella. Parasites, most commonly *Entamoeba histolytica,* also should be considered.

Insufficient time for absorption of nutrients may be caused by intestinal bypass operation, gastric surgery, hyperthyroidism, and vagotomy. These may speed up transit time. Generally, diarrhea that is due to involvement of the small intestine or the proximal colon will be more profuse, watery, and usually nonbloody. With large amounts of fluid loss, electrolytes are also lost, causing particular concern in the young and the elderly. Because of interference in digestion and absorption, the stool may contain undigested food or be greasy and foul smelling. When the pathology is in the distal colon or rectum the defecation reflex is activated, often releasing frequent, small volumes of stool that often are accompanied by flatulence. The stool is not usually foul smelling, but it may contain mucus or blood.

EVALUATION

History

Usually a well-elicited history will quickly pinpoint the cause of acute diarrhea in terms of a general cause (Table 34–1). More specific delineation requires laboratory evaluation of the stool; this is rarely indicated, however, unless the diarrhea is chronic or recurrent. From a historical perspective, determination of an offending substance or organism is gained by the distinction of the amount of stool, the presence of blood or mucus, and a detailed ingestion inventory.

Combinations of findings suggest a cause. For example, if the patient has large amounts of diarrhea (high fluid content) that is unrelieved by fasting, it is likely that the patient has a secretory diarrhea most commonly caused by bacterial toxins, viruses, laxative abuse, and hormones. Toxin-mediated diarrhea is usually due to small-bowel irritation. Bacterial and viral etiologies will usually have accompanying symptoms such as fever, abdominal pain, vomiting, and other symptoms. Hormonal causes are often linked to cancers. This type is rare in the chiropractic office. Laxative abuse may not be elicited on the history, but laboratory testing may uncover a surreptitious cause.

Infectious diarrhea is primarily due to colonic mucosal invasion referred to as dysentery (tenesmus, fever, abdominal pain, and bloody stools). This type of diarrhea is also characterized by early-morning rushes of diarrhea. The stool is often soft and contains mucus.

With acute diarrhea it is important to determine whether other individuals have similar symptoms (ie, diarrhea, vomiting, or abdominal pain). Food poisoning is likely when the same food was eaten. When the diarrhea is not associated with same-food eating, but occurs in the same family or daycare facility, a viral cause is likely. A traveling history is helpful in determining the acquisition of *E coli* or parasitic infection.

It is always important to obtain a complete drug history, including prescription and nonprescription drugs. Many drugs can cause diarrhea. The primary drugs are magnesium-containing antacids, antibiotics, β-blockers, digitalis, methyldopa, alcohol, phenothiazine, and high doses of pain medications (unless a sedative). Laxative abuse should be suspected when other historical clues are negative or in the unlikely event the patient volunteers the information. Some patients may be unaware of the abuse and feel that it is necessary for "normal" bowel movements (see Chapter 33). Antibiotics can also allow overgrowth of *C difficile,* which then produces irritating toxins. The timing of drug ingestion is often helpful, for example, if the diarrhea began after the initiation of a drug regimen. With antibiotics, however, there is often a delayed response.

When a patient has a complaint of chronic diarrhea, the separation of bloody from nonbloody types is an important first step. Bloody diarrhea that is constant or recurrent is highly indicative of inflammatory bowel disease. The historical distinction between ulcerative colitis (UC) and Crohn's disease is not always clear.[2] Both often begin at a young age (< 30 years of age). It is more likely, because of the small-bowel involvement usually found with Crohn's disease, that there will be associated weight loss and, because of the obstruction, perianal fistulas. Patients with Crohn's disease usually have more persistent symptoms and are more likely to have a fever. Bloody diarrhea is possible but less common

Table 34–1 History Questions for Diarrhea

Primary Question	*What Are You Thinking?*	*Secondary Questions*	*What Are You Thinking?*
Is the diarrhea of recent onset?	Viral gastroenteritis, foreign travel (parasites), drug reaction or side effect	Did others in your family or did your friends have similar symptoms?	Viral gastroenteritis is likely.
		Have you just returned from a trip to another country or back from a camping trip?	Parasitic infection, or "traveler's diarrhea."
		Do you take magnesium-containing antacids, laxatives, antibiotics, β-blockers, digitalis, or high doses of pain medication?	All may cause diarrhea.
Do you have recurrent bouts of diarrhea?	Irritable bowel disease, inflammatory bowel disease, lactose intolerance	Do you have alternating bouts of constipation and diarrhea, especially in the morning?	Irritable bowel syndrome likely.
		Do you have recurrent bouts of bloody diarrhea often associated with stress?	Ulcerative colitis is possible, especially with an onset in the 20s or 30s.
		Have you noticed an association with dairy products and have associated complaints of bloating and gas?	Lactose intolerance likely.
		Ask CAGE questions for alcoholism.	Alcohol-related.
		Do you have any diagnosed conditions?	Diabetes, hyperthyroidism, cancer.

than with UC. UC is more likely to present with bloody diarrhea. Stressful life events tend to activate the process.[3] Abdominal pain is more common with Crohn's disease than with UC. The final determination is made with barium studies and colonoscopy.

Patients who complain of early-morning constipation (marble-sized stool) and subsequent diarrhea that is recurrent are likely to have irritable bowel syndrome (IBS). It is important, though, that as many other clues be obtained as possible prior to jumping to this conclusion. These patients often have difficulty with specific foods that they can identify for the doctor. The stool is nonbloody, but it may have mucus. If there are associated hemorrhoids, the stool may be blood-tinged.

Other clues may suggest less common causes such as venereal-related diarrhea and diarrhea secondary to other diseases:

- Patients with known diabetes or complaints of numbness/tingling in the extremities, frequent vaginal yeast infections, or orthostatic hypotension should be evaluated for diabetic autonomic involvement.
- Patients with a history of hyperthyroidism or having complaints of heat intolerance, exophthalmos, or fine hand tremors should be evaluated for the secondary effects of hyperthyroidism on increased metabolism.
- Patients involved in unprotected sex, in particular anal sex, should be evaluated for possible venereal disease

with diarrhea as part of the symptom complex. Also these patients are at higher risk for acquired immunodeficiency syndrome (AIDS).

- Foul-smelling, light-colored stool that floats is suggestive of pancreatic disease or small-bowel disease.

Examination

The majority of important indicators are historical. With acute diarrhea, an abdominal examination should be performed to determine acute inflammatory processes. A rectal examination should be performed in patients with chronic diarrhea.

Laboratory evaluation of the stool should be performed in all patients with severe, chronic, or bloody diarrhea. Stool samples are tested for blood and for polymorphonuclear leukocytes (PMNs) by staining the sample (Gram stain or methylene blue). Fecal PMNs are highly suggestive of an enteroinvasive bacterial cause such as *Campylobacter, Shigella*, or enteroinvasive *E coli*.[4] When fecal PMNs are found, the laboratory should be instructed to culture the stool in an effort to identify the causative organism. Given that the isolation rate of bacteria in stool cultures is under 3% with acute diarrhea, it is unnecessary and expensive to order stool culture in those patients. When giardiasis is suspected, the laboratory should be instructed to look for cysts.

Patients with chronic diarrhea should be screened historically for identifiable causes prior to resorting to laboratory evaluation.

- If medications appear to be the culprit, discontinue if OTC or refer the patient back to the prescribing physician.
- If the patient has a diagnosis of diabetes, hyperthyroidism, pancreatic disease, or other conditions that may cause diarrhea, refer the patient to the primary provider without further laboratory testing.
- If the patient is suspected of having lactose intolerance, recommend a lactose-free diet or an OTC lactase product prior to further laboratory testing.

When a patient is suspected of having an inflammatory bowel disorder, refer to a physician for GI imaging studies or proctosigmoidoscopy. If the patient is suspected of having a metabolic disorder, order laboratory tests specific to the disorder (ie, serum glucose for diabetes, suprasensitive [thyroid stimulating hormone [TSH] for thyroid disorders). If maldigestion is evident in the history (ie, weight loss, vitamin deficiency, and osmotic diarrhea), quantification of fecal fat should be ordered; fatty acids suggest malabsorption.

MANAGEMENT

Antibiotic treatment is needed only in selected cases. In those patients who are immunosuppressed, antibiotics may protect against complications of a bacterial-caused diarrhea. Most acute diarrhea resolves in 2 days and therefore does not need antibiotic management. Viral and bacterial toxin-mediated diarrhea is not responsive to antibiotics. Antibiotic therapy is recommended for shigellosis and for any patient with severe enteroinvasive diarrhea.[5] Infections with parasites such as *Giardia* and *E histolytica* often require metronidazole (Flagyl).

The OTC drug approach to diarrhea is often effective. However, it is important to remember that diarrhea is often the body's attempt to rid itself of infectious agents. Using these agents too early in the course may be counterproductive and may prolong the infection. There are generally three types of medications available[6]:

1. Antimotility drugs—Loperamide (Imodium) is the most common type and quite effective (codeine is an effective prescription drug).
2. Antisecretory drugs—Bismuth subsalicylate (Pepto-Bismol) reduces diarrhea through prostaglandin inhibition (aspirin has some effect).
3. Absorbents—Kaopectate (mainly clay and pectin from apples/citrus fruits) bulks up the stool.

The primary goal of treatment is to maintain proper glucose and electrolytes. Sports drinks are not appropriate because the fluid must be hypoosmolar. For infants, several OTC drinks are available, such as Pedialyte. A simple home concoction is a mixture of ½ tsp salt, 1 tsp baking soda, 8 tsp sugar, and 8 oz of orange juice diluted in water to produce 1 L of liquid.[7]

Persons traveling to foreign countries should pack an antidiarrheal compound and, if concerned, ask their physicians about newer antibacterial agents.[8]

Algorithms

Algorithms for evaluation and management of acute and chronic diarrhea are presented in Figures 34–1 and 34–2.

Figure 34–1

ACUTE DIARRHEA—ALGORITHM.

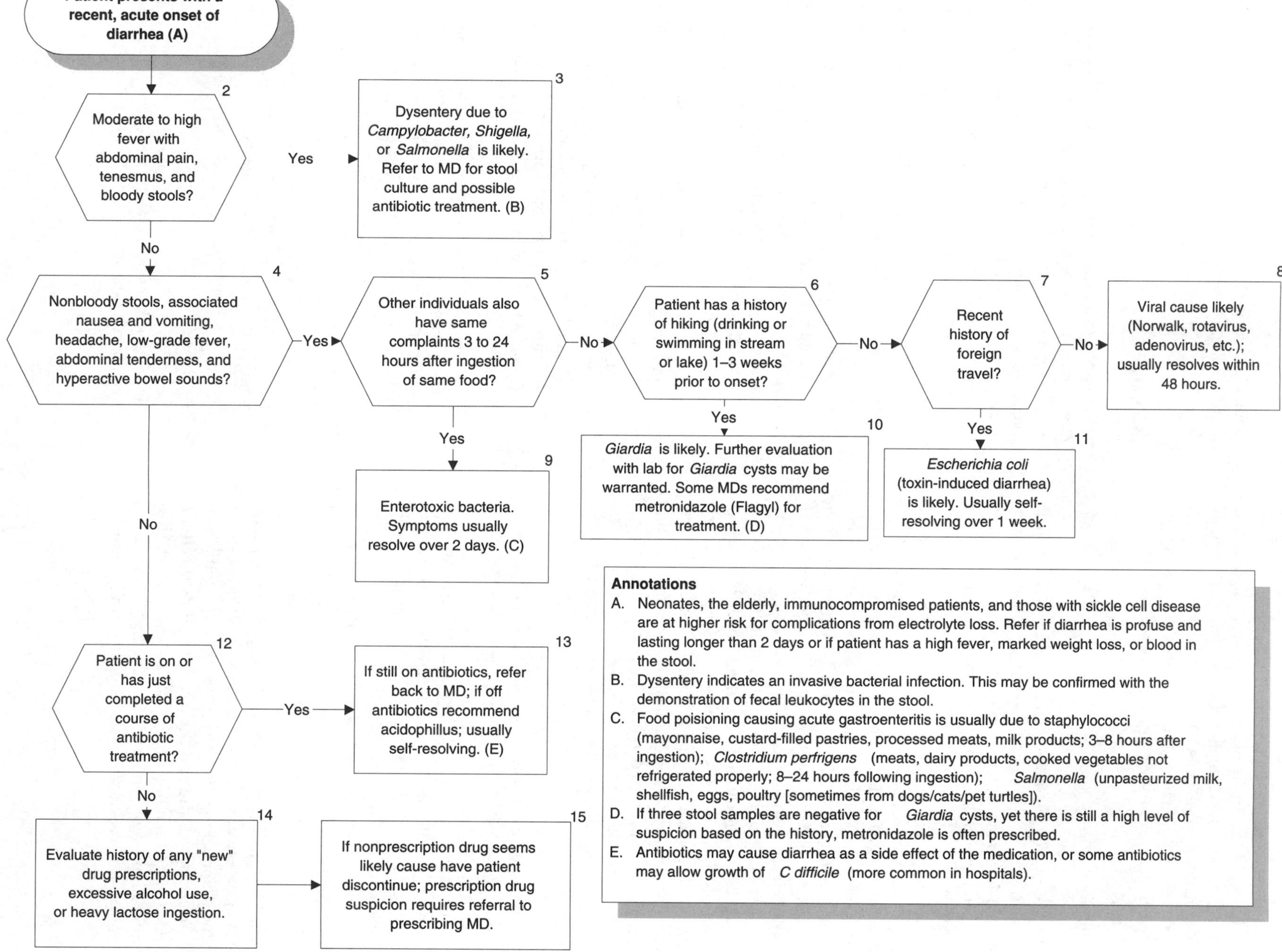

Annotations

A. Neonates, the elderly, immunocompromised patients, and those with sickle cell disease are at higher risk for complications from electrolyte loss. Refer if diarrhea is profuse and lasting longer than 2 days or if patient has a high fever, marked weight loss, or blood in the stool.

B. Dysentery indicates an invasive bacterial infection. This may be confirmed with the demonstration of fecal leukocytes in the stool.

C. Food poisioning causing acute gastroenteritis is usually due to staphylococci (mayonnaise, custard-filled pastries, processed meats, milk products; 3–8 hours after ingestion); *Clostridium perfrigens* (meats, dairy products, cooked vegetables not refrigerated properly; 8–24 hours following ingestion); *Salmonella* (unpasteurized milk, shellfish, eggs, poultry [sometimes from dogs/cats/pet turtles]).

D. If three stool samples are negative for *Giardia* cysts, yet there is still a high level of suspicion based on the history, metronidazole is often prescribed.

E. Antibiotics may cause diarrhea as a side effect of the medication, or some antibiotics may allow growth of *C difficile* (more common in hospitals).

Figure 34–2

CHRONIC DIARRHEA—ALGORITHM.

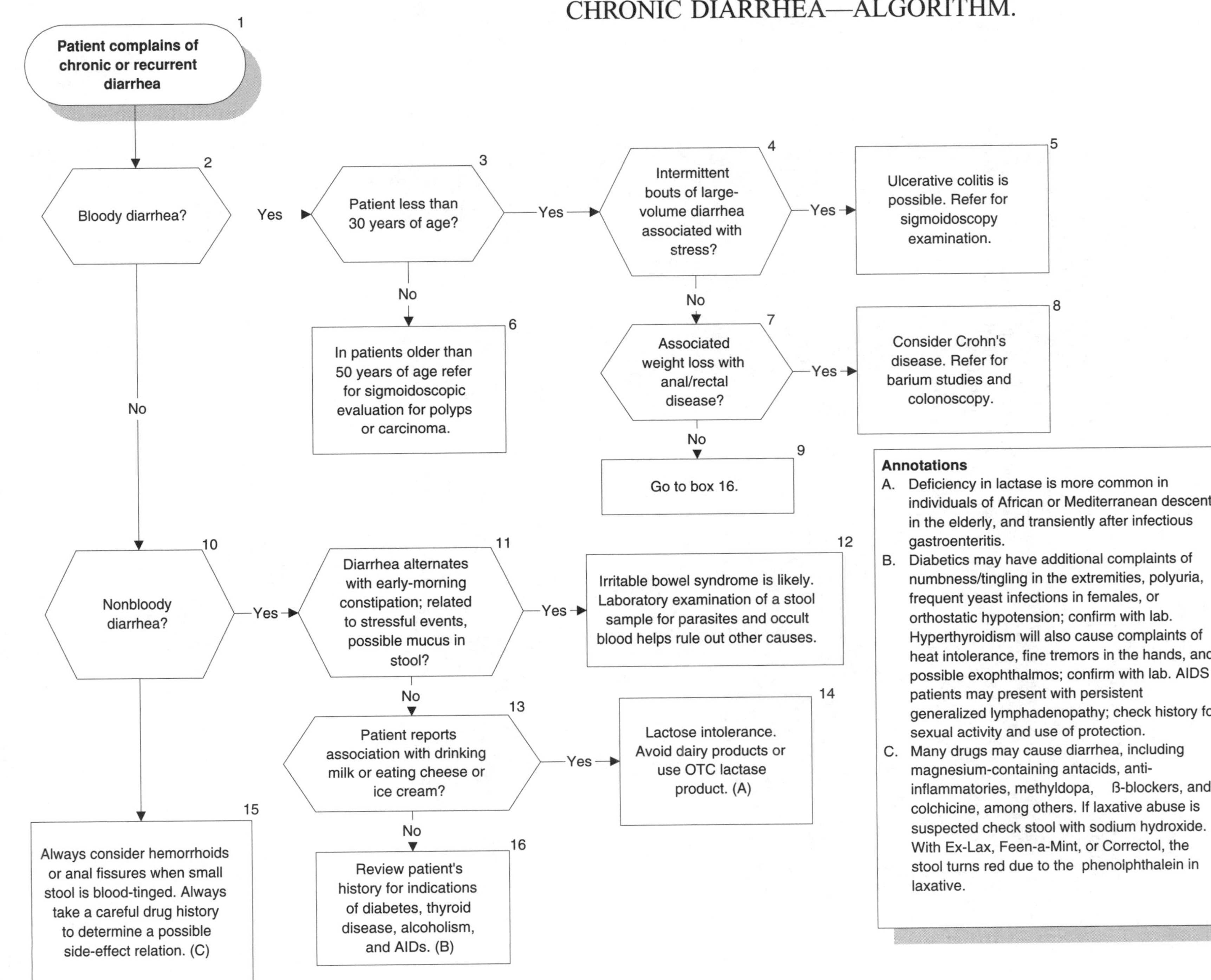

Annotations

A. Deficiency in lactase is more common in individuals of African or Mediterranean descent, in the elderly, and transiently after infectious gastroenteritis.

B. Diabetics may have additional complaints of numbness/tingling in the extremities, polyuria, frequent yeast infections in females, or orthostatic hypotension; confirm with lab. Hyperthyroidism will also cause complaints of heat intolerance, fine tremors in the hands, and possible exophthalmos; confirm with lab. AIDS patients may present with persistent generalized lymphadenopathy; check history for sexual activity and use of protection.

C. Many drugs may cause diarrhea, including magnesium-containing antacids, anti-inflammatories, methyldopa, β-blockers, and colchicine, among others. If laxative abuse is suspected check stool with sodium hydroxide. With Ex-Lax, Feen-a-Mint, or Correctol, the stool turns red due to the phenolphthalein in laxative.

REFERENCES

1. Baldassano RN, Liacouras CA. Chronic diarrhea: a practical approach for the pediatrician. *Pediatr Clin North Am.* 1991;38:667–687.
2. Farmer RG. Differentiating Crohn's disease from ulcerative colitis. *Diagnosis.* 1987;7:66–74.
3. Levenstein Sprantera C, Varvo V, et al. Psychological stress and disease activity in ulcerative colitis: a multidimensional cross-sectional study. *Am J Gastroenterol.* 1994;89:1219–1225.
4. Ritka P, Banwell JG. Laboratory workup of the patient with diarrhea. *Diagnosis.* 1986;12:22–38.
5. Park SI, Gianella RA. Approach to the adult patient with acute diarrhea. *Gastroenterol Clin North Am.* 1993;22:483.
6. Reilly BM. Diarrhea. In: *Practical Strategies in Outpatient Medicine.* 2nd ed. Philadelphia: W.B. Saunders; 1991:856.
7. McQuaid KR. Alimentary tract: acute diarrhea. In: Tierney LM Jr, McPhee SJ, Papadakis MA, eds. *Current Medical Diagnosis & Treatment 1995.* 3rd ed. Norwalk, CT: Appleton & Lange; 1995: 485.
8. Scarpignato C, Rampal P. Prevention and treatment of traveler's diarrhea: a clinical pharmacological approach. *Chemotherapy.* 1995;41:48–81.

PART V

Genitourinary Complaints

Chapter 35

Urinary Incontinence and Voiding Dysfunction

CONTEXT

Although 10 million individuals in the United States have urinary incontinence, it often remains a secret to loved ones and the patients' doctors.[1] It is estimated that in the elderly, 15% to 30% who live at home have urinary incontinence. This percentage increases in the acute care setting to one third, and up to one half of all the elderly in extended care facilities are incontinent.[2]

Because of the associated embarrassment, incontinence is rarely volunteered by the patient if incontinence is not a chief complaint. It is important, especially in the elderly and in women over age 40 years, to question the patient about loss of bladder control. It is unfortunate that many women consider incontinence as "normal."

For the chiropractor, it is important to realize that a full evaluation involves examination of the genital and perianal regions in both males and females. This may not be a comfortable scenario for the chiropractor if his or her training is not extensive for this area of investigation. Historical clues, though, can narrow down the diagnosis to the type of incontinence (or whether there is incontinence) and facilitate proper referral. For those who perform a thorough examination, it is important to realize that a complete evaluation for some types of incontinence requires ultrasound and/or urodynamic studies. These are the domain of the urologist.

GENERAL STRATEGY

History

Determine the following:

- whether the patient has signs of irritative bladder (urgency, increased frequency, nocturia, dysuria) or obstructive bladder (decreased stream, dribbling, hesitancy, or intermittent stream) dysfunction
- whether the patient has any known diseases such as Parkinson's disease, diabetes, multiple sclerosis, or others
- what, when, and how much fluid the patient drinks (large intake of diuretic fluids such as coffee, tea, colas, alcohol, or large amounts of water [especially before bed] may cause nocturia)
- whether the patient is taking any over-the-counter or prescription medications that may influence micturition (loop diuretics, α-adrenergic blockers, calcium channel blockers, cold capsules or nasal decongestants, haloperidol, or others)
- whether there are positions in which the incontinence is most likely to occur (stress incontinence usually occurs standing [unless patient laughs], nycturia occurs while recumbent)
- whether coughing, sneezing, laughing, exercising, or jumping causes loss of small amounts of urine (common with stress incontinence)
- whether the patient's mental state or mobility is a factor
- whether there is a history of past surgeries or radiation therapy

Examination

- Determine whether the patient has any signs of neurologic dysfunction; test for perianal reflex and lower extremity reflexes.
- Evaluate the perianal area for signs of fistulas or prolapse.
- Perform a prostate examination on men; a vaginal examination on women.

- Perform a urinalysis on all patients in an attempt to determine renal function or indicators of urinary tract infection (UTI).
- Refer for urodynamic testing by a urologist if incontinence is severe.

Management

- For patients with stress incontinence, prescription of exercises and behavioral training may be effective; if not, refer for medication or, in rare cases, surgery.
- For patients with diabetes mellitus, comanage with the medical doctor.
- For patients with prostate hypertrophy, manage with behavioral training and some dietary recommendations; if ineffective, refer for medication or possible surgery.

RELEVANT ANATOMY AND PHYSIOLOGY

Bladder control is an intricate balance among several neural systems. The tension within the bladder that is generated by filling must be balanced by restriction of outflow at the bladder neck. The primary innervation of the body of the bladder is parasympathetic (pudendal nerve S2-4). Therefore, parasympathetic stimulation facilitates urination by causing contraction of the body of the bladder (detrusor muscle) and urinary sphincter relaxation. Sympathetic innervation is via the hypogastric nerve plexus with nerve cell bodies at T11-L2. β-Adrenergic (sympathetic) stimulation causes detrusor muscle relaxation during filling. α-Adrenergic (sympathetic) stimulation at the bladder neck (which acts as an internal urethral sphincter) acts to prevent urination.

The micturition center is located in the pons and acts to inhibit urination. Cortical override occurs through connections from the frontal lobe, corpus callosum, and cingulate gyrus, which generally inhibit the pontine micturition center.

Various forms of dysfunction can affect this intricate balance. Involuntary contractions of the detrusor muscle may occur as a result of irritation or neurologic disease. This hyperreflexia is referred to as detrusor instability, or an unstable bladder. A different type of dysfunction occurs when the force of contraction of the bladder is too weak to expel all the urine, leading to residual retention and subsequent irritation or infection. This also may occur with any bladder outlet obstruction, such as prostatic hypertrophy or urethral stricture, when the ability to overcome this added resistance from obstruction is exceeded. When there is pelvic floor weakness and secondarily hypermobility of the urethra, an unequal pressure is created. Maneuvers that increase intraabdominal pressure cause bladder pressure to exceed urethral sphincter resistance, and urine is lost.

Urinary incontinence has been divided into several major types,[3] as follows:

- Urge incontinence—A sudden, uncontrollable urge to void is created by bladder irritation or neurologic dysfunction with urge incontinence. The most common cause is benign prostatic hypertrophy or urinary tract infection.
- Stress incontinence—Stress incontinence occurs when actions such as laughing, coughing, sneezing, or jumping cause loss of a small amount of urine. The most common cause is pelvic floor weakness in women.
- Mixed incontinence—This is a combination of urge and stress incontinence, often occurring in the elderly. Also, two thirds of men with prostatic hypertrophy have obstruction and detrusor hyperactivity.
- Overflow incontinence—Overflow incontinence occurs when an overdistended bladder exceeds the resistance of the urethral sphincter, and urine is lost. This is often due to detrusor weakness and/or outflow obstruction.
- Total incontinence—Total incontinence is the loss of urine at all times regardless of body position. Rarely would it be seen undiagnosed in the chiropractic setting. It is usually due to serious neurologic or structural abnormalities.

EVALUATION

History

The distinction between irritative and obstructive symptoms may give valuable clues to an underlying etiology. For example, if the patient complains of dysuria, urgency, increased frequency, and nocturia, an irritative cause is likely. Further investigation with urinalysis for a UTI is essential. For patients complaining of a decreased stream, hesitancy, dribbling, and a sense of incomplete emptying, an obstructive problem is likely. With men the most common problem is prostate hypertrophy, warranting a digital rectal examination.

The timing of incontinence onset with regard to childbirth, surgery, radiation therapy, low back pain, or medication ingestion often will provide valuable clues.

Important clues to differentiation among the various types of incontinence are the amount of fluid lost and the position or circumstances surrounding the loss. Patients who have problems only with increased abdominal pressure from laughing, sneezing, coughing, or jarring and subsequently void small amounts are likely to have stress incontinence. If patients are unable to stop voiding in midstream, stress incontinence is suggested. Patients who have a sense of uncontrollable urge without regard to body position are likely to have urge incontinence. A large amount of fluid loss associated with a large fluid intake is highly suggestive of diabetes, although some non-diabetic patients believe that an intake of more than eight glasses of water a day is necessary for optimal health.

If the patient complains mainly of nocturia it is critical to determine when the patient goes to bed, how often he or she actually gets up at night, how much is voided, and what his or her fluid intake is prior to going to bed. Patients who report voiding large amounts of fluid after 1 to 2 hours of recumbency are more likely to have nycturia. This reflects a shift in fluid from a lower extremity interstitial site to intravascular incorporation assisted by recumbency. This is seen with patients having right-sided heart failure, liver disease, or chronic venous insufficiency. Nocturia is often the continuation of a daily voiding problem caused by diabetes or renal failure.

If the patient is elderly, it is important to remember that there is a natural tendency to void most fluid after 9 PM. In younger patients, most fluid is voided prior to 9 PM. Additionally, the bladder capacity is reduced in the elderly.[4] If patients ingest water or beverages with xanthine, such as coffee, tea, and sodas, they will likely have to void more often.

Examination

General examination findings that might suggest an underlying cause for incontinence are lower extremity edema, mental status abnormalities, decreased reflexes, or sensory abnormalities. An elderly patient's ability to ambulate should be evaluated as an indicator of the ability to reach the bathroom when needed.

Specific focus is on the genital/rectal area. As mentioned previously, this may be uncomfortable for the chiropractor and especially the patient. If performed in the chiropractic setting, it is important to have a same-sex (as the patient) witness (if opposite sex doctor). The examination begins with an examination of the urethra in an effort to detect possible signs of infection. Rectal examination is used to determine prostate status in men and possible fecal impaction in both men and women. A pelvic examination in women may reveal a cystocele or a prolapse and the estrogen status (atrophic vaginitis). A urethrocele may be evident by bulging of the urethra with coughing. Another similar approach (for women) is to insert a cotton-tipped swab into the urethra and watch for movement of more than 30° from the horizontal with coughing or straining. This indicates a hypermobile urethra, which is associated with stress incontinence.

If the patient is cooperative, the doctor may watch the patient void (especially helpful in men) to determine the degree of hesitancy, the amount of stream, and the consistency of flow. With women it may be helpful to have the patient cough with a full bladder to determine whether there is any leaking. If there is immediate leaking, stress incontinence is likely. If there is a delay of a few seconds, detrusor instability is more likely. The bladder should be palpated in an effort to determine distention, although this may be difficult in many patients because of obesity or muscularity.

Neurologic status should also be checked, including rectal sphincter tone, by stroking the perianal area, looking for an anal "wink" that indicates an intact S2-S4 spinal cord level.

An essential in-office evaluation of urine is important to detect signs of UTI, renal dysfunction, or possible bladder cancer. A laboratory finding of greater than 5 white blood cells per high-power field is suggestive of a UTI, especially when accompanied with bacteriuria. A culture should be ordered. Glucosuria, proteinuria, or yeast suggests diabetes. Hematuria may indicate bladder cancer if associated with suprapubic pain (see algorithm for hematuria). Total and free prostate-specific antigen (PSA) should be included for males with suspicion of prostate cancer.

Special testing may be performed in a urologic setting. Urodynamic studies combine uroflowmetry and cystometry and/or videofluoroscopy. These studies are briefly listed as follows:

- Uroflowmeter—measures the urine flow in millimeters per second and is used in combination with postvoid residual urine volume to differentiate between obstruction and weak detrusor tone
- Cystoscopy—allows a direct visualization of the bladder and is used to determine any obstruction to outflow
- Cystometry—used to measure capacity and compliance, assess bladder sensation, and determine any voluntary or involuntary detrusor contractions
- Ultrasonography—used to measure postvoid residual (PVR) urine volume

PVR urine volume is often used to differentiate among the various types of incontinence. If the PVR volume is greater than 100 mL, impaired detrusor contraction is suspected. If the PVR volume is greater than 300 mL, overflow incontinence is likely. If the PVR volume is under 100 mL, stress or urgency incontinence is likely. If the uroflowmeter measurement is normal and the PVR volume is normal, obstruction is unlikely.

MANAGEMENT

Conservative nondrug, nonsurgical options may be helpful in patients with detrusor instability or stress incontinence. The basis of these behavioral approaches is bladder training for detrusor instability and Kegel (pelvic floor) exercises for stress incontinence. Additional approaches include biofeedback training, electrical stimulation, and vaginal cones. Conservative approaches require a compliant and highly motivated patient. The success rate with these conservative approaches is rather good when both cure rate and improved rate are combined. For urge incontinence, one study indicated a "success" rate of 87% (12% cured; 75% improved).[5] For stress incontinence the success rate with pelvic floor exercises was also 87% (12% cured; 75% improved); with bladder training, 70% (16% cured; 54% improved).

Bladder Training

Bladder training sets timed intervals for voiding. The patient is instructed to postpone voiding until the scheduled time. Starting with 1-hour intervals during the day, the patient is asked to increase the time interval gradually (over days) by 15 to 30 minutes. Over weeks, the patient should set a goal of 2½- to 3-hour intervals. In supporting this attempt, it is important to have the patient keep a diary. Another important factor is to have the patient time his or her drinking habits. Avoidance of intake of large amounts of water, coffee or tea, or carbonated drinks may help. A variation on this technique is timed voiding. With timed voiding the patient sets a schedule that fits his or her natural schedule instead of rigid timed intervals.

Pelvic Floor Exercises

Although Kegel exercises are traditionally used by women with stress incontinence, they may be helpful with urge incontinence and for men with incontinence after prostate surgery. The purpose of the exercises is to strengthen the pubococcygeus muscle and increase control over the periurethral and pelvic muscles. One reason for failure (other than noncompliance) is improper performance. In essence, the patient makes the mistake of performing a Valsalva maneuver. It is crucial to explain clearly and give written instructions on the performance of these exercises (or give an audiotape from Help for Incontinent People [HIP]). The patient must understand that the contractions are localized without concomitant contraction of the abdominal, gluteal, or thigh muscles. A good beginning exercise is to ask the patient to stop voiding in midstream. This can be accomplished only with the proper muscle recruitment. With the same focus, the patient should perform the exercise off the toilet and hold the contraction for approximately 10 seconds. The exercises should be performed religiously and often as many as 100 times per day. An adjunctive approach is to use vaginal cones for females. The cone is inserted and the patient attempts to hold it in place by contracting the pelvic floor muscles. This is performed twice a day for 15 minutes.

Augmented Voiding

For residual urine, it may be helpful to have the patient strain at the end of voiding or to have the patient press suprapubically in an attempt to add pressure to the bladder (Credé's maneuver). This technique also may be helpful with urge incontinence.

Other Options

Both biofeedback and electrical stimulation have been used for incontinence. Their efficacy is unknown; however, they appear promising with some patients who do not respond to other conservative approaches.

Two new devices have been approved for use as a mechanical block to urine flow. One is a short balloon-catheter device that, after insertion into the urethra, is inflated to block urine flow. The other is a shield device for women that cups over the vaginal area.

For the elderly it is important to focus on mobility issues. The proximity of bathroom facilities and the ease of arising from bed play an important role in preventing bed-wetting. A semirecumbent position, a walking device, rail support at the toilet, and the location of the bed may all assist in decreasing the time it takes to reach the bathroom, avoiding "accidents." Recommendation for protective pads or adult diapers may be needed.

When patients are unresponsive to conservative management or the incontinence is socially disabling, it is important to refer for medical approaches to care. The primary focus with medication is to select drugs that are specific to the cause. In other words, drugs that are helpful for one problem may have no effect or even aggravate incontinence due to another cause. For detrusor instability or hyperactivity, drugs that have anticholinergic effects are used. These block bladder contractions and so therefore may be contraindicated in patients with obstructive problems. Anticholinergics may also cause dry mouth, mental confusion, or constipation. The two classes of drugs that are used include tricyclic antidepressants (may cause orthostatic hypotension in the elderly) and propantheline.

For stress incontinence, the rationale is to access medically the α-adrenergic control of the bladder neck and proximal urethra. An α-adrenergic agonist such as phenylpropanolamine hydrochloride is often used. Oral and topical estrogens are also used. Topical estrogen is particularly useful for women with atrophic vaginitis because it reduces the incidence of infection and dysuria.

Surgical options include retropubic suspension and needle suspension for stress incontinence. For women with intrinsic sphincter deficiency, bulking with Teflon or collagen, a pubovaginal sling, and an artificial urinary sphincter replacement are options. It is extremely important that prior to these approaches a conservative approach with or without medication be attempted first. Also a thorough urodynamic evaluation preoperatively is extremely important for input in decision making regarding the best procedure to use.

Although it is often assumed that the primary cause of bladder outlet obstruction with prostate hypertrophy is mechanical blockage, a dynamic component based on increased sympathetic tone is probably the primary cause in many males. As a dynamic cause, the degree of obstruction and resulting symptoms vary based on external factors such as exposure to cold, over-filling of the bladder and resulting reflexes that affect urethral tension, stress, and anticholinergic medication (common ingredient in decongestants). Symptoms may then vary and often improve during periods of less stress or during warm weather. The medical approach to this sympathetic effect is to use sympathetic blockade as a strategy. The most common medications are alpha-1 adrenergic blockers.[6]

Prostate growth is governed by hormonal influences. Testosterone is converted to 5-alpha-dihydrotestosterone (DHT) in the prostate. This is accomplished through an enzyme 5-alpha-reductase. The medical approach to reducing DHT is to block the conversion of testosterone to DHT through the use of 5-alpha-reductase inhibitors. In this way the levels of testosterone are not affected.

These medical options are being used more frequently in place of transurethral excision of the prostate (TURP). Other surgical options include open prostatectomy, balloon dilation, stents, and newer techniques including laser ablation and microwave hyperthermia. Surgery should be reserved for those who do not respond to conservative or medical management or those with serious complications.

Although not always a cause of voiding dysfunction, it is important to mention prostate cancer. Prostate cancer is quite common in older males. The ethnic risk is more with African Americans and less with Asians. Factors that have been identified include a genetic predisposition and potentially some dietary factors. It is clear that dietary fat intake is an important factor. A high-fat diet increases the risk of prostate cancer.[7] Possible protective factors such as vitamins C, D, and E, beta-carotene, cadmium, and zinc are still being studied at this time.[8]

Beginning in their 40s, males should have an annual prostate examination. Complementing the digital prostate examination is evaluation of both total and free PSA. Through the use of this combination, false positives and negatives are less likely to occur.[9]

Algorithm

An algorithm for evaluation and management of urinary incontinence in adults is presented in Figure 35–1.

REFERENCES

1. Consensus Conference. Urinary incontinence in adults. *JAMA.* 1992;251:2685–2690.
2. Jolleyes J. Urinary incontinence. *Practitioner.* 1993;237:630–633.
3. Urinary Incontinence Guideline Panel. *Urinary Incontinence in Adults. Clinical Practice Guidelines.* AHCPR Publication No. 92-0038, Rockville, MD. U.S. Department of Health and Human Services. Public Health Service, Agency for Health Care Policy and Research, March 1992.
4. Hopkins TB. Dysfunctional voiding. In: Greene HL, Fincher RME, Johnson WP, et al., eds. *Clinical Medicine.* 2nd ed. St. Louis, MO: Mosby-Year Book; 1996:339–343.
5. Fantl JA, Wyman JF, McClish DK, et al. Efficacy of bladder training in older women with urinary incontinence. *JAMA.* 1991;265:609–613.
6. Cooper JW, Piepho RW. Cost-effective management of benign prostatic hyperplasia. *Drug Benefit Trends.* 1995;7:10–48.
7. Kolonel LN. Nutrition and prostate cancer. *Cancer Causes Control.* 1996;7:83–94.
8. Giovannucci E. How is individual risk for prostate cancer assessed? *Hematol Oncol Clin North Am.* 1996;10:537–548.
9. Catalona WJ. Clinical utility of measurements of free and total prostate-specific antigen (PSA): a review. *Prostate* (suppl). 1996;7:64–69.

Figure 35–1

URINARY INCONTINENCE IN ADULTS—ALGORITHM.

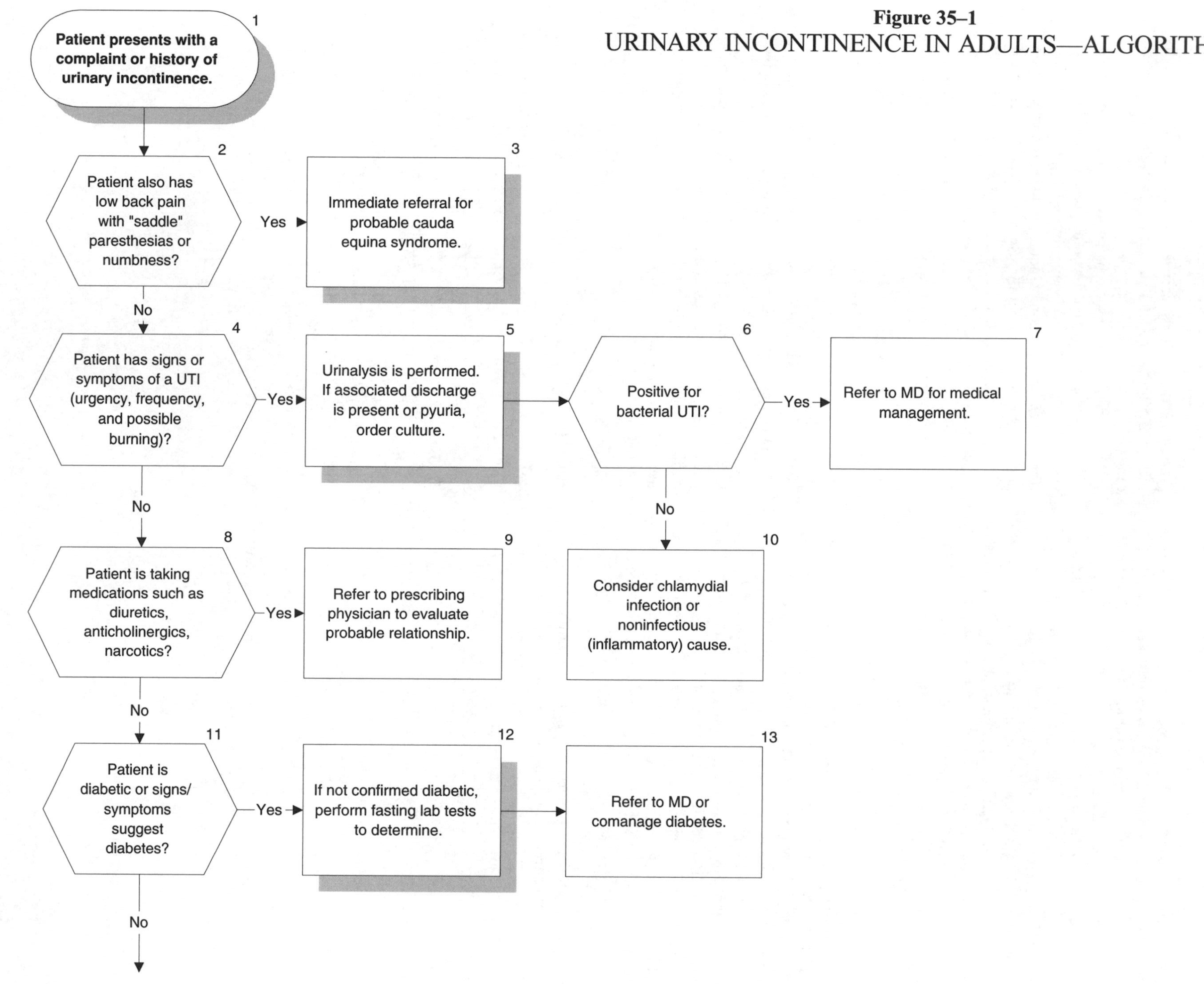

continues

Figure 35–1 continued

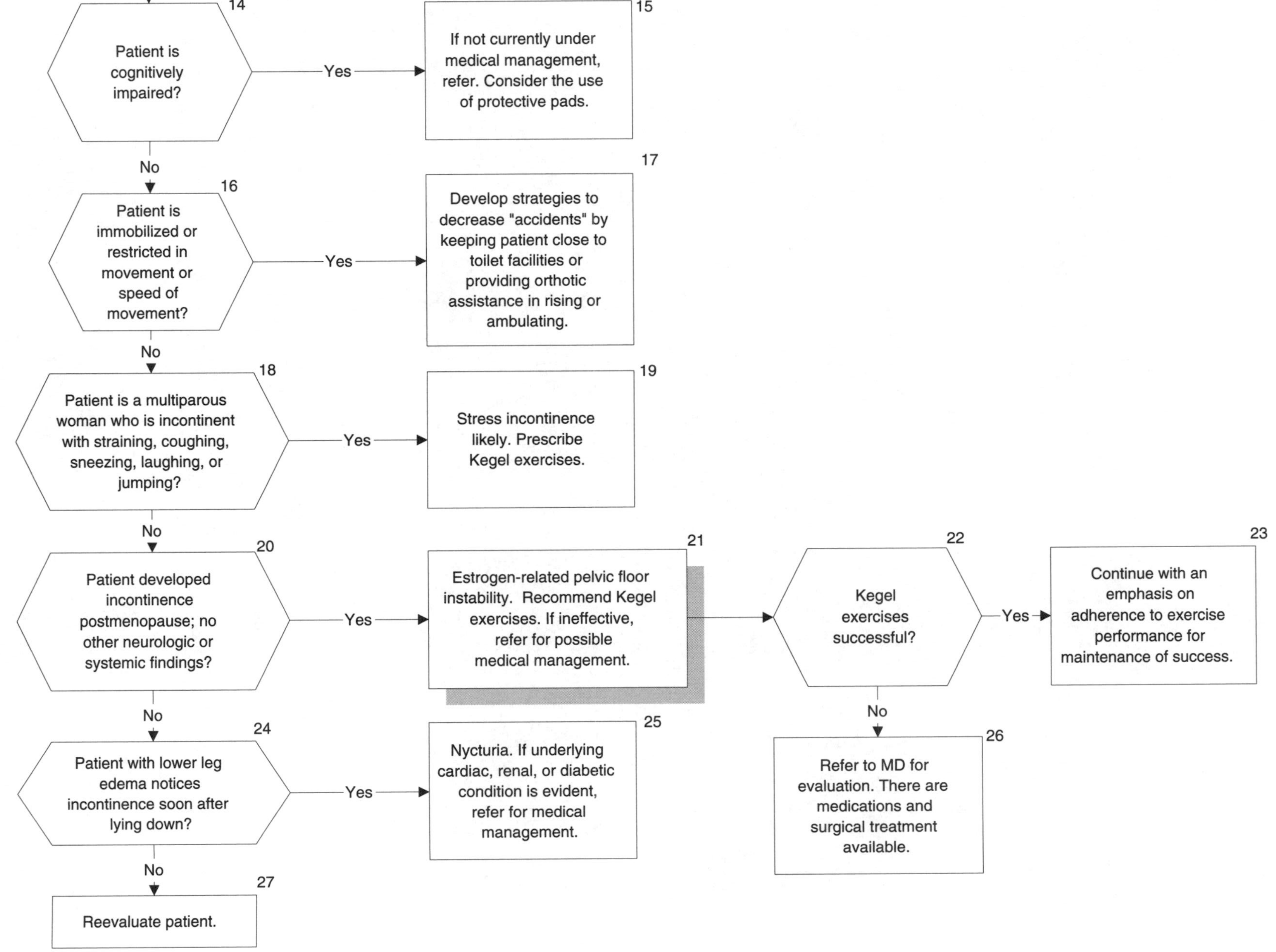

Chapter 36

Enuresis

CONTEXT

Nocturnal enuresis is a distressing disorder for parents and children. Approximately 5 to 7 million children in the United States are affected. It is more common in boys than in girls. Girls are more likely to have daytime incontinence, more often associated with bacteriuria. In a large study in Sweden, 2.9% of girls and 3.8% of boy school entrants reported bed-wetting once per week.[1]

Parents are often unaware of the natural history of continence development and expect their child to be continent at a relatively early age. One study indicated that between 30% and 70% of parents punish their children for bed-wetting.[2] Ironically, there is a strong genetic component. Children whose parents both have a history of enuresis as a child have a 77% chance of bed-wetting, 44% if only one parent has a positive history, and only a 15% if neither did.[3]

Parents seeking a nondrug, nonparent-intensive approach to bed-wetting seek a chiropractor's advice. The chiropractor may perform the initial evaluation to determine known causes such as urinary tract infection or diabetes. The nonpathologic, neurodevelopmental type of enuresis may be managed with conservative approaches. When these fail, referral for medication may be warranted.

Enuresis has been defined by the American Psychiatric Association as bed-wetting occurring in a child at age 5 years or above (and mental age of 4 years). The frequency is defined as two or more incontinent occurrences in a month between the ages of 5 and 6 or one or more occurrences after age 6 in children who do not have an associated physical disorder such as urinary tract infection (UTI), diabetes, or seizures.[4] At age 5 approximately 20% of children have enuresis, which decreases to 10% at age 10 and 1% at age 15.[5,6]

Enuresis is often categorized into primary and secondary causes. Primary causes include both functional and structural causes. Secondary enuresis is defined as the presence of a prior history of continence for more than a 6-month period. These patients often have a regression due to a stressful emotional event in the early years of life. Approximately 80% to 90% of childhood enuresis is the primary type.[7,8]

When not due to a structural cause, enuresis seems to follow a natural spontaneous remission. This natural history must be taken into account when it appears that a child is responding to a specific therapy. Without any specific therapy the natural history indicates that 50% of patients will become continent within 4 years. The prevalence of enuresis decreases with age at a rate of 10% to 20% per year after age 6.[9]

GENERAL STRATEGY

History

- Determine whether the patient fits the criteria for nocturnal enuresis.
- Determine identifiable causes such as a history or indications of diabetes, seizures, or other neuromuscular contributors.
- Determine the family history of enuresis.
- Determine the environmental and social history of the child with regard to changes in living environment, stresses, any psychologic problems, and parental punishment for enuresis.
- Determine any other treatment methods that have been attempted, and the patient/parent compliance.

Evaluation

- Evaluate the neurologic status of the child with emphasis on peripheral sensation and reflexes, genital sensation and perianal reflexes, and a search for any indications of congenital abnormalities such as clubfoot, spina bifida, or other.
- If there are associated complaints of frequent urination or irritation while urinating, obtain a urinalysis.
- Referral for specialized studies such as diagnostic ultrasound or cystourethrograms should be reserved for those patients who have daytime incontinence or signs of frequent UTI.

Management

- If chiropractic management is suggested to the patient, the rationale and literature support and other conservative options should be discussed, including their advantages and disadvantages.
- If food allergies are the cause of detrusor instability, advise the parents to eliminate dairy products, colas, chocolate, and citrus juices for several weeks to determine the effect.
- The bell and pad urine alarm method is probably the most effective approach.
- For those children with persistence and failure of conservative approaches, medical options may be considered; the natural course of enuresis, however, should be discussed with the parents.

RELEVANT ANATOMY AND PHYSIOLOGY

Bladder control is an intricate balance among several neural systems. The tension within the bladder that is generated by filling must be balanced by restriction of outflow at the bladder neck. The primary innervation of the body of the bladder is parasympathetic (pudendal nerve S2-4). Therefore, parasympathetic stimulation facilitates urination by causing contraction of the body of the bladder (detrusor muscle) and urinary sphincter relaxation. Sympathetic innervation is via the hypogastric nerve plexus with nerve cell bodies at T11-L2. β-Adrenergic (sympathetic) stimulation causes detrusor muscle relaxation during filling. α-Adrenergic (sympathetic) stimulation in the bladder neck (which acts as an internal urethral sphincter) acts to prevent urination.

The micturition center is located in the pons and acts to inhibit urination. Cortical override occurs through connections from the frontal lobe, corpus callosum, and cingulate gyrus, which generally inhibit the pontine micturition center.

There is a normal micturition maturation that occurs, paralleling changes in bladder capacity and neural development. In the first 2 years, a child has little control over urination, yet senses when the bladder is full. By the age of 3, a child should have some development of daytime control. By ages 4 and 5, the child should be able to control urination in midstream with starting and stopping at will. A delay in this normal maturation and a small bladder capacity (less than 50% of normal in 85% of enuretic children) seem to be the primary factors.[3] Another treatment-based theory centers around an abnormal diurnal rhythm of antidiuretic hormone (ADH) secretion.[10] If there is a decrease or absence during sleep, excessive amounts of unconcentrated urine accumulate.[11] This mechanism may account for enuresis in older children, given that one study found the bladder capacity of these children to be normal.[12]

EVALUATION

History

First, it is necessary to determine whether the child fits the criteria for enuresis. The child may, in fact, be too young or have infrequent occurrences. When these criteria are met, it is important to screen the child's history via the parent with regard to underlying psychiatric disorders or systemic disorders such as diabetes. If such disorders are not found, performing a review of systems should identify any suspicions with regard to urinary tract infections or diabetes.

Because of the strong familial tendency, it is crucial to identify a family history of enuresis. As mentioned above, the number of relatives (especially parents) with a history of enuresis has an effect on the tendency of a child to have enuresis. Beyond this observation, Ferguson et al.[13] noted that the number of first-order relatives with enuresis correlated with when a child would attain continence. Those with two or more first-order relatives were 1.5 years late in attaining control, compared with those with no family history.

Examination

The physical examination is often unrevealing. However, it is important to check genital sensation, perianal reflexes, and peripheral sensation and reflexes. Observation of voiding may be helpful in determining control, caliber of stream, and any associated discomfort.

A host of studies may be performed on the enuretic child, but urine screening tests may help obviate the need for further testing. Measurement for bacteriuria, glucose, blood, casts, and a first-morning urine sample for specific gravity will help disclose whether diabetes, renal disorders, or disorders of urine concentration, respectively, are involved in the patient's enuresis.

Further evaluation using voiding cystourethrograms, renal and pelvic ultrasound, or intravenous pyelograms should be reserved for those with daytime incontinence and associated signs of UTI. These tests are expensive and often are ordered prematurely in cases of primary nocturnal enuresis.

MANAGEMENT

The reality of primary nocturnal enuresis management is that no treatment has been found to be significantly superior to the natural history on a consistent basis.[14] Most forms of therapy may have an initially high success rate, yet relapse is extremely common. Methods that do work seem to be most effective in older children. Primary care physicians apparently rely more on a pharmacologic approach than a conditioning approach, with as many as 50% of them prescribing medication; 5% prescribe urine-alarm systems.[15]

The role of manipulative therapy has yet to be defined. Few studies have been performed. One or two case studies and two large studies have been published.[16–19] It is difficult to conclude that chiropractic manipulative therapy is effective, given the limitations of these studies. Unfortunately, most studies suffered for lack of long-term follow-up evaluation to determine maintenance of continence or relapse. In generalizing, the two larger studies indicated 15.5% and 25% improvement rates in the treatment groups. Given that the annual remission rate is between 10% and 20% per year, it does not appear that manipulation provides a significant effect over the natural history of the disorder. The one advantage may be that the effect may occur sooner than it would with natural history. Larger studies with longer follow-up periods are required to define more clearly chiropractic manipulation's role in enuresis management. One other difficulty is that the studies that have been performed and the textbooks that recommend specific treatment for enuresis are consistently inconsistent about which spinal levels to address. A side note is that some researchers have attempted to identify a relationship between spina bifida occulta and diurnal enuresis in children. This association seems related only when other clinical findings of neurologic abnormalities are apparent that suggest underlying lipoma or a tethered cord.[20]

It is generally agreed that the most effective therapy is conditioning therapy using a bell-and-pad urine alarm. The alarm system has been studied extensively and is consistently better than medication, desmopressin, and behavioral treatment.[21] Success rates average between 50% and 80% in children over 8 years of age if there is strict compliance for 4 to 6 months.[22] Unfortunately, the relapse rate is between 15% and 47%. Noncompliance occurs in at least 20% of cases. The intention of the alarm approach is to signal the child to awaken through an alarm that is set off by moisture sensors attached to the pajamas. The child is then instructed to finish voiding in the bathroom, change clothes and bedding, and reset the alarm.

It has been suggested that food allergies may play a role in detrusor instability.[23] Unfortunately, the studies have failed to identify specific foods or to use control groups to compare effect. Foods that have been suggested are dairy products, cola, chocolate, and citrus juices.[24] One study attempted to individualize the treatment approach by starting subjects on an oligoantigenic (few foods) diet.[25] When enuresis was improved, introduction of a single food at a time allowed identification of the antigenic food. This study focused on enuretic children with migraine or hyperkinetic behavior. Elimination diets have been proposed by others in the broader group of enuretic children.[26]

When conservative approaches fail, referral for medical management may be warranted. Two approaches are used. One is the administration of a tricyclic antidepressant, imipramine hydrochloride, for 2 to 3 months followed by gradual reduction over the following 3 to 4 months. The success rate is between 25% and 40% after withdrawal. Some studies have shown less dramatic success.[3,6,9] It is believed that the medication lightens sleep and improves voluntary control of the urethral sphincter with an associated increase in bladder capacity. The major concern with imipramine are side effects and—as one review paper suggests—accidental overdose.[27] The main side effects are dry mouth, blurred vision, lethargy and headaches, abdominal pain, mood and sleep disturbances, and in rare cases syncope and cardiac arrhythmias.[28]

Although intranasal ADH (desmopressin) has been advocated as a viable treatment option for enuresis, studies indicate that the numbers of children who improve are relatively small and that the relapse rate is quite high.[29] Additionally, the cost is high. When desmopressin is effective, it is usually evident within 2 weeks. The short-term success is as high as 70%; however, this is decreased to between 17% and 41% with drug withdrawal. Some studies indicate a higher success with older children. Most side effects are related to the portal of delivery. Nasal irritation, epistaxis, and headaches are the most common. Water intoxication may occur rarely and can be prevented with a serum electrolyte measurement taken at 1 week after therapy is initiated.

Algorithm

An algorithm for evaluation and management of enuresis in children is presented in Figure 36–1.

Figure 36–1

ENURESIS IN CHILDREN—ALGORITHM.

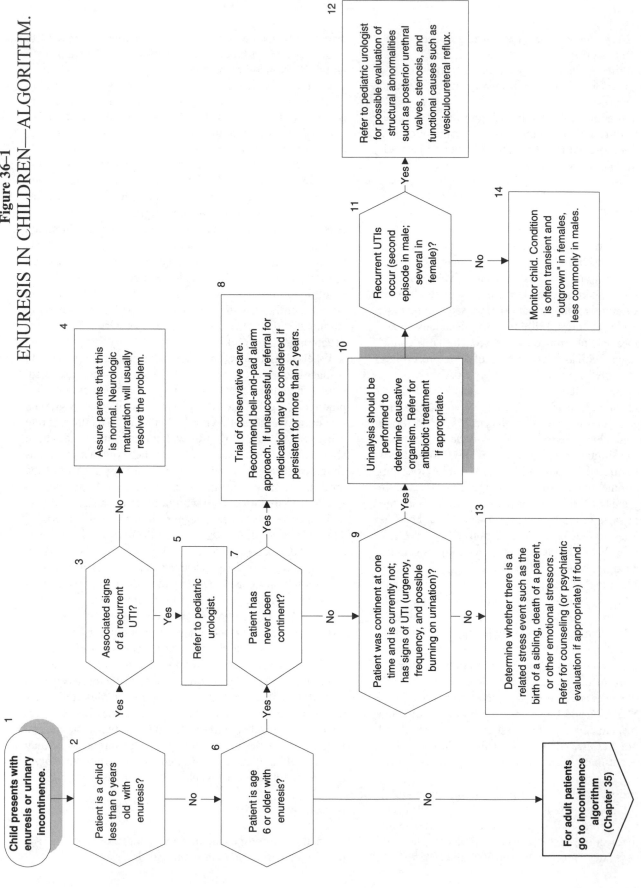

1 **Child presents with enuresis or urinary incontinence.**

2 Patient is a child less than 6 years old with enuresis?
- Yes → 3
- No → 6

3 Associated signs of a recurrent UTI?
- Yes → 5
- No → 4

4 Assure parents that this is normal. Neurologic maturation will usually resolve the problem.

5 Refer to pediatric urologist.

6 Patient is age 6 or older with enuresis?
- Yes → 7
- No → For adult patients go to incontinence algorithm (Chapter 35)

7 Patient has never been continent?
- Yes → 8
- No → 9

8 Trial of conservative care. Recommend bell-and-pad alarm approach. If unsuccessful, referral for medication may be considered if persistent for more than 2 years.

9 Patient was continent at one time and is currently not; has signs of UTI (urgency, frequency, and possible burning on urination)?
- Yes → 10
- No → 13

10 Urinalysis should be performed to determine causative organism. Refer for antibiotic treatment if appropriate. → 11

11 Recurrent UTIs occur (second episode in male; several in female)?
- Yes → 12
- No → 14

12 Refer to pediatric urologist for possible evaluation of structural abnormalities such as posterior urethral valves, stenosis, and functional causes such as vesiculoureteral reflux.

13 Determine whether there is a related stress event such as the birth of a sibling, death of a parent, or other emotional stressors. Refer for counseling (or psychiatric evaluation if appropriate) if found.

14 Monitor child. Condition is often transient and "outgrown" in females, less commonly in males.

For adult patients go to incontinence algorithm (Chapter 35)

REFERENCES

1. Hjalmas K. Functional daytime incontinence: definitions and epidemiology. *Scand J Urol Nephrol Suppl.* 1992;141:39–46.
2. Haque M, Ellerstein NS, Grandy JH. Parental perceptions of enuresis: a collaborative study. *Am J Dis Child.* 1981;135:809–811.
3. Friman PC. A preventative context for enuresis. *Pediatr Clin North Am.* 1986;33:871–876.
4. *Diagnostic and Statistical Manual of Mental Disorders.* 3rd rev. ed. Washington, DC: American Psychiatric Association; 1983;84–85.
5. Mann EM. Nocturnal enuresis. *West J Med.* 1991;155:520–521.
6. Rosenfeld J, Jerkins GR. The bed-wetting child: current management of a frustrating problem. *Postrgrad Med.* 1991;89:63–70.
7. Himsi KK, Hurwitz RS. Pediatric urinary incontinence. *Urol Clin North Am.* 1991;18:283–293.
8. Priman PC, Warzak WJ. Nocturnal enuresis: a prevalent, persistent, yet curable parasomnia. *Pediatrician.* 1990;17:38–45.
9. Novello AC, Novello JR. Enuresis. *Pediatr Clin North Am.* 1987;34:719–733.
10. Toffler WL, Weingarten F. A new treatment of nocturnal enuresis. *West J Med.* 1991;154:326–330.
11. Rittig S, Knudsen UB, Norgard JP, et al. Abnormal diurnal rhythm of plasma vasopresin and urinary output in patients with enuresis. *Am J Physiol.* 1989;256:664–671.
12. Norgard JP, Rittig S, Djurhuus JC. Nocturnal enuresis: an approach to treatment based on pathogenesis. *J Pediatr.* 1989;114(suppl):705–710.
13. Ferguson DM, Horwood LJ, Shannon FT. Factors related to the age of attainment of nocturnal bladder control: an eight-year longitudinal study. *Pediatrics.* 1986;78:884–890.
14. Monda JM, Jusmann DA. Primary nocturnal enuresis: a comparison among observation, imipramine, desmopressin acetate and bed-wetting alarm systems. *J Urol.* 1995;154:745–748.
15. Rushton HG. Nocturnal enuresis: epidemiology, evaluation, and currently available treatment options. *J Pediatr.* 1989;114:691–696.
16. Reed WR, Beavers S, Reddy SK, Kern G. Chiropractic management of primary nocturnal enuresis. *J Manipulative Physiol Ther.* 1994;17:596–600.
17. Leboeuf C, Brown P, Herman A, et al. Chiropractic care of children with nocturnal enuresis: a prospective outcome study. *J Manipulative Physiol Ther.* 1991;14:110–115.
18. Gemmel HA, Jacobson BH. Chiropractic management of enuresis: time series descriptive design. *J Manipulative Physiol Ther.* 1989;12:386–389.
19. Blomerth PR. Functional nocturnal enuresis. *J Manipulative Physiol Ther.* 1994;17:335–338.
20. Ritchey ML, Sinha A, DiPietro MA, et al. Significance of spina bifida occulta in children with diurnal enuresis. *J Urol.* 1994;152:815–818.
21. Alon US. Nocturnal enuresis. *Pediatr Nephrol.* 1995;9:94–103.
22. Devlin JB, O'Cathain C. Predicting treatment outcome in nocturnal enuresis. *Arch Dis Child.* 1990;65:1158–1161.
23. Zaleski A, Shokeir HK, Gerrard JW. Enuresis: familial incidence and relationship to allergic disorders. *Can Med Assoc J.* 1972;106:30–31.
24. Harrison A. Allergy and urinary infections: is there an association? *Pediatrics.* 1971;48:66–69.
25. Egger J, Carter CH, Soothill JF, Wilson J. Effect of diet treatment on enuresis in children with migraine or hyperkinetic behavior. *Clin Pediatr.* 1992;31:302–307.
26. Warady BA, Alon U, Hefferstein S. Primary nocturnal enuresis: current concepts about an old problem. *Pediatr Ann.* 1991;202:246–255.
27. Kreitz BG, Aker PD. Nocturnal enuresis: treatment implications for the chiropactor. *J Manipulative Physiol Ther.* 1994;17:465–473.
28. Ng KH. Nocturnal enuresis. *Singapore Med J.* 1994;35:198–200.
29. Evans JH, Meadow SR. Desmopressin for bed wetting: length of treatment, vasopressin secretion, and response. *Arch Dis Child.* 1992;67:184–188.

CHAPTER 37

Vaginal Bleeding

CONTEXT

A patient would rarely present to a chiropractor with a chief complaint of vaginal bleeding. However, with directed questioning on a review of systems, a complaint of abnormal bleeding may surface. The chiropractor's role in this scenario is to narrow the list of possibilities to determine whether there is a cause for concern and what that concern may be. Narrowing the list is primarily a historical process; however, some chiropractors trained in pelvic examination may extend the search through physical examination, adding more information to the referral.

GENERAL STRATEGY

History

- Determine the patient's staging with regard to her menstrual cycle.
- Determine whether the bleeding appears to be ovulatory or anovulatory.
- Determine whether there are any indicators of thyroid disease.
- Determine whether the patient is taking medications that interfere with menstrual function.
- Determine the patient's use of contraceptives, including an intrauterine device (IUD).
- Determine whether the patient might be pregnant.
- Determine whether the patient has any secondary signs of bleeding loss, such as anemia or iron deficiency.

Evaluation

For those chiropractors who have training and experience, perform a thorough pelvic examination.

Management

Refer the patient to her gynecologist with a letter or phone call explaining relevant findings.

RELEVANT ANATOMY AND PHYSIOLOGY

Menarche is not a fully matured occurrence. Maturation of the central nervous system (CNS)-hypothalamic-pituitary axis is the result of a complex triggering of hormonal release that, when not complete, may cause bleeding. The endometrium is the target site for the effect of this hormonal interplay. Three phases in the growth and subsequent degeneration of the endometrium are based on hormonal dominance. In the proliferative phase (days 5 to 14 of the cycle), the ovarian follicle secretes estrogen, which stimulates the growth of the endometrium. The secretory phase (days 15 to 28 of the cycle) is dominated by progesterone, which is released from the corpus luteum. Progesterone stops the development of the endometrium and stimulates differentiation to a secretory epithelium. Both progesterone and estrogen levels drop if conception does not occur by about day 23. This is due to the degeneration of the corpus luteum. The dramatic decrease in progesterone and estrogen trigger the release of follicle-stimulating hormone (FSH). FSH stimulation of ovarian follicle growth causes a concomitant rise in estrogen from the follicle. At the midcycle, a sudden rise in estradiol causes a rise in FSH and a surge of luteinizing hormone (LH), which leads to the formation of the corpus luteum. Without this LH surge, ovulation does not occur.

During adolescence, ovulation does not occur initially. Gonadotropin levels must reach a level high enough to stimulate development of ovarian follicles, which in turn produce estrogen, which in turn leads to the necessary LH surge leading to ovulation. This LH surge may not occur until as late as 5 years postmenarche.[1] Approximately 75% of abnormal bleeding in the adolescent is due to immaturity of this system.[2]

Dysfunctional bleeding occurs in the perimenopausal (before menopause) woman because of the decreased sensitivity of the ovary to FSH and LH. The resulting decrease in estrogen prevents the LH surge necessary for ovulation. However, similar to the adolescent, there is still enough estrogen being produced to stimulate endometrial growth. Without the balance of progesterone that would normally be produced by the corpus luteum, the endometrium becomes extremely vascular and friable, leading to intermittent sloughing. This type of bleeding is often referred to as estrogen withdrawal bleeding. Estrogen breakthrough bleeding may be due to (1) constant low levels of estrogen, causing portions of the endometrium to degenerate (often seen with low-dose oral contraceptive use); and (2) high levels of estrogen, which allow the endometrium to become hyperplastic and outgrow its blood supply, leading to degeneration and often profuse bleeding. Another type of hormonal imbalance bleeding is progesterone withdrawal and breakthrough bleeding. This is usually the result of exogenous administration of progesterone.

EVALUATION

Vaginal bleeding is usually due to uterine bleeding. The causes of vaginal bleeding are limited and are usually the result of trauma or atrophic vaginitis found in elderly women. Uterine bleeding should be correlated with the woman's menstrual history in an attempt to place her in a stage of menstrual development. Chronologically, a woman's reproductive system's development may be divided into the following five stages:[3]

1. premenarchal
2. menarche
3. the reproductive years
4. perimenopausal
5. postmenopausal

This categorization is useful in considering the most likely causes in each stage of development. Bleeding in stages 1 and 5 is abnormal and warrants investigation. In premenarchal years, the most common cause is direct trauma and/or sexual abuse. In postmenopausal years, any bleeding that appears to be uterine should be suspected to be cancerous in origin. Irregular bleeding during menarche and perimenopausal stages is often the natural consequence of fluctuations in hormonal balance. However, one fifth of abnormal bleeding during menarche is due to a bleeding diathesis. During the reproductive years, the major concerns are that there may be excessive bleeding and there may be bleeding during pregnancy. Alterations in the degree and timing of bleeding related to the menstrual cycle are defined by specific terms as follows:

- polymenorrhea—more frequent than every 20 days
- oligomenorrhea—less often than every 42 days
- menorrhagia—bleeding lasting longer than 8 days
- metrorrhagia—bleeding between periods

The time limits listed above are generalizations and may vary with other text definitions by a few days.

The major differential pivot point is whether bleeding is ovulatory or anovulatory. Ovulatory bleeding is cyclic and is associated with dysmenorrhea and some premenstrual symptoms. In general, the cause is usually a pelvic lesion such as endometriosis, fibroids, an IUD, pelvic inflammatory disease (PID), or pelvic tumors. Anovulatory bleeding is irregular and usually painless; it is often heavy. Endocrine dysfunction or contraceptive use is often the cause. Anovulation often is due to lack of production of LH during the midcycle. The type of bleeding may suggest an underlying cause. If bleeding is bright red with associated clots, a nonmenstrual flow is suggested.

The examination is limited to determination of endocrine causes or a bleeding tendency. An evaluation for thyroid dysfunction is prudent. Pelvic examination should be performed by chiropractors with training in a search for a bleeding source such as tumors. Laboratory evaluation may be helpful in determining whether the patient is anemic.

MANAGEMENT

After performing a thorough history and brief examination, the patient should be given an explanation as to the different types of bleeding and what is specifically suggested in her case. Referral should be made with a letter explaining the doctor's rationale or recommendations.

If a structural lesion is not found to be the source of bleeding, an attempt at controlling the bleeding and normalizing the cycle are made. The standard form of treatment is prescription of oral contraceptive pills (OCPs) or nonsteroidal antiinflammatory drugs (NSAIDs). Both OCPs and NSAIDs can reduce bleeding by up to 50% (NSAIDs usually are a little less effective).[4,5] NSAIDs have a strong vasoconstrictive effect. A side benefit is possible reduction of any associated dysmenorrhea. A small number of women may have an increase in bleeding.

Algorithm

An algorithm for evaluation and management of vaginal bleeding is presented in Figure 37–1.

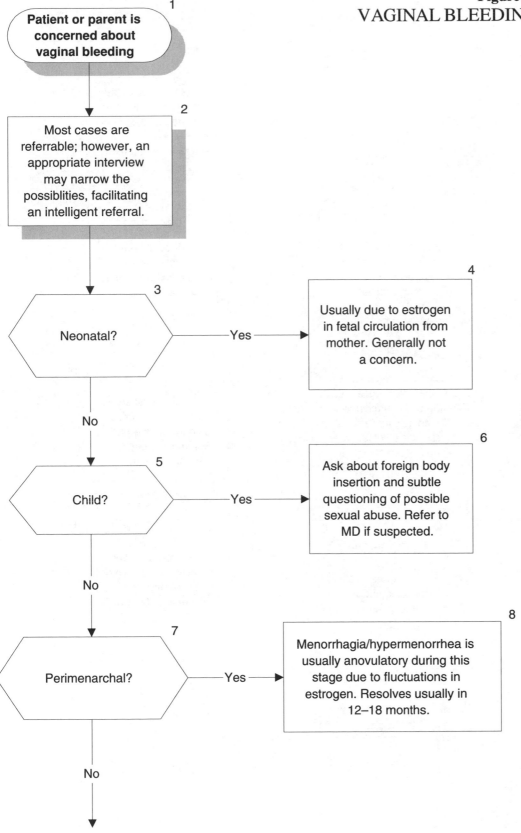

Figure 37–1
VAGINAL BLEEDING—ALGORITHM.

1 **Patient or parent is concerned about vaginal bleeding**

↓

2 Most cases are referrable; however, an appropriate interview may narrow the possiblities, facilitating an intelligent referral.

↓

3 Neonatal?

- Yes → 4 Usually due to estrogen in fetal circulation from mother. Generally not a concern.
- No ↓

5 Child?

- Yes → 6 Ask about foreign body insertion and subtle questioning of possible sexual abuse. Refer to MD if suspected.
- No ↓

7 Perimenarchal?

- Yes → 8 Menorrhagia/hypermenorrhea is usually anovulatory during this stage due to fluctuations in estrogen. Resolves usually in 12–18 months.
- No ↓

continues

Figure 37–1 continued

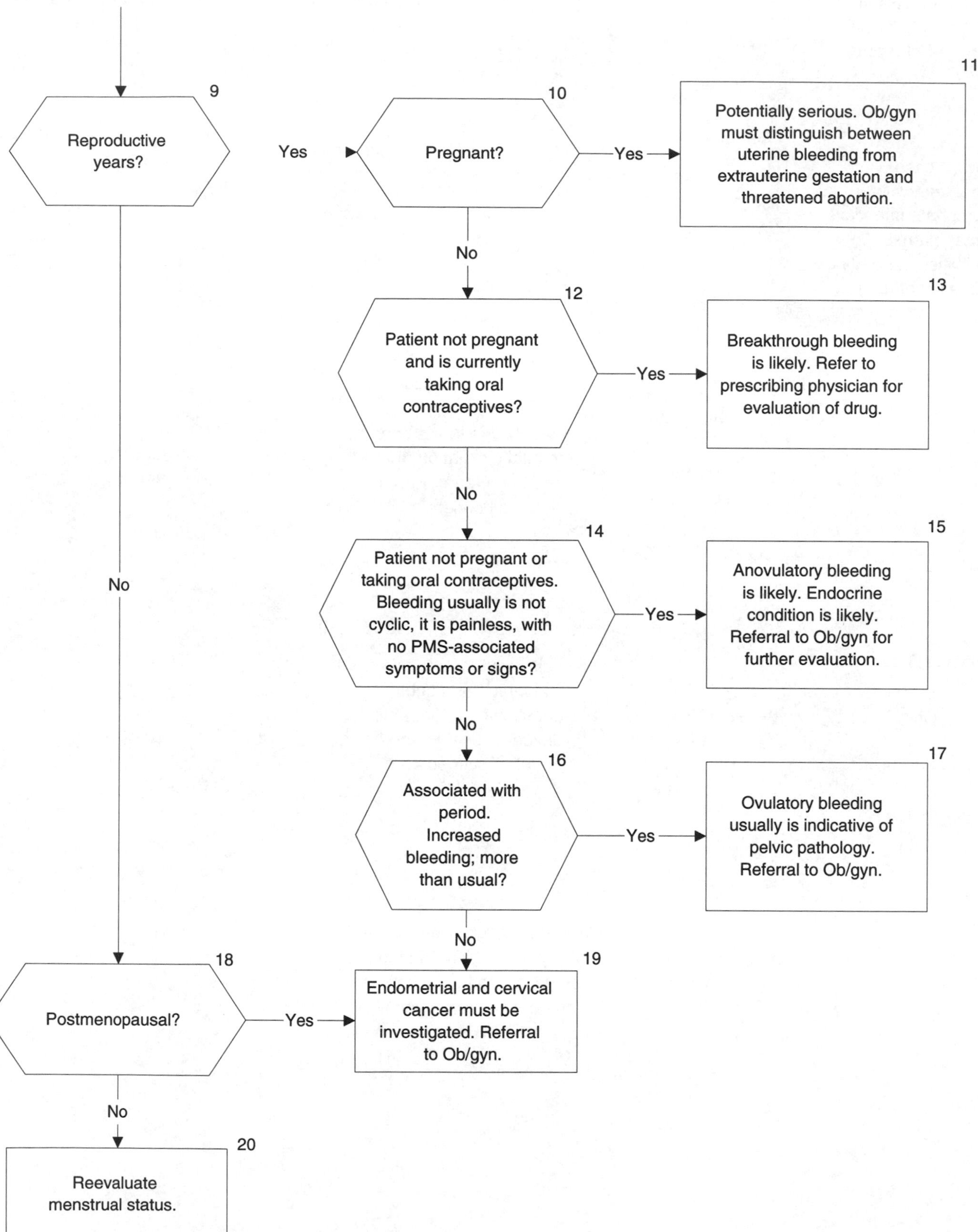

REFERENCES

1. Hertweck SP. Dysfunctional uterine bleeding. *Obstet Gynecol Clin North Am.* 1992;19:129–148.
2. Neinstein LS. Menstrual dysfunction in pathophysiologic states. *West J Med.* 1985;143:476–484.
3. Deprez DP. Abnormal vaginal bleeding. In: Greene HL, Fincher RME, Johnson WP, et al., eds. *Clinical Medicine*. 2nd ed. St. Louis, MO: Mosby-Year Book; 1996:821.
4. Nilsson L, Rybo G. Treatment of menorrhagia. *Am J Obstet Gynecol.* 1971;110:713–720.
5. van Eijkeren MA, Cristiaens GC, Scholten PC, et al. Menorrhagia: current drug treatment concepts. *Drugs.* 1992;43:201–209.

PART VI

Cardiopulmonary Complaints

CHAPTER 38

Syncope/Presyncope

CONTEXT

Although it is not a common primary complaint in the chiropractic setting, syncope is often a secondary concern or is evident on a past history review. Generally, the patient will ignore an infrequent sense of almost fainting (presyncope); however, he or she will be quite concerned with actual fainting if not obviously associated with a stressful, painful, or "sickening" scenario.

The most common cause in younger individuals is vasovagal faint. In the elderly, cardiac dysfunction and carotid sinus hypersensitivity are high on the list of causes.

GENERAL STRATEGY

History

- Determine whether the patient has actually fainted or has almost fainted (syncope versus presyncope).
- If the patient did faint, determine whether he or she or a witness can answer questions regarding how long the loss of consciousness (LOC) lasted and whether there were accompanying convulsions or any significant warning symptoms or postfaint signs or symptoms (distinguish between syncope and seizure).
- Determine the frequency of these events.
- Determine the patient's medication history (alcohol, diuretics, vasodilators, antidepressants, sedatives, or sympatholytic drugs).
- Determine whether there was an associated historical trigger such as heat (vasodilation), prolonged standing (pooling effect), sudden pain, emotional stress, tight collar (carotid sinus syndrome), turning the head to one side (carotid sinus syndrome), exercise (hypertrophic subaortic stenosis or vascular pooling), coughing (cough syncope), urinating (micturition syncope), a frightening/nauseating situation (vasovagal), or anxiety (hyperventilation).

Evaluation

- Test the patient with supine and standing blood pressure measurements (orthostatic hypotension).
- Perform or refer for ECG.
- Evaluate the patient with laboratory tests to determine whether anemia or diabetes is present.
- When the diagnosis is not clear, consider referral for tilt-table testing (vasovagal syncope).

Management

- If triggers are avoidable, give the patient advice regarding a defensive approach.
- Give the patient strategy options for when the sensation of fainting first recurs.
- Refer cases that seem to be medication-related or are unexplained/frequent episodes.

RELEVANT PHYSIOLOGY

Syncope or presyncope is often the result of a pooling effect of either prolonged standing or extreme heat, or the vasodilative effects of many medications. Interference with the normal functioning of cerebral blood pressure may be the result of a dysfunctional neuronal reflex. This occurs in the elderly, those with diabetes, and those with a dysfunctional adrenal gland. With the elderly, a combination of hypersensitivity of the carotid sinus and decreased neuronal conduction may contribute to a decrease in blood pressure upon rising, referred to as orthostatic hypotension. This may be potentiated by certain medications known to blunt the sympathetic response, such as β-blockers. Also, patients with volume depletion caused by diuretics, vomiting, or diarrhea may develop orthostatic hypotension.

Patients with orthostatic syncope appear to have neurocardiogenic dysfunction due to autonomic dysfunction. They demonstrate β-adrenergic hypersensitivity.[1] Patients who become faint with exercise or fasting may have vasodepressor syncope. This has been shown to occur following a rise in β-endorphin concentration just before syncope. These endogenous opiates have an inhibitory effect on sympathetic tone.[2] Another suggested cause in exercise-induced presyncope or syncope is inappropriate peripheral vasodilation due to ventricular mechanoreceptor stimulation. This was found in patients who had no discernible cardiac structural abnormalities.[3] These two theories obviously may overlap. Another theory to consider is that these individuals have a failure to decrease parasympathetic tone.[4]

Obviously, any decrease in blood supply to the head is a potential syncope cause. Therefore, a consideration of the pulmonary and cardiovascular systems structurally, functionally, and physiologically is needed. Blockage of outflow due to aortic (or subaortic) stenosis will decrease blood supply to the brain. Severe atherosclerosis is also a consideration. Functionally, the heart must pump effectively to maintain cerebral perfusion. Arrhythmias and heart block may result in hypoxia and syncope in some patients. Anemia is rarely a cause of syncope; with severe blood loss or severe anemia due to other causes, however, exertional syncope may occur. In particular with chronic obstructive pulmonary disease, decreased perfusion or oxygenation may result in a relative cerebral hypoxia.

EVALUATION

History

The initial focus of the history is to attempt to differentiate between syncope and seizure (Table 38–1). This is not as clear-cut as first assumed. One study demonstrated that, when syncope was induced through a combination of hyperventilation, Valsalva maneuver, and orthostasis, myoclonic activity occurred in 90% of those who fainted. Additionally, head turns, automatisms, and righting movements were observed in 79% of patients who fainted.[5] An important clue is the length of LOC. With a simple faint, the patient is often conscious within seconds. This may be extended in some instances, such as with hypoglycemia. When an epileptic seizure is the cause of LOC, the patient is usually unconscious for much longer; when there is convulsive activity, it usually lasts for several minutes. With a simple (vasovagal) faint, most patients have a warning with prodromal symptoms such as nausea, yawning, or belching with accompanying symptoms of lightheadedness, sweatiness, and cold hands. After fainting, the patient with vasovagal syncope is usually able to become functional in a short period of time. Those with seizure-associated LOC take much longer to regain function and often are disoriented after regaining consciousness. In addition, there may be signs of incontinence, extreme tiredness, and general body aching after a seizure episode (postictal). Eyewitnesses often are necessary to document the length of LOC and the associated patient activity during the attack.

A determination of whether the patient was standing, sitting, or lying down at the time of syncope is often revealing. Patients who faint when lying down are almost always suffering from a cardiac condition such as an arrhythmia or heart block. If the patient faints when in an upright position, vasovagal syncope is the most likely cause. This may be precipitated by prolonged standing, causing pooling of blood in the lower half of the body, or by heat, causing vasodilation. If the patient reports the occurrence only when rising from a recumbent position, orthostatic hypotension is most likely the mechanism. The normal sympathetic response from lying to standing causes splanchnic vasoconstriction (mainly venous) to prevent venous pooling in the abdominal area and increases the force of contraction of the heart. If the sympathetic effect is blocked by some medications or the autonomic nervous system is dysfunctional, this protective response is blunted. The most common drugs involved are those that decrease fluid volume (diuretics), cause vasodilation (many antihypertensives), decrease the nervous system response (sedatives and sympatholytics), and antidepressants and antipsychotic medications. Some simple physiologic causes should also be suspected with orthostatic hypotension, such as prolonged recumbency or prolonged standing, the augmenting effects of pregnancy (vascular pooling), and volume depletion from prolonged vomiting or diarrhea and possibly an associated sodium depletion.

The relationship of syncope to exercise may also be an important clue. If fainting occurs with exertion, severe aortic stenosis (particularly in the elderly) or pulmonary hypertension should be suspected. If the syncope is postexertional (particularly in a young man) subaortic hypertrophic cardiomyopathy should be investigated. If the syncope occurs after a prolonged endurance event, many other factors, such as volume depletion and heat exhaustion, must be taken into account.

There appear to be a few neurally mediated causes of syncope that are rare but worth mentioning because of strong historical clues. If syncope occurs with coughing, an exag-

Table 38–1 History Questions for Syncope

Primary Question	*What Are You Thinking?*	*Secondary Questions*	*What Are You Thinking?*
What position were you in when you fainted?	Recumbent suggests cardiac.	Were you doing anything just before fainting?	Twisting/turning head suggests subclavian steal syndrome.
	Upright suggests vasovagal.		Coughing suggests Valsalva response.
	Rising suggests orthostatic hypotension.		Urinating suggests micturition syncope.
How did you feel just prior to fainting?	Sweating, lightheadedness, or queasiness suggests vasovagal.	How did you feel after fainting?	Confusion with possible incontinence suggests seizure rather than vasovagal or cardiac syncope.
	Visual, auditory, or olfactory prodrome suggests an aura (seizure). Vision "closing in" or going dark suggests cardiac or orthostatic.		
How quickly did you regain consciousness?	Less than a minute suggests vasovagal. Five to 15 minutes is more common with epilepsy.	Were there witnesses?	Try to determine whether there was seizure activity.
Are you taking any medications?	Medications that vasodilate (antihypertensives), deplete fluid (diuretics), or cause nervous system depression (sedatives) are high on the list.	Have you been diagnosed with a condition for which medication was prescribed, but you do not take the medication?	Diabetes. Arrhythmia.
Is this related to exertion?	Cardiopulmonary dysfunction.	Did the fainting occur with exertion or after exertion?	With exertion, cardiopulmonary status should be checked; aortic stenosis, anemia, or pulmonary hypertension.
	Extreme exertion with volume depletion or in extreme heat.		After a strenuous event, rule out dehydration or heat exhaustion, then consider hypertrophic cardiomyopathy.
Were you emotionally stressed?	Most common cause is simple (vasovagal) faint.	Were there symptoms prior to fainting?	Nausea, lightheadedness, sweating/clamminess, and cold hands suggest simple faint.
	Anxiety-related hyperventilation.		Numbness, paresthesias, and cold hands suggest hyperventilation.

gerated vagal response is likely. If syncope occurs post-urination a similar mechanism may be in effect. This type usually occurs in elderly men at night. If syncope is associated with facial pain provoked by swallowing or yawning, glossopharyngeal syncope is likely, due to a reflex mechanism. If the patient notices that syncope occurs while wearing a tight collar or when turning the head, carotid sinus syndrome is likely.

If the patient appears anxious or volunteers an association of presyncope with anxiousness, ask about associated symptoms such as numbness, paresthesias, and coldness in the extremities. Similar symptoms may occur with hypoglycemia; therefore, it is important to ask about the relation to meals, use of insulin, or use of hypoglycemic medications.

Examination

Initial evaluation involves a search for cardiopulmonary disease through auscultation for carotid bruits, heart murmurs, or indications of congestive heart failure. Often the physical examination is unrevealing in those with a complaint of fainting or near-fainting. Most valuable is a search for orthostatic hypotension. The patient's blood pressure is taken supine and then standing after 3 minutes. A decrease of greater than 20 mm Hg in the systolic blood pressure or 10 mm Hg in the diastolic blood pressure is suggestive of orthostatic hypotension and warrants an investigation into volume depletion and neuronal dysfunction due to adrenal, medication, or diabetic causes. Carotid sinus sensitivity is often tested with carotid massage. This is probably not prudent in the chiropractor's office in the event of complications. Many times this potential cause may be suspected from a historical report of tight collar or neck rotational provocation. Laboratory testing may be helpful in detecting an underlying problem with anemia, hyponatremia, diabetes, or more specific testing for endocrine dysfunction. Electrocardiographic evaluation or Holter monitoring may uncover an underlying arrhythmia as the cause, especially in those with a concomitant complaint of palpitations or in patients who faint while lying. In patients who faint after exertion it is important to obtain an echocardiogram to evaluate subaortic hypertrophic cardiomyopathy. If the patient appears to have a history of anxiety-related presyncope or syncope, perform a hyperventilation test whereby the recumbent patient hyperventilates for approximately 1 minute while the examiner appears to be auscultating the chest. If the patient becomes faint, a suspicion of hyperventilation as the cause is appropriate unless the patient has underlying cardiopulmonary disease.

Recently, upright tilt testing has been increasingly utilized for evaluation of vasovagal syncope. This test incorporates varying degrees of tilt for varying amounts of time to provoke syncope. A comprehensive literature review of upright tilt testing suggests that although isoproterenol is often used to augment the effect, its use is usually unnecessary, adding to cost, complexity, and a higher associated false-positive response. The recommended protocol is passive testing at 60° for 45 to 60 minutes. This approach seems to have a higher overall specificity than other methods.[6]

MANAGEMENT

Referral is warranted for patients who appear to have any of the following:

- epilepsy
- a cardiac or pulmonary cause
- medication-induced syncope

For patients with orthostatic hypotension unrelated to medication, for patients who have an underlying disease that is managed by a medical doctor, or for patients with vasovagal syncope the following suggestions may be helpful:

- Avoid dehydration, fever, excessive heat, prolonged standing, prolonged recumbency, large meals, skipping meals, alcohol and unnecessary drugs, and quick standing.
- Rise slowly from a lying or sitting posture, maintain adequate fluid and salt intake, maintain physical conditioning, and support the lower extremities with elastic garments if venous insufficiency is a contributing factor.

REFERENCES

1. Balaju S, Oslizlok PC, Allen MC, et al. Neurocardiogenic syncope in children with a normal heart. *J Am Coll Cardiol.* 1994;23:779–785.
2. Wallbridge DR, MacIntyre HE, Gray CE, et al. Increase in plasma beta endorphins precedes vasodepressor syncope. *Br Heart J.* 1994;71:446–448.
3. Sneddon JF, Scalia G, Ward DE. Exercise induced vasodepressor syncope. *Br Heart J.* 1994;71:554–557.
4. Lippman N, Stein KM, Lerman BB. Failure to decrease parasympathetic tone during upright tilt predicts a positive tilt-table test. *Am J Cardiol.* 1995;75:591–595.
5. Lempert T, Bauer M, Schmidt D. Syncope: a videometric analysis of 56 episodes of transient cerebral hypoxia. *Ann Neurol.* 1994;36:233–237.
6. Kapoor WN, Smith MA, Miller NL. Upright tilt testing in evaluating syncope: a comprehensive literature review. *Am J Med.* 1994;97:78–88.

Chapter 39

Chest Pain

CONTEXT

Chest pain can be a frightening event. Patients often associate chest pain with the heart and experience enough concern to see a medical physician. The majority of patients with chest pain who present to a chiropractic office setting suspect that their pain is musculoskeletal or know from past diagnoses that their pain is cardiac and are being managed by a medical doctor. However, with some patients, there may be few historical clues or the pain is mild, leaving the patient unaware of an underlying problem of a potentially serious nature. Conversely, noncardiac pain may be frighteningly convincing as a cardiac impersonator. The primary role of the chiropractor as a first-contact physician is to differentiate between cardiac (ischemic) pain and noncardiac pain. This is also often the difference between a referable condition and a nonreferable condition. It is crucial, however, that the chiropractor be aware of the important role he or she can play in management of the patient with angina. The long-term quality of a patient's life and perhaps his or her prognosis may be affected through a lifestyle management approach with emphasis on diet, exercise, and stress management.[1]

Chest pain that appears to be cardiac may in fact be from another source. Studies indicate that 30% of patients who have catheterization for anginalike pain have no abnormalities angiographically. Of these patients, 50% may have pain due to esophageal disorders. The remainder may have microangiographic involvement not visible on angiography (syndrome X). It is estimated that musculoskeletal causes of chest pain account for approximately 13% to 30% of cases.[2,3]

GENERAL STRATEGY

History

- Attempt to distinguish between cardiac and noncardiac pain (Exhibit 39–1 and Table 39–1).
- Use the history to develop a high level of suspicion for cardiac pain—diffuse, substernal pain with radiation into the arm (medial) or jaw, lasting between 10 and 60 minutes (Table 39–2).
- In those suspected of having angina, check the history for risk factors, triggers, and other indicators.
- Check the drug history of all patients to determine use of cocaine or other stimulants, and response to nitroglycerin in patients who previously have been diagnosed with angina; some patients do not take their medication properly.

Evaluation

- Attempt to distinguish among the various causes of noncardiac chest pain—visceral, musculoskeletal, skin, psychogenic, referred, or local.
- Auscultate, obtain a screening electrocardiogram (ECG), and consider a chest radiograph when cardiac causes are suggested.
- With suspicion of musculoskeletal conditions, incorporate a mechanical challenge (stretch, compression, and palpation) in an attempt to reproduce the complaint.

Management

- Refer cardiac-caused pain for comanagement (input on proper diet and exercise if pain is anginal).
- Manage musculoskeletal causes conservatively based on the tissue involved.

RELEVANT ANATOMY AND PHYSIOLOGY

Cardiac pain is essentially ischemic pain. The degree of ischemia extends from mild, transient decrease of coronary blood flow to life-threatening infarction. Decrease in coronary artery blood flow (CABF) is generally due to atherosclerosis; however, other processes such as vasospasm (Prinzmetal's or variant angina) are also possible as pure or overlapping causes. CABF is also dependent on the status of the heart and its ability to pump an adequate supply of blood.[4] Specifically, the status of the aortic valve is important. If the aortic valve is stenotic, less blood leaves the heart. This is also true with aortic incompetence, where blood that would normally drain to the coronaries is allowed to return to the left ventricle. This in turn places a high demand on the heart to pump blood from a double source. Over 50% of patients with calcific aortic stenosis and angina have significant coronary artery disease.[5] Hypertrophic obstructive cardiomyopathy (HOCM) is a rare problem that in effect blocks off the aortic exit from the heart, often leading to sudden death. While it is developing it may give a prewarning with chest pain due to ischemia. Through a somewhat similar mechanism, mitral valve prolapse syndrome may cause atypical chest pain because of ischemia. Additionally, anemia may be a factor due to the decreased oxygen carrying capacity of the blood. Other stimulators are increased sympathetic activity from mechanical or environmental stresses such as anxiety, cold, and exercise.

Chest pain is rarely lung pain because the sensitivity of the lungs to pain has been delegated to the endemic vasculature and surrounding pleura. This is why a patient may have bronchogenic carcinoma or other lung processes such as chronic obstructive pulmonary disease (COPD) without any signal of pain until well late in the process.

Pleural pain illustrates an important concept with regard to pulmonary conditions. Processes that affect the pleura such as pleurisy, pneumothorax, pulmonary embolism, and cancer cause pain that is relatively well localized. This is because the parietal pleura is a somatic structure and therefore is innervated by unilateral spinal nerves, making possible localization in vertical and horizontal planes. This also explains why positions such as side bending and lying on the involved side may increase the pain. The pericardium may also react similarly and cause a more localized, left-sided chest pain.

Visceral chest pain is often central, reflecting the embryologic arrangement of most thoracic and abdominal organs. As organs migrate during development, the brain does not receive their forwarding address. As originally midline structures, these organs have a bilateral innervation not capable of providing localizing information. Therefore, a painful stimulus of an organ is not perceived as being on the right or the left. Confounding this natural neural bias is the fact that there is an overlap of sensory innervation to organs that are geographically related (see Figure 39–1). For example, the upper two thirds of the esophagus, the lungs, trachea, bronchi, and heart are innervated by thoracic spinal cord segments T1 through T4 or T5. Overlap continues, with the lower third of the esophagus, stomach, duodenum, liver, gallbladder, pancreas, and part of the small intestine all being innervated by the segments from T5 through T10. Therefore, pathology in one structure is difficult to localize from others when interpreted by the brain at the conscious level. Visceral afferent receptors primarily serve the goal of gathering information about function in an effort to maintain homeostasis. Therefore, information about distention and blood supply governs responses that help maintain normal functioning of these systems. The same pain-producing stimuli for somatic structures apparently do not elicit pain in deep visceral structures. Pain in somatic structures is a stimulus for survival, avoiding the external, potential risk of damage or death. So, although cutting, burning, stabbing, or pinching of somatic structures causes pain, it is not perceptible when applied to deep organs. Pressure and in particular ischemia, however, do cause pain (Table 39–3).

Esophageal causes of chest pain are thought to be due to a dysfunction in visceral sensory perception.[6] Either motility or acid sensitivity may play a role in a hypersensitivity reaction or a lowering of the pain sensitivity threshold. The motility disorders are represented by the nutcracker esophagus (NCE) and esophageal spasm. NCE is an occurrence of high-amplitude peristaltic contractions. Esophageal spasm is due to simultaneous contractions of the esophagus. Some theorize that these disorders and acid hypersensitivity do not cause chest pain but are markers for a propensity toward a dysfunctional visceral sensory system.[5]

Referred pain from the cervical or thoracic spine is possible. Biliary disorders such as cholelithiasis and cholecystitis also can cause pain in the chest. Finally, any irritation of the pleura and the distention by gas of the hepatic or splenic flexures of the colon may cause chest pain.

Exhibit 39–1 Differentiating between Cardiac Pain and Noncardiac Pain

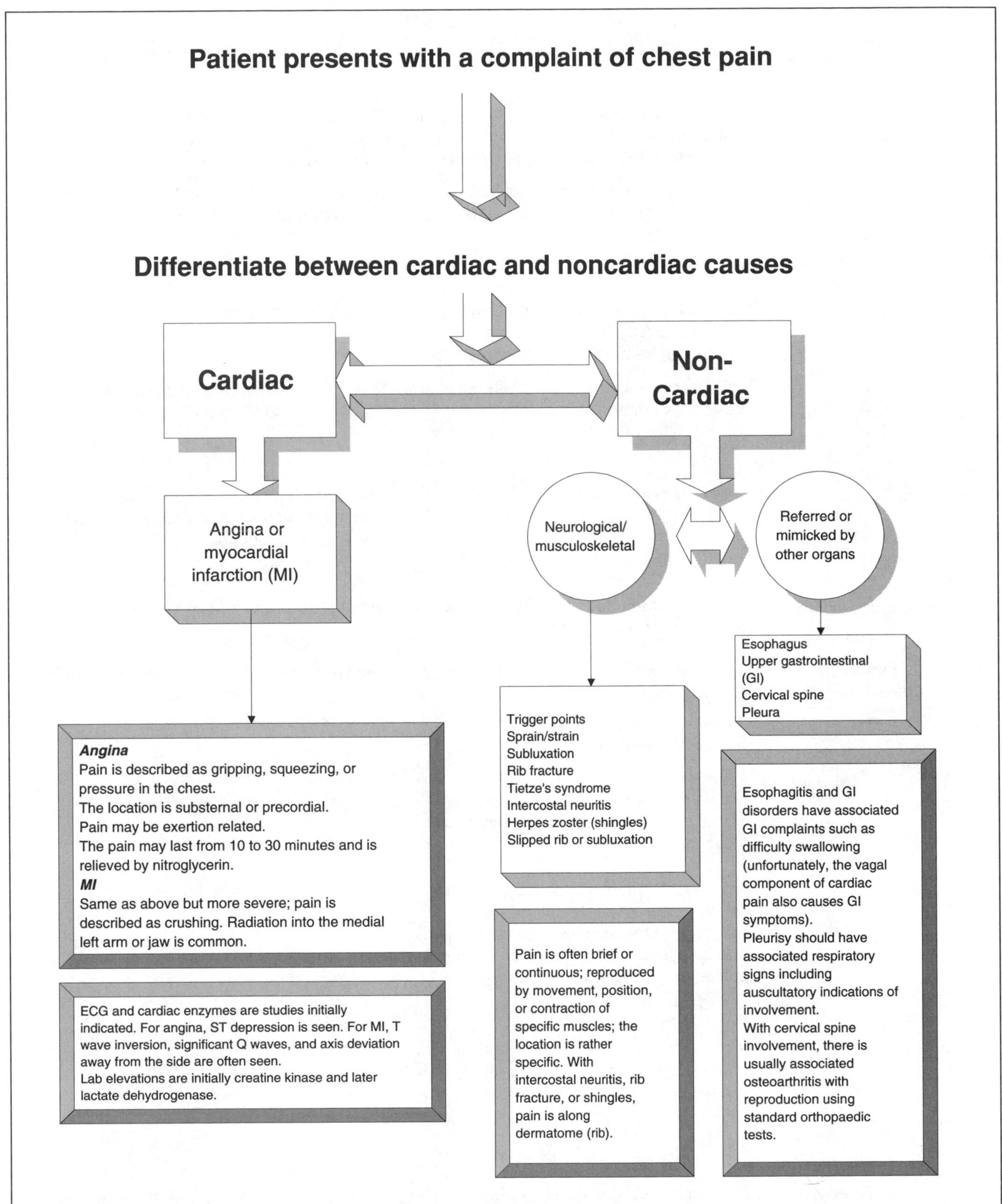

Patient presents with a complaint of chest pain
Differentiate between cardiac and noncardiac causes
Cardiac
Non-Cardiac
Angina or myocardial infarction (MI)
Neurological/ musculoskeletal
Referred or mimicked by other organs
Esophagus
Upper gastrointestinal (GI)
Cervical spine
Pleura
Angina
Pain is described as gripping, squeezing, or pressure in the chest.
The location is substernal or precordial.
Pain may be exertion related.
The pain may last from 10 to 30 minutes and is relieved by nitroglycerin.
MI
Same as above but more severe; pain is described as crushing. Radiation into the medial left arm or jaw is common.
Trigger points
Sprain/strain
Subluxation
Rib fracture
Tietze's syndrome
Intercostal neuritis
Herpes zoster (shingles)
Slipped rib or subluxation
Esophagitis and GI disorders have associated GI complaints such as difficulty swallowing (unfortunately, the vagal component of cardiac pain also causes GI symptoms).
Pleurisy should have associated respiratory signs including auscultatory indications of involvement.
With cervical spine involvement, there is usually associated osteoarthritis with reproduction using standard orthopaedic tests.
ECG and cardiac enzymes are studies initially indicated. For angina, ST depression is seen. For MI, T wave inversion, significant Q waves, and axis deviation away from the side are often seen.
Lab elevations are initially creatine kinase and later lactate dehydrogenase.
Pain is often brief or continuous; reproduced by movement, position, or contraction of specific muscles; the location is rather specific. With intercostal neuritis, rib fracture, or shingles, pain is along dermatome (rib).

Table 39–1 Differentiating Noncardiac Causes of Chest Pain

Cause	*Significant History Findings*	*Provocative Maneuvers, Special Exams*
Visceral		
Pleural	History may include pneumonia, pneumothorax, tuberculosis, bronchogenic carcinoma, etc.; pain is sharp	Deep breathing, bending toward same side may aggravate complaint; auscultate/ radiograph
Esophageal	May or may not have dysphagia; pain is substernal or radiates to central back	Hot or cold food may trigger pain; manometry/ barium x-ray may be necessary
Neuromusculoskeletal		
Nerve		
Herpes zoster	Often unilateral, dermatomal pattern; hypersensitivity followed vesicle formation; burning, sharp pain; recurrent	Hypersensitive to palpation
Intercostal neuritis	Similar to herpes presentation without vesicles; common causes include osteophytes and diabetes	May reproduce on rib separation or compression of intercostal space
Bone		
Rib Fracture	Usually history of trauma	Reproduce on compression anterior to posterior (if posterolateral); tuning fork, oblique radiographs
Joint		
Costochondral junction	Tietze's syndrome found in older women; higher ribs; unilateral; sharp pain	Direct pressure of junction or between ribs
Costovertebral or costotransverse	May or may not be traumatic; pain radiates along rib	Pressure over affected joint causes radiation
Cervical spine	Referral from osteophytic involvement; usually in older patients	Compression/distraction tests
Muscle		
Sprain	Possible history of overuse or trauma; usually, pectorals, serratus anterior, or intercostals	Stretch, contract, combine
Trigger point	Many causative factors, including visceral referral zone; possible autonomic nervous system changes; no neurologic changes; sternocleidomastoid, pectorals, scalenes, sternalis all possible	Sustained pressure on trigger point
Other		
Anxiety related	Patient may appear anxious or depressed; pain is often over heart and is often either quick/stabbing (seconds) or "heavy"/ constant	Psychologic evaluation may be necessary; may be aggravated by deep breathing

Source: Reprinted with permission from T.A. Souza, *Topics in Clinical Chiropractic,* Vol. 1, No. 1, p. 2, 1994, Aspen Publishers, Inc.

Table 39–2 History Questions for Chest Pain: Cardiac or NonCardiac?

Primary Question	*What Are You Thinking?*	*Secondary Questions*	*What Are You Thinking?*
Can you point to where it hurts?	If they can, it is unlikely that there is a cardiac cause.	Were you hit in the chest, back, or side?	Possible rib fracture, especially if worse with deep breathing or lying on the same side.
		Have you had a chest cold or flu?	Pleurisy possible, especially in elderly.
		Is it worse with arm movements; especially overhead or trunk bending?	Muscular cause is more likely; pleurisy is possible with trunk bending.
Is it more diffuse or hard to pinpoint?	Cardiac or esophageal, especially if substernal or precordial. Pressure type pain often described.	Did it occur after exertion and was relieved with rest?	Stable angina likely.
		Does it occur at rest?	Unstable or Prinzmetal's (variant) angina.
		Does it radiate down your inner arm or to your jaw?	Angina or pre–myocardial infarction likely.
		Does it radiate along your rib?	Intercostal neuritis, diabetes, shingles (with skin lesions), thoracic osteoarthritis.
		Does it radiate to your back?	Esophageal pathology or aortic aneurysm.
How long does it last?	Distinguish among brief, continuous, or a timed period.	Is it continuous (all the time)?	Cardiac unlikely.
		Does it last less than half an hour?	Cardiac more likely.
		Is it a split-second jab (sharp) pain?	Cardiac unlikely; probably short muscle spasm.
Is it relieved by nitroglycerin?	Angina or esophageal spasm.	How long does it take after taking nitroglycerin?	Should take a few minutes, not seconds to relieve angina.
		Do you have difficulty swallowing at times?	Esophageal spasm possible.
Do you smoke?	Lung cancer.	How long have you smoked?	Years of heavy smoking are usually needed.
		Do you have any difficulty swallowing or notice any prolonged hoarseness?	Indirect signs of tumor compression.
Any other associated complaints?	Depression/anxiety, collagen/vascular disorders, osteoarthritis.	Do you find your relationships and hobbies still exciting?	Depression.
		Any past diagnosis of collagen diseases?	Lupus, sarcoidosis.
		Is there any neck pain?	Osteoarthritis.

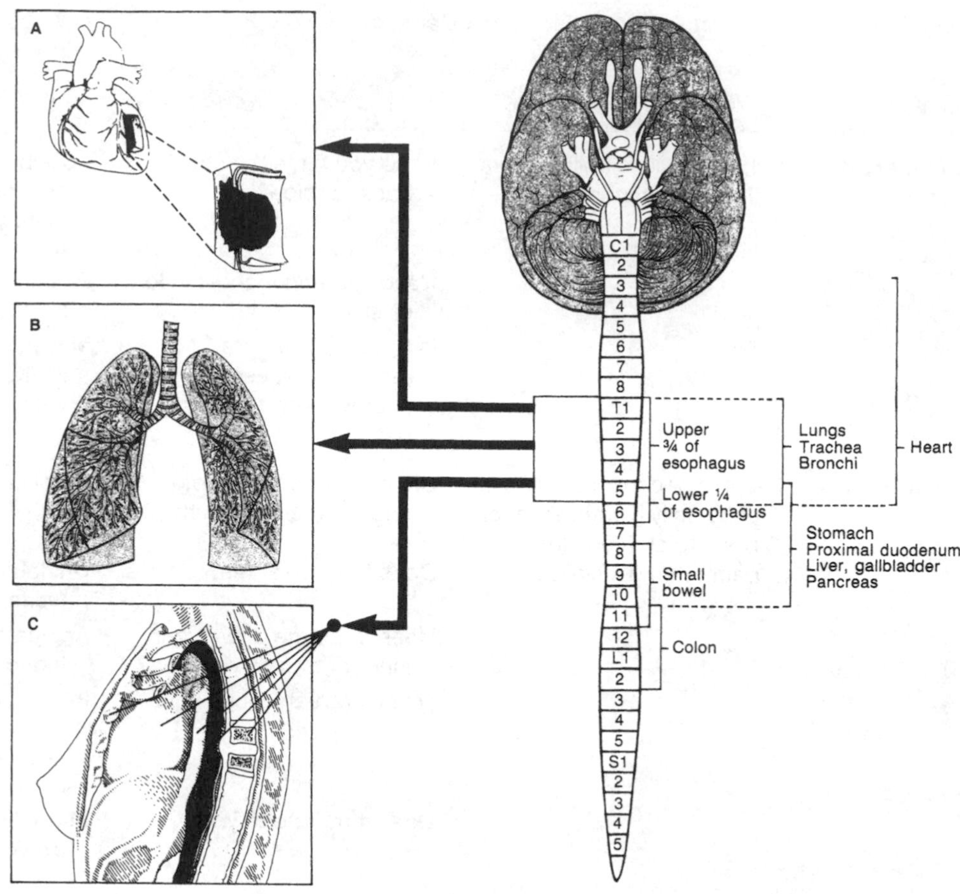

Figure 39–1 Segmental overlap in visceral sensory nerve supply. The poor correlation between referred pain and its site of origin necessitates a thorough history and a careful screening of the differential possibilities. Cardiac ischemic pain (**A**) is transmitted via the upper four or five thoracic spinal segments (as well as cervical levels). Sensory impulses from the lungs and bronchi (**B**) as well as the esophagus, aorta, and body walls (**C**), however, share the same spinal segments, making the diagnosis difficult in many cases. Reprinted with permission from Kerr RM. The GI tract as a cause of chest pain. *Source:* Reprinted by permission of QUADRANT HEALTHCOM Inc. from "The GI Tract as a Cause of Chest Pain," *Hospital Medicine,* Vol. 19, No. 2, p. 188, Copyright 1983 by QUADRANT HEALTHCOM Inc.

EVALUATION

History

The presentation with cardiac pain is often one of concern. Usually, the severity of the pain and the incapacitation with myocardial infarction will result in an emergency department visit or a 911 call. Therefore, most cardiac pain in an ambulatory setting is anginal. The characteristic attributes of cardiac pain are as follows:

- substernal or precordial in location
- diffuse (patient cannot point to a discrete spot)
- a dull, squeezing, or pressure sensation
- radiation to the medial side of the left arm or to the jaw
- relieved by rest
- pain usually lasts between 10 and 60 minutes
- body position has no obvious effect on improving or increasing the pain (with the possible exception of angina, where many patients are often reluctant to be recumbent)
- ischemic pain is usually relieved by nitroglycerin

Cardiac pain is often the result of coronary artery occlusion caused by atherosclerosis or vasospasm. Given that atherosclerosis is a slowly accumulating process, it is logical to assume cardiac disease in older patients who have chest pain. The classic presentation of an older man with retrosternal pain relieved by 5 to 15 minutes of rest is so

Table 39–3 Differentiation of Somatic and Visceral Pain Based on General Characteristics

Character	*Superficial Somatic*	*Deep Somatic*	*Visceral*
Neurology	Spinal nerves (unilateral innervation)	Spinal nerves (unilateral innervation)	Visceral afferents (bilateral innervation)
Structures	Skin, superficial fasciae, tendon sheaths, periosteum	Muscles, fasciae, tendons, joint capsules, ligaments, periosteum	Hollow organs, parenchymatous organs
Quality	Sharp	Aching, dull	Aching, dull
Localization	Yes (lateralizes)	Fairly good; refers often	Difficult; perceived away from organ site; often central
Main stimuli	Cutting, compression, burning	Cutting, compression, burning ischemia	Distention, inflammation, ischemia
Movement	Pain often increases	Pain often increases	Activity often has no effect

Source: Reprinted with permission from T.A. Souza, *Topics in Clinical Chiropractic,* Vol. 1, No. 1, p. 2, 1994, Aspen Publishers, Inc.

characteristic of coronary heart disease (CHD) that the patient has a 94% probability of having at least 75% occlusion of one coronary artery on angiography.[7] The opposite is also true; a young woman with chest pain that is not typical cardiac pain has a less than 1% chance of coronary artery occlusion.

Musculoskeletal and somatic chest pain has a broader range of attributes; however, it often presents as follows:

- localized pain
- pain that is often stabbing or sharp, but deep, dull, aching pain is also possible
- no radiation unless along a rib or between ribs (dermatomal)
- pain is either brief, lasting as little as a few seconds, or continuous
- the pain is made worse by specific body positions that stretch, contract, or compress the involved area
- a history of overuse or trauma may be found

When a history of trauma is given (fall or blow to the chest), a suspicion of rib fracture is high. Rib fractures generally feel worse with deep inspiration, coughing, sneezing, and while lying supine. Rib fractures may be the result of abuse, and eliciting a clear history is often difficult. Instead, the patient may claim an "accident." It is important to look for other clues of abuse during the examination, such as bruises and scars or radiographically for past fractures.

Overuse may be obvious, such as starting a new exercise or workout routine, or as subtle as doing housework, yardwork, or helping someone move furniture. If the pain is sharp and felt unilaterally at the costosternal junction, Tietze's syndrome should be considered. Other causes include repeated coughing or vomiting.

By focusing on the standard approach to history of a chief complaint questioning a rather accurate distinction can usually be made between cardiac and noncardiac pain. Further distinction between cardiac and other visceral sources may be more clouded. Substernal pain is also possible with esophageal disorders such as reflux or esophageal spasm.[8] Questions pertaining to swallowing and relationship to meals is often revealing. If swallowing is difficult, it is important to ask about the relationship to hot, cold, solid, and liquid foods. If the pain begins after drinking or eating very hot or cold foods and is associated with difficulty swallowing both solids and liquids, esophageal spasm must be considered a likely possibility. Pain that is worse with recumbency, especially after meals or with wearing a tight belt, is indicative of reflux. Reflux may also be associated with the ingestion of certain foods such as chocolate, fats, caffeine, orange juice, onions, and garlic. It is important to note, however, that patients with cardiac pain often have associated epigastric complaints.

The distinction between superficial and deep pain helps first to distinguish between cardiac and noncardiac pain. It also helps in distinguishing among various noncardiac sources of pain. If the patient complains of a superficial sensation of burning or hypersensitivity along a patch of skin, herpes zoster (shingles) should be suspected. This is confirmed within a few days with the appearance of a vesicular rash roughly following a dermatome (not necessarily the entire dermatome). This same superficial sensation may be the result of irritation from osteophytic impingement of a thoracic nerve root or may be due to diabetes. Another rare possibility is Mondor's disease. This occurs in women as a superficial thrombophlebitis of the thoracoepigastric vein. The patient feels a tender cordlike swelling beneath the breast.

Chest pain associated with difficulty breathing is common. If there are no indicators of an underlying respiratory infection, several possibilities to consider are the following:[9]

- A sudden onset of chest pain associated with dyspnea and fever suggests a pulmonary embolism, especially in a patient who was immobilized, is taking oral contraceptives, or has antecedent calf pain. Immediate referral is necessary.
- Dyspnea preceding chest pain and associated with lightheadedness, dizziness, or syncope, especially in a younger male athlete, suggests HOCM.[10] Referral for ECG or ultrasound evaluation is necessary.
- Sharp pains localized to the posterior chest that are made worse with respiration, there is no history of trauma, and there are no signs of infection suggest the possibility of spontaneous pneumothorax, especially if the patient is young and tall with a history of an exerting activity such as backpacking or exercise. Chest films are necessary.

A psychogenic cause should be suspected in patients with multiple body complaints that appear unrelated, in patients with a past or current psychiatric diagnosis (especially depression), and in those who appear to have anxiety reactions to stressful situations. It is important not to "excuse" the complaint without a thorough evaluation. Hyperventilation is often found with anxious patients.

Examination

Cardiac involvement is discovered largely through the history. Signs of cardiac involvement are rarely found when the patient is asymptomatic. These signs, when present, would largely be found on an ECG. Changes in the ST segment may reflect underlying ischemia. Depending on severity, either ST elevation or ST depression may be indicative of an ischemic cardiac problem. Given that a resting ECG can provide information only over a short period of time, a Holter monitor (portable recording unit) is often prescribed in an attempt to match the patient's symptoms to a recorded ECG abnormality. Further monitoring with a stress ECG should be done through referral and consultation with a cardiologist.

Indirect implications are generated through auscultatory findings such as murmurs or lung congestion. Hypertension also may be an indirect indicator of systemic atherosclerosis suggesting coronary involvement. Other indicators of atherosclerotic involvement are signs of intermittent claudication in the lower or upper extremities. This is characterized by pain and weakness/tiredness when exercising the extremity that is promptly relieved by rest.

Musculoskeletal involvement may be exposed, reproducing mechanically the patient's complaint with regard to location and quality. Muscles are challenged through a procedure involving contraction, stretch, and contraction in a stretched position. Palpation is used to localize tenderness and in a search for nodules or referred pain upon palpation of specific trigger points. The most common muscles that can cause chest pain are those that are geographically situated in close proximity: the pectoralis major, pectoralis minor, serratus anterior, and intercostals. Following are positions and contraction patterns that may stretch or contract these structures:

- The pectoralis muscles are stretched by elevation of the arms coupled with horizontal abduction (arms brought behind the back); contraction from this position with the patient attempting to adduct the arms horizontally is sufficiently specific to elicit pain when these muscles are involved.
- The serratus anterior can be stretched with the arm abducted and the trunk passively stretched to the opposite side; contraction is accomplished through either protraction maneuvers such as wall push-ups or high arm elevation against resistance.
- The intercostals can be challenged by having the patient seated, arms overhead, while the examiner contacts each rib individually and passively stretches the patient away from and to the involved side in an effort to stretch and compress the area.

Rib involvement is challenged by anterior to posterior and transverse pressure to the chest, being careful not to apply direct pressure at the painful area. Additional testing may involve the use of a tuning fork. Using a nonvibrating tuning fork, tenderness is checked in areas along the rib distal to the main site of pain. With this baseline reading, applying the vibrating probe of the tuning fork to the same area may cause a jump reaction due the vibrating fracture area. Radiographs for rib fractures must include oblique views because of the overlap that occurs on regular anterior to posterior and lateral views.

Chest films should be reserved for cases of suspected pneumothorax, pleurisy, congestive heart failure, and rib fracture. Following are some guidelines:

- Patients with suspected rib fracture should have a posterior to anterior (PA) chest film ordered in search of an associated pneumothorax, and oblique films localized to the area of complaint.
- Patients with suspected pleurisy should have a PA chest film and a lateral recumbent view ordered in search of an air-fluid level.
- With a posterior chest pain complaint it is important for the chiropractor not to rely on a collimated thoracic anterior to posterior view because significant pathology may be obscured.

MANAGEMENT

Although cardiac-caused pain should be referred for medical evaluation, comanagement may be helpful when attempting to change the patient's lifestyle, including diet, exercise, and stress management.[11] Noncardiac causes are managed based on the underlying tissue involved. See Selected Causes of Chest Pain for more detailed recommendations for listed conditions.

Algorithm

An algorithm for initial screening of chest pain is presented in Figure 39–2.

SELECTED CAUSES OF CHEST PAIN*

CARDIAC

Angina

Classic Presentation

The patient complains of a squeezing or pressure sensation in the chest. It came on rather suddenly after exertion. The patient said that after resting for several minutes the sensation went away. This was not the first time it had happened. He also noticed that there was an aching pain felt down the left inside arm to the fingers.

Cause

Angina is usually due to atherosclerosis; however, a variant of angina is related to vasospasm that may occur in isolation or with atherosclerosis (Prinzmetal's angina). Patients with Prinzmetal angina often have an atypical presentation in that they may be women under age 50 with angina that occurs at night (involves the right coronary most often). Another entity is called syndrome X in which there is no apparent coronary atherosclerosis. It is believed that there are microvascular abnormalities in these patients.[12] The threshold for angina may be decreased by factors such as anemia, valvular disorders (especially aortic stenosis), or conduction problems. Cocaine may also provoke an attack.[13] When atherosclerosis is excessive, angina may occur at rest without provocation (unstable angina). These attacks tend to be longer and may be a portent of impending myocardial infarction.

Evaluation

The history of a pressure or squeezing pain lasting for several minutes to 30 minutes with possible radiation to the arm or jaw is characteristic of angina. If the pain occurs at rest or without provocation, unstable angina is likely, indicating more occlusion. Given

*See also Chapter 40, Palpitations, and Chapter 41, Dyspnea.

Figure 39–2
CHEST PAIN: INITIAL SCREENING—ALGORITHM.

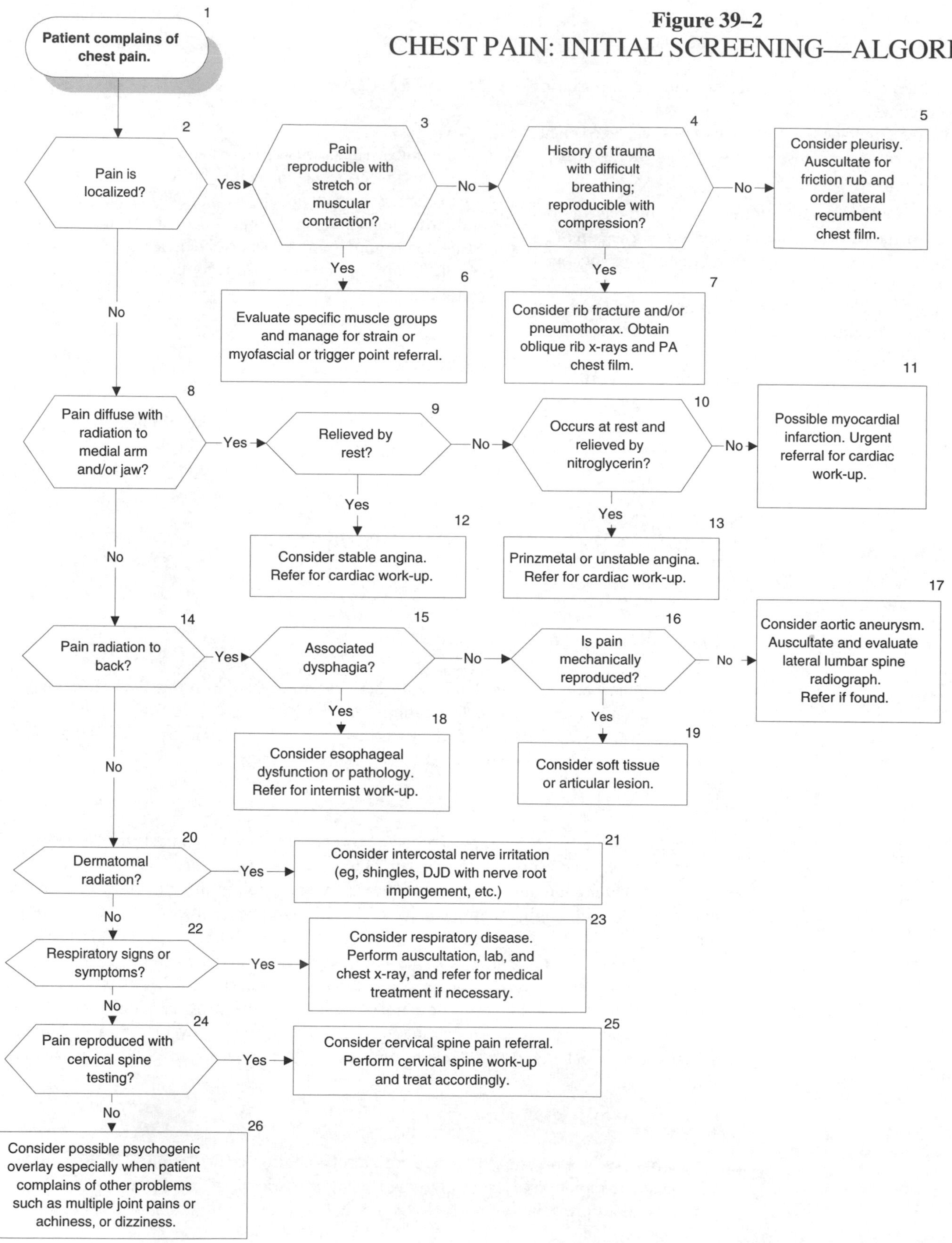

1 Patient complains of chest pain.
2 Pain is localized?
Yes
3 Pain reproducible with stretch or muscular contraction?
No
4 History of trauma with difficult breathing; reproducible with compression?
No
5 Consider pleurisy. Auscultate for friction rub and order lateral recumbent chest film.
Yes
6 Evaluate specific muscle groups and manage for strain or myofascial or trigger point referral.
Yes
7 Consider rib fracture and/or pneumothorax. Obtain oblique rib x-rays and PA chest film.
No
8 Pain diffuse with radiation to medial arm and/or jaw?
Yes
9 Relieved by rest?
No
10 Occurs at rest and relieved by nitroglycerin?
No
11 Possible myocardial infarction. Urgent referral for cardiac work-up.
Yes
12 Consider stable angina. Refer for cardiac work-up.
Yes
13 Prinzmetal or unstable angina. Refer for cardiac work-up.
No
14 Pain radiation to back?
Yes
15 Associated dysphagia?
No
16 Is pain mechanically reproduced?
No
17 Consider aortic aneurysm. Auscultate and evaluate lateral lumbar spine radiograph. Refer if found.
Yes
18 Consider esophageal dysfunction or pathology. Refer for internist work-up.
Yes
19 Consider soft tissue or articular lesion.
No
20 Dermatomal radiation?
Yes
21 Consider intercostal nerve irritation (eg, shingles, DJD with nerve root impingement, etc.)
No
22 Respiratory signs or symptoms?
Yes
23 Consider respiratory disease. Perform auscultation, lab, and chest x-ray, and refer for medical treatment if necessary.
No
24 Pain reproduced with cervical spine testing?
Yes
25 Consider cervical spine pain referral. Perform cervical spine work-up and treat accordingly.
No
26 Consider possible psychogenic overlay especially when patient complains of other problems such as multiple joint pains or achiness, or dizziness.

Key: DJD, Degenerative joint disease.

Source: Reprinted from T.A. Souza, *Topics in Clinical Chiropractic*, Vol. 1, No. 1, p. 67, © 1994, Aspen Publishers, Inc.

that it is rarely possible to examine a patient during an attack, most findings such as hypertension are indirect indicators of underlying atherosclerosis. Valvular abnormalities such as aortic stenosis in older patients and mitral valve prolapse in younger patients may be found. ECG findings are nonspecific except during the attack, when either ST depression or, with more severe ischemia, ST elevation is found. Provocation with exercise testing includes an ECG. Based on these findings scintigraphic or echocardiographic studies may be added.[14] Ambulatory monitoring with a Holter device may be used, especially if an underlying arrhythmia is suspected. Coronary angiography should be used in selected patients only.

Management

Nitroglycerin is used for symptomatic management of angina. It decreases contraction of the heart and causes vasodilation. It is usually taken sublingually and takes a minute or two to work. With more fulminant involvement of the coronaries, angioplasty or surgery may be suggested to the patient. It is important to advise patients with mild symptoms that supervised lifestyle changes including a healthful diet and exercise may decrease the need of nitroglycerin and, in some patients, reverse the underlying process. This is a comanagement scenario in which the medical doctor, chiropractor, and patient work together.

Myocardial Infarction

Classic Presentation

Not all patients with myocardial infarction (MI) are unconscious or in severe pain, although the majority of patients have pain severe enough to warrant a trip to the emergency department or a 911 call. It is possible to have a patient complain about pain that is often preceded by a history of angina. The substernal pain is more severe and often builds up over a few minutes. Nitroglycerin does not help. The pain lasts longer than 30 minutes. Twenty percent of individuals die before reaching the hospital. Approximately 25% of infarctions are silent, appearing inadvertently on an ECG.[15]

Cause

Usually MI is due to coronary thrombus or vasospasm. Blockage of a specific coronary artery causes damage to the area supplied. For example, blockage of the anterior descending branch of the left coronary artery causes infarction of the anterior left ventricle and interventricular septum. The extent of damage is subendocardial with some transmural extension evident in most cases. Extension of infarcted tissue increases after the occlusion and may be diminished by prompt thrombolytic therapy.

Evaluation

The evaluation of a patient suspected of having an MI is primarily a check for shock. Further evaluation is performed in the hospital with a check for associated arrhythmias. There are large variations at presentation with regard to heart rate, advential respiratory sounds, and general status of the patient. Laboratory testing performed within the first few hours will reveal an elevation of creatine kinase (CK) that peaks in about 12 to 24 hours. The isoenzyme CK-MB is specific for the heart. The level of CK elevation correlates to the degree of damage. Lactate dehydrogenase (LDH), especially the isoenzyme 1, may still be elevated 5 to 7 days later. ECG findings involve a sequence of hyperacute T waves, progressing to ST elevation, to Q wave development, to T wave inversion. When found, Q waves are diagnostic for MI; however, 30% to 50% of patients do not have them.[16]

Management

It is important for chiropractors to maintain cardiopulmonary resuscitation (CPR) certification (or knowledge). Although rare, it may be necessary to perform CPR in or out of the office. Initial treatment is crucial for survival and to diminish the extent of damage. Thrombolytic therapy must be given within the first 1 to 3 hours for best results.[17] This includes streptokinase, tissue plasminogen activator (t-PA), or anistreplase. Post-MI it is important for the chiropractor to work closely with the patient and cardiologist to maintain a program of prevention, including diet and exercise.

Pericarditis

Classic Presentation

The patient usually complains of chest pain and difficulty breathing that is worse with lying down; it is better seated. The pain is substernal, often radiating to the neck or shoulder. There may be a history of a preceding respiratory infection, renal failure, or cancer.

Cause

The pericardium is the double-layered sac covering and stabilizing the heart. Infiltration with infections or other inflammatory process decreases the available space and movement of the heart. Viral organisms such as coxsackievirus, Epstein-Barr, mumps, varicella, or HIV may be the cause. It can also be associated with hepatitis, tuberculosis, uremia from kidney failure, neoplasms, post-MI, or radiation treatment.[18]

Evaluation

The presentation may be very similar to that of an acute MI. The characteristic finding is a pericardial friction rub heard on auscultation. ECG findings are similar to those of an MI, including ST elevation or T wave inversion.

Management

Management is dependent on the underlying cause; however, it should be managed medically. Aspirin or NSAIDs are given for viral etiologies, antituberculin therapy for TB, and chemotherapy for neoplastic causes.

Hypertrophic Cardiomyopathy

Classic Presentation

The patient may be a young athlete complaining of exercise-induced chest pain and difficulty breathing. More important, there may be a report of postexercise syncope. Unfortunately, the first presentation may be sudden death.

Cause

HOCM is a nonfunctional ventricular wall enlargement (not due to increased pressure or volume of blood). This enlargement can involve mainly the interventricular septum, causing an outflow blockage during systole. This diminished outflow leads to ischemia with syncope as the clearest indicator. HOCM may be inherited as an autosomal dominant trait. HOCM is one of the leading causes of sudden death in young athletes.[19] It may also occur in the elderly.

Evaluation

The evaluation begins as a preventive measure on preparticipation screenings. Although it is still difficult to identify susceptible individuals, a history of chest pain, dyspnea, and/

or syncope related to exercise, and a family history of HOCM or sudden death in a close relative are indicators for further evaluation. The only physical examination finding that is suggestive of HOCM is a systolic murmur that is made worse with a Valsalva maneuver; it is improved with squatting. However, this is found only with patients having an outflow tract obstruction, who are the minority. ECG changes usually show ventricular hypertrophy. The echocardiogram is the definitive tool demonstrating asymmetric left ventricular hypertrophy.

Management

Management depends on the degree of involvement. β-Blockers or calcium channel blockers may be used for symptom relief. More severe problems may require excision of part of the enlarged myocardium.

NONCARDIAC, MUSCULOSKELETAL

Muscle Strain

Classic Presentation

The patient usually will recall a single event or repetitive overuse event. This may include weight lifting, or in many patients, cleaning the house or moving furniture.

Cause

Exceeding the limits of a muscle's ability to withstand a given load or overstretching the muscle may cause damage to the muscle or tendon.

Evaluation

Evaluation of muscle injury involves palpation for tender areas and referral zones from these areas, contraction in midrange and in a stretched position, and stretching the muscle passively. The main muscles to consider in the chest are the pectoralis major and minor, the serratus anterior, and the intercostals.

Management

Myofascial work in the form of trigger point massage and myofascial release techniques are most appropriate. Gradual retraining of the muscle should proceed from isometrics to isotonics and, depending on the need, isokinetics.

Rib Fracture

Classic Presentation

The patient will report either a direct blow to the chest or a fall onto the chest. The most common location of fracture is posterolateral.

Cause

Direct trauma is needed to break the ribs in adults. In seniors and those with underlying disease processes that result in osteoporosis or lytic processes, minor events may cause a fracture. The rib may be only partially fractured and is referred to as a "cracked" rib. Associated with complete rib fractures is pneumothorax, in which air enters the pleural space.

Evaluation

The patient has guarded respiration and finds it more difficult to lie supine. Pressure directed anterior to posterior or transversely (taking care not to apply pressure directly to the site of involvement) will often cause a sharp increase in pain. Tuning fork application may increase the pain dramatically. It is important to apply a nonvibrating tuning fork first to ascertain a baseline level for tenderness. Applying the vibrating tuning fork should be at a site along the rib away from the suspected fracture site. Radiographs should include a PA chest film and oblique films of the painful area. The PA chest film is necessary to evaluate for a coexisting pneumothorax. Radiographic evidence of fracture is often subtle and may take 2 to 3 weeks for callus formation to uncover the site. With cracked ribs, this may not be apparent.

Management

Multiple rib fractures are best managed medically. Cracked ribs or small single fractures can be managed conservatively with rest, pain medication, recommendations to avoid sleeping on the back, laughing, coughing, and sneezing. Immobilization with a rib belt or taping is not recommended because of the inhibitory effect it may have on breathing. Gradual stretching should be introduced to avoid contracture and its effect on respiration. Slow, deep breathing should be attempted when possible. Pain is often present for approximately 1 to 2 months. In sports, intercostal blocks are often used to allow the player to return to play. This is a medical decision that carries with it possible medlegal consequences.

Tietze's Syndrome

Classic Presentation

The patient is often a woman over age 50 years who complains of a moderate to severe pain in the upper part of the chest on one side. She points to the second and third costochondral junctions.

Cause

The cause is unknown. There appears to be an inflammatory reaction at the costochondral and, occasionally, chondrosternal, sternoclavicular, or manubriosternal areas. There may be an overexertion history of prolonged coughing or moving furniture. It is bilateral in 30% of cases.[20]

Evaluation

The area (usually upper chondrocostal junction) is tender, as is the adjacent intercostal area. There is swelling but no associated warmth or erythema.

There are no radiographic findings; however, in the differential diagnosis of rheumatoid conditions, radiographs may be needed. In rare cases, a bone scan may show abnormal uptake at the involved site. Chiropractic evaluation of rib and rib articulation movement is important.

Management

The condition is benign and self-resolves in about 6 months. During the symptomatic period, chiropractic mobilization or adjusting may help (or aggravate) the condition. Failure to respond may require medical referral for an anesthetic/corticosteroid injection, which is 90% effective.

Costochondritis

Classic Presentation

The patient is usually young, with a complaint of anterior chest pain that is bilateral and affects the middle ribs close to the sternum.

Cause

The cause is unknown. This term is also used to describe Tietze's syndrome; however, costochondritis appears to be a distinct entity because of the more common bilateral involvement of multiple rib articulations.[21] Trauma is suspected as the underlying cause. There are no consistent pathologic findings.

Evaluation

Tenderness without swelling is found at the costal junction of ribs two through five most commonly. A "crowing rooster" position with the patient's cervical spine extended and his or her flexed elbows extended upward behind the body may stretch the involved area and increase pain. Another position that may increase pain is forced horizontal adduction while the patient turns the head to the ipsilateral side. Chiropractic evaluation of the rib and rib articulation is an important aspect of the evaluation. Radiographs are unrevealing and usually unnecessary. Laboratory testing is reserved for those individuals suspected of having an underlying rheumatoid etiology.

Management

Moist heat and NSAIDs may help in this self-resolving, benign condition. It may be necessary to refer for an anesthetic and/or corticosteroid injection.

Slipped Rib

Classic Presentation

The patient complains of a popping or clunking sensation in the lower ribs, usually associated with an exertion maneuver such as a bench press or other lifting maneuver. The patient may report that the rib pops in and out with a specific type of maneuver.

Cause

Loosening of the lower costal cartilages, often due to direct trauma or constant overcontraction of the chest muscles, allows the rib tip to curl upward. Chest pain may result if this impinges on the superior rib or intercostal nerve.[22]

Evaluation

Palpation of the involved area is usually unrevealing unless the patient can reproduce the problem with a specific maneuver. Chiropractic evaluation of costovertebral accessory motion may indicate involvement.

Management

Avoidance of the causative maneuver is important for stabilization. Adjustment of the involved ribs may help the patient temporarily; however, in most cases the condition is recurrent if the patient continues the inciting activity.

Fibromyalgia

Classic Presentation

The patient is often a woman (5:1) and complains of an aching, fatigued, and stiff sensation in multiple muscle groups.

Cause

The cause is unknown. It is believed that there is some relationship to a disturbance in NREM sleep.[23] Cold, damp weather, fatigue, a sedentary position or overexertion, mental stress, and poor posture may make it worse.

Evaluation

The standard evaluation is to find a minimum of 11 of 18 bilateral tender areas designated by the American College of Rheumatology.[24]

Management

The conservative approach is to use local application of dry heat, mild to moderate exercise, and stress reduction. It may be necessary to refer for a trial of minidosing of tricyclic antidepressants, which are believed to assist in restoring normal NREM sleep.

Intercostal Neuritis

Classic Presentation

The patient complains of pain that is unilateral, extending in a band around the chest.

Cause

Intercostal neuritis may be idiopathic, or the result of herpes zoster (shingles), diabetes, osteophytic encroachment, or rib subluxation. Herpes zoster is due to a varicella virus infection. The organism's residence is the dorsal root ganglion. During periods of emotional or mechanical stress the organism becomes active.

Evaluation

In a diabetic patient with poor glycemic control diabetic neuropathy is likely. For patients with shingles, the pain is followed in 3 to 5 days by a vesicular rash along part of the dermatome. Rib subluxation may be determined by palpation of the movement of the rib and at the costotransverse articulation.

Management

For shingles, avoidance of emotional and mechanical stresses is recommended. When the infection is active, the use of lysine and the avoidance of caffeine may help. For more involved or resistant cases acyclovir may be prescribed by a medical doctor. Rib subluxations should be adjusted. Patients with suspected osteoarthritic involvement should be adjusted cautiously. Low-force techniques may be more appropriate. Adjusting also may be beneficial for the idiopathic and diabetic cases. Control of the underlying diabetes is the long-term goal.

NONCARDIAC, VISCERAL

Pleurisy

Classic Presentation

The patient presents with sharp pains in the chest that seem related to coughing, sneezing, and positions such as bending to the same side or lying on the involved side. The patient often will have a coexisting or recent history of a respiratory infection.

Cause

Pleurisy is usually associated with pleural effusion. Effusion is categorized as a transudate or exudate based mainly on the protein content. Transudates are more the result of congestive heart failure or hypoalbuminemia (loss of onconic pressure). Exudates are usually due to bacterial pneumonia or cancer. Other causes include empyema (direct infection of the pleural space), hemothorax (blood in the pleural space), or chyliform (chyle in the pleural space).

Evaluation

Physical examination findings (and symptoms) are dependent on the underlying cause and the degree of effusion. A pleural friction rub may be heard. With large effusion there may be a decreased fremitus, dullness to percussion, and an increase or decrease in breath sounds. Chest films may reveal large pleural effusions. Smaller effusions are visible with a lateral recumbent view.

Management

Small, transudate effusions are often managed conservatively. Larger effusions may require thoracentesis. When cancer is suspected, biopsy is often indicated. Treatment of the underlying condition is the primary feature of management.

Esophageal

Classic Presentation

The patient may complain of substernal chest pain associated with recumbency, dysphagia, and heartburn.

Cause

Convergence of afferents for both the heart and esophagus may explain why esophageal pain may be a cardiac imitator. There are numerous theories and categories of esophageal dysfunction. Currently there is much disagreement as to the cause and relative importance of these conditions. The three syndromes suggested are an acid-sensitive esophagus including gastroesophageal reflux disease (GERD) (20% of patients), a mechanicosensitive esophagus (including motility disorders such as esophageal spasm) (15% of patients), and an irritable esophagus seen as a combination of the other groups (25% of patients).[25] Chest pain of undetermined origin is believed to be due to esophageal disorders in 50% to 60% of patients.[26] Approximately 85% of patients with manometrically demonstrated esophageal abnormalities have a psychiatric abnormality.[27] A connecting hypothesis is that the esophageal disorders may represent a marker for individuals who have a dysfunctional visceral sensory mechanism wherein physiologic or pathophysiologic events may trigger pain, perhaps by lowering the threshold.[28]

Evaluation

After cardiac diseases have been evaluated and ruled out, evaluation for esophageal disorders is begun, yet is varied depending on the suspected underlying dysfunction. Some physicians use a proton-pump medication as an initial test for GERD, looking for relief as a positive test. The most sensitive test for GERD is 24-hour pH monitoring. Further testing may involve using balloon distention, the Bernstein acid perfusion test, or endoscopy. If esophageal motility is the underlying problem, manometry is often indicated.[29]

Management

Conservative treatment for GERD consists mainly of dietary and positional advice. It would seem logical that patients with motility disorders would improve with the use of smooth muscle relaxants or calcium channel blockers; however, even though often they are objectively improved with manometry, symptoms do not abate. These patients are usually reassured that they have a benign problem and often are given similar advice to that given the GERD patient, including stress relaxation approaches. Patients with an underlying psychiatric problem may benefit from psychiatric counseling or medication.

REFERENCES

1. Ornish DM, Scherwitz LW, Doody RS, et al. Effects of stress management training and dietary changes in treating ischemic heart disease. *JAMA*. 1983;249:54–59.
2. Levine RP, Mascette AM. Musculoskeletal chest pain in patients with angina: a prospective study. *South Med J*. 1989;82:580.
3. Lee TH, Cook EF, Weisberg M. Acute chest pain in the emergency room: identification and examination of low risk patients. *Arch Intern Med*. 1985;145:65.
4. Masseri A. Mechanisms and significance of cardiac ischemic pain. *Prog Cardiovasc Dis*. 1992;35:1.
5. Lombard JT, Selzer A. Valvular aortic stenosis: a clinical and hemodynamic profile of patients. *Ann Intern Med*. 1987;106:292.
6. Fennerty MB. Esophageal causes of noncardiac chest pain. *Hosp Med*. 1995;10:15–24.
7. Diamond GA, Forrester JS. Analysis of probability as an aid in the clinical diagnosis of coronary artery disease. *N Engl J Med*. 1979;300:1350.
8. Anselmino M, Clark GWB, Hinder RA. Esophageal chest pain: state of the art. *Surg Annu*. 1993;25(pt 1):193–210.
9. Wasserman K. Dyspnea on exertion: is it the heart or the lungs? *JAMA*. 1982;248:2039.
10. Louie EK, Edwards LC. Hypertrophic cardiomyopathy. *Prog Cardiovasc Dis*. 1994;36:275.
11. Ornish D. *Dr. Dean Ornish's Program for Reversing Heart Disease*. New York: Ivy Books; 1996.
12. Cannon RD. Microvascular angina: cardiovascular investigations regarding pathophysiology and management. *Med Clin North Am*. 1991;75:1097.
13. Gitter MJ. Cocaine and chest pain: clinical features and outcome of patients hopitalized to rule out myocardial infarction. *Ann Intern Med*. 1991;115:277.
14. Shub C. Stable angina pectoris, 1: clinical patterns; 2: cardiac evaluation and diagnostic testing. *Mayo Clin Proc*. 1990;65:233, 243.
15. Reeder GS, Gersh BJ. Modern management of acute myocardial infarction. *Curr Probl Cardiol*. 1993;18:81.
16. Schweitzer P. The electrocardiographic diagnosis of acute myocardial infarction: the thrombolytic era. *Am J Heart J*. 1990;119:642.
17. Anderson HB, Willerson JT. Thrombolysis in acute myocardial infarction. *N Engl J Med*. 1993;329:703.
18. Shabetai R. Disease of the pericardium. *Cardiol Clin*. 1990;8:579.
19. Maron BJ, Epstein SE, Roberts WC. Causes of sudden death in competitive athletes. *J Am Coll Cardiol*. 1986;204:214.
20. Kaye BR. Chest pain: not always a cardiac problem. *J Musculoskel Med*. 1993;10:37.
21. Mukerji B, Alpert MA, Mukerji G. Musculoskeletal causes of chest pain. *Hosp Med*. 1994;11:26–39.
22. Heinz GJ, Javala DC. Slipped rib syndrome: diagnosis using the "hooking maneuver." *JAMA*. 1977;237:794.
23. Bennet RM. Nonarticular rheumatism and spondyloarthropathies—similarities and differences. *Postgrad Med*. 1990;87:97–104.
24. Wolfe F, Smyth HA, Yunus MB, et al. The American College of Rheumatology 1990 criteria for the classification of fibromyalgia: report of the Multicenter Criteria Committee. *Arthritis Rheum*. 1990;33:160–172.
25. Janssens JP, Vantrappen G. Irritable esophagus. *Am J Med*. 1992;92(5A):27S.
26. Assey ME. The puzzle of normal coronary arteries in the patient with chest pain: what to do? *Clin Cardiol*. 1993;16:170.
27. Clouse RE, Lustman PJ. Psychiatric illness and contraction abnormalities of the esophagus. *N Engl J Med*. 1983;309:1337.
28. Lynn RB. Mechanisms of esophageal pain. *Am J Med*. 1992;92:11S.
29. Browning TH, Earnest DL, Balint JS. Diagnosis of chest pain of esophageal origin: a guideline of the Patient Care Committee of the American Gastroenterology Association. *Dig Dis*. 1990;35:289.

CHAPTER 40

Palpitations

CONTEXT

Although patients may not describe their complaints as palpitations, they may describe an uncomfortable awareness of the heart pounding, fluttering, stopping, skipping a beat, or racing. It is important to note that, although this would logically suggest a structural heart problem, the majority of cases represent physiologic reactions or normal fluctuations perceived as abnormal, or are augmented by psychologic overlay.[1] One study suggests that approximately 16% of outpatients present with a complaint of palpitations.[2] This percentage is likely less in the chiropractic setting. The role of the chiropractor is somewhat limited if an electrocardiogram (ECG) is not available in-office; however, defining the patient's concerns often may reveal an obvious benign cause or suggest the appropriate referral for further evaluation.

There is great variation in an individual's ability to perceive heart rate and rhythm. Common augmenting effects of normal heart activity include a quiet environment (more obvious when going to bed), lying on the left side with the ear against the mattress (sound transmitted through the mattress), and a conduction hearing problem (augments sound in the involved ear). Conditions that cause an increased stroke volume, such as regurgitant murmurs, functional hyperfunction as occurs with anemia, thyrotoxicosis, and hypertension, may augment the sensation of a palpitation due to cardiac movement. Although it may seem logical that an arrhythmia could be perceived as a palpitation, many patients do not "feel" the arrhythmic occurrence. When patients with palpitations were monitored over 24 hours with an ECG, an arrhythmia was found in a range of 39% to 85% of patients.[3–7] Only about 15% of patients' arrhythmias correlate with a complaint of palpitations. When not correlated, palpitations are unlikely to be due to cardiac pathology.

GENERAL STRATEGY

History

- Obtain a more defined description of the complaint (heart racing, pounding, stopping, etc.).
- Determine the timing and frequency with relation to exercise, stress, medication intake, and environment (eg, more in a quiet place versus any environment).
- Determine whether there are any related symptoms or signs (chest pain, presyncope, syncope, diaphoresis).
- Determine any past evaluation or diagnosis of the complaint and any coexisting diagnoses (ie, diabetes, hyperthyroidism, coronary artery disease, anemia, depression, panic disorder).

Evaluation

- Evaluate through auscultation, blood pressure measurement, and a 12-lead ECG.
- Laboratory testing should be reserved for patients suspected of having an underlying electrolyte, anemic, hypoglycemic, or endocrine abnormality.

Management

- Referral for further testing should be made with symptomatic patients (chest pain, syncope/presyncope) or asymptomatic patients who are suspected of having an underlying conduction or structural cardiac abnormality.
- The remainder of patients, therefore, will have an identifiable benign problem that can be modified or elimi-

nated, such as by eliminating caffeine use or recreational drug use, or will have no identifiable problem. Psychologic referral may be necessary for some of the remaining patients.

RELEVANT ANATOMY AND PHYSIOLOGY

Normal transmission of the pacemaking impulse from the sinoatrial (SA) node to the atrioventricular (AV) node and continuing propagation to the bundle of His and Purkinje fibers is reliant on autonomic nervous system integrity, proper electrolyte balance, proper blood supply, absence of accessory neural pathways, and nonpathologic cardiac structure. Generally, dysfunctional transmission is due to disorders of impulse formation/automaticity, abnormal conduction, reentry, and "triggered" activity. Cardiac cells have an inherent ability to act as a pacemaker. When this occurs, ectopic generation of impulses is possible, leading to flutter, fibrillation, and reentry phenomena. Impulse blockage, often due to organic disease, electrolyte imbalance, or the effects of medication, leads to various degrees of heart block in which impulse propagation from the AV node to the ventricles is prevented.

Reentry is one of the most common causes of arrhythmias, causing tachycardias, premature beats, and atrial flutter. Reentry occurs when an impulse is transmitted to a neural fork in the road, which allows travel down one path only. The signal participates in normal activation yet continues to travel in a circuit back to (retrograde transmission) the blocked path. Since blockage is antegrade only, this circle-around-the-back impulse is able to reenter the original open path and cause restimulation.

EVALUATION

History

Identify the patient who needs further work-up, such as the following:

- any patient with symptoms such as chest pain or syncope/presyncope
- any patient who has frequent attacks or attacks with exercise
- any patient with known cardiac disease or an immediate family member who died of cardiac disease before age 50 years

Also determine the following:

- any relationship to eating, exercise, or stress/anxiety
- any relationship to medications or ingestion of stimulants
- whether the patient has been diagnosed with or has symptoms of metabolic disorders involving diabetes, hypo- or hyperthyroidism, or depression/anxiety

Patients may describe their concerns many different ways. One study indicated that when patients used the descriptors *racing* or *pounding*, it was unlikely that there was an underlying associated arrhythmia.[8] When patients described the sensation as heart stopping, however, there was a high correlation with an ECG documentation of preventricular premature contractions. A description of an irregular heartbeat or fluttering was often associated with an associated arrhythmia. Neck palpitations or poundings are caused by simultaneous contraction of the atria and ventricles, which leads to reflux into the superior vena cava. This occurs with some forms of supraventricular and ventricular tachycardias. Ventricular tachycardias are more likely to cause symptoms such as syncope; palpitations are not often reported, probably because of the associated small stroke volume.

It is often difficult for the patient to describe palpitations with respect to regularity or rate. As few as one third of patients were able to do so in a study by Reid.[9] His solution was to have the patient tap out what is felt. Harvey,[10] however, suggests that the examiner simulate different arrhythmias in a sequential manner on the patient's chest. He starts with a quick tap followed by a pause to simulate a premature beat. If this does not represent the patient's sensation, a simulation of bigeminy or trigeminy is attempted. Failure to reproduce the correct simulation sequences requires further simulation of other tachycardias. The first is a simulated sinus tachycardia, similar to what occurs with normal stress. The tapping is gradually accelerated to about 100 beats per minute, keeping the rhythm regular. The examiner describes this to the patient as the sensation he or she might feel in an anxious scenario. If this is not the correct simulation, faster tapping is employed, first with a regular rhythm, then an irregular rhythm, in an attempt to simulate paroxysmal sinus tachycardia and atrial fibrillation, respectively. There are no studies to indicate the reliability or validity of this approach, yet it would seem to assist in narrowing the myriad of possibilities in some patients.

A fruitful avenue of questioning is whether there is overuse of drugs such as alcohol, caffeine, tobacco (smoking or snuff), amphetamines, over-the-counter cold/sinus/allergy medications (ephedrine), or illicit stimulants such as cocaine. Ironically, antiarrhythmic medication can eliminate or facilitate arrhythmias. Facilitation may occur with class I agents, which prolong the Q-T interval, predisposing the patient to ventricular tachycardias. Other cardiac or antihypertensive agents may precipitate bradycardia or tachycardias. It is important to warn patients that sudden withdrawal from these medications may cause arrhythmias and to consult with the prescribing physician before attempting to discontinue medication.

General assumptions may be helpful in discriminating between benign and clinically significant causes of palpitations. Often information by which to make these assumptions is not available at the time of evaluation; however, a well-trained patient may be able to provide these data with any future events.

- If a tachycardia is a possible cause have the patient palpate the pulse during an attack. If the pulse is regular with a rate greater than 160 beats per minute, it is likely to be supraventricular.
- If a tachycardia is a possible cause have the patient perform a Valsalva maneuver or press lightly over the carotid sinus to determine whether it abates an attack. If it does, the cause is likely supraventricular (the patient may report that induced vomiting eliminates the tachycardia, also suggestive of a supraventricular origin).

The relationship to eating may be helpful. If the arrhythmias occur several hours after eating (often late afternoon and early evening) reactive hypoglycemia is possible and can be evaluated via glucose tolerance testing. A similar presentation with diabetic use of insulin occurs at the time of maximum insulin activity. Both types of hypoglycemic responses often are accompanied with sweating and tremors and are often supraventricular in origin. A somewhat similar presentation may occur in the anxious patient, who often complains of difficulty breathing, dizziness, and paresthesias of the hands or face. These are associated with hyperventilation, which may or may not be apparent to the patient.

The relationship to exercise may also be a helpful discriminator with premature ventricular contractions. Palpitations that increase with exercise are likely to be cardiac in origin and require stress testing. Those that decrease with exercise are generally benign. ECG documentation and echocardiography is warranted, however, if the "palpitations" are frequent to rule out hypertrophic cardiomyopathy and other life-threatening conditions.

When otherwise healthy patients describe palpitations as rare or infrequent and there are no associated symptoms, the patient probably is not in need of further work-up. At this point in the evaluation, the patient may be reassured that it is unlikely that any significant problem exists. Patient monitoring of the problem; keeping a diary of events with the recommendation to return if the frequency of occurrence increases or to seek medical attention if there are any associated symptoms such as chest pain, dizziness, or fainting; and taking the pulse at the time of the next attack are usually sufficient.

Examination

It is unlikely that the patient will have the sensation of palpitations at the time of examination. If palpitations do occur, palpation for heart rate and rhythm and, if possible, an ECG would be helpful discriminators between cardiac and noncardiac causes. Some common findings on ECG are listed in Table 40–1. If the heart rate, rhythm, and ECG are normal, a cardiac condition is unlikely. Atrial fibrillation may be suspected if the heart rate is grossly irregular and a pulse deficit or auscultated beat that fails to present peripherally is detected. Examination of the jugular venous pulse is subtle; however, it may provide information regarding dissociation (atrial and ventricular activation are independent of each other). If the atria and ventricle contract simultaneously, blood is refluxed by atrial contraction against a closed tricuspid valve, which results in a large or canon A wave at the jugular vein. This may occur with ventricular tachycardia. In patients with a slow heart rate, canon A waves may suggest heart block. Large A waves with each heartbeat occur with retrograde AV, junctional or ventricular tachycardia. No A waves are present during atrial fibrillation because of inefficient atrial contraction.

Being less fortunate, the physician is more often indirectly evaluating cardiovascular function in a patient who is not at the time of presentation symptomatic, in an attempt to identify a potential cause of the patient's complaint. When other systemic problems are suggested by the history, a search for clues to hyperthyroidism, anemia, or sick sinus syndrome should be followed.

Laboratory testing is valuable when a specific suspicion is generated by the history. The following are examples:

- hypoglycemia—5-hour glucose tolerance testing
- diabetes—serum glucose testing (>140 mg/dL on 2 lab tests)
- illicit drug use—drug screen
- thyroid dysfunction—ultrasensitive thyrotropin (TSH)
- anemia—complete blood count (CBC) or anemia panel
- volume depletion from vomiting, diarrhea, or diuresis—electrolyte panel

When the initial evaluation is unrevealing, it is necessary to evaluate with a Holter monitor. The doctor attempts to correlate any symptom complaints temporally with any abnormal electrophysiologic events. If no correlation is found, the patient's problem presumably is not cardiac. For patients with less frequent yet troublesome events, a cardiac event recorder is given to the patient for a period of 1 month. The patient is taught to activate the device anytime he or she feels symptoms. The information can be transmitted or stored for analysis. Some devices will store information just prior to activation to catch premature events.

Table 40–1 Arrhythmias

Classification/Pathology	*ECG Findings*	*Treatment*
Arrhythmias Originating in the Atrium		
Sinus Bradycardia: Increased parasympathetic (vagal) tone causes heart to beat at < 60 beats per minute. Depolarization originates from sinoatrial node (hence the name sinus).	Slow, but regular rate on rhythm strip.	Not treated if asymptomatic. If patient develops angina, hypotension, heart failure or other symptoms, treated with **Atropine** **Isoproterenol** **Epinephrine** (Each of these drugs induces sympathetic predominance.)
Sinus Tachycardia: Increased sympathetic tone causes heart to race (100–160 beats per minute). Depolarization originates from sinoatrial node.	Rapid, but regular rate on rhythm strip.	Not treated if asymptomatic. If treatment is necessary: **Propranolol** (because it decreases catecholamine-induced firing rate of SA node and slows conduction through AV node.)
Multifocal Atrial Tachycardia: Depolarization originates from several atrial foci at irregular intervals. Rate is rapid (100–200 beats per minute) and irregular.	P waves are present, but are morphologically different from one another. P-R interval varies.	Correct precipitating factor(s). Once underlying cause is corrected, may initiate: **Verapamil** **Quinidine** (Both slow conduction velocity of cells that are abnormally pacing.)
Premature Atrial Depolarization (PAT): Heart beats prematurely because a focus of atrial cells fires spontaneously before the SA node is ready to fire.	Interruption of regular rhythm by an early P wave. P wave may be followed by a normal QRS if the SA node and ventricle have had time to repolarize.	Not treated if asymptomatic. If symptomatic, treated with Class Ia antiarrhythmics: **Quinidine** **Procainamide** **Disopyramide**
Atrial Flutter: Ectopic focus of atrial cells generates 250–350 impulses per minute. The ventricle responds to every second or third impulse. Both atrial and ventricular rhythm are regular.	Series of 2–4 closely spaced P waves followed by a normal QRS complex.	1) Control ventricular response by suppressing AV node conduction. Suitable agents are: **Digoxin** **Propranolol** **Verapamil** 2) Convert atrial rhythm to sinus rhythm **IV Procainamide**
Atrial Fibrillation: Multiple ectopic foci of atrial cells generate 350–450 impulses per minute. The ventricle responds to an occasional impulse. Both atrial and ventricular rhythm are irregular.	P waves can not be discerned. Baseline is irregular with unevenly spaced QRS complexes.	1) If hemodynamically stable, control ventricular response by suppressing AV node: **Digoxin** **Propranolol** **Verapamil** 2) Convert to sinus rhythm: **Ia antiarrhythmics** **IV Procainamide**

continues

Table 40–1 continued

Classification/Pathology	*ECG Findings*	*Treatment*
Arrhythmias Involving the AV Junction		
AV Reentry: AV node is split into a pathway that conducts toward the ventricle and a pathway that conducts the impulse back to the atrium. Reentry of the impulse into the atrium causes the atrium and ventricle to contract simultaneously.	Generally normal QRS complexes following normal P waves. The inverted P wave (retrograde atrial contraction) is buried in the QRS. Rate is 150–250/minute.	Carotid sinus massage may suppress tachycardia by increasing vagal tone. Alternatively: **Verapamil** **Propranolol** **Digoxin**
Wolff-Parkinson-White: A strip of conducting tissue (other than the AV node) connects the atrium and ventricle. Impulses reaching the ventricle via the AV node circle back to the atrium via the accessory pathway. Alternatively, the circuit may be reversed.	Each P wave is followed rapidly by a QRS. A "delta wave" leads into the QRS. Rate can exceed 300 beats/minute.	If symptomatic, either slow AV conduction with: **Verapamil** **Propranolol** **Digoxin** or slow accessory pathway conduction: **Lidocaine** **Procainamide**
Arrhythmias Originating in the Ventricle		
Ventricular Premature Depolarization: Spontaneous depolarization of ectopic focus in the ventricle. Considered benign if fewer than six per minute.	Wide, tall QRS complexes that are not associated with a P wave. A prominent T wave often points in the opposite direction as the QRS complex.	Usually not treated if asymptomatic. If treatment is necessary: **IV Lidocaine** **IV Procainamide** Long-term suppression may be achieved with: **Class I agents**
Ventricular Tachycardia: Usually secondary to reentry circuit. Both AV reentry and Wolff-Parkinson-White may progress to ventricular tachycardia.	Wide QRS complexes with abnormal S-T segment and T wave deflections (opposite in direction to QRS). AV dissociation and right bundle branch block are often associated.	Acute treatment involves one of the following: **IV Lidocaine** **IV Procainamide** **IV Bretylium** Oral drugs are used for chronic therapy **Quinidine** **Procainamide** **Disopyramide** **Flecanide, Encainide, Tocainide, Mexiletine**
Ventricular Fibrillation: Erratic discharge from many ectopic foci in the ventricle. Rate is 350–450 beats/min. Rhythm is irregular.	Completely erratic. Cannot distinguish normal waves or complexes.	Life threatening. If cardioversion fails, **Epinephrine** is given prior to defibrillation. If this fails combine **IV Lidocaine** and defibrillation. Either additional doses of lidocaine or **Bretylium** can then be used with defibrillation.

Source: Reprinted with permission from J. Olson, *Clinical Pharmacology Made Ridiculously Simple,* pp. 74–75, © 1994, MedMaster.

Patients who have historical or physical examination clues of mitral valve prolapse or structural problems often will be referred for echocardiography. Those patients with exertion-induced palpitations are sent for stress testing. Invasive electrodiagnostic studies are rarely needed to diagnosis the cause of palpitations; however, patients with suspected anomalous pathways or underlying cardiac structural abnormalities may be candidates.

MANAGEMENT

If the chiropractor either does not have direct access to ECG with medical interpretation or there is evidence of underlying systemic or cardiovascular disease, referral to a cardiologist is recommended. There is a general consensus that medical treatment of arrhythmias is not warranted with the following asymptomatic presentations:

- unsustained supraventricular tachycardia
- unsustained ventricular tachycardia in the absence of structural cardiac disease
- Wolff-Parkinson-White syndrome

Algorithms

Algorithms for evaluation of pulse rate, ECG for palpitations, and palpitations in general are presented in Figures 40–1 to 40–3.

POSSIBLE CAUSES OF PALPITATIONS

PAROXYSMAL SINUS TACHYCARDIA

Classic Presentation

Patients report a sudden, unprovoked, onset of a racing heart. This split-second onset lasts for 15 minutes to several hours and just as suddenly stops. Other symptoms may be lightheadedness, dyspnea, or weakness; syncope is rare. Depending on the cause and length, atypical chest pain may be felt. Patients are often young, with no cardiac pathology. Heart rate is regular and occurs at 160 to 220 beats per minute.

Cause

The most common reason for paroxysmal attacks is reentry, which ironically can be initiated or abated by a premature atrial contraction (PAC) or a premature ventricular contraction (PVC). This anomalous circuit may involve the SA, AV, or accessory pathways. Approximately 33% of patients have these accessory bundles in the ventricles. Mainly in men, Wolff-Parkinson-White (WPW) syndrome should be considered. WPW syndrome may also cause atrial fibrillation or flutter. In women, consideration of mitral valve prolapse syndrome is warranted. In the elderly, sick sinus syndrome should be considered, where a "tachy-brady syndrome" is possible.

Evaluation

It is difficult to catch these often short-lived attacks clinically. ECG evidence is often absent, but WPW syndrome may demonstrate a delta wave or other combination of findings. Mitral valve prolapse (MVP) syndrome usually has no associated findings. Echocardiography for MVP and stress testing for WPW may be necessary.

Management

Management is largely dependent on the underlying cause. MVP and WPW are often monitored if there are no associated symptoms or findings of underlying cardiac pathology. Sick sinus syndrome or drug-induced paroxysmal tachycardia is managed medically.

Figure 40–1
PULSE RATE—ALGORITHM.

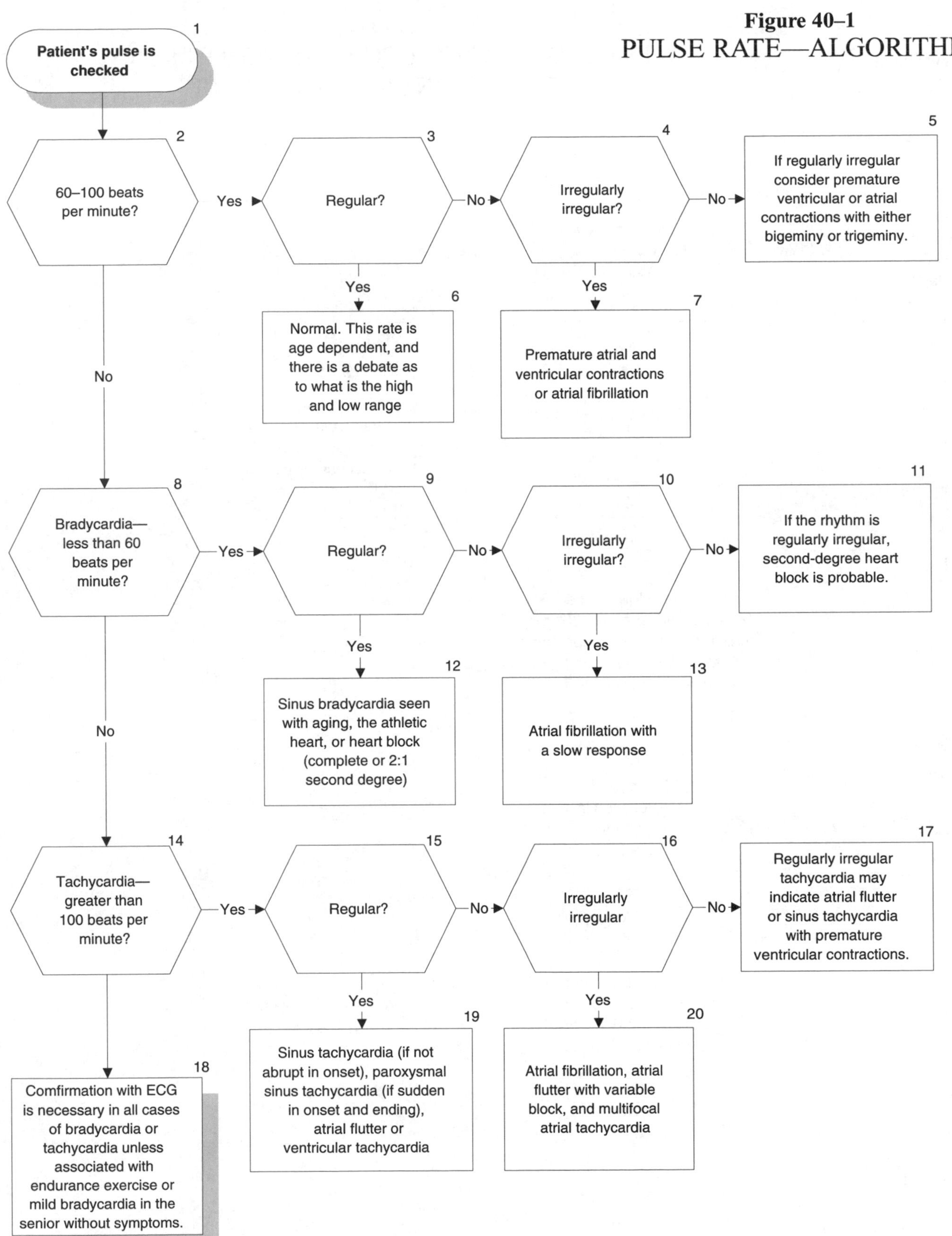

1
Patient's pulse is checked
2
60–100 beats per minute?
Yes
3
Regular?
No
4
Irregularly irregular?
No
5
If regularly irregular consider premature ventricular or atrial contractions with either bigeminy or trigeminy.
Yes
6
Normal. This rate is age dependent, and there is a debate as to what is the high and low range
Yes
7
Premature atrial and ventricular contractions or atrial fibrillation
No
8
Bradycardia—less than 60 beats per minute?
Yes
9
Regular?
No
10
Irregularly irregular?
No
11
If the rhythm is regularly irregular, second-degree heart block is probable.
Yes
12
Sinus bradycardia seen with aging, the athletic heart, or heart block (complete or 2:1 second degree)
Yes
13
Atrial fibrillation with a slow response
No
14
Tachycardia—greater than 100 beats per minute?
Yes
15
Regular?
No
16
Irregularly irregular
No
17
Regularly irregular tachycardia may indicate atrial flutter or sinus tachycardia with premature ventricular contractions.
Yes
19
Sinus tachycardia (if not abrupt in onset), paroxysmal sinus tachycardia (if sudden in onset and ending), atrial flutter or ventricular tachycardia
Yes
20
Atrial fibrillation, atrial flutter with variable block, and multifocal atrial tachycardia
18
Comfirmation with ECG is necessary in all cases of bradycardia or tachycardia unless associated with endurance exercise or mild bradycardia in the senior without symptoms.

Note: Abnormalities need further evaluation with ECG or Holter monitoring. With the exception of sinus tachycardia (due to pain, fever, exercise, anxiety, etc.) all other causes require medical evaluation.

Figure 40–2
12-LEAD RESTING ECG EVALUATION FOR "PALPITATIONS"—ALGORITHM.

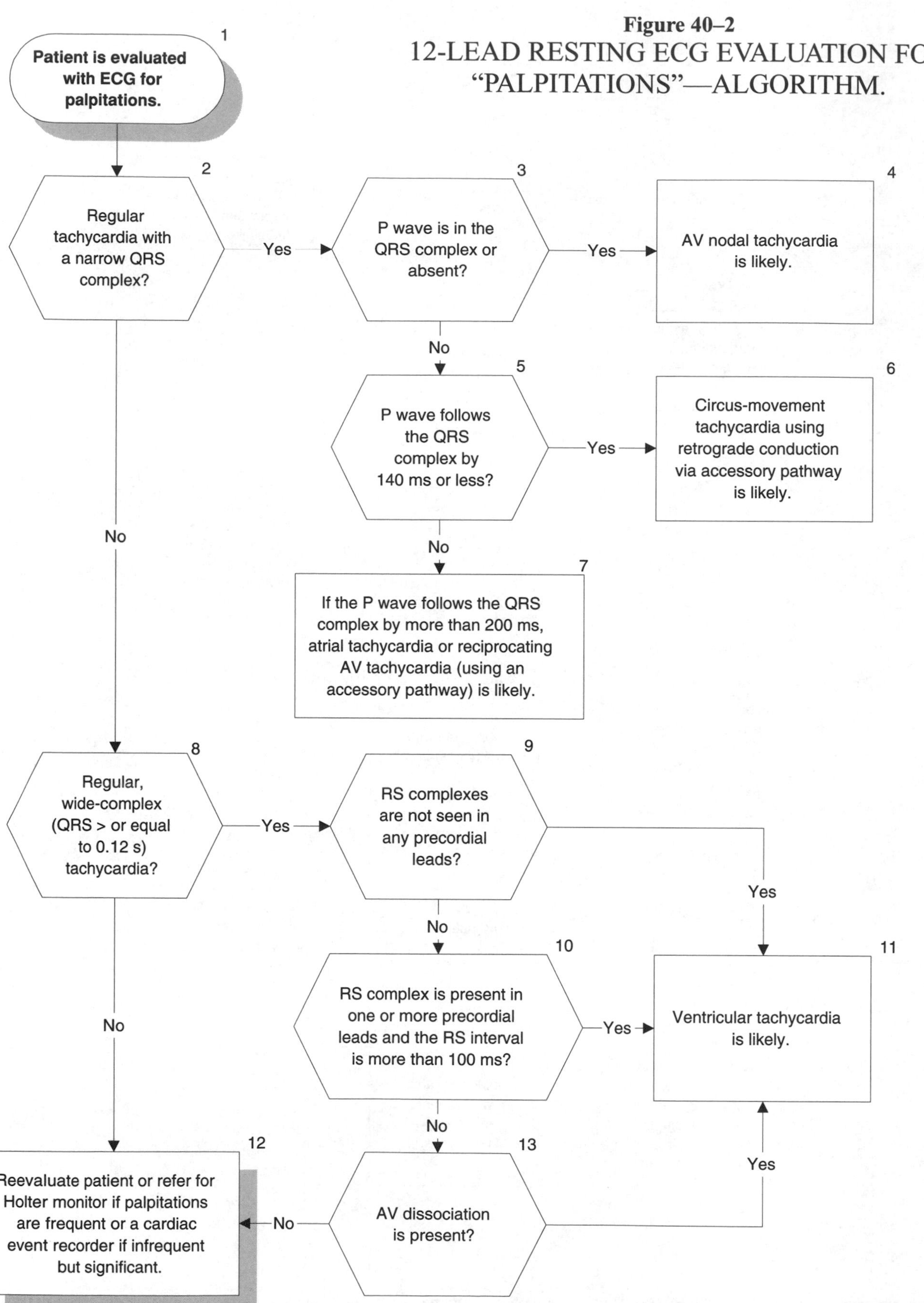

1
Patient is evaluated with ECG for palpitations.
2
Regular tachycardia with a narrow QRS complex?
Yes
3
P wave is in the QRS complex or absent?
Yes
4
AV nodal tachycardia is likely.
No
5
P wave follows the QRS complex by 140 ms or less?
Yes
6
Circus-movement tachycardia using retrograde conduction via accessory pathway is likely.
No
7
If the P wave follows the QRS complex by more than 200 ms, atrial tachycardia or reciprocating AV tachycardia (using an accessory pathway) is likely.
No
8
Regular, wide-complex (QRS > or equal to 0.12 s) tachycardia?
Yes
9
RS complexes are not seen in any precordial leads?
Yes
No
10
RS complex is present in one or more precordial leads and the RS interval is more than 100 ms?
Yes
11
Ventricular tachycardia is likely.
No
13
AV dissociation is present?
Yes
No
No
12
Reevaluate patient or refer for Holter monitor if palpitations are frequent or a cardiac event recorder if infrequent but significant.

Figure 40–3
PALPITATIONS—ALGORITHM.

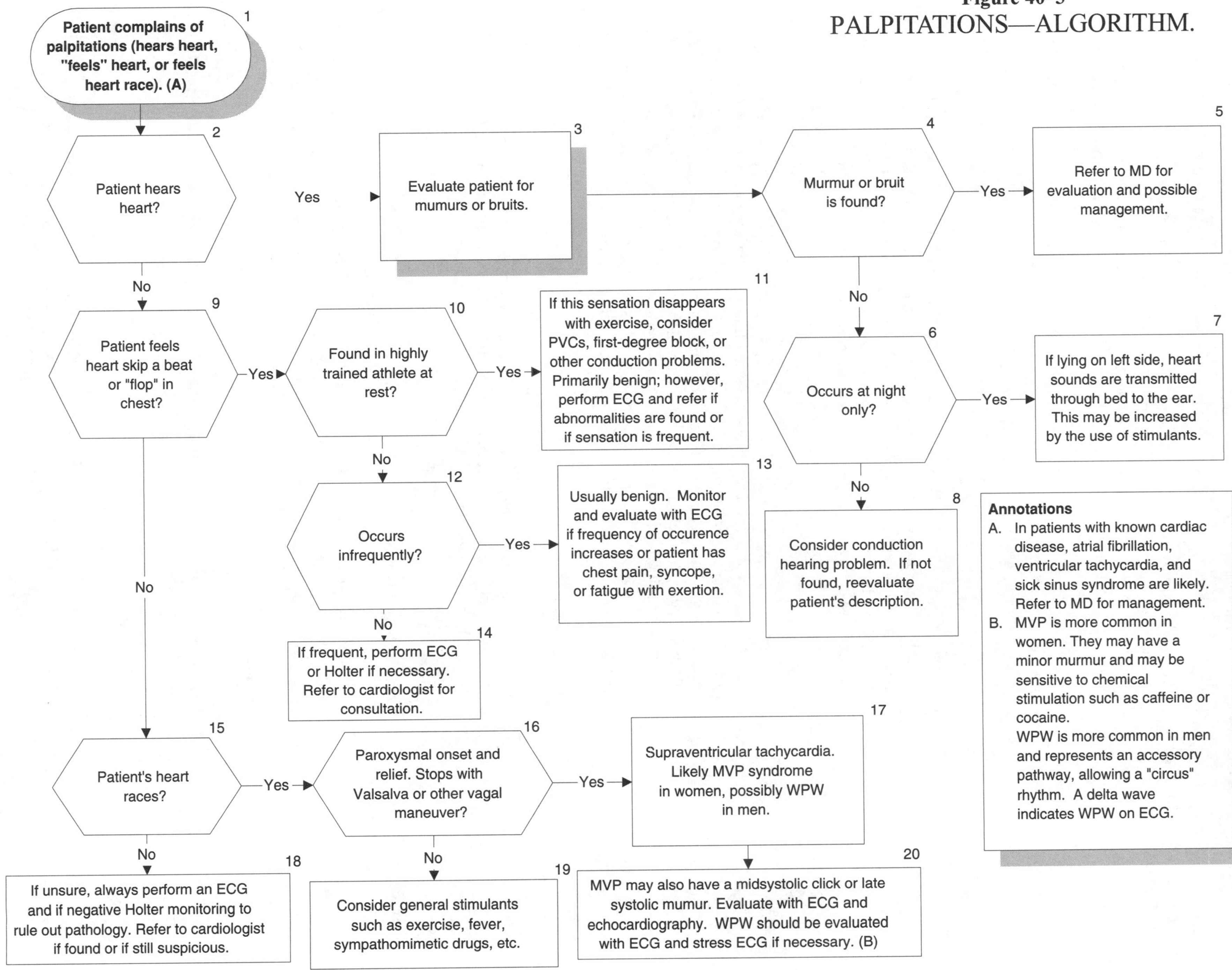

1 Patient complains of palpitations (hears heart, "feels" heart, or feels heart race). (A)
2 Patient hears heart?
Yes
3 Evaluate patient for mumurs or bruits.
4 Murmur or bruit is found?
Yes
5 Refer to MD for evaluation and possible management.
No
6 Occurs at night only?
Yes
7 If lying on left side, heart sounds are transmitted through bed to the ear. This may be increased by the use of stimulants.
No
8 Consider conduction hearing problem. If not found, reevaluate patient's description.
No
9 Patient feels heart skip a beat or "flop" in chest?
Yes
10 Found in highly trained athlete at rest?
Yes
11 If this sensation disappears with exercise, consider PVCs, first-degree block, or other conduction problems. Primarily benign; however, perform ECG and refer if abnormalities are found or if sensation is frequent.
No
12 Occurs infrequently?
Yes
13 Usually benign. Monitor and evaluate with ECG if frequency of occurence increases or patient has chest pain, syncope, or fatigue with exertion.
No
14 If frequent, perform ECG or Holter if necessary. Refer to cardiologist for consultation.
No
15 Patient's heart races?
Yes
16 Paroxysmal onset and relief. Stops with Valsalva or other vagal maneuver?
Yes
17 Supraventricular tachycardia. Likely MVP syndrome in women, possibly WPW in men.
20 MVP may also have a midsystolic click or late systolic mumur. Evaluate with ECG and echocardiography. WPW should be evaluated with ECG and stress ECG if necessary. (B)
No
19 Consider general stimulants such as exercise, fever, sympathomimetic drugs, etc.
No
18 If unsure, always perform an ECG and if negative Holter monitoring to rule out pathology. Refer to cardiologist if found or if still suspicious.
Annotations
A. In patients with known cardiac disease, atrial fibrillation, ventricular tachycardia, and sick sinus syndrome are likely. Refer to MD for management.
B. MVP is more common in women. They may have a minor murmur and may be sensitive to chemical stimulation such as caffeine or cocaine.
WPW is more common in men and represents an accessory pathway, allowing a "circus" rhythm. A delta wave indicates WPW on ECG.

Key: PVC, Premature ventricular contraction; MVP, mitral valve prolapse; WPW, Wolff-Parkinson-White syndrome.

MITRAL VALVE PROLAPSE SYNDROME

Classic Presentation

Although MVP may occur at any age and in either sex, most commonly the patient is a woman of childbearing years who complains of palpitations, easy fatigability, or dyspnea. On rare occasions chest pain may be felt. The patient is often thin; more than half of patients may have associated chest wall deformities, including scoliosis, straight back (loss of kyphosis), or pectus excavatum.

Cause

The cause is unknown. However, there is usually one of several features, including redundant mitral valve leaflets, elongated chordae tendinaea, an enlarged mitral annulus, and an abnormal ventricular wall motion. MVP is associated with other conditions such as Marfan's syndrome, atrial septal defect, and coronary artery disease. Apparently, MVP patients have decreased parasympathetic and increased α-adrenergic tone.[11]

Evaluation

As mentioned above, thoracic cage abnormalities may be evident on observation. The cardiac exam may reveal midsystolic click(s) and a late systolic murmur best heard at the apex. These findings are often intermittent; they are not consistent. Maneuvers that may help are standing (decreased ventricular size), which moves the click and murmur closer to S1, and hand gripping or squatting (increased ventricular size), which moves the click and murmur toward late systole. A combination of M-mode and two-dimensional echocardiography will usually demonstrate abnormal valve movement.

Management

Patients who are asymptomatic or have infrequent attacks of tachycardias are usually watched, yet not medically managed. The only recommendation is prophylactic antibiotics for dental work to avoid the risk of subacute bacterial endocarditis. Those with chest pain are sometimes given β-blockers.

WOLFF-PARKINSON-WHITE SYNDROME

Classic Presentation

The WPW syndrome is similar in presentation to MVP, except the patient is more often male. The patient presents with a complaint of palpitations that occur suddenly and without provocation. Twenty to thirty percent of patients have atrial flutter or fibrillation.[1]

Cause

Anomalous pathways connecting the atria to ventricles (Kent bundles) allow reentry-based tachycardias.

Evaluation

The primary diagnostic tool is the ECG, which may demonstrate a delta wave. ECG criteria based on the QRS complex morphology seems to be a more sensitive approach. St. George's and Skeberi's methods are the most accurate.

Management

Given the natural history of WPW in most patients, ablation of the anomalous pathways is reserved for those with severe disease reflected in symptomatology and ECG criteria. Narrow-wave (antegrade conduction through the node) reentry WPW is managed pharmacologically, whereas patients with atrial flutter or fibrillation with RR cycle length are at risk for sudden death and are treated with radiofrequency catheter ablation therapy. This approach is 90% effective with antegrade conduction. Failure of ablation therapy forces surgical correction of the problem.[12]

REFERENCES

1. Weitz HH, Weinstock PJ. Approach to the patient with palpitations. *Med Clin North Am.* 1995;79:449–456.
2. Kroenke K, Arrington M, Mangelsdorff A. The prevalence of symptoms in medical outpatients and the adequacy of therapy. *Arch Intern Med.* 1990;150:1685–1689.
3. Clark P, Glasser S, Spoto E. Arrhythmias detected by ambulatory monitoring. *Chest.* 1980;77:722–725.
4. Goldberg A, Rafferty E, Cashman P. Ambulatory ECG records in patients with transient cerebral attacks of palpitations. *Br Med J.* 1975;4:569–571.
5. Goodman R, Capone R, Most A. Arrhythmia surveillance by transtelephonic monitoring. *Am Heart J.* 1979;98:459–464.
6. Lipski J, Cohen L, Espinoz J, et al. Value of Holter monitoring in assessing cardiac arrhythmias in symptomatic patients. *Am J Cardiol.* 1976;37:102–107.
7. Zeldis S, Levine BJ, Michelson EL, et al. Cardiovascular complaints: correlation with cardiac arrhythmias on 25-hour ECG monitoring. *Chest.* 1980;78:456–462.
8. Barsky A, Cleary P, Barnett M, et al. The accuracy of symptom reporting by patients complaining of palpations. *Am J Med.* 1994;97:214–221.
9. Reid P. Indications for intracardiac eletrophysiologic studies in patients with unexplained palpitations. *Circulation.* 1987;75(suppl 3):154–158.
10. Harvey W. Cardiac pearls. *Dis Mon.* 1994;40:41–113.
11. Fontana ME. Mitral valve prolapse and the mitral valve prolapse syndrome. *Curr Probl Cardiol.* 1991;16:311.
12. Arai A, Kron J. Current management of the Wolff-Parkinson-White syndrome. *West J Med.* 1990;152:383.

CHAPTER 41

Dyspnea (Difficulty Breathing)

CONTEXT

Difficulty breathing (dyspnea) is usually a chronic complaint in the context of a chiropractic office setting. Patients are more likely to present with "acceptable" nondisabling dyspnea or a past history of paroxysmal dyspnea suggestive of asthma. Acute distressing dyspnea is usually due to a severe asthma attack, myocardial infarct, or pulmonary embolism.

Although there are a number of disorders that have dyspnea as one of the complaint symptoms, two thirds of patients with dyspnea as the main complaint have either a pulmonary or a cardiac disorder.[1] It is important then to differentiate cardiopulmonary disease from other causes in an effort to determine referrable disorders from those that are manageable or comanageable.

GENERAL STRATEGY

History

Determine the following:

- what the patient means when he or she complains of difficulty breathing: painful inspiration, tightness in the chest, unable to catch breath, etc. (Exhibit 41–1)
- whether it is positionally related: worse while lying, lying on the side, or standing
- whether it is related only to exertion, the degree of exertion, and the general fitness level of the patient
- whether there was an antecedent respiratory infection
- whether the patient has a diagnosis or signs of depression
- whether the patient was in a setting that produced anxiety prior to the onset of dyspnea
- whether the patient had any previous calf pain and whether he or she was either immobilized for a long period or is taking birth control pills

Evaluation

- Auscultate the heart and lungs listening for any murmurs or adventitial sounds (rales, rhonchi, or wheezes)
- Order a chest film; if rib fracture is suspected order anterior-posterior (AP) and oblique views of the involved area.
- If available, perform spirometry to determine pulmonary function (a simple, yet less accurate, monitoring approach is a peak flow meter).
- Order a general screening lab test to determine whether the red blood cell (RBC)/hematocrit (anemia), blood gases, and glucose (diabetes) levels are normal.

Management

- Refer the patient if pulmonary embolism, pneumothorax, pulmonary hypertension, pleurisy, infection, or tumor is suspected.
- Possible comanagement conditions include asthma, emphysema, congestive heart failure, and rib fractures or the myofascial/subluxation-related elements of these conditions.
- Manage "cracked" ribs (rest and time), vertebral or rib subluxations (chiropractic manipulation), and myofascial disorders (myofascial-release techniques or massage and stretching).
- Management of asthma is controversial, yet some practitioners report control with chiropractic manipulation;

Exhibit 41–1 Clarification of Difficulty Breathing

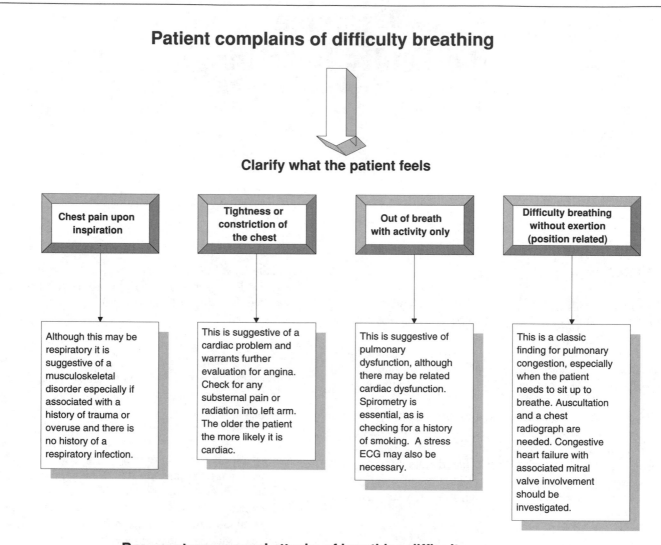

Patient complains of difficulty breathing

Clarify what the patient feels

Chest pain upon inspiration

Although this may be respiratory it is suggestive of a musculoskeletal disorder especially if associated with a history of trauma or overuse and there is no history of a respiratory infection.

Tightness or constriction of the chest

This is suggestive of a cardiac problem and warrants further evaluation for angina. Check for any substernal pain or radiation into left arm. The older the patient the more likely it is cardiac.

Out of breath with activity only

This is suggestive of pulmonary dysfunction, although there may be related cardiac dysfunction. Spirometry is essential, as is checking for a history of smoking. A stress ECG may also be necessary.

Difficulty breathing without exertion (position related)

This is a classic finding for pulmonary congestion, especially when the patient needs to sit up to breathe. Auscultation and a chest radiograph are needed. Congestive heart failure with associated mitral valve involvement should be investigated.

Recurrent paroxysmal attacks of breathing difficulty are characteristic of asthma and hyperactive airway disease. Both should be evaluated with spirometry and possibly bronchoprovocation challenge if necessary.

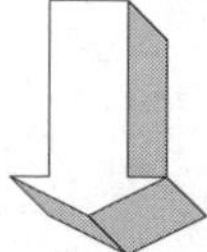

A sudden onset of difficulty breathing associated with chest pain is suggestive of pulmonary embolism, myocardial infarction, or pneumothorax (spontaneous). This demands immediate medical evaluation.

the issues are medication changes in those diagnosed with asthma prior to presentation and unavailability of medication in the event of an acute attack with those who have not received medical evaluation and prescription.

RELEVANT ANATOMY AND PHYSIOLOGY

Dyspnea is a conscious sensation and as such is a variable impression based on an individual's comparison to what is considered normal. In other words, although someone may feel an increased workload going up a flight of stairs, he or she would not report this as dyspnea unless it was felt to be an "unexpected" amount of effort. A variety of tissues with different receptors may convey information that is eventually interpreted as dyspnea; however, it is not clear how much each contributes. It does seem clear that respiratory muscle contractions play a predominant role. Following are some possible factors.

Acid-base balance serves as the primary stimulus for ventilation; however, it is not clear how much decrease in oxygen or increase in partial pressure of carbon dioxide (Pco_2) contributes to the sensation of dyspnea.[2] The carotid bodies sense pH and oxygen/carbon dioxide levels stimulating breathing when levels are perceived as unbalanced. However, hypercapnia associated with breath holding can be eliminated as a stimulus for breathing by neuromuscular blockade.[3] This allows discomfort-free breath holding.

Several intrapulmonary receptors play a role. Irritant and C-fiber receptors react to chemical and physical irritants.[4] Slowly adapting pulmonary stretch receptors respond to large increases in lung volume. This afferent information is carried via autonomic pathways. These receptors may be partially blocked by lidocaine or morphine, decreasing some of the severity of dyspnea.[5] However, patients with heart-lung transplantation (denervated lungs) can still sense dyspnea. Also, bilateral vagal block does not totally eliminate the perception of dyspnea.[6]

The key may lie in the sensory receptors of respiratory muscles. Muscle spindles and tendon organs are found mainly in the intercostal muscles. The diaphragm contains mainly tendon organs. These sensory organs are sensitive to increased muscle work. It appears that acid-base balance and irritant receptor stimulation play a contributory role through stimulation of muscular contraction. The increased muscular effort conveys the sense of dyspnea.[2,3]

Blockage to inspiration occurs with extrathoracic (upper airway) disorders. Blockages by inflammation acutely with anaphylaxis and more subacutely associated with mononucleosis or pertussis are serious causes requiring immediate treatment. Blockage due to foreign body aspiration is also a common serious cause in children and in the immunocompromised. With upper airway obstruction, stridor is often heard if the blockage is not complete. Intrathoracic obstruction has more of an effect on expiratory effort. Blockages from bronchoconstriction, mucosal edema, and mucus production are seen primarily with asthma with some overlapping with other chronic obstructive pulmonary disease (COPD) such as chronic bronchitis and emphysema. When both inspiration and expiration are affected, restrictive lung disorders should be considered. These include intrinsic lung disorders such as pneumonia, fibrotic lung disease, and pulmonary hypertension/edema. Extrathoracic causes of restriction include musculoskeletal disorders such as severe kyphoscoliosis, pectus excavatum, flail chest, and muscular dystrophy. Neurologic depression from central (tumor or stroke) or peripheral (Guillain-Barré, poliomyelitis, or myasthenia gravis) nervous system dysfunction also may cause dyspnea. Myasthenia gravis may simulate cardiac or lung disorders in some patients.[7]

EVALUATION

History

It is important to distinguish between general fatigue and dyspnea. Of course, these two possibilities may overlap; however, with chronic fatigue, depression, or metabolic/endocrine disorders, the patient will likely feel a more constant, yet nonthreatening, sense of dyspnea unless associated with anxiety or hyperventilation.

A patient's description of what he or she means by difficulty breathing, coupled with the context of when this occurs, is often the compass point needed for directing further evaluation.

- Painful breathing—Patients who feel that breathing is difficult solely because of painful restriction on inspiration are likely to have a somatic problem such as a musculoskeletal cause or pleurisy (parietal pleural irritation). This is differentiated by determining whether there was a history of trauma or respiratory infection, respectively. Rib subluxations are often nontraumatic, whereas rib fractures are usually due to direct chest trauma. If the patient has no history of a respiratory infection or trauma, spontaneous pneumothorax should be considered. This disorder occurs without warning and appears to be more common in young, tall men, often after exertion (although it may occur at rest). This disorder is also a possibility in those patients with COPD who develop a sudden, sharp, unilateral chest pain that is worse with inspiration. These same patients may have a rib subluxation due to chronic coughing. Relatively recent additions to the literature are reports of diaphragmatic spasm.[8] This condition will present with an abrupt onset of chest pain and dyspnea with no obvious provocation or triggering event. Some patients will report the ability to eliminate the pain and dyspnea with a forced, full expiratory effort.

- Chest tightness—If a patient complains of chest tightness and/or substernal discomfort or pain, angina should be considered as a strong possibility, especially if relieved by rest (or nitroglycerin). Patients who appear depressed or anxious may complain of a similar sensation. Further questioning regarding emotional context is important.
- Dyspnea at night—Difficulty breathing while sleeping suggests congestive heart failure (CHF)/pulmonary hypertension, or asthma. Patients with CHF often are awakened with dyspnea (paroxysmal nocturnal dyspnea) and find they have to prop themselves up with pillows (redistributes blood and decreases visceral compression on the diaphragm). Patients with asthma may have attacks at around 12 to 4 AM because of changes in sympathetic activity and cortisol levels.
- Dyspnea with exertion—Difficulty breathing with exertion is suggestive of cardiopulmonary or pulmonary disease (especially asthma or hyperactive airway disease). With CHF or pulmonary hypertension, minor effort is enough to bring on shortness of breath. With asthmatics, dyspnea usually occurs after 10 to 15 minutes into intense exercise and/or after exercise in general. The recovery period with CHF and pulmonary hypertension would generally take longer.

If dyspnea appears to be position-related, a clue to underlying causes may be found. Common terms used and conditions associated with position-related dyspnea include the following:

- Trepopnea—occurs in one lateral position; if lying on the involved side improves breathing a pleural effusion or internal lung disorder is likely because of the increased perfusion created by gravity; if breathing is made worse by lying on the same side, a somatic problem such as rib fracture or pleurisy is more likely.
- Orthopnea—occurs when lying supine; it is usually relieved by sitting up and is characteristic of left ventricular failure and sometimes with COPD or weakness of the respiratory muscles.
- Platypnea—occurs in the standing position, is relieved by lying down; this is suggestive of right-to-left shunt in the heart or pulmonary vascular shunting of venous blood.

A history of prolonged immobilization, use of birth control pills, or prior calf pain suggests the possibility of pulmonary embolism, especially in a patient with a mild fever. A history of prolonged smoking would steer the investigation toward COPD. An associated history of a chronic productive cough suggests chronic bronchitis. If the patient appears to be in respiratory distress, having to lean forward to breathe through pursed lips and using the secondary muscles of respiration (like someone who has just finished a race), emphysema is likely. A history of smoking with a recent history of weight loss warrants a suspicion of lung cancer. It is important to determine prolonged occupational exposure to various dust particulates in an effort to uncover a possible pneumoconiosis such as asbestosis or silicosis.

When dyspnea is gradual and constant, progressive cardiac or pulmonary disease is likely. Other possibilities include deconditioning and obesity. When dyspnea is characterized by recurrent attacks with resolution into symptom-free periods, asthma is likely. Questioning regarding family history of asthma or allergies and any triggering events or substances (allergens, drugs, or pollutants) is important. Cold and dry environments are more likely to trigger an asthmatic reaction, especially in an athlete. Allergies to pollen, pets, dust mites, foods, clothing, and medications (aspirin or NSAIDs) are common in asthmatics. Emotional triggering with stressful events is known to occur with asthma.

Most other causes are due to conditions that have enough premonitory signs or symptoms prior to dyspnea that the diagnosis is already made. For example, a patient with Guillain-Barré syndrome will almost always present with an ascending weakness starting in the legs. This usually gives ample time for the diagnosis and preparation for ventilation support. The same is true of polio (associated muscle weakness), myasthenia gravis (weakness of cranial muscle first with repetitive use), and other disorders.

Examination

Although there are classic examination techniques recommended in the evaluation of pulmonary and cardiac conditions, a review of a large literature base on sensitivity, specificity, and reliability is disappointing. One common examination technique is percussion, used to detect various lung pathologies and in estimating heart size and diaphragmatic excursion.[9] Although factors such as the speed of the stroke of the plexor finger, the speed at which the finger is withdrawn, and the degree of force (light or heavy) are determinants of the sensitivity and accuracy of percussion, it appears that their value has been overestimated. It is generally believed that percussion travels several centimeters through the body, and the result is a sound whose pitch and quality reflect the density of tissue directly under the percussion. There is poor literature support for this belief. In several studies, chest percussion revealed large pleural effusions; however, smaller lesions such as granulomas or deep nodules were undetected.[10,11]

Traditionally, diaphragmatic excursion is evaluated by chest percussion. Several difficulties with this approach exist. There is a high interexaminer disagreement,[12] and, radiographically, differences between bedside percussion and chest film measurements are as much as 3 cm.[13,14] This means that the difference between rating a patient normal or abnormal with percussion is often not possible.

As long ago as 1899, the accuracy of percussion for delineating cardiac size was challenged. Through comparisons with cardiac weight at autopsy it was discovered that only about half of moderately enlarged hearts and less than one third of mildly enlarged hearts had been discovered and noted by clinicians. More recent studies indicate a generally good correlation between a displaced left-sided heart border detected by percussion and an enlarged cardiothoracic ratio on a chest radiograph.[15] The only problem is that patient outcome is poorly correlated with this measure. Other factors are more predictive of patient outcome, such as left ventricular end-diastolic volume and left ventricular mass. Percussion was sensitive (0.91) to these two measures, but not specific (0.30).[16]

A chest radiograph is important in the evaluation of cardiac size and the status of the lungs. Following are some classic findings and associated disorders:

- Haziness of vascular markings with an associated cardiomegaly may be evident with CHF.
- Diffuse granulomatous involvement of the lungs may suggest a fungal disorder and, if more apical, tuberculosis.
- Decreased markings suggest emphysema.
- Hyperlucency (no markings) and/or shifting of the trachea suggest pneumothorax.
- Lobar consolidation suggests pneumonia.
- Evidence of an air-fluid line would suggest pleural effusion.
- Perihilar opacities may suggest sarcoidosis or lung cancer.

Pulmonary function testing is essential in patients with a complaint of dyspnea. Peak expiratory flow rate (PEFR) can be measured using a peak flow meter. This is an inexpensive device that measures the patient's ability to expire. It is an acceptable monitoring device; however, it is effort-dependent, and decreases are found with many disorders. Age-, gender-, and height-matched standards are used as optimal comparison values. Spirometry is more sophisticated and may give more specific clues. If the forced expiratory volume in 1 second (FEV_1) or maximum midexpiratory flow rate ($FEF_{25\%-75\%}$) is decreased, COPD is likely. If this response is reversed with a bronchodilator or made worse by a bronchoconstrictor (methacholine challenge), asthma is likely. Measurements of lung volumes or diffusing capacity are expensive and should be reserved for the specialist. When a pulmonary embolism is suspected, referral for lung perfusion scanning or digital subtraction angiography is needed.

Laboratory testing is usually unnecessary unless anemia, diabetes, or endocrine disorders are suspected. In children with asthma, it is important to obtain skin-allergy test results. This may direct the development of an avoidance program if necessary.

MANAGEMENT

Management of the acutely dyspneic patient is better managed medically in an effort to provide any supportive emergency efforts when needed. The patient with a more chronic or mild complaint may be amenable to comanagement. Specific management approaches are discussed under selected causes of Dyspnea. In general, the chiropractic approach may include cervical or thoracic manipulation, myofascial work, stretching, and breathing exercises.

A controversial issue is the management of asthma or asthmalike conditions with chiropractic manipulation. The current literature support is still slim; however, there is a suggestion that there is a possible benefit.[17,18] More research is needed prior to making claims of consistent success. Like many conditions, there are multifactorial causes and, therefore, multiple aspects of management. The approach to many conditions is avoidance of triggers. This is certainly part of chiropractic management also. Additionally, there may be reflex mechanisms that either simulate or worsen an asthma attack. Perhaps these are important aspects that can be addressed through chiropractic manipulation. The major concern with sole management of asthma is the unavailability of abortive medication in the event of a severe attack. Attacks occur without warning, or with little warning, and the opportunity to get to the chiropractor (or the emergency department if severe) in time may be unrealistic. Therefore, comanagement is a safer approach for the patient. There are, however, many younger patients with either cough-variant asthma or minor episodes, solely related to upper respiratory infections, for whom dyspnea is not the prominent component. Initial management of these cases over several weeks of an active, symptomatic period may be appropriate. If there appears to be no improvement, especially in peak-flow or spirometry measurement, comanagement is suggested.

The underlying mechanism with asthma appears to be a chronic inflammatory process. The medical approach is to reduce this underlying inflammation through the use of anti-inflammatory medications (eg, aerosol corticosteroids) in an effort to decrease this predispositional state. The medical literature also seems to support an earlier resolution in asthma patients. In other words, those treated seemed to recover entirely from their asthma at an earlier age with less complications.[19]

Algorithm

An algorithm for evaluation and management of dyspnea is presented in Figure 41–1.

SELECTED CAUSES OF DYSPNEA*

ASTHMA

Classic Presentation

The presentation is variable depending on type. In a child with an allergic form of asthma, the presentation will be one of recurrent episodes of wheezing, cough, dyspnea, and a feeling of chest tightness. These attacks may be related to exposure to an environmental allergen or may be aggravated by stress or exercise. The patient may notice attacks occurring in the early morning. In an adult, it is more common to have a patient with similar symptoms; however, the patient will not be aware of allergies. There is often a history of a prolonged respiratory infection and/or a history of smoking.

Cause

It is believed that asthma is due to an underlying subacute inflammatory disease of the airways. With the allergic form, there are sensitized mast cells that degranulate during an acute episode, releasing histamine, bradykinin, and other factors that lead to acute-phase and late-phase reactions.[19] During an attack, bronchoconstriction, mucus production, mucosal edema, and underlying inflammation join together to cause wheezing with associated dyspnea. In addition to this immediate response, there is often a late response 4 to 6 hours later. There are many triggers, including cold/dry air (eg, exercise induced), allergens, dusts and sulfur dioxide fumes, emotional stress, upper respiratory infections, and medications such as aspirin, β-blockers, NSAIDs, and angiotensin-converting enzyme (ACE) inhibitors. In about 25% of patients, the primary complaint is coughing. This is referred to as cough-variant asthma.

Evaluation

An investigation for historical clues such as family history of allergies (extrinsic asthma), triggers to attacks, and severity of attacks is helpful to establish a high index of suspicion. Auscultation may detect wheezes. Simple pulmonary function testing with a hand-held device such as a peak flow meter may detect a decrease in peak expiratory flow rate when compared with age-, sex-, and height-matched values. Spirometry testing focuses on detecting a decrease in forced expiratory volume in 1 second (FEV_1). If there is no decrease, two other functional tests are possible. The first is a provocation test, often with methacholine (a bronchoconstrictor). A hyperresponsive reaction will significantly reduce expiratory measurements (eg, a decrease of 20% or greater in FEV_1). The opposite approach is the use of a bronchodilator to measure improvement in pulmonary function (improvement of 15% or greater in FEV_1).[20] Ancillary tests include laboratory evaluation of sputum to detect Curschmann's spirals, eosinophils, or Charcot-Leyden crystals. Skin testing for allergens is particularly helpful in younger patients with extrinsic asthma. Radioallergosorbent (RAST) testing is usually too expensive and less sensitive than skin allergen testing.

Management

There are anecdotal reports of success with chiropractic management. Some studies and a literature review provide mixed results, but suggest the need for further research.[17,18] It is

*See also Chapter 39, Chest Pain, and Chapter 42, Cough.

Figure 41–1
DYSPNEA (DIFFICULTY BREATHING)—ALGORITHM.

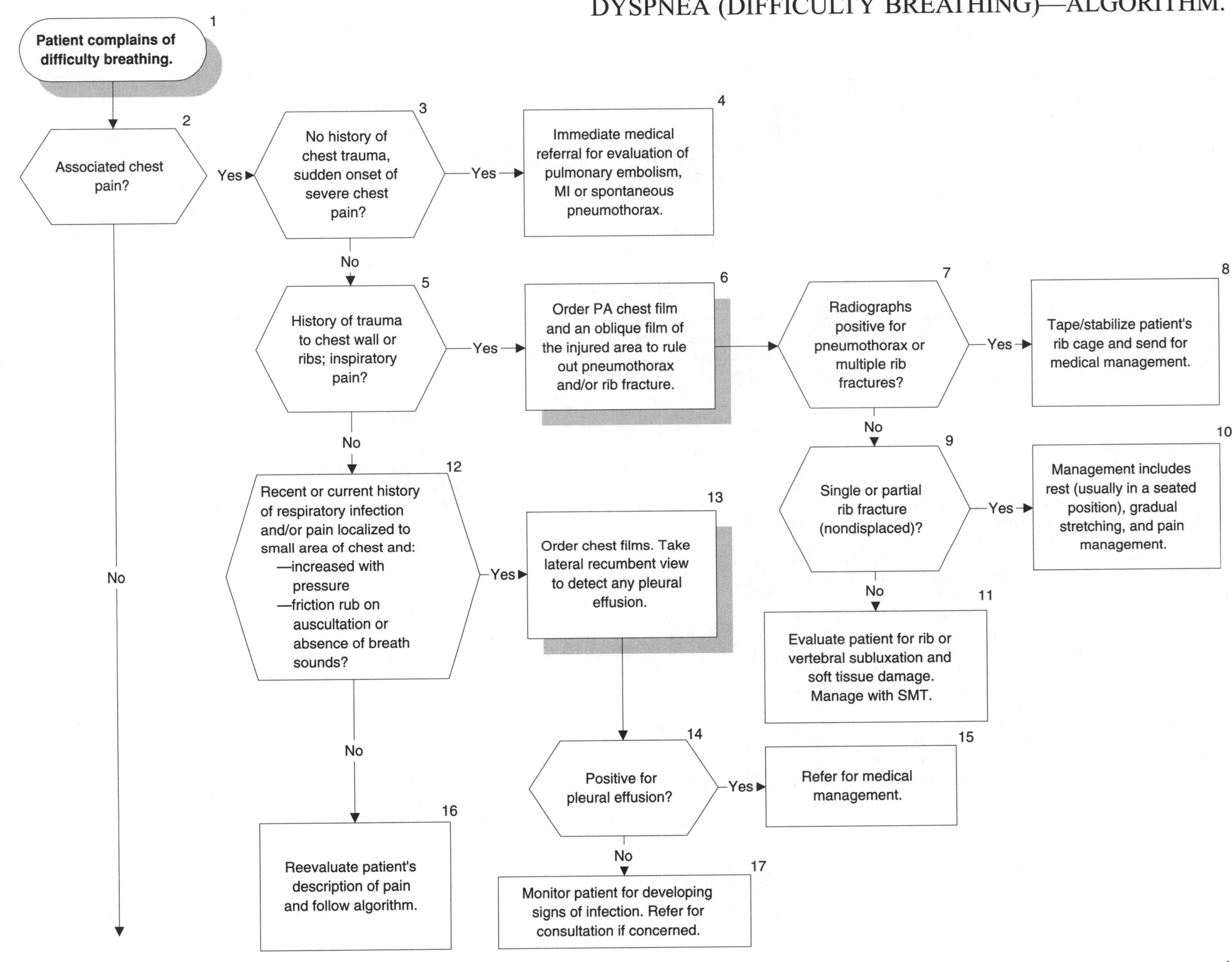

continues

Figure 41–1 continued

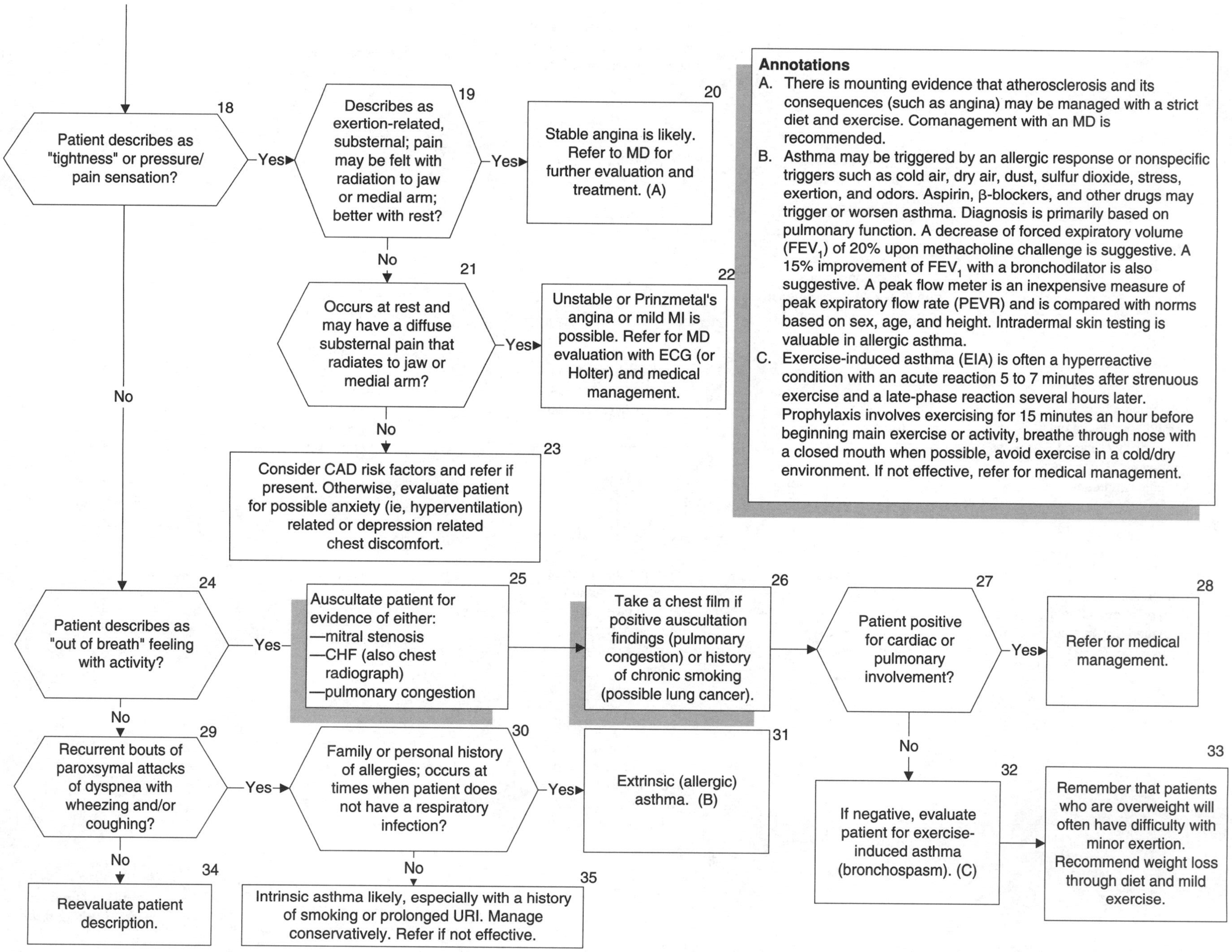

18 Patient describes as "tightness" or pressure/ pain sensation?
- Yes → 19
- No → 24

19 Describes as exertion-related, substernal; pain may be felt with radiation to jaw or medial arm; better with rest?
- Yes → 20
- No → 21

20 Stable angina is likely. Refer to MD for further evaluation and treatment. (A)

21 Occurs at rest and may have a diffuse substernal pain that radiates to jaw or medial arm?
- Yes → 22
- No → 23

22 Unstable or Prinzmetal's angina or mild MI is possible. Refer for MD evaluation with ECG (or Holter) and medical management.

23 Consider CAD risk factors and refer if present. Otherwise, evaluate patient for possible anxiety (ie, hyperventilation) related or depression related chest discomfort.

24 Patient describes as "out of breath" feeling with activity?
- Yes → 25
- No → 29

25 Auscultate patient for evidence of either:
—mitral stenosis
—CHF (also chest radiograph)
—pulmonary congestion

26 Take a chest film if positive auscultation findings (pulmonary congestion) or history of chronic smoking (possible lung cancer).

27 Patient positive for cardiac or pulmonary involvement?
- Yes → 28
- No → 32

28 Refer for medical management.

29 Recurrent bouts of paroxysmal attacks of dyspnea with wheezing and/or coughing?
- Yes → 30
- No → 34

30 Family or personal history of allergies; occurs at times when patient does not have a respiratory infection?
- Yes → 31
- No → 35

31 Extrinsic (allergic) asthma. (B)

32 If negative, evaluate patient for exercise-induced asthma (bronchospasm). (C)

33 Remember that patients who are overweight will often have difficulty with minor exertion. Recommend weight loss through diet and mild exercise.

34 Reevaluate patient description.

35 Intrinsic asthma likely, especially with a history of smoking or prolonged URI. Manage conservatively. Refer if not effective.

Annotations

A. There is mounting evidence that atherosclerosis and its consequences (such as angina) may be managed with a strict diet and exercise. Comanagement with an MD is recommended.

B. Asthma may be triggered by an allergic response or nonspecific triggers such as cold air, dry air, dust, sulfur dioxide, stress, exertion, and odors. Aspirin, β-blockers, and other drugs may trigger or worsen asthma. Diagnosis is primarily based on pulmonary function. A decrease of forced expiratory volume (FEV_1) of 20% upon methacholine challenge is suggestive. A 15% improvement of FEV_1 with a bronchodilator is also suggestive. A peak flow meter is an inexpensive measure of peak expiratory flow rate (PEVR) and is compared with norms based on sex, age, and height. Intradermal skin testing is valuable in allergic asthma.

C. Exercise-induced asthma (EIA) is often a hyperreactive condition with an acute reaction 5 to 7 minutes after strenuous exercise and a late-phase reaction several hours later. Prophylaxis involves exercising for 15 minutes an hour before beginning main exercise or activity, breathe through nose with a closed mouth when possible, avoid exercise in a cold/dry environment. If not effective, refer for medical management.

Key: PA, posterior to anterior; SMT, spinal manipulative therapy; URI, upper respiratory infection; MI, myocardial infarction.

important to realize that the chiropractor cannot make recommendations to parents or patients on medication regarding a change in the prescribed use; consultation with the prescribing physician is necessary. If a treatment trial is initiated, it is extremely important to use spirometry or a peak flow meter to measure function when the patient is not symptomatic. Comanagement is recommended in cases where asthma is severe or the patient is already under the management of a physician.

Medication is used to abort an attack and manage acute reactions, and another group of medications is used as prophylactics. β-Agonist medications such as albuterol (Ventolin) are used during an attack. Antiinflammatory drugs, such as aerosol corticosteroids, are used to control the underlying inflammation that exists between attacks. A mast cell stabilizer (cromolyn sodium) is used to prevent degranulation and release of histamine and other mediators.

EMPHYSEMA

Classic Presentation

The patient has a history of smoking and has noticed gradual difficulty breathing. If the emphysema is advanced the patient will appear barrel chested and will demonstrate the use of accessory muscles of respiration, or breathing through pursed lips. When advanced, the patient is often thin and frail.

Cause

Destruction of alveolar walls due to the release and deregulation of proteases from neutrophils and macrophages leads to a decrease in the available cross-sectional area available for gas exchange. The cause appears to be smoking and, in a small percentage of patients, a deficiency in α-1-antiprotease (an inhibitory enzyme for proteases). As a result of the destruction of the elastin portion of the lung matrix, the natural elastic recoil response with expiration is lost, forcing the patient to work hard to expel air. The inefficient expiratory effort leads to an increase in residual air in the lungs. The patient is forced to expend a majority of his or her body energy just for breathing, and often will become a respiratory cripple. It is most common to find chronic bronchitis and emphysema coexisting in most patients.

Evaluation

The patient's appearance is characteristic when presenting in the later stages. This is often referred to as a "pink-puffer" (breathing through pursed lips to create a positive back pressure, opening the airways and making breathing less laborious). The patient in the later stages will have hyperresonant lungs on percussion coupled with diminished breath sounds on auscultation. The chest radiograph will reveal diminished markings in the periphery with associated low and flat hemidiaphragms.

Management

The patient must cease smoking. This may require outside support. Additionally, referral to a respiratory therapist is necessary to prevent the cycling of decreased function that leads to the "respiratory cripple." Chiropractic management of associated musculoskeletal complaints would be beneficial logically.

PULMONARY EMBOLISM

Classic Presentation

Although it is unlikely that a patient will present with an acute attack of pulmonary embolism, the patient would be in distress with chest pain, dyspnea, cough, and diaphoresis.

Cause

Thrombi that develop in the lower extremity, particularly in the calves, travel to the lungs, causing vascular blockage and/or infarction.

Evaluation

In addition to the above-mentioned appearance, patients often will have a history suggesting predisposition, including prolonged bed rest, childbirth, prolonged use of oral contraceptives, hip or femur fractures, surgery, or recent myocardial infarction. Tachycardia, tachypnea, and associated low-grade fever are often found. Shock is unusual. Although a chest radiograph may reveal a triangular density with the base at the pleura and point in the direction of the hilus (Hampton's lump), this is an unusual finding. Other findings are nonspecific. The patient should be evaluated with a ventilation/perfusion lung scan.

Management

Antithrombolytic therapy with streptokinase, urokinase, or recombinant tissue plasminogen activator (TPA) is used in an acute event. Preventive therapy incorporates anticoagulant therapy with heparin or warfarin.[21]

PNEUMOTHORAX

Classic Presentation

There are different types of pneumothorax, each with a different patient presentation. The patient with spontaneous pneumothorax (SPT) is often a tall, thin male between 20 and 40 years of age with an acute onset of sharp, unilateral chest pain with dyspnea. It often occurs at rest or when sleeping. Traumatic pneumothorax is often the consequence of rib fracture. The presentation would be one of someone who presents with a blow or a fall to the chest. Pneumothorax can also occur as a consequence to COPD, asthma, cystic fibrosis, or TB.

Cause

Pneumothorax is an accumulation of air in the pleural space. With spontaneous pneumothorax, it appears that subpleural apical blebs rupture spontaneously. Traumatic pneumothorax is usually due to outside air entering the pleural space. This may progress to tension pneumothorax if air is allowed in with each respiration, but on expiration air is trapped (check-valve mechanism).

Evaluation

The patient may have complaints mild enough to wait several days before being evaluated. The patient may have a family history of spontaneous pneumothorax or a history of smoking. Unilateral, sharp chest pain without a history of trauma, no recent or current signs of a respiratory infection, and no signs of other pulmonary disease should raise the suspicion of spontaneous pneumothorax. Severe tachycardia and mediastinal or tracheal shift are not likely to occur unless the pneumothorax is massive, as may occur gradually in tension pneumothorax. Also, the signs of decreased fremitus and breath sounds are detectable only in a large pneumothorax. Chest films may reveal a visceral pleural line (especially on expiration). If a film is taken supine, a "deep sulcus" sign may be evident as an unusually radiolucent costophrenic sulcus. If thoracic films are used for chiropractic evaluation, it is important not to collimate out the lungs.

Management

It is important to distinguish SPT from a rib subluxation. Because the pain of SPT is pleuritic, it may be reproducible mechanically. If the patient is found to have pneumothorax, he or she is hospitalized and monitored. If the pneumothorax is small (< 15%) the air is often absorbed over time. However, if it is larger, tube thoracostomy is performed.

CONGESTIVE HEART FAILURE

Classic Presentation

The patient complains of bilateral leg edema. He or she has associated complaints of difficulty breathing with exertion or lying fully supine at night (orthopnea).

Cause

Right-sided heart failure is often secondary to left-sided failure. Pressure increases into the venous system, delaying return to the heart from the lower extremities.

Evaluation

The edema is reduced by elevation of the legs. Rales are often apparent on auscultation. The chest radiograph provides important confirmation of cardiac failure with a demonstration of cardiomegaly, dilation of the upper lobe veins, haziness of vessel outlines, and interstitial edema. Electrocardiography may reveal associated arrhythmias or hypertrophy.

Management

Comanagement is recommended. The standard approach is the use of diuretics for early-stage failure. However, long-term management should include a change to a strict, low-fat diet, with gradual supervised exercise.

REFERENCES

1. Gillespie DJ, Staats BA. Unexplained dyspnea. *Mayo Clin Proc.* 1994;69:657–663.
2. Wasserman K, Casaburi R. Dyspneic physiological and pathophysiological mechanisms. *Annu Rev Med.* 1988;39:503–515.
3. Killian KJ, Jones NL. Respiratory muscles and dyspnea. *Clin Chest Med.* 1988;9:237–248.
4. Tobin MJ. Dyspnea: pathophysiologic basis, clinical presentation, and management. *Arch Intern Med.* 1990;150:1604–1613.
5. Schwartzstein RM, Manning HL, Weiss JW, et al. Dsypnea: a sensory experience. *Lung.* 1990;4:185–199.
6. Burki NK. Dyspnea. *Lung.* 1987;165:269–277.
7. Hopkins LC. Clinical features of myasthenia gravis. *Neurol Clin.* 1994;12:243–261.
8. Wolf SG. Diaphragmatic spasm: a neglected cause of dyspnea and chest pain. *Integr Physiol Behav Sci.* 1994;29:74–76.
9. McGee SR. Percussion and physical diagnosis: separating myth from science. *Dis Mon.* 1995;10:641–692.
10. Bohadana AB, Coimbra FTV, Santiago JRF. Detection of lung abnormalities by auscultatory percussion: a comparative study with conventional percussion. *Respiration.* 1986;50:218–225.
11. Bourke S, Nunes D, Stafford F, et al. Percussion of the chest revisited: a comparison of the diagnostic value of auscultatory and conventional chest percussion. *Ir J Med Sci.* 1989;158:82–84.
12. Badgett RG, Tanaka DJ, Hunt DK, et al. Can moderate chronic obstructive pulmonary disease be diagnosed by historical and physical findings alone? *Am J Med.* 1993;94:188–196.
13. Williams TJ, Ahmad D, Morgan WKC. A clinical and roentgenographic correlate of diaphragmatic movement. *Arch Intern Med.* 1981;141:878–880.
14. Cole MB, Hummel JV, Manginelli VW, Lawton AH. Bedside versus laboratory estimations of timed and total vital capacity and diaphragmatic height and movement. *Dis Chest.* 1970;38:519–521.
15. Karnegis JN, Kadri N. Accuracy of percussion of the left cardiac border. *Int J Cardiol.* 1992;37:361–364.
16. Heckerling PS, Wiener SL, Moses VK, et al. Accuracy of precordial percussion in detecting cardiomegaly. *Am J Med.* 1991;91:328–334.
17. Ziegler R, Carpenter D. The chiropractic approach to the treatment of asthma: a literature review. *J Chiro.* 1992;29:71.
18. Renand CI, Pichette D. Chiropractic management of bronchial asthma: a literature review. *ACA J Chiro.* 1990;27:25–26.
19. McFadden ER Jr, Gilbert IA. Asthma (current concepts). *N Engl J Med.* 1992;327:1928.
20. National Asthma Education Program, National Heart, Lung, and Blood Institute. Executive Summary. *Guidelines for the Diagnosis and Management of Asthma.* National Institutes of Health Publication No. 91-3042A, June 1991.
21. Hirsh J. Oral anticoagulant drugs. *N Engl J Med.* 1991;324:1865.

Chapter 42

Cough

CONTEXT

Everyone coughs at some time. Coughing is a natural defense mechanism used to clear the airways. Most individuals accept this as a naturally occurring component to most respiratory infections and assume that it is self-limiting to a week or two. When the cough is persistent, individuals are more likely to seek attention. In a primary care setting, cough is the fifth most common presenting complaint in adults.[1] This accounts for 30 million office visits per year. In children, the numbers may be higher.[2] As a common complaint, it is not surprising that approximately $600 million is spent per year in the United States alone on prescription and over-the-counter (OTC) cough medications.[3]

Chiropractors are probably more inadvertently involved in the evaluation of a patient with cough. Most patients would first seek medical consultation with a chronic cough. However, the chiropractor is well positioned to evaluate and diagnose a patient with cough and offer suggestions regarding conservative approaches that may benefit. Patients with chronic cough may also have musculoskeletally related complaints due to the constant strain on the chest and thoracic spine and musculature.

The majority of acute cough is due to viral infection or smoking.[4] Other causes include bacterial pneumonias, inhaled irritants, allergies, and medications. Chronic cough is most often due to one of a short list of causes.[5,6] The following is a hierarchical list of these causes:

1. postnasal drip—40% of cases (87% in one study)
2. asthma—25% to 35% of cases (cough is the only presenting complaint in up to 25% of asthmatics)[7]
3. gastroesophageal reflux (GER)—20% of cases
4. chronic bronchitis—5% to 10% of cases
5. bronchiectasis—4% of cases

However, it is important to consider that smoking may be the underlying initiator of many of the above causes. Most important, a history of chronic smoking should raise the concern of bronchogenic carcinoma. Tuberculosis (TB) should also be considered when a low-grade upper respiratory infection (URI) seems to persist or there is known exposure to a TB carrier. Rarer causes of chronic cough are subdiaphragmatic abscess or tumors.

GENERAL STRATEGY

Acute Cough (< 3 weeks)

Determine the following:

- whether the patient has been exposed to any chemicals—occupational or home cleaning solutions
- whether the patient could have aspirated food or liquid—infants, seniors, alcoholics, or sedated individuals
- whether the patient has additional signs of a URI and possible history of exposure to others with similar symptoms—viral infection most common; consider TB also
- whether the patient smokes or is exposed to a smoker
- whether the patient is taking medications that may provoke cough—angiotensin-converting enzyme (ACE) inhibitors, other antihypertensives, and some antiasthmatic medications such as albuterol (Ventolin) or cromolyn (drying of airways)
- response to OTC drugs—often ineffective, yet patient overutilizes
- whether the cough is positionally related—cough that increases with recumbency indicates postnasal drip, pulmonary vascular congestion, or asthma (if at night)

- whether there are any associated complaints such as fainting, incontinence, rib or chest pain, headaches, nausea/vomiting, hernias, or low back pain with radicular symptoms

Chronic Cough

Determine the following:

- whether initial signs of a URI resolved within 2 weeks, but cough is persistent—possible viral infection, superinfection with bacteria, or TB
- whether the cough is recurrent and appears to be either seasonal or associated with eye itching or stuffy nose—allergies, possible postnasal drip
- whether the patient has to clear the throat often—postnasal drip
- whether the patient is a smoker or is exposed to a smoker—chronic bronchitis
- whether the cough is worse with recumbency and is associated with a tickling in the upper throat—postnasal drip
- whether the cough is worse when recumbent and possibly associated with epigastric discomfort or a sour taste in the mouth—GER
- whether the cough is worse with exertion or associated with shortness of breath—cough-variant asthma
- whether there are any associated complaints such as fainting, incontinence, rib or chest pain, headaches

Evaluation

- Auscultate for wheezes, rales, or other adventitial sounds.
- If TB, congestive heart failure, fungal infection, pleurisy, or lung cancer is suspected, order a chest film.
- Laboratory testing may help differentiate bacterial causes from viral causes.
- Pulmonary function testing is particularly important when asthma or chronic bronchitis is suspected.

Management

- Depending on underlying cause, hydration and brief OTC medication are all that are needed for acute cough.
- When GER is suspected, changes in the types of food eaten, quantity of food, avoidance of lying down after large meals, and loss of weight will all be of benefit.
- For chronic bronchitis, smoking cessation is most important.
- A short course of manipulative therapy may be applied for uncomplicated asthma, comanagement is suggested.

RELEVANT ANATOMY AND PHYSIOLOGY

Cough receptors are ubiquitous. They are found in the nose, pharynx, larynx, trachea, bronchi, pleura, diaphragm, stomach, esophagus, also the tympanic membrane and external auditory canal. Within the tracheobronchial tree there are several types of receptors: (1) slowly adapting stretch receptors; (2) rapidly adapting, irritant receptors; (3) pulmonary C-fiber receptors (J receptors); and (4) bronchial C-fibers.[8] The stretch and irritant receptors are myelinated. The rapidly adapting receptors are probably the main group associated with coughing. The C-fiber receptors are sensitive to inflammation and toxins or other noxious substances. Receptors in the external auditory meatus are sensitive to hair or cerumen and may be the cause of cough in some individuals.

The medullary cough center modulates the cough reflex via afferent vagal, glossopharyngeal, trigeminal, and phrenic nerves and efferent vagal, phrenic, and spinal accessory nerves.[9] Coughing is a rather violent act requiring several simultaneous participants. First, inspiration prior to coughing stretches the lungs, taking advantage of an elastic recoil effect. Next, a Valsalva maneuver occurs with closing of the glottis and contraction of the muscles of the abdomen, chest, and diaphragm. This is followed by an expiratory blast occurring with abduction of the glottis. This is then followed by a deep inspiration. During the cough phase, flow rate is as high as 600 L/min at speeds of up to 500 miles/h.[10]

Interference of coughing may be caused by position, weakened musculature, pain, or an overwhelmed mucociliary ladder. The inability to expel foreign material or mucus can result in atelectasis and/or infection. Chronic smoking is known to inhibit the mucociliary ladder and cause metaplasia of the cells in the smaller bronchioles. Normally, the cells of the smaller airways secrete a clear, nonviscous fluid. Chronic smoking causes these cells to transform into mucus-producing cells called Clara cells. It is much more difficult to clear the smaller airways except through coughing.

Sometimes associated with cough is a tendency toward thoracic flexion. This is an important consideration in older osteoporotic patients who may cause a compression fracture while coughing.

EVALUATION

History

The history will provide a high level of suspicion in most cases (Table 42–1). A search for external irritants should in-

Table 42–1 History Questions for Cough

Primary Question	*What Are You Thinking?*	*Secondary Questions*	*What Are You Thinking?*
Have you had the cough less than 3 weeks?	Consider common causes such as viral or bacterial URI, bronchitis, or pneumonia.	Is there someone you have been in contact with who has similar symptoms?	Determine contact's symptoms. Common infection likely.
		Associated signs of sore throat, low-grade fever, stuffy nose, malaise?	Viral cause likely.
		Associated signs of high-grade fever, chills, or rigors (shaking, teeth chattering) in addition to above list?	Bacterial cause likely. Does the patient have other predisposing conditions such as AIDS, diabetes, chronic obstructive pulmonary disease (COPD)?
Does the cough occur only with or soon after exertion?	Asthma, hyperactive airway disease, and cardiopulmonary causes.	Worse in dry, cold environment?	Asthma and hyperactive airways disease more likely. Look for auscultation findings if cardiopulmonary cause is suspected.
Have you had the cough longer than 3 weeks?	Causes of chronic cough include postnasal drip, COPD, esophageal reflux, and bacterial complication of viral disorder.	Is the cough worse when you are lying down at night?	Consider postnasal drip; if associated with difficulty breathing, orthopnea (cardiopulmonary); with meals, consider esophageal reflux.
		Is the cough productive?	A productive cough would suggest bacterial infection.
		Do you smoke?	COPD; with isolated wheeze consider bronchogenic carcinoma.
Does the cough occur intermittently (off and on)?	Occupational or environmental exposure. Also consider medications such as ACE inhibitors, beta-blockers, and some asthma medications.	Does the cough happen without other signs/ symptoms?	Probably environmental.
		Does it occur only at work?	Ask about occupational exposure, relationship to eating, etc.
		Does it occur after returning home but before bed?	May be allergic if patient lives in rural area and works in urban area.

clude smoking, exposure to smoke, occupational dust exposure, apparent pet allergies, and smog. Given that the most common cause of acute cough is a viral infection, questioning regarding associated signs of fever, runny or stuffy nose, and lethargy are helpful. In older patients and immunocompromised patients, a concern for the possibility of an underlying pneumonia is warranted.

A drug history, especially in those with a diagnosis of hypertension or asthma, is often revealing. ACE inhibitors are known as potential cough stimulators in some patients.[11] This is believed to be due to either stimulation of C-fibers through an ACE inhibitor effect of accumulation of kinins (ie, bradykinin) or secondarily through production of a postnasal drip. Unfortunately, the association may not be clearly evident because the reported reaction may occur 3 to 4 weeks and as much as 1 year following initial usage. ACE inhibitor cough may also be worse in the supine position, probably related to the above-mentioned secondary effect.[12] Other medications include β-blockers (especially nonselective) that may, through a bronchoconstricting effect, irritate an asthmatic or those with hyperresponsive airways.[13] Ironically, asthmatics taking β-agonists such as albuterol or cromolyn sodium (Intal) or corticosteroids may develop a nonproductive cough due to irritation or drying of the bronchial membranes.[14]

If the cough is present only under stressful circumstances, both cough-variant asthma and psychogenic cough should be considered, especially in the adolescent. If the cough is provoked by exertion, exercise-induced asthma should be considered.[15]

If the cough appears or is made worse by recumbency, consider the following:

- Chronic cough occurring after lying down after a large meal and/or association with epigastric discomfort is probably GER.
- Recurrent cough occurring while lying flat and improved by support of the body or head at an angle is suggestive of postnasal drip or congestive heart failure (pulmonary vascular congestion).
- If the cough is worse while lying flat and is associated with dyspnea (orthopnea), congestive heart failure is more likely.
- Chronic cough that becomes worse in the middle of the night and is not always position dependent is likely to be asthma.

The distinction between a productive and a nonproductive cough is helpful. Productive coughs usually imply infection. Nonproductive coughs are often the result of irritation such as with the underlying inflammation of asthma, postnasal drip, and external irritants such as from allergies or smoke. Questions regarding the color and consistency of phlegm are traditionally asked; however, they probably contribute little to the diagnosis. The typical assumption is that yellow or green phlegm is found often with bacterial or viral infections. A clear or mucuslike phlegm is suggestive of allergy or viral infection. Blood in the sputum (hemoptysis) is an indication of erosion or trauma from coughing found with pulmonary infarct, TB, bronchiectasis, and bronchogenic carcinoma.

Patients with a productive cough on the majority of days for 3 consecutive months occurring over 2 or more consecutive years are likely to have chronic bronchitis. This is particularly true in chronic smokers.

Examination

The primary focus of the examination is observation of the nose and throat and auscultation of the lungs. A cobblestone appearance of the oropharyngeal mucosa or direct visualization of mucoid secretions may be seen with postnasal drip.

Auscultation for wheezes may provide clues to an underlying chronic obstructive lung disorder (COPD) such as asthma, chronic bronchitis, or emphysema. A localized wheeze is suggestive of bronchogenic carcinoma in a patient who is a chronic smoker. Always check for a prominent supraclavicular lymph node (sentinel or Virchow's node). Extrathoracic wheezing—stridor—is associated with whooping cough (pertussis) in infants and children. This must be differentiated from blockage by a foreign object. When further testing is requested, supportive historical and/or physical examination findings must be present, as follows:

- Only when suspicion is high for pneumonia, TB fungal infection, or cancer does a chest film need to be ordered.
- When perinasal tenderness, positionally related nose stuffiness, or transillumination of the sinuses is positive, skull radiographs for sinus infection should be considered.
- If asthma is suggested by the history, spirometry testing with a focus on forced expiratory volume should be performed or ordered (peak flow meter evaluation is an inexpensive, but less sensitive measurement tool).
- Laboratory studies are rarely needed. The most common scenarios are with the suspected asthmatic patient in whom skin testing or pulmonary function testing is needed. A search for eosinophilia is not warranted given the nonspecificity of this finding. Sputum evaluation for Charcot-Leyden crystals or Curschmann spirals is rarely performed or needed.

MANAGEMENT

Conservative management of cough should be pursued in both a generic and specialized approach. The generic approach focuses on environmental factors that are modifiable, including the following:

- Ensure adequate hydration—8 oz of water every waking hour. Use of a humidifier/vaporizer may be helpful, but some asthmatics respond poorly to humidified air. Humidifiers must be thoroughly and properly cleaned to avoid spread of other allergens or infectious agents.
- Avoid smoking or being in a smoke-filled environment.
- Ensure that the house environment is clean. Change or clean furnace filters regularly. Use a vacuum cleaner that does not recycle room air.
- Avoid any potential allergens including grasses, plants, animals, or foods.
- Avoid supine positions; elevate the head of the bed or prop up the head and upper trunk with pillows.
- Consider supplementation with antioxidants such as vitamins A (β-carotene 20,000 IU/day), C (100 mg/waking hour), and E (400 to 800 IU/d).

Specific musculoskeletal approaches may include the following:

- Perform spinal and costovertebral adjusting to allow unrestricted movement while breathing.
- Perform deep trigger point work or myofascial release to the trapezius, serratus anterior, intercostals, pectorals, and midscapular muscles, and cervical spine musculature when the need is determined.
- Educate the patient to breathe through use of the diaphragm, and to breathe through the nose when possible; breathing should be deep and relaxed.

When GER is the cause, avoidance of large, heavy meals and foods such as chocolate, caffeine, alcohol, fat, onions, garlic, and orange juice will usually help. Avoidance of a supine position, especially after eating, is a requisite.

Pharmacologic treatment of cough should be tempered with the knowledge that, initially, cough serves a protective function. Inhibition of this function should be considered in patients only under the following conditions:

- when it interrupts sleep (which is necessary for recovery of an underlying infection)
- when there is the potential of damage, such as in osteoporotic patients or postsurgery
- in those patients with spinal pain and radicular symptoms
- in patients with hernias, stress incontinence, or syncope
- when the cough is incapacitating

Pharmacologic treatment is based on several approaches. Interruption of the cough reflex may occur peripherally, by acting on sensory receptors, or centrally, by acting on the cough center in the medulla and nucleus tractus solitarius. Antitussive (anticough) medications are generally divided into (1) central suppressants, (2) expectorants, (3) mucolytics, and (4) peripheral anesthetics (benzonate). The primary prescription suppressant is codeine, a narcotic. Because it is so effective, OTC (nonnarcotic) medications pale in comparison. OTC medications are a confusing array of mixtures with unproven effectiveness. When looking for or recommending an effective OTC antitussive, check for one of two ingredients: dextromethorphan or diphenhydramine. The combination of antihistamines, cough suppressants, and expectorants is probably useless or counterproductive.

Expectorants theoretically stimulate submucosal gland fluid secretion, rendering mucus less viscous and easier to clear. The primary approach to accomplishing this task is proper hydration, orally and via a humidifier. When ineffective, OTCs with guaifenesin (glycerol gualacolate) or iodinated glycerol are sometimes effective. It is interesting to note that there is no evidence that these medications are any more effective than home remedies such as garlic, horseradish, pepper, or chicken soup. In patients with thicker sputum unresponsive to expectorants (rarely seen in a chiropractic office) a mucolytic agent, *N*-acetylcysteine may be prescribed.

The common OTC approach of using cough lozenges is probably no more effective than sucking on candy. However, the psychologic effect of the sensation provided by camphor, menthol, or eucalyptus oil is soothing enough to continue sales.

Preventive measures should be encouraged when an infectious cause of cough is suspected. This includes washing one's hands after sneezing, nose blowing, or coughing. Use disposable tissues rather than handkerchiefs. Coughing into a flexed elbow or sleeve may also prevent direct spread through hand contact with others.

Patients suspected of having ACE inhibitor-provoked cough should be referred back to the prescribing physician. It is important to note that switching to another ACE inhibitor usually is not effective. Therefore, a switch to another antihypertensive is usually necessary.

Sinusitis may benefit from myofascial work over the temporal and masseter muscles, acupressure perinasally, or moist heat over the sinuses. Congestion-provoking positions should be avoided. Diathermy may be helpful in some cases. Patients suspected of having a sinus infection based on clinical examination and radiographs usually require referral for a decongestant and antibiotics. Some chiropractors employ a nasal-specific balloon therapy to drain the sinuses. It is anecdotally reported to be effective when performed by a chiropractor trained specifically in this approach.

Algorithm

An algorithm for evaluation and management of chronic cough is presented in Figure 42–1.

SELECTED CAUSES OF COUGH*

PNEUMONIA

Classic Presentation

The patient appears to have a respiratory infection with an associated productive cough and fever. The specificity of the presentation is increased by knowing whether the patient is immunocompromised, elderly, alcoholic, or a chronic smoker.

Cause

Inhalation or aspiration of oropharyngeal secretions containing microorganisms leads to lung infection. There are numerous causes, each with its own clinical presentation and treatment. Generalization will be made to assist in the distinction of pneumonia from other causes of respiratory infection.

Evaluate

In general, if the pneumonia is bacterial, the patient will appear to be more sick, with a higher fever and possibly chills. This is not always true, especially in the elderly and immunocompromised. Viral causes are usually more mild with a low-grade fever; however, the symptoms are more prolonged. Radiographs may be helpful, but there is no consistent pattern in all cases of any one cause. However, finding abnormal findings on a chest radiograph, such as lobar consolidation, patchy infiltrate, or pleural effusion, are characteristic of pneumonia and would warrant referral. Rales are often heard.

Management

Antibiotic treatment is necessary with bacterial pneumonia. Viral causes are not responsive. However, mycoplasma pneumonia may be responsive because it is an atypical organism.

PULMONARY TUBERCULOSIS

Classic Presentation

Patients with primary infection are often asymptomatic unless immunocompromised. Patients who are symptomatic usually have reactivated TB. The patient will complain of fatigue, weight loss, low-grade fever, chronic cough, and night sweats.

Cause

Inhalation of mycoplasma tuberculosis will result in widespread lymphatic or hematogenous spread and an immune response that results in granulomatous walling-off of the organism. Primary TB rarely progresses to symptomatic presentation unless the patient is immunocompromised, such as the elderly or those with HIV infection (with or without

*See also Chapter 41, Dyspnea, for asthma and Chapter 39, Chest Pain, for gastroesophageal reflux.

Figure 42–1
CHRONIC COUGH—ALGORITHM.

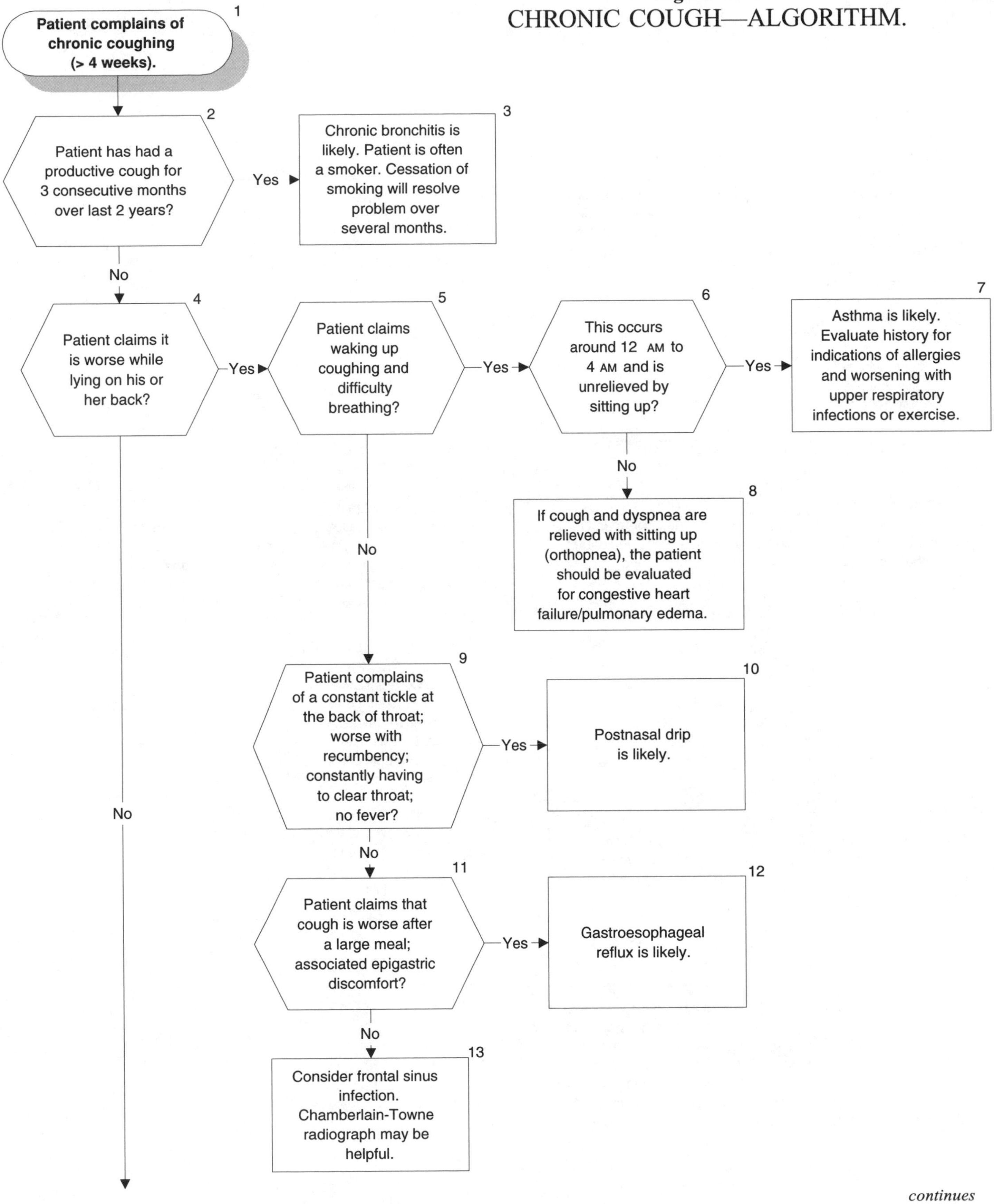

1. **Patient complains of chronic coughing (> 4 weeks).**

2. Patient has had a productive cough for 3 consecutive months over last 2 years?
   - Yes → 3. Chronic bronchitis is likely. Patient is often a smoker. Cessation of smoking will resolve problem over several months.
   - No → 4

4. Patient claims it is worse while lying on his or her back?
   - Yes → 5
   - No ↓

5. Patient claims waking up coughing and difficulty breathing?
   - Yes → 6
   - No → 9

6. This occurs around 12 AM to 4 AM and is unrelieved by sitting up?
   - Yes → 7. Asthma is likely. Evaluate history for indications of allergies and worsening with upper respiratory infections or exercise.
   - No → 8. If cough and dyspnea are relieved with sitting up (orthopnea), the patient should be evaluated for congestive heart failure/pulmonary edema.

9. Patient complains of a constant tickle at the back of throat; worse with recumbency; constantly having to clear throat; no fever?
   - Yes → 10. Postnasal drip is likely.
   - No → 11

11. Patient claims that cough is worse after a large meal; associated epigastric discomfort?
   - Yes → 12. Gastroesophageal reflux is likely.
   - No → 13. Consider frontal sinus infection. Chamberlain-Towne radiograph may be helpful.

continues

Figure 42–1 continued

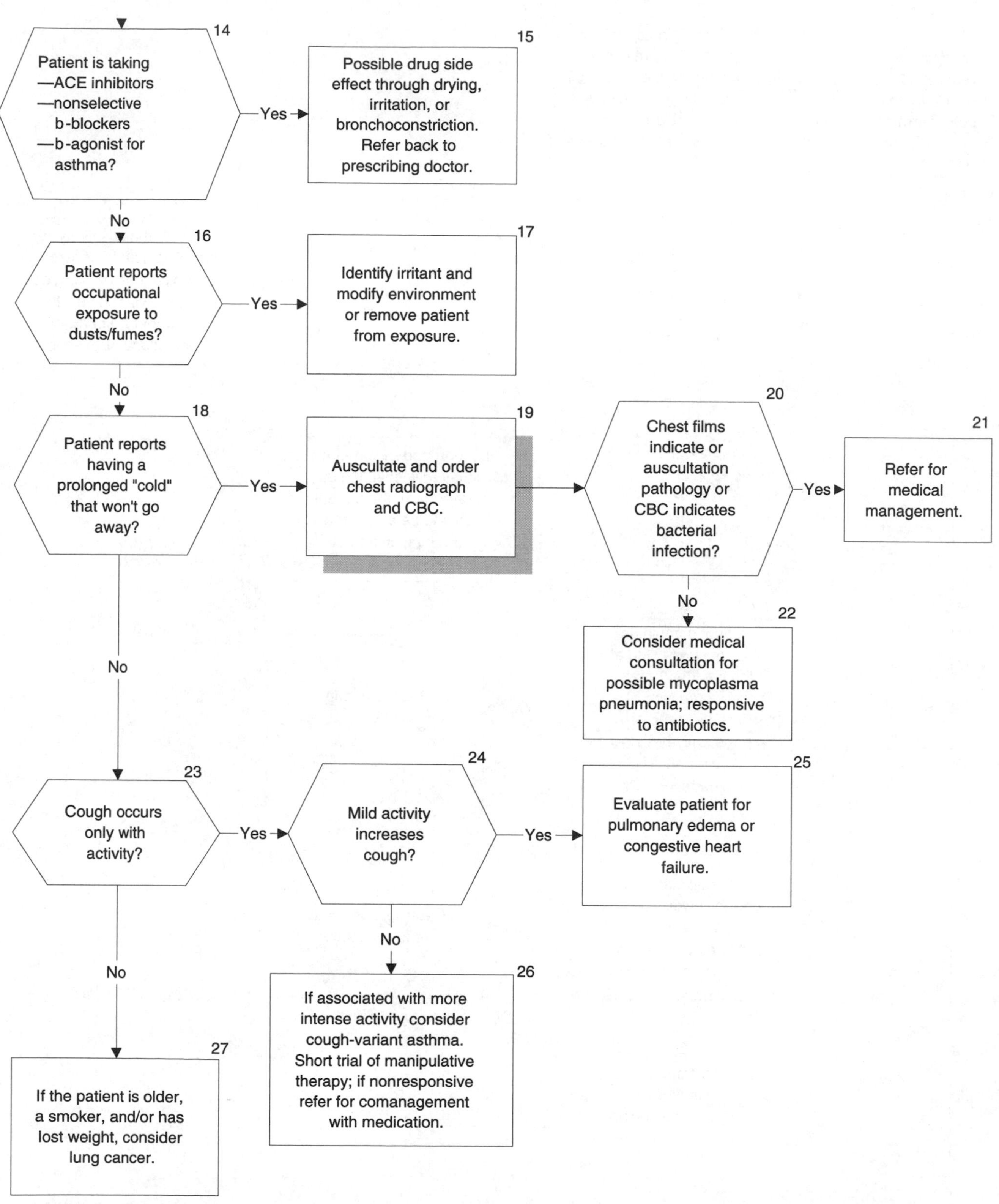

Key: CBC, complete blood count.

AIDS).[16] An increase in the number of TB cases is due to those with HIV, immigrants, and prisoners. Dissemination throughout the lungs is often called miliary TB.

Evaluation

The patient presentation is not always classic. Patients known to be infected with HIV, immigrants, and the elderly should always be monitored for the development of pulmonary or other organ involvement. Auscultation may reveal posttussive apical rales. Radiographs may demonstrate nodules or infiltrates in the apical or posterior segments in the upper lobes. However, there is much variation. Calcified areas (Ghon lesion) indicate healed primary TB. The definitive diagnostic tool is sputum stain (Kinyoun or Ziehl-Neelsen) and culture. Fiberoptic bronchoscopy may be necessary if not enough sputum is available. Skin testing is unable to distinguish active, current disease from past infection. The multiple-puncture test is used for group screening or the Mantoux test is used for individual testing.

Management

Referral for medical management is necessary. All cases demonstrating positive findings and those in whom there is a high suspicion must be reported to local and state public health departments. This is best left to the treating physician. Because of the development of TB-resistant organisms, the Centers for Disease Control and Prevention have developed a new strategy that involves multiple drug application and monitoring. Isoniazid and rifampin are supported by other medications such as pyrazinamide and streptomycin.

POSTNASAL DRIP

Classic Presentation

The patient complains of a chronic cough that seems worse while lying down (supine). The patient reports a dry or nonproductive cough. He or she may also notice a persistent tickle at the back of the throat, requiring frequent clearing of the throat.

Cause

There are a variety of causes, including upper respiratory infection, sinusitis, allergies, drugs (eg, ACE inhibitors), smoking, and environmental pollutants. Chronic irritation of the pharyngeal and tracheal membranes initiates the cough reflex. Postnasal drip is by far the most common cause of chronic cough.

Evaluation

Classically, there will be a cobblestone appearance of the posterior mucosa; however, this is a nonspecific finding. Primarily, it is necessary to identify the underlying cause through a history. If there is associated nasal congestion, a suspicion of sinusitis warrants sinus evaluation with skull radiographs.

Management

The patient is instructed to avoid any identifiable triggering stimuli. OTC nasal decongestants or antihistamines used for a short course may be effective. If a prescribed medication is the suspect, such as an ACE inhibitor, referral back to the prescribing physician is necessary. Failure to respond to conservative measures requires referral for prescribed decongestants or antihistamines. An evaluation of sinusitis is warranted if this treatment trial fails. There is a nasal-specific technique used by some chiropractors for the treatment of sinusitis; however, it should be used only by those with special training and experience. Physicians often will use a trial of antibiotics first before more invasive procedures.

CHRONIC BRONCHITIS

Classic Presentation

The patient complains of a chronic productive cough for 3 months or more in at least 2 consecutive years. The patient is a smoker.

Cause

Airway blockage occurs as a result of metaplasia of cells, smooth muscle hypertrophy, and increased mucus production. It appears that chronic cigarette smoking is the major risk factor. However, air pollution, respiratory infections, and allergies have all been implicated as contributory. Chronic bronchitis and emphysema often coexist in the later stages of COPD.

Evaluation

Initially, the patient is asymptomatic. Unlike the purely emphysematous patient, the patient with chronic bronchitis is often overweight and may show some degree of cyanosis. Dyspnea is primarily exertion related. The prominent feature at presentation is a chronic productive cough. Auscultation often will reveal rhonci or wheezes. Chest films will show an increase in markings with an associated cardiomegaly. ECG changes may indicate right ventricular hypertrophy.

Management

The primary treatment is the same for prevention: cessation of smoking and avoidance of any known irritants such as dusts or other pollutants. Complications such as associated asthmatic reaction or infections warrant comanagement with a medical physician.

BRONCHOGENIC CARCINOMA

Classic Presentation

The patient is older than 40, has a history of smoking, and complains of a persistent cough, hemoptysis, weight loss, and anorexia.

Cause

Primary lung cancer is due most often to cigarette smoking. Additional causes include exposure to therapeutic radiation, heavy metals, or industrial toxins such as asbestos. Bronchogenic carcinoma is classified according to cell type, including squamous cell, adenocarcinoma, small cell, and large cell carcinomas. In general, squamous cell and small cell carcinomas are more central in location, demonstrating a tendency for widespread metastasis. Adenocarcinoma and large cell carcinoma are usually more peripherally located in the lungs. Because the lungs themselves are insensitive to pain, widespread involvement may occur without symptoms. Until bronchi are compressed or eroded or the pleura is involved, the patient is usually asymptomatic.

Evaluation

By the time obvious symptoms and signs are evident, the cancer has often reached a stage that is not amenable to treatment. About one fifth of cases may demonstrate lymphadenopathy, splenomegaly, and clubbing of the fingers.

Horner's syndrome (miosis, ptosis, and anhydrosis) from a Pancoast (apical) tumor is seen in a small number of cases (<5%). Auscultation may reveal a solitary wheeze or nothing at all. Laboratory tests may reveal nonspecific but incriminating evidence of metastasis, including increased calcium, alkaline phosphatase, or anemia. Sputum cytologic examination will confirm the diagnosis in over half of cases if the cancer is centrally located. Chest radiographs usually will demonstrate nonspecific yet important clues, including hilar masses, atelectasis, pleural effusions, or mediastinal widening. If suspicious findings are evident computed tomography or magnetic resonance imaging is helpful in determining the degree of involvement and may suggest the type based on location and pathologic process viewed.

Management

Treatment includes surgery, chemotherapy, and radiation therapy based on the type and staging of disease. Although the overall 5-year survival rate is less than 15%, patients with early squamous cell cancer may have a much higher rate (35% to 40%).[17] Chiropractors treating patients with lung cancer or other cancers that metastasize should be concerned about spinal or joint pains. These may indicate metastasis and warrant first a radiograph of the area and then possible referral for bone scan coordinated with the patient's oncologist.

REFERENCES

1. Irwin RS, Curley FJ, French CL. Chronic cough: the spectrum and frequency of causes, key components of the diagnostic evaluation, and outcomes of specific therapies. *Am Rev Respir Dis.* 1990;141:640.
2. Kamei RK. Chronic cough in children. *Pediatr Clin North Am.* 1991;38:593–604.
3. Corrao WM. Chronic cough: an approach to management. *Comp Ther.* 1986;12:14.
4. Irwin RS, Rosen, MJ, Braman SS. Cough: a comprehensive review. *Arch Intern Med.* 1977;137:1186–1191.
5. Pratter MR, Bartter T, Akers S, et al. An algorithmic approach to chronic cough. *Ann Intern Med.* 1993;119:977–983.
6. Irwin RS, Curley FJ. The diagnosis of chronic cough. *Hosp Pract.* 1988;11:82.
7. Seaton A. The management of cough in clinical practice. *Scott Med J.* 1977;22:99.
8. Adcock JJ. Peripheral opioid receptors and the cough reflex. *Respir Med.* 1991;(suppl A)85:43–46.
9. Korpas J, Widdicombe JG. Aspects of the cough reflex. *Respir Med.* 1991;85:3–5.
10. Fuller RW. Physiology and treatment of cough. *Thorax.* 1990;44:425.
11. Sesoko S, Kaneko Y. Cough associated with use of captopril. *Arch Intern Med.* 1985;145:1324.
12. Karlberg BE. Cough and inhibition of the renin-angiotensin system. *J Hypertens.* 1993;11:549–552.
13. Braman SS, Corao WM. Cough: differential diagnosis and treatment. *Clin Chest Med.* 1987;8:177.
14. Zervanos NJ, Shute KM. Acute, disruptive cough. *Postgrad Med.* 1994;95:153.
15. Johnson D, Osborne LM. Cough-variant asthma: a review of the clinical literature. *J Asthma.* 1991;28:85–90.
16. Barnes PF, Barrows SA. Tuberculosis in the 1990's. *Ann Intern Med.* 1993;119:400.
17. Matthay RA. Lung cancer. *Clin Chest Med.* 1993;14:1.

Part VII

Head and Face Complaints

CHAPTER 43

Eye Complaints

CONTEXT

The prevalence of undetected vision problems appears to be between 5% and 10% in preschool children.[1] Of these, approximately 2% to 5% have amblyopia, "lazy eye."[2] Left uncorrected, vision loss may be permanent. Ninety to ninety-five percent of school-age children have "normal" eyesight.[3] The majority of the children with eyesight problems have refractory errors.

In the elderly, vision loss is more common. In one large study approximately 70% of the nursing home residents over the age of 65 had good vision.[4] Approximately 15% had adequate vision (15/50 to 15/70). Fifteen percent had poor vision of 15/100 or worse (1% had no light perception). Sixty percent of people over the age of 65 have some opacification of the ocular lens, although they are not necessarily impaired. Past the age of 75, 5% of all individuals have exudative macular degeneration (another 25% have the dry, less severe form)[5] and 5% have glaucoma.[6] Approximately 50% have significant cataracts (higher frequency in women). Whites have a higher incidence of macular degeneration, whereas blacks have a higher incidence of untreated cataract, open-angle glaucoma, and diabetic retinopathy.[7] Up to 25% of those wearing glasses had inappropriate visual correction.[8]

Vision loss in the elderly can be a significant factor in fatal car crashes. States that require vision testing for those over the age of 65 have a lower incidence.[9] It is also important to recognize the increased risk of falling when eyesight is poor. Proprioceptive compensation is often diminished in the elderly; therefore, maneuvering in dimly lighted areas places the low-vision senior at risk.

Eye complaints may reflect local pathology in the eye, a reaction to systemic infection or metabolic abnormalities, or vascular/neurologic pathology (Figure 43–1). Most causes of visual loss that are not congenital are treatable or curable. To facilitate an organized approach, each eye complaint is discussed separately under each section. The following is a list of common patient complaints and possible causes:

- loss of vision—may be due to vascular disease (local cause due to retinal infarct; central processes such as stroke are usually associated with other findings), increased intraocular pressure (glaucoma), increased opacification of the lens (cataract), retinal detachment (trauma, vitreoretinal traction, or neovascularization), tumors (distinguished by type of visual field defect and associated cranial nerve findings)
- blurred vision—refractory error (near- or farsightedness), cataracts
- diplopia—monocular (cataract or refractory error), binocular (cranial nerve problem due to tumor, drugs, myasthenia gravis, diabetes, or drugs)
- flashing lights—migraine prodrome, vitreoretinal detachment, epilepsy
- floaters—usually benign unless sudden onset of many may indicate retinal detachment
- photophobia—certain medications, migraine, corneal inflammation, iritis, albinism, fever
- dry eyes—aging, medications (diuretics and anticholinergics), Sjögren's syndrome, Bell's palsy
- eye pain—acute-angle glaucoma, foreign body
- red or pink eye—conjunctivitis, iritis, or uveitis
- itchy eyes—allergies

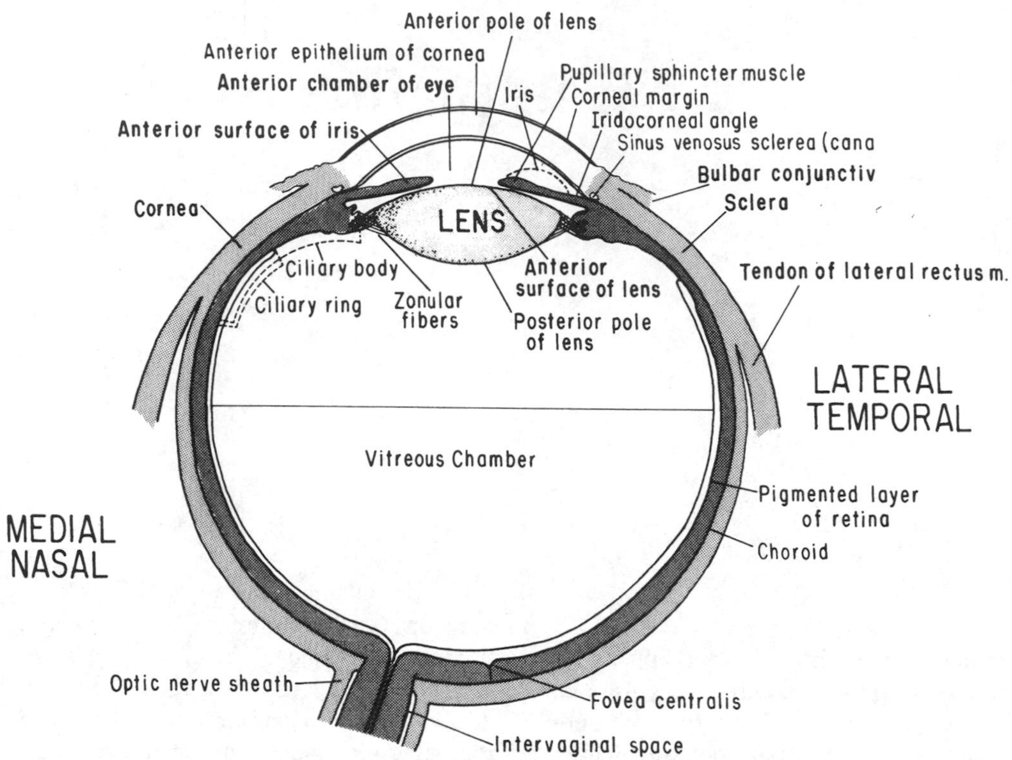

Figure 43–1 Anatomy of the eye, as seen in cross-section. *Source:* Reprinted with permission from B.M. Reilly, *Practical Strategies in Outpatient Medicine*, 2nd ed, p. 36, © 1991, W.B. Saunders Company.

REVIEW OF GENERAL TERMINOLOGY

- Accommodation—to focus on near objects the eyes "accommodate" through contraction of the ciliary muscles, increasing the curvature (convexity) of the lens
- Presbyopia—loss of accommodation with aging
- Amblyopia—loss of vision due to disuse ("lazy eye")
- Myopia—nearsighted; the eye is longer; light rays focus in front of the retina (requires a concave or diverging lens to move the focal point back)
- Hyperopia—farsighted; the eye is shorter; light rays focus at a point behind the retina (if they could pass through) (requires a convex or converging lens to move the focal point forward)
- Astigmatism—the refractory errors in the vertical and horizontal axes differ, requiring a cylindric lens for correction
- Strabismus—deviation of the eye; esotropia = internal deviation; exotropia = external deviation (strabismus may lead to permanent vision loss through cortical suppression of the weak eye)
- Exophthalmos—abnormal protrusion of the eye usually caused by hyperthyroidism due to proteinaceous buildup behind the eye
- Nystagmus—a rhythmic beating movement of the eyes comprised of a fast and slow movement

GENERAL STRATEGY

History

Vision Loss

Determine whether

- The vision loss is acute (often vascular or traumatic) or chronic (macular degeneration, presbyopia), transient (amaurosis fugax, multiple sclerosis, papilledema) or permanent (macular degeneration, retinitis pigmentosa, stroke).
- The vision loss is painful (traumatic or acute-angle glaucoma) or painless (macular degeneration, cataract, open-angle glaucoma, amaurosis fugax). If the vision loss is painless, does the patient have indicators of hypertension, diabetes, or a history of smoking (amaurosis fugax, diabetic retinopathy)?
- The vision loss is unilateral (vascular or neurologic; may eventually become bilateral) or bilateral (usually glaucoma or cataracts).

- The vision loss is central (cataract or macular degeneration [slow onset] or retinal detachment [sudden onset usually]) or peripheral (glaucoma in initial stages or retinitis pigmentosa).
- The vision loss is associated with a headache (migraine [transient prior to headache usually] or temporal arteritis [permanent]).

Blurred Vision

Determine whether

- blurriness is in one or both eyes
- onset is sudden or gradual
- the patient is diabetic (in addition to diabetic retinopathy, diabetics have an increased risk of glaucoma and cataract formation)
- distant or near vision is affected
- corrective lenses have improved vision (last change in prescription)

Diplopia

Determine whether

- patient has monocular (refractory error or cataract) or binocular (vascular, cranial tumor, myasthenia gravis, drug effect, or multiple sclerosis), diplopia
- binocular, whether patient has indicators of tumor, diabetes, or multiple sclerosis

Flashing Lights and/or Floaters

Determine whether

- flashing lights are associated with a headache
- floaters are acute (possible retinal detachment if sudden onset of many) or chronic (usually benign)

Photophobia

Determine whether

- there are associated complaints such as redness or itchiness, or headache
- the patient is taking any medications that may cause photophobia
- the patient has a fever

Dry or Gritty Eyes

Determine whether

- the patient has indicators of hyperthyroidism (exophthalmos may prevent proper lubrication)
- the patient has indicators of Sjögren's syndrome

Eye Pain (without Vision Loss)

Determine whether

- it is felt superficially (local pathology) or behind the eye (referred pain from headache or tumor)
- there are accompanying signs or symptoms such as a urinary tract infection (Reiter's syndrome)

Red or Pink Eye

Determine whether

- the redness occurred suddenly without associated itching or pain (subconjunctival hemorrhage from coughing or sneezing)
- there is associated debris and itching (conjunctivitis)
- there are associated signs of allergies

Examination

- Observe and inspect for redness, dryness, eye deviation, lid lag, and exophthalmos.
- Perform a battery of tests to check for extraocular muscle weakness, symmetry of the eyes, a cover test.
- Test for pupillary reaction and accommodation.
- Test for visual acuity with a Snellen eye chart or Jaeger chart with adults; with children, picture cards or oriented E charts are valuable.
- Test for color perception in male children and those not previously tested.
- Examine the anterior chamber with a temporally positioned light.
- Refer for slit-lamp or flourescein stain if corneal abrasion or foreign body is suspected.
- Refer for tonometry when glaucoma is suspected.

EVALUATION

History

Vision Loss

Although it may appear that by simply asking the patient whether he or she has difficulty seeing would be an effective screen for vision loss, studies have shown that it is not. It is estimated that 1 million individuals have glaucoma and are unaware of significant vision loss. When adult patients were asked, "Do you have difficulty seeing distant objects?" the sensitivity for detecting vision worse than 20/40 was only 28%.[10] The question, "Can you see well enough to recognize a friend across the street (while wearing glasses)?" had a sensitivity of only 48%.[11]

When vision loss is sudden, a vascular cause is likely. When there are other associated neurologic signs, a site proximal to the eye is the cause. When vision loss is the only neurologic sign and its appearance is without pain, amaurosis fugax (microembolism from carotid arteries) or retinal detachment is likely. The patient will often describe either occurrence as "a curtain was pulled down over my eye." The difference is that amaurosis fugax usually lasts only for minutes while vision loss from retinal detachment does not improve without treatment. The vision loss from temporal arteritis is also painless and often sudden or over a few days due to infarction of the optic nerve head. Associated signs of temporal arteritis are a temporal headache, neck and upper trunk myopathy (polymyalgia rheumatica), and general arthralgia prior to the loss of vision.

Other than trauma, acute, painful loss of vision is usually due to acute-angle glaucoma. Associated indicators are age over 60 years, a family history, nausea and vomiting, provocation from prolonged periods in a dark environment, and drugs that cause dilation of the pupils, such as anticholinergics (antiparkinsonian drugs, antidepressants, and some gastrointestinal drugs).

Gradually developing vision loss or blurriness is common with progressive refractory errors, glaucoma, cataracts, diabetic retinopathy, and macular degeneration. With chronic open-angle glaucoma, the patient often will have a bilateral peripheral vision loss (often in the nasal field). Historical indicators of predisposition to glaucoma include a family history (occasionally), topical or systemic corticosteroid use, prior surgery or trauma to the eye, and diabetes. Cataracts are also seen in the elderly, producing a gradual loss of central vision. Associated indicators include a change in color vision and halos around lights, affecting the patient's ability to drive at night. There are different types of cataracts; however, with nuclear cataracts, some patients report an improvement with near vision early in the course of the disorder. Macular degeneration is usually bilateral with progressive central vision loss.

Red Eye

Patients complaining of itchy eyes, a foreign-body sensation, tearing, and eyelid edema likely have bacterial or viral conjunctivitis, especially if the symptoms occurred in one eye and over the following 2 days involved both eyes. When the complaint is bilateral from the onset, allergic conjunctivitis is more likely. The discharge is purulent and more profuse with a viral or bacterial cause and more watery with allergic conjunctivitis.

Examination

Some initial observational clues that are helpful include the following:

- Groping, squinting, or craning of the neck often will indicate loss of vision.
- Eye deviation (strabismus), unequal or absent movement of the eyes, ptosis (Horner's or oculomotor nerve), or inability to close the eyes (facial nerve) are indicators of nerve damage.
- Exophthalmos or lid lag indicates hyperthyroidism.
- Loss of the outer eyebrows indicates hypothyroidism; scaling of the eyebrows indicates seborrhea.
- Red or pink eyes with discharge suggest conjunctivitis; without discharge and with pain suggest acute uveitis.

A general screen for the eye should include visual acuity testing, extraocular muscle function, tests for eye position with a light and cover card, pupillary reflex, a corneal status check with a flashlight, accommodation, and color vision testing in male children or those not tested in the past. Following is a brief discussion of each:

- Extraocular muscle function is tested in several ways. By shining a light about 1 ft away from the patient's eyes the corneal light reflex (Hirschberg test) determines whether the light shines on the same sport on each eye. If not, there is deviation of one of the eyes. Next, the cover test is performed. Have the patient look straight ahead and cover one eye. With the macular image suppressed, the covered eye will drift into a relaxed position. If, when the examiner uncovers the eye, a jump is noted it indicates that a weakness is present and the eye needed to reestablish fixation. Finally, the six-cardinal positions of gaze are tested by holding an object such as a pencil approximately 1 ft away and having the patient track movement into up and out, straight lateral, and down and out paths on both sides. Third-nerve palsy is indicated by deviation that is generally down and out; however, with complete involvement there is paralysis of the eyelid, and lifting the lid by the examiner is necessary to see the deviation. Esotropia and inability to abduct the eye is indicative of sixth nerve involvement. The patient may rotate his or her head to the weak side. A torsional or oblique deviation with head tilt away from the involved side is found with fourth-nerve palsy. In general, when a muscle is weak, the image separation will be greatest while looking into the normal direction of action. Many of these nerve palsies are associated with diplopia. In particular the diplopia will be binocular, meaning that diplopia is present with both eyes open and disappears when either eye is covered. Diplopia that is monocular, meaning that it is present only when the involved eye is open and disappears when it is closed, indicates a refractive error in most cases.
- The pupillary light reflex tests the function of both the second and third cranial nerves. By having the patient

look into the distance, normal eyes will have pupils that dilate. By shining a light from the side, two reactions should occur: (1) pupillary constriction on the side tested and (2) constriction on the opposite side (consensual reflex). If a pupil is large and poorly reactive, a third-nerve palsy is likely. If it is small and poorly reactive, a Horner's syndrome may be present. Fixed and constricted pupils (meiosis) are seen with glaucoma treatment, use of narcotics, or damage to the pons. Fixed and dilated pupils (mydriasis) are seen with severe brain damage or deep anesthesia. Unequal pupils seen without light stimulation that react equally to light are probably anisocoria, a normal variant.

- Accommodation is tested by having the patient look in the distance and then introducing an object in his or her field of gaze. The normal response is pupillary constriction and convergence of the eyes.
- A simple test to observe the anterior chamber is to shine a light from the side across the eye. A nasal shadow across the iris due to a shallow anterior chamber may be seen with glaucoma. Diffuse redness indicates conjunctivitis. Occasionally, corneal lesions or scarring may be seen. For a complete evaluation, referral for slit-lamp evaluation and fluorescein stain are necessary.
- Color blindness affects about 8% of white males (only 4% of black males). Females are only affected 0.4% of the time. Testing should be performed on boys ages 4 to 8 with an Ishihara's test comprising a series of polychromatic cards. The child must identify a pattern made up of a single color of dots against a multicolored background.

A funduscopic examination is more difficult for the chiropractor because tropicamide dilation drops cannot be used. However, with careful observation, some abnormalities may still be visible. A list of possible findings follows:

- disc pallor—optic nerve atrophy
- papilledema—increased intracranial pressure
- vessel nicking, narrowed arteries, silver-wire arteries, and copper-wire arteries—usually due to hypertension
- microaneurysms—seen with diabetes
- soft exudates (cotton-wool patches)—fluffy and irregular; seen with diabetes, hypertension, lupus, subacute bacterial endocarditis, and papilledema
- fatty exudates—well defined, small, regular, and often seen in clusters; found in diabetic and hypertensive retinopathy
- hard exudates (drusen)—normal with aging

Visual Acuity Testing

Screening tests for children between the ages of 3 and 5 years should include inspection, the cover test, visual acuity tests, and stereo vision assessment. Taken together, an estimated negative predictive value of 99% for amblyopia, strabismus, and/or high refractive problems may be achieved.[12,13] Unfortunately, stereo vision testing is not available in most chiropractic offices. For children, the Snellen eye chart is relatively insensitive (25% to 37%).[14] Other visual acuity tests include the Landolt C, the tumbling E, Allen picture cards (familiar objects or animals), and others.[15] The advantage of these tests is that the ability to read is not tested as much as the ability to determine orientation of a letter or recognition of an object or animal.

Snellen eye charts should always be used as the initial screening for visual acuity in adults. With the Snellen eye chart test, the patient is expected to read with one eye at a time, covering the other with a card. The patient should keep his or her glasses (unless they are reading glasses) or contacts on. Encourage patients to read to the smallest line possible. The recorded measurement includes two numbers. The first number represents the distance the patient was standing (20 = 20 ft) and the second number indicates the distance at which a normal eye could read that specific line (lettersize = 20 micrometers) (20 = a normal eye could see this line at 20 ft). For patients who have difficulty reading, a hand-held version such as the Jaeger card may be used. In the United States, an individual is legally blind if vision is 20/200 or less in the better eye with correction. If peripheral vision is reduced to 10° or less in both eyes (tested on perimetry) the patient is also considered legally blind even if his or her central vision is better than 20/200.

A simple test for visual acuity that tests for refractory errors is the pinhole test. Repeating the Snellen test with the patient looking through a 2-mm pinhole in a card will improve performance if the cause is a refractory error. The patient may state that the image is dimmer (this is due to less light being allowed into the eye).

Confrontation testing is used to test for visual field defects. All fields are the same for the examiner (except in the temporal field). Therefore, when a patient is asked to say "now" when a finger or object enters his or her visual perception, the examiner should see it at the same time. With a temporal field examination it is necessary to start with the finger or object behind the patient and advance it forward. The patient should see it at approximately 90°. Visual field testing may indicate where the problem is in the vision relay system. Following is a brief, generalized list:

- central scotoma—optic nerve involvement
- nasal quadrant deficits—glaucoma is a common cause
- bilateral temporal field deficits—compression at the optic chiasma (often from a tumor)
- homozygous hemianopic deficit (same side in both eyes)—optic tract to the calcarine cortex

Red or Pink Eye

When there is purulent discharge associated with eyelid involvement with crusted material and no associated preauricular lymph node involvement, the patient will probably have a bacterial conjunctivitis requiring referral. When crusting of the eyelids is a predominant finding, a blepharitis (bacterial infection of the sebaceous follicles and meibomian glands) has occurred through extension of the conjunctivial infection. When the conjunctivitis is more watery or mucuslike, with no crusting, and associated with preauricular node involvement, a viral cause (usually adenovirus) is likely. Other conditions, such as corneal abrasion or infection, often will be accompanied by pain, impaired vision, light sensitivity, and unequal pupils. These added findings dictate referral to an ophthalmologist for further evaluation. Also, patients with eye inflammation who have had prior eye surgery, wear contact lenses, or have a history of herpes simplex keratitis should also be referred to an ophthalmologist.

A similar presentation may occur with the use of eye drops (prescribed or over-the-counter [OTC]). This is usually bilateral and is a diagnosis of exclusion. Referral back to a prescribing physician for evaluation or discontinuing an OTC eyedrop is usually effective.

MANAGEMENT

Immediate referral to an ophthalmologist is needed in the following cases:

- acute glaucoma
- abrasion of the cornea or foreign body implantation
- temporal arteritis
- retinal detachment
- suspicion of bacterial conjunctivitis
- acute cerebrovascular event

Nonemergent referral to an ophthalmologist is needed in the following cases:

- suspicion of open-angle glaucoma, age-related macular degeneration, cataracts
- cases where there is progressive loss of vision without a known cause
- patients interested in radiokeratotomy or laser ablation therapy

Referral to an optometrist (with the possibility of comanagement) should be made in the following cases:

- children age 4 years and over with vision 20/40 or worse in either eye or difference between two eyes of one line or more on the Snellen eye chart
- all patients with indication of diabetic retinopathy (to determine need for ophthalmologic referral)
- patients who wear glasses but have lost the corrective ability of the lenses

Recommendations for prevention of vision loss include the following:

- All children between ages 3 and 4 years should have a visual screening.
- All individuals over 40 (particularly blacks) should have a tonometry and ophthalmoscopic examination every 3 to 5 years to detect glaucoma.
- All diabetics should be closely monitored for any vision changes and have a minimum of an annual eye examination; emphasis on control of diabetes is crucial to the prevention of diabetic retinopathy.
- All hypertensive patients should be educated regarding the higher probability of vision loss with chronic hypertension, and a program to reduce hypertension should be strictly adhered to.

Therefore, the chiropractor may act as a screening source for many eye problems. Although there are anecdotal and in some cases paper presentations of recovery of eyesight with chiropractic care, it is too early to recommend this approach as an isolated attempt.[16] Comanagement with an optometrist or ophthalmologist is highly suggested for purposes of both patient safety and documentation. Although older theories focused on a proposed sympathetic nervous system irritation, a more convincing theory suggests cerebral hibernation as a cause, with manipulation "reviving" the quiescent nerve cells. The theory is based on an observation that when cerebral blood flow is deprived from an area of the brain, cell death occurs. However, if the vascular reduction is less than that causing death, a protective cellular hibernation with no apparent electrical activity occurs. When the blood flow is returned to the area, cellular function returns.[17] One study claims such a response in cerebral blood flow following manipulative therapy.[18] With regard to lesser vision problems such as phorias and tropias, there is a theory that the relationship between cervical input into the vestibular nuclei and other connections may have an effect on cranial nerves or extraoccular muscle function. There have been two small studies of patients without glaucoma who demonstrate a reduction in intraocular pressure after spinal manipulation.[19,20] Unfortunately, tonometry is known to be quite variable, and the results might be flawed by this deficiency.

Patients who are classified as legally blind are not able to obtain a driver's license and have some restrictions in contact or vehicle-operated sports. These individuals are eligible for assistance with education, visual aids, and seeing-eye dogs.

Algorithm

An algorithm for evaluation and management of vision problems in the elderly is presented in Figure 43–2.

Figure 43–2

VISION PROBLEMS IN THE ELDERLY—ALGORITHM.

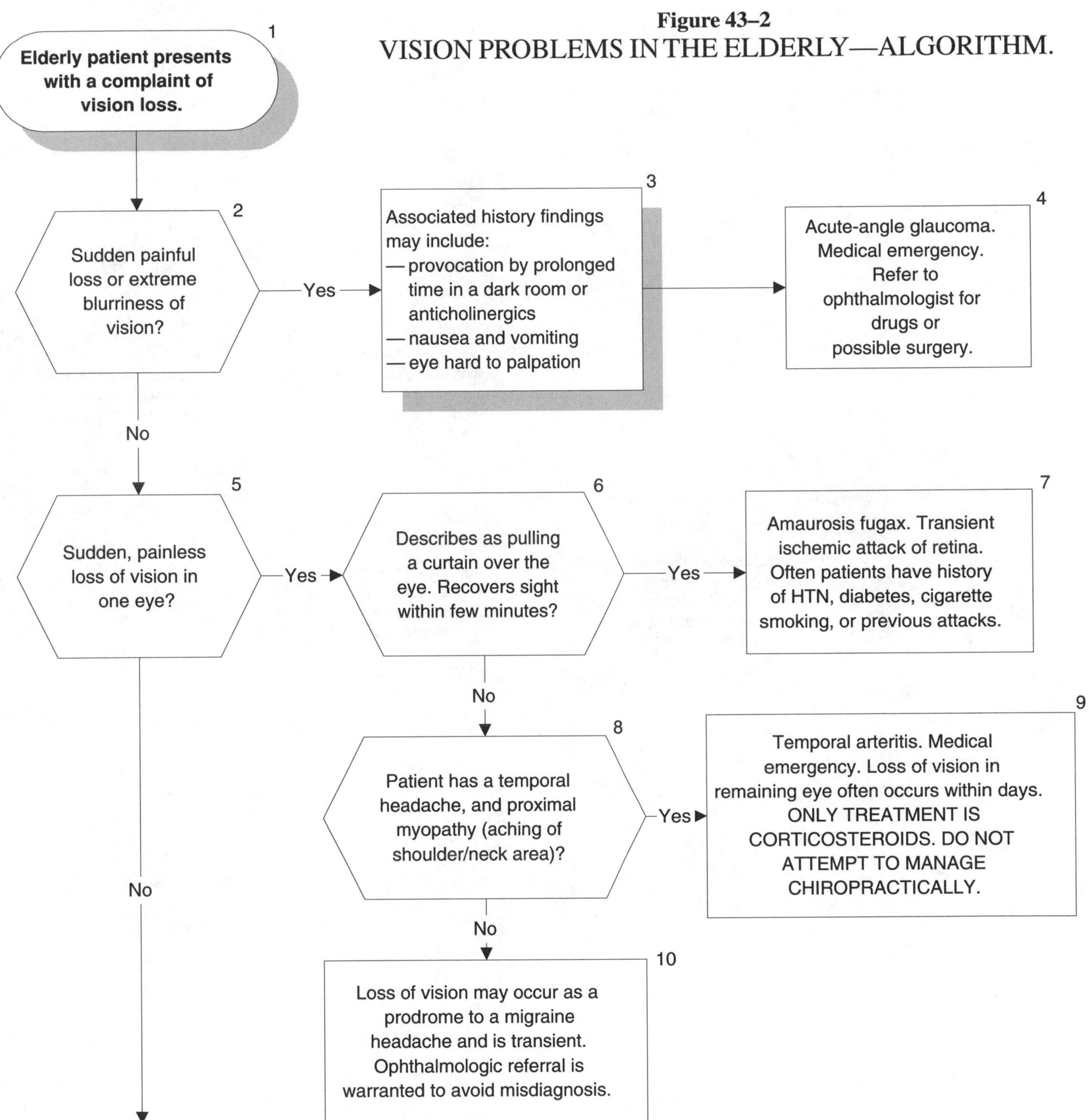

1
Elderly patient presents with a complaint of vision loss.
2
Sudden painful loss or extreme blurriness of vision?
Yes
3
Associated history findings may include:
— provocation by prolonged time in a dark room or anticholinergics
— nausea and vomiting
— eye hard to palpation
4
Acute-angle glaucoma. Medical emergency. Refer to ophthalmologist for drugs or possible surgery.
No
5
Sudden, painless loss of vision in one eye?
Yes
6
Describes as pulling a curtain over the eye. Recovers sight within few minutes?
Yes
7
Amaurosis fugax. Transient ischemic attack of retina. Often patients have history of HTN, diabetes, cigarette smoking, or previous attacks.
No
8
Patient has a temporal headache, and proximal myopathy (aching of shoulder/neck area)?
Yes
9
Temporal arteritis. Medical emergency. Loss of vision in remaining eye often occurs within days. ONLY TREATMENT IS CORTICOSTEROIDS. DO NOT ATTEMPT TO MANAGE CHIROPRACTICALLY.
No
10
Loss of vision may occur as a prodrome to a migraine headache and is transient. Ophthalmologic referral is warranted to avoid misdiagnosis.
No

continues

Figure 43–2 continued

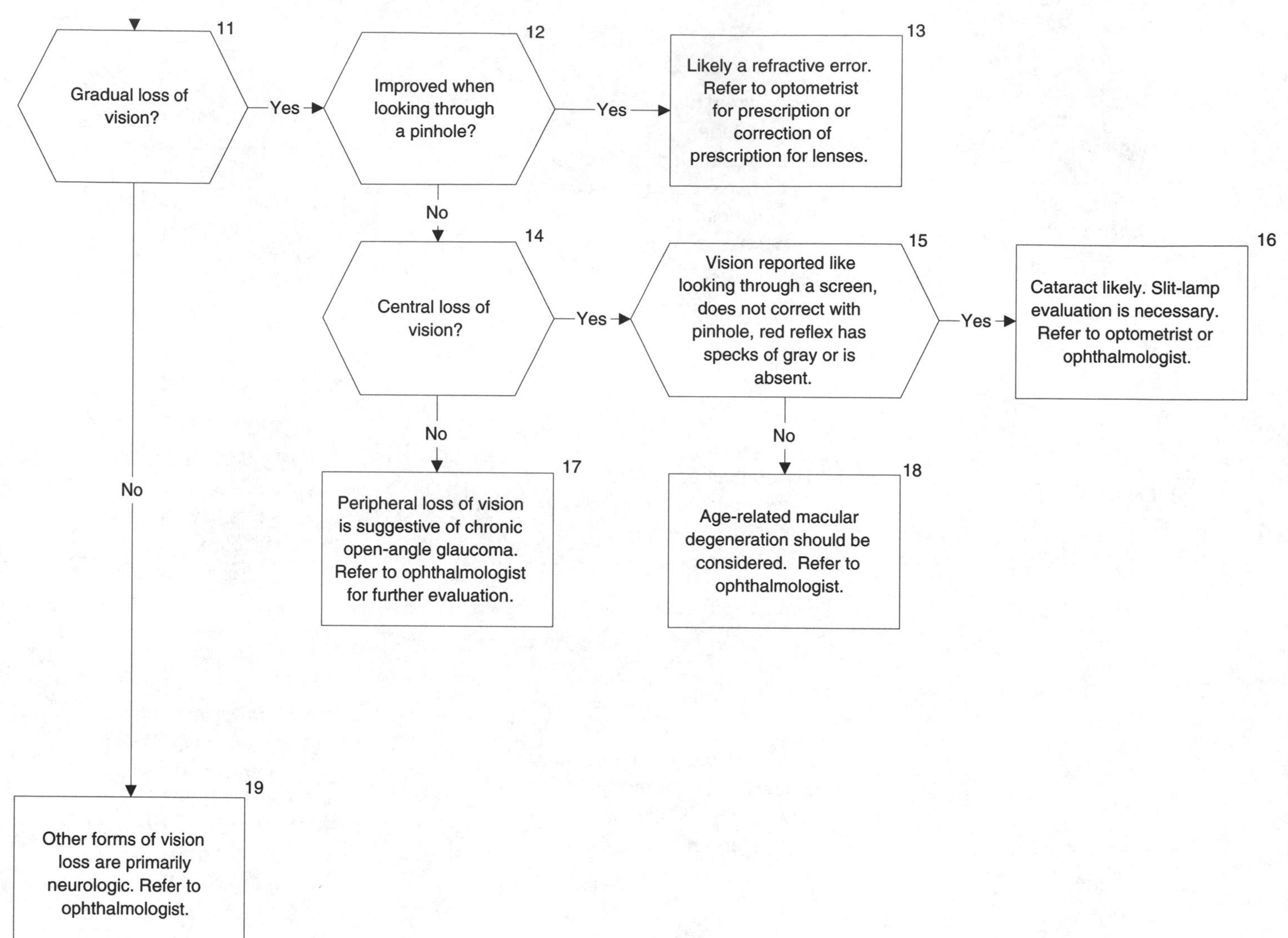

Key: HTM, hypertension.

SELECTED CAUSES OF VISION LOSS

ACUTE ANGLE-CLOSURE GLAUCOMA

Classic Presentation

A patient with acute glaucoma is likely to seek emergency care because of severe pain. If a patient presents to a chiropractic office, the presentation would be eye pain associated with a complaint of halos around light, blurred unilateral vision, and possibly nausea and vomiting. The patient may report having been in a prolonged dark environment such as a movie theater, during stress, or having had his or her eyes dilated for medical purposes. The patient is usually a senior with a positive family history for acute angle-closure glaucoma.[6]

Cause

Blocked outflow of aqueous humor from the anterior chamber causes increased pressure and severe pain. The "angle" is formed between the cornea and the root of the iris. The outflow canal that is blocked consists of a trabecular network and the canal of Schlemm. Preexisting narrow angles are found in the elderly (due to lens enlargement), patients with hyperopia, and Asians.[7] Fortunately, acute-angle glaucoma accounts for less than 10% of all glaucoma cases.

Evaluation

Because the patient is likely to see an emergency physician, examination is not commonly necessary. However, if less acute, the chiropractor should be aware of acute glaucoma as a possible cause of eye pain. The patient will have eye redness (ciliary flush) and a cloudy-looking cornea. The depth of the anterior chamber can be assessed with a penlight. Shining the penlight from the side, a shadow will be visible over the nasal half of the iris. The eye is hard to palpation.

Management

This is a medical emergency. A permanent correction may be accomplished with laser peripheral iridectomy. Left untreated, the patient will have permanent vision loss in 3 to 5 days.

OPEN-ANGLE GLAUCOMA

Classic Presentation

Unfortunately, a patient with early open-angle glaucoma has no warning symptoms. If undetected, a patient would present with a complaint of a peripheral visual field "cut," usually the nasal half.

Cause

The cause is unknown; however, a surfacing theory is that glaucoma is an optic nerve disease that may be related to specific vascular changes.[21] Additionally, these vascular changes may be caused by free radicals (as in stroke or similar diseases). The intraocular pressure is chronically elevated in patients with this type of glaucoma, yet the cause is unknown. It is usually bilateral and seen earlier in blacks than other ethnic groups. The patient may be genetically predisposed to an adverse reaction to topical or oral corticosteroids, leading to the development of glaucoma. Past eye surgery or trauma may also predispose the patient.

Evaluation

The evaluation for glaucoma in the chiropractic setting is difficult. There would have to be a high level of suspicion (given most patients are asymptomatic) and the tools and expertise to perform a comprehensive examination. These include tonometry (the measurement of intraocular pressure), ophthalmoscopic visualization of specific changes, and visual field testing. If the glaucoma is advanced, visual field testing may reveal an upper nasal field cut. Ophthalmoscopic changes include cupping of the disc and nasal displacement of the vessels.

Management

Ophthalmoscopic referral is necessary. Initial treatment is with medication. Failure to improve usually requires a referral for laser trabeculoplasty.

CATARACTS

Classic Presentation

The patient is usually a senior complaining of progressive, painless, central vision loss or blurred vision. Ironically, some patients may report an improvement in close vision in the initial stages of cataract formation.

Cause

A cataract is due to opacification of the lens. There are several different types and causes, including congenital (often due to rubella and cytomegalovirus intrauterine infection), secondary to diabetes, chronic corticosteroid use, or uveitis. However, the most common type is that associated with aging—senile cataract. Chronic ultraviolet light exposure appears to be the main cause with aging. Most patients over the age of 50 have some degree of lens opacification, yet not all have a visual impairment. Risk factors include cigarette smoking or alcohol abuse.[22,23]

Evaluation

The vision loss is central and not improved by looking through a pinhole. There is a normal pupillary reaction. Ophthalmoscopic examination may reveal flecks of gray appearing with the red reflex, or obliteration of the red reflex in advanced cases. Visualization of the opacity is possible in later stages, but a slit-lamp examination is necessary to locate it (and therefore the type of cataract).

Management

The decision to have cataracts removed must be a weighted process, taking into account the age of the patient, the degree of cataract formation, and most important the effect on function. For example, an 80-year-old patient confined to bed may not have the same benefits as a younger, more active patient. Surgery involves one of two procedures: (1) extracapsular surgery and (2) phacoemulsification. Extracapsular surgery leaves the posterior capsule of the lens intact, providing a firm anchoring for the implant. Phacoemulsification, called no-stitch surgery, involves fractionation of the lens with sound waves. Future use of lasers for the same procedure is being researched. Foldable silicone implants have been developed that can be inserted through smaller incisions and with newer techniques can be implanted with no sutures. Bifocal or multifocal lenses are also available in some locations.[24]

AGE-RELATED MACULAR DEGENERATION

Classic Presentation

The patient may present differently based on the underlying type. A patient with atrophic (dry) degeneration will complain of slowly developing, painless, central vision loss. A patient with the disciform (wet) degeneration presents with sudden, painless loss of vision. Prior to loss the patient may notice parts of words missing or straight lines appearing crooked.

Cause

Age-related macular degeneration (ARMD) is the leading cause of blindness in the geriatric population. It affects up to 30% of the elderly to varying degrees. Ninety percent of cases are the dry, slowly progressive form.[5] Associated risk factors include smoking and a family history of ARMD. Asians have a very low risk; whites a higher risk. Individuals with light blue or green irises or exposure to intense blue light are also at risk. The layer between the retinal pigmented epithelium and choriocapillaries is called Bruch's membrane. Degeneration of this membrane and the retinal pigmented epithelium results in the atrophic form. If degeneration allows ingrowth of new vessels (neovascularization) the exudative or wet form occurs.

Evaluation

Funduscopic findings include drusen (yellow-white spots) and hyper- or hypopigmentation of the fundi with the atrophic form. Hemorrhages and exudates are seen. Patients at risk for ARMD are often told to use a straight line or Ansler grid to detect any new distortion, which would require immediate consultation with an ophthalmologist.

Management

There is no treatment for the dry form of ARMD, yet low-vision aids and adaptation to gradual loss are usually sufficient to allow mobility. Patients with the wet form of ARMD often require laser photocoagulation to ablate the neovascular membrane. The location of the membrane affects the success of the laser ablation. In some cases, restoration of some central vision may reduce general vision, yet, ironically, prevent blindness. Up to 60% of patients need repeat treatment because of regrowth. It appears that a diet high in vitamin A and antioxidants (large amounts of fruits and vegetables) may reduce the risk of developing ARMD.[25]

RETINITIS PIGMENTOSA

Classic Presentation

The patient is often a youngster who notices (or a parent notices) poor night vision.

Cause

This disorder is hereditary, with recessive, autosomal dominant, and X-linked modes identified. It may also occur as part of Bassen-Kornzweig syndrome or Laurence-Moon-Biedl syndrome. Degeneration of the retina, particularly the retinal rods, occurs. This is why night vision loss is one of the earliest signs. A peripheral-ring scotoma usually expands to include some central vision by middle age.

Evaluation

Funduscopic examination will reveal dark pigmentation in the equatorial region of the retina, often associated with a yellow, waxy disk. Definitive diagnosis requires specialized testing that includes dark adaptation, electroretinography, and electrooculography.

Management

No treatment is currently effective. Genetic counseling is recommended in those affected. Retinoid supplementation is advocated by many, yet the results have not been clearly reproducible. In the future it is hoped that genetic engineering may allow replacement of the defective gene. Retinal transplantation is currently being researched.

AMAUROSIS FUGAX

Classic Presentation

The patient is usually over the age of 50 years and complains of an episode of vision loss in one eye that lasted a few minutes and then the vision returned. The patient often describes the loss and recovery of vision like a shade being pulled down and raised, respectively. There is often a history of diabetes, hypertension, or smoking.

Cause

Emboli originating in the ipsilateral internal carotid travel to the retina via branches of the ophthalmic artery, causing a "fleeting blindness," amaurosis fugax. The same risk factors for atherosclerosis are found, such as hypertension, diabetes, and chronic cigarette smoking.

Evaluation

An ipsilateral carotid bruit may be heard. Funduscopic examination will usually reveal signs of hypertensive disease. Additionally, whitish emboli and/or refractive cholesterol emboli may be seen. Patients should be sent for Doppler studies and possibly angiography to determine the extent of stenosis.

Management

After an attack, the patient should be warned of a predisposition to stroke or loss of vision if a subsequent attack occurs (16% of patients).[26] Aspirin and antiplatelet drugs are used in patients with mild stenosis. Endarterectomy has a high success rate in patients with severe stenosis. There is a subgroup of patients who are younger and have no signs of atherosclerosis or stenosis. The belief is that these patients may suffer from retinal artery spasm. These patients will be placed on a calcium channel blocker. For obvious reasons, patients who have had an attack of amaurosis fugax are probably at somewhat greater risk with cervical adjustments. Other techniques should be employed.

OPTIC NEURITIS

Classic Presentation

The patient presents with an abrupt loss of vision in one eye. Central vision is affected and may progressively worsen over the next 2 days. If the patient presents 2 to 3 weeks later the vision often has returned to normal. However, now the patient has some eye pain associated with eye movement.

Cause

Inflammation of the optic nerve is usually due to demyelinating disorders, specifically multiple sclerosis (MS). It may occur less commonly with a host of other problems such as infection (mumps, measles, influenza, or varicella virus), autoimmune disorders (lupus), bee sting, meningitis, or infarction from temporal arteritis.

Evaluation

Opthalmoscopic evaluation by a specialist is required.

Management

In the past, oral prednisone was used; however, it has been discovered that this approach, in addition to not being effective, doubled the risk of recurrence in the following 2 years in the same or opposite eye.[27] Currently, intravenous methylprednisolone sodium succinate, followed by oral prednisone, effects a quicker recovery and has a fortuitous side effect of delaying the onset of MS in some patients.[28]

REFERENCES

1. National Center for Health Statistics. *Refraction Status and Motility Defects of Persons 4–74 Years, 1971–1972. US Vital Health Statistics*, Series II; 1978.
2. Ehrlich MI, Reinecke RD, Simons K. Preschool vision screening for amblyopia and strabismus: Programs, methods, guidelines. *Surv Ophthalmol.* 1983;28:145–163.
3. Hevlston EM, Weber JC, Miller K, et al. Visual function and academic performance. *Am J Ophthalmol.* 1985;99:346–355.
4. Tielsch JM, Javitt JC, Coleman A, et al. The prevalence of blindness and visual impairment among nursing home residents in Baltimore. *N Engl J Med.* 1995;332:1205–1209.
5. Klein R, Klein BE, Linton KL. Prevalence of age-related maculopathy: the Beaver Dam eye study. *Ophthalmology.* 1992; 99:933–943.
6. Klein BE, Klein R, Sponsel WE, et al. Prevalence of glaucoma: the Beaver Dam eye study. *Ophthalmology.* 1992;99:1499–1504.
7. Sommer A, Tiesch JM, Katz J, et al. Racial differences in the cause-specific prevalence of blindness in East Baltimore. *N Engl J Med.* 1991;325:1412–1417.
8. Stults BM. Preventive health care for the elderly. *West J Med.* 1984;141:832–845.
9. Nelson DE, Sacks JJ, Chorba TI. Required vision testing for older drivers. *N Engl J Med.* 1992;326:1784–1785.
10. Stone DH, Shannon DJ. Screening for impaired vision in middle age in general practice. *Br Med J.* 1978;2:859–861.
11. Haase KW, Bryant EE. Development of a scale designed to measure functional vision loss using an interview technique. *Proc Am Stat Assoc.* 1973;(SS):274–279.
12. De Becker I, MacPherson HJ, LaRoche GR, et al. Negative predictive value of a population-based preschool vision screening program. *Ophthalmology.* 1992;99:998–1003.
13. MacPherson H, Braunsetin J, LaRoche GR. Utilizing basic screening principles in the design and evaluation of vision screening programs. *Am Orthopt J.* 1991;41:110–121.
14. Lieberman S, Cohen AH, Stolzberg M, Ritty JM. Validation study of the New York State Optometric Association (NYSOA) vision screening battery. *Am J Optom Physiol Optics.* 1985;62:165–168.
15. Fern KD, Manney RE. Visual acuity of the preschool child: a review. *Am J Optom Physiol Optics.* 1986;63:319–345.
16. Terrett AGJ, Gorman RF. The eye, cervical spine, and spinal manipulative therapy: a review of the literature. *Chiro Tech.* 1995;7: 43–54.
17. Astrup J, Siesjo BK, Symon L. Thresholds in cerebral ischemia: the ischemic prenumbra. *Stroke.* 1981;12:723–725.
18. Zhang C, Wang Y, Lu W, et al. Study on cervical visual disturbance and its manipulative treatment. *J Tradid Chin Med.* 1984;4: 205–210.
19. Cipolla Vtdubrow CM, Schuller EA. Preliminary study: an evaluation of the effects of osteopathic manipulative therapy on intraocular pressure. *J Am Osteopath Assoc.* 1975;74:147–151.
20. Beckenstein L. Glaucoma: detection and management. *J Chiro.* 1969;6:525–527.
21. Drance SM. Glaucoma: changing concepts. *Eye.* 1992;6:337.
22. Ritter LL. Alcohol use and lens opacities in the Beaver Dam eye study. *Arch Ophthalmology.* 1993;111:113.
23. Christin WG. A prospective study of cigarette smoking and risk of cataract in men. *JAMA.* 1992;268:989.
24. Sher NA, Trobe JD, Weingeist TA. New options for vision loss. *Patient Care.* 1995;9:55–76.
25. Seddon JM, Ajani UA, Sperduto RD, et al. Dietary carotenoids: vitamins A, C, and E, and advanced age-related macular degeneration. *JAMA.* 1994;272:1413–1420.
26. Li L. Vision problems in the elderly. In: Greene HL, Fincher RME, Johnson WP, et al, eds. *Clinical Medicine.* 2nd ed. St. Louis, MO: Mosby-Year Book; 1996;678–682.
27. Beck RW, Cleary PA, Anderson MM Jr, et al. A randomized, controlled trial of corticosteroids in the treatment of acute optic neuritis. *N Engl J Med.* 1992;326:581–588.
28. Beck RW, Cleary PA, Trobe JD, et al. The effect of corticosteroids for acute optic neuritis on the subsequent development of multiple sclerosis. *N Engl J Med.* 1993;329:1764–1769.

CHAPTER 44

Facial Pain

CONTEXT

Initial distinction between facial pain and headache is necessary. Facial pain may arise from several anatomic sources, including the ears, oral cavity, sinuses, cervical spine, and eyes. Although there is obvious overlap and the possibility of referral, patient localization and associated findings are usually revealing.[1] Facial pain is best approached from a temporal perspective. Sudden onset with recurrent attacks is typical of several neuralgias. Deep, boring, aching pain is more characteristic of oral, ear, eye, and sinus problems, and intracranial pathology. Dental causes are often distinguished by oral stimuli such as cold, hot, sweetness, or pressure.

GENERAL STRATEGY

History

- Distinguish among facial, ear, eye, oral, and headache pain.
- Determine whether the onset is sudden and recurrent (neuralgic) or chronic (intracranial or eyes, ears, nose, and throat [EENT]).
- Determine the quality of pain; sharp, lancinating pain of relatively short duration suggests neuralgias; deep, boring pain is more characteristic of dental, sinus, and intracranial masses.

Neuralgias

- Determine whether the pain is acute or chronic.
- If acute, determine whether there are any triggers such as shaving, cold, eating, or other (trigeminal neuralgia).
- Determine whether the pains are sharp and stabbing in the mouth and awaken the person at night (possible glossopharygenal neuralgia).
- Determine whether there are any associated neurologic symptoms (neuralgia secondary to other processes such as multiple sclerosis).

Oral Cavity

- Determine whether there has been any recent prolonged dental work and/or last dental examination.
- Determine whether pain is related to eating cold, hot, or sweet foods.

Sinus

- Determine whether there is a prior or current history of a upper respiratory infection.
- Determine whether there are positional exacerbations of the pain (ie, bending forward or lying down).

Temporomandibular Joint

- Determine whether opening the mouth increases the pain.
- Determine whether there is a history of grinding teeth.
- Determine whether there is a history of popping or clicking at the temporomandibular joint (TMJ).

Myofascial

- Determine whether the pain location includes the periaural or temporal area.
- Determine whether the pain is in the region of the masseter (cheeks) and associated with prolonged opening of the mouth or movement of the jaw.

Psychologic

- Determine whether the patient may be depressed or have periods of stress, drug addiction, or a dysfunctional home environment.
- Determine whether there is a family history of similar complaints.

Evaluation

- Examine the eyes, ears, nose, throat, and TMJ for any obvious pathology with a focus on dental abnormalities.
- When a sinusitis is suspected, transillumination or specific skull radiographs may be helpful in determining involvement.
- When a diagnosis is not clear, referral for special imaging is warranted.

Management

- If tolerable, patients with neuralgias may benefit from a trial treatment with manipulative therapy; if unresponsive after 2 to 3 weeks, referral for medical management is suggested.
- Sinus pain is often self-resolving, but the patient may benefit from facial massage, cervical adjustments, and physical therapy; over-the-counter decongestants have some value with limited use; failure to respond is suggestive of a sinus infection that may require antibiotic management.

RELEVANT NEUROLOGY

The trigeminal nerve is responsible for general sensation of the head and face. The skin of the face and forehead are supplied by three divisions of the trigeminal nerve. The nose, forehead, and scalp to the vertex of the skull are supplied by the ophthalmic (V1) division; the cheek and below the nose to the lip is supplied by the maxillary (V2) division; the jaw to the front of the ear is supplied by the mandibular (V3) division. The trigeminal nerve also supplies the mucosa of the oral and nasal cavities, the paranasal sinuses, the teeth, and most of the dura. The angle of the jaw and scalp of the back of the head are supplied by C2 and C3. Bogduk and Marsland[2] demonstrated that referral pain overlapping the V1 division of the trigeminal nerve may be due to facet irritation.

EVALUATION

History

Neuralgias

Generally, neuralgias are differentiated by a classic onset in older patients (after age 50 years) with a description of sharp, excruciating jolts of facial (or oral) pain that are recurrent and often progressive. The same presentation in a younger patient would suggest other conditions such as multiple sclerosis, a trigeminal neuroma, and, more rarely, an acoustic neuroma.

Trigeminal neuralgia is the most common facial neuralgia. The short, sudden, electric shock–like pains usually follow either the second or third trigeminal branch. Trigger areas may be reported by the patient. Even light touch to, for example, the nasolabial fold or upper lip may trigger an onset if the maxillary branch is involved. An area lateral to the lower lip may trigger an attack with mandibular division involvement.

When the less common glossopharyngeal neuralgia is the cause, pain is felt deep in the oral cavity and palate. Pain often occurs during the night, awakening the patient. Triggers involve relatively common benign activities such as talking, swallowing, yawning, or eating. It appears that salty, spicy, or bitter foods may be triggers. Postnasal drip is occasionally found as a trigger for some patients. Patients may also report having fainted upon coughing or yawning.[3]

Dental

When dental pulp is inflamed (pulpitis) as a result of caries, trauma, or dental surgery, pain is provoked by hot or cold foods and sweets. When the pulp undergoes necrosis, local gas is produced, which, when expanded by heat, increases pressure and causes pain. Cold decreases the gas pressure and relieves the pain. There are apical foramina that connect the pulp to the periodontal ligament and periapical alveolar bone. Infection or inflammation may spread through this connection, leading to a tooth that is sensitive to compressive pressure from chewing or percussion. This is also found with a cracked tooth.

Myofascial

Myofascially related temporomandibular problems are often evident from a history of early-morning jaw pain or if the patient is aware of grinding the teeth throughout the night or day. Other indicators may be pain upon opening the mouth. The pain is often felt at the pretragus area or temporalis muscle and may radiate into the face (see Chapter 3).

Sinus

In many cases there may be a history of an upper respiratory problem currently or preceding the development of facial pain. It may be possible to localize which sinuses are involved by questions regarding positional exacerbation or relief. The pain from frontal sinus involvement is relieved by standing or sitting. It is likely that the patient will report worse pain at night or when lying down and improvement after arising in the morning or as the day progresses. Those patients with maxillary sinus involvement may report the opposite: relief when lying down, which allows better drainage. Sphenoid sinusitis is unusual in that it may refer to the vertex of the skull, the eye, or the neck.

Examination

The examination for facial pain should focus on a detailed examination of the mouth, paying particular attention to dental status and any oral lesions. The examination continues with palpation of facial structures in an attempt to reproduce pain. Patients with neuralgias may have their pain triggered by light touch around the mouth or cheek areas. Palpation of the TMJ while the patient opens and closes the mouth will usually localize the problem. Further evaluation is discussed in Chapter 3.

Acute sinusitis is usually quite obvious, with localized tenderness to either palpation or percussion over the involved sinus. Bending forward may increase pressure and therefore pain in the sinus. When the maxillary sinus is involved, referral to the teeth may produce a complaint of toothache, and percussion of the maxillary teeth may produce discomfort. Transillumination of the sinuses may be decreased. Radiographic evaluation of the sinuses includes the following views (Figure 44–1):[4]

- Waters' view for maxillary sinuses
- Caldwell view for ethmoid sinuses
- Chamberlain-Towne view for frontal sinuses

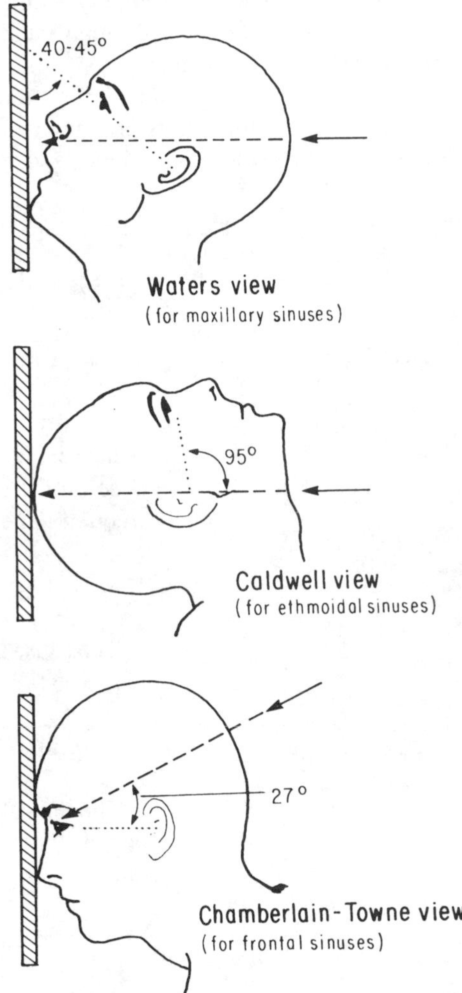

Figure 44–1 Radiographic views of the maxillary, ethmoid, and frontal sinuses. *Source:* Reprinted with permission from B.M. Reilly, *Practical Strategies in Outpatient Medicine*, 2nd ed, p. 137, © 1991, W.B. Saunders Company.

MANAGEMENT

Chiropractic management of facial pain is based entirely on the suspected source. If there is a dental source, referral to a dentist is appropriate. If the patient appears to have one of the neuralgias, such as trigeminal neuralgia, a brief treatment trial of chiropractic care may be attempted if the patient is amenable; however, there are no studies indicating success with the facial neuralgias in the chiropractic literature. The rationale for this approach is the anatomic relationship between the spinal nucleus of the trigeminal nerve and the upper spinal nerves in the trigeminocervical nucleus. Medical management of trigeminal neuralgia is with an antiseizure medication such as carbamazepine (Tegretol). If this is unsuccessful, surgical decompression may be effective in cases where anomalous blood vessels are pressing on the trigeminal nerve. Recently, implanted electrical stimulation devices have shown some success.[5] Radiofrequency rhizotomy is reserved for patients with a limited life expectancy. Glossopharyngeal neuralgia is managed similarly. Microvascular decompression appears to be very successful.[6]

Sinusitis pain is often self-resolving. This may be aided by moist heat and possibly aided through facial massage. Cranial manipulation is advocated by some osteopaths and chiropractors. When there is an underlying infection, conservative measures to reduce sinus pressure will often fail and require medical referral for antibiotics and in rare cases drainage.

The reader is referred to Chapter 3 for appropriate patients.

Algorithm

An algorithm for evaluation and management of facial pain is presented in Figure 44–2.

FACIAL PAIN CAUSED BY NEURALGIAS

TRIGEMINAL

Classic Presentation

Usually a middle-aged or older (>50) patient (usually female) presents with a complaint of sharp, electric shock–like pains that start at the mouth and shoot toward the ear, eye, or nose on the same side. The attacks are recurrent and often progressively become more frequent. The patient is often distraught and may be considering suicide.

Cause

The cause is unknown. Triggers include sensory stimulation from touch, the wind, shaving, or eating.

Evaluation

The neurologic examination is negative. If positives are found, especially in a younger patient, suspect multiple sclerosis. Other causes include trigeminal neuroma and other tumors. If suspected, referral for imaging studies may be necessary.

Management

Current medical management includes carbamazepine. Surgical decompression may be effective if anomalous blood vessels are pressing on the trigeminal nerve. Radiofrequency rhizotomy is reserved for those individuals with limited life expectancy. Acupuncture is often tried as an alternative. Implanted electrical stimulation devices may be of benefit.[5]

GLOSSOPHARYNGEAL

Classic Presentation

Patient presents with a complaint of deep, stabbing, or electric shock–like pain in the mouth (tongue, tonsils, throat, or sometimes ear). It may awaken the patient at night. There may be a history of syncope from coughing.

Cause

The cause is unknown. Triggers may include swallowing, yawning, talking, or chewing.

Evaluation

Neurologic examination is negative.

Figure 44–2
FACIAL PAIN—ALGORITHM.

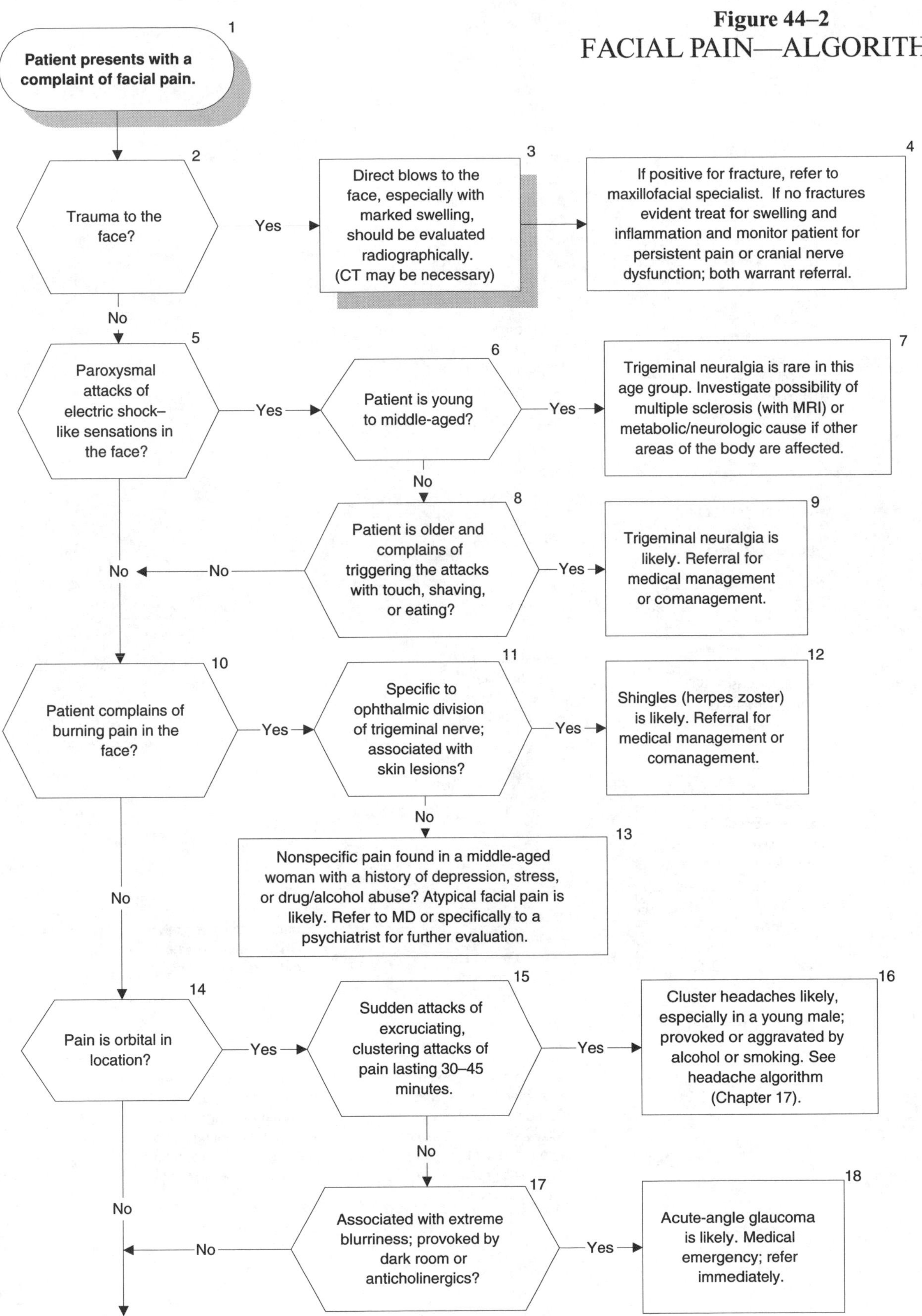

1
Patient presents with a complaint of facial pain.
2
Trauma to the face?
Yes
3
Direct blows to the face, especially with marked swelling, should be evaluated radiographically. (CT may be necessary)
4
If positive for fracture, refer to maxillofacial specialist. If no fractures evident treat for swelling and inflammation and monitor patient for persistent pain or cranial nerve dysfunction; both warrant referral.
No
5
Paroxysmal attacks of electric shock–like sensations in the face?
Yes
6
Patient is young to middle-aged?
Yes
7
Trigeminal neuralgia is rare in this age group. Investigate possibility of multiple sclerosis (with MRI) or metabolic/neurologic cause if other areas of the body are affected.
No
8
Patient is older and complains of triggering the attacks with touch, shaving, or eating?
Yes
9
Trigeminal neuralgia is likely. Referral for medical management or comanagement.
No
No
10
Patient complains of burning pain in the face?
Yes
11
Specific to ophthalmic division of trigeminal nerve; associated with skin lesions?
Yes
12
Shingles (herpes zoster) is likely. Referral for medical management or comanagement.
No
13
Nonspecific pain found in a middle-aged woman with a history of depression, stress, or drug/alcohol abuse? Atypical facial pain is likely. Refer to MD or specifically to a psychiatrist for further evaluation.
No
14
Pain is orbital in location?
Yes
15
Sudden attacks of excruciating, clustering attacks of pain lasting 30–45 minutes.
Yes
16
Cluster headaches likely, especially in a young male; provoked or aggravated by alcohol or smoking. See headache algorithm (Chapter 17).
No
17
Associated with extreme blurriness; provoked by dark room or anticholinergics?
Yes
18
Acute-angle glaucoma is likely. Medical emergency; refer immediately.
No
No

continues

Figure 44–2 continued

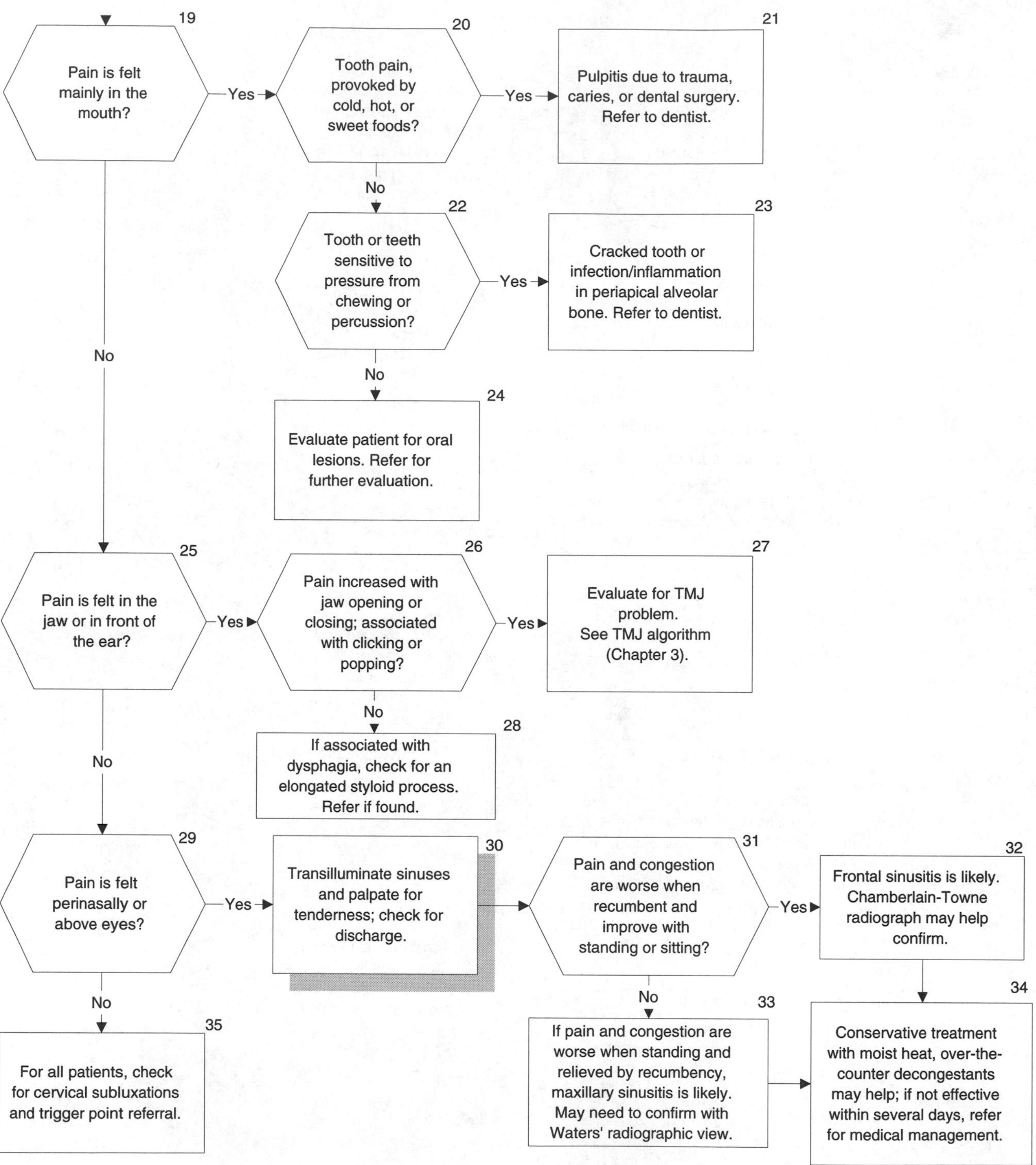

Management

Management is the same as for trigeminal neuralgia—carbamazepine. Surgical microvascular decompression appears to be an effective treatment.[6]

ATYPICAL FACE PAIN

Classic Presentation

A middle-aged woman (between 30 and 50 years of age) complains of constant facial pain that is described as burning. The women often will have a history of psychiatric problems, depression, drug addiction, high-stress personal life, and a positive family history (60% of patients).

Cause

The cause is unknown.

Evaluation

Neurologic examination is negative. If suspected, evaluation for depression may be appropriate.

Management

Cervical spine manipulation theoretically may be of benefit, but there are no reports in the literature. Analgesics should be tried first; if not effective, referral for stronger medication.

REFERENCES

1. Green DB. Orofacial and craniofacial pain: primary care concerns. *Postgrad Med.* 1992;57:64.
2. Bogduk N, Marsland A. The cervical zygapophyseal joints as a source of neck pain. *Spine.* 1988;13:610.
3. Aminoff MJ. Nervous system. In: Tierney LM, McPhee SJ, Papadakis MA, eds. *Current Medical Diagnosis & Treatment.* 34th ed. Norwalk, CT: Appleton & Lange; 1995:831.
4. Yochum TR, Rowe LJ. *Essentials of Skeletal Radiology.* 2nd ed. Baltimore: Williams & Wilkins; 1996;1:12–19.
5. Young RF. Electrical stimulation of the trigeminal nerve root for the treatment of chronic facial pain. *J Neurosurg.* 1995;83:72–78.
6. Resnick DK, Jannetta PJ, Bissonnette D, et al. Microvascular decompression for glossopharyngeal neuralgia. *Neurosurgery.* 1995;36:64–68.

Chapter 45

Ear Pain

CONTEXT

A complaint of ear pain usually raises the concern of an ear infection. It is interesting to note that although commonly a cause in children, in adults, one study indicated that ear pain was referred in 60% of patients. Even more interesting is that 80% of those with referred pain were found to have temporomandibular (TMJ), cervical spine, or a dental (50%) pathology or dysfunction.[1] Therefore, it appears that ear pain is often best evaluated and treated by one of three specialists: the chiropractor, the pediatrician, or the dentist.

Otitis media is the most common diagnosis in children and the second most common diagnosis in medicine, with approximately two thirds of all children in the United States being affected by age 2.[2,3] Depending on the type (acute otitis, recurrent acute otitis, otitis media with effusion, chronic otitis media), management may include antibiotics, decongestants, tympanostomy tubes, or other surgical procedures. The major medical concern with otitis media with effusion is that it is believed that associated hearing loss in infants can impair language development.[4,5] Other studies have criticized the methodology used in studies that claim risk.[6] Most cases of hearing loss associated with otitis media with effusion resolve spontaneously in 6 to 8 weeks.[7]

GENERAL STRATEGY

History

- Determine whether the pain is due to trauma (lacerations, hematoma, temporal bone fracture).
- Determine whether the pain is superficial (skin lesions) or deep (otitis externa, media, or cholesteatoma).
- Determine whether the pain is unilateral or bilateral (bilateral is more common with otitis externa).
- Determine whether there are associated auditory or vestibular symptoms (otitis media, labyrinthitis, cholesteatoma).
- Determine whether there are associated signs or symptoms of infection (acute otitis media).
- Determine whether there are any oral, TMJ, cervical spine, or facial symptoms.

Evaluation

- Evaluate the outside of the ear and palpate for tenderness; otoscopically evaluate the ear.
- Examine the TMJ, cervical spine, and mouth.

Management

- Refer for obvious cases of bacterial infection.
- Follow Agency for Health Care Policy and Research guidelines with regard to otitis media with effusion.
- Refer to dentist for dental pathology.
- Manage TMJ and cervical spine problems initially; refer if unsuccessful.

RELEVANT ANATOMY AND PHYSIOLOGY

The external ear is innervated by several sensory nerves, as follows:

- Arnold's nerve (sensory branch of the vagus)
- Jacobson's nerve (sensory branch of the glossopharyngeal)

- auriculotemporal nerve (sensory branch of the trigeminal; V3)
- a branch of the facial nerve
- greater auricular and lesser occipital nerves (C2 and C3)

However, the common end-point for central projections from the primary neurons of the above nerves is in the spinal nucleus of cranial nerve V. This spinal nucleus merges with the dorsal horn of C1 through C3 in the trigeminocervical nucleus. This convergence explains why referred pain to the ear is so common.

A central concept in ear complaints and disorders is dysfunction of the eustachian (auditory) tube. The eustachian tube is extremely important in that it provides a drainage and ventilation source for the middle ear via a communication with the nasopharynx.[8] Normally, the eustachian tube remains closed except when swallowing or yawning. Narrowing or blockage of the tube may occur through tube lining edema. This is often due to viral infections or allergies. Congenital narrowing of the canal may also occur. In children, the canal is usually narrow and more horizontal than it is in adults, leading to an age-related predisposition to eustachian tube involvement. A temporal sequence of dysfunction may occur. If the blockage is temporary or partial, air in the middle ear is trapped and absorbed, with a resultant negative pressure. This may be visible otoscopically as a retracted tympanic membrane. If transient, yawning, swallowing, or autoinflation (forced exhalation through closed nostrils) will cause a popping or crackling sound with some relief. If more chronic, the negative pressure will draw fluid into the ear, causing a serous otitis media. If the fluid becomes infected, the patient may develop acute otitis media.

EVALUATION

History

The history can quickly determine whether the cause is due to barotrauma effects, infection, or referral from the teeth, TMJ, or cervical spine (Table 45–1). Bilateral pain indicates external otitis. Other clues include whether the person has recently gone swimming, cleans the ears by overinserting cotton swabs, or sticks other foreign objects in the ears, such as pencils.

Young children with signs of an upper respiratory infection with fever may have a bacterially caused, acute otitis media. Associated temporary conductive hearing loss is common. Left untreated, the pain may migrate to behind the ear when the mastoid air cells become involved. The pain is often severe and causes disruption of sleep. Infants may constantly grab their ears. If ear pain is associated with vertigo and hearing loss, consider labyrinthitis.

If the pain is better with swallowing, chewing, or yawning, barotrauma or serous otitis media is possible. If the pain occurs with air travel only or diving, barotrauma is likely the cause. With air travel the pain is often worse on descent. Sharp, stabbing pains are felt deep in the ear.

Pain made worse with chewing or yawning is suggestive of a TMJ disorder. Associated complaints will include clicking or popping of the jaw or occasional locking of the jaw. The pain is often unilateral. Dental pathology is also a possible cause of referral. When dental pulp is inflamed (pulpitis) as a result of caries, trauma, or dental surgery, pain is provoked by hot or cold foods and sweets. When the pulp undergoes necrosis, local gas is produced, which, when expanded by heat, increases pressure and causes pain. Cold decreases the gas pressure and relieves the pain. There are apical foramina that connect the pulp to the periodontal ligament and periapical alveolar bone. Infection or inflammation may spread through this connection, leading to a tooth that is sensitive to compressive pressure from chewing or percussion. This is also found with a cracked tooth.

Examination

A general screen of the patient with ear pain consists of the following:

- Observe the area for lacerations, skin lesions, or discharge from the ear canal.
- Take the patient's temperature.
- Otoscopically evaluate the canal for inflammation, obstruction, infection, or fluid distention.
- Screen for possible TMJ referral pain.
- Screen the cervical spine with palpation, compression, and distraction.
- Evaluate the teeth and palpate/percuss for tenderness, especially in the molar region.

Otoscopic evaluation of the ear will often reveal an underlying cause. Following are some classic otoscopic appearances:

- otitis externa—erythema and edema of the ear canal with a purulent discharge
- acute otitis media—absent or distorted light reflex indicating bulging of the tympanic membrane; the tympanic membrane may be hypomobile with pneumatic challenge
- serous otitis media—tympanic membrane may appear yellow-amber in color; air-fluid level or air bubbles may be evident
- chronic otitis media—diminished or absent landmarks on the tympanic membrane; perforation is often seen

Table 45–1 History Questions for Ear Pain

Primary Question	*What Are You Thinking?*	*Secondary Questions*	*What Are You Thinking?*
Did the pain occur after being hit in the ear?	Lacerations, fracture, hematoma, perforated ear drum, perilymphatic fistula.	Any fluid leaking from the ear?	Fracture.
		Pain associated with dizziness or tinnitus?	Perilymphatic fistula or perforated ear drum.
Did the pain occur after or during flying or scuba diving?	Barotrauma, eustachian tube dysfunction.	Severe pain felt mainly on the descent?	Eustachian tube dysfunction, especially in a patient with an upper respiratory infection or allergies.
Was the pain felt after swimming?	Otitis externa, ruptured tympanic membrane.	Past history of severe or recurrent ear infections?	Ruptured tympanic membrane.
		Ear is painful to touch and/or itchy?	Otitis externa.
Do you have a cough or fever and/or other signs of a respiratory infection?	Acute otitis, labyrinthitis.	Are you also dizzy or have any hearing loss?	Labyrinthitis more likely (rare).
		Is the pain associated with a fullness with a "blocked" ear sensation?	Acute otitis more likely.
Do you insert anything into your ears such as paper clips, pencils, cotton-tipped swabs, towel tips?	Foreign body, otitis externa.	Is your ear tender to touch or itchy?	Otitis externa likely.
Is the pain made worse with jaw motion?	TMJ, dental problem, elongated styloid.	Is the pain worse when eating cold, hot, or sweet foods?	Cavity or pulpitis likely.
		Is the pain worse with biting down?	TMJ or cracked tooth.
		Is the pain worse with opening the mouth wide or associated with popping and clicking of the jaw?	TMJ likely.
		Is the pain in front of the ear and worse while opening?	Elongated styloid.
Is the pain worse with neck movement?	Cervical spine dysfunction.	Do you have associated neck pain?	Cervical spine arthritis or subluxation.

Numerous skin lesions may affect the ear. Following is a list of some of the more common:

- Furuncles from infected hair follicles may appear.
- Polyps due to granulomatous processes may appear in the ear canal.
- Keloid is an overgrowth of scar tissue that is often the result of trauma (often due to ear piercing), more commonly seen in blacks.
- Sebaceous cysts are more common behind the lobule of the ear; they have a central black punctum (indicates blocked sebaceous gland).
- Tophi are small, whitish-yellow nodules found on the helix or antihelix in individuals with gout; they are usually hard and nontender.
- Chondrodermatitis presents as painful nodules on the rim of the helix.

When results of the otoscopic examination and outer inspection of the ear are normal, referral pain is likely. Focus on a thorough examination of the teeth, TMJ, and cervical spine.

MANAGEMENT

There is much debate with regard to the management of otitis media. With acute otitis, it is generally accepted that antibiotics are warranted because of the bacterial etiology. If the otitis is in fact viral (recurrent otitis or otitis media with effusion), however, the approach is not clear. It is known that otitis media with effusion will self-resolve in 6 to 8 weeks. However, when recurrent, it is often suggested to use drainage tubes (tympanostomy tubes). The evidence for their effectiveness has come under criticism. One study indicated that more than half of these procedures were either inappropriate or had equivocal clinical indications.[9] Clarification has come from recommendations for otitis media with effusion made by the Agency for Health Care Policy and Research (AHCPR) guidelines of 1994.[10] If the child has no craniofacial or neurologic abnormalities or sensory deficits, the AHCPR panel recommends initial treatment to consist of observation or antibiotic treatment. The panel recommends against myringotomy with or without tympanostomy tubes. After 3 months, antibiotics or tubes are recommended in children with a bilateral hearing deficit of 20-dB hearing threshold level or worse. One environmental influence that can be modified includes avoidance of exposure to cigarette smoking. There also appears to be an association with daycare facilities and bottle-feeding in infants. The panel also found that decongestants and/or antihistamines, corticosteroids, and tonsillectomy were ineffective treatments for otitis media with effusion.

The following are brief recommendations for ear pain based on condition.

Barotrauma

- Swallow, yawn, and autoinflate often during a flight descent.
- Decongestants should be taken several hours before arrival.
- Nasal decongestants should be administered 1 hour before arrival.
- Do not sleep during the descent phase (leads to markedly negative pressure).
- Diving is contraindicated for individuals who have tympanic membrane perforation because of the unbalanced thermal stimulation that may lead to vertigo.
- Individuals with one ear with normal hearing should avoid diving because of the risk of otologic injury to the good ear.
- Patients with upper respiratory infections should avoid diving.

Otitis Externa

- Patients should be instructed to keep the ear dry, and to avoid overinsertion or cleaning with cotton swabs and scratching the ears.
- Avoid swimming in potentially contaminated water.

There is a belief among some chiropractors that otitis media is best managed conservatively with cervical spine manipulation and/or massage and diet recommendations. The effectiveness of chiropractic manipulation requires research. A review of these concepts can be found in articles by Hendricks and Larkin-Thier,[11] Hobbs and Rasmussen,[12] and Philips.[13]

Algorithm

An algorithm for evaluation and management of ear pain is presented in Figure 45–1.

Figure 45–1

EAR PAIN—ALGORITHM.

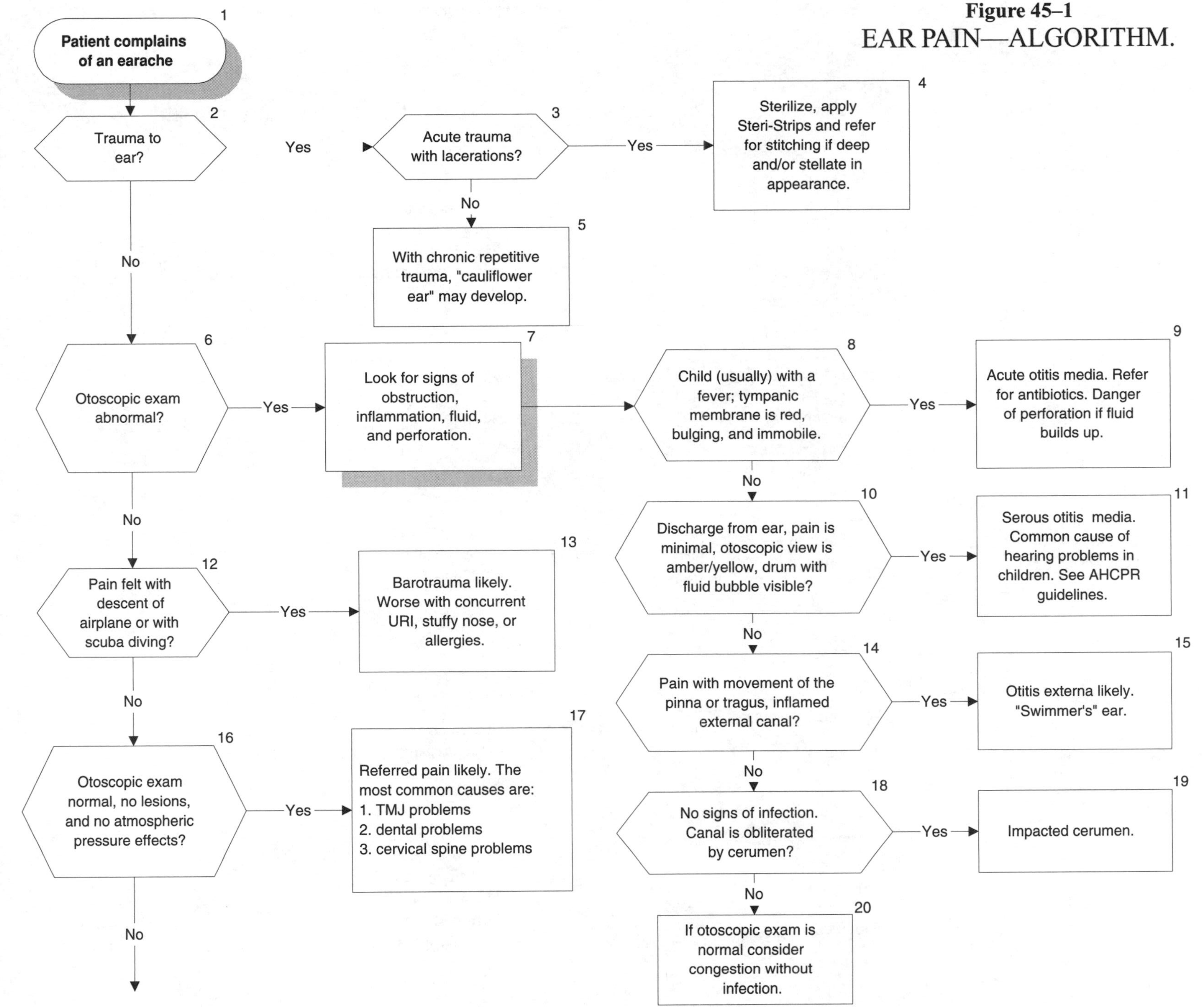

continues

Figure 45–1 continued

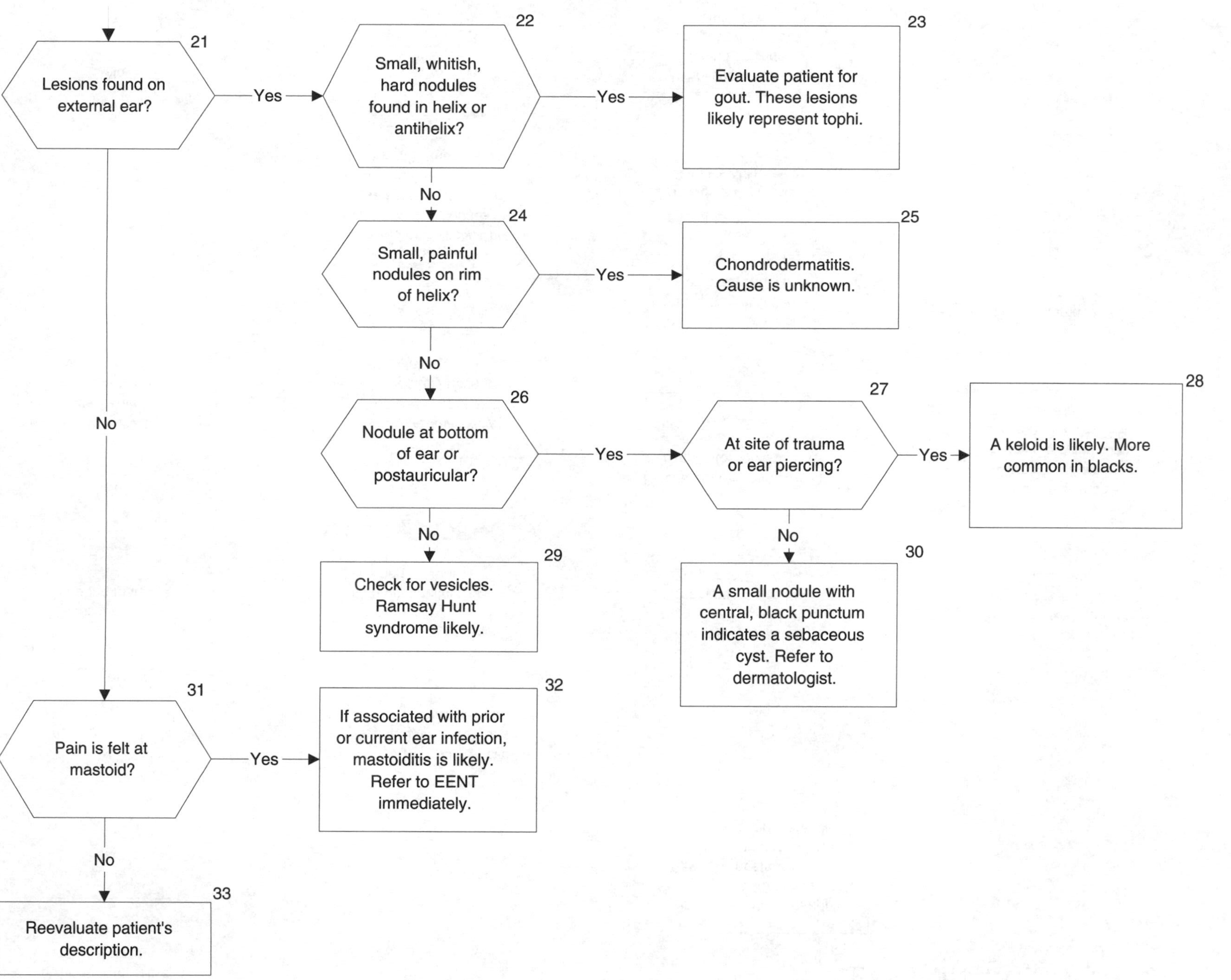
21
Lesions found on external ear?
Yes
22
Small, whitish, hard nodules found in helix or antihelix?
Yes
23
Evaluate patient for gout. These lesions likely represent tophi.
No
24
Small, painful nodules on rim of helix?
Yes
25
Chondrodermatitis. Cause is unknown.
No
26
Nodule at bottom of ear or postauricular?
Yes
27
At site of trauma or ear piercing?
Yes
28
A keloid is likely. More common in blacks.
No
30
A small nodule with central, black punctum indicates a sebaceous cyst. Refer to dermatologist.
No
29
Check for vesicles. Ramsay Hunt syndrome likely.
No
31
Pain is felt at mastoid?
Yes
32
If associated with prior or current ear infection, mastoiditis is likely. Refer to EENT immediately.
No
33
Reevaluate patient's description.

Key: URI, upper respiratory infection; EENT, eyes, ears, nose, and throat.

SELECTED CAUSES OF EAR PAIN

BAROTRAUMA

Classic Presentation

The patient complains of severe ear pain on airplane descent. A sharp, stabbing pain in the ear may be felt. Another presentation is a patient who feels a similar sharp pain with underwater diving. The pain is usually felt within the first 15 feet of descent.

Cause

The cause is failure of equalization of pressure in the middle ear by a narrowed eustachian tube. This is usually due to mucosal edema from an upper respiratory infection or allergy or from a congenitally narrowed tube.

Evaluation

Otoscopic evaluation should be performed to determine whether there is any associated rupture of the tympanic membrane or otitis externa or media.

Management

Suggestions to the airplane traveler are to use frequent yawning, swallowing, and autoinflation (forced exhalation against closed nostrils) during the descent. If unsuccessful, the use of a systemic decongestant several hours before descent and a nasal decongestant 1 hour before descent is usually successful. In recalcitrant cases, myringotomy or the insertion of ventilating tubes is necessary, or the avoidance of flying altogether. Serous otitis media may follow an episode of barotrauma.

SEROUS OTITIS MEDIA

Classic Presentation

A patient presents with a complaint of fullness, and possible hearing loss or pain associated with an upper respiratory infection or barotrauma.

Cause

A persistently closed eustachian tube allows a negative pressure to develop in the middle ear, which then causes transudation of fluid into the middle ear space. This is more common in children because of a more horizontal canal, and in both adults and children because of infection, allergy, or barotrauma.

Evaluation

Otoscopic evaluation will reveal a dull, hypomobile tympanic membrane. Occasionally, bubbles may be visible. Hearing loss, if present, is conductive.

Management

Although a short course of corticosteroids or antibiotics is often prescribed, there appears to be little long-term benefit. A conservative approach is to use over-the-counter systemic or nasal decongestants. If ineffective, refer for medical management. Medical recommendations for typanostomy tubes for the treatment of recurrent otitis have been questioned. It is estimated that the recommendations in more than half of cases are either inappropriate (23%) or based on equivocal indications (35%).[9] (For a discussion of chiropractic management, see references 11–13.) In adults, persistent otitis media may be an indication of nasopharyngeal carcinoma.[14]

ACUTE OTITIS MEDIA

Classic Presentation

The patient is often a child or infant (although adults are affected) who complains of deep ear pain, a pressure sensation, and decreased hearing.

Cause

Acute otitis often represents the next stage after serous otitis in eustachian tube involvement. Middle ear fluid resulting from a negative pressure is subsequently infected. Common organisms are *Streptococcus pneumoniae, Haemophilus influenzae*, and *Streptococcus pyogenes*.

Evaluation

The patient will often have a fever. The tympanic membrane will appear erythematous and be hypomobile. Bullae may also be seen. When empyema occurs, the tympanic membrane may bulge, indicating impending perforation.

Management

Referral for antibiotic treatment is warranted because of the bacterial cause. Several weeks of untreated or inadequately treated acute otitis can lead to acute mastoiditis with serious consequences.

CHRONIC OTITIS MEDIA

Classic Presentation

The patient presents with a history of recurrent acute ear infections. Currently, he or she complains of ear discharge that is worse with colds and swimming. There is little pain, but often a complaint of some hearing loss.

Cause

Chronic infection of the middle ear and mastoid may lead to perforation of the tympanic membrane and degeneration of the tympanic membrane or ossicles. This results in a conductive hearing loss. Common organisms include *Pseudomonas aeruginosa, Proteus*, and *Staphylococcus aureus*.

Evaluation

Otoscopy often reveals perforation of the tympanic membrane and discharge. Tests for hearing reveal a conductive hearing loss.

Management

Initial treatment consists of antibiotic drops to the ears, systemic antipseudomonal antibiotics, removal of infected debris, and either avoidance of swimming or the use of ear plugs. Surgery eventually may be necessary to reconstruct the tympanic membrane.

CHOLESTEATOMA

Classic Presentation

The patient presents similarly to the patient with chronic otitis media; however, the patient may have more dizziness or pain.

Cause

With a chronic dysfunction of the eustachian tube, negative pressure pulls the upper tympanic membrane inward to form a sac, which can grow and become infected. If the cholesteatoma enlarges it may erode or compress the tympanic membrane, ossicles, or the mastoid.

Evaluation

Otoscopic evaluation may reveal a retraction pocket and exudate. Hearing loss is conductive.

Management

The treatment of choice is surgical removal and sometimes a surgically created connection between the ear canal and mastoid.

OTITIS EXTERNA

Classic Presentation

The patient is often a swimmer complaining of ear pain, itching, and discharge. The patient is more likely to present during warm, humid weather.

Cause

Infection of the ear or ear canal is caused by exposure to infected water or is caused by scratching or overaggressive use of cotton applicators. The infection is usually due to bacteria such as *Pseudomonas* or *Proteus* or fungi such as *Aspergillus*. The fungal growth is assisted by excessive moisture in the ear.

Evaluation

Pain is produced by pulling on the ear. The ear canal demonstrates erythema and edema, associated sometimes with a purulent discharge.

Management

Referral for antibiotic drops is necessary. Additional preventive advice includes keeping the ear dry and avoidance of cotton swabs or other mechanical trauma (eg, pencils) in the ear canal.

REFERENCES

1. Thaller SR, Thaller JL. Head and neck symptoms: is the problem in the ear, face, neck, or oral cavity? *Postgrad Med.* 1990;87:75–77, 83–86.
2. Lohr KN, Beck S, Kamberg KJ, et al. *Measurement of Physiologic Health for Children: Middle Ear Disease and Hearing Impairment.* Santa Monica, CA: Rand Health Experiment Series; 1983.
3. Shappert SM. *Office Visits for Otitis Media: United States, 1975–1990: Advance Data.* Hyattsville, MD: National Center for Health Statistics; 1992:214.
4. Teele DW, Klein JO, Rosner RA, et al. Greater Boston Otitis Media Study Group: otitis media with effusion during the first three years of life and development of speech and language. *Pediatrics.* 1984;74:282–287.
5. Rach GH, Ziethuis GA, VanBaarle PW, et al. The effect of treatment with ventilating tubes on language development in preschool children with otitis media with effusion. *Clin Otolaryngol.* 1991;16: 128–132.
6. Paradise JL. Otitis media during early life: how hazardous to development? A critical review of the evidence. *Pediatrics.* 1981;68: 869–873.
7. Cross AW. Health screening in schools. *J Pediatr.* 1985;107 (pt 1):487–494.
8. Bluestone CD, Doyle WJ. Anatomy and physiology of eustachian tube and middle ear related to otitis media. *Allerg Clin Immmunol.* 1988;81:997.
9. Kleinmann LC, Kosecoff J, Dubois R, Brook RH. The medical appropriateness of tympanostomy tubes proposed for children younger than 16 years in the United States. *JAMA.* 1994;271:1250–1255.
10. Stool SE, Berg AO, Berman S, et al. *Managing Otitis Media with Effusion in Young Children: Quick Reference Guide for Clinicians.* AHCPR Publication No. 94 0623. Rockville, MD: Agency for Health Care Policy and Research, Public Health Service, US Dept of Health and Human Services, July 1994.
11. Hendricks CL, Larkin-Thier SM. Otitis media in young children. *Chiro J Chiro Res Study.* 1989;2:9–13.
12. Hobbs DA, Rasmussen SA. Chronic otitis media: a case report. *J Chiro.* 1991;28:67–68.
13. Philips NJ. Vertebral subluxation and otitis media: a case study. *Chiro J Chiro Res Study.* 1992;8:38–39.
14. Sham JST. Serous otitis media: an opportunity for early recognition of nasopharyngeal carcinoma. *Arch Otolaryngol.* 1992;118:794.

CHAPTER 46

Hearing Loss

CONTEXT

Hearing loss is a frightening occurrence, which, when sudden, would cause most patients to seek the attention of a medical doctor or emergency department. The acuteness and degree of loss would be steering factors that would influence a patient's decision to seek immediate attention. Mild to moderate loss, especially over time, or if assumed to be related to congestion from a respiratory infection, post–airline flight, or cerumen would allow most patients to adopt a "wait-and-see" attitude for at least several days. Another context is the patient who is not aware of the degree of loss because of the chronicity of the problem or he or she assumes that it is related to aging. The chiropractor is more likely to see these patients with chronic, mild loss or those unaware of loss. If a screening examination for hearing loss is conducted on patients complaining of loss and on the elderly, most cases can be discovered. Although some causes of hearing loss are nonrecoverable, those that cause sudden loss often spontaneously recover over 7 to 10 days.[1,2]

Although chiropractic was launched from an anecdotal reporting of hearing recovery, it is unfortunate that the literature is barren of any significant case reports or large studies. Nonetheless, there are still anecdotal reports, often given at seminars and among colleagues, warranting at least a consideration for study.

GENERAL STRATEGY

History and Examination

- Determine whether the hearing loss was sudden (trauma, viral, or vascular) or chronic/insidious.
- Determine whether there are any underlying systemic or whole-body processes such as diabetes, multiple sclerosis, or Paget's disease.
- Determine whether there was an associated event such as trauma or infection.
- Differentiate between conductive and sensorineural loss with simple tuning fork tests.
- Refer for audiologic or imaging studies when hearing loss is evident.

Management

- Refer to otolaryngologist or neurologist when appropriate. Some examples include the following:
  1. ear infection or mastoid involvement
  2. suspected medication-induced hearing loss from prescribed ototoxic medication
  3. possible acoustic neuroma or other tumor
  4. perilymphatic fistula that is interfering with patient's lifestyle
- Refer for hearing aid if the following circumstances apply:
  1. patient has a diagnosis of presbycusis and hearing loss is interfering with lifestyle
  2. patient has had surgical correction for otosclerosis and now suffers some sensorineural loss
- Use a trial treatment with spinal manipulative therapy (SMT) when it appears that a complex of symptoms such as postwhiplash syndrome is apparent or when medical management offers no clear-cut solution.

RELEVANT ANATOMY/PHYSIOLOGY

Hearing is a remarkable sense that performs a transformation of mechanical vibration into electric potentials that are then processed and integrated into a composite impression of one's environment. The interface of this transformation is the fluid environment of the middle ear. The structural components of this system are the ear canal, the eardrum, and the bony ossicles. The efficiency of this impedance-matching system may be compromised, leading to a decrease in the perception of loudness but leaving the quality of the sound unaffected. This is referred to as a conduction hearing loss. Dampening of sound may occur with blockage of the ear canal by cerrumen or a foreign body, or by middle ear effusion. If the ossicles are sclerotic (otosclerosis) or damaged due to trauma/pathology, sound is not transmitted efficiently.

Pathology of the hair cells of the organ of Corti, the cochlear nerve, or in rarer cases, the central transmission of these signals will result in a sensorineural loss that is clinically represented by both a decrease in loudness and a distortion of sound quality.

Hearing is not only a function of loudness threshold and frequency perception; a patient's individual requirements (eg, a musician), the ability to concentrate, environmental distraction, and central processing are also factors. The audible range of frequencies is between approximately 16 and 16,000 Hz, with the majority of speech limited to 300 to 3,000 Hz. The overtones that affect the quality of speech, however, are above 3,000 Hz. Loudness is measured in decibels (dB). This is a logarithmic scale, not linear. Therefore, a 20-dB tone carries 100 times the energy of a 1-dB tone; a 30-dB tone, 1,000 times that of a 1-dB tone. The threshold level is an important indicator of hearing loss. Normally, a whisper can be heard, indicating a hearing threshold of between 0 and 20 dB. Normal speaking is between 40 and 60 dB; a shout is 80 dB or above. A 10- to 15-dB threshold loss is often not noticed. Generally, a loss averaging between 20 and 25 dB between 300 and 3,000 Hz (speech frequencies) is noticed by the patient. A loss exceeding 30 to 40 dB is a significant handicap for conversation.

EVALUATION

History

In obtaining the history (Table 46–1), determine the following:

- whether the patient has had a sudden or insidious loss and whether it is bilateral
- any specific event onset such as past infection or trauma, including head trauma and barotrauma from scuba diving or airplane travel
- whether the patient has been prescribed any ototoxic medications
- past or current history of occupational or recreational noise exposure
- functional impact on patient's life (social and occupational)
- whether there are any previous diagnoses or treatment, including hearing aids or surgeries

Age of onset, acuteness of onset, and associated signs are extremely valuable in narrowing the diagnosis. Hearing deficits in an infant or young child should suggest congenital deafness or the sequelae to infection or ototoxic medication. Insidious onset in the middle-aged patient is suggestive of otosclerosis. In the elderly patient, various forms of presbycusis are the first suspicion. When sudden and associated with signs of infection, transient benign processes that are viral are suggested. When the hearing loss is more profound and permanent, a bacterial etiology is more likely. Accumulated otologic trauma from environmental noise should be sought in the middle-aged and elderly. Common sources are loud machinery and loud music (concerts or headphones). Hearing loss may be a complication of many disorders; especially noted are collagen vascular diseases, vasculitis, multiple sclerosis, osteogenesis imperfecta, and compression from Paget's disease.

Conductive hearing loss generally does not interfere with speech discrimination. The patient even may be able to hear better in noisy environments. This is due to the blockage of low-frequency sounds. This phenomenon is analogous to wearing earplugs, when the general loudness is attenuated, but the distinctness of the sound may be increased because of the blockage of other frequencies. The patient with a sensorineural deficit usually will have difficulty with speech discrimination. Patients often note that women's voices and British accents pose more of a problem. They especially find it difficult to screen out ambient noise in a noisy environment. Their hearing loss is generally in the higher ranges, whereas most environmental noise is low frequency, the range they hear best.

Sudden loss with accompanying vertigo is suggestive of labyrinthine etiology. If the attacks are recurrent with progressive hearing loss, Meniere's disease is suspected. If the vertigo gradually improves over several weeks, bacterial labyrinthitis is most likely.

Examination

- Examine the ear for signs of lesions, cerumen impaction, or infection.
- Screen with tuning fork tests, including Weber and Rinne tests.
- Use an otoscope/audiometer combination, if available, to screen for loss within speech frequency ranges.
- Refer for audiologic testing if a deficit is found.

Table 46–1 History of Questions for Hearing Loss

Primary Question	*What Are You Thinking?*	*Secondary Questions*	*What Are You Thinking?*
Was the hearing loss sudden?	Trauma, vascular, or viral infection.	Was there an injury to the head?	Fracture of the temporal bone.
		Was there trauma to the ear?	Barotrauma to the tympanic membrane or a perilymphatic fistula.
		Is there a recent history of coronary bypass surgery or a history of stroke or transient ischemic attacks?	Vascular infarction of cochlear nerve (usually would involve other areas with other signs or symptoms).
		(If appropriate) Did the hearing loss resolve within 10 days?	Viral infection likely.
Does the hearing loss fluctuate (come and go)?	Meniere's, recurrent otitis media, cerumen impaction, eustachian tube dysfunction.	Hearing loss associated with recurrent bouts of dizziness?	Meniere's disease is likely.
		Recurrent ear infections?	Chronic otitis media.
		History of allergies and/or extreme pain with airplane descent, bilateral?	Auditory tube dysfunction.
Is the hearing loss chronic?	Presbycusis, otosclerosis, congenital acoustic neuroma, ototoxicity, noise pollution.	Is it difficult to hear on the phone? No problem in noisy rooms?	Otosclerosis is likely.
		(With an older patient) Difficulty carrying on a conversation in crowded rooms or understanding women's voices or those with accents?	Presbycusis is likely.
		Are you taking high doses of aspirin or other "pain killers," chemotherapy, or antibiotics (aminoglycosides)?	Ototoxicity is likely.
		Do you or have you worked with loud power tools or in a loud machinery environment?	Sensorineural loss due to hair cell trauma.

Examination of the ear with an otoscope focuses on a search for signs of impacted cerumen, otitis media, vesicles (Ramsay Hunt syndrome), cotton swab injury, cholesteatoma, and any other obvious pathology. Hearing may be tested with two tuning fork tests, Weber and Rinne, to attempt to differentiate between conductive and sensorineural loss. Recommended are 512-Hz and 1,024-Hz tuning forks. The Weber's test is performed several ways. The vibrating tuning fork is applied to the middle forehead, glabella, or middle incisors (some authors have the patient bite on the vibrating handle). With a conduction loss, the sound is heard more loudly in the affected ear. It is heard equally in both ears with normal patients and in patients with bilateral sensorineural loss (eg, presbycusis). A conductive loss of only 5 dB will cause sound to localize to the "bad" ear. The Rinne's test evaluates bone versus air conduction. The vibrating tuning fork is applied to the patient's mastoid. The patient is instructed to indicate when the sound disappears. At this point the examiner places the tines of the tuning fork approximately 1 cm from the patient's ear. The sound should now be audible for about twice as long as when applied to the mastoid (bone). Air conduction is usually twice as long as bone conduction. Masking of the opposite ear with a noise box or any other external sound source such as compressed air or suction may help. A conductive loss of at least 20 dB is necessary to cause a negative response; sound is not longer with air conduction. Therefore, less severe hearing loss is not detectable with the Rinne test.

An in-office audiologic evaluation may be performed with an otoscope containing a built-in audiometer. The otoscope/audiometer uses 40 dB at 1,000 and 2,000 Hz (common frequencies needed to understand speech). The sensitivity for detecting hearing loss is 94%. Interestingly, the specificity is 72% in a standard physician's office and 90% in an audiologist's office.[3]

Audiologist referral is helpful when a hearing loss has been detected or in the case of infants and others unable to communicate effectively. The general evaluation will determine decibel threshold, frequency range, and, more specifically, speech discrimination ability. Loss of speech discrimination ability is highly suggestive of a central cause of hearing loss. Additional testing to differentiate between central and peripheral causes of hearing loss consist of the following:

- Small-tone increment discrimination—Small differences in frequency are appreciated with more sensitivity with a peripheral cause than in the normal ear.
- Tone decay—When a tone is played over earphones, the tone appears to diminish in intensity when, in fact, it remains the same; this occurs with a central cause.
- Recruitment—Loud sounds are heard normally. This occurs with a peripheral cause.

Further testing not requiring a patient response is the brain stem auditory-evoked potential (BAEP). Surface electrodes are placed over the scalp and ears. A high-frequency click at a fixed rate and intensity is delivered and the electrical responses are measured. Seven short-latency waves can be measured within 10 milliseconds of the click. The latency of response may be able to localize the lesion site. For acoustic neuroma the true-positive rate is high at 98% (false-positive about 1%).

MANAGEMENT

- If there is a buildup of cerumen, suggest over-the-counter ear wax dissolvers; if ineffective, refer to primary care physician for ear lavage.
- If an acoustic neuroma, tumor, infection, or systemic process is suspected as the cause, refer to appropriate specialist for management.
- Treatment may be warranted when there are associated signs of headache, dizziness, and neck pain postwhiplash (assuming more serious causes have been ruled out).
- Comanagement with an audiologist is appropriate when hearing loss is affecting lifestyle, all serious causes have been ruled out, and the patient is likely to have presbycusis.

Management will vary depending on scope of practice restrictions and interest. Referral is often necessary. However, if the hearing loss is either the result of cerumen impaction or a transient phenomenon from a whiplash injury with concomitant headache, dizziness, and/or neck pain, the chiropractor may be helpful. With presbycusis, comanagement with an audiologist for prescription of a hearing aid is appropriate.

Algorithm

An algorithm for evaluation and management of hearing loss is presented in Figure 46–1.

Figure 46–1

HEARING LOSS—ALGORITHM.

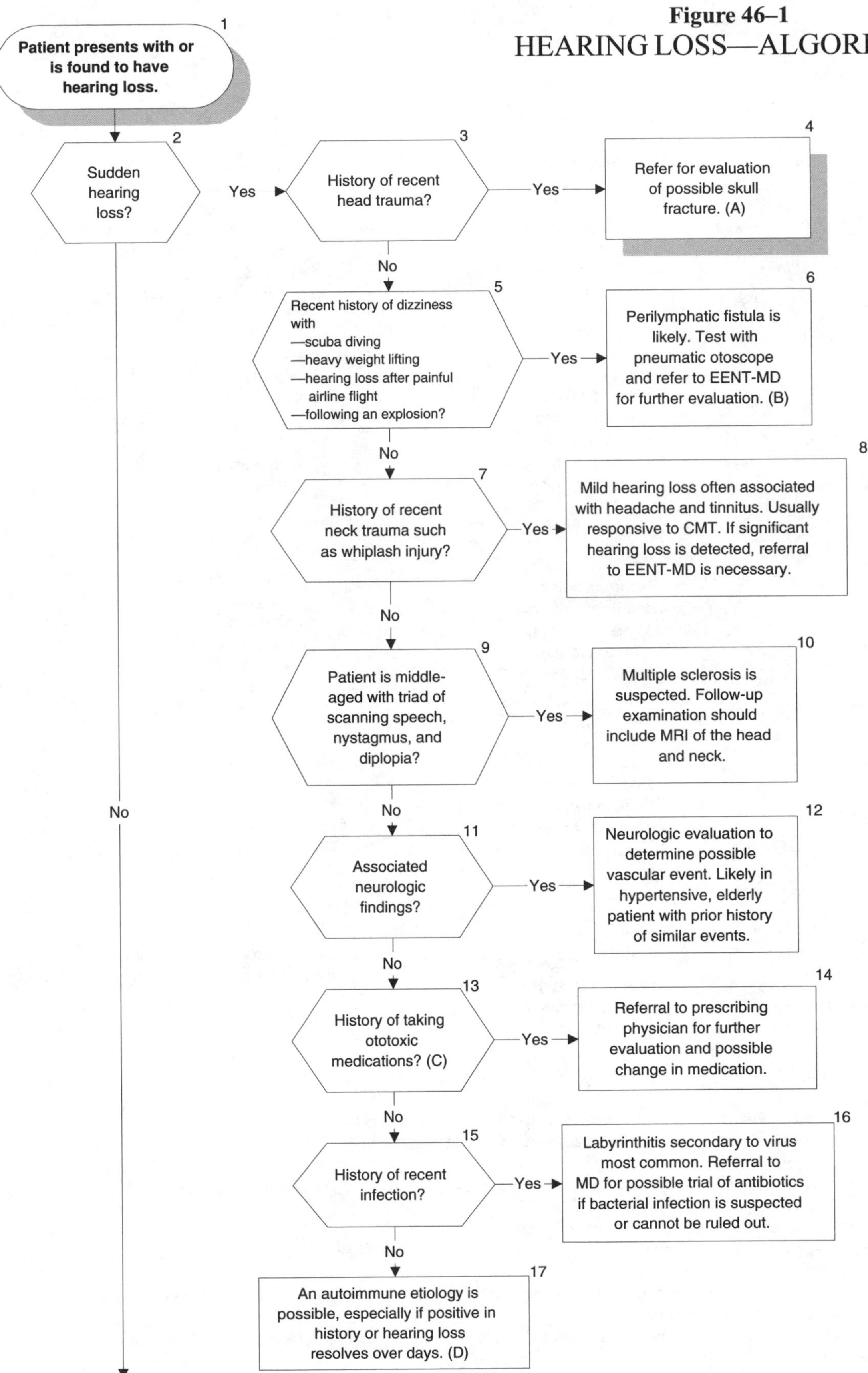

1
Patient presents with or is found to have hearing loss.
2
Sudden hearing loss?
Yes
No
3
History of recent head trauma?
Yes
4
Refer for evaluation of possible skull fracture. (A)
No
5
Recent history of dizziness with
—scuba diving
—heavy weight lifting
—hearing loss after painful airline flight
—following an explosion?
Yes
6
Perilymphatic fistula is likely. Test with pneumatic otoscope and refer to EENT-MD for further evaluation. (B)
No
7
History of recent neck trauma such as whiplash injury?
Yes
8
Mild hearing loss often associated with headache and tinnitus. Usually responsive to CMT. If significant hearing loss is detected, referral to EENT-MD is necessary.
No
9
Patient is middle-aged with triad of scanning speech, nystagmus, and diplopia?
Yes
10
Multiple sclerosis is suspected. Follow-up examination should include MRI of the head and neck.
No
11
Associated neurologic findings?
Yes
12
Neurologic evaluation to determine possible vascular event. Likely in hypertensive, elderly patient with prior history of similar events.
No
13
History of taking ototoxic medications? (C)
Yes
14
Referral to prescribing physician for further evaluation and possible change in medication.
No
15
History of recent infection?
Yes
16
Labyrinthitis secondary to virus most common. Referral to MD for possible trial of antibiotics if bacterial infection is suspected or cannot be ruled out.
No
17
An autoimmune etiology is possible, especially if positive in history or hearing loss resolves over days. (D)

continues

Figure 46–1 continued

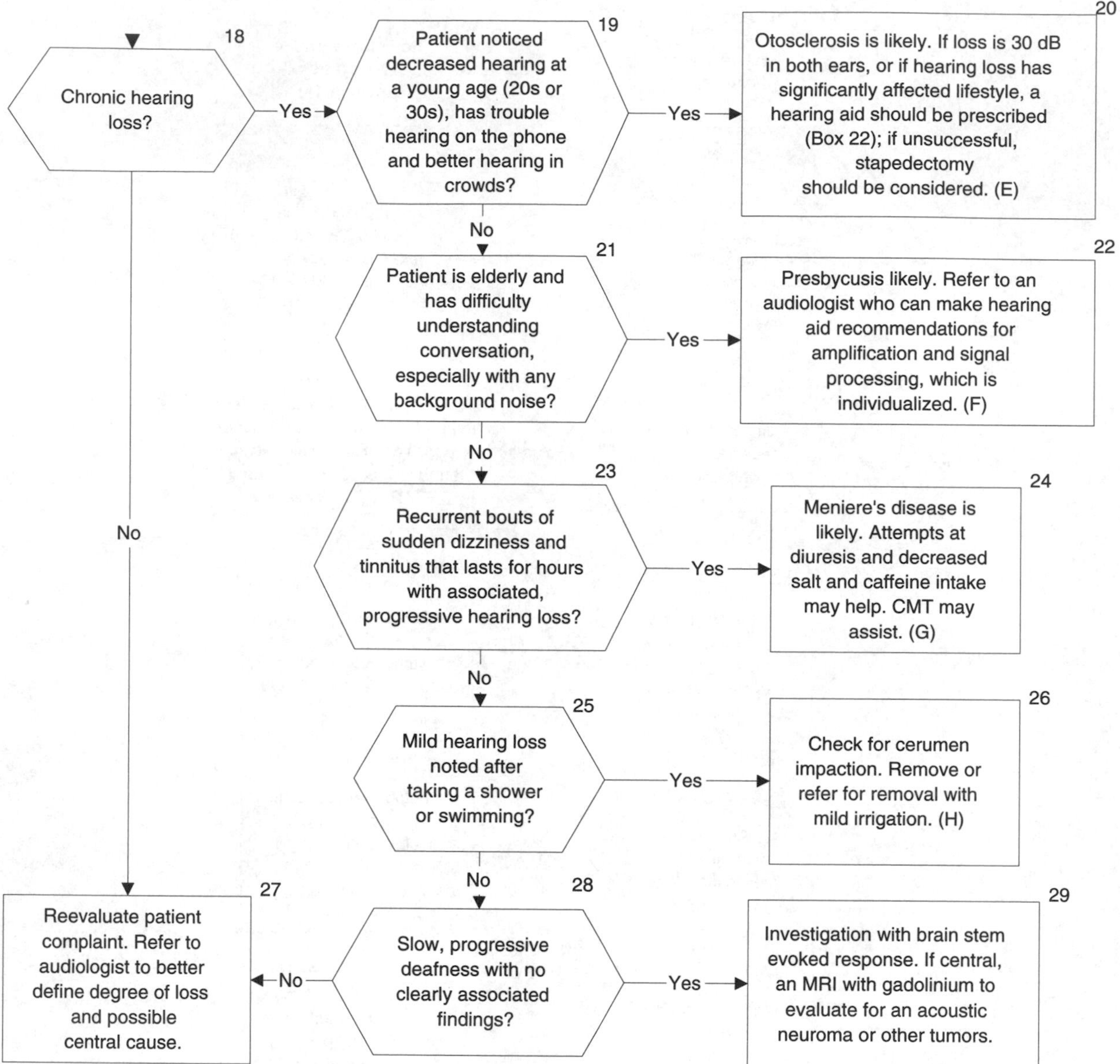

Annotations

A. Hearing loss subsequent to fracture is usually due to a transverse fracture of the temporal bone.

B. A perilymphatic fistula is a defect in the round window that allows communication between the inner and middle ear. Surgery is often necessary.

C. Some common ototoxic drugs include salicylates, aminoglycosides, loop diuretics, and some anticancer medications such as cisplatin.

D. A short course of corticosteroids is often used with acute hearing loss.

E. Otosclerosis is a progressive, conductive hearing loss disorder characterized by sclerosis of the bony capsule and ear ossicles, leading to a conductive hearing loss.

F. Presbycusis is a progressive sensory hearing loss that is age related. There is a selective deterioration of high-frequency hearing with an associated loss of hair cells of the organ of Corti.

G. Meniere's is a disease characterized by an increase in endolymphatic fluid pressure. There is a selective loss of low frequencies early in the course of the disease.

H. Cerumen (wax) absorbs water and expands, causing a conductive hearing loss. With swimmers check for otitis externa (swimmer's ear); often in need of antibiotic drops.

SELECTED CAUSES OF HEARING LOSS*

OTOSCLEROSIS

Classic Presentation

A patient in his or her 20s or 30s presents with a complaint of difficulty hearing on the telephone. Ironically, he or she notices that there is no difficulty hearing a conversation in a noisy room or environment. The patient may note a similar history in a parent. The difficulty hearing is usually bilateral.

Cause

The cause is unknown; however, there is a familial tendency with onset occurring in the late teenage years to the 30s. There is a progressive sclerosis of the bony capsule and ear osicles with a consequent decreased mechanical transmission of sound, producing a conductive hearing loss. The stapes is often the first bone to be affected, with the foot plate being fixed to the oval window. However, if the lesions are large enough to compress the cochlea, a sensory hearing loss will occur that is often permanent. Some practitioners feel that otosclerosis is caused by an inflammatory reaction to the measles virus.[4]

Examination

Evaluate for other causes of obstruction such as cerumen or exostoses/osteomas, which may block the ear canal. With the Rinne test, bone conduction is louder and longer than air conduction. The Weber test will localize to the involved ear if unilateral. Referral for audiologic testing is important.

Treatment

Although 10% of the white population has some degree of otosclerosis, only a small percentage develop appreciable hearing loss. Those who do may benefit from microsurgical techniques. Others decide to live with the problem.

PRESBYCUSIS

Classic Presentation

An elderly patient presents with a complaint of hearing difficulty. He or she may notice that hearing is worse in noisy environments such as crowded rooms. Other complaints may be difficulty hearing women's voices or people with British or other accents. There may also be an associated increase in tinnitus.

Cause

It is believed that there is damage to the hair cells of the organ of Corti, producing a selective high-tone frequency hearing loss, usually bilateral. The contribution of noise trauma to presbycusis varies among individuals. It is particularly hard to hear consonants.

*See also Chapter 18, Dizziness, and Chapter 45, Ear Pain.

Evaluation

Standard Rinne and Weber testing may demonstrate a conductive hearing loss if there is cerumen or a middle ear effusion. However, the hearing loss from presbycusis is a sensorineural loss. Referral for audiologic testing is warranted if the hearing loss is a concern.

Management

There are numerous types of hearing aids available. With newer technology, some of the older complaints have been decreased or eliminated. It is important that the patient work with the audiologist to develop a strategy for determining the degree of amplification and signal processing needed. New programmable devices allow for more sound filtering and can be set for different environmental scenarios.[5]

REFERENCES

1. Grandis JR. Treatment of idiopathic sudden sensorineural hearing loss. *Am J Otol*. 1993;14:183.
2. Farrior JB. Sudden hearing loss. *Emerg Med*. 1994;2:60–74.
3. Katz MS, Gerety MB, Lichtenstein MJ. Gerontology and geriatric medicine. In: Stein JH, ed. *Internal Medicine*. St. Louis, MO: Mosby-Year Book; 1994:2834.
4. Niedermeyer HP, Arnold W. Otosclerosis: a measles virus associated inflammatory disease. *Acta Otolaryngol (Stockh)*. 1995; 115:300–303.
5. Gantz BJ, Schindler RA, Snow JB. Adult hearing loss: some tips and pearls. *Patient Care*. 1995;9:77.

Chapter 47

Tinnitus

CONTEXT

Tinnitus is a relatively common symptom with approximately 6.4% of the population affected.[1] Although the most common presentation is a patient who complains of "ringing" in the ears, there are numerous sounds that a patient may complain of that fit under the umbrella term *tinnitus*. These include clicking, rushing, echoing, fluttering, and hissing. Ringing in the ears is a ubiquitous symptom and is unavoidable, yet the question for the chiropractor is whether it is temporary or permanent, and whether there are any clear clues as to its cause. Additionally, distinguishing among the other sounds the patient may be hearing may lead to an identifiable vascular, toxic, cochlear, small muscle spasm, or cervicogenic etiology.

Tinnitus may be categorized by some simple differentiations. First, is the tinnitus localized to an ear or ears or is it more central and diffuse? *Tinnitus cerebri* is the term used for the latter and may represent organic pathology. Therefore, referral for medical evaluation is appropriate. The localization to one or both ears is called tinnitus aurium and is further divided into subjective and objective. Is the patient hearing sounds appreciable only by them or are they sounds that are audible to the examiner? Subjective tinnitus is audible only to the patient and is probably the most common (99% of patients), yet the most difficult type to identify as to cause. Objective tinnitus may sometimes be appreciated by the examiner and usually represents various vascular sounds.

GENERAL STRATEGY

- Have the patient describe what he or she is hearing.
- Determine whether the patient hears the sounds in the ears or as central or diffuse sounds in the head.
- Determine whether the patient has associated hearing loss or vertigo.
- Determine whether the patient is taking salicylates or indomethacin.
- Determine whether the patient is taking any ototoxic medications such as aminoglycoside antibiotics.
- Determine whether the patient has been exposed to environmental noise such as machinery, loud music, or earphones.
- Determine whether the patient has been diagnosed with any endocrine, vascular, neurologic, or otologic diseases.
- Determine whether the patient experienced trauma to the head or ear.

RELEVANT ANATOMY AND PHYSIOLOGY

Although the ear is designed to monitor the external environment, it is capable of perceiving internal "noise," especially when the outside environment is muted or eliminated. Most objective tinnitus is due to this phenomenon and requires a search for the internal sound source. Most of these sounds are the result of vascular turbulence or small muscle spasm in close proximity to the ear.

Subjective tinnitus of neural origin is extremely difficult to explain and to cure. Although it would seem logical to assume that part of the labyrinth system or the neural connections to the cortex are damaged, labyrinthectomy or cochlear division may still leave a patient with subjective tinnitus.[2] This phantom aural sensation has no known anatomic or physiologic substrate. Theoretically, the auditory epithelium, basilar membrane, or endolymph may be damaged or altered in a way to send a continuous stream of mechanical stimulus, which is interpreted as a high-frequency background hiss, yet this has not been demonstrated. This is, in fact, the theory behind excessive loud noise exposure, when the basilar membrane is forced to vibrate continuously beyond its normal amplitude.[3] The result is that there is a spontaneous discharge in the high-frequency range. It is known that patients who develop hearing loss often have accompanying tinnitus. Other theories focus on a decrease in vertebral artery blood flow[4] and, most recently, a proposed deficiency or dysfunction of serotonin.[5] It is known than serotonin acts as a sensory "suppressor," preventing hypersensitivity to light and sound.

Although a sympathetic nervous system dysfunction with consequent vertebral blood flow reduction has seemed attractive, the findings of Bogduk et al.[6] significantly decrease this possibility as a consideration. A spinal connection to tinnitus may be the relationship of the trigeminal nerve to the ear and the upper cervical spinal segments.

EVALUATION

History

Subjective tinnitus is by far the most common type. When related to systemic causes such as medications or the aging process, it is often continuous, high-pitched, and bilateral. Questioning with regard to medication is helpful when the latter description is a relatively recent phenomenon. When long-standing, otosclerosis or presbycusis should be suspected, especially when associated with bilateral hearing loss. Unilateral tinnitus with associated hearing loss and recurrent vertigo should suggest Meniere's disease or multiple sclerosis. When unilateral, continuous, and associated with hearing loss, an acoustic neuroma is more likely.

There are some characteristic descriptions that may identify the underlying cause when objective tinnutus is suspected, as follows:

- pulsating or rushing—vascular (cardiac murmurs, bruits, ateriovenous malformations [AVM], glomus tumors)
- humming—venous (cervical venous hum)
- low-pitched clicking or fluttering—muscular spasm (stapedius, tensor tympani, or tensor palati)

Examination

Physical examination of the patient with tinnitus centers on the ear and auscultation for a vascular etiology. It is likely that the examination will reveal few if any clues as to the patient's complaint, yet an attempt is made to determine whether secondary causes or primary ear pathology may be contributing. When the patient complains of local ear pain, vertigo, or hearing loss, a thorough investigation of the ear should be performed, including standard Rinne and Weber hearing tests and a search for the following:

- cerrumen impaction
- otitis media
- otosclerosis

Physical examination for the source of objective tinnitus centers on auscultation for the following:

- orbital, cranial, or carotid bruits
- cardiac murmurs
- venous hum

By connecting the tubing of one stethoscope to another, the doctor can hear what the patient hears if the cause is objective. Additional examination procedures include evaluating the palate for spasm and checking the temporomandibular joint for clicking or popping. A pulsatile type of tinnitus relieved by pressure on the jugular vein confirms a venous hum.

MANAGEMENT

When other auditory and other sensory stimuli are reduced, the tinnitus may be unbearable for some patients. These patients often attempt sensory distraction by leaving the radio or television on when trying to sleep. Other solutions include biofeedback, which appears to have a relatively good initial response rate, and the use of a tinnitus masker (worn like a hearing aid).[7] Patients with hearing loss often find that the tinnitus improves with the use of a hearing aid. If the tinnitus is postwhiplash (acceleration/deceleration injury to the neck) or associated with other indicators of vertebrogenic vertigo, chiropractic manipulative treatment may be helpful in resolving the complaint.[8]

Although a number of drugs are used in the treatment of tinnitus, there is little consistent evidence of success. Patients with intractable tinnitus often undergo surgical procedures. When the tinnitus is associated with vertigo or hearing loss, surgery may be helpful.[9] Cochlear nerve section is used for those with isolated or intractable tinnitus, with the obvious trade-off of permanent hearing loss.[2] However, for some patients who are so disabled that suicide is considered, this surgery may be an attractive alternative.

Algorithm

An algorithm for evaluation and management of tinnitus is presented in Figure 47–1.

Figure 47–1
TINNITUS—ALGORITHM.

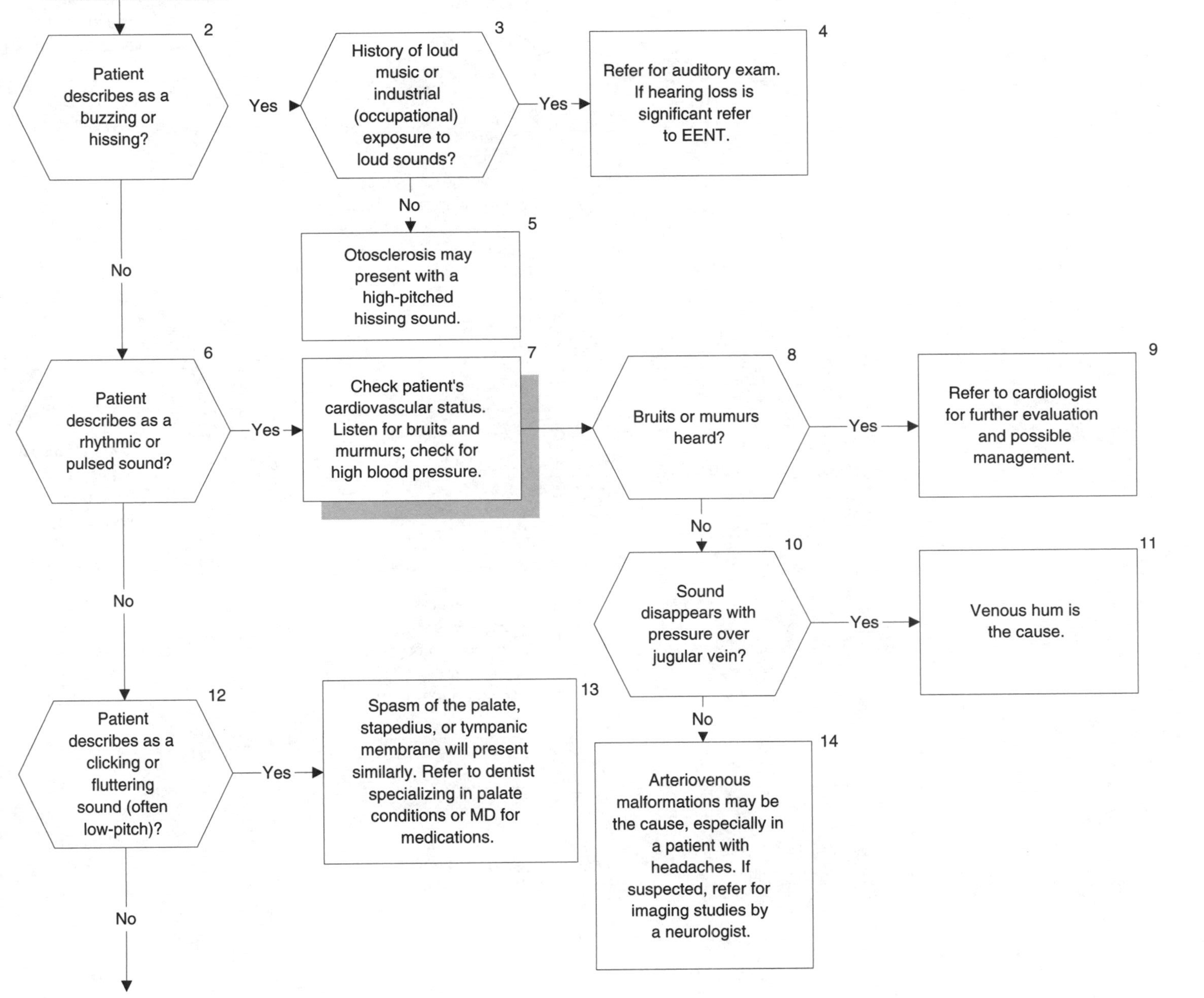

1
Patient complains of hearing abnormal sounds in the ears.
2
Patient describes as a buzzing or hissing?
Yes
3
History of loud music or industrial (occupational) exposure to loud sounds?
Yes
4
Refer for auditory exam. If hearing loss is significant refer to EENT.
No
5
Otosclerosis may present with a high-pitched hissing sound.
No
6
Patient describes as a rhythmic or pulsed sound?
Yes
7
Check patient's cardiovascular status. Listen for bruits and murmurs; check for high blood pressure.
8
Bruits or mumurs heard?
Yes
9
Refer to cardiologist for further evaluation and possible management.
No
10
Sound disappears with pressure over jugular vein?
Yes
11
Venous hum is the cause.
No
14
Arteriovenous malformations may be the cause, especially in a patient with headaches. If suspected, refer for imaging studies by a neurologist.
No
12
Patient describes as a clicking or fluttering sound (often low-pitch)?
Yes
13
Spasm of the palate, stapedius, or tympanic membrane will present similarly. Refer to dentist specializing in palate conditions or MD for medications.
No

continues

Figure 47–1 continued

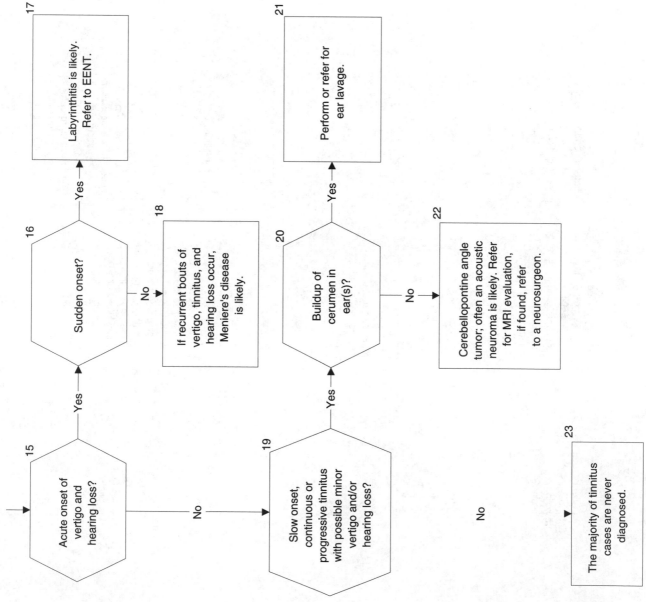

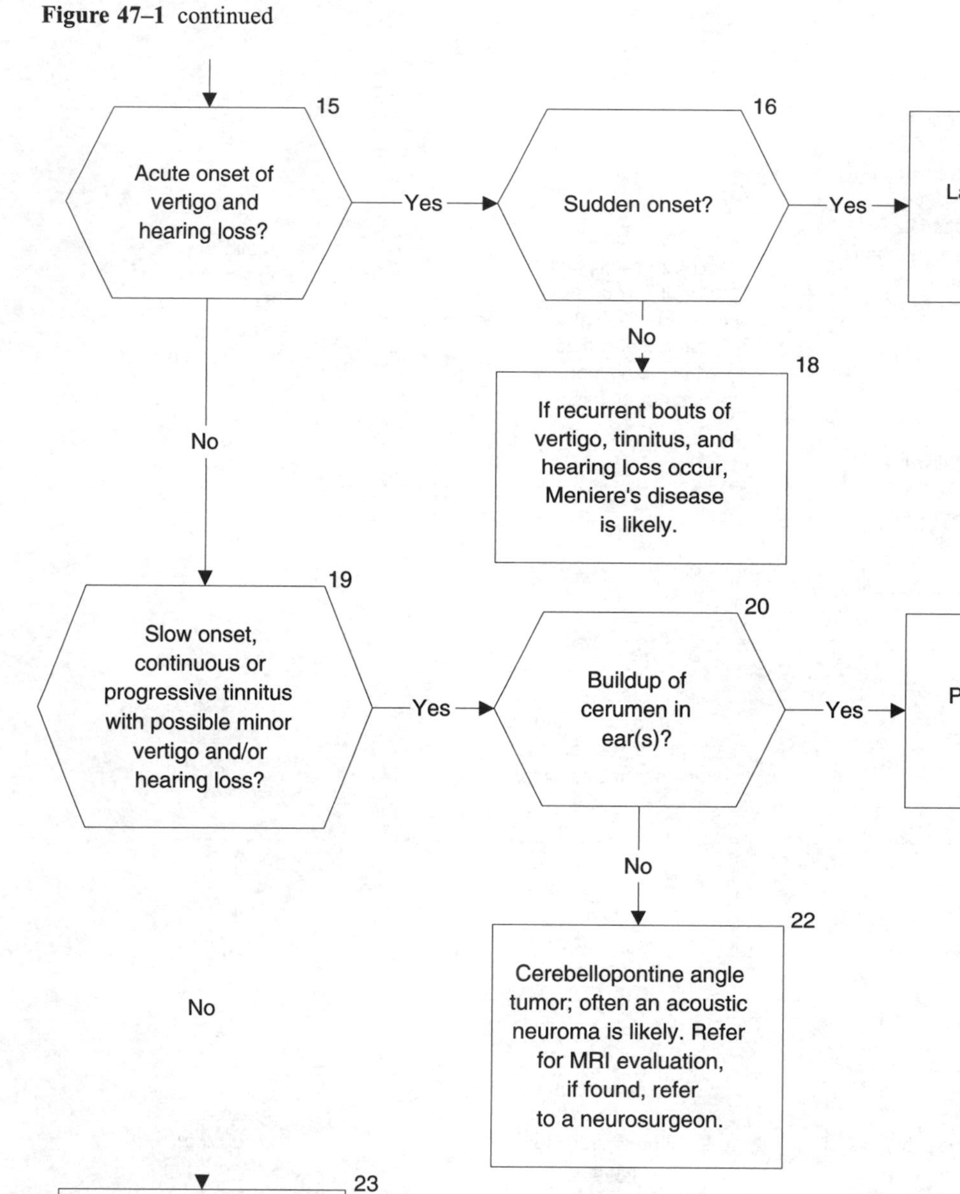

15
Acute onset of vertigo and hearing loss?
Yes
16
Sudden onset?
Yes
17
Labyrinthitis is likely. Refer to EENT.
No
18
If recurrent bouts of vertigo, tinnitus, and hearing loss occur, Meniere's disease is likely.
No
19
Slow onset, continuous or progressive tinnitus with possible minor vertigo and/or hearing loss?
Yes
20
Buildup of cerumen in ear(s)?
Yes
21
Perform or refer for ear lavage.
No
22
Cerebellopontine angle tumor; often an acoustic neuroma is likely. Refer for MRI evaluation, if found, refer to a neurosurgeon.
No
23
The majority of tinnitus cases are never diagnosed.

REFERENCES

1. Hughes JP. Tinnitus. In: Greene HL, Fincher RME, Johnson WP, et al, eds. *Clinical Medicine*. 2nd ed. St. Louis, MO: Mosby-Year Book; 1996:791.
2. Pulec JL. Cochlear nerve section for intractable tinnitus. *Ear Nose Throat J.* 1995;74:468–476.
3. Mitchell CR, Creedon TA. Psychophysical tuning curves in subjects with tinnitus suggest outer hair cell lesions. *Otolaryngol Head Neck Surg*. 1995;113:223–233.
4. Koyuncu M, Celik O, Luleci C, et al. Doppler sonography of vertebral arteries in patients with tinnitus. *Auris Nasus Larynx*. 1995;22: 24–28.
5. Marriage J, Barnes NM. Is central hyperacusis a symptom of 5-hydroxytryptamine (5-HT) dysfunction? *J Laryngol Otol*. 1995;109: 915–921.
6. Bogduk N, Lambert G, Duckworth JW. The anatomy and physiology of the vertebral nerve and its relation to cervical migraine. *Cephalalgia*. 1981;1:1–14.
7. Anderson RG. Tinnitus. In: Holt GR, et al, eds. *Decision Making in Otolaryngology*. Toronto: BC Decker; 1984.
8. Terrett AGJ. Tinnitus, the cervical spine, and spinal manipulative therapy. *Chiro Tech*. 1989;1:41–45.
9. Henrich DE, McCabe BF, Gantz BJ. Tinnitus and acoustic neuromas: analysis of the effect of surgical excision on postoperative tinnitus. *Ear Nose Throat J.* 1995;74:462–466.

Chapter 48

Epistaxis (Nosebleed)

CONTEXT

Nasal bleeding (epistaxis) is a common, usually benign, phenomenon that warrants little concern. Occasionally, however, patients seek help when bleeding is severe and uncontrollable or when it is recurrent. Approximately 25% of the time, epistaxis cannot be tied to a specific etiology.[1] Most benign causes are easily identifiable, often due to drying, irritation, or inflammation of the vessel-rich nasal musoca. These are probably more often seen in children, in whom nose blowing, wiping, and picking account for 95% of common initiators.[2] Another common cause is the drying effect of house heating during winter months. Trauma from a blow to the nose is quite obvious and often benign; however, if the severity of trauma is significant, underlying fracture should be investigated. A particular concern is the hypertensive patient who presents with nosebleeds. These are often profuse and poorly controlled without medical management. More rarely, bleeding dyscrasias may present with nasal bleeding. A major concern in children is the possibility of acute leukemia. This is manifested by a recently sick child with epistaxis and gingival and subcutaneous bleeding.

GENERAL STRATEGY

Acute and Profuse

If simple measures to control bleeding are not effective, referral for medical management is important. This will usually involve the use of silver nitrate sticks or electrocoagulation and packing.

Acute with Minimal Bleeding

- Control with slight pinching of the nose with the head held in neutral, not extended. In extension, blood may be swallowed, leading to nausea and/or vomiting.
- If significant trauma occurred, consider radiographs to rule out an associated fracture.

History of Recurrent Nose Bleeds

- Determine the frequency, amount of bleeding, and length of attacks.
- Determine whether there are any obvious causes with respect to allergies or nasal trauma from picking, blowing, or wiping; or whether the patient lives in a house where home heating produces a low-humidity environment (especially when the heater runs all night).
- In adults, determine whether the patient is hypertensive.
- Evaluate the patient for any other signs of bleeding tendencies, such as easy bruising.
- If recurrent and no obvious cause can be identified, lab tests may indicate any underlying blood dyscrasia.
- Refer if the suspected underlying cause is hypertension, mitral stenosis, a bleeding disorder, or drug related (chemotherapy, anticoagulant therapy for thrombophlebitis, etc.).

RELEVANT ANATOMY

Nasal bleeding is rather common because of an abundant and redundant blood supply and the vulnerability of the nose to trauma. Both the internal and external carotid arteries supply branches that feed the nasal mucosa. Epistaxis is classified as either anterior or posterior. Bleeding is most common anteriorly because of the abundance of vessels in Kiesellbach's plexus. Bleeding posteriorly is less common and more likely to be profuse. The blood vessels are quite superficial and vulnerable to various environmental factors as a result of allergies, infections, low humidity, and trauma.

EVALUATION

History

A focused history addresses common causes associated with nasal trauma, such as chronic blowing of the nose, nose picking or wiping, and direct trauma from blows. It is particularly important to determine the humidity of the patient's living or working environment. Specifically, when heating is used all night in the winter months, the nasal mucosa dries and leaves the area susceptible to bleeding from minor trauma.

A drug history is important. The use of anticoagulant or antiplatelet drugs, such as warfarin sodium (commonly used for deep vein thrombosis) or aspirin on a long-term basis, may predispose the patient. Drug-induced thrombocytopenia may occur with chemotherapy. Use of cocaine will cause nasal vasospasm and eventual tissue necrosis leading to bleeding (ironically, cocaine may be used in the acute management of nasal bleeding due to the vasoconstrictive effects). A family history of bleeding may indicate a rare hereditary hemorrhagic telangiectasia (Rendu-Osler-Weber syndrome). Determine whether the patient has a history of hypertension that is poorly controlled. Also investigate any possibility of advanced liver disease.

Examination

At the time of bleeding it is important to distinguish anterior from posterior bleeding.[3] This is often difficult because of the amount of bleeding. Posterior bleeding is classically profuse and difficult to control without silver nitrate sticks or electrocoagulation and nose packing. If trauma was involved, a close check for nasal or facial fracture is warranted. Radiographs or computed tomography may be needed to determine the extent of a facial fracture. For patients with recurrent or profuse bleeding, the evaluation should include the following:

- nasal mucosa inspection
- blood pressure measurement
- a complete blood cell count to determine thrombocytopenia (more extensive testing, including liver function tests, should be reserved for those suspected from history) or pancytopenia

MANAGEMENT

- Patients with thrombocytopenia or pancytopenia have serious disease and require immediate medical referral.
- Nasal hygiene is important to convey to children and their parents to eliminate common benign causes. When house humidity is suspected as the cause, two suggestions should be given. First, reduce the thermostat at night so that the heater is not used often during the evening. Second, apply a lubricant such as Vaseline around the nose before going to bed, which helps to moisten incoming air.
- For children who do not have a nasal hygiene cause, it may help to address the possibility of dairy product allergies through a trial of elimination for several weeks if the bleeding is recurrent.
- Persistent epistaxis with associated signs of bruising, fatigue, or weight loss may suggest an underlying leukemia warranting further medical evaluation.
- For patients with hypertension, referral for medical management is imperative. This type of bleeding may be potentially life threatening if the underlying hypertension is not controlled.

REFERENCES

1. Hughes JP. Nose bleed (epistaxis). In: Greene HL, Fincher RME, Johnson WP, et al, eds. *Clinical Medicine.* 2nd ed. St. Louis, MO: Mosby-Year Book; 1996:793.
2. Davis WE. Epistaxis. In: Holt GR, et al, eds. *Decision Making in Otolaryngology.* Toronto: BC Decker; 1984.
3. Josephson JD, Codley FA, Stierna P. Practical management of epistaxis. *Med Clin North Am.* 1991;75:1311.

CHAPTER 49

Sore Throat

CONTEXT

Although sore throat is one of the five most common complaints in a primary care setting,[1] presentation in a chiropractic setting is far less common. This is largely based on an assumption by the patient that antibiotics will be given for his or her problem and that drug prescription is not within the scope of chiropractors. The rationale for antibiotic treatment of pharyngitic sore throat, however, is not so much to treat for cure of the primary infection (there is no strong evidence indicating improvement of the sore throat with antibiotic treatment beyond the natural history), but to prevent the serious complication of streptococcal throat infection—rheumatic fever. It is interesting to note, though, that fewer than 15% of adults and 40% of children with sore throat have group A β-hemolytic *Streptococcus pyogenes* infection; the main cause of "strep" throat.[2] Viral causes account for about 50% of pharyngitis. Therefore, it is important to distinguish the patient with a nonstrep cause from the patient who is likely to have a viral (nonantibiotic treatable) cause of sore throat.

The two primary management issues with the indiscriminate use of antibiotics for sore throat (accounts for 50% of antibiotic prescription in outpatient clinics) are the inappropriate use of antibiotics, resulting in resistant bacterial strains, and the cost.[3] It would seem that such a common complaint as sore throat would have a clear-cut gold standard for evaluation or at least a classic presentation that would nail down the diagnosis. However, presentation varies, and the distinction between viral and bacterial pharyngitis is not always clear. There is no gold standard for the diagnosis of *S pyogenes*. With a suggestive history and examination coupled with the appropriate use of a rapid screen for antibodies to group A streptococcus and/or throat culture, the diagnosis should be evident in the majority of patients. Ironically, one study indicated that although primary care physicians who were educated regarding probabilities of strep throat improved in their diagnosis (decreased overestimation tendencies), they had a slight trend toward increasing prescription of antibiotics.[4] The study concludes that it is difficult to change treatment tendencies even with an improved ability to make treatment decisions.

In general, those patients at high risk for *S pyogenes* or its complications should be referred for antibiotic treatment. Others may be managed for symptoms and monitored for symptom persistence and severity. Failure to improve (or if the patient worsens) warrants referral for further testing or antibiotic treatment. As a potential first-contact doctor, chiropractors should have available the ability to perform a rapid antibody test for strep in an effort to save the patient from an unnecessary visit to his or her medical doctor.

GENERAL STRATEGY

History

Determine whether the patient has the following:

- indicators of high risk for *S pyogenes* or its complications (diabetes, prior rheumatic fever, strep throat in a close-contact individual)
- recurrent attacks that are relatively mild (allergic pharyngitis)
- history of orogenital sex or other indicators of gonorrhea

Examination

Determine or perform the following:

- whether the patient has a fever and/or rash
- whether the patient has signs of a respiratory infection
- examine sinuses for indication of infection (transilluminate)
- whether the patient has associated anterior or posterior lymph node involvement (anterior suggests bacterial, posterior suggests viral)
- whether there are any lesions in the mouth or oropharynx (examine the teeth and gums, tongue, palate, and pharynx)
- check the thyroid gland
- perform a rapid determination for streptococcus antigen if patient appears to have either strep or viral pharyngitis; if negative, yet history and exam are highly suggestive, perform a throat culture
- perform a screening lab test for patients suspected of having mononucleosis (Monospot in 2 weeks if still unsure)

Management

- Refer patients who are at high risk for strep.
- Refer patients who have a positive strep antigen test or throat culture for group A β-hemolytic strep.
- Manage patients symptomatically who have mononucleosis (unless extremely painful on swallowing or difficulty breathing).
- Manage patients for symptoms if a viral cause is suspected; monitor for worsening or persistence.

EVALUATION

History

The focus of the history is to determine whether patients have been exposed to strep throat and those who may be predisposed. Children are more likely to acquire strep throat than adults. A positive history of exposure to a schoolmate or a family member is often found. It is important to confirm that the contact individual has had positive tests for streptococcus and was not simply treated with antibiotics as a gunshot approach. It is also important to determine whether the patient has had prior rheumatic fever or a current history of diabetes; both predispose the individual to streptococcal infection.

The next step is to determine whether there are historical indicators of other causes of sore throat.

- With diabetics, the immunosuppressed, or those taking oral corticosteroids (inflammatory diseases) or inhaled corticosteroids (asthma) there is a higher risk for candidiasis.
- Patients (in particular homosexual men) who engage in orogenital sex are more likely to acquire oral gonorrhea.
- Patients who report a mild sore throat that is recurrent and unassociated with a fever are likely to have allergic pharyngitis (unless following a more severe initial attack). There is often an associated complaint of a chronic cough or sinus congestion.
- Patients who have had extensive dental procedures who complain of difficulty swallowing and an associated sore throat may have a retropharyngeal abscess (visible only with a lateral cervical spine radiograph).

Examination

One of the key findings is a pharyngeal exudate. Unfortunately, taken alone, this is a relatively nonspecific finding, occurring in as many as 65% of patients with viral pharyngitis and 40% of patients with mycoplasma infection. Following are some classic descriptions for various causes of exudates (it is recommended to examine a color atlas to gain better recognition):

- Streptococcal—tonsils are covered with a loose yellow exudate; tonsils are swollen.
- Herpangina—due to coxsackie virus infection; there are multiple, small (1 to 2 mm), painful ulcerations (often in children) of the soft palate and pharynx (a similar condition called hand-foot-and-mouth disease is caused by coxsackie virus but also involves the palms and soles of the feet).
- Herpes simplex—similar to herpangina in appearance; there are multiple, small (1 to 2 mm) vesicles that rupture in a few days to produce painful ulcerations; however, they may involve the lips, gingivae, or palate.
- Herpes zoster—the lesions are usually unilateral, involving the lip, tongue, or buccal mucosa; lesions are usually larger (2 to 4 mm) and go through vesiculation.
- Candidiasis—usually produces white, curdy patches on the tongue or mucosa.
- Mononucleosis—palatine petechiae are virtually diagnostic with small, red lesions with small, white bases.
- Vincent's angina (necrotizing ulcerative gingivostomatitis)—caused by fusobacterium or *Borrelia vincetii;* begins as a fulminant gingivitis with bleeding, ulcerations, and a grayish covering that spreads to the posterior pharynx; there is an associated foul breath.

In addition to examination of the mouth and throat, it is important to palpate for lymphadenopathy. Anterior lymph node enlargement is suggestive of a bacterial cause of pharyngitis. Posterior lymph node involvement suggests a viral source. Regional node enlargement in the axillary and inguinal regions in association with posterior neck involvement suggests mononucleosis. With a suspicion of mononucleosis it is always important to check for splenomegaly. In patients with no obvious oral involvement, palpation of the thyroid gland should be included. A scarlatiniform rash is strong evidence for streptococcal infection.

A temperature greater than 101°F is found more commonly with a streptococcal infection or a complication, peritonsillar abscess, involving unilateral swelling of a tonsil (a referral condition). Mild fever is more suggestive of a viral infection.

Unfortunately, the classic findings of fever, pharyngeal exudate, and anterior adenopathy without cough are not always found in all patients with strep throat (found in only 56% of patients). These findings are also nonspecific, occurring with other causes of pharyngitis. This, taken together with expediency issues, leads to a tendency toward overestimation of strep throat when the patient presents with pharyngitis. Reliance on clinical impression alone leads to an overestimation rate of between 80% and 95% by experienced clinicians.[5] For this reason laboratory evaluation is necessary.

There are two general approaches to detection of group A streptococcus. First is an in-office (or referral) check for rapid strep antigen. This approach has an estimated sensitivity of 79% to 88% and a specificity of about 95%.[5] Newer optical methods approach the 94% to 96% sensitivity level. Specificity was similar to that in the older methods. Based on these generalizations, it is suggested that patients with a positive test be referred for antibiotic treatment. The difficulty is the patient who appears to have strep throat, yet has a negative rapid antigen test. Most physicians would still order a culture, but would not treat until the results indicated infection with *S pyogenes*. Given the high specificity, some physicians would not culture. This is based solely on a cost-effectiveness decision.

In a patient with mononucleosis a complete blood count will demonstrate a lymphocytosis greater than 50% or atypical lymphocytes greater than 10%. A Monospot test should be ordered for confirmation after 1 week or 3 weeks if the first test is negative.

MANAGEMENT

- Refer patients who are at high risk for streptococcal infection.
- Refer patients who have a positive strep antigen test or throat culture for group A β-hemolytic streptococci.
- Manage patients symptomatically who have mononucleosis (unless extremely painful on swallowing or difficulty breathing).
- Manage patients for symptoms if a viral cause is suspected; monitor for worsening or persistence. Symptomatic management includes hydration and throat lozenges; cervical adjusting and massage may help with lymphatic drainage.

REFERENCES

1. Winters TH. Sore throat. In: Greene HL, Fincher RME, Johnson WP, et al, eds. *Clinical Medicine.* 2nd ed. St. Louis, MO: Mosby-Year Book; 1996:794.
2. Vukmir RB. Adult and pediatric pharyngitis: a review. *J Emerg Med.* 1992;10:607–616.
3. Pichichero ME. Explanations and therapies for penicillin failure in streptococcal pharyngitis. *Clin Pediatr.* 1992;31:642.
4. Poses RM, Cebul RD, Wigton RS. You can lead a horse to water: improving physicians' knowledge of probabilities may not affect their decisions. *Med Decis Making.* 1995;15:65–75.
5. Pichichero ME. Group A-streptococcal tonsillopharyngitis: cost-effective diagnosis and treatment. *Ann Emerg Med.* 1995;25:390–403.

Part VIII

Special Conditions

CHAPTER 50

Diabetes Mellitus

CONTEXT

Diabetes mellitus is a disorder that results in chronic hyperglycemia due to absence of insulin, decreases in insulin, and/or decreased sensitivity of insulin receptors. Diabetes mellitus (DM) generally is evident in two major forms: (1) type I, insulin-dependent diabetes mellitus (IDDM), and (2) type II, non–insulin-dependent diabetes mellitus (NIDDM). Generally, IDDM becomes apparent in childhood or adolescence, while NIDDM is not evident until later in life (over the age of 40). NIDDM may affect as many as 20% of the senior US population (ages 65 to 74 years). These two disorders are not always clearly defined by age, with some older patients developing IDDM and some younger patients developing NIDDM. Ninety to ninety-five percent of diabetics in the United States have NIDDM.[1] There is an ethnic distinction in that Scandinavians have a much higher proportion of patients with IDDM (20%). In Japan and China, only 1% of diabetic patients have IDDM.

The major complications of a chronic hyperglycemic state (and associated abnormalities) are macrovascular and microvascular disease. As a result, several complications of diabetes make it an extremely important disease to control. The major complications include the following:

- Death—DM significantly increases the risk of atherosclerosis-related death (seventh leading cause of death in the United States).[2] Seventy-five percent of DM-related deaths are due to this macrovascular manifestation. Two thirds of adult patients with DM have hypertension.
- Blindness—DM is the leading cause of blindness in the United States in patients between the ages of 20 and 74.[3]
- Renal failure—DM is the leading cause of end-stage renal disease in the United States; 25% to 30% of patients receiving some form of renal replacement therapy are diabetic.[4]
- Neuropathy—DM is the most common cause of polyneuropathy, affecting 50% of all diabetics within 25 years (20% of patients with NIDDM are affected).[5]
- Gangrene of the feet—Diabetics have an incidence 20 times higher than the nondiabetic population. This may lead to amputation. Smoking increases the risk.

Because of these and other complications, the estimated total annual price tag for the United States alone is estimated at $100 billion.[6]

The Diabetes Complication and Control Trial (DCCT) publication studied patients with IDDM and demonstrated a reduction in microvascular complications in patients who were tightly controlled (hyperglycemia controlled).[7] These included diabetic retinopathy, nephropathy, and neuropathy. There was also a reduction in macrovascular complications, such as atherosclerosis, that result in coronary artery disease. Although this study focused on IDDM, it is generally assumed that these beneficial effects will also occur in patients with NIDDM.

The chiropractor will often have diabetic patients present with various musculoskeletal and neurologic complaints. It is important to place the evaluation and management of these complaints in the context of a diabetic patient. In other words, if a diabetic patient presents with numbness, tingling, or pain in the lower extremity associated (or not associated) with low back pain, the question is whether the lower extremity problem is a complication of the diabetes or due to some other nondiabetic etiology. More important, only half of patients with diabetes are aware of their disorder.[8] This means that if a patient complains of symptoms of a neuropathy and no history of a diabetes diagnosis, the chiropractor could be unaware of an important component for decision making in the patient's management and prognosis.

Therefore, the chiropractor who uses laboratory facilities is in an advantageous position to detect the diabetic patient. In addition, if a patient is discovered to have NIDDM, comanagement with a strong emphasis on dietary and exercise control should be the focus of the chiropractor's involvement. Diabetic management is complex and difficult with regard to patient compliance, given that many patients may be asymptomatic. If the patient has a supportive network, including the chiropractor, the medical doctor, and the family, his or her chances for conservative control of NIDDM are increased.

GENERAL STRATEGY

History

Determine whether

- the patient has risk factors, such as being older and obese; a family history of diabetes; signs and symptoms such as blurred vision or numbness and tingling in the extremities; or polyphagia, polyuria, or polydypsia
- the patient has a history or signs and symptoms of other disorders that may cause hyperglycemia (Cushing's disease, pheochromocytoma) or whether he or she is taking medications that may cause hyperglycemia or worsen diabetes (corticosteroids, diuretics causing hypokalemia)
- the patient is a known diabetic—is the patient taking medication (insulin or a hypoglycemic agent), following a dietary program, following an exercise program, monitoring his or her blood glucose level, being monitored with a glycosolated hemoglobin?

Evaluation

- Pay particular attention to weight, blood pressure, and vision (patients with NIDDM are often overweight and hypertensive).
- Check for secondary signs of diabetes, including an ophthalmoscopic examination, a check of the skin and nails, and a neurologic check for vibration or sensory deficits.
- Screen high-risk patients (see risk factors above), preferably with a fasting laboratory test; if not being performed by primary care giver, screen for gestational diabetes in pregnant women between weeks 24 and 28, using a 1-hour glucose tolerance test.
- In known diabetics use a glycosolated hemoglobin to check control of diabetes (coordinate with medical doctor if necessary).

Management

- IDDM should be managed by the patient's medical doctor; however, the chiropractor can provide a supportive role with the medical doctor to better guarantee tight glycemic control and prevention of complications.
- NIDDM should be comanaged with a strong emphasis on a specific dietary and exercise program.
- Monitor all patients for clinical indicators of progressive macrovascular and microvascular complications.

RELEVANT PHYSIOLOGY

Glycemic metabolism is controlled by the interaction of insulin (which has mainly a hypoglycemic function) and hormones that are referred to as counterregulatory. These counterregulatory hormones include glucagon, epinephrine/norepinephrine (catecholamines), cortisol, and growth hormone. In general, these hormones act to stimulate glycogenolysis and gluconeogenesis. Catecholamines, in particular, suppress insulin secretion and stimulate hepatic glucose production. The hypoglycemic function of insulin is the result of several mechanisms, including promoting the uptake of glucose by mainly muscle and adipose tissue, inhibiting the breakdown of glycogen (promotes glycogen stores), and inhibiting the production of other sources of energy such as from free fatty acids. Both chromium and potassium are needed for the proper functioning of insulin.

There are two circadian effects that influence diabetes.[9] The Somogyi effect begins with a nocturnal hypoglycemia that occurs with type I diabetes. This may stimulate an overproduction of counterregulatory hormones leading to hyperglycemia by 7:00 AM. Another effect is called the dawn phenomenon.[10] This phenomenon occurs in most diabetic and nondiabetic individuals with a reduced tissue sensitivity to insulin between 5:00 AM and 8:00 AM. These effects and exercise may have an effect on the timing and need for insulin.

During exercise, insulin need is diminished. This is due to the enhanced insulin binding at receptor sites, so that glucose uptake is increased without an increase in insulin (insulin demand reduced). Also, because the amount of circulating plasma glucose is quite small and unable to meet the demands of exercise, the inhibitory effects of insulin on liver glucose production are inhibited by the counterregulatory hormones, in particular, glucagon and the catecholamines.

Patients with a level of plasma glucose high enough to exceed the renal threshold for glucose will have a spillover into the urine. This causes an osmotic diuresis (polyuria) leading to dehydration. This will lead to increased thirst—polydipsia. When glucose uptake in the peripheral sites is decreased, patients will often feel a lack of energy or feel fatigued. This relative "cell starvation" may lead to a desire to eat—polyphagia.

Type I diabetes is due to the failure of the beta cells of the pancreas to produce and secrete insulin. It is currently believed that this is due to an autoimmune response that is genetically predetermined. It is proposed that either through an infectious or toxic environmental stimulus, the body produces an autoimmune response against either altered pancreatic beta cell antigens or against part of the beta cell that resembles a viral protein. As a result, 85% of patients with type I diabetes have circulating islet cell antibodies, with the majority having antiinsulin antibodies detected. Some of the suspected viral causes are the mumps and coxsackievirus B4. With type I IDDM, patients may become ketotic and subsequently develop life-threatening metabolic acidosis.

Type II NIDDM represents a range of glycemic disorders that are due mainly to tissue insensitivity to insulin, a blunted beta-cell response to glucose, and an increase in hepatic production of glucose. These patients usually have enough insulin to prevent ketoacidosis, but do not have enough to prevent the consequences of chronic hyperglycemia. The increase in liver production appears to be due to an increased circulating level of glucagon. Most patients in the United States with type II DM are obese. Those who are not obese may represent a subcategory of IDDM because they often eventually need insulin. There appears to be a pattern of inheritance with NIDDM that appears to be autosomal dominant.

The relationship to obesity appears to be predominantly associated with an abdominal fat distribution. Apparently, fat that is in the extremities or distributed superficially in the abdomen has less an effect on hepatic production of glucose than does fat that is "visceral."[11] This visceral type of fat is distributed mainly in the omental and mesenteric regions. Both insulin resistance and hepatic glucose production are increased with this type of obesity.

The relationship between NIDDM and associated hypertension, hyperlipidemia, hyperglycemia, and hyperinsulinemia has led to a proposed syndrome called insulin resistance syndrome, syndrome X, or CHAOS.[12] CHAOS is an acronym for coronary artery disease, hypertension, atherosclerosis, obesity, and stroke. This acronym represents the clinical consequences of insulin resistance. It is known that the conditions associated with syndrome X are interdependent to some degree and that a reduction in one of them will have a beneficial effect on reducing risk for CHAOS.

Gestational diabetes is diabetes that is first detected during pregnancy. It carries with it the risk of fetal abnormalities, including neural tube deficits (folic acid helps), macrosomia, and fetal death. A well-controlled blood glucose level (mainly through diet) can substantially reduce the risk.

Cause of Clinical Manifestations

Diabetic neuropathy presents in various clinical forms, including poly- and mononeuropathies (Exhibit 50–1). The underlying cause is uncertain. However, with acute onset of symptoms, the suspicion is that there is an infarction of one or several branches of the vasonervorum (the arteries feeding the nerves), so the cause is actually vascular. When progression is slower it is believed that there is a gradual deterioration that causes the sensory aberrations seen in many long-term or poorly controlled diabetics. The cause appears to be excess sorbitol formation in Schwann cells or nerve trunks in reaction to chronic hyperglycemia.

Diabetic retinopathy is due to deterioration of the microcirculation to the retina, resulting in microaneurysms. Tight glycemic control may decrease the rate of these microaneurysms. The microaneurysms may progress to the development of exudates and punctate hemorrhages, together called background retinopathy. Although relatively stable, background retinopathy may progress to large hemorrhages with subsequent scarring. Following scarring, angiogenesis factor released by the ischemic retina leads to a proliferation of new blood vessels called neovascularization. As these contract into the vitreous, the retina may become detached, causing blindness.

The lens is also affected in many diabetics. Chronic hyperglycemia may lead to a change in lens shape, resulting in visual acuity that fluctuates. It usually takes 6 to 8 weeks of tight glycemic control to correct the problem. Additionally, chronic hyperglycemia may also cause excess sorbitol deposition in the lens. This creates an osmotic gradient, drawing in extracellular waste products and leading to the development of a cataract. Unfortunately, tight glycemic control does not seem to prevent or reverse this process. Glaucoma is also more common in diabetics (occurring in 6% of diabetics), apparently because of scar formation at the canal of Schlemm.

Diabetic nephropathy leads to hyperfiltration and microalbuminuria. Decreasing renal function leads to glomerulopathy and subsequent renal failure. Factors that increase the rate of failure are hypertension and a high-protein diet.

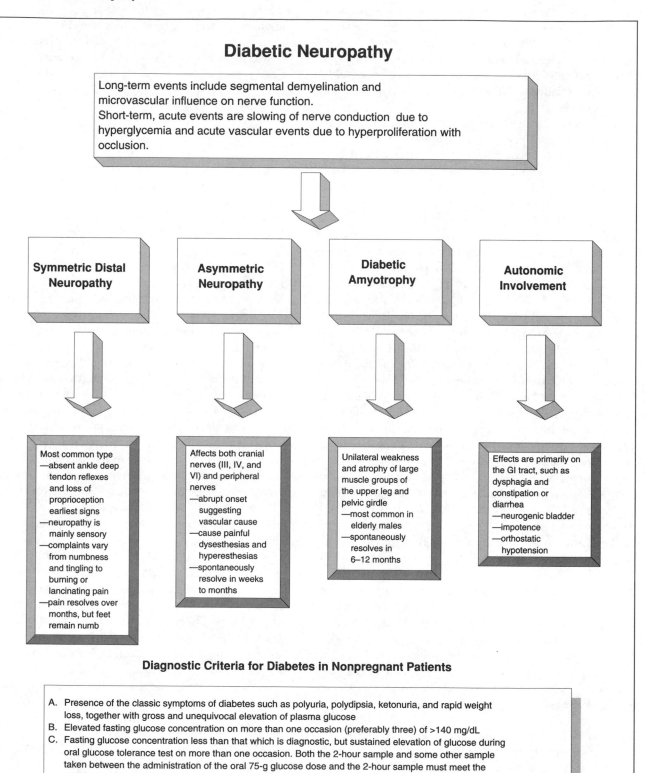

Exhibit 50–1 Diabetic Neuropathy

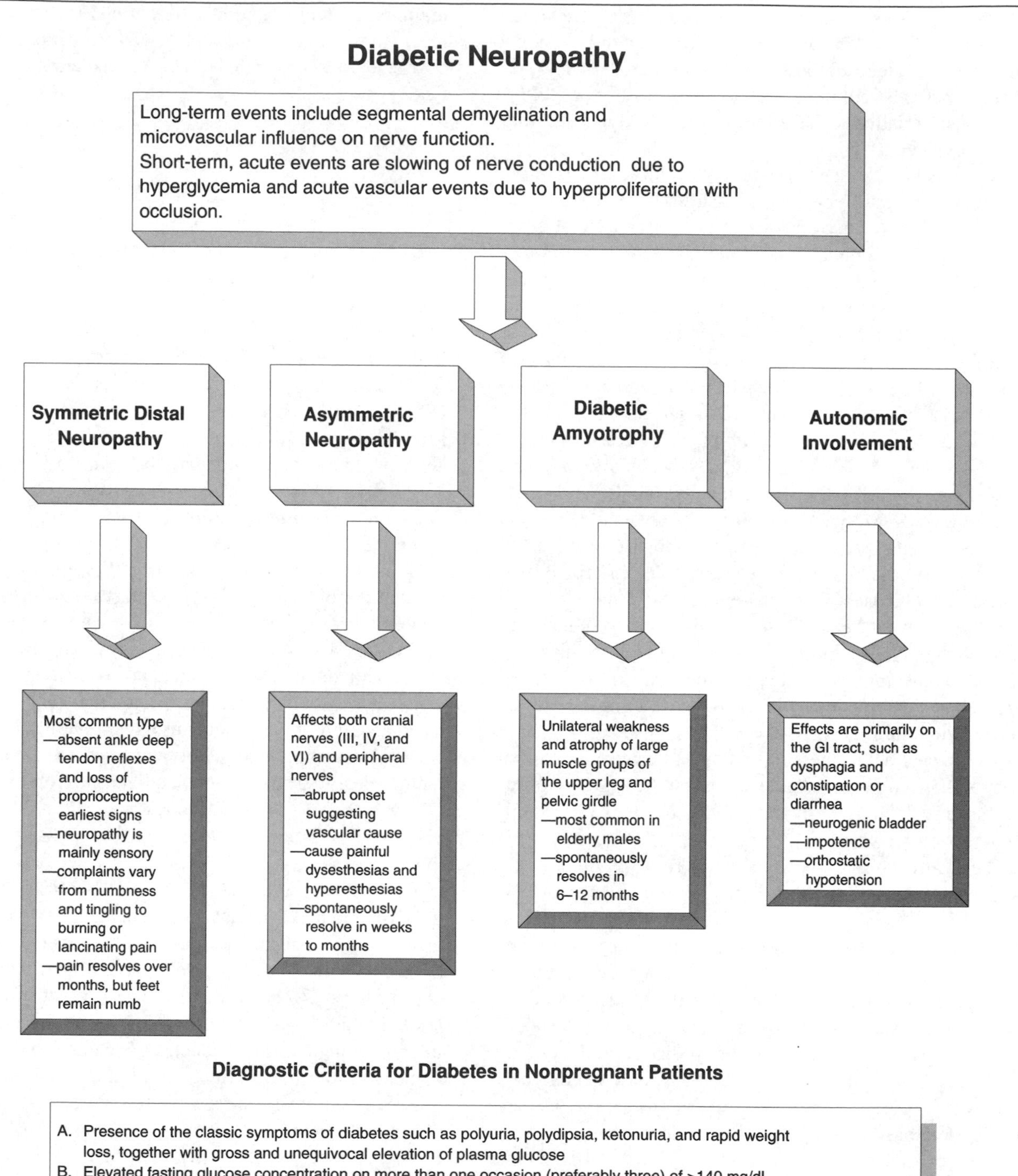

Diabetic Neuropathy
Long-term events include segmental demyelination and microvascular influence on nerve function.
Short-term, acute events are slowing of nerve conduction due to hyperglycemia and acute vascular events due to hyperproliferation with occlusion.
Symmetric Distal Neuropathy
Asymmetric Neuropathy
Diabetic Amyotrophy
Autonomic Involvement
Most common type
—absent ankle deep tendon reflexes and loss of proprioception earliest signs
—neuropathy is mainly sensory
—complaints vary from numbness and tingling to burning or lancinating pain
—pain resolves over months, but feet remain numb
Affects both cranial nerves (III, IV, and VI) and peripheral nerves
—abrupt onset suggesting vascular cause
—cause painful dysesthesias and hyperesthesias
—spontaneously resolve in weeks to months
Unilateral weakness and atrophy of large muscle groups of the upper leg and pelvic girdle
—most common in elderly males
—spontaneously resolves in 6–12 months
Effects are primarily on the GI tract, such as dysphagia and constipation or diarrhea
—neurogenic bladder
—impotence
—orthostatic hypotension

Diagnostic Criteria for Diabetes in Nonpregnant Patients

A. Presence of the classic symptoms of diabetes such as polyuria, polydipsia, ketonuria, and rapid weight loss, together with gross and unequivocal elevation of plasma glucose
B. Elevated fasting glucose concentration on more than one occasion (preferably three) of >140 mg/dL
C. Fasting glucose concentration less than that which is diagnostic, but sustained elevation of glucose during oral glucose tolerance test on more than one occasion. Both the 2-hour sample and some other sample taken between the administration of the oral 75-g glucose dose and the 2-hour sample must meet the criteria of > 200 mg/dL.

EVALUATION

History

The Undiagnosed Diabetic

A high level of suspicion is raised when a patient with a family history of diabetes presents with a complaint of bilateral (or unilateral) numbness or tingling in the feet or hands. Complaints such as blurring vision, polyuria, and polydipsia (increased thirst) in an older patient with associated weight gain are also highly suggestive. Symptoms of hypoglycemia following meals or simply generalized fatigue in an older patient warrants evaluation for diabetes. Hypertension, obesity, hyperlipedemia, and smoking are important as potential risk factors (or possibly associated factors). A thorough drug history is crucial to determine a contributing or unmasking effect on diabetes. These drugs include thiazide diuretics that may cause chronic potassium deficiency.

One of the first signs of NIDDM in women is pruritus or signs of vaginitis. Frequent candida (yeast) infections are also suggestive. Women who have given birth to large babies (greater than 9 lb) or who have experienced preeclampsia or unexplained fetal death also should be screened for diabetes. Pregnant women should be questioned regarding gestational diabetes screening.

The Diagnosed Diabetic

IDDM—Assuming that the patient is presenting with a neuromusculoskeletal complaint, it is important to determine how well the IDDM patient is controlled. It may well be that a complaint of radicular pain into the extremities or localized in the extremities may be a manifestation of diabetic neuropathy. This will strongly influence interpretation of examination findings, management, and prognosis (many are self-resolving). History questions regarding age at diagnosis, type of insulin, frequency of visits to the physician, development of diabetic complications, exercise and diet history, and current medication history are necessary to gauge where a patient stands with regard to risk.

NIDDM—The main concern with the NIDDM patient is adherence to a diet/exercise regimen. Questions regarding general well-being and/or the development of any diabetes-related neurovascular problems should be included. It is important to determine whether the patient has been given all the available patient information provided by the American Diabetes Association. It is also important to determine how often the patient is being evaluated for glycosolated hemoglobin. The chiropractor may provide this service if more convenient or cost effective than through the patient's primary physician.

Examination

The physical examination of all patients with diabetes or suspected diabetes should focus first on the associated comorbidity problems of obesity (in NIDDM), hypertension, retinopathy, and neuropathy. Therefore, blood pressure measurement (supine and standing); an ophthalmoscopic examination; deep tendon reflexes; and distal vibration, proprioception, and touch should be evaluated.

In known diabetics, it is important to screen the status of the teeth/gums, toes/toenails (in particular between the toes), and skin (especially skin injection sites).

The laboratory evaluation begins with the determination of diabetes in undiagnosed patients. The criteria for diabetes is a plasma glucose level of 140 mg/dL or higher on a fasting lab specimen on more than one occasion. Because of the difficulties in interpreting glucose tolerance tests, they are not recommended for general screening. For patients with apparent signs of diabetes with a glucose level below 140 mg/dL, an oral glucose tolerance test may be ordered. When checking for gestational diabetes, a 1-hour glucose tolerance test between weeks 24 and 28 should be ordered.

Additional findings suggestive of diabetes are

- proteinuria (albumin)
- ketonuria
- budding yeasts on urinalysis
- hyperlipidemia

In the known diabetic, it is not necessary or desirable to test for a fasting glucose level. Diabetics self-monitor their blood glucose levels often. It is more important to gain a sense of whether or not there is glycemic control. This is accomplished with a nonfasting test called glycosylated hemoglobin. Since glycosylated hemoglobin is a measure of the amount of glucose attached to red blood cells (RBCs), it gives a good estimate of glycemic status over the preceding 8 to 12 weeks (the life of the RBC). Adequate control of glucose is indicated by an average glucose level of 150 mg/dL or a hemoglobin A_{1c} of 7% to 8%.[13] Levels above 10% are poorly controlled and at greater risk of developing complications.

MANAGEMENT

Management of the diabetic patient is a complex, time-consuming program for both the patient and the doctor. For IDDM patients, control through injection is required. Medical instruction in delivery with regard to timing and injection site are necessary. In addition, instructions on proper care of the feet to avoid gangrenous complications is also necessary. The patient usually is sent to a dietitian to explain a comprehensive diet, including the American Diabetic Association exchange lists, the need for fiber, and artificial sweeteners as a substitute for table sugar.

For NIDDM patients, the focus is on diet control and exercise. Unfortunately about half of all diabetics do not follow their diets. The main role of the diet is to reduce weight in NIDDM patients. For medical doctors managing NIDDM, it is important to keep in mind that correction of hypertension may raise lipid levels if diuretics or β-blockers are used. Or in an attempt to correct hyperlipidemia, prescription of niacin is given, leading to an increased insulin resistance.

Specific complications of diabetes and their management are briefly listed, as follows:

- Diabetic nephropathy—To prevent progressive deterioration, a low-protein diet, combined with hypertension control using an angiotensin-converting inhibitor has been proven effective.
- Diabetic retinopathy—Good glycemic control, management of hypertension, and avoidance of smoking may help prevent the development of retinal changes. If neovascularization occurs, photocoagulation with an argon laser is often effective.
- Diabetic neuropathy—Good glycemic control and avoidance of smoking are essential. Most of the poly- and mononeuropathies will self-resolve in 6 to 12 months.

Algorithm

An algorithm for evaluation and management of the diabetic patient is presented in Figure 50–1.

REFERENCES

1. National Diabetes Information Clearinghouse. *Diabetes Statistics*. Bethesda, MD: National Institutes of Diabetes and Digestive and Kidney Diseases; 1994. (NIH publication No. 94-3822).
2. American Diabetes Association. *Diabetes—1996 Vital Statistics*. Alexandria, VA: American Diabetes Association; 1995.
3. Centers for Disease Control and Prevention. Public health focus: prevention of blindness associated with diabetic retinopathy. *MMWR*. 1993;42:191–195.
4. Breyer JA. Diabetic nephropathy in insulin-dependent patients. *Am J Kidney Dis*. 1992;20:533–547.
5. Harati Y. Diabetic peripheral neuropathies. *Ann Intern Med*. 1987;107:546–559.
6. American Diabetes Association. *Direct and Indirect Costs of Diabetes in the United States in 1992*. Alexandria, VA: American Diabetes Association; 1993.
7. Diabetes Complication and Control Trial Research Group. The effect of intensive treatment of diabetes on the development and progression of long-term complications in insulin-dependent diabetes mellitus. *N Engl J Med*. 1993;329:977.
8. Harris MI. Undiagnosed NIDDM: clinical and public health issues. *Diabetes Care*. 1993;16:642–652.
9. Karam JH. Diabetes mellitus and hypoglycemia. In: Tierney LM, McPhee SJ, Papadakis MA, eds. *Current Medical Diagnosis and Treatment*. 34th ed. Norwalk, CT: Appleton & Lange; 1995:1022.
10. Bolli GB, Gerich JE. The "dawn phenomenon"—a common occurrence in both non-insulin dependent and insulin-dependent diabetes. *N Engl J Med*. 1984;310:746.
11. Bjorntorp P. Metabolic implications of body fat distribution. *Diabetes Care*. 1991;14:1132.
12. Karam JH. Type II diabetes and syndrome X: Pathogenesis and glycemic management. *Endocrinol Metab Clin North Am*. 1992;21:329.
13. Fore WW. Noninsulin-dependent diabetes mellitus: the prevention of complications. *Med Clin North Am*. 1995;79:287–298.

Figure 50–1

THE DIABETIC PATIENT—ALGORITHM.

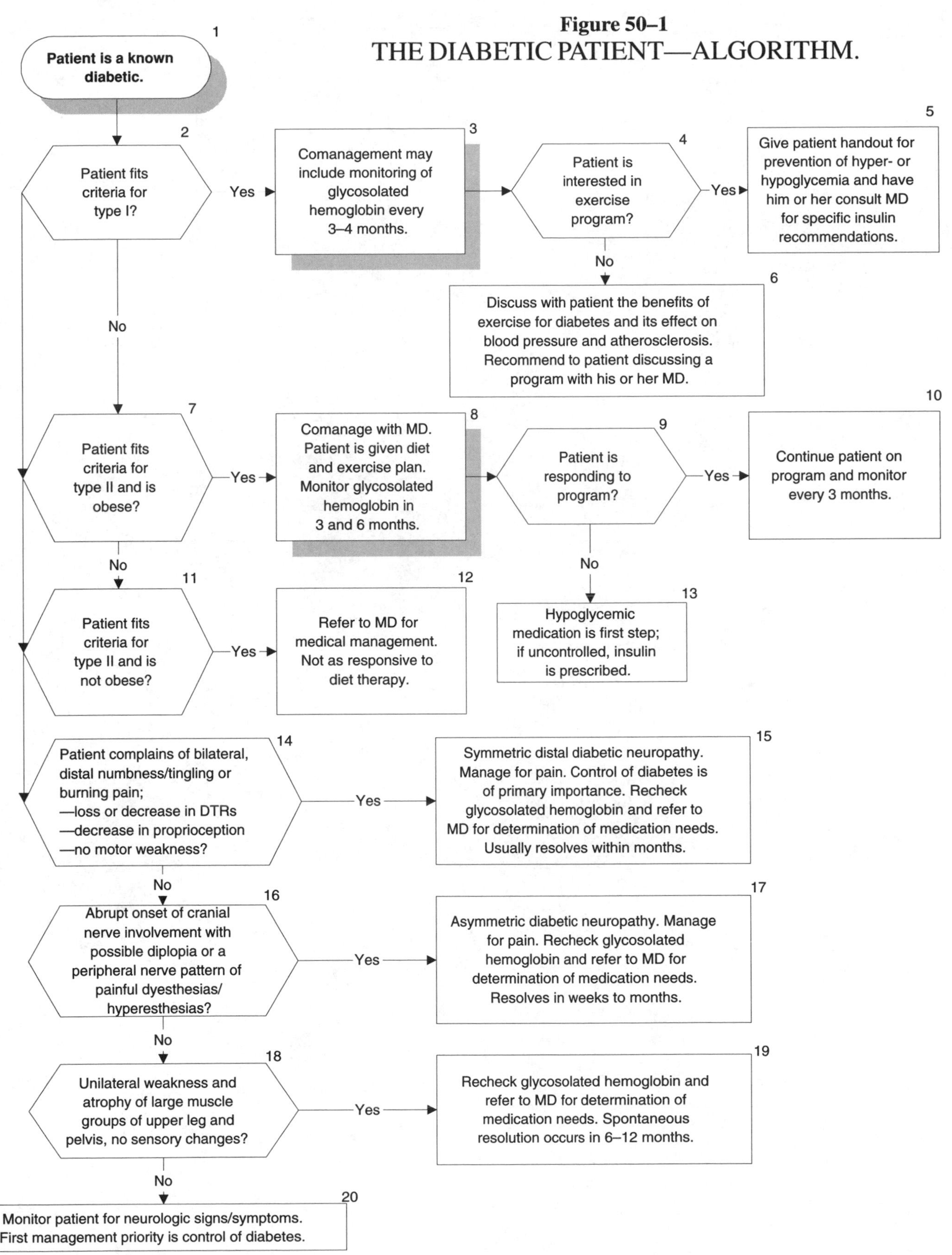

1 Patient is a known diabetic.
2 Patient fits criteria for type I?
Yes
No
3 Comanagement may include monitoring of glycosolated hemoglobin every 3–4 months.
4 Patient is interested in exercise program?
Yes
5 Give patient handout for prevention of hyper- or hypoglycemia and have him or her consult MD for specific insulin recommendations.
No
6 Discuss with patient the benefits of exercise for diabetes and its effect on blood pressure and atherosclerosis. Recommend to patient discussing a program with his or her MD.
7 Patient fits criteria for type II and is obese?
Yes
8 Comanage with MD. Patient is given diet and exercise plan. Monitor glycosolated hemoglobin in 3 and 6 months.
9 Patient is responding to program?
Yes
10 Continue patient on program and monitor every 3 months.
No
13 Hypoglycemic medication is first step; if uncontrolled, insulin is prescribed.
No
11 Patient fits criteria for type II and is not obese?
Yes
12 Refer to MD for medical management. Not as responsive to diet therapy.
14 Patient complains of bilateral, distal numbness/tingling or burning pain; —loss or decrease in DTRs —decrease in proprioception —no motor weakness?
Yes
15 Symmetric distal diabetic neuropathy. Manage for pain. Control of diabetes is of primary importance. Recheck glycosolated hemoglobin and refer to MD for determination of medication needs. Usually resolves within months.
No
16 Abrupt onset of cranial nerve involvement with possible diplopia or a peripheral nerve pattern of painful dyesthesias/ hyperesthesias?
Yes
17 Asymmetric diabetic neuropathy. Manage for pain. Recheck glycosolated hemoglobin and refer to MD for determination of medication needs. Resolves in weeks to months.
No
18 Unilateral weakness and atrophy of large muscle groups of upper leg and pelvis, no sensory changes?
Yes
19 Recheck glycosolated hemoglobin and refer to MD for determination of medication needs. Spontaneous resolution occurs in 6–12 months.
No
20 Monitor patient for neurologic signs/symptoms. First management priority is control of diabetes.

Key: DTR, deep tendon reflex.

CHAPTER 51

Thyroid Dysfunction

CONTEXT

Patients with thyroid dysfunction often have signs and symptoms that are suggestive of other disorders, including fatigue, depression, or other metabolic problems. Determination of the appropriate patient to screen for thyroid disease is based on either a clinical presentation of overt disease or high-risk categories for asymptomatic patients. There is a general consensus that screening all patients for thyroid dysfunction is not cost-effective because of the low yield and the difficulty with sorting out small increases and decreases that may reflect a euthyroid state (temporary change with no thyroid pathology).[1,2] Thyroid dysfunction is found in approximately 1% to 4% of the adult population of the United States with an annual incidence of 0.08% for hypothyroidism and 0.05% for hyperthyroidism.[2] Epidemiologic studies have determined several groups of patients who are at higher risk. Those patients who are symptomatic often will have a constellation of signs of symptoms; however, there are a number of individuals who are subclinically dysfunctional. A percentage of these patients will progress onto overt hypo- or hyperthyroidism. These categories include the following:

Those with a risk 20 times that of the general population:[3]

- patients who have had radioisotope or radiation therapy
- patients with other automimmune disorders
- patients with first-degree relatives with thyroid disease
- patients taking amiodarone hydrochloride

Those with a risk 8 times that of the general population:[4–6]

- the elderly

Those with a risk 4 times that of the general population:[7]

- women over 40

Consideration for screening in patients with minor risk:

- psychiatric patients[8]
- those patients taking lithium or have a quickly fluctuating bipolar disorder

Neonatal testing is required in all states. This is due less to the risk (1 of 3,500 to 4,000 births) than to the devastating effects of not detecting what will become cretinism with its associated mental retardation and other neuropsychologic effects.

Although there are a number of thyroid disorders and even temporal sequencing of hyper- and hypothyroidism with the same named condition, the majority of patients fit into two categories: (1) hyperthyroidism—most often due to Graves' disease, and (2) hypothyroidism—most often due to Hashimoto's disease. Hypothyroidism also may be due to treatment for hyperthyroidism with either radioactive iodine therapy or surgery. There are also age-related changes in thyroid physiology, which is why patients over age 65 years, especially women, must be considered for screening. Thyroid dysfunction may also be due to secondary (pituitary) and tertiary (hypothalamic) disorders. Specific thyroid disorders and how they differ are listed under Selected Thyroid Disorders.

GENERAL STRATEGY

History

- Determine whether the patient has been diagnosed with a thyroid disorder or has had treatment for a thyroid disorder.
- Determine whether the patient has any complaints of fatigue, intolerance to heat or cold, tremors, or eye problems.

Evaluation

- Determine whether a goiter is present.
- Determine whether there are secondary signs of hypothyroidism, including dry skin, loss of outer third of eyebrows, weight gain, slow speech, a decrease in deep tendon reflexes, or the more classic facial appearance of cretinism.
- Determine whether there are secondary signs of hyperthyroidism, including increased pulse rate and blood pressure, increased respiration, increase in deep tendon reflexes, detection of a fine tremor, exophthalmos, or lid lag.
- Screen asymptomatic patients at higher risk based on the above-listed categories.
- Run an ultrasensitive thyrotropin (uTSH) or thyroid panel on patients believed to have a thyroid disorder.

Management

- Refer patients who fit classic laboratory criteria for overt thyroid disease.
- Educate patients who have subclinical thyroid disease about the pros and cons of treatment and refer to a medical doctor for a second opinion.

RELEVANT PHYSIOLOGY

A feedback loop controls thyroid hormone production. When circulating thyroid hormone levels are low, pituitary thyrotroph cells are stimulated by hypothalmaic thyrotropin-releasing hormone (TRH). TSH (thyrotropin) is then secreted from the pituitary to initiate several steps in the production of active thyroid hormone. Iodine is trapped and linked to tyrosine by perioxidase. Next, coupling of monoiodotyrosine and diiodotyrosine form T_3 (triiodotyrosine) and T_4 (thyroxine). The thyroid gland then secretes T_4 and a very small amount of T_3. T_3 is the most active form of thyroid hormone. Most of the circulating T_3 is, in fact, produced via peripheral deiodination of T_4 in the liver. Reverse T_3, an inactive form, is also produced. Thyroid-binding globulin (TBG) binds 99.95% of thyroid hormones. Therefore, any condition that affects protein levels will affect total thyroid hormone levels. These conditions include liver disease, pregnancy, estrogen levels, starvation, and acute or chronic illness. With severe illness the peripheral conversion of T_4 to T_3 is reduced even though there is no thyroid organ pathology.

EVALUATION

History

Signs and symptoms suggestive of hyperthyroidism include nervousness, irritability, tremor, muscle weakness, heat intolerance, change in appetite, decreased or dysfunctional menstrual flow, and increased frequency of bowel movements. Many of these complaints are the result of increased metabolism. The patient may also notice a change in appearance, such as a neck mass, enlarged or more prominent eyes and associated eye irritation. Only 5% to 10% develop severe eye changes. Lymphocytic infiltration is the cause of exophthalmos and occasionally diplopia when the extraocular muscles become entrapped by infiltrates.

Patients with hypothyroidism may have complaints similar to those with hyperthyroidism. Complaints include weakness, tiredness, fatigue, depression, weight gain (true obesity is unusual), cold intolerance, dry skin, hoarseness, impaired mental function, joint pains and muscle cramps, and menstrual difficulties such as anovulatory bleeding and infertility. An enlarged gland may be apparent to the patient.

Examination

The physical examination focuses on possible enlargement of the thyroid gland and the secondary effects of thyroid dysfunction on skin/hair, weight, myxoid deposition, and the cardiovascular system. The first aspect of evaluation of thyroid size and contour is inspection. Viewing the patient from the front and having him or her extend the neck often provides a better visualization of the thyroid. Cross-lighting may be helpful to better delineate contour. Next, viewing from the side, determine if there is any protrusion between the cricoid cartilage and the suprasternal notch. Palpation of the thyroid has been described many different ways. Some of the variations are whether to palpate from behind or in front of the patient and whether to use the ipsilateral or opposite hand. No studies indicate any specific method as superior. The location of the thyroid gland is determined in relation to the thyroid and cricoid cartilage. Normally the thyroid gland is palpable on either side of the distal half of the thyroid cartilage down to the upper trachea. Palpation is facilitated by relaxing the sternocleidomastoids. This is accomplished by having the patient flex and rotate the head to the ipsilateral side of palpation. It is often recommended that having the patient swallow may assist in determining size and possibly reveal a low-lying gland. It is important to have the patient swallow a sip of water, only because the larger the amount of water, the more the excursion, the more difficult the task of discrimination from other structures.

Some individuals are difficult to palpate. These include the obese, the elderly, and those with chronic pulmonary disease, where the neck is relatively short. Errors may occur due to misinterpretation in the following patients:[9]

- overestimation of size in thin individuals or those with long, slender necks (Modigliani syndrome)
- overestimation due to a more superior location (normal variant)
- misidentification of a fat pad in the anterior and lateral neck as a goiter (pseudogoiter) found in the obese and those of normal weight (in particular young women) (the fat pad does not move with swallowing and the texture is different from that of the thyroid)
- underestimation due to a low-lying thyroid (can be retrosternal)
- underestimation due to sternocleidomastoid interference

Interexaminer agreement on the detection of a goiter and whether individual lobes are enlarged has been demonstrated to be very good.[10,11]

Additional maneuvers such as measuring neck circumference and determining mobility, modularity, and texture are more subtle and not necessarily consistently rated by examiners. Auscultation for bruits may provide a clue to a hyperfunctioning gland. It is important to remember that a goiter may appear with either hyper- or hypothyroidism and does not help to distinguish between them. It is also possible to have no enlargement and have either disorder.

Patients with hyperthyroidism may have a widened pulse pressure and tachycardia. Approximately 10% to 25% of patients will have atrial fibrillation. Confirmation with an electrocardiogram is needed. In postmenopausal women, bone loss is increased and may be confirmed with dual-photon absorptiometry.

LABORATORY TESTING AND MANAGEMENT

Laboratory testing for thyroid dysfunction can be extremely confusing. However, in the context of chiropractic practice, most cases of dysfunctional thyroid can be detected by running a uTSH test.[12] The advantages of this test are that it can discriminate between euthyroidism (increased levels due to an underlying disorder/disease), which is transient, and overt thyroid dysfunction. When the TSH is elevated, it should be rerun adding FT_4 and a thyroid autoantibody panel. If the TSH is high and the FT_4 is low, the patient is hypothyroid. If there is an elevation of antimicrosomal antibodies, it is likely the patient has Hashimoto's disease. If the TSH is high and the FT_4 is normal, the patient is considered to be subclinically hypothyroid. Recommendations are to recheck TSH levels every 3 to 6 months for the first year and every 6 to 12 months thereafter. Referral for medical management is suggested by some practitioners, especially when there is a high level of autoantibodies.

When the TSH is low, rerun with FT_4 and FT_3 with a thyroid autoantibody panel. If the TSH is low and either the FT_4 or FT_3 is elevated, the patient is hyperthyroid. If there is an elevation of thyroid antibodies, it is likely that the patient has Graves' disease. If the TSH is low and the FT_3 and FT_4 are normal, the patient is considered subclinically hyperthyroid. If the TSH is low, or if it is minimally high or normal with a low T_4, a search for hypothalamic or pituitary disease is necessary. It is important to note that thyroid function tests are often abnormal in hospitalized and severely ill patients. This may represent a temporary dysfunction and cannot be viewed with the same degree of trust as with the ambulatory patient.

Additional findings with hypothyroidism include macrocytic anemia, increased creatinine phosphatase, and hyperlipidemia. Hyperthyroidism may also demonstrate hypercalcemia, increased alkaline phosphatase, anemia, and decreased granulocytes.

Algorithm

An algoritm for thyroid lab evaluation is presented in Figure 51–1.

Figure 51–1

THYROID LAB EVALUATION—ALGORITHM.

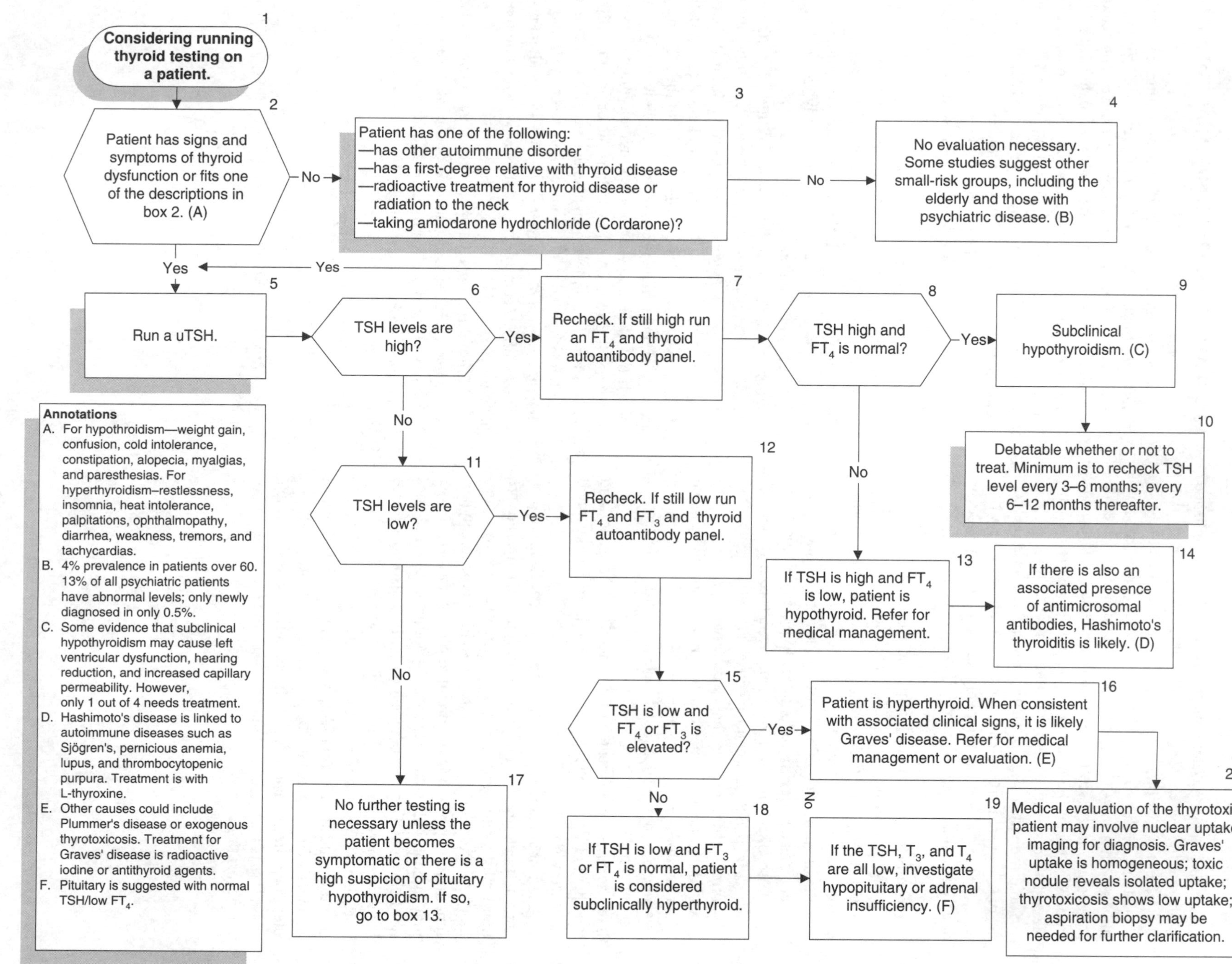

1 Considering running thyroid testing on a patient.
2 Patient has signs and symptoms of thyroid dysfunction or fits one of the descriptions in box 2. (A)
No
3 Patient has one of the following:
—has other autoimmune disorder
—has a first-degree relative with thyroid disease
—radioactive treatment for thyroid disease or radiation to the neck
—taking amiodarone hydrochloride (Cordarone)?
No
4 No evaluation necessary. Some studies suggest other small-risk groups, including the elderly and those with psychiatric disease. (B)
Yes
Yes
5 Run a uTSH.
6 TSH levels are high?
Yes
7 Recheck. If still high run an FT_4 and thyroid autoantibody panel.
8 TSH high and FT_4 is normal?
Yes
9 Subclinical hypothyroidism. (C)
10 Debatable whether or not to treat. Minimum is to recheck TSH level every 3–6 months; every 6–12 months thereafter.
No
No
11 TSH levels are low?
Yes
12 Recheck. If still low run FT_4 and FT_3 and thyroid autoantibody panel.
13 If TSH is high and FT_4 is low, patient is hypothyroid. Refer for medical management.
14 If there is also an associated presence of antimicrosomal antibodies, Hashimoto's thyroiditis is likely. (D)
No
15 TSH is low and FT_4 or FT_3 is elevated?
Yes
16 Patient is hyperthyroid. When consistent with associated clinical signs, it is likely Graves' disease. Refer for medical management or evaluation. (E)
17 No further testing is necessary unless the patient becomes symptomatic or there is a high suspicion of pituitary hypothyroidism. If so, go to box 13.
No
18 If TSH is low and FT_3 or FT_4 is normal, patient is considered subclinically hyperthyroid.
No
19 If the TSH, T_3, and T_4 are all low, investigate hypopituitary or adrenal insufficiency. (F)
20 Medical evaluation of the thyrotoxic patient may involve nuclear uptake imaging for diagnosis. Graves' uptake is homogeneous; toxic nodule reveals isolated uptake; thyrotoxicosis shows low uptake; aspiration biopsy may be needed for further clarification.
Annotations
A. For hypothroidism—weight gain, confusion, cold intolerance, constipation, alopecia, myalgias, and paresthesias. For hyperthyroidism–restlessness, insomnia, heat intolerance, palpitations, ophthalmopathy, diarrhea, weakness, tremors, and tachycardias.
B. 4% prevalence in patients over 60. 13% of all psychiatric patients have abnormal levels; only newly diagnosed in only 0.5%.
C. Some evidence that subclinical hypothyroidism may cause left ventricular dysfunction, hearing reduction, and increased capillary permeability. However, only 1 out of 4 needs treatment.
D. Hashimoto's disease is linked to autoimmune diseases such as Sjögren's, pernicious anemia, lupus, and thrombocytopenic purpura. Treatment is with L-thyroxine.
E. Other causes could include Plummer's disease or exogenous thyrotoxicosis. Treatment for Graves' disease is radioactive iodine or antithyroid agents.
F. Pituitary is suggested with normal TSH/low FT_4.

SELECTED THYROID DISORDERS

GRAVES' DISEASE

Classic Presentation

A woman (8:1 ratio to men) between the ages of 20 and 40 years presents with complaints of nervousness, weight loss, palpitations, fatigue, heat intolerance, or menstrual irregularities.

Cause

Graves' disease (also called Basedow's disease) is an autoimmune disorder. Autoantibodies are formed that bind to the TSH receptors, stimulating hyperactivity of the thyroid gland. Antimicrosomal and antithyroglobulin antibodies are also found. A familial tendency with an association with HLA-B8 and HLA-DR3 has been found.

Evaluation

Hyperthyroidism is usually evident on examination because of the hypermetabolic state and ophthalmopathy. Tachycardia and atrial fibrillation are possible findings and should be evaluated with an ECG.[13,14] A fine resting tremor, hyperreflexia, fine hair, and moist, warm skin are often found. The eyes may appear protuberant (exophthalmos) and this may be associated with other eye signs, including lid lag and diplopia due to lymphocytic infiltration. The eye changes are not an indication of the severity of the disease.[15] Exophthalmos may be unilateral or bilateral. Pretibial "myxedema" is found in about 3% of patients with Graves' disease. This is an infiltrate on top of the tibia that has the texture of the skin of an orange.

Management

Treatment involves symptomatic management with β-blockers and the use of drugs that inhibit function, such as methimazole or propylthiouracil.[16] The latter drugs are commonly used in children and pregnant women. Alternatives include radioactive iodine treatment and surgery. Radioactive iodine treatment is contraindicated in pregnancy. Opponents feel that radioactive iodine will predispose the individual to cancer or damage an individual's genetic pool. Surgery is used less often than radioactive iodine and is more likely offered as an alternative for pregnant women unresponsive to medication.[17] When surgery is performed, the patient must be made euthyroid with medication if possible. Complications with surgery can include recurrent laryngeal nerve damage, leading to vocal cord paralysis, and damage to the parathyroid gland, which may lead to hypoparathyroidism.

HASHIMOTO'S DISEASE

Classic Presentation

The patient with overt hypothyroidism presents with multiple body complaints including weakness, fatigue, arthralgias, constipation, and cold intolerance. Other complaints may include headache, menstrual dysfunction, thinning hair, dry skin, and mental difficulties. The only helpful differentiation from many other similar presentations is a goiter. The patient may present first with a goiter and no other complaints.

Cause

Hashimoto's disease is an autoimmune disorder characterized by lymphocytic infiltration of the thyroid. Antibodies against thyroglobulin and the microsomal portion of thyroid cells is found. Hashimoto's disease is more common in women and demonstrates a familial relationship.

Evaluation

Signs may be subtle. Check for loss of lateral third of eyebrows, bradycardia, an enlarged tongue, and decreased deep tendon reflexes. A goiter may or may not be palpable due to individual and disease variation.

Management

Levothyroxine replacement therapy is used for primary hypothyroidism. Reevaluation is performed at 6- to 8-week intervals until the TSH levels have normalized. After normalization of TSH, the level should be checked every 6 to 12 months.

SUBACUTE THYROIDITIS (DE QUERVAIN'S THYROIDITIS)

Classic Presentation

The patient is more likely white or Chinese and presents with a complaint of anterior neck pain that followed a viral prodrome (myalgia, low-grade fever, sore throat, and tiredness), often in the summer or fall. Associated symptoms may be palpitations, diaphoresis, and tachycardia.

Cause

Apparently viral in origin, subacute thyroiditis is an acute, self-limited inflammatory disorder of the thyroid. There appears to be an autoimmune abnormality and an association with HLA-Bw35 in white and Chinese patients. Women are more commonly affected (range from 3:1 to 6:1), with an onset between ages 30 and 50 years.[18]

Evaluation

Palpation usually reveals a very tender, nodular goiter, but a goiter is not always found. Thyroid function tests indicate hyperthyroidism; however, a coupled finding of a reduced radioactive iodine uptake is diagnostic. A normal thyroglobulin level generally rules out primary hyperthyroidism.

Management

Referral for medical management is necessary, although many patients are treated with aspirin in the initial stages. Occasionally, patients with dysphagia due to an enlarged gland need prednisone (20% experience rebound swelling when drug is withdrawn).[19] β-Blockers are occasionally used for the hypermetabolic symptoms. Antithyroid drugs are useless; the disorder has nothing to do with synthesis of thyroid hormone, only release of existing preformed hormones. Recovery is common in 3 to 6 weeks; however, 30% of patients develop hypothyroidism due to follicular cell destruction. Ninety percent of these patients recover in 4 to 6 weeks. Ten percent are permanently hypothyroid.[20]

SILENT THYROIDITIS

Classic Presentation

A women who is 4 to 8 weeks postpartum presents with complaints of nervousness and palpitations.

Cause

Antithyroid antibodies are found in 50% to 80% of patients, suggesting an autoimmune process. Although this entity may occur in men and women, the most common form is found in women (4:1). Thyroiditis may occur sporadically in either gender, but postpartum presentation is common in women. Hormonal shifts postpartum may act as a trigger. The postpartum and sporadic types account for between 5% and 20% of all hyperthyroidism. Six percent of patients may have persistent hypothyroidism.[21]

Evaluation

Thyroid palpation will reveal a nontender goiter in almost 50% of patients. Other findings are secondary to an initial hyperthyroidism for a few weeks, which may be followed by a 4- to 16-week period of hypothyroidism in 40% of patients. There is a low radioactive uptake in this disorder, distinguishing it from true hyperthyroidism.

Management

Generally reassurance is all that is needed. However, in some patients, referral may be necessary for medical management of transient symptoms, including β-blockers. There is no place for antithyroid medication in the treatment of silent thyroiditis.

ACUTE THYROIDITIS

Classic Presentation

Patients present with an abrupt onset of intense anterior neck pain with associated signs of fever and chills; it occurs more often in women.

Cause

Sometimes referred to as suppurative thyroiditis, this rare disorder is usually due to *Staphylococcus aureus, Streptococcus pyrogens,* or pneumonia, although parasites and fungi are possible causes. Infection is hematogenous, lymphatic, or through a persistent thyroglossal duct. Fifty percent of patients have a history of thyroid disease.

Evaluation

Acute thyroiditis is usually apparent because of the abrupt onset and a tender thyroid. Laboratory results indicate normal thyroid function, an elevated white blood cell count with a shift to the left, and a normal radioactive iodine uptake.

Management

Refer for medical management of underlying infection.

RIEDEL'S THYROIDITIS

Classic Presentation

A middle-aged or elderly woman presents with a slowly enlarging, hard anterior neck mass that is not tender.

Cause

This extremely rare condition is due to replacement of thyroid tissue with dense fibrous tissue.

Evaluation

Palpation reveals a very hard thyroid gland. Laboratory tests usually reveal a normally functioning gland. In some patients, complete replacement of thyroid tissue will result in hypothyroidism evident on laboratory tests.

Management

Generally, the patient is monitored for progression to hypothyroidism, at which time thyroid replacement therapy is necessary. Surgical treatment is reserved for those with compressive complaints due to thyroid enlargement.

THYROID CANCER

Classic Presentation

A patient with a past history of irradiation of the head or neck presents with a painless swelling in the region of the thyroid.

Cause

Papillary carcinoma or mixed papillary/follicular cancer accounts for 70% of all thyroid cancers, yet it is the least aggressive. Follicular cancer accounts for about 15% of cancers and is responsible for more metastases. Thyrotoxicosis rarely occurs with thyroid cancer.

Evaluation

Palpation of the thyroid will reveal a hard nodule in an enlarged gland and in some cases, palpable lymph nodes. Fine-needle biopsy is most useful in distinguishing benign (70% of time) from malignant (5%) tumors.[22] Thyroid function tests are usually normal. Occasionally, calcitonin levels are elevated. Radioiodine uptake testing usually demonstrates malignancies as "cold" lesions representing nonfunctioning tissue. Fine-needle aspiration is the test of choice. Metastatic lesions may be visible on radiographs or bone scans.

Management

Refer to oncologist.

REFERENCES

1. Surks MI, Chopra IJ, Mariash CN, Nicoloff JT, Solomon DH. American Thyroid Association guidelines for use of laboratory tests in thyroid disorders. *JAMA*. 1990;263:1529–1532.
2. US Preventative Services Task Force. Screening for thyroid disease: In: *Guide to Clinical Preventive Services*. Baltimore: Williams & Wilkins; 1996:209.
3. Ladenson PW: Diagnosis of hypothyroidism. In: Braverman LE, Unger RD, eds. *Werner and Ingbar's The Thyroid: A Fundamental and Clinical Text.* 6th ed. Philadelphia: JB Lippincott; 1991:1092–1098.
4. Berlowitz I, Ramot Y, Rosenberg T, et al. Prevalence of thyroid disorders among the elderly in Israel. *Isr J Med Sci.* 1990;26:496–498.
5. Sobel R. Screening for thyroid disease (editorial). *Isr J Med Sci.* 1990;26:516–517.
6. Helfand M, Crapo LM. Screening for thyroid disease. *Ann Intern Med.* 1990;112:840–849.
7. DeGroot LJ, Mayor G. Admission screening by thyroid function tests in an acute general care teaching hospital. *Am J Med.* 1992;93:558–564.
8. Enns M, Ross C, Clark P. Thyroid screening tests in psychiatric inpatients. *Gen Hosp Psychiatry.* 1992;14:334–349.
9. Siminoski K. Does this patient have a goiter? *JAMA.* 1995;273:813–817.
10. Kilpatrick R, Milne JS, Rushbrooke M, Wilson ESB. A survey of thyroid enlargement in two general practices in Great Britain. *Br Med J.* 1963;1:29–34.
11. Dingle PR, Ferguson A, Horn DB, Tubmen J, Hall R. The incidence of thyroglobulin antibodies and thyroid enlargement in a general practice in Northeast England. *Clin Exp Immunol.* 1966;1:277–284.

12. Brody MB, Reichard RA. Thyroid screening: how to interpret and apply results. *Postgrad Med.* 1995;98:54–66.
13. Woeber KA. Thyrotoxicosis and the heart. *N Engl J Med.* 1992;327:94.
14. Sawin CT, Geller A, Wolf PA, et al. Low serum thyrotropin concentration as a risk factor for atrial fibrillation in older persons. *N Engl J Med.* 1994;331:1249–1252.
15. Barrie WE. Graves' ophthalmopathy. *West J Med.* 1993;158:591.
16. Singer PA, Cooper DS, Levy EG, et al. Treatment guidelines for patients with hyperthyroidism and hypothyroidism. *JAMA.* 1995;273:808–812.
17. Patwardham NA, Moroni M, Rao S, et al. Surgery still has a role in Graves' hyperthyroidism. *Surgery.* 1993;114:1108–1113.
18. Sakiyama R. Thyroiditis: a clinical review. *Am Fam Physician.* 1993;48:615–621.
19. Singer PA. Thyroiditis: acute, subacute, and chronic. *Med Clin North Am.* 1991;75:61–77.
20. DeGroot LJ, Larsen PR, Refetoff S, et al. Acute and subacute thyroiditis. In Braverman LE, Utiger RD, eds. *The Thyroid and Its Dseases.* 5th ed. New York: John Wiley & Sons; 1984: 717–727.
21. Schubert MF, Kountz DS. Thyroiditis: a disease with many faces. *Postgrad Med.* 1995;98:101–112.
22. Gharib H, Goellner JR. Fine needle aspiration biopsy of the thyroid: an appraisal. *Ann Intern Med.* 93:118:282.

Chapter 52

Hyperlipidemia

CONTEXT

The leading cause of death in the United States is coronary artery (heart) disease (CAD or CHD).[1] The primary modifiable risk factors are high cholesterol, smoking, and hypertension. The second leading cause of death by disease is cancer; the third is diabetes.[2] There is evidence to suggest that some cancers are linked to high-fat diets. Adult-onset diabetes is strongly linked to diet. It would seem that the philosophy of prevention held by the chiropractic profession would dictate that part of a patient's care must involve intervention in areas such as these that do not require (and may prevent) the use of drugs or surgery and may prevent morbidity and mortality. Realistically, changes in diet and smoking habits are some of the most difficult to effect. Yet, the chiropractor is ideally positioned to provide either a direct or indirect comprehensive "wellness" program for his or her patients. Promotion of healthful eating and exercise should be a cornerstone in the treatment of all patients, regardless of current CHD status.

There are at least 10 meta-analysis studies of randomized trials that have attempted to address the effectiveness of cholesterol reduction and its effect on CHD.[3–5] It appears that for each 1% decrease in serum cholesterol, there is a 2% to 3% reduction in risk for CHD. This occurred in trials using drugs or diet. There is some controversy regarding the use of drugs in patients without CHD regarding cost and an interesting increase in noncoronary mortality.[6] However, most agree that symptomatic men unresponsive to diet will benefit from drug intervention if it is monitored and reduced when appropriate. The reduction of serum cholesterol and decrease in CHD risk is not as clear in women. Women statistically have their onset of CHD approximately 10 years later than men, beginning at age 45. This delay is probably related to the protective effects of estrogen.[7] However, 49% of all CHD-related deaths in the United States are women.[1]

GENERAL STRATEGY

- Screening of all individuals is not recommended. Men aged 35 years and over, women aged 45 years and older, those with CHD or more than two risk factors, and children with a familial predisposition should be screened. Further testing is based on baseline results.
- Determine an individual's risk factors for CHD, including age, gender, smoking, obesity, hypertension, and diabetes.
- If the patient is at risk for CHD or has known CHD, order a lipid panel that includes total cholesterol, high-density lipoprotein cholesterol (HDLc), low-density lipoprotein cholesterol (LDLc), and triglycerides.
- Combine findings from the lipid panel with risk factors and make treatment/referral decisions.
- If patients have an isolated elevation of triglycerides, suggestive of a familial disorder, order lipoprotein electrophoresis.
- For those patients without CHD or less than two risk factors, diet and exercise are the main approach; for those with CHD or two or more risk factors, a trial of diet therapy is usually attempted for 3 to 6 months; when not responsive, drug therapy may be indicated.

RELEVANT PHYSIOLOGY

Cholesterol is not in and of itself bad. It is, in fact, essential to the body for the production of bile and the construction of cell membranes, myelin, and steroid hormones. The liver produces half the body's cholesterol; the remainder is acquired through the diet.[8] There are two main fats carried in the blood: cholesterol and triglycerides. They are packaged with proteins (apoproteins) into lipoproteins. The lipoproteins are classified based on density. The higher the triglyceride content, the least dense. The three main lipoproteins are HDLs, LDLs, and very-low-density lipoproteins (VLDLs). Therefore, LDLs contain about 75% lipid and 25% protein, whereas HDLs contain about an equal ratio. The general sequence of interaction is that VLDLs produced in the liver transport triglycerides to cells. When the VLDLs have lost a sufficient amount of triglyceride, they become LDL particles. LDL then provides cholesterol to the cells. Any excess of LDLs is metabolized in the liver, providing cholesterol for bile. LDLs that are oxidized are potentially more harmful because of the direct effects on the arterial wall, and possibly through antibodies developed against the oxidized LDLs.[9] HDLs are produced in the liver and assist in transfer of apoproteins among the other lipoproteins. It is well known that HDLs may be protective through a mechanism referred to as reverse cholesterol transport—carrying excess cholesterol to other lipoproteins or to the liver.[10]

Hyperlipidemia is a term used to describe an increase in either plasma cholesterol or plasma triglycerides. These may occur in combination or in pure forms. Generally there are three main causes: (1) dietary, (2) genetic, and (3) secondary to other diseases or drugs. One distinction is that the dietary forms are generally more mild than the genetic forms. In effect, hyperlipidemia is the same as hyperlipoproteinemia because there is always a problem with one of the steps in lipoprotein metabolism. For example, there may be a problem with the production, lipolysis, removal, or conversion of VLDL. The diagnosis is usually made when a lipid electrophoresis reveals an abnormally high fraction or combination of fractions of the lipoprotein pool.

One cause of high LDLc is familial hypercholesterolemia.[11] It is believed to be due to a defect in the LDL receptor gene, resulting in a reduced ability to process LDLc particles. This results in an LDLc level that is approximately twice normal. Many patients have an additional contribution to high LDLc from high dietary intake. These patients have an increased risk of developing CHD in their 30s and 40s. They are more likely to need drug therapy, especially if their LDLc levels remain above 190 mg/dL. Patients with a rare homozygous (two abnormal genes) form have absent surface receptors for LDLc and have extremely high levels of LDLc, with atherosclerosis development in childhood.

Another condition is called either mixed hyperlipidemia, metabolic syndrome X, or familial hyperlipidemia (although these are not always synonymous). Most patients show a central obesity, hyperinsulinemia, hypertension, elevated triglycerides, low HDLc, and elevation of small LDL subfractions. Because these patients are prone toward diabetes and hypertension, they should be evaluated and monitored for these conditions. Patients with mixed hyperlipidemia respond favorably even to small decreases in weight. One ironic complication is that if total fat is reduced below 30% of total calories, there may be a compensatory increase in carbohydrate intake that may then stimulate the production of VLDLc.

Triglycerides are more subject to changes in food consumption prior to laboratory investigation. An isolated increase (ie, cholesterol, LDLc, and HDLc are normal) is often due to a patient's not fasting or perhaps drinking coffee with cream prior to giving the laboratory sample. There are a number of lipid disorders that result in isolated triglyceride elevation. Usually the triglyceride levels are 1000 mg/dL or above while the LDLc levels are often low or normal. Although there appears to be a genetic component, poor diet and lack of exercise seem to make the disorder more obvious. These patients can have a predisposition to pancreatitis, especially if they drink alcohol. Therefore, questioning regarding abdominal pain and counseling against excessive alcohol ingestion are warranted. Exercise and weight loss are the main treatment approaches. If unsuccessful, referral for medical management is necessary. There is disagreement as to the risk for patients with an isolated triglyceride elevation without a concomitant LDLc elevation. Many studies indicate that the risk may not be substantial.

EVALUATION

History

The history is important in determining the level of concern with any individual cholesterol level. There are specific risk factors that significantly affect management decisions. Nonmodifiable, but significant, factors include age (45 years or older in men; 55 years or older in women), male gender, and a family history of premature CHD (myocardial infarction or sudden death before age 55 years in a parent or sibling). The modifiable risk factors include cigarette smoking (more than 10 per day), obesity (more than 130% of ideal total body weight), hypertension, physical inactivity, an HDLc level below 35 mg/dL, and diabetes mellitus. It is interesting to note that with the exception of smoking, the other risk factors are often interdependent. In other words, a patient who is inactive is more likely to become obese. Being obese is a predisposition for adult-onset diabetes, which is associated with hypertension. The other modifiable factor is diet. Although diet cannot always lower cholesterol levels, a low-fat diet is often instrumental in controlling obesity, diabetes, and hypertension.[12] Therefore, a careful diet history is important in determining the level of daily fat intake and its possible relationship to high levels of cholesterol and LDLc.

Laboratory Evaluation

There is some basic agreement as to who should be screened for high blood cholesterol. Men between the ages of 35 and 65 and women between the ages of 45 and 65 should be screened with either a fasting or nonfasting specimen to obtain a baseline reading.[13] The recommendation for how often these individuals should be screened varies. The strictest guidelines are from the National Cholesterol Education Program (NCEP) Adult Treatment Panel II, which recommends screening of nonfasting total cholesterol and HDLc every 5 years in all asymptomatic individuals aged 20 and older.[14] These are similar to the recommendations of the American Academy of Family Physicians and the American College of Obstetricians and Gynecologists.[15,16] Most groups recommend selective screening of children and adolescents based on risk factors.[17,18] Children with a parental history of hypercholesterolemia should be screened with a nonfasting test for total cholesterol. Those with a family history of premature CHD should be screened with a fasting lipid profile. Children with multiple risk factors such as obesity and smoking should be considered for a screening lab test. Most groups agree that screening of individuals over the age of 75 years is not warranted.[19]

Interpretation of laboratory results is not a simple process of using a high cut-off value; for example, all levels above 240 mg/dL are bad. The relationship of cholesterol to risk is multivariable, including modifiable and nonmodifiable factors as discussed above. It is also important to refer to a cholesterol result as fitting into a range as opposed to a specific value. The reason for this caution is that cholesterol levels vary with many "outside" influences such as minor illness, stress, posture, and season.[20] This variation may be as much as 4% to 11% for an individual. Additionally, laboratory values may not reflect a "true" cholesterol. Laboratory error and variation in equipment or operation of the equipment may affect readings. Finger-stick methods are biased toward a high range averaging between 4% and 7% more than a venipuncture specimen.[21] New desktop machines have been introduced that produce reliable readings, however, some machines do not meet required standards. Given the possible influences on a specific reading, the variation in an individual can be as high as 14%. It is important to note that reliability for HDLc is less than that for total cholesterol, with an average variation as much as 10% from a reference standard. Triglycerides are even less reliable. Therefore, a single measure is insufficient if high, and consideration of rechecking with a second sample is often suggested. If the two measurements (performed on different days) differ by more than 16%, a third sample is recommended.

Generally, if a patient's total cholesterol is 240 mg/dL or above or the level is between 200 and 239 mg/dL with known CHD or two risk factors, a lipid panel (cholesterol LDLc, HDLc, and triglycerides) should be performed. Based on the LDLc levels, decisions regarding diet or medication can be made.

MANAGEMENT

Using only total cholesterol measurements to make management decisions may lead to unwarranted concern or confidence. As discussed above, high-normal levels may be the result of lab error or variation. More important, some individuals, especially women, may have a high total cholesterol level, in part, because of a high proportion of HDLc. On the other hand, approximately 20% of men with confirmed CHD have a cholesterol below 200 mg/dL with an HDLc below 35 mg/dL. It is clear that women with high cholesterol levels, especially those who appear healthy, should not be assumed to be at risk unless confirmed with an associated low HDLc. Men who have a low cholesterol level but either are symptomatic or have significant risk factors should be tested for a low HDLc. In the past, a simple ratio was used between total cholesterol and HDLc, but this may be misleading. For example, two individuals may have a ratio of 5:1. In one individual the total cholesterol is 240 mg/dL with an HDLc of 48 mg/dL; the other individual has a total cholesterol of 150 mg/dL with an HDLc of 30 mg d/L. The second individual may be at more of a risk than the first based on the low HDLc, especially when other risk factors are added.

Level of risk is known to increase by approximately 3% for each 1% increase in total cholesterol for middle-aged men. Although it is difficult to quantify other risk factors, it can be generally assumed that each additional risk factor doubles the risk for CHD. Joining these generalizations together, a formula may be used to gain a general degree of prognostication for an individual patient. For example, a 55-year-old man who smokes, has hypertension, diabetes, and a low HDLc concentration would have a 30-fold (ie, 2×2×2×2×2) increase of risk compared with a woman with no risk factors at the same cholesterol level. An additional suggestion is to subtract one risk factor if the HDLc is above 50 mg/dL and two risk factors if the HDLc is above 70 mg/dL. These simple calculations may be helpful in defining risk for the patient and illustrate how significant each additional risk factor becomes.

In practical application, the level of concern for two patients with a cholesterol level of 240 mg/dL is different. If the patient is a middle-aged man with any risk factors, monitoring levels while applying intervention with diet or medication is warranted, whereas a woman with the same cholesterol level and a high HDLc would warrant less concern.

The NCEP guidelines are a good reference source for managing patients found to have high LDLc levels. The recommendations divide management into diet and drug treatment categories based on a coupling of LDLc with CHD and risk factors. In general, patients without CHD or without two risk factors with an LDLc level at or above 160 mg/dL should be managed initially with diet. Patients with CHD or two risk factors may be managed initially with diet if the level is 130 to 160 mg/dL. Those patients without CHD or two risk factors with LDLc levels 190 mg/dL or above should be considered for drug therapy. Patients with CHD or two risk factors with levels above 160 mg/dL should also be considered for referral for drug therapy.

Diet therapy centers around a reduction in dietary fat. The NCEP two-step program is a staged approach to this reduction.[22] The step-one diet is to reduce dietary fat to less than 30% of total calories (saturated fat less than 10% of total calories). If after a 3-month trial the step-one diet is unsuccessful, the step-two diet is implemented. This diet restricts saturated fats to 7% of total calories and dietary cholesterol to 200 mg/d. It begins with a focus on healthful choices. A list of foods that are high in fat and a substitute for that food allows for an educated participation by the patient rather than a strict diet menu. The goal of the step-one diet is to reduce the total serum cholesterol by 30 to 40 mg/dL. Reduction from the step-two diet is targeted at an additional 15%. Reduction in LDLc is based on the baseline measure. Generally, if the level is above 160 mg/dL, a goal is simply to achieve levels below this. For those between 130 and 159 mg/dL, the goal is to reach 130 mg/dL if there are two risk factors or 100 mg/dL if the patient has CHD. Failure to achieve these goals after 6 months of using the step-one and step-two diet plans may indicate an individual who is noncompliant or unresponsive to diet therapy. Referral for drug management may be appropriate.

Another recommended approach is the Ornish program.[23] Ornish has demonstrated that a low-fat diet can reverse some CHD and help prevent development of CHD. His program is divided into a reversal diet and a prevention diet. The reversal diet is for those who have CHD and restricts fat to less than 10% of total calories; protein, 15% to 20%; and carbohydrates (complex), 70% to 75%.[24] Cholesterol is limited to 5 mg/d. The prevention diet is less strict, but it is still more conservative than the NCEP guidelines. Ornish recommends the prevention diet for those with cholesterol levels above 150 mg/dL or if the total cholesterol to HDLc ratio is greater than 3.0. With the prevention diet, fat is still restricted to no more than 20% of total calories. Ornish also recommends other lifestyle changes, such as avoidance of caffeine and other stimulants, inclusion of exercise, and meditation.

Other nutritional factors that may be of benefit include diets high in or supplementation with vitamin E and omega-3 fatty acids. Vitamin E supplementation at 200 to 400 IU/day may be beneficial.[25] The benefit is derived mainly from prevention of free-radical damage that may lead to atherosclerosis. Other antioxidants include vitamin C and bioflavinoids.[26] For omega-3 fatty acids, 8 mg of eicosapentaenoric acid (EPA) and docosahexaenoic acid (DHA) have been demonstrated to have a protective effect.[27] This protective effect is believed to be due to several actions. First, it is believed that omega-3 fatty acids prevent oxidation of LDL. Second, they may protect against CHD by reducing clot formation and coronary artery spasm through a reduction in production of thromboxane and an increase in prostacyclin and tissue plasminogen activator production. Foods high in omega-3s are fish oil, whole grains, beans, seaweed, and soybean.

Medications

There are several classifications of drugs used to lower lipids.

- bile acid–binding resins (cholestyramine [Questran] and colestipol [Colestid])
- nicotinic acid (niacin)
- 3-hydroxy-3-methylglutaryl coenzyme A (HMG CoA) reductase inhibitors ("statins" such as lovastatin)
- fibric acid derivatives (gemfibrozil [Lopid])
- probucol (Lorelco)

The use of these drugs is somewhat controversial given that there are, as with most drugs, contraindications to their use, side effects, and cost considerations. Lovastatin, for example, has been estimated to cost approximately $1 million dollars if taken for life by a 35-year-old woman. In general, in patients with isolated LDLc elevations, bile acid–binding resins or statins would be used first. For those with mixed hyperlipidemia, nicotinic acid (if tolerated) would be the first drug; if not effective, gemfibrozil or one of the statins would be used. For isolated triglyceride elevation, niacin is used. However, niacin can unmask or increase the risk of developing diabetes.

Comanagement with a team including the chiropractor, dietitian, and medical doctor is recommended when a patient is noncompliant or does not seem to respond to individual provider recommendations with diet and exercise.

Algorithm

An algorithm for hypercholesterolemia management is presented in Figure 52–1.

Figure 52–1

HYPERCHOLESTEROLEMIA MANAGEMENT—ALGORITHM.

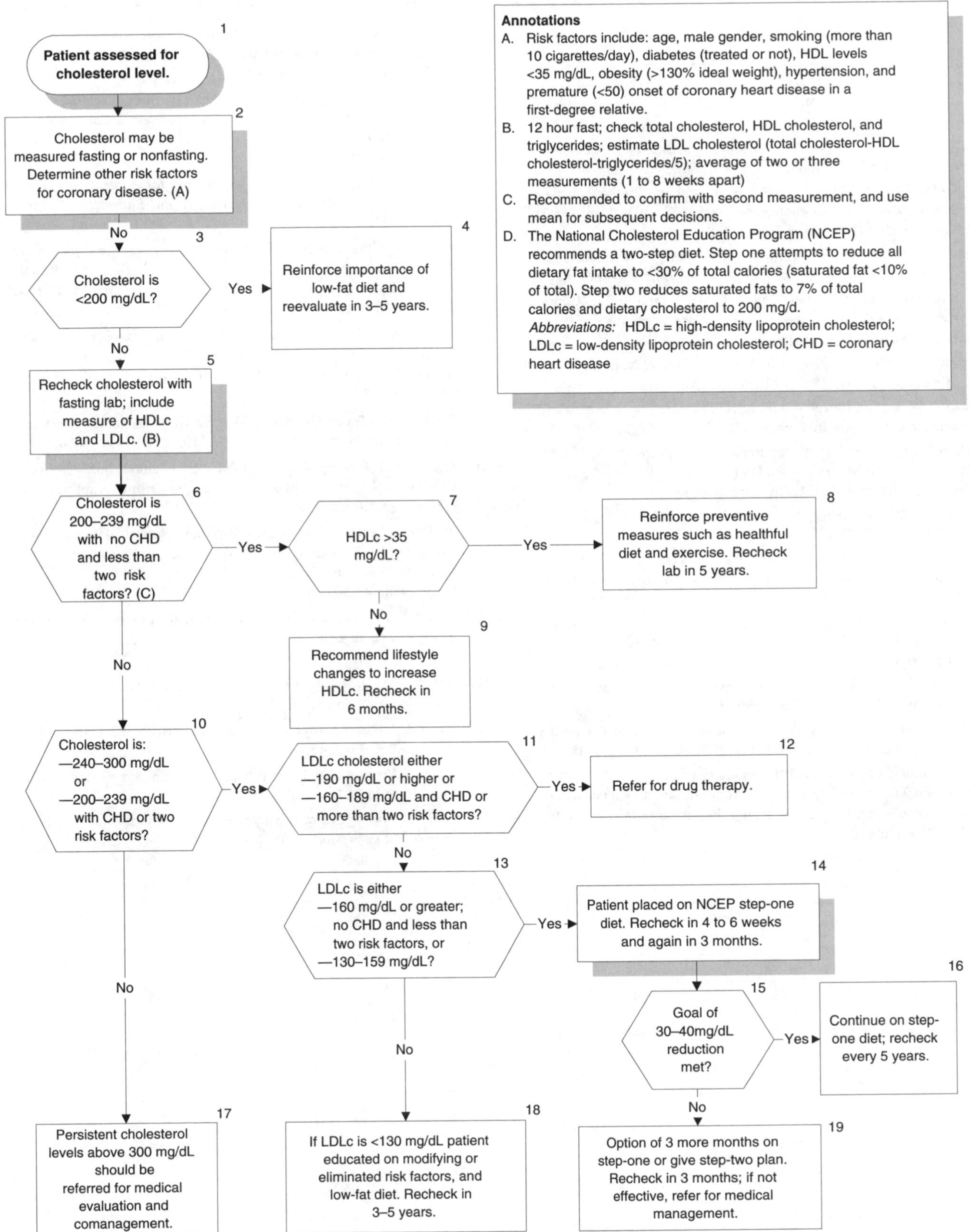

1
Patient assessed for cholesterol level.
2
Cholesterol may be measured fasting or nonfasting. Determine other risk factors for coronary disease. (A)
No
3
Cholesterol is <200 mg/dL?
Yes
4
Reinforce importance of low-fat diet and reevaluate in 3–5 years.
No
5
Recheck cholesterol with fasting lab; include measure of HDLc and LDLc. (B)
6
Cholesterol is 200–239 mg/dL with no CHD and less than two risk factors? (C)
Yes
7
HDLc >35 mg/dL?
Yes
8
Reinforce preventive measures such as healthful diet and exercise. Recheck lab in 5 years.
No
9
Recommend lifestyle changes to increase HDLc. Recheck in 6 months.
No
10
Cholesterol is:
—240–300 mg/dL
or
—200–239 mg/dL with CHD or two risk factors?
Yes
11
LDLc cholesterol either
—190 mg/dL or higher or
—160–189 mg/dL and CHD or more than two risk factors?
Yes
12
Refer for drug therapy.
No
13
LDLc is either
—160 mg/dL or greater; no CHD and less than two risk factors, or
—130–159 mg/dL?
Yes
14
Patient placed on NCEP step-one diet. Recheck in 4 to 6 weeks and again in 3 months.
15
Goal of 30–40mg/dL reduction met?
Yes
16
Continue on step-one diet; recheck every 5 years.
No
No
No
17
Persistent cholesterol levels above 300 mg/dL should be referred for medical evaluation and comanagement.
18
If LDLc is <130 mg/dL patient educated on modifying or eliminated risk factors, and low-fat diet. Recheck in 3–5 years.
19
Option of 3 more months on step-one or give step-two plan. Recheck in 3 months; if not effective, refer for medical management.

Annotations

A. Risk factors include: age, male gender, smoking (more than 10 cigarettes/day), diabetes (treated or not), HDL levels <35 mg/dL, obesity (>130% ideal weight), hypertension, and premature (<50) onset of coronary heart disease in a first-degree relative.

B. 12 hour fast; check total cholesterol, HDL cholesterol, and triglycerides; estimate LDL cholesterol (total cholesterol-HDL cholesterol-triglycerides/5); average of two or three measurements (1 to 8 weeks apart)

C. Recommended to confirm with second measurement, and use mean for subsequent decisions.

D. The National Cholesterol Education Program (NCEP) recommends a two-step diet. Step one attempts to reduce all dietary fat intake to <30% of total calories (saturated fat <10% of total). Step two reduces saturated fats to 7% of total calories and dietary cholesterol to 200 mg/d.

Abbreviations: HDLc = high-density lipoprotein cholesterol; LDLc = low-density lipoprotein cholesterol; CHD = coronary heart disease

REFERENCES

1. National Center for Health Statistics. Annual summary of births, marriages, divorces, and deaths: United States; 1993. Monthly vital statistics report. Vol. 42, No. 13. Hyattsville, MD: US Public Health Service; 1994.
2. La Vecchia C. Cancers associated with high-fat diets. *Monogr Natl Cancer Inst.* 1992;12:79–85.
3. Law MR, Waid NJ, Thompson SC. By how much and how quickly does reduction in serum cholesterol lower risk of ischemic heart disease? *Br Med J.* 1994:308:367–373.
4. Law MR, Thompson SC, Waid NJ. Assessing possible hazards of reducing serum cholesterol. *Br Med J.* 1994;344:1833–1839.
5. Gordon DJ. Cholesterol lowering and total mortality. In: Rifkind BM, et al. *Lowering Cholesterol in High-Risk Individuals and Populations.* New York: Marcel Dekker; 1995:333–348.
6. Heady JA, Morris JN, Oliver MF. WHO clofibrate/cholesterol trial: clarifications. *Lancet.* 1992;340:1405–1406.
7. Bush TL, Fried LE, Barrett-Connor E. Cholesterol, lipoproteins, and coronary heart disease in women. *Clin Chem.* 1988;34:B60–B70.
8. Mayes PA. Cholesterol synthesis, transport, and excretion. In: Murray RK, Granner DK, Mayes PA, Rodwell VW, eds. *Harper's Biochemistry.* 23rd ed. Norwalk, CT: Appleton & Lange; 1993.
9. Lipscomb TA. Antibodies to oxidized LDL in atherosclerosis. *Lancet.* 1992;339:899.
10. Franceschini G, Maderna P, Sirtori CR. Reverse cholesterol transport: physiology and pharmacology. *Atherosclerosis.* 1991;88:99–107.
11. Fredrickson DS, Levy R. Familial hyperlipoproteinemia. In: Stanbury JB, Wyngarden JB, Fredrickson DS, eds. *The Metabolic Basis of Inherited Disease.* 5th ed. New York: McGraw-Hill; 1982.
12. Vanltallie TB. Health implications of overweight and obesity in the United States. *Ann Intern Med.* 1985;103:983–988.
13. US Preventive Services Task Force. *Guide to Clinical Preventive Services.* 2nd ed. Baltimore: Williams & Wilkins; 1996:15–38.
14. NCEP Adult Treatment Panel II. Summary of the Second Report of the National Cholesterol Education Program Expert Panel on detection, evaluation, and treatment of high blood cholesterol in adults. *JAMA.* 1993;269:3015.
15. American Academy of Family Physicians. Age charts for periodic health examination. Kansas City, MO: American Academy of Family Physicians; 1994 (reprint no. 510).
16. American College of Obstetricians and Gynecologists. *The Obstetrician–Gynecologist in Primary Preventive Health Care: A Report of the ACOG Task Force on Primary and Preventive Health Care.* Washington, DC: ACOG; 1993.
17. American Medical Association. *Guidelines for Adolescent Preventive Services (GAPS): Recommendations and Rationale.* Chicago: AMA; 1994.
18. National Cholesterol Education Program. *Report of the Expert Panel on Blood Cholesterol Levels in Children and Adolescents.* Bethesda, MD: National Institutes of Health, National Heart, Lung, and Blood Institute; 1991. (NIH Publication No. 91-2732).
19. American College of Physicians. Serum cholesterol, high-density lipoprotein cholesterol, and triglyceride screening tests for the prevention of coronary heart disease in adults. *Ann Intern Med.* 1996;124:327.
20. Copper GR, Meyers GL, Smith SJ, et al. Blood lipid measurements: variations and practical utility. *JAMA.* 1992;267:1652–1660.
21. Greenland P, Bowley NL, Meikljohn P, et al. Blood cholesterol concentration: fingerstick plasma vs. venous serum sampling. *Clin Chem.* 1990;36:628–630.
22. National Cholesterol Education Program. Report of the National Cholesterol Education Program expert panel on detection, evaluation, and treatment of high blood cholesterol in adults. *Arch Intern Med.* 1988;148:360–369.
23. Ornish DM, Scherwitz LW, Brown SE, et al. Adherence to lifestyle changes and reversal of coronary atherosclerosis. *Circulation.* 1989;80:11–57.
24. Ornish DM. *Dr. Dean Ornish's Program for Reversing Heart Disease.* New York: Ivy Books; 1990.
25. Byers T. Vitamin E supplements and coronary heart disease. *Nutr Rev.* 1993;51:333–345.
26. Simon J. Vitamin C and cardiovascular disease: a review. *J Am Coll Nutr.* 1992;11:107.
27. Leaf A, Weber PC. Cardiovascular effects of omega-3 fatty acids: an update. *N Engl J Med.* 1988;318:549–557.

Chapter 53

Anemia

CONTEXT

Although the Job Analysis on Chiropractic Report from the National Board of Chiropractic Examiners[1] indicates that few chiropractors order laboratory studies on their patients, all chiropractic colleges teach students that laboratory studies are a diagnostic tool to be used when appropriate. This discrepancy probably occurs for several reasons. One is that students often feel that they have not had enough exposure in the college setting to feel comfortable ordering labs. There is often the concern of reimbursement. This is easily defended (as for any procedure) with an explanation of why the test was ordered. Also, the vast majority of patients are probably being seen by a medical doctor and it is often the assumption of the chiropractor that any appropriate laboratory work will be ordered by the MD, and in fact, the chiropractor refers the patient to the MD for the lab work and follow-up. Yet, there is a significant group of patients who request and/or need laboratory work for screening of certain values such as cholesterol/triglyceride levels, prostate-specific antigen, urinalysis with symptoms of a urinary tract infection, and a cross-check with complaints of fatigue. These are easy tests to order and generally easy to interpret. It is important to remember that the patient population seen by chiropractors is an ambulatory population—not hospitalized. From a cost-effectiveness perspective, it may be less expensive for the patient within the context of the smaller chiropractic setting.

There is often an assumption that all patients with anemia will present as pale, fatigued, clay-eating individuals. It is far more common for a patient to be unaware of an underlying anemia. The absence of pallor and other physical signs of anemia as a diagnostic rationale for ruling out anemia has a false-negative value of between 45% and 55%.[2] If fatigue is present, it is initially felt only with exertion. If the patient is not in a position to exert himself or herself, anemia may remain silent. It is also crucial to regard anemia as a sign of disease rather than a disease in itself. In other words, the doctor is only half finished with the evaluation process when anemia is discovered on laboratory testing. The next step in the process is to determine why. Anemia, in general, is due to one of three processes: (1) decreased production, (2) increased breakdown, and (3) blood loss. With each there is a limited number of common causes, and significant associated laboratory findings usually aid in the diagnosis.

GENERAL STRATEGY

History

- Determine whether there are any clear historical clues of anemia such as blood loss, dietary deficiencies, ethnic or familial predispositions, pregnancy or alcoholism, or past history of anemia; obtain a thorough drug history.
- Determine whether there are any secondary clues such as tiredness with exertion, gastrointestinal (GI) pains (GI bleeding source), heavy menstrual flow, pallor, pica (dirt/clay eating, ice eating, or starch eating), or bone pain (sternal pain in particular).

Examination

- Examine the patient for signs of tachycardia, systolic flow murmurs, a loud S1 and S2, a widened pulse pressure, a venous hum, and pale conjunctivae.
- If screening for a specific anemia, order an anemia panel that best demonstrates that anemia; if screening the pa-

tient generally, order a complete blood count (CBC), blood chemistry, and urinalysis.
- Interpret the lab with a focus on the size (combined findings of mean corpuscular volume [MCV] and a morphologic description such as microcytosis or macrocytosis) and shape of the red blood cells (RBC), the RBC distribution width (RDW), and a search for signs of hemolysis (increased bilirubin, lactate dehydrogenase [LDH], and/or potassium), or blood loss (increase in reticulocytosis).
- Combine the laboratory and historical findings to determine a working diagnosis.

Management

- Iron deficiency anemia requires a further determination of a bleeding (and more rarely a dietary) source; if not an occult process, use iron supplementation for 2 weeks; a recheck for response is necessary.
- Thalassemia minor is usually asymptomatic and not in need of intervention except to counsel parents who both have the same thalassemia (trait or minor) about risk for their children and also prenatal counseling.
- A patient with macrocytic anemia due to pernicious anemia is referred for cyanocobalamin (vitamin B_{12}) injections; temporary deficiencies not associated with a loss of intrinsic factor may be managed nutritionally.
- Folic acid deficiencies are usually dietary and respond to supplementation; a trial of 100 mg for 10 days and a check for a reactive reticulocytosis helps distinguish between vitamin B_{12} and folate deficiency.

RELEVANT PHYSIOLOGY

Anemia is an indication of an underlying disorder, not a disease itself. Anemia indicates a decreased ability of oxygen-carrying capacity and will usually result in attempts by the body to compensate. These compensations may be an increase in heart rate and/or an increase in RBC production. Anemia has been described several ways. However, anemia usually involves a decrease in hematocrit, hemoglobin, or RBCs. All of these are not necessarily decreased when anemia is present. In adult women a hemoglobin of less than 12 g/dL is considered anemia; in men, less than 13.5 g/dL. Hematocrit values indicating anemia are less than 36% in adult women and less than 39% in adult men. These values were established by the World Health Organization (WHO) and are guidelines, not absolutes.[3]

Decreased Production

Although a decrease in production is 50% of the time idiopathic, there are some common, identifiable reasons. Many of these aplastic anemias are pancytopenic, meaning there is a concomitant decrease in white blood cells (WBCs) and platelets. Chemotherapeutic agents and other drugs are often the cause. A distinction between blood loss and decreased production is the reticulocyte count. The reticulocyte count (or index) is a reflection of new RBC production in response to a loss of blood. This does not occur with aplastic disorders.[4]

Increased Breakdown

Breakdown of RBCs is either intravascular or extravascular (within the cells of the reticuloendothelial system [RES]). Intravascular hemolysis is rare in the ambulatory patient, usually due to a transfusion reaction, extensive burns, aortic valve prosthesis, or acute glucose-6-dehydrogenase deficiency. Intravascular hemolysis leaves a trail of clues. With RBC breakdown there is an increase in the released constituents such as bilirubin (indirect), LDH, and potassium. These same findings may occur if there was mishandling of the blood sample with consequent hemolysis but to a lesser degree. Urine hemosiderin may be found several days after intravascular hemolysis has occurred. Extravascular hemolysis, not occurring within the vascular system but within the cells of the RES, leaves few clues. However, most causes can be determined by an abnormality in the hemoglobin or shape of the RBC. Other causes are autoimmune. These are determined by the Coombs' test. A history of transfusion or pregnancy is often found.

Blood Loss

When blood is lost, a historical report of a bleeding source is not always obvious. Abortions, stab wounds, and surgeries are obvious causes. Yet the majority of patients in an ambulatory setting have less obvious causes. The most common cause is heavy menstrual flow in women. Occult sites of bleeding are often gastrointestinal. GI bleeding may be frank, as with hemorrhoids; however, higher GI bleeding is often not evident in the stool without guaiac testing. Associated GI symptoms such as upper GI pain associated with meals or lower GI pain with a change in bowel habits may be the only clues.

Laboratory Evaluation

The distinction among the various major types of anemia begins with an evaluation of size. This is done two ways: (1) indices, mainly the MCV, and (2) RBC morphology. These two values often coincide. For example, small cells are morphologically described as microcytic and are usually associated with a decreased MCV. Conversely, large cells are referred to as macrocytes and are accompanied by an increased MCV.

Microcytic Anemia

Microcytic anemia is mainly due to iron deficiency anemia (IDA) and thalassemia minor. Anemia of chronic disease may present as normocytic or microcytic. IDA has some characteristic associated findings that often will cinch the diagnosis. RDW is the coefficient of variation of RBCs. This is determined by dividing the standard deviation of the erythrocyte volume distribution by the MCV. The result is then multiplied by 100 and expressed as a percentage. RDW is either normal or increases. There is no known disease that will decrease the value. An RDW increase often precedes changes in the MCV because the MCV is sensitive to large RBC population changes in the small (or large) cell population. The sensitivity of RDW in diagnosing IDA is between 87% and 100%.[5] The RDW is normal with thalassemia minor (except in rare cases of severe anemia).

Serum ferritin is highly specific for IDA (99% to 100%). Therefore, IDA is diagnosed by finding a microcytic anemia with a combination of a decrease in RBCs and an increase in RDW that is confirmed by a concomitant decrease in serum ferritin. Other supportive findings are a decreased hemoglobin, an increased total iron-binding capacity (TIBC), and a decreased transferrin percent saturation.

Patients with thalassemia minor are usually asymptomatic. Although the anemia is microcytic and hypochromic, the serum ferritin is usually normal or slightly elevated, distinguishing it from IDA. More important, an elevated RBC count is virtually diagnostic, being 75% sensitive and 97% specific for thalassemia syndromes. Further confirmation may be necessary with hemoglobin electrophoresis.

Anemia of chronic disease (ACD) may present in a pure form or associated with IDA. ACD is microcytic in only 25% of cases.[6] When microcytic, the MCV rarely is below 78 fL. When ACD is pure, the distinction between IDA is clearer. A decrease in TIBC, an increase in ferritin, and often an increase in the erythrocyte sedimentation rate (ESR) are found with pure ACD. Serum ferritin is often increased because it is an acute-phase reactant; it is increased in inflammatory diseases. Total serum iron is low in both ACD and IDA. IDA and ACD may coexist for various reasons. One is that patients with rheumatoid arthritis, for example, may be taking medications that cause GI bleeding and an associated IDA. The serum ferritin will then be low or borderline.

Macrocytic Anemia

The most common causes of macrocytic anemia are vitamin B_{12} deficiency, folate deficiency, alcoholism, hypothyroidism, and liver disease. A distinction is made between megaloblastic and nonmegaloblastic anemia. This requires a bone marrow aspirate. This is rarely needed, however, because of the sensitivity and specificity of other laboratory values, coupled with the history. When the MCV is greater than 130 fL the probability is 100% for vitamin B_{12} or folate deficiency (magaloblastic).[7] Levels below 95 fL equal a 0.1% probability. Antimetabolite or antifolate drugs may also cause a megaloblastic anemia. A mild elevation in the range of 100 to 110 fL is suggestive of other causes, such as alcoholism, liver disease, or hypothyroidism. Further laboratory testing for liver enzymes and ultrasensitive thyrotropin (TSH) will differentiate these possibilities.

Some lab values are elevated in both vitamin B_{12} and folate deficiencies, such as RDW. Also, RBC folate concentrations are low and serum homocysteine levels are elevated with both vitamin B_{12} and folate deficiencies.

A differentiation between vitamin B_{12} deficiency and folate deficiency is important because of the potential neurologic consequences of vitamin B_{12} deficiency. In other words, folate supplementation will not correct the neurologic abnormalities of vitamin B_{12} deficiency. Also, vitamin B_{12} deficiency is less often a "nutritional" deficiency and more often a lack of intrinsic factor. This usually requires lifelong intramuscular injections as opposed to temporary oral supplementation.

Serum levels of vitamin B_{12} and folate may be measured. Additionally, serum methylmalonic acid and total homocysteine levels are high in patients with vitamin B_{12} deficiency (95% sensitive).[8,9] Folate deficiency will usually raise the homocysteine level. RBC folate is less valuable in distinguishing between the two anemias because it is often found to be low in both vitamin B_{12} and folate deficiency. RBC folate is better used as an indicator of tissue stores.

A therapeutic trial may be acceptable as an initial attempt to differentiate between vitamin B_{12} and folate deficiency. Oral folate at 100 μg/d for 10 days is prescribed. The patient's reticulocyte response is then measured. If the underlying cause of macrocytic anemia is folate deficiency, there will be an increase in reticulocytes; however, there will be no increase in patients with a vitamin B_{12} deficiency.

MANAGEMENT

Dietary management of anemias through supplementation must be preceded by a thorough diagnostic search that provides sufficiently convincing information that there is not an underlying cause that needs comanagement or referral. For example, IDA may be a dietary issue in pregnant women, infants, and adolescent or adult athletes. Dietary supplementation (or an iron-enriched formula for infants) is appropriate. However, in the case of occult GI bleeding, heavy menstrual flow, and urinary loss, referral for determination of underlying pathology is needed prior to institution of dietary correction. ACD also requires at the minimum a consultation with the physician treating the primary disorder. Vitamin B_{12} deficiency that is due to a strictly vegetarian diet is responsive to a change in diet or supplementation; patients with pernicious anemia should be referred for lifelong treatment with injectable vitamin B_{12}. There is some evidence from Swedish studies, however, that daily supplementation of 1,000 μg (2,000 μg twice daily for the first month) is sufficient to cover the variable absorption rate in some individuals. There are no toxic effects known.[10] The main reasons given for not using this approach are compliance and cost. The cost currently is not a consideration.

Following are some basic recommendations for dietary supplementation when appropriate.[11]

Iron Deficiency Anemia

- For adults, ferrous sulfate (or ferrous forms of lactate, fumarate, gluconate, glycine sulfate, or glutamate), 200 mg/d, is given for 6 to 12 months after hemoglobin levels are normal (the dose is dependent on patient tolerance).
- Side effects may be decreased by starting with a lower dosage and slowly increasing gradually over several days or by taking the supplement in three divided doses.

Dietary recommendations include the following:

- Avoid substances that may affect iron absorption, including tea, coffee, milk or dairy products, calcium, and some medications at least for 1 hour before and after ingestion of iron supplementation.
- Include a source of vitamin C at every meal.
- Include foods rich in iron, such as dried beans and peas, poultry, seafood, and red meat.
- Increase dietary fiber moderately to offset the possible side effect of constipation associated with iron supplements.

Folate Deficiency

- Oral folic acid at 1 to 5 mg/d for 2 to 3 weeks is necessary to replenish tissues.
- Maintaining levels requires 50 to 100 ug/d.
- Foods high in folic acid include orange juice, asparagus, beef liver, wheat germ, red beans, and peanut butter.

Vitamin B_{12} Deficiency Anemia

- Very large doses are necessary to compensate for the 1% to 3% of vitamin B_{12} that does not require intrinsic factor; doses at 1,000 μg/d are necessary.
- Dietary sources include liver, beef, pork, eggs, milk and milk products.

Algorithm

An algorithm for microcytic anemia is presented in Figure 53–1.

SELECTED ANEMIAS

MICROCYTIC AND NORMOCYTIC ANEMIAS

Iron Deficiency Anemia

Classic Presentation

Most patients are initially asymptomatic. When symptomatic, the patient may present with symptoms related to a decreased oxygen-carrying capacity of the blood, such as fatigue (mainly upon exertion), orthopnea, headaches, dizziness, learning disability/decreased attention span (in children), syncope/presyncope, or angina (if predisposed with coronary artery disease).

Causes

IDA is the most common hematologic disorder, affecting as many as 30% of the world's population. However, in the United States, it affects 0.2% to 2% of adult males and 2% to 10% (one study indicated up to 20%[12]) of adult females.[13] The likelihood of IDA development is increased in certain patient populations: pregnant women, 60%; heavily menstruating women, 80%; and individuals with pica symptoms, 90%. Other groups at risk in-

Figure 53–1

ANEMIA—ALGORITHM.

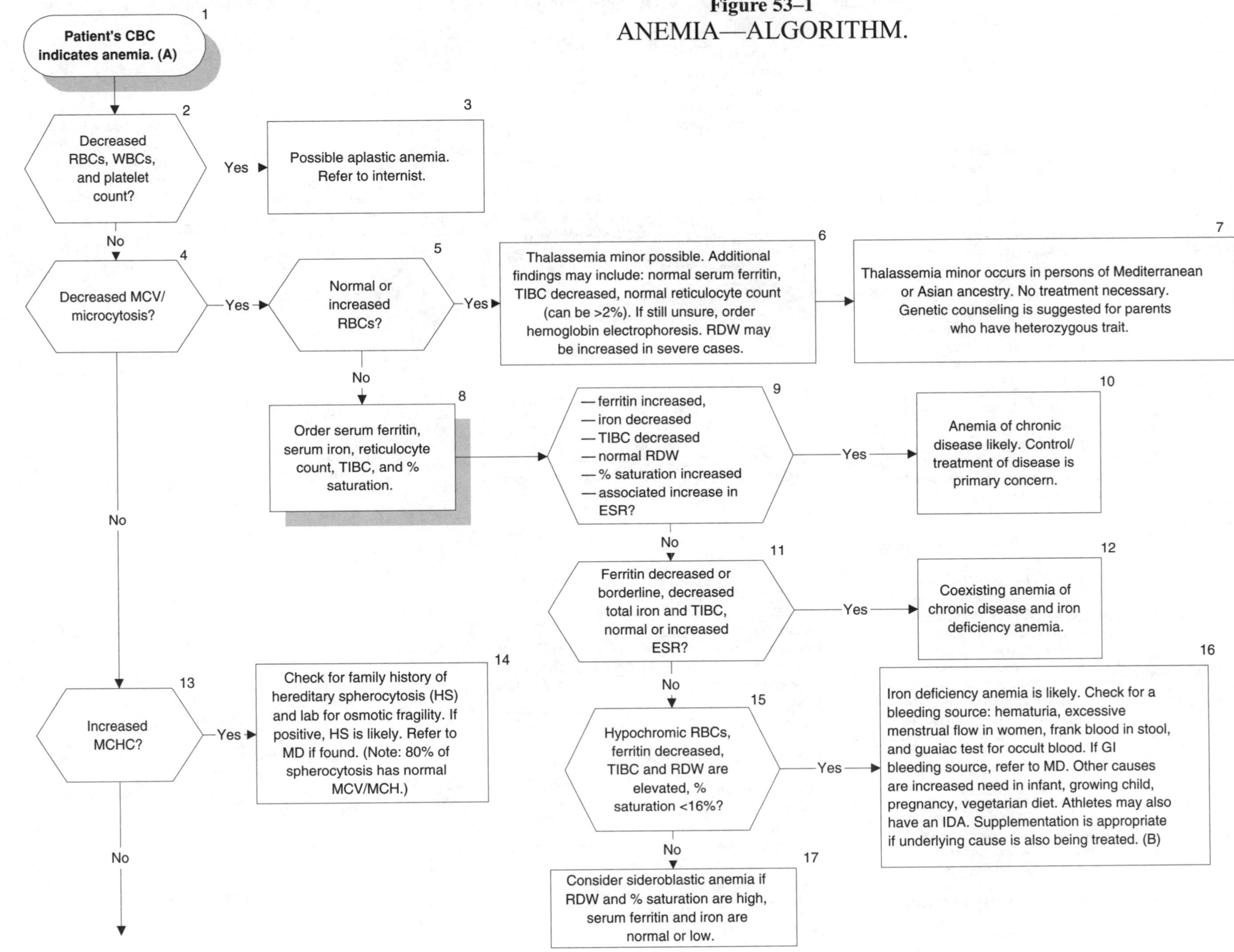

continues

Figure 53–1 continued

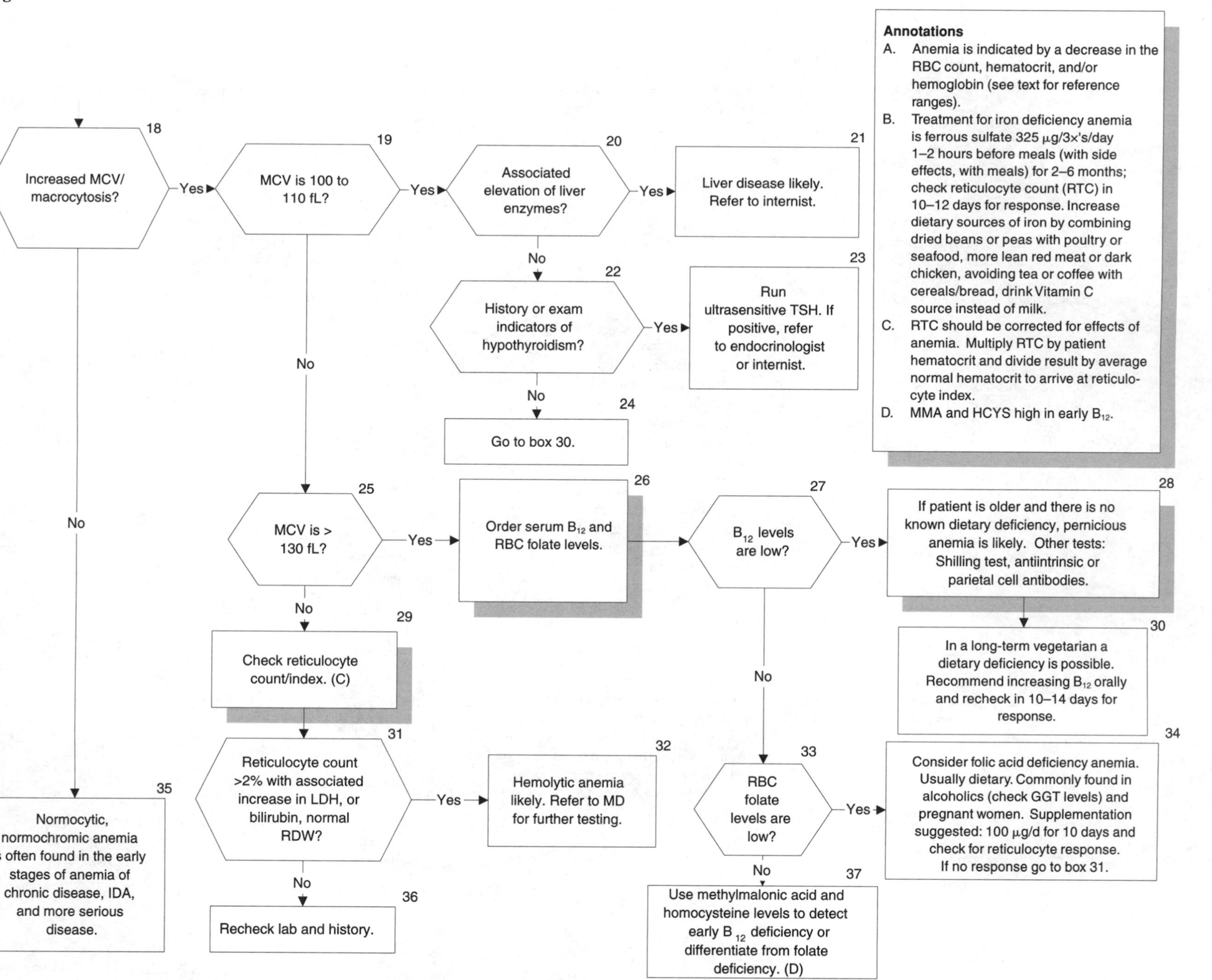

Key: MCHC, Mean corpuscular hemoglobin concentration; GGT, γ-glutamyltransferase; MMA, methylmalonic acid; HCYS, homocysteine.

clude infants to age 4 years, adolescents who exercise heavily, long-distance runners, and patients with chronic diseases (ie, rheumatoid arthritis, cancer).[14]

Anemia is not the first sign of iron deficiency. There are generally five stages: (1) depletion of storage iron, (2) decreased serum iron, (3) anemia with normal cells, (4) microcytosis, then hypochromia, and (5) symptoms and signs of IDA. The main cause of IDA is blood loss. When IDA is diagnosed, a search for a bleeding source is a requisite prior to treatment. However, nutritional demand for and availability of iron at varying stages of life is a factor for individuals without blood loss.

Evaluation

In the early stage of iron deficiency, there are no signs or symptoms. When a patient has reached the later stages, patients with chronic IDA often will have an unusual craving 50% of the time, referred to as pica (craving for ice, clay/dirt, or starch); pagophagia (ice eating) is most common.[15] Chronic, severe IDA may have signs, including spoon-shaped nails (koilonychia), brittle nails, skin cracking at the corners of the mouth (angular stomatitis), a smooth tongue (atrophic glositis), or blue sclerae.[16] Remember that these signs and symptoms are the last clinical indicator of IDA. Laboratory evaluation can detect anemia prior to the development of these indicators. The classic laboratory presentation is a decrease in RBCs and hemoglobin, microcytosis, and a decreased MCV with an increase in the RDW. Specific indicators include a decrease in serum ferritin (< 10 ng/mL), increase in total TIBC, and a decrease in transferrin saturation (< 16%). Other indicators are due to blood loss, such as increase of blood or RBCs in the urine, or a positive guaiac test for occult blood. If IDA is discovered, a thorough search for a source of blood loss must be made. The most common will be heavy menstruation, GI loss from an ulcer or cancer, and urinary/renal pathology.

Management

The first decision to make before treatment is whether IDA is caused by nutritional need due to increased demand or due to blood loss. Blood loss from heavy menstruation should be comanaged with a gynecologist to determine whether there is an underlying hormonal imbalance. If occult blood is found, referral for medical evaluation should occur. Nutritional causes may be managed with dietary supplementation. Between 200 and 325 mg of ferrous sulfate per day for 10 to 14 days should be prescribed (higher doses may be necessary in some individuals).[17] At about 2 weeks the reticulocyte count is checked to determine a response (increase). The hemoglobin concentration should increase to normal in 6 to 8 weeks. If responsive, continue for a total of 6 months. If not, consider another cause. Remember to counsel and possibly screen high-risk individuals (or their parents).

Thalassemia Minor

Classic Presentation

The patient is usually asymptomatic.

Causes

Thalassemia (TS) is the second most common anemia in humans and the most common genetic disorder. The thalassemias are characterized by a reduction in globin chains that results in reduced hemoglobin synthesis. There are different types with varying degrees of severity. α-Thalassemia trait and β-thalassemia minor (heterozygous) are by far the most common. α-TS is more common in individuals from Asia/China and in blacks. β-TS is more common in persons of Italian or Greek ancestry and less common in blacks and Asians/Chinese. Thalassemia major is quite rare in the United States, representing less than 1,000 cases. These patients are homozygous and develop severe life-threatening problems within the first year of life.

Evaluation

An elevated RBC count with a low MCV is 75% sensitive and 95% specific for thalassemia syndromes. This combination distinguishes TS from IDA in most cases. Other findings may include microcytosis, target cells (basophilic stippling with β-TS), a normal serum ferritin, TIBC normal or decreased, and a reticulocyte count that is normal or slightly elevated. It is important to recognize that a patient suspected of having IDA yet is unresponsive to iron supplementation may have an underlying TS.

Management

Patients with α-TS trait or β-TS minor need no treatment. It is important to note that both parents who are heterozygous for a specific TS (ie, both parents have TS minor or both parents have α-TS trait) are at risk of producing a homozygous (TS major) child. Given the severity and poor prognosis for a TS child, genetic counseling should be suggested and the option of prenatal diagnosis should be discussed with those already pregnant.

Anemia of Chronic Disease

Classic Presentation

Patients with ACD usually have rheumatoid arthritis (RA), cancer, chronic infection or inflammation, or liver disease.

Causes

The cause is unknown. Several theories have been proposed: (1) impairment of protein synthesis (decrease in transferrin, albumin, and erythropoietin), (2) activation of macrophages or reticuloendothelial (RE) cells, and (3) an impaired ability to recirculate iron from phagocytosed RBC. Iron deficiency often coexists with ACD. A distinction is made between ACD and that caused by chronic renal failure; however, the mechanisms may overlap.

Evaluation

Coexisting indications or diagnosis of an underlying chronic disease help in the diagnosis. Laboratory diagnosis is sometimes confusing because values are similar for ACD and IDA. This is often due to the fact that they coexist (especially in patients with RA). ACD is usually normochromic and normocytic (75% of the time). Twenty-five percent of the time ACD is microcytic with an associated decrease in the MCV. Classically, the hematocrit is rarely below 25% and there is a decreased TIBC. While serum iron may be decreased, RDW is usually normal unless there is coexisting iron depletion that would lead to an elevated RDW. The likelihood of ACD is strong when there is a normal or increased serum ferritin and a decreased TIBC.

Management

Usually treatment of the underlying disease is mainly what is necessary. If there is an associated IDA, iron supplementation may be beneficial. In severe cases, transfusion or erythropoietin injection may be necessary.

MACROCYTIC ANEMIAS

Vitamin B_{12} Deficiency

Classic Presentation

In the early stages, most patients are asymptomatic. In later stages, the patient may complain of general weakness, shortness of breath, numbness and tingling, difficulty walking, or a swollen tongue.

Causes

Vitamin B_{12} (cyanocobalamin) is a water-soluble vitamin that requires a glycoprotein, intrinsic factor, for absorption in the terminal ileum. Vitamin B_{12} stores in the liver are usually sufficient for 3 to 5 years. Vitamin B_{12} is a coenzyme in DNA synthesis and important for myelin production. It is found in dairy products and meats. With pernicious anemia (PA) and atrophic gastritis, intrinsic factor is unavailable, making vitamin B_{12} unabsorbable (except for 1% to 3%). PA is due to an autoimmune response against the parietal cells and intrinsic factor, leading to atrophic gastritis. Although the classic presentation of a gray-haired, middle-aged, northern European has been the standard description of a person with PA, PA is found in all ethnic groups; it is found more often in older patients[18] and young (<40 years old) black women.[19] Malabsorption of vitamin B_{12} due to lack of intrinsic factor is the most common cause of vitamin B_{12} deficiency; malabsorption from blind loop syndrome, fish tapeworm, and certain drugs is less common. Nutritional deficiency is most common in chronic alcoholics and vegetarians. Vitamin B_{12} deficiency in vegetarians is not inevitable if they eat a balanced diet. It would take 3 to 5 years of a diet free of dairy products and meat before clinical signs are evident.

Evaluation

Differentiation between vitamin B_{12} and other causes of macrocytic anemia is necessary. A history of alcoholism, nutritional deficiency, or gastric surgery may be helpful. Laboratory diagnosis is based on several classic findings: an MCV greater than 130 fL is 100% sensitive for vitamin B_{12} and folic deficiency. Further distinction is that vitamin B_{12} deficiency is associated with a low serum vitamin B_{12}, and a high serum or urine methylmalonic acid (MMA) (95% sensitive).[20] MMA is not elevated with folic acid deficiency. Further testing with a Schilling test is not usually needed. Coexisting IDA and PA occurs 20% to 25% of the time.[21] This may result in a normal MCV.

Management

Folic acid replacement will correct the anemia of vitamin B_{12} deficiency; however, there will be no reticulocyte count increase in response to folic acid supplementation. Vitamin B_{12} deficiency due to PA requires lifelong injections (daily injections for 1 week, weekly injections for 1 month, monthly injections for life). Oral supplementation requires very large dosages (1,000 μg/d) and strict patient compliance (1% to 3% is absorbed without intrinsic factor).[10] It is not currently practical to rely on oral supplementation treatment for PA. Early treatment of PA may prevent or reverse neurologic manifestations. PA patients with neurologic findings less than 3 months before treatment may have these findings reversed. This may take between 6 and 18 months. Hematologic response is with an increased reticulocyte count in 10 days, correction within 6 weeks. Patients generally feel physically better almost immediately. It is recommended that because of a higher predisposition to gastric carcinoma, PA patients should be examined with endoscopy every 5 years.

Folate Deficiency

Classic Presentation

Early folate (folic acid) deficiency is asymptomatic. The patient is often either an alcoholic or is pregnant and is complaining of generalized fatigue.

Causes

Folate is a water-soluble vitamin needed for DNA synthesis and erythropoiesis. Folate stores last for 3 to 6 months. It is found in most fruits and vegetables (especially citrus fruits and green leafy vegetables). There are numerous causes of deficiency. Inadequate intake is found in infants, adolescents, the elderly, and chronic alcoholics. Increased need is found in pregnant women. Malabsorption syndromes and drugs such as oral contraceptives and phenytoin interfere with absorption. Smoking appears to be a risk factor with folate deficiency. Overcooking foods and lack of vitamin C may also contribute to a deficiency.[22] It is important to note that low folate levels may be associated with an increased risk of colorectal and cervical cancer.[23] There may also be a relationship to chronic fatigue.[24] Low folate levels during pregnancy may result in neural tube defects in the fetus.

Evaluation

Folate deficiency is difficult to differentiate from early vitamin B_{12} deficiency. There are no neurologic findings with either. Eventually vitamin B_{12} deficiency might develop neurologic manifestations. Laboratory evaluation is helpful. Shared findings include an MCV > 130 fL, macrocytosis, and decreased hemoglobin. Specific findings include low levels of serum and RBC folate. Although RBC folate is the better test, it may not indicate folate deficiency for several months. A trial of oral folate at 100 μg/d for 10 days followed by a check for a reticulocyte count increase helps to differentiate between vitamin B_{12} deficiency and folate deficiency. At this level of supplementation there will not be a response with vitamin B_{12} deficiency.[25]

Management

When dietary deficiency or increased demand is the cause, supplementation at 1 to 2 mg/d for 2 to 3 weeks is needed. The reticulocyte response is within 10 days. Unresponsiveness suggests other causes. Daily supplementation of between 50 and 100 μg is needed. This can be achieved through diet with orange juice, asparagus, red beans, peanut butter, and beef liver.

REFERENCES

1. National Board of Chiropractic Examiners. *Job Analysis of Chiropractic*. Greeley, CO: National Board of Chiropractic Examiners; 1993.
2. Nardonne DA, Roth KM, Mazur DJ, McAfee JH. Usefulness of physical examination in detecting the presence or absence of anemia. *Arch Intern Med*. 1990;150:201.
3. Djulbegovic B. Anemia: diagnosis. In: *Reasoning and Decision Making in Hematology*. New York: Churchill Livingstone; 1992: 13–17.
4. Crosby WH. Reticulocyte counts. *Arch Intern Med*. 1981;147:1747.
5. Witte DL, Kraemer DF, Johnson GF, et al. Prediction of bone marrow findings from tests performed on peripheral blood. *Am J Clin Pathol*. 1986;85:202.
6. Schilling RF. Anemia of chronic disease: a misnomer. *Ann Intern Med*. 1991;115:572.
7. Scates S, Glaspy J. The macrocytic anemias. *Lab Med*. 1990;21:736.
8. Green R. Metabolic assays in cobalamin and folate deficiency. *Baillieres Clin Haematol*. 1995;8:533–566.
9. Stabler SP, Lindenbaum J, Allen RH. The use of homocysteine and other metabolites in the specific diagnosis of vitamin B12 deficiency. *J Nutr*. 1996:126:126–127.
10. Berlin H, Berlin R, Brante G. Oral treatment of pernicious anemia with high doses of vitamin B12 without intrinsic factor. *Acta Med Scand*. 1968;184:247–258.
11. Branson RA, Bowers LJ. Nutritional anemia: iron, cobalamin, or folate deficiency? *Top Clin Chiro*. 1995;2(4):33–42.
12. Scrinshaw NS. Iron deficiency. *Sci Am*. 1991;265:46–52.
13. Djulbegovic B. Iron deficiency anemia. In: *Reasoning and Decision Making in Hematology*. New York: Churchill Livingstone; 1992:21–24.
14. Williams SR. *Nutrition and Diet Therapy*. 7th ed. St. Louis, MO: Mosby-Year Book; 1993.
15. Hamilton HK. *Professional Guide to Diseases*. 2nd ed. Springhouse, PA: Springhouse Corp; 1987.
16. Robbins SL. *Robbin's Pathologic Basis of Disease*, 4th ed. Philadelphia: WB Saunders; 1989.
17. Brigden ML. Iron deficiency anemia. *Postgrad Med*. 1993;93: 181–192.
18. Pippard JD. Megaloblastic anemia: geography and diagnosis. *Lancet*. 1994;344:6–7.
19. Carmel R, Johnson CS. Racial patterns in pernicious anemia: early age at onset and increased frequency of intrinsic-factor antibody in black women. *N Engl J Med*. 1978;298:647.
20. Pruthi RK, Tefferi A. Pernicious anemia revisited. *Mayo Clin Proc*. 1994;69:144–150.
21. Chanarin I. Pernicious anemia. *Br Med J*. 1992;304:1584–1585.
22. Bailey LB. Folate status assessment. *J Nutr*. 1990;120:1508–1511.
23. Butterworth CE Jr, Hutch KD, Macaloso M, et al. Folate deficiency and cervical dysplasia. *JAMA*. 1992;267:528–533.

24. Jacobson W, Saich T, Borysiewicz LK, Behan WM, et al. Serum folate and chronic fatigue syndrome. *Neurology*. 1993;43: 2645–2647.

25. Speicher CE. Hematological diseases. In: *The Right Test: A Physician's Guide to Laboratory Medicine*. 2nd ed. Philadelphia: WB Saunders; 1993:208.

Index

E

F

G

H

P

Q

R

S

T